THE
PUBLIC GENERAL ACTS

AND GENERAL SYNOD MEASURES

1992

[IN FIVE PARTS]

PART V

TABLES & INDEX

LONDON: HMSO

1993

£345·00 net

HMSO publications are available from:

HMSO Publications Centre
(Mail, fax and telephone orders only)
PO Box 276, London SW8 5DT
Telephone orders 071-873 9090
General enquiries 071-873 0011
(queuing system in operation for both numbers)
Fax orders 071-873 8200

HMSO Bookshops
49 High Holborn, London WC1V 6HB
071-873 0011 Fax 071-873 8200 (Counter service only)
258 Broad Street, Birmingham B1 2HE
021-643 3740 Fax 021-643 6510
33 Wine Street, Bristol BS1 2BQ
0272 264306 Fax 0272 294515
9-21 Princess Street, Manchester M60 8AS
061-834 7201 Fax 061-833 0634
16 Arthur Street, Belfast BT1 4GD
0232 238451 Fax 0232 235401
71 Lothian Road, Edinburgh EH3 9AZ
031-228 4181 Fax 031-229 2734

HMSO's Accredited Agents
(see Yellow Pages)

and through good booksellers

ISBN 0 11 840323 0

c

THIS PUBLICATION

relates to

the Public General Acts

and General Synod Measures

which received the Royal Assent in 1992

in which year ended the FORTIETH

and began the FORTY-FIRST YEAR

of the Reign of HER MAJESTY

QUEEN ELIZABETH THE SECOND

and

ended the Fifth session

of the Fiftieth Parliament

and began the First session of the Fifty-First Parliament

of the United Kingdom of Great Britain

and Northern Ireland.

d

PRINTED IN THE UNITED KINGDOM BY PAUL FREEMAN
Controller and Chief Executive of HMSO and
Queen's Printer of Acts of Parliament

e

CONTENTS

PART I

PART II

PART III

PART IV

PART V

TABLE I
Alphabetical List of
the Public General Acts of 1992

TABLE II

Chronological List of
the Public General Acts of 1992

*Consolidation Act

TABLE III

Alphabetical List of
the Local and Personal Acts of 1992

There were no personal acts passed during the year 1992

TABLE IV

Chronological List of
the General Synod Measures of 1992

Measure passed by the General Synod of the Church of England which received the Royal Assent during the year 1992

TABLE V

Tables of the Derivations and Destinations of the Consolidation Acts of 1992.

These Tables have no official status. They are intended only as a help in tracing the derivation of the Consolidation Acts and the destinations of the enactments consolidated.

CONTENTS

SOCIAL SECURITY CONTRIBUTIONS AND BENEFITS ACT 1992 (c. 4)

TABLE OF DERIVATIONS

(for Table of Destinations see page v)

Note:

1. The following abbreviations are used in this Table:—

1975(1) =	Social Security Act 1975 (c.14)
1975(2) =	Social Security Pensions Act 1975 (c.60)
1975(3) =	Child Benefit Act 1975 (c.61)
1975 (Old Cases) =	Industrial Injuries and Diseases (Old Cases) Act 1975 (c.16)
1977 =	Social Security (Miscellaneous Provisions) Act 1977 (c.5)
1978 =	Employment Protection (Consolidation) Act 1978 (c.4)
1979 =	Social Security Act 1979 (c.18)
1980(1) =	Social Security Act 1980 (c.30)
1980(2) =	Social Security (No.2) Act 1980 (c.39)
1981(1) =	Social Security (Contributions) Act 1981 (c.1)
1981(2) =	Social Security Act 1981 (c.33)
1982(1) =	Social Security (Contributions) Act 1982 (c.2)
1982(2) =	Social Security and Housing Benefits Act 1982 (c.24)
1983 =	Health and Social Services and Social Security Adjudications Act 1983 (c.41)
1984 =	Health and Social Security Act 1984 (c.48)
1985 =	Social Security Act 1985 (c.53)
1986 =	Social Security Act 1986 (c.50)
1987 =	Social Fund (Maternity and Funeral Expenses) Act 1987 (c.7)
1988(1) =	Social Security Act 1988 (c.7)
1988(2) =	Local Government Finance Act 1988 (c.41)
1989 =	Social Security Act 1989 (c.24)
1990 =	Social Security Act 1990 (c.27)
1991(1) =	Statutory Sick Pay Act 1991 (c.3)
1991(2) =	Disability Living Allowance and Disability Working Allowance Act 1991 (c.21)
1991(3) =	Social Security (Contributions) Act 1991 (c.42)
R followed by a number =	the Law Commission recommendation of that number

2. The Table does not contain any entries in respect of section 66(2) of the Social Security Pensions Act 1975 (c.60) which provides that, with certain exceptions, that Act and the Social Security Act 1975 (c.14) shall have effect as if the provisions of the Social Security Pensions Act 1975 were contained in the Social Security Act 1975. The effect is that the general provisions of the Social Security Act 1975 apply to the provisions of the Social Security Pensions Act 1975.

3. Numerous sums specified in this Act are subject to frequent alteration by statutory instrument. There are three relevant statutory instruments in force—

(a) The Social Security (Contributions) (Re-rating) (No. 2) Order 1991 (S.I. 1991/2909), ("the Contributions Order");

SOCIAL SECURITY CONTRIBUTIONS AND BENEFITS ACT—*continued.*

(b) The Social Security Benefits (Up-rating) (No. 2) Order 1991 (S.I. 1991/2910), ("the Benefits Order");

(c) The Statutory Sick Pay (Rate of Payment) (No. 2) Order 1991 (S.I. 1991/2911), ("the Sick Pay Order");

The order in which the provisions amended by the Benefits Order are consolidated is not identical with the order in which they appear in the Social Security Act 1975.

4. The Table does not show the effect of transfer of functions orders.

Section of 1992 Act	Derivation
1(1)	1975(1) s.1(1); 1990 s.16(1),(2)
(2)	1975 s.1(2); 1991(3) s.1(2)
(3)	1975(1) s.1(3); 1985 s.29(1), Sch.5, para.5
(4)	1975(1) s.1(4); 1991(3) s.2(1)(a)
(5)	1975(1) s.1(4A); 1990 s.16(2); 1991(1) s.1(4)
(6)	1975(1) s.1(6); 1991(3) s.1(3)
2	1975(1) s.2
3(1)	1975(1) s.3(1)
(2), (3)	1975(1) s.3(2), (3)
4(1)	1975(1) s.3(1A); 1982(2) ss.23, 37(1); 1986 s.49, Sch.4, para.10
(2), (3)	1975(1) s.3(1B),(1C); 1982(2) s.37(1)
(4)	1975(1) s.3(1D); 1989 s.31(1), Sch.8, para.1
(5)	1975(1) s.3(4); 1982(2) s.48(5), Sch.4, para.8
5(1)	1975(1) s.4(1); 1975(2) ss.1(1), 65(1), Sch.4, para.36(a); 1985 s.7(1)
(2)	1975(2) s.1(2); 1986 s.74(6)
(3)	1975(2) s.1(3)
6(1)	1975(1) s.4(2); Education (School-Leaving Dates) Act 1976 (c.5) s.2(4)
(2)	1975(2) s.4(1); 1984 s.21, Sch.7, para.3(a)
(3)	1975(1) s.4(3); 1989 s.26, Sch.7, para.2(1)
(4)	1975(1) s.4(2)
(5)	1975(1) s.4(7); 1979 s.14(1); 1985 s.8(1)
(6)	1986 s.74(5)
7	1975(1) s.4(4),(5)
8(1)—(3)	1975(1) s.4(6), (6A), (6B); 1989 s.1(1)
(4)	1986 s.74(5)
9(1)	1975(1) s.4(6C); 1985 s.7(2); 1989 s.26, Sch.7, para.2(2)
(2)	1975(1) s.4(6D); 1985 s.7(2)
(3)	1975(1) s.4(6E); 1985 s.7(2); Contributions Order art.2(2)
(4)	1975(1) s.4(6C), (6E); 1985 s.7(2)
(5)	1986 s.74(5)
10	1975(1) s.4A; 1991(3) s.1(5)

SOCIAL SECURITY CONTRIBUTIONS AND BENEFITS ACT—*continued.*

Section of 1992 Act	Derivation
11(1)	1975(1) s.7(1); Education (School-Leaving Dates) Act 1976 (c.5) s.2(4); 1984 s.17(1); Contributions Order art.3(a)
(2)	1975(2) s.4(2)
(3)	1975(1) s.7(4)
(4)	1975(1) s.7(5) Contributions Order art.3(b)
(5)	1975(1) s.7(6)
12(1),(2)	1975(1) s.7A(1),(2); 1984 s.17(2)
(3)	1975(1) s.7A(3); 1984 s.17(2); 1989 s.26, Sch.7, para.3(b), (c); The Social Security (Contributions and Credits) (Transitional and Consequential Provisions) Regulations 1985 (S.I.1985/1398) reg.4(2)
(4)—(8)	1975(1) s.7A(4)—(8); 1984 s.17(2)
13(1)	1975(1) s.8(1); Education (School-Leaving Dates) Act 1976 (c.5) s.2(4); 1984 s.18(1)(a) Contributions Order art.4
(2)	1975(1) s.8(2)
(3)	1975(1) s.8(2)(a)
(4)	1975(1) s.8(2A); 1984 s.18(1)(b), (3)
(5)	1975(1) s.8(2B); 1984 s.18(3)
(6)	1975(1) s.8(2C); 1984 s.18(3); 1989 s.26, Sch.7, para.4; The Social Security (Contributions and Credits) (Transitional and Consequential Provisions) Regulations 1985 (S.I.1985/1398) reg.4(3)
(7)	1975(1) s.8(2D); 1984 s.18(3)
14(1)	1975(2) s.5(1); 1986 s.75, Sch.8, para.6
(2), (3)	1975(2) s.5(2); 1977 s.1(5)
15(1), (2)	1975(1) s.9(1); 1989 s.26, Sch.7, para.5(a),(b)
(3)	1975(1) s.9(2); Social Security (Contributions, Re-rating) Order 1982 (S.I.1982/1790) art.5(a) Contributions Order art.5
(4)	Income and Corporation Taxes Act 1988 (c.1) s.844, Sch.29, para.14
(5)	1975(1) s.9(1); 1989 s.26, Sch.7, para.5(c)
16(1),(2)	1975(1) s.9(3)
(3)	1975(1) s.9(4)
(4)	1975(1) s.9(5); 1990 s.17(1)
(5)	1975(1) s.9(6); 1990 s.17(2)
17(1), (2)	1975(1) s.9(7), (8)
(3) - (6)	1975(1) s.9(9)
18(1)	1975(1) s.10(1); Social Security (Contributions, Re-rating) Order 1982 (S.I. 1982/1790) art.5(a) Contributions Order art.5
(2)	1975(1) s.10(2)
19(1)—(3)	1975(1) s.11

SOCIAL SECURITY CONTRIBUTIONS AND BENEFITS ACT—*continued.*

Section of 1992 Act	Derivation
(4), (5)	1975(2) s.3(2), (3)
(6)	1975(2) s.3(4); 1986 s.75, Sch.8, para.5
20(1)	1975(1) s.12(1); 1975(?) s.65(1), Sch.4, para.37; 1984 s.13, Sch.5, para.2(a); 1986 s.86, Sch.10, para.63; 1989 s.26, Sch.7, para.6
(2) "long-term benefit"	1975(1) s.168(1), Sch.20, "long-term benefit"; 1975(2) s.65(1), Sch.4, para.64
"short-term benefit"	1975(1) s.12(2)
(3)	Drafting
21(1), (2)	1975(1) s.13(1); 1986 s.86, Sch.10, para.64
(3)	1975(1) s.13(6)
(4)	1975(1) s.13(8); 1986 s.86, Sch.10, para.72(b)
(5)	1975(1) s.13(6); 1986 s.75, Sch.8, para.2(6)
(6)	1975(1) s.13(7)
22(1), (2)	1975(1) s.13(2); 1975(2) s.65(1), Sch.4, para.38(a); 1986 ss.18(1), 75, 86, Sch.8, para.2(1), Sch.10, para.72
(3)	1975(1) s.13(5); 1986 s.75, Sch.8, para.2(4)(c); 1989 s.26, Sch.7, para.7
(4)	1975(1) s.13(3); 1975(2) s.65(1), Sch.4, para.38(b); 1986 s.75, Sch.8, para.2(2)
(5)	1975(1) s.13(4); 1986 s.75, Sch.8, para.2(3)
(6)	1975(1) s.13(5AA); 1989 s.4(3)
(7)	1977 s.2
23(1)	1975(1) s.13(5); 1979 s.21(4), Sch.3, para.5; 1986 s.75, Sch.8, para.2(4)(a); 1988(1) s.9, Sch.2, para.1(1)(a)
(2)	1975(1) s.13(5ZA); 1988(1) s.9, Sch.2, para.1(1)(b)
(3)	1975(1) s.13(5); 1989 s.4(2)
(4)	1975(1) s.13(5A); 1985 s.29(1), Sch.5, para.6(b); R1
24(1)	1975(1) s.13(5B); 1986 s.75, Sch.8, para.2(5)
(2)	1975(1) s.13(5C); 1989 s.4(4)
25(1)	1975(1) s.14(1)
(2)	1975(1) s.14(2); 1989 s.7, Sch.1, para.4(1)
(3)	1975(1) s.14(3)
(4)	1975(1) s.14(4); 1975(2) s.18(1)
(5), (6)	1975(1) s.14(6); 1975(2) s.65(1), Sch.4, para.39(b); 1979 s.21(4), Sch.3, para.6; 1986 s.86, Sch.10, para.83
(7)	1975(1) s.14(8)
26(1)	1975(1) s.18(1)
(2) - (4)	1975(1) s.18(2) - (2B); 1989 s.11

SOCIAL SECURITY CONTRIBUTIONS AND BENEFITS ACT—*continued.*

Section of 1992 Act	Derivation
(5)	1975(1) s.18(3)
(6)	1975(1) s.18(4); 1986 s.43(1)
27(1), (2)	1975(1) s.19(1), (1A); 1986 s.44(1)
(3)	1975(1) s.19(2)
28(1)	1975(1) s.20(1); Employment Act 1988 (c.19) s.27(2); 1989 s.12(1); Unemployment Benefit (Disqualification Period) Order 1988 (S.I.1988/487) art.2
(2)	1975(1) s.20(1A); 1986 s.43(3)(a)
(3)	1975(1) s.20(3)
(4)	1975(1) s.20(3A); 1985 s.10
(5)	1975(1) s.20(4); 1989 s.12(3)
(6)	Education (Scotland) Act 1962 (c.47) s.145(16); Local Government (Scotland) Act 1973 (c.65) s.129, Sch.11, para.12; 1975(1) s.20(5); Employment Act 1988 (c.19) s.27(3)
29	1975(1) s.20A; 1989 s.12(4)
30(1)	1980(2) s.5(1); 1988(1) s.7(a); 1989 s.9(1)
(2)	1980(2) s.5(1A); 1982(2) s.48(5), Sch.4, para.34(2)
(3)	1980(2) s.5(2); 1982(2) s.48(5), Sch.4, para.34(3); 1989 s.9(1)
(4) "employer"	1980(2) s.5(3) "employer"
"employment"	1980(2) s.5(3) "employment"
"modifications"	1980(2) s.5(3) "modifications"
31(1)	1975(1) s.14(1)
(2)	1975(1) s.14(2); 1989 s.7, Sch.1, para.4(1)
(3)	1975 s.14(2A); 1982(2) s.39(3)
(4)	1975(1) s.14(3)
(5)	1975(1) s.14(4); 1975(2) s.18(1); 1982(2) s.48(5), Sch.4, para.9
(6), (7)	1975(1) s.14(6); 1975(2) s.65(1), Sch.4, para.39(b); 1979 s.21(4), Sch.3, para.6; 1986 s.86, Sch.10, para.83
(8)	1975(1) s.14(8)
32(1), (2)	1975(1) s.20(2), (3)
(3)	1975(1) s.20(5)(d) "week"
33(1)	1975(1) s.15(1); 1989 s.7, Sch.1, para.5(1)
(2)	1975(1) s.15(2); 1989 s.7, Sch.1, para.5(2)
(3)	1975(1) s.15(3); 1975(2) ss.14, 65(1), Sch.4, para.40(b); 1990 s.4(1)
(4), (5)	1975(1) s.15(4); 1975(2) s.65(1), Sch.4, para.40(c); 1979 ss.5, 21(4), Sch.1, para.1, Sch.3, para.7; 1986 s.86, Sch.10, para.83
(6)	1975(1) s.15(5)
(7), (8)	1975(1) s.15(5A), (5B); 1991(2) s.9(1)
(9)	1975(1) s.15(6); 1982(2) s.48(5), Sch.4, para.10

SOCIAL SECURITY CONTRIBUTIONS AND BENEFITS ACT—*continued.*

Section of 1992 Act	Derivation
(10), (11)	1975(1) s.15A(1), (2); 1985 s.18(3)
34(1), (2)	1975(1) s.16(1); 1985 s.9(1)(a)
(3)	1975(1) s.16(2); 1979 s.5, Sch.1, para.10(a)
(4)	1975(1) s.16(2B)(a); 1985 s.9(1)(b); 1986 s.18(1)
(5)	1975(1) s.16(2C)(a); 1985 s.9(1)(b); 1986 s.18(1)
(6)	1975(1) s.16(2D)(a); 1985 s.9(1)(b); 1986 s.18(1)
(7)	1975(1) s.16(3); 1985 s.9(1)(c)
35(1) - (3)	1975(1) s.22(1) - (3); 1986 s.49(2), Sch.4, para.13
(4)	1975(1) s.22(4A); 1988(1) s.16, Sch.4, para.5(b)
(5)	1975(1) s.22(5); 1986 s.49(2), Sch.4, para.13
(6)	1975(1) s.22(6); 1986 ss.49(2), 50, Sch.4, para.13
(7)	1975(1) s.22(7); 1986 s.49(2), Sch.4, para.13
36(1), (2)	1975(1) s.24(1), (2); 1986 s.36(1)
(3)	1975(1) s.24(3); 1989 s.26, Sch.7, para.8
37(1)	1975(1) s.25(1); 1975(2) s.65(1), Sch.4, para.41; 1975(3) s.21(1), Sch.4, para.9(a); Human Fertilisation and Embryology Act 1990 (c.37) s.49, Sch.4, para.2
(2)	1975(1) s.25(2); 1975(3) s.21(1), Sch.4, para.9(b)
(3), (4)	1975(1) s.25(3), (4); 1989 s.31(1), Sch.8, para.4(1)
38(1)	1975(1) s.26(1); 1975(2) s.65(1), Sch.4, para.42; 1986 s.36(3)(a)
(2), (3)	1975(1) s.26(3), (4); 1989 s.31(1), Sch.8, para.4(2)
(4)	1989 s.6(1)
39(1)	1975(2) s.13(1), (3)
(2)	1975(2) s.13(2)
(3)	1986 s.19(1)(c)
(4), (5)	1975(1) s.26(2); 1986 s.36(3)(b)
(6)	1989 s.6(1)
40(1)	1975(2) s.15(1); 1986 s.86, Sch.10, para.70(a)
(2)	1975(2) s.15(1A); 1989 s.26, Sch.7, para.20(1)
(3)	1975(2) s.15(2); 1986 s.86, Sch.10, para.70(b)
(4)	1975(2) s.15(3)
(5)	1975(2) s.15(4); 1986 s.86, Sch.10, para.70(c); 1990 s.4(2)
(6)	1977 s.17(6)
(7)	1975(2) s.15(5); 1977 s.4(4); 1989 s.7, Sch.1, para.10(1)
(8)	1975(2) s.15(6)
(9)	1977 s.24(1) "modifications"
41(1)	1975(2) s.16(1); 1979 s.5, Sch.1, para.18

SOCIAL SECURITY CONTRIBUTIONS AND BENEFITS ACT—*continued.*

Section of 1992 Act	Derivation
(2), (3)	1975(2) s.16(2), (3)
(4), (5)	1975(2) s.16(4); 1990 s.4(3)
(6)	1986 s.19(1)(d)
(7)	1975(2) s.16(5); 1977 s.4(4); 1989 s.7, Sch.1, para.10(2)
(8)	1975(2) s.16(6)
42	1975(2) s.16A; 1991(2) s.9(3)
43(1)	1975(1) s.27(6)
(2)	1977 s.4(1); 1979 s.5, Sch.1, para.8
(3), (4)	1975(2) s.25(1)
(5)	1975(2) s.25(2)
44(1)	1975(1) s.28(1); 1975(2) s.65(1), Sch.4, para.43; 1989 s.31(1), Sch.8, para.4(3)
(2)	1975(1) s.28(1A); 1989 s.31(1), Sch.8, para.4(4)
(3), (4)	1975(2) s.6(1); 1986 s.18(1); Benefits Order art.4(2)
(5)	1975(2) s.6(4); 1979 s.21(4), Sch.3, para.14
(6)	1975(2) s.6(5); 1986 s.75, Sch.8, para.7(1)(a); 1989 s.26, Sch.7, para.19
(7)	1975(2) s.6(6)
(8)	Transitional
45(1)	1975(2) s.6(2); 1986 s.18(1), (2)
(2), (3)	1975(2) s.6(2A); 1986 s.18(3)
(4), (5)	1975(2) s.6(2B); 1986 s.18(3)
(6), (7)	1975(2) ss.6(3), 60A; 1979 s.18; 1986 s.18(4)
(8)	Drafting
46(1)	1986 s.18(6)
(2)	1986 s.18(5)
47(1)	1975(1) s.28(7); 1980(2) s.3(3); 1985 s.9(2)(a),(b)
(2)	1975(1) s.28(7A)(a); 1985 s.9(2)(c); 1986 s.18(1)
(3)	1975(1) s.28(7B)(a); 1985 s.9(2)(c); 1986 s.18(1)
(4)	1975(1) s.28(7C)(a); 1985 s.9(2)(c); 1986 s.18(1)
(5)	1975(1) s.28(8)
(6)	1980(2) s.3(4)
48(1)	1975(2) s.20(1); 1979 s.5, Sch.1, para.5
(2)	1979 s.5, Sch.1, para.20
(3)	1975(2) s.20(2)
49(1)	1975(1) s.29(1)
(2), (3)	1975(1) s.29(2), (3); 1989 s.7(3)(a)

SOCIAL SECURITY CONTRIBUTIONS AND BENEFITS ACT—*continued.*

Section of 1992 Act	Derivation
(4)	1975(1) s.29(4)
(5)	1975(1) s.29(5)
(6)	1975(1) s.29(6)
(7), (8)	1975(1) s.29(9), (9A); 1989 s.31(1), Sch.8, para.4(5)
50(1)	1975(1) s.29(7); 1975(2) s.65(1), Sch.4, para.44
(2)	1975(1) s.29(8); 1985 s.9(3)
(3),(4)	1975(2) s.7
(5)	1986 s.19(1)(a)
51(1)	1975(2) s.8(1); 1979 s.5, Sch.1, paras.4, 14
(2)	1975(2) s.8(2)
(3)	1986 s.19(1)(b)
(4)	1975(2) s.8(3); 1989 s.7, Sch.1, para.9(2)
52(1)	1975(2) s.9(1)
(2), (3)	1975(2) s.9(2), (3); 1986 s.18(1)
(4)	1979 s.5, Sch.1, para.15
53(1)	1975(2) s.10(1)
(2)	1975(2) s.10(2); 1986 s.18(1)
(3)	1979 s.5, Sch.1, para.16
54(1), (2)	1975(1) s.30(3)
(3)	1975(1) s.30(4); 1975(2) s.65(1), Sch.4, para.45
(4)	1975(1) s.30(5); 1989 s.7, Sch.1, para.2(2)
55	1975(2) s.12; 1989 s.7(4)
56(1), (2)	1975(1) s.31; 1975(3) s.21(1), Sch.4, para.10; 1977 s.22(2)
(3), (4)	1975(1) s.43(1); 1975(3) s.21(1), Sch.4, para.15(a)
(5)	1975(1) s.43(2); 1975(3) s.21(1), Sch.4, para.15(b); 1977 s.22(3)
(6)	1986 s.40
57(1)	1975(1) s.17(1); 1980(2) s.3(1); 1989 s.10(2)
(2)	1975(1) s.22(4); 1986 s.49, Sch.4, para.13; 1988(1) s.16, Sch.4, para.5(a)
(3)	1975(1) s.17(2); 1989 s.10(3); R2
(4)	1975(1) s.17(2A); 1988(1) s.16, Sch.4, para.4
(5)	1975(1) s.17(2B); 1989 s.10(4)
(6), (7)	1975(1) s.17(2C), (2D); 1989 s.31(1), Sch.8, para.3
(8)	1975(1) s.17(3)
(9), (10)	1975(1) s.17(4), (5); 1980(2) s.3(4); 1981(2) s.5
58(1)	1989 s.31(1), Sch.8, para.2(1)

SOCIAL SECURITY CONTRIBUTIONS AND BENEFITS ACT—_continued._

Section of 1992 Act	Derivation
(2)	1989 s.31(1), Sch.8, para.2(2), (6) "incapacity benefit"; 1990 s.21(1), Sch.6, para.30(2)
(3)	1989 s.31(1), Sch.8, para.2(3)
(4)	1989 s.31(1), Sch.8, para.2(6); Local Government and Housing Act 1989 (c.42) s.194, Sch.11, para.113; 1990 s.21(1), Sch.6, para.30(4)
(5)	1989 s.31(1), Sch.8, para.2(7)
59(1), (2)	1975(1) s.20(2), (3)
(3)	1975(1) s.20(5)(d) "week"
60(1)	1975(1) s.33(1), (2)
(2), (3)	1986 s.39, Sch.3, para.10; 1988(1) s.2, Sch.1, para 5(b)
(4) - (6)	1975(1) s.33(3); 1975(2) s.65(1), Sch.4, para.46; 1990 s.21(1), Sch.6, para.3(1)
(7)	1975(1) s.33(4); 1975(2) s.19(5); 1986 s.18(1)
(8)	1988(1) s.2, Sch.1, para.5(a)
61(1)	1977 s.8(1); 1986 s.18(1); 1990 s.21(1), Sch.6, para.3(3)
(2)	1977 s.8(2); 1986 s.18(1); 1990 s.21(1), Sch.6, para.3(4)
62(1)	1975(2) s.24(1)(b), (c)
(2)	1975(2) s.24(2)
63	1975(1) s.34; 1984 s.11, Sch.4, para.3; 1990 s.2(3); 1991(2) s.1(1)
64	1975(1) s.35(1); 1988(1) s.1(1); 1991(2) s.2(1)
65(1)	1975(1) s.35(2); 1979 s.2(2); 1989 s.31(1), Sch.8, para.5(2)
(2)	1975(1) s.35(2A); 1979 s.2(3)
(3)	1975(1) s.35(3); 1991(2) s.4, Sch.2, para.3(2)
(4)	1975(1) s.35(4); 1989 s.31(1), Sch.8, para.5(3); 1991(2) s.4, Sch.2, para.3(3)
(5)	1975(1) s.35(4A); 1980(1) s.2, Sch.1, para.8; 1989 s.31(1), Sch.8, para. 5(4); 1991(2) s.4, Sch.2, para.3(3)
(6)	1975(1) s.35(4)(a); 1979 s.2(5); 1989 s.31(1), Sch.8, para.5(3); 1990 s.1(2)
66	1975(1) s.35(2B), (2C); 1990 s.1(1); 1991(2) s.4, Sch.2, para.3(1)
67(1)	1975(1) s.35(5A); 1979 s.2(6)
(2)	1975(1) s.35(6); National Health Service Act 1977 (c.49) s.129, Sch.15, para.63; 1991(2) s.4, Sch.2, para.3(4)
68(1)—(4)	1975(1) s.36; 1984 s.11(1)
(5)	1975(1) s.36(4A); 1985 s.21, Sch.4, para.3
(6), (7)	1975(1) s.36(5), (6); 1984 s.11(1)
(8), (9)	1975(1) s.36(6A), (6B); 1989 s.31(1), Sch.8, para.6
(10)	1975(1) s.36(6C); 1991(2) s.9(2)
(11)	1975(1) s.36(7); 1984 s.11(1); 1989 s.31(1), Sch.8, para.2(5); 1990 s.21(1), Sch.6, para.30(5)

SOCIAL SECURITY CONTRIBUTIONS AND BENEFITS ACT—*continued.*

Section of 1992 Act	Derivation
(12)	1989 s.31(1), Sch.8, para.2(4)
(13)	1975(1) s.36(8); 1984 s.11(1); 1989 s.31(1), Sch.8, para.2(6) "coun-cillor"; "pre-commencement period", (7)
69	1975(1) s.36A; 1990 s.2(1)
70(1)	1975(1) s.37(1)
(2)	1975(1) s.37(2); 1991(2) s.4, Sch.2, para.4.
(3) - (5)	1975(1) s.37(3) - (5)
(6)	1975(1) s.37(6); 1989 s.26, Sch.7, para.10
(7) - (9)	1975(1) s.37(7) - (9)
(10)	1975(1) s.37(6)
71	1975(1) s.37ZA; 1991(2) s.1(2)
72	1975(1) s.37ZB; 1991(2) s.1(2)
73	1975(1) s.37ZC; 1991(2) s.1(2)
74(1)	1977 s.13(1); 1991(2) s.4, Sch.2, para.7
(2)	1977 s.13(3)
75	1975(1) s.37ZD; 1991(2) s.1(2)
76	1975(1) s.37ZE; 1991(2) s.1(2)
77(1)	1975(1) s.38(1); 1975(3) s.21(1), Sch.4, para.12(a)
(2), (3)	1975(1) s.38(2), (3)
(4), (5)	1975(1) s.43(1); 1975(3) s.21(1), Sch.4, para.15(a)
(6)	1975(1) s.43(2); 1975(3) s.21(1), Sch.4, para.15(b); 1977 s.22(3)
(7)	1975(1) s.38(1)
(8)	1975(1) s.38(4)
(9)	1975(1) s.38(5); 1975(3) s.21(1), Sch.4, para.12(c)
(10)	1975(1) s.38(6); 1986 s.45(a)
(11)	1975(1) s.38(7); 1986 s.45(b)
78(1), (2)	1975(1) s.39(1)(a), (b)
(3), (4)	1975(1) s.39(1)(c); 1979 s.5, Sch.1, para.2; 1986 s.18(1)
(5)	1975(1) s.39(2)
(6)	1975(1) s.39(2A); 1985 s.12(1)(b)
(7), (8)	1975(1) s.39(3), (3A); 1989 s.31(1), Sch.8, para.4(6)
(9)	1975(1) s.39(4)
79	1975(1) s.40
80(1)	1975(1) s.41(1); 1975(3) s.21(1), Sch.4, para.13
(2)	1975(1) s.41(2); 1984 s.13, Sch.5, para.3(a)
(3)	1975(1) s.41(2A); 1984 s.13, Sch.5, para.3(c)

Tables of Derivations and Destinations

SOCIAL SECURITY CONTRIBUTIONS AND BENEFITS ACT—*continued.*

Section of 1992 Act	Derivation
(4)	1975(1) s.41(2B); 1984 s.13, Sch.5, para.3(c); Benefits Order 1991 art.11
(5), (6)	1975(1) s.41(4), (5); 1975(3) s.21(1), Sch.4, para.13
(7)	1975(1) s.41(2D); 1984 s.13, Sch.5, para.3(c)
81(1), (2)	1975(1) s.43(1); 1975(3) s.21(1), Sch.4, para.15(a)
(3)	1975(1) s.43(2); 1975(3) s.21(1), Sch.4, para.15(b); 1977 s.22(3)
82(1)	1975(1) s.44(1); 1975(3) s.22(1), Sch.4, para.16(a); 1980(1) s.21, Sch.1, para.5(2); 1988(1) s.16, Sch.4, para.16(a)
(2)	1975(1) s.44(2); 1975(3) s.22(1), Sch.4, para.16(a); 1980(1) s.21, Sch.1, para.5(2)
(3)	1975(1) s.44(3)(a); 1988(1) s.16, Sch.4, para.16(b)
(4)	1975(1) s.44(3)(c); 1975(3) s.22(1), Sch.4, para.16(b); 1980(1) s.2, Sch.1, para.4(a)
(5)	1975(1) s.44(4)
83(1)	1975(1) s.45(1)
(2)	1975(1) s.45(2); 1975(3) s.21(1), Sch.4, para.17; 1988(1) s.16, Sch.4, para.7(a)
(3)	1975(1) s.45(2A); 1985 s.13(1)
84(1)	1975(1) s.45A(1); 1984 s.12; 1985 s.13(2)(a)
(2)	1975(1) s.45A(2); 1985 s.13(2)(b); 1988(1) s.16, Sch.4, para.8(a)
(3)	1975(1) s.45A(3); 1985 s.13(2)(b)
85(1)	1975(1) s.46(1)
(2)	1975(1) s.46(2); 1975(3) s.21(1), Sch.4, para.18; 1980(1) s.2, Sch.1, para.4(b)
(3)	1975(1) s.46(3)
(4)	1975(1) s.46(4); 1985 s.13(3)
86(1)	1975(1) s.47(1); 1975(3) s.21(1), Sch.4, para.19; 1980(1) s.2, Sch.1, para.5(2); 1989 s.31(1), Sch.8, para.7(1)
(2)	1975(1) s.47(1A); 1985 s.13(4)(b)
87(1)	1975(1) s.47A(a); 1980(1) s.2, Sch.1, para.5(1); 1990 s.21(1), Sch.6, para.3(2)
(2)	1975(1) s.47A(b); 1990 s.21(1), Sch.6, para.3(2)
88	1975(1) s.48(1)
89	1975(1) s.47B; 1984 s.14(a); 1989 s.9(3)
90	1975(1) s.49; 1984 s.11, Sch.4, para.3
91	1975(1) s.49A; 1986 s.44(2)
92	1975(1) s.84A; 1989 s.31, Sch.8, para.7(2)
93	1991(2) s.9(5)
94(1)	1975(1) s.50(1); 1986 s.39, Sch.3, para.2
(2)	1975(1) s.50(1A); 1988(1) s.16, Sch.4, para.11
(3)	1975(1) s.50(3)
(4)	1975(1) s.50(4); 1982(2) s.48(5), Sch.4, para.12(2)

SOCIAL SECURITY CONTRIBUTIONS AND BENEFITS ACT—*continued.*

Section of 1992 Act	Derivation
(5)	1975(1) s.50(5)
(6)	1975(1) s.50(6); 1982(2) s.48(5), Sch.4, para.12(3)
95(1) - (3)	1975(1) s.51
(4), (5)	1977 s.17(3)
96	1975(1) s.157
97	1975(1) s.156
98 - 101	1975(1) ss.52 - 55
102(1), (2)	1975(1) s.50A(1), (2); 1982(2) s.39(4)
(3)	1975(1) s.50A(3); 1982(2) s.39(4); 1989 s.7, Sch.1, para.8(1)
103(1)	1975(1) s.57(1); 1986 s.39, Sch.3, para.3(1)
(2) - (4)	1975(1) s.57(1A) - (1C); 1986 s.39, Sch.3, para.3(2)
(5)	1975(1) s.57(3)
(6)	1975(1) s.57(4); 1982(2) s.39(2); 1989 s.26, Sch.7, para. 12
(7), (8)	1975(1) s.57(6); 1986 s.39, Sch.3, para.3(4)
104(1), (2)	1975(1) s.61(1), (2)
(3), (4)	1975(1) s.61(3), (4); 1986 s.39, Sch.3, para.6
105	1975(1) s.63
106	Drafting
107(1)	1975(1) s.91(1); 1982(2) s.48(5), Sch.4, para.15
(2)	1975(1) s.91(2); R3
108(1) - (4)	1975(1) s.76(1) - (4)
(5)	1975(1) s.76(4A); 1990 s.21(1), Sch.6, para.4(1)
(6)	1975(1) s.76(5)
109(1)	1975(1) s.77(1)
(2)	1975(1) s.77(2); 1990 ss.3(7), 21(1), Sch.6, para.4(2)
(3)	1975(1) s.77(3)
(4) - (6)	1975(1) s.77(4); 1986 s.39, Sch.3 para.13
(7)	1975(1) s.77(5); 1986 s.39, Sch.3 para.13
110	1975(1) s.78
111	Drafting
112(1), (2)	1977 s.18(1)
(3)	1977 s.18(2); Employment Protection (Consolidation) Act 1978 (c.44) s.159, Sch.16, para.29(d); 1986 s.86, Sch.10, para.74
113(1), (2)	1975(1) s.82(5), (6)
(3)	1975(1) s.83; 1985 s.29(1), Sch.5, para.8
114(1), (2)	1975(1) s.84(1), (2)

SOCIAL SECURITY CONTRIBUTIONS AND BENEFITS ACT—*continued.*

Section of 1992 Act	Derivation
(3)	1975(1) s.84(4); 1985 s.13(6)
(4)	1975(1) s.84(5); 1985 s.13(8); 1986 s.39, Sch.3, paras.4, 16
115(1)	1975(1) s.127(1)
(2), (3)	1975(1) s.127(2)
(4)	Drafting
116	1975(1) s.128(1) - (3)
117	1975(1) s.129
118	1975(1) s.130
119	1975(1) s.131
120(1)	1975(1) s.132(1)
(2)	1975(1) s.132(2); Oil and Gas (Enterprise) Act 1982 (c.23) s.37, Sch.3, para.21
(3)	1975(1) s.132(3)
121	1975(1) s.162
122(1) "beneficiary"	1975(1) s.168(1), Sch.20, "beneficiary"
"benefit"	1975(1) s.168(1), Sch.20, "benefit"
"child"	1975(1) s.168(1), Sch.20, "child"; 1975(3) s.21(1), Sch.4, para.38
"claim"	1975(1) s.168(1), Sch.20, "claim"
"claimant"	1975(1) s.168(1), Sch.20, "claimant"
"contract ofservice"	1975(1) s.168(1), Sch.20, "contract of service"
"current"	1975(1) s.168(1), Sch.20, "current"
"day of incapacity for work"; "day ofinterruption of employment"; "deferred"; "period of deferment"; "earnings"; "earner"; "employed earner"	Drafting
"employment"; "employed"	1975(1) s.168(1), Sch.20, "employment"; "employed"
"entitled"	1975(1) s.168(1), Sch.20, "entitled"; 1985 s.29(1), Sch.5, para. 14; 1990 s.5(2)
"industrial injuries benefit"	1975(1) s.168(1), Sch.20, "industrial injuries benefit"

SOCIAL SECURITY CONTRIBUTIONS AND BENEFITS ACT—*continued.*

Section of 1992 Act	Derivation
"initial primary percentage"	1975(1) s.168(1), Sch.20, "initial primary percentage"; 1989 s.1(9)
"the Inland Revenue"	1975(1) s.168(1), Sch.20, "the Inland Revenue"
"late husband"	1975(1) s.168(1), Sch.20, "late husband"
"long-term benefit"	Drafting
"loss of physical faculty"	1975(1) s.168(1), Sch.20, "loss of physical faculty"; 1984 s.11, Sch.4, para.11(a)
"lower earnings limit", "upper earnings limit"	1975(1) s.168(1), Sch.20, "lower earnings limit", "upper earnings limit"
"main primary percentage"	1975(1) s.168(1), Sch. 20, "main primary percentage"; 1989 s.1(9)
"medical examination"	1975(1) s.168(1), Sch.20, "medical examination"
"medical treatment"	1975(1) s.168(1), Sch.20, "medical treatment"
"the Northern Ireland Department"	1975(1) s.168(1), Sch.20, "the Northern Ireland Department"
"Old Cases payments"	Drafting
"payments by way of occupational or personal pension"	1975(1) s.168(1), Sch.20 "payments by way of occupational or personal pension"; 1980(2) s.5(3) "payments by way of occupational or personal pension"; 1984 s.21, Sch.7, para.2; 1989 s.9(2), (4)
"pensionable age"	1975(1) ss.27(1), 168(1), Sch.20, "pensionable age"
"pneumoconiosis"	1975(1) s.168(1), Sch.20, "pneumoconiosis"
"prescribe"	1975(1) s.168(1), Sch.20, "prescribe"
"primary percentage"	1975(1) s.168(1), Sch.20, "primary percentage"; 1989 s.1(9)
"qualifying earnings factor""	1975(1) s.168(1), Sch.20, "qualifying earnings factor"; am. 1975(2) s.65, Sch.4, para.64
"relative"	1975(1) s.168(1), Sch.20, "relative"
"relevant accident"	1975(1) s.168(1), Sch.20, "relevant accident"
"relevant injury"	1975(1) s.168(1), Sch.20, "relevant injury"
"relevant loss of faculty"	1975(1) s.168(1), Sch.20, "relevant loss of faculty"; 1984 s.11, Sch.4, para.11(b)

SOCIAL SECURITY CONTRIBUTIONS AND BENEFITS ACT—_continued._

Section of 1992 Act	Derivation
"self-employed earner"; "short-term benefit"	Drafting
"tax week"	1975(1) s.168(1), Sch.20, "tax week"
"tax year"	1975(1) s.168(1), Sch.20, "tax year"; 1990 s.21(1), Sch.6, para.11
"trade or business"	1975(1) s.168(1), Sch.20, "trade or business"
"trade union"	1975(1) s.168(1), Sch.20, "trade union"
"week"	1975(1) s.168(1), Sch.20, "week"; 1991(2) s.9(4)
(2)	1975(1) s.168(1), Sch.20, "employment"; 1989 s.12(5)
(3)	1977 s.22(1)
(4), (5)	1975(1) s.168(1), Sch.20, "entitled to child benefit"; 1975(3) s.21(1), Sch.4, para.38
(6)	1975(1) s.168(1), Sch.20, "permanently incapable of self support"; 1980(1) s.2, Sch.1, para.7
123(1)	1986 s.20(1); 1988(2) s.135, Sch.10, para.2(2); 1991(2) s.6(2)
(2)	1986 s.20(2); 1991(2) s.6(3); S.I.1988/1843 Sch.3, para.4(c)
(3)	1986 s.31(4)
(4) - (6)	1986 s.31G(4) - (6); 1988(2) s.135, Sch.10, para.6
124(1)	1986 s.20(3); 1988(1) s.4(1); 1989 s.13(1)
(2)	1986 s.20(4N); 1988(1) s.4(2)
(3)	1986 s.20(4)
(4)	1986 s.21(1); 1988(1) s.16, Sch.4, para.23(1)
(5), (6)	1986 s.21(1A), (1B); 1988(1) s.16, Sch.4, para.23(2)
125(1) - (4)	1986 s.20(4A) - (4D); 1988(1) s.4(2)
(5)	1986 s.20(4N); 1988(1) s.4(2)
126(1) - (4)	1986 s.23(1) - (4)
(5)	1986 s.23(5); Income and Corporation Taxes Act 1988 (c.1) s.844, Sch.29, para.32
(6)	1986 s.23(5A); 1988(1) s.16, Sch.4, para.24(1)
(7)	1986 s.23(6); 1990 s.21(1), Sch.6, para.17(2) Benefits Order art.16
(8)	1986 s.23(7); 1990 s.21(1), Sch.6, para.17(3)
127	1986 s.23A; 1988(1) s.16, Sch.4, para.25; 1989 s.31(1), Sch.8, para.16
128(1)	1986 s.20(5), (5A); 1988(1) s.3(a); 1991(2) s.8(1)
(2)	1986 s.21(2), (3)
(3)	1986 s.20(6); 1989 s.31(1), Sch.8, para.15(1)
(4)	1986 s.20(10); 1991(2) s.8(2)
(5)	1986 s.21(6)(a)

SOCIAL SECURITY CONTRIBUTIONS AND BENEFITS ACT —*continued.*

Section of 1992 Act	Derivation
(6)	1986 s.79(3)
129(1)	1986 s.20(6A), (6D); 1991(2) s.6(4)
(2), (3)	1986 s.20(6B), (6C); 1991(2) s.6(4)
(4)	1986 s.20(6E); 1991(2) s.6(4)
(5)	1986 s.21(3A), (3B); 1991(2) s.6(8)
(6)	1986 s.20(6F); 1991(2) s.6(4)
(7)	1986 s.27B(4); 1991(2) s.7(1)
(8)	1986 s.21(6)(aa); 1991(2) s.6(9)
(9)	1986 s.79(3); 1991(2) s.7, Sch.3, para.7
130(1), (2)	1986 s.20(7), (8)
(3)	1986 s.21(4), (5)
(4), (5)	1986 s.21(6); Housing (Scotland) Act 1988 (c.43) s.70(3); Housing Act 1988 (c.50) s.121(4)
131(1)	1986 s.20(8A); 1988(2) s.135, Sch.10, para.2(3)
(2)	1986 s.20(8AA); 1989 s.31(1), Sch.8, para.9(2)
(3) - (9)	1986 s.20(8B) - (8H); 1988(2) s.135, Sch.10, para.2(3)
(10), (11)	1986 s.21(5A), (5B); 1988(2) s.135, Sch.10, para.3(2)
(12)	1986 s.21(6)(c); 1988(2) s.135, Sch.10, para.3(3)
132	1986 s.22A; 1988(2) s.135, Sch.10, para.5
133(1)	1986 s.22B(1); 1988(2) s.135, Sch.10, para.5; 1989 s.31(1), Sch.8, para.9(3)
(2) - (4)	1986 s.22B(2) - (4); 1988(2) s.135, Sch.10, para.5
134(1)	1986 s.22(6)
(2)	1986 s.20(9)
(3)	1986 s.20(9A); 1988(2) s.135, Sch.10, para.2(4)
(4)	1986 s.21(7)
135(1), (2)	1986 s.22(1), (2)
(3), (4)	1986 s.22(2A), (2B); 1990 s.9
(5)	1986 s.22(3); 1988(2) s.135, Sch.10, para.4(2)
(6)	1986 s.22(4)
136(1)	1986 s.22(5)
(2), (3)	1986 s.22(7), (8)
(4)	1986 s.22(8A); 1988(2) s.135, Sch.10, para.4(3)
(5)	1988 s.22(9)
137(1) "charging authority"	1986 s.20(11) "charging authority"; 1988(2) s.135, Sch.10, para.2(5)
"child"	1986 s.20(11) "child"; 1989 s.5(1)

SOCIAL SECURITY CONTRIBUTIONS AND BENEFITS ACT—*continued.*

Section of 1992 Act	Derivation
"contribution period"	1986 s.20(11) "contribution period"; 1988(2) s.135, Sch.10, para.2(5)
"dwelling"	1986 s.84(1) "dwelling"
"family"	1986 s.20(11) "family"
"industrial injuries scheme"	1986 s.20(11) "industrial injuries scheme"; 1991(2) s.6(6)(a)
"levying authority"	1986 s.20(11) "levying authority"; 1988(2) s.135, Sch.10, para.2(5)
"married couple"	1986 s.20(11) "married couple"
"the 1987 Act", "the 1988 Act"	Drafting
"prescribed"	1986 s.84(1) "prescribed"
"unmarried couple"	1986 s.20(11) "unmarried couple"
"war pension scheme"	1986 s.20(11) "war pension scheme"; 1991(2) s.6(6)(b)
"week"	1986 s.20(11) "week"; 1988(2) s.135, Sch.10, para.2(5)
(2)	1986 s.20(12); 1989 s.13(2); 1991(2) s.6(7)
138(1)	1986 s.32(2); 1987 s.1
(2)	1986 s.32(2A); 1988(1) s.11, Sch. 3, para. 2
(3)	1986 s.33(1A); 1988(1) s.11, Sch. 3, para. 10
(4)	1986 s.84(1) "prescribed"
139(1) - (3)	1986 s.33(2) - (4)
(4)	1986 s.33(4A); 1988(1) s.11, Sch. 3, para. 11
(5)	1986 s.33(11)
140(1)	1986 s.33(9); 1988(1) s.11, Sch. 3, para. 12
(2)	1986 s.33(10)
(3)	1986 s.33(10ZA); 1990 s.10(3)
(4)	1986 s.33(10A); 1988(1) s.11, Sch. 3, para.13; 1990 s.10(4)
(5)	1986 s.32(11); 1988(1) s.11, Sch.3, para.7
141	1975(3) s.1(1)
142(1)	1975(3) s.2(1); 1986 s.70(1)(a); 1988(1) s.4(3)
(2), (3)	1975(3) s.2(1A), (1B); 1986 s.70(1)(b)
(4), (5)	1975(3) s.2(2), (3)
143(1), (2)	1975(3) s.3(1), (2)

SOCIAL SECURITY CONTRIBUTIONS AND BENEFITS ACT—*continued.*

Section of 1992 Act	Derivation
(3)	1975(3) s.3(3); National Health Service and Community Care Act 1990 (c.19) s.66(1), Sch.9, para.15
(4), (5)	1975(3) s.3(4), (5)
144(1), (2)	1975(3) s.4(1); 1988(1), s.4(4)
(3)	1975(3) s.4(2)
145(1) - (4)	1975(3) s.5(1) - (4)
(5)	1975(3) s.22(1)(a)
(6)	1975(3) s.22(8)
(7)	1975(3) s.22(9)
146	1975(3) s.13
147(1) "prescribed"	1975(3) s.24(1) "prescribed"
"recognised educational establishment"	1975(3) s.24(1) "recognised educational establishment"
"voluntary organisation"	1975(3) s.24(1) "voluntary organisation"
"week"	1975(3) s.24(1) "week"
(2)	1975(3) s.24(2)
(3)	1975(3) s.24(3)(b)
(4)	1975(3) s.24(4)
(5)	1975(3) s.9(2)
(6)	1975(3) s.24(5)
148	1986 s.66, Sch.6, para.2
149	1986 s.66, Sch.6, para.3
150(1)	1986 s.66, Sch.6, para.1(1)
(2) "attendance allowance"	1986 s.66, Sch.6, para.1(2) "attendance allowance"; 1991(2) s.4, Sch.2, para.16
"pensionable age"	1986 s.66, Sch.6, para.1(2) "pensionable age"
"retirement pension"	1986 s.66, Sch.6, para.1(2) "retirement pension"
"unemployability supplement or allowance"	1986 s.66, Sch.6, para.1(2) "unemployability supplement or allowance"; Income and Corporation Taxes Act 1988 (c.1) s.844, Sch.29, para.32, Table
"war disablement pension"	1986 s.84(1) "war disablement pension"; Income and Corporation Taxes Act 1988 s.844, Sch.29, para.32, Table
"war widow's pension"	1986 s.84(1) "war widow's pension"; Income and Corporation Taxes Act 1988 s.844, Sch.29, para.32, Table

SOCIAL SECURITY CONTRIBUTIONS AND BENEFITS ACT—*continued.*

Section of 1992 Act	Derivation
(3)	1986 s.66, Sch.6, para.1(2) "married couple"; "unmarried couple"
(4)	1986 s.66, Sch.6, para.1(3)
151(1), (2)	1982(2) s.1(1), (2)
(3)	1982(2) s.23A(1); 1984 s.21, Sch.7, para.8
(4), (5)	1982(2) s.1(3), (4)
(6)	1982(2) s.1(5); 1986 s.68
152(1), (2)	1982(2) s.2(1), (2)
(3)	1982(2) s.2(3); The Statutory Sick Pay (General) Regulations 1982 (S.I.1982/894) reg.2A; The Statutory Sick Pay (General) Amendment Regulations 1986 (S.I.1986/477) reg.2
(4)	1982(2) s.2(3A); 1985 s.18(4)
(5), (6)	1982(2) s.2(4), (5)
153(1) - (4)	1982(2) s.3(1) - (4)
(5)	1982(2) s.3(4A); 1985 s.18(5)
(6), (7)	1982(2) s.3(5), (6)
(8), (9)	1982(2) s.3(6A), (6B); 1985 s.29(1), Sch.4, para.4
(10), (11)	1982(2) s.3(7), (8)
(12)	1982(2) s.3(9); 1986 s.86, Sch.10, para.77
154(1)	1982(2) s.4(1)
(2)	1982(2) s.4(2); 1984 s.21, Sch.7, para.7
(3), (4)	1982(2) s.4(3), (4)
155(1) - (3)	1982(2) s.5(1) - (3)
(4)	1982(2) s.5(4); 1985 s.18(1)
(5)	1982(2) s.5(5)
156	1982(2) s.6
157(1)	1982(2) s.7(1) Sick Pay Order reg.2
(2)	1982(2) s.7(1A); 1986 s.67(1); 1990 s.21(1), Sch.6, para.15(1)
(3)	1982(2) s.7(2)
158(1)	1982(2) s.9(1); 1991(1) s.1(1)
(2)	1982(2) s.9(1B); 1991(1) s.2(1)
(3)	1982(2) s.9(1D); 1991(1) s.2(1)
(4)	1982(2) s.9(2); 1991(1) s.2(2)
(5)	1982(2) s.9(3)(b), (c); 1991(1) s.1(3)
(6)	1982(2) s.9(6)
(7)	1991(1) s.2(5)
159	1982(2) s.9(1C); 1991(1) s.2(1)

SOCIAL SECURITY CONTRIBUTIONS AND BENEFITS ACT—*continued.*

Section of 1992 Act	Derivation
160	Drafting
161(1), (2)	1982(2) s.27(1), (2)
(3)	1982(2) s.27(3); 1989 s.26, Sch.7, para.23
162	1982(2) s.22; Oil and Gas (Enterprise) Act 1982 (c.23) s.37, Sch.3, para.44; R4
163(1) "contract of service"	1982(2) s.26(1) "contract of service"
"employee"	1982(2) s.26(1) "employee"
"employer"	1982(2) s.26(1) "employer"; 1985 s.29(1), Sch.4 para.6
"period of entitlement"; "period of incapacity for work"; "period of interruption of employment"	Drafting
"prescribed"	1982(2) s.26(1) "prescribed"
"qualifying day"	Drafting
"week"	1982(2) s.26(1) "week"
(2)	1982(2) s.26(2); 1985 s.29(1), Sch.4, para.7
(3) - (5)	1982(2) s.26(3) - (5)
(6)	1982(2) s.26(5A); 1990 s.21(1), Sch.6, para.16
(7)	1982(2) s.26(6)
164(1) - (5)	1986 s.46(1) - (5)
(6), (7)	1982(2) s.23A(1); 1984 s.21, Sch.7, para.8; 1986 s.46(6)
(8)	1986 s.46(7)
(9)	1986 s.46(8); 1988(1) s.16, Sch.4, para.16(1)
(10)	1986 s.46(9); 1988(1) s.16, Sch.4, para.16(2)
165(1) - (6)	1986 s.47(1) - (6)
(7)	1986 s.47(7); 1989 s.26, Sch.7, para.25
166(1)	1986 s.48(1)
(2)	1986 s.48(2); 1988(1), s.16, Sch.4, para.17
(3) - (8)	1986 s.48(3) - (8)
167(1)	1986 s.49, Sch.4, para.1
(2)	R5
(3)	1986 s.49, Sch.4, para.2
(4)	1986 s.49, Sch.4, para.5
168	Drafting

SOCIAL SECURITY CONTRIBUTIONS AND BENEFITS ACT—*continued.*

Section of 1992 Act	Derivation
169	1986 s.79(4)
170	1986 s.80; R4
171(1) "confinement"	1986 s.50(1) "confinement"
"dismissed"	1986 s.50(1) "dismissed"
"employee"	1986 s.50(1) "employee"
"employer"	1986 s.50(1) "employer"
"maternity pay period"	Drafting
"modifications"	1986 s.84(1) "modifications"
"prescribed"	1986 s.84(1) "prescribed"
"week"	1986 s.50(1) "week"
(2)	1986 s.50(2)
(3)	1986 s.50(2A); 1990 s.21(1), Sch.6, para.22
(4) - (6)	1986 s.50(3) - (5)
172	1982(2) ss.26(7), 44(1)(b), (c), (d), (2)(a), (b); 1986 s.84(4)
173	1975(1), s.168(1), Sch.20 "age"; 1980(1), s.18; 1980(2) s.5(6); 1991(1) s.3(1)(b)
174	Drafting
175(1)	1975(1) s.168(1), Sch.20 "regulations"; 1975(3) s.22(1)(b); 1977 s.24(1) "regulations"; 1980(2) ss.3(4), 5(3) "regulations"; 1982(2) s.47 "regulations"; 1986 s.84(1) "regulations"; 1989 s.30(1) "regulations"
(2)	1975(1) s.166(1); 1975 (Old Cases) ss.4(8), 8(1); 1975(3) s.22(2); 1977 s.24(3); 1980(2) s.7(3); 1982(2) s.45(2); 1986 s.83(1); 1989 s.29(1); 1990 s.21(1), Sch.6, paras. 8(7), 12
(3)	1975(1) ss.162, 166(2); 1975(3) s.22(6); 1977 s.24(3); 1980(2) s.7(3); 1982(2) s.45(1); 1986 s.83(1); 1989 s.29(1)
(4)	1975(1) s.166(3); 1975(3) s.22(7); 1977 s.24(3); 1980(2) s.7(3); 1982(2) s.45(1); 1986 s.83(1); 1989 ss.29(1), 31(1), Sch.8, para.10(1); R6
(5)	1975(1) s.166(3A); 1975(3) s.22(7A); 1977 s.24(3); 1986 ss.62(1), (2), 83(1); 1989 s.29(1)
(6)	1986 s.83(2); 1988(2) s.135, Sch.10, para.11(2)
(7)	1975(1) s.166(5); 1977 s.24(3); 1982(2) s.45(1); 1986 s.83(6); 1989 s.29(6); R7
(8)	1975(1) s.166(6)
(9)	1975(1) s.166(7)
(10)	1975(1) s.168(4)
176(1)	1975(1) s.167(1); 1975(2) s.62(1); 1975(3) s.22(3); 1980(2) s.5(4); 1982(2) ss.7(1B), 9(1F); 1986 ss.43(3)(b), 62(3), 67(1), 83(3)(e); 86, Sch.10, para.65; 1989 s.9(1); 1990 s.21(1), Sch.6, paras.8(2), (3), (5), 15(2); 1991(1) s.2(1); R15
(2)	1975(1) s.167(2); 1975(3) s.22(4); 1990 s.21(2), Sch.6, para.8(1), (3)

SOCIAL SECURITY CONTRIBUTIONS AND BENEFITS ACT—*continued.*

Section of 1992 Act	Derivation
(3)	1975(1) s.167(3); 1975 (Old Cases) ss.4(8), 8(1); 1975(3) s.22(5); 1977 s.24(5); 1980(2) s.7(4); 1982(2) s.45(2); 1986 s.83(4); 1989 s.29(3); 1990 s.21(1), Sch.6, para.8(1), (3), (4), (6), (7), (9), (12)
177(1)	Short title
(2)	Commencement
(3), (4)	1975(1) ss.9(3), 169(2)
Sch. 1	
para.1(1)	1975(1) s.1(4), Sch.1, para.1(1); 1977 s.1(3)
(2)	1975(1) s.1(4), Sch.1, para.1(1A); 1980(1) s.2, Sch.1, para.16; 1985 s.29(1), Sch.5, para.13(a)
(4)	1975(1) s.1(4), Sch.1, para.1(1B), (1C); 1985 s.29(1), Sch.5, para.13(b)
(5)	1986 s.74(5)
(6)	1975(1) s.1(4), Sch.1 para.1(1D); 1985 s.29(1), Sch.5, para.13(b)
(7), (8)	1975(1) s.1(4), Sch.1, para.1(2), (3)
para.2	1975(1) s.1(4), Sch.1, para.2
para.3(1)	1975(1) s.1(4), Sch.1, para.3(1)
(2)	1975(1) s.1(4), Sch.1, para.3(2); Criminal Justice Act 1982 (c.48) ss.38, 46, 54; Criminal Procedure (Scotland) Act 1975 (c.21) ss.289F, 289G
(3)	1975(1) s.1(4), Sch.1, para.3(3)
para.4	1975(1) s.1(4), Sch.1, para.4; 1977 s.1(4)
para.5	1975(1) s.1(4), Sch.1, para.4A; 1991(3) s.2(2)
para.6(1)	1975(1) s.1(4), Sch.1, para.5(1); 1991(3) s.2(3)(a)
(2)	1975(1) s.1(4), Sch.1, para.5(1A); 1990 s.17(5); 1991(3) s.2(3)(b)
(3), (4)	1975(1) s.1(4), Sch.1, para.5(1B), (1C); 1990 s.17(5)
(5)	1982(2) s.9(4); 1986 s.49, Sch.4, para.3
(6)	1982(2) s.9(5); 1985 s.19; 1986 s.49, Sch.4, para.4
(7)	1975(1) s.1(4), Sch.1, para.5(2)
(8)	1975(1) s.1(4), Sch.1, para.5(3); 1990 s.17(6)
para.7(1) - (10)	1975(1) s.1(4), Sch.1, para.5A(1) - (10); 1990 s.17(7), Sch.5
(11)	1975(1) s.1(4), Sch.1, para.5A(11); 1990 s.17(7), Sch.5; 1991(3) s.2(4)
(12), (13)	1975(1) s.1(4), Sch.1, para.5A(12), (13); 1990 s.17(7), Sch.5
para.8(1)(a)	1975(1) s.1(4), Sch.1, para.6(1)(a)
(b)	1975(1) s.1(4), Sch.1, para.6(1)(aa); 1991(3) s.2(5)(a)
(c) - (f)	1975(1) s.1(4), Sch.1, para.6(1)(b) - (e)
(g)	1975(1) s.1(4), Sch.1, para.6(1)(f); 1975(2) s.65(1), Sch.4, para.61
(h)	1975(1) s.1(4), Sch.1, para.6(1)(gg); 1989 s.2
(i)	1975(1) s.1(4), Sch.1, para.6(1)(ggg); 1991(3) s.2(5)(c)

SOCIAL SECURITY CONTRIBUTIONS AND BENEFITS ACT—*continued.*

Section of 1992 Act	Derivation
(j), (k)	1975(1) s.1(4), Sch.1, para.6(1)(gh), (gj); 1990 s.21(1), Sch.6, para.9
(l)	1975(1) s.1(4), Sch.1, para.6(1)(g); 1991(3) s.2(5)(b)
(m)	1975(1) s.1(4), Sch.1, para.6(1)(h); 1986 s.86, Sch.10, para.10
(n) - (q)	1975(1) s.1(4), Sch.1, para.6(1)(j) - (m)
(2), (3)	1975(1) s.1(4), Sch.1, para.6(2), (3)
paras.9, 10	1975 (1) s.1(4), Sch.1, paras.7, 8
para.11	1975(1) s.1(4), Sch.1, para.9; 1982(2) s.37(2)
Sch. 2	
para.1	Drafting
para.2	1975(1) s.9(4), Sch.2, para.2; Capital Allowances Act 1990 (c.1) s.164, Sch.1, para.2
para.3(1), (2)	1975(1) s.9(4), Sch.2, para.3(1), (2); Income and Corporation Taxes Act 1988 s.844, Sch.29, para.32, Table
(3)	1975(1) s.9(4), Sch.2, para.3(3)
(4)	1975(1) s.9(4), Sch.2, para.3(3); Finance Act 1988 (c.39) s.35, Sch.3, para.31
(5)	1975(1) s.9(4), Sch.2, para.3(4); Income and Corporation Taxes Act 1988 s.844, Sch.29, para.32, Table
paras.4, 5	1975 (1) s.9(4), Sch.2, paras.5, 6; Income and Corporation Taxes Act 1988 s.844, Sch.29, para.32, Table
para.6(1)	1975(1) s.9(4), Sch.2, para.7(1); Income and Corporation Taxes Act 1988, s.844, Sch.29, para.32, Table; 1990 s.17(8)
(2)	1975(1) s.9(4), Sch.2, para.7(2); 1990 s.17(9)
paras.7, 8	1975(1) s.9(4), Sch.2 paras.8, 9
para.9	1975(1) s.9(4), Sch.2, para.4; Income and Corporation Taxes Act 1988 s.844, Sch.29, para.32, Table; Finance Act 1988 (c.39) s.145, Sch.14, Part VIII and Note 6
Sch. 3	
para.1(1)	1975(1) s.13(6), Sch.3, para.1(1)
(2)	1975(1) s.13(6), Sch.3, para.1(2); 1986 s.75, Sch.8, para.3(1); 1988(1) s.6(2)(a)
(3)	1975(1) s.13(6), Sch.3, para.1(3); 1986 s.75, Sch.8, para.3(2), (3); 1988(1) s.6(2)(b)
(4)	1975(1) s.13(6), Sch.3, para.1(2)(b)(i); 1986 s.75, Sch.8, para.3(1)
(5)	1975(1) s.13(6), Sch.3, para.1(3)(b)(i); 1986 s.75, Sch.8, para.3(3)
(6)	1975(1) s.13(6), Sch.1, para.1(4)
para.2(1)	1975(1) s.13(6), Sch.3, para.1(1)
(2)	1975(1) s.13(6), Sch.3, para.1(2); 1986 s.75, Sch.8, para.3(1); 1988(1) s.6(2)(a)
(3)	1975(1) s.13(6), Sch.3, para.1(3); 1986 s.75, Sch.8, para.3(2), (3); 1988(1) s.6(2)(b)
(4)	1975(1) s.13(6), Sch.3, para.1(2)(b)(ii); 1986 s.75, Sch.8, para.3(1)
(5)	1975(1) s.13(6), Sch.3, para.1(3)(b)(ii); 1986 s.75, Sch.8, para.3(3)

SOCIAL SECURITY CONTRIBUTIONS AND BENEFITS ACT—*continued.*

Section of 1992 Act	Derivation
(6)	1975(1) s.13(6), Sch.1, para.1(4)
para.3(1)	1975(1) s.13(6), Sch.3, para.3(1); 1986 s.49, Sch.4, para.14; 1990 s.21(1), Sch.6, para.10(1)
(2), (3)	1975(1) s.13(6), Sch.3, para.3(2), (3); 1990 s.21(1), Sch.6, para.10(2)
para.4(1), (2)	1975(1) s.13(6), Sch.3, para.4(1); 1986 ss.75, 86, Sch.8, para.3(4), Sch.10, para.66(a)
(3)	1975(1) s.13(6), Sch.3, para.4(2)
para.5(1)	1975(1) s.13(6), Sch.3, para.5(1)
(2)	1975(1) s.13(6), Sch.3, para.5(2); 1975(2) s.19(2); 1986 s.75 Sch.8, para.3(5)
(3), (4)	1975(1) s.13(6), Sch.3, para.5(3); 1986 s.75, Sch.8, para.3(6)
(5), (6)	1975(1) s.13(6), Sch.3, para.5(4), (5)
(7)	1975(1) s.13(6), Sch.3, para.5(6); 1979 s.5, Sch.1, para.3
(8)	1975(1) s.27(2)
para.6	1975(1) s.31(6), Sch.3, para.6
para.7(1)	1975(1) s.13(8), Sch.3, para.8(1); 1989 s.26, Sch.7, para.16
(2)	1975(1) s.13(8), Sch.3, para.8(2); 1986 s.86, Sch.10, para.66(b)
(3), (4)	1975(1) s.13(8), Sch.3, para.8(3); 1979 s.21(4), Sch.3, para.10; 1986 ss.75, 86, Sch.8, para.3(7), Sch.10, para.66(b)
para.8	1975(1) s.13(8), Sch.3, para.10
para.9	1975(1) s.13(8), Sch.3, para.13; 1986 s.86, Sch.10, para.66(c)
Sch. 4	
Part I	
para.1	1975(1) s.14, Sch.4, Part I, para.1(a); Benefits Order art.3(2), (3), Sch.1
para.2	1975(1) s.14, Sch.4, Part I, para.1(b); Benefits Order art.3(2), (3), Sch.1
para.3	1975(1) s.16, Sch.4, Part I, para.3; Benefits Order art.3(2), (3), Sch.1
para.4	1975(1) s.22, Sch.4, Part I, para.4; Benefits Order art.3(2), (3), Sch.1
para.5	1975(1) s.29(7), Sch.4, Part I, para.9; 1975(2), s.65(1), Sch.4, para.62; Benefits Order art.3(2), (3), Sch.1
para.6	1975(1) s.31, Sch.4, Part I, para.10; Benefits Order art.3(2), (3), Sch.1
Part II	1975(1) s.24, Sch.4, Part IA; 1986 s.36(2)
Part III	
para.1	1975(1) s.35, Sch.4, Part III, para.1; Benefits Order art.3(2), (3), Sch.1
para.2	1975(1) s.36, Sch.4, Part III, para.2; 1984 s.11, Sch.4, para.3; Benefits Order art.3(2), (3), Sch.1
para.3	1975(1) s.36A, Sch.4, Part III, para.2A; 1990 s.2(2); Benefits Order art.3(2), (3), Sch.1
para.4	1975(1) s.37, Sch.4, Part III, para.3; Benefits Order art.3(2), (3), Sch.1
para.5	1975(1) s.38, Sch.4, Part III, para.4; Benefits Order art.3(2), (3), Sch.1

SOCIAL SECURITY CONTRIBUTIONS AND BENEFITS ACT—*continued.*

Section of 1992 Act	Derivation
para.6	1975(1) s.39, Sch.4, Part III, para.5; Benefits Order art.3(2), (3), Sch.1
para.7	1975(1) s.39, Sch.4, Part III, para.5A; 1985 s.12(2); Benefits Order art.3(2), (3), Sch.1
para.8	1975(1) s.40, Sch.4, Part III, para.6
Part IV	
col.(1)	1975(1) ss.41-49, Sch.4, Part IV, col.(1); 1984 s. 11, Sch.4, para.3; Benefits Order art.3(2), (3), Sch.1
col.(2)	1975 ss.41-49, Sch.4, Part IV, col.(2); Benefits Order art.3(2), (3), Sch.1
col.(3)	1975(1) ss.41-49, Sch.4, Part IV, col.(3); Benefits Order art.3(2), (3), Sch.1
Part V	
para.1	1975(1) s.57(6), Sch.4, Part V, para.3; Benefits Order art.3(2), (3), Sch.1
para.2	1975(1) s.61, Sch.4, Part V, para.7; Benefits Order art.3(2), (3), Sch.1
para.3	1975(1) s.63, Sch.4, Part V, para.8; Benefits Order art.3(2), (3), Sch.1
para.4	1975(1) s.91, Sch.4, Part V, para.16; Benefits Order art.3(2), (3), Sch.1
para.5	1975(1) s.58, Sch.4, Part V, para.4; Benefits Order art.3(2), (3), Sch.1
para.6	1975(1) s.59, Sch.4, Part V, para.5; 1979 s.5, Sch.1, para.13; Benefits Order art.3(2), (3), Sch.1
para.7	1975(1) s.64, Sch.4, Part V, para.10; Benefits Order art.3(2), (3), Sch.1
para.8	1975(1) s.66(2), Sch.4, Part V, para.12; Benefits Order art.3(2), (3), Sch.1
para.9	1975(1) s.57(5), Sch.4, Part V, para.2; Benefits Order art.3(2), (3), Sch.1
para.10	1975(1) s.68, Sch.4, Part V, para.13; 1975(2) s.65(1), Sch.4, para.63; Benefits Order art.3(2), (3), Sch.1
para.11	1975(1) s.69, Sch.4, Part V, para.14; Benefits Order art.3(2), (3), Sch.1
para.12	1975(1) s.70, Sch.4, Part V, para.15; Benefits Order art.3(2), (3), Sch.1
Sch. 5	
para.1	1975(2) s.12, Sch.1, para.1; 1989 s.7, Sch.1, para.3(1)
para.2(1)	1975(2) s.12, Sch.1, para.2(1); 1989 s.7, Sch.1, para.3(2)
(2)	1975(2) s.12, Sch.1, para.2(2); 1989 s.7, Sch.1, para.3(3)
(3)	1975(2) s.12, Sch.1, para.2(3); 1977 s.3(1)(b); 1989 s.7, Sch.1, para.3(4)
(4)	1975(2) s.60A; 1979 s.18
(5)	1975(2) s.12, Sch.1, para.2(4); 1977 s.3(1)(c); 1980(1) s.3(11)
(6)	1975(2) s.12, Sch.1, para.2(4A); 1985 s.9(5)
(7)	1975(2) s.12, Sch.1, paras.2(5); 1986 s.86, Sch.10, para.95(a); 1989 s.7, Sch.1, para.3(5)
(8)	1975(2) s.12, Sch.1, para.2(6); 1977 s.3(1)(d); 1989 s.7, Sch.1, para.3(6)
para.3	1975(2) s.12, Sch.1, para.3; 1977 s.3(1)(e); 1989 s.7, Sch.1, para.3(7)

SOCIAL SECURITY CONTRIBUTIONS AND BENEFITS ACT—*continued.*

Section of 1992 Act	Derivation
para.4(1)	1975(2) s.12, Sch.1, para.4(1); 1979 s.21(4), Sch.3, para.23; 1986 s.19(2)(a); 1989 s.7, Sch.1, para.3(8)
(2)	1975(2) s.12, Sch.1, para.4(2); 1979 s.21(4), Sch.3, para.23; 1986 s.19(2)(a); 1989 s.7, Sch.1, para.3(8)
(3)	1975(2) s.12, Sch.1, para.4(2A); 1986 s.19(2)(b)
(4)	1975(2) s.12, Sch.1, para.4(3); 1979 s.5, Sch.1, para.6; 1986 s.86, Sch.10, para.95(a)
(5)	1975(2) s.12, Sch.1, para.4(4); 1979 s.5, Sch.1, para.22
para.5(1), (2)	1975(2) s.12, Sch.1, para.4A(1); 1979 s.5, Sch.1, para.7; 1986 s.19(3)
(3)	1975(2) s.12, Sch.1, para.4A(1A); 1986 s.19(4)
para.6(1), (2)	1975(2) s.12, Sch.1, para.4A(2); 1979 s.5, Sch.1, para.7; 1986 s.19(5)
(3)	1975(2) s.12, Sch.1, para.4A(2A)(a); 1986 s.19(6)
(4)	1975(2) s.12, Sch.1, para.4A(2A)(b); 1986 s.19(6)
para.7(1)	1975(2) s.12, Sch.1, para.4A(3); 1979 s.5, Sch.1, para.7; 1986 s.86, Sch.10, para.95(b)
(2)	1975(2) s.60A; 1979 s.18
para.8(1), (2)	1975(2) s.12, Sch.1, para.5(1), (2); 1989 Sch.1, para.3(9)
(3)	1975(2) s.12, Sch.1, para.5(3); 1989 s.7, Sch.1, para.3(10)
(4)	1975(2) s.12, Sch.1, para.5(4)
para.9	Drafting
Sch. 6	
para.1	1975(1) s.57(3), Sch.8, para.1; 1984 s.11, Sch.4, para.10(a)
paras.2, 3	1975(1) s.57(3), Sch.8, paras.2, 3
para.4	1975(1) s.57(3), Sch.8, para.4A; 1984 s.11, Sch.4, para.10(b)
para.5	1975(1) s.57(3), Sch.8, para.5A; 1984 s.11, Sch.4, para.10(c)
para.6(1), (2)	1975(1) s.57(3), Sch.8, para.4(1); 1982(2) s.48(5), Sch.4, para.17
(3) - (5)	1975(1) s.57(3), Sch.8, para.4(2) - (4); 1989 s.21, Sch.3, para.13(1)
para.7	1975(1) s.57(3), Sch.8, para.5; 1989 s.21, Sch.3, para.13(2)
para.8	1975(1) s.57(3), Sch.8, para.6
Sch. 7	
Part I	
para.1	1986 s.39, Sch.3, para.4
para.2	1975(1) s.58
para.3(1)	1975(1) s.59(1); 1985 s.9(4)(a); 1986 s.39, Sch.3, para.4
(2)	1975(1) s.59(1A)(a); 1985 s.9(4)(b); 1986 s.18(1)
(3)	1975(1) s.59(1B)(a); 1985 s.9(4)(b); 1986 s.18(1)
(4)	1975(1) s.59(1C)(a); 1985 s.9(4)(b); 1986 s.18(1)

SOCIAL SECURITY CONTRIBUTIONS AND BENEFITS ACT—*continued.*

Section of 1992 Act	Derivation
(5), (6)	1975(1) s.59(2), (3)
(7), (8)	1975(1) s.59(4); 1980(2) s.3(3)
(9)	1980(2) s.3(4)
(10)	1975(1) s.59(5)
(11)	Drafting
para.4(1)	1975(1) s.64(1); 1975(3) s.21(1), Sch.4, para.21(a); 1986 s.39, Sch.3, para.4
(2)	1975(1) s.64(2)
(3)	1975(1) s.64(1A); 1984 s.13, Sch.5, para.4
(4)	1975(1) s.64(1B); 1984 s.13, Sch.5, para.4; Social Security (Industrial Injuries) (Dependency) (Permitted Earnings Limits) Order 1991 (S.I.1991/546) art.2
(5), (6)	1975(1) s.64(1C), (1D); 1984 s.13, Sch.5, para.4
para.5(1)	1975(1) s.65(1); 1975(3) s.21(1), Sch.4, para.22(a); 1986 s.39, Sch.3, para.4
(2)	1975(1) s.65(2); 1975(3) s.21(1), Sch.4, para.22(b); 1977 s.22(3)
para.6(1)	1975(1) s.66(1); 1975(3) s.21(1), Sch.4, para.23; 1980(1) s.5, Sch.1, paras.4 and 6; 1986 s.39, Sch.3, para.4
(2)	1975(1) s.66(2)
(3) - (6)	1975(1) s.66(3) - (6); 1985 s.13(5)
(7)	1975(1) s.66(7)
para.7	1975(1) s.66A; 1984 s.14(b); 1989 s.9(3)
para.8	1975(1) s.84A; 1989 s.31, Sch.8, para.7(2)
Part II	
para.9(1), (2)	1975(1) s.57(1), (5); 1986 s.39, Sch.3, para.3(3)
(3)	1975(1) s.57(4); 1982(2) s.39(2); 1989 s.26, Sch.7, para.12
Part III	
para.10(1)	1986 s.39, Sch.3, para.7
(2), (3)	1975(1) s.62
Part IV	
para.11(1)	1975(1) s.59A(1), (10B); 1986 s.39, Sch.3, para.5(1); 1989 s.26, Sch.7, para.13; 1990 s.3(1), (4)
(2), (3)	1975(1) s.59A(1A), (1B); 1990 s.3(2)
(4) - (7)	1975(1) s.59A(2) - (5); 1986 s.39, Sch.3, para.5(1)
(8)	1975(1) s.59A(6); 1986 s.39, Sch.3, para.5(1); 1990 s.3(3)
(9)	1975(1) s.59A(7); 1986 s.39, Sch.3, para.5(1)
(10)	1975(1) s.59A(8); 1986 s.39, Sch.3, para.5(1); 1988(1) s.16, Sch.4, para.12(a)
(11)	1988(1) s.2(3)
(12)	1975(1) s.59A(9); 1986 s.39, Sch.3, para.5(1)

SOCIAL SECURITY CONTRIBUTIONS AND BENEFITS ACT—*continued.*

Section of 1992 Act	Derivation
(13)	1975(1) s.59A(10); 1986 s.39, Sch.3, para.5(1)
(14)	1975(1) s.59A(10A); 1988(1) s.16, Sch.4, para.12(b)
para.12(1), (2)	1988(1) s.2(4), (5)
(3), (4)	1988(1) s.2(5A), (5B); 1989 s.17(5)
(5)	1988(1) s.2(6)
(6)	1988(1) s.2(7); 1989 s.17(6)
Part V	
para.13(1)	1975(1) s.59B(1); 1988(1) s.2(1); 1989 s.7, Sch.1, para.8(2)
(2), (3)	1975(1) s.59B(2), (3); 1988(1) s.2(1)
(4)	1975(1) s.59B(5); 1988(1) s.2(1); 1989 s.7, Sch.1, para.8(5); Benefits Order art.3(4) Sch.1
(5)	1975(1) s.59B(5A); 1989 s.17(3)
(6)	1975(1) s.59B(6); 1988(1) s.2(1)
(7)	Drafting
(8), (9)	1975(1) s.59B(7), (8); 1989 s.7, Sch.1, para.8(6)
(10)	1975(1) s.59B(9); 1990 s.3(6)
(11)	1975(1) s.59A(10A); 1988(1) s.16, Sch.4, para.12(b)
Part VI	
para.14(1)	1988(1) s.2, Sch.1, paras.2, 3
(2)	1975(1) s.168(1), Sch.20 "deceased"
para.15(1) - (3)	1975(1) s.67(1), (2); 1977 s.22(4); 1988(1) s.2, Sch.1, para.2
(4)	1975(1) s.67(3)
para.16	1975(1) s.68; 1988(1) s.2, Sch.1, para.2
para.17	1975(1) s.69; 1988(1) s.2, Sch.1, para.3
para.18	1975(1) s.70; 1984 s.13, Sch.5, para.5; 1988(1) s.2, Sch.1, para.2
para.19	1975(1) s.70, Sch.9, para.1; 1988(1) s.2, Sch.1, para.2
para.20	1975(1) s.75; 1988(1) s.2, Sch.1, paras.2, 6(a)
para.21	1977 s.9; 1988(1) s.2, Sch.1, para.6(b)
Sch. 8	
Part I	
para.1	1975 (Old Cases) s.1
para.2(1)	1975 (Old Cases) s.2(1); 1990 s.16(8)(a)
(2) - (5)	1975 (Old Cases) s.2(2) - (5)
(6), (7)	1975 (Old Cases) s.2(6); The Social Security Act 1986 (Commencement No.5) Order 1987 (S.I.1987/354) art.3; Benefits Order art.6
(8)	1975 (Old Cases) s.2(7)

SOCIAL SECURITY CONTRIBUTIONS AND BENEFITS ACT—*continued.*

Section of 1992 Act	Derivation
para.3	1975 (Old Cases) s.3
para.4(1)	1975 (Old Cases) s.5(1); 1990 s.16(8)(a)
(2) - (4)	1975 (Old Cases) s.5(2) - (4)
para.5(1)	1975 (Old Cases) s.6(1)
(2)	1975 (Old Cases) s.6(2); 1980(1) s.4(3)
(3), (4)	1975 (Old Cases) s.6(3), (4)
(5)	1977 s.10, Sch.1, para.6
para.6(1)	1975 (Old Cases) s.7(1)
(2), (3)	1975 (Old Cases) s.7(2); The Social Security Act 1986 (Commencement No.5) Order 1987 (S.I.1987/354) art.3; Benefits Order art.6
(4)	1975 (Old Cases) s.7(3); 1982(2) s.48(5), Sch.4, para.18(2); 1984 s.13, Sch.5, para.8(a); 1986, s.86(1), Sch.10, para.68(2)(a)
(5)	1975 (Old Cases) s.7(4); 1984 s.13, Sch.5, para.8(b); 1986 s.86, Sch.10, para.68(2)(b)
(6)	1975 (Old Cases) s.7(5)
Part II	
para.7(1)	1975(1) s.159(1)
(2)	1975(1) s.159(3)
Part III	
para.8(1) "corresponding disablement pension rate"	1975 (Old Cases) s.14(1) "corresponding disablement pension rate"
"the 1967 Act"	Drafting
"injury pension"	1975(1) s.159(2) "injury pension"
"the original Industrial Injuries Act"	Drafting
"prescribed"	1975 (Old Cases) s.14(1) "prescribed"
"workmen's compensation"	1975 (Old Cases) s.14(1) "workmen's compensation"
"the Workmen's Compensation Acts"	1975 (Old Cases) s.14(1) "the Workmen's Compensation Acts"
(2)	1975 (Old Cases) s.14(1) "pneumoconiosis"
(3), (4)	1975 (Old Cases) s.14(2), (3)
(5)	1975 (Old Cases) s.14(4); 1977 s.11(5)
(6)	1986 s.39, Sch.3, para.16
Sch. 9	
paras.1 - 4	1975(3) s.4(1), Sch.1, paras.1 - 4

SOCIAL SECURITY CONTRIBUTIONS AND BENEFITS ACT—*continued.*

Section of 1992 Act	Derivation
para.5	1975(3) s.4(1), Sch.1, para.5; 1984 s.11, Sch.4, para.13
Sch. 10	1975(3) s.4(2), Sch.2
Sch. 11	
paras.1 - 4	1982(2) s.3(3), Sch.1, paras.1 - 4
para.5	1982(2) s.3(3), Sch.1, para.5; 1984 s.11, Sch.4, para.15(b)
paras.6 - 8	1982(2) s.3(3), Sch.1, paras.6 - 8
Sch. 12	
para.1	1982(2) s.10, Sch.2, para.1; 1985 s.18(6)(a)
paras.2 - 4	1982(2) s.10, Sch.2, paras.2 - 4
para.5	1982(2) s.10, Sch.2, para.1A; 1985 s.18(6)(b)
para.6	1982(2) s.10, Sch.2, para.6
Sch. 13	
para.1	1986 s.49, Sch.4, para.11; 1988(1) s.16, Sch.4, para.19(1)
para.2	1986 s.49, Sch.4, para.11A; 1988(1) s.16, Sch.4, para.19(2)
para.3	1986 s.49, Sch.4, para.12

SOCIAL SECURITY ADMINISTRATION ACT 1992 (c. 5)

TABLE OF DERIVATIONS

(for Table of Destinations see page v)

Note:

1. Abbreviations used in this Table are the same as those used in the Table of Derivations for the Social Security Contributions and Benefits Act. They are set out at the beginning of that Table.

2. The Table does not acknowledge the general changes made by paragraph 1 of Schedule 8 to the Health and Social Services and Social Security Adjudications Act 1983. That paragraph transferred adjudication functions to adjudication officers and social security appeal tribunals.

3. The Table does not contain any entries in respect of section 66(2) of the Social Security Pensions Act 1975 (c.60) which provides that, with certain exceptions, that Act and the Social Security Act 1975 (c.14) shall have effect as if the provisions of the Social Security Pensions Act 1975 were contained in the Social Security Act 1975. The effect is that the general provisions of the Social Security Act 1975 apply to the provisions of the Social Security Pensions Act 1975.

4. The Table does not show the effect of transfer of functions orders.

Section of 1992 Act	Derivation
1(1)	1975(1) s.165A(1); 1986 s.86(1), Sch.10, para.87; 1989 s.31(1), Sch.8, para.9(1); 1990 s.6(1)(a)
(2)	1975(1) s.165A(2); 1986 s.86(1), Sch.10, para.87; 1990 s.6(1)(b)
(3)	1975(1) s.165A(3); 1990 s.1(6); 1991(2) s.4, Sch.1, para.19
(4)	1975(1) s.165A(1); 1986 s.86, Sch.10, para.48(b); 1990 s.5(4)
(5), (6)	Drafting
2(1)	1975(1) s.165B(1); 1990 s.5(1)
(2), (3)	1975(1) s.165B(2); 1990 s.5(1)
(4), (5)	1975(1) s.165B(3), (4); 1990 s.5(1)
3	1975(1) s.165C; 1990 s.6(2)
4	1990 s.21(1), Sch.6, para.27(2)
5(1)(a)—(h)	1986 s.51(1)(a)—(h)
(i)—(r)	1986 s.51(1)(k)—(t)
(2)	1986 s.51(2); 1988(1) s.11, Sch.3, para.16; 1991(2) s.7, Sch.3, para.1
(3)	Housing Act 1988 (c.50) s.121(6)
(4), (5)	1986 s.51(3),(4)
6(1)(a) - (k)	1986 s.51A(1)(a) - (k); 1988(2) s.135, Sch.10, para.8
(l)	1986 s.51A(1)(kk); 1989 s.31(1), Sch.8, para.9(6)(a)
(m) - (p)	1986 s.51A(1)(l) - (o); 1988(2) s.135, Sch.10, para.8
(q)	1986 s.51A(1)(oo); 1989 s.31(1), Sch.8, para.9(6)(b)
(r) - (u)	1986 s.51A(1)(p) - (s); 1988(2) s.135, Sch.10, para.8
(2),(3)	1986 s.51A(2),(3); 1988(2) s.135, Sch.10, para.8
7	1986 s.51B; 1988(2) s.135, Sch.10, para.8
8	1975(1) s.88
9	1975(1) s.89
10(1)	1975(1) s.90(2); 1988(1) s.2, Sch.1, para.6

SOCIAL SECURITY ADMINISTRATION ACT—*continued.*

Section of 1992 Act	Derivation
(2)	1975(1) s.90(3); 1986 s.86, Sch.10, para.85
(3)	1975(1) s.90(4)
11	1986 s.27B(1) - (3); 1991(2) s.7(1)
12(1)	1986 s.33(1); 1988(1) s.11, Sch.3, para.9
(2)	1986 s.33(13); 1990 s.10(5)
13(1)	1975(3) s.6(1); 1989 s.26, Sch.7, para.22
(2)	1975(3) s.6(3)
14(1)	1982(2) s.17(2)
(2)	1982(2) s.17(2A); 1985 s.20
(3)	1982(2) s.17(3)
15(1)	1986 s.49, Sch.4, para.6
(2)	1986 s.49, Sch.4, para.7
16	1988(1) s.8
17(1)(a),(b)	1975(1) s.93(1)(a),(b)
(c)	1975(1) s.93(1)(bb); 1991(3) s.3(1)
(d)	1975(1) s.93(1)(d)
(e)	1975(1) s.93(1)(e); 1977 s.22(5)
(f)	1975(2) s.60(1)(a)
(g)(i) - (iv)	1986 s.52(2), Sch.5, Part II, para.(b)(i) - (iv)
(v)	1986 s.52(2), Sch.5, Part II, para.(b)(vi); 1991(1) s.2(3)
(vi)	1986 s.52(2), Sch.5, Part II, para.b(v)
(h)	1986 s.52(2), Sch.5, Part II, para.(c)
(2)	1975(1) s.93(2)
(3)	1975(1) s.93(2A); 1989 s.21, Sch.3, para.1(1); R8
(4)	1975(1) s.93(3); R8
18(1)	1975(1) s.94(1); R8
(2) - (5)	1975(1) s.94(2) - (5)
(6), (7)	1975(1) s.94(7), (8)
19(1)	1975(1) s.96(1); 1986 s.52(1), Sch.5, para.3; R8
(2), (3)	1975(1) s.96(2); 1980(1) ss.2, 21, Sch.1, para.9
20(1)	1975(1) s.98(1); 1991(2) s.4, Sch.1, para.2
(2)	1975(1) s.98(2); 1986 s.52(1), Sch.5, para.4
(3)	1975(1) s.98(1); 1986 s.52(3), (7)(a); 1991(2) s.4, Sch.2, para.15(a)
(4)	1975(1) s.98(2A); 1986 s.52(1), Sch.5, para.4
(5)	1975(1) s.98(3)

SOCIAL SECURITY ADMINISTRATION ACT—*continued.*

Section of 1992 Act	Derivation
(6)	1975(1) s.98(1); 1986 s.52(3)(a), (3A), (6); 1988(1), s.11, Sch.3, para.16; 1991(2) ss.4, 7, Sch.2, para.15(a), Sch.3, para.3(1)
21(1)	1975(1) s.99(1); 1991(2) s.4, Sch.1, para.3(1)
(2)	1975(1) s.99(2); 1986 s.52(1), Sch.5, para.5; 1991(2) s.4, Sch.1, para.3(2)
(3)	1975(1) s.99(2A); 1986 s.52(3A); 1991(2) ss.4, 7, Sch.1, para.3(3), Sch.3, para.3(1)
(4), (5)	1975(1) s.99(3); 1986 s.52(7)(b)
(6)	1975(1) s.99(4); 1989 s.21, Sch.3, para.2
22(1)	1975(1) s.100(1); 1986 s.52(3A), (7)(c)(i); 1991(2) ss.4, 7, Sch.1, para.4(a), Sch.3, para.3(1)
(2)	1975(1) s.100(2); 1986 s.52(1), (7)(c)(ii), Sch.5, para.6(b); 1991(2) s.4, Sch.1, para.4(b)
(3)	1975(1) s.100(3); 1986 s.52(1), Sch.5, para.6(c)
(4)	1975(1) s.100(4); 1986 s.52(1), Sch.5, para.6(d)
(5)	1975(1) s.100(7); 1986 s.52(1), (7)(c)(iii), Sch.5, para.6(e); 1991(2) s.4, Sch.1, para.4(c)
(6), (7)	1975(1) s.100(8),(9); 1990 s.21(1), Sch.6, para.6(1)
23(1)	1975(1) s.101(1); 1986 s.52(1), Sch.5, para.7(1)
(2)	1975(1) s.101(2); 1986 s.52(7)(d)
(3)	1975(1) s.101(2)(a), (b), (c), (d); 1986 s.52(1), Sch.5, para.7(2)
(4)	1975(1) s.101(2)(bb); 1990 s.21(1), Sch.6, para.6(2)
(5)	1975(1) s.101(3); 1990 s.21(1), Sch.6, para.6(3)
(6)	1975(1) s.101(4)
(7), (8)	1975(1) s.101(5); 1986 s.52(1), Sch.5, para.7(3); 1989 s.21, Sch.3, para.6
(9), (10)	1975(1) s.101(5A), (5B); 1986 s.52(1), Sch.5, para.7(3)
24(1) - (5)	1980(1) s.14(1)—(5)
(6)	1980(1) s.14(8)(a); The Transfer of Functions (Social Security Commissioners) Order 1984 (S.I.1984/1818) art.3
25(1)	1975(1) s.104(1); 1986 s.52(1), (3)(a), (3A), (6) Sch.5, para.10(a); 1988(1) ss.11, 16, Sch.3, para.16, Sch.4, para.14; 1989 ss.10(5), 21, Sch.3, para.11(1); 1991(2) ss.4, 7, Sch.1, para.8(a), Sch.3, para.3(1)
(2)	1975(1) s.104(1A); 1983 s.25, Sch.8, para.3; 1986 s.52(3A); 1991(2) ss.4, 7, Sch.1, para.8(b), Sch.3, para.3(1)
(3)	1975(1) s.104(1); 1986 s.52(1), Sch.5, para.10(a)
(4)	1986 s.52(8); R9
(5)	1975(1) s.104(1ZA); 1989 s.25, Sch.3, para.11(2)
26(1),(2)	1975(1) s.104(2),(3)
(3)	1975(1) s.104(3A); 1986 s.52(1), Sch.5, para.10(c)
27(1)	1975(1) s.104(5); 1986 s.52(1), Sch.5, para.10(d); 1989 s.21, Sch.3, para.11(4)

SOCIAL SECURITY ADMINISTRATION ACT—*continued.*

Section of 1992 Act	Derivation
(2)	1975(1) s.104(6); 1990 s.6(3)
28	1975(1) s.104(4)
29	1975(1) s. 104(3B); 1989 s.21, Sch.3, para.7
30(1)	1975(1) s.100A(1); 1986 s.52(3A), (10); 1991(2) ss.4, 7, Sch.1, para.5, Sch.3, para.3(1), (3)
(2)	1975(1) s.100A(2); 1991(2) s.4, Sch.1, para.5
(3)	1975(1) s.100A(3); 1991(2) s.4, Sch.1, para.5
(4)	1975(1) s.100A(4); 1991(2) s.4, Sch.1, para.5
(5)	1975(1) s.100A(2); 1986 s.52(3A), (9)(a), (b), (10); 1991(2) ss.4, 7, Sch.1, para.5, Sch.3, para.3(1), (3)
(6) - (11)	1975(1) s.100A(5) - (10); 1986 s.52(3A); 1991(2) ss.4, 7, Sch.1, para.5, Sch.3, para.3(1)
(12)	1975(1) s.100A(11); 1991(2) s.4, Sch.1, para.5
(13)	1975(1) s.100A(12); 1986 s.52(3A); 1991(2) ss.4, 7, Sch.1, para.5, Sch.3, para.3(1)
31	1975(1) s.100B; 1986 s.52(3A); 1991(2) ss.4, 7, Sch.1, para.5, Sch.3, para.3(1)
32(1)	1975(1) s.100C(1); 1986 s.52(3A); 1991(2) ss.4, 7, Sch.1, para.5, Sch.3, para.3(1)
(2) - (5)	1975(1) s.100C(2) - (5); 1991(2) s.4, Sch.1, para.5
(6), (7)	1975(1) s.100C(6), (7); 1986 s.52(3A); 1991(2) ss.4, 7, Sch.1, para.5, Sch.3, para.3(1)
(8)	1975(1) ss.100C(8)(a), 104(5)(b); 1986 s.52(3A); 1991(2) ss.4, 7, Sch.1, para.5, Sch.3, para.3(1)
(9), (10)	1975(1) s.100C(9), (10); 1986 s.52(3A); 1991(2) ss.4, 7, Sch.1, para.5, Sch.3, para.3(1)
33	1975(1) s.100D(1) - (6); 1986 s.52(3A); 1991(2) ss.4, 7, Sch.1, para.5, Sch.3, para.3(1)
34(1)	1975(1) s.101(1); 1986 s.52(3A); 1991(2) ss.4, 7, Sch.1, para.6(a), Sch.3, para.3(1)
(2)	1975(1) s.101(2), (3); 1986 s.52(3A); 1991(2) s.7, Sch.3, para.3(1)
(3)	1975(1) s.101(4); 1986 s.52(3A); 1991(2) s.7, Sch.3, para.3(1)
(4)	1975(1) s.101(5) - (5B); 1991(2) s.7, Sch.3, para.3(1)
(5)	1980(1) s.14(1) - (5), (8)(a)
35(1), (2)	1975(1) s.104A(1), (2); 1991(2) s.4, Sch.1, para.9
(3)	1975(1) s.104A(1); 1986 s.52(3A), (9)(a), (b), (10); 1991(2) ss.4, 7, Sch.1, para.9, Sch.3, para.3(1), (3)
(4)	1975(1) s.104A(3); 1986 s.52(3A); 1991(2) ss.4, 7, Sch.1, para.9, Sch.3, para.3(1)
(5)	1975(1) ss.104(3A), 104A(9); 1986 s.52(3A), (9)(c); 1991(2) ss.4, 7, Sch.1, para.9, Sch.3, para.3(1), (3)(c)

SOCIAL SECURITY ADMINISTRATION ACT—*continued.*

Section of 1992 Act	Derivation
(6) - (9)	1975(1) s.104A(4) - (7); 1986 s.52(3A); 1991(2) ss.4, 7, Sch.1, para.9, Sch.3, para.3(1)
(10)	1975(1) ss.104(5)(b), 104A(9)(c); 1986 s.52(3A), (9)(c); 1991(2) ss.4, 7, Sch.1, para.9, Sch.3, para.3(1), (3)(c)
(11)	1975(1) ss.104(1ZA), 104A(9)(a); 1991(2) s.4, Sch.1, para.9
(12)	1975(1) s.104A(8); 1986 s.52(3A); 1991(2) ss.4, 7, Sch.1, para.9, Sch.3, para.3(1)
36(1)	1975(1) s.102(1), (2); 1986 s.52(1), Sch.5, para.8; 1991(2) s.4, Sch.1, para.7(1)
(2)	1975(1) s.102(3); 1991(2) s.4, Sch.1, para.7(2)
37(1)	1975(1) s.103(1); 1986 s.52(1) Sch.5, para.9
(2)	1975(1) 103(2); 1986 s.52(1), Sch.5, para.9; 1989 s.21, Sch.3, para.15
(3)	1975(1) s.103(3); 1986 s.52(1), Sch.5, para.9
38(1)	1975(1) s.97(1); 1983 s.25, Sch.8, para.2; 1990 s.21(1), Sch.6, para.5(1)
(2)	1975(1) s.97(1A); 1983 s.25, Sch.8, para.2
39	1975(1) s.97(1B)—(1E); 1983 s.25, Sch.8, para.2
40(1)	1975(1) s.97(4), Sch.10, para.1(1); 1983 s.25, Sch.8, para.7
(2), (3)	1975(1) s.97(4), Sch.10, para.1(2), (2A); 1984 s.16(b)
(4)	1975(1) s.97(4), Sch.10, para.1(6); 1983 s.25, Sch.8, para.7
41(1)	1975(1) s.97(2); 1983 s.25, Sch.8, para.2
(2)	1975(1) s.97(2A); 1984 s.16(a)
(3), (4)	1975(1) s.97(2C),(2D); 1983 s.25, Sch.8, para.2
(5)	1975(1) s.97(2E); 1983 s.25, Sch.8, para.2; Courts and Legal Services Act 1990 (c.41) s.71(2), Sch.10, para.37(1)
(6)	1975(1) s.97(4), Sch.10, para.1(8); 1983 s.25, Sch.8, para.7
(7)	Drafting
42(1) - (5)	1975(1) s.100D(7), Sch.10A, paras.3 - 7; 1991(2) s.4, Sch.1, paras.5, 16
(6)	1975(1) ss.97(4), 100D(7), Sch.10, para.1(2A); Sch.10A, para.8; 1991(2) s.4, Sch.1, paras.5, 16
(7)	1975(1) ss.97(4), 100D(7), Sch.10, para.1(6); Sch.10A, para.8; 1991(2) s.4, Sch.1, paras.5, 16
43(1)	1975(1) s.100D(7), Sch.10A, para.1; 1991(2) s.4, Sch.1, paras.5, 16
(2), (3)	1975(1) s.100D(7), Sch.10A, paras.9, 10; 1991(2) s.4, Sch.1, paras.5, 16
(4)—(6)	1975(1) ss.97(2C)—(2E), 100D(7), Sch.10A, para.2; 1991(2) s.4, Sch.1, paras.5, 16
(7), (8)	1975(1) s.100D(7), Sch.10A, paras.12, 13; 1991(2) s.4, Sch.1, paras.5, 16
(9)	Drafting
44(1)—(3)	1975(1) s.107(1)—(3)
(4), (5)	1975(1) s.107(4); 1988 s.2, Sch.1, para.6

SOCIAL SECURITY ADMINISTRATION ACT—*continued.*

Section of 1992 Act	Derivation
(6)	1975(1) s.107(5)
(7)	1975(1) s.107(6); 1986 s.52(1), Sch.5, para.12(a)
45(1)	1975(1) s.108(1); 1984 s.11(2), Sch.4, para.5; 1986 s.39, Sch.3, para.14(a); 1989 s.21, Sch.3, para.12(1)
(2)	1975(1) s.108(2); 1983 s.25, Sch.8, para.21(1); 1984 s.11(2), Sch.4, para.6
(3)	1975(1) s.108(4); 1983, s.25, Sch.8, para.21(3)
(4), (5)	1975(1) s.108(4A),(4B); 1989 s.21, Sch.3, para.12(2)
(6)	1975(1) s.108(5); 1983 s.25, Sch.8, para.21(3)
46(1)	1975(1) s.109(1); 1983 s.25, Sch.8, para.22(a); 1984, s.11(2), Sch.4, para.7
(2)	1975(1) s.109(2); 1983 s.25, Sch.8, para.22(b)(i)
(3)	1975(1) s.109(3); 1983 s.25, Sch.8, para.22(c); 1986 s.52(1), Sch.5, para.13
47(1)	1975(1) s.110(1); 1979 s.21(4), Sch.3, para.8; 1983 s.25, Sch.8, para.23(a)
(2),(3)	1975(1) s.110(1A),(1B); 1986 s.52(1), Sch.5, para.14(b)
(4)	1975(1) s.110(2); 1983 s.25, Sch.8, para.23(b)
(5)—(7)	1975(1) s.110(3)—(5)
(8)	1975(1) s.110(6); 1983 s.25, Sch.8, para.23(c); 1984 s.11(2), Sch.4, para.8(a)
(9)	1975(1) s.110(7); 1983 s.25, Sch.8, para.23(d); 1984 s.11(2), Sch.4, para.8(b)
(10)	Social Security (Consequential Provisions) Act 1975 (c.18) ss.2, 4, Sch.3, para.20
48(1)	1975(1) s.112(1); 1984 s.11(2), Sch.4, para.9; 1986 s.52(1), Sch.5, para.15(a)
(2)	1975(1) s.112(2)
(3)	1975(1) s.112(3); 1986 s.52(1), Sch.5, para.15(b)
(4)	1975(1) s.112(5)
(5), (6)	1975(1) s.112(6), (7); 1989 s.21, Sch.3, para.9(2)
49(1)	1975(1) s.108(3), Sch.12, para.1; 1983 s.25, Sch.8, paras.21(2), 27(a)
(2)	1975(1) s.108(3), Sch.12, para.3; 1983 s.25, Sch.8, paras.21(2), 27(b)
50(1)	1975(1) s.108(3), Sch.12, para.2(1); 1983 s.25, Sch.8, paras.9, 21(2)
(2)	1975(1) s.108(3), Sch.12, para.2(2); 1983 s.25, Sch.8, paras.9, 21(2); 1986 s.52(1), Sch.5, para.18
(3), (4)	1975(1) s.108(3), Sch.12, para.2(3), (4); 1983 s.25, Sch.8, paras.9, 21(2)
(5)	1975(1) s.108(3), Sch.12, para.2(5); 1983 s.25, Sch.8, paras.9, 21(2); 1989 ss.21, 26, Sch.3, para.18, Sch.7, para.17; Courts and Legal Services Act 1990 (c.41) s.71(2), Sch.10, para.37(4)
(6)	1975(1) s.108(3), Sch.12, para.3; 1983 s.25, Sch.8, paras.21(2), 27(b)
(7)	Drafting
51(1)	1975(1) s.97(4), Sch.10 para.1A(1); 1991(2) s.4, Sch.1, para.15
(2)	1975(1) s.97(4), Sch.10, para.1A(2); 1983 s.25, Sch.8, para.8; Courts and Legal Services Act 1990 (c.41) s.71(2), Sch.10, para.37(2)

SOCIAL SECURITY ADMINISTRATION ACT—*continued.*

Section of 1992 Act	Derivation
(3)	1975(1) s.97(4), Sch.10, para.1A(3); 1983 s.25, Sch.8, para.8; Courts and Legal Services Act 1990 (c.41) s.71(2), Sch.10, para.37(3)
(4)	Drafting
52(1)	1975(1) s.97(3); 1980(1) s.12; Courts and Legal Services Act 1990 (c.41) s.71(2), Sch.10, para.36
(2)	1980(1) s.13(5); Courts and Legal Services Act 1990 (c.41) s.71(2), Sch.10, para.46
(3)	1980(1) s.13(6)
(4)	Drafting
53(1)	1975(1) s.115A(1); 1989 s.21, Sch. 3, para. 3(1)
(2)	1975(1) s.115A(2); 1989 s.21, Sch. 3, para. 3(1); 1991(2) s.4, Sch.1, para.11
(3), (4)	1975(1) s.115A(3), (4); 1989 s.21, Sch. 3, para. 3(1)
54(1), (2)	1975(1) s.115C(1), (2); 1986 s.52(3A); 1991(2) ss.4, 7, Sch.1, para.13, Sch.3, para.3(1)
(3)	1975(1) s.115C(3); 1991(2) s.4, Sch.1, para.13
(4)	1975(1) s.115C(3); 1986 s.52(3A), (9)(d); 1991(2) s.7, Sch.3, para.3(1), (3)
(5)	1975(1) s.115C(4); 1986 s.52(3A), (9)(b); 1991(2) ss.4, 7, Sch.1, para.13, Sch.3, para.3(1), (2)
(6)	1975(1) s.115C(5); 1991(2) s.4, Sch.1, para.13
(7)	1975(1) s.115C(5); 1986 s.52(3A), (9)(e); 1991(2) s.7, Sch.3, para.3(1), (3)
(8)	1975(1) s.115C(6); 1986 s.52(3A); 1991(2) ss.4, 7, Sch.1, para.13, Sch.3, para.3(1)
55	1975(1) s.115D; 1986 s.52(3A)(c); 1991(2) ss.4, 7, Sch.1, para.13, Sch.3, para.3(1)
56(1)	1975(1) s.115B(1); 1989 s.21, Sch.3, para.3(1)
(2)	1975(1) s.115B(2); 1989 s.21, Sch.3, para.3(1); 1991(2) s.4, Sch.1, para.12
57(1)	1975(1) s.116(1); 1980(1) s.12
(2)	1975(1) s.116(2)
58(1), (2)	1975(1) s.114(1); 1986 s.52(3)(b), (3A), (6); 1988(1) s.11, Sch.3, para.16; 1991(2) s.7, Sch.3, para.3(1)
(3)	1975(1) s.114(2)
(4)	1975(1) s.114(2A); Employment Protection (Consolidation) Act 1978 (c.44) s.159, Sch.16, para.19(1)
(5) - (7)	1975(1) s.114(2B) - (2D); 1986 s.52(1), Sch.5, para.16(a)
(8)	1975(1) s.114(5)
59(1)	1975(1) s.115(1), (2); 1986 s.52(3)(c), (3A) (6); 1988(1) s.11, Sch.3, para.16; 1991(2) s.7, Sch.3, para.3(1)
(2)	1975(1) s.115(3); 1986 s.52(4); 1991 s.7, Sch.3, para.3(2)
(3)	1975(1) s.115(4)
(4)	1975(1) s.115(4A); 1991(3) s.3(2)

SOCIAL SECURITY ADMINISTRATION ACT—*continued.*

Section of 1992 Act	Derivation
(5)	1975(1) s.115(5)
(6)	1975(1) s.115(6); 1989 s.21, Sch.3, para.1(2)
(7)	1975(1) s.115(7)
60(1)	1975(1) s.117(1); 1983 s.25, Sch.8, para.6; 1986 s.52(3)(d), (3A), (6); 1988(1) s.11, Sch.3, para.16; 1991(2) s.7, Sch.3, para.3(1)
(2)	1975(1) s.117(2)
(3)	1975(1) s.117(3); 1983 s.25, Sch.8, para. 26
(4)	1975(1) s.117(4); 1988(1) s.2, Sch.1, para.6
(5)	1975(1) s.117(5); 1988(1) s.2, Sch.1, para.6
61(1)	1975(1) s.119(3)
(2)	1975(1) s.119(4)(a)
(3)	1977 s.17(5)
(4)	1975(1) s.119(3); 1986 s.52(3)(e), (3A), (6); 1988(1) s.11, Sch.3, para.16; 1991(2) s.7, Sch.3, para.3(1)
62(1)	1975(1) s.113(1)
(2)	1975(1) s.113(2)(a), (b); 1983 s.25, Sch.8, para.24(a)
63(1)	1986 ss.29(1), 31C(1); 1988(2) s.135, Sch.10, para.6
(2)	1986 ss.29(2), 31C(2); 1988(2) s.135, Sch.10, para.6
(3)	1986 ss.29(3), 31C(3); 1988(2) s.135, Sch.10, para.6
64(1), (2)	1986 s.32(8),(9)
(3)	1986 s.32(10); 1988(1) s.11, Sch.3, para.7; 1990 s.10(2)
65	1986 s.35
66(1) - (8)	1986 s.34
(9), (10)	1986 s.32(11), (12); 1988(1) s.11, Sch.3, para.7
67	1986 s.66, Sch.6, para.4
68(1)—(3)	1975(1) s.165D(1)—(3); 1990 s.21(1), Sch.6, para.7(2)
(4)	1975(1) s.165D(4); 1986 s.86, Sch.10, para.48(c); 1990 s.21(1), Sch.6, para.7(2), (3); 1991(2) s.4, Sch.2, para.5
(5), (6)	1975(1) s.165D(5), (6); 1990 s.21(1), Sch.6, para.7(2)
69(1)	1975(1) ss.100C(8)(b), 104(7); 1986 s.52(3)(a), (3A); 1990 s.21(1), Sch.6, para.7(1); 1991(2) ss.4, 7, Sch.1, para.5, Sch.2, para.15(a), Sch.3, para.3(1)
(2) - (4)	1975(1) s.104(8) - (10); 1990 s.21(2), Sch.6, para.7(1)
70(1)	National Insurance Act 1974 (c.14) s.6(1)
(2)	National Insurance Act 1974 s.6(3)
(3)	National Insurance Act 1974 s.6(1); Social Security (Consequential Provisions) Act 1975 (c.18) s.1(3), Sch.2, para.70; 1975(2) s.65, Sch.4, para.35; 1975(3) s.21(1), Sch.4, para.8; Supplementary Benefits Act 1976

SOCIAL SECURITY ADMINISTRATION ACT—*continued.*

Section of 1992 Act	Derivation
	(c.71) s.35(2), Sch.7, para.36; 1990 s.21(1), Sch.6, para.31(a); 1991(1) s.3(1)(a); 1991(2) s.15(1); 1991(3) s.6(1)
71(1)	1986 s.53(1)
(2)	1986 s.53(1A); 1989 s.21, Sch.3, para.14(1)
(3), (4)	1986 s.53(2), (3)
(5)	1986 s.53(4); 1989 s.21, Sch.3, para.14(2)
(6) - (8)	1986 s.53(5)—(7)
(9), (10)	1986 s.53(8), (9)
(11)	1986 s.53(10); 1988(1) ss.11, 16, Sch.3, para.16, Sch.4, para.30(1); 1991(2) s.7, Sch.3, para.4
72(1)	1986 s.20(4E); 1988(1) s.4(2)
(2)	1986 s.20(4H); 1988(1) s.4(2)
(3)—(6)	1986 s.20(4J)—(4M); 1988(1) s.4(2)
(7), (8)	1986 s.20(4F),(4G); 1986 s.53(10A); 1988(1) ss.4(2), 16, Sch.4, para.30(2)
73(1)	1975(1) s.85(1)
(2)	1975(1) s.85(2); 1975(3) s.21(1), Sch.4, para.28
(3)	1975(1) s.85(3)
(4), (5)	1975(1) s.85(4), (5); 1979 s.15(1)
74	1986 s.27
75	1986 s.29(4)—(7)
76(1), (2)	1986 s.31D(1), (2); 1988(2) s.135, Sch.10, para.6
(3)	1986 s.31D(3); 1988(2) s.135, Sch.10, para.6; 1989 s.31(1), Sch.8, para.9(4)
(4)	1986 s.31D(4); 1988(2) s.135, Sch.10, para.6
(5)	1986 s.31D(5); 1988(2) s.135, Sch.10, para.6; 1989 s.31(1), Sch.8, para.9(4)
(6) - (8)	1986 s.31D(6) - (8); 1988(2) s.135, Sch.10, para.6
77	1986 s.31E; 1988(2) s.135, Sch.10, para.6
78(1) - (3)	1986 s.33(5) - (7)
(4)	1986 s.32(4)
(5)	1986 s.33(12)
(6)	1986 ss.26(3), 33(8); 1989 s.5(2)
(7)	1986 ss.26(4), 33(8); Family Law Reform Act 1987 (c.42) s.33(1), Sch.2, para.93; 1989 s.5(3)
(8)	1986 ss.26(5), 33(8); 1989 s.5(4)
(9)	1986 ss.26(6), 33(8)
79(a)	1986 s.53(7A); 1988 s.16, Sch.4, para.28
(b)	1986 s.29(8); 1988 s.16, Sch.4, para.26
(c)	1986 s.33(8A); 1988 s.16, Sch.4, para.27

SOCIAL SECURITY ADMINISTRATION ACT—*continued.*

Section of 1992 Act	Derivation
80	1975(3) s.4A; 1979 s.15(3)
81(1) "benefit"	1989 s.22(3) "benefit"; 1991(1) s.1(5)
"certificate of deduction"	1989 s.22(3) "certificate of deduction"
"certificate of total benefit"	1989 s.22(3) "certificate of total benefit"
"compensation payment"	1989 s.22(3) "compensation payment"; 1990 s.7, Sch.1, para.1(1)
"compensation scheme for motor accidents"	1989 s.22(3) "compensation scheme for motor accidents"; 1990 s.7, Sch.1, para.1(2)
"compensator"; "victim"; "intended recipient"	Drafting
"payment"	1989 s.22(3) "payment"
"relevant deduction"	1989 s.22(7), Sch.4, para.1(1) "relevant deduction"
"relevant payment"	1989 s.22(7), Sch.4, para.1(1) "relevant payment"
"relevant period"	1989 s.22(3) "relevant period"
"total benefit"	1989 s.22(7), Sch.4, para.1(1) "total benefit"
(2)	1989 s.22(3A); 1991(1) s.1(5)
(3) - (5)	1989 s.22(4) - (6)
(6)	1989 s.22(7), Sch.4, para.1(2)
(7)	1989 s.22(8)
82	1989 s.22(1), (2)
83	1989 s.22(7), Sch.4, para.2
84	1989 s.22(7), Sch.4, para.3
85	1989 s.22(7), Sch.4, para.4
86	1989 s.22(7), Sch.4, para.5
87	1989 s.22(7), Sch.4, para.6
88	1989 s.22(7), Sch.4, para.7
89	1989 s.22(7), Sch.4, para.8
90	1989 s.22(7), Sch.4, para.9
91	1989 s.22(7), Sch.4, para.10
92	1989 s.22(7), Sch.4, para.11
93(1)	1989 s.22(7), Sch.4, para.12(1)
(2)	1989 s.22(7), Sch.4, para.12(2); 1990 s.7, Sch.1, para.2(1)
(3), (4)	1989 s.22(7), Sch.4, para.12(3), (4)
(5)	1989 s.22(7), Sch.4, para.12(5); 1990 s.7, Sch.1, para.2(2)
(6)	1989 s.22(7), Sch.4, para.12(6); 1990 s.7, Sch.1, para.2(3)
(7)	1989 s.22(7), Sch.4, para.12(6A); 1990 s.7 Sch.1, para.2(4)

SOCIAL SECURITY ADMINISTRATION ACT—*continued.*

Section of 1992 Act	Derivation
(8), (9)	1989 s.22(7), Sch.4, para.12(7), (8)
94(1), (2)	1989 s.22(7), Sch.4, para.13(1), (2)
(3)	1989 s.22(7), Sch.4, para.13(2A); 1990 s.7, Sch.1, para.1(4)
(4) - (6)	1989 s.22(7), Sch.4, para.13(3) - (5)
95	1989 s.22(7), Sch.4, para.14
96	1989 s.22(7), Sch.4, para.15
97	1989 s.22(7), Sch.4, para.16
98(1), (2)	1989 s.22(7), Sch.4, para.17(1), (2)
(3)	1989 s.22(7), Sch.4, para.17(3); 1990 s.7, Sch.1, para.3
(4) - (10)	1989 s.22(7), Sch.4, para.17(4) - (10)
(11)	1989 s.22(7), Sch.4, para.17(11); 1990 s.7, Sch.1, para.4
(12)	1989 s.22(7), Sch.4, para.17(12)
99	1989 s.22(7), Sch.4, para.18
100	1989 s.22(7), Sch.4, para.19
101	1989 s.22(7), Sch.4, para.20A; 1990 s.7, Sch.1, para.5(1)
102(1)	1989 s.22(7), Sch.4, para.21(1); 1990 s.7, Sch.1, para.5(2)
(2)	1989 s.22(7), Sch.4, para.21(2)
103	1989 s.22(7), Sch.4, para.24; 1990 s.7, Sch.1, para.6
104	1989 s.27
105(1), (2)	1986 s.26(1), (2)
(3)	1986 s.26(3) - (6); 1990 s.8(3)
106(1)	1986 s.24(1)
(2) - (4)	1986 s.24(4)—(6)
(5)	1986 s.24(7); Family Law Reform Act 1987 (c.42) s.33(1), Sch.2, para.91
(6),(7)	1986 s.24(8),(9)
107(1)—(4)	1986 s.24A (1) - (4); 1990 s.8(1)
(5)	1986 s.24A(4A); Maintenance Enforcement Act 1991 (c.17) s.9(1)
(6) - (8)	1986 s.24A(5) - (7); 1990 s.8(1)
(9) - (11)	1986 s.24A(7A) - (7C); Maintenance Enforcement Act 1991 s.9(2)
(12) - (15)	1986 s.24A(8) - (11); 1990 s.8(1)
108	1986 s.24B; 1990 s.8(1)
109	1986 s.25A; Debtors (Scotland) Act 1987 (c.18) s.68
110(1)	1986 s.58(1)
(2)	1986 s.58(2); 1989 s.22, Sch.4, para.20(2),(3)
(3)	1986 s.58(3); 1989 s.22, Sch.4, para.20(4)
(4),(5)	1986 s.58(4),(5)

SOCIAL SECURITY ADMINISTRATION ACT—*continued.*

Section of 1992 Act	Derivation
(6)	1986 s.58(6); 1989 s.22, Sch.4, para.20(5)
(7)	1986 s.58(7); 1989 s.22, Sch.4, para.20(6)
(8)	1986 s.84(1) "the benefit Acts"
(9) "relevant benefit"	1986 s.58(2)(b)(ll), (10); 1989 s.22, Sch.4, para.20(2), (7)
"relevant payment"	1986 s.58(c)(iii), (6)(a)(iii), (7)(e), (10); 1989 s.22, Sch.4, para.20(3), (5) - (7)
111	1986 s.58(8), (9); R10
112	1986 s.55
113	1986 s.54
114(1)	1975(1) s.146(1); Criminal Procedure (Scotland) Act 1975 (c.21) s.289G; Criminal Justice Act 1982 (c.48) ss.46, 54
(2)	1975(1) s.1(4), Sch.1, para.5(2)
(3)	1975(1) s.146(2)
(4)	1975(1) s.146(3); Criminal Procedure (Scotland) Act 1975 (c.21) s.289G; Criminal Justice Act 1982 (c.48) ss.46, 54
(5), (6)	1975(1) s.146(4)
115	1986 s.57
116(1)	1986 s.56(1)
(2)	1986 s.56(2); 1988(2) s.135, Sch.10, para.9(2)
(3)	1986 s.56(3)
(4)	1986 s.56(4); 1988(2) s.135, Sch.10, para.9(3)
(5)	1986 s.56(4A), 1988(2) s.135, Sch.10, para.9(4)
(6)	1986 s.56(4B); 1990 s.21(1), Sch.6, para.5(2)
(7)	1986 s.56(5); 1988(2) s.135, Sch.10, para.9(5)
117(1)	1975(1) s.148(1); 1986 s.52(5); R8
(2), (3)	1975(1) s.148(2), (3)
118	1975(1) s.149
119	1975(1) s.150
120(1), (2)	1975(1) s.151(1), (2)
(3)	1975(1) s.151(3); 1991(3) s.2(6)(a)
(4)	1975(1) s.151(3A); 1991(3) s.2(6)(b)
(5)	1975(1) s.151(4)
(6)	1975(1) s.151(5); 1991(3) s.2(6)(c)
121(1)	1975(1) s.152(1); Magistrates' Courts Act 1980 (c.43) s.154, Sch.7, para.135
(2)	1975(1) s.152(2); 1975(2) s.65, Sch.4, para.67
(3)	1975(1) s.152(3)
(4) - (6)	1975(1) s.152(5) - (7)
122(1)	1986 s.59(1); 1989 s.20(a)

SOCIAL SECURITY ADMINISTRATION ACT—*continued.*

Section of 1992 Act	Derivation
(2)	1986 s.59(2); 1989 s.20(b)
(3)	1986 s.59(3)
123(1)—(6)	1989 s.19(1)—(6)
(7)	1989 s.19(7); 1990 s.21(1), Sch.6, para.28(1)
(8)	1989 s.19(8)
(9)	1989 s.19(9); 1990 s.21(1), Sch.6, para.28(2)
(10)	1989 s.19(10); 1990 s.21(1), Sch.6, para.28(3)
124(1), (2)	1975(1) s.160(1); 1975 (Old Cases) s.11; 1986 s.52(3)(f), (3A) (6); 1988(1) s.11, Sch.3, para.16; 1991(2) s.7, Sch.3, para.3(1)
(3)	1975(1) s.160(2); Registration of Births, Deaths and Marriages (Fees) (No.2) Order 1990 (S.I.1990/2515) art.2, Sch.; Registration of Births, Deaths and Marriages (Fees) (Scotland) Order 1990 (S.I.1990/2637) art.2, Sch.
(4), (5)	1975(1) s.160(3), (4)
125	1986 s.60
126	1986 s.27A; 1989 s.31(1), Sch.8, para.17
127	1986 s.31(1)—(3)
128	1986 s.31G(1)—(3); 1988(2), s.135, Sch.10, para.6
129	1982(2) s.17(1)
130(1)	1982(2) s.18(1); 1984 s.11, Sch.4, para.15(a)
(2), (3)	1982(2) s.18(2), (3)
(4)(a), (b)	1982(2) s.17(4)
(c)	1982(2) s.9(3)(a)
131	1986 s.49, Sch.4, para.9
132(1), (2)	1986 s.49, Sch.4, para.8A; 1989 s.31(1), Sch.8, para.18;
(3)	1986 s.49, Sch.4, para.8
133	1975(1) s.161(1)
134(1)	1986 s.28(1); 1990 s.21(1), Sch.6, para.18
(2)	1986 s.28(1A); 1989 s.14(1)
(3)—(6)	1986 s.28(2) - (5)
(7)	1986 s.28(5A); 1990 s.21(1), Sch.6, para.18
(8) - (12)	1986 s.28(6) - (10)
(13)	1986 s.84(1) "modifications"
135(1)	1986 s.30(1)
(2), (3)	1986 s.30(2); Local Government and Housing Act 1989 (c.42) s.81(1); The Housing Benefit (Transitional) Amendment Regulations 1988 reg.3 (S.I.1988/458)
(4)	1986 s.30(2ZA); 1990 s.21(1), Sch.6, para.19(1)

SOCIAL SECURITY ADMINISTRATION ACT—*continued.*

Section of 1992 Act	Derivation
(5)	1986 s.30(3)
(6), (7)	1986 s.30(5); Housing (Scotland) Act 1988 (c.43) ss. 1, 3, Sch.2, para.1; Local Government and Housing Act 1989 s.81(2)
(8), (9)	1986 s.30(6); Local Government and Housing Act 1989 s.81(3)
(10)	1986 s.30(7); R11
(11)	1986 s.30(8); 1989 s.15(2)
(12)	1986 s.30(9)
(13)	1986 s.84(3)
(14)	1986 s.84(1) "modifications"
136(1)	1986 s.30(2A); 1989 s.15(1); 1990 s.21(1), Sch.6, para.19(2)
(2)—(4)	1986 s.30(2B), (2C); 1989 s.15(1)
137	1986 s.30(8A)—(8F); 1989 s.15(2)
138(1),(2)	1986 s.31A(1),(2); 1988(2) s.135, Sch.10, para.6; 1990 s.21(1), Sch.6, para.20
(3)—(9)	1986 s.31A(3)—(9); 1988(2) s.135, Sch.10, para.6
139(1)—(5)	1986 s.31B(1)—(5); 1988(2) s.135, Sch.10, para.6
(6)	1986 s.31B(6); 1988(2) s.135, Sch.10, para 6; the Community Charge Benefits (General) Regulations 1989 reg.11(1) (S.I.1989/1321)
(7)—(10)	1986 s.31B(7)—(10); 1988(2) s.135, Sch.10, para.6
(11)	1986 s.84(1) "modifications", "war disablement pension", "war widow's pension"; the Income and Corporation Taxes Act 1988 (c.1) s.844, Sch.29, para. 32, Table; the Community Charge Benefits (General) Regulations 1989 reg.11(2)
140(1),(2)	1986 s.31F(1),(2); 1988(2) s.135, Sch.10, para.6
(3)	1986 s.31F(3); 1990 s.21(1), Sch.6, para.21(1)
(4), (5)	1986 s.31F(4),(5); 1988(2) s.135, Sch.10, para.6
(6)	1986 s.31F(5A); 1990 s.21(1), Sch.6, para.21(2)
(7)	1986 s.31F(6); 1990 s.21(1), Sch.6, para.21(3)
(8)	1986 s.31F(7); 1988(2) s.135, Sch.10, para.6
141(1)	1975(1) s.120(2); 1975(2) s.65(1), Sch.4, para.50(b)
(2) - (6)	1975(1) s.120(3) - (7)
(7)	Transitional
142(1)	1975(1) ss.121(1), 165
(2)	1975(1) s.121(2)
(3)	1975(1) s.121(3); 1990 s.21(1), Sch.6, para.1(2)(a)
143(1)	1975(1) s.122(1); 1985 s.29(1), Sch.5, para.9(a); 1989 s.1(3)
(2)	1975(1) s.122(2)
(3)	1975(1) s.122(3)(a)

SOCIAL SECURITY ADMINISTRATION ACT—*continued.*

Section of 1992 Act	Derivation
(4)	1975(1) s.122(6); 1980(1) s.2, Sch.1, para.13; 1989 s.1(5)
144(1)	1975(1) ss.123(2), 165
(2)	1975(1) s.123(3); 1990 s.21(1), Sch.6, para.1(2)(b)
145(1)	1975(1) s.123A(1); 1989 s.1(6)
(2)	1975(1) s.123A(2); 1985 s.7(5)
(3)	1975(1) s.123A(3); 1985 s.7(5); 1989 s.1(7)
(4)	1975(1) s.123A(4); 1985 s.7(5)
146	1975(1) s.4(6F); 1985 s.7(2)
147(1)	1975(1) ss.4(6G), 123A(5); 1985 s.7(2), (5)
(2)	1975(1) ss.4(6HH), 123A(6A), 165; 1986 s.74(1), (2)
(3)	1975(1) ss.4(6J), 123A(7); 1985 s.7(2),(5)
(4), (5)	1975(1) ss.4(6K), 123A(8); 1985 s.7(2),(5); 1990 s.21(1), Sch.6, para.1(1), (2)(c)
148(1)	1975(2) s.21(1); 1985 s.4, Sch.3, para.1; 1986 s.18(1)
(2)	1975(2) s.21(2); 1979 s.10(2)
(3), (4)	1975(2) s.21(3); 1979 s.10(3); 1980(1) s.3(3)
(5)	1975(2) s.21(4)
(6)	1975(2) s.21(5); 1980(1) s.3(3)
(7)	Transitional
149	1982(2) s.9(1E); 1991(1) s.2(1)
150(1)(a)(i)	1986 s.63(1)(a)(i)
(ii)	1986 s.63(1)(a)(iv)
(iii)	1986 s.63(1)(a)(iii)
(b)	1986 s.63(1)(aa); 1991(2) s.4, Sch.2, para.16(a)
(c) - (f)	1986 s.63(1)(b) - (e)
(g)	1986 s.63(1)(ee); 1988(1) s.2(2)(a)
(h)	1986 s.63(1)(i); 1991(2) s.7, Sch.3, para.5(a)
(i)	1986 s.63(1)(f)
(j)	1986 s.63(1)(g), (h)
(2)	1986 s.63(2)
(3)	1986 s.63(3); 1988(1) s.2(2)(b); 1991(2) s.4, Sch.2, para.16(b)
(4) - (6)	1986 s.63(4)—(6)
(7)	1986 s.63(10); Social Security Act 1986 (Consequential) Amendment Regulation 1988 (S.I.1988/961) reg.2(a)
(8)	1986 s.63(11); 1990 s.21(1), Sch.6, para.23
(9)	1986 s.63(12)
(10)	1986 s.63(13); 1989 s.31(1), Sch.8, para.15(2); 1991(2) s.7, Sch.3, para.5(b)

SOCIAL SECURITY ADMINISTRATION ACT   *continued.*

Section of 1992 Act	Derivation
(11)	1975(2) s.24(1)(a); 1986 s.86, Sch.10, para.92
151(1)	1975(2) s.23(2); 1986 ss.18(1), 86, Sch.10, para.91
(2)	1975(2) s.23(3); 1986 s.86, Sch.10, para.91
(3) - (5)	1986 s.63(7) - (9)
(6)	1986 s.63(10A); Social Security Act 1986 (Consequential) Amendment Regulation 1988 (S.I.1988/961) reg.2(b)
152	1986 s.63A; 1989 s.17(1)
153	1988(1) s.5
154	1975(3) s.17(1), (2)
155(1)	1986 s.64(1); 1989 s.17(2)(a)
(2)	1986 s.64(6)
(3) - (6)	1986 s.64(2) - (5)
(7)	1975(2) s.24(1)(a); 1986 s.86, Sch.10, para.92
156	1975(2) s.23(2A); 1989 s.31(1), Sch.8, para.11
157(1)	1975(3) s.5(6), Sch.3, paras.1, 2; 1986 s.86, Sch.10, para.97
(2)	1975(3) s.5(6), Sch.3, para.3
158	1977 s.17(4)
159	1986 s.64A; 1989 s.18
160	1986 s.64B; 1990 s.21(1), Sch.6, para.24
161(1), (2)	1975(1) s.133(1), (2)
(3)	1975(1) s.133(3); Finance Act 1980 (c.48) s.120, Sch.19, para.5(4)
(4)	1975(1) s.133(4)
162(1)	1975(1) s.134(1)(a)
(2)	1975(1) s.134(2); 1989 s.26, Sch.7, para.15
(3)	1975(1) s.134(2A); 1990 s.16(3)
(4)	1975(1) s.134(2B); 1990 s.17(3)
(5)(a)	1975(1) s.134(4)(a); 1985 s.29(1), Sch. 5, para.11; 1989 s.1(8); The Social Security (Contributions and Allocation of Contributions) (Re-rating) Order 1989 (S.I.1989/26) art.6
(b)	1975(1) s.134(4)(b); 1985 s.29(1), Sch.5, para.11; The Social Security (Contributions and Allocation of Contributions) (Re-rating) Order 1989 (S.I.1989/26) art.6
(c)	1975(1) s.134(4)(bb); 1991(3) s.4(a)
(d) - (f)	1975(1) s.134(4)(c) - (e); 1985 s.29(1), Sch.5, para.11; The Social Security (Treasury Supplement to and Allocation of Contributions)(Re-rating) Order 1987 (S.I.1987/48) art.3
(6)	1975(1) ss.134(4), 165; 1985 s.29(1), Sch.5, para.11
(7)	1975(1) s.134(4A); 1981(1) s.3(3)

SOCIAL SECURITY ADMINISTRATION ACT—*continued.*

Section of 1992 Act	Derivation
(8)(a)	1975(1) s.134(4B)(a); 1981(1) s.3(3)
(b)	1975(1) s.134(4B)(aa); 1991(3) s.4(b)
(c), (d)	1975(1) s.134(4B)(b), (c); 1981(1) s.3(3)
(9)—(11)	1975(1) s.134(5)
(12)	1975(1) s.134(6); 1979 s.14(2)
163(1)(a), (b)	1975(1) s.135(1), (2); 1975(2) s.65(1), Sch.4, para.52; 1984 s.11, Sch.4, para.3; 1990 s.16(4); 1991(2) s.4, Sch.1, para.17
(c)	1986 s.85(3)(d)
(d)	1982(2) ss.1(6), 9(7); 1985 s.19; 1986 ss.68, 85(3)(c)
(e)	1989 s.28(4)(b)
(2)(a)	1975(1) s.135(3)(a); 1975(2) s.64(1)(a); 1975(3) s.23(1)(a); 1977 s.23(1)(a); 1980(1) s.19(1); 1982(2) s.46(1)(a); 1986 s.85(1)(e), (f); 1988(1) s.15(1)(a); 1989 s.28(1)(a); 1990 s.18(1)(a); 1991(1) s.4(3)
(b)	1975(1) s.135(2)(a) - (f), (3)(b); 1984 s.11, Sch.4, para.3; 1991(2) s.4, Sch.1, para.18
(c)	1975(1) ss.135(2)(h), (3)(b), 159(4); 1975 (Old Cases) ss.2(1), 5(1); 1990 s.16(4), (7), (8)(a)
(d)	1986 s.85(1)(a); 1988(2) s.135, Sch.10, para.12; 1991(2) s.7, Sch.3, para.8(a)
(e)	1986 s.85(1)(b)
(f)	1975(3) s.1(2)
(g)	1986 s.85(1)(c)
(h)	1986 s.85(1)(d)
(i)	1989 s.28(4)(a)
(3)	1975(1) s.135(4); 1982(2) s.46(2)
(4)	1977 s.1(2)
(5)	1975(1) s.135(7); 1990 s.17(4)
164(1) - (3)	1986 s.85(5) - (7)
(4)	1975 (Old Cases) s.4(4)(e); 1990 s.16(8)(b)
(5)	1975(1) s.113(2)(b); 1983 s.25, Sch.8 para.24; 1986 s.85(8)
(6)	1989 s.28(3)
165(1)	1975(1) s.133(5); 1986 s.85(9); 1991(2) s.7, Sch.3, para.8(b)
(2) - (4)	1975(1) s.133(6); 1975(3) s.23(4); 1986 s.85(10)
(5)	1975(1) s.135(5); 1975(2) s.64(2); 1975(3) s.23(4); 1977 s.23(2); 1980(1) s.19(3); 1980(2) s.7(1); 1986 s.85(4); 1988(1) s.15(2); 1989 s.28(2); 1990 ss.16(5), 18(2)
166(1)—(3)	1975(1) ss.137(2), 165
(4), (5)	1975(1) ss.137(3), (4), 165
167(1)	1986 s.32(1)

SOCIAL SECURITY ADMINISTRATION ACT—*continued.*

Section of 1992 Act	Derivation
(2)—(4)	1986 s.32(5)—(7)
(5), (6)	1986 s.32(7A), (7B); 1988(1) s.11, Sch.3, para.4
168(1) - (4)	1986 s.32(8A)—(8D); 1988(1) s.11, Sch.3, para.6
(5)	1986 s.32(8E); 1990 s.10(1)
169	1986 s.85(11), (12)
170(1) - (4)	1980(1) s.9(1) - (4)
(5)	1980(1) s.9(7); 1982(2) s.48(5), Sch.4, para.30; 1991(1) s.3(1)(b); R12
171(1), (2)	1975(1) s.141(1)
(3)	1975(1) s.141(3)
(4)	1975(1) s.141(4); 1982 s.48(5), Sch.4, para.16
172(1)	1980(1) s.10(1); 1986 s.86, Sch.10, para.98(a)
(2)	1975(1) s.141(2); 1981(2) s.8, Sch.2, para.2; 1986 s.86, Sch.10, para.86
(3)	1980(1) s.10(2)
(4)	1975(1) s.141(2)
(5)	1980(1) s.10(9)
173(1), (2)	1986 s.61(1), (2)
(3)	1986 s.61(3); 1989 s.26, Sch.7, para.27
(4)	1986 s.61(4)
(5)	1986 s.61(5); 1989 s.31(1), Sch.8, para.12(3)
(6)	1980(1) s.10(9)
(7)	1986 s.61(10) "regulations"; 1989 s.31(1), Sch.8, para.12(4)
174(1) - (3)	1980(1) s.10(3) - (5)
(4)	1980(1) s.10(9)
175	1991(2) s.3(1) - (6)
176(1)	1986 s.61(7); 1988(2) s.135, Sch.10, para.10
(2), (3)	1986 s.61(8), (9)
177(1) - (3)	1975(1) s.142(1) - (3)
(4)	1975(1) s.142(4); 1975(2) s.65(2), Sch.4, para.66; 1986 s.65(1)
(5)	1975(1) s.142(1)
178(1), (2)	1975(3) s.14(1); 1986 s.65(4); 1991(2) s.7, Sch.3, para.6
(3)	1975(3) s.14(2)
179(1)	1975(1) s.143(1); 1975(3) s.15(1); 1977 s.20(1), (2); 1986 s.65(2)(a)
(2)	1975(1) s.143(1A); 1975(3) s.15(1A); 1981(2) s.6(1), (2)
(3)	1975(1) s.143(2); 1975(3) s.15(2)
(4)	1975(1) s.143(1); 1975(3) s.15(1); 1986 s.65(4); 1991(2) s.7, Sch.3, para.6
(5)	1975(3) s.15(1); 1986 s.65(4); 1991(2) s.7, Sch.3, para.6

SOCIAL SECURITY ADMINISTRATION ACT—*continued.*

Section of 1992 Act	Derivation
180	1986 s.78
181	Supplementary Benefits Act 1976 (c.71) s.22; 1980(1) s.6(1), (3), Sch.2, Part I, para.21, Part II; Criminal Procedure (Scotland) Act 1975 (c.21) s.298G; Criminal Justice Act 1982 (c.48) ss.46, 54; The Transfer of Functions (Health and Social Security) Order 1988 (S.I.1988/1843) Sch.3, para.2(c)
182	Supplementary Benefits Act 1976 s.23; 1980(1) s.6(3), Sch.2, Part II; Criminal Procedure (Scotland) Act 1975 s.298G; Criminal Justice Act 1982 ss.46, 54; The Transfer of Functions (Health and Social Security) Order 1988 Sch.3, para.2(c)
183	1975(1) s.154
184	1975(1) s.155
185(1)	Drafting
(2)	1975(1) s.159(3)(c)
186	Drafting
187(1)	1975(1) s.87(1); 1975(3) s.12(1); 1986 s.86, Sch.10, para.48(a)
(2)	1975(1) s.87(2); 1975(3) s.12(2); Solicitors (Scotland)) Act 1980 (c.46) s.66, Sch.6, para.2
(3)	1975(1) s.87(3)
188(1), (2)	1975(1) s.163
(3)	1975 (Old Cases) s.12
189(1), (2)	1975(1) s.168(1), Sch.20, "regulations"; 1975(3) s.22(1); 1977 s.24(1) "regulations"; 1982(2) s.47 "regulations"; 1986 ss.52, 84(1) "regulations", Sch.5, para.20, 1989 s.30(1) "regulations"; 1991(2) s.3(8)
(3)	1975(1) s.166(1); 1975(3) s.22(2); 1977 s.24(3); 1980(1) s.14(8); 1982(2) s.45(2); 1986 s.83(1); 1989 s.29(1); 1990 s.21(1), Sch.6, para.8(7); 1991(2) s.3(8)
(4)	1975(1) s.166(2); 1975(3) s.22(6); 1977 s.24(3); 1982(2) s.45(1); 1986 s.83(1); 1989 s.29(1)
(5)	1975(1) ss.113(2)(c), 166(3); 1975(3) s.22(7); 1977 s.24(3); 1982(2) s.45(1); 1986 s.83(1); 1989 ss.29(1), 31(1), Sch.8, para.10(1); 1991(2) s.3(7); R6
(6)	1975(1) s.166(3A); 1975(3) s.22(7A); 1977 s.24(3); 1986 ss.62(1), (2), 83(1); 1989 s.29(1)
(7)	1986 s.83(2); 1988(2) s.135, Sch.10, para.11(2)
(8)	1975(1) s.133(6); 1986 s.83(5); 1988(2) s.135, Sch.10, para.11(4); 1989 ss.17(2)(c), s.9(5)
(9)	1975(1) s.166(5); 1977 s.24(3); 1982(2) s.45(1); 1986 s.83(6); 1989 s.29(6); 1991 s.12(3)
(10)	1975(1) s.166(5A); 1986 s.52(1), Sch.5, para.17
(11)	1975(1) s.166(7); 1975(3) ss.14(3), 15(3); 1986 s.65(4); 1991(2) s.7, Sch.3, para.6
(12)	1975(1) s.168(4)

SOCIAL SECURITY ADMINISTRATION ACT—*continued.*

Section of 1992 Act	Derivation
190(1)	1975(1) s.167(1)(b); 1975(3) s.22(3); 1981(1) s.4(5)(b), 1986 ss.62(3), 83(3)(d); 1989 ss.17(2)(b), 29(2)(h)
(2)	1975(3) s.22(4); 1990 s.21(1), Sch.6, para.8(3)
(3)	1975(1) s.167(3); 1975(3) s.22(5), 1977 s.24(5); 1982(2) s.45(2); 1986 s.83(4); 1989 s.29(3); 1990 s.21(1), Sch.6, para.8(1), (3), (4), (7), (9), (12); 1991(2) s.12(2)
(4)	1975(1) s.167(4); 1980(1) s.14(8); 1990 s.21(1), Sch.6, para.8(1); R13
191	
"the 1975 Act"; "the 1986 Act"; "benefit"	Drafting
"chargeable financial year"; "charging authority"	1986 s.20(11), "chargeable financial year"; "charging authority"; 1988(2) s.135, Sch.10, para.2(5)
"Christmas bonus"	Drafting
"claim"	1975(1) s.168(1), Sch.20, "claim"
"claimant"	1975(1) s.168(1), Sch.20, "claimant"
"Commissioner"; "compensation payment"; "compensator"; "the Consequential Provisions Act"; "contribution card"; "the Contributions and Benefits Act"; "disablement benefit"; "the disablement questions"	Drafting
"dwelling"	1986 s.84(1) "dwelling"
"5 year general qualification"	Drafting
"housing authority"	1986 s.84(1) "housing authority"; Housing (Scotland) Act 1988 (c.43) ss. 1, 3, Sch.2, para.1
"housing benefit scheme"	1986 s.84(1) "housing benefit scheme"
"income-related benefit"	Drafting
"industrial injuries benefit"	1975(1) s.168(1), Sch.20, "industrial injuries benefit"
"invalidity benefit"	Drafting
"levying authority"	1986 s.20(11) "levying authority"; 1988(2) s.135, Sch.10, para.2(5)
"local authority"	1986 s.84(1) "local authority"
"medical examination"	1975(1) s.168(1), Sch.20, "medical examination"
"medical practitioner"	1975(1) s.168(1), Sch.20, "medical practitioner"
"medical treatment"	1975(1) s.168(1), Sch.20, "medical treatment"

SOCIAL SECURITY ADMINISTRATION ACT—*continued.*

Section of 1992 Act	Derivation
"new town corporation"	1986 s.84(1) "new town corporation"
"the Northern Ireland Department"	1975(1) s.168(1), Sch.20, "the Northern Ireland Department"
"the Northern Ireland Administration Act"; "occupational pension scheme"; "the Old Cases Act"; "Old Cases payments"; "the Pensions Act"; "personal pension scheme"	Drafting
"prescribe"	1975 s.168(1), Sch.20, "prescribe"
"President"	1975(1) s.168(1), Sch.20 "President"; 1991(2) s.4, Sch.1, para.20
"rate rebate"; "rent rebate"; "rent allowance"	Drafting
"rates"	1986 s.84(1) "rates"; Abolition of Domestic Rates Etc. (Scotland) Act 1987 (c.47) s.26(2)(a)
"rating authority"	1986 s.84(1) "rating authority"
"tax year"	1975(1) s.168(1), Sch.20, "tax year"
"10 year general qualification"	Drafting
"widow's benefit"	Drafting
192	Short title, commencement and extent
Sch. 1	
para.1	1975(1) s.165A; 1985 ss.17, 32(3)
para.2	1975(1) s.165A; 1985 s.17; 1986 s.86, Sch.10, para.88; Social Security Act 1986 (Commencement No.1) Order 1986 (S.I.1986/1609)
para.3	1975(1) s.165A; 1986 s.86, Sch.10, para.87; Social Security Act 1986 (No.4) Commencement Order 1986 (S.I.1986/1959)
para.4	1975(1) s.165A; 1986 s.86, Sch.10, para.87; 1989 ss.31(1), 33(2), (3), Sch.8, para.9(1)
para.5	1975(1) s.165A; 1986 s.86, Sch.10, para.87; 1989 s.31(1), Sch.8, para.9(1); 1990 ss.6(1), 23(2), (3)
Sch. 2	
para.1(1)	1975(1) s.97(4), Sch.10, para.1A(4); 1983 s.25, Sch.8, para.8
(2) - (4)	1975(1) s.97(4), Sch.10, para.1A(5) - (7); 1980(1) s.13(1) - (3); 1983 s.25, Sch.8, para.8
(5)	1975(1) s.97(4), Sch.10, para.1A(9); 1980(1) s.13(6); 1983 s.25, Sch.8, para.8
(6)	1980(1) s.13(5)(a); Judicial Pensions Act 1981 (c.20) s.36, Sch.3, para.10
(7)	1980(1) s.13(1)

SOCIAL SECURITY ADMINISTRATION ACT—*continued.*

Section of 1992 Act	Derivation
para.2	1975(1) s.97(4), Sch.10, para.1A(10); 1983 s.25, Sch.8, para.8
para. 3	1975(1) ss.97(4), 100D(7), 108(3), Sch. 10, para.1A(11), Sch.10A, para.11, Sch.12, paras.5A, 7; 1983 s.25, Sch.8, paras.8, 10; 1991(2) s.4, Sch.1, paras.5, 16
para.4(1), (2)	1975(1) ss.97(4), 100D(7), Sch.10, paras.1B, 1C, Sch.10A, para.11; 1983 s.25, Sch.8, para.8; 1991(2) s.4, Sch.1, paras.5, 16
para.5	1975(1) ss.97(4), 100D(7), 108(3), Sch.10, para.1D, Sch.10A, para.11, Sch.12, para.9; 1983 s.25, Sch.8, paras.8, 11; 1991(2) ss.4, Sch.1, paras.5, 16
para.6	1975(1) s.97(4), Sch.10, para.4; 1980(1) s.12; The Transfer of Functions (Social Security Commissioners) Order 1984 (S.I.1984/1818) art.3
para.7	1975(1) ss.97(4), 100D(7), 108(3), 113(3), Sch.10, para.3, Sch.10A, para.11, Sch.12, paras.4, 5, 6, 7; 1983 s.25, Sch.8, para.27(b); 1991(2) s.4, Sch.1, paras.5, 16
para.8	1980(1) s.17; 1991(2) s.4, Sch.2, para.10
Sch. 3	
para.1	1975(1) s.115(2) "competent tribunal"; 1983 s.25, Sch.8, paras.5, 25; 1991(2) s.4, Sch.1, para.10
para.2	1975(1) s.115, Sch.13, para.1; 1989 s.21, Sch.3, para.4
para.3	1975(1) s.115, Sch.13, para.1A; 1986 s.52(1), Sch.5, para.19(a)
paras.4 - 9	1975(1) s.115, Sch.13, paras.2 - 7
para.10	1975(1) s.115, Sch.13, para.7A; 1989 s.21, Sch.3, para.10; 1991(2) s.4, Sch.1, para.17
para.11	1975(1) s.115, Sch.13, para.10; 1986 s.52(1), Sch.5, para.19(b)
para.12	1975(1) s.115, Sch.13, para.11
Sch. 4	
Part I	1989 s.19, Sch.2, Part I; 1990 s.21(1), Sch.6, para.28(4), (5); 1991(2) s.4, Sch.2, para.19
Part II	1989 s.19, Sch.2, Part II; 1990 s.21(1), Sch.6, para.28(6)
Sch. 5	
para.1	1980(1) s.9(2), Sch.3, para.1; 1982(2) s.48(5), Sch.4, para.32(2)
para.2	1980(1) s.9(2), Sch.3, para.2; 1982(2) s.48(5), Sch.4, para.32(3)
paras.3 - 10	1980(1) s.9(2), Sch.3, paras.3 - 10
Sch. 6	1975(1) s.141, Sch.16, Part 1
Sch. 7	
Part I	
para.1	1980(1) s.10(2), Sch.3, para.12(4); 1991(2) s.4, Sch.2, para.11
para.2	1980(1) s.10(2), Sch.3, para.12(1)
para.3	1980(1) s.10(2), Sch.3, para.12(2); 1986 s.86, Sch.10, para.99
para.4	1980(1) s.10(2), Sch.3, para.13(1)

SOCIAL SECURITY ADMINISTRATION ACT—*continued.*

Section of 1992 Act	Derivation
para.5	1980(1) s.10(2), Sch.3, para.13(1A); 1986 s.86, Sch.10, para.106
paras.6, 7	1980(1) s.10(2), Sch.3, para.14
para.8	1980(1) s.10(2), Sch.3, paras.15A, 15AA; 1982(2) s.48(5), Sch.4, para.33(3); 1986 s.86, Sch.10, para.107; 1989 s.31(1), Sch.8, para.12(6)
paras.9, 10	1980(1) s.10(2), Sch.3, paras.19, 20
Part II	R14
para.11	1975(1) s.141, Sch.16, para.5
para.12	1975(1) s.141, Sch.16, para.8; 1986 s.86, Sch.10, para.90
paras.13 - 15	1975(1) s.141, Sch.16, paras.9 - 11
para.16	1980(1) s.11(2)(a)
para.17	1975(1), s.141, Sch.16, para.12
Sch. 8	1975(1) s.142(2); Sch.17
Sch. 9	
para.1(1)	1975 (Old Cases) s.4(1)
(2)	1975 (Old Cases) s.4(2); 1989 s.31(1), Sch.8, para.10(1)
(3)	1975 (Old Cases) s.4(3)
(4)	1975 (Old Cases) s.4(4); 1977 s.11(1)(a); 1990 s.16(8)(b)
(5) - (7)	1975 (Old Cases) s.4(5) - (7)
paras.2, 3	1975 (Old Cases) ss.8, 9
para.4	1986 s.53(11)
Sch. 10	
para.1	Drafting
para.2	1986 s.73, Sch.7, para.3
para.3(1)	1986 s.73, Sch.7, para.4(1); 1991(2) s.4, Sch.2, para.15(b)
(2)	1986 s.73, Sch.7, para.4(2)
para.4(1)	1986 s.73, Sch.7, para.5(1)
(2)	1986 s.73, Sch.7, para.2
(3)	1986 s.73, Sch.7, para.5(2)
para.5	1986 s.73, Sch.7, para.7
para.6	1986 s.73, Sch.7, para.6

SOCIAL SECURITY ACTS CONSOLIDATION
TABLE OF DESTINATIONS

1. The legislation relating to social security is consolidated into three Acts—
    (a) the Social Security Contributions and Benefits Act (c. 4);
    (b) the Social Security Administration Act (c. 5); and
    (c) the Social Security (Consequential Provisions) Act (c. 6).
They are respectively referred to in this Table as CB, A and SS CP.

2. Notes 1 to 4 at the beginning of the Table of Derivations for the Social Security Administration Act apply to this Table as well.

Section of Act	Subject matter	Section of 1992 Act	Remarks
	NATIONAL INSURANCE ACT 1974 (c. 14)		
6(1)	Regulations as to correction of errors etc.	A70(1), (3)	Am. Social Security (Consequential Provisions) Act 1975 (c. 18) s. 1(3), Sch. 2, para. 70; 1975(2) s. 65, Sch. 4, para. 35; 1975(3) s. 21(1), Sch. 4, para. 8; Supplementary Benefits Act 1976 (c. 71) s. 35(2), Sch. 7, para. 36; 1990 s. 21(1), Sch. 6, para. 31(a); 1991(1) s. 3(1)(a); 1991(2) s. 15(1); 1991(3) s. 6(1).
(3)	—	See A70(2), 189	—
	SOCIAL SECURITY ACT 1975 (c. 14)		
1	Outline of contributory system.		
(1)	—	CB1(1)	Rep. in part 1986 s. 86, Sch. 11; 1990 s. 21(2), Sch. 7; Employment Act 1990 (c. 38) s. 16(2), Sch. 3; am. 1990 s. 16(1), (2), (10).
(2)	—	CB1(2)	Am. 1991(3) s. 1(2).
(3)	—	CB1(3)	Am. 1985 s. 1(2), Sch. 5, para. 5.
(4)	—	CB1(4)	Am. 1991(3) s. 2(1)(a).
(4A)	—	CB1(5)	Inserted 1990 s. 16(2); am. 1991(1) s. 1(4).
(5), (5A)	—	—	Rep. 1989 s. 31(2), Sch. 9.
(6)	—	CB1(6)	Am. 1991(3) s. 1(3).
2	Categories of earners.	CB2	—
3	"Earnings".	—	—
(1)	—	CB3(1)	—
(1A)–(1C)	—	CB4(1)–(3)	Inserted 1982(2) s. 37(1).
(1D)	—	CB4(4)	Inserted 1989 s. 31(1), Sch. 8, para. 1.
(2), (3)	—	CB3(2), (3)	—
(4)	—	CB4(5)	Inserted 1982(2) s. 48(5), Sch. 4, para. 8.

SOCIAL SECURITY ACTS CONSOLIDATION—*continued.*

Section of Act	Subject matter	Section of 1992 Act	Remarks

SOCIAL SECURITY ACT 1975 (c. 14)—*continued.*

Section of Act	Subject matter	Section of 1992 Act	Remarks
4	Class 1 contributions.	—	—
(1)	—	CB5(1)	Am. 1985 s. 7(1).
(2)	—	CB6(1)	Rep. in part 1982(2) s. 48(6), Sch. 5.
(3)	—	CB6(3)	Subst. 1989 s. 26, Sch. 7, para. 2.
(4), (5)	—	CB7	—
(6)–(6B)	—	CB8(1)–(3)	Subst. 1989 s. 1(1).
(6C)	—	CB9(1), (4)	Inserted 1985 s. 7(2); am. 1989 s. 26, Sch. 7, para. 2(2).
(6D)	—	CB9(2)	Inserted 1985 s. 7(2).
(6E)	—	CB9(3), (4)	Inserted 1985 s. 7(2).
(6F)	—	A146	Inserted 1985 s. 7(2); rep. in part 1989 s. 1(2).
(6G)	—	A147(1)	Inserted 1985 s. 7(2).
(6H)	—	A190(1)	Inserted 1985 s. 7(2).
(6HH)	—	A147(2)	Inserted 1986 s. 74(1), (2).
(6J)	—	A147(3)	Inserted 1985 s. 7(2).
(6K)	—	A147(4), (5)	Inserted 1985 s. 7(2); am. 1990 s. 21(1), Sch. 6, para. 1(1).
(7)	—	CB6(5)	Inserted 1979 s. 14(1); am. 1985 s. 8(1).
4A	Class 1A contributions.	CB10	Inserted 1991(3) s. 1(5).
5, 6	—	—	Rep. 1975(2) s. 65(3), Sch. 5.
7	Class 2 contributions.	—	—
(1)	—	CB11(1)	Am. Education (School-Leaving Dates) Act 1976 (c. 5) s. 2(4), 1984 s. 17(1).
(2), (3)	—	—	Rep. 1975(2), s. 65(3), Sch. 5.
(4)–(6)	—	CB11(3)–(5)	—
7A	Late paid Class 2 contributions.	CB12	Inserted 1984 s. 17(2); subsection (3) partly subst. SI 1985/1398.
8	Class 3 contributions.		
(1)	—	CB13(1)	Am. Education (School-Leaving Dates) Act 1976 s. 2(4), 1984 s. 18(1)(a).
(2)	—	CB13(2)	—
(2)(a)	—	CB13(3)	1975(1) s. 8(2)(b) rep. 1975(2), s. 65(3), Sch. 5.
(2A)	—	CB13(4)	Inserted 1984 s. 18(1)(b); words added 1984 s. 18(3).
(2B)	—	CB13(5)	Inserted 1984 s. 18(3).

SOCIAL SECURITY ACTS CONSOLIDATION—*continued.*

Section of Act	Subject matter	Section of 1992 Act	Remarks
	SOCIAL SECURITY ACT 1975 (c. 14)—*continued.*		
(2C)	—	CB13(6)	Added 1984 s. 18(3); amended SI 1985/1398 and 1989 s. 26, Sch. 7, para. 4.
(2D)	—	CB13(7)	Inserted 1989 s. 18(3).
(3)	—	—	Rep. 1975(2) s. 65(3) Sch. 5.
9	Class 4 contributions.	—	—
(1)	—	CB15(1), (2), (5)	Am. 1989 s. 26, Sch. 7, paras. (a)–(c).
(2)	—	CB15(3)	—
(3)	—	CB16(1), (2), (6)	—
(4)	—	CB16(3)	—
(5)	—	CB16(4)	Am. 1990 s. 17(1).
(6)	—	CB16(5)	Am. 1990 s. 17(2).
(7), (8)	—	CB17(1), (2)	—
(9)	—	CB17(3)–(6)	—
10	Class 4 contributions recoverable under regulations.	CB18	—
11	General power to regulate liability for contributions.	CB19(1)–(3)	—
12	Descriptions of contributory benefits.	—	—
(1)	—	CB20(1)	Rep. in part 1980(2) s. 7(6), Sch., 1986 s. 86, Sch. 11; am. 1975(2) s. 65(1), Sch. 4, para. 37, 1984 s. 13, Sch. 5, para. 2(a), 1986 s. 86, Sch. 10, para. 63, 1989 s. 26, Sch. 7, para. 6.
(2)	—	CB20(2)	Rep. in part 1980(1) s. 5(1)(i), 1986 s. 86, Sch. 11.
(3)	—	—	Rep. 1986 s. 86, Sch. 11.
13	Contribution conditions and the earnings factor.	—	—
(1)	—	CB21(1), (2)	Rep. in part 1980(1) s. 5(1)(ii), 1986 s. 86, Sch. 11; am. 1986 s. 86, Sch. 10, para. 64.
(2)	—	CB22(1), (2)	Rep. in part 1980(2) s. 7(6), Sch; am. 1975(2) s. 65, Sch. 4, para. 38(a), 1986 ss. 18(1), 75, 86, Sch. 8, para. 2(1), Sch. 10, para. 72(a).
(3)	—	CB22(4)	Am. 1975(2) s. 65, Sch. 4, para. 38(b), 1986 s. 75, Sch. 8, para. 2(2).
(4)	—	CB22(5)	Rep. in part 1980(2) s. 7(6), Sch.; am. 1986 s. 75, Sch. 8, para. 2(3).

SOCIAL SECURITY ACTS CONSOLIDATION—*continued.*

Section of Act	Subject matter	Section of 1992 Act	Remarks

SOCIAL SECURITY ACT 1975 (c. 14)—*continued.*

Section of Act	Subject matter	Section of 1992 Act	Remarks
(5)	—	CB22(3), 23(1), (3)	Am. 1979 s. 21(4), Sch. 3, para. 5, 1986 s. 75, Sch. 8, para. 2(4), 1988(1) s. 9, Sch. 2, para. 1(1)(a), 1989 ss. 4(2), 26, Sch. 7, para. 7.
(5ZA)	—	CB23(2)	Inserted 1988(1) s. 9, Sch. 2, para. 1(1)(b).
(5A)	—	CB23(4)	Affected by R1; inserted 1985 s. 29(1), Sch. 5, para. 6(b).
(5AA)	—	CB22(6)	Inserted 1989 s. 4(3).
(5B)	—	CB24(1)	Inserted 1986 s. 75, Sch. 8, para. 2(5).
(5C)	—	CB24(2)	Inserted 1989 s. 4(4).
(6)	—	CB21(3), (5)	Am. 1986 s. 75, Sch. 8, para. 2(6).
(7)	—	CB21(6)	—
(8)	—	CB21(4)	Am. 1986 s. 86, Sch. 10, para. 72(b).
14	Unemployment benefit and sickness benefit.	—	—
(1)	—	CB25(1), 31(1)	—
(2)	—	CB25(2), 31(2)	Am. 1989 s. 7(6), Sch. 1, para. 4(1).
(2A)	—	CB31(3)	Inserted 1982(2) s. 39(3).
(3)	—	CB25(3), 31(4)	—
(4)	—	CB25(4), 31(5)	Substituted 1975(2) s. 18(1); am. 1982(2) s. 48(5), Sch. 4, para. 9.
(5)	—	—	Subsection (4) substituted for subsections (4) and (5); see above.
(6)	—	CB25(5), (6), 31(6), (7)	Rep. in part 1989 s. 7, Sch. 1, para. 4(2); am. 1975(2) s. 65, Sch. 4, para. 39(b), 1979 s. 21(4), Sch. 3, para. 6, 1986 s. 86, Sch. 10, para. 83.
(7)	—	—	Rep. 1980(2) s. 7(6), Sch.
(8)	—	CB25(7), 31(8)	—
15	Invalidity pension.	—	—
(1)	—	CB33(1)	Am. 1989 s. 7, Sch. 1, para. 5(1).
(2)	—	CB33(2)	Inserted 1989 s. 7, Sch. 1, para. 5(2).
(3)	—	CB33(3)	Am. 1975(2) s. 65, Sch. 4, para. 40(b).

SOCIAL SECURITY ACTS CONSOLIDATION—*continued.*

Section of Act	Subject matter	Section of 1992 Act	Remarks

SOCIAL SECURITY ACT 1975 (c. 14)—*continued.*

Section of Act	Subject matter	Section of 1992 Act	Remarks
(4)	—	CB33(4), (5)	Am. 1975(2) s. 65, Sch. 4, para. 40(c), 1979 ss. 5, 21(4), Sch. 1, para. 1, Sch. 3, para. 7, 1986 s. 86, Sch. 10, para. 83.
(5)	—	CB33(6)	—
(5A), (5B)	—	CB33(7), (8)	Inserted 1991(2) s. 9(1).
(6)	—	CB33(9)	Inserted 1982(2) s. 48(5), Sch. 4, para. 10.
15A	Statutory sick pay and entitlement to invalidity pension.	CB33(10), (11)	Section inserted 1985 s. 18(3)
16	Invalidity allowance.	—	—
(1)	—	CB34(1), (2)	Am. 1985 s. 9(1)(a).
(2)	—	CB34(3)	Am. 1979 s. 5, Sch. 1, para. 10(a).
(2A)	—	—	Spent; inserted 1979 s. 5, Sch. 1, para. 10(b).
(2B)–(2D)	—	CB34(4)–(6)	Inserted 1985 s. 9(1)(b); am. 1986 s. 18(1); see also SS CP s. 4, Sch. 2, para. 23 (1975(2) s. 29A).
(3)	—	CB34(7)	Am. 1985 s. 9(1)(c); see also SS CP s. 4, Sch. 2, para. 23 (1975(2) s. 29A(4)).
17	Determination of days for which benefit is payable.	—	—
(1)	—	CB57(1)	Am. 1980(2) s. 3(1), 1989 s. 10(2).
(2)	—	CB57(3)	Affected by R2; am. 1989 s. 10(3).
(2A)	—	CB57(4)	Inserted 1988(1) s. 16, Sch. 4, para. 4.
(2B)	—	CB57(5)	Inserted 1989 s. 10(4).
(2C), (2D)	—	CB57(6), (7)	Inserted 1989 s. 31(1), Sch. 8, para. 3
(3)	—	CB57(8)	Rep. in part 1980(2) s. 7(6). Sch.
(4), (5)	—	CB57(9), (10)	Inserted 1981(2) s. 5.
18	Duration of unemployment benefit.	—	—
(1))	—	CB26(1)	—
(2)–(2B)	—	CB26(2)–(4)	Substituted 1989 s. 11.
(3)	—	CB26(5)	—
(4)	—	CB26(6)	Substituted 1986 s. 43(1).

SOCIAL SECURITY ACTS CONSOLIDATION—*continued.*

Section of Act	Subject matter	Section of 1992 Act	Remarks
	SOCIAL SECURITY ACT 1975 (c. 14)—*continued.*		
19	Loss of employment due to stoppage of work.	—	—
(1), (1A)	—	CB27(1), (2)	Substituted 1986 s. 44(1).
(2)	—	CB27(3)	—
20	Other disqualifications.	—	—
(1)	—	CB28(1)	Rep. in part Employment Act 1988 (c. 19) s. 33(2), Sch. 4; amended Employment Act 1988 s. 27(2), 1989 s. 12(1), Unemployment Benefit (Disqualification Period) Order 1988 (S.I. 1988/487) art. 2.
(1A)	—	CB28(2)	Inserted 1986 s. 43(3)(a); rep. in part 1989 s. 12(2).
(2)	—	CB32(1), 59(1)	—
(3)	—	CB28(3), 32(2), 59(2)	—
(3A)	—	CB28(4)	Inserted 1985 s. 10.
(4)	—	CB28(5)	Substituted 1989 s. 12(3).
(5)	—	CB28(6), 32(3), 59(3)	Rep. in part Employment Act 1989 (c. 38) s. 29(4), Sch. 7; am. Employment Act 1988 (c. 19) s. 27(3).
20A	Exemptions from disqualification for unemployment benefit.	CB29	Inserted 1989 s. 12(4).
21	—	—	Rep. 1980(1) s. 5(1)(iii), 1986 s. 38(1), (2)(a)(i).
22	State maternity allowance.	—	Section 22 substituted for sections 22 and 23 1986 s. 49, Sch. 4, para. 13.
(1)–(3)	—	CB35(1)–(3)	—
(4)	—	CB57(2)	Am. 1988(1) s. 16, Sch. 4, para. 5(a).
(4A)	—	CB35(4)	Inserted 1988(1) s. 16, Sch. 4, para. 5(b).
(5)–(7)	—	CB35(5)–(7)	—
24	Widow's payment.	—	Section substituted 1986 s. 36(1).
(1), (2)	—	CB36(1), (2)	—
(3)	—	CB36(3)	Added 1989 s. 26, Sch. 7, para. 8.

SOCIAL SECURITY ACTS CONSOLIDATION—*continued.*

Section of Act	Subject matter	Section of 1992 Act	Remarks
	SOCIAL SECURITY ACT 1975 (c. 14)—*continued.*		
25	Widowed mother's allowance.	—	—
(1)	—	CB37(1)	Am. 1975(2) s. 65, Sch. 4, para. 41, 1975(3) s. 21(1), Sch. 4, para. 9(a), Human Fertilisation and Embryology Act 1990 (c. 37) s. 49, Sch. 4, para. 2.
(2)	—	CB37(2)	Substituted 1975(3) s. 21, Sch. 4, para. 9(b).
(3), (4)	—	CB37(3), (4)	Substituted 1989 s. 31(1), Sch. 8, para. 4(1).
26	Widow's pension.	—	—
(1)	—	CB38(1)	Am. 1975(2) s. 65, Sch. 4, para. 42, 1986 s. 36(3)(a).
(2)	—	CB39(4), (5)	Am. 1986 s. 36(3)(b).
(3), (4)	—	CB38(2), (3)	Substituted 1989 s. 31(1), Sch. 8, para. 4(2).
27	Matters affecting entitlement to pension.	—	—
(1)	—	CB122(1) "pension-able age"	—
(2)	—	CB Sch. 3 para. 5(8)	—
(3)–(5)	—	—	Rep. 1989 s. 7, Sch. 1, para. 1.
(6)	—	CB43(1)	Rep. in part 1975(2) s. 65, Sch. 5.
28	Category A retirement pension.	—	—
(1)	—	CB 44(1)	Rep. in part 1989 s. 7(2); am. 1975(2) s. 65, Sch.4, para. 43, 1989 s. 31(1), Sch. 8, para. 4(3).
(1A)	—	CB 44(2)	Inserted 1989 s. 31(1), Sch. 8, para. 4(4).
(2)	—	—	Rep. 1985 s. 29(2), Sch. 6.
(3)–(6)	—	—	Rep. 1975(2) s. 65(3), Sch. 5.
(7)	—	CB 47(1)	Am. 1980(2) s. 3(3), 1985 s. 9(2)(a), (b).
(7A)–(7C)	—	CB 47(2)–(4)	Inserted 1985 s. 9(2)(c); am. 1986 s. 18(1); see also SS CP s. 4, Sch. 2, para. 23 (1975(2) s. 29B).
(8)	—	CB 47(5)	Rep. in part 1975(2) s. 65(3), Sch. 5.
29	Category B retirement pension.	—	—

SOCIAL SECURITY ACTS CONSOLIDATION—*continued.*

Section of Act	Subject matter	Section of 1992 Act	Remarks

SOCIAL SECURITY ACT 1975 (c. 14)—*continued.*

Section of Act	Subject matter	Section of 1992 Act	Remarks
(1)	—	CB 49(1)	—
(2), (3)	—	CB 49(2), (3)	Am. 1989 s. 7(3)(a).
(4)	—	CB 49(4)	—
(5)	—	CB 49(5)	Rep. in part 1989 s. 7(3)(b).
(6)	—	CB 49(6)	—
(7)	—	CB 50(1)	Am. 1975(2) s. 65, Sch. 4, para. 44.
(8)	–	CB 50(2)	Am. 1985 s. 9(3).
(9), (9A)	—	CB 49(7), (8)	Inserted 1989 s. 31(1), Sch. 8, para. 4(5).
(10)–(12)	—	—	Rep. 1975(2) s. 65(3), Sch. 5.
30	Category A and B pension (supplementary).	—	—
(1)	—	—	Rep. 1989 s. 7(1).
(2)	—	—	Spent.
(3)	—	CB 54(1), (2)	Rep. in part 1989 s. 7, Sch. 1, para. 2(1).
(4)	—	CB 54(3)	Am. 1975(2) s. 65, Sch. 4, para. 45.
(5)	—	CB 54(4)	Substituted 1989 s. 7, Sch. 1, para. 2(2).
(6)	—	—	Affected by R15; see SS CP s. 3(2); inserted 1979 s. 4(1);p rep. in part 1989 s. 7, Sch. 1, para. 2(3); am. 1989 s. 26, Sch. 7, para. 9.
31	Child's special allowance.	CB 56(1), (2)	Am. 1975(3) s. 21(1), Sch. 4, para. 10; 1977 s. 22(2).
32	—	—	Rep. 1986 s. 86, Sch. 11.
33	Partial satisfaction of contribution conditions.	—	—
(1), (2)	—	CB 60(1), (2)	Rep. in part 1986 s. 42.
(3)	—	CB 60(4)–(6)	Am. 1975(2) s. 65, Sch. 4, para. 46; 1990 s. 21(1), Sch. 6, para. 3(1).
(4)	—	CB 60(7)	Inserted 1975(2) s. 19(5); am. 1986 s. 18(1).
34	Descriptions of non-contributory benefits.	—	—
(1)	—	CB 63	Rep. in part 1991(2) s. 10, Sch. 4; am. 1984 s. 11, Sch. 4, para. 3, 1990 s. 2(3); 1991(2) s. 1(1).
(2)	—	—	Rep. 1986 s. 86, Sch. 11.

SOCIAL SECURITY ACTS CONSOLIDATION—*continued.*

Section of Act	Subject matter	Section of 1992 Act	Remarks

SOCIAL SECURITY ACT 1975 (c. 14)—*continued.*

Section of Act	Subject matter	Section of 1992 Act	Remarks
35	Attendance allowance.	—	—
(1)	—	CB 64	Am. 1988(1) s. 1(1); 1991(2) s. 2(1).
(2)	—	CB 65(1)	Rep. in part 1991(2) s. 10, Sch. 4; am. 1979 s. 2(1), 1989 s. 31(1), Sch. 8, para. 5(2).
(2A)	—	CB 65(2)	Inserted 1979 s. 2(3).
(2B)	—	CB 66(1)	Inserted 1990 s. 1(1); rep. in part 1991(2) s. 10, Sch. 4; am. 1991(2) s. 4, Sch. 2, para. 3(1).
(2C)	—	CB 66(2)	Inserted 1990 s. 1(1).
(3)	—	CB 65(3)	Substituted 1991(2) s. 4, Sch. 2, para. 3(2).
(4)	—	CB65(4), (6)	Rep. in part 1991(2) s. 10, Sch. 4; am. 1979 s. 2(5), 1989 s. 31(1), Sch. 8, para. 5(3), 1990 s. 1(2), 1991(2) s. 4, Sch. 2, para. 3(3).
(4A)	—	CB65(5)	Inserted 1980(1) s. 2, Sch. 1, para. 8; am. 1989 s. 31(1), Sch. 8, para. 5(4), 1991(2) s. 4, Sch. 2, para. 3(3).
(5)	—	—	Rep. 1991(2) s. 10, Sch. 4.
(5A)	—	CB67(1)	Inserted 1979 s. 2(6).
(6)	—	CB67(2)	Rep. in part 1991(2) s. 10, Sch. 4; am. National Health Service Act 1977 (c. 49) s. 129, Sch. 15, para. 63, 1991(2) s. 4, Sch. 2, para. 3(4).
36	Severe disablement allowance.	—	Section substituted 1984 s. 11(1).
(1)–(4)	—	CB68(1)–(4)	—
(4A)	—	CB68(5)	Inserted 1985, s. 21, Sch. 4, para. 3.
(5), (6)	—	CB68(6), (7)	—
(6A), (6B)	—	CB68(8), (9)	Inserted 1989 s. 31(1), Sch. 8, para. 6.
(6C)	—	CB68(10)	Inserted 1991(2) s. 9(2).
(7)	—	CB68(11)	Rep. in part 1989 s. 31(2), Sch. 9; am. 1989 s. 31(1), Sch. 8, para. 2(5), 1990 s. 21(1), Sch. 6, para. 30(5).
(8)	—	CB68(13)	—

SOCIAL SECURITY ACTS CONSOLIDATION—*continued.*

Section of Act	Subject matter	Section of 1992 Act	Remarks
	SOCIAL SECURITY ACT 1975 (c. 14)—*continued.*		
36A	Severe disablement allowance: age related addition.	CB69	Section inserted 1990 s. 2(1).
37	Invalid care allowance.	—	—
(1)	—	CB70(1)	—
(2)	—	CB70(2)	Am. 1991(2) s. 4, Sch. 2, para. 4.
(3)	—	CB70(3)	Rep. in part 1986 s. 37(1).
(4)	—	CB70(4)	—
(5)	—	CB70(5)	—
(6)	—	CB70(6), (10)	Am. 1989 s. 26, Sch. 7, para. 10.
(7)–(9)	—	CB70(7)–(9)	—
37ZA	Disability living allowance.	CB71	Section inserted 1991(2) s. 1(2).
37ZB	The care component.	CB72	Section inserted 1991(2) s. 1(2).
37ZC	The mobility component.	CB73	Section inserted 1991(2) s. 1(2).
37ZD	Persons 65 or over.	CB75	Section inserted 1991(2) s. 1(2).
37ZE	Disability living allowance— supplementary.	CB76	Section inserted 1991(2) s. 1(2).
37A	Mobility allowance.	—	Rep. 1991(2) s. 2(3).
38	Guardian's allowance.	—	—
(1)	—	CB77(1), (7)	Am. 1975(3) s. 21(4), Sch. 4, para. 12(a).
(2), (3)	—	CB77(2), (3)	—
(4)	—	CB77(8)	Rep. in part 1975(3) s. 21(2), Sch. 5.
(5)	—	CB77(9)	Substituted 1975(3) s. 21(1), Sch. 4, para. 12(c).
(6)	—	CB77(10)	Am. 1986 s. 45(a).
(7)	—	CB77(11)	Inserted 1986 s. 45(b).
39	Retirement benefits for the aged.	—	—
(1)(a)	—	CB78(1)	—
(1)(b)	—	CB78(2)	Rep. in part 1989 s. 7, Sch. 1, para. 6.
(1)(c)	—	CB78(3), (4)	Am. 1979 s. 5, Sch. 1, para. 2; 1986 s. 18(1).
(2)	—	CB78(5)	—
(2A)	—	CB78(6)	Inserted 1985 s. 12(1)(b).
(3), (3A)	—	CB78(7), (8)	Substituted 1989 s. 31(1), Sch. 8, para. 4(6).
(4)	—	CB78(9)	—
40	Age addition.	CB79	—
41	Beneficiary's dependent children.	—	—

SOCIAL SECURITY ACTS CONSOLIDATION—*continued.*

Section of Act	Subject matter	Section of 1992 Act	Remarks
	SOCIAL SECURITY ACT 1975 (c. 14)—*continued.*		
(1)	—	CB80(1)	Rep. in part 1989 s. 31(2), Sch. 9; am. 1975(3) s. 21(1), Sch. 4, para. 13.
(2)	—	CB80(2)	Rep. in part 1984 s. 24, Sch. 8, 1986 s. 86, Sch. 11; am. 1984 s. 13, Sch. 5, para. 3(a).
(2A)	—	CB80(3)	Inserted 1984 s. 13, Sch. 5, para. 3(c).
(2B)	—	CB80(4)	Inserted 1984 s. 13, Sch. 5, para. 3(c).
(2C)	—	—	Rep. 1986 s. 86, Sch. 11.
(2D)	—	CB80(7)	Inserted 1984 s. 13, Sch. 5, para. 3(c).
(3)	—	—	Rep. 1984 s. 24, Sch. 8.
(4), (5)	—	CB80(5), (6)	Am. 1975 (3) s. 13, Sch. 4, para. 13.
(6)	—	—	Rep. 1980(1) s. 21, Sch. 5.
42	—	—	Rep. 1975(3) s. 21(2), Sch. 5.
43	Limits of increase for dependent children.	—	—
(1)	—	CB81(1), (2)	Rep. 1975(3) s. 21(2), Sch. 5; am. 1975 (3) s. 21(1), Sch. 4, para. 15(a).
(2)	—	CB81(3)	Am. 1975 (3) s. 21(1), Sch. 4, para. 15(b); 1977 s. 22(3).
(3), (4)	—	—	Rep. 1975(3) s. 21(2), Sch. 5.
44	Short-term benefit increase for adult dependants.	—	—
(1)	—	CB82(1)	Am. 1975 (3) s. 22(1), Sch. 4, para. 16(a); 1980(1) s. 21, Sch. 1, para. 5(2); 1988(1) s. 16, Sch. 4, para. 16(a).
(2)	—	CB82(2)	Am. 1975(3) s. 22(1), Sch. 4, para. 16(a), 1980(1) s. 21, Sch. 1, para. 5(2).
(3)(a)	—	CB82(3)	Am. 1988(1) s. 16, Sch. 4, para. 6(b).
(3)(b)	—	—	Rep. 1980(1) s. 21, Sch. 5.
(3)(c)	—	CB82(4)	Am. 1975(3) s. 22(1), Sch. 4, para. 16(b); 1980(1) s. 2, Sch. 1, para. 4(a).
(4)	—	CB82(5)	—
(5), (6)	—	—	Rep. 1980(1) s. 21, Sch. 5.
45	Pension increase (wife).	—	—
(1)	—	CB83(1)	—

SOCIAL SECURITY ACTS CONSOLIDATION—*continued.*

Section of Act	Subject matter	Section of 1992 Act	Remarks
	SOCIAL SECURITY ACT 1975 (c. 14)—*continued.*		
(2)	—	CB83(2)	Am. 1975(3) s. 21(1), Sch. 4, para. 17; 1988(1) s. 16, Sch. 4, para. 7(a).
(2A)	—	CB83(3)	Inserted 1985 s. 13(1); rep. in part 1988(1) s. 16, Sch. 4, para. 7(b).
(3), (4)	—	—	Rep. 1985 s. 29(2), Sch. 6.
45A	Pension increase (husband).	—	Section inserted 1984 s. 12.
(1)	—	CB84(1)	Am. 1985 s. 13(2)(a).
(2)	—	CB84(2)	Substituted 1985 s. 13(2)(b); am. 1988(1) s. 16, Sch. 4, para. 8(a).
(3)	—	CB84(3)	Substituted 1985 s. 13(2)(b); rep. in part 1988(1) s. 16, Sch. 4, para. 8(b).
46	Pension increase (person with care of children).	—	—
(1)	—	CB85(1)	—
(2)	—	CB85(2)	Am. 1975(3) s. 21(1), Sch. 4, para. 18; 1980(1) s. 2, Sch. 1, para. 4(b).
(3)	—	CB85(3)	—
(4)	—	CB85(4)	Substituted 1985 s. 13(3); rep. in part 1988(1) s. 16, Sch. 4, para. 9.
47	Invalidity pension (dependent relative).	—	—
(1)	—	CB86(1)	Rep. in part 1980(1) s. 21, Sch. 5; am. 1975(3) s. 21(1), Sch. 4, para. 19; 1980(1) s. 2, Sch. 1, para. 5(2); 1985 s. 13(4); 1989 s. 31(1), Sch. 8, para. 7(1).
(1A)	—	CB86(2)	Inserted 1985 s. 13(4)(b).
(2)	—	—	Rep. 1980(1) s. 21, Sch. 5.
47A	Rate of increase where associated retirement pension is attributable to reduced contributions.	—	Section inserted 1980(1) s. 2, Sch. 1, para. 5(1).
(a)	—	CB87(1)	Am. 1990 s. 21(1), Sch. 6, para. 3(2).
(b)	—	CB87(2)	Inserted 1990 s. 21(1), Sch. 6, para. 3(2).
47B	Earnings to include occupational and personal pensions for purposes of benefits.	—	Section inserted 1984 s. 14(a).
(1)	—	CB89(1)	Rep. in part 1988(1) s. 16, Sch. 5; am. 1989 s. 9(3).

SOCIAL SECURITY ACTS CONSOLIDATION— *continued.*

Section of Act	Subject matter	Section of 1992 Act	Remarks
	SOCIAL SECURITY ACT 1975 (c. 14)—*continued.*		
(2)	—	CB89(2)	Am. 1989 s. 9(3).
48	Pensions increases: supplementary provisions.	CB88	Subsections (2) and (3) rep. 1989 s. 7, Sch. 1, para. 7.
49	Beneficiaries under ss. 36 and 37.	CB90	Am. 1984 s. 11, Sch. 4, para. 3.
49A	Effect of trade disputes on entitlement to increases.	CB91	Section inserted 1986 s. 44(2).
50	Descriptions of industrial injuries benefits.	—	—
(1)	—	CB94(1)	Substituted 1986 s. 39, Sch. 3, para. 2.
(1A)	—	CB94(2)	Substituted 1988(1) s. 16, Sch. 4, para. 11.
(2)	—	—	Rep. 1982 s. 48(6), Sch. 5, 1986 s. 86, Sch. 11.
(3)	—	CB94(3)	—
(4)	—	CB94(4)	Substituted 1982(2) s. 48(5), Sch. 4, para. 12(2).
(5)	—	CB94(5)	Affected by R21.
(6)	—	CB94(6)	Substituted 1982(2) s. 48(5), Sch. 4, para. 12(3).
50A	Sickness benefit in respect of industrial injury.	—	Section inserted 1982(2) s. 39(4).
(1), (2)	—	CB102(1), (2)	—
(3)	—	CB102(3)	Am. 1989 s. 7, Sch. 1, para. 8(1).
51	Relevant employments.	CB95	—
52	Earner acting in breach of regulations, etc.	CB98	—
53	Earner travelling in employer's transport.	CB99	—
54	Accidents happening while meeting emergency.	CB100	—
55	Accident caused by another's misconduct, etc.	CB101	—
56	—	—	Rep. 1982(2) s. 48(6), Sch. 5.
57	Disablement gratuity and pension.	—	—
(1)	—	CB103(1), Sch. 7, para. 9(1)	Am. 1986 s. 39, Sch. 3, para. 3(1).
(1A)–(1C)	—	CB103(2)– (4)	Inserted 1986 s. 39, Sch. 3, para. 3(2).
(2)	—	—	Rep. 1984 s. 24, Sch. 8.
(3)	—	CB103(5)	—

SOCIAL SECURITY ACTS CONSOLIDATION—*continued.*

Section of Act	Subject matter	Section of 1992 Act	Remarks
		SOCIAL SECURITY ACT 1975 (c. 14)—*continued.*	
(4)	—	CB103(6), Sch. 7, para. 9(3)	Substituted 1982(2) s. 39(2); am. 1989 s. 26, Sch. 7, para. 12.
(5)	—	CB Sch. 7, para. 9(1), (2)	—
(6)	—	CB103(7), (8)	Am. 1986 s. 39, Sch. 3, para. 3(4).
58	Unemployability supplement.	CB Sch. 7, para. 2.	—
59	Increase of unemployability supplement.	—	—
(1)	—	CB Sch. 7, para. 3(1)	Proviso spent; proviso inserted 1979 s. 5, Sch. 1, para. 12; am. 1985 s. 9(4)(a).
(1A)–(1C)	—	CB Sch. 7, para. 3(2)–(4)	Inserted 1985 s. 9(4)(b); am. 1986 s. 18(1); see also SS CP s. 4, Sch. 2, para. 23 (1975(2) s, 29C).
(2)–(3)	—	CB Sch. 7, para. 3(5), (6)	—
(4)	—	CB Sch. 7, para. 3(7), (8)	Am. 1980(2) s. 3(3).
(5)	—	CB Sch. 7, para. 3(10)	
59A	Reduced earnings allowance.	—	—
(1)	—	CB Sch. 7, para. 11(1)	Inserted 1986 s. 39, Sch. 3, para. 5(1); am. 1989 s. 26, Sch. 7, para. 13, 1990 s. 3(1).
(1A), (1B)	—	CB Sch. 7, para. 11(2), (3)	Inserted 1990 s. 3(2).
(2)–(5)	—	CB Sch. 7, para. 11(4)–(7)	Inserted 1986 s. 39, Sch. 3, para. 5(1).
(6)	—	CB Sch. 7, para. 11(8)	Inserted 1986 s. 39, Sch. 3, para. 5(1); am. 1990 s. 3(3).
(7)	—	CB Sch. 7, para. 11(9)	Inserted 1986 s. 39, Sch. 3, para. 5(1).
(8)	—	CB Sch. 7, para. 11(10), (11)	Inserted 1986 s. 39, Sch. 3, para. 5(1); am. 1988(1) ss. 2(3), 16, Sch. 4, para. 12(a).
(9)	—	CB Sch. 7, para. 11(12)	Inserted 1986 s. 39, Sch. 3, para. 5(1).

SOCIAL SECURITY ACTS CONSOLIDATION—*continued.*

Section of Act	Subject matter	Section of 1992 Act	Remarks
	SOCIAL SECURITY ACT 1975 (c. 14)—*continued.*		
(10)	—	CB Sch. 7, para. 11(14)	Inserted 1986 s. 39, Sch. 3, para. 5(1).
(10A)	—	CB Sch. 7, paras. 11(15), 13(11)	Inserted 1988(1) s. 16, Sch. 4, para. 12(b).
(10B)	—	CB Sch. 7, para. 11(1)	Inserted 1990 s. 3(4).
(11)	—	—	Rep. 1988(1) s. 16, Sch. 5.
59B	Retirement allowance.	—	Section inserted 1988(1) s. 2(1).
(1)	—	CB Sch. 7, para. 13(1)	Rep. in part 1990 s. 3(5)(a); am. 1989 s. 7, Sch. 1, para. 8(2).
(2)	—	CB Sch. 7, para. 13(2)	
(3)	—	CB Sch. 7, para. 13(3)	Rep. in part 1990 s. 3(5)(b).
(4)	—	—	Rep. 1990 s. 3(5)(c).
(5)	—	CB Sch. 7, para. 13(4)	Am. 1989 s. 7, Sch. 1, para. 8(5).
(5A)	—	CB Sch. 7, para. 13(5)	Inserted 1989 s. 17(3).
(6)	—	CB Sch. 7, para. 13(6)	
(7)	—	CB Sch. 7, para. 13(8)	Inserted 1989 s. 7, Sch. 1, para. 8(6).
(8)	—	CB Sch. 7, para. 13(9)	Inserted 1989 s. 7, Sch. 1, para. 8(6); rep. in part 1990 s. 21(2), Sch. 7.
(9)	—	CB Sch. 7, para. 13(10)	Inserted 1990 s. 3(6).
60	—	—	Rep. 1986 s. 39, Sch. 3, para. 5(2).
61	Increase where constant attendance needed.		
(1), (2)	—	CB104(1), (2)	—
(3), (4)	—	CB104(3), (4)	Inserted 1986 s. 39, Sch. 3, para. 6.

SOCIAL SECURITY ACTS CONSOLIDATION—*continued.*

Section of Act	Subject matter	Section of 1992 Act	Remarks

SOCIAL SECURITY ACT 1975 (c. 14)—*continued.*

Section of Act	Subject matter	Section of 1992 Act	Remarks
62	Increase during hospital treatment.	CB Sch. 7, para. 10(2), (3)	—
63	Increase for exceptionally severe disablement.	CB 105	—
64	Beneficiary's dependent children.	—	—
(1)	—	CB Sch. 7, para. 4(1)	Rep. in part 1982(2) s. 48(6), Sch. 5; am. 1975(3), s. 21(1), Sch. 4, para. 21(a).
(1A)–(1D)	—	CB Sch. 7, para. 4(3)–(6)	Inserted 1984 s. 13, Sch. 5, para. 4.
(2)	—	CB Sch. 7, para. 4(2)	Rep. in part 1982(2) s. 48(6), Sch. 5.
(3), (4)	—	—	Rep. 1975(3) s. 21(2), Sch. 5.
65	Additional provisions as to increase under s. 64.	—	—
(1)	—	CB Sch. 7, para. 5(1)	Am. 1975(3) s. 21(1), Sch. 4, para. 22(a).
(2)	—	CB Sch. 7, para. 5(2)	Am. 1975(3) s. 21(1), Sch. 4, para. 22(b); 1977 s. 22(3).
66	Adult dependents.	—	—
(1)	—	CB Sch. 7, para. 6(1)	Rep. in part 1980(1) s. 21, Sch. 5, 1982(2) s. 48(6), Sch. 5; am. 1975(3) s. 21(1) s. 5, Sch.1, paras. 4(a), 6.
(2)	—	CB Sch. 7, para. 6(2)	Rep. in part 1982(2) s. 48(6), Sch. 5.
(3)	—	CB Sch. 7, para. 6(3)	Substituted 1985 s. 13(5); rep. in part 1988(1) s. 16, Sch. 4, para. 13(a).
(4)	—	CB Sch. 7, para. 6(4)	Substituted 1985 s. 13(5); rep. in part 1988(1) s. 16, Sch. 4, para. 13(b).
(5), (6)	—	CB Sch. 7, para. 6(5), (6)	Substituted 1985 s. 13(5).
(7)	—	CB Sch. 7, para. 6(7)	—
(8)	—	—	Rep. 1980(1) s. 21, Sch. 5.
66A	Earnings to include occupational pensions for purposes of disablement pension.	CB Sch. 7, para. 7.	Section inserted 1984 s. 14(b); am. 1989 s. 9(3).
67	Widow's benefit (entitlement).		
(1)	—	CB Sch. 7, para. 15(1)	

SOCIAL SECURITY ACTS CONSOLIDATION—*continued.*

Section of Act	Subject matter	Section of 1992 Act	Remarks
	SOCIAL SECURITY ACT 1975 (c. 14) —*continued.*		
(2)	—	CB Sch. 7, para. 15(2), (3)	Rep. in part 1986 s. 39, Sch. 3, para. 8; am. 1977 s. 22(4).
(3)	—	CB Sch. 7, para. 15(4)	
68	Widow's benefit (rate).		
(1)	—	CB Sch. 7, para. 16(1)	
(2)	—	CB Sch. 7, para. 16(2)	Rep. in part 1975(3) s. 21(1), Sch. 4, para. 24.
(3)	—	CB Sch. 7, para. 16(3)	
69	Widower's benefit (entitlement and rate).	CB Sch. 7, para. 17	
70	Children of deceased's family.	CB Sch. 7, para. 18	Section substituted 1984 s. 13, Sch. 5, para. 5.
71, 72	—	—	Rep. 1986 s. 39, Sch. 3, para. 8.
73	—	—	Rep. 1975(3) s. 21(2), Sch. 5, 1986 s. 39, Sch. 3, para. 8.
74	—	—	Rep. 1986 s. 39, Sch. 3, para. 8.
75	Death of person with constant attendance allowance.	CB Sch. 7, para. 20	
76	Benefit in respect of industrial disease, etc.		
(1)–(4)	—	CB 108(1)–(4)	
(4A)	—	CB 108(5)	Inserted 1990 s. 21(1), Sch. 6, para. 4(1).
(5)	—	CB108(6)	
77	General provisions as to benefit under s. 76.		
(1)	—	CB109(1)	
(2)	—	CB109(2)	Rep. in part 1982(2) s. 48(6), Sch. 5; am. 1990 ss. 3(7), 21(1), Sch. 6, para. 4(2).
(3)	—	CB109(3)	
(4)	—	CB109(4) (6)	Inserted 1986 s. 39, Sch. 3, para. 13.
(5)	—	CB109(7)	Inserted 1986 s. 39, Sch. 3, para. 13.
78	Respiratory diseases.		
(1)–(3)	—	CB110(1)–(3)	
(4)	—	CB110(4)	Rep. in part 1982(2) s. 48(6), Sch. 5.

SOCIAL SECURITY ACTS CONSOLIDATION—*continued.*

Section of Act	Subject matter	Section of 1992 Act	Remarks
	SOCIAL SECURITY ACT 1975 (c. 14)—*continued.*		
79	—	—	Rep. 1980(2) s. 7(6), Sch., 1985 s. 29(2), Sch. 6, 1986 s. 86, Sch. 11.
80, 81	—	—	Rep. 1986 s. 86, Sch. 11.
82	Disqualification for and suspension of benefits.		
(1), (2)	—	—	Rep. 1985 s. 29(2), Sch. 6
(3), (4)	—	—	Rep. 1986 s. 86, Sch. 11
(5)	—	CB113(1)	
(6)	—	CB113(2)	Rep. in part 1986 s. 86, Sch. 11.
83	Disqualifications disregarded for certain purposes.	CB113(3)	Section substituted 1985 s. 29(1), Sch. 5, para. 8.
84	Persons maintaining dependents, etc.		
(1), (2)	—	CB114(1), (2)	
(3)	—	—	Rep. 1986 s. 86, Sch. 11.
(4)	—	CB114(3)	Am. 1985 s. 13(6).
(5)	—	CB114(4)	Substituted 1985 s. 13(8).
84A	Dependency increases; continuation of awards in cases of fluctuating earnings.	CB92, Sch. 7, para. 8.	Section inserted 1989 s. 31(1), Sch. 8, para. 7(2).
85	Overlapping benefits.		
(1)	—	A73(1)	
(2)	—	A73(2)	Rep. in part 1975(3) s. 21(1), Sch. 4, para. 28; am. 1975(3) s. 21(1), Sch. 4, para. 28.
(3)	—	A73(3)	
(4), (5)	—	A73(4), (5)	Inserted 1979 s. 15(1).
87	Benefit to be inalienable.	A187	.
88	Notification of accidents, etc.	A8	
89	Medical examination and treatment.		
(1)	—	A9(1)	Rep. in part 1986 s. 86, Sch. 11.
(2)	—	A9(2)	
90	Obligations of claimants.		
(1)	—	—	Rep. 1982(2) s. 48(6), Sch. 5.
(2)	—	A10(1)	Rep. in part 1982(2) s. 48(6), Sch. 5.
(3)	—	A10(2)	Substituted 1986 s. 86, Sch. 10, para. 85.
(4)	—	A10(3)	Rep. in part 1982(2) s. 48(6), Sch. 5.
91	Adjustments for successive accidents.		

SOCIAL SECURITY ACTS CONSOLIDATION—*continued.*

Section of Act	Subject matter	Section of 1992 Act	Remarks
	SOCIAL SECURITY ACT 1975 (c. 14)—*continued.*		
(1)	—	CB107(1)	Rep. in part 1982 s. 48(6), Sch. 5; am. 1982(2) s. 48(5), Sch. 4, para. 15.
(2)	—	CB107(2)	Affected by R3.
93	Principal questions for Secretary of State.		
(1)	—	A 17(1)	Rep. in part 1975(3) s. 21(2), Sch. 5; am. 1977 s. 22(5), 1991(3) s. 3(1).
(2)	—	A 17(2)	—
(2A)	—	A 17(3)	Inserted 1989 s. 21, Sch. 3, para. 1(1); affected by R8.
(3)	—	A 17(4).	Affected by R8.
94	Appeal on question of law.		
(1)–(5)	—	A 18(1)–(5)	Affected by R8.
(6)	—	—	Rep. Supreme Court Act 1981 (c. 54) s. 152(4), Sch. 7.
(7), (8)	—	A 18(6), (7)	
95	Other questions for Secretary of State.	—	Rep. 1986 s. 52, Sch. 5, para. 2.
96	Review of decisions under ss. 93, 95.		
(1)	—	A 19(1)	Subst. 1986 s. 52(1), Sch. 5, para. 3; affected by R8.
(2)	—	A 19(2), (3)	Am. 1980(1) ss. 2, 21, Sch. 1, para. 9.
97	Adjudication officers and bodies.		
(1)	—	A 38(1)	Subst. 1983 s. 25, Sch. 8, para. 2; am. 1990 s. 21(1), Sch. 6, para. 5(1).
(1A)	—	A 38(2)	Subst. 1983 s. 25, Sch. 8, para. 2.
(1B)–(1E)	—	A 39	Subst. 1983 s. 25, Sch. 8, para. 2.
(2)	—	A 41(1)	Subst. 1983 s. 25, Sch. 8, para. 2.
(2A)	—	A 41(2)	Subst. 1984 s. 16(a).
(2C), (2D)	—	A 41(3), (4)	Subst. 1983 s. 25, Sch. 8, para. 2.
(2E)	—	A 41(5)	Subst. 1983 s. 25, Sch. 8, para. 2; am. Courts and Legal Services Act 1990 (c. 41) s. 71(2), Sch. 10, para. 37(1).
(3)	—	A 52(1)	Am. 1980 s. 12; Courts and Legal Services Act 1990 s. 71(2), Sch. 10, para. 36.

SOCIAL SECURITY ACTS CONSOLIDATION—*continued.*

Section of Act	Subject matter	Section of 1992 Act	Remarks

SOCIAL SECURITY ACT 1975 (c. 14)—*continued.*

Section of Act	Subject matter	Section of 1992 Act	Remarks
(4)	—	See A 41(7), 43(8), 50(7), 51(4), 52(4).	
98	Claims and questions to be submitted to adjudication officer.		
(1)	—	A 20(1)	Am. 1991(2) s. 4, Sch. 1, para. 2.
(2)	—	A 20(2)	Subst. 1986 s. 52, Sch. 5, para. 4.
(2A)	—	A 20(4)	Inserted 1986 s. 52, Sch. 5, para. 4.
(3)	—	A 20(5)	
99	Decision of adjudication officer.		
(1)	—	A 21(1)	Am. 1991(2) s. 4, Sch. 1, para. 3(1).
(2)	—	A 21(2)	Subst. 1986 s. 52(1), Sch. 5, para. 5; am. 1991(2) s. 4, Sch. 1, para. 3(2).
(2A)	—	A 21(3)	Inserted 1991(2), s. 4, Sch. 1, para. 3(3).
(3)	—	A 21(4), (5)	
(4)	—	A 21(6)	Inserted 1989 s. 21, Sch. 3, para. 2.
100	Appeal to social security appeal tribunal.		
(1)	—	A 22(1)	Rep. in part 1986 s. 52, Sch. 5, para. 6(a); am. 1991(2), s. 4, Sch. 1, para. 4(a).
(2)	—	A 22(2)	Am. 1986 s. 52, Sch. 5, para. 6(b), 1991(2), s. 4, Sch. 1, para. 4(b).
(3)	—	A 22(3)	Am. 1986 s. 52, Sch. 5, para. 6(c); rep. in part 1989 s. 21, Sch. 3, para. 5.
(4)	—	A 22(4)	Subst. 1986 s. 52, Sch. 5, para. 6(d).
(5), (6)	—	—	Rep. 19869 s. 86, Sch. 11.
(7)	—	A 22(5)	Subst. 1986 s. 52, Sch. 5, para. 6(e); am. 1991(2) s. 4, Sch. 1, para. 4(c).
(8), (9)	—	A 22(6), (7)	Inserted 1990 s. 21(1), Sch. 6, para. 6(1).
100A	Reviews of decisions of adjudication officers as to attendance allowance or		Section inserted 1991 (2), s. 4, Sch. 1, para. 5.

SOCIAL SECURITY ACTS CONSOLIDATION—*continued.*

Section of Act	Subject matter	Section of 1992 Act	Remarks
	SOCIAL SECURITY ACT 1975 (c. 14)—*continued.*		
	disability living allowance.		
(1)–(4)	—	A 30(1)–(4)	
(5)–(12)	—	A 30(6)–(13)	
100B	Further reviews of decisions as to attendance allowance or disability living allowance.	A 31	Section inserted 1991 (2), s. 4, Sch. 1, para. 5.
100C	Reviews of decisions as to attendance allowance or disability living allowance: supplementary.	A 32	Section inserted 1991 (2), s. 4, Sch. 1, para. 5.
100D	Appeals following reviews of decisions as to attendance allowance or disability living allowance.	A 33	Section inserted 1991 (2), s. 4, Sch. 1, para. 5.
101	Appeal from social security appeal tribunal to Commissioner.		
(1)	—	A 23(1)	Am. 1986 s. 52, Sch. 5, para. 7(1); 1991(2), s. 4, Sch. 1, para. 6(a).
(2)	—	A 23(3), (4)	Am. 1986 s. 52, Sch. 5, para. 7(2); 1990 s. 21(1), Sch. 6, para. 6(2).
(3)	—	A 23(5)	Rep in part 1986 s. 86, Sch. 11, am. 1990 s. 21(1), Sch. 6, para. 6(3).
(4)	—	A 23(6)	
(5)	—	A 23(7), (8)	Subst. 1986 s. 52, Sch. 5, para. 7(3); am. 1989 s. 21, Sch. 3, para. 6.
(5A)	—	A 23(9)	Subst. 1986 s. 52, Sch. 5, para. 7(3); rep. in part 1991(2), ss. 4, 10, Sch. 1, para. 6(b), Sch. 4.
(5B)	—	A 23(10)	Subst. 1986 s. 52, Sch. 5, para. 7(3).
(6), (7)	—	—	Rep. 1989 s. 21, Sch. 3, para. 3(2)(a).
102	Questions first arising on appeal.		
(1)	—	A 36(1)	Am. 1991(2), s. 4, Sch. 1, para. 7(1).
(2)	—	A 36(1)	Substituted 1986 s. 52, Sch. 5, para. 8.
(3)	—	A 36(2)	Inserted 1991(2) s. 4, Sch. 1, para. 7(2).
103	Reference of special questions.		Section substituted 1986 s. 52, Sch. 5, para. 9.
(1)	—	A 37(1)	
(2)	—	A 37(2)	Am. 1989 s. 21, Sch. 3, para. 15.

SOCIAL SECURITY ACTS CONSOLIDATION—*continued.*

Section of Act	Subject matter	Section of 1992 Act	Remarks
	SOCIAL SECURITY ACT 1975 (c. 14)—*continued.*		
(3)	—	A 37(3)	
104	Review of decisions.		
(1)	—	A 25(1), (3)	Subst. 1986, s. 52, Sch, 5, para. 10(a); am. 1988 s. 16, Sch. 4, para. 14; 1989 ss. 10(5), 21, Sch. 3, para. 11(1); 1991(2) s. 4, Sch. 1, para. 8(a).
(1ZA)	—	A 25(5)	Inserted 1989 s. 21, Sch. 3, para. 11(2).
(1A)	—	A 25(2)	Inserted 1983 s. 25, Sch. 8, para. 3; rep. in part 1986 s. 52, Sch. 5, para. 10(b); am. 1991(2), s. 4, Sch. 1, para. 8(b).
(2), (3)	—	A 26(1), (2)	
(3A)	—	A 26(3)	Inserted 1986 s. 52, Sch, 5, para. 10(c).
(3B)	—	A 29	Subst. 1989 s. 21, Sch. 3, para. 7.
(4)	—	A 28	
(5)	—	A 27(1)	Inserted 1986 s. 52, Sch. 5, para. 10(d); am. 1989 s. 21, Sch. 3, para. 11(3), (4).
(6)	—	A 27(2)	Inserted 1990 s. 6(3).
(7)–(10)	—	A 69	Inserted 1990 s. 21(1), Sch. 6, para. 7(1).
104A	Reviews of decisions on appeal as to attendance allowance and disability living allowance.	—	Section inserted 1991(2) s. 4, Sch. 1, para. 9.
(1), (2)	—	A 35(1), (2)	
(3)	—	A 35(4)	
(4)–(7)	—	A 35(6)–(9)	
(8)	—	A 35(12)	
(9)	—	A 35(5), (10), (11)	
105, 106	—	—	Rep. 1991(2) s. 10, Sch. 4.
107	Declaration that accident is an industrial accident.		
(1)–(3)	—	A 44(1)–(3)	
(4)	—	A 44(4), (5)	Rep. in part 1986 s. 86, Sch. 11; subject to saving in 1988(1), s. 2, Sch. 1, para. 6.
(5)	—	A 44(6)	

SOCIAL SECURITY ACTS CONSOLIDATION—*continued.*

Section of Act	Subject matter	Section of 1992 Act	Remarks
	SOCIAL SECURITY ACT 1975 (c. 14)—*continued.*		
(6)	—	A 44(7)	Rep. in part 1986 s. 52, Sch. 5, para. 12(b); am. 1986 s. 52, Sch. 5, para. 12(a).
108	Disablement questions.		
(1)	—	A 45(1)	Am. 1984 s. 11, Sch. 4, para. 5; 1986 s. 39, Sch. 3, para. 14(a); 1989 s. 21, Sch. 3, para. 12(1).
(2)	—	A 45(2)	Subst. 1983 s. 25, Sch. 8, para. 21(1); am. 1984 s. 11, Sch. 4, para. 6.
(3)	—	A 49, 50	
(4)	—	A 45(3)	Subst. 1983 s. 25, Sch. 8 para. 21(3); am. 1983 s. 25, Sch. 8, para. 1(1), (3).
(4A)	—	A 45(4)	Subst. 1989 s. 21, Sch. 3, para. 12(2).
(4B)	—	A 45(5)	Inserted 1989 s. 21, Sch. 3, para. 12(2).
(5)	—	A 45(6)	Inserted 1983 s. 25, Sch. 8, para. 21(3).
109	Medical appeals and references.		
(1)	—	A 46(1)	Am. 1983 s. 25, Sch. 8, para. 22(a); 1984 s. 11, Sch. 4, para. 7.
(2)	—	A 46(2)	Am. 1983 s. 25, Sch. 8, para. 22(b).
(3)	—	A 46(3)	Am. 1983 s. 25, Sch. 8, para. 22(c); 1986 s. 52(1), Sch. 5, para. 13.
110	Review of medical decisions.		
(1)	—	A 47(1)	Am. 1979 s. 21(4), Sch. 3, para. 8; 1983 s. 25, Sch. 8, para. 23(a); 1986 s. 52(1), Sch. 5, para. 14(a).
(1A), (1B)	—	A 47(2), (3)	Inserted 1986 s. 52(1), Sch. 5, para. 14(b).
(2)	—	A 47(4)	Am. 1983 s. 25(1), Sch. 8, para. 23(b).
(3)–(5)	—	A 47(5)–(7)	
(6)	—	A 47(8)	Am. 1983 s. 25(1), Sch. 8, para. 23(c); 1984 s. 11, Sch. 4, para. 8(a).
(7)	—	A 47(9)	Am. 1983 s. 25(1), Sch. 8, para. 23(d); 1984 s. 11, Sch. 4, para. 8(b).
111		—	—	Rep. 1983 s. 30, Sch. 11.

SOCIAL SECURITY ACTS CONSOLIDATION—*continued.*

Section of Act	Subject matter	Section of 1992 Act	Remarks
	SOCIAL SECURITY ACT 1975 (c. 14)—*continued.*		
112	Appeal etc on question of law to Commissioner.		
(1)	—	A 48(1)	Am. 1984 s. 11, Sch. 4, para. 9; 1986 s. 52(1), Sch. 5, para. 15(a).
(2)	—	A 48(2)	
(3)	—	A 48(3)	Am. 1986 s. 52(1), Sch. 5, para. 15(b).
(4)	—	—	Rep. 1989 s. 21, Sch. 3, para. 9(1).
(5)	—	A 48(4)	Rep. in part 1989 s. 21, Sch. 3, para. 9(1).
(6), (7)	—	A 48(5), (6)	Inserted 1989 s. 21, Sch, 3, para. 9(2).
113	Adjudication as to industrial diseases.		
(1)	—	A 62(1)	
(2)(a), (b)	—	A 62(2), 164(5)(a)	Am. 1983 s. 25(1), Sch. 8, para. 24(a), (b).
(c)	—	A 189(5)	
(3)	—	A Sch. 2, para. 7	
114	Regulations as to determination of questions.		
(1)	—	A 58(1), (2)	
(2)	—	A 58(3)	
(2A)	—	A 58(4)	Inserted 1978 s. 159, Sch. 16, para. 19(1).
(2B)–(2D)	—	A 58(5)–(7)	Inserted 1986 s. 52(1), Sch. 5, para. 16(a).
(3), (4)	—	—	Rep. 1986 s. 52(1), Sch. 5, para. 16(b).
(5)	—	A 58(8)	
115	Procedure.		
(1)	—	A 59(1)	
(2)	—	A 59(1), Sch, 3, para. 1	Am. 1983 s. 25(1), Sch. 8, paras. 5, 25; 1991(2), s. 4. Sch. 1, para. 10.
(3), (4)	—	A 59(2), (3)	
(4A)	—	A 59(4)	Inserted 1991(3), s. 3(2).
(5)	—	A 59(5)	
(6)	—	A 59(6)	Am. 1989 s. 21, Sch. 3, para. 1(2).
(7)	—	A 59(7)	

SOCIAL SECURITY ACTS CONSOLIDATION—*continued.*

Section of Act	Subject matter	Section of 1992 Act	Remarks
	SOCIAL SECURITY ACT 1975 (c. 14)—*continued.*		
115A	Power of adjudicating authorities to refer matters to experts.		Section inserted 1989 s. 21, Sch. 3, para. 3(1); subs (2) am. 1991(2) s. 4, Sch. 1, para. 11.
115B	Assessors.	A 56	Section inserted 1989 s. 21, Sch. 3, para. 3(1); am. 1991(2) s. 4, Sch. 1, para. 12.
115C	References of claims relating to attendance allowance and disability living allowance to medical practitioners and Disability Living Allowance Advisory Board.	A 54	Section inserted 1991(2), s. 4, Sch. 1, para. 13.
115D	Medical examination etc. in relation to appeals to disability appeal tribunals.	A 55	Section inserted 1991(2), s. 4, Sch. 1, para. 13.
116	Tribunal of 3 Commissioners.		
(1)	—	A 57(1)	Am. 1980 s. 12.
(2)	—	A 57(2)	
117	Finality of decisions.		
(1)	—	A 60(1)	Am. 1983 s. 25(1), Sch. 8, para. 6.
(2)	—	A 60(2)	
(3)	—	A 60(3)	Am. 1983 s. 25(1), Sch. 8, para. 26.
(4)	—	A 60(4)	Rep. 1986 s. 86, Sch. 11; subject to saving in 1988(1), s. 2, Sch. 1, para. 6.
(5)	—	A 60(5)	Rep. in part 1986 s. 86, Sch. 11; subject to saving in 1988(1) s. 2, Sch. 1, para. 6.
118	—	—	Rep 1975(3) s. 21, Sch. 5.
119	Effect of adjudication on payment and recovery.		
(1)–(2A)	—	—	Rep. 1986 s. 86, Sch. 11 with savings.
(3)	—	A 61(1), (3)	Rep. in part 1986 s. 86, Sch. 11.
(4)	—	A 61(2)	Rep. in part 1986 s. 86, Sch. 11.
(5), (6)	—	—	Rep. 1986 s. 86, Sch. 11 with savings.
120	Annual review of contributions.		
(1)	—	—	Spend.
(2)	—	A 141(1)	Am. 1975(2) Sch. 48 para. 50(b).
(3)–(7)	—	A 141(2)-(6)	
121	Orders under s. 120 (supplementary).		
(1),(2)	—	A	

SOCIAL SECURITY ACTS CONSOLIDATION—*continued.*

Section of Act	Subject matter	Section of 1992 Act	Remarks
	SOCIAL SECURITY ACT 1975 (c. 14)—*continued.*		
		142(1),(2)	
(3)	—	A 142(3)	Am. 1990 s. 21(1), Sch. 6 para. 1(2)(a).
122	Additional power to alter contributions.		
(1)	—	A143(1)	Am. 1985 s. 29(1), Sch. 5, para. 9(a); 1989 s. 1(3).
(2), (3)(a)	—	A143(2),(3)	
(b)	—	—	Rep. Employment Act 1990 (c. 38) s. 16, Sch. 3.
(4)	—	—	Rep. Employment Act 1990 s. 16, Sch. 3.
(5)	—	—	Rep. 1989 s. 31, Sch. 8, para. 8(1), Sch. 9.
(6)	—	A143(4)	Am. 1980(1) s. 2, Sch. 1 Pt II para. 13; 1989 s. 1(5).
123	Orders under s. 122 (supplementary).		
(1)	—	A190(1)	
(2)	—	A144(1)	Rep. in part Employment Act 1990 (c. 38) s. 16, Sch. 3.
123A	Further power to alter certain contributions.	—	Section inserted 1985 s. 7(5).
(1)	—	A145(1)	Subst. 1989 s. 1(6).
(2)	—	A145(2)	
(3)	—	A145(3)	Am. 1989 s. 1(7).
(4)	—	A145(4)	
(5)	—	A147(1)	
(6)	—	A190(1)	
(6A)	—	A147(2)	Inserted 1986 s. 74(1).
(7)	—	A147(3)	
(8)	—	A147(4),(5)	Am. 1990 s. 21(1), Sch. 6 para 1(2)(c).
124—126A	—	—	Rep. 1986 s. 86, Sch. 11.
127	Crown employment.		
(1)	—	CB 115(1)	
(2)	—	CB 115(2), (3)	
128(1)-(3)	Her Majesty's forces.	CB 116.	
(4)	—	CB 177(3)	See also SS CP Sch. 2, para. 14.

SOCIAL SECURITY ACTS CONSOLIDATION—*continued.*

Section of Act	Subject matter	Section of 1992 Act	Remarks
	SOCIAL SECURITY ACT 1975 (c. 14)—*continued.*		
129	Mariners, airmen, etc.		
(1),(2)	—	CB 117	
(3)	—	—	Rep. 1977 s. 24, Sch. 2.
130	Married women and widows.		
1	—	CB 118	
(2), (3)	—	—	Rep. 1977(2), s. 65, Sch. 5.
131	Persons outside Great Britain.	CB 119	
132	Employment at sea (Continental shelf operations).		
(1)	—	CB 120(1)	
(2)	—	CB 120(2)	Am. Oil and Gas (Enterprise) Act 1982 (c. 23) Sch. 3 para. 21.
(3)	—	CB 120(3)	
133	National Insurance Fund.		
(1),(2)	—	A161(1), (2)	
(3)	—	A161(3)	Am. Finance Act 1980 (c. 48) s. 120, Sch. 19 para. 5(4).
(4)	—	A161(4)	
(5)	—	A165(1)	
(6)	—	A165(2)- (4), 189(8)	
134	Destination of contributions and Treasury supplements.		
(1)	—	A162(1)	
(2)	—	A162(2)	Am. 1989 s. 26, Sch. 7 para. 15.
(2A)	—	A162(3)	Inserted 1990 s. 16(3).
(2B)	—	A162(4)	Inserted 1990 s. 17(3); see also SS CP Sch. 4 para. 17.
(3)	—	—	Rep. 1989 s. 31, Sch. 9.
(4)	—	A162(5), (6)	Am. 1991(3) s. 4(a).
(4A)	—	A162(7)	Inserted 1981(1) s. 3(3).
(4B)	—	A162(8)	Inserted 1981(1) s. 3(1); am. 1991(3) s. 4(b).
(5)	—	A162(9)- (11)	Rep. in part Employment Act 1990 (c.38) s. 16, Sch. 3.
(5A)-(5D)	—	—	Rep. Employment Act 1990 s. 16, Sch. 3.
(6)	—	A162(12)	Am. 1979 s. 14(2).

SOCIAL SECURITY ACTS CONSOLIDATION—*continued.*

Section of Act	Subject matter	Section of 1992 Act	Remarks
	SOCIAL SECURITY ACT 1975 (c. 14)—*continued.*		
135	General financial arrangements.		
(1)-(3)	—	A163(1), (2)	1975(1) s. 135(2); am. 1984 s. 11, Sch. 4, para. 3, 1990 s. 16(4), 1991(2) s. 4, Sch. 1, para. 18; rep. in part 1986 s. 86 Sch. 11, 1991(2) s. 10, Sch. 4.
(4)	—	A163(3)	
(5)	—	A165(5)	Am. 1990 s. 16(5).
(6)	—	—	Rep. 1986 s. 86, Sch. 11; see SS CP Sch. 4, para. 19.
(7)	—	A163(5)	Inserted 1990 s. 17(4); see also SS CP Sch. 4 para. 18.
136	—	—	Rep. 1986 s. 86, Sch. 11.
137	Financial review and report.		
(1)	—	—	Spent.
(2)-(4)	—	A166	
138	National Insurance Advisory Committee.	—	Rep. 1980(1) s. 21, Sch. 5.
139	Committee to be consulted as to regulations.	—	Rep. 1980(1) s. 21, Sch. 5.
140	—	—	Rep. 1986 s. 86 Sch. 11.
141	Industrial Injuries Advisory Council.		
(1)	—	A171(1), (2)	
(2)	—	A172(2), (4)	Subst. 1981 s. 8, Sch. 2, para. 2; am. 1986 s. 75, Sch. 10, para. 86; rep. in part 1986 s. 86 Sch. 11.
(3)	—	A171(3)	
(4)	—	A171(4)	Inserted 1982 s. 48(5), Sch. 4, para. 16.
142	Co-ordination with Northern Ireland.		
(1)	—	A177(1), (5)	
(2)-(4)	—	A177(2)-(4)	Am. 1975(2) s. 65(2), Sch. 4, para. 66; 1986 s. 65(1).
(5)	—	—	See SS CP Sch.2, para. 13
143	Reciprocity with other countries.		
(1)	—	A 179(1), (4)	Am. 1977 s. 20(1); 1986 s. 65(2)(a); rep. in part 1986 ss. 65(2)(b), 86, Sch. 11.
(1A)	—	A 179(2)	Inserted 1981(2) s. 6(1).
(2)	—	A 179(3)	
144, 145	—	—	Rep. 1986 s. 86, Sch. 11.

SOCIAL SECURITY ACTS CONSOLIDATION—*continued.*

Section of Act	Subject matter	Section of 1992 Act	Remarks
			SOCIAL SECURITY ACT 1975 (c. 14)—*continued.*
146	Offences and Penalties.	—	See also SS CP Sch. 2 para. 35 (1975(2) s. 60ZB).
(1)	—	A 114(1)	Rep. in part 1986 s. 86 Sch. 11.
(2)	—	A 114(3)	
(3)	—	A 114(4)	Rep. in part 1986 s. 86 Sch. 11.
(4)	—	A 114(5), (6)	
(5)	—	—	Rep. 1986 s. 86 Sch. 11.
147	—	—	Subss. (1) - (5) and (7) rep. 1986 s. 86, Sch. 11; subs. (6) rep. Criminal Justice (Scotland) Act 1980 (c. 62) s. 83, Sch. 8; Police and Criminal Evidence Act 1984 (c. 60) s. 119, Sch. 7.
148	Questions arising in proceedings.	A 117	See also SS CP Sch. 2, para. 35 1975(2) s. 60ZC); affected by R8.
149	Evidence of non-payment.	A 118	
150	Recovery on prosecution.	A 119	See also SS CP Sch. 2, para. 35 (1975(2) s. 60ZD)
151	Proof of previous offences.	A 120	Am. 1991(3) s. 2(6); see also SS CP Sch. 2 para. 35 (1975(2) s. 60ZE).
152	Provisions supplementary of ss. 150, 151.	—	See also SS CP Sch. 2, para. 35 (1975(2) s. 60ZF).
(1)	—	A 121(1)	Am. Magistrates' Courts Act 1980 (c. 43) s. 154 Sch. 7 para. 135.
(2), (3)	—	A 121(2), (3)	Am. 1975(2) s. 65, Sch. 4, para. 67.
(4)	—	—	Rep. Insolvency Act 1985 (c. 65) s. 216, Sch. 10, Pt. IV.
(5) - (7)	—	A 121(4) - (6)	
(8)	—	—	Substituted 1975(2) s. 65, Sch. 4, para. 60; rep. in part 1986 s. 86, Sch. 11; see SS CP Sch. 2, para. 33 (1975(2) s. 60ZF(5)).
153	—	—	Rep. Insolvency Act 1985 (c. 65) s. 216, Sch. 10, Pt. IV.
154	Research on industrial injuries, etc.	A 183	
155	Control of pneumoconiosis.	A 184	
156	Accidents in course of illegal employment.	CB 97	

SOCIAL SECURITY ACTS CONSOLIDATION—*continued.*

Section of Act	Subject matter	Section of 1992 Act	Remarks
	SOCIAL SECURITY ACT 1975 (c. 14)—*continued.*		
157	Persons treated as employers for certain purposes.	CB 96	
158	—	—	Rep. 1980(1) s. 21, Sch. 5
159	Payments for pre- 1948 cases.		
(1)	—	CB Sch. 8 para. 7(1)	
(2)	—	CB Sch. 8 para. 8(1)	
(3)	—	CB Sch. 8 para. 7(2)	
(4)	—	A 163(2)(c)	Am. 1990 s. 16(7)
160	Provisions relating to age, death and marriage.		
(1)	—	A 124(1), (2)	
(2) - (4)	—	A 124(3) - (5)	
161	Furnishing of addresses for maintenance proceedings etc.		
(1)	—	A 133	
(2)	—	—	Unnecessary; see Family Law Reform Act 1987 (c. 42).
162	Treatment of certain marriages.	CB 121, 175(3) (b)(ii)	
163	Exemption from stamp duty.	A 188(1), (2)	
164	—	—	Rep. 1986 s. 86, Sch. 11.
165	Deputy Government Actuary.	A 142(1), 144(1), 147(2)	
165A	General provision as to necessity of claim for entitlement to benefit.		
(1)	—	A 1(1), (4)	Subst. 1986 s. 86(1), Sch. 10, para. 87; am. 1989 s. 31(1), Sch. 8, para. 9(1); 1990 s. 6(1)(a).
(2)	—	A 1(2)	Subst. 1986 s. 86(1), Sch. 10, para. 87; am. 1990 s. 6(1)(b).
(3)	—	A 1(3)	Added 1990 s. 1(6); am. 1991 (2) s. 5, Sch. 1, para. 19.

SOCIAL SECURITY ACTS CONSOLIDATION—*continued.*

Section of Act	Subject matter	Section of 1992 Act	Remarks
	SOCIAL SECURITY ACT 1975 (c. 14)—*continued.*		
165B	Retrospective effect of s. 165A.		Section inserted 1990 s. 5(1).
(1)	—	A 2(1)	
(2)	—	A 2(2), (3)	
(3), (4)	—	A 2(4), (5)	
(5)	—		
(6)	—		
165C	Late claims for widowhood benefits where death is difficult to establish.	A 3	Section inserted 1990 s. 6(2).
165D	Restrictions on entitlement to benefit in certain cases of error.	A 68	Section inserted 1990 s. 21(1), Sch. 6, para. 7(2); subs. (4) am. 1991 (2) s. 4 Sch. 2, para. 5.
166	Orders and regulations (general provisions).		
(1)	—	CB 175(2), A 189(3)	
(2)	—	CB 175(3), A 189(4)	
(3)	—	CB 175(4), A 189(5)	Am. 1989 s. 31(1), Sch. 8, para. 10(1).
(3A)	—	CB 175(5), A 189(6)	Inserted 1986 s. 62(1).
(4)	—	—	Unnecessary – see Interpretation Act 1978 (c. 30) s. 14.
(5)	—	CB 175(7), A 189(9)	See also SS CP Sch. 2, para. 12; affected by R7.
(5A)	—	A 189(10)	Inserted 1986 s. 52, Sch. 5, para. 17.
(6)	—	CB 175(8)	
(7)	—	CB 175(9), A 189(11)	
167	Parliamentary control of orders and regulations.		
(1)	—	CB 176(1), A 190(1)	Am. 1979 s. 4(2)(a); 1981(1) s. 4(5)(b); 1986 ss. 43(3)(b), 62(3), 86, Sch. 10, para. 65; rep. in part 1975(2) s. 65(3), Sch. 5; 1989 s. 31(1), Sch. 9; Employment Act 1990 (c. 38) s. 16, Sch. 3; affected by R15.
(2)	—	CB 176(2)	Substituted 1990 s. 21(1), Sch. 6, para. 8(1).
(3)	—	CB 176(3), A 190(3)	Substituted 1990 s. 21(1), Sch. 6, para. 8(1); affected by R15.

SOCIAL SECURITY ACTS CONSOLIDATION—*continued.*

Section of Act	Subject matter	Section of 1992 Act	Remarks
	SOCIAL SECURITY ACT 1975 (c. 14)—*continued.*		
(4)	—	A 190(4)	Substituted 1990 s. 21(1), Sch. 6, para. 8(1).
168	Interpretation.		
(1)	—	—	Gives effect to Schedule 20.
(2)	—	—	Unnecessary – see Interpretation Act 1978 s. 20.
(3)	—	—	Unnecessary.
(4)	—	CB 175(10), A 189(12)	
169	Citation, extent and commencement.	—	
Sch. 1	Supplementary provisions relating to contributions of classes 1, 1A, 2 and 3		Heading am. 1991(3) s. 2(1)(b)
Para. 1(1)	—	CB Sch. 1, para. 1(1)	
(1A)	—	CB Sch. 1, para. 1(2)	Inserted 1980(1) s. 2, Sch. 1, para. 16; am. 1985 s. 29(1), Sch. 5, para. 13(a)
(1B), (1C)	—	CB Sch. 1, para. 1(3), (4)	Inserted 1985 s. 29(1), Sch. 5, para. 13(b)
(1D)	—	CB Sch. 1, para. 1(6)	Inserted 1985 s. 29(1), Sch. 5, para. 13(b)
(2), (3)	—	CB Sch. 1, para. 1(7), (8)	
2	—	CB Sch. 1, para. 2	
3	—	CB Sch. 1, para. 3	
4	—	CB Sch. 1, para. 4	Am. 1977 s. 1(4)
4A	—	CB Sch. 1, para. 5	Inserted 1991(3) s. 2(2)
5(1)	—	CB Sch. 1, para. 6(1)	Am. 1991(3) s. 2(3)(a)
(1A)	—	CB Sch. 1, para. 6(2)	Inserted 1990 s. 17(5); am. 1991(3) s. 2(3)(b); see also SS CP Sch. 4, para. 6
(1B), (1C)	—	CB Sch. 1, para. 6(3), (4)	Inserted 1990 s. 17(5); see also SS CP Sch. 4, para. 6
(2)	—	CB Sch. 1, para. 6(7)	
(3)	—	CB Sch. 1, para. 6(8)	Am. 1990 s. 17(6); see also SS CP Sch. 4, para. 7

SOCIAL SECURITY ACTS CONSOLIDATION—*continued.*

Section of Act	Subject matter	Section of 1992 Act	Remarks
		SOCIAL SECURITY ACT 1975 (c. 14)—*continued.*	
5A	—	CB Sch. 1, para. 7	Inserted 1990 s. 17(7), Sch. 5; sub-paragraph (11) am. 1991(3) s. 2(4)
6(1)(a)	—	CB Sch. 1, para. 8(1)(a)	
(aa)	—	CB Sch. 1, para. 8(1)(b)	Inserted 1991(3) s.2(5)(a)
(b)–(e)	—	CB Sch. 1, para. 8(1)(c)-(f)	
(f)	—	CB Sch. 1, para. 8(1)(g)	Am. 1975(2) s. 65(1), Sch. 4, para. 61
(g)	—	CB Sch. 1, para. 8(1)(l)	Am. 1991(3) s. 2(5)(b)
(gg)	—	CB Sch. 1, para. 8(1)(h)	Inserted 1989 s. 2
(ggg)	—	CB Sch. 1, para. 8(1)(i)	Inserted 1991(3) s.2(5)(c)
(gh), (gj)	—	CB Sch. 1, para. 8(1)(j), (k)	Inserted 1990 s. 21(1), Sch. 6, para. 9
(h)	—	CB Sch. 1, para. 8(1)(m)	Am. 1986 s.86, Sch. 10, para. 10
(j)-(m)	—	CB Sch. 1, para. 8(1)(j)-(m)	—
(2), (3)	—	CB Sch. 1, para. 8(2), (3)	
7, 8	—	CB Sch. 1, paras. 9, 10	
9	—	CB Sch. 1, para. 11	Inserted 1982(2) s. 37(2)
Sch. 2	Levy of class 4 contributions with income tax		
Para. 1	—	CB Sch. 2, para. 1	Am. Income and Corporation Taxes Act 1988 (c. 1) s. 844, Sch. 29, para. 32, Table; Capital Allowances Act 1990 (c. 1) s. 164, Sch. 1, para. 2.

SOCIAL SECURITY ACTS CONSOLIDATION—*continued.*

Section of Act	Subject matter	Section of 1992 Act	Remarks
		SOCIAL SECURITY ACT 1975 (c. 14)—*continued.*	
2	—	CB Sch. 2, para. 2	Am. Capital Allowances Act 1990 s. 164, Sch. 1, para. 2.
3(1),(2)	—	CB Sch. 2, para. 3(1), (2)	Am. Income and Corporation Taxes Act 1988 (c. 1) s. 844, Sch. 29, para. 32, Table.
(3)	—	CB Sch. 2, para. 3(3), (4)	Substituted for 1990–1991 onwards Finance Act 1988 (c. 39) s. 35, Sch. 3, para. 31.
(4)	—	CB Sch. 2, para. 3(5)	Am. Income and Corporation Taxes Act 1988 (c. 1) s. 844, Sch. 29, para. 32, Table.
4	—	CB Sch. 2, para. 9	Am. Income and Corporation Taxes Act 1988 s. 844, s. 844, Sch. 29, para. 32, Table; Finance Act 1988 s. 145, Sch. 14, Part VIII and Note 6.
5,6	—	CB Sch. 2, para. 4, 5	Am. Income and Corporation Taxes Act 1988 s. 844, Sch. 29, para. 32, Table.
7(1)	—	CB Sch. 2, para. 6(1)	Am. 1990 s. 17(8); see also SS CP Sch. 4, para. 8.
(2)	—	CB Sch. 2, para. 6(2)	Inserted 1990 s. 17(9); see also SS CP Sch. 4, para. 9.
8, 9	—	CB Sch. 2, paras. 7, 8	
Sch. 3	Contribution conditions for entitlement to benefit		
Para 1(1)	—	CB Sch. 3, paras. 1(1), 2(1)	
(2)	—	CB Sch. 3, paras. 1(2), (4), 2(2), (4)	Am. 1986 s. 75, Sch. 8, para. 3(1), 1988(1) s. 6(2)(a).
(3)	—	CB Sch. 3, paras. 1(3), (5), 2(3), (5)	Am. 1986 s. 75, Sch. 8, para. 3(2), (3), 1988(1) s. 6(2)(b).
(4)	—	CB Sch. 1, paras. 1(6), 2(6)	Rep. in part 1988(1) s. 16, Sch. 5.
2	—	—	Rep. 1980(1) s. 5.
3(1)	—	CB Sch. 3, para. 3(1)	Paragraph substituted 1986 s. 49, Sch. 4, para. 14; am. 1990 s. 21(1), Sch. 6, para. 10(1).
(2), (3)	—	CB Sch. 3, para. 3(2), (3)	Inserted 1990 s. 21(1), Sch. 6, para. 10(2).

SOCIAL SECURITY ACTS CONSOLIDATION—*continued.*

Section of Act	Subject matter	Section of 1992 Act	Remarks
		SOCIAL SECURITY ACT 1975 (c. 14)—*continued.*	
4(1)	—	CB Sch. 3, para. 4(1), (2)	Am. 1986 ss. 75, 86, Sch. 8, para. 3(4), Sch. 10, para. 66(a).
(2)	—	CB Sch. 3, para. 4(3)	
5(1)	—	CB Sch. 3, para. 5(1)	
(2)	—	CB Sch. 3, para. 5(2)	Am. 1975 (2) s. 19(2), 1986 s. 75, Sch. 8, para. 3(5).
(3)	—	CB Sch. 3, para. 5(3), (4)	Am. 1986 s. 75, Sch. 8, para. 3(6).
(4), (5)	—	CB Sch. 3, para. 5(5), (6)	
(6)	—	CB Sch. 3, para. 5(7)	Substituted 1979 s. 5, Sch. 1, para. 3.
6	—	CB Sch. 3, para. 6	
7	—	—	Rep. 1986 s. 86, Sch. 11.
8(1)	—	CB Sch. 3, para. 7(1)	Am. 1989 s. 26, Sch. 7, para. 16.
(2)	—	CB Sch. 3, para. 7(2)	Para. (a) unnecessary; rep. in part 1986 s. 86, Sch. 11; am. 1986 s. 86, Sch. 10, para. 66(b).
(3)	—	CB Sch.3, para.7(3), (4)	Substituted 1979 s.21(4), Sch.3, para.10; rep. in part 1988(1) s.6(3); am. 1986 ss.75,86, Sch.8, para 3(7), Sch.10, para.66(b)
9	—	—	Rep. 1988(1) s.6(4)
10	—	CB Sch.3, para.8	Rep. in part 1986 s.86, Sch.11
11	—	—	Rep. 1980(1) s.5
12	—	—	Rep. 1986 s.86, Sch.11
13	—	CB Sch.3, para.9	Substituted 1986 s.86, Sch.10, para.65(c)
Sch.4	Rates of benefits, grants and increases for dependents		
Part I	—		
Para.1(a)	—	Sch.4, Part I, para.1	
1(b)	—	CB Sch.4, Part I, para.2	

SOCIAL SECURITY ACTS CONSOLIDATION—*continued.*

Section of Act	Subject matter	Section of 1992 Act	Remarks
		SOCIAL SECURITY ACT 1975 (c. 14)—*continued.*	
3	—	CB Sch.4, Part I, para.3	
4	—	CB Sch.4, Part I, para.4	
9	—	CB Sch.4, Part I, para.5	
10	—	CB Sch.4, Part I, para.6	
Part IA	—	CB Sch.4, Part II	Inserted 1986 s.36(2)
Part III			
Paras.1, 2	—	CB Sch.4, Part III, paras.1,2	
2A	—	CB Sch.4, Part III, para.3	Inserted 1990 s.2(2)
3	—	CB Sch.4, Part III, para.4	
4	—	CB Sch.4, Part III, para.5	
5	—	CB Sch.4, Part III, para.6	
5A	—	CB Sch.4, Part III, para.7	
6	—	CB Sch.4, Part III, para.8	
Part IV	—	—	
Paras.1–3	—	CB Sch.4, Part IV, paras.1–3	
5–10	—	CB Sch.4, Part IV, paras.4–9	
Part V			
Para.2	—	CB Sch.4, Part V, para.9	

SOCIAL SECURITY ACTS CONSOLIDATION—*continued.*

Section of Act	Subject matter	Section of 1992 Act	Remarks

SOCIAL SECURITY ACT 1975 (c. 14)—*continued.*

Section of Act	Subject matter	Section of 1992 Act	Remarks
3	—	CB Sch.4, Part V, para.1	
4	—	CB Sch.4, Part V, para.5	
5	—	CB Sch.4, Part V, para.6	
7,8	—	CB Sch.4, Part V, paras 2,3	
10,12	—	CB Sch.4, Part V, paras.7, 8	
13, 14	—	CB Sch. 4, Part V, paras. 10, 11	
15	—	CB Sch. 4, Part V, para. 12	
16	—	CB Sch. 4, Part V, para. 4	
Sch. 5	Meaning of "unemployability supplement or allowance".	—	Unnecessary.
Sch. 6	—	—	Rep. 1980(2) s. 7(6), Sch.
Sch. 7	—	—	Rep. 1975(2) s. 65(3), Sch. 5.
Sch. 8			
Para. 1	—	CB Sch. 6, para. 1	Am. 1984 s. 11, Sch. 4, para. 10(a).
2,3	—	CB Sch. 6, paras. 2, 3	
4(1)	—	CB Sch. 6, para. 6(1), (2)	Para. renumbered by 1986 s. 39, Sch. 3, para. 15; am 1982(2) s. 48(5), Sch. 4, para. 17.
(2)–(4)	—	CB Sch. 6, para. 6(3)-(5)	Substituted 1989 s. 21, Sch. 3, para. 13(1).
4A	—	CB Sch. 6, para. 4	Paragraph inserted 1984 s. 11, Sch. 4, para. 10(b).
5	—	CB Sch. 6, para. 7	Rep. in part 1986 s. 86, Sch. 11; am. 1989 s. 21, Sch. 3, para. 13(2).
5A	—	CB Sch. 6, para. 5	Inserted 1984 s. 11, Sch. 4, para. 10(c).

SOCIAL SECURITY ACTS CONSOLIDATION—*continued.*

Section of Act	Subject matter	Section of 1992 Act	Remarks

SOCIAL SECURITY ACT 1975 (c. 14)—*continued.*

Section of Act	Subject matter	Section of 1992 Act	Remarks
6	—	CB Sch. 6, para. 8	
Sch. 9	Limits of entitlement to industrial death benefit.		
Para. 1	—	CB Sch. 7, para. 19	Rep. in part 1975(3) s. 21(2), Sch. 5.
2–8	—	—	Affected by R16; see SS CP s. 3(2).
Sch. 10	Supplementary provisions as to social security appeal tribunals, Commissioners etc.		
Para. 1(1)	—	A40(1), (2)	Subst. 1983 s. 25, Sch. 8, para. 7.
(2), (2A)	—	A40(2), (3)	Subst. 1984 s. 16(b).
(6)	—	A40(4)	Subst. 1983 s. 25, Sch. 8, para. 7.
(7)	—	—	Rep. 1989 s. 21 Sch. 3 para. 17, Sch. 9.
(8)	—	A41(6)	Subst. 1983 s. 25, Sch. 8, para. 7.
1A(1)	—	A51(1)	Inserted 1983 s. 25, Sch. 8, para. 8; substituted 1991(2) s. 4, Sch. 1, para. 15.
(2)	—	A51(2)	Inserted 1983 s. 25, Sch. 8, para. 8; am. Courts and Legal Services Act 1990 (c. 41) s. 71, Sch. 10, para. 37(2).
(3)	—	A51(3)	Inserted 1983 s. 25, Sch. 8, para. 8; am. Courts and Legal Services Act 1990 s. 71, Sch. 10, para. 37(3).
(4)–(7)	—	A Sch. 2, para. 1(1)-(4)	Inserted 1983 s. 25, Sch. 8, para. 8.
(8)	—	—	Rep. Courts and Legal Services Act 1990 s. 125, Sch. 20.
(9)	—	A Sch. 2, para. 1(5)	Inserted 1983 s. 25, Sch. 8, para. 7.
(10), (11)	—	A Sch. 2, paras. 2,3	Inserted 1983 s. 25, Sch. 8, para. 7.
1B, 1C	—	A Sch. 2, para. 4	Inserted 1983 s. 25, Sch. 8, para. 7.
1D	—	A Sch. 2, para. 5	Inserted 1983 s. 25, Sch. 8, para. 7.

SOCIAL SECURITY ACTS CONSOLIDATION—*continued.*

Section of Act	Subject matter	Section of 1992 Act	Remarks
	SOCIAL SECURITY ACT 1975 (c. 14)—*continued.*		
2(1)	—	—	Affected by R18; see SS CP s. 3(2).
(2)	—	—	Rep. 1989 s. 21, Sch. 3, para. 9, Sch. 9.
3	—	A Sch. 2, para. 7	
4	—	A Sch. 2, para. 6	
5, 6	—	—	Rep. Judical Pensions Act 1981 (c. 20) s. 36, Sch. 4.
Sch. 10A	Disability appeal tribunals.	—	Sch. inserted 1991(2) s. 4, Sch. 1, para. 16.
para. 1	—	A 43(1)	
para. 2	—	A 43(4)–(6)	
3–7	—	A 42(1)–(5)	
8	—	A 42(6), (7)	
9, 10	—	A 43(2), (3)	
11	—	A Sch. 2, paras. 3–5, 7	Affected by R18.
12, 13	—	A 43(7), (8)	
Sch. 11	—	—	Rep. 1991(2) s. Sch. 4
Sch. 12	Medical boards and medical appeal tribunals.		
Para. 1	—	A 49(1)	Subst. 1983 s. 25. Sch. 8, para. 27(a).
2(1)	—	A 50(1)	Subst. 1983 s. 25, Sch. 8, para. 9.
(2)	—	A 50(2)	Subst. 1983 s. 25, Sch. 8, para. 9; am. 1986 s. 52, Sch. 5, para. 18.
(3), (4)	—	A 50(3), (4)	Subst. 1983, s. 25, Sch. 8, para. 9.
(5)	—	A 50(5)	Am. 1989 s. 21, Sch. 3, para. 18, Courts and Legal Services Act 1990 (c. 41) s. 71, Sch. 10, para. 37(4).
3	—	A 50(6)	Subst. 1983 s. 25, Sch. 8, para. 9.
4, 5	—	A Sch. 2, para. 7	

SOCIAL SECURITY ACTS CONSOLIDATION—*continued.*

Section of Act	Subject matter	Section of 1992 Act	Remarks
	SOCIAL SECURITY ACT 1975 (c. 14)—*continued.*		
5A	—	A Sch. 2, para. 3	Inserted 1983 s. 25, Sch. 8, para. 10.
6–8	—	A Sch. 2, para. 7	
9	—	A Sch. 2, para. 5	Added 1983 s. 25, Sch. 8, para. 11.
Sch. 13	Provision which may be made by procedure regulations.		
Para. 1	—	A Sch. 3, para. 2	Am. 1989 s. 21, Sch. 3, para. 4.
1A	—	A Sch. 3, para. 3	Inserted 1986 Sch. 5, para. 19(a).
2–7	—	A Sch. 3, paras. 4–9	
7A	—	A Sch. 3, para. 10	Inserted 1989 s. 21, Sch. 3, para. 10; am. 1991(2) s. 4, Sch. 1, para. 17.
8, 9	—	—	Rep. 1989 s. 21, Sch. 3, para. 3(2)(c), Sch. 9.
10	—	A Sch. 3, para. 11	Am. 1986 s. 52, Sch. 5, para. 19(b).
11	—	A Sch. 3, para. 12	
Sch. 14	—	—	Rep. 1986 s. 86, Sch. 11.
Sch. 15	—	—	Rep. 1980(1) s. 21, Sch. 5.
Sch. 16	Industrial Injuries Advisory Council.		
Part I	Constitution of Council.		
para. 1, 2	—	A Sch. 6	
Part II	Regulations not requiring prior submission to Council.		
3	—	—	Affected by R14.
4	—	—	Rep. 1986 s. 86, Sch. 11.
5	—	A Sch. 7, para. 11	
6	—	—	Spent.
7	—	—	Rep. 1991(2) s. 10, Sch. 4.
8	—	A Sch. 7, para. 12	Am. 1986 s. 86, Sch. 10, para. 90.

SOCIAL SECURITY ACTS CONSOLIDATION—*continued.*

Section of Act	Subject matter	Section of 1992 Act	Remarks

SOCIAL SECURITY ACT 1975 (c. 14)—*continued.*

Section of Act	Subject matter	Section of 1992 Act	Remarks
9–11	—	A Sch. 7, paras. 13-15	
12	—	A Sch. 7, para. 17	
Sch. 17	Constitution etc of Joint Authority for Great Britain and Northern Ireland.	A Sch. 8	
Sch. 18	—	—	Rep. Insolvency Act 1985 (c. 65) s. 235, Sch. 10, Pt. IV.
Sch. 19	—	—	Rep. 1980(1) s. 21, Sch. 5.
Sch. 20	Glossary of expressions.		
"the 1973 Act."	—	—	Unnecessary.
"adjudicating medical practitioner"	—	—	Unnecessary; inserted 1983 s. 25, Sch. 8, para. 28.
"age"	—	CB173	
"appropriate employment protection allocation"	—	—	Rep. Employment Act 1990 (c. 38) s. 16(2), Sch. 3.
"assessed"	—	CB103(5)	
"beneficiary", "benefit"	—	CB122(1) "beneficiary" "benefit"	
"benefit year", "capable of work"	—	—	Unnecessary.
"child"	—	CB 122(1) "child"	Inserted 1975(3) s. 21(1), Sch. 4, para. 38.
"the Child Benefit Act"	—	—	Unnecessary; inserted 1975(3) s. 21(1), Sch. 4, para. 38.
"child of family"	—	—	Rep. 1975(3) s. 21(1), Sch. 4, para. 38.
"claim"	—	CB122(1), A191 "claim"	
"claimant"	—	CB122(1), A191 "claimant"	
"Commissioner"	—	A191 "Commissioner"	Am. 1980(1) s. 12.
"confinement", "date of confinement", "confined"	—	—	Unnecessary.

SOCIAL SECURITY ACTS CONSOLIDATION—*continued.*

Section of Act	Subject matter	Section of 1992 Act	Remarks
SOCIAL SECURITY ACT 1975 (c. 14)—*continued.*			
"contract of service"	—	CB122(1) "contract of service"	
"contribution card"	—	—	Unnecessary.
"current"	—	CB122(1) "current"	
"day of incapacity for work", "day of interruption of employment"	—	CB122(1) "day of incapacity for work", "day of interruption of employment."	
"the deceased."	—	CB Sch. 7, para. 14(2)	
"deferred", "period of deferment"	—	CB122(1) "deferred", "period of deferment"	Inserted 1989 s. 7, Sch. 1, para. 3(11).
"disablement questions"	—	—	Unnecessary.
"earner", "earnings"	—	CB122(1) "earner", "earnings"	
"earnings factor"	—	—	Unnecessary.
"employed", "employment"	—	CB122(1) "employed", "employment", (2)	Am. 1989 s. 12(5).
"employed earner"	—	CB122(1) "employed earner"	
"entitled"	—	CB122(1) "entitled"	Inserted 1985 s. 29(1), Sch. 5, para. 14; a.m. 1990 s. 5(2)(b).
"entitled to child benefit"	—	CB122(4), (5)	Inserted 1975(3) s. 21(1), Sch. 4, para. 38.
"family allowance", "Family Allowances Act"			Rep. 1975(3) s. 21(1), Sch. 4, para. 38.

SOCIAL SECURITY ACTS CONSOLIDATION—*continued.*

Section of Act	Subject matter	Section of 1992 Act	Remarks
SOCIAL SECURITY ACT 1975 (c. 14)—*continued.*			
"former Industrial Injuries Act", "former principal Act"	—	—	Unnecessary.
"friendly society"	—	—	Unnecessary.
"hovercraft"	—	—	Unnecessary.
"incapable of work", "incapacity for work", "industrial death benefit"	—	—	Unnecessary.
"industrial injuries benefit"	—	CB122(1), A199 "industrial injuries benefit"	
"initial primary percentage", "main primary percentage", "primary percentage"		CB122(1) "initial primary percentage", "main primary percentage", "primary percentage"	Inserted 1989 s. 1(9).
"the Inland Revenue"	—	CB122(1) "the Inland Revenue"	
"late husband"	—	CB122(1) "late husband"	
"living with", "living together"	—	—	Unnecessary.
"long-term benefit"	—	CB20(2)	Inserted 1975(2) s. 65, Sch. 4, para. 64.
"loss of physical faculty"	—	CB 122(1) "loss of physical faculty"	Inserted 1984 s. 11, Sch. 4, para. 11(a).

SOCIAL SECURITY ACTS CONSOLIDATION—*continued.*

Section of Act	Subject matter	Section of 1992 Act	Remarks

SOCIAL SECURITY ACT 1975 (c. 14)—*continued.*

Section of Act	Subject matter	Section of 1992 Act	Remarks
"lower earnings limit", "upper earnings limit"	—	CB 122(1) "lower earnings limit"; "upper earnings limit"	
"main primary percentage"	—	CB 122(1) "main primary percentage"	Inserted 1989 s. 1(9).
"medical examination", "medical practitioner", "medical treatment"	—	CB 122(1) "medical examination", "medical treatment", A 191 "medical examination", "medical practitioner", "medical treatment"	
"the Northern Ireland Department"	—	CB 122(1), A 191 "the Northern Ireland Department"	
"the Old Cases Act"	—	CB 174, A 191 "the Old Cases Act"	
"payments by way of occupational or personal pension"	—	CB 122(1) "payments by way of occupational or personal pension"	Inserted 1984 s. 21, Sch. 7, para. 2; am. 1989 s. 9(4).

SOCIAL SECURITY ACTS CONSOLIDATION—*continued.*

Section of Act	Subject matter	Section of 1992 Act	Remarks
		SOCIAL SECURITY ACT 1975 (c. 14)—*continued.*	
"the Pensions Act"	—	CB 174, A 191 "the Pensions Act"	Inserted 1975(2) s. 65, Sch 4, para. 64.
"pensionable age"	—	CB 122(1) "pensionable age"	
"permanently incapable of self support"	—	CB 122(6)	Inserted 1980(1) s. 2, Sch. 1, para. 7.
"pneumoconiosis", "prescribe"	—	CB 122(1) "pneumoconiosis", "prescribe"	
"President"	—	A 191 "President"	Inserted 1983 s. 25, Sch. 8, para. 13; am. 1991 (2) s. 4, Sch. 1, para. 20.
"primary percentage"	—	CB 122(1) "primary percentage"	Inserted 1989 s. 1(9).
"procedure regulations"	—	—	Unnecessary.
"qualifying earnings factor"	—	CB 122(1) "qualifying earnings factor"	Inserted 1975(2) s. 65, Sch. 4, para. 64.
"regulations"	—	CB 175(1), A189(1), (2)	Substituted 1986 s. 52, Sch. 5, para. 20
"relative"	—	CB 122(1) "relative"	Rep. in part Children Act 1975 (c.72) s. 108, Sch. 4, Pt. I, 1986 s. 86, Sch. 11
"relevant accident", "relevant injury"	—	CB 122(1) "relevant accident", "relevant injury"	
"relevant loss of faculty"	—	CB 122(1) "relevant loss of faculty"	Am. 1984 s. 11, Sch. 4, para. 11(b)
"residing with", "residing together"	—	—	Rep. 1977 s. 22(1)

SOCIAL SECURITY ACTS CONSOLIDATION—*continued.*

Section of Act	Subject matter	Section of 1992 Act	Remarks
		SOCIAL SECURITY ACT 1975 (c. 14)—*continued.*	
"Reserve pension Fund", "reserve scheme contributions", "reserve scheme premiums"	—	—	Rep. 1975(2) s. 65(3), Sch. 5
"school-leaving age"	—	—	Rep. Education (School-Leaving Dates) Act 1976 (c. 5) s. 3(3), Sch.
"self-employed earner"	—	CB 122(1) "self-employed earner"	—
"short-term benefit"	—	CB 122(1) "short-term benefit"	Rep. in part 1980(1) s. 5, 1986 s. 86, Sch. 11
"supplementary scheme"	—	—	Obsolete
"tax week"	—	CB 122(1) "tax week"	—
"tax year"	—	CB 122(1) "tax year"	Am. 1990 s. 21(1), Sch. 6, para. 11
"trade or business", "trade union"	—	CB 122(1) "trade or business", "trade union"	—
"unemployability supplement"	—	—	Unnecessary
"unmarried couple"	—	—	Inserted 1984 s. 13, Sch. 5, para. 7(b)
"upper earnings limit"	—	—	Unnecessary
"up-rating order"	—	—	Rep. s. 86, Sch. 11
"week"	—	CB 122(1) "week"	Rep. in part 1989 ss. 26, 31(2), Sch. 7, para. 18, Sch. 9; am. 1975(2) s. 65, Sch. 4, para. 64, 1984 s. 13, Sch. 5, para. 7(a), 1991(2) s. 9(4)
"working life"	—	—	Unnecessary

SOCIAL SECURITY ACTS CONSOLIDATION—*continued.*

Section of Act	Subject matter	Section of 1992 Act	Remarks

SOCIAL SECURITY ACT 1975 (c. 14)—*continued.*

INDUSTRIAL INJURIES AND DISEASES (OLD CASES) ACT 1975 (c. 16)

Section of Act	Subject matter	Section of 1992 Act	Remarks
1	Continuation of workmen's compensation in certain cases	CB Sch. 8 para. 1	
2	Schemes for supplementing workmen's compensation		
(1)	—	CB Sch. 8, para. 2(1), A 163(2)(-c)	Am. 1990 s.16(8)(a).
(2) - (5)	—	CB Sch. 8, para. 2(2) - (5)	
(6)	—	CB Sch. 8, para. 2(6), (7)	Rep. in part 1986 s. 86, Sch. 10, para. 67 with savings; by S.I. 1987/354, art. 3; am. S.I. 1990/320.
(7)	—	CB Sch. 8, para. 2(8)	
3	Provisions supplementary to s. 2	CB Sch. 8, para. 3	
4	Provisions as to schemes under s. 2		
(1)	—	A Sch. 9, para. 1(1)	
(2)	—	A Sch. 9, para. 1(2)	Am. 1989 s. 31(1), Sch. 8, para. 10(1).
(3)	—	A Sch. 9, para. 1(3)	
(4)	—	A 164(4), Sch. 9, para. 1(4)	Rep. in part 1986 s. 86, Sch. 11; am. 1977 s. 11(1)(a); 1990 s. 16(8)(b).
(5)	—	A Sch. 9, para. 1(5)	Rep. in part 1977 s. 11(1)(b).
(6)	—	A Sch. 9, para. 1(6)	
(7)	—	A Sch. 9, para. 1(6)	
(8)	—	CB 175(2), 176(3)	Inserted 1990 s. 21(1), Sch. 6, para. 12.
5	Industrial diseases benefit schemes		
(1)	—	CB Sch. 8, para. 4(1), A 163(2) (-c)	Am. 1990 s. 16(8)(a).

SOCIAL SECURITY ACTS CONSOLIDATION—*continued.*

Section of Act	Subject matter	Section of 1992 Act	Remarks

INDUSTRIAL INJURIES AND DISEASES (OLD CASES) ACT 1975 (c. 16)—*continued.*

Section of Act	Subject matter	Section of 1992 Act	Remarks
(2) - (4)	—	CB Sch. 8, para. 4(2) - (4)	
6	Restrictions on scope of schemes under s. 5		
(1)	—	CB Sch. 8, para. 5(1)	
(2)	—	CB Sch. 8, para. 5(2)	Rep. in part 1980(1) ss. 8, 21, Sch. 5; am. 1980(1) s. 4(3).
(3), (4)	—	CB Sch. 8, para. 5(3), (4)	
(5)	—	—	Rep. 1980(1) ss. 8, 21, Sch. 5.
7	Nature and amount of benefit under s. 5		
(1)	—	CB Sch. 8, para. 6(1)	
(2)	—	CB Sch. 6, para. 6(2)	Rep. in part 1986 s. 86, Sch. 10, para. 67 with savings; by S.I. 1987/354 Art. 3; am. S.I. 1990/320.
(3)	—	CB Sch. 8, para. 6(4)	Am. 1982(2) s. 48(5), Sch. 4, para. 18(2); 1984 s. 13, Sch. 5, para. 8(a); 1986 s. 86, Sch. 10, para. 68(2)(a).
(4)	—	CB Sch. 8, para. 6(5)	Substituted 1984 s. 13, Sch. 5, para. 8(b); am. 1986 s. 86, Sch. 10, para. 68(2)(b).
(5)	—	CB Sch. 8. para. 6(6)	Rep. in part 1977 s. 11(3).
8	Ancillary provisions to s. 5		
(1), (2)	—	CB 175(2), 176(3), A Sch. 9, para. 2(1), (2)	
(3)	—	A Sch. 9, para. 2(3)	Rep. in part 1977 s. 24(6), Sch. 2.
(4)	—	A Sch. 9, para. 2(4)	
(5), (6)	—	—	Rep. 1977 s. 24(6), Sch. 2.
9	Adjustment of benefit in certain cases.		
(1), (2)	—	A Sch. 9, para. 3	
(3)	—	—	Rep. 1986 s. 86, Sch. 11.
10(1) - (3)	—	—	Rep. 1986 s. 86, Sch. 11.

SOCIAL SECURITY ACTS CONSOLIDATION—*continued.*

Section of Act	Subject matter	Section of 1992 Act	Remarks
INDUSTRIAL INJURIES AND DISEASES (OLD CASES) ACT 1975 (c. 16)—*continued.*			
(4)	—	—	Rep. (England and Wales) Police and Criminal Evidence Act 1984 s. 119, Sch. 7; (for Scotland, The Criminal Justice (Scotland) Act 1980 (c. 62) s. 29).
11	Proof of age, death and marriage.	A 124	
12	Exemption from stamp duty.	A 188(3)	
13	Reciprocal arrangements with Northern Ireland.	—	Rep. 1990 s. 16(8)(c).
14	Interpretation.		
(1)	—	CB Sch. 8, para. 8(1), (2)	
(2), (3)	—	CB Sch. 8, para. 8(3), (4)	
(4)	—	CB Sch. 8, para. 8(5)	Am. 1977 s. 8(5).
(5)	—	—	Unnecessary; see Interpretation Act 1978 (c. 30) s. 20(2).
15	Citation, extent and commencement	—	
SOCIAL SECURITY (CONSEQUENTIAL PROVISIONS) ACT 1975 (c. 18)			
Sch. 2	Amendments.		
Paras. 6, 8, 9, 11, 69, 70	—	—	Spent.
Sch. 3	Transitional Provisions and Savings.		
Paras. 1, 2	—	—	Spent.
3 - 5	—	SS CP Sch. 3, paras. 11 - 13	
6	—	—	Spent.
7, 8	—	SS CP Sch. 3, paras. 14, 15	
9, 10	—	—	Spent.
11(1)	—	SS CP Sch. 3, para. 16	
(2)	—	SS CP Sch. 3, para. 22(2) - (4), (7)	Rep. in part 1980(1) s. 21, Sch. 5.

SOCIAL SECURITY ACTS CONSOLIDATION—*continued.*

Section of Act	Subject matter	Section of 1992 Act	Remarks
SOCIAL SECURITY (CONSEQUENTIAL PROVISIONS) ACT 1975 (c. 18)—*continued.*			
12 - 17	—	—	Spent.
18	—	SS CP Sch. 4, para. 20	
19	—	—	Spent.
20	—	A 47(10)	
SOCIAL SECURITY PENSIONS ACT 1975 (c. 60)			
1	Earnings limits.		
(1)	—	CB 5(1)	Am. 1985 s. 29(1), Sch. 5, para. 15.
(2)	—	CB5 (2)	Am. 1986 s. 74(6).
(3)	—	CB5 (3)	
2	—	—	Rep. 1977 s. 24(6), Sch. 2.
3	Married women and widows.		
(1)	Repeal.	—	Spent.
(2), (3)	—	CB 19(4), (5)	
(4)	—	CB 19(6)	Am. 1986 s. 75, Sch. 8, para. 5.
4	Persons over pensionable age.		
(1)	—	CB 6(2)	Rep. in part 1984 s. 24, Sch. 8; am. 1984 s. 21, Sch. 7, para. 3(a).
(2)	—	CB 11(2)	
(3)	Amendment.	CB 17(2)	
5	Voluntary contributions.		
(1)	—	CB 14(1)	Am. 1986 s. 75. Sch. 8, para. 6.
(2)	—	CB 14(3), (4)	
(3)	—	CB 14(2)	
6	Rate of Category A retirement pension.		
(1)	—	CB 44(3), (4)	Am. 1986 s. 18(1).
(2)	—	CB 45(1)	Rep. in part 1986 s. 86, Sch. 11; am. 1986 s. 18(1), (2).
(2A), (2B)	—	CB 45(2) – (5)	Inserted 1986 s. 18(3).
(3)	—	CB 45(6)	Rep. in part 1979 s. 21(4), Sch. 3, para. 13; am. 1986 s. 18(4).
(4)	—	CB 44(5)	Am. 1979 s. 21(4), Sch. 3, para. 14.

SOCIAL SECURITY ACTS CONSOLIDATION—*continued.*

Section of Act	Subject matter	Section of 1992 Act	Remarks
	SOCIAL SECURITY PENSIONS ACT 1975 (c. 60)—*continued.*		
(5)	—	CB 44(6)	See also SS CP Sch. 4, para. 2; rep. in part 1986 s. 86, Sch. 11; am. 1985 s. 29(1), Sch. 5, para. 16(a); 1986 s. 75, Sch. 8, para. 7(1)(a); 1989 s. 26, Sch. 7, para. 19.
(5A)	—	—	See SS CP Sch. 4, para. 3; inserted 1985 s. 29(1), Sch. 5, para. 16(b); rep. 1986 s. 75, Sch. 8, para. 7(1)(b).
(6)	—	CB 44(7)	
7	Rate of widow's Category B retirement pension.	CB 50(3), (4)	
8	Category B retirement pension for widower.		
(1)	—	CB 51(1)	Rep. in part 1989 s. 7, Sch. 1, para. 9(1); am. 1979 s. 5, Sch. 1, para. 4.
(2)	—	CB 51(2)	
(3)	—	CB 51(4)	Substituted 1989 s. 7, Sch. 1, para. 9(2).
9	Special provision for surviving spouses.		
(1)	—	CB 52(1)	
(2), (3)	—	CB 52(2), (3)	Am. 1986 s. 18(1)
10	Special provision for married women.	CB 53(1), (2)	
12	Increase of retirement pension where entitlement is deferred.	CB 55	Substituted 1989 s. 7(4).
13	Rate of widowed mother's allowance and widow's pension.	CB 39(1), (2)	Am. 1986 s. 86, Sch. 10, para. 69.
14	Rate of invalidity pension for persons under pensionable age.	CB 33(3)	Am. 1990 s. 4(1).
15	Invalidity pension for widows.		
(1)	—	CB 40(1)	Am. 1986 s. 86, Sch. 10, para. 70(a).
(1A)	—	CB 40(2)	Inserted 1989 s. 26, Sch. 7, para. 20(1).
(2)	—	CB 40(3)	Am. 1986 s. 86, Sch. 10, para. 70(b).
(3)	—	CB 40(4)	
(4)	—	CB 40(5)	Am. 1986 s. 86, Sch. 10, para. 70(c); 1990 s. 4(2).
(5)	—	CB 40(7)	Am. 1977 s. 4(4); 1989 s. 7, Sch. 1, para. 10(1).
(6)	—	CB 40(8)	

SOCIAL SECURITY ACTS CONSOLIDATION—*continued.*

Section of Act	Subject matter	Section of 1992 Act	Remarks
	SOCIAL SECURITY PENSIONS ACT 1975 (c. 60)—*continued.*		
16	Invalidity pension for widowers.		
(1) – (3)	—	CB 41(1) – (3)	
(4)	—	CB 41(4), (5)	Substituted 1990 s. 4(3).
(5)	—	CB 41(7)	Am. 1977 s. 4(4); 1989 s. 7, Sch. 1, para. 10(2).
(6)	—	CB 41(8)	
16A	Entitlement to invalidity pension on termination of employment after a period of entitlement to disability working allowance.	CB 42	Inserted 1991(2) s. 9(3).
18	Rate of unemployment and sickness benefit for persons under pensionable age.		
(1)	Amendment	CB 25(4), 31(4)	
(2)	—	—	Spent.
19	Contribution conditions for retirement pensions, widowed mother's allowance and widow's pension.		
(1), (2)	Amendment	CB Sch. 3, para. 5(2)(b)	
(3)	—	—	Spent.
(4)	Repeal.	—	Spent.
(5)	—	CB 60(7)	
20	Use of former spouse's contributions.		
(1)	—	CB 48(1)	Am. 1979 s. 5, Sch. 1, para. 5.
(2)	—	CB 48(3)	
(3)	Repeal.	—	Spent.
21	Revaluation of earnings factors.		
(1)	—	A 148(1)	Am. 1985 s. 4, Sch. 3, para. 1; 1986 s. 18(1).
(2)	—	A 148(2)	Am. 1979 s. 10(2).
(3)	—	A 148(3), (4)	Substituted 1979 s. 10(3); am. 1980(1) s. 3(3).
(4)	—	A 148(5)	
(5)	—	A 148(6)	Am. 1980(1) s. 3(3).
(6)	—	—	Rep. 1980(1) s. 21, Sch. 5.
(7)	—	—	Substituted 1979 s. 10(4); spent.

SOCIAL SECURITY ACTS CONSOLIDATION—*continued.*

SOCIAL SECURITY PENSIONS ACT 1975 (c. 60)—*continued.*

Section of Act	Subject matter	Section of 1992 Act	Remarks
23	Increase of long-term benefits.		
(1)	—	—	Rep. 1986 s. 86, Sch. 11.
(2)	—	A 151(1)	Am. 1986 ss. 18(1), 86, Sch. 10, para. 91.
(2A)	—	A 156	Inserted 1989 s. 31(1), Sch. 8, para. 11.
(3)	—	A 151(1)	Am. 1986 s. 86, Sch. 10, para. 91.
(4)	—	—	Rep. 1980(1) s. 21, Sch. 5.
(5)	—	—	Rep. 1986 s. 86, Sch. 11.
24	Power to modify provisions about graduated retirement benefit.		
(1)(a)	—	A 150(11)	Am. 1986 s. 86, Sch. 10, para. 92.
(b), (c)	—	CB 62(1)	
(2)	—	CB 62(2)	
25	Simultaneous entitlement to more than one pension.	CB 43(3) - (5)	
51A(13)	—	—	See SS CP Sch. 2, para. 36 (1975(2) s. 61A(1)).
60(1)(a)	Determination of questions.	A 17(1)(f).	Affected by R8.
60A	Treatment of insignificant amounts.	CB 45(7), Sch. 5, paras. 2(4), 7(2).	Inserted 1979 s. 18.
62(1)	Other provisions about regulations and orders.	CB 176(1)(a).	Substituted 1990 s. 21(1), Sch. 6, para. 8(2).
(3)	—	—	See SS CP Sch. 2, para. 36 (1975(2) s. 61B(1)).
64(2)	—	—	Only partly repealed; unnecessary.
65(4)	References to benefit.	—	Spent.
66(2)	Interpretation	—	Only partly consolidated; spent.
Sch. 1	Increase of pension where entitlement is deferred.		
para. 1	—	CB Sch. 5, para. 1	Am. 1989 s. 7, Sch. 1, para. 3(1).
2(1)	—	CB Sch. 5, para. 2(1)	Am. 1989 s. 7, Sch. 1, para. 3(2).
(2)	—	CB Sch. 5, para. 2(2)	Substituted 1989 s. 7, Sch. 1, para. 3(3).
(3)	—	CB Sch. 5, para. 2(3)	Am. 1977 s. 3(1); 1989 s. 7, Sch. 1, para. 3(4).

SOCIAL SECURITY ACTS CONSOLIDATION—*continued.*

Section of Act	Subject matter	Section of 1992 Act	Remarks
	SOCIAL SECURITY PENSIONS ACT 1975 (c. 60)—*continued.*		
(4)	—	CB Sch. 5, para. 2(5)	Am. 1977 s. 3(1); 1980(1) s. 3(11)
(4A)	—	CB Sch. 5, para. 2(6)	Inserted 1985 s. 9(5).
(5)	—	CB Sch. 5, para. 2(7)	Rep. in part 1977 s. 3(1); am. 1986 s. 86, Sch. 10, para. 95(a); 1989 s. 7, Sch. 1, para. 3(5).
(6)	—	CB Sch. 5, para. 2(8)	Inserted 1977 s. 3(1); am. 1989 s. 7, Sch. 1, para. 3(6).
3	—	CB Sch. 5, para. 3	Substituted 1977 s. 3(1); am. 1989 s.7, Sch. 1, para. 3(7).
4(1)	—	CB Sch. 5, para. 4(1)	Am. 1979 s. 21(4), Sch. 3, para. 23; 1986 s. 19(2)(a); 1989 s. 7, Sch. 1, para. 3(8).
(2)	—	CB Sch. 5, para. 4(2)	Am. 1979 s. 21(4), Sch. 3, para. 23; 1986 s. 19(2)(a); 1989 s. 7, Sch. 1, para. 3(8).
(2A)	—	CB Sch. 5, para. 4(3)	Inserted 1986 s. 19(2)(b).
(3)	—	CB Sch. 5, para. 4(4)	Inserted 1979 s. 5, Sch. 1, para. 6; am. 1986 s. 86, Sch. 10, para. 95(a).
(4)	—	CB Sch. 5, para. 4(5)	Inserted 1979 s. 5, Sch. 1, para. 22.
4A(1)	—	CB Sch. 5, para. 5(1), (2)	Paragraph inserted 1979 s. 5, Sch. 1, para. 7; amended 1986 s. 19(3).
(1A)	—	CB Sch. 5, para. 5(3)	Inserted 1986 s. 19(4).
(2)	—	CB Sch. 5, para. 6(1), (2)	Am. 1986 s. 19(5).
(2A)	—	CB Sch. 5, para. 6(3), (4)	Inserted 1986 s. 19(6).
(3)	—	CB Sch. 5, para. 7(1)	Am. 1986 s. 86, Sch. 10, para. 95(b).
5(1), (2)	—	CB Sch. 5, para. 8(1), (2)	Substituted 1989 s. 7, Sch. 1, para. 3(9).
(3)	—	CB Sch. 5, para. 8(3)	Am. 1989 s. 7, Sch. 1, para. 3(10).
(4)	—	CB Sch. 5, para. 8(4)	
Sch. 4 para. 35	Amendments of enactments. —	—	Spent.

SOCIAL SECURITY ACTS CONSOLIDATION—*continued.*

Section of Act	Subject matter	Section of 1992 Act	Remarks
	SOCIAL SECURITY PENSIONS ACT 1975 (c. 60)—*continued.*		
36(a)	—	CB 5(1)	
(b)	—	—	Spent.
37	—	CB 20(1)	
38(a)	—	CB 22(2)	
(b)	—	CB 22(4)	
39(a)	—	—	Rep. 1989 s. 31(2), Sch. 9
(b)	—	CB 25(6), 31(7).	
40(a)	—	—	Spent.
(b)	—	CB 33(3)	
(c)	—	CB 33(5)	
41	—	CB 37(1)	Affected by R21.
42	—	CB 38(1)	Affected by R21.
43	—	CB 44(1)	
44	—	CB 50(1)	
45	—	CB 54(3)	
46	—	CB 60(4)	
49	—	—	Spent.
50(a)	—	—	Spent.
(b)	—	A141(1)	
(c)	—	—	Spent.
53	—	—	Spent.
54	—	—	Spent.
55	—	—	Spent.
56	—	—	See 1975(2) s. 60ZB inserted SS CP Sch. 2, para. 35.
57	—	—	See 1975(2) s. 60ZC inserted SS CP Sch. 2, para. 35.
58	—	—	See 1975(2) s. 60ZD inserted SS CP Sch. 2, para. 35.
59	—	—	See 1975(2) s. 60ZE inserted SS CP Sch. 2, para. 35.
60	—	—	See 1975(2) s. 60ZF(5) inserted SS CP Sch. 2, para. 35.
61	—	CB Sch. 1, para. 8(1)(g)	
62	—	CB Sch. 4, Part I, para. 5	
63	—	CB Sch. 4, Part V, para. 10	

SOCIAL SECURITY ACTS CONSOLIDATION—*continued.*

Section of Act	Subject matter	Section of 1992 Act	Remarks
SOCIAL SECURITY PENSIONS ACT 1975 (c. 60)—*continued.*			
64	—	CB 20(2) "long-term benefit", CB 174, A191 "Pensions Act", CB 122(1) "qualifying earnings factor", CB 122(1) "week"	
66	—	A177(4)	
67	—	A119(2)	
CHILD BENEFIT ACT 1975 (c. 61)			
1	Child benefit.		
(1)	—	CB 141	
(2)	—	A163(2)(f)	
(3)	—	—	Spent.
2	Meaning of "child".		
(1)	—	CB 142(1)	Am. 1986 s. 70(1)(a); 1988 s. 4(3).
(1A), (1B)	—	CB 142(2), (3)	Inserted 1986 s. 70(1)(b).
(2)	—	CB 142(4)	
(3)	—	CB 142(5)	Rep. in part 1980(1) s. 21, Sch. 5.
3	Meaning of "person responsible for child"		
(1), (2)	—	CB 143(1), (2)	
(3)	—	CB 143(3)	Am. National Health Service Act 1977 (c.49) s. 129, Sch. 15, para.67; National Health Service (Scotland) Act 1978 (c. 29) s. 109, Sch. 15, para.2; National Health Service and Community Care Act 1990 (c. 19) s. 661(1), Sch. 9, para. 15; the Children Act 1989 (Consequential Amendment of Enactments) Order 1991 art. 2 (S.I.1991/1881); see also SS CP Sch. 4, para. 5.

SOCIAL SECURITY ACTS CONSOLIDATION—*continued.*

Section of Act	Subject matter	Section of 1992 Act	Remarks
	CHILD BENEFIT ACT 1975 (c. 61)—*continued.*		
(4), (5)	—	CB 143(4), (5)	
4	Exclusions and priority.		
(1)	—	CB 144(1), (2)	Am. 1988(1) s. 4(4).
(2)	—	CB 144(3)	
4A	Overlap with benefits under legislation of other member States.	A 80	Section inserted 1979 s. 15(3).
5	Rate of child benefit.		
(1) - (4)	—	CB 145(1)-(4)	
(5)	—	—	Rep. 1986 s. 86, Sch. 11.
(6)	—	A 157	
6	Claims and payment.		
(1)	—	A 13(1)	Am. 1989 s. 26, Sch. 7, para. 22.
(2)	—	—	Rep. 1986 s.86, Sch. 11.
(3)	—	A 13(2)	
(4), (5)	—	—	Rep. 1986 s. 86, Sch. 11.
7,8	—	—	Rep. 1986 s. 86, Sch. 11.
9	Age, marriage and death.		
(1)	—	—	Rep. 1986 s. 86, Sch. 11.
(2)	—	CB 147(5)	
10	—	—	Rep. 1986 s. 86, Sch. 11.
11(1)–(7)	—	—	Rep. 1986 s. 86, Sch. 11.
(8)	—	—	Rep. (Scotland) Criminal Justice (Scotland) Act 1980 c. 62 s. 83, Sch. 8, (England and Wales) Police and Criminal Evidence Act 1984 (c.60) s. 119, Sch. 7.
12	Benefit to be inalienable.	A 187(1). (2)	
13	Persons outside Great Britain.	CB 146	
14	Reciprocal arrangements with Northern Ireland.		
(1), (2)	—	A 178(1)-(3)	
(3)	—	A 189(11)	
15	Reciprocal arrangements with countries outside the United Kingdom.		
(1)	—	A 179(1), (4), (5).	Rep. in part 1986 s. 86, Sch. 11; 1977 s. 20(2).
(1A)	—	A 179(2)	Inserted 1981 s. 6(2).
(2)	—	A 179(3)	

SOCIAL SECURITY ACTS CONSOLIDATION—*continued.*

Section of Act	Subject matter	Section of 1992 Act	Remarks
	CHILD BENEFIT ACT 1975 (c. 61)—*continued.*		
(3)	—	A 189(11)	
16	—	—	Rep. 1975(3) s. 21, Sch. 5.
17	Social security benefits in respect of children.		
(1), (2)	—	A 154	Partly spent.
(3)–(6)	—	—	Rep. 1986 s. 86, Sch. 11.
20	Transitional provisions.	—	See SS CP Sch. 3, paras.4, 6.
21	Consequential amendments and repeals.		
(1)–(4)	—	—	Spent.
(5)	—	—	Rep. 1975(3) s. 21(2), Sch. 5.
(6), (7)	—	—	Spent.
22	Regulations and orders.		
(1)	—	CB 145(5), 175(1), A 189(1)	
(2)	—	CB 175(2), A 189(3)	
(3)	—	CB 176(1) (a), A 190(1)(–b)	Subst. 1990 s. 21, Sch. 6, para. 8(3).
(4)	—	CB 176(2) (b), A 190(2)	Subst. 1990 s. 21, Sch. 6, para 8(3).
(5)	—	CB 176(3), A 190(3)	Subst. 1990 s. 21, Sch. 6, para 8(3).
(6)	—	CB 175(3), A 189(4)	
(7)	—	CB 175(4), A 189(5)	Affected by R6.
(7A)	—	CB 175(5), A 189(6)	Inserted 1986 s. 62(2).
(8)	—	CB 145(6)	Otherwise unnecessary or spent.
(9)	—	CB 145(7)	Otherwise spent.
23	Financial provisions.		
(1)	—	A 163(2)(a)	
(2)	—	—	Unnecessary.
(3)	—	—	Spent.
(4)	—	A 165(2), (3)(b)	
24	Interpretation.		
(1)	—	CB147(1)	Rep. in part 1983 s. 30, Sch. 10; 1986 s. 86, Sch. 11.

SOCIAL SECURITY ACTS CONSOLIDATION—*continued.*

Section of Act	Subject matter	Section of 1992 Act	Remarks
	CHILD BENEFIT ACT 1975 (c. 61)—*continued.*		
(2)	—	CB147(2)	
(3)	—	CB147(3)	Rep. in part Children Act 1975 (c. 72), s. 108, Sch. 4; see also Family Law Reform Act 1989 (c. 42).
(4)	—	CB147(4)	
(5)	—	CB147(6)	
(6)	—	—	Unnecessary.
25	Short title and extent.		
Sch. 1	Exclusions from entitlement.		
Paras. 1–4	—	CB Sch. 9 paras. 1–4	
5	—	CB Sch. 9 para. 5	Am. 1984 s. 11, Sch. 4, para. 13.
Sch. 2	Priority between persons entitled.	CB Sch. 10	
Sch. 3	Increases in rate of benefit.		
Paras. 1, 2	—	A157(1)	Am. 1986 s. 86, Sch. 10, para. 97.
3	—	A157(2)	
Sch. 4	Consequential amendments.		
Paras. 1, 2	—	—	Rep. Supplementary Benefits Act 1976 (c. 71) s. 35(3), Sch. 8.
3–6	—	—	Rep. 1986 s. 86, Sch. 11.
7	—	—	Rep. Supplementary Benefits Act 1976 (c. 71) s. 35(2), Sch. 8.
8	—	A70(3)	
9	—	CB37(1), (2)	
10	—	CB56(1)	
11	—	—	Rep. 1986 s. 86, Sch. 11.
12	—	CB77(1), (9)	
13	—	CB80(1), (5), (6)	Paragraphs (a), (b) and (c) amend respectively 1975(1) s. 41(1), (4) and (5).
14	Repeal.	—	Spent.
15	—	CB81(1)–(3)	
16	—	CB82(1), (2), (4)	
17	—	CB83(2)	
18	—	CB85(2)	
19	—	CB86(1)	

Tables of Derivations and Destinations

SOCIAL SECURITY ACTS CONSOLIDATION—*continued.*

Section of Act	Subject matter	Section of 1992 Act	Remarks
		CHILD BENEFIT ACT 1975 (c. 61)—*continued.*	
20	—	—	Spent.
21	—	CB Sch. 7, para. 4(1)	
22	—	CB Sch. 7, para. 5(1), (2)	
23	—	CB Sch. 7, para. 6(1)	
24	—	CB Sch. 7, para. 16(2)(a)	
25	—	—	Rep. 1984 s. 24, Sch. 8.
26	—	—	Spent.
27	—	—	Rep. 1986 s. 86, Sch. 11.
28	—	A73(2)	
29	—	—	Rep. 1986 s. 86, Sch. 11.
30	—	A17(1)	
31	—	—	Rep. 1986 s. 86, Sch. 11.
32	—	—	Spent.
33	—	—	Rep. 1986 s. 86, Sch. 11.
34	—	CB Sch. 4, Parts IV, V	
35	—	CB Sch. 4, Part V, para. 12	Otherwise spent.
36	—	—	Rep. 1980(1) s. 21, Sch. 5.
37	—	A Sch. 7, Part II	
38	—	A122(4)–(5)	
39	—	—	Rep. 1982(2) s. 48(6), Sch. 5.
Sch. 5	Repeals.	—	Spent.
		EDUCATION (SCHOOL-LEAVING DATES) ACT 1976(c. 5)	
2(4)	Social security amendments.	CB6(1), 11(1), 13(1)	
		SUPPLEMENTARY BENEFITS ACT 1976 (c. 71)	
22	Impersonation of officers.	A181	Rep. in part 1980(1) ss. 6(1), 21(4), Sch. 2, para. 21, Sch. 5; am. 1980(1) s. 6(1), Sch. 2, para. 21; SI 1988/1843, Sch. 3, para. 2(c).

SOCIAL SECURITY ACTS CONSOLIDATION—*continued.*

Section of Act	Subject matter	Section of 1992 Act	Remarks
	SUPPLEMENTARY BENEFITS ACT 1976 (c. 71)—*continued.*		
23	Illegal possession of documents.	A182	Am. S.I. 1988/1843, Sch. 3, para. 2(c).
Sch. 7, para. 36	Amendment.	A70(3)	
	SOCIAL SECURITY (MISCELLANEOUS PROVISIONS) ACT 1977 (c. 5)		
1	Amendments relating to contributions.		
(1)	—	—	Spent.
(2)	—	A163(4)	
(3)	—	CB Sch. 1, para. 1(1)	
(4)	—	CB Sch. 1, para. 4	
(5)	—	CB14(3), (4)	
(6), (7)	—		Spent.
2	Amendment of regulations for crediting contributions.	CB22(7)	
3	Increments of retirement pension for deferred retirement etc.		
(1)(a)	—	—	Spent.
(b)	—	CB Sch. 5, para. 2(3)	
(c)	—	CB Sch. 5, para. 2(5)	
(d)	—	CB Sch. 5, para. 2(8)	
(e)	—	CB Sch. 5, para. 3(1)	
4	Other amendments relating to retirement pensions.		
(1)	—	CB43(2)	
(2), (3)	—	—	Spent.
(4)	—	CB40(7), 41(7)	
5	Alteration of earnings rules.		
(1)	—	—	Spent.
(2)	—	—	Rep. 1979 s. 21(4), Sch. 3, para. 29(b).
6	Review of earnings rule operation.	—	Spent.
8	Adjustments of benefit.		
(1)	—	CB61(1)	Am. 1990 s. 21(1), Sch. 6, para. 3(3).
(2)	—	CB61(2)	Am. 1990 s. 21(1), Sch. 6, para. 3(4).
(3)	—	—	Rep. 1980(1) s. 21, Sch. 5.

Tables of Derivations and Destinations

SOCIAL SECURITY ACTS CONSOLIDATION—*continued.*

Section of Act	Subject matter	Section of 1992 Act	Remarks
	SOCIAL SECURITY (MISCELLANEOUS PROVISIONS) ACT 1977 (c. 5)—*continued.*		
9	Industrial death benefit in certain cases of death from pulmonary disease.	CB Sch. 7, para. 21	
10	Revocation of Silicosis Schemes and abolition of boards administering Pneumoconiosis etc. and Supplementation Schemes.		
(1)	—	—	Spent except as to para. 6 of Sch. 1.
(2)	—	—	Spent.
11	Miscellaneous amendments of Old Cases Act.		
(1)(a)	—	A Sch. 9, para. 4(4)(a).	
(b)	Repeal.	—	Spent.
(2)	—	—	Rep. 1980(1)s. 21, Sch. 5.
(3), (4)	Repeals.	—	Spent.
(5)	Amendment.	CB Sch. 8, para. 11(5)(b).	
(6)	—	—	Spent.
13	Mobility allowances for certain persons eligible for invalid carriages.		
(1)	—	CB 74(1)	Am. 1991(2) s. 4, Sch. 2, para. 8.
(2)	—	—	Rep. 1979 s. 21(4), Sch. 3, para. 29(c).
(3)	—	CB74(2)	
17	Amendments relating to benefit.		
(1)	—	—	Spent.
(2)	—	—	Rep. 1986 s. 86, Sch. 11.
(3)	—	CB 95(4), (5)	
(4)	—	A 158	
(5)	—	A 61(3)	
(6)	—	CB 40(6)	
18	Certain sums to be earnings for social security purposes.	CB 112	Rep. in part 1986 s. 86, Sch. 11; am. Employment Protection (Consolidation) Act 1978 (c. 44) s. 159, Sch. 16, para. 29(d), 1986 s. 86, Sch. 10, para. 74.
20	Reciprocal arrangements		
(1),(2)	—	A 179(1)	
22	Miscellaneous amendments.		

SOCIAL SECURITY ACTS CONSOLIDATION—*continued.*

Section of Act	Subject matter	Section of 1992 Act	Remarks
SOCIAL SECURITY (MISCELLANEOUS PROVISIONS) ACT 1977 (c. 5)—*continued.*			
(1)	—	CB 122(3)	
(2)	—	CB 56(2)(b)	Part spent.
(3)	—	CB 81(3), Sch. 7, para. 5(2).	
(4)	—	CB Sch. 7, para. 15(3).	Otherwise spent.
(5)	—	A 17(1)(e)	
23(2)	—	—	Only partly repealed; unnecessary.
24(1)	Supplemental.	—	Certain words only; spent.
(2)	—	—	See SS CP Sch. 2, para. 43(2); otherwise unnecessary.
(4)	—	—	Spent.
Sch. 1	Provisions connected with revocation of Silicosis Schemes and abolition of boards administering Pneumoconiosis etc and Supplementation Schemes.	CB Sch. 8, para. 5(5)	Otherwise spent.
NATIONAL HEALTH SERVICE ACT 1977 (c. 49)			
Sch. 15, paras. 63, 64, 67	Consequential amendments.	CB 67(2)	Part spent.
NATIONAL HEALTH SERVICE (SCOTLAND) ACT 1978 (c. 29)			
Sch. 16, para. 40	Consequential amendments of enactments.	—	Spent.
EMPLOYMENT PROTECTION (CONSOLIDATION) ACT 1978 (c.44)			
Sch. 16	Consequential amendments		
Para. 19(1)	—	A58(4)	
(2)	—	—	Spent.
29	—	CB112	
SOCIAL SECURITY ACT 1979 (c.18)			
2	Attendance allowance.		
(1)	—	—	Drafting.
(2)	—	CB65(1)(b)	
(3)	—	CB65(2)	
(4)	—	—	Rep. 1991(2) s. 10, Sch. 4.
(5)	—	CB65(6)	
(6)	—	CB67(1)	
4	Amendment of provisions relating to earnings after retirement age.		
(1)	—	—	Affected by R15.

SOCIAL SECURITY ACTS CONSOLIDATION—*continued.*

Section of Act	Subject matter	Section of 1992 Act	Remarks
	SOCIAL SECURITY ACT 1979 (c.18)—*continued.*		
(2)	—	—	Para. (a) spent; para. (b) rep. 1990 s. 21(2), Sch. 7.
(3)	—	—	Rep. 1980(1) s. 21, Sch. 5.
5	Amendment of principal Act, Pensions Act and Act of 1977.	—	Gives effect to Schedule 1.
9(1)	Amendment.	—	Spent.
10	Amendments.		
(1)	—	—	Drafting.
(2)	—	A148(2)	
(3)	—	A148(3), (4)	
(4)	—	—	Spent.
14	Amendments.		
(1)	—	CB6(5)	
(2)	—	A162(12)	
15	Amendments.		
(1)	—	A73(4), (5)	
(2)	—	—	Rep. 1980(1) s. 21, Sch. 5
(3)	—	A80	
19	Enactment of same provisions for Northern Ireland.	—	Unnecessary.
20(3)	Financial provisions	—	Unnecessary.
Sch. 1	Amendment of principal Act, Pensions Act and Act of 1977.		
Para. 1	—	CB33(5)	
2	—	CB78(4)	
3	—	CB Sch. 3, para. 5(7)	
4	—	CB51(1)	
5	—	CB48(1)	
6	—	CB Sch. 5, para. 4(4)	
7	—	CB Sch. 5, paras. 5(1), (2), 6(1), (2), 7(1)	
8	—	CB43(2)	
9	—	—	Drafting.
10(a)	—	CB34(3)	
(b)	—	—	Spent.
11	—	—	Rep. 1985 s. 29(2), Sch. 6.
12	—	—	Spent.

SOCIAL SECURITY ACTS CONSOLIDATION—*continued.*

Section of Act	Subject matter	Section of 1992 Act	Remarks

SOCIAL SECURITY ACT 1979 (c.18)—*continued.*

Section of Act	Subject matter	Section of 1992 Act	Remarks
13	—	CB Sch. 4, Part V, para. 6	
14	Modification.	CB51(1)(a)	
15	—	CB52(4)	
16	—	CB53(3)	
17	—	—	Rep. 1989 s. 26, Sch. 7, para. 20(2).
18	—	CB41(1)	
19	Repeal.	—	Spent.
20	Modification.	CB48(2)	
21	Amendment.	—	Spent.
22	—	CB Sch.5, para.4(5)	
Sch.2	Amendment.	—	Spent.
Sch.3	Amendments.		
Para.4	—	—	Spent.
5	—	CB23(1)	
6	—	CB25(6), 31(7)	
7	—	CB33(5)	
8	—	A47(1)	
10	—	CB Sch.3, para. 7(3), (4)	
11	—	—	Spent.
13	Repeal.	—	Part only repealed.
14	—	CB44(5)	
15	—	—	Spent.
23	—	CB Sch.5, para.4(1), (2)	
29	Repeals.	—	Spent.
31	Revocation.	—	Spent.
32	Amendment.	—	Spent.

SOCIAL SECURITY ACT 1980 (c.30)

Section of Act	Subject matter	Section of 1992 Act	Remarks
2	Amendments.	—	Introduces Schedule.
3	Amendments.		
(1)	—	—	Spent.
(2)	—	—	Spent.
(3)	—	A148(3), (6)	

SOCIAL SECURITY ACTS CONSOLIDATION—*continued.*

Section of Act	Subject matter	Section of 1992 Act	Remarks
	SOCIAL SECURITY ACT 1980 (c.30)—*continued.*		
(11)	—	CB Sch.5, para.2(5)	
4	Amendments.		
(3)	—	CB Sch.8, para.5(2)	
(5)	—	CB142(5)	
(6)	—	—	Unnecessary.
5(1)	Maternity grant.	—	Spent.
6	Amendments.		
(2)	—	—	Spent.
(4)	—	—	Spent.
9	Social Security Advisory Committee.		
(1)–(4)	—	A170(1)–(4)	See also the Northern Ireland consolidation.
(5)	—	—	See SS CP Sch.3, paras.4, 6.
(7)	—	A170(5)	Affected by R12; rep. in part 1986 s.86, Sch.11, Sch.10 to S.I. 1986/1888 (N.I. 18); am. 1982(2) s.48(5), Sch.4, para.30, 1989 s.31(1), Sch.8, para.12(2), 1990 s.21(1), Sch.6, para.31(b), 1991(3) s.3(1)(b), S.I. 1982/1084 (N.I. 16) Sch.4, para.17, S.I. 1989/1342 (N.I. 13) Sch.8, para.11(1), S.I. 1990/1511 (N.I. 15) Sch.6, para.20.
10	Consultation with Committee on proposals for regulations.	—	See also SS CP Sch.2, para.36 (1975(2) s.61A) and the Northern Ireland consolidation.
(1)	—	A127(1)	Am. 1986 s.86, Sch10, para.98(a), S.I. 1986/1888 (N.I. 18) Sch.9, para.64(a).
(2)	—	A172(3)	Rep. in part 1989 s.31(1), Sch.8, para.12(5), S.I. 1986/1888 (N.I. 18), Sch.10; partly otiose.
(3)–(5)	—	A174(1)–(3)	
(9)	—	A172(5), 173(6), 174(4)	Only partly repealed.
11	Exclusion of requirements to consult Industrial Injuries Advisory Committees.		

SOCIAL SECURITY ACTS CONSOLIDATION—*continued.*

Section of Act	Subject matter	Section of 1992 Act	Remarks
	SOCIAL SECURITY ACT 1980 (c.30)—*continued.*		
(1)	—	—	Rep. Social Security (Advisory Committees) Transitional Regulations 1980 (S.I. 1980/1874) reg.3.
(2)(a)	—	A Sch.7, para.16	
(b)	—	—	Spent.
13	Tenure of office of Commissioner.	—	See also Northern Ireland consolidation.
(1)–(3)	—	A Sch.2, para. 1(2)–(4), (7)	
(5)	—	A52(2)	Am. Courts and Legal Services Act 1990 s. 71(2). Sch. 10, para. 46.
(a)	—	A Sch. 2, para. 1(6)	Am. Judicial Pensions Act 1981 (c. 20) s. 36, Sch. 3, para. 10, Courts and Legal Services Act 1990 s. 125(3), Sch. 18, para. 24.
(b)	—	—	See House of Commons Disqualification Act 1975 (c. 24) Sch. 1, Part I amended by SS CP Sch. 2, para. 16 and Northern Ireland Assembly Disqualifications Act 1975 (c. 25) Sch. 1, Part I amended SS CP Sch. 2, para. 17.
(6)	—	A52(3), Sch. 2, para. 1(5)	
14	Appeal from Commissioners etc. on point of law.	—	See also Northern Ireland consolidation.
(1)–(5)	—	A24(1)–(5), 34(5)	
(6)	—	—	Rep. 1986 s. 86, Sch. 11.
(7)	—	—	Rep. 1989 s. 31(2), Sch.9; see SS CP Sch. 4, para. 12.
(8)	—	A24(6), 190(4)	Am. 1986 s. 82, Sch 9, para. 11(c); affected by R13.
17	Proof of decisions of statutory authorities.	A Sch.2, para. 8	Am. 1991(2) s. 4, Sch. 2, para. 10.

SOCIAL SECURITY ACTS CONSOLIDATION—*continued.*

Section of Act	Subject matter	Section of 1992 Act	Remarks

SOCIAL SECURITY ACT 1980 (c.30)—*continued.*

Section of Act	Subject matter	Section of 1992 Act	Remarks
18	Computations of age in Scotland.	CB173	Rep. in part 1986 s. 86, Sch. 11.
19(3)	Expenses.	A165(5)	
Sch. 1	Amendments.		
Paras. 1–3	—	—	Spent.
4	—	CB82(4), 85(2). Sch. 7. para. 6(1)	Partly spent.
5(1)	—	CB87(1)	Partly spent.
(2)	—	CB82(1), (2), 86(1)	
6	—	CB Sch. 7, para. 6(1)	
7	—	CB122(6)	Partly spent.
8	—	CB65(5)	
9	—	A19(2), (3)	Rep. in part 1986 s. 86, Sch. 11.
10	—	—	Rep. 1986 s. 86, Sch. 11.
11	—	—	Spent.
12	—	—	Rep. 1986 s. 86, Sch. 11.
13	—	A143(4)	
14	—	—	Spent.
15	—	—	Spent.
16	—	CB Sch. 1, para. 1(2)	
Sch. 2, para. 21	Amendment.	A181	
Sch. 3	Social Security Advisory Committee.		
Part I	Constitution etc of Committee.		
para. 1	—	A Sch. 5, para. 1	Am. 1982(2) s. 48(5), Sch. 4, para. 32(2).
2	—	A Sch. 5, para. 2	Am. 1982(2) s. 48(5), Sch. 4, para. 32(3).
3–10	—	A Sch. 5, paras. 3–10	
Part II	Regulations not requiring prior submission to Committee.	—	See also Northern Ireland consolidation.
11	—	—	Rep. 1986 s. 86, Sch. 11.
12(1)	—	A Sch. 7, Part I, para. 2	

SOCIAL SECURITY ACTS CONSOLIDATION—*continued.*

Section of Act	Subject matter	Section of 1992 Act	Remarks
		SOCIAL SECURITY ACT 1980 (c.30)—*continued.*	
(2)	—	A Sch. 7, Part I, para. 3	Am. 1982(2) s. 42(2), 1986 s. 86, Sch. 10, para. 99.
(3)	—	—	Inserted 1991(2) s. 4, Sch. 2, para. 11; see Northern Ireland consolidation.
(4)	—	A Sch. 7, Part I, para. 1	Inserted 1991(2) s. 4, Sch. 2, para. 11.
13(1)	—	A Sch. 7, Part I, para. 4	
(1A)	—	A Sch. 7, Part I, para. 5	Inserted 1986 s. 86, Sch. 10, para. 106, am. S.I. 1986/1888 (N.I. 18) Sch. 9, para. 73.
(2)	—	—	See A 170(5) definition of "relevant enactments" and SS CP Sch. 2, para. 36 (1975(2) s. 61A(1)); am. 1982(2) s. 48(5), Sch. 4, para. 33(2), S.I. 1982/1084 (N.I. 16) Sch. 4, para. 18(2).
14	—	A Sch. 7, Part I, paras. 6, 7	
15	—	—	Rep. 1986 s. 86, Sch. 11.
15A	—	A Sch. 7, Part I, para. 8	Inserted 1982(2) s. 48(5), Sch. 4, para. 33(3).
15AA	—	A Sch. 7, Part I, para. 8	Inserted 1989 s. 31(1), Sch. 8, para. 12(6); am. S.I. 1989/1342 (N.I. 13) Sch. 8, para. 11(3).
15B–18	—	—	Rep. 1986 s. 86, Sch. 11.
19, 20	—	A Sch. 7, Part I, paras. 9, 10	
21	—	—	See Northern Ireland consolidation; am. 1986 s. 82, Sch. 9, para. 12.
Sch. 4	Amendments.		
para. 10	—	—	Spent.
14	—	—	Spent.

SOCIAL SECURITY ACTS CONSOLIDATION—*continued.*

Section of Act	Subject matter	Section of 1992 Act	Remarks
	SOCIAL SECURITY (No. 2) ACT 1980 (c. 39)		
1	Reduction of compulsory uprating of certain benefits.	—	Rep. 1986 s. 86, Sch. 11.
2	Abolition of compulsory uprating of amount certain pensioners may earn without abating pensions.	—	Rep. 1986 s. 86, Sch. 11.
3	Alteration of period of interruption of employment and of periods relating to invalidity allowance and unemployability supplement.		
(1)	Amendment.	CB57(1)(d)	
(2)	—	—	Rep. 1982(2) s. 48(6), Sch. 5.
(3)	—	CB47(1), Sch. 7, para. 3(8)	
(4)	Regulations.	CB47(6), 57(9)(a), 175(1), Sch. 7, para. 3(9)	
4	Reduction and abolition of earnings-related supplement and addition.	—	Spent.
5	Abatement of unemployment benefit on account of payments of occupational or personal pension.		
(1)	—	CB30(1)	Am. 1988(1) s. 7(a), 1989 s. 9(1).
(1A)	—	CB30(2)	Inserted 1982(2) s. 48(5), Sch. 4, para. 34(2).
(2)	—	CB30(3)	Am. 1982(2) s. 48(5), Sch. 4, para. 34(3); 1989 s. 9(1).
(3)	—	CB 30(4), 122(1) "payments by way of occupational or personal pension", "prescribe", 175(1)	Am. 1989 s. 9(2).
(4)	—	CB 176(1)(b)	Am. 1989 s. 9(1), 1990 s. 21(1), Sch. 6, para. 8(5).
(5)	—	—	Spent or unnecessary.
(6)	—	CB 173	

SOCIAL SECURITY ACTS CONSOLIDATION—*continued.*

Section of Act	Subject matter	Section of 1992 Act	Remarks
	SOCIAL SECURITY (No. 2) ACT 1980 (c. 39)—*continued.*		
6	Supplementary benefit in cases affected by trade disputes.	—	Rep. 1986 s. 86, Sch. 11.
7	Supplemental.		
(1)	—	A 165(5)	
(2)	—	—	See SS CP Sch. 3, paras. 4, 6.
(3)	—	CB 175(2)-(4)	
(4)	—	CB 176(3)	Inserted 1990 s. 21(1), Sch. 6, para. 8(6).
(5), (6)	—	—	Spent.
(7)	—	—	Rep. Employment Act 1988 (c. 19) s. 33, Sch. 4.
8	Citation, commencement and extent.	—	
Sch.	Repeals.	—	Spent.
	MAGISTRATES' COURTS ACT 1980 (c. 43)		
65(1) (m)	—	—	See paragraph of section 65(1) of Magistrates' Courts Act 1980 inserted by SS CP Sch. 2, para. 59; otherwise spent.
Sch. 7 para. 135	Amendment.	A 121(1)	
	FINANCE ACT 1980 (c. 48)		
Sch. 19, para. 5(4)	Amendment.	A 161(3)	Certain words only.
	SOCIAL SECURITY (CONTRIBUTIONS) ACT 1981 (c. 1)		
1	Increase in contributions.	—	Rep. 1982(1) s. 4(3), Sch. 2.
2	Alteration of Treasury supplement to contributions.	—	Rep. 1982 s. 4(3), Sch. 2; 1989 s. 31(2), Sch. 9.
3	Amendments.		
(1)	—	—	Drafting.
(2)	—	—	Spent.
(3)	—	A 162(7), (8)	
4	Supplemental.		
(1), (2)	—	—	Unnecessary.
(3), (4)	—	—	Rep. 1982(1) s. 4(3), Sch. 2.
(5)	Amendment.	A 190(1)	Para. (a) rep. by 1989 s. 31(2), Sch. 9.
(6)	—	—	Rep. Employment Act 1990 (c. 38) s. 16(2), Sch. 3.

SOCIAL SECURITY ACTS CONSOLIDATION—*continued.*

Section of Act	Subject matter	Section of 1992 Act	Remarks

SOCIAL SECURITY (CONTRIBUTIONS) ACT 1981 (c. 1)—*continued.*

Section of Act	Subject matter	Section of 1992 Act	Remarks
(7)	—	—	Rep. 1982(1) s. 4(3), Sch. 2.
5	Short title and extent.		

JUDICIAL PENSIONS ACT 1981 (c. 20)

| Sch. 3, para. 10 | Amendment. | A Sch. 2, para. 1(6) | |

SOCIAL SECURITY ACT 1981 c. 33

5	Amendment.	CB 57(9)(b), (10)	
6	Reciprocity with other countries.		
(1)	Amendment.	A179(2)	
(2)	—	A179(2)	
(3)	—	—	Spent.
(4)	—	—	Spent.
8(2)	Northern Ireland.	—	Spent.
Sch. 1, para. 3(a)	Amendments.	—	Spent.
6	—	A181	
7	—	A182(3)	
Sch. 2, para. 2	Amendment.	A172(2)	Spent.

SOCIAL SECURITY (CONTRIBUTIONS) ACT 1982 (c. 2)

1	Increase in contributions.		Spent, so far as unrepealed.
2	Alteration of Treasury supplement to contributions.		Spent.
3	Allocation of contributions.	—	Spent, so far as unrepealed.
4	Supplemental.	—	Spent, so far as unrepealed.
5	Short title and extent.		
Sch. 1	Consequential amendments.		Spent, so far as unrepealed.

OIL AND GAS (ENTERPRISE) ACT 1982 (c. 23)

| Sch. 3, para. 21 | Amendments. | CB120(3) | |
| 44 | — | CB120(2), 162(1)(c) | |

SOCIAL SECURITY AND HOUSING BENEFITS ACT 1982 (c. 24)

1	Employer's liability.		
(1), (2)	—	CB151(1), (2)	
(3), (4)	—	CB151(4), (5)	
(5)	—	CB151(6)	Inserted 1986 s. 68.
(6)	—	A163(1)(d)	Inserted 1986 s. 68.
2	Period of incapacity for work.		
(1), (2)	—	CB152(1), (2)	

SOCIAL SECURITY ACTS CONSOLIDATION—*continued.*

Section of Act	Subject matter	Section of 1992 Act	Remarks
		SOCIAL SECURITY AND HOUSING BENEFITS ACT 1982 (c. 24)—*continued.*	
(3)		CB152(3)	Am. S.I. 1982/894 reg. 2A inserted S.I. 1986/477 reg. 2.
(3A)	—	CB152(4)	Inserted 1985 s. 18(4).
(4), (5)	—	CB152(5), (6)	
3	Period of entitlement.		
(1)–(4)	—	CB153(1)–(4)	
(4A)	—	CB153(5)	Inserted 1985 s. 18(5).
(5), (6)	—	CB153(6), (7)	
(6A), (6B)	—	CB153(8), (9)	Inserted 1985 s. 21(1), Sch. 4, para. 4.
(7), (8)	—	CB153(10), (11)	
(9)	—	CB153(12)	Substituted 1986 s. 86, Sch. 10, para. 77.
4	Qualifying days.		
(1)	—	CB154(1)	
(2)	—	CB154(2)	Am. 1984 s. 21, Sch. 7, para. 7.
(3), (4)	—	CB154(3), (4)	
5	Limitations on entitlement.		
(1)	—	CB155(1)	
(2)	—	CB155(2)	Rep. in part 1985 ss. 18, 29(2), Sch. 6.
(3)	—	CB 155(3)	Rep. in part 1985 ss. 18, 29(2), Sch. 6.
(4)	—	CB 155(4)	Am. 1985 s. 18(1).
(5)	—	CB 155(5)	Rep. in part 1985 ss. 18, 29(2), Sch. 6.
6	Notification of incapacity for work.	CB 156	
7	Rate of payment.		
(1)		CB 157(1)	Subst. S.I. 1990/257 reg. 2; am. S.I. 1991/506 art. 2 subject to saving in art. 3.
(1A)	—	CB 157(2).	Inserted 1986 s. 67(1); am. 1990 s. 21(1), Sch. 6, para. 15(1).
(1B)	—	CB 176(1)(c)	Inserted 1986 s. 67(1); am. 1990 s. 21(1), Sch. 6, para. 15(2)
(2)	—	CB 157(3)	
(3) - (10)	—	—	Rep. 1986 s. 86, Sch. 11.
9	Recovery by employers of amounts paid by way of statutory sick pay.		

SOCIAL SECURITY ACTS CONSOLIDATION—*continued.*

Section of Act	Subject matter	Section of 1992 Act	Remarks
	SOCIAL SECURITY AND HOUSING BENEFITS ACT 1982 (c. 24)—*continued.*		
(1)	—	CB 158(1)	Am. 1991(1) s. 1(1).
(1A)	—	—	Rep. 1991(1) s. 1(2), Sch.
(1B)	—	CB 158(2)	Inserted 1991(1) s. 2(1).
(1C)	—	CB 159	Inserted 1991(1) s. 2(1).
(1D)	—	CB 158(3)	Inserted 1991(1) s. 2(1).
(1E)	—	A 149	Inserted 1991(1) s. 2(1).
(1F)	—	CB 176(1)(a), (c)	Inserted 1991(1) s. 2(1).
(2)	—	CB 158(4)	Am. 1991(1) s. 2(2).
(3)	—	CB 158(5), A 130(4)(c)	Am. 1991(1) s. 1(3); rep. in part 1991(1) s. 3(6) Sch.
(4)	—	CB Sch. 1 para. 5(5)	
(5)	—	CB Sch. 1 para. 5(6)	Rep. in part 1991(1) s. 3(6), Sch.
(6)	—	CB 158(6)	
(7)	—	A 163(1)	Rep. in part 1991(1) s. 3(2), Sch.
(8) - (10)	—	—	Rep. 1986 s. 86, Sch. 11.
17	Provision of information: general.		
(1)	—	A 129	
(2)	—	A 14(1)	
(2A)	—	A 14(2)	Inserted 1985 s. 20.
(3)	—	A 14(3)	
(4)		A 130(4) (a), (b)	
18	Claims for sickness and other benfits: provision of information by employers.		
(1)	—	A 130(1)	Am. 1984 s. 11, Sch. 4, para. 15(a).
(2), (3)	—	A 130(2), (3)	
22	Modification of provisions of Part I.		
(1), (2)	—	CB 162	Am. Oil and Gas (Enterprise) Act 1982 (c. 23), s. 37, Sch. 3, para. 44; affected by R4.
(3)	—	CB 120(2), 162(1)(c)	
23	Statutory sick pay to count as remuneration for principal Act.		
23A	Deductions from sick pay.		Section inserted 1984 s. 21, Sch. 7, para. 8.
(1)	—	CB 151(3)	

SOCIAL SECURITY ACTS CONSOLIDATION—*continued.*

Section of Act	Subject matter	Section of 1992 Act	Remarks
	SOCIAL SECURITY AND HOUSING BENEFITS ACT 1982 (c. 24)—*continued.*		
(2)	—	—	Rep. Wages Act 1986 (c. 48) s. 32(2), Sch.5.
26	Interpretation of Part I and supplementary provisions.	—	—
(1)	—	CB 163(1)	Am. 1985 s. 21, Sch. 4, para. 6; repealed in part 1983 s. 30, Sch. 10.
(2)	—	CB 163(2)	Am. 1985 s. 21, Sch. 4, para. 7.
(3)—(5)	—	CB 163(3)-(5)	
(5A)	—	CB 163(6)	Inserted 1990 s. 21(1), Sch. 6, para. 16.
(6)	—	CB 163(7)	
(7)	—	CB 172(a)	
27	Crown employment.		
(1), (2)	—	CB 161(1) (2)	
(3)	—	CB 161(3)	Inserted 1989 s. 26, Sch. 7 para. 23.
37	Amendments.		
(1)	—	CB 4(2)-(4)	
(2)	—	CB Sch.1, para.11	
39	Industrial injuries.		
(1)	—	—	Spent.
(2)	Amendment.	CB 103(6)	
(3)	—	CB 31(3)	
(4)	—	CB 192	
44	Application of social security legislation in relation to territorial waters.		
(1), (2)	—	CB 172	Subs. (1) rep. in part 1986 s. 86, Sch. 11.
(3), (4)	—	—	Rep. 1989 s. 26, Sch. 7, para. 24.
46(2)	Cost of inquiries.	A163(3)	
48(2)	Northern Ireland.	—	Spent.
Sch. 1	Circumstances in which periods of entitlement do not arise.		
Para. 1	—	CB Sch. 11, para. 1	
2	—	CB Sch. 11, para. 2	Rep. in part 1985 ss. 18(2)(d), 29(2), Sch. 6.
3, 4	—	CB Sch. 11, paras. 3, 4	

SOCIAL SECURITY ACTS CONSOLIDATION—*continued.*

Section of Act	Subject matter	Section of 1992 Act	Remarks

SOCIAL SECURITY AND HOUSING BENEFITS ACT 1982 (c. 24)—*continued.*

Section of Act	Subject matter	Section of 1992 Act	Remarks
5	—	CB Sch. 11, para. 5	Am. 1984 s. 11, Sch. 4, para. 15(b)
6	—	CB Sch. 11, para. 6	
7	—	CB Sch. 11, para. 7	Rep. in part 1989 s. 31(1), Sch. 8, para. 14.
8	—	CB Sch. 11, para. 8	
Sch. 2	Relationship with benefits and other payments, etc.		
Para. 1	—	CB Sch. 12, para. 1	Am. 1985 s. 18(6)(a).
1A	—	CB Sch. 12, para. 5	Inserted 1985 s. 18(6)(b).
2-4	—	CB Sch. 12, paras. 2-4	
Sch. 4	Amendments and transitional provisions.		
Para. 7	—	A70(3)	—
8	—	CB s. 4(5)	
9	—	CB s. 31(5)	—
10	—	CB s. 33(9)	—
12	—	CB 94(4), (6)	—
13	—	—	Spent.
15	—	CB 107(1)(b)	—
16	—	A 171(4)	
17	—	CB Sch. 6 para. 6(1)	—
18	—	CB Sch. 8 para. 6(4)	—
30	—	A 170(5)	Amendment of 1980(1) s. 9(7).
31	—	—	Spent.
32	—	A Sch. 5 paras, 1, 2	—
33	—	A Sch 7 para. 8	Amendment of 1980(1) Sch. 3 Part II.
34	—	CB 30(2), (3)	
39	Transitional regulations.	—	Spent.

SOCIAL SECURITY ACTS CONSOLIDATION—*continued.*

Section of Act	Subject matter	Section of 1992 Act	Remarks
Sch. 8	Social security adjudications.	—	
Para. 1(1),(2)	—	—	See Note to Table of Derivations for A.
(3)(b)	—	—	Spent.
(4)	—	—	Introduces Parts II to V of Sch.
2	Amendments.	A 38, 39, 41(1), (3)–(5)	Part spent.
3	—	A 25(2)	
4	—	—	Spent.
5	—	A Sch. 3, para 1	
6	—	A 60(1)	
7	—	A 40(1), (4), 41(6)	Part spent.
8	—	A 51(1)-(3),Sch. 2, para. 1(1)-(5),2,4	Part spent.
9	—	A 50(1)-(5)	
10	—	A Sch. 2, para. 3	
11	—	A Sch. 2, para. 5	
12	—	—	Spent.
13	—	A 191 "President"	
14-18	—	—	Rep. 1986 s. 86. Sch 11.
19, 20	—	—	Spent.
21(1)	—	A 45(2)	
(2)	—	A 49, 50	
(3)	—	A 45(3), (6)	
22	—	A 46	
23(a)	—	A 47(1)	
(b)	—	A 47(4)	
(c), (d)	—	A 47(8), (9)	
24(a), (b)	—	A 62(2)	
(c)	—	A Sch. 2, para. 7	
25	—	A Sch. 3, para. 1	

SOCIAL SECURITY ACTS CONSOLIDATION—*continued.*

Section of Act	Subject matter	Section of 1992 Act	Remarks
	**HEALTH AND SOCIAL SERVICES AND SOCIAL SECURITY ADJUDICATIONS ACT 1983 (c. 41)—*continued.***
26	—	A 60(3), (4)	
27(a)	—	A 49(1)	
(b)	—	A 49(2), Sch. 2, para. 7	
28	—	—	Unnecessary.
30	—	—	Spent.
31(1), (2)	—	—	See SS CP Sch. 3, paras. 4, 6.
(3)	—	—	Rep. 1986 s. 86, Sch. 11.
(4)	—	—	Unnecessary.
(5)	—	—	See SS CP Sch. 3, paras. 4, 6.
(6)	—	—	Spent.
	**HEALTH AND SOCIAL SECURITY ACT 1984 (c. 48)**
11	Severe disablement allowance.		
(1)	—	CB 68	
(2)	—	—	Introduces Sch. 4.
12	Pension increase in respect of husbands	CB 84	—
13	Dependent children.	—	Introduces Sch.5.
14	Earnings to include occupational pensions for purposes of benefits in respect of dependents.		
(a)	—	CB 89	
(b)	—	CB Sch. 7,para.7	
16	Constitution of panel for social security appeal tribunals.		
(a)	—	A 41(2)	
(b)	—	A 40(2),(3)	
17	Late paid Class 2 contributions.		
(1)	—	CB 11(1)	
(2)	—	CB 12	
18	Class 3 contributions.		
(1)(a)	—	CB 13(1)	
(b)	—	CB 13(4)	
(2)	—	—	Spent.
(3)	—	CB 13(4)— (7)	
Sch.4	Severe disablement allowance.		
1,2	—	—	Spent.

SOCIAL SECURITY ACTS CONSOLIDATION—*continued.*

Section of Act	Subject matter	Section of 1992 Act	Remarks

HEALTH AND SOCIAL SECURITY ACT 1984 (c. 48)—*continued.*

Section of Act	Subject matter	Section of 1992 Act	Remarks
3	—	CB 63, 90,A 163(2),CB Sch. 4,Part III,para. 2,Part IV,para. 8	
4	—	—	See entries for provisions amended.
5	—	A 45(1)	
6	—	A 45(2)(d)	
7	—	A 46(1)	
8	—	A 47(8),(9)	
9	—	A 48(1)(c)	
10(a)	—	CB Sch. 6,para.1	
(b),(c)	—	CB Sch. 6,paras. 4, 5	
11	—	CB 122(1)	
12	—	—	Spent.
13	—	CB Sch.9, para.5	
14	—	—	Spent.
15(a)	—	A 130(1)(e)	
(b)	—	CB Sch.11, para.5	
16, 17	—	—	Spent.
Sch. 5	Dependent children.	—	
1	—	—	Drafting
2	—	CB 20(1)	
3(a)	—	CB 80(2)	
(b)	—	—	Spent.
(c)	—	CB 80(3),(4),(7)	
4	—	CB Sch. 7, para. 4 (3)–(6)	
5	—	CB Sch. 7, para. 18	
6	—	CB Sch. 4, Part V, para. 12	
7	—	CB 122(1)	Otherwise unnecessary.

SOCIAL SECURITY ACTS CONSOLIDATION—*continued.*

Section of Act	Subject matter	Section of 1992 Act	Remarks

HEALTH AND SOCIAL SECURITY ACT 1984 (c. 48)—*continued.*

Section of Act	Subject matter	Section of 1992 Act	Remarks
		"week"	
8(a)	—	CB Sch. 8, para. 6(4)(c)	
(b)	—	CB Sch. 8, para. 6(5)	
Sch. 7	Miscellaneous social security amendments.		
1	—	—	Spent.
2	—	CB 122(1) "payments by way of occupational pension"	
3	—	CB 6(2)	
6	—	—	Spent.
7	—	CB 154(2)	
8	—	CB 151(3)	Part spent.

SOCIAL SECURITY ACT 1985 (c.53)

Section of Act	Subject matter	Section of 1992 Act	Remarks
7	Calculation of contributions.		
(1)	—	CB 5(1)	
(2)	—	CB 9(1) - (3), (5), A146,147(1), (3),(4),(5), 190(1)(a).	Part spent.
(3), (4)	—	—	Spent.
(5)	—	A 145	
8(1)	Dock workers.	CB 6(5)	
9	Abatement of invalidity allowance etc., where beneficiary entitled to additional pension or to guaranteed minimum pension.		
(1)(a)	—	CB 34(1)	
(b)	—	CB 34(4) - (6)	
(c)	—	CB 34(7)	
(2)(a), (b)	—	CB 47(1)	
(c)	—	CB 47(2) - (4)	
(3)	—	CB 50(2)	
(4)(a)	—	CB Sch. 7,para. 3(1)	

SOCIAL SECURITY ACTS CONSOLIDATION—*continued.*

Section of Act	Subject matter	Section of 1992 Act	Remarks
	SOCIAL SECURITY ACT 1985 (c.53)—*continued.*		
(b)	—	CB Sch. 7para. 3(2) -(4)	
(5)	—	CB Sch. 5para. 2(6)	
(6) - (9)	—	—	Spent.
10	Voluntary redundancy - entitlement to unemployment benefit.		
11	Entitlement of married women to Category A retirement pensions.	—	Spent.
12	Abolition of lower rate for Category. D retirement pension.		
(1)	—	CB 78(6)	
(2)	—	CB Sch. 4,Part III,para. 7	
13	Pension increase in respect of adult dependants - equal treatment for males and females etc.		
(1)	—	CB 83(3)	
(2)(a)	—	CB 84(1)	
(b)	—	CB 84(2),(3)	
(3)	—	CB 85(4)ʳ	
(4)(a)	—	—	Rep. 1988(1) s. 16, Sch. 5.
(b)	—	CB 86(2)	
(5)	—	CB Sch. 7 para. 6(3) –(6)	
(6), (7)	—	CB 114(3), (4)	
18	Period of entitlement to statutory sick pay.		
(1)	—	CB 155(4)	
(2)	—	—	Spent.
(3)	—	CB 33(10), (11)	
(4)	—	CB 152(4)	
(5)	—	CB 153(5)	
(6)	—	CB Sch. 12 paras. 1, 5	
20	Medical evidence	A14(2)	
27	Regulations–miscellaneous.		
(1), (2)	—	—	Spent.

SOCIAL SECURITY ACTS CONSOLIDATION—*continued.*

Section of Act	Subject matter	Section of 1992 Act	Remarks

SOCIAL SECURITY ACT 1985 (c.53)—*continued.*

Section of Act	Subject matter	Section of 1992 Act	Remarks
(3), (4)	—	—	Rep. 1990 s. 21(1), Sch. 6, para. 8(8).
(5)-(8)	—	—	Spent.
30	Northern Ireland.	—	Spent.
Sch. 3	Earnings factors and guaranteed minimum pensions.		
Para. 1	—	A 14(8)	
Sch. 4	Miscellaneous amendments relating to statutory sick pay.		
Para. 3	—	CB 68(5)	—
4	—	CB 153(8), (9)	
5	Repeals.	—	Spent.
6	—	CB 163(1)	
7	—	CB 163(2)	
Sch. 5	Minor and consequential amendments.		
5	—	CB 1(3)	
8	—	CB 113(3)	
9	—	A 143(1)	Para. (a) part spent; para. (b) spent.
11	—	A 162(5), (6)	Part spent.
13(a)	—	CB Sch. 1 para. 1(2)	
(b)	—	CB Sch. 1 paras. 1(3), (4), (6)	
14	—	CB 122(1) "entitled"	
15	—	CB 5(1)	

SOCIAL SECURITY ACT 1986 (c. 50)

Section of Act	Subject matter	Section of 1992 Act	Remarks
18	Amendments.		
(2)	—	CB 45(1)	
(3)	—	CB 45(2)-(5)	
(4)	—	CB 45(6)	
(5)	Calculation of additional pension.	CB 46(2)	
(6)	—	CB 46(1)	
19	Additional pensions—supplementary		
(1)	—	CB 39(3), 41(6), 50(5), 51(3)	

SOCIAL SECURITY ACTS CONSOLIDATION—*continued.*

Section of Act	Subject matter	Section of 1992 Act	Remarks
	SOCIAL SECURITY ACT 1986 (c. 50)—*continued.*		
(2)	Amendment.	CB Sch. 5, para. 4(1)-(3)	
(3)	—	CB Sch. 5, para. 5(1)	
(4)	—	CB Sch. 5, para. 5(3)	
(5)	—	CB Sch. 5, para. 6(1)	
(6)	—	CB Sch. 5, para. 6(3), (4)	
20	Income-related benefits.		
(1)	—	CB 123(1)	Am. 1988(2) s. 135 Sch. 10, para. 2(2), 1991(2) s. 6(2).
(2)	—	CB 123(2)	Am. 1991(2) s. 6(3).
(3)	—	CB 124(1)	Am. 1988(1) s. 4(1), 1989 s. 13(1).
(4)	—	CB 124(3)	
(4A)-(4D)	—	CB 125(1)-(4)	Inserted 1988(1) s. 4(2).
(4E)	—	A72(1)	Inserted 1988(1) s. 4(2).
(4F), (4G)	—	A72(7), (8)	Inserted 1988(1) s. 4(2).
(4H)-(4M)	—	A72(2)-(6)	Inserted 1988(1) s. 4(2).
(4N)	—	CB 125(5)	Inserted 1988(1) s. 4(2).
(5)	—	CB 128(1)	Am. 1991(2) s. 8(1).
(5A)	—	CB 128(1)	Inserted 1988(1) s. 3(a).
(6)	—	CB 128(3)	Rep. in part 1988(1) s 3(b); am. 1989 s. 31(1), Sch. 8, para. 15(1).
(6A)	—	CB 129(1)	Inserted 1991(2) s. 6(4).
(6B), (6C)	—	CB 129(2), (3)	Inserted 1991(2) s. 6(4).
(6D)	—	CB 129(1)	Inserted 1991(2) s. 6(4).
(6E)	—	CB 129(4)	Inserted 1991(2) s. 6(4).
(6F)	—	CB 129(6)	Inserted 1991(2) s. 6(4).

SOCIAL SECURITY ACTS CONSOLIDATION—*continued.*

Section of Act	Subject matter	Section of 1992 Act	Remarks

SOCIAL SECURITY ACT 1986 (c. 50)—*continued.*

Section of Act	Subject matter	Section of 1992 Act	Remarks
(7)	—	CB 130(1)	Am. Housing Benefit (Social Security Act 1986 Modifications) (Scotland) Regulations 1988 reg. 3(a) (S.I. 1988/1483); amendment not relevant to consolidation.
(7A)	—	—	Inserted Housing Benefit (Social Security Act 1986 Modifications) (Scotland) Regulations 1988 reg. 3(b) (S.I. 1988/1483); not relevant to consolidation.
(8)	—	CB 130(2)	
(8A)	—	CB 131(1)	Inserted 1988(2) s. 135, Sch. 10, para. 2(3).
(8AA)	—	CB 131(2)	Inserted 1989(2) s. 31(1), Sch. 8, para. 9(2).
(8B)-(8H)	—	CB 131(3)-(9)	Inserted 1988(2) s. 135, Sch. 10, para. 2(3).
(9)	—	CB 134(2)	
(9ZA)	—	—	Inserted Housing Benefit (Social Security Act 1986 Modifications) (Scotland) Regulations 1988 reg. 3(c) (S.I. 1988/1483); not relevant to consolidation.
(9A)	—	CB 134(3)	Inserted 1988(2) s. 135, Sch. 10, para. 2(4).
(10)	—	CB 128(4)	Am. 1991(2) s. 8(2).
(11)	Definitions.		
"chargeable financial year"	—	A 191 "chargeable financial year"	Inserted 1988(2) s. 135, Sch. 10, para. 2(5).
"charging authority"	—	CB 137(1), A 191 "charging authority"	Inserted 1988(2) s. 135 Sch. 10, para. 2(5).
"child"	—	CB 137(1) "child"	Substituted 1989 s. 5(1).

SOCIAL SECURITY ACTS CONSOLIDATION—*continued.*

Section of Act	Subject matter	Section of 1992 Act	Remarks
SOCIAL SECURITY ACT 1986 (c. 50)—*continued.*			
"community charge rebate"	—		Inserted Housing Benefit (Social Security Act 1986 Modifications) (Scotland) Regulations 1988 reg. 3(d) (S.I. 1988/1483); not relevant to consolidation.
"contribution period"	—	CB 137(1) "contribution period"	Inserted 1988(2) s. 135, Sch. 10, para. 2(5).
"family"	—	CB 137(1) "family"	
"industrial injuries scheme"	—	CB137(1) "industrial injuries scheme"	Inserted 1991(2) s. 6(6)(a)
"levying authority"	—	CB137(1), A191 "levying authority"	Inserted 198(2) s. 135, Sch. 10, para. 2(5)
"married couple"	—	CB137(1) "married couple"	
"personal community charge"		—	Inserted Housing Benefit (Social Security Act 1986 Modifications) (Scotland) Regulations 1988 reg. 3(d) (S.I. 1988/1483); not relevant to consolidation
"the 1987 Act", "the 1988 Act"	—	CB 137(1) "the 1987 Act", "the 1988 Act"	Inserted 1988(2) s. 135, Sch. 10, para. 2(5)
"un-married couple"	—	CB 137(1) "un-married couple"	
"war pension scheme"	—	CB 137(1) "war pension scheme"	Inserted 1991(2) s. 6(6)(b)
"week"	—	CB 137(1) "week"	Inserted 1988(2) s. 135, Sch. 10, para. 2(5)
(12)	—	CB 137(2)	Am. 1989 s.13(2), 1991(2) s.6(7)
21	Amount etc.		
(1)	—	CB 124(4)	Am. 1988(1) s.16, Sch. 4, para. 23(1)
(1A), (1B)	—	CB 124(5), (6)	Inserted 1988(1) s.16, Sch. 4, para. 23(2)

SOCIAL SECURITY ACTS CONSOLIDATION—*continued.*

Section of Act	Subject matter	Section of 1992 Act	Remarks
	SOCIAL SECURITY ACT 1986 (c. 50)—*continued.*		
(2), (3)	—	CB 128(2)	
(3A), (3B)	—	CB 129 (5)	Inserted 1991(2) s.6(8)
(4), (5)	—	CB 130(3)	
(5A), (5B)	—	CB 131 (10), (11)	Inserted 1988(2) s. 135, Sch. 10, para. 3(2)
(6)	—	CB 128(5), 129(8), 130(4), (5), 131(12)	Am. 1988(2) s. 135, Sch. 10, para. 3(3), Housing (Scotland) Act 1988 (c. 43) s. 70(3), Housing Act 1988 (c.50) s. 121(4), 1991(2) s. 6(9)
(7)	—	CB 134(4)	
22	Calculation		
(1), (2)	—	CB 135(1), (2)	
(2A), (2B)	—	CB 135(3), (4)	Inserted 1990 s. 9; see also SS CP Sch. 4, para. 4
(3)	—	CB 135(5)	Am. 1988(2) s. 135, Sch. 10, para 4(2)
(4)	—	CB 135(6)	
(5)	—	CB 136(1)	
(6)	—	CB 134(1)	
(7), (8)	—	CB 136(2), (3)	
(8A)	—	CB 136(4)	Inserted 1988(2) s. 135, Sch. 10, para. 4(3)
(9)	—	CB 136(5)	
22A	Couples	CB 132	Inserted 1988(2) s. 135, Sch. 10, para. 5
22B	Polygamous marriages		Section inserted 1988(2) s. 135, Sch. 10, para 5
(1)	—	CB 133(1)	Am. 1989 s. 31(1), Sch. 8, para. 9(3)
(2)-(4)	—	CB 133(2)-(4)	
23	Trade disputes		
(1)-(4)	—	CB 126(1)-(4)	
(5)	—	CB 126(5)	Am. Income and Corporation Taxes Act 1988 (c.1) s. 944, Sch. 29, para. 32, Table
(5A)	—	CB 126(6)	Inserted 1988(1) s. 16, Sch. 4, para. 24(1)
(6)	—	CB 126(7)	Substituted 1990 s. 21(1), Sch. 6, para. 17(2)

SOCIAL SECURITY ACTS CONSOLIDATION—*continued.*

Section of Act	Subject matter	Section of 1992 Act	Remarks
	SOCIAL SECURITY ACT 1986 (c. 50)—*continued.*		
(7)	—	CB 126(8)	Am. 1990 s.21(1), Sch. 6, para. 17(3)
(8)	—	—	Rep. 1988(1) s. 16, Sch. 5
23A	Effect of return to work.	CB127	Inserted 1988(1) s. 16, Sch. 4, para. 25, am. 1989 s. 31(1), Sch. 8, para. 16.
24	Recovery of expenditure on benefit from person liable for maintenance.		
(1)	—	A106(1)	
(2), (3)	—	—	Rep. Family Law Reform Act 1987 (c. 42) s. 33(1), Sch. 2, para 91.
(4)-(6)	—	A106(2)-(4)	
(7)	—	A106(5)	Substituted Family Law Reform Act 1987 (c. 42) s. 33(1), Sch. 2, para. 91.
(8), (9)	—	A106(6), (7)	
24A	Recovery of expenditure on income support: additional amounts and transfer of orders.		Section inserted 1990 s. 8(1).
(1)-(4)	—	A107(1)-(4)	
(4A)	—	A107(5)	Inserted Maintenance Enforcement Act 1991 (c. 17) s. 9(1); see SS CP Sch. 4, para.14.
(5)-(7)	—	A107(6)-(8)	
(7A)-(7C)	—	A107(9)-(11)	Inserted Maintenance Enforcement Act 1991 s. 9(2); see SS CP Sch. 4, para.15.
(8)-(11)	—	A107(12)-(15)	
24B	Reduction of expenditure on income support: certain maintenance orders to be enforceable by the Secretary of State.	A108	Inserted 1990 s. 8(1).
25	Affiliation orders.	—	Rep. Family Law Reform Act 1987 (c. 42) s. 33(1), Sch. 2, para. 92.
25A	Diversion of arrested earnings to Secretary of State.	A109	Inserted Debtors (Scotland) Act 1987 (c. 18) s. 68.
26	Failure to maintain-general.		
(1), (2)	—	A105(1), (2)	

SOCIAL SECURITY ACTS CONSOLIDATION—*continued.*

Section of Act	Subject matter	Section of 1992 Act	Remarks
	SOCIAL SECURITY ACT 1986 (c. 50)—*continued.*		
(3)	—	A105(3)	Rep. in part 1989 s. 31(2), Sch. 9; a.m. 1989 s. 5(2), 1990 s. 8(3).
(4)	—	A105(3)	Substituted Family Law Reform Act 1987 (c. 42) s. 33(1), Sch. 2, para. 93; am. 1989 s. 5(3).
(5)	—	A105(3)	Am. 1989 s. 5(4).
(6)	—	A105(3)	
27	Prevention of duplication of payments.	A74	
27A	Personal representatives to give information about the estate of a deceased benificiary.	A126	Inserted 1989 s. 31(1), Sch. 8, para. 17.
27B	Supplementary provisions about disability working allowance.		Section inserted 1991(2) s. 7(1)
(1)-(3)	—	A11	
(4)	—	CB 129(7)	
28	Arrangements for housing benefit.		
(1)	—	A134(1)	Am. 1990 s. 21(1), Sch. 6, para. 18, Housing Benefit (Social Security Act 1986 Modifications) (Scotland) Regulations 1988 reg. 4(a) (S.I. 1988/1483); amendment not relevant to consolidation.
(1A)	—	A134(2)	Inserted 1989 s. 14.
(2)	—	A134(3)	
(2A)	—	—	Inserted Housing Benefit (Social Security Act 1986 Modifications) (Scotland) Regulations 1988 reg. 4(b) (S.I. 1988/1483); not relevant to consolidation.
(3)	—	A134(4)	
(3A)	—	—	Inserted Housing Benefit (Social Security Act 1986 Modifications) (Scotland) Regulations 1988 reg. 4(c) (S.I. 1988/1483); not relevant to consolidation.
(4), (5)	—	A134(5), (6)	
(5A)	—	A134(7)	Inserted 1990 s. 21(1), Sch. 6, para. 18.

SOCIAL SECURITY ACTS CONSOLIDATION —*continued.*

Section of Act	Subject matter	Section of 1992 Act	Remarks

SOCIAL SECURITY ACT 1986 (c. 50)—*continued.*

Section of Act	Subject matter	Section of 1992 Act	Remarks
(6) – (10)	—	A134(8) – (12)	
(11)	—	—	Inserted Housing Benefit (Social Security Act 1986 Modifications) (Scotland) Regulations 1988 reg. 4(d) (S.I. 1988/1483); not relevant to consolidation.
29	Adjudication and overpayments.		
(1) – (3)	—	A63	
(4) – (7)	—	A75	
(8)	—	A79(b)	Inserted 1988(1) s. 16, Sch. 4, para. 26.
30	Housing benefit finance.		
(1)	—	A135(1)	Am. Housing Benefit (Social Security Act 1986 Modifications) (Scotland) Regulations 1988 reg. 5(a) (S.I. 1988/1483); amendment not relevant to consolidation.
(1A)	—	—	Inserted Housing Benefit (Social Security Act 1986 Modifications) (Scotland) Regulations 1988 reg. 5(b) (S.I. 1988/1483); not relevant to consolidation.
(2)	—	A135(2), (3)	Rep. in part 1989 s. 15(1); am. Local Government and Housing Act 1989 (c. 42) s. 81(1), The Housing Benefit (Transitional) Amendment Regultions 1988 reg. 3 (S.I. 1988/458), Housing Benefit (Social Security Act 1986 Modifications) (Scotland) Regulations 1988 reg. 5(c) (S.I. 1988/1483); amendment by 1988/1483 not relevant to consolidation.
(2ZA)	—	A135(4)	Inserted 1990 s. 21(1), Sch. 6, para. 19(1).
(2A)	—	A136(1)	Inserted 1989 s. 15(1); am. 1990 s. 21(1), Sch. 6, para. 19(2).
(2B)	—	A136(2)	Inserted 1990 s. 15(1).
(2C)	—	A136(3), (4)	Inserted 1989 s. 15(1).

SOCIAL SECURITY ACTS CONSOLIDATION—*continued.*

Section of Act	Subject matter	Section of 1992 Act	Remarks
	SOCIAL SECURITY ACT 1986 (c. 50)—*continued.*		
(3)	—	A135(5)	Am. Housing Benefit (Social Security Act 1986 Modifications) (Scotland) Regulations 1988 reg. 5(c) (S.I. 1988/1483); amendment not relevant to consolidation.
(4)	—	—	Spent.
(5)	—	A135(6), (7)	Am. Housing (Scotland) Act 1988 (c. 43) ss. 1, 3, Sch. 2, para. 1; Local Government and Housing Act 1989 (c. 42) s. 81(2).
(6)	—	A135(8), (9)	Am. Local Government and Housing Act 1989 s. 81(3).
(7)	—	A135(10)	Affected by R11.
(8)	—	A135(11)	Substituted 1989 s. 15(2).
(8A) -(8F)	—	A137	Substituted 1989 s. 15(2).
(9)	—	A135(12)	
(11)	—	SS CP Sch. 3 para. 17	Inserted 1988(1) s. 16, Sch. 4, para. 20.
31	Information.		
(1) - (3)	—	A127	
(4)	—	CB123(3)	
(5)	—	—	See Rent Act 1977 (c. 42) s. 72A inserted SS CP Sch. 2, para. 46, Housing (Scotland) Act 1988 (c. 43) s. 48A inserted SS CP Sch. 2, para. 99, Housing Act 1988 (c. 50) s. 41A inserted SS CP Sch. 2, para. 100.
31A	Nature of community charge benefits.		Section inserted 1988(2) s. 135, Sch. 10, para. 6.
(1), (2)	—	A138(1), (2)	Am. 1990 s. 21(1), Sch. 6, para. 20.
(3) - (9)	—	A138(3) - (9)	
31B(1) – (5)	Arangements for community charge benefits.	A139(1) - (5)	Section inserted 1988(2) s. 135, Sch. 10, para. 6.

SOCIAL SECURITY ACTS CONSOLIDATION—*continued.*

Section of Act	Subject matter	Section of 1992 Act	Remarks
		SOCIAL SECURITY ACT 1986 (c. 50)—*continued.*	
(6)	—	A139(6)	Am. the Community Charge Benefits (General) Regulations 1989 reg. 11 (S.I. 1989/1321).
(7) - (10)	—	A139(7) - (10)	
31C	Adjudication.	A63	Section inserted 1988(2) s. 135, Sch. 10, para. 6.
31D	Excess community charge benefits.		Section inserted 1988(2) s. 135, Sch. 10, para. 6.
(1), (2)	—	A76(1), (2)	
(3)	—	A76(3)	Am. 1989 s. 31(1), Sch. 8, para. 9(4).
(4)	—	A76(4)	
(5)	—	A76(5)	Am. 1989 s. 31(1), Sch. 8, para. 9(4).
(6) - (8)	—	A76(6) - (8)	
31E	Shortfall in community charge benefits.	A77	Section inserted 1988(2) s. 135, Sch. 10, para. 6.
31F	Community charge benefit finance.		Section inserted 1988(2) s. 135, Sch. 10, para. 6.
(1), (2)	—	A140(1), (2)	
(3)	—	A140(3)	Substituted 1990 s. 21(1), Sch. 6, para. 21(1).
(4), (5)	—	A140(4), (5)	
(5A)	—	A140(6)	Inserted 1990 s. 21(1), Sch. 6, para. 21(2).
(6)	—	A140(7)	Substituted 1990 s. 21(1), Sch. 6, para. 21(3).
(7)	—	A140(8)	
31G	Community charge benefits—information.		Section inserted 1988(2) s. 135, Sch. 10, para. 6.
(1) - (3)	—	A128	
(4) - (6)	—	CB123(4)-(6)	
32	The social fund and social fund officers.		
(1)	—	A167(1)	
(2)	—	CB138(1)	Am. 1987 s. 1.

Tables of Derivations and Destinations

SOCIAL SECURITY ACTS CONSOLIDATION—*continued.*

Section of Act	Subject matter	Section of 1992 Act	Remarks
			SOCIAL SECURITY ACT 1986 (c. 50)—*continued.*
(2A)	—	CB138(2)	Inserted 1988(1) s. 11, Sch. 3, para. 2.
(3)	—	—	Rep. 1988(1) s. 11, Sch. 3, para. 3.
(4)	—	A78(4)	Rep. in part 1988(1) s. 16, Sch. 5.
(5) - (7)	—	A167(2) - (4)	
(7A), (7B)	—	A167(5), (6)	Inserted 1988(1) s. 11, Sch. 3, para. 4.
(8)	—	A64(1)	Rep. in part 1988(1) ss. 11, 16, Sch. 3, para. 5, Sch. 5.
(8A) - (8D)	—	A168(1) - (4)	Inserted 1988(1) s. 11, Sch. 3, para. 6.
(8E)	—	A168(5)	Inserted 1990 s. 10(1).
(9)	—	A64(2)	
(10)	—	A64(3)	Inserted 1988(1) s. 11, Sch. 3, para. 7; am. 1990 s. 10(2).
(11)	—	CB140(5), A66(9)	Inserted 1988(1) s. 11, Sch. 3, para. 7
(12)	—	A66(10)	Inserted 1988(1) s. 11, Sch. 3, para. 7.
33	Awards by social fund officers.		
(1)	—	A12(1)	Rep. in part 1988(1) s. 16, Sch. 5; am. 1988(1) s. 11, Sch. 3, para. 9.
(1A)	—	CB138(3)	Inserted 1988(1) s. 11, Sch. 3, para. 10.
(2)–(4)	—	CB139(1)–(3)	
(4A)	—	CB139(4)	Inserted 1988(1) s. 11, Sch. 3, para. 11.
(5)–(7)	—	A78(1)–(3)	
(8)	—	A78(6)–(9)	
(8A)	—	A79(c)	Inserted 1988(1) s. 16, Sch. 4, para. 27.
(9)	—	CB140(1)	Am. 1988(1) s. 11, Sch. 3, para. 12.
(10)	—	CB140(2)	
(10ZA)	—	CB140(3)	Inserted 1990 s. 10(3).
(10A)	—	CB140(4)	Inserted 1988(1) s. 11, Sch. 3, para. 13; rep. in part 1990 s. 21(2), Sch. 7; am. 1990 s. 10(4).

SOCIAL SECURITY ACTS CONSOLIDATION—*continued.*

Section of Act	Subject matter	Section of 1992 Act	Remarks
	SOCIAL SECURITY ACT 1986 (c. 50)—*continued.*		
(11)	—	CB139(5)	
(12)	—	A78(5)	
(13)	—	A12(2)	Inserted 1990 s. 10(5).
34	Reviews.		
(1)	—	A66(1)	Rep. in part 1988(1) ss. 11, 16, Sch. 3, para. 15, Sch. 5.
(2)–(8)	—	A66(2)–(8)	
35	The social fund Commissioner.	A65	
36	Amendments.		
(1)	—	CB36(1), (2)	
(2)	—	CB Sch. 4, Part II	
(3)	—	CB38(I), 39(4)	
37(1)	—	CB70(3)	
38	Abolition of maternity grant.		Spent.
40	Abolition of child's special allowance except for existing beneficiaries.	CB56(6)	
41	Abolition of death grant.	—	Spent.
42	Repeal.	—	Spent.
43	Amendments.		
(1)	—	CB26(6)	
(2)	—	—	Spent.
(3)(a)	—	CB28(2)	
(b)	—	CB176(1)(c)	
44	Amendments.		
(1)	—	CB27(1), (2)	
(2)	—	CB91	
45	Amendments.		
(a)	—	CB77(10)	
(b)	—	CB77(11)	
46	Statutory maternity pay-entitlement and liability to pay.		
(1)–(5)	—	CB164(1)–(5)	
(6)	—	CB164(6), (7)	
(7)	—	CB164(8)	
(8)	—	CB164(9)	Am. 1988(1) s. 16, Sch. 4, para. 16(1).

SOCIAL SECURITY ACTS CONSOLIDATION—*continued.*

Section of Act	Subject matter	Section of 1992 Act	Remarks
	SOCIAL SECURITY ACT 1986 (c. 50)—*continued.*		
(9)	—	CB164(10)	Inserted 1988(1) s. 16, Sch. 4, para. 16(2).
47	The maternity pay period.		
(1)–(6)	—	CB165(1)–(6)	
(7)	—	CB164(7)	Am. 1989, s. 26, Sch. 7, para. 25.
48	Rates of payment.		
(1)	—	CB166(1)	
(2)	—	CB166(2)	Am. 1988(1) s. 16, Sch. 4, para. 17.
(3)–(8)	—	CB166(3)-(8)	
49	Further provisions relating to statutory maternity pay etc.	—	Gives effect to Schedule 4.
50	Interpretation of Part V.		
(1) "confinement", "dismissed", "employee"	—	CB171(1) "confinement", "dismissed", "employee"	
"employer"	—	CB171(1) "employer"	Rep. in part 1988(1) s. 16, Sch. 4, para. 18.
"maternity pay period"	—	CB171(1) "employer"	
"week"	—	CB171(1) "week"	Rep. in part 1989 s. 26, Sch. 7, para. 26.
(2)	—	CB171(2)	
(2A)	—	CB171(3)	Inserted 1990 s. 21(1), Sch. 6, para. 22.
(3)–(5)	—	CB171 (4)-(6)	
51	Regulations about claims for and payments of benefit.		
(1)(a)–(h)	—	A5(1) (a)–(h)	
(j)	—	—	Rep. 1988(2) s. 135, Sch. 10, para. 7.
(k)–(t)	—	A5(1)(i)–(r)	
(u)	—	—	Rep. 1988(2) s. 135, Sch. 10, para. 7.

SOCIAL SECURITY ACTS CONSOLIDATION—*continued.*

Section of Act	Subject matter	Section of 1992 Act	Remarks
	SOCIAL SECURITY ACT 1986 (c. 50)—*continued.*		
(2)	—	A5(2)	Rep, in part 1988(1) s. 16, Sch. 5; am. 1988(1) s. 11, Sch. 3, para. 16, 1991(2) s. 7, Sch. 3, para. 2.
(3),(4)	—	A5(4), (5)	
51A	Community charge benefits: administration.		Section inserted 1988(2) s. 135, Sch. 10, para. 8.
(1)(a)–(k)	—	A6(1) (a)– (k)	
(kk)	—	A6(1)(l)	Inserted 1989 s. 31(1), Sch. 8, para. 9(6)(a).
(l)–(o)	—	A6(1) (m)–(p)	
(oo)	—	A6(1)(q)	Inserted 1989 s. 31(1), Sch. 8, para. 9(6)(b).
(p)–(s)	—	A6(1) (r)–(u)	
(2), (3)	—	A6(2), (3)	
51B	Administration of benefits: general.	A7	Section inserted 1988(2) s. 135, Sch. 10, para. 8.
52	Adjudication.		
(3)	—	—	See note to Table; am. 1991(2) s. 4, Sch. 2, para. 15(a).
(3A)	—	—	See note to Table; inserted 1991(2) s. 7, Sch. 3, para. 3(1).
(4)	—	A59(2)	Am. 1991(2) s. 7, Sch. 3, para. 3(2).
(5)	—	A117(1)	
(6)	—	—	See note to Table.
(7)(a)	—	A20(3)	
(b)	—	A21(4)	
(c)	—	22(1), (2), (5)	
(d)	—	A23(2)	
(8)	—	A25(4)	Affected by R9.
(9)(a)	—	A30(5)(b), 35(3)(b)	Subsection inserted 1991(2) s. 7, Sch. 3, para. 3(3).
(b)	—	—	See A Part II generally.

SOCIAL SECURITY ACTS CONSOLIDATION—*continued.*

Section of Act	Subject matter	Section of 1992 Act	Remarks

SOCIAL SECURITY ACT 1986 (c. 50)—*continued.*

Section of Act	Subject matter	Section of 1992 Act	Remarks
(c)	—	—	See A35.
(d)	—	A54(4)	
(e)	—	A54(7)	
(10)	—	A30(1), (5)(b), 35(3)(b)	Inserted 1991(2) s. 7, Sch. 3, para. 3(3).
53	Overpayments.		
(1)	—	A71(1)	
(1A)	—	A71(2)	Inserted 1989 s. 21, Sch. 3, para. 14(1).
(2), (3)	—	A71(3), (4)	
(4)	—	A71(5)	Am. 1989 s. 21, Sch. 3, para. 14(2).
(5)–(7)	—	A71(6)–(8)	—
(7A)	—	A79(a)	Inserted 1988(1) s. 16, Sch. 4, para. 28.
(8), (9)	—	A71(9), (10)	
(10)	—	A71(11)	Rep. in Part 1988(1) s. 16 Sch. 5; am. 1988(1) ss. 11, 16, Sch. 3, para. 16, Sch. 4, para. 30(1), 1991(2) s. 7, Sch. 3, para. 4.
(10A)	—	A72(7), (8)	Inserted 1988(1) s. 16, Sch. 4, para. 30(2).
(11)	—	A Sch. 9, para. 4	
54(2)	Breach of regulations.	A113	
55	False representations for obtaining benefit etc.	A112	
56(2)(a)	Legal proceedings.	A116(2)(a)	Am. 1988(2) s. 135, Sch. 10, para. 9(2).
(2)(b)	—	A116(2)(b)	Am. 1988(2) s. 135, Sch. 10, para. 9(2).
(3)(b)	—	A116(3)(b)	
(4)	—	A116(4)	Am. 1988(2) s. 135, Sch. 10, para. 9(3).
(4A)	—	A116(5)	Inserted 1988(2) s. 135, Sch. 10, para. 9(4).

SOCIAL SECURITY ACTS CONSOLIDATION—*continued.*

Section of Act	Subject matter	Section of 1992 Act	Remarks
	SOCIAL SECURITY ACT 1986 (c. 50)—*continued.*		
(4B)	—	A116(6)	Inserted 1990 s. 21(1), Sch. 6, para. 5(2).
58	Inspection.		
(1)	—	A110(1)	
(2)	—	A110(2)	Am. 1989 s. 22, Sch. 4, para. 20(2), (3).
(3)	—	A110(3)	Am. 1989 s. 22, Sch. 4, para. 20(4).
(4), (5)	—	A110(4), (5)	
(6)	—	A110(6)	Am. 1989 s. 22, Sch. 4, para. 20(5).
(7)	—	A110(7)	Am. 1989 s. 22, Sch. 4, para. 20(6).
(8), (9)	—	A111	Affected by R10.
(10)	—	—	Unnecessary; inserted 1989 s. 22, Sch. 4, para. 20(7).
60	Regulations as to notification of deaths.	A125	
61	Consultations on subordinate legislation.		
(1)	—	A173(1)	Part repeal only.
(3)	—	A173(3)	Part repeal only; substituted 1989 s. 26, Sch. 7, para. 27.
(4)	—	A173(4)	Part repeal only.
(5)	—	A173(5)	Part repeal only; substituted 1989 s. 31(1), Sch. 8, para. 12(3).
(7)	—	A176(1)	Am. 1988(2) s. 135, Sch. 10, para. 10.
(8), (9)	—	A176(2), (3)	
(10)	—	A173(7)	Am. 1989 s. 31(1), Sch. 8, para. 12(4).
62	Amendments.		
(1)	—	CB175(5), A189(6)	
(2)	—	CB175(5), A189(6)	
(3)	—	CB176(1), A190(1)	

SOCIAL SECURITY ACTS CONSOLIDATION—*continued.*

Section of Act	Subject matter	Section of 1992 Act	Remarks
	SOCIAL SECURITY ACT 1986 (c. 50)—*continued.*		
63	Annual up-rating of benefits.		
(1)(a)(i)	—	A150(1)(a) (i)	
(ii)	—	—	Rep. 1989 s. 31(2), Sch. 9.
(iii)	—	A150(1)(a) (i-ii)	
(iv)	—	A150(1)(a) (i-i)	
(aa)	—	A150(1)(b)	Inserted 1991(2) s. 4, Sch. 2, para. 16(a).
(b)–(e)	—	A150(1)(c) –(f)	
(ee)	—	A150(1)(g)	Inserted 1988(1) s. 2(2)(a).
(f)	—	A150(1)(i)	
(g), (h)	—	A150(1)(j)	
(i)	—	A150(1)(h)	Am. 1991(2) s. 7, Sch. 3, para. 5(a).
(2)	—	A150(2)	
(3)	—	A150(3)	Am. 1988(1) s. 2(2)(b), 1991(2) s. 4, Sch. 2, para. 16(b).
(4)–(6)	—	A150(4)– (6)	
(7)	—	A151(3)	Rep. in part 1988(1) s. 16, Sch. 5.
(8), (9)	—	A151(4), (5)	
(10)	—	A150(7)	Am. Social Security Act 1986 (Consequential) Amendment Regulation 1988 (S.I. 1988/961) reg. 2(a).
(10A)	—	A151(6)	Inserted S. I. 1988/961 reg. 2(b)
(11)	—	A150(8)	Am. 1990 s. 21(1), Sch. 6, para. 23.
(12)	—	A150(9)	
(13)	—	A150(10)	Am. 1989 s. 31(1), Sch. 8, para. 15(2), 1991(2) s. 7, Sch. 3, para. 5(b).
63A	Rectification of mistakes in orders under section 63.	A152	Inserted 1989 s. 17(1)
64	Effect of alteration of rates of benefit.		
(1)	—	A155(1)	Am. 1989 s. 17(2)(a).
(2)–(5)	—	A155 (3)–(6)	
(6)	—	A155(2)	

SOCIAL SECURITY ACTS CONSOLIDATION—*continued.*

Section of Act	Subject matter	Section of 1992 Act	Remarks
	SOCIAL SECURITY ACT 1986 (c. 50)—*continued.*		
64A	Effect of alteration in the component rates of income support.	A159	Inserted 1989 s. 18
64B	Implementation of increases in income support due to attainment of particular ages.	A160	Inserted 1990 s. 21(1), Sch.6, para. 24.
65	Amendments.		
(1)	—	A177(4)	
(2)	—	A179(1)	
(3)	Repeal.		Spent.
(4)	—	A178(2), 179(4), (5)	Am. 1991(2) s. 7, Sch. 3, para. 6.
66	Pensioners' Christmas bonus.	—	Gives effect to Schedule 6.
67	Amendments.		
(1)	—	CB157(2), 176(1)(c)	
(2)	—	—	Rep, 1991(1) s. 3(2), Sch.
68	Amendments.	CB151(6), A163(1) (–d)	
69	Repeal of section 92 of Social Security Act 1975.	—	Spent.
70(1)(a)	Amendment.	CB142(1)	
(b)	—	CB142(2), (3)	
73	Application of provisions of Act to supplementary benefit etc.	—	Gives effect to Schedule 7.
74	Amendments.		
(1), (2)	—	A147(2)	
(3), (4)	—	—	Rep. Employment Act 1990 c. 38 s. 16(2), Sch. 3.
(5)	—	CB9(5), Sch. 1, para. 1(5)	
(6)	—	CB5(2)	
78	Travelling expenses	A180	
79(3)	Crown employment.	CB128(b) 129(9)	Am. 1991(2) s. 7, Sch. 3, para. 7.
(4)	—	CB169	Rep. in part 1990 s. 21(2), Sch. 7.
80(1)	Application of Parts I and V to special cases.	CB170	Only part repealed; affected by R4.
81	Orders in Council making corresponding provision for Northern Ireland.	—	Spent.

SOCIAL SECURITY ACTS CONSOLIDATION—*continued.*

Section of Act	Subject matter	Section of 1992 Act	Remarks

SOCIAL SECURITY ACT 1986 (c. 50)—*continued.*

Section of Act	Subject matter	Section of 1992 Act	Remarks
83(2)	Orders and regulations (general provisions).	CB175(6), A189(7), SS CP Sch. 3, para. 17(3)	Am. 1988(2) s. 135, Sch 10, para. 11(2).
(3)(b)-(ccc)	—	—	Spent; paras. (cc), (ccc) inserted 1988(2) s. 135, Sch. 10, para. 11(4).
(d)	—	A190(1)(a)	Am. 1989 s.17(2)(b)
(e)	—	CB176 (1)(c)	
(5)	—	A189(8)	Only partly repealed; am. 1988(2) s. 135, Sch. 10, para. 11(4), 1989 s. 17(2)(c).
84	Interpretation.		
(1) "applicable amount-"	—	—	Unnecessary.
"benefit Acts"	—	—	Only partly rep.
"dwelling"	—	CB137(1), A191 "dwelling"	
"housing authority"	—	A191 "housing authority"	Am. Housing (Scotland) Act 1988 (c. 43) ss. 1, 3, Sch. 2, para. 1.
"housing benefit scheme"	—	—	Unnecessary.
"Housing Revenue Account dwelling"	—	—	Unnecessary; am. Local Government and Housing Act 1989 (c. 42) s. 81 (5).
"income related benefit"	—	A191 "income-related benefit"	
"local authority"	—	A191 "local authority"	
"long-term benefit"	—	—	Unnecessary.
"new town corporation"	—	A191 "new town corporation"	

SOCIAL SECURITY ACTS CONSOLIDATION—*continued.*

Section of Act	Subject matter	Section of 1992 Act	Remarks
	SOCIAL SECURITY ACT 1986 (c. 50)—*continued.*		
"primary Class 1 contributions", "secondary Class 1 contributions", "qualifying benefit"	—	—	Unnecessary.
"rate rebate", "rent rebate", "rent allowance"	—	A191 "rate rebate", "rent rebate", "rent allowance"	
"rates"	—	A191 "rates"	Am. Abolition of Domestic Rates Etc. (Scotland) Act 1987 (c. 47) s. 26(2)(a).
"rating authority	—	A191 "rating authority"	
"trade dispute"	—	—	Unnecessary.
"war disablement pension", "war widow's pension"	—	CB150(2) "war disablement pension", "war widow's pension" A139(11) "war disablement pension", "war widow's pension"	Am. Income and Corporation Taxes Act 1988 (c. 1) s. 844, Sch. 29, para. 32, Table.
(3)	—	A135(13)	
85(1)(a)	Financial provision.	A163(2)(d)	Am. 1988(2) s. 135, Sch 10, para. 12, 1991(2) s. 7, Sch. 3, para. 8(a), Housing Benefit (Social Security Act 1986 Modifications) (Scotland) Regulations 1988 reg. 6 (S.I. 1988/1483); amendment by 1988/1483 not relevant to consolidation.
(b)	—	A163(2)(e)	
(c), (d)	—	A163(2) (g), (h)	

SOCIAL SECURITY ACTS CONSOLIDATION—*continued.*

Section of Act	Subject matter	Section of 1992 Act	Remarks
	SOCIAL SECURITY ACT 1986 (c. 50)—*continued.*		
(f)	—	A163(2)(a)	
(3)(c)	—	A163(1)(d)	
(d)	—	A163(1)(c)	
(4)	—	A165(5)	Rep. in part 1990 s.16(9).
(5)	—	—	See repeal of 1986 s. 85(7).
(7)	—	A164(3)	
(8)	—	A164(5)(b)	Only partly rep.
(9)	—	A165(1)	Am. 1991(2) s. 7, Sch. 3, para. 8(b).
(10)	—	A165 (2)–(4)	
(11), (12)	—	A169	
Sch. 3	Amendments.		
1	—	—	Drafting.
2	—	CB94(1)	
3(1)	—	CB103(1)	
(2)	—	CB103 (2)–(4)	
(3)	—	CB Sch. 7, para. 9(1)(a)	
(4)	—	CB103(7), (8)	Amendment of 1975(1) s. 57(6).
4	—	CB Sch. 7, para. 1	
5(1)	—	CB Sch. 7, para. 11	
(2)	Repeal.	—	Spent.
(3)–(8)	—	—	Rep. 1988(1) s. 16, Sch. 5.
6	Amendments.	CB104(3), (4)	
7	—	CB Sch. 7, para. 10(1)	
8	Repeals.	—	See 1988(1) Sch. 1.
9	—	—	Rep. 1988(1) s. 2, Sch. 1, para. 4.
10	Failure to satisfy contribution conditions.	CB60(2), (3)	Am. 1988(1) s. 2, Sch. 1, para. 5.
11	—	—	Rep. 1988(1) s. 16, Sch. 5.
12	—	SS CP Sch. 3, para. 18	
13	—	CB 109(4)–(6)	

SOCIAL SECURITY ACTS CONSOLIDATION—*continued.*

Section of Act	Subject matter	Section of 1992 Act	Remarks
	SOCIAL SECURITY ACT 1986 (c. 50)—*continued.*		
14	—	A45(1)	Para. (b) spent.
15	—	—	Para.(b) rep. 1989 s.31(2), Sch.9; para.(a) unnecessary
16	—	CB Sch.8, para.8(6)	
Sch.4	Statutory maternity pay etc.		
Part I	Provisions supplementary to Part V		
1	—	CB167(1)	
2	—	CB167(3)	
3, 4	—	CB Sch.1, para.6(5), (6)	
5	—	CB167(4)	
6, 7	—	A15	
8	—	A132(3)	
8A	—	A132(1), (2)	Inserted 1989 s.31(1), Sch.8, para.18.
9	—	A131	
10	—	CB4(1)	
11	—	CB Sch.13, para.1	Am. 1988(1) s.16, Sch.4, para.19(1).
11A	—	CB Sch.13, para.2	Inserted 1988(1) s.16, Sch.4, para.19(2).
12	—	CB Sch.13, para.3	
Part II	Amendments of Social Security Act 1975.		
13	—	CB35	
14	—	CB Sch.3, para.3	
Part III	Abolition of maternity pay and winding-up of maternity pay fund.		
15–17	—	—	Spent.
Sch. 5	Ajudication.		
Part I	Amendments.		
2	Repeal	—	Spent.
3	Amendment.	A96(1)	
4	—	A20(2),(4)	
5	—	A21(2)	
6(a)	Repeal.	—	Spent.

SOCIAL SECURITY ACTS CONSOLIDATION—*continued.*

Section of Act	Subject matter	Section of 1992 Act	Remarks

SOCIAL SECURITY ACT 1986 (c. 50)—*continued.*

Section of Act	Subject matter	Section of 1992 Act	Remarks
(b)	Amendment.	A22(2)	
(c)	—	A22(3)	
(d)	—	A22(4)	
(e)	—	A22(5)	
7(1)	—	A23(1)	
(2)	—	A23(3)(d)	
(3)	—	A23(7)-(10)	
(8)	—	A36(1)	
(9)	—	A37	
10(a)	—	A25(1), (3)	
(b)	Repeal.	—	Spent.
(c)	Amendment.	A26(3)	
(d)	—	A27(1)	
11	—	—	Rep. 1991(2) s. 10, Sch. 4
12	—	A44(7)	
13	—	A46(3)	
14(a)	—	A47(1)	
(b)	—	A47(2), (3)	
15(a)	—	A48(1)	
(b)	—	A48(3)	
16	—	A58(5) - (7)	Para. (b) spent
17	—	A189(10)	
18	—	A50(2)	
19(a)	—	A Sch. 3, para. 3	
(b)	—	A Sch. 3, para. 11	
20	—	A189(1), (2)	
Part II	Questions for determination by Secretary of State.	A17(1) (g), (h)	Am. 1991(1) s. 2(3); paragraph (a) not repealed.
Sch. 6	Christmas bonus for pensioners.		
1	Interpretation.		
(1)	—	CB150(1)	
(2)	—	CB150(2)	Am. 1991(2) s. 4, Sch. 2, para. 17.
"attendance allowance"	—	"attendance allowance"	

SOCIAL SECURITY ACTS CONSOLIDATION—*continued.*

Section of Act	Subject matter	Section of 1992 Act	Remarks

SOCIAL SECURITY ACT 1986 (c. 50)—*continued.*

Section of Act	Subject matter	Section of 1992 Act	Remarks
"married couple", "un-married couple"	—	CB150(3)	
"pensionable age", "retirement pension"	—	CB150(2) "pension-able age", "retire-ment pension"	
"unemploy-ability sup-plement or allowance"	—	CB150(2) "un-employ-ability supple-ment or allow-ance"	Am. Income and Corporation Taxes Act 1988 (c. 1) s. 844, Sch. 29, para. 32, Table.
(3)	—	CB150(4)	
2	—	CB148	
3	Supplementary.		
(1)	—	CB149(1)	
(2)	—	CB149(2)	Rep. in part 1990 s. 21(1), Sch. 6, para. 26(1)(a).
(3)	—	CB149(3)	Rep. in part 1989 ss. 26, 31(2), Sch. 7, para. 28, Sch. 9, 1990 s. 21(1). (2), Sch. 6, para. 26(1)b, Sch. 7.
(4)	—	CB149(4)	Rep. in part 1989 s. 31(2), Sch. 9.
4	Administration of payments.	A67	
Sch. 7	Supplementary benefit etc.		
para. 1	—	—	Drafting.
2	—	A Sch. 10, para. 4(2)	
3	—	A Sch. 10, para. 2	
4	—	A Sch. 10, para. 3	Am. 1991(2) s. 4, Sch. 2, para. 15(b).
5(1)	—	A. Sch. 10, para. 4(1)	
(2)	—	A Sch. 10, para. 4(3)	

SOCIAL SECURITY ACTS CONSOLIDATION—*continued.*

Section of Act	Subject matter	Section of 1992 Act	Remarks

SOCIAL SECURITY ACT 1986 (c. 50)—*continued.*

Section of Act	Subject matter	Section of 1992 Act	Remarks
6	—	A Sch. 10, para. 6	
7	—	A Sch. 10, para. 5	
8	—	—	Spent.
Sch. 8	Amendments.		
1	—	—	Drafting.
2(1)	—	CB22(1), (2)	
(2)	—	CB22(4)	
(3)	—	CB22(5)	
(4)	—	CB22(3), 23(1), (3)	
(5)	—	CB24(1)	
(6)	—	CB21(3), (5)	
3(1)	—	CB Sch. 3, paras. 1(4)(a), 2(4)(a)	
(2)	—	CB Sch. 3, paras. 1(3)(a), 2(3)(a)	
(3)	—	CB Sch.3, paras. 1(5)(a), 2(5)(a)	
(4)	—	CB Sch.3, para. 4 (1), (2)	
(5)	—	CB Sch. 3, para. 5(2)	
(6)	—	CB Sch. 3, para. 5 (4)(a)	
(7)	—	CB Sch.3, para. 7 (4)(a)	
5	—	CB19(6)	
6	—	CB14(1)	
7	—	CB44(6)	See also SS CP Sch. 4, para. 2

SOCIAL SECURITY ACTS CONSOLIDATION—*continued.*

Section of Act	Subject matter	Section of 1992 Act	Remarks

SOCIAL SECURITY ACT 1986 (c. 50)—*continued.*

Section of Act	Subject matter	Section of 1992 Act	Remarks
Sch.10	Amendments		
10	—	CB Sch.1, para. 8 (1)(m)	
34, 40	—	—	Spent
48	—	A1(4)(b), 68(4) "benefit", 187 (1)(b),	Am. 1990 s. 21(1), Sch. 6, para. 7(3)
54	—	—	See Magistrates' Court Act 1980 (c.43) s. 65(1)(n) inserted SS CP Sch. 2, para. 59
62	—	—	Drafting
63	—	CB20(1)	
64	—	CB21(1),(2)	
65	—	CB176(1) (a)	
66(a)	—	CB Sch.3, para. 4 (1)	
(b)	—	CB Sch.3, para. 7 (2)–(4)	
(c)	—	CB Sch.3, para. 9	
67	Repeal.	—	Spent.
68(2)	—	CB Sch.8, para. 6 (4), (5)	
69	—	CB39(1)	
70(a)	—	CB40(1)	
(b)	—	CB40(3)	
(c)	—	CB40(5)	
72(a)	—	CB22(2)(a)	
(b)	—	CB21(4)	
74	—	See 1977 s.18	
77	—	CB153 (12)	
83	—	CB25(6) (d), 31 (7)(c), 33(5) (d)	

SOCIAL SECURITY ACTS CONSOLIDATION—*continued.*

Section of Act	Subject matter	Section of 1992 Act	Remarks
	SOCIAL SECURITY ACT 1986 (c. 50)—*continued.*		
84	Repeal.	—	Spent.
85	—	A10(2)	
86	—	A172(2)	
87	—	A Sch.1, para. 3	
88	—	A Sch.1, para. 2	
90	—	A Sch.7, para. 12	
91	—	A151(1)	
92	—	A150(11)	
95	—	CB Sch.5, paras. 2 (7), 4 (4), 7(1)	
97	—	A157(1)	
98(a)	—	A172(1)	
(b)	—	A173(6)	
99	—	A Sch.7, Part I, para.3	
100	—	—	Spent.
103(a)	—	A70(3)	
(b)	—	A170(5), CB 173	
104	—	—	Spent.
105	—	—	Spent
106	—	A Sch.7, Part I, para.5	
107	—	—	Unnecessary
108(a)	—	—	Spent
	SOCIAL FUND (MATERNITY AND FUNERAL EXPENSES) ACT 1987 (c. 7)		
1	Amendment of Section 32(2) of Social Security Act 1986.	CB 128(1)	
2	Short title etc.	—	
	DEBTORS (SCOTLAND) ACT 1987 (c. 18)		
68	Diversion of arrested earnings to Secretary of State	A109	
	FAMILY LAW REFORM ACT 1987 (c. 42)		
2(1)(g)	Construction of enactments relating to parental rights and duties (1986 s.26)3))	A78(7)	

SOCIAL SECURITY ACTS CONSOLIDATION—*continued.*

Section of Act	Subject matter	Section of 1992 Act	Remarks
FAMILY LAW REFORM ACT 1987 (c. 42)—*continued.*			
Sch. 2	Amendments		
Para. 59	—	—	Spent
91	—	A106(5)	
92	Repeal	—	Spent
93	—	A 105(3)	
INCOME AND CORPORATION TAXES ACT 1988 (c. 1)			
Sch 29	Consequential amendments		
Para. 14	—	CB 15 (4)	
32	—	See entries relating to amendment provisions.	Amends 1975(1) Sch.2
SOCIAL SECURITY ACT 1988 (c. 7)			
1	Amendments		
(1)	—	CB 64(1)	
(2)	—	SS CP Sch. 3, para. 19	
2	Amendments		
(1)	—	CB Sch. 7 para. 13 (1), (2), (5), (6)	
(2)	—	A 150(1)(g), (3)(b)	
(3)	—	CB Sch. 7, para. 11 (11),	
(4), (5)	—	CB Sch. 7, para. 12 (1), (2)	
(5A), (5B)	—	CB Sch. 7, para. 12 (3), (4)	Inserted 1989 s.17(5)
(6)	—	CB Sch. 7, para. 12 (6)	
(7)	—	CB Sch. 7, para. 12 (7)	Am. 1989 s.17(6)
(8)	—	—	Substituted 1989 s.7, Sch. 1, para. 8(7); rep. 1990 s.3(8)

SOCIAL SECURITY ACTS CONSOLIDATION—*continued.*

Section of Act	Subject matter	Section of 1992 Act	Remarks

SOCIAL SECURITY ACT 1988 (c. 7)—*continued.*

Section of Act	Subject matter	Section of 1992 Act	Remarks
(8A)	—	—	Inserted 1989 s. 7, Sch. 1, para. 8(7); rep. 1990 s.3(8)
(9)	—	—	See SS CP Sch. 4, paras 10, 11; rep. 1989 s.7, Sch. 1, para. 8(8).
(10)	—	—	Introduces Sch. 1.
3	Amendment		
(a)	—	CB 128(1)	
(b)	—	—	Spent.
4	Income support and child benefit.		
(1)	—	CB 124(1)	
(2)	—	CB 125, A 72	
(3)	—	CB 142(1)(b)	
(4)	—	CB 144(1)	
5	Annual review of child benefit.	A 153	See also SS CP Sch. 4, para. 16.
6	Contribution conditions for short-term benefits.		
(1)	—	—	Drafting.
(2)(a)	—	CB Sch. 3, para. 1(2), 2(2).	
(b)	—	CB Sch. 3 paras. 2(2), 3(2).	
(3), (4)	Repeals.	—	Spent.
7	Unemployment benefit and occupational pension.	—	
(a)	—	CB 30(1), 137	
(b)	—	CB 137	
8	Emergency payments of benefits by local authorities and other bodies.	A 8	
10	Increase and reduction of benefits by reference to earnings.	—	Affected by R17; see also SS CP s. 3(2).
11	Amendments relating to the social fund.	—	Gives effect to Schedule 3.
17	Northern Ireland.	—	Spent.
18(2)	Commencement.	—	Spent; only partly rep.
Sch. 1	Industrial death benefit.		
Para. 1	—	—	Spent.
2, 3	—	CB Sch. 7, para. 14(1)	
4	—	—	Spent.
5(a)	Amendment.	CB 60(8)	

SOCIAL SECURITY ACTS CONSOLIDATION—*continued.*

Section of Act	Subject matter	Section of 1992 Act	Remarks
	SOCIAL SECURITY ACT 1988 (c. 7)—*continued.*		
(b)	—	CB 60(3)(d)	
6	—	CB Sch. 7 paras. 20, 21; see also A 10(1)(a), 44(5), 60(4), (5)(a)	
Sch. 2	Earnings factors and transfer values.		
Para. 1(1)(a)	—	CB 23(1)	
(b)	—	CB 23(2)	
Sch. 3	The social fund.		
Para. 1	—	—	Drafting.
2	—	CB 138(2)	
3	—	—	Spent.
4	—	A 167(5), (6)	
5	—	—	Spent.
6	—	A 168(1)–(4)	
7	—	A 64(3), 66(9), (10)	
8	—	—	Drafting.
9	—	A 12(1)	
10	—	CB 138(3)	
11	—	CB 139(4)	
12	—	CB 140(1)	
13	—	CB 140(4)	
14	—	—	Drafting.
15	—	—	Spent.
16	—	A 5(2)(b), 20(6)(e), 61(4), 71(11)(e)	
Sch 4	Minor and consequential amendments.		
Para. 3	—	—	Drafting.
4	—	CB 57(4)	
5(a)	—	CB 57(2)	
(b)	—	CB 35(4)	

SOCIAL SECURITY ACTS CONSOLIDATION—*continued.*

Section of Act	Subject matter	Section of 1992 Act	Remarks
	SOCIAL SECURITY ACT 1988 (c. 7)—*continued.*		
6(a)	—	CB 82(1)(b)	
(b)	—	CB 82(3)(a)	
7(a)	—	CB 83(2)(b)	
(b)	—	—	Spent.
8(a)	—	CB 84(2)(b)	
(b)	—	—	Spent.
9	—	—	Spent.
10	—	CB 86(1)(a)	
11	—	CB 94(2)	
12(a)	—	CB Sch. 7 para. 11(10)	
(b)	—	CB Sch. 7 para. 11(15)	
13	—	—	Spent.
14	—	A 25(1)(e)	
15	—	—	Drafting.
16(1)	—	CB 164(9)	
(2)	—	CB 164(10)	
17	—	CB 166(2)	
18	—	—	Spent.
19(1)	—	CB Sch. 13 para. 1	
(2)	—	CB Sch. 13 para. 2	
20	—	SS CP Sch. 3. para. 17	
23(1)	—	CB 124(4)	
(2)	—	CB 124(5), (6)	
24	—	CB 126(6), (7)	
25	—	CB 127	
26	—	A 79(b)	
27	—	A 79(c)	
28	—	A 79(a)	

SOCIAL SECURITY ACTS CONSOLIDATION—*continued.*

Section of Act	Subject matter	Section of 1992 Act	Remarks

SOCIAL SECURITY ACT 1988 (c. 7)—*continued.*

Section of Act	Subject matter	Section of 1992 Act	Remarks
29	—	—	See SS CP Sch. 3, para. 4.
30	—	A 72(7), (8)	

EMPLOYMENT ACT 1988 (c. 19)

Section of Act	Subject matter	Section of 1992 Act	Remarks
27	Amendment of the Social Security Act 1975 with respect to the refusal of training etc.		
(1)	—	—	Drafting.
(2)	—	CB 28(1)	
(3)	—	CB 28(6)	

LEGAL AID ACT 1988 (c. 34)

Section of Act	Subject matter	Section of 1992 Act	Remarks
34(14)	Regulations.	—	Unnecessary: see SS CP Sch. 2, para. 94.

FINANCE ACT 1988 (c. 39)

Section of Act	Subject matter	Section of 1992 Act	Remarks
Sch. 3, para. 31	Amendment.	CB Sch. 2, para. 3(4)	

LOCAL GOVERNMENT FINANCE ACT 1988 (c. 41)

Section of Act	Subject matter	Section of 1992 Act	Remarks
Sch. 4, para. 28(2)	Community charges: enforcement.	—	Only partly repealed.
Sch. 10	Amendments.		
2(1)	—	—	Drafting.
(2)	—	CB 123(1)	
(3)	—	CB 131(1), (3) - (9)	
(4)	—	CB 134(3)	
(5)	—	CB 137(1), A 191	
3(1)	—	—	Drafting
(2)	—	CB 131(10), (11)	
(3)	—	CB 131(12)	
4(1)	—	—	Drafting
(2)	—	CB 135(5)	
(3)	—	CB 136(4)	
5	—	CB 132, 133	
6	—	CB 123(4) - (6), A 63, 76, 77, 128, 138, 139, 140	

SOCIAL SECURITY ACTS CONSOLIDATION—*continued.*

Section of Act	Subject matter	Section of 1992 Act	Remarks
\multicolumn{4}{c}{LOCAL GOVERNMENT FINANCE ACT 1988 (c. 41)—*continued.*}			
7	Repeal	—	Spent
8	—	A6, 7	
9(2)	—	A 116(2)	
(3)	—	A 116(4)	
(4)	—	A 116(5)	
10	—	A 176(1)	
11(1)	—	—	Drafting
(2)	—	CB 175(6), A 189(7)	
(3)	—	—	Spent
(4)	—	A 189(8)	
12	—	A 163(2)(d)	
\multicolumn{4}{c}{HOUSING ACT 1988 (c. 50)}			
121	Rent officers: Additional functions relating to housing benefit etc.		
(4)	—	CB 130(5)	
(5)	—	—	Spent
(6)	—	A 5(3)	
\multicolumn{4}{c}{SOCIAL SECURITY ACT 1989 (c. 24)}			
1	Amendments relating to primary Class 1 contributions.		
(1)	—	CB 8(1) - (3)	
(2)	—	—	Spent
(3)	—	A 143(1)	
(4)	—	—	Rep. Employment Act 1990 (c. 38) s. 16(2), Sch. 3
(5)	—	A 143(4)	
(6)	—	A 145(1)	
(7)	—	A 145(3)	
(8)	—	A 162(5)(a)	
(9)	—	CB 122(1) "initial primary percent-age", "main primary percent-age", "primary percent-age"	

SOCIAL SECURITY ACTS CONSOLIDATION—*continued.*

Section of Act	Subject matter	Section of 1992 Act	Remarks
	SOCIAL SECURITY ACT 1989 (c. 24)—*continued.*		
2	Repayment of contributions where earnings become repayable.	CB Sch. 1, para. 8(1)(h)	
3	Abolition of Treasury supplement to contributions.	—	Spent
4	Earnings factors		
(1)	—	—	Drafting
(2)	—	CB 23(3)(a)	
(3)	—	CB 22(6)	
(4)	—	CB 24(2)	
5	Liability of parents to maintain children under the age of nineteen in respect of whom income support is paid.		
(1)	—	CB 137(1)	
(2)-(4)	—	A 76(6) - (8)	
6(1)	Benefits for women widowed before 11th April 1988.	CB 38(4), 39(6)	
7	Abolition of earnings rule etc.		
(1), (2)	—	—	Spent.
(3)(a)	—	49(2)(a), (3)(a)	
(b)	—	—	Spent.
(4)	—	CB 55	
(5)	—	—	Spent.
9	Extension to personal pensions of occupational pension provisions relating to the abatement of unemployment benefit and the meaning of "earnings".		
(1)	—	CB 30(1), (3)(d), 176(1)(b)	
(2)	—	CB 122(1)	
(3)	—	CB 89(1), (2)	
(4)	—	CB 122(1) "payments by way of occupational or personal pension"	

SOCIAL SECURITY ACTS CONSOLIDATION—*continued.*

Section of Act	Subject matter	Section of 1992 Act	Remarks
	SOCIAL SECURITY ACT 1989 (c. 24)—*continued.*		
10	Unemployment benefit: requirement to seek employment actively.		
(1)	—	—	Unnecessary.
(2), (3)	—	CB 57(1)(a)(i), (2)(b)	
(4)	—	CB 57(5)	
(5)	—	A 25(1)(c)	
11	Requalification for unemployment benefit.	CB 26(2)-(4)	
12	Disqualification for unemployment benefit.		
(1)	—	CB 28(1)	
(2)	—	—	Spent.
(3)	—	CB 28(5)	
(4)	—	CB 29	
(5)	—	CB 122(2)	
(6)	—	—	Spent.
13	Income support and unemployment.		
(1)	—	CB 124(1)(d)	
(2)	—	CB 137(2)(d)	
14	Housing benefit to take the form of payments or reductions.		
(1)	—	A 134(2)	
(2)	—	—	See SS CP Sch. 3, para. 4
15	Housing benefit subsidy.		
(1)	—	A 136	
(2)	—	A 137	
16	Expenses of Secretary of State in making transitional payments relating to income support and housing benefit.	SS CP Sch. 3, para. 20	
17	Rectification of mistakes in uprating orders.		
(1)	—	A 152	
(2)(a)	—	A 155(1)(b)	
(b)	—	A 190(1)(a)	
(c)	—	A 189(8)	
(3)	—	CB Sch. 7 para. 13(5)	

SOCIAL SECURITY ACTS CONSOLIDATION—*continued.*

Section of Act	Subject matter	Section of 1992 Act	Remarks
SOCIAL SECURITY ACT 1989 (c. 24)—*continued.*			
(4)	—	—	Drafting.
(5)	—	CB Sch. 7, para. 12(3), (4)	
(6)	—	CB Sch. 7, para. 12(6)	
(7)	—	—	See SS CP Sch. 3, para. 4.
18	Effect of alteration in the component rates of income support.	A 159	
19	Unauthorised disclosure of information relating to particular persons.		
(1) - (6)	—	A 123(1) - (6)	
(7)	—	A 123(7)	Am. 1990 s. 21(1) Sch. 6, para. 28(1).
(8)	—	A 123(8)	
(9)	—	A 123(9)	Am. 1990 s. 21(1) Sch. 6, para. 28(2).
(10)	—	A 123(10)	Am. 1990 s. 21(1) Sch. 6, para. 28(3).
(11)	—	—	See SS CP Sch. 3, para. 4.
21	Miscellaneous amendments relating to adjudication.	—	Gives effect to Schedule 3.
22	Recovery of sums equivalent to benefit from compensation payments in respect of accidents, injuries and diseases.		
(1), (2)	—	A 82(1), (2)	
(3)	—	A 81(1)	Am. 1990 s. 7, Sch. 1, para. 1(1), (2), 1991(1) s. 1(5); rep. in part para. 1(3); "costs" unnecessary.
(3A)	—	A 81(2)	Inserted 1991(1) s. 1(5).
(4) - (6)	—	A 81(3) - (5)	
(8)	—	A 81(7)	
27	Application to the Crown.	A 104	See also SS CP Sch. 4, para. 13.
28	Financial provisions.		
(2)	—	A 165(5)	Only partly repealed.
(3)	—	A 164(6)	
(4)	—	A 163(1)(e), (2)(i)	

SOCIAL SECURITY ACTS CONSOLIDATION—*continued.*

Section of Act	Subject matter	Section of 1992 Act	Remarks
	SOCIAL SECURITY ACT 1989 (c. 24)—*continued.*		
29	Regulations and orders: general provisions.		
(2)	—	A 190(1)(b)	Otherwise spent.
(5)	—	A 189(8)	
(6)	—	CB175(7), A 189(9)	
30(1)	Interpretation.	—	Spent; only partly repealed.
32	Corresponding provision for Northern Ireland.	—	Spent.
Sch. 1	Amendments and repeals.		
Para. 1	—	—	Spent.
2(1)	—	—	Spent.
(2)	—	CB 54(4)	
(3)	—	—	Spent.
3(1)	—	CB Sch. 5, para. 1	
(2)	—	CB Sch. 5, para. 2(1)	
(3)	—	CB Sch. 1, para. 2(2)	
(4)	—	CB Sch. 5, para. 2(3)	
(5)	—	CB Sch. 5, para. 2(7)	
(6)	—	CB Sch. 5, para. 2(8)	
(7)	—	CB Sch. 5, para. 3(1)	
(8)	—	CB Sch. 5, para. 4(1) (b)(ii), (2)(c)(ii)	
(9)	—	CB Sch.5, para. 8(1), (2)	
(10)	—	CB Sch. 5, para. 8(3)	
(11)	—	—	Unnecessary.
4(1)	—	CB 25(2)	
(2)	Repeal.	—	Spent.
5(1), (2)	Amendment.	CB 33(1), (2)	
(3)	Repeal.	—	Spent.
6	—	—	Spent.

SOCIAL SECURITY ACTS CONSOLIDATION—*continued.*

Section of Act	Subject matter	Section of 1992 Act	Remarks

SOCIAL SECURITY ACT 1989 (c. 24)—*continued.*

Section of Act	Subject matter	Section of 1992 Act	Remarks
7	—	—	Spent.
8(1)	—	CB 102(3)(b)	
(2)	—	CB Sch. 7, para. 13(1)	
(4)	—	—	Spent.
(5)	—	CB Sch. 7, para. 13(4)	
(6)	—	CB Sch. 7, para. 13(7), (8)	
(7)	—	—	Rep. 1990 s. 3(8)(b).
(8)	—	—	See SS CP Sch. 4, paras. 10, 11.
9(1)	—	—	Spent.
(2)	—	CB 51(4)	
10(1)	—	CB 40(7)	
(2)	—	CB 41(7)	
Sch. 2	Persons employed in social security administration or adjudication.		
Part I	The specified persons.	A Sch. 4 Part I	Am. 1990 s. 21(1) Sch. 6, para. 28(4), (5), 1991(2) s. 4, Sch. 2, para. 19.
Part II	Construction of references to Government Departments etc.		
Paras. 1,2	—	A Sch. 4, Part II, paras. 1, 2	
3	—	A Sch. 4, Part II, para. 3	Substituted 1990 s. 21(1), Sch. 6, para. 28(6).
4	—	CB Sch. 4, Part II, para. 4	Rep. in part 1990 s. 21(1), Sch. 6, para. 28(7)
5	—	A Sch. 4, Part II, para. 5	Inserted 1990 s. 21(1), Sch. 6, para. 28(7)
Sch. 3	Amendments		
Para. 1(1)	—	A 17(3)	
(2)	—	A 59(6)	
2	—	A 21(6)	
3(1)	—	A 53, 56	
(2)	Repeals	—	Spent.
4	—	A Sch. 3, para. 2	
5	Repeal	—	Spent.

SOCIAL SECURITY ACTS CONSOLIDATION—_continued._

Section of Act	Subject matter	Section of 1992 Act	Remarks
	SOCIAL SECURITY ACT 1989 (c. 24)—_continued._		
6(a)	—	A 23(7)	
(b)	—	A 23(8)	
7	—	A 29	
8	—	—	Rep. 1991(2) s. 10, Sch. 4.
9(1)	Repeals	—	Spent
(2)	—	A 48(5), (6)	
10	—	A Sch. 3, para. 10	
11(1)	—	A 25(1)(c)	
(2)	—	A 25(5)	
(3)	—	A 27(1)(a)	
(4)	—	A 27(1)(b)	
12(1)	—	A 45(1)	
(2)	—	A 45(4), (5)	
13(1)	—	CB Sch. 6, para. 6(3) – (5)	
(2)	—	CB Sch. 6, para. 7	
14(1)	—	A 71(2)	
(2)	—	A 71(5)	
15	—	A 37(2)	
16	—	—	Rep. 1990 s. 21(2), Sch. 7.
17	Repeals	—	Spent
18	—	A 50(5)	
19	Repeal	—	Spent
Sch. 4	Recovery of sums equivalent to benefit from compensation payments in respect of accidents etc: supplementary provision.		
Para. 1(1) "the recoupment provisions"	—	—	Unnecessary.
"the relevant deduction", "relevant payment", "total benefit"	—	A 81(1) "relevant deduction", "relevant payment", "total benefit"	

SOCIAL SECURITY ACTS CONSOLIDATION—*continued.*

Section of Act	Subject matter	Section of 1992 Act	Remarks
	SOCIAL SECURITY ACT 1989 (c. 24)—*continued.*		
(2)	—	A 81(6)	
(3)	—	—	Unnecessary.
2 – 11	—	A 83 – 92	
12(1)	—	A 93(1)	
(2)	—	A 93(2)	Am. 1990 ss. 7, Sch. 1, para. 2(1).
(3), (4)	—	A 93(3), (4)	
(5)	—	A 93(5)	Am. 1990 s. 7, Sch. 1, para. 2(2).
(6)	—	A 93(6)	Am. 1990 s. 7, Sch. 1, para. 2(3).
(6A)	—	A 93(7)	Inserted 1990 s. 7, Sch. 5, para. 2(4).
(7), (8)	—	A 93(8), (9)	
13(1), (2)	—	A 94(1), (2)	
(2A)	—	A 94(3)	Inserted 1990 s. 7, Sch. 1, para. 1(4).
(3) – (5)	—	A 94(4) – (6)	
14 – 16	—	A 95 – 97	
17(1), (2)	—	A 98(1), (2)	
(3)	—	A 98(3)	Am. 1990 s. 7, Sch. 1, para. 3.
(4) – (10)	—	A 98(4) – (10)	
(11)	—	A 98(11)	Am. 1990 s. 7, Sch. 1, para. 4.
(12)	—	A 98(12)	
18, 19	—	A99, 100	
20	Amendments		
(1), (2)	—	A 110(2), (3)	
(4)	—	A 110(3)	
(5)	—	A 110(6)	
(6)	—	A 110(7)	
(7)	—	—	Unnecessary.
20A(1) – (6)	—	A 101	Paragraph inserted 1990 s. 7, Sch. 1, para. 5(1).
(7)	—	A 192(3)	
21(1)	—	A 102(1)	Am. 1990 s. 7, Sch. 1, para. 5(2).
(2)	—	A 102(2)	
24	—	A 103	Inserted 1990 s. 7, Sch. 1, para. 6.

SOCIAL SECURITY ACTS CONSOLIDATION—*continued.*

Section of Act	Subject matter	Section of 1992 Act	Remarks

SOCIAL SECURITY ACT 1989 (c. 24)—*continued.*

Section of Act	Subject matter	Section of 1992 Act	Remarks
Sch. 7	Pre-consolidation amendments.		
Para. 2(1)	—	CB6(3)	
(2)	—	CB 9(1)	
3	—	CB 12(3)	
4	—	CB 13(6)	
5(a),(b)	—	CB 15(1)	
(c)	—	CB 15(5)	
6	—	CB 20(1)	
7	—	CB 22(3)	
8	—	CB 36(3)	
9	—	—	Amends provision to be omitted in pursuance of R15.
10	—	CB 70(6)	
11	—	—	Spent.
12	—	CB (6), Sch. 7 para. 9(3)	
13	—	CB Sch. 7 para 11(1)	
15	—	A 162(2)	
16	—	CB Sch. 3 para (1)	
17	—	A 50(5)	
18	—	—	Spent.
19	—	CB 44(6)	
20(1)	—	CB 40(2)	
(2)	—	—	Spent.
22	—	A 13(1)	
23	—	CB 161(3)	
24	—	—	Spent.
25	—	CB 165(7)	
26	—	—	Spent.
28	—	—	Spent.
Sch. 8	Amendments.		
1	—	CB 4(5)	
2	Incapacity for work: work as councillor to be disregarded.		
(1)	—	CB 58(1)	
(2)	—	CB 58(2)	Am. 1990 s. 21(1), Sch. 6, para. 30(2).
(3)	—	CB 58(3)	
(4)	—	CB 68(12)	

SOCIAL SECURITY ACTS CONSOLIDATION—*continued.*

Section of Act	Subject matter	Section of 1992 Act	Remarks
	SOCIAL SECURITY ACT 1989 (c. 24)—*continued.*		
(5)	—	CB 68(11)(d)	
(6)	—	CB 58(2), (4), 68(13)	Am. Local Government and Housing Act 1989 (c. 42) s. 194, Sch. 11, para. 113, 1990 s. 21(1), Sch. 6, para. 30(3); rep. in part 1990 s. 21(1), Sch. 6, para. 30(4).
(7)	—	CB 58(5), 68(13)	
3	Amendments.	CB 57(6), (7)	
4(1)	—	CB 37(3), (4)	
(2)	—	CB 38(2), (3)	
(3)	—	CB 44(1)	
(4)	—	CB 44(2)	
(5)	—	CB 49(7), (8)	
(6)	—	CB 78(7), (8)	
5(1)	—	—	Drafting.
(2)	—	CB 65(1)	
(3)	—	CB 65(4), (6)	
(4)	—	CB 65(5)	
6	—	CB 68(8), (9)	
7(1)	—	CB 86(1)	
(2)	—	CB 92, Sch. 7, para. 8	
9(1)	—	A 1(1)	
(2)	—	CB 131(2)	
(3)	—	CB 133(1)	
(4)	—	A 76(3), (5)	
(5)	—	—	Spent.
(6)	—	A 6(1)(l), (q)	
10(1)	—	CB 175(3), A 189(5), Sch. 1, para. 1(2)	
11	—	A 156	

SOCIAL SECURITY ACTS CONSOLIDATION—*continued.*

Section of Act	Subject matter	Section of 1992 Act	Remarks
	SOCIAL SECURITY ACT 1989 (c. 24)—*continued.*		
12(2)	—	A 170(5)	
(5)	Repeal	—	Spent.
(6)	—	A Sch. 7, Part I, para. 8	
14	Repeal	—	Spent.
15(1)	—	CB 128(3)	
(2)	—	A 150(10)	
16	—	CB 127(c)	
17	—	A 126	
18	—	A 132(1), (2)	
19(a)	—	A 70(3)	
(b)	—	A 170(5), CB 173	
	LOCAL GOVERNMENT AND HOUSING ACT 1989 (c. 42)		
81	Amendments		
(1)	—	A 135(2), (3)	
(2)	—	A 135(6)(a)	
(3)	—	A 135(8)	
(4)	Repeal		Spent.
(5)	—	—	Amends 1986 s. 84(1) definition of "Housing Revenue Account dwelling".
Sch. 11, para. 113	Amendment	CB 58(4)	
	CAPITAL ALLOWANCES ACT 1990 (c. 1)		
Sch. 1, para. 2	Amendments	CB Sch. 2, paras. 1, 2	
	NATIONAL HEALTH SERVICE AND COMMUNITY CARE ACT 1990 (c. 19)		
Sch. 9, para. 5	Amendment	CB 143(3)(c)	See also SS CP Sch. 4, para. 5.
	SOCIAL SECURITY ACT 1990 (c. 27)		
1	Amendments		
(1)	—	CB 66(1),(2)	
(2)	—	CB 65(6)	
(3)–(5)	—	—	Rep. 1991(2) s.10, Sch.4.
(6)	—	A 1(3)	
(7)	—	—	Spent.
2	Amendments		
(1)	—	CB 69	

SOCIAL SECURITY ACTS CONSOLIDATION—*continued.*

Section of Act	Subject matter	Section of 1992 Act	Remarks
		SOCIAL SECURITY ACT 1990 (c. 27)—*continued.*	
(2)	—	CB Sch.4, Part III, para. 3	
(3)	—	CB 63	
3	Amendments		
(1)	—	CB Sch. 7, para. 11(1)	
(2)	—	CB Sch. 7, para. 11(2), (3)	
(3)	—	CB Sch. 7, para. 11(8)	
(4)	—	CB Sch. 7, para. 11(1)	
(5)	Repeals	—	Spent.
(6)	—	CB Sch. 7, para. 13(10)	See also SS CP Sch. 3, para. 4.
(7)	—	CB 109(2)	
(8)	Repeals	—	Spent.
4	Amendments		
(1)	—	CB 33(3)	
(2)	—	CB 40(5)	
(3)	—	CB 41(4),(5)	
5	Amendments		
(1)	—	A2	
(2)	—	CB 122(1) "entitled"	
(3)	Repeal.	—	Spent.
(4), (5)	Amendment.	A 1(4)(b)	See also SS CP Sch.3, para.4.
6	Amendments.		
(1)	—	A 1(1), (2)	
(2)	—	A 3	
(3)	—	A 27(2)	
8	Amendments.		
(1)	—	A 107, 108	
(2)	—	—	See SS CP Sch. 4, para. 22.
(3)	—	A 105(3)	
9	Amendments.	CB 135(3), (4)	See also SS CP Sch. 4, para. 4.
10	Amendments.		
(1)	—	A 168(5)	
(2)	—	A 64(3)	

SOCIAL SECURITY ACTS CONSOLIDATION—*continued.*

Section of Act	Subject matter	Section of 1992 Act	Remarks

SOCIAL SECURITY ACT 1990 (c. 27)—*continued.*

Section of Act	Subject matter	Section of 1992 Act	Remarks
(3)	—	CB 140(3)	
(4)	—	CB 140(4)	
(5)	—	A 12(2)	
16	Amendments.		
(1)	—	CB 1(1)	
(2)	—	CB 1(1), (5)	
(3)	—	A 162(3)	
(4)	—	A 163(2)(c)	
(5)	—	A 165(5)	
(6)	Repeal.	—	Spent.
(7)	—	A 163(2)(c)	
(8)(a)	—	A 168(2)(c)	
(b)	—	A Sch.9, para.1(4)	
(c)	Repeal.	—	Spent.
(9)	Repeals.	—	Spent.
(10)	—	—	See SS CP Sch. 3, para. 4.
17	Amendment.		
(1)	—	CB 16(4)	
(2)	—	CB 16(5)	
(3)	—	A 162(4)	See also SS CP Sch. 4, para. 17.
(4)	—	A 163(5)	See also SS CP Sch. 4, para. 18.
(5)	—	CB Sch. 1, para. 6(2)-(4)	See also SS CP Sch. 4, para. 6.
(6)	—	CB Sch. 1, para. 6(8)	See also SS CP Sch. 4, para. 7.
(7)	—	CB Sch. 1, para. 7	
(8)	—	CB Sch. 2, para. 6(1)	See also SS CP Sch. 4, para. 8.
(9)	—	CB Sch. 2, para. 6(2)	See also SS CP Sch. 4, para. 9.
20 "the 1982 Act", "the 1986 Act", "the 1989 Act", "the Old Cases Act"	Interpretation.	—	Unnecessary.

SOCIAL SECURITY ACTS CONSOLIDATION—*continued.*

Section of Act	Subject matter	Section of 1992 Act	Remarks
	SOCIAL SECURITY ACT 1990 (c. 27)—*continued.*		
22(1)	Provision for Northern Ireland.	—	Spent.
Sch. 1	Amendments.		
Para. 1(1)-(3)	—	A 81(1)	
(4)	—	A 94(3)	
2(1)	—	A 93(2)	
(2)	—	A 93(5)	
(3)	—	A 93(6)	
(4)	—	A 93(7)	
3	—	A 98(3)	
4	—	A 98(11)	
5(1)	—	A 101, 192(3)	
(2)	—	A 102(1)	
6	—	A 103	
Sch. 5	Amendments.	CB Sch. 1, para. 7	
Sch. 6	Amendments.		
Para. 1(1)	—	A 147(4)	
(2)(a)	—	A 142(3)	
(b)	—	A 144(1)	
(c)	—	A 147(4)	
3(1)	—	CB 60(5)	
(2)	—	CB 87(1), (2)	
(3)	—	CB 61(1)	
(4)	—	CB 61(2)	
4(1)	—	CB 108(5)	
(2)	—	CB 109(2)	
5(1)	—	A 38(1)	
(2)	—	A 116(6)	
6(1)	—	A 22(6), (7)	
(2)	—	A 23(4)	
(3)	—	A 23(5)(c)	
(4)	—	—	See SS CP Sch. 3, para. 4.
7(1)	—	A 69	
(2)	—	A 68	
(3)	—	A 68(4) definition of "benefit"	
8(1)	—	CB 176(2), A 190(2)	

SOCIAL SECURITY ACTS CONSOLIDATION—*continued.*

Section of Act	Subject matter	Section of 1992 Act	Remarks
		SOCIAL SECURITY ACT 1990 (c. 27)—*continued.*	
(2)	—	CB 176(1)(a)	See also 1975(2) s. 62(2) inserted SS CP Sch. 2, para. 37.
(3)	—	CB 176(1)(a), (2)(b), A 190(1)(b), (2), (3)	
(5)	—	CB 176(1)(b)	
(7)	—	CB 175(1), 176(2)	
(8)	Repeal.	—	Spent.
(11)	Repeals.	—	Spent.
9	—	CB Sch. 1, para. 8(1)(j), (k)	
10(1)	—	CB Sch. 3, para. 3(1)	
(2)	—	CB Sch. 3, para. 3(2), (3)	
11	—	CB 122(1) "tax year"	
12	—	CB 176(3)	
14	—	—	Spent: amendments deemed never to have had effect.
15(1)	—	CB 157(2)	
(2)	—	CB 176(1)(c)	
16	—	CB 163(6)	
17(1)	—	—	Drafting.
(2)	—	CB 126(7)	
(3)	—	CB 126(8)	
18	—	A 134(1), (7)	
19(1)	—	A 135(4)	
(2)	—	A 136(1)	
20	—	A 138(1), (2)	
21(1)	—	A 140(3)	
(2)	—	A 140(6)	
(3)	—	A 140(7)	
22	—	CB 171(3)	
23	—	A 150(8)	

SOCIAL SECURITY ACTS CONSOLIDATION—*continued.*

Section of Act	Subject matter	Section of 1992 Act	Remarks
SOCIAL SECURITY ACT 1990 (c. 27)—*continued.*			
24	—	A 160	
25	Repeal.	—	Spent.
26	Repeals.	—	Spent; see also SS CP Sch. 3, para. 4.
27(2)	—	A 4	
28(1)	—	A 123(7)	
(2)	—	A 123(9)	
(3)	—	A 123(10)	
(4), (5)	—	A Sch. 4, Part I	
(6)	—	A Sch. 4, Part II, para. 3	
(7)	—	A Sch. 4, Part II, para. 5	
30(1)	—	—	Drafting.
(2)	—	CB 58(2)	
(3)	Repeal.	—	Spent.
(4)	—	CB 58(4)	
(5)	—	CB 68(11)	
31(a)	—	A 70(3)	
(b)	—	CB 173, A 170(5)	
HUMAN FERTILISATION AND EMBRYOLOGY ACT 1990 (c. 37)			
Sch. 4, para. 2	Amendment.	CB 37(1)	
COURTS AND LEGAL SERVICES ACT 1990 (c. 41)			
Sch. 10	Amendments.		
Para. 36	—	A 52(1)	
37(1)	—	A 41(5)	
(2)	—	A 51(2)	
(3)	—	A 51(3)	
(4)	—	A 50(5)	
46	—	A 52(2)	
Sch. 11, words in entry beginning "Social Security Commissioner"	—	—	Unnecessary.
Sch. 18, para. 24	Amendment.	A Sch. 2, para. 1(6)	

SOCIAL SECURITY ACTS CONSOLIDATION—*continued.*

Section of Act	Subject matter	Section of 1992 Act	Remarks
	STATUTORY SICK PAY ACT 1991 (c. 3)		
1	Amendments.		
(1)	—	CB 158(1)	
(2)	Repeal.	—	Spent.
(3)	—	CB 158(5)	
(4)	—	CB 1(5)	
(5)	—	A 81(1) "benefit", (2)	
2	Amendments.		
(1)	—	CB 158(2), (3), 159, 176(1)(a), (c), A 149	
(2)	—	CB 158(4)	
(3)	—	A 17(1)(g)(v)	
(4)	—	—	Spent.
(5)	—	CB 158(7)	
3	Consequential amendments, repeals and supplementary provisions.		
(1)(a)	—	A 70(3)	
(b)	—	CB 173, A 170(5)	
(3)–(5)	—	—	See SS CP Sch. 3, paras. 4,6.
4(5)	Northern Ireland.	—	Spent.
	MAINTENANCE ENFORCEMENT ACT 1991 (c. 17)		
9	Amendments.		
(1)	—	A 107(5)	See also SS CP Sch. 4, para. 14.
(2)	—	A 107(9)–(11)	See also SS CP Sch. 4, para. 15.
	DISABILITY LIVING ALLOWANCE AND DISABILITY WORKING ALLOWANCE ACT 1991 (c. 21)		
1	Amendments.		
(1)	—	CB 63	
(2)	—	CB 71–73, 75, 76	
2(1)	Amendment.	CB 64	
3	Disability Living Allowance Advisory Board.		
(1) - (6)	—	A 175	
(7)	—	A 189(5)	
(8)	—	A 189(1), (3)	

SOCIAL SECURITY ACTS CONSOLIDATION—*continued.*

Section of Act	Subject matter	Section of 1992 Act	Remarks
\multicolumn{4}{c}{DISABILITY LIVING ALLOWANCE AND DISABILITY WORKING ALLOWANCE ACT 1991 (c. 21)—*continued.*}			
4(1)	Management of disability living allowance and attendance allowance etc.	—	Gives effect to Schedule 1.
5	Regulations supplementary to ss.1 to 4.		
(1) - (3)	—	SS CP Sch. 3, para. 21	
(4)	—	SS CP Sch. 3, para. 22(2), (3), (5)	
6	Introduction of disability working allowance.		
(1)	—	—	Drafting.
(2)	Amendment.	CB 123(1)(c)	
(3)	—	CB 123(2)	
(4)	—	CB 129(1) - (4), (6)	
(5)	Transition from mobility allowance.	SS CP Sch. 4, para. 21	
(6)	Amendments.	CB 137(1) "industrial injuries scheme", "war pension scheme"	
(7)	—	CB 137(2)	
(8)	—	CB 129(5)	
(9)	—	CB 129(8)	
7(1)	Amendments.	CB 129(7), A 11	
8	Amendments.		
(1)	—	CB 128(1)	
(2)	—	CB 128(4)	
9	Entitlement to other benefits after termination of entitlement to disability working allowance.		
(1)	Amendment.	CB 33(7), (8)	
(2)	—	CB 68(10)	
(3)	—	CB 42	
(4)	—	CB 122(1) "week"	
(5)	Dependency increases.	CB 93	
11	Supplementary.	—	See SS CP Sch, 3, paras, 4,6.

SOCIAL SECURITY ACTS CONSOLIDATION—*continued.*

Section of Act	Subject matter	Section of 1992 Act	Remarks
	DISABILITY LIVING ALLOWANCE AND DISABILITY WORKING ALLOWANCE ACT 1991 (c. 21)—*continued.*		
12	Regulations.		
(1)	—	—	Spent.
(2)	—	A 190(3), SS CP Sch. 3, para. 22(7)	
(3)	—	A 189(9), SS CP Sch. 3, para. 22(6)	
13	Provision for Northern Ireland.	—	Spent.
14	Administrative expenses.	A 163(2)(a)	
Sch. 1	Amendments.		
Para. 1	—	—	Drafting.
2	—	A 20(1)	
3(1)	—	A 21(1)	
(2)	—	A 21(2)	
(3)	—	A 21(3)	
4(a)	—	A 22(1)	
(b)	—	A 22(2)	
(c)	—	A 22(5)	
5	—	A 30 - 33	
6(a)	—	A 23(1)	
(b)	Repeal.	—	Spent.
7(1)	—	A 36(1)	
(2)	—	A 36(2)	
8(a)	—	A 25(1)	
(b)	—	A 25(2)	
9	—	A 35	
10	—	A Sch. 3, para. 1(c)	
11	—	A 53(2)(e)	
12	—	A 56(2)(d)	
13	—	A 54, 55	
14	—	—	Spent.
15	—	A 51(1)	
16	—	A 42, 43, Sch. 2, paras. 3 - 5, 7	
17	—	A Sch, 3, para. 10	
18	—	A	

SOCIAL SECURITY ACTS CONSOLIDATION—*continued.*

Section of Act	Subject matter	Section of 1992 Act	Remarks
		163(2)(b)	

DISABILITY LIVING ALLOWANCE AND DISABILITY WORKING ALLOWANCE ACT 1991 (c. 21)—*continued.*

Section of Act	Subject matter	Section of 1992 Act	Remarks
19	—	A 1(3)	
20	—	A 191 "President"	
Sch. 2	Amendments.		
Para. 2(2)	—	—	Spent: see SS CP Sch. 2, para. 9.
3(1)	—	CB 66(1)	
(2)	—	CB 65(3)	
(3)	—	CB 65(4), (5)	
(4)	—	CB 67(2)	
4	—	CB 70(2)	
5	—	A 68(4)	
8	—	CB 74(1)	
10	—	A Sch. 2, para. 8	
11	—	A Sch. 7, Part I, para. 1	See also entry for 1980 Sch. 3, para. 12(3).
15	—	A Sch. 10, para. 3	See also entry for 1986 s. 52(3).
16(a)	—	A 150(1)(b)	
(b)	—	A 150(3)	
17	—	CB 150(2) "attend-ance allow-ance"	
19	—	A Sch. 4, Part I	
Sch. 3	Amendments.		
Part I	Amendments of 1986 Act.		
Para. 1	—	—	Drafting.
2	—	A 5(2)(d)	
3(1)	—	—	See Entry for 1986 s. 52(3A).
(2)	—	A 59(2)	
(3)	—	—	See entries for 1986 s. 52(9), (10).
4	—	A 71(11)	
5(a)	—	A 150(1)(h)	
(b)	—	A 150(10)	
6	—	A 178(2)(c), 179(4), (5)(c)	

SOCIAL SECURITY ACTS CONSOLIDATION—*continued.*

Section of Act	Subject matter	Section of 1992 Act	Remarks
\multicolumn{4}{c}{DISABILITY LIVING ALLOWANCE AND DISABILITY WORKING ALLOWANCE ACT 1991 (c. 21)—*continued.*}			
7	—	CB 129(9)	
8(a)	—	A 163(2)(d)	
(b)	—	A 165(1)	
\multicolumn{4}{c}{SOCIAL SECURITY (CONTRIBUTIONS) ACT 1991 (c. 42)}			
1	Amendments.		
(1)	—	—	Drafting.
(2)	—	CB 1(2)	
(3)	—	CB 1(6)	
(4)	—	—	Amendment of heading.
(5)	—	CB 10	
2	Amendments.		
(1)	—	CB 1(4)	Also amends heading.
(2)	—	CB Sch. 1, para. 5	
(3)(a)	—	CB Sch. 1, para. 6(1)	
(b)	—	CB Sch. 1, para. 6(2)	See also SS CP Sch. 4, para. 6.
(4)	—	CB Sch. 1, para. 7(11)	
(5)(a)	—	CB Sch. 1, para. 8(1)(b)	
(b)	—	CB Sch. 1, para. 8(1)(1)	
(c)	—	CB Sch. 1, para. 8(1)(i)	
(6)(a)	—	A 120(3)	
(b)	—	A 120(4)	
(c)	—	A 120(6)	
3	Amendments.		
(1)	—	A 17(1)	
(2)	—	A 59(4)	
4	Amendments.		
(a)	—	A 162(5)(c)	
(b)	—	A 162(8)(b)	
5	Provision for Northern Ireland.	—	Spent.
6	Short title, commencement, financial provision and extent.	—	Unnecessary.
\multicolumn{4}{c}{CHILD SUPPORT ACT 1991 (c. 48)}			
Sch. 3, words in paras. 1(1), 3(2)(c)	—	—	Unnecessary.

SOCIAL SECURITY CONTRIBUTIONS AND BENEFITS
(NORTHERN IRELAND) ACT 1992 (c. 7)

TABLE OF DERIVATIONS

(for Table of Destinations see page ccxvi)

Note:

1. The following abbreviations are used in this Table:—

1975	= The Social Security (Northern Ireland) Act 1975 (c. 15)
1975OC	= The Industrial Injuries and Diseases (Northern Ireland Old Cases) Act 1975 (c.17)
1975P	= The Social Security Pensions (Northern Ireland) Order 1975 (NI 15)
1975CB	= The Child Benefit (Northern Ireland) Order 1975 (NI 16)
1976	= The Social Security and Family Allowances (Northern Ireland) Order 1976 (NI 9)
1976IR	= The Industrial Relations (Northern Ireland) Order 1976 (NI 16)
1977	= The Social Security (Miscellaneous Provisions) (Northern Ireland) Order 1977 (NI 11)
1977A	= The Social Security (Miscellaneous Provisions) Act 1977 (c. 5)
1977SB	= The Supplementary Benefits (Northern Ireland) Order 1977 (NI 27)
1979	= The Social Security (Northern Ireland) Order 1979 (NI 5)
1980	= The Social Security (Northern Ireland) Order 1980 (NI 8)
1980(2)	= The Social Security (No. 2) (Northern Ireland) Order 1980 (NI 13)
1980A	= The Social Security Act 1980 (c. 30)
1981C	= The Social Security (Contributions) (Northern Ireland) Order 1981 (NI 9)
1981	= The Social Security (Northern Ireland) Order 1981 (NI 25)
1981MC	= The Magistrates' Courts (Northern Ireland) Order 1981 (NI 26)
1982	= The Social Security (Northern Ireland) Order 1982 (NI 16)
1982A	= The Social Security and Housing Benefits Act 1982 (c. 24)
1982SR	= The Social Security (Contributions, Re-rating) Order (Northern Ireland) 1982 (SR 1982 No. 413)
1983	= The Social Security Adjudications (Northern Ireland) Order 1983 (NI 17)
1984	= The Health and Social Security (Northern Ireland) Order 1984 (NI 8)
1984F	= The Fines and Penalties (Northern Ireland) Order 1984 (NI 3)
1985	= The Social Security (Northern Ireland) Order 1985 (NI 16)
1985SR	= The Social Security (Contributions and Credits) (Transitional and Consequential Provisions) Regulations (Northern Ireland) 1985 (SR 1985 No. 260)
1986	= The Social Security (Northern Ireland) Order 1986 (NI 18)
1986A	= The Social Security Act 1986 (c. 50)
1987	= The Social Fund (Maternity and Funeral Expenses) (Northern Ireland) Order 1987 (NI 8)
1988	= The Social Security (Northern Ireland) Order 1988 (NI 2)
1988E	= The Employment and Training (Amendment) (Northern Ireland) Order 1988 (NI 10)
ICTA 1988	= The Income and Corporation Taxes Act 1988 (c. 1)
1989	= The Social Security (Northern Ireland) Order 1989 (NI 13)
1990	= The Social Security (Northern Ireland) Order 1990 (NI 15)
1991C	= The Social Security (Contributions) (Northern Ireland) Order 1991 (NI 22)
1991D	= The Disability Living Allowance and Disability Working Allowance (Northern Ireland) Order 1991 (NI 17)

SOCIAL SECURITY CONTRIBUTIONS AND BENEFITS
(NORTHERN IRELAND) ACT—*continued.*

1991R   = The Social Security (Contributions) (Re-rating) (No. 2) Order (Northern Ireland) 1991
                 (SR 1991 No. 542)

1991RF   = The Redundancy Fund (Abolition) (Northern Ireland) Order 1991 (NI 2)

1991SP   = The Statutory Sick Pay (Northern Ireland) Order 1991 (NI 9)

1992CP   = The Social Security (Consequential Provisions) Act 1992 (c. 6)

1992U   = The Social Security Benefits Up-rating Order (Northern Ireland) 1992 (SR 1992 No.
                 18)

M (followed   = The paragraph in the Memorandum under the Consolidation of Enactments
by a   (Procedure) Act 1949
number)

2. The Table does not contain any entries in respect of Article 2(3) of the Social Security Pensions
(Northern Ireland) Order 1975 (NI 15) under which, with certain exceptions, that Order and the Social
Security (Northern Ireland) Act 1975 (c. 15) have effect as if the provisions of the Order were contained
in the Social Security (Northern Ireland) Act 1975. The effect is that the general provisions of the Social
Security (Northern Ireland) Act 1975 apply to the provisions of that Order.

3. The Table does not show the effect of transfer of functions orders.

Section of 1992 Act	Derivation
1(1)	1975 s. 1(1); Industrial Relations (No. 2) (NI) Order 1976 (NI 28) art. 20(2); 1986 Sch. 10; 1989 Sch. 9; 1990 art. 18(1), (2); 1991RF Sch. 2
(2)	1975 s. 1(2); 1991C art. 3(2)
(3)	1975 s. 1(3)
(4)	1975 s. 1(4); 1991C art. 4(1)
(5)	1975 s. 1(4A); 1990 art. 18(2); 1991SP art. 3(4)
(6)	1975 s. 1(6); 1991C art. 3(3)
2	1975 s. 2
3	1975 s. 3(1), (2), (3)
4(1)	1975 s. 3(1A); 1982 arts. 25, 30(1); 1986 Sch. 4 para. 10
(2), (3)	1975 s. 3(1B), (1C); 1982 art. 30(1)
(4)	1975 s. 3(1D); 1989 Sch. 8 para. 1
(5)	1975 s. 3(4); 1982 Sch. 4 para. 4
5(1)	1975 s. 4(1); 1975P art. 3(1), Sch. 5 para. 18(a); 1985 art. 9(1), Sch. 5 para. 7
(2), (3)	1975P art. 3(2), (3); 1986 art. 75(4)
6(1)	1975 s. 4(2); 1976 art. 3(1); 1982 Sch. 5
(2)	1975P art. 6(1); 1984 Sch. 5 para. 4
(3)	1975 s. 4(3); 1989 Sch. 7 para. 1(1)
(4)	1975 s. 4(2)
(5)	1975 s. 4(7); 1979 art. 11(2); 1985 art. 10
(6)	1986 art. 75(3)
7	1975 s. 4(4), (5)
8(1) - (3)	1975 s. 4(6), (6A), (6B); 1989 art. 3(1)
(4)	1986 art. 75(3)
9(1) - (3)	1975 s. 4(6C) - (6E); 1985 art. 9(2); 1989 Sch. 7 para. 1(2); SR 1991 No. 73 art. 2; 1991R art. 2
(4)	1975 s. 4(6C), (6E); 1985 art. 9(2)
(5)	1986 art. 75(3)
10	1975 s. 4A; 1991C art. 3(5)
11(1)	1975 s. 7(1); 1976 art. 3(1); 1984 art. 11(1); 1991R art. 3(a)
(2)	1975P art. 6(2)
(3)	1975 s. 7(4)

SOCIAL SECURITY CONTRIBUTIONS AND BENEFITS
(NORTHERN IRELAND) ACT—*continued.*

Section of 1992 Act	Derivation
(4)	1975 s. 7(5); 1991R art. 3(b)
(5)	1975 s. 7(6)
12	1975 s. 7A; 1984 art. 11(2); 1985SR reg. 4(2); 1989 Sch. 7 para. 2, Sch. 9
13(1)	1975 s. 8(1); 1976 art. 3(1); 1984 art. 12(1)(a); 1991R art. 4
(2)	1975 s. 8(2); 1975P Sch. 6
(3)	1975 s. 8(2)(a); 1975P Sch. 6
(4)	1975 s. 8(2A); 1984 art. 12(1)(b), (3)
(5) - (7)	1975 s. 8(2B) - (2D); 1984 art. 12(3); 1985SR reg. 4(3); 1989 Sch. 7 para. 3
14(1)	1975P art. 7(1); 1986 Sch. 8 para. 4
(2)	1975P art. 7(3)
(3)	1975P art. 7(2)
(4)	1975P art. 7(2); 1977 art. 3(6)
15(1), (2)	1975 s. 9(1); 1989 Sch. 7 para. 4(a), (b)
(3)	1975 s. 9(2); 1982SR art. 5(a); 1991R art. 5
(4)	ICTA 1988 Sch. 29 para. 14
(5)	1975 s. 9(1); 1989 Sch. 7 para. 4(c)
16	1975 s. 9(3)
17(1)	1975 s. 9(4)
(2)	1975 s. 9(5); 1975P Sch. 6
(3) - (6)	1975 s. 9(6)
18	1975 s. 10; 1982SR art. 5(a); 1991R art. 5
19(1) - (3)	1975 s. 11
(4) - (6)	1975P art. 5(2) - (4); 1986 Sch. 8 para. 3
20	1975 s. 12; 1975P Sch. 5 para. 19; 1980 art. 6(1)(i); 1984 Sch. 3 para. 1; 1986 art. 41, Sch. 9 para. 39, Sch. 10; 1989 Sch. 7 para. 5
21(1), (2)	1975 s. 13(1); 1980 art. 6(1)(ii); 1986 Sch. 9 para. 40, Sch. 10
(3)	1975 s. 13(6)
(4)	1975 s. 13(8); 1986 Sch. 9 para. 46(b)
(5)	1975 s. 13(6); 1986 Sch. 8 para. 1(6)
(6)	1975 s. 13(7)
22(1)	1975 s. 13(2); 1986 Sch. 8 para. 1(1)
(2)	1975 s. 13(2); 1975P Sch. 5 para. 20(a); 1980(2) Sch.; 1986 Sch. 9 para. 46(a)
(3)	1975 s. 13(5); 1986 Sch. 8 para. 1(4)(c); 1989 Sch. 7 para. 6
(4)	1975 s. 13(3); 1975P Sch. 5 para. 20(b); 1986 Sch. 8 para. 1(2)
(5)	1975 s. 13(4); 1980(2) Sch.; 1986 Sch. 8 para. 1(3)
(6)	1975 s. 13(5AA); 1989 art. 6(3)
(7)	1977 art. 18(25)
23(1)	1975 s. 13(5); 1979 Sch. 3 para. 4; 1986 Sch. 8 para. 1(4)(a); 1988 Sch. 2 para. 1(1)(a)
(2)	1975 s. 13(5ZA); 1988 Sch. 2 para. 1(1)(b)
(3)	1975 s. 13(5); 1989 art. 6(2)
(4)	1975 s. 13(5A); 1985 Sch. 5 para. 1(b); M1, M12
24(1)	1975 s. 13(5B); 1986 Sch. 8 para. 1(5)
(2)	1975 s. 13(5C); 1989 art. 6(4)
25(1)	1975 s. 14(1)
(2)	1975 s. 14(2); 1989 Sch. 1 para. 4(1)
(3)	1975 s. 14(3)
(4)	1975 s. 14(4); 1975P art. 20(1); 1982 Sch. 4 para. 5
(5), (6)	1975 s. 14(6); 1975P Sch. 5 para. 21(b); 1979 Sch. 3 para. 5; 1986 Sch. 9 para. 53; 1989 Sch. 9
(7)	1975 s. 14(8)

SOCIAL SECURITY CONTRIBUTIONS AND BENEFITS
(NORTHERN IRELAND) ACT—*continued.*

Section of 1992 Act	Derivation
26(1)	1975 s. 18(1)
(2) - (4)	1975 s. 18(2) - (2B); 1989 art. 13
(5)	1975 s. 18(3)
(6)	1975 s. 18(4); 1986 art. 44(1); 1989 Sch. 7 para. 7
27(1), (2)	1975 s. 19(1), (1A); 1986 art. 45(1)
(3)	1975 s. 19(2)
28(1)	1975 s. 20(1); 1986 art. 44(2)(a); Unemployment Benefit (Disqualification Period) Order (NI) 1988 (SR 1988 No. 83) art. 2; 1988E arts. 5(2), 6(a); 1989 art. 14(1)
(2)	1975 s. 20(1A); 1986 art. 44(3)(a); 1989 Sch. 9
(3)	1975 s. 20(3)
(4)	1975 s. 20(3A); 1985 art. 12
(5)	1975 s. 20(4); 1989 art. 14(3)
(6)	1975 s. 20(5); 1988E art. 5(3)
29	1975 s. 20A; 1989 art. 14(4)
30(1)	1980(2) art. 5(1); 1988 art. 8; 1989 art. 11(1)
(2)	1980(2) art. 5(1A); 1982 Sch. 4 para. 19
(3)	1980(2) art. 5(2); 1989 art. 11(1)
(4)	1980(2) art. 5(3)
31(1)	1975 s. 14(1)
(2)	1975 s. 14(2); 1989 Sch. 1 para. 4(1)
(3)	1975 s. 14(2A); 1982 art. 32(3)
(4)	1975 s. 14(3)
(5)	1975 s. 14(4); 1975P art. 20; 1982 Sch. 4 para. 5
(6), (7)	1975 s. 14(6); 1975P Sch. 5 para. 21(b); 1979 Sch. 3 para. 5; 1986 Sch. 9 para. 53; 1989 Sch. 9
(8)	1975 s. 14(8)
32(1), (2)	1975 s. 20(2), (3)
(3)	1975 s. 20(5)(c)
33(1)	1975 s. 15(1); 1989 Sch. 1 para. 5(1)
(2)	1975 s. 15(2); 1989 Sch. 1 para. 5(2)
(3)	1975 s. 15(3); 1975P art. 16, Sch. 5 para. 22(b); 1990 art. 6(1)
(4), (5)	1975 s. 15(4); 1975P Sch. 5 para. 22(c); 1979 Sch. 1 para. 1, Sch. 3 para. 6; 1986 Sch. 9 para. 53
(6)	1975 s. 15(5)
(7), (8)	1975 s. 15(5A), (5B); 1991D art. 11(1)
(9)	1975 s. 15(6); 1982 Sch. 4 para. 6
(10), (11)	1975 s. 15A(1), (2); 1985 art. 18(3)
34(1), (2)	1975 s. 16(1); 1985 art. 11(1)(a)
(3)	1975 s. 16(2); 1979 Sch. 1 para. 10
(4) - (6)	1975 s. 16(2B) - (2D); 1985 art. 11(1)(b); 1986 art. 19(1)(b)
(7)	1975 s. 16(3); 1985 art. 11(1)(c)
35(1) - (3)	1975 s. 22(1) - (3); 1986 Sch. 4 para. 13
(4)	1975 s. 22(4A); 1988 Sch. 4 para. 2(b)
(5) - (7)	1975 s. 22(5) - (7); 1986 Sch. 4 para. 13
36(1), (2)	1975 s. 24(1), (2); 1986 art. 37(1)
(3)	1975 s. 24(3); 1989 Sch. 7 para. 8
37(1)	1975 s. 25(1); 1975P Sch. 5 para. 23; 1975CB Sch. 4 para. 10(a); Human Fertilisation and Embryology Act 1990 (c. 37) Sch. 4 para. 3
(2)	1975 s. 25(2); 1975CB Sch. 4 para. 10(b)
(3), (4)	1975 s. 25(3), (4); 1989 Sch. 8 para. 4(1)
38(1)	1975 s. 26(1); 1975P Sch. 5 para. 24; 1986 art. 37(3)

SOCIAL SECURITY CONTRIBUTIONS AND BENEFITS
(NORTHERN IRELAND) ACT—*continued.*

Section of 1992 Act	Derivation
(2), (3)	1975 s. 26(3), (4); 1989 Sch. 8 para. 4(2)
(4)	1989 art. 8(1)
39(1)	1975P art. 15(1), (3)
(2)	1975P art. 15(2)
(3)	1986 art. 20(1)(c)
(4), (5)	1975 s. 26(2); 1986 art. 37(3)(b)
(6)	1989 art. 8(1)
40(1)	1975P art. 17(1); 1986 Sch. 9 para. 45(a)
(2)	1975P art. 17(1A); 1989 Sch. 7 para. 17
(3)	1975P art. 17(2); 1986 Sch. 9 para. 45(b)
(4)	1975P art. 17(3)
(5)	1975P art. 17(4); 1986 Sch. 9 para. 45(c); 1990 art. 6(2)
(6)	1977 art. 13(6)
(7)	1975P art. 17(5); 1977 art. 5(4); 1989 Sch. 1 para. 10(1)
(8)	1975P art. 17(6)
41(1)	1975P art. 18(1); 1979 Sch. 1 para. 18
(2), (3)	1975P art. 18(2), (3)
(4), (5)	1975P art. 18(4); 1990 art. 6(3)
(6)	1986 art. 20(1)(d)
(7)	1975P art. 18(5); 1977 art. 5(4); 1989 Sch. 1 para. 10(2)
(8)	1975P art. 18(6)
42	1975P art. 18A; 1991D art. 11(3)
43(1)	1975 s. 27(6)
(2)	1977 art. 5(1); 1979 Sch. 1 para. 8
(3) - (5)	1975P art. 27
44(1)	1975 s. 28(1); 1975P Sch. 5 para. 25; 1989 Sch. 8 para. 4(3)
(2)	1975 s. 28(1A); 1989 Sch. 8 para. 4(4)
(3), (4)	1975P art. 8(1); 1992U art. 4(2)
(5)	1975P art. 8(4); 1979 Sch. 3 para. 16
(6)	1975P art. 8(5); 1986 Sch. 8 para. 5(1)
(7)	1975P art. 8(6)
(8)	Transitional
45(1)	1975P art. 8(2); 1986 art. 19(2)
(2), (3)	1975P art. 8(2A); 1986 art. 19(3)
(4), (5)	1975P art. 8(2B); 1986 art. 19(3)
(6), (7)	1975P arts. 8(3), 70A; 1979 art. 14; 1986 art. 19(4)
(8)	Drafting
46(1)	1986 art. 19(6)
(2)	1986 art. 19(5)
47(1)	1975 s. 28(7); 1980(2) art. 3(3); 1985 art. 11(2)(a), (b)
(2) - (4)	1975 s. 28(7A) - (7C); 1985 art. 11(2)(c); 1986 art. 19(1)(b)
(5)	1975 s. 28(8)
(6)	1980(2) art. 3(4)
48(1)	1975P art. 22(1); 1979 Sch. 1 para. 5
(2)	1979 Sch. 1 para. 20
(3)	1975P art. 22(2)
49(1)	1975 s. 29(1)
(2), (3)	1975 s. 29(2), (3); 1989 art. 9(3)(a)
(4)	1975 s. 29(4)
(5)	1975 s. 29(5); 1989 art. 9(3)(b)

SOCIAL SECURITY CONTRIBUTIONS AND BENEFITS
(NORTHERN IRELAND) ACT—*continued.*

Section of 1992 Act	Derivation
(6)	1975 s. 29(6)
(7), (8)	1975 s. 29(9), (9A); 1989 Sch. 8 para. 4(5)
50(1)	1975 s. 29(7); 1975P Sch. 5 para. 26
(2)	1975 s. 29(8); 1985 art. 11(3)
(3), (4)	1975P art. 9
(5)	1986 art. 20(1)(a)
51(1)	1975P art. 10(1); 1979 Sch. 1 paras. 4, 14
(2)	1975P art. 10(2)
(3)	1986 art. 20(1)(b)
(4)	1975P art. 10(3); 1989 Sch. 1 para. 9(2)
52(1) - (3)	1975P art. 11(1) - (3); 1986 art. 19(1)
(4)	1979 Sch. 1 para. 15
53(1), (2)	1975P art. 12; 1986 art. 19(1)(a)
(3)	1979 Sch. 1 para. 16
54(1), (2)	1975 s. 30(3); 1989 Sch. 9
(3)	1975 s. 30(4); 1975P Sch. 5 para. 27
(4)	1975 s. 30(5); 1989 Sch. 1 para. 2(2)
55	1975P art. 14; 1989 art. 9(4)
56(1), (2)	1975 s. 31; 1975CB Sch. 4 para. 11; 1977 art. 18(2)
(3), (4)	1975 s. 43(1); 1975CB Sch. 4 para. 16(a)
(5)	1975 s. 43(2); 1975CB Sch. 4 para. 16(b); 1977 art. 18(3)
(6)	1986 art. 41
57(1)	1975 s. 17(1); 1980(2) art. 3(1); 1989 art. 12(2)
(2)	1975 s. 22(4); 1986 Sch. 4 para. 13; 1988 Sch. 4 para. 2(a)
(3)	1975 s. 17(2); 1989 art. 12(3); M2
(4)	1975 s. 17(2A); 1988 Sch. 4 para. 1
(5)	1975 s. 17(2B); 1989 art. 12(4)
(6), (7)	1975 s. 17(2C), (2D); 1989 Sch. 8 para. 3
(8)	1975 s. 17(3)
(9), (10)	1975 s. 17(4), (5); 1980(2) art. 3(4); 1981 art. 6
58(1)	1989 Sch. 8 para. 2(1)
(2)	1989 Sch. 8 para. 2(2); 1990 Sch. 6 para. 19(2)
(3)	1989 Sch. 8 para. 2(3)
(4)	1989 Sch. 8 para. 2(6); 1990 Sch. 6 para. 19(3)
(5)	1989 Sch. 8 para. 2(7)
59(1), (2)	1975 s. 20(2), (3)
(3)	1975 s. 20(5)(c)
60(1)	1975 s. 33(1), (2)
(2), (3)	1986 Sch. 3 para. 10; 1988 Sch. 1 para. 5
(4) - (6)	1975 s. 33(3); 1975P Sch. 5 para. 28; 1990 Sch. 6 para. 1(1)
(7)	1975 s. 33(4); 1975P art. 21(5); 1986 art. 19(1)
(8)	1986 Sch. 3 para. 10; 1988 Sch. 1 para. 5
61(1)	1977 art. 7(1); 1986 art. 19(1)(a); 1990 Sch. 6 para. 1(3)
(2)	1977 art. 7(2); 1986 art. 19(1)(a); 1990 Sch. 6 para. 1(4)
62	1975P art. 26
63	1975 s. 34; 1975P Sch. 5 para. 29; 1984 Sch. 2 para. 2; 1990 art. 4(3); 1991D art. 3(1), Sch. 4
64	1975 s. 35(1); 1988 art. 3; 1991D art. 4(1)
65(1)	1975 s. 35(2); 1979 art. 3(2); 1989 Sch. 8 para. 5(2)
(2)	1975 s. 35(2A); 1979 art. 3(3)
(3)	1975 s. 35(3); 1991D Sch. 2 para. 2(2)

SOCIAL SECURITY CONTRIBUTIONS AND BENEFITS
(NORTHERN IRELAND) ACT—*continued.*

Section of 1992 Act	Derivation
(4)	1975 s. 35(4); 1989 Sch. 8 para. 5(3)(a); 1991D Sch. 2 para.2(3)
(5)	1975 s. 35(4A); 1980 Sch. 1 para. 8; 1989 Sch. 8 para. 5(4); 1991D Sch. 2 para. 2(3)
(6)	1975 s. 35(4); 1979 art. 3(5); 1989 Sch. 8 para. 5(3)(b); 1990 art. 3(2); 1991D Sch. 4
66	1975 s. 35(2B), (2C); 1990 art. 3(1); 1991D Sch. 2 para. 2(1)
67(1)	1975 s. 35(5A); 1979 art. 3(6)
(2)	1975 s. 35(6)
68(1) - (4)	1975 s. 36(1) - (4); 1984 art. 5(1)
(5)	1975 s. 36(4A); 1985 Sch. 4 para. 2
(6), (7)	1975 s. 36(5), (6); 1984 art. 5(1)
(8), (9)	1975 s. 36(6A), (6B); 1989 Sch. 8 para. 6
(10)	1975 s. 36(6C); 1991D art. 11(2)
(11)	1975 s. 36(7); 1984 art. 5(1); 1989 Sch. 8 para. 2(5); 1990 Sch. 6 para. 19(4)
(12)	1989 Sch. 8 para. 2(4)
(13)	1975 s. 36(8); 1984 art. 5(1); 1989 Sch. 8 para. 2(6) (part), (7)
69	1975 s. 36A; 1990 art. 4(1)
70(1)	1975 s. 37(1)
(2)	1975 s. 37(2); 1991D Sch. 2 para. 3
(3) - (5)	1975 s. 37(3) - (5)
(6)	1975 s. 37(6)
(7) - (9)	1975 s. 37(7) - (9)
(10)	1975 s. 37(6)
71	1975 s. 37ZA; 1991D art. 3(2)
72	1975 s. 37ZB; 1991D art. 3(2)
73	1975 s. 37ZC; 1991D art. 3(2)
74(1)	1977 art. 10(1); 1991D Sch. 2 para. 7
(2)	1977 art. 10(3)
75	1975 s. 37ZD; 1991D art. 3(2)
76	1975 s. 37ZE; 1991D art. 3(2)
77(1)	1975 s. 38(1); 1975CB Sch. 4 para. 13(a)
(2), (3)	1975 s. 38(2), (3)
(4), (5)	1975 s. 43(1); 1975CB Sch. 4 para. 16(a)
(6)	1975 s. 43(2); 1975CB Sch. 4 para. 16(b); 1977 art. 18(3)
(7)	1975 s. 38(1)
(8)	1975 s. 38(4)
(9)	1975 s. 38(5); 1975CB Sch. 4 para. 13(c)
(10)	1975 s. 38(6); 1986 art. 46(a)
(11)	1975 s. 38(7); 1986 art. 46(b)
78(1), (2)	1975 s. 39(1)(a), (b)
(3), (4)	1975 s. 39(1)(c); 1979 Sch. 1 para. 2; 1986 art. 19(1)(b)
(5)	1975 s. 39(2)
(6)	1975 s. 39(2A); 1985 art. 14(1)(b)
(7), (8)	1975 s. 39(3), (3A); 1989 Sch. 8 para. 4(6)
(9)	1975 s. 39(4)
79	1975 s. 40
80(1)	1975 s. 41(1); 1975CB Sch. 4 para. 14(a)
(2)	1975 s. 41(2); 1984 Sch. 3 para. 2(a)
(3)	1975 s. 41(2A); 1984 Sch. 3 para. 2(c)
(4)	1975 s. 41(2B); 1984 Sch. 3 para. 2(c); 1992U art. 11
(5), (6)	1975 s. 41(4), (5); 1975CB Sch. 4 para. 14(b), (c)

SOCIAL SECURITY CONTRIBUTIONS AND BENEFITS
(NORTHERN IRELAND) ACT—*continued.*

Section of 1992 Act	Derivation
(7)	1975 s. 41(2D); 1984 Sch. 3 para. 2(c)
81(1), (2)	1975 s. 43(1); 1975CB Sch. 4 para. 16
(3)	1975 s. 43(2); 1975CB Sch. 4 para. 16(b); 1977 art. 18(3)
82(1)	1975 s. 44(1); 1975CB Sch. 4 para. 17(a); 1980 Sch. 1 para. 5(2); 1988 Sch. 4 para. 3(a)
(2)	1975 s. 44(2); 1975CB Sch. 4 para. 17(a); 1980 Sch. 1 para. 5(2)
(3)	1975 s. 44(3)(a); 1988 Sch. 4 para. 3(b)
(4)	1975 s. 44(3)(c); 1975CB Sch. 4 para. 17(b); 1980 Sch. 1 para. 4
(5)	1975 s. 44(4)
83(1)	1975 s. 45(1)
(2)	1975 s. 45(2); 1975CB Sch. 4 para. 18; 1988 Sch. 4 para. 4(a)
(3)	1975 s. 45(2A); 1985 art. 15(1)
84(1)	1975 s. 45A(1); 1984 art. 6; 1985 art. 15(2)(a)
(2)	1975 s. 45A(2); 1985 art. 15(2)(b); 1988 Sch. 4 para. 5(a)
(3)	1975 s. 45A(3); 1985 art. 15(2)(b)
85(1)	1975 s. 46(1)
(2)	1975 s. 46(2); 1975CB Sch. 4 para. 19; 1980 Sch. 1 para. 4(b)
(3)	1975 s. 46(3)
(4)	1975 s. 46(4); 1985 art. 15(3)
86(1)	1975 s. 47(1); 1975CB Sch. 4 para. 20; 1980 Sch. 1 para. 5(2); 1989 Sch. 8 para. 7(1)
(2)	1975 s. 47(1A); 1985 art. 15(4)(b)
87(1)	1975 s. 47A; 1980 Sch. 1 para. 5; 1990 Sch. 6 para. 1(2)
(2)	1975 s. 47A; 1990 Sch. 6 para. 1(2)
88	1975 s. 48(1)
89	1975 s. 47B; 1984 art. 8(a); 1989 art. 11(3)
90	1975 s. 49; 1984 Sch. 2 para. 2
91	1975 s. 49A; 1986 art. 45(2)
92	1975 s. 84A; 1989 Sch. 8 para. 7(2)
93	1991D art. 11(5)
94(1)	1975 s. 50(1); 1986 Sch. 3 para. 2
(2)	1975 s. 50(1A); 1988 Sch. 4 para. 8
(3)	1975 s. 50(3)
(4)	1975 s. 50(4); 1982 Sch. 4 para. 8(2)
(5)	1975 s. 50(5)
(6)	1975 s. 50(6); 1982 Sch. 4 para. 8(3)
(7)	1986 Sch. 10
95(1) - (3)	1975 s. 51
(4), (5)	1977 art. 13(3)
96	1975 s. 148
97	1975 s. 147
98 - 101	1975 ss. 52 - 55
102(1), (2)	1975 s. 50A(1), (2); 1982 art. 32(4)
(3)	1975 s. 50A(3); 1982 art. 32(4); 1989 Sch. 1 para. 8(1)
103(1)	1975 s. 57(1); 1986 Sch. 3 para. 3(1)
(2) - (4)	1975 s. 57(1A) - (1C); 1986 Sch. 3 para. 3(2)
(5)	1975 s. 57(3)
(6)	1975 s. 57(4); 1982 art. 32(2); 1989 Sch. 7 para. 11
(7), (8)	1975 s. 57(6); 1986 Sch. 3 para. 3(4)
104(1), (2)	1975 s. 61(1), (2)
(3), (4)	1975 s. 61(3), (4); 1986 Sch. 3 para. 6

SOCIAL SECURITY CONTRIBUTIONS AND BENEFITS
(NORTHERN IRELAND) ACT—*continued.*

Section of 1992 Act	Derivation
105	1975 s. 63
106	Drafting
107	1975 s. 91; 1982 Sch. 4 para. 11, Sch. 5; M4
108(1) - (4)	1975 s. 76(1) - (4)
(5)	1975 s. 76(4A); 1990 Sch. 6 para. 2(1)
(6)	1975 s. 76(5)
109(1), (2)	1975 s. 77(1), (2); 1990 art. 5(7), Sch. 6 para. 2(2)
(3)	1975 s. 77(3)
(4) - (6)	1975 s. 77(4); 1986 Sch. 3 para. 13
(7)	1975 s. 77(5); 1986 Sch. 3 para. 13
110	1975 s. 78
111	Drafting
112(1), (2)	1977 art. 14(1); 1977SB Sch. 7; 1986 Sch. 10
(3)	1977 art. 14(2); 1986 Sch. 9 para. 49, Sch. 10
113(1), (2)	1975 s. 82(5), (6)
(3)	1975 s. 83; 1985 Sch. 5 para. 3
114(1), (2)	1975 s. 84(1), (2)
(3)	1975 s. 84(4); 1985 art. 15(6)
(4)	1975 s. 84(5); 1985 art. 15(8); 1986 Sch. 3 paras. 4, 15
115(1), (2)	1975 s. 122(1), (2)
(3)	1975 s. 122(2)
(4)	Drafting
116	1975 s. 123
117 - 119	1975 ss. 124 - 126
120	1975 s. 152
121	1975 Sch. 17; 1975P Sch. 5 para. 44; 1975CB Sch. 4 para. 37; 1977 art. 18(1); 1980 Sch. 1 para. 7; 1984 Sch. 2 para. 9; 1985 Sch. 5 para. 6; 1986 Sch. 10; 1989 arts. 3(3), 11(2), 14(5), Sch. 1 para. 3(11); 1990 Sch. 6 para. 9; 1991D art. 11(4); drafting
122(1), (2)	1986 art. 21(1), (2); 1991D art. 8(2), (3)
(3)	1986 art. 32(4)
123(1)	1986 art. 21(3); 1988 art. 6(1); 1989 art. 15(1)
(2)	1986 art. 21(4N); 1988 art. 6(2)
(3)	1986 art. 21(4)
(4)	1986 art. 22(1); 1988 Sch. 4 para. 16(1)
(5), (6)	1986 art. 22(1A), (1B); 1988 Sch. 4 para. 16(2)
124(1) - (4)	1986 art. 21(4A) - (4D); 1988 art. 6(2)
(5)	1986 art. 21(4N); 1988 art. 6(2)
125(1) - (4)	1986 art. 24(1) - (4)
(5)	1986 art. 24(5); ICTA 1988 Sch. 29 para. 32
(6)	1986 art. 24(5A); 1988 Sch. 4 para. 17(1)
(7)	1986 art. 24(6); 1990 Sch. 6 para. 12(2); 1992U art. 15
(8)	1986 art. 24(7); 1990 Sch. 6 para. 12(3)
126	1986 art. 24A; 1988 Sch. 4 para. 18; 1989 Sch. 8 para. 15
127(1)	1986 art. 21(5), (5A); 1988 art. 5(1); 1991D art. 10(1)
(2)	1986 art. 22(2), (3)
(3)	1986 art. 21(6); 1989 Sch. 8 para. 14
(4)	1986 art. 21(10); 1991D art.10(2)
(5)	1986 art. 22(6)(a)
(6)	1986 art. 79(3)
128(1)	1986 art. 21(6A), (6D); 1991D art. 8(4)

SOCIAL SECURITY CONTRIBUTIONS AND BENEFITS
(NORTHERN IRELAND) ACT—*continued.*

Section of 1992 Act	Derivation
(2), (3)	1986 art. 21(6B), (6C); 1991D art. 8(4)
(4)	1986 art. 21(6E); 1991D art. 8(4)
(5)	1986 art. 22(3A), (3B); 1991D art. 8(8)
(6)	1986 art. 21(6F); 1991D art. 8(4)
(7)	1986 art. 28B(4); 1991D art. 9(1)
(8)	1986 art. 22(6); 1991D art. 8(9)
(9)	1986 art. 79(3); 1991D Sch. 3 para. 6
129(1), (2)	1986 art. 21(7), (8)
(3)	1986 art. 22(4), (5)
(4)	1986 art. 22(6)(b)
130(1)	1986 art. 23(6)
(2)	1986 art. 21(9)
(3)	1986 art. 22(7)
131(1), (2)	1986 art. 23(1), (2)
(3), (4)	1986 art. 23(2A), (2B); 1990 art. 11
(5), (6)	1986 art. 23(3), (4)
132(1)	1986 art. 23(5)
(2), (3)	1986 art. 23(7), (8)
(4)	1986 art. 23(9)
133(1)	1986 arts. 2(2), 21(11), 29(1)(b); 1991D art. 8(6); drafting
(2)	1986 art. 21(12); 1989 art. 15(2); 1991D art. 8(7)
134(1)	1986 art. 33(2); 1987 art. 3
(2)	1986 art. 33(2A); 1988 Sch. 3 para. 1
(3)	1986 art. 34(1A); 1988 Sch. 3 para. 8
(4)	1986 art. 2(2)
135(1) - (3)	1986 art. 34(2) - (4)
(4)	1986 art. 34(4A); 1988 Sch. 3 para. 9
(5)	1986 art. 34(11)
136(1)	1986 art. 34(9); 1988 Sch. 3 para. 10
(2)	1986 art. 34(10)
(3)	1986 art. 34(10ZA); 1990 art. 12(3)
(4)	1986 art. 34(10A); 1988 Sch. 3 para. 11; 1990 art. 12(4)
(5)	1986 art. 33(11); 1988 Sch. 3 para. 6
137	1975CB art. 3(1)
138(1)	1975CB art. 4(1); 1986 art. 71(1)(a); 1988 art. 6(3)
(2), (3)	1975CB art. 4(1A), (1B); 1986 art. 71(1)(b)
(4), (5)	1975CB art. 4(2), (3)
139	1975CB art. 5
140(1), (2)	1975CB art. 6(1); 1988 art. 6(4)
(3)	1975CB art. 6(2)
141(1) - (4)	1975CB art. 7(1) - (4)
(5)	1975CB art. 24(1)(a)
142	1975CB art. 15
143(1)	1975CB art. 2(2)
(2) - (4)	1975CB art. 2(3) - (5)
(5)	1975CB art. 11
(6)	1975CB art. 2(6)
144	1986 Sch. 6 para. 2
145	1986 Sch. 6 para. 3
146(1)	1986 Sch. 6 para. 1(1)

SOCIAL SECURITY CONTRIBUTIONS AND BENEFITS
(NORTHERN IRELAND) ACT—*continued.*

Section of 1992 Act	Derivation
(2)	1986 art. 2(2), Sch. 6 para. 1(2); ICTA 1988 Sch. 29 para. 32; 1991D Sch.2 para. 12
(3)	1986 Sch. 6 para. 1(2)
(4)	1986 Sch. 6 para. 1(3)
147(1), (2)	1982 art. 3(1), (2)
(3)	1982 art. 25A(1); 1984 Sch. 5 para. 8
(4), (5)	1982 art. 3(3), (4)
(6)	1982 art. 3(5); 1986 art. 69
148(1), (2)	1982 art. 4(1), (2)
(3)	1982 art. 4(3); Statutory Sick Pay (General) (Amendment) Regulations (NI) 1986 (SR 1986 No. 83) reg. 2(1)
(4)	1982 art. 4(3A); 1985 art. 18(4)
(5), (6)	1982 art. 4(4), (5)
149(1) - (4)	1982 art. 5(1) - (4)
(5)	1982 art. 5(4A); 1985 art. 18(5)
(6), (7)	1982 art. 5(5), (6)
(8), (9)	1982 art. 5(6A), (6B); 1985 Sch. 4 para. 4
(10), (11)	1982 art. 5(7), (8)
(12)	1982 art. 5(9); 1986 Sch. 9 para. 50
150(1)	1982 art. 6(1)
(2)	1982 art. 6(2); 1984 Sch. 5 para. 7
(3), (4)	1982 art. 6(3), (4)
151(1) - (3)	1982 art. 7(1) - (3)
(4)	1982 art. 7(4); 1985 art. 18(1)
(5)	1982 art. 7(5)
152	1982 art. 8
153(1)	1982 art. 9(1); Statutory Sick Pay (Rate of Payment) Order (NI) 1992 (SR 1992 No. 27) art. 2
(2)	1982 art. 9(1A); 1986 art. 68(1); 1990 Sch. 6 para. 11(1)
(3)	1982 art. 9(2)
154(1)	1982 art. 11(1); 1991SP art. 3(1)
(2)	1982 art. 11(1B); 1991SP art. 4(1)
(3)	1982 art. 11(1D); 1991SP art. 4(1)
(4)	1982 art. 11(2); 1985 art. 19(1)(b); 1991SP art. 4(2)
(5)	1982 art. 11(3)(b), (c); 1991SP art. 3(3)
(6)	1982 art. 11(6)
(7)	1991SP art. 4(5)
155	1982 art. 11(1C); 1991SP art. 4(1)
156	Drafting
157	1982 art. 29(1) - (3); 1989 Sch. 7 para. 20
158	1982 art. 24; M9
159(1)	1982 art. 28(1); 1985 Sch. 4 para. 6
(2)	1982 art. 28(2); 1985 Sch. 4 para. 7
(3) - (5)	1982 art. 28(3) - (5)
(6)	1982 art. 28(5A); Health and Personal Social Services (NI) Order 1991 (NI 1) Sch. 5 Part II
(7)	1982 art. 28(6)
160(1) - (6)	1986 art. 47(1) - (6)
(7)	1982 art. 25A(1); 1984 Sch. 5 para. 8; 1986 art. 47(6)
(8)	1986 art. 47(7)
(9)	1986 art. 47(8); 1988 Sch. 4 para. 12(1)

SOCIAL SECURITY CONTRIBUTIONS AND BENEFITS
(NORTHERN IRELAND) ACT—*continued.*

Section of 1992 Act	Derivation
(10)	1986 art. 47(9); 1988 Sch. 4 para. 12(2)
161	1986 art. 48; 1989 Sch. 7 para. 22
162(1)	1986 art. 49(1)
(2)	1986 art. 49(2); 1988 Sch. 4 para. 13
(3) - (8)	1986 art. 49(3) - (8)
163(1)	1986 Sch. 4 para. 1
(2)	M11
(3)	1986 Sch. 4 para. 2
(4)	1986 Sch. 4 para. 5
164	Drafting
165	1986 art. 79(4)
166	1986 art. 80; M9
167(1), (2)	1986 arts. 2(1), 51(1), (2); 1988 Sch. 5; 1989 Sch. 9
(3)	1986 art. 51(2A); Health and Personal Social Services (NI) Order 1991 (NI 1) Sch. 5 Part II
(4) - (6)	1986 art. 51(3) - (5)
168	1982 arts. 28(7), 35(1)(b), (d), (2)(a), (b); 1986 art. 2(4)
169	1975 Sch. 17
170	Drafting
171(1)	1975 Sch. 17; 1986 Sch. 5 para. 17
(2)	1975 s. 155(1); Statutory Rules (NI) Order 1979 (NI 12) Sch. 4 para. 16; 1988 art. 15A; 1990 Sch. 6 para. 6(9)
(3)	1975 s. 155(2); 1977A Sch. 2
(4)	1975 s. 155(3); 1977A Sch. 2; 1989 Sch. 8 para. 9
(5)	1975 s. 155(3A); 1975CB art. 24(5A); 1986 art. 63(1), (2)
(6)	1986 art. 81(2)
(7)	1975 s. 155(5); 1986 Sch. 10; 1991RF Sch. 2
(8)	1975 s. 155(6)
(9)	1975 s. 155(7); 1977A Sch. 2
(10)	1975 s. 155(8); 1982 art. 29(4); 1986 Sch. 9 para. 70; 1989 Sch. 7 para. 20
(11)	1975 s. 155(4A); 1992CP Sch. 2 para. 11
(12)	1975 s. 157(4); 1977A Sch. 2
172(1)	1975 s. 156(1)
(2)	1975 s. 156(2); 1975P Sch. 6; 1979 art. 5(2); 1981C art. 6(1); 1986 arts. 44(3)(b), 63(3), Sch. 9 para. 41, Sch. 10; 1989 Sch. 9; 1991RF Sch. 2; M3
(3)	1975 s. 156(3); 1990 Sch. 6 para. 6(1)
(4)	1975 s. 156(4)
(5)	1975 s. 156(5)
(6)	1990 Sch. 6 para. 6(12), (17)
(7)	1990 Sch. 6 para. 6(13)
(8)	1975 s. 156(6)
(9)	1975 s. 155A; 1992CP Sch. 2 para. 12
(10)	1990 Sch. 6 para. 6(14), (17)
(11)	1990 Sch. 6 para. 6(15)
(12)	1975 s. 156(4); 1990 Sch. 6 para. 6(12); drafting
173(1)	Short title, etc.
(2)	Commencement
(3), (4)	1975 s. 158(2), (2A); 1992CP Sch. 2 para. 12
Sch. 1	
para. 1(1)	1975 Sch. 1 para. 1(1); 1977 art. 3(4)
(2)	1975 Sch. 1 para. 1(1A); 1980 Sch. 1 para. 15; 1985 Sch. 5 para. 5(a)

SOCIAL SECURITY CONTRIBUTIONS AND BENEFITS
(NORTHERN IRELAND) ACT—*continued.*

Section of 1992 Act	Derivation
(3), (4)	1975 Sch. 1 para. 1(1B), (1C); 1985 Sch. 5 para. 5(b)
(5)	1986 art. 75(3)
(6)	1975 Sch. 1 para. 1(1D); 1985 Sch. 5 para. 5(b)
(7), (8)	1975 Sch. 1 para. 1(2), (3)
para. 2	1975 Sch. 1 para. 2
para. 3	1975 Sch. 1 para. 3
para. 4	1975 Sch. 1 para. 4; 1977 art. 3(5)
para. 5	1975 Sch. 1 para. 4A; 1991C art. 4(2)
para. 6(1)	1975 Sch. 1 para. 5(1); 1991C art. 4(3)(a)
(2) - (4)	1975 Sch. 1 para. 5(1A) - (1C); 1990 art. 19(3); 1991C art. 4(3)(b)
(5)	1982 art. 11(4); 1986 Sch. 4 para. 3
(6)	1982 art. 11(5); 1986 Sch. 4 para. 4
(7)	1975 Sch. 1 para. 5(2)
(8)	1975 Sch. 1 para. 5(3); 1990 art. 19(4)
para. 7	1975 Sch. 1 para. 5A; 1990 Sch. 5; 1991C art. 4(4)
para. 8	1975 Sch. 1 para. 6; 1975P Sch. 5 para. 41; 1986 Sch. 9 para. 1; 1989 art. 4; 1990 Sch. 6 para. 7; 1991C art. 4(5)
paras. 9, 10	1975 Sch. 1 paras. 7, 8; 1982 art. 30(2)
Sch. 2	
paras. 1 - 3	1975 Sch. 2 paras. 1-3; ICTA 1988 Sch. 29 para. 32; Finance Act 1988 (c. 39) Sch. 3 para. 31; Capital Allowances Act 1990 (c. 1) Sch. 1 para. 2
paras. 4, 5	1975 Sch. 2 paras. 5, 6; ICTA 1988 Sch. 29 para. 32
para. 6	1975 Sch. 2 para. 7; ICTA 1988 Sch. 29 para. 32; Social Security Act 1990 (c. 27) s. 17(8), (9)
paras. 7, 8	1975 Sch. 2 paras. 8, 9
para. 9	1975 Sch. 2 para. 4; ICTA 1988 Sch. 29 para. 32; Finance Act 1988 (c. 39) Sch. 14 Part VIII and Note 6
Sch. 3	
para. 1(1)	1975 Sch. 3 para. 1(1)
(2)	1975 Sch. 3 para. 1(2); 1986 Sch. 8 para. 2(1); 1988 art. 7(2)(a)
(3)	1975 Sch. 3 para. 1(3); 1986 Sch. 8 para. 2(2), (3); 1988 art. 7(2)(b)
(4)	1975 Sch. 3 para. 1(2)(b); 1986 Sch. 8 para. 2(1)
(5)	1975 Sch. 3 para. 1(3)(b); 1986 Sch. 8 para. 2(3)
(6)	1975 Sch. 3 para. 1(4)
para. 2(1)	1975 Sch. 3 para. 1(1)
(2)	1975 Sch. 3 para. 1(2); 1986 Sch. 8 para. 2(1); 1988 art. 7(2)(a)
(3)	1975 Sch. 3 para. 1(3); 1986 Sch. 8 para. 2(2), (3); 1988 art. 7(2)(b)
(4)	1975 Sch. 3 para. 1(2)(b); 1986 Sch. 8 para. 2(1)
(5)	1975 Sch. 3 para. 1(3)(b); 1986 Sch. 8 para. 2(3)
(6)	1975 Sch. 3 para. 1(4)
para. 3	1975 Sch. 3 para. 3; 1986 Sch. 4 para. 14; 1990 Sch. 6 para. 8
para. 4(1)	1975 Sch. 3 para. 4(1); 1986 Sch. 9 para. 42(a)
(2)	1975 Sch. 3 para. 4(1)(b); 1986 Sch. 8 para. 2(4)
(3)	1975 Sch. 3 para. 4(2)
para. 5(1)	1975 Sch. 3 para. 5(1)
(2)	1975 Sch. 3 para. 5(2); 1975P art. 21(2); 1986 Sch. 8 para. 2(5)
(3), (4)	1975 Sch. 3 para. 5(3); 1986 Sch. 8 para. 2(6)
(5), (6)	1975 Sch. 3 para. 5(4), (5)
(7)	1975 Sch. 3 para. 5(6); 1979 Sch. 1 para. 3
(8)	1975 s. 27(2)
para. 6	1975 Sch. 3 para. 6

SOCIAL SECURITY CONTRIBUTIONS AND BENEFITS
(NORTHERN IRELAND) ACT—*continued.*

Section of 1992 Act	Derivation
para. 7(1)	1975 Sch. 3 para. 8(1); 1989 Sch. 7 para. 14
(2)	1975 Sch. 3 para. 8(2); 1986 Sch. 9 para. 42(b)
(3), (4)	1975 Sch. 3 para. 8(3); 1979 Sch. 3 para. 10; 1986 Sch. 8 para. 2(7), Sch. 9 para. 42(b)
para. 8	1975 Sch. 3 para. 10
para. 9	1975 Sch. 3 para. 13; 1986 Sch. 9 para. 42(c)
Sch. 4	
Part I	
para. 1	1975 Sch. 4 Part I para. 1(a); 1992U Sch. 1
para. 2	1975 Sch. 4 Part I para. 1(b); 1992U Sch. 1
para. 3	1975 Sch. 4 Part I para. 3; 1992U Sch. 1
para. 4	1975 Sch. 4 Part I para. 4; 1992U Sch. 1
para. 5	1975 Sch. 4 Part I para. 9; 1975P Sch. 5 para. 42; 1992U Sch. 1
para. 6	1975 Sch. 4 Part I para. 10; 1992U Sch. 1
Part II	1975 Sch. 4 Part IA; 1986 art. 37(2)
Part III	
para. 1	1975 Sch. 4 Part III para. 1; 1992U Sch. 1
para. 2	1975 Sch. 4 Part III para. 2; 1984 Sch. 2 para. 2; 1992U Sch. 1
para. 3	1975 Sch. 4 Part III para. 2A; 1990 art. 4(2); 1992U Sch. 1
para. 4	1975 Sch. 4 Part III para. 3; 1992U Sch. 1
para. 5	1975 Sch. 4 Part III para. 4; 1992U Sch. 1
para. 6	1975 Sch. 4 Part III para. 5; 1992U Sch. 1
para. 7	1975 Sch. 4 Part III para. 5A; 1985 art. 14(2)
para. 8	1975 Sch. 4 Part III para. 6
Part IV	
col. (1)	1975 Sch. 4 Part IV col. (1); 1984 Sch. 2 para. 2; 1986 Sch. 10
col. (2)	1975 Sch. 4 Part IV col. (2); 1975CB Sch. 4 para. 35(a); 1986 Sch. 10; 1992U Sch. 1
col. (3)	1975 Sch. 4 Part IV col. (4); 1975CB Sch. 4 para. 35(b), (c); 1992U Sch. 1
Part V	
para. 1	1975 Sch. 4 Part V para. 3; 1992U Sch. 1
para. 2	1975 Sch. 4 Part V para. 7; 1992U Sch. 1
para. 3	1975 Sch. 4 Part V para. 8; 1992U Sch. 1
para. 4	1975 Sch. 4 Part V para. 16; 1992U Sch. 1
para. 5	1975 Sch. 4 Part V para. 4; 1986 Sch. 3 paras. 4, 15; 1992U Sch. 1
para. 6	1975 Sch. 4 Part V para. 5; 1979 Sch. 1 para. 13; 1986 Sch. 3 paras. 4, 15; 1992U Sch. 1
para. 7	1975 Sch. 4 Part V para. 10; 1986 Sch. 3 paras. 4, 15; 1992U Sch. 1
para. 8	1975 Sch. 4 Part V para. 12; 1986 Sch. 3 paras. 4, 15; 1992U Sch. 1
para. 9	1975 Sch. 4 Part V para. 2; 1986 Sch. 3 para. 3(3); 1992U Sch. 1
para. 10	1975 Sch. 4 Part V para. 13; 1986 Sch. 3 para. 8; 1988 Sch. 1 para. 2; 1992U Sch. 1
para. 11	1975 Sch. 4 Part V para. 14; 1986 Sch. 3 para. 11; 1988 Sch. 1 para. 1; 1992U Sch. 1
para. 12	1975 Sch. 4 Part V para. 15; 1986 Sch. 3 para. 8; 1988 Sch. 1 para. 2; 1992U Sch. 1
Sch. 5	
para. 1	1975P Sch. 1 para. 1; 1989 Sch. 1 para. 3(1)
para. 2(1)	1975P Sch. 1 para. 2(1); 1989 Sch. 1 para. 3(2)
(2)	1975P Sch. 1 para. 2(2); 1989 Sch. 1 para. 3(3)
(3)	1975P Sch. 1 para. 2(3); 1977 art. 4(1)(b); 1989 Sch. 1 para. 3(4)

SOCIAL SECURITY CONTRIBUTIONS AND BENEFITS
(NORTHERN IRELAND) ACT—*continued.*

Section of 1992 Act	Derivation
(4)	1975P art. 70A; 1979 art. 14
(5)	1975P Sch. 1 para. 2(4); 1977 art. 4(1)(c); 1980 art. 4(10)
(6)	1975P Sch. 1 para. 2(4A); 1985 art. 11(5)
(7)	1975P Sch. 1 para. 2(5); 1986 Sch. 9 para. 59(a); 1989 Sch. 1 para. 3(5)
(8)	1975P Sch. 1 para. 2(6); 1977 art. 4(1)(d); 1989 Sch. 1 para. 3(6)
para. 3	1975 Sch. 1 para. 3; 1977 art. 4(1)(e); 1989 Sch. 1 para. 3(7)
para. 4(1)	1975P Sch. 1 para. 4(1); 1979 Sch. 3 para. 22; 1986 art. 20(2); 1989 Sch. 1 para. 3(8)
(2)	1975P Sch. 1 para. 4(2); 1979 Sch. 3 para. 22; 1986 art. 20(2); 1989 Sch. 1 para. 3(8)
(3)	1975P Sch. 1 para. 4(2A); 1986 art. 20(2)
(4)	1975P Sch. 1 para. 4(3); 1979 Sch. 1 para. 6; 1986 Sch. 9 para. 59(a)
(5)	1975P Sch. 1 para. 4(4); 1979 Sch. 1 para. 22
para. 5(1), (2)	1975P Sch. 1 para. 4A(1); 1979 Sch. 1 para. 7; 1986 art. 20(3)
(3)	1975P Sch. 1 para. 4A(1A); 1986 art. 20(4)
para. 6(1), (2)	1975P Sch. 1 para. 4A(2); 1979 Sch. 1 para. 7; 1986 art. 20(5)
(3)	1975P Sch. 1 para. 4A(2A)(a); 1986 art. 20(6)
(4)	1975P Sch. 1 para. 4A(2A)(b); 1986 art. 20(6)
para. 7(1)	1975P Sch. 1 para. 4A(3); 1979 Sch. 1 para. 7; 1986 Sch. 9 para. 59(b)
(2)	1975P art. 70A; 1979 art. 14
para. 8(1), (2)	1975P Sch. 1 para. 5(1), (2); 1989 Sch. 1 para. 3(9)
(3)	1975P Sch. 1 para. 5(3); 1989 Sch. 1 para. 3(10)
(4)	1975P Sch. 1 para. 5(4)
para. 9	Drafting
Sch. 6	
para. 1	1975 Sch. 8 para. 1; 1984 Sch. 2 para. 8(a)
paras. 2, 3	1975 Sch. 8 paras. 2, 3
para. 4	1975 Sch. 8 para. 4A; 1984 Sch. 2 para. 8(b)
para. 5	1975 Sch. 8 para. 5A; 1984 Sch. 2 para. 8(c)
para. 6(1)	1975 Sch. 8 para. 4(1); 1982 Sch. 4 para. 12
(2)	1975 Sch. 8 para. 4(1) proviso
(3) - (5)	1975 Sch. 8 para. 4(2) - (4); 1989 Sch. 3 para. 13(1)
para. 7	1975 Sch. 8 para. 5; 1989 Sch. 3 para. 13(2)
para. 8	1975 Sch. 8 para. 6
Sch. 7	
para. 1	1986 Sch. 3 para. 4
para. 2	1975 s. 58
para. 3(1)	1975 s. 59(1); 1985 art. 11(4)(a)
(2) - (4)	1975 s. 59(1A) - (1C); 1985 art. 11(4)(b)
(5) - (7)	1975 s. 59(2) - (4)
(8)	1975 s. 59(4); 1980(2) art. 3(3)
(9)	1980(2) art. 3(4)
(10)	1975 s. 59(5)
(11)	Drafting
para. 4(1)	1975 s. 64(1); 1975CB Sch. 4 para. 22(a); 1986 Sch. 3 para. 4
(2)	1975 s. 64(2)
(3)	1975 s. 64(1A); 1984 Sch. 3 para. 3
(4)	1975 s. 64(1B); 1984 Sch. 3 para. 3; Social Security (Industrial Injuries) (Dependency) (Permitted Earnings Limits) Order (NI) 1991 (SR 1991 No. 72) art. 2
(5), (6)	1975 s. 64(1C), (1D); 1984 Sch. 3 para. 3

SOCIAL SECURITY CONTRIBUTIONS AND BENEFITS
(NORTHERN IRELAND) ACT—*continued.*

Section of 1992 Act	Derivation
para. 5(1)	1975 s. 65(1); 1975CB Sch. 4 para. 23(a)
(2)	1975 s. 65(2); 1975CB Sch. 4 para. 23(b); 1977 art. 18(3)
para. 6(1)	1975 s. 66(1); 1975CB Sch. 4 para. 24; 1980 Sch. 1 paras. 4, 6; 1986 Sch. 3 paras. 4, 15
(2)	1975 s. 66(2)
(3) - (6)	1975 s. 66(3) - (6); 1985 art. 15(5)
(7)	1975 s. 66(7)
para. 7	1975 s. 66A; 1984 art. 8(b); 1989 art. 11(3)
para. 8	1975 s. 84A; 1989 Sch. 8 para. 7(2)
para. 9(1), (2)	1975 s. 57(1), (5); 1986 Sch. 3 para. 3(3)
(3)	1975 s. 57(4); 1982 art. 32(2); 1989 Sch. 7, para. 11
para. 10(1)	1986 Sch. 3 para. 7
(2), (3)	1975 s. 62
para. 11(1)	1975 s. 59A(1), (10B); 1986 Sch. 3 para. 5(1); 1989 Sch. 7 para. 12; 1990 art. 5(1), (4)
(2), (3)	1975 s. 59A(1A), (1B), (10B); 1990 art. 5(2), (4)
(4) - (7)	1975 s. 59A(2) - (5); 1986 Sch. 3 para. 5(1)
(8)	1975 s. 59A(6); 1986 Sch. 3 para. 5(1); 1990 art. 5(3)
(9)	1975 s. 59A(7); 1986 Sch. 3 para. 5(1)
(10)	1975 s. 59A(8); 1986 Sch. 3 para. 5(1); 1988 Sch. 4 para. 9(a)
(11)	1988 art. 4(2)
(12)	1975 s. 59A(9); 1986 Sch. 3 para. 5(1)
(13)	1975 s. 59A(10); 1986 Sch. 3 para. 5(1)
(14)	1975 s. 59A(10A); 1988 Sch. 4 para. 9(b)
para. 12(1)	1988 art. 4(3)
(2)	1988 art. 4(4)
(3), (4)	1988 art. 4(4A), (4B); 1989 art. 19(5)
(5), (6)	1988 art. 4(5), (6); 1989 art. 19(6)
para. 13(1)	1975 s. 59B(1); 1988 art. 4(1); 1989 Sch. 1 para. 8(2)
(2)	1975 s. 59B(2); 1988 art. 4(1)
(3)	1975 s. 59B(3); 1988 art. 4(1)
(4)	1975 s. 59B(5); 1988 art. 4(1); 1989 Sch. 1 para. 8(5)
(5)	1975 s. 59B(5A); 1989 art. 19(3)
(6)	1975 s. 59B(6); 1988 art. 4(1)
(7)	Drafting
(8), (9)	1975 s. 59B(7), (8); 1989 Sch. 1 para. 8(6)
(10)	1975 s. 59B(9); 1990 art. 5(6)
(11)	1975 s. 59A(10A); 1988 Sch. 4 para. 9(b)
para. 14(1)	1988 Sch. 1 paras. 2, 3
(2)	1975 Sch. 17
para. 15	1975 s. 67; 1977 art. 18(4); 1986 Sch. 3 para. 8(a); 1988 Sch. 1 para. 2
para. 16	1975 s. 68; 1975CB Sch. 5; 1986 Sch. 3 para. 8(a); 1988 Sch. 1 para. 2
para. 17	1975 s. 69; 1986 Sch. 3 para. 11; 1988 Sch. 1 para. 3
para. 18	1975 s. 70; 1984 Sch. 3 para. 4; 1986 Sch. 3 para. 8(b); 1988 Sch. 1 para. 2
para. 19	1975 Sch. 9 para. 1; 1986 Sch. 3 para. 8(c); 1988 Sch. 1 para. 2
para. 20	1975 s. 75; 1986 Sch. 3 para. 8(b); 1988 Sch. 1 paras. 2, 6(2)(a)
para. 21	1977 art. 8; 1986 Sch. 10; 1988 Sch. 1 para. 6(2)(b)
Sch. 8	
para. 1	1975OC s. 1
para. 2	1975OC s. 2; 1990 art. 18(7)(a); 1992U art. 6
para. 3	1975OC s. 3

SOCIAL SECURITY CONTRIBUTIONS AND BENEFITS
(NORTHERN IRELAND) ACT—*continued.*

Section of 1992 Act	Derivation
para. 4(1)	1975 s. 150(1)
(2)	1975 s. 150(3)
para. 5(1)	1975 s. 150(2); 1975OC s. 9(1)
(2)	1975OC s. 9(2); 1977 art. 9(1)
(3)	1986 Sch. 3 para. 15
Sch. 9	1975CB Sch. 1; 1980 art. 5(6); Treatment of Offenders (NI) Order 1980 (NI 10) art. 3, Sch. 1 para. 1; 1984 Sch. 2 para. 11
Sch. 10	1975CB Sch. 2
Sch. 11	1982 Sch. 1; 1984 Sch. 2 para. 13(2)
Sch. 12	
para. 1	1982 Sch. 2 para. 1; 1985 art. 18(6)(a)
paras. 2 - 4	1982 Sch. 2 paras. 2 - 4
para. 5	1982 Sch. 2 para. 1A; 1985 art. 18(6)(b)
para. 6	1982 Sch. 2 para. 6
Sch. 13	
para. 1	1986 Sch. 4 para. 11; 1988 Sch. 4 para. 15(1)
para. 2	1986 Sch. 4 para. 11A; 1988 Sch. 4 para. 15(2)
para. 3	1986 Sch. 4 para. 12

SOCIAL SECURITY ADMINISTRATION (NORTHERN IRELAND) ACT 1992 (c. 8)

TABLE OF DERIVATIONS

(for Table of Destinations see page ccxvi)

Note:

1. Abbreviations used in this Table are the same as those used in the Table of Derivations for the Social Security Contributions and Benefits (Northern Ireland) Act. They are set out at the beginning of that Table.

2. The Table does not acknowledge the general changes made by Articles 3 and 4 of the Social Security Adjudications (Northern Ireland) Order 1983. Those Articles transferred adjudication functions to adjudication officers, social security appeal tribunals and adjudicating medical practitioners.

3. The Table does not contain any entries in respect of Article 2(3) of the Social Security Pensions (Northern Ireland) Order 1975 (NI 15) under which, with certain exceptions, that Order and the Social Security (Northern Ireland) Act 1975 (c. 15) have effect as if the provisions of the Order were contained in the Social Security (Northern Ireland) Act 1975. The effect is that the general provisions of the Social Security (Northern Ireland) Act 1975 apply to the provisions of the Social Security Pensions (Northern Ireland) Order 1975.

4. The Table does not contain any entries for Transfer of Functions Orders.

Section of 1992 Act	Derivation
1(1), (2)	1975 s. 154A(1), (2); 1986 Sch. 9 para. 56; 1989 Sch. 8 para. 8; 1990 art. 8(1)
(3)	1975 s. 154A(3); 1990 art. 3(6); 1991D Sch. 1 para. 19
(4)	1975 s. 154A(1); 1986 Sch. 9 paras. 32(b), 56; 1990 art. 7(4)
(5), (6)	Drafting
2	1975 s. 154B; 1990 art. 7(1)
3	1975 s. 154C; 1990 art. 8(2)
4	1990 Sch. 6 para. 16(2)
5(1)	1986 art. 52(1)
(2)	1986 art. 52(2); 1988 Sch. 3 para. 13, Sch. 5; 1991D Sch. 3 para. 2
(3), (4)	1986 art. 52(3), (4)
6	1975 s. 88; 1986 Sch. 10
7	1975 s. 89; 1982 Sch. 5
8	1975 s. 90; 1982 Sch. 5; 1985 Sch. 6; 1986 Sch. 9 para. 55, Sch. 10
9	1986 art. 28B(1) - (3); 1991D art. 9(1)
10(1)	1986 art. 34(1); 1988 Sch. 3 para. 7, Sch. 5
(2)	1986 art. 34(13); 1990 art. 12(5)
11(1)	1975CB art. 8(1); 1989 Sch. 7 para. 19
(2)	1975CB art. 8(3)
12(1)	1982 art. 19(2)
(2)	1982 art. 19(2A); 1985 art. 20
(3)	1982 art. 19(3)
13	1986 Sch. 4 paras. 6, 7
14	1988 art. 9
15(1)(a), (b)	1975 s. 93(1)(a), (b)
(c)	1975 s. 93(1)(bb); 1991C art. 5(1)
(d)	1975 s. 93(1)(d)
(e)	1975 s. 93(1)(e); 1977 art. 18(5)
(f)	1975P art. 70(1)(a); M5
(g)(i) - (iv)	1986 Sch. 5 Part II para. (b)(i) - (iv); M5
(v)	1986 Sch. 5 Part II para. (b)(vi); 1991SP art. 4(3); M5
(vi)	1986 Sch. 5 Part II para. (b)(v); M5
(h)	1986 Sch. 5 Part II para. (c); M5
(2), (3)	1975 s. 93(2), (2A); 1989 Sch. 3 para. 1(1)
(4)	1975 s. 93(3); M6

SOCIAL SECURITY ADMINISTRATION (NORTHERN IRELAND) ACT— *continued.*

Section of 1992 Act	Derivation
16	1975 s. 94; M5
17(1)	1975 s. 96(1); 1986 Sch. 5 para. 2; M6
(2), (3)	1975 s. 96(2); 1980 Sch. 1 para. 9
18(1), (2)	1975 s. 98(1), (2); 1986 Sch. 5 para. 3; 1991D Sch. 1 para. 2
(3)	1975 s. 98(1); 1986 art. 53(3), (7)(a); 1991D Sch. 2 para. 11(a)
(4)	1975 s. 98(2A); 1986 Sch. 5 para. 3
(5)	1975 s. 98(3)
(6)	1975 s. 98(1); 1986 art. 53(3)(a), (3A), (6); 1988 Sch. 3 para. 13; 1991D Sch. 2 para. 11, Sch. 3 para. 3(1)
19(1), (2)	1975 s. 99(1), (2); 1986 Sch. 5 para. 4; 1991D Sch. 1 para. 3(1), (2)
(3)	1975 s. 99(2A); 1986 art. 53(3A); 1991D Sch. 1 para. 3(3), Sch. 3 para. 3(1), (2)
(4), (5)	1975 s. 99(3); 1986 art. 53(7)(b)
(6)	1975 s. 99(4); 1989 Sch. 3 para. 2
20(1)	1975 s. 100(1); 1986 art. 53(3A), (7)(c)(i); 1991D Sch. 1 para. 4(a), Sch. 3 para. 3(1)
(2)	1975 s. 100(2); 1986 art. 53(7)(c)(ii), Sch. 5 para. 5(b); 1991D Sch. 1 para. 4(b)
(3)	1975 s. 100(3); 1986 Sch. 5 para. 5(c); 1989 Sch. 3 para. 5
(4)	1975 s. 100(4); 1986 Sch. 5 para. 5(d)
(5)	1975 s. 100(6); 1986 art. 53(7)(c)(iii), Sch. 5 para. 5(e); 1991D Sch. 1 para. 4(c)
(6), (7)	1975 s. 100(7), (8); 1990 Sch. 6 para. 4(1)
21(1)	1975 s. 101(1); 1986 Sch. 5 para. 6(1)
(2)	1975 s. 101(2); 1986 art. 53(3), (7)(d)
(3)	1975 s. 101(2); 1986 art. 53(3), Sch. 5 para. 6(2)
(4)	1975 s. 101(2)(bb); 1990 Sch. 6 para. 4(2)
(5)	1975 s. 101(3); 1986 Sch. 10; 1990 Sch. 6 para. 4(3)
(6)	1975 s. 101(4)
(7) - (10)	1975 s. 101(5) - (5B); 1986 Sch. 5 para. 6(3); 1989 Sch. 3 para. 6
22(1) - (5)	1980A s. 14(1) - (5)
(6)	1980A s. 14(8)(a); 1986A Sch. 9 para. 11(c)(i)
23(1)	1975 s. 104(1); 1986 art. 53(3), (3A), Sch. 5 para. 9(a); 1988 Sch. 3 para. 13, Sch. 4 para. 11; 1989 art. 12(5), Sch. 3 para. 11(1); 1991D Sch. 1 para. 8(a), Sch. 3 para. 3(1)
(2)	1975 s. 104(1A); 1983 Sch. 1 para. 2; 1986 art. 53(3A), Sch. 10; 1991D Sch. 1 para. 8(b), Sch. 3 para. 3(1)
(3)	1975 s. 104(1); 1986 Sch. 5 para. 9(a)
(4)	1986 art. 53(8); M10
(5)	1975 s. 104(1ZA); 1989 Sch. 3 para. 11(2)
24(1), (2)	1975 s. 104(2), (3)
(3)	1975 s. 104(3A); 1986 Sch. 5 para. 9(c)
25(1)	1975 s. 104(5); 1986 Sch. 5 para. 9(d); 1989 Sch. 3 para. 11(3), (4)
(2)	1975 s. 104(6); 1990 art. 8(3)
26	1975 s. 104(4)
27	1975 s. 104(3B); 1989 Sch. 3 para. 7
28(1)	1975 s. 100A(1); 1986 art. 53(3A), (10); 1991D Sch. 1 para. 5, Sch. 3 para. 3(1), (3)
(2) - (4)	1975 s. 100A(2) - (4); 1991D Sch. 1 para. 5
(5)	1975 s. 100A(2); 1986 art. 53(3A), (9)(a), (b), (10); 1991D Sch. 1 para. 5, Sch. 3, para. 3(1), (3)
(6) - (11)	1975 s. 100A(5) - (10); 1986 art. 53(3A); 1991D Sch. 1 para. 5, Sch. 3 para. 3(1)
(12)	1975 s. 100A(11); 1991D Sch. 1 para. 5
(13)	1975 s. 100A(12); 1986 art. 53(3A); 1991D Sch. 1 para. 5, Sch. 3 para. 3(1)

SOCIAL SECURITY ADMINISTRATION (NORTHERN IRELAND) ACT—*continued.*

Section of 1992 Act	Derivation
29	1975 s. 100B; 1986 art. 53(3A); 1991D Sch. 1 para. 5, Sch. 3 para. 3(1)
30(1)	1975 s. 100C(1); 1986 art. 53(3A); 1991D Sch. 1 para. 5, Sch. 3 para. 3(1)
(2) - (5)	1975 s. 100C(2) - (5); 1991D Sch. 1 para. 5
(6), (7)	1975 s. 100C(6), (7); 1986 art. 53(3A); 1991D Sch. 1 para. 5, Sch. 3 para. 3(1)
(8)	1975 s. 100C(8)(a), 104(5)(b); 1986 art. 53(3A), Sch. 5 para. 9(d); 1991D Sch. 1 para. 5, Sch. 3 para. 3(1)
(9), (10)	1975 s. 100C(9), (10); 1986 art. 53(3A); 1991D Sch. 1 para. 5, Sch. 3 para. 3(1)
31	1975 s. 100D(1) - (6); 1986 art. 53(3A); 1991D Sch. 1 para. 5, Sch. 3 para. 3(1)
32(1) - (4)	1975 s. 101; 1986 art. 53(3A), Sch. 5 para. 6; 1991D Sch. 1 para. 6, Sch. 3 para. 3(1)
(5)	1980A s. 14(1) - (4), (8)(b)
33(1), (2)	1975 s. 104A(1), (2); 1991D Sch. 1 para. 9
(3)	1975 s. 104A(1); 1986 art. 53(3A), (9)(a), (b), (10); 1991D Sch. 1 para. 9, Sch. 3 para. 3(1), (3)
(4)	1975 s. 104A(3); 1986 art. 53(3A); 1991D Sch. 1 para. 9, Sch. 3 para. 3(1)
(5)	1975 ss. 104(3A), 104A(9)(b); 1986 art. 53(3A), (9)(c), Sch. 5 para. 9(c); 1991D Sch. 1 para. 9, Sch. 3 para. 3(1), (3)
(6) - (9)	1975 s. 104A(4) - (7); 1986 art. 53(3A); 1991D Sch. 1 para. 9, Sch. 3 para. 3(1)
(10)	1975 ss. 104(5)(b), 104A(9)(c); 1986 art. 53(3A), (9)(c); 1991D Sch. 1 para. 9, Sch. 3 para. 3(1), (3)
(11)	1975 ss. 104(1ZA), 104A(9)(a); 1991D Sch. 1 para. 9
(12)	1975 s. 104A(8); 1986 art. 53(3A); 1991D Sch. 1 para. 9, Sch. 3 para. 3(1)
34(1)	1975 s. 102(1), (2); 1986 Sch. 5 para. 7; 1991D Sch. 1 para. 7(1)
(2)	1975 s. 102(3); 1991D Sch. 1 para. 7(2)
35	1975 s. 103; 1986 Sch. 5 para. 8; 1989 Sch. 3 para. 15
36	1975 s. 97(1), (1A); 1983 Sch. 1 para. 1; 1990 Sch. 6 para. 3(1)
37	1975 s. 97(1B) - (1E); 1983 Sch. 1 para. 1
38(1)	1975 Sch. 10 para. 1(1); 1983 Sch. 1 para. 5
(2), (3)	1975 Sch. 10 para. 1(2), (2A); 1984 art. 10(b)
(4)	1975 Sch. 10 para. 1(6); 1983 Sch. 1 para. 5
39(1), (2)	1975 s. 97(2), (2A); 1983 Sch. 1 para. 1; 1984 art. 10(a)
(3), (4)	1975 s. 97(2C) - (2D); 1983 Sch. 1 para. 1
(5)	1975 Sch. 10 para. 1(8); 1983 Sch. 1 para. 5
(6)	Drafting
40	1975 Sch. 10 para. 1(2), (2A), Sch. 10A paras. 3 - 8; 1984 art.10(b); 1991D Sch. 1 para. 16
41(1) - (3)	1975 Sch. 10A paras. 1, 9, 10; 1983 Sch. 1 para. 1; 1991D Sch. 1 para. 16
(4), (5)	1975 s. 97(2C), (2D), Sch. 10A para. 2; 1984 art. 10(a); 1991D Sch. 1 para. 16
(6), (7)	1975 Sch. 10A paras. 12, 13; 1991D Sch. 1 para. 16
(8)	Drafting
42	1975 s. 107; 1986 Sch. 5 para. 11, Sch. 10; 1988 Sch. 1 para. 6
43(1), (2)	1975 s. 108(1), (2); 1983 Sch. 2 para. 1(1); 1984 Sch. 2 paras. 4, 5; 1986 Sch. 3 para. 14(a); 1989 Sch. 3 para. 12(1)
(3) - (6)	1975 s. 108(4) - (5); 1983 Sch. 2 para. 1(3); 1989 Sch. 3 para. 12(2)
44	1975 s. 109; 1983 Sch. 2 para. 2, Sch. 3; 1984 Sch. 2 para. 6; 1986 Sch. 5 para. 12
45(1) - (9)	1975 s. 110; 1979 Sch. 3 para. 7; 1983 Sch. 2 para. 3; 1984 Sch. 2 para. 7; 1986 Sch. 5 para. 13, Sch. 10
(10)	Social Security (Consequential Provisions) Act 1975 (c. 18) Sch. 3 paras. 20, 31
46(1) - (4)	1975 s. 112A(1) - (5); 1986A Sch. 9 para. 1; 1989 Sch. 9
(5), (6)	1975 s. 112A(5A), (5B); 1989 Sch. 3 para. 9(2)
47(1), (2)	1975 Sch. 12 para. 1; 1983 Sch. 2 para. 7(a)

SOCIAL SECURITY ADMINISTRATION (NORTHERN IRELAND) ACT—*continued.*

Section of 1992 Act	Derivation
(3)	1975 Sch. 12 para. 3; 1983 Sch. 2 para. 7(b)
48(1) - (4)	1975 Sch. 12 para. 2(1) - (4); 1983 Sch. 1 para. 6; 1986 Sch. 5 para. 15
(5)	1975 Sch. 12 para. 2(6); 1983 Sch. 1 para. 6
(6)	1975 Sch. 12 para. 3; 1983 Sch. 2 para. 7(b)
(7)	Drafting
49(1) - (3)	1975 s. 97(2D)(a), Sch. 10 para. 1A(1) - (3); 1983 Sch. 1 paras. 1, 5; 1991D Sch. 1 para. 15
(4)	1975 s. 97(2E), Sch. 10A para. 2, Sch. 12 para. 2(5); 1983 Sch. 1 paras. 1, 6; 1991D Sch. 1 para. 16
(5)	Drafting
50(1)	1975 s. 97(3); 1979 s. 9(2)
(2)	1980A s. 13(5); Courts and Legal Services Act 1990 (c. 41) Sch. 10 para. 46
(3)	Drafting
51	1975 s. 115A; 1989 Sch. 3 para. 3(1); 1991D Sch. 1 para. 11, Sch. 4
52(1), (2)	1975 s. 115C(1), (2); 1986 art. 53(3A); 1991D Sch. 1 para. 13, Sch. 3, para. 3(1)
(3)	1975 s. 115C(3); 1991D Sch. 1, para. 13
(4)	1975 s. 115C(3); 1986 art. 53(3A), (9)(d); 1991D Sch. 1 para. 13, Sch. 3 para. 3(1), (3)
(5)	1975 s. 115C(4); 1986 art. 53(3A), (9)(b); 1991D Sch. 1 para. 13, Sch. 3 para. 3(1)
(6)	1975 s. 115C(5); 1991D Sch. 1 para. 13
(7)	1975 s. 115C(5); 1986 art. 53(3A), (9)(e); 1991D Sch. 1 para. 13, Sch. 3 para. 3(1), (3)
(8)	1975 s. 115C(6); 1986 art. 53(3A); 1991D Sch. 1 para. 13, Sch. 3 para. 3(1)
53	1975 s. 115D; 1986 art. 53(3A)(c); 1991D Sch. 1 para. 13, Sch. 3 para. 3(1)
54	1975 s. 115B; 1989 Sch. 3 para. 3(1); 1991D Sch. 1 para. 12, Sch. 4
55	1975 s. 116; 1980A s. 12
56(1), (2)	1975 s. 114(1); 1986 art. 53(3)(b), (3A), (6); 1988 Sch. 3 para. 13; 1991D Sch. 3 para. 3(1)
(3)	1975 s. 114(2)
(4)	1976IR art. 72(3)
(5) - (7)	1975 s. 114(2A) - (2C); 1986 Sch. 5 para. 14
(8)	1975 s. 114(5)
57(1), (2)	1975 s. 115(1) - (3); 1986 art. 53(3)(c), (3A), (4), (6); 1988 Sch. 3 para. 13; 1991D Sch. 3 para. 3(1)
(3)	1975 s. 115(4)
(4)	1975 s. 115(4A); 1991C art. 5(2)
(5), (6)	1975 s. 115(5); 1989 Sch. 3 para. 1(2)
58(1)	1975 s. 117(1); 1983 Sch. 1 para. 4; 1986 art. 53(3), (3A), (6); 1991D Sch. 3 para. 3(1)
(2)	1975 s. 117(2); 1986 art. 53(3), (3A), (6); 1991D Sch. 3 para. 3(1)
(3)	1975 s. 117(3); 1983 Sch. 2 para. 6
(4)	1975 s. 117(4); 1988 Sch. 1 para. 6
(5)	1975 s. 117(5)
59(1), (2)	1975 s. 119(3), (4)(a)
(3)	1977 art. 13(5)
(4)	1986 art. 53(3)(e), (3A), (6); 1988 Sch. 3 para. 13; 1991D Sch. 3 para. 3(1)
60	1975 s. 113(1), (2)(a), (b); 1983 Sch. 2 para. 4
61	1986 art. 30(1) - (3)
62(1), (2)	1986 art. 33(8), (9); 1988 Sch. 5
(3)	1986 art. 33(10); 1988 Sch. 3 para. 6; 1990 art. 12(2)
63	1986 art. 36

SOCIAL SECURITY ADMINISTRATION (NORTHERN IRELAND) ACT—*continued.*

Section of 1992 Act	Derivation
64(1) - (8)	1986 art. 35; 1988 Sch. 5
(9), (10)	1986 art. 33(11), (12); 1988 Sch. 3 para. 6
65	1986 Sch. 6 para. 4
66(1) - (3)	1975 s. 154D(1) - (3); 1990 Sch. 6 para. 5(2)
(4)	1975 s. 154D(4); 1986 Sch. 9 para. 32; 1990 Sch. 6 para. 5(2), (3); 1991D Sch. 2 para. 4
(5), (6)	1975 s. 154D(5), (6); 1990 Sch. 6 para. 5(2)
67	1975 s. 104(7) - (10); 1986 art. 53(3); 1990 Sch. 6 para. 5(1); 1991D Sch. 2 para. 11, Sch. 3 para. 3(1)
68	National Insurance Measure (NI) 1974 (c. 4) s. 5(1), (4)
69(1)	1986 art. 54(1)
(2)	1986 art. 54(1A); 1989 Sch. 3 para. 14(1)
(3) - (10)	1986 art. 54(2) - (9); 1989 Sch. 3 para. 14(2)
(11)	1986 art. 54(10); 1988 Sch. 3 para. 13, Sch. 4 para. 23(1), Sch. 5; 1991D Sch. 3 para. 4
70(1), (2)	1986 art. 21(4E), (4H); 1988 art. 6(2)
(3) - (6)	1986 art. 21(4J) - (4M); 1988 art. 6(2)
(7), (8)	1986 arts. 21(4F), (4G), 54(10A); 1988 art. 6(2), Sch. 4 para. 23(2)
71	1975 s. 85; 1975CB Sch. 4 para. 29, Sch. 5; 1979 art. 12
72	1986 art. 28
73	1986 art. 30(4) - (7)
74(1) - (3)	1986 art. 34(5) - (7)
(4)	1986 art. 33(4); 1988 Sch. 5
(5)	1986 art. 34(12)
(6) - (8)	1986 arts. 27(3) - (5), 34(8); 1989 art. 7(2), (3), Sch. 9; 1990 art. 10(2)
75	1986 arts. 30(8), 54(7A); 1988 Sch. 4 paras. 19, 21
76	1975CB art. 6A; 1979 art. 12(2)
77(1)	1989 art. 24(3), Sch. 4 para. 1(1); 1990 Sch. 1 para. 1(1) - (3); 1991SP art. 3(5)
(2)	1989 art. 24(3A); 1991SP art. 3(5)
(3) - (5)	1989 art. 24(4) - (6)
(6)	1989 Sch. 4 para. 1(2)
(7)	1989 art. 24(8)
78	1989 art. 24(1), (2)
79	1989 Sch. 4 para. 2
80	1989 Sch. 4 para. 3
81	1989 Sch. 4 para. 4
82	1989 Sch. 4 para. 5
83	1989 Sch. 4 para. 6
84	1989 Sch. 4 para. 7
85	1989 Sch. 4 para. 8
86	1989 Sch. 4 para. 9
87	1989 Sch. 4 para. 10
88	1989 Sch. 4 para. 11
89	1989 Sch. 4 para. 12; 1990 Sch. 1 para. 2
90	1989 Sch. 4 para. 13; 1990 Sch. 1 para. 1(4)
91	1989 Sch. 4 para. 14
92	1989 Sch. 4 para. 15
93	1989 Sch. 4 para. 16
94	1989 Sch. 4 para. 17; 1990 Sch. 1 paras. 3, 4
95	1989 Sch. 4 para. 18
96	1989 Sch. 4 para. 19

SOCIAL SECURITY ADMINISTRATION (NORTHERN IRELAND) ACT—*continued.*

Section of 1992 Act	Derivation
97	1989 Sch. 4 para. 21
98	1989 Sch. 4 para. 23; 1990 Sch. 1 para. 5
99	1989 art. 28
100	1986 art. 27; 1989 art. 7(2), (3); 1990 art. 10(2)
101	1986 art. 25
102	1986 art. 25A; 1990 art. 10(1)
103	1986 art. 25B; 1990 art. 10(1)
104(1) - (8)	1986 art. 59(1) - (7); 1989 Sch. 4 para. 20(1) - (6)
(9)	1986 art. 59(10); 1989 Sch. 4 para. 20(3), (7)
105	1986 art. 59(8), (9)
106	1986 art. 56
107	1986 art. 55
108(1)	1975 s. 137(1); 1975P Sch. 5 para. 36; 1984F arts. 5(2), 6(1), (3)
(2)	1975 s. 1(4), Sch. 1 para. 5(2)
(3)	1975 s. 137(2)
(4)	1975 s. 137(3); 1981 Sch. para. 3(a); 1986 Sch. 10
(5), (6)	1975 s. 137(4)
109	1986 art. 58
110(1) - (3)	1986 art. 57(1) - (3)
(4)	1986 art. 57(3A); 1990 Sch. 6 para. 3(2)
(5), (6)	1986 art. 57(4), (5)
111	1975 s. 139; 1986 art. 53(5); M6
112	1975 s. 140
113	1975 s. 141
114(1), (2)	1975 s. 142(1), (2); 1975P Sch. 5 para. 39; 1986 Sch. 10
(3)	1975 s. 142(3); 1991C art. 4(6)(a)
(4)	1975 s. 142(3A); 1991C art. 4(6)(b)
(5)	1975 s. 142(4)
(6)	1975 s. 142(5); 1991C art. 4(6)(c)
115(1)	1975 s. 143(7); Criminal Justice (NI) Order 1980 (NI 6) Sch. 1 para. 72; 1981MC Sch. 6 para. 35
(2) - (6)	1975 s. 143(1), (3), (4), (5); 1990 Sch. 7
116	1986 art. 60; 1989 art. 22
117	1989 art. 21; 1990 Sch. 6 para. 17
118	1986 art. 61
119	1986 art. 28A; 1989 Sch. 8 para. 16
120	1986 art. 32(1) - (3)
121	1982 art. 19(1)
122(1) - (3)	1982 art. 20; 1984 Sch. 2 para. 13(1)
(4)	1982 arts. 11(3)(a), 19(4)
123	1986 Sch. 4 para. 9
124(1), (2)	1986 Sch. 4 para. 8A; 1989 Sch. 8 para. 17
(3)	1986 Sch. 4 para. 8
125	1975 s. 151; Adoption (NI) Order 1987 (NI 22) Sch. 5
126(1)	1986 art. 29(1)
(2)	1986 art. 29(1A); 1989 art. 16(1)
(3) - (6)	1986 art. 29(2) - (5)
127(1), (2)	1986 art. 31(1), (2)
(3)	1986 art. 31(4); 1989 art. 17
128	1986 art. 31(5) - (8); 1989 art. 17
129	1975 s. 120; 1979 Sch. 3 para. 9; 1985 art. 9(5)

SOCIAL SECURITY ADMINISTRATION (NORTHERN IRELAND) ACT—*continued.*

Section of 1992 Act	Derivation
130	1975P art. 23; 1985 Sch. 3 para. 1
131	1982 art. 11(1E); 1991SP art. 4(1)
132	1986 art. 64
133	1975 art. 64A; 1989 art. 19(1)
134(1), (2)	1975CB art. 19(1), (2)(a) - (e)
135	1986 art. 65; 1989 art. 19(2)(a)
136	1975P art. 11(3A); 1989 Sch. 8 para. 10
137(1)	1975CB art. 7(5), Sch. 3 paras. 1, 2; 1986 Sch. 9 para. 62
(2)	1975CB Sch. 3 para. 3
138	1977 art. 13(4)
139	1986 art. 65A; 1989 art. 20
140	1986 art. 65B; 1990 Sch. 6 para. 13
141	1975 s. 127(1) - (4); Finance Act 1980 (c. 48) Sch. 19 para. 5(4)
142(1), (2)	1975 s. 128(1), (2); 1991R Sch. 2
(3)	1975 s. 128(2A); 1990 art. 18(3)
(4)	1975 s. 128(2B); 1990 art. 19(1)
(5)	1975 ss. 128(4); 1981 art. 5(2)(b), (c), (3); 1982 art. 5(2); 1985 Sch. 5 para. 4; Social Security (Consolidated Fund of Northern Ireland Supplements to, and Allocation of, Contributions) (Re-rating) Order (NI) 1987 (SR 1987 No. 25) art. 3(2); 1989 art. 3(2); Social Security (Contributions and Allocation of Contributions) (Re-rating) Order (NI) 1989 (SR 1989 No. 89) art. 6(2); 1991RF Sch. 2; 1991C art. 6(a)
(6)	1975 s. 128(4); 1985 Sch. 5 para. 4
(7), (8)	1975 s. 128(4A), (4B); 1981C art. 5(3)
(9) - (11)	1975 s. 128(5)
(12)	1975 s. 128(6); 1979 art. 11(3)
143(1)(a), (b)	1975 ss. 1(5), 129(1), (2); 1975P Sch. 5 para. 32; 1986 Sch. 10; 1990 art. 18(4); 1991D Sch. 1 para. 18
(c)	1986 art. 82(1)(c)
(d)	1982 art. 11(7); 1985 art. 19(1)(d); 1986 art. 82(1)(c)
(e)	1989 art. 29(3)(b)
(2)	1975 s. 129(2), (3); 1984 Sch. 2 para. 2; 1989 art. 29(3); 1990 art. 18(4); 1991D Sch. 1 para. 18
(3)	1975 s. 129(4)
(4)	1977 art. 3(2)
(5)	1975 s. 129(7); 1990 art. 19(2)
144(1) - (3)	1986 art. 82(3) - (5)
(4)	1975OC s. 4(3)(e); 1990 art. 18(7)(b)
(5)	1975 s. 113(2)(b); 1983 Sch. 2 para. 4(b); 1986 art. 82(6)
(6)	1989 art. 29(2)
145(1)	1975 s. 127(5); 1986 art. 82(7); 1991D Sch. 3 para. 7
(2) - (4)	1975 s. 127(6); 1975CB art. 25; 1986 art. 82(8)
(5)	1975 s. 129(5); 1975P art. 73(1); 1977 art. 20; 1980 art. 14; 1982 art. 37; 1986 art. 82(2); 1988 art. 15; 1989 art. 29(1); 1990 arts. 18(5), 20(2)
146(1)	1986 art. 33(1)
(2) - (4)	1986 art. 33(5) - (7)
(5), (6)	1986 art. 3(7A), (7B); 1988 Sch. 3, para. 3
147(1) - (4)	1986 art. 33(8A) - (8D); 1988 Sch. 3 para. 5
(5)	1986 art. 33(8E); 1990 art. 12(1)
148	1986 art. 82(9), (10)
149	1980A ss. 9(3), 10; 1986 Sch. 9 para. 64; 1991SP art. 5(1)(b)

SOCIAL SECURITY ADMINISTRATION (NORTHERN IRELAND) ACT—*continued*.

Section of 1992 Act	Derivation
150(1) - (4)	1986 art. 62(1) - (4)
(5)	1986 art. 62(5); 1989 Sch. 8 para. 11(2)
(6)	1986 art. 62(6); 1989 Sch. 8 para. 11(2)
151	1980A s. 10(3), (6), (8), (9)
152	1991D art. 5(1) - (6)
153	1975 s. 133; Social Security Pensions Act 1975 (c. 60) Sch. 4 para. 69; 1986 art. 66(1)
154	1975CB art. 16; 1986 art. 66(4); 1991D Sch. 3 para. 5
155(1)	1975 s. 134(1); 1975CB art. 17(1); 1977A s. 20(3); 1977 art. 16; 1986 art. 66(2), Sch. 10
(2)	1975 s. 134(1A); 1975CB art. 17(1A); 1981 art. 7(1), (2)
(3)	1975 s. 134(2); 1975CB art. 17(2)
(4)	1975 s. 134(1); 1975CB art. 17(1); 1986 art. 66(4); 1991D Sch. 3 para. 5
(5)	1975CB art. 17(3); 1986 art. 66(4); 1991D Sch. 3 para. 6
(6)	1975CB arts. 16(3), 17(3)
156	1986 art. 78
157	1977SB art. 28; 1984F arts. 4, 6(1), (3)
158	1977SB art. 29; 1984F arts. 4, 6(1), (3)
159	1975 s. 145
160	1975 s. 146
161(1)	Drafting
(2)	1975 s. 150(3)(c)
162	Drafting
163(1)	1975 s. 87(1); 1975CB art. 14; 1986 Sch. 9 para. 32(a)
(3)	1975 s. 87(3); Judgments Enforcement (Northern Ireland Consequential Amendments) Order 1981 (SI 1981/234) art. 5; 1981MC Sch. 6 para. 34
164(1), (2)	1975 s. 153
(3)	1975OC s. 7
165(1)	1975 Sch. 17; 1986 Sch. 5 para. 17
(2)	1975 Sch. 17; 1986 Sch. 5 para. 17
(3)	1975 s. 155(1); 1986 art. 81(1); 1989 art. 30(1); 1991D art. 13(2)
(4)	1975 s. 155(2); 1982 art. 36(1); 1986 art. 81(1); 1989 art. 30(1); 1991D art. 13(2)
(5)	1975 ss. 13(2)(c), 155(3); 1975CB art. 24(5); 1982 art. 36(1); 1986 art. 81(1); 1989 art. 30(1), Sch. 8 para. 9(1); M8
(6)	1975 s. 155(3A); 1975CB art. 24(5A); 1986 arts. 63(1), (2), 81(1); 1989 art. 30(1); 1991D art. 13(2)
(7)	1986 art. 81(2)
(8)	1986 art. 81(5)
(9)	1975 s. 127(6); 1986 art. 81(6); 1989 art. 30(5)
(10)	1975 s. 155(5); 1982 art. 36(1); 1986 art. 81(7)
(11)	1975 s. 155(7); 1975CB arts. 16(3), 17(3); 1977A Sch. 2; 1986 art. 66(4); 1991D Sch. 3 para. 5
(12)	1975 s. 157(4); 1977A Sch. 2
166(1)	1975 s. 156(1)
(2)	1975 s. 156(2); 1975CB art. 24(2); 1982 art. 11(1F); 1986 art. 81(3)(c); 1989 art. 30(2)(h); 1991SP art. 4(1)
(3)	1975 s. 156(3)(c); 1975CB art. 24(3); 1990 Sch. 6 para. 6(1)
(4)	1975 s. 156(4); 1975OC s. 4(9); 1975CB art. 24(4); 1977 arts. 9(2), 19(3); 1982 art. 36(2); 1986 art. 81(4); 1988 art. 15A(2); 1989 art. 30(3); 1990 Sch. 6 para. 6(4), (6), (8), (11)
(5)	1975 s. 156(5A); 1989 Sch. 3 para. 16; 1990 Sch. 6 para. 6(16)

Tables of Derivations and Destinations

SOCIAL SECURITY ADMINISTRATION (NORTHERN IRELAND) ACT—*continued.*

Section of 1992 Act	Derivation
(6)	s. 156(5)
(7)	1990 Sch. 6 para. 6(12), (17)
(8)	1990 Sch. 6 para. 6(13)
(9)	1990 Sch. 6 para. 6(14), (17)
(10)	1990 Sch. 6 para. 6(15)
(11)	1975 s. 156(6)
(12)	1975 s. 156(4); 1980A s. 14(8); 1986A Sch. 9 para. 11(c); 1990 Sch. 6 para. 6(12)(a)
167	1975 Sch. 17
168	Short title, etc.
Sch. 1	
para. 1	1975 s. 154A; 1985 art. 17
para. 2	1975 s. 154A; 1985 art. 17; 1986 Sch. 9 para. 57; Social Security (1986 Order) (Commencement No. 1) Order (NI) 1986 (SR 1986 No. 339)
para. 3	1975 s. 154A; 1986 Sch. 9 para. 56; Social Security (1986 Order) (Commencement No. 3) Order (NI) 1987 (SR 1987 No. 21)
para. 4	1975 s. 154A; 1986 Sch. 9 para. 56; 1989 arts. 1(2), (3), Sch. 8 para. 8(1)
para. 5	1975 s. 154A; 1986 Sch. 9 para. 56; 1989 Sch. 8 para. 8(1); 1990 arts. 1(3), (4), 8(1)
Sch. 2	
para. 1(1)	1975 Sch. 10 para. 1A(4); 1983 Sch. 1 para. 5
(2)	1975 Sch. 10 paras. 1A(5), 5; 1980A s. 13(1); 1983 Sch. 1 para. 5
(3) - (5)	1975 Sch. 10 para. 1A(6) - (8); 1980A s. 13(2); 1983 Sch. 1 para. 5
(6)	1980A s. 13(5)(a); Judicial Pensions Act 1981 (c. 20) Sch. 3 para. 10
para. 2	1975 Sch. 10 para. 2(1); Sch. 10A para. 11; 1991D Sch. 1 para. 16
para. 3	1975 Sch. 10 para. 1A(9); 1983 Sch. 1 para. 5
para. 4	1975 Sch. 10 para. 1A(10), Sch. 10A para. 11; Sch. 12 para. 5A; 1983 Sch. 1 paras. 5, 7; 1991D Sch. 1 para. 16
para. 5	1975 Sch. 10 paras. 1B, 1C, Sch. 10A para. 11; 1983 Sch. 1 para. 5; 1991D Sch. 1 para. 16
para. 6	1975 Sch. 10 para. 1D, Sch. 10A para. 11, Sch. 12 para. 9; 1983 Sch. 1 para. 5; 1991D Sch. 1 para. 16
para. 7	1975 Sch. 10 para. 4; 1986A Sch. 9 para. 10(1)(a), (b)
para. 8	1975 s. 113(3), Sch. 10 para. 3, Sch. 10A para. 11, Sch. 12 paras. 4 - 7; 1983 Sch. 2 para. 7(b); 1991D Sch. 1 para. 16
para. 9	1980 art. 12; 1991D Sch. 2 para. 9
Sch. 3	
para. 1	1975 s. 115(2); 1983 Sch. 1 para. 3, Sch. 2 para. 5; 1991D Sch. 1 para. 10
para. 2	1975 Sch. 13 para. 1; 1989 Sch. 3 para. 4
para. 3	1975 Sch. 13 para. 1A; 1986 Sch. 5 para. 16(a)
paras. 4 - 9	1975 Sch. 13 paras. 2 - 7
para. 10	1975 Sch. 13 para. 7A; 1989 Sch. 3 para. 10; 1991D Sch. 1 para. 17
para. 11	1975 Sch. 13 para. 10; 1986 Sch. 5 para. 16(b); 1991D Sch. 2 para. 13
para. 12	1975 Sch. 13 para. 11
Sch. 4	1989 Sch. 2; 1990 Sch. 5 para. 17(4); 1991D Sch. 2 para. 13
Sch. 5	
para. 1	1980A Sch. 3 para. 12(4); 1991D Sch. 2 para. 8(b); Disability Living Allowance and Disability Working Allowance Act 1991 (c. 21) Sch. 2 para. 10
para. 2	1980A Sch. 3 para. 12(1)
para. 3	1980A Sch. 3 para. 12(2); 1982A s. 42(2); 1986A Sch. 10 para. 99
para. 4	1980A Sch. 3 para. 13(1)

SOCIAL SECURITY ADMINISTRATION (NORTHERN IRELAND) ACT—*continued*.

Section of 1992 Act	Derivation
para. 5	1980A Sch. 3 para. 13(1A); 1986A Sch. 10 para. 106; 1986 Sch. 9 para. 73
paras. 6, 7	1980A Sch. 3 para. 14
para. 8	1980A Sch. 3 paras. 15A, 15AA; 1982 Sch. 4 para. 18(3); 1982A Sch. 4 para. 33(3); 1989 Sch. 8 para. 11(3); Social Security Act 1989 (c. 24) Sch. 8 para. 12(6)
paras. 9, 10	1980A Sch. 3 paras. 20, 21; 1986A Sch. 9 para. 13
Sch. 6	
para. 1	1975OC s. 4
para. 2	1975OC s. 5
para. 3	1986 art. 54(11)
Sch. 7	
para. 1	1986 Sch. 7 paras. 1, 3
para. 2	1986 Sch. 7 para. 4; 1991D Sch. 2 para. 11(b)
para. 3	1986 Sch. 7 para. 5
para. 4	1986 Sch. 7 para. 7
para. 5	1986 Sch. 7 para. 6

SOCIAL SECURITY (NORTHERN IRELAND) ACTS CONSOLIDATION

TABLE OF DESTINATIONS

1. The legislation relating to social security is consolidated into three Acts—
   (a) the Social Security Contributions and Benefits (Northern Ireland) Act (c. 7);
   (b) the Social Security Administration (Northern Ireland) Act (c. 8); and
   (c) the Social Security (Consequential Provisions) (Northern Ireland) Act (c. 9).
They are respectively referred to in this Table as CB, A and CP.

2. Notes 1 and 2 at the beginning of the Table of Derivations for the Social Security Contributions and Benefits (Northern Ireland) Act apply to this Table as well.

Section of Act, etc.	Subject matter	Section of 1992 Act	Remarks
NATIONAL INSURANCE MEASURE (NORTHERN IRELAND) 1974 (c. 4)			
5	Supplementary provisions and minor amendments.		
(1)		A 68(1), (3)	Am. 1975P Sch. 5 para. 17, 1975CB Sch. 4 para. 9, 1977SB Sch. 6 para. 19, 1982 Sch 4 para. 3, 1991SP art. 5(1)(a); rep. in part 1975CB Sch 5.
(3)		A 166(4)	Rep. in part Social Security (Consequential Provisions) Act 1975 (c. 18) Sch. 1.
(4)		A 68(2)	
SOCIAL SECURITY (NORTHERN IRELAND) ACT 1975 (c. 15)			
1	Outline of the contributory system.		
(1)		CB 1(1)	Am. 1990 art. 18(1), (2); rep. in part 1989 Sch. 9, 1986 Sch. 19; 1990 Sch. 7; 1991RF Sch. 2.
(2)		CB 1(2)	Am. 1991C art. 3(2).
(3)		CB 1(3)	
(4)		CB 1(4)	Am. 1991C art. 4(1)(a).
(4A)		CB 1(5)	Inserted 1990 art 18(2); am. 1991SP art. 3(4).
(5)		—	Rep. 1989 Sch. 9.
(5A)		—	Inserted 1981C art. 4(2); rep. 1989 Sch. 9.
(6)		CB 1(6)	Am. 1991C art. 3(3).
2	Categories of earners.	CB 2	
3	"Earnings".		
(1)		CB 3(1)	
(1A)–(1C)		CB 4(1)–(3)	Inserted 1982 art. 30(1).
(1D)		CB 4(4)	Inserted 1989 Sch. 8 para. 1.
(2)		CB3(2)	
(3)		CB 3(3)	
(4)		CB 4(5)	Added 1982 Sch. 4 para. 4.
4	Class 1 contributions.		
(1)		CB 5(1)	Am. 1975P Sch. 5 para. 18(a); 1985 art. 9(1).

SOCIAL SECURITY (NORTHERN IRELAND) ACTS CONSOLIDATION—*continued.*

Section of Act, etc.	Subject matter	Section of 1992 Act	Remarks

SOCIAL SECURITY (NORTHERN IRELAND) ACT 1975 (c. 15)—*continued.*

Section of Act, etc.	Subject matter	Section of 1992 Act	Remarks
(2)		CB 6(1), (4)	Am. 1976 art. 3(1); rep. in part 1982 Sch. 5.
(3)		CB 6(3)	Subst. 1989 Sch. 7 para. 1(1).
(4)		CB 7(1)	
(5)		CB 7(2)	
(6)–(6B)		CB 8(1)–(3)	Subst. 1989 art. 3(1).
(6C)–(6E)		CB 9(1)–(4)	Subst. 1985 art. 9(2); am. 1989 Sch. 7 para. 1(2); S.R. 1991 No. 73 art. 2; 1991R art. 2.
(7)		CB 6(5)	Added 1979 art. 11(2); am. 1985 art. 10.
4A	Class 1A contributions	CB 10	Inserted 1991C art. 3(5).
5, 6	—	—	Rep. 1975P Sch. 6.
7	Class 2 contributions.		
(1)		CB 11(1)	Am. 1976 art. 3(1); 1984 art. 11(1); 1991R.
(2), (3)		—	Rep. 1975P Sch. 6.
(4)–(6)		CB 11(3)–(5)	Am. 1991R art. 3(b).
7A	Late paid Class 2 contributions.	CB 12	Inserted 1984 art. 11(2); subs. (3) am. 1985SR reg. 4(2); 1989 Sch. 7 para. 2; rep. in part 1989 Sch. 9.
8	Class 3 contributions.		
(1)		CB 13(1)	Am. 1976 art. 3(1); 1984 art. 12(1)(a); 1991R art. 4.
(2)		CB 13(2)	
(a)		CB 13(3)	
(b)		—	Rep. 1975P Sch. 6.
(2A)		CB 13(4)	Inserted 1984 art. 12(1)(b); am. art. 12(3).
(2B)		CB 13(5)	Added 1984 art. 12(3).
(2C)		CB 13(6)	Added 1984 art. 12(3); am. 1985SR reg. 4(3); 1989 Sch. 7 para.3.
(2D)		CB 13(7)	Added 1984 art. 12(3).
(3)		—	Rep. 1975P Sch. 6.
9	Class 4 contributions.		
(1)		CB 15(1), (2), (5)	Am. 1889 Sch. 7 para. 4.
(2)		CB 15(3)	Am,. 1982SR art. 5(a); 1991R art. 5.
(3)		CB 16	

SOCIAL SECURITY (NORTHERN IRELAND) ACTS CONSOLIDATION—*continued.*

Section of Act, etc.	Subject matter	Section of 1992 Act	Remarks
	SOCIAL SECURITY (NORTHERN IRELAND) ACT 1975 (c. 15)—*continued.*		
(4)		CB 17(1)	
(5)		CB 17(2)	Rep. in part 1975P Sch. 6.
(6)		CB 17(3)–(6)	
10	Class 4 contributions recoverable under regulations.	CB 18	Am. 1982SR art. 5(a); 1991R art. 5.
11	General power to regulate liability for contributions.	CB 19(1)–(3)	
12	Descriptions of contributory benefits.	CB 20	Am. 1975P Sch. 5 para. 19; 1984 Sch. 3 para. 1(a); 1986 Sch. 9 para. 39; 1989 Sch. 7 para. 5; rep. in part 1980 art. 6(1)(i); 1980(2) Sch.; 1984 Sch. 3 para. 1(b), Sch. 6 Part II; 1986 Sch. 10.
13	Contribution conditions and the earnings factor.		
(1)		CB 21(1), (2)	Am. 1986 Sch. 9 para. 40; rep. in part 1980 art. 6(1)(ii), 1986 Sch. 10.
(2)		CB 22(1), (2)	Am. 1975P Sch. 5 para. 20(a); 1986 art. 19(1)(b); Sch. 8 para. 1(1), Sch. 9 para. 46(a); rep. in part 1980(2) Sch.
(3)		CB 22(4)	Am. 1975P Sch. 5 para. 20(b); 1986 Sch. 8 para. 1(2); rep. in part 1980(2) Sch.
(4)		CB 22(5)	Am. 1986 Sch. 8 para. 1(3); rep. in part 1980(2) Sch.
(5)		CB 22(3), 23(1), (3)	Am. 1979 Sch. 3 para. 4; 1986 Sch. 8 para. 1(4); 1988 Sch. 2 para. 1(1)(a); 1989 art 6(2), Sch. 7 para. 6; rep. in part 1986 Sch. 10.
(5ZA)		CB 23(2)	Inserted 1988 Sch. 2 para. 1(1)(b), (3).
(5A)		CB 23(4)	Inserted 1985 Sch. 5 para. 1(b); am. M 1; rep. in 1986 Sch. 10 omitted by M 12.
(5AA)		CB 22(6)	Inserted 1989 art. 6(3).
(5B)		CB 24(1)	Inserted 1986 Sch. 8 para. 1(5).
(5C)		CB 24(2)	Inserted 1989 art. 6(4).
(6)		CB 21(3), (5)	Am. 1986 Sch. 8 para. 1(6).
(7)		CB 21(6)	
(8)		CB 21(4)	AM. 1986 Sch. 9 para. 46(b).

SOCIAL SECURITY (NORTHERN IRELAND) ACTS CONSOLIDATION—*continued.*

Section of Act, etc.	Subject matter	Section of 1992 Act	Remarks
	SOCIAL SECURITY (NORTHERN IRELAND) ACT 1975 (c. 15)—*continued.*		
14	Unemployed benefit and sickness benefit.		
(1)		CB 25(1), 31(1)	
(2)		CB 25(2), 31(2)	Paras. (b)(c) sub. 1989 Sch. 1 para. 4(1).
(2A)		CB 31(3)	Inserted 1982 art. 32(3).
(3)		CB 25(3), 31(4)	
(4)		CB 25(4), 31(5)	Subst. 1975P art. 20(1); am. 1982 Sch. 4 para. 5.
(5)		—	Subst. as for subs. (4).
(6)		CB 25(5), (6), 31(6), (7)	Am. 1975P Sch. 5 para. 21(b); 1979 Sch. 3 para. 5; 1986 Sch. 9 para. 53; rep. in part 1989 Sch. 9.
(7)		—	Rep. 1980(2) Sch.
(8)		CB 25(7), 31(8)	
15	Invalidity pension.		
(1)		CB 33(1)	Am. 1989 Sch. 1 para. 5(1).
(2)		CB 33(2)	Subst. 1989 Sch. 1 para. 5(2).
(3)		CB 33(3)	Am. 1975P art. 16, Sch. 5 para. 22(b), 1990 art. 6(1).
(4)		CB 33(4), (5)	Am. 1975P Sch. 5 para. 22(c); 1979 Sch. 1 para. 1, Sch. 3 para. 6; 1986 Sch. 9 para. 53.
(5)		CB 33(6)	
(5A), (5B)		CB 33(7), (8)	Inserted 1991 D art. 11(1).
(6)		CB 33(9)	Added 1992 Sch. 4 para. 6; rep. in part 1989 Sch. 9.
15A	Statutory sick pay and entitlemen to invalidity pension.	CB 33(10), (11)	Inserted 1985 art. 18(3).
16	Invalidity allowance.		
(1)		CB 34(1), (2)	Am. 1985 art. 11(1).
(2)		CB 34(3)	Am. 1979 Sch. 1 para. 10.
(2A)		—	Inserted 1979 Sch. 1 para. 10(b); spent.

SOCIAL SECURITY (NORTHERN IRELAND) ACTS CONSOLIDATION—*continued.*

Section of Act, etc.	Subject matter	Section of 1992 Act	Remarks
	SOCIAL SECURITY (NORTHERN IRELAND) ACT 1975 (c. 15)—*continued.*		
(2B)–(2D)		CB 34(4)–(6)	Inserted 1985 art. 11(1)(b); 1986 art. 19(1)(b); see also 1975P art. 31A inserted, CP Sch. 2 para. 14(9).
(3)		CB 34(7)	Am. 1985 art. 11(1)(c); see also 1975P art. 31A(4).
17	Determination of days for which benefit is payable.		
(1)		CB 57(1)	Am. 1980(2) art. 3(1); 1989 art. 12(2).
(2)		CB 57(3)	Am. 1989 art. 12(3); part omitted M 2.
(2A)		CB 57(4)	Inserted 1988 Sch. 4 para. 1.
(2B)		CB 57(5)	Inserted 1989 art. 12(4).
(2C), (2D)		CB 57(6), (7)	Inserted 1989 Sch. 8 para. 3.
(3)		CB 57(8)	Rep. in part 1980(2) Sch.
(4), (5)		CB 57(9)(b), 57(10)	Added 1981 art. 6.
18	Duration of unemployment benefit.		
(1)		CB 26(1)	
(2)–(2B)		CB 26(2)–(4)	Subst. 1989 art. 13.
(3)		CB 26(5)	
(4)		CB 26(6)	Subst. 1986 art. 44(1); am. 1989 Sch. 7 para. 7.
19	Loss of employment due to stoppage at work.		
(1), (1A)		CB 27(1), (2)	Subst. 1986 art. 45(1).
(2)		CB 27(3)	
20	Other disqualifications, etc.		
(1)		CB 28(1)	Am. 1986 art. 44(2)(a); Unemployment Benefit (Disqualification Period) Order (NI) 1988 (SR 1988 No. 83); 1988E art. 5(2); 1989 art. 14(1); rep. in part 1988E art. 6(a).
(1A)		CB 28(2)	Inserted 1986 art. 44(3)(a); rep. in part 1989 Sch. 9.

SOCIAL SECURITY (NORTHERN IRELAND) ACTS CONSOLIDATION—*continued.*

Section of Act, etc.	Subject matter	Section of 1992 Act	Remarks
	SOCIAL SECURITY (NORTHERN IRELAND) ACT 1975 (c. 15)—*continued.*		
(2)		CB 32(1), 59(1)	
(3)		CB 28(3), 32(2), 59(2)	
(3A)		CB 28(4)	Inserted 1985 art. 12
(4)		CB 28(5)	Subst. 1989 art. 14(3).
(5)(a), (b), (bb)		CB 28(6)(a), (b), (c)	Am. 1988E art. 5(3).
(c)		CB 28(6)(d), 32(3), 59(3)	
20A	Exemptions from disqualification for unemployment benefit.	CB 29	Inserted 1989 art. 14(4).
21	Maternity Grant.	—	Rep. 1986 Sch. 10.
22	State maternity allowance.		Subst. for ss. 22, 23, 1986 Sch. 4 para 13.
(1)–(3)		CB 35(1)–(3)	
(4)		CB 57(2)	Am. 1988 Sch. 4 para. 2(a).
(4A)		CB 35(4)	Inserted 1988 Sch. 4 para. 2(b).
(5)–(7)		CB 35(5)–(7)	
23	Supplementary provisions as to maternity benefit.	—	See entry for s. 22.
24	Widow's payment.		Subst. 1986 art. 37(1).
(1), (2)		CB 36(1), (2)	
(3)		CB 36(3)	Added 1989 Sch. 7 para. 8.
25	Widowed mother's allowance.		
(1)		CB 37(1)	Am. 1975P Sch. 5 para. 23; 1975CB Sch. 4 para. 10(a); Human Fertilisation and Embryology Act 1990 (c. 37) Sch. 4 para. 3.
(2)		CB 37(2)	Subst. 1975CB Sch. 4 para. 10(b).
(3), (4)		CB 37(3), (4)	Subst. 1989 Sch. 8 para. 4(1).
26	Widow's pension.		
(1)		CB 38(1)	Am. 1975P Sch. 5 para. 24; 1986 art. 37(3)(a).
(2)		CB 39(4), (5)	Am. 1986 art. 37(3)(b).
(3), (4)		CB 38(2), (3)	Subst. 1989 Sch. 8 para. 4(2).

SOCIAL SECURITY (NORTHERN IRELAND) ACTS CONSOLIDATION—*continued.*

Section of Act, etc.	Subject matter	Section of 1992 Act	Remarks

SOCIAL SECURITY (NORTHERN IRELAND) ACT 1975 (c. 15)—*continued.*

Section of Act, etc.	Subject matter	Section of 1992 Act	Remarks
27	Matters affecting entitlement to pension.		
(1)		CB 121(1)	
(2)		CB Sch. 3 para. 5(8)	
(3)–(5)		—	Rep. 1989 Sch. 9.
(6)		CB 43(1)	Rep. in part 1975P Sch. 6.
28	Category A retirement pension.		
(1)		CB 44(1)	Am. 1975P Sch. 5 para. 25; 1989 Sch. 8 para. 4(3); rep. in part 1989 Sch. 9.
(1A)		CB 44(2)	Inserted 1989 Sch. 8 para 4(4).
(2)–(6)		—	Rep. 1975P Sch. 6; 1985 Sch 6.
(7)		CB 47(1)	Am. 1980(2) art. 3(3); 1985 art. 11(2)(a), (b).
(7A)–(7C)		CB 47(2)–(4)	Inserted 1985 art. 11(2)(c); see also 1975P art. 31B inserted, CP Sch 2 para. 14(9).
(8)		CB 47(5)	Rep. in part 1975P Sch. 6.
29	Category B retirement pension.		
(1)		CB 49(1)	
(2), (3)		CB 49(2), (3)	Am. 1989 art. 9(3)(a).
(4)		CB 49(4)	
(5)		CB 49(5)	Rep. in part 1989 Sch. 9.
(6)		CB 49(6)	
(7)		CB 50(1)	Am. and rep. in part 1975P Sch. 5 para. 26, Sch. 6.
(8)		CB 50(2)	Am. 185 art. 11(3).
(9), (9A)		CB 49(7), (8)	Subst. 1989 Sch. 8 para. 4(5).
(10)–(12)		—	Rep. 1975P Sch. 6.
30	Category A and B pensions (supplementary).		
(1)		—	Rep. 1989 Sch. 9.
(2)		—	Spent.
(3)		CB 54(1), (2)	Rep. in part 1989 Sch. 9.
(4)		CB 54(3)	Am. 1975P Sch. 5 para. 27.
(5)		CB 54(4)	Subst. 1989 Sch. 1 para. 2(2).
(6)		CB 54(5)	Added 1979 art. 5(1); am. 1989 Sch. 7 para. 9; rep. in part 1989 Sch. 9; part omitted M 3.

SOCIAL SECURITY (NORTHERN IRELAND) ACTS CONSOLIDATION—*continued.*

Section of Act, etc.	Subject matter	Section of 1992 Act	Remarks
	SOCIAL SECURITY (NORTHERN IRELAND) ACT 1975 (c. 15)—*continued.*		
31	Child's special allowance.	CB 56(1), (2)	Am. 1975CB Sch. 4 para. 11; 1977 art. 18(2); restricted 1986 art. 41.
32	Death grant.	—	Rep. 1986 Sch. 10.
33	Partial satisfaction of contribution conditions.		
(1), (2)		CB 60(1)	Rep. in part 1986 Sch. 10.
(3)		CB 60(4)–(6)	Am. 1975P Sch. 5 para. 28; 1990 Sch. 6 para. 1(1).
(4)		CB 60(7)	Added 1975P art. 21(5).
34	Descriptions of non-contributory benefits.		
(1)		CB 63	Am. 1975P Sch. 5 para. 29; 1984 Sch. 2 para. 2; 1990 art. 4(3); 1991D art. 3(1); rep. in part 1991D Sch. 4.
(2)		—	Rep. 1986 Sch. 10.
35	Attendance allowance.		
(1)		CB 64	Am. 1988 art. 3(1); 1991D art. 4(1).
(2)		CB 65(1)	Am. 1979 art. 3(2); 1989 Sch. 8 para. 5(2); rep. in part 199D Sch. 4.
(2A)		CB 65(2)	Inserted 1979 art. 3(3).
(2B), (2C)		CB 66	Inserted 1990 art. 3(1); am. 1991D Sch. 2 para. 2(1); rep. in part 1991D Sch 4.
(3)		CB 65(3)	Subst. 1991D Sch. 2 para. 2(2).
(4)		CB 65(4), (6)	Am. 1979 art. 3(5); 1989 Sch. 8 para. 5(3); 1990 art. 3(2); 1991D Sch. 2 para. 2(3); rep. in part 1991D Sch 4.
(4A)		CB 65(5)	Inserted 1980 Sch. 1 para. 8; am. 1989 Sch. 8 para. 5(4), 1991D Sch. 2 para. 2(3).
(5)		—	Rep. 1991D Sch. 4.
(5A)		CB 67(1)	Inserted 1979 art. 3(6).
(6)		CB 67(2)	Rep. in part 1991D Sch. 4.
36	Severe disablement allowance.		Subst. 1984 art. 5(1).
(1)–(4)		CB 68(1)–(4)	
(4A)		CB 68(5)	Inserted 1985 Sch. 4 para. 2.
(5), (6)		CB 68(6), (7)	

SOCIAL SECURITY (NORTHERN IRELAND) ACTS CONSOLIDATION—*continued.*

Section of Act, etc.	Subject matter	Section of 1992 Act	Remarks

SOCIAL SECURITY (NORTHERN IRELAND) ACT 1975 (c. 15)—*continued.*

Section of Act, etc.	Subject matter	Section of 1992 Act	Remarks
(6A), (6B)		CB 68(8), (9)	Inserted 1989 Sch. 8 para. 6.
(6C)		CB 86(10)	Inserted 1991D art. 11(2).
(7)		CB 68(11)	Am. 1989 Sch. 8 para. 2(5); 1990 Sch. 6 para. 19(4); rep. in part 1989 Sch. 9.
(8)		CB 68(6), (12)	
36A	Severe disablement allowance: age related addition.	CB 69	Inserted 1990 art. 4(1).
37	Invalid care allowance.		
(1)		CB 70(1)	
(2)		CB 70(2)	Am. 1991D Sch. 2 para. 3.
(3)		CB 70(3)	Rep. in part 1986 Sch. 10.
(4), (5)		CB 70(4), (5)	
(6)		CB 70(6), (10)	
(7)–(9)		CB 70(7)–(9)	
37ZA	Disability living allowance.	CB 71	Inserted 1991D art. 3(2).
37ZB	The care component.	CB 72	Inserted 1991D art. 3(2).
37ZC	The mobility component.	CB 73	Inserted 1991D art. 3(2).
37ZD	Persons 65 or over.	CB 75	Inserted 1991D art. 3(2).
37ZE	Disability living allowance— supplementary.	CB 76	Inserted 1991D art. 3(2).
37A	Mobility allowance.	—	Rep. 1991D Sch. 4.
38	Guardian's allowance.		
(1)		CB 77(1), (7)	Am. 1975CB Sch. 4 para. 13(a).
(2), (3)		CB 77(2), (3)	
(4)		CB 77(8)	Rep. in part 1975CB Sch. 4 para. 13(b), Sch. 5.
(5)		CB 77(9)	Subst. 1975CB Sch. 4 para. 13(c).
(6)		CB 77(10)	Am. 1986 art. 46(a).
(7)		CB 77(11)	Inserted 1986 art. 46(b).
39	Retirement benefits for the aged.		
(1)(a)		CB 78(1)	
(1)(b)		CB 78(2)	Rep. in part 1989 Sch. 9.
(1)(c)		CB 78(3), (4)	Am. 1979 Sch. 1 para. 2; 1986 art. 19(1).
(2)		CB 78(5)	Rep. in part 1985 Sch. 6.

SOCIAL SECURITY (NORTHERN IRELAND) ACTS CONSOLIDATION—*continued.*

Section of Act, etc.	Subject matter	Section of 1992 Act	Remarks
	SOCIAL SECURITY (NORTHERN IRELAND) ACT 1975 (c. 15)—*continued.*		
(2A)		CB 78(6)	Inserted 1985 art. 14(1)(b).
(3), (3A)		CB 78(7), (8)	Subst. 1989 Sch. 8 para. 4(6).
(4)		CB 78(9)	
40	Age addition.	CB 79	
41	Beneficiary's dependent children.		
(1)		CB 80(1)	Am. 1975CB Sch. 4 para. 14(a); rep. in part 1989 Sch. 9.
(2)		CB 80(2)	Am. 1984 Sch. 3 para. 2(a); rep. in part 1984 Sch. 6; 1986 Sch. 10.
(2A)		CB 80(3)	Inserted 1984 Sch. 3 para. 2(c).
(2B)		CB 80(4)	Inserted 1984 Sch. 3 para. 2(c); am. 1992U art. 11.
(2C)		—	Rep. 1986 Sch. 10.
(2D)		CB 80(7)	Inserted 1984 Sch. 3 para. 2(c).
(3)		—	Rep. 1984 Sch. 6.
(4), (5)		CB 80(5), (6)	Am. 1975 Sch. 4 para. 14(b), (c).
(6)		—	Rep. 1980 Sch. 4.
42	Additional provisions as to increase under s. 41.	—	Rep. 1975CB Sch. 5.
43	Limits of increase for dependent children.		
(1)		CB 81(1), (2)	Am. 1975CB Sch. 4 para. 16(a); rep. in part 1975CB Sch. 5.
(2)		CB 81(3)	Am. 1975CB Sch. 4 para. 16(b); 1977 art. 18(3).
(3), (4)		—	Rep.1975CB Sch. 5.
44	Short term benefit increase for adult dependants.		
(1)		CB 82(1)	Am. 1975CB Sch. 4 para. 17(a); 1980 Sch. 1 para. 5(2); 1988 Sch. 4 para. 3(a).
(2)		CB 82(2)	Am. 1975CB Sch. 4 para. 17(a); 1980 Sch. 1 para. 5(2).
(a)		CB 82(3)	Am. 1988 Sch. 4 para. 3(b).
(b)		—	Rep. 1980 Sch. 4.
(3)(c)		CB 82(4)	Am. 1975CB Sch. 4 para. 17(b); 1980 Sch. 1 para. 4.
(4)		CB 82(5)	
(5), (6)		—	Rep. 1980 Sch. 1 para. 5(1)(a), Sch. 4 Part II.
45	Pension increase (wife).		

SOCIAL SECURITY (NORTHERN IRELAND) ACTS CONSOLIDATION—*continued.*

Section of Act, etc.	Subject matter	Section of 1992 Act	Remarks
	SOCIAL SECURITY (NORTHERN IRELAND) ACT 1975 (c. 15)—*continued.*		
(1)		CB 83(1)	
(2)		CB 83(2)	Am. 1975CB Sch. 4 para. 18; 1988 Sch. 4 para. 4(a).
(2A)		CB 83(3)	Inserted 1985 art. 15(1); rep. in part 1988 Sch. 5.
(3), (4)		—	Rep. 1985 Sch. 6.
45A	Pension increase (husband).		Inserted 1984 art. 6.
(1)		CB 84(1)	Am. 1985 art. 15(2)(a).
(2)		CB 84 (2)	Subst. 1985 art. 15(2)(b); am. 1988 Sch. 4, para 5(a).
(3)		CB 84(3)	Subst. 1985 art. 15(2)(b); rep. in part 1988 Sch. 5.
46	Pension increase (person with care of children).		
(1)		CB 85(1)	
(2)		CB 85(2)	Am. 1975CB Sch. 4 para. 19; 1980 Sch. 1 para.4.
(3)		CB 85(3)	
(4)		CB 85(4)	Subst. 1985 art. 15(3); rep. in part 1988 Sch. 5.
47	Invalidity pension (dependent relative).		
(1)		CB 86(1)	Am. 1975CB Sch. 4 para. 20; 1980 Sch. 1 para. 5(2); 1989 Sch. 8 para. 7(1); rep. in part 1980 Sch. 4 Part II.
(1A)		CB 86(2)	Inserted 1985 art. 15(4)(b).
(2)		—	Rep. 1980 Sch. 4 Part II.
47A	Rate of increase where associated retirement pension is attributable to reduced contributions.	CB 87	Inserted 1980 Sch. 1 para. 5(1); am. 1990 Sch. 6 para. 1(2).
47B	Earnings to include occupational pensions for purposes of benefits.	CB 89	Inserted 1984 art. 8(a); am. 1989 art. 11(3); rep. in part 1988 Sch. 5.
48	Pension increases: supplementary provisions.		
(1)		CB 88	
(2), (3)		—	Rep. 1989 Sch. 9.
49	Beneficiaries under sections 36 and 37.	CB 90	Am. 1984 Sch. 2 para. 2.
49A	Effect of trade disputes on entitlement to increases.	CB 91	Inserted 1986 art. 45(2).

SOCIAL SECURITY (NORTHERN IRELAND) ACTS CONSOLIDATION—*continued.*

SOCIAL SECURITY (NORTHERN IRELAND) ACT 1975 (c. 15)—*continued.*

Section of Act, etc.	Subject matter	Section of 1992 Act	Remarks
50	Descriptions of industrial injuries benefits.		
(1)		CB 94(1)	Subst. 1986 Sch. 3 para. 2.
(1A)		CB 94(2)	Inserted 1988 Sch. 4 para. 8.
(2)		—	Rep. 1986 Sch. 10.
(3)		CB 94(3)	
(4)		CB 94(4)	Subst. 1982 Sch. 4 para. 8(2).
(5)		CB 94(5)	Rep. 1986 Sch. 10 (see CB 94(7)).
(6)		CB 94(6)	Inserted 1982 Sch. 4 para. 8(3).
50A	Sickness benefit in respect of industrial injury.		Inserted 1982 art. 32(4).
(1), (2)		CB 102(1), (2)	
(3)		CB 102(3)	Am. 1989 Sch. 1 para. 8(1).
51	Relevant employments.	CB 95(1)–(3)	
52	Earner acting in breach of regulations, etc.	CB 98	
53	Earner travelling in employer's transport.	CB 99	
54	Accidents happening while meeting emergency.	CB 100	
55	Accidents caused by another's misconduct, etc.	CB 101	
56	Injury benefit.	—	Rep. 1982 Sch. 5
57	Disablement gratuity and pension.		
(1)		CB 103(1), Sch. 7 para. 9(1)	Am. 1986 Sch. 3 para. 3(1).
(1A)–(1C)		CB 103 (2)–(4)	inserted 1986 Sch. 3 para. 3(2).
(2)		—	Rep. 1984 Sch. 6 Part II:
(3)		CB 103(5)	
(4)		CB 103(6), Sch. 7 para. 9(3)	Subst. 1982 art. 32(2); am. 1989 Sch. 7 para. 11.
(5)		CB Sch. 7 para. 9(1), (2)	
(6)		CB 103 (7), (8)	Am. 1986 Sch. 3 para. 3(4).
58	Unemployability supplement.	CB Sch. 7 para. 2	

SOCIAL SECURITY (NORTHERN IRELAND) ACTS CONSOLIDATION—*continued.*

Section of Act, etc.	Subject matter	Section of 1992 Act	Remarks

SOCIAL SECURITY (NORTHERN IRELAND) ACT 1975 (c. 15)—*continued.*

Section of Act, etc.	Subject matter	Section of 1992 Act	Remarks
59	Increase of unemployability supplement.		Rep. 1986 Sch. 10, with saving in 1986 Sch. 3 para. 4.
(1)		CB Sch. 7 para. 3(1)	Am. 1979 Sch. 1 para. 12; am. 1985 art. 11(4)(a); proviso spent.
(1A)–(1C)		CB Sch. 7 para. 3 (2)–(4)	Inserted (with saving) 1985 art. 11(4)(b); am. 1986 art. 19 (1); see also 1979P art. 31C inserted, CP Sch. 2 para. 14 (9).
(2), (3)		CB Sch. 7 para. 3 (5),(6)	
(4)		CB Sch. 7 para. 3 (7), (8)	Am. 1980 (2) art. 3(3).
(5)		CB Sch. 7 para. 3 (10)	
59A	Reduced earnings allowance.		Inserted 1986 Sch. 3 para. 5 (1).
(1)		CB Sch. 7 para. 11 (1)	Am. 1989 Sch. 7 para. 12; 1990 art. 5(1).
(1A), (1B)		CB Sch. 7 para. 11 (2), (3)	Inserted 1990 art. 5(2).
(2)–(5)		CB Sch. 7 para. 11 (4), (7)	
(6)		CB Sch. 7 para. 11 (8)	Am. 1990 art. 5(3).
(7)		CB Sch. 7 para. 11 (9)	
(8)		CB Sch. 7 para. 11 (10), (11)	Am. 1988 art. 4(2), Sch. 4 para. 9(a).
(9)		CB Sch. 7 para. 11 (12)	
(10)		CB Sch. 7 para. 11 (13)	Added 1986 Sch. 3 para. 5(1).
(10A)		CB Sch. 7 paras. 11 (14), 13 (11)	Inserted 1988 Sch. 4 para. 9(b).

SOCIAL SECURITY (NORTHERN IRELAND) ACTS CONSOLIDATION—*continued.*

Section of Act, etc.	Subject matter	Section of 1992 Act	Remarks
	SOCIAL SECURITY (NORTHERN IRELAND) ACT 1975 (c. 15)—*continued.*		
(10B)		CB Sch. 7 para. 11 (1)	Inserted 1990 art. 5(4).
(11)		—	Rep. 1988 Sch. 5
59B	Retirement allowance		Inserted 1988 art. 4(1).
(1)		CB Sch. 7 para. 13 (1)	Am. 1989 Sch. 1 para. 8(2); rep. in part 1990 Sch. 7.
(2)		CB Sch. 7 para. 13 (2)	
(3)		CB Sch. 7 para. 13 (3)	Rep. in part 1990 Sch. 7.
(4)		—	Rep. 1990 Sch. 7.
(5)		CB Sch. 7 para. 13 (4)	Am. 1989 Sch. 1 para. 8(5).
(5A)		CB Sch. 7 para. 13(5)	Inserted 1989 art. 19(3).
(6)		CB Sch. 7 para 13 (6)	
(7), (8)		CB Sch. 7 para. 13 (8), (9)	Added 1989 Sch. 1 para 8(6); rep in part 1990 Sch. 7.
(9)		CB Sch. 7 para. 13(10)	Added 1990 art. 5(6).
60	Increase of disablement pension for special hardship.	—	Rep. 1986 Sch. 10.
61	Increase where constant attendance needed.		
(1), (2)		CB 104(1), (2)	
(3), (4)		CB 104(3), (4)	Inserted 1986 Sch. 3 para. 6.
62	Increase during hospital treatment.	CB Sch. 7 para. 10(2), (3)	Rep. 1986 Sch. 10, with saving in 1986 Sch. 3 para. 7.
63	Increase for exceptionally severe disablement.	CB 105	
64	Beneficiary's dependent children.		Rep. 1986 Sch. 10, with saving in 1986 Sch. 3 para. 4.
(1)		CB Sch. 7 para. 4(1)	Am. 1975CB Sch. 4 para. 22(a); rep in part 1982 Sch. 5.

SOCIAL SECURITY (NORTHERN IRELAND) ACTS CONSOLIDATION—*continued.*

Section of Act, etc.	Subject matter	Section of 1992 Act	Remarks
SOCIAL SECURITY (NORTHERN IRELAND) ACT 1975 (c. 15)—*continued.*			
(1A)-(1D)		CB Sch. 7 para. 4(3)–(6)	Inserted 1984 Sch. 3 para. 3; subs. (1B) am. Social Security (Industrial Injuries) (Dependency) (Permitted Earnings Limits) Order (NI) 1991 (SR 1991 No. 72) art. 2.
(2)		CB Sch. 7 para. 4(2)	Rep. in part 1982 Sch. 5.
(3), (4)		—	Rep. 1975CB Sch. 5 Part I.
65	Additional provisions as to increase under section 64.		Rep. 1986 Sch. 10, with saving in 1986 Sch. 3 para. 4.
(1)		CB Sch. 7 para. 5(1)	Am. 1975CB Sch. 4 para. 23(a).
(2)		CB Sch. 7 para. 5(2)	Am. 1975CB Sch. 4 para. 23(b); 1977 art. 18(3).
(3)		—	Rep. 1975CB Sch. 5 Part I.
(4)		—	Rep. 1980 Sch. 4 Part II.
66	Adult dependants.		Rep. 1986 Sch. 10, with saving in 1986 Sch. 3 para. 4.
(1)		CB Sch. 7 para. 6(1)	Am. 1975CB Sch. 4 para. 24; 1980 Sch. 1 paras. 4, 6; rep. in part 1980 Sch. 4 Part II; 1982 Sch. 5.
(2)		CB Sch. 7 para. 6(2)	Rep. in part 1982 Sch. 5.
(3)–(6)		CB Sch. 7 para. 6(3)–(6)	Subst. 1985 art. 15(5); subs. (3), (4) rep. in part 1988 Sch. 5.
(7)		CB Sch. 7 para. 6(7)	
(8)		—	Rep. 1980 Sch. 4 Part II
66A	Earnings to include occupational and personal pensions for purposes of disablement pension.	CB Sch. 7 para. 7	Inserted 1984 art. 8(b) Am. 1989 art. 11(3).
67	Industrial death benefit.		
(1)		CB Sch. 7 para. 15(1)	
(2)		CB Sch. 7 para. 15(2), (3)	Am. 1977 art. 18(4); rep. in part 1986 Sch. 10.
(3)		CB Sch. 7 para. 15(4)	
68	Widow's benefit.		
(1)		CB Sch. 7 para. 16(1)	
(2)		CB Sch. 7 para. 16(2)	Rep. in part 1975CB Sch. 5.

SOCIAL SECURITY (NORTHERN IRELAND) ACTS CONSOLIDATION—*continued.*

Section of Act, etc.	Subject matter	Section of 1992 Act	Remarks
	SOCIAL SECURITY (NORTHERN IRELAND) ACT 1975 (c. 15)—*continued.*		
(3)		CB Sch. 7 para. 16(3)	
69	Widower's benefit (entitlement and rate).	CB Sch. 7 para. 17	
70	Children of deceased's family.	Sch. 7 para. 18	Subst. 1984 Sch. 3 para. 4.
71	Parents.	—	Rep. 1986 Sch. 10.
72	Relatives.	—	Rep. 1986 Sch. 10.
73	Woman having care of deceased's children.	—	Rep. 1986 Sch. 10.
74	Beneficiary previously maintained by deceased.	—	Rep. 1986 Sch. 10.
75	Death of person with constant attendance allowance.	CB Sch. 7 para. 20	
76	Benefit in respect of industrial disease, etc.		
(1)–(4)		CB 108(1)–(4)	
(4A)		CB 108(5)	Inserted 1990 Sch. 6 para. 2(1).
(5)		CB 108(6)	
77	General provision as to benefit under s. 76.		
(1)		CB 109(1)	
(2)		CB 109(2)	AM. 1990 art. 5(7), Sch. 6 para. 2(2) rep. in part 1982 Sch. 5.
(3)		CB 109(3)	
(4), (5)		CB 109(4)–(7)	Inserted 1986 Sch. 3 para. 13.
78	Respiratory diseases.	CB 110	
79–81	—	—	Rep. 1986 Sch. 10.
82	Disqualification and suspension.		
(1), (2)		—	Rep. 1985 Sch. 6.
(3), (4)		—	Rep. 1986 Sch. 10.
(5)		CB 113(1)	
(6)		CB 113(3)	Rep. in part 1986 Sch. 10.
83	Disqualifications disregarded for certain purposes.	CB 113(3)	Subst. 1985 Sch. 5 para. 3.
84	Persons maintaining dependants, etc.		
(1), (2)		CB 114(1), (2)	
(3)		—	Rep. 1986 Sch. 10.
(4)		CB 114(3)	Am. 1985 art. 15(6).
(5)		CB 114(4)	Subst. 1985 art. 15(8).

SOCIAL SECURITY (NORTHERN IRELAND) ACTS CONSOLIDATION—*continued.*

Section of Act, etc.	Subject matter	Section of 1992 Act	Remarks

SOCIAL SECURITY (NORTHERN IRELAND) ACT 1975 (c. 15)—*continued.*

Section of Act, etc.	Subject matter	Section of 1992 Act	Remarks
84A	Dependency increases: continuation of awards in cases of fluctuating earnings.		
85	Overlapping benefits.		
(1)		A 71(1)	Am. 1975CB Sch. 4 para. 29.
(2)		A 71(2)	Am. 1975CB Sch. 4 para. 29; rep. in part 1975CB Sch. 5.
(3)		A 71(3)	
(4), (5)		A 71(4), (5)	Inserted 1979 art. 12(1)
86	Set-off of overpayments.		Rep. 1975CB Sch. 5, 1986 Sch. 10.
87(1)	Benefit to be inalienable.	A 163(1)	Extended 1986 Sch. 9 para. 32(a).
(2)		A 163(2)	
(3)		A 163(3)	Am. Judgments Enforcement (Northern Ireland Consequential Amendments) Order 1981 (SI 1981/234) art. 5; 1981MC Sch. 6 para. 34(b); rep. in part 1982 Sch.5.
88	Notification of accidents.	A 6	Rep. in part 1986 Sch. 10.
89	Medical examination and treatment.	A 7	Rep. in part 1982 Sch. 5.
90	Obligations of claimants.		
(1)		—	Rep. 1982 Sch. 5.
(2)		A 8(1)	Rep. in part 1982 Sch. 5; 1986 Sch. 10 (with saving in 1988 Sch. 1 para. 6).
(3)		A 8(2)	Subst. 1986 Sch. 9 para. 55; rep. in part 1985 Sch. 6.
(4)		A 8(3)	Rep. in part 1982 Sch. 5.
91	Adjustments for successive accidents.		
(1)		CB 107(1)	Am. 1982 Sch. 4 para. 11; rep. in part 1982 Sch. 5.
(2)		CB 107(2)	Omitted in part M 4.
92	Benefit forgone for unabated sick pay.		Rep. 1986 Sch. 10.
93	Principal questions for Department.		
(1)		A 15(1)	Am. 1977 art. 18(5); 1986 art. 53(2), Sch. 5 Part II, 1991SP art. 4(3), 1991C art. 5(1); rep. in part 1975CB Sch. 5.
(2)		A 15(2)	
(2A)		A 15(3)	Inserted 1989 Sch. 3 para. 1; am. M 5.
(3)		A 15(4)	

SOCIAL SECURITY (NORTHERN IRELAND) ACTS CONSOLIDATION—*continued.*

Section of Act, etc.	Subject matter	Section of 1992 Act	Remarks
	SOCIAL SECURITY (NORTHERN IRELAND) ACT 1975 (c. 15)—*continued.*		
94	Appeal on question of law.	A 16	Am. M 6.
95	Other questions for Department.	—	Rep. 1986 Sch. 10.
96	Review of decisions under ss. 93, 95.		
(1)		A 17(1)	Subst. 1986 Sch. 5 para. 2; am. M 6.
(2)		A 17(2), (3)	Am. 1980 Sch. 1 para. 9.
97	Adjudicating officials and bodies.		
(1)		A 36(1)	Subst. 1983 Sch. 1 para. 1; am. 1990 Sch. 6 para. 3(1).
1A)		A 36(2)	Subst. 1983 Sch. 1 para. 1.
(1B)-(1E)		A 37	Subst. 1983 Sch. 1 para. 1.
(2)		A 39(1)	Subst. 1983 Sch. 1 para. 1.
(2A)		A 39(2)	Subst. (for (2A), (2B)) 1984 art. 10(a).
(2C)-(2D)		A 39(3), (4), 41(4), (5), 49(1)-(3)	Subst. 1983 Sch. 1 para. 1.
(2E)		A 49(4)	Subst. 1983 Sch. 1 para. 1.
(3)		A 50(1)	Am. Social Security Act 1979 (c. 18) s. 9(2), 1980A s. 12.
(4)		—	Introduces Sch. 10.
98	Claims and questions to be submitted to adjudication officers.		
(1)		A 18(1)	Am. 1991D Sch. 1 para. 2.
(2), (2A)		A 18(2), (4)	Subst. 1986 Sch. 5 para. 3.
(3)		A 18(5)	
99	Decision of adjudication officer.		
(1)		A 19(1)	Am. 1991D Sch. 1 para. 3(1).
(2)		A 19(2)	Subst. 1986 Sch. 5 para. 4; am. 1991D Sch. 1 para. 3(2).
2A)		A 19(3)	Inserted 1991D Sch. 1 para. 3(3).
(3)		A 19(4), (5)	Am. 1986 s. 53(7)(c).
(4)		A 19(6)	Inserted 1989 Sch. 3 para. 2.
100	Appeal to social security appeal tribunal.		
(1)		A 20(1)	Modified for certain benefits, 1986 art. 53(3), (7)(c); am. 1991D Sch. 1 para. 4(a); rep. in part 1986 Sch. 10.

SOCIAL SECURITY (NORTHERN IRELAND) ACTS CONSOLIDATION—*continued.*

Section of Act, etc.	Subject matter	Section of 1992 Act	Remarks
	SOCIAL SECURITY (NORTHERN IRELAND) ACT 1975 (c. 15)—*continued.*		
(2)		A 20(2)	Modified 1986 art. 53(7); am. 1986 Sch. 5 para. 5(b); am. 1991D Sch. 1 para. 4(b).
(3)		A 20(3)	Am. 1986 Sch. 5 para. 5(c); rep. in part 1989 Sch. 9.
(4)		A 20(4)	Subst. 1986 Sch. 5 para. 5(d).
(5)			Rep. 1986 Sch. 10.
(6)		A 20(5)	Subst. 1986 art. 53(7), Sch. 5 para. 5(e); am. 1991D Sch. 1 para. 4(c).
(7), (8)		A 20(6), (7)	Inserted 1990 Sch. 6 para. 4(1).
100A	Reviews of decisions by adjudication officers as to attendance allowance or disability living allowance.	A 28	Inserted 1991D Sch. 1 para. 5.
100B	Further reviews of decisions as to attendance allowance or disability living allowance.	A 29	Inserted 1991D Sch. 1 para. 5.
100C	Reviews of decisions as to attendance allowance or disability living allowance: supplementary.	A 30	Inserted 1991D Sch. 1 para. 5.
100D	Appeals following reviews of decisions as to attendance allowance or disability living allowance.	A 31, 41	Inserted 1991D Sch. 1 para. 5.
101	Appeal from social security appeal tribunal to Commissioner.		
(1)		A 21(1), 32(1)	Am. 1986 Sch. 5 para. 6(1).
(2)		A 21(2), (3), (4), 32(2)	Am. 1986 Sch. 5 para. 6(2); 1990 Sch. 6 para. 4(2); 1991D Sch. 1 para. 6(a).
(3)		A 21(5), 32(2)	Am. 1990 Sch. 6 para. 4(3); rep. in part 1986 Sch. 10.
(4)		A 21(6), 32(3)	
(5)		A 21(7), (8), 32(4)	Subst. 1986 Sch. 5 para. 6(3); am. 1989 Sch. 3 para. 6.
(5A)		A 21(9), 32(4)	Subst. 1986 Sch. 5 para. 6(3); rep. in part 1991D Sch. 4.
(5B)		A 21(10), 32(4)	Subst. 1986 Sch. 5 para. 6(3).
(6), (7)		—	Rep. 1989 Sch. 9.
102	Questions first arising on appeal.	A 34	Am. 1986 Sch. 5 para. 7; 1991D Sch. 1 para. 7.
103	Reference of special questions.	A 35	Subst. 1986 Sch. 5 para. 8; am. 1989 Sch. 3 para. 15(1)
104	Review of decisions.		

SOCIAL SECURITY (NORTHERN IRELAND) ACTS CONSOLIDATION—*continued.*

Section of Act, etc.	Subject matter	Section of 1992 Act	Remarks
	SOCIAL SECURITY (NORTHERN IRELAND) ACT 1975 (c. 15)—*continued.*		
(1)		A 23(1), (3)	Subst. 1986 Sch. 5 para. 9; am. 1988 Sch. 4 para.11; 1989 art. 12(5), Sch. 3 para. 11(1), 1991D Sch. 1 para. 8(a).
(1ZA)		A 23(5), 33(11)	Inserted 1989 Sch. 3 para. 11(2).
(1A)		A 23(2)	Inserted 1983 Sch. 1 para. 2; rep. in part 1986 Sch. 10.
(2), (3)		A 24(1), (2)	
(3A)		A 24(3), 33(5)	Inserted 1986 Sch. 5 para. 9.
(3B)		A 27	Inserted 1989 Sch. 3 para 7.
(4)		A 26	
(5)		A 25(1), 33(10)	Inserted 1986 Sch. 5 para. 9(d); am. 1989 Sch. 3 para. 11(3), (4).
(6)		A 25(2)	Inserted 1990 art. 8(3).
(7)-(10)		A 67	Inserted 1990 Sch. 6 para. 5(1).
104A	Reviews of decisions on appeal as to attendance allowance and disability living allowance.		
(1), (2)		A 33(1), (2)	Inserted 1991D Sch. 1 para. 9.
(4)-(7)		A 33(6)-(9)	Inserted 1991D Sch. 1 para. 9.
(8)		A 33(12)	Inserted 1991D Sch. 1 para. 5.
(9)		A 33(5), (10), (11)	Inserted 1991D Sch. 1 para. 9.
105, 106	Attendance Allowance Board for Northern Ireland etc.	—	Rep. 1991D Sch. 4.
107	Declaration that accident is an industrial accident.		
(1)-(3)		A 42(1)-(3)	
(4)		A 42(4), (5)	Rep. in part 1986 Sch. 10 subject to saving in 1988 Sch. 1 para. 6.
(5)		A 42(6)	
(6)		A 42(7)	Am. 1986 Sch. 5 para. 11; rep. in part 1986 Sch. 10.
108	Disablement questions.		
(1)		A 43(1)	Am. 1984 Sch. 2 para. 4; 1986 Sch. 3 para. 14(a); 1989 Sch 3 para. 12(1).
(2)		A 43(2)	Subst. 1983 Sch. 2 para. 1(1); am. 1984 Sch. 2 para.5.
(3)		—	Introduces Sch. 12.

SOCIAL SECURITY (NORTHERN IRELAND) ACTS CONSOLIDATION—*continued.*

Section of Act, etc.	Subject matter	Section of 1992 Act	Remarks
	SOCIAL SECURITY (NORTHERN IRELAND) ACT 1975 (c. 15)—*continued.*		
(4)		A 43(3)	Subst. 1983 Sch. 2 para. 1(3).
(4A), (4B)		A 43(4), (5)	Subst. 1989 Sch. 3 para. 12(2).
(5)		A 43(6)	Subst. 1983 Sch. 2 para. 1(3).
109	Medical appeals and references.		
(1)		A 44(1)	Am. 1983 Sch. 2 para. 2; 1984 Sch. 2 para. 6.
(2)		A 44(2)	Rep. in part 1983 Sch. 3.
(3)		A 44(3)	Am. 1983 Sch. 2 para. 2; 1986 Sch. 5 para. 12.
110	Review of medical decisions.		
(1)		A 45(1)	Am. 1979 Sch. 3 para. 7; rep. in part 1986 Sch. 10.
(1A), (1B)		A 45(2), (3)	Inserted 1986 Sch. 5 para. 13(b).
(2)		A 45(4)	Am. 1983 Sch. 2 para. 3(b).
(3)–(5)		A 45(5)–(7)	
(6)		A 45(8)	Am. 1983 Sch. 2 para. 3(c); 1984 Sch. 2 para. 7(a).
(7)		A 45(9)	Am. 1983 Sch. 2 para. 3(d); 1984 Sch. 2 para. 7(b).
111, 112		—	Rep. 1983 Sch.3.
112A	Appeal etc. on question of law to Commissioner.		Inserted 1986A Sch. 9 para. 1.
(1)–(3)		A 46(1)–(3)	
(4)		—	Rep. 1989 Sch. 9.
(5)		A 46(4)	Rep. in part 1989 Sch. 9.
(5A), (5B)		A 46(5), (6)	Inserted 1989 Sch. 3 para. 9(2).
(6)		—	Spent.
113	Adjudication as to industrial diseases.		
(1)		A 60(1)	
(2)(a), (b)		A 60(2; A 144(5)	Am. 1983 Sch. 2 para. 4.
(2)(c)		A 165(5)	
(3)		A Sch. 2 para. 8	Am. 1983 Sch. 2 para. 4.

SOCIAL SECURITY (NORTHERN IRELAND) ACTS CONSOLIDATION—*continued.*

Section of Act, etc.	Subject matter	Section of 1992 Act	Remarks
	SOCIAL SECURITY (NORTHERN IRELAND) ACT 1975 (c. 15)—*continued.*		
114	Regulations as to determinations of questions.		
(1), (2)		A 56(1)–(3)	
(2A)–(2C)		A56(5)–(7)	Inserted 1986 Sch. 5 para. 14.
(3), (4)			Rep. 1986 Sch. 10.
(5)		A56(8)	
115	Procedure.		
(1)		A57(1)	
(2)		A57(1), Sch. 3 para. 1	Am. 1983 Sch. 1 para. 3, Sch. 2 para. 5; 1991D Sch. 1 para. 10.
(3), (4)		A57(2), (3)	
(4A)		A57(4)	Inserted 1991C art. 5(2).
(5)		A57(5)	Am. 1989 Sch. 3 para. 1(2).
(6)		A57(6)	
115A	Power of adjudicating authorities to refer matters to experts.	A51	Inserted 1989 Sch. 3 para. 3(1); rep. in part 1991D Sch. 4.
115B	Assessors.	A54	Inserted 1989 Sch. 3 para. 3(1); rep. in part 1991D Sch. 4.
115C	References of claims relating to attendance allowance and disability living allowance to medical practitioners and Disability Living Allowance Advisory Board.	A52	Inserted 1991D Sch. 1 para. 13.
115D	Medical examination etc. in relation to appeals to disability appeal tribunals.	A53	Inserted 1991D Sch. 1 para. 13.
116	Tribunals of 2 or 3 Commissioners.	A55	Am. 1980A s. 12.
117	Finality of decisions.		
(1)		A58(1)	Am. 1983 Sch. 1 para. 4.
(2)		A58(2)	
(3)		A58(3)	Am. 1983 Sch. 2 para. 6.
(4)		A58(4)	Rep. 1986 Sch. 10, subject to saving in 1988 Sch. 1 para. 6.
(5)		A58(5)	Rep. in part 1986 Sch. 10, subject to saving in 1988 Sch. 1 para. 6.
118	Question as to child of family.	—	Rep. 1975CB Sch. 5.
119	Effect of adjudication on payment and recovery.		
(1)–(2A)		—	Rep. 1986 Sch. 10.
(3)		A59(1)	
(4)		A59(2)	Rep. in part 1986 Sch. 10.
(5)		—	Rep. 1986 Sch. 10.

SOCIAL SECURITY (NORTHERN IRELAND) ACTS CONSOLIDATION—*continued.*

Section of Act, etc.	Subject matter	Section of 1992 Act	Remarks
	SOCIAL SECURITY (NORTHERN IRELAND) ACT 1975 (c. 15)—*continued.*		
120	Amendments following alterations in Great Britain.	A129	Am. 1979 Sch. 3 para. 9, 1985 art. 9(5); rep. in part 1977 Sch., 1986 Sch. 10, 1991RF Sch. 2.
121	Supplementary provisions as to up-rating.	—	Rep. 1986 Sch. 10.
122	Crown employment.	CB115	
123	Her Majesty's forces.	CB116	
124	Mariners, airmen, etc.		
(1), (2)		CB117(1), (2)	
(3)		—	Rep. 1977 Sch. 2.
125	Married women and widows.		
(1)		CB118	
(2), (3)			Rep. 1975P Sch. 6.
126	Persons outside Northern Ireland.	CB119	
127	National Insurance Fund.		
(1), (2)		A141(1), (2)	
(3)		A141(3)	Am. Finance Act 1980 (c. 48) Sch. 19 para. 5(4).
(4)		A141(4)	
(5)		A145(1)	
(6)		A145(2)–(4)	Rep. in part 1975P Sch. 6.
128	Destination of contributions and supplements.		
(1)		A142(1)	Rep. in part 1991RF Sch. 2.
(2)		A142(2)	
(2A)		A142(3)	Inserted 1990 art. 18(3).
(2B)		A142(4)	Inserted 1990 art. 19(1).
(3)		—	Rep. 1989 Sch. 9.
(4)		A142(5), (6)	Am. 1985 Sch. 5 para. 4, SR 1987 No. 25, SR 1989 No. 9, 1989 art. 3(2), 1991C art. 6; repealed in part 1991RF Sch. 2.
(4A), (4B)		A142(7), (8)	Inserted 1981C art. 5; am. 1991C art. 6(b).
(5)		A142(9)–(11)	Rep. in part 1991RF Sch. 2.
(5A)–(5D)			Rep. 1991RF Sch. 2.
(6)		A142(12)	Am. 1979 art. 11.
129	General financial arrangements.		
(1)		A143(1)	

SOCIAL SECURITY (NORTHERN IRELAND) ACTS CONSOLIDATION—*continued.*

Section of Act, etc.	Subject matter	Section of 1992 Act	Remarks
	SOCIAL SECURITY (NORTHERN IRELAND) ACT 1975 (c. 15)—*continued.*		
(2), (3)		A143(2)	Am. 1984 Sch. 2 para. 2, 1989 art. 29(3), 1990 art. 18(4), 1991D Sch. 1 para. 18; rep. in part 1991D Sch. 4.
(3)		A143(3)	
(5)		A145(5)	Am. 1990 art. 18(5); rep. in part 1990 Sch. 7.
(6)		—	Rep. 1986 Sch. 10.
(7)		A143(5)	Added 1990 art. 19(2).
130	Payments for purposes of s. 92.	—	Rep. 1986 Sch. 10.
131		—	Rep. 1980 Sch. 4.
132	Advisory functions in relation to attendance allowance.	—	Rep. 1991D Sch. 4.
133	Co-ordination with Great Britain.	A 153	Am. Social Security Pensions Act 1975 (c. 60) Sch. 4 para. 69; 1986 art. 66(1).
134	Reciprocity with other countries.		
(1)		A 155(1), (4)	Am. 1977A s. 20(3); 1986 art. 66(2)(a); rep. in part 1986 Sch. 10.
(1A)		A 155(2)	Inserted 1981 art. 7(1).
(2)		A 155(3)	
135, 136		—	Rep. 1986 Sch. 10.
137	Offences and penalties		
(1)		A 108(1)	Am. 1975P Sch. 5 para. 36; rep. in part 1986 Sch. 10; see also 1975P art. 70ZB, inserted by CP Sch. 2 para. 14(20).
(2)		A 108(3)	
(3)		A 108(4)	Am. 1981 Sch. para. 3(a); rep. in part 1986 Sch. 10
(4)		A 108(5), (6)	
(5)		—	Rep. 1986 Sch.10.
138	General provisions as to prosecutions.	—	Rep. 1986 Sch.10.
139	Questions arising in proceedings.	A 111.	Am. 1975P Sch. 5 para. 37, M 5; extended 1986 art. 53(5); see also 1975P art. 70ZC, inserted by CP Sch. 2 para. 14(20).

SOCIAL SECURITY (NORTHERN IRELAND) ACTS CONSOLIDATION—*continued.*

Section of Act, etc.	Subject matter	Section of 1992 Act	Remarks
	SOCIAL SECURITY (NORTHERN IRELAND) ACT 1975 (c. 15)—*continued.*		
140	Evidence of non-payment.	A 112	
141	Recovery on prosecution.	A 113	Am. 1975P Sch. 5 para. 38; see also 1975P art. 70ZD, inserted by CP Sch. 2 para. 14(20).
142	Proof of previous offences.	A 114	Am. 1975P Sch. 5 para. 39, 1991C art. 4(6); rep. in part 1986 Sch. 10; see also 1975P art. 70ZE, inserted by CP Sch. 2 para. 14(20).
143	Provisions supplementary to ss. 141, 142.		
(1)		A 115(2)	
(2)		—	Rep. Insolvency (Northern Ireland) Order 1989 (NI 19) Sch. 10.
(3), (4)		A 115(3), (4)	
(5)		A 115(5)	Rep. in part 1990 Sch. 7.
(6)		A 115(6)	Am. 1975 Sch. 5 para. 40; rep. in part 1986 Sch. 10; see also 1975P art. 70ZF, inserted by CP Sch. 2 para. 14(20).
(7)		A 115(1)	Inserted Criminal Justice (NI) Order 1980 (NI 6) Sch. 1 para. 72; am. 1981MC Sch. 6 para. 35.
144	Priority in bankruptcy, etc.	—	Rep. Insolvency (Northern Ireland) Order 1989 (NI 19) Sch. 10.
145	Research on industrial injuries, etc.	A 159	
146	Control of pneumoconiosis.	A 160	Rep. in part 1983 Sch. 3.
147	Accidents in course of illegal employment.	CB 97	
148	Persons treated as employers for certain purposes.	CB 96	
149	Supplementary schemes.	—	Rep. 1980 Sch. 4.
150	Payments for pre-1948 cases.		
(1), (2)		CB Sch. 8 para. 7(1)	
(3)		CB Sch. 8 para. 7(2); A 161(2)	
(4)		CB Sch. 8 Part II, A 143(2)(c)	Am. 1990 art. 18(6).

SOCIAL SECURITY (NORTHERN IRELAND) ACTS CONSOLIDATION—*continued.*

Section of Act, etc.	Subject matter	Section of 1992 Act	Remarks
	SOCIAL SECURITY (NORTHERN IRELAND) ACT 1975 (c. 15)—*continued.*		
151	Furnishing of addresses for maintenance proceedings, etc.	A 125	Rep. in part Adoption (NI) Order 1987 (NI 22) Sch. 5.
152	Treatment of certain marriages.	CB 120	
153	Exemption from stamp duty.	A 164(1), (2)	
154	Disclosure of information by Inland Revenue.	—	Rep. 1986 Sch. 10.
154A	General provision as to necessity of claim for entitlement to benefit.		
(1), (2)		A 1(1), (2). Sch. 1	Inserted 1986 Sch. 9 para. 56; am. 1989 Sch. 8 para. 8; 1990 art. 8(1).
(3)		A 1(3), Sch. 1	Inserted 1990 art. 3(6); am. 1991D Sch. 1 para. 19.
154B	Retrospective effect of s. 154A.	A 2	Inserted 1990 art. 7(1).
154C	Late claims for widowhood benefits where death is difficult to establish.	A 3	Inserted 1990 art. 8(2).
154D	Restriction on entitlement to benefit in certain cases of error.	A 66	Inserted 1990 Sch. 6 para. 5(2); 1991D Sch. 2 para. 4; rep. in part 1991D Sch. 4.
155	Orders and regulations (general provisions).		
(1)		A 165(3), CB 171(2)	Am. Statutory Rules (NI) Order 1979 (NI 12) Sch. 4 para. 16.
(2)		A 165(4), CB 171(3)	Rep. in part 1977A Sch. 2.
(3)		A 165(5), CB 171(4)	Am. 1989 Sch. 8 para. 9(1); rep. in part 1977A Sch. 2.
(3A)		A 165(6), CB 171(5)	Inserted 1986 art. 63(1).
(4)		—	Unnecessary: Interpretation Act 1978 (c. 30) ss. 14, 24(3).
(5)		A 165(10), CB 171(7)	Rep. in part 1977A Sch. 2, 1991RF Sch. 2.
(6)		CB 171(8)	
(7)		A 165(11), CB 171(9)	Rep. in part 1977A Sch.2.
(8)		CB 171(10)	Am. 1986 Sch. 9 para. 70.
156	Orders and regulations (control by Northern Ireland Assembly).	CB 171(10)	Am. 1986. Sch. 9 para. 70.
(1)		A 166(1), CB 172(1)	

SOCIAL SECURITY (NORTHERN IRELAND) ACTS CONSOLIDATION—*continued.*

Section of Act, etc.	Subject matter	Section of 1992 Act	Remarks
	SOCIAL SECURITY (NORTHERN IRELAND) ACT 1975 (c. 15)—*continued.*		
(2)		A 166(2), CB 172(2)	Am. 1981C art. 6, 1986 arts. 44(3)(b), 63(3), 75(2), Sch. 9 para. 41; rep. in part 2975P Sch. 6, 1986 Sch. 10, 1989 Sch. 9, 1991RF Sch. 2
(3)		A 166(3), CB 172(3)	Subst. 1990 Sch. 6 para. 6(1).
(4)		A 166(4), CB 172(4), (12)	
(5)		A 166(5), CB 172(5)	
(5A)		A 166(5)	Inserted 1989 Sch. 3 para. 16; am. 1990 Sch. 6 para. 6(16)
(6)		A 166(11), CB 172(8)	
157	Interpretation.		
(1)		—	Unnecessary.
(2)		—	Unnecessary–see Interpretation Act 1978 s. 20.
(3)		—	Unnecessary.
(4)		A 165(12), CB 171(12)	Rep. in part 1977A Sch. 2.
158	Citation, extent and commencement.	—	
Sch. 1	Supplementary provisions relating to contributions of classes 1, 2 and 3.		
para. 1(1)		CB Sch. 1 para. 1(1)	
(1A)		CB Sch. 1 para. 1(2)	Inserted 1980 Sch. 1 para. 15; am. 1985 Sch. 5 para. 5(a)
(1B)–(1D)		CB Sch. 1 para. 1(3), (4), (6)	Inserted 1985 Sch. 5 para. 5(b).
(2), (3)		CB Sch. 1 para. 1(7), (8)	
2, 3		CB Sch. 1 paras. 2, 3	
4		CB Sch. 1 para. 4	Am. 1977 art. 3(5)
4A		CB Sch. 1 para. 5	Inserted 1991C art. 4(2)
5(1)		CB Sch. 1 para. 6(1)	Am. 1991C art. 4(3)(a)

SOCIAL SECURITY (NORTHERN IRELAND) ACTS CONSOLIDATION—*continued.*

Section of Act, etc.	Subject matter	Section of 1992 Act	Remarks
	SOCIAL SECURITY (NORTHERN IRELAND) ACT 1975 (c. 15)—*continued.*		
(1A)		CB Sch. 1 para. 6(2)	Inserted 1990 art. 19(3); am. 1991C art. 4(3)(b)
(1B), (1C)		CB Sch. 1 para. 6(3), (4)	Inserted 1990 art. 19(3)
(2)		CB Sch. 1 para. 6(7)	
(3)		CB Sch. 1 para. 6(8)	Am. 1990 art. 19(4)
5A		CB Sch. 1 para. 7	Inserted 1990 Sch. 5; am. 1991C art. 4(4)
6(1)		CB Sch. 1 para. 8(1)	Am. 1975P Sch. 5 para. 41, 1986 Sch. 9 para. 1, 1989 art. 4, 1990 Sch. 6 para. 7, 1991C art. 4(5)
(2), (3)		CB Sch. 1 para. 8(2), (3)	
7		CB Sch. 1 para. 9	
8		CB Sch. 1 para. 10	Inserted 1982 art. 30(2).
Sch. 2	Levy of class 4 contributions with income tax.		
para 1.		CB Sch. 2 para. 1	Am. ICTA 1988 Sch. 29 para. 32; Capital Allowances Act 1990 (c.1) Sch. 1 para. 2.
2		CB Sch. 2 para. 2	Am. Capital Allowances Act 1990 Sch. 1 para. 2
3(1)		CB Sch. 2 para. 3(1)	Am. ICTA 1988 Sch. 29 para. 32.
(2)		CB Sch. 2 para. 3(2)	Am. Finance Act 1985 (c. 54) s. 42(2), ICTA 1988 Sch. 29 para. 32.
(3)		CB Sch. 2 para. 3(3)	Subst. for 1990-91 on, Finance Act 1988 (c. 39) Sch. 3 para. 31
(4)		CB Sch. 2 para. 3(5)	Am. ICTA 1988 Sch. 29 para. 32.
4		CB Sch. 2 para. 9	Am. ICTA 1988 Sch. 29 para. 32; Finance Act 1988 Sch. 14 Part VIII, note 6.
5		CB Sch. 2 para. 4	Am. ICTA 1988 Sch. 29 para. 32.
6		CB Sch. 2 para. 5	Am. ICTA 1988 Sch. 29 para. 32.

SOCIAL SECURITY (NORTHERN IRELAND) ACTS CONSOLIDATION—*continued.*

Section of Act, etc.	Subject matter	Section of 1992 Act	Remarks

SOCIAL SECURITY (NORTHERN IRELAND) ACT 1975 (c. 15)—*continued.*

Section of Act, etc.	Subject matter	Section of 1992 Act	Remarks
7(1)		CB Sch. 2 para. 6(1)	Am. 1990A s. 17(8).
(2)		CB Sch. 2 para. 6(2)	Inserted 1990A s. 17(9)
8, 9		CB Sch. 2 paras. 7, 8	
Sch. 3	Contribution conditions for entitlement to benefit.		
para. 1(1)		CB Sch. 3 paras. 1(1), 2(1)	
(2)		CB Sch. 3 paras. 1(2), (4), 2(2),(4)	Am. 1986 Sch. 8 para. 2(1), 1988 art. 7(2)(a).
(3)		CB Sch. 3 paras. 1(3), (5), 2(3), (5)	Am. 1986 Sch. 8 para. 2(3), 1988 art. 7(2)(b).
(4)		CB Sch. 3 paras. 1(6), 2(6)	Rep. in part 1988 Sch. 5.
2		—	Rep. 1980 art. 6(1)(v)
3(1)		CB Sch. 3 para. 3(1)	Subst. 1986 Sch. 4 para. 14; Am. 1990 Sch. 6 para. 8(1)
(2), (3)		CB Sch. 3 para. 3(2), (3)	Inserted 1990 Sch. 6 para. 8(2).
4(1)		CB Sch. 3 para. 4(1), (2)	Am. 1986 Sch. 8 para. 2(4), Sch. 9 para. 42(a)
(2)		CB Sch. 3 para. 4(3)	
5(1)		CB Sch. 3 para. 5(1)	
(2)		CB Sch. 3 para. 5(2)	Am. 1975P art. 21(2), 1986 Sch. 8 para. 2(5).
(3)		CB Sch. 3 para. 5(3), (4)	Am. 1986 Sch. 8 para. 2(6).
(4), (5)		CB Sch. 3 para. 5(5), (6)	
(6)		CB Sch. 3 para. 5(7)	Inserted 1979 Sch. 1 para. 3.
6		CB Sch. 3 para. 6	

SOCIAL SECURITY (NORTHERN IRELAND) ACTS CONSOLIDATION—*continued.*

Section of Act, etc.	Subject matter	Section of 1992 Act	Remarks

SOCIAL SECURITY (NORTHERN IRELAND) ACT 1975 (c. 15)—*continued.*

Section of Act, etc.	Subject matter	Section of 1992 Act	Remarks
7		—	Rep. 1986 Sch. 10
8(1)		CB Sch. 3 para. 7(1)	Am. 1989 Sch. 7 para. 14
(2)		CB Sch. 3 para. 7(2)	Am. 1986 Sch. 9 para. 42(b); rep.in part 1986 Sch. 10.
(3)		CB Sch. 3 para. 7(3), (4)	Subst. 1979 Sch. 3 para. 10; am. 1986 Sch. 8 para. 2(7), Sch. 9 para. 42(b); rep. in part 1988 Sch. 5
9		—	Rep. 1988 Sch. 5
10		CB Sch. 3 para. 8	Rep. in part 1986 Sch. 10.
11		—	Rep. 1980 art. 6(1)(v)
12		—	Rep. 1986 Sch. 10
13		CB Sch. 3 para. 9	Subst. 1986 Sch. 9 para. 42(c)
Sch. 4	Rates of benefits, grants and increases for dependants.		See 1992U Sch. 1
Part 1		CB Sch. 4 Part 1	Para. 2 rep. 1975P Sch. 6; para. 5 rep. 1986 Sch. 10; paras. 6-8 rep. 1975P Sch. 6.
Part IA		CB Sch. 4 Part II	Inserted 1986 art. 37(2)
Part II		—	Rep. 1986 Sch. 10.
Part III		CB Sch. 4 Part III	Am. 1990 art. 4(2); para. 3A rep. 1991D Sch. 4.
Part IV		CB Sch. 4 Part IV	Para. 4 rep. 1986 Sch. 10
Part V		CB Sch. 4 Part V	Paras. 1, 9, 11 rep. 1985 Sch. 5; para. 6 rep. 1986 Sch. 10.
Sch. 5	Meaning of "unemployability supplement or allowance".	—	Unnecessary.
Sch. 6	Earnings-related supplement and addition.	—	Rep. 1980(2) Sch.
Sch. 7	Method of treating deceased husband's contributions as those of his widow, so as to entitle her to Category A retirement pension.		Rep. 1975P. Sch. 6.
Sch. 8	Assessment of extent of disablement.		
para. 1		CB Sch. 6 para. 1	Am. 1984 Sch. 2 para. 8(a)
2, 3		CB Sch. 6 paras. 2, 3	
4(1)		CB Sch. 6 para. 6(1), (2)	Am. 1982 Sch. 4 para. 12, 1986 Sch. 3 para. 16(a).

SOCIAL SECURITY (NORTHERN IRELAND) ACTS CONSOLIDATION—*continued.*

Section of Act, etc.	Subject matter	Section of 1992 Act	Remarks
	SOCIAL SECURITY (NORTHERN IRELAND) ACT 1975 (c. 15)—*continued.*		
(2)-(4)		CB Sch. 6 para. 6(3)-(5)	Subst. 1989 Sch. 3 para. 13(1)
4A		CB Sch. 6 para. 4	Inserted 1984 Sch. 2 para. 8(b).
5		CB Sch. 6 para. 7	Am. 1989 Sch. 3 para. 13(2); rep. in part 1986 Sch. 10.
5A		CB Sch. 6 para. 5	Inserted 1984 Sch. 2 para. 8(c)
6		CB Sch. 6 para. 8	
Sch. 9	Limits of entitlement to industrial death benefit.		
para. 1		CB Sch. 7 para. 19	Rep. in part 1975CB Sch. 5.
2–8		—	Omitted M 7.
Sch. 10	Supplementary provisions as to local tribunals, commissioners etc.		
para. 1			Subst. 1983 Sch. 1 para. 5.
(1)		A 38(1)	Rep. in part 1984 Sch. 6.
(2), (2A)		A 38(2), (3), (4)	Subst. 1984 art. 10(b)
(3)–(5)		—	Replaced by (2), (2A).
(6)		A 38(4)	
(7)		—	Rep. 1989 Sch. 9.
(8)		A 39(5)	
1A			Inserted 1983 Sch. 1 para. 5.
(1)		A 49(1)	Subst. 1991D Sch. 1 para. 15.
(2), (3)		A 49(2), (3)	
(4)–(8)		A Sch. 2 para. 1(1)–(5)	
(9), (10)		A Sch. 2 paras. 3, 4	
1B–1D		A Sch. 2 paras. 5, 6	
2(1)		A Sch. 2 para. 2	
(2)		—	Rep. 1989 Sch. 9.
3		A Sch. 2 para. 8	

SOCIAL SECURITY (NORTHERN IRELAND) ACTS CONSOLIDATION—*continued.*

Section of Act, etc.	Subject matter	Section of 1992 Act	Remarks
		SOCIAL SECURITY (NORTHERN IRELAND) ACT 1975 (c. 15)—*continued.*	
4		A Sch. 2 para. 7	Am. 1986 Sch. 9 para. 10(1).
5(1)		A Sch. 2 para. 1(2)	
Sch. 10A	Disability appeal tribunals.	A 40, 41, Sch. 2	Inserted 1991D Sch. 1 para. 15.
Sch. 11	Attendance Allowance Board for Northern Ireland.	—	Rep. 1991D Sch. 4.
Sch. 12	Medical boards and medical appeal tribunals.		
para. 1		A 47(1), (2)	Subst. 1983 Sch. 2 para. 7(a).
2		A 48(1)–(5), 49(4)	Subst. 1983 Sch. 1 para. 6; am. 1986 Sch. 5 para. 15; 1989 Sch. 3 para. 18, Sch. 7 para. 15.
3		A 47(3), 48(6)	Subst. 1983 Sch. 2 para. 7(b).
4, 5		A Sch. 2 para. 8	Subst. 1983 Sch. 2 para. 7(b).
5A		A Sch. 2 para. 4	Inserted 1983 Sch. 1 para. 7.
6		A Sch. 2 para. 8(1)(c)	Subst. 1983 Sch. 2 para. 7(b).
7		A Sch. 2 para. 8(1)	
8		A Sch. 2 para. 8(6)	
9		A Sch. 2 para. 5	Inserted 1983 Sch. 1 para. 8.
Sch. 13	Provision which may be made by procedure regulations		
para. 1		A Sch. 3 para. 2	Am. 1989 Sch. 3 para. 4.
1A		A Sch. 3 para. 3	Inserted 1986 Sch. 5 para. 16(a).
2–7		A Sch. 3 paras. 4–9	
7A		A Sch. 3 para. 10	Inserted 1989 Sch. 3 para. 10; am. 1991D Sch. 1 para. 17.
8, 9		—	Rep. 1989 Sch. 9.

SOCIAL SECURITY (NORTHERN IRELAND) ACTS CONSOLIDATION—*continued.*

Section of Act, etc.	Subject matter	Section of 1992 Act	Remarks
	SOCIAL SECURITY (NORTHERN IRELAND) ACT 1975 (c. 15)—*continued.*		
10, 11		A Sch. 3 paras. 11, 12	Am. 1986 Sch. 5 para. 16(b).
Sch. 14	Provisions applicable on alteration of benefit rates.	—	Rep. 1986 Sch. 10.
Sch. 15	Priority of debts in cases of personal and company insolvency.	—	Rep. Insolvency (Northern Ireland) Order 1990 (NI 19) Sch. 10.
Sch. 16	Supplementary schemes.	—	Rep. 1980 Sch. 4.
Sch. 17	Glossary of expressions.	CB 20(2), 103(5), 121, 167, 170, 171(1), Sch. 7 para. 14(2), A 167.	
	INDUSTRIAL INJURIES AND DISEASES (NORTHERN IRELAND OLD CASES) ACT 1975 (c. 17)		
1	Continuation of workmen's compensation in certain cases.	CB Sch. 8 para. 1	
2	Regulations to provide for supplementing workmen's compensation.		
(1)		CB Sch. 8 para. 2(1); A 143(2)	Am. 1990 art. 18(7)(a).
(2)–(5)		CB Sch. 8 para. 2(2)–(5)	
(6)		CB Sch. 8 para. 2(6), (7)	Rep. in part 1986 Sch. 10; am. 1992U art. 6.
(7)		CB Sch. 8 para. 2(8)	
3	Provisions supplementary to s. 2.	CB Sch. 8 para. 3	
4	Provisions as to the regulations.		
(1)		A 165(5)	
(2)		A Sch. 6 para. 1(2)	Am. 1989 Sch. 8 para. 9(1).
(3)		A Sch. 6 para. 1(3)	
(4)		A 144(4), Sch. 6 para. 1(4)	Am. 1990 art. 18(7)(b).

SOCIAL SECURITY (NORTHERN IRELAND) ACTS CONSOLIDATION—*continued.*

Section of Act, etc.	Subject matter	Section of 1992 Act	Remarks
INDUSTRIAL INJURIES AND DISEASES (NORTHERN IRELAND OLD CASES) ACT 1975 (c. 17)—*continued.*			
(5)–(7)		A Sch. 6 para. 1(5)–(7)	
(8)		A 165(3)	Am. Statutory Rules (N.I.) Order 1979 (N.I. 12) Sch. 4 para. 17.
(9)		A 166(4)	Inserted 1977 art. 9(2).
5(1), (2)	Adjustment of benefit in certain cases.	A Sch. 6 para. 2(1), (2)	
(3)		—	Rep. 1986 Sch. 10.
6	Offences, penalties, etc.	—	Rep. 1986 Sch. 10.
7	Exemptions from stamp duty.	A 164(3)	
8	Reciprocal arrangements with Great Britain.	—	Rep. 1990 Sch. 7.
9	Interpretation.		
(1)		CB Sch. 8 para. 5(1)	
(2)		CB Sch. 8 para. 5(1), (2)	Am. 1977 art. 9(1).
(3)		—	Unnecessary; Interpretation Act 1978 (c. 30) s. 20(2).
(4)			Unnecessary.
SOCIAL SECURITY (CONSEQUENTIAL PROVISIONS) ACT 1975 (c. 18)			
Sch. 2	Amendments.		
paras. 73,74			See CP Sch. 2 para. 2.
77			See CP Sch. 2 para. 3(3).
80			Spent.
87			See CP Sch. 2 para. 5.
108			See CP Sch. 2 para. 8(2).
110			See CP Sch. 2 para. 9.
112		—	Spent.
Sch. 3	Transitional provisions and savings.		
para. 31		A 45(10)	Spent (repeal of part only).
NORTHERN IRELAND ASSEMBLY DISQUALIFICATION ACT 1975 (c. 25)			
Sch. 1	Offices disqualifying for membership.		
Part II		—	Unnecessary.
SOCIAL SECURITY PENSIONS ACT 1975 (c. 60)			
Sch. 4	Amendments.		
para. 68		—	Spent.

SOCIAL SECURITY (NORTHERN IRELAND) ACTS CONSOLIDATION—*continued.*

Section of Act, etc.	Subject matter	Section of 1992 Act	Remarks
	SOCIAL SECURITY PENSIONS ACT 1975 (c. 60)—*continued.*		
69		A 153	
70,71(a)(b)		—	Spent.
	SOCIAL SECURITY PENSIONS (NORTHERN IRELAND) ORDER 1975 (N.I. 15)		
2	Interpretation.		
(3)		—	Detailed consequential repeal.
3	Earnings limits.		
(1)		CB 5(1)	Am. 1985 Sch. 5 para. 7.
(2)		CB 5(2)	Am. 1986 art. 75(4).
(3)		CB 5(3)	
4	Rates of contributions in respect of employed earners.		
5	Married women and widows.		
(1)	Repeals.	—	Spent.
(2), (3)		CB 19(4), (5)	
(4)		CB 19(6)	Am. 1986 Sch. 8 para. 3.
6	Persons over pensionable age.		
(1)		CB 6(2)	Am. 1984 Sch. 5 para. 4(a); rep. in part 1984 Sch. 6.
(2)		CB 11(2)	
(3)	Amends 1975 s. 9(5)(b).	CB 17(2)	
7	Voluntary contributions.		
(1)		CB 14(1)	Am. 1986 Sch. 8 para. 4.
(2)		CB 14(3), (4)	
(3)		CB 14(2)	
8	Rate of Category A retirement pension.		
(1)		CB 44(3), (4)	Am. 1986 art. 19(1), 1992U art. 4(2).
(2)		CB 45(1)	Am. 1986 art. 19(2); rep. in part 1986 Sch. 10.
(2A), (2B)		CB 45(2)–(5)	Inserted 1986 art. 19(3).
(3)		CB 45(6)	Am. 1986 art. 19(4); rep. in part 1979 Sch. 3.
(4)		CB 44(5)	Am. 1979 Sch. 3 para. 16.
(5)		CB 44(6)	Am. 1985 Sch. 5 para. 8(a); 1986 Sch. 8 para. 5(1)(a); rep. in part 1986 Sch. 10; see also CP Sch. 4 para. 2.
(5A)			Inserted 1985 Sch. 5 para. 8(b); see also CP Sch. 4 para. 3.

SOCIAL SECURITY (NORTHERN IRELAND) ACTS CONSOLIDATION—*continued.*

Section of Act, etc.	Subject matter	Section of 1992 Act	Remarks
	SOCIAL SECURITY PENSIONS (NORTHERN IRELAND) ORDER 1975 (N.I. 15)—*continued.*		
(6)		CB 44(7)	
9	Rate of widow's Category B retirement pension.	CB 50(3), (4)	
10	Category B retirement pension for widower.		
(1)		CB 51(1)	Am. 1979 Sch. 1 para. 4; rep. in part 1989 Sch. 9.
(2)		CB 51(2)	
(3)		CB 51(4)	Subst. 1989 Sch. 1 para. 9(2).
11	Special provision for surviving spouses.		
(1)		CB 52(1)	
(2), (3)		CB 52(2), (3)	Am. 1986 art. 19(1).
(3A)		A 136	Inserted 1989 Sch. 8 para. 10.
12	Special provision for married women.		
(1)		CB 53(1)	
(2)		CB 53(2)	Am. 1986 art. 19(1).
14	Deferred retirement.	CB 55	Subst. 1989 art. 9(4).
15	Rate of widowed mother's allowance and widow's pension.	CB 39(1), (2)	Am. 1986 Sch. 9 para. 44.
16	Rate of invalidity pension for persons under pensionable age.	CB 33(3)	Am. 1990 art. 6(1).
17	Invalidity pension for widows.		
(1)		CB 40(1)	Am. 1986 Sch. 9 para. 45(a).
(1A)		CB 40(2)	Inserted 1989 Sch. 7 para. 17.
(2)		CB 40(3)	Am. 1986 Sch. 9 para. 45(b).
(3)		CB 40(4)	
(4)		CB 40(5)	Am. 1986 Sch. 9 para. 45(c); 1990 art. 6(2).
(5)		CB 40(7)	Am. 1977 art. 5(4); 1989 Sch. 1 para. 10(1).
(6)		CB 40(8)	
18	Invalidity pension for widowers.		
(1)–(3)		CB 41(1)–(3)	
(4)		CB 41(4), (5)	Am. 1990 art. 6(3).
(5)		CB 41(7)	Am. 1977 art. 5(4); 1989 Sch. 1 para. 10(2).
(6)		CB 41(8)	
18A	Entitlement to invalidity pension after termination of entitlement to disability working allowance.	CB 42	Inserted 1991D art. 11(2).

SOCIAL SECURITY (NORTHERN IRELAND) ACTS CONSOLIDATION—*continued.*

Section of Act, etc.	Subject matter	Section of 1992 Act	Remarks
SOCIAL SECURITY PENSIONS (NORTHERN IRELAND) ORDER 1975 (N.I. 15)—*continued.*			
19	Invalidity allowance and disablement pension.	—	Rep. 1979 Sch. 1 para. 10.
20	Rate of unemployment and sickness benefit for persons under pensionable age.		
(1)		CB 25(4), 31(4)	Amends 1975 s. 14(4), (5).
(2)		—	Spent.
21	Contribution conditions for retirement pensions, widowed mother's allowance and widow's pension.		
(1), (2)	Amends 1975 Sch. 3 para. 5(2), (3); rep. in part 1986 Sch. 10.	CB Sch. 3 para. 5(2)	
(3)		—	Spent.
(4)	Repeal.		Spent.
(5)		CB 60(7)	Inserts 1975 s. 33(4).
22	Use of former spouse's contributions.		
(1)		CB 48(1)	Am. 1979 Sch. 1 para. 5.
(2)		CB 48(3)	
(3)	Repeal.	—	Spent.
23	Revaluation of earnings factors.	A 130	Am. 1985 Sch. 3 para. 1, 1986 art. 19(1).
24	Mobility allowance.	—	Rep. 1991D Sch. 4.
25	Increase of long-term benefits.	—	Rep. 1986 Sch. 10.
26	Power to modify provisions about graduated retirement benefit.		
(1)		CB 62(1)	
(2)		CB 62(2)	
27	Simultaneous entitlement to more than one pension.	CB 43(3)–(5)	
52A(13)			See 1975P art. 71A(1) inserted by CP Sch. 2 para. 14(22).
70	Determination of questions.		
(1)(a)		A 15(1)(f)	
70A	Treatment of insignificant amounts.	CB 45(7), Sch. 5 paras. 2(4), 7(2)	Inserted 1979 art. 14; only partly consolidated.
71(1)	Regulations and orders.	—	Partial repeal only.
74(3)	References to benefit.	—	Spent.

SOCIAL SECURITY (NORTHERN IRELAND) ACTS CONSOLIDATION—*continued.*

Section of Act, etc.	Subject matter	Section of 1992 Act	Remarks
\multicolumn{4}{l}{SOCIAL SECURITY PENSIONS (NORTHERN IRELAND) ORDER 1975 (N.I. 15)—*continued.*}			
Sch. 1	Deferred retirement.		
para. 1		CB Sch. 5 para. 1	Subst. 1989 Sch. 1, para. 3(1).
2(1)		CB Sch. 5 para. (2)1	Am. 1989 Sch. 1, para. 3(2).
(2)		CB Sch. 5 para. 2(2)	Subst. 1989 Sch. 1 para. 3(3).
(3)		CB Sch. 5 para. 2(3)	Am. 1977 art. 4(1)(b); 1989 Sch. 1 para. 3(4).
(4)		CB Sch. 5 para. 2(5)	Am. 1977 art. 4(1)(c); 1980 art. 4(10).
(4A)		CB Sch. 5 para. 2(6)	Inserted 1985 art. 11(5).
(5)		CB Sch. 5 para. 2(7)	Am. 1986 Sch. 9 para. 59(a); 1989 Sch. 1 para. 3(5); rep. in part 1977 Sch.
(6)		CB Sch. 5 para. 2(8)	Am. 1977 art. 4(1)(d); 1989 Sch. 1 para. 3(6).
3		CB Sch. 5 para. 3	Subst. 1977 art. 4(1)(e); am. 1989 Sch. 1 para. 3(7).
4(1), (2)		CB Sch. 5 para. 4(1), (2)	Am. 1979 Sch. 3 para. 22; 1986 art. 20(2); 1989 Sch. 1 para. 3(8).
(2A)		CB Sch. 5 para. 4(3)	Inserted 1986 art. 20(2).
(3)		CB Sch. 5 para. 4(4)	Am. 1979 Sch. 1 para. 6; 1986 Sch. 9 para. 59(a).
(4)		CB Sch. 5 para. 4(5)	Inserted 1979 Sch. 1 para. 22.
4A			Inserted 1979 Sch. 1 para. 7.
(1)		CB Sch. 5 para. 5(1), (2)	Am. 1986 art. 20(3).
(1A)		CB Sch. 5 para. 5(3)	Inserted 1986 art. 20(4).
(2)		CB Sch. 5 para. 6(1), (2)	Am. 1986 art. 20(5).
(2A)		CB Sch. 5 para. 6(3), (4)	Inserted 1986 art. 20(6).
(3)		CB Sch. 5 para. 7(1)	Am. 1986 Sch. 9 para. 59(b).
5(1), (2)		CB Sch. 5 para. 8(1), (2)	Subst. 1989 Sch. 1 para. 3(9).

SOCIAL SECURITY (NORTHERN IRELAND) ACTS CONSOLIDATION—*continued.*

Section of Act, etc.	Subject matter	Section of 1992 Act	Remarks

SOCIAL SECURITY PENSIONS (NORTHERN IRELAND) ORDER 1975 (N.I. 15)—*continued.*

Section of Act, etc.	Subject matter	Section of 1992 Act	Remarks
(3)		CB Sch. 5 para. 8(3)	Am. 1989 Sch. 1 para. 3(10).
(4)		CB Sch. 5 para. 8(4)	
Sch. 5	Amendments.		
para. 17		A 68(1)	
18(a)		CB 5(1)	
(b)		—	Spent.
19		CB 20	
20		CB 22(2), (4)	
21(a)		—	Rep. 1989 Sch. 9.
(b)		CB 25(6), 31(7)	
22(a)		—	Rep. 1989 Sch. 9.
(b)		CB 33(3)	
(c)		CB 33(5)	
23		CB 37(1)	
24		CB 38(1)	
25		CB 44(1)	
26		CB 50(1)	
27		CB 54(3)	
28		CB 60(4)	
29		—	Rep. 1991D Sch. 4.
30		—	Rep. 1975CB Sch. 5.
31		A 59(2)	
32		—	Rep. 1991D Sch. 4.
33		A 155(1)	
34, 35		—	Rep. 1986 Sch. 10.
36		A 108(1)	See also 1975P art. 70ZB inserted by CP Sch. 2 para. 14(20).
37		A 111(1)	See 1975P art. 70ZC inserted by CP Sch. 2 para. 14(20).
38		A 113(1)	See 1975P art. 70ZD inserted by CP Sch. 2 para. 14(20).
39		A 114	See 1975P art. 70ZE inserted by CP Sch. 2 para. 14(20).
40		A 115(4)	See 1975P art. 70ZF inserted by CP Sch. 2 para. 14(20).
41		CB Sch. 1 para. 8(1)	

SOCIAL SECURITY (NORTHERN IRELAND) ACTS CONSOLIDATION—*continued.*

Section of Act, etc.	Subject matter	Section of 1992 Act	Remarks
SOCIAL SECURITY PENSIONS (NORTHERN IRELAND) ORDER 1975 (N.I. 15)—*continued.*			
42		CB Sch. 4, Part I, para. 5	
43		—	Rep. 1986 Sch. 10.
44		CB 121	
CHILD BENEFIT (NORTHERN IRELAND) ORDER 1975 (N.I. 16)			
1	Title and commencement.	—	Unnecessary.
2	General interpretation.		
(1)		—	Unnecessary.
(2)		CB 143(1), A 167	Rep. in part 1983 Sch. 3, 1986 Sch. 10.
(3)–(5)		CB 143(2)–(4)	
(6)		CB 143(6)	
3	Child benefit.		
(1)		CB 137	
(2)		CB 141(1)	
(3)		—	Spent.
4	Meaning of "child".		
(1)		CB 138(1)	Am. 1986 art. 71(1)(a), 1988 art. 6(3).
(1A), (1B)		CB 138(2), (3)	Inserted 1986 art. 71(1)(b).
(2)		CB 138(4)	
(3)		CB 138(5)	Rep. in part 1980 Sch. 4.
5	Meaning of "person responsible for child".	CB 139	
6	Exclusions and priority.		
(1)		CB 140(1), (2)	Am. 1988 art. 6(4).
(2)		CB 140(3)	
6A	Overlap with benefits under legislation of other member States.	A 76	Inserted 1979 art. 12(2).
7	Rate of child benefit.		
(1)–(4)		CB 141(1)–(4)	
(5)		A 137(1)	
8	Claims and payment.		
(1)		A 11(1)	Am. 1989 Sch. 7 para. 19.
(2)		—	Rep. 1986 Sch. 10.
(3)		A 11(2)	
(4), (5)		—	Rep. 1986 Sch. 10.

SOCIAL SECURITY (NORTHERN IRELAND) ACTS CONSOLIDATION—*continued.*

Section of Act, etc.	Subject matter	Section of 1992 Act	Remarks
	CHILD BENEFIT (NORTHERN IRELAND) ORDER 1975 (N.I. 16)—*continued.*		
9	Determination of questions.		Rep. 1986 Sch. 10.
10	Suspension, and effect of adjudication on payment and recovery.	—	Rep. 1986 Sch. 10.
11	Treatment of certain marriages.	CB 143(5)	
12	Disclosure of information by Inland Revenue.	—	Rep. 1986 Sch. 10.
13	Offences and prosecutions.	—	Rep. 1986 Sch. 10.
14	Benefit to be inalienable.	A 163(1), (2)	Am. 1981MC Sch. 6 para. 135.
15	Persons outside Northern Ireland.		
(1)		CB 142(1)	
(2), (3)		CB 142(2), (3)	
16	Reciprocal arrangements with Great Britain.	A 154, 165(11)	
17	Reciprocal arrangements with countries outside the United Kingdom.		
(1)		A 155(1), (4)	Am. 1977 art. 16; rep. in part 1986 Sch. 10.
(1A)		A 155(2)	Inserted 1981 art. 7(2).
(2)		A 155(3)	
(3)		A 165(11)	
18	Interim benefit for unmarried or separated parents with children.	—	Rep. 1975CB Sch. 5.
19	Social security benefits in respect of children.		
(1), (2)		A 134	
(3)–(6)		—	Rep. 1986 Sch. 10.
20	Provisions as to the exclusion from a family for family allowances purposes of children entitled to non-contributory invalidity pension.	—	Rep. 1975CB Sch. 5.
21	Abolition of wage-stop.	—	Rep. 1977SB Sch. 7.
22	Transitional provisions.	—	Spent.
23	Amendments and repeals.	—	Spent.
24	Regulations and orders.		
(1)		CB 141(5), A 165(1)	
(2)		CB 172(1), A 166(2)	
(3)		CB 172(3)	
(4)		CB 172(4), A 166(4)	

SOCIAL SECURITY (NORTHERN IRELAND) ACTS CONSOLIDATION—*continued.*

Section of Act, etc.	Subject matter	Section of 1992 Act	Remarks
	CHILD BENEFIT (NORTHERN IRELAND) ORDER 1975 (N.I. 16)—*continued.*		
(5)		CB 171(4), A 165(5)	Am. M 8.
(5A)		CB 171(5), A 165(6)	Inserted 1986 art. 63(2).
25	Financial provisions.	A 145(2)	
Sch. 1	Exclusions from entitlement.		
para. 1(1)		CB Sch. 9 para. 1(1)	
(2)		CB Sch. 9 para. 1(2)	Subst. 1980 art. 5(6).
2–4		CB Sch. 9 paras. 2–4	
5		CB Sch. 9 para. 5	Am. 1984 Sch. 2 para. 11.
Sch. 2	Priority between persons entitled.	CB Sch. 10	
Sch. 3	Increase in rates of benefit.		
paras. 1, 2		A 137(1)	Am. 1986 Sch. 9 para. 62.
3		A 137(2), (3)	
Sch. 4	Amendments.		
para. 1			See CP Sch. 2 para. 4.
2, 3		—	Rep. 1977SB Sch. 7.
4		—	Rep. Births and Deaths Registration (NI) Order 1976 (NI 14) Sch. 2.
5–7		—	Rep. 1986 Sch. 10.
8		—	Rep. 1977SB Sch. 7.
9		A 68(1), (3)	
10(a)		CB 37(1)	
(b)		CB 37(2)	
(c)		—	
11		CB 56(1)	
12		—	Rep. 1986 Sch. 10.
13(a)		CB 77(1)	
(b)	Repeal.	—	Spent.
(c)		CB 77(9)	
14(a)		CB 80(1)	
(b), (c)		CB 80(5), (6)	
15	Repeal.	—	Spent.
16(a)		CB 56(4), 77(5), 81(2)	

SOCIAL SECURITY (NORTHERN IRELAND) ACTS CONSOLIDATION—*continued.*

Section of Act, etc.	Subject matter	Section of 1992 Act	Remarks
CHILD BENEFIT (NORTHERN IRELAND) ORDER 1975 (N.I. 16)—*continued.*			
(b)		CB 56(5), 77(6), 81(3)	
(c)	Repeal.	—	Spent.
17		CB 82(1), (2), (4)	
18		CB 83(2)	
19		CB 85(2)	
20		CB 86(1)	
21		—	Rep. 1982 Sch. 5.
22		CB Sch. 7 para. 4(1)	
23		CB Sch. 7 para. 5(1), (2)	
24		CB Sch. 7 para. 6(1)	
25	Repeal.		Spent.
26		—	Rep. 1984 Sch. 6.
27, 28		—	Rep. 1986 Sch. 10.
29		A 71(1), (2)	
30		—	Rep. 1986 Sch. 10.
31		—	Spent.
32		—	Rep. 1986 Sch. 10.
33		—	Spent.
34		—	Rep. 1986 Sch. 10.
35(a), (b)		—	Spent.
(c)		CB Sch. 4 Part IV	
(d)		CB Sch. 4 Part IV	
36		CB Sch. 4, Part V, para. 12; otherwise spent	
37		CB 121	
Sch. 5	Repeals.	—	Spent.
INDUSTRIAL RELATIONS (NORTHERN IRELAND) ORDER 1976 (N.I. 16)			
72(3)	Clarification of 1975 s. 114.	A 56(4)	
SOCIAL SECURITY (MISCELLANEOUS PROVISIONS) ACT 1977 (c. 5)			
20	Modifications of principal Act etc. in connection with reciprocal agreements.		

SOCIAL SECURITY (NORTHERN IRELAND) ACTS CONSOLIDATION—*continued.*

Section of Act, etc.	Subject matter	Section of 1992 Act	Remarks
SOCIAL SECURITY (MISCELLANEOUS PROVISIONS) ACT 1977 (c. 5)—*continued.*			
(3)		A 155(1)	
(4)		—	Spent.
SOCIAL SECURITY (MISCELLANEOUS PROVISIONS) (NORTHERN IRELAND) ORDER 1977 (NI 11)			
2(3)	Interpretation.	—	—
3	Amendments relating to contributions.		
(1)		—	Spent.
(2), (3)		A 143(4)	
(4)		CB Sch. 1 para. 1(1)	
(5)		CB Sch. 1 para. 4	Amends 1975 Sch. 1 para. 4(a).
(6)		CB 14(3), (4)	
(7)		—	Spent.
(8)		—	Rep. 1990 Sch. 7.
4	Increments of retirement pension for deferred retirement etc.		
(1)		CB Sch. 5 paras. 2(3), (5), (8), 3(1)	
5	Other amendments relating to retirement pensions.		
(1)		CB 43(2)	
(2), (3)		—	Spent.
(4)		CB 40(7), 41(7)	
6	Alteration of earnings rule.		
(1)		—	Spent.
(2)		—	Rep. 1979 Sch. 3 para. 8.
7	Other adjustments of benefit.		
(1)		CB 61(1)	Am. 1990 Sch. 6 para. 1(3).
(2)		CB 61(2)	Am. 1990 Sch. 6 para. 1(4).
(3)		—	Rep. 1980 Sch. 4.
8	Industrial death benefit in certain cases of death from pulmonary disease.	CB Sch. 7 para. 21	
9	Miscellaneous amendments of the Old Cases Act.		
(1)	Amends 1975OC s. 9(2).	CB Sch. 8 para. 5(2)(b)	
(2)	Amends 1975OC s. 4.	A 166(4)	

SOCIAL SECURITY (NORTHERN IRELAND) ACTS CONSOLIDATION—*continued.*

Section of Act, etc.	Subject matter	Section of 1992 Act	Remarks
SOCIAL SECURITY (MISCELLANEOUS PROVISIONS) (NORTHERN IRELAND) ORDER 1977 (NI 11)—*continued.*			
10	Mobility allowances for certain persons eligible for invalid carriages.		
(1)		CB 74(1)	Am. 1991D Sch. 2 para. 7.
(2)		—	Rep. 1979 Sch. 3 para. 28.
(3)		CB 74(2)	
11	Amendments of the 1966 Act.	—	Rep. 1977 Sch. 7.
13	Other amendments relating to benefit.		
(1)		—	Spent.
(2)		—	Rep. 1986 Sch. 10.
(3)		CB 95(4), (5)	
(4)		A 138	
(5)		A 59(3)	
(6)		CB 40(6)	
14	Certain sums to be earnings for social security purposes.		
(1)		CB 112(1), (2)	Rep. in part 1977SB Sch. 7, 1986 Sch. 10.
(2)		CB 112(3)	Am. 1986 Sch. 9 para. 49; rep. in part 1986 Sch. 10.
(3)	Repeal.	—	Spent.
15	Inspectors for the purposes of the 1966 Act and the Family Income Supplements Act (N.I.) 1971.	—	Rep. 1986 Sch. 10.
16	Modification of the Child Benefit (N.I.) Order 1975 in connection with reciprocal agreements.	A155(1)	
18	Other miscellaneous amendments.		
(1)		CB 121(3)	
(2)		CB 56(1)	
(3)		CB 56(5), 77(6), 81(3), Sch. 7 para. 5(1)	
(4)		CB Sch. 7 para. 15	
(5)		A 15(1)(e)	
(16)		—	Spent.
(17)		A 145(1)	
(25)		—	Spent.

SOCIAL SECURITY (NORTHERN IRELAND) ACTS CONSOLIDATION—*continued.*

Section of Act, etc.	Subject matter	Section of 1992 Act	Remarks
SOCIAL SECURITY (MISCELLANEOUS PROVISIONS) (NORTHERN IRELAND) ORDER 1977 (NI 11)—*continued.*			
19(3)		A 166(4), CB 172(4)	
SUPPLEMENTARY BENEFITS (NORTHERN IRELAND) ORDER 1977 (N.I. 27)			
28	Impersonation of officers.	A 157	See also 1984F arts. 4, 6(1), (3).
29	Illegal possession of documents.	A 158	See also 1984F arts. 4, 6(1), (3).
JUDICATURE (NORTHERN IRELAND) ACT 1978 (c. 23)			
Sch. 5 Part II	Amendments.	A 16	repeal of one entry.
SOCIAL SECURITY ACT 1979 (c. 18)			
9(2)	Amendments.	A 50(1)	
SOCIAL SECURITY (NORTHERN IRELAND) ORDER 1979 (N.I. 5)			
3	Attendance allowance.		
(1)		—	Introductory.
(2)		CB 65(1)	
(3)		CB 65(2)	
(4)		—	Rep. 1991D Sch. 4.
(5)		CB 65(6)	
(6)		CB 67(1)	Inserts 1975 s. 35(5A).
4	Mobility allowance.	—	Rep. 1991D Sch. 4.
5(1)	Amendment of provisions relating to earnings after retirement age.	—	Rep. 1989 Sch. 9; M3.
(2)		A 166(2)	
6	Amendment of principal Act, Pensions Order and Order of 1977.	—	Introduces Schedule 1.
11	Adjustment of secondary Class 1 contributions for exceptions to redundancy provisions.		
(1)			Introductory.
(2)		—	Adds 1975 s. 4(7).
(3)	Amends 1975 s. 128(6).	A 142(12)	
12	Overlap with benefits under legislation of other member States.		
(1)		A 71(4), (5)	
(2)		A 74(6)	
13	Criminal proceedings.	—	
15	Financial provisions.	A 143(2)	
Sch. 1	Amendment of principal Act, Pensions Order and Order of 1977.		
para. 1		CB 33(4), (5)	

SOCIAL SECURITY (NORTHERN IRELAND) ACTS CONSOLIDATION—*continued.*

Section of Act, etc.	Subject matter	Section of 1992 Act	Remarks
		SOCIAL SECURITY (NORTHERN IRELAND) ORDER 1979 (N.I. 5)—*continued.*	
2		CB 78(4)	
3		CB Sch. 3 para. 5(7)	
4		CB 51(1)	
5		CB 48(1)	
6		CB Sch. 5 para. 4(4)	
7		CB Sch. 5 paras. 5(1) (2), 6(1), (2), 7(1)	
8		CB 43(2)	
9			Drafting.
10		CB 34(3)	
11		—	Rep. 1985 Sch. 6.
12		—	Spent.
13		CB Sch. 4 Pt. V para. 6	
14		CB 51(1)	
15		CB 52(4)	
16		CB 53(3)	
17		—	Rep. 1989 Sch. 9.
18		CB 41(1)	
19		—	Spent.
20		CB 48(2)	
21		—	Spent.
22		CB Sch. 5 para. 4(5)	
Sch. 3	Minor and consequential amendments and repeals.		
para. 3		—	Spent.
4		CB 23(1)	
5		CB 25(6), 31(7)	
6		CB 35(5)	
7		A 45(1)	
9			Indirectly rep. by 1986 Sch. 10.
10		CB Sch. 3 para. 7(3)	
11		—	Spent.
12		—	Unnecessary.

SOCIAL SECURITY (NORTHERN IRELAND) ACTS CONSOLIDATION—*continued.*

Section of Act, etc.	Subject matter	Section of 1992 Act	Remarks
	SOCIAL SECURITY (NORTHERN IRELAND) ORDER 1979 (N.I. 5)—*continued.*		
15		—	Spent.
16		CB 44(5)	
22		CB Sch. 5 para. 4(1), (2)	
23		—	Superseded 1986 Sch. 9 para. 33(b).
28		—	Spent.
	STATUTORY RULES (NORTHERN IRELAND) ORDER 1979 (N.I. 12)		
Sch. 4 para. 16	Amendments.	A 165(3), CB 171(2)	
	SOCIAL SECURITY ACT 1980 (c. 30)		
9	Social Security Advisory Committee.		
(3)		A 149(1)	
(4)		A 149(4)	
10	Consultation with Committee on proposals for regulations.		
(1)		A 149(2)	Am. 1986 Sch. 9 para. 64.
(2)		A 149(3)	
(3), (6)		A 151(1), (2)	
(8), (9)		A 151(3), (4)	
13	Tenure of office of Commissioners.		
(1)–(3)		A Sch. 2 para. 1(2)–(4)	
(4)		—	Rep. Courts and Legal Services Act 1990 (c. 41) Sch. 20.
(5)		A 50(2)	
(a)		A Sch. 2 para. 1(6)	Am. Courts and Legal Services Act 1990 (c. 41) Sch. 10 para. 46.
(b)			See CP Sch. 2 paras. 12(a), 13(a).
(6)		—	Does not extend.
(7)(a)		—	Spent.
(b), (c)			See CP Sch. 2 para. 10(2).
14	Appeal from Commissioners etc. on point of law.		
(1)–(5)		A 22(1)–(5), 32(5)	
(6)		—	Rep. 1986A Sch. 11

Tables of Derivations and Destinations

SOCIAL SECURITY (NORTHERN IRELAND) ACTS CONSOLIDATION—*continued.*

Section of Act, etc.	Subject matter	Section of 1992 Act	Remarks
	SOCIAL SECURITY ACT 1980 (c. 30)—*continued.*		
(7)			Spent.
(8)		A 22(6), 32(5), 165(2), 166(5), (12)	Amends 1986A Sch. 9 para. 11(c).
Sch. 3	Social Security Advisory Committee.		
Part II		A Sch. 5	
	SOCIAL SECURITY (NORTHERN IRELAND) ORDER 1980 (N.I. 8)		
2	Interpretation.		
(2)			Unnecessary definitions.
3	Amendments of the Social Security (Northern Ireland) Act 1975.	—	Introduces Schedule 1.
4	Amendments of the Social Security Pensions (Northern Ireland) Order 1975.		
(1)	Repeal.	—	Spent.
(10)		CB Sch. 5 para. 2(5)	
5	Miscellaneous amendments.		
(2)			See CP Sch. 2 para. 14(21).
(5)	Repeal.	—	Spent.
(6)		CB Sch. 9 para. 1(2)	
(7)			Unnecessary.
6	Maternity grant.		
(1)		—	Spent.
7	Amendments of the Supplementary Benefits (Northern Ireland) Order 1977.		
(2)–(4)		—	Spent.
9	Provisions supplementary to Articles 7 and 8.		Spent.
10	Repeal of certain provisions of the Payments for Debt (Emergency Provisions) Act (Northern Ireland) 1971.	—	Spent.
12	Proof of decisions of statutory authorities.	A Sch. 2 para. 9	Am. 1991D Sch. 2 para. 9.
13	Regulations and orders.		Spent.
15(2)	Transitional.		Spent.
Sch. 1	Amendments of the principal Act.		
paras. 1–3		—	Spent.

SOCIAL SECURITY (NORTHERN IRELAND) ACTS CONSOLIDATION—*continued.*

Section of Act, etc.	Subject matter	Section of 1992 Act	Remarks
	SOCIAL SECURITY (NORTHERN IRELAND) ORDER 1980 (N.I. 8)—*continued.*		
4		CB 82(4), 85(2), Sch. 7 para. 6(1)	
5(1)		CB 87(1), (6)	
(2)		CB 82(1), (2), 86(1)	
6		CB Sch. 7 para. 6(1)	
7		CB 121(6)	
8		CB 65(5)	
9		A 17(2), (3)	Rep. in part 1986 Sch. 10.
10		—	Rep. 1986 Sch. 10.
11		—	Spent.
12		—	Rep. 1986 Sch. 10.
13, 14	Repeals.	—	Spent.
15		—	Rep. 1983 Sch. 3.
16		—	Rep. 1986 Sch. 3.
Sch. 2	Amendments of the Supplementary Benefits (Northern Ireland) Order 1977.		Spent.
Part II	Sets out 1977SB (since rep.) as am.	—	Spent.
Sch. 3	Consequential and minor amendments.		
8		—	Spent.
	SOCIAL SECURITY (No. 2) (NORTHERN IRELAND) ORDER 1980 (N.I. 13)		
1	Title, citation and commencement.	—	Unnecessary.
2	Interpretation.	—	Unnecessary.
3	Alteration of period of interruption of employment and of periods relating to invalidity allowance and unemployability supplement.		
(1)		CB 57(1)	
(2)		—	Rep. 1982 Sch. 5.
(3)		CB 47(1), Sch. 7 para. 3(8)	Rep. in part 1986 Sch. 10.
(4)		CB 47(6), 57(9), Sch. 7 para. 3(9)	

SOCIAL SECURITY (NORTHERN IRELAND) ACTS CONSOLIDATION—*continued.*

Section of Act, etc.	Subject matter	Section of 1992 Act	Remarks
SOCIAL SECURITY (No. 2) (NORTHERN IRELAND) ORDER 1980 (N.I. 13)—*continued.*			
4	Reduction and abolition of earnings-related supplement and addtion.	—	Spent.
5	Abatement of unemployment benefit on account of payments of occupational or personal pension.		
(1)		CB 30(1)	Am. 1988 art. 8; 1989 art. 11(1).
(1A)		CB 30(2)	Inserted 1982 Sch. 4.
(2)		CB 30(3)	Am. 1989 art. 11(1).
(3)		CB 30(4), 121(4)	Am. 1989 art. 11(2).
(4)		A 149(2)	Am. 1989 art. 11(1).
6	Supplementary benefit in cases affected by trade disputes.	—	Rep. 1986 Sch. 10.
7	Supplementary provisions.		
(1), (2)		—	Spent.
(3)		CB 171(3), (4)	
(4)		CB 172(2)	
(5), (6)		—	Spent.
(7)		—	Rep. 1988E art. 6(c).
Sch.	Repeals.	—	Spent.
SOCIAL SECURITY (CONTRIBUTIONS) (NORTHERN IRELAND) ORDER 1981 (N.I. 9)			
1	Title and commencement.	—	Unnecessary.
2	Interpretation.	—	Unnecessary.
3	Increase in contributions.	—	Rep. 1982 Sch. 2.
4	Alteration of Consolidated Fund supplement to contributions.	—	Rep. 1989 Sch. 9.
5	Allocation of contributions.		
(1)		—	Introductory.
(2)			Spent.
(3)		A 147(6), (8)	
6	Supplementary provisions.		
(1)		A 166(2)	
(2)	Revocations.	—	Spent.
Sch.	Revocations.	—	Spent.
SOCIAL SECURITY (NORTHERN IRELAND) ORDER 1981 (N.I. 25)			
1	Title, citation and commencement.	—	Unnecessary.
2	Interpretation.	—	Unnecessary.
3	Maternity pay.	—	Rep. 1986 Sch. 10.
4	Increases in certain penalties.	—	Introduces Sch. 1 and effects repeal.

SOCIAL SECURITY (NORTHERN IRELAND) ACTS CONSOLIDATION—*continued.*

Section of Act, etc.	Subject matter	Section of 1992 Act	Remarks
	SOCIAL SECURITY (NORTHERN IRELAND) ORDER 1981 (N.I. 25)—*continued.*		
5	Payment of supplementary benefit after return to full-time employment following trade dispute.		Rep. 1986 Sch. 10.
6	Determination of days for which sickness or invalidity benefit is payable.	CB 57(9)(b), (10)	
7	Reciprocity with other countries.		
(1)		A 155(2)	
(2)		A 155(2)	
(3)		—	Spent.
(4)			Spent.
Sch. 1	Increase in penalties.		
Paras. 1, 2			Rep. 1986 Sch. 10.
3		A 108(3)	Rep. in part 1986 Sch. 10.
4, 5		—	Rep. 1986 Sch. 10.
6, 7		A 157, 158(3)	
8, 9		—	Rep. 1986 Sch. 10.
	MAGISTRATES' COURTS (NORTHERN IRELAND) ORDER 1981 (N.I. 26)		
Sch. 6	Amendments.		
para. 34		A 163(3)	
35		A 115(1)	
135		A 163(2)	
	FORFEITURE (NORTHERN IRELAND) ORDER 1982 (N.I. 14)		
6(5)	Definition.		See CP Sch. 2 para. 26(3).
	SOCIAL SECURITY (CONTRIBUTIONS) (NORTHERN IRELAND) ORDER 1982 (N.I. 4)		
1	Title and commencement.	—	Unnecessary.
2	Interpretation.	—	Unnecessary.
3	Increase in contributions.	—	Spent so far as unrepealed.
4	Alteration of Consolidated Fund supplement to contributions.	—	Rep. 1989 Sch. 9.
5	Allocation of contributions.		
(1)		—	Introductory.
(2),(3)		—	Spent so far as unrepealed.
6	Supplementary provisions.	—	Spent so far as unrepealed.
Sch. 1	Consequential amendments.		
Para. 1(1)		—	Rep. 1991 RF Sch. 2.
(2)		—	Spent.

SOCIAL SECURITY (NORTHERN IRELAND) ACTS CONSOLIDATION—*continued.*

Section of Act, etc.	Subject matter	Section of 1992 Act	Remarks

SOCIAL SECURITY (CONTRIBUTIONS) (NORTHERN IRELAND) ORDER 1982 (N.I. 4)—*continued.*

Section of Act, etc.	Subject matter	Section of 1992 Act	Remarks
Sch. 2	Repeals		Spent.

SOCIAL SECURITY (NORTHERN IRELAND) ORDER 1982 (N.I. 16)

Section of Act, etc.	Subject matter	Section of 1992 Act	Remarks
3	Employer's liability.		
(1)–(4)		CB 147(1), (2), (4), (5)	
(5)		CB 147(6)	Inserted 1986 art. 69.
(6)		A 143(1)(d)	Inserted 1986 art. 69.
4	Period of incapacity for work.		
(1)–(3)		CB 148(1)–(3)	
(3A)		CB 148(4)	Inserted 1985 art. 18(4).
(4), (5)		CB 148(5), (6)	
5	Period of entitlement.		
(1)–(4)		CB 149(1)–(4)	
4(A)		CB 149(5)	Inserted 1985 art. 18(5).
(5), (6)		CB 149(6), (7)	
(6A), (6B)		CB 149(8), (9)	Inserted 1985 Sch. 4 para. 4.
(7), (8)		CB 149(10), (11)	
(9)		CB 149(12)	Substituted 1986 Sch. 9 para. 50.
6	Qualifying days.		
(1)		CB 150(1)	
(2)		CB 150(2)	Am. 1984 Sch. 5 para. 7.
(3), (4)		CB 150(3), (4)	
7	Limitations on entitlement.		
(1)		CB 151(1)	
(2), (3)		CB 151(2), (3)	Rep. in part 1985 Sch. 6.
(4)		CB 151(4)	Am. 1985 art. 18(1).
(5)		CB 151(5)	Rep. in part 1985 Sch. 6.
8	Notification of incapacity for work.	CB 152	

SOCIAL SECURITY (NORTHERN IRELAND) ACTS CONSOLIDATION—*continued.*

Section of Act, etc.	Subject matter	Section of 1992 Act	Remarks
	SOCIAL SECURITY (NORTHERN IRELAND) ORDER 1982 (N.I. 16)—*continued.*		
9	Rate of payment.		
(1)		CB 153(1)	Subst. Statutory Sick Pay (Rate of Payment) Order (NI) 1992 (SR 1992 No. 27), subject to saving in art. 3
(1A)		CB 153(2)	Inserted 1986 art. 68(1); am. 1990 Sch. 6 para. 11(1).
(1B)		CB 172(1)	Inserted 1986 art. 68(1); am. 1990 Sch. 6 para. 11(2).
(2)		CB 153(3)	
(3), (4)		—	Rep. 1986 Sch. 10.
11	Recovery by employers of amounts paid by way of statutory sick pay.		
(1)		CB 154(1)	Am. 1991 SP art. 3(1).
(1A)		—	Rep. 1991 SP Sch.
(1B)–(1D)		CB 154(2), (3), 155(1), (2), 159, 172(2), A 131, 166(2)	Inserted 1991 SP art. 4(1).
(2)		CB 154(4)	Am. 1985 art. 19(1), 1991 SP art. 4(2).
(3)		CB 154(5)	Am. 1991 SP art. 3(3); rep. in part 1991 SP Sch.
(4)		CB Sch. 1 para. 6(5)	
(5)		CB Sch. 1 para. 6(6)	Am. 1985 art. 19(1); rep. in part 1991 SP Sch.
(6)		CB 154(6)	
(7)		A 143(1)	Am. 1985 art. 19(1); rep. in part 1991 SP Sch.
(8)—(10)		—	Rep. 1986 Sch. 10.
12	Relationship with benefits and other payments etc.	See CB 156	
19	Provision of information: general.		
(1)		A 121	
(2)		A 12(1)	
(2A)		A 12(2)	Inserted 1985 art. 20.
(3)		A 12(3)	
(4)		A 122(4)	
20	Claims for sickness and other benefits: provision of information by employers.		

SOCIAL SECURITY (NORTHERN IRELAND) ACTS CONSOLIDATION—*continued.*

SOCIAL SECURITY (NORTHERN IRELAND) ORDER 1982 (N.I. 16)—*continued.*

Section of Act, etc.	Subject matter	Section of 1992 Act	Remarks
(1)		A 122(1)	Am. 1984 Sch. 2 para. 13(1).
(2), (3)		A 122(2), (3)	
24	Modification of provisions of Part I.	CB 158	Am. M9.
25	Statutory sick pay to count as remuneration for principal Act.	CB 4(1)	
25A	Deductions from statutory sick pay.		Inserted 1984 Sch. 5, para. 8.
(1)		CB 147(3)	
(2)		—	Rep. Wages (NI) Order 1988 (NI 7), Sch. 5.
28	Interpretation of Part II and supplementary provisions.		
(1)		CB 159(1)	Am. 1985 Sch. 4, para. 6(1); rep. in part 1983 Sch. 3.
(2)		CB 159(2)	Am. 1985 Sch. 4, para. 7.
(3)–(5)		CB 159(3)–(5)	
(5A)		CB 159(6)	Inserted Health and Personal Social Services (NI) Order 1991 (NI 1)Sch. 5.
(6)		CB 159	
(7)		CB 168(a)	
29	Crown employment.		
(1), (2)		CB 157(1), (2)	
(3)		CB 157(3)	Inserted 1989 Sch. 7, para. 20.
(4)		CB 171(10), 172(9)	Inserted 1989 Sch. 7, para. 20.
30	Sick pay to count as remuneration for principal Act.		
(1)	Inserts 1975 s. 3(1A)–(1C).	CB 4(1)(b), (2), (3)	
(2)		CB Sch. 1, para. 10	Inserts 1975 Sch. 1, para. 8.
32	Industrial Injuries.		
(1)	Repeal	—	Spent.
(2)	Substitutes 1975 s. 57(4).	CB 103(6), Sch. 7, para. 9(3)	
(3)		CB 31(3)	
(4)		CB 102	
(5)		—	Spent.

SOCIAL SECURITY (NORTHERN IRELAND) ACTS CONSOLIDATION—*continued.*

Section of Act, etc.	Subject matter	Section of 1992 Act	Remarks
	SOCIAL SECURITY (NORTHERN IRELAND) ORDER 1982 (N.I. 16)—*continued.*		
35	Application of social security legislation in relation to territorial waters.		
(1), (2)		CB 168	Subs. (1) rep. in part 1986 Sch. 10.
(3), (4)		—	Rep. 1989 Sch. 9.
36	Regulations and orders.		
(1)		CB 171, A 165	
(2)		CB 172(4), A 166(4)	Subst. 1990 Sch. 6, para. 6(6).
Sch. 1	Circumstances in which periods of entitlement do not arise.		
Para. 1		CB Sch. 11, para. 1	
2		CB Sch. 11, para. 2	Rep. in part 1985 Sch. 6.
3, 4		CB Sch. 11, paras. 3,4	
5		CB Sch, 11, para. 5	Am. 1984 Sch. 2, para. 13(2).
6		CB Sch. 11, para. 6	
7		CB Sch, 11, para. 7	Rep. in part 1989 Sch. 9.
8		CB Sch. 11, para. 8	
Sch. 2	Relationships with benefits and other payments, etc.		
Para. 1		CB Sch. 12, para. 1	Am. 1985 art. 18(6)(a).
1A		CB Sch. 12, para. 5	Inserted 1985 art. 18(6)(b).
2-4		CB Sch. 11, paras. 2–4	
6		CB Sch. 12, para. 6	
Sch. 4	Amendments and transitional provisions.		
Para. 3		—	Superseded.
4		CB 4(5)	
5		CB 31(5)	
6		CB 33(9)	

SOCIAL SECURITY (NORTHERN IRELAND) ACTS CONSOLIDATION—*continued.*

Section of Act, etc.	Subject matter	Section of 1992 Act	Remarks
\multicolumn{4}{c}{SOCIAL SECURITY (NORTHERN IRELAND) ORDER 1982 (N.I. 16)—*continued.*}			
8		CB 94(4), (6)	
12		CB Sch. 6, para. 6(1)	
17		A 149(5)	
18		A Sch. 5 para. 8; see CP Sch. 2 para. 14(22)	
19		CB 30(2)	
\multicolumn{4}{c}{SOCIAL SECURITY ADJUDICATIONS (NORTHERN IRELAND) ORDER 1983 (N.I. 17)}			
3	Adjudicating officers and social security appeal tribunals.		
(1)–(3)			See note 2 to A.
(4)		—	Introduces Sch. 1.
4	Adjudicating medical practitioners.		
(1),(2)			See note 2 to A.
(3)			Consequential amendment.
(4)		—	Introduces Sch. 2.
5	Transitional provisions and savings.	—	Spent.
Sch. 1	Amendments relating to adjudication officers, etc.		
para. 1		A 36, 37, 39	
2		A 23(2)	
3		A Sch. 3, para. 1	
4		A 58(1)	
5		A 38, 39(5), 49(1), Sch. 2, paras. 1–5	Am. 1984 art. 10(b).
6		A 48. 49(3)	
7		A Sch. 2, para. 4	
8		A Sch. 2, para. 6	
9		—	Rep. 1989 Sch. 9.
10		A 167(1)	

SOCIAL SECURITY (NORTHERN IRELAND) ACTS CONSOLIDATION—*continued.*

Section of Act, etc.	Subject matter	Section of 1992 Act	Remarks
	SOCIAL SECURITY ADJUDICATIONS (NORTHERN IRELAND) ORDER 1983 (N.I. 17)—*continued.*		
11–13		—	Spent.
14, 15		—	Rep. 1986 Sch. 10.
16			See CP Sch. 2, para. 13(e), (f).
17–19			Rep. 1986 Sch. 10.
Sch. 2	Amendments relating to adjudicating medical practitioners, etc.		
para. 1(1)		A 43(2)	
(2)		—	Unnecessary.
(3)		A 43(3), (6)	
2(a)		A 44(1)	
(b)		A 44(2)	
(c)		A 44(3)	
3(a)		A 45(1)	
(b)		A 45(4)	
(c)		A 45(8)	
(d)		A 45(9)	
4(a), (b)		A 60(2)(a), (b), 144(5)	
(c)		A Sch. 2, para. 8	
5		A Sch. 3, para. 1	
6		A 58(3)(4)	
7(a)		A 47(1), (2)	
(b)		A 47(3), 48(6), Sch. 2, paras. 4, 8	
8		—	Unnecessary.
	HEALTH AND SOCIAL SECURITY (NORTHERN IRELAND) ORDER 1984 (N.I. 8)		
5	Severe disablement allowance.		
(1)	Substitutes 1975 s. 36.	CB 68	
(2)		—	Introduces Sch. 2.
6	Pension increase in respect of husbands.	CB 84	
7	Dependent children.	—	Introduces Sch. 3.
8	Earnings to include occupational pensions for purposes of benefits in respect of dependents.		
(a)		CB 89	

SOCIAL SECURITY (NORTHERN IRELAND) ACTS CONSOLIDATION—*continued.*

Section of Act, etc.	Subject matter	Section of 1992 Act	Remarks
	HEALTH AND SOCIAL SECURITY (NORTHERN IRELAND) ORDER 1984 (N.I. 8)—*continued.*		
(b)		CB Sch. 7, para. 7	
10	Constitution of panel for social security appeal tribunals.		
(a)		A 39(1), (2)	
(b)		A 38(2), (3)	
11	Late paid Class 2 contributions.		
(1)		—	Unnecessary.
(2)		CB 12	
12	Class 3 contributions.		
(1)(a)		CB 13(1)	
(b)		CB 13(4)	
(2)		—	See CP Sch. 3, para. 4.
(3)		CB 13(5)–(7)	
Sch. 2 para. 1	Severe disablement allowance.	—	Rep. 1989 Sch. 9.
2		CB 63, 90 Sch. 4 Parts III, IV; A 143(2)	
3		—	Spent – amends superseded enactments.
4		A 43(1)	
5		A 43(2)(d)	
6		A 44(1)	
7		A 45(8), (9)	
8a		CB Sch. 6 para. 1	
(b), (c)		CB Sch. 6 paras. 4, 5	
9		CB 121(1)	
10			Rep. 1986 Sch.10.
11		CB Sch. 9 para. 5	
12		—	Rep. 1986 Sch. 10.
13(1)		A 122(1)(e)	
(2)		CB Sch. 11 para. 5(1)(a)	

SOCIAL SECURITY (NORTHERN IRELAND) ACTS CONSOLIDATION—*continued.*

Section of Act, etc.	Subject matter	Section of 1992 Act	Remarks
	HEALTH AND SOCIAL SECURITY (NORTHERN IRELAND) ORDER 1984 (N.I. 8)—*continued.*		
14, 15			Unnecessary.
Sch.3	Dependent children		
para. 1		CB 20(1)	
2(a)		CB 80(2)	
(b)		—	Spent.
(c)		CB 80(3), (4), (7)	
3		CB Sch. 7 para. 4(3)–(6)	
4		CB Sch. 7 para. 18	
5		CB Sch. 4, Part V, para. 12	
6		—	Unnecessary definition.
Sch. 5	Miscellaneous social security amendments		
para. 1		—	Spent – amends repealed enactment
2			Unnecessary.
4		CB 6(2)	
7		CB 150(2)	
8		CB 147(3)	Spent in part.
9		—	Spent
9	Calculation of Contributions.		
(1)		CB 5(1)	
(2)		CB 9(1) - (4)	Spent in part.
(3), (4)		—	Spent.
(5)		A 129	
10	Regulations reducing Class I Contributions in certain cases.	CB 6(5)	
11	Abatement of invalidity allowance etc., where beneficiary entitled to additional component in pension or to guaranteed minimum pension		
(1)		CB 34(1), (2), (4)-(6)	
(2)		CB 47(1), (2)-(4)	
(3)		CB 50(2)	
(4)		CB Sch. 7 para. 3(1)–(4)	

SOCIAL SECURITY (NORTHERN IRELAND) ACTS CONSOLIDATION—*continued.*

Section of Act, etc.	Subject matter	Section of 1992 Act	Remarks
	HEALTH AND SOCIAL SECURITY (NORTHERN IRELAND) ORDER 1984 (N.I. 8)—*continued.*		
(5)		CB Sch. 5 para. 2(6)	
(6)–(9)			Spent.
12	Voluntary redundancy–entitlement to unemployment benefit.	CB 28(4)	
13	Entitlement of married women to Category A retirement pensions.	—	Spent.
14	Abolition of lower rate for Category D retirement pension.		
(1)		CB 78(5), (6)	
(2)		CB Sch. 4 Pt.III para. 7	
15	Pension increases in respect of adult dependants–equal treatment for males and females etc.		
(1)		CB 83(3)	
(2)		CB 84(1)–(3)	
(3)		CB 85(4)	
(4)		CB 86(2)	Rep. in part 1988 Sch. 5.
(5)		CB Sch. 7 para. 6(3)–(6)	
(6), (7)		CB 114(3)	
(8)		CB 114(4)	
18	Period of entitlement.		
(1)		CB 151(4)	
(2)	Repeal		Spent.
(3)		CB 33(10), (11)	
(4)		CB 148(4)	
(5)		CB 149(5)	
(6)		CB Sch. 12 paras. 1, 5	
19	Right of employers to amounts in respect of contributions.	—	Rep. 1991 SP Sch.
20	Medical evidence.	A 12(2)	Inserts 1982 art. 19(2A).
23	Regulations.	—	Spent.
Sch. 3	Earnings factors and guaranteed minimum pensions		

SOCIAL SECURITY (NORTHERN IRELAND) ACTS CONSOLIDATION—*continued.*

Section of Act, etc.	Subject matter	Section of 1992 Act	Remarks
	HEALTH AND SOCIAL SECURITY (NORTHERN IRELAND) ORDER 1984 (N.I. 8)—*continued.*		
Para. 1		A 130	
Sch. 4	Miscellaneous amendments relating to statutory sick pay		
para. 2		CB 68(5)	
4		CB 149(8), (9)	
5	Repeal.	—	Spent.
6, 7		CB 159	
Sch. 5	Minor and consequential amendments		
para, 3		CB 113(3)	
4		A 142(5), (6)	
5		CB Sch. 1 para. 1(2) (4),–(6)	
6		—	Unnecessary
7		CB 5(1)	
8			See CP sch. 4 paras. 2, 3.
	SOCIAL SECURITY ACT 1986 (c. 50)		
Sch. 9	Northern Ireland		
para. 1		A 46	
3(1)(c)		—	
(2)(a)–(g)(i)			See entries for provisions mentioned
11		A 22(6), 166(5)	
12		A Sch. 5 para. 10	
	SOCIAL SECURITY (NORTHERN IRELAND) ORDER 1986 (N.I. 18)		
2	Interpretation		
(2)		A 167(1), CB 146(2)	Relevant definitions only
19	Additional pensions.		
(2)		CB 45(1)	
(3)		CB 45(2)–(5)	
(4)		CB 45(6)	
(5)		CB 46(2)	
(6)		CB 46(1)	

SOCIAL SECURITY (NORTHERN IRELAND) ACTS CONSOLIDATION—*continued.*

Section of Act, etc.	Subject matter	Section of 1992 Act	Remarks
	SOCIAL SECURITY (NORTHERN IRELAND) ORDER 1986 (N.I. 18)—*continued.*		
20	Additional pensions-supplementary		
(1)		CB 39(3), 41(6), 50(5), 51(3)	
(2)		CB sch. 5 para. 4(1)–(3)	
(3)		CB sch. 5 para. 5(1)	
(4)		CB Sch. 5 para. 5(3)	
(5)		CB Sch. 5 para. 6(1)	
(6)		CB Sch. 5 para. 6(3), (4)	
21	Income-related benefits		
(1), (2)		CB 122(1), (2)	Am. 1991D art. 8(2), (3).
(3)		CB 123(1)	Am. 1988 art. 6(1), 1989 art. 15(1).
(4)		CB 123(3)	
(4A)–(4D)		CB 124(1)–(4)	Inserted 1988 art. 6(2).
(4E)		A 70(1)	Inserted 1988 art. 6(2).
(4F), (4G)		A 70(7), (8)	Inserted 1988 art. 6(2).
(4H)–(4M)		A 70(2)–(6)	Inserted 1988 art. 6(2).
(4N)		CB 123(2)	Inserted 1988 art. 6(2).
(5)		CB 127(1)	Am. 1991D art. 10(1)
(5A)		CB 127(1)	Inserted 1988 art. 5(a)
(6)		CB 127(3)	Am. 1989 sch. 8 para. 14, rep. in part 1988 Sch. 5.
(6A)–(6F)		CB 128(1)–(4), (6)	Inserted 1991D art. 8(4)
(7), (8)		CB 129(1), (2)	
(9)		CB 130(2)	
(10)		CB 127(4)	Am. 1991D art. 10(2)
(11)		CB 133(1)	Am. 1989 art. 7(1), 1991D art. 8(6).
(12)		CB 133(2)	Am. 1989 art. 15(2), 1991D art. 8(7).

SOCIAL SECURITY (NORTHERN IRELAND) ACTS CONSOLIDATION—*continued.*

Section of Act, etc.	Subject matter	Section of 1992 Act	Remarks
	SOCIAL SECURITY (NORTHERN IRELAND) ORDER 1986 (N.I. 18)—*continued.*		
22	Amount, etc		
(1)		CB 123(4)	Am. 1988 Sch. 4 para. 16(1).
(1A), (1B)		CB 123(5), (6)	Inserted 1988 Sch. 4 para. 16(2)
(2), (3)		CB 127(2)	
(3A), (3B)		CB 128(5)	Inserted 1991 D art. 8(8).
(4), (5)		CB 129(3)	
(6)		CB 127(5), 128(8), 129(4)	Am. 1991D art. 8(9).
(7)		CB 130(3)	
23	Calculation.		
(1), (2)		CB 131(1), (2)	
(2A), (2B)		CB 131(3), (4)	Inserted 1990 art. 11.
(3), (4)		CB 131(5), (6)	
(5)		CB 132(1)	
(6)		CB 130(1)	
(7)–(9)		CB 132(2)–(4)	
24	Trade disputes.		
(1)–(4)		CB 125(1)–(4)	
(5)		CB 125(5)	ICTA 1988 Sch. 29 para. 32, Table.
(5A)		CB 125(6)	Inserted 1988 Sch. 4 para. 17.
(6), (7)		CB 125(7), (8)	Subst. 1990 Sch. 6 para. 12(2), (3).
(8)			Rep. 1988 Sch. 5.
24A	Effect of return to work.	CB 126	Inserted 1988 Sch. 4 para. 18; am. 1989 Sch. 8 para. 15.
25	Recovery of expenditure on benefit from person liable for maintenance.	A 101	
25A	Recovery of expenditure on income support: additional amounts and transfer of orders.	A 102	Inserted 1990 art. 10(1).
25B	Reduction of expenditure on income support: certain maintenance orders to be enforceable by the Department.	A 103	Inserted 1990 art. 10(1).

SOCIAL SECURITY (NORTHERN IRELAND) ACTS CONSOLIDATION—*continued.*

Section of Act, etc.	Subject matter	Section of 1992 Act	Remarks
	SOCIAL SECURITY (NORTHERN IRELAND) ORDER 1986 (N.I. 18)—*continued.*		
27	Failure to maintain—general.		
(1), (2)		A 100(1), (2)	Am. 1989 art. 7(2), (3), 1990 art. 10(2).
(3)		A 74(6), 100(3)	Am. 1989 art. 7(2), 1989 art. 7(3); rep. in part 1989 Sch. 9.
(4)		A 74(7), 100(3)	Am. 1989 art. 7(3).
(5)		A 74(8), 100(3)	
28	Prevention of duplication of payments.	A 72	
28A	Personal representatives to give information about the estate of a deceased beneficiary.	A 119	Inserted 1989 Sch. 8 para. 16.
28B	Supplementary provisions about disability working allowance.		Inserted 1991D art. 9(1).
(1)–(3)		A 9	
(4)		CB 128(7)	
29	Arrangements for housing benefit.		
(1)		A 126(1)	
(1A)		A 126(2)	Inserted 1989 art. 16(1).
(2)–(5)		A 126(3)–(6)	
30	Adjudication and over-payments.		
(1)–(3)		A 61	
(4)–(7)		A 73	
(8)		A 75(b)	Added 1988 Sch. 4 para. 19.
31	Housing benefit finance.		
(1), (2)		A 127(1), (2)	
(3)		—	Spent.
(4)		A 127(3)	Subst. 1989 art. 17.
(5)–(8)		A 128	Subst. 1989 art. 17.
32	Information.		
(1)–(3)		A 120	
(4)		CB 122(3)	
(5)			See CP Sch. 2 para. 19.
33	The social fund and social fund officers.		
(1)		A 146(1)	
(2)		CB 134(1)	Am. 1987 art. 3.
(2A)		CB 134(2)	Inserted 1988 Sch. 3 para 1.
(3)		—	Rep. 1988 Sch. 5.
(4)		A 74(4)	Rep. in part 1988 Sch. 5.

SOCIAL SECURITY (NORTHERN IRELAND) ACTS CONSOLIDATION—*continued.*

SOCIAL SECURITY (NORTHERN IRELAND) ORDER 1986 (N.I. 18)—*continued.*

Section of Act, etc.	Subject matter	Section of 1992 Act	Remarks
(5)–(7)		A 146(2)–(4)	
(7A), (7B)		A 146(5), (6)	Inserted 1988 Sch. 3 para. 3.
(8)		A 62(1)	Rep. in part 1988 Sch. 5.
(8A)–(8D)		A 147(1)–(4)	Inserted 1988 Sch. 3 para. 5.
(8E)		A 147(5)	Inserted 1990 art. 12(1).
(9)		A 62(2)	
(10)		A 62(3)	Added 1988 Sch. 3 para. 6; am. 1990 art. 12(3).
(11)		A 64(9), CB 136(5	Added 1988 Sch. 3 para. 6.
(12)		A 64(10)	Added 1988 Sch. 3 para. 6.
34	Awards by social fund officers.		
(1)		A 10(1)	Amended 1988 Sch. 3, para. 7, rep. in part 1988 Sch. 5.
(1A)		CB 134(3)	Inserted 1988 Sch. 3, para. 8.
(2)–(4)		CB 135(1)–(3)	
(4A)		CB 134(4)	Inserted 1988 Sch. 3, para. 9.
(5)–(7)		A 74(1)–(3)	
(8)		A 74(6)–(9)	
(8A)		A 75(c)	Inserted 1988 Sch. 4, para. 20.
(9)		CB 136(1)	Am. 1988 Sch. 3, para. 10.
(10)		CB 136(2)	
(10ZA)		CB 136(3)	Inserted 1990 art. 12(3).
(10A)		CB 136(4)	Inserted 1988 Sch. 3, para. 11, am. 1990 art. 12(4), rep, in part 1990 Sch. 7.
(11)		CB 135(5)	
(12)		A 74(5)	
(13)		A 10(2)	Inserted 1990 art. 12(5).
35	Reviews.		
(1)		A 64(1)	Rep. in part 1988 Sch. 5.
(2)–(8)		A 64(2)–(8)	
36	The social fund Commissioner.	A 63	
37	Widowhood.		
(1)		CB 36(1), (2)	
(2)		CB Sch. 4, Part II	

SOCIAL SECURITY (NORTHERN IRELAND) ACTS CONSOLIDATION—*continued.*

Section of Act, etc.	Subject matter	Section of 1992 Act	Remarks
	SOCIAL SECURITY (NORTHERN IRELAND) ORDER 1986 (N.I. 18)—*continued.*		
(3)		CB 38(1), 39(4)	
38	Invalid care allowance for women.		
(1)	Repeal.		Spent.
39	Abolition of maternity grant.	—	Spent.
41	Abolition of child's special allowance except for existing beneficiaries.	CB 56(6)	
42	Abolition of death grant.	—	Spent.
43	Abolition of reduced rate of short-term benefits.	—	Spent.
44	Unemployment benefit—disqualification.		
(1)		CB 26(6)	
(2)		—	Spent.
(3)(a)		CB 28(2)	
(b)		CB 172(2)	
45	Unemployment benefit—trade disputes.		
(1)		CB 27(1), (2)	
(2)		CB 91	
46	Guardian's allowance—adoption.		
(a)		CB 77(10)	
(b)		CB 77(11)	
47	Statutory maternity pay—entitlement to pay.		
(1)–(7)		CB 160(1)–(8)	
(8)		CB 160(9)	Am. 1988 Sch. 4, para. 12(1).
(9)		CB 160(10)	Inserted 1988 Sch. 4, para. 12(2).
48	The maternity pay period.		
(1)–(6)		CB 161(1)–(6)	
(7)		CB 161(7)	Am. 1989 Sch. 7, para. 22.
49	Rates of payment		
(1)		CB 162(1)	
(2)		CB 162(2)	Am. 1988 Sch. 4, para. 13.
(3)–(8)		CB 162(3–(8)	
50	Further provisions relating to statutory maternity pay, etc.		
51	Interpretation of Part I.		
(1)		CB 167(1)	Rep. in part 1988 Sch. 5, 1989 Sch. 9.

SOCIAL SECURITY (NORTHERN IRELAND) ACTS CONSOLIDATION—*continued.*

Section of Act, etc.	Subject matter	Section of 1992 Act	Remarks
	SOCIAL SECURITY (NORTHERN IRELAND) ORDER 1986 (N.I. 18)—*continued.*		
(2)		CB 167(2)	
(2A)		CB 167(3)	Inserted Health and Personal Social Services (NI) Order 1991 (NI 1) Sch. 5.
(3)–(5)		CB 167(4)–(6)	
52	Regulations about claims for and payment of benefit.		
(1)–(4)		A5(1)-(4)	Am. 1988 Sch. 3, para. 13, 1991D Sch. 3, para. 2; rep. in part 1988 Sch. 5.
53	Adjudication.		
(3)		A 18(3), (6), 23(1), 59(4)	Am. 1988 Sch. 3, para. 13, 1991D Sch. 2, para. 11(a).
(3A)		A 18(6), 28(1), 29, 30, 31, 32, 33, 59(4)	Inserted 1991D Sch. 3, para. 3(1).
(4)		A 57(2)	Am. 1991D Sch. 3, para. 3(2).
(5)		A 115(1)	
(6)			See subs. (3).
(7)(a)		A 18(3)	
(b)		A 19(4)	
(c)		A 20(1), (2),(5)	
(d)		A 21(2)	
(8)		A 23(4)	Am. M 10.
(9)(a)		A 28(5)(b), 33(3)(b)	Sub-para. (9) inserted 1991D Sch. 3 para. 3(3).
(b)		—	See A Part II.
(c)		—	See A 33.
(d)		A 52(3)	
(e)		A 52(7)	
(10)		A 28(1), (5)(b), 33(3)(b)	Inserted 1991D Sch. 3 para. 3(3).
54	Overpayments		
(1)		A 69(1)	
(1A)		A 69(2)	Inserted 1989 Sch. 3 para. 14(1).
(2), (3)		A 69(3), (4)	
(4)		A 69(5)	Am. 1989 Sch. 3 para. 14(2).

SOCIAL SECURITY (NORTHERN IRELAND) ACTS CONSOLIDATION—*continued.*

Section of Act, etc.	Subject matter	Section of 1992 Act	Remarks
	SOCIAL SECURITY (NORTHERN IRELAND) ORDER 1986 (N.I. 18)—*continued.*		
(5)–(7)		A 69(6)–(8)	
(7A)		A 75(a)	Inserted 1988 Sch. 4 para. 21.
(8), (9)		A 69(9), (10)	
(10)		A 69(11)	Am. 1988 Sch. 3 para. 4, Sch. 4 para. 23(1), 1991D Sch. 3 para. 4; rep. in part 1988 Sch. 5.
(10A)		A 70(7), (8)	Inserted 1988 Sch. 4 para. 23(2).
(11)		A Sch. 6 para. 3	
56	False representations for obtaining benefit etc.	A 106	
57	Legal proceedings		
(1)–(3)		A 110(1)–(3)	Partial repeals only.
(3A)		A 110(4)	Added 1990 Sch. 6 para. 32.
59	Inspection		
(1)		A 104(1)	
(2), (3)		A 104(2), (3)	Am. 1989 Sch. 4 para.20(2)–(4).
(4), (5)		A 104(4), (5)	
(6), (7)		A 104(6), (7)	Am. 1989 Sch. 4 para. 20(5), (6).
(8), (9)		A 105	
(10)		A 104(9)	Added 1989 Sch. 4 para. 20(7).
61	Regulations as to notification of deaths	A 118	
62	Consultations on subordinate legislation		
(1)–(4)		A 150(1)–(4)	
(5), (6)		A 150(5), (6)	Subst. 1989 Sch. 8 para. 11(2).
63	Subordinate legislation-miscellaneous		
(1), (2)		A 165(6), CB 171(5)	
(3)		A 166(2); CB 172(2)	
64	Annual uprating of benefits	A 132	
64A	Retification of mistakes in orders under Article 64	A 133	Inserted 1989 art. 19(1).

SOCIAL SECURITY (NORTHERN IRELAND) ACTS CONSOLIDATION—*continued.*

Section of Act, etc.	Subject matter	Section of 1992 Act	Remarks
	SOCIAL SECURITY (NORTHERN IRELAND) ORDER 1986 (N.I. 18)—*continued.*		
65	Effect of alteration of rates of benefit		
(1)		A 135(1)	Am. 1989 art. 19(2).
(2)-(6)		A 135(2)-(6)	
65A	Effect of alteration in the component rates of income support	A 139	Inserted 1989 art. 20.
65B	Implementation of increases in income support due to attainment of particular ages.	A 140	Inserted 1990 Sch. 6 para. 13.
66	Reciprocal arrangements		
(1)		A 153(3)(b)	
(2)		A 155(1)(a)	
(3)		—	Spent.
(4)		A 154(2), (5)	
67	Pensioners' Christmas bonus	—	Introduces Sch.6.
68	Rates of payments of statutory sick pay and provisions as to recovery.		
(1)		CB 153(2), 172(1)	
(2)		—	Rep. 1991SP Sch.
69	Liability of Department to pay statutory sick pay in prescribed circumstances.	CB 147(6), A 143(1)(d)	
70	Repeal of s. 92 of principal Act	—	Spent.
71(1)	Child benefit in respect of children educated otherwise than at educational establishments.	CB 138(1)	
74	Application of provisions of Order to supplementary benefit, etc.	—	Unnecessary.
75	National insurance contributions.		
(1),(2)		—	Rep. 1991RF Sch. 2
(3)		CB 6(6), 8(4), 9(5), Sch. 1 para. 1(5)	
(4)		CB 5(2)	
78	Travelling expenses.	A 156	
79	Crown Employment		
(3)		CB 127(6), 128(9)	Am. 1991D Sch. 3 para. 6.
(4)		CB 165	Rep. in part 1990 Sch. 7.
80(1) (part)	Application of Parts II and VI to special cases.	CB 166	

SOCIAL SECURITY (NORTHERN IRELAND) ACTS CONSOLIDATION—*continued.*

Section of Act, etc.	Subject matter	Section of 1992 Act	Remarks
	SOCIAL SECURITY (NORTHERN IRELAND) ORDER 1986 (N.I. 18)—*continued.*		
81	Orders and regulations (general provisions).		
(2)		CB 171(6), A165(7)	
(4)		CB 172(4), A166(4)	
(5)		A 165(8)	
(6)		A 165(9)(c)	
82	Financial provision.		
(1)(c), (d)		A 143(1)(c), (d)	
(2)		A 145(5)	Rep. in part 1990 Sch. 7.
(3)		—	Detailed consequential repeal.
(5)		A 144(3)	
(6) (part)		A 144(5)(b)	
(7)		A 145(1), 165(10)	Am. 1991D Sch. 3 para. 7.
(8)		A 145(2)	
(9), (10)		A 148	
Sch. 3	Industrial injuries and diseases.		
para. 1		—	Introductory.
2		CB 94(1)	
3(1)		CB103(1)	
(2)		CB 103(2)–(4)	
(3)		CB Sch. 7 para. 9(1)(a)	
(4)		CB 103(7), (8)	
4		CB Sch. 7 para. 1	
5(1)		CB Sch. 7 para. 11	
(2)	Repeal.	—	Spent.
6		CB 104(3), (4)	
7		CB Sch. 7 para. 10(1)	—
8	Spent.	—	
9		—	Rep. 1988 Sch. 5.
10		CB 60(2), (3)	

SOCIAL SECURITY (NORTHERN IRELAND) ACTS CONSOLIDATION—*continued.*

Section of Act, etc.	Subject matter	Section of 1992 Act	Remarks
SOCIAL SECURITY (NORTHERN IRELAND) ORDER 1986 (N.I. 18)—*continued.*			
11		—	Rep. 1988 Sch. 5.
12		CP Sch. 3 para. 27	—
13		CB 109(4)–(7)	
14(a)		A 43(1)	
(b)		—	Rep. 1989 Sch. 9.
15		CB Sch. 8 para. 5(3)	
16		—	Rep. in part 1989 Sch. 5, balance spent.
Sch. 4	Statutory maternity pay etc.		
para. 1		CB 163(1)	Am. M 11.
2		CB 163(3)	
3, 4		CB Sch. 1 para. 6(5), (6)	
5		CB 163(4)	
6, 7		A 13	
8		A 124(3)	
8A		A 124(1), (2)	Inserted 1989 Sch. 8 para 17.
9		A 123	
10		CB 4(1)	
11		CB Sch. 13 para. 1	Am. 1988 Sch. 4 para. 15(1).
11A		CB Sch. 13 para. 2	Inserted 1988 Sch. 4 para. 15(2).
12		CB Sch. 13 para. 3	
13		CB 35	
14		CB Sch. 3 para. 3	
15–17		—	Spent.
Sch. 5			
para. 1		—	Spent.
2		A 17(1)	
3		A 18(2), (4)	
4		A 19(2)	
5(a)			—Spent.
(b), (c)		A 20(2),(3)	
(d), (e)		A (20)(4), (5)	

SOCIAL SECURITY (NORTHERN IRELAND) ACTS CONSOLIDATION—*continued.*

Section of Act, etc.	Subject matter	Section of 1992 Act	Remarks
SOCIAL SECURITY (NORTHERN IRELAND) ORDER 1986 (N.I. 18)—*continued.*			
6(1)		A 21(1)	
(2)		A (21)(3)(d)	
(3)		A (21)(7)–(10)	
7		A 34(1)	
8		A 35	
9			
(a)		a 23(1), (3)	
(b)	Repeal.	—	Spent.
(c), (d)		A 24(3), 25(1)	
10		—	Rep. 1991D Sch. 4.
11		A 42(7)	
12		A 44(3)	
13		A 45(2), (3)	
14		A 56(4)–(6)	
15		A 48(2)	
16		A Sch. 3, paras. 3,11	
17		A 167(1)	
Part II			
(b), (c)		A 15(1)(g), (h)	Am. 1991SP art. 4(3).
Sch. 6	Christmas bonus for pensioners.		
Para. 1(1)		CB 146(1)	
(2)		CB 146(2), (3)	Am. 1991D Sch. 1, para. 12.
(3)		CB 146(4)	
2		CB 144	
3(1)		CB 145(1)	
(2)		CB 145(2)	Rep. in part 1989 Sch, 9, 1990 Sch. 6
(3)		CB 145(3)	Rep. in part 1989 Sch. 9.
(4)		CB 145(4)	
(5), (6)		CB 145(5), (6)	
4		A 65	
Sch. 7	Supplementary benefit, etc.		
1		A Sch. 7, para. 1(3)	
2		A Sch. 7, para. 3(2)	

SOCIAL SECURITY (NORTHERN IRELAND) ACTS CONSOLIDATION—*continued.*

Section of Act, etc.	Subject matter	Section of 1992 Act	Remarks
SOCIAL SECURITY (NORTHERN IRELAND) ORDER 1986 (N.I. 18)—*continued.*			
3		A Sch. 7, para. 1(1), (2)	
4		A Sch. 7, para. 2	Am. 1991D Sch. 2, para. 11(6).
5(1)		A Sch. 7, para. 3(1)	
(2)		A Sch. 7, para. 3(3)	
6		A Sch. 7, para. 5	
7		A Sch. 7, para. 4	
Sch. 8	Earnings factors		
Para. 1(1)–(3)		CB 22(1), (4), (5)	
(4)		CB 22(3), 23	
(5)		CB 24(1)	
(6)		CB 21(5)	
2(1)		CB Sch. 3, paras. 1(4)(a), 2(4)(a)	
(2)		CB Sch. 3, paras. 1(3)(a), 2(3)(a)	
(3)		CB Sch, 3, paras. 1(5)(a), 2(5)(a)	
(4)		CB Sch. 3, paras. 4(1)(b), (2)	
(5)		CB Sch. 3. paras. 5(2)	
(6)		CB Sch. 3, para. 5(4)(a)	
(7)		CB Sch. 3. para 7(4)(a)	
3		CB 19(6)	
4		CB 14(1)	
5		CB 44(6)	See also CP Sch. 4, para. 2.
Sch. 9	Minor and consequential amendments.		

SOCIAL SECURITY (NORTHERN IRELAND) ACTS CONSOLIDATION—*continued.*

Section of Act, etc.	Subject matter	Section of 1992 Act	Remarks
SOCIAL SECURITY (NORTHERN IRELAND) ORDER 1986 (N.I. 18)—*continued.*			
Para. 1		CB Sch. 1, para. 8(1)(m)	
27(b)			See CP Sch. 2, para. 6.
28–30		—	Spent.
32		A 1(4)(b), 66(4), 163(1)(b)	Am. 1990 Sch. 6, para. 5(3).
36(2)			See CP Sch. 2, para. 24.
37, 38			See CP Sch. 2, para. 25.
39		CB 20	
40		CB 21(1)	
41		CB 172(2)	
42		CB Sch. 3, para. 4(1), 7(2), (3), (9)	
43	Repeal	—	Spent.
44		CB 39(1)	
45		CB 40(1), (3), (5)	
46(a)		CB 22(2)	
(b)		CB 21(4)	
49		CB 112(3)	
50		CB 149(12)	
51	Repeal	—	Spent.
52			See CP Sch. 2, para. 4.
53		CB 25(6), 31(5), 33(9)	
54	Repeal.	—	Spent.
55		A 8(2)	
56		A 1(1), (2), Sch. 1 paras. 3, 4	
57			Unnecessary.
59		CB Sch. 5 paras. 2(7), 4(4), 7(1)	
62		A 137(1)	
63			See CP Sch. 2 para. 15.
64		A 150(1), 151(4)	
65			Spent.
67		CP Sch. 2 para. 7	

SOCIAL SECURITY (NORTHERN IRELAND) ACTS CONSOLIDATION—*continued.*

Section of Act, etc.	Subject matter	Section of 1992 Act	Remarks

SOCIAL SECURITY (NORTHERN IRELAND) ORDER 1986 (N.I. 18)—*continued.*

Section of Act, etc.	Subject matter	Section of 1992 Act	Remarks
68		A 68(1), (3)	
69		—	Superseded by 1989 art. 3(1).
70		CB 171(10)	
71		—	Spent.
72		A 149(5)	
73		A Sch. 5 para. 4	
74			Spent.

SOCIAL FUND (MATERNITY AND FUNERAL EXPENSES) (NORTHERN IRELAND) ORDER 1987 (N.I. 8)

1,2		—	Unnecessary.
3	Amendment of Article 33(2) of the 1986 Order.	CB 134(1)	

INCOME AND CORPORATION TAXES ACT 1988 (c. 1)

Sch. 29	Amendments.		
para. 14		CB 15(4)	
32(part)		See provisions amended	

FINANCE ACT 1988 (c. 39)

Sch. 3	Married couples: minor and consequential provisions.		
para. 31		CB Sch. 2 para. 3(4)	

SOCIAL SECURITY (NORTHERN IRELAND) ORDER 1988 (N.I. 2)

1(4) (part)	Commencement.	—	Spent.
3	Attendance allowance.	CB 64(3)	Rep. in part 1991D Sch. 4.
4	Introduction of retirement allowance and other provisions relating to industrial benefit.		
(1)		CB Sch. 7 para. 13(1)–(4), (6)	
(2)		CB Sch. 8 para. 11(11)	
(3), (4)		CB Sch. 7 para. 12(1), (2)	
(4A), (4B)		CB Sch. 7 para. 12(3), (4)	Inserted 1989 art. 19(5).

SOCIAL SECURITY (NORTHERN IRELAND) ACTS CONSOLIDATION—*continued.*

Section of Act, etc.	Subject matter	Section of 1992 Act	Remarks
	SOCIAL SECURITY (NORTHERN IRELAND) ORDER 1988 (N.I. 2)—*continued.*		
(5)		CB Sch. 7 para. 12(5)	
(6)		CB Sch. 7 para. 12(6)	Am. 1989 art. 19(6).
(7), (7A)		—	Rep. 1990 Sch. 7.
(8)		—	Rep. 1989 Sch. 9.
(9)		—	Introduces Sch. 1.
5	Commencement of payment of family credit.		
(a)		CB 127(1)	
(b)		—	Spent.
6	Income support and child benefit.		
(1)		CB 123(1)	
(2)		CB 124; A 70	
(3)		CB 138(1)(b)	
(4)		CB 140(1)	
7	Contribution conditions for short-term benefits.		
(1)		—	Introductory.
(2)(a)		CB Sch. 3 paras. 1(2), 2(2)	
(b)		CB Sch. 3 paras. 1(3), 2(3)	
(3), (4)		—	Spent.
8	Unemployment benefit and occupational pension.	CB 30(1)	
9	Emergency payments.	A 14	
11	Increase and reduction of benefit by reference to earnings.	—	Introduces Sch. 2 Part I; omitted M 13.
12	Amendments relating to the social fund.	—	Introduces Sch. 3.
15	Financial provision.	A 145(5)	
16(1)	Minor and consequential amendments.	—	Spent.
Sch. 1	Industrial death benefit.		
para. 1		—	Spent.
2		CB Sch. 7 para. 14(1)	Savings for certain repeals by 1986.
3		—	Spent.
4		—	Spent.

SOCIAL SECURITY (NORTHERN IRELAND) ACTS CONSOLIDATION—*continued.*

Section of Act, etc.	Subject matter	Section of 1992 Act	Remarks
	SOCIAL SECURITY (NORTHERN IRELAND) ORDER 1988 (N.I. 2)—*continued.*		
5(a)		CB 60(8)	
(b)		CB 60(3)(d)	
6	Savings for certain repeals by 1986.	CB Sch. 7 paras. 20, 21; see also A (8)(1)(a), 42(5), 58(4), (5)(a)	
Sch. 2	Earnings factors and transfer values.		
para. 1(1)		CB 23(1), (2)	
Sch. 3	The social fund.		
para. 1		CB 134(2)	
2		—	Spent.
3		A 146(5), (6)	
4		—	Spent.
5		A 147(1)–(4)	
6		A 62(3), 64(9), (10)	
7		A 10(1)	
8		CB 134(3)	
9		CB 135(4)	
10		CB 136(1)	
11		CB 136(4)	
12		—	Spent.
13		A 5(2)(e), 18(6)(e), 59(4), 62(11)(e), 69(11)	
Sch. 4	Minor and consequential amendments.		
para. 1		CB 57(4)	
2(a)		CB 57(2)	
(b)		CB 35(4)	
3(a)		CB 82(1)(b)	
(b)		CB 82(3)(a)	
4		CB 83(2)	Spent in part.
5		CB 84(2)	Spent in part.

SOCIAL SECURITY (NORTHERN IRELAND) ACTS CONSOLIDATION—*continued.*

Section of Act, etc.	Subject matter	Section of 1992 Act	Remarks
SOCIAL SECURITY (NORTHERN IRELAND) ORDER 1988 (N.I. 2)—*continued.*			
6		—	Spent.
7		CB 86(1)	
8		CB 94(2)	
9		CB Sch. 7 para. 11(14), 13(11)	
10		—	Spent.
11		A 23(1)(e)	
12		CB 160(9), (10)	
13		CB 162(2)	
14		—	Spent.
15(1)		CB Sch. 13 para. 1	
(2)		CB Sch. 13 para. 2	
16(1)		CB 123(4)	
(2)		CB 123(5), (6)	
17(1)		CB 125(6)	
(2)		—	Rep. 1990 Sch. 7.
18		CB 126	
19–21		A 75	
22		—	CP Sch. 3 para. 4.
23		A 69(11), 70(7), (8)	
EMPLOYMENT AND TRAINING (AMENDMENT) (NORTHERN IRELAND) ORDER 1988 (N.I. 10)			
5	Amendment of Social Security (N.I.) Act 1975 with respect to training.		
(1)		—	Introductory.
(2)		CB 28(1)	
(3)		CB 28(6)	
6	Repeals.	—	Spent.
SOCIAL SECURITY (NORTHERN IRELAND) ORDER 1989 (N.I. 13)			
2(2) part	Interpretation.	—	Spent definitions.
3	Amendments relating to primary Class 1 contributions.		
(1)		CB 8(1)–(3)	
(2)		A 142(5)	
(3)		—	Unnecessary.

SOCIAL SECURITY (NORTHERN IRELAND) ACTS CONSOLIDATION—*continued.*

Section of Act, etc.	Subject matter	Section of 1992 Act	Remarks
	SOCIAL SECURITY (NORTHERN IRELAND) ORDER 1989 (N.I. 13)—*continued.*		
4	Repayment of contributions where earnings become repayable.	CB Sch. 1 para. 8(1)	
5	Abolition of Consolidated Fund supplement to contributions.	—	Spent.
6	Earnings factors.		
(1)		—	Introductory.
(2)		CB 23(3)(a)	
(3)		CB 22(6)	
(4)		CB 24(2)	
7	Liability of parents to maintain children under the age of 19 in respect of whom income support is paid.		
(1)		CB 133(1) "child"	
(2), (3)		A 74(6), (7)	
8(1)	Necessity for claim.	A Sch. 1 para. 5	
9	Abolition of earnings rule etc.		
(1), (2)		—	Spent.
(3)(a)		CB 49(2), (3)	
(b)		—	Spent.
(4)		CB 55	
(5)			See CP Sch. 3 para. 4.
11	Extension to personal pensions of occupational pension provisions relating to the abatement of unemployment benefit and the meaning of "earnings".		
(1)		CB 30(1), (3)(d), 172(2)	
(2)		CB 121(1)	
(3)		CB 89(1), (2)	
(4)		—	Unnecessary.
12	Unemployment benefit: requirement to seek employment actively.		
(1)		—	Introductory.
(2), (3)		CB 57(1), (3)(b)	
(4)		CB 57(5)	
(5)		A 23(1)(c)	

SOCIAL SECURITY (NORTHERN IRELAND) ACTS CONSOLIDATION—*continued.*

Section of Act, etc.	Subject matter	Section of 1992 Act	Remarks
	SOCIAL SECURITY (NORTHERN IRELAND) ORDER 1989 (N.I. 13)—*continued.*		
13	Requalification for unemployment benefit.	CB 26(2)–(4)	
14	Disqualifaction for unemployment benefit.		
(1)		CB 28(1)	
(2)		—	Spent.
(3)		CB 28(5)	
(4)		CB 29	
(5)		—	Unnecessary.
(6)		—	Spent.
15	Income support and unemployment.		
(1)		CB 123(1)(d)	
(2)		CB 133(2)(d)	
16	Housing benefit to take the form of payments or deducations.		
(1)		A 126(2)	
(2)		—	See CP Sch. 3 para. 4.
17	Housing benefit grant.	A 127(3), 128	
18	Expenses in making transitional payments relating to income support and housing benefit.	—	Spent.
19	Rectification of mistakes in uprating orders.		
(1)		A 133	
(2)		A 135(1); A 166(2)	
(3)		CB Sch. 7 para. 13(5)	
(4)		—	Introductory.
(5)		CB Sch. 7 para. 12(3), (4)	
(6)		CB Sch. 7 para. 12(6)	
(7)			See CP Sch. 3 para. 4.
20	Effect of alteration in the component rates of income support.	A 139	
21	Unauthorised disclosure of information relating to particular persons.	A 117	Am. 1990 Sch. 6 para. 17.

SOCIAL SECURITY (NORTHERN IRELAND) ACTS CONSOLIDATION—*continued.*

Section of Act, etc.	Subject matter	Section of 1992 Act	Remarks
	SOCIAL SECURITY (NORTHERN IRELAND) ORDER 1989 (N.I. 13)—*continued.*		
22	Disclosure of information by Inland Revenue for social security purposes.	A 116	
23	Miscellaneous amendments relating to adjudication.	—	Introduces Sch. 3.
24	Recovery of sums equivalent to benefit from compensation payments in respect of accidents, injuries and diseases.		
(1),(2)		A 78(1)–(8)	
(3)		A 77(1)	Am. 1990 Sch. 1 para. 1, 1991SP art. 3(5); rep. in part 1990 Sch. 7.
(3A)		A 77(2)	Inserted 1991SP art. 3(5).
(4)–(6)		A 77(3)–(5)	
(8)		A 77(7)	
27	Pre-consolidation amendments.	—	Unnecessary.
28	Application to the Crown.	A 99	
29	Financial provisions.		
(2)		A 144(6)	
(3)		A 143(1)(e), (2)(d)	
30	Regulations and orders: general provisions.		
(2)		A 166(2)	
(3)		—	Partial repeal—consequential.
(5)		A 165(9)	
Sch. 1	Abolition of earnings rule, etc.		
para. 1		—	Spent.
2(1)		—	Spent.
(2)		CB 54(4)	
(3)		—	Spent.
3(1)		CB Sch. 5 para. 1	
(2)–(4)		CB Sch. 5 para. 2(1)–(3)	
(5), (6)		CB Sch. 5 para. 2(7), (8)	
(7)		CB Sch. 5 para. 3(1)	
(8)		CB Sch. 5 para. 4	

SOCIAL SECURITY (NORTHERN IRELAND) ACTS CONSOLIDATION—*continued.*

Section of Act, etc.	Subject matter	Section of 1992 Act	Remarks
	SOCIAL SECURITY (NORTHERN IRELAND) ORDER 1989 (N.I. 13)—*continued.*		
(9), (10)		CB Sch. 5 para. 8(1)–(3)	
(11)		—	Unnecessary.
4(1)		CB 25(2)	
(2)		—	Spent.
5(1)		CB 33(1)	
(2)		CB 33(2)	
(3)		—	Spent.
6, 7		—	Spent.
8(1)		CB 102(3)	
(2)		CB Sch. 7 para. 13(1)	
(3), (4)		—	Rep. 1990 Sch. 7.
(5)		CB Sch. 7 para. 13(4)	
(6)		CB Sch. 7 para. 13(8), (9)	
(7)		—	Rep. 1990 Sch. 7.
(8)		—	Spent.
9(1)		—	Spent.
(2)		CB 51(4)	
10(1)		CB 40(7)	
(2)		CB 41(7)	
Sch. 2	Persons employed in social security administration or adjudication.	A Sch. 4 Part I	Am. 1990 Sch. 6 para. 17(4), 1991D Sch. 2 para. 13; rep. in part 1991D Sch. 4.
Sch. 3	Adjudication.		
para. 1(1)		A 15(3)	
(2)		A 57(5)(b)	
2		A 19(5)	
3(1)		A 51, A 54	
(2)		—	Spent.
4		A Sch. 3 para. 2	
5		—	Spent.
6		A21(7), (8)	
7		A 27	
8		—	Rep. 1991D Sch. 4
9(1)		—	Spent.

SOCIAL SECURITY (NORTHERN IRELAND) ACTS CONSOLIDATION—*continued.*

Section of Act, etc.	Subject matter	Section of 1992 Act	Remarks

SOCIAL SECURITY (NORTHERN IRELAND) ORDER 1989 (N.I. 13)—*continued.*

Section of Act, etc.	Subject matter	Section of 1992 Act	Remarks
(2)		A 46(5), (6)	
10		A Sch. 3 para. 9	
11(1)		A 23(1)(c)	
(2)		A 23(5)	
(3), (4)		A 25(1)	
12(1)		A 43(1)	
(2)		A 43(4), (5)	
13(1)		CB Sch. 6 para. 6(3)–(5)	
(2)		CB Sch. 6 para. 7	
14(1)		A 69(2)	
(2)		A 69(5)	
15		A 35(2)	
16		A 166(6)	
17		—	Spent.
18		A 49(4)	
Sch. 4	Recovery of sums equivalent to benefit from compensation payments in respect of accidents, etc. supplementary provision.		
para. 1(1)		A 77(1) (part)	Am. Social Security Act 1990 (c. 27) Sch. 1 para. 5(4)(a).
(2)		A 77(6)	
(3)		—	Unnecessary.
2–11		A 79–88	
12		A 89	Am. 1990 Sch. 1 para. 2.
13		A 90	Sub-para. (2A) inserted 1990 Sch. 1 para. 1(4).
14–16		A 91–93	
17		A 94	Am. 1990 Sch. 1 paras. 3, 4.
18, 19		A 95, 96	
20(1)		—	Introductory.
(2)–(4)		A 104(2), (3)	
(5), (6)		A 104(6), (7)	
(7)		A 104(9)	
21		A 97	
23		A 98	Inserted 1990 Sch. 1 para. 5.

SOCIAL SECURITY (NORTHERN IRELAND) ACTS CONSOLIDATION—*continued.*

Section of Act, etc.	Subject matter	Section of 1992 Act	Remarks
	SOCIAL SECURITY (NORTHERN IRELAND) ORDER 1989 (N.I. 13)—*continued.*		
Sch. 7	Pre-consolidation amendments.		
para. 1(1)		CB 6(3)	
(2)		CB 9(1)	
2		CB 12(3)	
3		CB 13(6)	
4		CB 15(1), (2), (5)	
5		CB 20	
6		CB 22(3)	
7		CB 26(6)	
8		36(3)	
9		—	Spent, see M 3.
10		—	Spent.
11		CB 103(6)	
12		CB Sch. 7 para. 11(1)	
13		—	Rep. 1991D Sch. 4.
14		CB Sch. 3 para. 7(1)	
15		A 49(4)	
16		—	Unnecessary.
17(1)		CB 40(2)	
(2)		—	Spent.
19		A 11(1)	
20		CB 157(3), 171(10), 172(9)	
21		—	Spent.
22		CB 161	
23, 24		—	Spent.
Sch. 8	Minor and consequential amendments.		
para. 1		CB 4(4)	
2(1)		CB 58(1)	
(2)		CB 58(2)	Am. 1990 Sch. 6 para. 19(2).
(3)		CB 58(3)	
(4)		CB 68(12)	
(5)		CB 68(11)(d)	
(6)		CB 58(4)	Am. 1990 Sch. 6 para. 19(3)
(7)		CB 58(5)	
3		CB 57(6), (7)	

SOCIAL SECURITY (NORTHERN IRELAND) ACTS CONSOLIDATION—*continued.*

Section of Act, etc.	Subject matter	Section of 1992 Act	Remarks
	SOCIAL SECURITY (NORTHERN IRELAND) ORDER 1989 (N.I. 13)—*continued.*		
4(1)		CB 37(3), (4)	
(2)		CB38(2), (3)	
(3)		CB 44(1)	
(4)		CB 44(2)	
(5)		CB 49(7), (8)	
(6)		CB 78(7), (8)	
5(1)		—	Introductory.
(2)		CB 65(1)	
(3)		CB 65(4), (6)	
(4)		CB 65(5)	
6		CB 68(8), (9)	
7(1)		CB 86(1)	
(2)		CB Sch. 7 para. 8	
8		A 1(1), (2)	
9(1)		A 165(5), CB 171(4)	
10		A 136	
11(1)		A 149(3)	
(2)		A 150(5)	
(3)		A Sch. 5 para. 8	
13		—	Spent.
14		CB 127(3)	
15		CB 126(c)	
16		A 119	
17		CB 124(1), (2)	
18(a), (b)		—	
	HUMAN FERTILISATION AND EMBRYOLOGY ACT 1990 (c. 37)		
Sch. 4 para. 3	Amendments.	CB 37(1)	
	SOCIAL SECURITY (NORTHERN IRELAND) ORDER 1990 (N.I. 15)		
2(2) (part)	Interpretation	—	Partial repeal: unnecessary.
3	Attendance allowance for people who are terminally ill.		

SOCIAL SECURITY (NORTHERN IRELAND) ACTS CONSOLIDATION—*continued.*

Section of Act, etc.	Subject matter	Section of 1992 Act	Remarks
	SOCIAL SECURITY (NORTHERN IRELAND) ORDER 1990 (N.I. 15)—*continued.*		
(1)		CB 66(1), (2)	
(2)		CB 65(6)	
(3)–(5)		—	Rep. 1991D Sch. 4.
(6)		A 1(3)	
4	Severe disablement allowance: age related addition.		
(1)		CB 69	
(2)		CB Sch. 4 Part III, para. 3	
(3)		CB 63	
5	Reduced earnings allowance and retirement allowance.		
(1)		CB Sch. 7 para. 11(1)	
(2)		CB Sch. 7 para. 11(2), (3)	
(3)		CB Sch. 7 para. 11(8)	
(4)		CB Sch. 7 para. 11(1)	
(5)		—	Spent.
(6)		CB Sch. 7 para. 13(10)	
(7)		CB 109(2)	
(8)		—	Spent.
6	Computation of additional pension for purposes of invalidity pension etc.		
(1)		CB 33(3)	
(2)		CB 40(5)	
(3)		CB 41(4), (5)	
7	Retrospective effect of section 154A of the principal Act.		
(1)		A 2	
(2)			
(3)		—	Spent.
(4), (5)		A 1(4)(b)	

SOCIAL SECURITY (NORTHERN IRELAND) ACTS CONSOLIDATION—*continued.*

Section of Act, etc.	Subject matter	Section of 1992 Act	Remarks
	SOCIAL SECURITY (NORTHERN IRELAND) ORDER 1990 (N.I. 15)—*continued.*		
8	Late claims for widowhood benefits where death is difficult to establish.		
(1)		A 1(1), (2), Sch. 1 para. 5	
(2)		A 3	
(3)		A 25(2)	
10	Liability to maintain dependants.		
(1)		A 102, 103	
(2)		A 74(6), 100(3)	
11	Income support in respect of accommodation charges for persons in nursing homes, etc.	CB 131(3), (4)	
12	Amendments relating to the social fund		
(1)		A 147(5)	
(2)		A 62(3)	
(3)		CB 136(3)	
(4)		CB 136(4)	
(5)		A 10(2)	
18	Removal of certain liabilities from the National Insurance Fund.		
(1)		CB 1(1)	
(2)		CB 1(1), (5)	
(3)		A 142(3)	
(4), (5)		A 143(2), (5), 145(5)	
(6)		A 143(2)(c)	
(7)(a)		A 143(2)(c)	
(b)		A 144(4), Sch. 5 para. 1(3)(c)	
(c)	Repeal.	—	Spent.
(8)		—	Spent.
(9)		—	See CP Sch. 3 para. 4.
19	Interest and penalties in respect of certain contributions.		
(1)		A 142(4)	
(2)		A 143(5)	
(3)		CB Sch. 1 para. 6(2)–(4)	

SOCIAL SECURITY (NORTHERN IRELAND) ACTS CONSOLIDATION—*continued.*

Section of Act, etc.	Subject matter	Section of 1992 Act	Remarks
	SOCIAL SECURITY (NORTHERN IRELAND) ORDER 1990 (N.I. 15)—*continued.*		
(4)		CB Sch. 1 para. 6(8)	
(5)		—	Introduces Sch. 5.
20	General financial provisions.	A 145(5)	
Sch. 1	Amendments relating to the recovery from damages etc. of sums equivalent to benefit.		
para. 1		A 77(1), 78(1)–(8), 90	
2		A 89	
3, 4		A 94	
5		A 98	
Sch. 5	Special penalties in the case of certain returns.	CB Sch. 1 para. 7	
Sch. 6	Minor and consequential amendments.		
para. 1(1)		CB 60(5)	
(2)		CB 87(1), (2)	
(3)		CB 61(1)	
(4)		CB 61(2)	
2(1)		CB 108(5)	
(2)		CB 109(2)	
3(1)		A 36(1)	
(2)		A 110(4)	
4(1)		A 20(6), (7)	
(2)		A 21(4)	
(3)		A 21(5)	
(4)		—	Spent.
5(1)		A 67	
(2)		A 66	
(3)		A 66(4)	
6(1)		A 166(3), CB 172(3)	
(2)			See 1975P art. 71(1), (3) inserted by CP Sch. 2 para. 14(21).
(3)		A 166(2), CB 172(2)	
(4)		A 166(4), CB 172(4)	
(5)		CB 172(6)	

SOCIAL SECURITY (NORTHERN IRELAND) ACTS CONSOLIDATION—*continued.*

Section of Act, etc.	Subject matter	Section of 1992 Act	Remarks
	SOCIAL SECURITY (NORTHERN IRELAND) ORDER 1990 (N.I. 15)—*continued.*		
(7)	Repeal.	—	Spent.
(8)		A 166(4), CB 172(4)	
(10)	Repeal.	—	Spent.
(16)		A 166(6)	
(17)		—	Partial repeal–unnecessary.
7		CB Sch. 1 para. 8(1)	
8(1)		CB Sch. 3 para. 3(1)	
(2)		CB Sch. 3 para. 3(2), (3)	
9		CB 121(1)	
10		—	Spent.
11		CB 153(2), 172(1)	
12(1)		—	Introductory.
(2), (3)		CB 125(7), (8)	
13		A 140	
14, 15		—	Spent.
16(2)		A 4	
17(1)–(4)		A 117(7)(b), (9)(d), (10)(d)	
(4)		A Sch. 4 Part I	
19(1)		—	Introductory.
(2), (3)		CB 58(2), (4)	
(4)		CB 68(11)	
	STATUTORY SICK PAY (NORTHERN IRELAND) ORDER 1991 (N.I. 9)		
3	Reduction in the amounts recoverable by employers who have paid statutory sick pay.		

SOCIAL SECURITY (NORTHERN IRELAND) ACTS CONSOLIDATION—*continued.*

Section of Act, etc.	Subject matter	Section of 1992 Act	Remarks
STATUTORY SICK PAY (NORTHERN IRELAND) ORDER 1991 (N.I. 9)—*continued.*			
(1)		CB 154(1)	
(2)		—	Spent.
(3)		CB 154(5)	
(4)		CB 1(5)	
(5)		A 77(1) "benefit", (2)	
4	Small employers' relief.		
(1)		CB154(2), (3), 155, 172(2), A 131, 166(2)	
(2)		CB 154(4)	
(3)		A 15(1)(g)(v)	
(4)		—	Spent.
5	Consequential amendments, repeals and supplementary provisions.		
(1)(a)		A 68(3)	
(b)		A 149(2)	
(3)			See CP Sch. 3 para. 6.
(4), (5)		—	Spent.

DISABILITY LIVING ALLOWANCE AND DISABILITY WORKING ALLOWANCE (NORTHERN IRELAND) ORDER 1991 (N.I. 17)

Section of Act, etc.	Subject matter	Section of 1992 Act	Remarks
3	Introduction of disability living allowance.		
(1)		CB 63	
(2)		CB 71–73, 75, 76	
4	Attendance allowance and mobility allowance.		
(1)		CB 64	
5	Disability Living Allowance Advisory Board for Northern Ireland.		
(1)–(6)		A 152	
(7), (8)		A 165(1), (5)	

SOCIAL SECURITY (NORTHERN IRELAND) ACTS CONSOLIDATION—*continued.*

Section of Act, etc.	Subject matter	Section of 1992 Act	Remarks
	DISABILITY LIVING ALLOWANCE AND DISABILITY WORKING ALLOWANCE (NORTHERN IRELAND) ORDER 1991 (N.I. 17)—*continued.*		
6	Management of disability living allowance and attendance allowance, etc.		
(1)		—	Introductory.
7	Regulations supplementary to Articles 3 to 6		
(1)–(3)			See CP Sch. 3 para. 20.
(4)			See CP Sch. 3 para. 21(2), (3), (5).
8	Introduction of disability working allowance.		
(1)		—	Introductory.
(2)		CB 122(1)(c)	
(3)		CB 122(2)	
(4)		CB 128(1)–(4), (6)	
(5)			See CP Sch. 4 para. 16.
(6)		CB 133(1) "industrial injuries regulations", "war pension scheme".	
(7)		CB 133(2)	
(8)		CB 128(5)	
(9)		CB 128(8)	
9	Disability working allowance—supplementary.		
(1)		CB 128(7), A 11	
10	Effect on entitlement to family credit of entitlement to disability working allowance.		
(1)		CB 127(1)	
(2)		CB 127(4)	

SOCIAL SECURITY (NORTHERN IRELAND) ACTS CONSOLIDATION—*continued.*

DISABILITY LIVING ALLOWANCE AND DISABILITY WORKING ALLOWANCE (NORTHERN IRELAND) ORDER 1991 (N.I. 17)—*continued.*

Section of Act, etc.	Subject matter	Section of 1992 Act	Remarks
11	Entitlement to other benefits after termination of entitlement to disability working allowance.		
(1)		CB 33(7), (8)	
(2)		CB 68(10)	
(3)		CB 42	
(4)		CB 121(1)	
(5)		CB 83	
13	Supplementary.		
(1)			See CP Sch. 3 para. 4.
(2)			Spent.
14	Regulations.		
(1)		—	Spent.
(2)		A 166(4), CB 172(4)	
(3)		A 165(10), CB 171(7)	
Sch. 1	Management of disability living allowance and attendance allowance.		
Para. 1		—	Introductory.
2		A 18(1)	
3		A 19(1)	
4		A 20(1), (2), (5)	
5		A 28–31	
6		A 21(3), (4)	
7		A 34	
8		A 23(1), (3), 32(1)–(4)	
9		A 33	
10		A Sch. 3 para. 1	
11		A 51	
12		A 54	
13		A 52, 53	
14		—	Spent.
15		A 49(1)	

SOCIAL SECURITY (NORTHERN IRELAND) ACTS CONSOLIDATION—*continued.*

Section of Act, etc.	Subject matter	Section of 1992 Act	Remarks
DISABILITY LIVING ALLOWANCE AND DISABILITY WORKING ALLOWANCE (NORTHERN IRELAND) ORDER 1991 (N.I. 17)—*continued.*			
16		A 40, 41, Sch. 2 paras. 2–6, 8	
17		A Sch. 3 para. 10	
18		A 143(2)	
19		A 1(3)	
20			Unnecessary.
Sch. 2	Disability living allowance and attendance allowance: amendments.		
Para. 2			See destinations of enactments amended.
3		CB 70(2)	
4		A 66	
6	Assembly disqualification.		See CP Sch. 2 para. 13(e), (f).
7		CB 74(1)	
8		A Sch. 5	
9		A Sch. 2 para. 9	
11		A 18(6), Sch. 7 para. 2	
12		CB 146(2)	
13		A Sch. 4 Part I	
Sch. 3	Disability working allowance: amendments.		
Para. 1			Introductory.
2		A 5(2)	
3			See destinations of enactments amended.
4		A 69(11)	
5		A 154(2), (5)	
6		CB 128(9)	
7		A 145(1)	
SOCIAL SECURITY (CONTRIBUTIONS) (NORTHERN IRELAND) ORDER 1991 (N.I. 22)			
1	Citation, financial and commencement.		Unnecessary.
2	Interpretation.	—	Unnecessary.

SOCIAL SECURITY (NORTHERN IRELAND) ACTS CONSOLIDATION—*continued.*

Section of Act, etc.	Subject matter	Section of 1992 Act	Remarks
	SOCIAL SECURITY (CONTRIBUTIONS) (NORTHERN IRELAND) ORDER 1991 (N.I. 22)—*continued.*		
3	Class 1A contributions.		
(1)		—	Introductory.
(2), (3)		CB 1(2), (6)	
(4), (5)		CB 5, 10	
4	Computation, collection and recovery.		
(1)		CB 1(4)	
(2)		CB Sch. 1 para. 5	
(3)		CB Sch. 1 para. 6	
(4)		CB Sch. 1 para. 7(11)	
(5)		CB Sch. 1 para. 8(1)	
(6)		A 114	
5	Determination of questions.		
(1)		A 15(1)	
(2)		A 57(4)	
6	Health service allocation.		
(a)		A 142(5)	
(b)		A 142	
	SOCIAL SECURITY (CONSEQUENTIAL PROVISIONS) ACT 1992 (c. 9)		
Sch. 2	Consequential amendments.		
para. 12		CB 171(11)	
13		CB 172(9)	
14		CB 173(4)	

TAXATION OF CHARGEABLE GAINS ACT 1992 (c. 12)

TABLE OF DERIVATIONS

(for Table of Destinations see page cccxxv)

Note: The following abbreviations are used in this Table:

1970	=	Income and Corporation Taxes Act 1970 c. 10.
1970(F)	=	Finance Act 1970 c. 24.
1973	=	Finance Act 1973 c. 51.
HA1974	=	Housing Act 1974 c. 44.
1975(2)	=	Finance (No. 2) Act 1975 c. 45.
1976	=	Finance Act 1976 c. 40.
1977	=	Finance Act 1977 c. 36.
1979	=	Capital Gains Tax Act 1979 c. 14.
1979(2)	=	Finance (No. 2) Act 1979 c. 47.
1980	=	Finance Act 1980 c. 48.
1981	=	Finance Act 1981 c. 35.
1982	=	Finance Act 1982 c. 39
AJA1982	=	Administration of Justice Act 1982 c. 53.
1983(2)	=	Finance (No. 2) Act 1983 c. 49.
LRTA1984	=	London Regional Transport Act 1984 c. 32.
1984	=	Finance Act 1984 c. 43.
ITA	=	Inheritance Tax Act 1984 c. 51.
CCCPA	=	Companies Consolidation (Consequential Provisions) Act 1985 c. 9.
1985	=	Finance Act 1985 c. 54.
HCPA	=	Housing (Consequential Provisions) Act 1985 c. 71.
1986	=	Finance Act 1986 c. 41.
PCA	=	Parliamentary Constituencies Act 1986 c. 56.
1987	=	Finance Act 1987 c. 16.
1987(2)	=	Finance (No. 2) Act 1987 c. 51.
ICTA	=	Income and Corporation Taxes Act 1988 c. 1.
1988	=	Finance Act 1988 c. 39.
CDPA1988	=	Copyright, Designs and Patents Act 1988 c. 48.
HA1988	=	Housing Act 1988 c. 50.
1989	=	Finance Act 1989 c. 26.
CAA	=	Capital Allowances Act 1990 c. 1.
1990	=	Finance Act 1990 c. 29.
DLA1991	=	Disability Living Allowance and Disability Working Allowance Act 1991 c. 21 Sch. 2 §9; Disability Living Allowance and Disability Working Allowance (Northern Ireland Consequential Amendments) Order 1991 Art. 2.
1991	=	Finance Act 1991 c. 31.
SSCP	=	Social Security (Consequential Provisions) Act 1992 c. 6; Security Security (Consequential Provisions) Act (Northern Ireland) 1992 c. 9.
SI 1988/744	=	The Finance (No. 2) Act 1987 (Commencement) Order 1988.
SI 1989/1299	=	The Income Tax (Stock Lending) Regulations 1989.
SI 1989/1788	=	The Finance Act 1989 (Repeal of Tithe Redemption Enactments) (Appointed Day) Order 1989.
SI 1991/736	=	Capital Gains (Annual Exempt Amount) Order 1991.

Section of 1992 Act	Derivation
1	1979 s. 1.
2(1)	1979 s. 2.
(2)	1979 s. 4(1).
(3)	1979 s. 29(5).
3(1)	1979 s. 5(1); 1980 s. 77(2); 1982 s. 80(1).
(2)-(4)	1979 s. 5(1A), (1B), (1C); 1982 s. 80(2); S.I. 1991/736.
(5), (6)	1979 s. 5(4), (5); 1982 s. 80(1).

TAXATION OF CHARGEABLE GAINS ACT—*continued.*

Section of 1992 Act	Derivation
(7)	1979 Sch. 1 §4.
(8)	1979 s. 5(6).
4	1988 s. 98.
5	1988 s. 100.
6	1988 s. 102; 1991 Sch. 6 §6.
7	1979 s. 7; 1980 s. 61(2).
8	ICTA s. 345, 834.
9	1979 s. 18(1)-(3).
10(1)	1979 s. 12(1).
(2)	1979 s. 12(1A); 1989 s. 128(2).
(3)	ICTAs. 11(2)(b), 6(4).
(4)	1979 s. 12(2).
(5)	1979 s. 12(2A); 1989 s. 126(2).
(6)	1979 s. 12(3).
11	1979 s. 18(5)-(8); ICTA Sch. 29 §16.
12	1979 s. 14.
13(1)-(9)	1979 s. 15(1)-(9).
(10)	1981 s. 85.
(11)	1979 s. 15(10).
14	1979 s. 16.
15	1979 s. 28(1), (2), 30; 1982 s. 86.
16	1979 s. 29(1)-(4).
17	1979 s. 29A(1), (2); 1981 s. 90.
18	1979 s. 62; 1981 s. 90(3)(a), (b).
19	1985 s.71(1)-(4), (6), (7).
20	1985 Sch. 21.
21	1979 s. 19(1), (2).
22	1979 s. 20.
23	1979 s. 21.
24	1979 s. 22.
25	1989 s. 127; 1990 Sch. 9 §2.
26	1979 s. 23.
27	1979 s. 24.
28	1979 s. 27.
29	1979 s. 25.
30(1)	1979 s. 26(1); 1989 s. 135(1).
(2)	1979 s. 26(1A); 1989 s. 135(1).
(3)-(7)	1979 s. 26(2)–(6).
(8)	1979 s. 26(7); 1989 s. 135(2).
(9)	1979 s. 26(8); 1989 s. 135(3).

TAXATION OF CHARGEABLE GAINS ACT—*continued.*

Section of 1992 Act	Derivation
31	1979 s. 26A; 1989 s. 136.
32	1979 s. 26B; 1989 s. 136.
33	1979 s. 26C; 1989 s. 136.
34	1979 s. 26D; 1989 s. 137.
35	1988 s. 96; Sch.8 §1(3); 1989 Sch. 15 §4(2); 1990 s. 70(7)(b), Sch. 12 §2(2); 1979 s. 28(3); 1991 s. 78(7).
36	1988 s. 97.
37(1)-(3)	1979 s. 31(1)-(3); CAA Sch. 1 §3.
(4)	1979 s. 31(4); ICTA Sch. 29 §17.
38	1979 s. 32.
39	1979 s. 33; ICTA Sch. 29 §19.
40	1970 s. 269; 1981 s. 38(3), (4).
41	1979 s. 34; 1988 Sch. 13 §16; CAA Sch. 1 §3.
42	1979 s. 35.
43	1979 s. 36.
44	1979 s. 37.
45	1979 s. 127.
46	1979 s. 38.
47	1979 s. 39.
48	1979 s. 40(2).
49	1979 s. 41.
50	1979 s. 42.
51	1979 s. 19(4), (5).
52	1979 s. 43.
53	1982 s. 86(2)-(4), (6); 1985 Sch. 19 §1.
54	1982 s. 87; 1985 Sch. 19 §2.
55(1)	1985 s. 68(4).
(2)	1985 s. 68(5); 1988 Sch. 8 §11.
(3)	1985 s. 68(5A); 1988 s. 118.
(4)	1985 s. 68(6).
(5)	1985 s. 68(7), (7A); 1988 s. 118; 1989 Sch. 15 §4; 1990 s. 70(7); 1991 s. 78(6), 99(1).
(6)	1985 s. 68(8).
56(1)	1982 Sch. 13 §1; 1985 Sch. 19 §5(1).
(2)	1982 Sch. 13 §2; 1985 Sch. 19 §5(2)(b).
57	1982 Sch. 13 §4.
58	1979 s. 44.
59	1979 s. 60.
60	1979 s. 46.
61	1979 s. 99; AJA 1982 s. 46(2)(f).
62	1979 s. 49; 1981 s. 90(3)(a).

TAXATION OF CHARGEABLE GAINS ACT—*continued.*

Section of 1992 Act	Derivation
63	1979 s. 50.
64	1979 s. 47.
65	1979 s. 48.
66	1979 s. 61.
67	1980 s. 79; 1979 s. 56A; 1982 s. 84; 1989 s. 124(3).
68	1979 s. 51.
69	1979 s. 52.
70	1979 s. 53; 1981 s. 86.
71	1979 s. 54; 1981 s. 87.
72	1979 s. 55(1),(3)-(6); 1982 s. 84.
73(1)	1979 s. 56(1); 1981 s. 87.
(2), (3)	1979 s. 56(1A), (1B); 1982 s. 84(2).
74	1979 s. 56A; 1982 s. 84; 1989 Sch. 14 §6(1).
75	1979 s. 57.
76	1979 s. 58.
77	1988 Sch. 10 §1-4.
78(1), (2)	1988 Sch. 10 §5(1), (2).
(3)	1988 Sch. 10 §5(3); 1991 s. 89(3).
79	1988 Sch. 10 §6-9.
80	1991 s. 83.
81	1991 s. 84.
82	1991 s. 85.
83	1991 s. 86.
84	1991 s. 87.
85(1)	1981 s. 88(1).
(2)-(9)	1991 s. 88(1)-(8).
86(1)-(3)	1991 Sch. 16 §1(1)-(3).
(4)	1991 Sch. 16 §2.
(5)	—
87(1), (2)	1981 s. 80(1), (2).
(3)	1980 s. 80(2A); 1991 s. 89(2).
(4)-(7)	1981 s. 80(3)-(6).
(8)	1981 s. 80(6A); 1991 Sch. 18 §1.
(9)	1981 s. 80(7).
(10)	1981 s. 80(1), (8); 1984 s. 70(3).
88	1981 s. 80A; 1991 Sch. 18 §2.
89	1981 s. 81; 1991 Sch. 18 §3.
90	1981 s. 82.
91	1991 Sch. 17 §4.
92(1)	1991 Sch. 17 §2(3).

TAXATION OF CHARGEABLE GAINS ACT—*continued.*

Section of 1992 Act	Derivation
(2)	1991 Sch. 17 §2(2), (4), (5).
(3)	1991 Sch. 17 §3(1), (2).
(4)-(6)	1991 Sch. 17 §3(3)-(5).
93(1)	1991 Sch. 17 §5(1)(a), (b), (d), 6(1)(a), (b), (d).
(2)	1991 Sch. 17 §5(1)(c), (2), (3).
(3)	1991 Sch. 17 §6(1)(c), (2), (3).
(4)	1991 Sch. 17 §7.
94	1991 Sch. 17 §8.
95	1991 Sch. 17 §9.
96	1981 s. 82A; 1991 Sch. 18 §4.
97(1)(a)	1981 s. 83(1), (11); 1991 Sch. 17 §1(c), 18 §6(2).
(b)	1981 s. 83(1A); 1991 Sch. 18 §6(3).
(2)-(6)	1981 s. 83(2)-(6); 1990 Sch. 14 §18; 1991 Sch. 18 §6(4), (5).
(7)	1981 s. 83(7); 1984 s. 71; 1991 Sch. 18 §6(5).
(8)-(10)	1981 s. 83(8)-(10); 1991 Sch. 18 §5.
98	1981 s. 84.
99(1)	1979 s. 93.
(2)	1979 s. 92(1)(a), (b); 1987 s. 40(3).
(3)	1979 s. 92(2), (3)(a); 1987 s. 40(4).
100(1)	1980 s. 81(1).
(2)	1979 s. 96.
(3)	1979 s. 92(1)(d).
101	1979 s. 98; 1980 s. 81.
102	1989 s. 140.
103	1990 s. 54.
104(1), (2)	1985 Sch. 19 §8, 9(1), 17(1).
(3)	1979 s. 66(3), (4); 1985 s. 68(9), (10), Sch. 19 §8(1)(c), 9(3).
(4)	1985 Sch. 19 §8(2).
(5)	1985 Sch. 19 §8(3).
(6)	1985 Sch. 19 §10.
105	1979 s. 66(1), (2); 1985 Sch. 19 §17(2).
106	1975(2) s. 58; 1979 Sch. 7.
107(1), (2)	1985 Sch. 19 §16(1), (2).
(3)-(6)	1985 Sch. 19 §18
(7)-(9)	1985 Sch. 19 §19.
108	1982 s. 88; 1985 Sch. 19 §3.
109(1)-(3)	1982 Sch. 13 §6(1), (2), 7(1), 8(1), (2)(a), (3), 9, 10.
(4), (5)	1985 Sch. 19 §6(3), (4).
(6)	1985 Sch. 19 §7(2), (3).
110(1)-(3)	1985 Sch. 19 §11.

TAXATION OF CHARGEABLE GAINS ACT—*continued.*

Section of 1992 Act	Derivation
(4)	1985 Sch. 19 §12.
(5)-(9)	1985 Sch. 19 §13.
(10), (11)	1985 Sch. 19 §14.
111	1988 s. 113.
112	1985 Sch. 19 §21(2), (3), 20.
113	1982 Sch. 13 §6, 1985 Sch. 19 §5(5).
114	1985 Sch. 19 §15.
115	1979 s. 67; 1986 s. 59.
116(1)	1984 s. 64(7)
(2)-(4)	1984 Sch. 13 §7.
(5)-(8)	1984 Sch. 13 §8.
(9)	1984 Sch. 13 §9.
(10), (11)	1984 Sch. 13 §10; 1985 s. 67(2)(c); 1989 s. 139; 1990 s. 70(6).
(12)-(14)	1984 Sch. 13 §11.
(15)	1984 Sch. 13 §12; 1990 s. 85.
117(1)	1984 s. 64(2)(b), (c), (2A); 1991 s. 98.
(2)	1984 s. 64(3).
(3)	1984 s. 64(3A)-(3D); 1989 s. 139; 1990 Sch. 10 §28.
(4)-(6)	1984 s. 64(3E)-(3G); 1991 Sch. 10 §1.
(7), (8)	1984 s. 64(4), (5); 1989 Sch. 14 §6(4).
(9)	1984 s. 64(5A)-(5D); 1989 s. 139; 1990 Sch. 10 §28.
(10)	1984 s. 64(6); 1989 s. 139.
(11)(a)	1984 s. 64(8).
(11)(b), (12)	1984 s. 64(9)-(11); 1991 Sch. 10 §1.
(13)	1991 Sch. 10 §1(5).
118	1979 s. 132A; ICTA Sch. 29 §23; 1989 s. 96(3).
119	1979 s. 33A; ICTA Sch. 29 §20.
120(1)	1988 s. 84.
(2)-(7)	1979 s. 32A; ICTA Sch. 29 §18.
121	1979 s. 71.
122	1979 s. 72
123	1979 s. 73.
124	1979 s. 74.
125	1979 s. 75; 1988 Sch. 8 §7.
126	1979 s. 77; 1982 Sch. 13 §5(3).
127	1979 s. 78.
128(1)	1979 s. 79(1).
(2)	1979 s. 79(1), first and second provisos; 1981 s. 91.
(3), (4)	1979 s. 79(2), (3).
129	1979 s. 80.

TAXATION OF CHARGEABLE GAINS ACT—*continued.*

Section of 1992 Act	Derivation
130	1979 s. 81.
131	1982 Sch. 13 §5(1), (2).
132	1979 s. 82; 1982 Sch. 13 §5(3).
133	1979 s. 83.
134(1)	1979 s. 84(1).
(2)	1979 s. 84(2), (3).
(3)	1979 s. 84(4); 1985 s. 67(2).
(4)-(6)	1979 s. 84(5)-(7).
135	1979 s. 85; 1982 Sch. 13 §5(3).
136	1979 s. 86.
137	1979 s. 87; 1987(2) Sch. 6 §5.
138	1979 s. 88.
139(1), (2)	1970 s. 267(1), (2); 238(4).
(3)	1970 s. 267(2A); 1990 s. 65(1).
(4)	1970 s. 267(3); 1980 s. 81(2).
(5)-(7)	1970 s. 267(3A)-(3C); 1977 s. 41.
(8)	1987(2) Sch. 6 §2.
(9)	1970 s. 267(4).
140	1970 s. 268A; 1977 s. 42.
141	1979 s. 89; 1981 s. 91(2).
142	1979 s. 90; 1981 s. 90(3).
143(1), (2)	1985 s. 72(1), (2); 1987(2) s. 81(1), (2).
(3), (4)	1985 s. 72(2A), (2B); 1987(2) s. 81(3).
(5), (6)	1985 s. 72(3), (4).
144(1)-(4)	1979 s. 137(1)-(4); 1987(2) s. 81.
(5)-(9)	1979 s. 137(6)-(10); 1987(2) s. 81.
145	1982 Sch. 13 §7.
146	1979 s. 138; 1980 s. 84(5), (6); 1987(2) s. 81.
147	1979 s. 139.
148	1991 s. 102.
149	1991 Sch. 10 §4.
150	1979 s. 149C; 1985 Sch. 19 §16(3); ICTA Sch. 29 §26; 1990 Sch. 14 §17; 1991 s. 99(2).
151(1), (2)	1979 s. 149D(1), (2); ICTA Sch. 29 §26.
(3)	1979 s. 149D(2A); 1988 s. 116.
152(1), (2)	1979 s. 115(1), (2).
(3), (4)	1979 s. 115(3).
(5)-(8)	1979 s. 115(4)-(7).
(9)	1979 s. 115(7A); 1988 Sch. 8 §9.
(10), (11)	1979 s. 115(8), (9).
153	1979 s. 116.

TAXATION OF CHARGEABLE GAINS ACT—*continued.*

Section of 1992 Act	Derivation
154(1), (2)	1979 s. 117(1), (2); 1990 s. 40(2).
(3), (4)	1979 s. 117(2A), (3); 1990 s. 40(3), (4).
(5)-(7)	1979 s. 117(4)-(6).
155	1979 s. 118; 1988 s. 112.
156	1979 s. 119.
157	1979 s. 120; 1985 s. 70(9).
158	1979 s. 121.
159	1989 s. 129.
160	1989 s. 133.
161	1979 s. 122.
162	1979 s. 123.
163	1985 s. 69; 1991 s.100.
164	1985 s. 70(1)-(8); 1991 s. 100.
165(1), (2)	1979 s. 126(1), (1A); 1989 Sch. 14 §1.
(3)	1979 s. 126(2); 1985 s. 70(9); 1989 Sch. 14 §1(3).
(4)-(6)	1979 s. 126(3)-(5).
(7)-(9)	1979 s. 126(6)-(8); 1981 s. 90(3)(a); 1985 s. 70(9).
(10), (11)	1979 s. 126(9), (10); 1989 Sch. 14 §1.
166	1979 s. 126A; 1989 Sch. 14 §2.
167	1979 s. 126B; 1989 Sch. 14 §2.
168	1981 s. 79; 1989 Sch. 14 §6; 1991 s. 92(2).
169	1986 s. 58; 1989 Sch. 14 §6.
170(1)	1970 s. 238(4); 1988 Sch. 14 Part V Note 3
(2)	1970 s. 272(1); 1989 s. 138(1); 1990 s. 70(2).
(3)-(8)	1970 s. 272(1A)-(1F); 1989 s. 138(2); 1990 s. 86.
(9)	1970 s. 272(2); 1987(2) s. 79; CCCPA Sch. 2.
(10), (11)	1970 s. 272(3), (4); 1989 s. 138(3), (4).
(12), (13)	1970 s. 272(5).
(14)	1970 s. 272(6); LRTA 1984 Sch. 6 §7.
171(1)	1970 s. 273(1).
(2)	1970 s. 273(2); 1980 s. 81(4); 1987(2) s. 64(3); 1990 s. 65(2).
(3)	1970 s. 273(2A); 1988 s. 115.
(4)	1970 s. 273(3).
172	1970 s. 273A; 1990 s. 70.
173	1970 s. 274.
174(1)-(3)	1970 s. 275(1), (1A), (1B); 1990 s. 70(3).
(4)	1970 s. 275(2).
(5)	1970 s. 275(3); 1980 s. 81(5).
175(1)	1970 s. 276(1); 1987(2) s. 64(4).
(2)	1970 s. 276(1A); 1987(2) s. 64(4); 1990 s. 65(3).

TAXATION OF CHARGEABLE GAINS ACT—*continued.*

Section of 1992 Act	Derivation
(3)	1970 s. 276(2).
(4)	1990 s. 65(6).
176	1970 s. 280, CCCPA Sch. 2; 1988 Sch. 8 §6.
177	1970 s. 281; 1990 s. 70(4).
178(1)-(3)	1970 s. 278(1)-(3).
(4)-(6)	1970 s. 278(3B)-(3D); 1989 s. 138(5).
(7)	1970 s. 278(3F); 1989 s. 138(5).
(8)-(10)	1970 s. 278(4)-(6).
179(1)-(3)	1970 s. 278(1)-(3); 1987(2) Sch. 6 §4(2).
(4)	1970 s. 278(3A); 1987(2) Sch. 6 §4(2).
(5)-(9)	1970 s. 278(3B)-(3F); 1989 s. 138(5).
(10)	1970 s. 278(4).
(11)	1970 s. 278(5); 1987(2) Sch. 6 §4(3).
(12)	1970 s. 278(5A); 1987(2) Sch. 6 §4(4).
(13)	1970 s. 278(6).
180(1), (2)	1970 s. 278(8); 1987(2) s. 95(2); 1989 s. 138(7).
(3)-(7)	1989 s. 138(8)-(12).
181	1970 s. 278A; 1970(F) s. 27.
182	1988 Sch. 11 §1, 2.
183	1988 Sch. 11 §3.
184	1988 Sch. 11 §4, 5, 6; 1990 s. 70(8).
185	1988 s. 105(1)-(5).
186	1988 s. 106.
187	1988 s. 107.
188	1989 s. 132.
189	ICTA s. 346.
190	ICTA s. 347.
191	1989 s. 134.
192	1980 s. 117, Sch. 18 §9, 10, 15, 23.
193	1987(2) s. 80.
194	1988 s. 62.
195	1988 s. 63.
196	1988 s. 64.
197	1984 s. 79.
198	1984 s. 80.
199	1989 s. 131.
200	1990 s. 64.
201(1), (2)	ICTA s. 122(1).
(3)	ICTA s. 122(3).
(4)	ICTA s. 122(8).

TAXATION OF CHARGEABLE GAINS ACT—*continued.*

Section of 1992 Act	Derivation
202(1), (2)	1970(F) s. 29(5), Sch. 6 §3.
(3), (4)	1970(F) Sch. 6 §4.
(5), (6)	1970(F) Sch. 6 §5.
(7), (8)	1970(F) Sch. 6 §6.
(9)-(11)	1970(F) Sch. 6 §7.
203	1970(F) s. 29(6), (7), (9), Sch. 6 §8, 9.
204	1979 s. 140, 149A(2).
205	1979 s. 141.
206	1979 s. 142; 1988 s. 101.
207(1)-(3)	1979 s. 142A(1)-(3); ICTA Sch. 29 §24.
(4), (5)	1979 s. 142A(4A), (4B); 1989 s. 91; S.I. 1989/1299.
(6)	1979 s. 142A(4).
208	1985 Sch. 19 §22, 23.
209	1979 s. 142A(5-7); 1989 s. 92.
210	1979 s. 143.
211	1970 s. 267A; 1990 Sch. 9 §1.
212	1990 s. 46; 1991 Sch. 7 §14.
213	1990 s. 47.
214	1990 Sch. 8; 1991 Sch. 7 §15.
215	1979 s. 149A(1); ICTA Sch. 29 §26.
216	1988 Sch. 12 §1, 4.
217	1988 Sch. 12 §5.
218	1970 s. 342; HCPA Sch. 2 §18; 1991 s. 95, 96.
219	1970 s. 342A; HA 1974 s. 11; HCPA Sch. 2 §18; 1991 s. 95, 96.
220	1970 s. 342B; 1984 s. 56(3).
221	1979 s. 123A; ICTA Sch. 29 §22.
222	1979 s. 101; ICTA Sch. 29 §21; 1991 s. 93.
223(1)-(3)	1979 s. 102(1)-(3); 1991 s. 94.
(4)	1980 s. 80(1); 1991 s. 94.
(5), (6)	1979 s. 102(5), (6); 1991 s. 94.
(7)	1979 s. 102(3), (4); 1988 Sch. 8 §8.
224	1979 s. 103.
225	1979 s. 104.
226(1), (2)	1979 s. 105(1), (2); 1988 s. 111(1), (2).
(3)	1988 s. 111(3).
(4)-(7)	1979 s. 105(3)-(6).
227	1990 s. 31.
228	1990 s. 32.
229	1990 s. 33.
230	1990 s. 34.

TAXATION OF CHARGEABLE GAINS ACT—*continued.*

Section of 1992 Act	Derivation
231	1990 s. 35.
232	1990 s. 36.
233	1990 s. 37.
234	1990 s. 38.
235	1990 s. 39.
236	1990 s. 40(5)-(8).
237	1979 s. 144.
238	1979 s. 144A; ICTA Sch. 29 §25.
239	1979 s. 149; 1981 s. 90(3); ITA Sch. 8 §11; CCCPA Sch. 2.
240	1979 s. 106, 129.
241(1)	1984 s. 50(1).
(2)	1984 s. 50(2)-(9).
(3)	1984 Sch. 11 §1; 1985 s. 70(10).
(4)-(8)	1984 Sch. 11 §4-7.
242	1979 s. 107; 1984 s. 63; 1986 s. 60.
243	1979 s. 108.
244	1979 s. 109.
245	1979 s. 110.
246	1979 s. 111.
247	1979 s. 111A; 1982 s. 83.
248	1979 s. 111B; 1982 s. 83.
249	1979 s. 112.
250	1979 s. 113; 1988 Sch. 6 §6(5).
251	1979 s. 134.
252	1979 s. 135.
253(1)-(5)	1979 s. 136(1)-(5).
(6)-(8)	1979 s. 136(5A)-(5C); 1990 s. 83.
(9)	1979 s. 136(6); 1990 s. 83.
(10)-(12)	1979 s. 136(7)-(9).
(13)	1979 s. 136(9A); 1990 s. 83.
(14), (15)	1979 s. 136(10), (11); 1989 Sch. 12 §6.
254	1979 s. 136A; 1990 s. 84.
255	1979 s. 136B; 1990 s. 84.
256	1979 s. 145.
257	1979 s. 146; 1981 s. 90; ITA Sch. 8 §9.
258	1979 s. 147; ITA Sch. 8 §10; 1985 s. 95(1)(b).
259	1979 s. 146A; 1989 s. 125.
260	1979 s. 147A; 1989 Sch. 14 §4.
261	1979 s. 147B; 1989 Sch. 14 §4.
262	1979 s. 128; 1989 s. 123.

TAXATION OF CHARGEABLE GAINS ACT—*continued.*

Section of 1992 Act	Derivation
263	1979 s. 130.
264	1983(2) s. 7; PCA Sch. 3 §6.
265	1984 s. 126; 1985 s. 96.
266	1976 s. 131.
267	1991 s. 78(1)-(3), (8).
268	1979 s. 131.
269	1979 s. 133.
270	1981 s. 135.
271	1979 s. 149B; ICTA Sch. 29 §26; 1988 Sch. 12 §7(b), Sch. 13 §17; 1990 s. 28(3), 81, Sch. 18 §3; 1991 s. 57(4).
272	1979 s. 150(1)-(4), (6).
273	1979 s. 152.
274	1979 s. 153.
275	1979 s. 18(4); 1984 s. 69; CDPA 1988 Sch. 7 §26.
276(1)	1973 s. 38(1); ICTA s. 830(1).
(2), (3)	1973 s. 38(2), (3).
(4)-(6)	1973 s. 38(3A)-(3C); 1984 s. 81(2); 1989 s. 130(1).
(7)	1973 s. 38(4); ICTA Sch. 29 §12.
(8)	1973 s. 38(5); 1984 s. 81.
277	1979 s. 10.
278	1979 s. 11.
279(1)-(6)	1979 s. 13; 1991 s. 97.
(7)	1988 s. 104.
(8)	1991 s. 97.
280	1979 s. 40(1).
281	1979 s. 7A; 1989 Sch. 14 §5.
282	1979 s. 59.
283(1)	1975(2) s. 47(1); 1989 s. 179(1).
(2)	1975(2) s. 47(4).
(3)	1975(2) s. 47(8).
(4), (5)	1975(2) s. 47(11),(12).
284	1979 s. 154.
285	1987(2) s. 73; ICTA s. 841(3).
286	1979 s. 63 ICTA Sch. 29 §15.
287	1979 s. 5(1C), 92(3), 102(5), (7), 137(10), 142A(5), 149D(3), Sch. 2 §1; 1984 s. 64(3F), (12), 126(1), (4); 1985 s. 96(1), Sch. 19 §21(4); 1987(2) s. 73, 81, 95(2), Sch. 6 §2, 4, 5; ICTA s. 828, Sch. 29 §24, 26; 1989 s. 92(6); 1990 s. 46(9); 1991 s. 94, Sch. 10 §1, Sch. 17 §4(8).
288	1979 s. 155; 1979 s. 64; 1984 s. 64; 1985 s. 72(6); ICTA Sch. 29 §27; 1988 Sch. 13 §18; 1989 Sch. 14 §6; 1990 s. 127(2).
289	—

TAXATION OF CHARGEABLE GAINS ACT—*continued.*

Section of 1992 Act	Derivation
290	—
291	—
Sch. 1	
§1(1)	1979 Sch. 1 §5(1); 1980 s. 77(4)(c); 1981 s. 89(2); DLA 1991.
(2)	1979 Sch. 1 §5(1A); 1981 s. 89(3).
(3)	1979 Sch. 1 §5(1B); 1981 s. 89(3); 1982 s. 80(3).
(4)	1979 Sch. 1 §5(1C); 1981 s. 89(3).
(5)	1979 Sch. 1 §5(1D); 1981 s. 89(3); 1982 s. 80(3).
(6)	1979 Sch. 1 §5(2); Mental Health Act 1983 Sch. 4 §49; 1981 s. 89(4); DLA 1991; SSCP.
(7)	1979 Sch. 1 §5(3); 1981 s. 89(5).
2(1)	1979 Sch. 1 §6(1); 1980 s. 78(2).
(2)	1979 Sch. 1 §6(2); 1980 s. 78(3); 1982 s. 80(3)(b), (d).
(3)	1979 Sch. 1 §6(3); 1980 s. 78(3); 1982 s. 80(3)(e).
(4)	1979 Sch. 1 §6(4); 1980 s. 78(3); 1982 s. 80(3)(c), (d).
(5)	1979 Sch. 1 §6(5); 1980 s. 78(3).
(6)	1979 Sch. 1 §6(6); 1980 s. 78(3); 1982 s. 80(3)(d).
(7)-(9)	1979 Sch. 1 §6(7)-(9); 1980 s. 78(3).
Sch. 2	
§1-3	1979 Sch. 5 §1-3; 1982 Sch. 13 §11.
4(1)	—
(2)	1979 Sch. 5 §4(1).
(3)-(7)	1979 s. 65.
(8)-(13).	1979 Sch. 5 §4(2)-(7).
5-8	1979 Sch. 5 §5-8.
9-15	1979 Sch. 5 §9, 10.
16	1979 Sch. 5 §11.
17	1979 Sch. 5 §12.
18	1979 Sch. 5 §13; 1982 Sch. 13 §11.
19-23	1979 Sch. 5 §14-18.
Sch. 3	
§1	1988 Sch. 8§1; 1989 Sch. 15§4(2); 1990 s. 70(7)(b), Sch. 12§2(2); 1991 s. 78(7).
2	1988 Sch. 8§2.
3	1988 Sch. 8§3.
4	1988 Sch. 8§4; 1989 Sch. 15§3.
5	1988 Sch. 8§5.
6	1988 Sch. 8§10.
7	1988 Sch. 8§12; 1990 s. 63.
8	1988 Sch. 8§13; 1989 Sch. 15§5.
9	1988 Sch. 8§14.

TAXATION OF CHARGEABLE GAINS ACT—*continued.*

Section of 1992 Act	Derivation
Sch. 4	
§1	1988 Sch. 9§1; 1991 s. 101(2).
2	1988 Sch. 9§2; 1991 s. 101(3), (4).
3	1988 Sch. 9§2A; 1991 s. 101(5).
4(1)-(4)	1988 Sch. 9§3; 1989 Sch. 15§2; 1991 s. 101(6)-(8)
(5)	1989 Sch. 15§1.
5-8	1988 Sch. 9§4-7.
9	1988 Sch. 9§8; 1991 s. 101(9).
Sch. 5	1991 Sch. 16§3-16.
Sch. 6	
§1-12	1985 Sch. 20§1-12; 1991 s. 100.
13	1985 Sch. 20§13; 1988 s. 110; 1991 s. 100.
14	1985 Sch. 20§14.
15	1985 Sch. 20§15; 1988 s. 110.
16	1985 Sch. 20§16; 1988 s. 110.
Sch. 7	
§1	1979 Sch. 4§1; ITA 1984 Sch. 8§12; 1989 Sch. 14§3(2).
2	1979 Sch. 4§2; 1989 Sch. 14§3(3).
3	1979 Sch. 4§3; ITA 1984 Sch. 8§12; 1989 Sch. 14§3(4).
4	1979 Sch. 4§4; 1989 Sch. 14§3(5).
5, 6	1979 Sch. 4§5, 6; 1989 Sch. 14§3(6).
7	1979 Sch. 4§7; 1989 Sch. 14§3(7).
8	1979 Sch. 4§8; 1985 s. 70(9).
Sch. 8	1979 Sch. 3.
Sch. 9	
§1-3	1979 Sch. 2§1-3.
Part II	1979 Sch. 2 Part II together with the securities specified in the Capital Gains Tax (Gilt-edged Securities) Orders 1979-1991 made under paragraph 1 of Schedule 2 to the 1979 Act; Gas Act 1986 (c. 44) s. 50(3).

TAXATION OF CHARGEABLE GAINS ACT 1992
TABLE OF DESTINATIONS

For a key to the abbreviations used in this Table, see the Table of Derivations

Section of Act		Section of 1992 Act	Remarks
	INCOME AND CORPORATION TAXES ACT 1970 c.10		
238(4)		170(1)	
267(1),(2)		139(1),(2)	
(2A)		139(3)	Added 1990 s.65.
(3)		139(4)	Am. 1980 s.81; rep. in part 1980 Sch. 20 Pt. X.
(3A)–(3C)		139(5)–(7)	Added 1977 s.41; 1987(2) Sch. 6 §2.
(4)		139(9), 288(1)	
267A		211	Added 1990 Sch. 9.
268A		140	Added 1977 s.42.
269		40	Rep. in part 1971 Sch. 14 Pt. III; am. 1981 s.38.
270(4)–(6)		—	Inserted in ICTA s S.126A: see Sch. 10 §14(6).
272(1)		170(2)	Am. 1989 s.138; 1990 s.70(2)(a); rep. in part 1990 Sch. 19 Pt. IV.
(1A)–(1F)		170(3)–(8)	Added 1989 s.138; am. 1990 s.86.
(2)		170(9)	Am. CCCPA Sch. 2; 1987(2) s.79; partly spent.
(3),(4)		170(10),(11)	Am. 1989 s.138.
(5)		170(12),(13)	
(6)		170(14)	Rep. in part & am. LRTA Sch. 6 §7 and Sch. 7.
273(1),(2)		171(1),(2)	Am. 1980 s.81(4) 1987(2) s.64(3); 1990 s.65.
(2A)		171(3)	Added 1988 s.115.
(3)		171(4)	
273A		172	Added 1990 s.70.
274		173	
275(1),(1A), (1B)		174(1)–(3)	Subst. 1990 s.70.
(2)		174(4)	
(3)		174(5)	Added 1980 s.81(5).
276(1)		175(1)	Am. 1987(2) s.64(4).
(1A)		175(2)	Added 1987(2) s.64(4); am. 1990 s.65.
(2)		175(3)	
277		—	Rep. ICTA Sch. 31.
278(1)–(3)		178(1)–(3), 179(1)–(3)	

TAXATION OF CHARGEABLE GAINS ACT 1992—*continued.*

Section of Act		Section of 1992 Act	Remarks
	INCOME AND CORPORATION TAXES ACT 1970 c.10—*continued.*		
(3A)		179(4)	Added 1987(2) Sch. 6 §4.
(3B)–(3D)		178(4)–(6), 179(5)–(7)	Added 1989 s.138(5).
(3E)		179(8)	Added 1989 s.138(5).
(3F)		178(7), 179(9)	Added 1989 s.138(5)
(4)		178(8), 179(10)	
(5)		178(9), 179(11)	
(5A)		179(12)	Added 1987(2) Sch. 6 §4.
(6)		178(10), 179(13)	Rep. in part 1987(2) Sch. 6 §4.
(7)		—	Spent.
(8)		180(1)	
278A		181	Added 1970(F) s.27.
279		—	Spent.
280(4)		176	Am. CCCPA Sch. 2; 1988 Sch. 8 §6; rep. in part 1988 Sch. 14 Pt. VII; 1974 Sch. 14 Pt. VI.
281		177	Am. 1990 s.70.
342		218	Am. HCPA Sch. 2; 1991 s.95, 96; rep. in part 1991 Sch. 19 Pt. VI.
342A		219	Added HA 1974 s.11; am. HCPA Sch. 2; 1991 s.95, 96.
342B		220	Added 1984 s.56.
	FINANCE ACT 1970 c.24		
27		181	
28		Sch.10	See ICTA s.126A.
29(5)		202(1),(2)	
(6)–(9)		203(1)	
Sch.3 §1,8		Sch. 11 §26, 27	
Sch.6 §3–9		202, 203	Rep. in part 1971 Sch. 14 Pt. III.
	FINANCE ACT 1973 c.51		
38(1)–(3)		276(1)–(3)	Rep. in part ICTA Sch. 31
(3A),(3B),(3C)		276(4)–(6)	Added 1984 s.81; am. 1989 s.130 rep. in part 1989 Sch. 17 Pt. VII.
(4)		276(7)	Subst. ICTA Sch. 29 §12. Partly spent.
(5)		276(8)	Am. 1984 s.81

TAXATION OF CHARGEABLE GAINS ACT 1992—*continued.*

Section of Act		Section of 1992 Act	Remarks
FINANCE (No. 2) ACT 1975 c.45			
47(1), (4), (8), (11), (12)		283	Rep. in part 1988 Sch. 14 Pt. IV; am. 1989 s.179
47(2),(3),(5)–(7), (9), (10)		—	Rep. 1988 Sch. 14 Pt. IV; 1989 Sch. 17 Pt. X.
58		106	Rep. in part 1985 Sch. 27 Pt. VII; 1990 Sch. 19 Pt. IV.
FINANCE ACT 1976 c. 40			
54		—	Spent.
131		266	
FINANCE ACT 1977 c. 36			
41		139(5)–(7)	
42		140	
CAPITAL GAINS TAX ACT 1979 c.14			
1		1	
2		2(1)	
3		—	Rep. 1988 Sch. 14, Pt. VII.
4(1)		2(2)	
(2)		—	Rep. 1988 Sch. 14, Pt. VIII.
5(1)		3(1)	Subst. 1980 s. 77(2); am. 1982 s. 80(1).
(1A), (1B), (1C)		3(2)–(4), 287	added 1982 s. 80(2); £5,500 fixed for 1991-92 by 1991/736.
(2), (3)			Replaced by subsection (1) in 1980.
(4), (5)		3(5), (6)	Am. 1980 s. 77(3); 1982 s. 80(1); rep. in part 1988 Sch. 14, Pt. VIII.
(6)		3(8)	
6		—	Rep. 1984 Sch. 23, Pt. VIII.
7		7	Am. 1980 s. 61(2).
7A		281	Added 1989 Sch. 14 §5.
8, 9		—	Rep. 1984 Sch. 23, Pt. VIII.
10		277	
11		278	
12(1)		10(1)	
(1A)		10(2)	Added 1989 s. 128(2).
(2)		10(4)	
(2A)		10(5)	Added 1989 s. 126(2).
(3)		10(6)	
13		279(1)–(6)	Am. 1991 s. 97.
14		12	Am. ICTA Sch. 29 §15.
15(1)–(9)		13(1)–(9)	
(10)		13(11)	

TAXATION OF CHARGEABLE GAINS ACT 1992—*continued.*

Section of Act		Section of 1992 Act	Remarks
	CAPITAL GAINS TAX ACT 1979 c.14—*continued.*		
16		14	
17		—	Rep. 1981 Sch. 19, Pt. VIII.
18(1)–(3)		9	
(4)		275	Am. 1984 s. 69; CDPA 1988 Sch. 7 §26.
(5)–(8)		11	Added ICTA Sch. 29 §16.
19(1), (2)		21	
(3)		—	Rep. 1981 Sch. 19, Pt. VIII.
(4)–(5)		51	
20		22	
21(1)–(5)		23(1)–(5)	
(6)		35(9)	
(7)		23(6)	
22		24	
23		26	
24		27	
25		29	
26		30	Am. 1989 s. 135.
26A		31	Added 1989 s. 136.
26B		32	Added 1989 s. 136.
26C		33	Added 1989 s. 136.
26D		34	Added 1989 s. 137.
27		28	
28(1), (2)		15	Am. 1982 s. 86(4).
(3)		35(9)	
29(1)–(4)		16	
(5)		2(3)	
29A(1), (2)		17	Added 1981 s. 90; rep. in part 1984 Sch. 23, Pt. VII.
(3)–(5)		—	Spent.
30		15(1)	
31		37	Am. ICTA Sch. 29 §17; CAA Sch. 1 §3.
32		38	Rep. in part 1984 Sch. 23 Pt. VIII.
32A		120(2)–(7)	Added ICTA Sch. 29 §18.
33		39	Am. ICTA Sch. 29 §19.
33A		119	Added ICTA Sch. 29 §20.
34		41	Am. and rep. in part CAA Sch. 1, 2; 1988 Sch. 13 §16.
35		42	
36		43	

TAXATION OF CHARGEABLE GAINS ACT 1992—*continued.*

Section of Act		Section of 1992 Act	Remarks
	CAPITAL GAINS TAX ACT 1979 c.14—*continued.*		
37		44	
38		46	
39		47	
40(1)		280	
40(2)		48	
41		49	
42		50	
43		52	
44		58	
45		—	Rep. 1988 Sch. 14, Pt. VIII.
46		60	
47		64	
48		65	
49		62	Am. 1981 s. 90.
50		63	
51		68	
52		69	
53		70	Am. 1981 s. 86.
54		71	Am. 1981 s. 87.
55(1)		72(1)	Am. 1982 s. 84.
(2)		—	Rep. 1982 Sch. 22, Pt. VI.
(3)–(6)		72(2)–(5)	
56(1)		73(1)	Am. 1981 s. 87.
(1A), (1B)		73(2), (3)	Added 1982 s. 84.
(2)		—	Rep. 1982 Sch. 22, Pt. VI.
56A		74	Added 1982 s. 84; am. 1989 Sch. 14 §6.
57		75	
58		76	
59		282	
60		59	
61		66	
62		18	Am. 1981 s. 90.
63		286	ICTA Sch. 29 §15.
64		288(1), (5), (8)	
65		Sch. 2§4	Partly spent.
66(1), (2)		105	Am. 1985 Sch. 19 §17(2).
(3), (4)		104(3)	Rep. in part 1985 Sch. 27 Pt. VII.
67		115	Subst. 1986 s. 59
68, 69, 70		—	Rep. 1985 Sch. 27, Pt. VII.

TAXATION OF CHARGEABLE GAINS ACT 1992—*continued.*

Section of Act		Section of 1992 Act	Remarks
	CAPITAL GAINS TAX ACT 1979 c.14—*continued.*		
71		121	
72		122	
73		123	Subsection (2) spent.
74		124	
75		125	Am. 1988 Sch. 8 §7.
76		—	Spent.
77		126	
78		127	
79(1)		128(1)	
1st Proviso		128(2)	
2nd Proviso		128(2)	Added 1981 s. 91.
(2), (3)		128(3), (4)	
80		129	
81		130	
82		132	
83		133	
84(1)		134(1)	
(2)		134(2)	
(3)		134(2)	Rep. in part 1985 Sch. 27, Pt. VII.
(4)		134(3)	Am. 1985 s. 67(2).
(5)-(7)		134(4)–(6)	
(8)		—	Spent.
85		135	
86		136	
87		137	Am. 1987(2) Sch. 6§5.
88		138	
89		141	Am. 1981 s. 91; rep. in part 1989 Sch, 17 Pt. V.
90		142	
91		—	Unnecessary.
92(1)		99(2), 100(3), 288(1), 8)	Am. 1987 s. 40.
(2), (3)		99(3), 287	Am. 1987 s. 40.
93		99(1)	
94, 95		—	Rep. 1980 Sch. 20 Pt. X.
96		100(2)	
97		—	Rep. 1980 Sch. 20 Pt. X.
98		101	Am. 1981 s. 81(3).
99		61	Am. AJA 1982 s. 46(2)(f).
100		—	Rep. 1980 Sch. 20, Pt. X.

TAXATION OF CHARGEABLE GAINS ACT 1992—*continued.*

Section of Act		Section of 1992 Act	Remarks

CAPITAL GAINS TAX ACT 1979 c.14—*continued.*

Section of Act		Section of 1992 Act	Remarks
101		222	Am. ICTA Sch. 29, §21; 1991 s. 93; rep. in part 1988 Sch. 14, Pt. VII.
102(1), (2)		223(1), (2)	Am. 1980 s. 80; 1991 s. 94.
(3)		223(3), (7)	
(4)		223(7)	Am. 1988 Sch. 8, §8.
(5), (6), (7)		223(5), (6), 287	Added 1991 s. 94.
103		224	
104		225	
105		226	Am. 1988 s. 111.
106		240	
107		242	Am. 1984 s. 63; 1986 s. 60; ICTA Sch. 29, §15.
108		243	
109		244	
110		245	
111		246	
111A		247	Added 1982 s. 83.
111B		248	Added 1982 s. 83.
112		249	
113		250	Am. 1988 Sch. §6.
114		—	Rep. 1985 Sch. 27, Pt. X.
115(1), (2)		152(1), (2)	
(3)		152(3), (4)	
(4)–(7)		152(5)–(8)	
(7A)		152(9)	Added 1988 Sch. 8, §9.
(8), (9)		152(10), (11)	
116		153	
117(1), (2)		154(1), (2)	Am. 1990 s. 40(2).
(2A)		154(3)	Added 1990 s. 40(3).
(3)–(6)		154(4)–(7)	Am. 1990 s. 40(4).
118		155	Am. 1988 s. 112.
119		156	
120		157	Am. 1985 s. 70(9).
121		158	
122		161	
123		162	
123A		221	Added ICTA Sch. 29, §22.
124, 125		—	Rep. 1985 Sch. 27, Pt. VII.
126(1), (1A)		165(1), (2)	Subst. 1989 Sch. 14, §1.

TAXATION OF CHARGEABLE GAINS ACT 1992—*continued.*

Section of Act		Section of 1992 Act	Remarks
CAPITAL GAINS TAX ACT 1979 c.14—*continued.*			
(2)–(8)		165(3)–(9)	Am. 1981 s. 90; 1985 s. 70(9); 1989 Sch. 14, §1; rep. in part 1989, Sch. 17 Pt. VII.
(9)–(10)		165(10), (11)	Added 1989 Sch. 14, §1.
126A		166	Added 1989 Sch. 14. §2.
126B		167	Added 1989 Sch. 14. §2.
126C		—	Rep. 1991 Sch. 19, Pt. VI.
127		45	
128		262	Am. 1989 s. 123.
129		240	
130		263	
131		268	
132		—	Unnecessary.
132A		118	Added ICTA Sch. 29 §23; am. 1989 s. 96(3).
133		269	
134		251	
135		252	
136(1)–(5)		253(1)–(5)	
(5A)–(5C)		253(6)–(8)	Added 1990 s. 83.
(6)–(9)		253(9)–(12)	Am. 1990 s.83.
(9A)		253(13)	Added 1990 s. 83.
(10),(11)		253(14), (15)	Am. 1989 Sch. 12, §6.
136A		254	Added 1990 s. 84.
136B		255	Added 1990 s. 84.
137(1)–(4)		144(1)–(4)	Am. 1987(2) s. 81.
(5)		—	Spent.
(6)–(8)		144(5)–(7)	
(9), (10)		144(8), (9), 287	Subst. 1987(2) s. 81.
138		146	Am. 1980 s. 84; 1987(2) s. 81.
139		147	
140		204(1), (2), (4)	
141		205	
142		206	Am. 1988 s. 101.
142A(1)–(3)		207(1)–(3)	Section 142A added ICTA Sch. 29 §24.
(4)		207(6)	
(4A), (4B)		207(4), (5)	Added 1989 s. 91.

TAXATION OF CHARGEABLE GAINS ACT 1992—*continued.*

Section of Act		Section of 1992 Act	Remarks
	CAPITAL GAINS TAX ACT 1979 c.14—*continued.*		
(5)		209(2), 287	Rep. in part 1989 Sch. 17, Pt. VII.
(6), (7)		209(6)	Added 1989 s. 92.
143		210	
144		237	
144A		238	Added ICTA Sch. 29 §25.
145		256	
146		257	Am. 1981 s. 90; ITA Sch. 8 §9; rep. in part 1982 Sch. 22, Pt. VI.
146A		259	Added 1989 s. 125.
147		258	Am. 1985 s. 95; ITA Sch. 8 §10.
147A		260	Added 1989 Sch. 14 §4.
147B		261	Added 1989 Sch. 14 §4.
148		—	Rep. 1984 Sch. 23, Pt. VIII.
149		239	Am. 1981 s. 90(3); ITA Sch. 8 §11; CCCPA Sch. 2.
149A		215, 204(3), 288(1)	Added ICTA Sch. 29 §26.
149B		271	Added ICTA Sch. 29 §26; am. 1988 Sch. 13 §17; 1990 s. 28(3), 81, Sch. 18 §3; 1991 S. 57(4).
149C		150	Added ICTA Sch. 29 §26; am 1990 Sch. 14 §17.
149D		151, 287	Added ICTA Sch. 29 §26; am. 1988 s. 116.
150		272	Rep. in part 1987 Sch. 16 Pt. XI.
151		—	Rep. 1985 Sch. 27 Pt. VII.
152		273	
153		274	
154		284	
155		288	Am. 1990 s. 127(2); 1989 Sch. 14 §6; ICTA Sch. 29 §27; 1985 s. 72(6); 1988 Sch. 13 §18.
156–160		—	Commencement, savings etc: for corresponding provisions see sections 289 to 291 and Part IV of Schedule 11.
Sch. 1			
§1		—	Unnecessary.
2, 3		—	Rep. 1988 Sch. 14 Pt. VIII.
4		3(7)	Am. 1980 s. 77(4)(c).

TAXATION OF CHARGEABLE GAINS ACT 1992—*continued.*

Section of Act		Section of 1992 Act	Remarks
	CAPITAL GAINS TAX ACT 1979 c.14—*continued.*		
5, 6		Sch. 1	Am. 1980 s. 77(4)(c); 1981 s.89; 1982 s. 80; Mental Health Act 1983 Sch. 4 §49; 1980 s. 78; SSCP Sch. 2.
Sch. 2		Sch. 9, 287	Rep. in part Gas Act 1986 Sch. 9 Pt. II; 1989 Sch. 17 Pt. XIV; S.I. 1989/1788; Electricity Act 1989 Sch. 18.
Sch. 3		Sch. 8	
Sch. 4		Sch, 7	Am. ITA Sch, 8 §12; 1989 Sch. 14 §3; rep. in part 1981 Sch. 19 Pt. VIII; 1982 Sch. 22 Pt. VI; 1989 Sch. 17 Pt. VII.
Sch. 5		Sch. 2	
Sch. 6		Sch. 11	
§1		§1	
2		§7, 8	
3		§6	
4		§1	
5, 6		§3	
7		§4	
8		§5	
9		§9	
10		§26	
11		§10(1)	
12, 13		§11,12	
14–16		—	Spent.
17–20		§13–16	
21		§17	
22		—	Unnecessary.
23		—	Spent.
24–26		§20–22	
27		—	Spent.
28, 29		§23, 25	
	FINANCE ACT 1980 c. 48		
61(2)		7	
77,78			See destinations of enactments amended.
79(5), (6)		67(2), (3)	Rep. 1989 Sch. 17, Pt. VII.
80(1)		223(4)	Am. 1991 s. 94.
(2)		—	Rep. 1991 Sch. 19, Pt. VI.
(3)		—	Spent.
81(1)		100(1)	

TAXATION OF CHARGEABLE GAINS ACT 1992—*continued.*

Section of Act		Section of 1992 Act	Remarks
FINANCE ACT 1980 c. 48—*continued.*			
(2)–(6)			See destinations of enactments amended.
(7)		—	Spent.
82		—	Rep. 1984 Sch. 23, Pt. VIII.
83,84			See destinations of enactments amended.
117		192(1)	
Sch. 18			
§9, 10, 15, 23		192	
1–8, 11–14		—	Rep. 1985 Sch. 27, Pt. X; 1986 Sch. 23, Pt. IX; 1988 Sch. 14, Pt. XI; ICTA Sch. 31.
FINANCE ACT 1981 c. 35			
38(3), (4)		40	
78		—	Rep. 1989 Sch. 17, Pt. VII.
79		168	Am. 1989 Sch. 14, §6; 1991 s. 92.
80(1), (2)		87(1), (2), (10)	
(2A)		87(3)	Added 1991 s. 89.
(3)–(6)		87(4)—(7)	
(6A)		87(8)	Added 1991 Sch. 18§1.
(7), (8)		87(9), (10)	Partly spent.
80A		88	Added 1991 Sch. 18 §2.
81		89	Am. 1991 Sch. 18 §3.
82		90	
82A		96	Added 1991 Sch. 18 §4.
83		97	Am. 1984 s. 71; 1990 Sch. 14 §18, 19; 1991 Sch. 18 §5, 6.
84		98	
85		13(10)	
86		70	
87		71, 73	
88(1)		85(1)	
(2)–(6)			Rep. 1991 Sch. 19, Pt. VI.
89–91			See destinations of enactments amended.
135		270	
FINANCE ACT 1982 c. 39			
80			See destinations of enactments amended.
83		247, 248	
84		72, 73,74	

TAXATION OF CHARGEABLE GAINS ACT 1992—*continued.*

Section of Act		Section of 1992 Act	Remarks
		FINANCE ACT 1982 c. 39—*continued.*	
85		—	Rep. 1984 Sch. 23, Pt. VIII.
86(1)		—	Rep. in part 1985 Sch. 27 Pt. VII.
(2), (3)		53(2), (3)	Am. 1985 Sch. 19, Pt. I.
(4)		53(1)	Am. 1985 Sch. 19, Pt. I.
(5)			Rep. 1985 Sch. 27, Pt. VII.
(6)		53(4)	
87		54	Am. 1985 Sch. 19, Pt. I; rep. in part 1985 Sch. 27, Pt. VII.
88		108	Am. 1985 Sch. 19, Pt. I; rep. in part 1985 Sch. 27, Pt. VII.
148		—	Spent.
Sch. 13			
§1, 2		56(1), (2)	Am. 1985 Sch. 19, Pt. I; rep. in part 1985 Sch. 27, Pt. VII.
3		—	Rep. 1985 Sch. 27, Pt. VII.
4		57	Rep. in part 1985 Sch. 27, Pt. VII.
5		131, 126, 132	
6		113	Am. 1985 Sch. 19, Pt. I.
7		145	Rep. in part 1985 Sch. 27, Pt. VII.
8–10		109	
11		Sch. 2 §2(2), 18(2).	
		FINANCE ACT 1983 c.28	
34, Sch. 6		—	Spent.
		FINANCE (No. 2) ACT 1983 c. 49	
7		264	AM. PCA Sch. 3 §6; rep. in part 1985 Sch. 27, Pt. VII.
		FINANCE ACT 1984 c. 43	
44		—	Spent.
50		24(1), (2)	
56(3), (4)		220	
63			See destinations of enactments amended.
64(1)		—	Unnecessary.
(2)		117(1)	Rep. in part 1989 Sch. 17, Pt. VII.
(2A)		117(1)	Added 1991 s. 98.
(3)		117(2)	

TAXATION OF CHARGEABLE GAINS ACT 1992—*continued.*

Section of Act		Section of 1992 Act	Remarks

FINANCE ACT 1984 c. 43—*continued.*

Section of Act		Section of 1992 Act	Remarks
(3A) (3C)		117(3)(a)(c)	Added 1989 s. 139.
(3D)		117(3)(d)	Added 1990 Sch. 10 §28.
(3E)–(3G)		117(4–(6))	Added 1991 Sch. 10 §1.
(4), (5)		117(7), (8)	Am. 1989 Sch. 14 §6.
(5A)–(5C)		117(9)(a)–(c)	Added 1989 s. 139.
(5D)		117(9)(d))	Added 1990 Sch. 10 §28.
(6)		117(10)	Am. 1989 s. 139.
(7)		116(1)	
(8)		117(11)(a)	
(9)–(12)		117(11)(b), (12), 287	Added 1991 Sch. 10 §1.
65		—	Rep. 1987(2) Sch. 9, Pt. II.
66		—	Spent.
67, 68		—	Spent.
69		275	
70		Sch. 11 §18	
71		97	
79(1)–(4)		197(1)–(4)	
(5)		Sch. 10, ICTA s. 502	Rep. in part 1987(2) Sch. 9, Pt. II; ICTA Sch. 31.
(6)–(9)		197(5)–(8)	
(10)		—	Unnecessary.
80		198	Am. 1988 Sch. 13 §22.
81		276	
126		265, 287	
Sch. 11		241	Rep in part ICTA Sch. 31.
Sch. 13			
§1		288(8)	
2–4		—	Rep. 1985 Sch. 27, Pt. VII; 1986 Sch. 23, Pt. VII.
5		—	Rep. ICTA Sch. 31.
6		—	Spent.
7		116(2)–(4)	
8		116(5)–(8)	
9		116(9)	Rep. in part 1985 Sch. 27, Pt. VII.
10		116(10), (11)	Am. 1985 s. 67; 1989 s. 139.
11		116(12), (13), (14)	

TAXATION OF CHARGEABLE GAINS ACT 1992—*continued.*

Section of Act		Section of 1992 Act	Remarks
	FINANCE ACT 1984 c. 43—*continued.*		
12		116(5)	Added 1990 s. 85.
Sch. 14		Sch. 11 §18	
	FINANCE ACT 1985 c. 54		
67			See destinations of enactment amended.
68(1)–(3)		–	Unnecessary.
(4)		55(1)	Rep. in part 1988 Sch. 14, Pt. VII.
(5)		55(2)	Subst. 1988 Sch. 8 §11.
(5A)		55(3)	Added 1988 s. 118.
(6), (7)		55(4), (5)	Am. 1988 s. 118.
(7A)		55(5)	Added 1988 s. 118; am. 1989 Sch. 15 §4; 1990 s. 70(7); 1991 s. 78(6), 99.
(8)		55(6)	
(9), (10)		104(3)	
69		163	Am. 1991 s. 100.
70(1)–(8)		164	Am. 1991 s. 100.
(9), (10)			See destinations of enactments amended.
71(1)–(4)		19(1)–(4)	
(5)		—	Spent.
(6), (7)		19(5), (6)	
(8)		—	Spent.
72(1), (2)		143(1), (2)	Am. 1987(2) s. 81; rep. in part ICTA Sch. 31.
(2A), (2B)		143(3), (4)	Added 1987(2) s. 81.
(3), (4)		143(5), (6)	
(5), (7)		—	Rep. 1987(2) Sch. 9, Pt. II; ICTA Sch. 31.
(6)		288(6), (7)	
Sch. 19			
Part I			See destinations of enactment amended.
Pt. II			
§6(1),(2)		109(1)	
(3),(4)		109(4),(5)	
7(1)		109(2)	
(2),(3)		109(6)	
Pt. III			
§8		104(3)–(5)	
9		104(1),(3)	
10		104(6)	

TAXATION OF CHARGEABLE GAINS ACT 1992—*continued.*

Section of Act		Section of 1992 Act	Remarks
	FINANCE ACT 1985 c. 54—*continued.*		
11		110(1) (3)	
12		110(4)	
13		110(5)–(9)	
14		110(10),(11)	
15		114	
Pt. IV			
§16		107(1),(2), 150(5)	
17		104(2)(b), 105(2)	
18,19		107(3)–(9)	
Pt. V			
§20,21		112,287	Partly spent.
Pt. VI			
§22,23		208	
Sch. 20		Sch. 6	Am. 1988 s. 110; 1991 s. 100; rep. in part 1988 Sch. 14 Pt. VII.
Sch. 21			
§1		20(1),(2)	
2		20(3)	
3		20(4),(5)	
4		20(6)–(9)	
	FINANCE ACT 1986 c. 41		
58		169	Am. 1989 Sch. 14 §6; rep. in part 1989 Sch. 17 Pt. VII; 1991 Sch. 19 Pt. VI.
59		115	
60		242	
	FINANCE ACT 1987 c. 16		
40		99(2),(3), 287	Rep. in part ICTA Sch. 31.
68(3)		Sch. 11§7	
	FINANCE (No. 2) ACT 1987 c. 51		
64		171(2), 175(2)	Partly spent.
73		285,287	
79		170(9)	
80		193	
81(1)-(3)		143	In force on 29.4.88: S.I.1988/744.
(4),(5)		144	
(6)		146(1)(b)	

TAXATION OF CHARGEABLE GAINS ACT 1992—*continued.*

Section of Act		Section of 1992 Act	Remarks
FINANCE (No. 2) ACT 1987 c. 51—*continued.*			
(7)		146(4)(a)	
(8)		—	Spent.
Sch. 6			
§2		139	
4		179	
5		137	
INCOME AND CORPORATION TAXES ACT 1988 c. 1			
122(1)(b),(3), (8)		201	
345		8	
346		189	
347		190	
761(4)		Sch. 10§14 (47)(b)	
Sch. 28			Spent.
§8(4),(5)		—	
FINANCE ACT 1988 c. 39			
62		194, Sch. 10§21	
63		195	
64		196, Sch. 10§21	Am. 1991 s. 67.
96		35	
97		36	
98		4	
99		—	Spent.
100		5	
101		206	
102(1)		6(1)	
(1A)		6(1)	Added 1991 Sch. 6 §6.
(2)–(4)		6(2)–(4)	S. 102(2)(a) rep. 1989 Sch. 17 Pt. V.
103		—	Spent.
104(1), (2)		—	Spent.
(3)		279(7)	
105		185	Partly spent.
106		186	
107		187	
108		—	Spent.
109		—	Unnecessary.
110		Sch. 6	
111		226	

TAXATION OF CHARGEABLE GAINS ACT 1992—*continued.*

Section of Act		Section of 1992 Act	Remarks
	FINANCE ACT 1988 c. 39—*continued.*		
112		155	
113		111	
114		—	Unnecessary.
115		171(3)	
116		151	
118		55	
Sch. 6			
§6(5)		250	
Sch. 8		Sch. 3, s. 35	Am. 1989 Sch. 15 §4(2); 1990 s. 63, 70(7)(b), Sch. 12 §2(2); 1991 s. 78(3). And see destinations of enactments amended.
Sch. 9			
§1, 2		Sch. 4§1, 2	Am. 1991 s. 101.
2A		Sch. 4§3	Added 1991 s. 101.
3		Sch. 4§4	Am. 1989 Sch. 15 §2; 1991 s. 101; rep. in part 1991 Sch. 19 Pt. VI.
4–7		Sch. 4§5–8	
8		Sch. 4§9	Am. 1991 s. 101.
Sch. 10			
§1–4		77	
5		78	Am. 1991 s. 89; rep. in part 1988 Sch. 14 Pt. VIII.
6–9		79	
10		—	Spent.
Sch, 11			
§1, 2		182	
3		183	
4–6		184	Am. 1990 s. 70.
7		—	Spent.
Sch. 12			
§4		216	
5		217	
7(b)		271(4)	
Sch. 13			
§16		41	
17		271(1)(c)	
18		288(3)	
	FINANCE ACT 1989 c. 26		
81(2)		—	Spent.
91(2)		207	

TAXATION OF CHARGEABLE GAINS ACT 1992—*continued.*

Section of Act		Section of 1992 Act	Remarks
	FINANCE ACT 1989 c. 26—*continued.*		
92(3)		209, 287	
96(3)		118	
122		—	Spent.
123			See destinations of enactments amended.
124		67	And see destinations of enactments amended.
125		259	
126		10	Partly spent.
127		25	Am. 1990 Sch. 9 §2.
128		10	
129		159	
130		276	
131		199	
132		188	
133		160	
134		191	
135		30	
136		31, 32, 33, Sch. 11 §10	
137		34, Sch. 11 §10	
138		170, 178, 179, 180	
139		117, 116(11), Sch. 11 §16(4)	
140		102	
141		—	Unnecessary.
Sch. 14			See destinations of enactments amended.
Sch. 15			
§1		Sch. 4 §4(5)	
2		Sch. 4 §4(1)	
3		Sch. 3 §4(2)	
4, 5			See destinations of enactments amended.
	FINANCE ACT 1990 c. 29		
28(3)		271(4)	
31–39		227–235	

TAXATION OF CHARGEABLE GAINS ACT 1992—*continued.*

Section of Act		Section of 1992 Act	Remarks
	FINANCE ACT 1990 c. 29—*continued.*		
40(1)(4)		154	
(5)–(8)		236	
46		212	Am. 1991 Sch. 7 §14.
47		213	
54		103	
63		Sch. 3 §7	
64		200	
65			See destinations of enactments amended.
70			See destinations of enactments amended.
72		—	Spent.
81(3), (6)		271(10), (11)	
83		253	
84		254, 255	
85		116	
86		170	
127(2)		288	
Sch. 8		214	Am. 1991 Sch. 7 §15.
Sch. 9			
§1, 2		211,25	
Sch. 10			
§28, 29		117, Sch. 11 §16	
Sch. 14			
§17, 18		97,150	
19(2)–(4)		—	Spent.
Sch. 18			
§3		271	
	FINANCE ACT 1991 c. 31.		
57(4)		271(9)	
67		Sch. 10 §21	
77(2)		Sch. 11 §16(4)	
78(1)–(3), (8)		267	And see destinations of enactments amended.
83		80	
84		81, 288(1)	
85		82	
86		83, 288(1)	
87		84,288(1)	

TAXATION OF CHARGEABLE GAINS ACT 1992—*continued.*

Section of Act		Section of 1992 Act	Remarks

FINANCE ACT 1991 c. 31.—*continued.*

Section of Act		Section of 1992 Act	Remarks
88		85(2)–(9)	
89(1)		—	Unnecessary.
(2)		87(3)	
(3)		78(3)	
90		—	Unnecessary.
91		—	Unnecessary.
92(1)		—	Spent.
(2)		168	
(3)–(7)		—	Spent.
93		222	
94		223	
95, 96		218, 219	
97		279	
98		117, Sch. 11 §16(4)	
99			See destinations of enactments amended.
100		163, 164, Sch. 6	
101(1)			Spent.
(2)		Sch. 4 §1(b)	
(3)		Sch. 4 §2(1)	
(4)		Sch. 4 §2(3), (4)	
(5)		Sch. 4 §3	
(6)		Sch. 4 §4(1)	
(7)		Sch. 4 §4(2)	
(8)		Sch. 4 §4(4)	
(9)		Sch. 4 §9	
(10)		—	Spent.
102		148	
Sch. 6			
§6		6(1)	
Sch. 10			
§1(1), (2)		117(4), (5), (6)	
(3)		288, 117(11), (12), 287	

TAXATION OF CHARGEABLE GAINS ACT 1992—*continued.*

Section of Act		Section of 1992 Act	Remarks
	FINANCE ACT 1991 c. 31.—*continued.*		
(4)		—	Spent.
(5)		117(13)	
4		149	
Sch. 16			
§1, 2		86(1)–(4), 288(1)	
3–16		Sch. 5	
17		Sch. 10 §2	
Sch. 17			
§1		97	Partly spent.
2		92(1), (2)	
3		92(3)–(6)	
4		91,287	
5		93(1), (2)	
6		93(1), (3)	
7		93(4)	
8		94	
9		95	
Sch. 18			
§1		87(8)	
2		88,288(1)	
3		89(1)	
4		96	
5		97(1), (8)–(10)	
6		97(1)–(7)	

PROTECTION OF BADGERS ACT 1992 (c.51)

TABLE OF DERIVATIONS

(for Table of Destinations see page cccxlviii)

Note:

The following abbreviations are used in this Table:—

1973	= The Badgers Act 1973 (c.57)
1975	= The Conservation of Wild Creatures and Wild Plants Act 1975 (c.48)
1981	= The Wildlife and Countryside Act 1981 (c.69)
1985	= The Wildlife and Countryside (Amendment) Act 1985 (c.31)
1986	= The Animals (Scientific Procedures) Act 1986 (c.14)
1990	= The Environmental Protection Act 1990 (c.43)
1991 (S)	= The Natural Heritage (Scotland) Act 1991 (c.28)
1991 (FP)	= The Badgers (Further Protection) Act 1991 (1991 c.35)
1991	= The Badgers Act 1991 (1991 c.36)

Section of 1992 Act	Derivation
1(1)	1973 s.1(1); 1985 s.1(1)(a)
(2)	1973 s.1(1A); 1985 s.1(1)(b)
(3)	1973 s.1(2); 1981, Sch.7, para 8
(4)	1973 s.1(3); 1981, Sch.7, para 8
(5)	1973 s.5
2(1)	1973 s.2(1); 1981, Sch.7, para 9(2); 1985 s.1(2)(a)
(2)	1973 s.2(2); 1985 s.1(2)(b)
3	1973 s.2(3); 1991 s.1
4	1973 s.3
5	1973 s.4
6	1973 s.8(1), (3); 1986, Sch.3, para 9
7	1973 s.8(1A), (1B); 1981, Sch.7, para 10(1)
8(1), (2)	1973 s.8(1A), (1B); 1981, Sch.7, para 10(1); 1991 s.2(1)
(3)	1973 s.8(4); 1991 s.2(2)
(4) to (9)	1973 s.8(5), (6); 1991 s.3
9	1973 s.8(2) (s.8(2)(a) spent); s.8(2)(c) rep. 1981, Sch.7, para 9(4), Sch.17, Part II)
10(1)(a)	1973 s.9(1)(a), (2)(a); 1991 s.4(a); 1991(S) Sch.2, para.5(2)
(b)	1973 s.9(1)(b), (2)(a)
(c)	1973 s.9(1)(c), (2)(a)
(d)	1973 s.9(1)(f), (2)(a); 1991 s.4 (d), (e)
(e)	1973 s.9(1)(j), (2)(a); 1991 s.4(d), (e)
(f)	1973 s.9(1)(i), (2)(a); 1991 s.4(d), (e)
(2)(a)	1973 s.9(1)(d), (2)(b); 1991 s.4(b)

PROTECTION OF BADGERS ACT—*continued.*

Section of 1992 Act	Derivation
(b)	1973 s.9(1)(e), (2)(b); 1981, Sch.7, para 10(2), (3); 1991 s.4(c)
(c)	1973 s.9(1)(g), (2)(b); 1991 s.4(d), (f)
(d)	1973 s.9(1)(h), (2)(b); 1991 s.4(d), (f)
(3)	1973 s.9(1)(k), (2)(c); 1991 s.4(d), (g)
(4)	1973 s.9(2)(a); 1990, Sch.9, para 6(2); 1991(S), Sch.2, para 5(2)
(5)	1973 s.9(2)(b); The Transfer of Functions (Wales) (No.1) Order 1978 (S.I. 1978/272)
(6), (7)	1973 s.9(4),(4A); 1981, Sch.7, para 10(4); 1990, Sch.9, para 6(3); 1991(S), Sch.2, para 5(3); 1991 s.4(h)
(8)	1973 s.9(3)
(9)	1973 s.9(6); 1991 s.4(i)
(10)	1973 s.9(4); 1975 s.16 (saved by 1981 s.73(4))
11	1973 s.10(1); 1981, Sch.7, para 11(1) (s.10(1)(b) repealed (E&W) by Police and Criminal Evidence Act 1984 (c.60), Sch.7, Part I)
12(1), (2), (3)	1973 s.10(2); 1981, Sch.7, para 11(2); Criminal Justice Act 1982 (c.48) s.46; Criminal Procedure (Scotland) Act 1975 (c.21) s.289G; Criminal Justice Act 1991 s.26(3); S.I. 1991/2208 art 2(3); S.I. 1991/2706 art.2(2); 1991(FP) s.1(7)
(4)	1973 s.10(3)
13	1991 (FP) s.1
14	1973 s.11; 1981, Sch.7, para 12; 1991 s.5
15(1)	—
(2)	—
(3)	—
(4)	1973 s.12(2); 1991 (FP) s.2(4)

PROTECTION OF BADGERS ACT1992 (c. 51)

TABLE OF DESTINATIONS

Notes:

1. The following abbreviations are used in this Table:—

1973	= The Badgers Act 1973 (c. 57).
1975	= The Conservation of Wild Creatures and Wild Plants Act 1975 (c. 48).
1981	= The Wildlife and Countryside Act 1981 (c. 69).
1985	= The Wildlife and Countryside (Amendment) Act 1985 (c. 31).
1986	= The Animals (Scientific Procedures) Act 1986 (c. 14).
1990	= The Environmental Protection Act 1990 (c. 43).
1991(S)	= The Natural Heritage (Scotland) Act 1991 (c. 28).
1991	= The Badgers Act 1991 (c. 36).

2. The functions of the Minister of Agriculture, Fisheries and Food under the Badgers Act 1973 so far as exercisable in relation to Wales were transferred to the Secretary of State by the Transfer of Functions (Wales) (No. 1) Order 1978 (S.I. 1978/272) Art. 2, Sch. 1.

Section of Act	Subject matter	Section of 1992 Act	Remarks
	THE BADGERS ACT 1973 (c. 57)		
1(1)	Taking badgers etc.	1(1)	Am. 1985 s. 1(1)(a).
(1A)		1(2)	Inserted 1985 s. 1(1)(b).
(2), (3)		1(3), (4)	Subst. 1981, Sch. 7 para. 8.
2(1)	Cruelty to badgers.	2(1)	Am. 1985, 1(2)(a).
(a)		2(1)(a)	
(b)		2(1)(b)	
(c)		2(1)(c)	Am. 1981 Sch. 7 para. 9(2).
(d)		2(1)(d)	
(2)		2(2)	Added 1985 s. 1(2)(b).
(3)		3	Added 1991 s. 1.
3	Selling and possession of badgers.	4	
4	Marking and ringing.	5	Reference to s. 8(2)(a) spent.
5	Offender required to quit land.	1(5)	
6	Special protection.	—	Rep. 1981, Sch. 7 para. 9(3), Sch. 17, Part II.
7	Exception for authorised persons.	—	Rep. 1981, Sch. 7 para. 9(1), Sch. 17, Part II.
8(1)	General exceptions.	6	
(1A), 1(B)		7, 8(1), (2)	Inserted 1981, Sch. 7 para. 10(1); am. 1991 s. 2(1).
(2)		9	Para. (a) spent and para. (c) rep. 1981, Sch. 7 para. 9(4), Sch. 17 Part II.
(3)		6(d)	Am. 1986 Sch. 3 para. 9.
(4)		8(3)	Added 1991 s. 2(2).
(5), (6)		8(4)–(9)	Added 1991 s. 3.
9(1)	Licences.	10(1), (2), (3)	
(a)		10(1)(a)	Am. 1991 s. 4(a).
(b)		10(1)(b)	
(c)		10(1)(c)	
(d)		10(2)(a)	Am. 1991 s. 4(b).

PROTECTION OF BADGERS ACT—*continued.*

Section of Act	Subject matter	Section of 1992 Act	Remarks
		THE BADGERS ACT 1973 (c. 57)—*continued.*	
(e)		10(2)(b)	Inserted 1981, Sch. 7 para. 10(2); am. 1991 s. 4(c).
(f)–(j)		10(1)(d), (e), (f), (2)(c), (d).	Inserted 1991, s. 4(d).
(k)		10(3)	Inserted 1991 s. 4(d).
(2)(a)		10(1), (4)	Am. 1990 Sch. 9 para. 6(2), 1991(S), Sch. 2, para. 5(2) and 1991 s. 4(e).
(b)		10(2), (5)	Am. 1981 Sch. 7 para. 10(3) and 1991 s. 4(f).
(c)		10(3)	Inserted 1991 s. 4(g); am. 1991(S) Sch. 2, para. 5(2).
(3)		10(8)	
(4)		10(6)	Inserted 1981, Sch. 7 para. 10(4); 1990, Sch. 9, para. 6(3); am. 1991 s. 4(h).
(4A)		10(6), (7)	Inserted 1991(S) Sch. 2, para. 5(3).
(4)		10(10)	Added 1975 s. 16 saved 1981 s. 73(4).
(6)		10(9)	Added 1991 s. 4(i).
10(1)(a)	Enforcement and penalties.	11(a)	
(b)		11(c)	Rep. (E & W) Police and Criminal Evidence Act 1984, Sch. 7 Part I.
(c)		11(b)	Am. 1981, Sch. 7, para. 11(1).
(2)		12(1), (2), (3)	Am. 1981 Sch. 7 para. 11(2); Criminal Justice Act 1982 (c. 48) s. 46; Criminal Procedure (Scotland) Act 1975 (c. 21) s. 289G; Criminal Justice Act 1991 (c. 53) s. 26(3); saved in part S.I. 1991/2208 art. 2(3), S.I. 1991/2706 art. 2(2).
(3)		12(4)	
11	Interpretation.	14	Rep. in part 1981, Sch. 7 para. 9(5), Sch. 17 Part II; am. 1981, Sch. 7 para. 12 and 1991 s.5.
12(1)	Short title.	—	
(2)	Extent.	15(4)	
(3)	Commencement.	—	
	THE WILDLIFE AND COUNTRYSIDE ACT 1981 (c. 69)		
73(4)	Saving for s.9(4) of 1973.	10(9)	
Sch. 7 para. 8	Possession of dead badgers.	1(3), (4)	Substitutes s.1(2), (3) in 1973.

PROTECTION OF BADGERS ACT—*continued.*

Section of Act	Subject matter	Section of 1992 Act	Remarks
THE WILDLIFE AND COUNTRYSIDE ACT 1981 (c. 69)—*continued.*			
para. 9(2)		2(1)(c)	Amends s.2(c) of 1973.
para. 10(1)	Exceptions.	7, 8(1), (2)	Inserts s.8(1A), (1B) in 1973.
(2)	Licences.	10(2)(b)	Inserts 9(1)(e) in 1973.
(3)		10(2)	Amends s.9(2)(b) of 1973.
(4)		10(6)	Inserts s.9(4) in 1973.
para. 11(1)	Powers of constables.	11(b)	Amends s.10(1)(c) of 1973.
(2)	Penalties.	12(1)	Amends s.10(2) of 1973.
para. 12	Definition of "sale"	14	
THE WILDLIFE AND COUNTRYSIDE (AMENDMENT) ACT 1985 (c. 31)			
1(1)	Killing etc. badgers.	1(2)	Amends s.1 of 1973.
(2)	Digging for badgers.	2(2)	Amends s.2 of 1973.
THE ANIMALS (SCIENTIFIC PROCEDURES) ACT 1986 (c. 14)			
Sch. 3 para. 9	Exceptions.	6(d)	Amends s.8(3) of 1973.
THE ENVIRONMENTAL PROTECTION ACT 1990 (c. 43)			
Sch. 9 para. 6	Licences.	10(4)	Amends s.9(2)(a), (4) of 1973.
THE NATURAL HERITAGE (SCOTLAND) ACT 1991 (c. 28)			
Sch. 2, para. 5	Licences.	10(4)	Amends s.9(2) and inserts s.9(4A) of 1973.
THE BADGERS (FURTHER PROTECTION) ACT 1991 (c. 35)			
1	Powers of court where dog used by a person for commission of offence.	12(1), 13	
2(1)	Short title.	—	
(2)	Saving.	—	
(3)	Commencement.	—	
(4)	Extent.	15(4)	
THE BADGERS ACT 1991 (c. 36)			
1	Protection of badger sets.	3	Adds subsection (3) to s.2 of 1973.
2	Exceptions.	8(1), (3)	Amends subsection (1A) of, and adds subsection (4) to s.8 of 1973.
3	Exceptions for fox-hunting activities.	8(4) to (9)	Adds subsection (5) and (6) to s.8 of 1973.
4(a)	Licences.	10(1)(a)	Amends s.9(1)(a) of 1973.
(b)		10(2)(a)	Amends s.9(1)(d) of 1973.
(c)		10(2)(b)	Amends s.9(1)(e) of 1973.
(d)		10(1)(d), (e), (f), (2)(c), (d), (3)	Inserts paras. (f) to(k) in s.9(1) of 1973.
(e)		10(1)	Amends s.9(2)(a) of 1973.
(f)		10(2)	Amends s.9(2)(b).

PROTECTION OF BADGERS ACT—*continued.*

Section of Act	Subject matter	Section of 1992 Act	Remarks

THE BADGERS ACT 1991 (c. 36)—*continued.*

Section of Act	Subject matter	Section of 1992 Act	Remarks
(g)		10(3)	Inserts s.9(2)(c) of 1973.
(h)		10(6)	Amends 1973 s.9(4).
(i)		10(9)	Adds 1973 s.9(6).
5	Interpretation.	14	Amends s.11 of 1973.
6(1)	Citation.	—	
(2)	Commencement.	—	

THE CRIMINAL JUSTICE ACT 1991 (c. 53)

Section of Act	Subject matter	Section of 1992 Act	Remarks
26(3)	Penalties.	12(1), (2), (3)	Amends s.12(2) of 1973 but see saving in S.I. 1991/2208 art. 2(3) and S.I. 1991/2706 art. 2(2).

TRADE UNION AND LABOUR RELATIONS (CONSOLIDATION) ACT 1992 (c. 52)

TABLE OF DERIVATIONS

(for Table of Destinations see page ccclxxvi)

The following abbreviations are used in this Table:—

1875	Conspiracy and Protection of Property Act 1875 (c. 86).
1913	Trade Union Act 1913 (2 & 3 Geo.5 c. 30).
1919	Industrial Courts Act 1919 (c. 69).
1964	Trade Union (Amalgamations, &c.) Act 1964 (c. 24).
1971	Industrial Relations Act 1971 (c. 72).
1974	Trade Union and Labour Relations Act 1974 (c. 52).
1975	Employment Protection Act 1975 (c. 71).
1976	Trade Union and Labour Relations (Amendment) Act 1976 (c. 7).
1978	Employment Protection (Consolidation) Act 1978 (c. 44).
1980	Employment Act 1980 (c. 42).
1982	Employment Act 1982 (c. 46).
1984	Trade Union Act 1984 (c. 49).
1988	Employment Act 1988 (c. 19).
1989	Employment Act 1989 (c. 38).
1990	Employment Act 1990 (c. 38).

Section of 1992 Act	Derivation
Part I, Chapter I.	
1	1913 s.2(1); 1964 s.9(1) "trade union"; 1974 s.28(1), Sch.3 paras.2(2), 10(8); 1975 s.126(1) "trade union"; 1978 s.153(1); 1980 s.3(9); 1982 s.18(2); 1984 ss.9(1), 10(5); 1988 ss.18(2), 32(1); 1990 ss.7(5), 8(7).
2(1)	1974 s.8(1), (2); 1975 Sch.16 Pt.III, para.1.
(2), (3)	1974 s.8(9); 1975 Sch.16 Pt.III, paras.1 and 4.
(4), (5), (6)	1974 s.8(10); 1975 Sch.16 Pt.III, paras.1 and 5.
3(1)	1974 s.8(3); 1975 Sch.16 Pt.III para.1.
(2)	1974 s.8(4); 1975 Sch.16 Pt.III para.1.
(3)	1974 s.8(3); 1975 Sch.16 Pt.III para.1.
(4)	1974 s.8(5); 1975 Sch.16 Pt.III para.1.
4(1), (2)	1974 s.8(6); 1975 Sch.16 Pt.III, para.1.
(3)	1974 s.8(6A); 1975 Sch.16 Pt.III, paras.1 and 2.
5	1974 s.30(1) "independent trade union"; 1975 s.126(1) "independent trade union", "independence" and "independent"; 1978 s.153(1) "independent trade union".
6(1)	1975 s.8(1), (2).
(2), (3)	1975 s.8(3), (4).
(4)	1975 s.8(6).
(5)	1975 s.8(5)(a),(b).
(6)	1975 s.8(5)(c).
7(1)	1975 s.8(7).
(2)	1975 s.8(3), (8).
(3)	1975 s.8(6), (8).
(4)	1975 s.8(5)(a),(b), (8).
(5)	1975 s.8(5)(c), (8).
(6)	1975 s.8(10).

TRADE UNION AND LABOUR RELATIONS (CONSOLIDATION) ACT—*continued.*

Section of 1992 Act	Derivation
8(1) to (3)	1975 s.8(11).
(4), (5)	1975 s.8(12).
9(1)	1974 s.8(7); 1975 Sch.16 Pt.III, para.3; 1978 s.136(3), Sch.16 para.18.
(2)	1975 s.8(9).
(3)	1974 s.8(7); 1975 s.8(9), Sch.16 Pt.III para.3.
(4)	1974 s.8(7); 1975 s.8(9), Sch.16 Pt.III para.3; 1978 s.136(3), Sch.16 paras.18 and 23(3).
Part I, Chapter II.	
10(1), (2)	1974 s.2(1)(a), (c), (d).
(3)	1974 s.2(2), (3); Interpretation Act 1978 (c.30) s.17(2)(a); Companies Consolidation (Consequential Provisions) Act 1985 (c.9) Sch.2.
11(1), (2)	1974 s.2(5).
12(1)	1974 s.2(1)(b).
(2)	1974 s.2(1)(e).
(3)	drafting.
13(1)	1974 s.4(1), (2), (3).
(2)	1974 s.4(1).
(3)	1974 s.4(3).
(4)	1974 s.4(1).
14(1) to (6)	1974 s.4(3) to (8)
15(1) to (4)	1988 s.8(1) to (4).
(5)	1988 s.8(4), (5).
(6)	1988 s.8(6).
(7)	1988 s.32(1) "member".
16(1) to (4)	1988 s.9(1) to (4).
(5)	1988 s.23(1), (2).
(6)	1988 s.9(5).
(7)	1988 s.32(1) "member".
17(1)	1974 Sch.1 para.31(1)(a).
(2), (3)	1974 Sch.1 para.31(2).
(4), (5)	1974 Sch.1 para.31(3).
(6)	1974 s.26(2), (3).
18(1)	1974 Sch.1 para.31(1)(b); Administration of Estates (Small Payments) (Increase of Limits) Order 1984 (S.I. 1984/539).
(2)	1974 Sch.1 para.31(3).
(3)	1974 s.26(2), (3).
(4)	1974 Sch.1 para.31(4); 1975 Sch.16, Pt.III, para.32.
19(1)	Industrial Assurance and Friendly Societies Act 1948 (c.39) ss.6(1), (2), 23(1)(d); 1974 Sch.3 para.5(2), (4).
(2)	Industrial Assurance and Friendly Societies Act 1948 (c.39) s.16(4); Friendly Societies Act 1974 (c.46) Sch.9 para.12; 1974 Sch.3 para.5(3).
(3)	Friendly Societies Act 1896 (c.25) s.22(2), (3); Friendly Societies Act 1974 (c.46) Sch.9 para.1; 1974 s.9(1).

TRADE UNION AND LABOUR RELATIONS (CONSOLIDATION) ACT—*continued.*

Section of 1992 Act	Derivation
20(1)	1974 s.13(1); 1982 s.15(2); 1990 s.6(2).
(2) to (4)	1982 s.15(3) to (3B); 1990 s.6(3).
(5)	1982 s.15(8).
(6)	1982 s.15(9); 1990 s.6(8).
(7)	1982 s.15(7) "rules".
21(1)	1982 s.15(4); 1990 s.6(4).
(2)	1982 s.15(5); 1990 s.6(5).
(3)	1982 s.15(5A); 1990 s.6(5).
(4)	1982 s.15(5B); 1990 s.6(5).
(5)	1982 s.15(6).
(6)	1982 s.15(6A); 1990 s.6(6).
(7)	1982 s.15(7) "commercial contract"; 1990 s.6(7).
22(1)	1982 s.16(1), (2); Consumer Protection Act 1987 (c.43) Sch.4 para.8.
(2)	1982 s.16(1), (3).
(3)	1985 s.16(4), (5)(b).
(4)	1982 s.16(5)(a).
(5)	1982 s.16(2)(b), (6).
23(1)	1982 s.17(1).
(2)	1982 s.17(2), (3) "political fund", "provident benefits fund".
(3)	1982 s.17(3) "provident benefits".
Part I, Chapter III.	
24(1), (2)	1984 s.4(1), (2).
(3), (4)	1984 s.4(2A); 1988 Sch.3 para. 5(3).
(5)	1984 s.9(1) "proper address".
(6)	1984 ss.5(10), 6(3).
25(1)	1984 s.5(1).
(2)	1984 s.5(3); s.6(5).
(3)	1984 s.5(4).
(4), (5)	1984 s.6(1), (2).
(6), (7)	1984 s.6(7), (8).
26(1)	1984 s.5(1).
(2)	1984 s.6(4).
(3)	1984 s.5(4).
(4)	1984 s.5(5), (6), (7), (9).
(5)	1984 s.5(11), (12).
(6)	1988 s.23(1), (2).
27	1974 s.11(4).
28(1)	1974 s.10(1), (2).
(2)	1974 s.10(3).
29(1)	1988 s.6(1), (9)(a).
(2)	1988 s.6(9)(a); drafting.
(3)	1988 s.6(2).
30(1)	1988 s.6(2), (10).

TRADE UNION AND LABOUR RELATIONS (CONSOLIDATION) ACT—*continued.*

Section of 1992 Act	Derivation
(2), (3)	1988 s.6(3), (4).
(4)	1974 Sch.2 para.6; Companies Consolidation (Consequential Provisions) Act 1985 (c.9), Sch.2; 1988 s.6(9)(c).
(5), (6)	1988 s.6(5), (6).
(7)	1988 s.32(1) "member".
31(1), (2)	1988 s.6(7).
(3)	1988 s.23(1), (2).
32(1)	1974 s.11(1), (2); 1975 Sch.16 Pt.III para.1.
(2)	1974 Sch.2 Pt.I para.1(1), (2).
(3)	1974 Sch.2 Pt.I paras. 2, 3 and 4.
(4)	1974 Sch.2 Pt.I para.5.
(5), (6)	1974 s.11(4), (5).
33(1)	1974 s.11(3).
(2)	1974 Sch.2 Pt.I para.22.
34(1)	1974 Sch.2 Pt.I paras.6, 7; Interpretation Act 1978 (c.30) s.17(2)(a); Companies Consolidation (Consequential Provisions) Act 1985 (c.9) Sch.2.
(2), (3)	1974 Sch.2 Pt.I para.9(1), (2).
(4)	1974 s.26(2), (3); 1974 Sch.2 Pt.I para.9(3).
(5)	1974 Sch.2 Pt.I para.10(1), (2).
35(1)	1974 Sch.2 Pt.I para.11, 12, 13(1).
(2)	1974 Sch.2 Pt.I para.12.
(3) to (5)	1974 Sch.2 Pt.I para.13(1) to (3).
(6)	1974 s.26(2), (3); 1974 Sch.2 Pt.I para.14.
(7), (8)	1974 Sch.2 Pt.I para.15(1), (2).
36(1)	1974 Sch.2 Pt.I para.18.
(2)	1974 Sch.2 Pt.I para.19.
(3), (4)	1974 Sch.2 Pt.I para.20.
37(1)	1974 Sch.2 Pt.I para.16.
(2)	1974 Sch.2 Pt.I para.21.
(3)	1974 Sch.2 Pt.I para.17.
38(1)	1974 Sch.2 Pt.II para.36(a).
(2)	1974 Sch.2 Pt.II paras.34, 35, 36(c).
39(1)	1974 Sch.2 Pt.II, para.27; 1975 Sch.16 Pt.III, para.1.
(2)	1974 Sch.2 Pt.II, paras.25, 27.
(3)	1974 Sch.2 Pt.II, para.28.
40(1), (2)	1974 Sch.2 Pt.II, para.32(1), (2).
(3)	1974 Sch.2 Pt.II, paras.24, 33.
(4)	1974 Sch.2 Pt.II, paras 25, 33.
(5), (6)	1974 Sch.2 Pt.II, paras.26, 33; 1975 Sch.16 Pt.III, para.1.
(7)	1974 Sch.2 Pt.II, paras.28, 33.
41(1)	1974 Sch.2 Pt.II, paras.30, 33A; 1975 Sch.16 Pt.III, para.1; 1980 Sch.1 para.3.
(2)	1974 Sch.2 Pt.II, paras.31, 33B; 1975 Sch.16 Pt.III, para.1; 1980 Sch.1 para.3.
(3)	1974 Sch.2 Pt.II, para.33B; 1980 Sch.1 para.3.
(4)	1974 Sch.2 Pt.II, para.32(3); 1975 Sch.16 Pt.III, para.1.

TRADE UNION AND LABOUR RELATIONS (CONSOLIDATION) ACT—*continued.*

Section of 1992 Act	Derivation
42	1974 Sch.2 Pt.II, para.36(b); 1975 Sch.16 Pt.III, para.1.
43(1)	1974 s.11(1).
(2)	1984 s.7(4) to (7).
44(1)	drafting.
(2)	1974 ss.10(4), 11(8).
(3)	1974 s.10(4), 11(8); 1984 s.4(3).
45(1) to (4)	1974 s.12(1) to (4); 1988 s.6(8).
(5)	1974 s.12(5); Criminal Justice Act 1982 (c.48) ss.38, 46; 1988 s.6(8).
Part I, Chapter IV.	
46(1), (2)	1984 s.1(1), (2), (6B); 1988 s.12(1), Sch.3 Pt.I para.5(1).
(3)	1984 s.1(6A); 1988 s.12(1).
(4)	1984 s.1(6C); 1988 s.12(1).
(5)	1984 s.1(7).
(6)	1984 s.1(1), (4).
47(1), (2)	1984 s.2(9), (10).
(3)	1984 s.2(11), (12).
48(1)	1988 s.13(2)(a), (b).
(2)	1988 s.13(2)(b), (4).
(3)	1988 s.13(3).
(4) to (6)	1988 s.13(2)(d) to (f).
(7)	1988 s.13(2)(c).
(8)	1988 s.13(5).
49(1)	1988 s.15(2)(a).
(2), (3)	1988 s.15(3), (4).
(4)	1988 s.15(2)(b).
(5)	1988 s.15(2)(bb); 1990 s.5(5).
(6), (7)	1988 s.15(2)(c), (d).
50(1), (2)	1984 s.2(1), (2).
(3)	1984 ss.2(3), (4)(a), 9(1) "section".
(4)	1984 s.2(4)(b).
51(1)	1984 s.2(5).
(2)	1984 s.2(5)(a), (b), (c); 1988 Sch.3 Pt.I para.5(2)(a); 1990 s.5(4).
(3), (4)	1984 s.2(6), (7).
(5)	1984 s.2(8)(a), (c).
(6)	1984 s.2(8).
(7)	1984 s.9(1) "single transferable vote".
52(1)	1988 s.15(5)(a) to (d).
(2)	1988 s.15(5)(e), (f), (6).
(3)	1988 s.15(7).
(4)	1988 s.15(7)(a).
(5)	1988 s.15(7)(b), (c).
53	1984 s.2(14).

TRADE UNION AND LABOUR RELATIONS (CONSOLIDATION) ACT—*continued.*

Section of 1992 Act	Derivation
54(1)	1984 ss.5(1), (10), 6(3); 1988 Sch.3 Pt.I para.5(4)(a).
(2)	1984 s.5(1)(a), (b), (12A); 1988 Sch.3 Pt.I para.5(4)(c).
(3)	1984 s.5(2).
55(1)	1984 s.5(1).
(2)	1984 ss.5(3), 6(5).
(3)	1984 s.5(4).
(4), (5)	1984 s.6(1), (2).
(6), (7)	1984 s.6(7), (8).
56(1)	1984 s.5(1); 1988 Sch.3 Pt.I para.5(4)(a).
(2)	1984 s.6(4).
(3)	1984 s.5(4).
(4)	1984 s.5(5) to (7), (9).
(5)	1984 s.5(8); 1988 Sch.3 Pt.1 para.5(4)(b).
(6)	1984 s.5(11) to (12A); 1988 Sch.3 Pt.I para.5(4)(c).
(7)	1988 s.23(1), (2).
57(1)	1984 s.7(4) to (7).
(2)	1988 s.12(2).
(3)	1984 s.7(8); 1988 s.12(2).
58(1)	1984 s.8(1).
(2)	1984 s.8(2); 1988 Sch.3 Pt.I para.5(5)(b)
(3)	Interpretation Act 1978 (c.30) s.17(2)(a); 1984 s.8(3).
59	1984 s.1(3).
60(1)	1984 s.2(13).
(2)	1984 s.9(1) "overseas member".
(3)	1984 s.2(13); 1988 Sch.3 Pt.I para.5(2)(b).
61(1)	1984 s.9(2).
(2)	1984 s.1(6).
Part I, Chapter V.	
62(1)	1988 s.1(1); 1990 Sch.2 para.3(2).
(2)	1988 s.1(5); 1990 Sch.2 para.3(5).
(3)	1988 s.1(2); 1990 Sch.2 para.3(3).
(4)	1988 s.23(1), (2).
(5)	1988 s.1(3); 1990 Sch.2 para.3(4).
(6)	1988 s.1(6), (7) "industrial action"; 1990 s.5(1).
(7)	1988 s.30(1).
(8)	1990 s.5(1).
(9)	1988 s.1(8).
63(1)	1988 s.2(4).
(2)	1988 s.2(1).
(3)	1988 s.2(3).
(4)	1988 s.2(2).
(5), (6)	1988 s.2(5), (6).
64(1)	1988 s.3(1).

TRADE UNION AND LABOUR RELATIONS (CONSOLIDATION) ACT—*continued.*

Section of 1992 Act	Derivation
(2)	1988 s.3(5).
(3)	1988 s.3(8).
(4), (5)	1988 s.3(7).
65(1)	1988 s.3(2), (3).
(2)	1988 s.3(3)(a) to (d), (f), (6) "enactment".
(3)	1988 s.3(3)(e).
(4)	1988 s.3(3)(g).
(5)	1988 s.3(3), closing words.
(6)	1988 s.3(4).
(7)	1988 s.3(3)(b),(d), (6) "representative".
(8)	1988 s.30(1)
66(1)	1988 s.4(1).
(2)	1988 s.4(2), (3).
(3)	1988 s.4(4).
(4)	1988 s.4(6).
67(1) to (9)	1988 s.5(1) to (9).
68(1)	1988 s.7(1).
(2), (3)	1988 s.7(2)(a), (b).
(4)	1988 s.7(3).
69	1974 s.7; 1976 s.3(1).
70	1988 s.32(1) "member".
Part I, Chapter VI.	
71(1), (2)	1913 s.3(1); 1971 Sch.8; 1974 Sch.3 para.2(3); 1975 Sch.16 Pt.IV para.2(2).
72(1) to (3)	1913 s.3(3) to (3B); 1984 s.17(1).
(4)	1913 s.3(3C); Films Act 1960 (c.57) s.38(4) "film"; 1984 s.17(1).
73(1)	1913 s.3(1); 1971 Sch.8; 1974 Sch.3 para.2(3).
(2)	1913 s.3(4); 1971 Sch.8; 1974 Sch.3 para.2(3).
(3)	1984 s.12(2)(a).
(4)	1984 s.12(2)(b), (4).
74(1)	1913 s.4(1); 1971 Sch.8; 1974 Sch.3 para.2(3); 1975 Sch.16 Pt.IV para.2(2).
(2)	1984 s.13(3).
(3)	1913 s.4(1); 1971 Sch.8; 1974 Sch.3 para.2(3); 1975 Sch.16 Pt.IV para.2(2); 1984 s.13(1); 1988 s.15(1)(a).
75(1)	1988 s.15(2)(a).
(2), (3)	1988 s.15(3), (4).
(4)	1988 s.15(2)(b).
(5)	1988 s.15(2)(bb); 1990 s.5(5).
(6), (7)	1988 s.15(2)(c), (d).
76	1913 s.4(1A); 1984 s.13(2).
77(1), (2)	1913 s.4(1B); 1984 s.13(2); 1988 Sch.3 para.1(1)(b); 1990 s.5(4).
(3)	1913 s.4(1C); 1984 s.13(2).

TRADE UNION AND LABOUR RELATIONS (CONSOLIDATION) ACT—*continued.*

Section of 1992 Act	Derivation
(4)	1913 s.4(1D); 1984 s.13(2); 1988 s.14(1).
(5)	1913 s.4(1E); 1984 s.13(2).
78(1), (2)	1988 s.15(5), (6).
(3) to (6)	1988 s.15(7).
79(1)	1984 ss.5(10), 6(3); 1988 s.16(4), Sch.3 para.5(4)(a).
(2), (3)	1988 s.16(2), (3).
80(1)	1988 s.16(1).
(2)	1984 ss.5(3), 6(5); 1988 s.16(4).
(3)	1984 s.5(4); 1988 s.16(4).
(4), (5)	1984 s.6(1), (2); 1988 s.16(4).
(6), (7)	1984 s.6(7), (8); 1988 s.16(4).
81(1)	1988 s.16(1).
(2)	1984 s.6(3), (4); 1988 s.16(4).
(3)	1984 s.5(4); 1988 s.16(4).
(4)	1984 s.5(5) to (7), (9); 1988 s.16(4).
(5)	1984 s.5(8); 1988 s.16(4)(b), Sch.3 para.5(4)(b).
(6)	1984 ss.5(11), 12; 1988 s.16(4).
(7)	1988 s.23(1), (2).
82(1)	1913 s.3(1); 1971 Sch.8; 1974 Sch.3 para.2(3).
(2) to (4)	1913 s.3(2); 1971 Sch.8; 1974 Sch.3 para.2(3); 1975 Sch.16 Pt.IV para.2(2).
83(1)	1984 s.14(1), (2)(a).
(2)	1984 s.14(2)(b).
(3)	1984 s.14(3), (4).
84(1) to (3)	1913 s.5(1), Sch.; 1971 Sch.8; 1974 Sch.3 para.2(3); 1975 Sch.16 Pt.IV para.2(2).
(4), (5)	1913 s.5(2); 1971 Sch.8; 1974 Sch.3 para 2(3); 1984 ss.13(9), (10) "new resolution".
85(1), (2)	1913 s.6; 1971 Sch.8; 1974 Sch.3 para 2(3).
86(1) to (3)	1984 s.18(1) to (3).
87(1), (2)	1984 s.18(4), (6).
(3)	1984 s.18(5).
(4)	1984 s.18(3).
88(1)	drafting.
(2)	Wages Act 1986 (c.48) s.1(6); 1988 Sch.3 para.6(1).
(3), (4)	Wages Act 1986 (c.48) s.5(3A); 1988 Sch.3 para.6(3)
89(1)	1984 s.15(10).
(2)	1984 s.15(1), (2).
(3)	1984 ss.14(2)(a), 15(5).
(4)	1984 s.14(2)(c).
(5)	1984 s.15(9).
90(1), (2)	1984 s.15(3)(a), (b).
(3)	1984 s.15(4).
(4)	1984 s.16(1).

TRADE UNION AND LABOUR RELATIONS (CONSOLIDATION) ACT—*continued.*

Section of 1992 Act	Derivation
(5)	1984 s.16(2) to (4).
(6)	1984 s.16(5).
91(1), (2)	1984 s.15(6), (7)(a), (10).
(3)	1984 s.15(7)(b).
(4)	1984 s.15(8).
92	1913 s.4(2); 1971 Sch.8; 1974 Sch.3 para 2(3); 1975 Sch.16 Pt.IV para.2(2).
93(1)	1964 s.5(4); 1971 Sch.8; 1974 Sch.3 para.10(2).
(2)	1984 s.12(5).
(3)	drafting.
94(1), (2)	1984 s.13(7), (8).
(3)	1984 ss.9(1) "overseas member", 13(10) "overseas member".
95	1913 s.5A; 1975 Sch.16 Pt.IV para. 2(3); 1978 s.136(2)(a), Sch.16 para.2.
96	1984 s.19(2) "date of the ballot".
Part I, Chapter VII.	
97(1), (2)	1964 s.1(1)(a), (b); 1971 Sch.8; 1974 Sch.3 para.10(2).
(3)	1964 s.1(6); 1971 Sch.8; 1974 Sch.3 para.10(2).
(4)	1964 s.2(1); 1971 Sch.8; 1974 Sch.3 para.10(2).
98(1)	1964 s.1(1)(a), (b), (4)(a); 1971 Sch.8; 1974 Sch.3 para.10(2); 1975 Sch.16, Pt.IV, para.10(2).
(2)	1964 s.1(3), (4)(a); 1971 Sch.8; 1974 Sch.3 para.10(2); 1975 Sch.16, Pt.IV, para.10(2).
99(1)	1964 s.1(2)(d); 1971 Sch.8; 1974 Sch.3 para.10(2); 1975 Sch.16, Pt.IV, para.10(2).
(2), (3)	1964 s.1(3)(a), (b).
(4)	1964 s.1(3).
(5)	1964 s.1(4)(b); 1971 Sch.8; 1974 Sch.3 para.10(2); 1975 Sch.16, Pt.IV, para.10(2).
100(1)	1964 s.1(1), (2); 1971 Sch.8; 1974 Sch.3 para.10(2); 1975 Sch.16 Pt.IV para.10(2).
(2)	1964 s.2(2); 1971 Sch.8; 1974 Sch.3 para.10(2).
(3), (4)	1964 s.2(3); 1971 Sch.8; 1974 Sch.3 para.10(2).
101(1), (2)	1964 s.1(5); 1975 Sch.16, Pt.IV, para.10(2).
102(1) to (3)	1964 s.3; 1971 Sch.8; 1974 Sch.3 para.10(2).
103(1)	1964 s.4(1); 1971 Sch.8; 1974 Sch.3 para.10(2); 1975 Sch.16, Pt.IV, para.10(2).
(2)	1964 s.4(2), (10); 1975 Sch.16, Pt.IV, para.10(2).
(3)	1964 s.4(3), (5); 1971 Sch.8; 1974 Sch.3 para.10(2); 1975 Sch.16, Pt.IV, para.10(2).
(4)	1964 s.4(4); 1975 Sch.16, Pt.IV, para.10(2).
(5)	1964 s.4(7); 1975 Sch.16, Pt.IV, para.10(2).
104	1964 s.4(8); 1975 Sch.16 Pt.IV para.10(3); 1978 Sch.16 para.5; 1978 s.136(2)(b).
105(1)	1964 s.5(1); 1971 Sch.8; 1974 Sch.3 para.10(2).
(2), (3)	1964 s.5(3)(a), (b); 1971 Sch.8; 1974 Sch.3 para.10(2).
(4)	1964 s.5(2).

TRADE UNION AND LABOUR RELATIONS (CONSOLIDATION) ACT—*continued.*

Section of 1992 Act	Derivation
106(1)	1964 s.10(2); 1971 Sch.8; 1974 Sch.3 para.10(2).
(2)	1964 Sch.2 para.2(1); 1971 Sch.8; 1974 Sch.3 para.10(2); 1975 Sch.16 Pt.IV para.10(2).
(3)	1964 Sch.2 para.4; 1971 Sch.8; 1974 Sch.3 para.10(2); 1975 Sch.16 Pt.IV para.10(2).
(4)	1964 Sch.2 paras.2(2), 3.
(5)	1964 Sch.2 para.1; 1971 Sch.8; 1974 Sch.3 para.10(2).
107(1)	1964 s.6(1).
(2), (3)	1964 s.6(2); 1974 Sch.3 para.10(5); 1975 Sch.16 Pt.IV para.10(2).
(4)	1964 s.6(3).
108(1)	1964 s.7(1); Secretary of State for Employment and Productivity Order 1968 (S.I. 1968/729); 1975 Sch.16 Pt.IV para.10(2).
(2)	1964 s.7(2); 1975 Sch.16 Pt.IV para.10(2).
(3), (4)	1964 s.7(3), (4).
Part I, Chapter VIII.	
109(1)	1988 s.20(7)(a) to (d).
(2)	1990 s.10(1) to (3), (4)(b).
(3)	1988 s.20(7)(e), (8).
110(1)	1988 s.20(1).
(2), (3)	1988 s.20(4), (5).
(4)	1990 s.10(5).
(5)	1988 s.20(2)(b).
111(1)	1988 s.20(2)(a)
(2)	1988 s.20(3).
(3)	1988 s.21(3).
(4)	1988 s.21(2).
(5), (6)	1988 s.21(4), (5).
112(1), (2)	1990 s.11(1), (2).
113(1), (2)	1988 s.21(1)
114(1)	1988 s.20(3)
(2)	1988 s.20(6)
(3)	1988 s.21(6)
Part I, Chapter IX.	
115(1)	1980 s.1(1).
(2)	1980 s.1(2) to (3A); Funds for Trade Union Ballots Order 1982 (S.I. 1982/953) art.2; 1984 s.20(2), (3).
(3)	1980 s.1(4).
(4)	1980 s.1(5); 1984 s.20(4).
(5)	1980 s.1(7).
116(1)	1980 s.2(1), (3)(a).
(2)	1980 s.2(2); 1984 s.20(5).

TRADE UNION AND LABOUR RELATIONS (CONSOLIDATION) ACT—*continued.*

Section of 1992 Act	Derivation
(3)	1980 s.2(1), (3)(b); 1988 Sch.3 para.3(1)(a).
(4) to (6)	1980 s.2(4) to (6).
(7)	1980 s.2(8).
117(1)	1974 s.30(1) "special register body"; Companies Consolidation (Consequential Provisions) Act 1985 (c.9) Sch.2.
(2)	drafting.
(3)	1974 ss.2(1), (2), (5), 4; 1982 s.15(7) "rules".
(4)	1974 s.11(9); 1989 (c.40) s.124.
(5)	1984 s.1(1), (2), (6A), (6B), (7); 1988 s.12(1).
118(1), (2)	drafting.
(3)	1982 s.16(7).
(4)	1974 ss.10(1), 11(1).
(5)	1988 s.6(9)(b).
(6)	1984 s.7(1) to (3).
(7)	1913 s.3(5).
119	
"branch or section"	1984 s.9(1) "section"; 1988 s.32(1) "branch or section".
"executive"	1984 ss.1(5), 9(1), 19(1) "principal executive committee"; 1988 s.12(6) "principal executive committee".
"general secretary"	1984 s.1(6B)(b); 1988 s.12(1).
"officer"	1974 s.30(1) "officer"; 1975 Sch.16 Pt.III para.7(5).
"official"	1974 s.30(1) "official"; 1975 s.126(1) "official"; 1978 s.153(1); 1988 s.32(1).
"president"	1984 s.1(6B)(a); 1988 s.12(1).
"rules"	1988 s.32(1) "rules".
120	1964 s.10(5), (6); Industrial Relations (Northern Ireland) Order 1992 (S.I. 1992/807 (N.I.5)).
121	drafting.
Part II	
122	1913 s.2(1A); 1964 s.9(1) "employers' association"; 1974 s.28(1), Sch.3 paras.2(2), 10(8).
123(1)	1974 s.8(1), (2); 1975 Sch.16 Pt.III, para.1.
(2), (3)	1974 s.8(9); 1975 Sch.16 Pt.III, paras.1 and 4.
(4), (5), (6)	1974 s.8(10); 1975 Sch.16 Pt.III, paras.1 and 5.
124(1)	1974 s.8(3); 1975 Sch.16 Pt.III para.1.
(2)	1974 s.8(4); 1975 Sch.16 Pt.III para.1.
(3)	1974 s.8(3); 1975 Sch.16 Pt.III para.1.
(4)	1974 s.8(5); 1975 Sch.16 Pt.III para.1.
125(1), (2)	1974 s.8(6); 1975 Sch.16 Pt.III, para.1.
(3)	1974 s.8(6A); 1975 Sch.16 Pt.III, paras.1 and 2.
126(1), (2)	1974 s.8(7); 1975 Sch.16 Pt.III, para.3.
(3)	1974 s.8(7); 1975 Sch.16 Pt.III para.3; 1978 s.136(3), Sch.16 para.23(3).
127(1)	1974 s.3(1).

TRADE UNION AND LABOUR RELATIONS (CONSOLIDATION) ACT—*continued.*

Section of 1992 Act	Derivation
(2)	1974 s.3(2)(a),(c),(d).
(3)	1974 s.3(4).
128(1), (2)	1974 s.3(5).
129(1)	1974 ss.3(2)(b), 4(1) to (8).
(2)	drafting
(3)	Friendly Societies Act 1896 (c.25) s.22(2), (3); Industrial Assurance and Friendly Societies Act 1948 (c.39) ss.6(1), (2), 16(4), 21(1)(d); Friendly Societies Act 1974 (c.46) Sch.9 paras.1, 12; 1974 s.9(1), Sch.3 para.5.
130(1)	1982 s.17(1).
(2)	1982 s.17(2)(a),(b),(c).
131(1)	1974 ss.10(1) to (4), 11(1) to (8), 12(1) to (5), Sch.2; Criminal Justice Act 1982 (c.48) ss.38, 46.
(2)	1974 s.11(9); 1989 (c.40) s.124.
132	1913 s.6A; 1974 Sch.3 para.2(5); 1984 s.19(4); 1988 ss.15(8), 16(5).
133	1964 s.1(1A); 1974 Sch.3 para.10(3).
134(1)	1964 ss.1(1A), 6(1); 1974 Sch.3 para.10(3).
(2), (3)	1964 s.6(2); 1974 Sch.3 para.10(5); 1975 Sch.16 Pt.IV para.10(2).
(4)	1964 ss.1(1A), 6(3); 1974 Sch.3 para.10(3).
(5)	1964 s.7(1) to (4); Secretary of State for Employment and Productivity Order 1968 (S.I. 1968/729); 1975 Sch.16 Pt.IV para.10(2).
135(1), (2)	drafting.
(3)	1974 ss.10(1), 11(1).
(4)	1913 s.3(5).
136	1974 s.30(1) "officer"; 1975 Sch.16 Pt.III para.7(5).
Part III 137(1) to (6)	1990 s.1(1) to (6).
(7)	1990 s.3(2).
(8)	1990 s.1(7).
138(1) to (5)	1990 s.2(1) to (5).
139(1) to (3)	1990 Sch.1 para.3(1) to (3).
140(1) to (4)	1990 Sch.1 para.5(1) to (4).
141(1) to (3)	1990 Sch.1 para.6(1) to (3).
142(1) to (4)	1990 Sch.1 para.7(1) to (4).
143(1)	1990 s.3(1).
(2), (3)	1990 s.3(3), (4).
(4)	1990 Sch.1 para.2(1), (2).
144	1982 s.12(1).

TRADE UNION AND LABOUR RELATIONS (CONSOLIDATION) ACT—*continued.*

Section of 1992 Act	Derivation
145(1)	1982 s.12(2), (7); drafting.
(2)	1982 s.12(2)(a), (4).
(3)	1982 s.12(2)(c), (3), (6).
(4)	1982 s.12(2)(b), (5).
(5)	1982 s.12(7).
146(1)	1978 s.23(1); 1982 s.10(4).
(2)	1978 s.23(2).
(3), (4)	1978 s.23(1A), (1B); 1982 s.10(3).
(5)	1978 s.24(1).
147	1978 s.24(2).
148(1), (2)	1978 s.25(1), (2).
149(1)	1978 s.24(3).
(2) to (4)	1978 s.26(1) to (3).
(5)	1978 ss.25(2), 26(4).
(6)	1978 s.26(5).
150(1)	1978 s.26A(1); 1982 s.11.
(2)	1978 ss.24(3), 26A(2); 1982 s.11.
(3)	1978 s.26A(3); 1982 s.11.
151(1)	1978 s.23(7); 1988 Sch.3 para.2(1).
(2)	1978 s.129.
152(1), (2)	1978 s.58(1), (2); 1982 s.3.
(3), (4)	1978 s.58(13), (14); 1988 Sch.3 para.2(2)(a).
153	1978 s.59; 1982 Sch.3 para.17.
154	1978 ss.64(3), 64A(2); 1980 s.8; 1982 Sch.3 paras.19, 20.
155(1)	1978 s.72A(1), (2); 1982 s.6.
(2)	1978 s.72A(2)(a), (3); 1982 s.6.
(3)	1978 s.72A(2)(b), (c); 1982 s.6.
156(1)	1978 s.73(4A); 1982 s.4(1); Unfair Dismissal (Increase of Limits of Basic and Special Awards) Order 1992 (S.I. 1992/313).
(2)	1978 s.73(7C); 1982 s.4(2).
157(1)	1978 s.72(c) and closing words; 1982 s.5(2).
(2)	1978 s.71(2)(b); 1982 s.5(1).
158(1) to (6)	1978 s.75A(1) to (6); 1982 s.5(3); Unfair Dismissal (Increase of Limits of Basic and Special Awards) Order 1992 (S.I. 1992/313).
159(1)	1978 ss.73(4B), 75A(7), 154(1); 1982 ss.4(1), 5(3).
(2)	1978 s.154(3).
(3)	1978 ss.73(4B), 75A(7); 1982 ss.4(1), 5(3).
160(1) to (3)	1978 s.76A(1) to (3); 1982 s.7.
161(1)	1978 s.77(1); 1982 s.8(1).

TRADE UNION AND LABOUR RELATIONS (CONSOLIDATION) ACT—*continued.*

Section of 1992 Act	Derivation
(2), (3)	1978 s.77(2); 1982 Sch.3 para.24(1).
(4) to (6)	1978 s.77(10), (11).
162(1)	1978 s.77(3); 1982 Sch.3 para.24(2).
(2), (3)	1978 s.77(3), (3A); 1982 s.8(2).
(4)	1978 s.77(4).
163(1), (2)	1978 s.77(5); 1982 Sch.3 para.24(3).
(3) to (6)	1978 s.77(6) to (9).
164(1)	1978 s.78(1).
(2), (3)	1978 s.78(2)
(4) to (7)	1978 s.78(3) to (6)
165(1), (2)	1978 s.79(1).
166(1), (2)	1978 s.79(2)
(3) to (5)	1978 s.79(3)
167(1) to (3)	drafting.
168(1)	1978 s.27(1)(a); 1989 s.14(a).
(2)	1978 s.27(1)(b); 1989 s.14(b).
(3)	1978 s.27(2).
(4)	1978 s.27(7).
169(1)	1978 s.27(3).
(2)	1978 s.27(3)(a).
(3)	1978 s.27(3)(b), (4).
(4)	1978 s.27(5), (6).
(5)	1978 s.27(7).
170(1)	1978 s.28(1), (2).
(2) to (4)	1978 s.28(2) to (4).
171	1978 s.30(1).
172(1), (2)	1978 s.30(2).
(3)	1978 s.30(3).
173(1)	1978 s.32(1); 1989 Sch.6 para.19.
(2)	1978 s.129.
174(1)	1980 s.4(1), (2).
(2), (3)	1974 s.30(1) "union membership agreement", (5A); 1976 s.3(3), (4); 1980 s.4(10).
(4)	1980 s.4(9).
(5), (6)	1980 s.4(4), (5).
175	1980 s.4(6).
176(1)	1980 s.4(7).
(2)	1980 s.5(1), (2).
(3)	1980 s.5(3).
(4)	1980 s.5(4)(a), (7).
(5)	1980 s.5(4)(b), (8).

TRADE UNION AND LABOUR RELATIONS (CONSOLIDATION) ACT—*continued.*

Section of 1992 Act	Derivation
(6), (7)	1980 s.5(5), (6).
(8)	1980 s.5(8A); 1988 Sch.3 para.3(2).
177(1)	1980 s.4(10).
(2), (3)	1980 s.4(3).
Part IV.	
178(1), (2)	1974 ss.29(1), 30(1) "collective agreement"; 1975 s.126(1) "collective agreement", "collective bargaining"; 1978 s.153(1).
(3)	1975 s.126(1) "recognition"; 1978 s.32(2); 1980 Sch.1 para.6; 1989 Sch.6 para.19..
179(1), (2)	1974 s.18(1), (2).
(3), (4)	1974 s.18(3).
180(1), (2)	1974 s.18(4).
(3)	1974 s.18(5).
181(1), (2)	1975 s.17(1), (2)(a).
(3) to (5)	1975 s.17(3) to (5).
182(1), (2)	1975 s.18(1), (2).
183(1)	1975 s.19(1).
(2)	1975 s.19(2), (3).
(3) to (6)	1975 s.19(4) to (7).
184(1) to (4)	1975 s.20(1) to (4).
185(1), (2)	1975 s.21(1), (2).
(3)	1975 s.21(3), (4).
(4)	1975 s.21(5)(a).
(5) to (7)	1975 s.21(6) to (8).
186	1982 s.13(1).
187(1)	1982 s.13(1) to (3).
(2)	1982 ss.12(2), 13(2).
(3)	1982 s.13(4).
188(1)	1975 s.99(1).
(2)	1975 s.99(3); Employment Protection (Handling of Redundancies) Variation Order 1979 (S.I. 1979/958).
(3) to (8)	1975 s.99(4) to (9).
189(1)	1975 s.101(1), (7).
(2) to (5)	1975 s.101(3) to (6).
(6)	1975 s.101(2).
190(1) to (3)	1975 s.102(1) to (3).
(4)	1975 s.102(4); 1978 Sch.16 para.23(4).
(5)	1975 s.106(3); 1978 Sch.16 para.23(6).
(6)	1975 Sch.12 para.7.
191(1) to (7)	1975 s.102(5) to (11).

TRADE UNION AND LABOUR RELATIONS (CONSOLIDATION) ACT— *continued.*

Section of 1992 Act	Derivation
192(1) to (3)	1975 s.103(1) to (3).
(4)	1975 s.108(1).
193(1), (2)	1975 s.100(1); Employment Protection (Handling of Redundancies) Variation Order 1979 (S.I. 1979/958).
(3), (4)	1975 s.100(2), (3).
(5)	1975 s.100(5).
(6)	1975 s.100(1), (4).
(7)	1975 s.100(6).
194(1)	1975 s.105(1); Criminal Justice Act 1982 (c.48) s.38.
(2)	1975 s.105(2), (3).
(3), (4)	1975 s.117(1), (2)
195(1)	1975 s.126(6).
(2)	1975 s.126(1) "business", (7).
(3)	1975 s.106(2).
196	1975 s.99(2).
197(1), (2)	1975 s.106(4), (5).
198(1), (2)	1975 s.107(1).
(3) to (5)	1975 s.107(2) to (4).
199(1)	1975 s.6(1).
(2), (3)	1975 s.6(2); 1978 Sch.16 para.23(2).
(4)	1975 s.6(10).
200(1)	1975 s.6(3), (10).
(2), (3)	1975 s.6(4), (5).
(4)	1975 s.6(6) to (8).
(5)	1975 s.6(5), (8), (9).
201(1)	1990 s.12(1), (2)(b).
(2), (3)	1990 s.12(4), (5).
(4)	1990 s.12(6), (9).
202(1)	1990 s.12(7), (9).
(2)	1990 s.12(8).
(3)	1990 s.12(7)(b).
203(1)	1980 s.3(1); 1988 s.18(1).
(2)	1980 s.3(6).
204(1)	1980 s.3(2), (3).
(2)	1980 s.3(4).
(3), (4)	1980 s.3(5).
205(1)	1990 s.12(1), (2)(a).
(2)	1990 s.12(3).
(3)	1990 s.12(5).
(4)	1990 s.12(6), (9).
206(1), (2)	1990 s.12(7), (9).

TRADE UNION AND LABOUR RELATIONS (CONSOLIDATION) ACT—*continued.*

Section of 1992 Act	Derivation
207(1)	1975 s.6(11); 1980 s.3(8).
(2)	1975 s.6(11).
(3)	1980 s.3(8).
208(1)	1975 s.6(10A); 1980 Sch.1 para.4.
(2)	1980 s.3(7).
(3)	1975 s.6(10A); 1980 s.3(7), Sch.1 para.4.
209	1975 s.1(2).
210(1) to (3)	1975 s.2(1) to (3).
211	1975 s.2(4).
212(1)	1975 s.3(1).
(2), (3)	1975 s.3(2).
(4)	1975 s.3(3), (4), (6).
(5)	1975 s.3(5).
213(1), (2)	1975 s.4(1).
(3)	1975 s.4(2).
214(1), (2)	1975 s.5(1), (2).
215(1)	1919 s.4(1).
(2)	1919 ss.4(1), 5(1).
(3), (4)	1919 s.5(2), (3).
(5)	1919 s.5(3), proviso.
(6)	1919 s.13.
216(1), (2)	1919 s.4(2), (3).
(3)	1919 s.4(1).
(4), (5)	1919 s.4(4), (5).
(6)	1919 s.9.
217	Administration of Justice (Scotland) Act 1972 (c.59) s.3(3); 1975 s.10(2); 1982 Sch.3 para.11(a), (b).
218(1) to (5)	1919 s.8 "trade dispute"; 1975 ss.126(1) "trade dispute", 126A(1) to (4), (6); 1982 Sch.3 paras.10, 13(2), (3).
Part V	
219(1)	1974 s.13(1); 1976 s.3(2).
(2)	1974 s.13(4).
(3)	1980 s.16(2).
(4)	drafting.
220(1), (2)	1974 s.15(1), (2); 1980 s.16(1).
(3)	1974 s.15(3); 1980 s.16(1); 1982 Sch.3 para.12.
(4)	1974 s.15(4); 1980 s.16(1).
221(1), (2)	1974 s.17(1), (2); 1975 Sch.16 Pt.III para.6.
222(1), (2)	1988 s.10(1), (2).

TRADE UNION AND LABOUR RELATIONS (CONSOLIDATION) ACT—*continued.*

Section of 1992 Act	Derivation
(3)	1982 s.14(1).
(4)	1988 s.10(3)(a).
(5)	1988 s.10(1), (2), (3)(b).
223	1990 s.9(2), (3).
224(1) to (6)	1990 s.4(1) to (6).
225(1)	1982 s.14(1).
(2)	1982 s.14(2), (3).
226(1)	1984 s.10(1); 1990 Sch.2 para.2(2).
(2)	1984 s.10(3), (4), (4A); 1988 Sch.3 para.5(7); 1990 Sch.2 para.2(3), (5), (6).
(3)	1984 s.10(3A); 1988 s.17(2); 1990 Sch.2 para.2(4).
(4)	1984 s.11(11); 1988 s.1(6), Sch.3 para.5(8)(f).
227(1)	1984 s.11(1); 1988 Sch.3 para.5(8)(a).
(2)	1984 s.11(2); 1988 Sch.3 para.5(8)(b).
228(1)	1984 s.11(1A); 1988 s.17(1).
(2)	1984 s.11(1B)(a); 1988 s.17(1).
(3)	1984 s.11(1B)(b), (c); 1988 s.17(1).
229(1)	1984 s.11(3).
(2)	1984 s.11(4); 1988 Sch.3 para.5(8)(d).
(3)	1984 s.11(4A); 1990 s.7(1).
(4)	1984 s.11(3); 1988 Sch.3 para.5(8)(c).
230(1)	1984 s.11(5).
(2)	1984 s.11(6)(a).
(3)	1984 s.11(6)(b).
(4)	1984 s.11(7).
231	1984 s.11(8).
232(1), (2)	1984 s.11(9), (10).
(3)	1984 ss.9(1), 11(11) "overseas member".
(4), (5)	1990 s.5(2), (3).
233(1)	1990 s.7(2).
(2)	1990 s.7(5) "specified person".
(3), (4)	1990 s.7(3), (4).
234(1) to (6)	1990 s.8(1) to (6).
235	1990 s.5(1).
236	1974 s.16.
237(1) to (6)	1978 s.62A(1) to (6); 1990 s.9(1).
238(1)	1978 s.62(1), (5); 1982 s.9(4); 1990 Sch.2 para.1(2).
(2)	1978 s.62(2); 1982 s.9(2).
(3)	1978 s.62(4)(b), (5); 1982 s.9(3), Sch.3 para.18; 1990 Sch.2 para.1(2).
(4)	1978 s.62(4)(c).

TRADE UNION AND LABOUR RELATIONS (CONSOLIDATION) ACT—*continued.*

Section of 1992 Act	Derivation
(5)	1978 s.62(4)(a).
239(1)	drafting.
(2)	1978 s.67(3); 1982 s.9(5).
(3)	1978 s.62(3); 1982 s.9(4).
240(1)	1875 s.5; Merchant Shipping Act 1970 (c.36) s.42(1).
(2)	Malicious Damage Act 1861 (c.97) s.58; 1875 s.15.
(3)	1875 s.5; Criminal Procedure (Scotland) Act 1975 (c.21) s.289C(4), (5), (8); Criminal Law Act 1977 (c.45) s.31(5), (6), (9), Sch.11 para.5.; Criminal Justice Act 1982 (c.48) ss.37, 46.
(4)	1875 s.16; Merchant Shipping Act 1970 (c.36) Sch.3 para.1.
241(1)	1875 s.7(1).
(2)	1875 s.7(1); Public Order Act 1986 (c.64) Sch.2 para.1(1).
(3)	1875 s.7(1); Public Order Act 1986 (c.64) Sch.2 para.1(2).
242(1)	Criminal Law Act 1977 (c.45) s.1(3).
(2)	Criminal Law Act 1977 (c.45) s.65(10).
243(1) to (4)	1875 s.3; 1974 Sch.3 para.1.
(5)	drafting.
244(1)	1974 s.29(1); 1982 s.18(2).
(2)	1974 s.29(2); 1982 s.18(3).
(3)	1974 s.29(3); 1982 s.18(4).
(4)	1974 s.29(5).
(5)	1974 s.29(6); 1982 s.18(6).
245	1988 s.30(1).
246	
"date of the ballot"	1984 s.10(5) "date of the ballot".
"place of work"	1984 s.10(5) "place of work"; 1988 s.17(3).
"strike"	1984 s.11(11) "strike".
"working hours"	1984 s.11(11) "working hours"; 1990 s.5(1).
Part VI	
247(1)	1975 s.1(1).
(2)	1975 Sch.1 para.1.
(3), (4)	1975 Sch.1 para.11(1), (2).
(5)	1975 Sch.1 para.12.
(6)	1975 Sch.1 para.9.
248(1)	1975 Sch.1 paras.1, 2(1).
(2)	1975 Sch.1 para.2(2).
(3)	1975 Sch.1 para.2(4).
(4)	1975 Sch.1 para.2(3).
(5), (6)	1975 Sch.1 para.4(1), (2).
(7)	1975 Sch.1 para.5.
249(1)	1975 Sch.1 para.3(1).
(2)	1975 Sch.1 paras.2(1),(3) and 3(3),(4).

TRADE UNION AND LABOUR RELATIONS (CONSOLIDATION) ACT—*continued.*

Section of 1992 Act	Derivation
(3)	1975 Sch.1 para.3(2).
(4)	1975 Sch.1 para.3(5),(6).
(5)	1975 Sch.1 para.3(7) to (9); Bankruptcy (Scotland) Act 1985 (c.66) s.75(10).
250(1)	1975 Sch.1 para.28(a).
(2)	1975 Sch.1 para.30.
(3)	1975 Sch.1 para.31.
(4)	1975 Sch.1 paras.28, 30, 31; Transfer of Functions (Minister for the Civil Service and Treasury) Order 1981 (S.I. 1981/1670).
251(1)	1975 Sch.1 para.6.
(2)	1975 Sch.1 para.7.
(3)	1975 Sch.1 paras.6, 7; Transfer of Functions (Minister for the Civil Service and Treasury) Order 1981 (S.I. 1981/1670).
(4)	1975 Sch.1 para.32; Transfer of Functions (Minister for the Civil Service and Treasury) Order 1981 (S.I. 1981/1670).
(5)	1975 Sch.1 para.10(1),(2).
252(1)	1975 Sch.1 para.33.
(2)	1975 Sch.1 para.29; Transfer of Functions (Minister for the Civil Service and Treasury) Order 1981 (S.I. 1981/1670).
253(1)	1975 Sch.1 para.13(1), (3).
(2)	1975 Sch.1 paras.34, 35(1).
(3), (4)	1975 Sch.1 para.35(2).
254(1), (2)	1975 s.7(1).
(3)	1975 s.7(4).
(4)	1964 s.8; 1974 Sch.3 para.10(7); 1975 s.7(5), (6).
(5)	1975 Sch.1 para.8.
(6)	1980 s.1(6).
255(1)	1975 Sch.1 para.28(c).
(2)	1975 Sch.1 para.30.
(3)	1975 Sch.1 para.31.
(4)	1975 Sch.1 paras.28, 30, 31; Transfer of Functions (Minister for the Civil Service and Treasury) Order 1981 (S.I. 1981/1670).
256(1), (2)	1988 s.22(1).
(3)	1988 s.22(2).
(4)	1975 Sch.1 para.32A; 1988 s.22(3).
257(1), (2)	1975 s.9(1), (2).
258(1)	1975 Sch.1 para.13(2), (3).
(2)	1975 Sch.1 para.35(1).
259(1)	1975 s.10(1).
(2)	1975 Sch.1 para.27.
(3)	1975 Sch.1 para.8.
260(1) to (3)	1975 Sch.1 para.14(1) to (3).
(4), (5)	1975 Sch.1 para.16(1), (2).
(6)	1975 Sch.1 para.21.

TRADE UNION AND LABOUR RELATIONS (CONSOLIDATION) ACT—*continued.*

Section of 1992 Act	Derivation
261(1) to (4)	1975 Sch.1 para.15(1) to (4).
(5)	1975 Sch.1 para.15(5), (6); Bankruptcy (Scotland) Act 1985 (c.66) s.75(10).
(6)	1975 Sch.1 para.15(7).
262(1)	1975 Sch.1 para.28(b).
(2)	1975 Sch.1 para.30.
(3)	1975 Sch.1 para.31.
(4)	1975 Sch.1 paras.28, 30, 31; Transfer of Functions (Minister for the Civil Service and Treasury) Order 1981 (S.I. 1981/1670).
263(1)	1975 Sch.1 para.17(1), (2).
(2)	1975 Sch.1 para.17(3).
(3)	1975 Sch.1 para.18.
(4)	1975 Sch.1 para.19.
(5)	1975 Sch.1 para.20.
(6)	Administration of Justice (Scotland) Act 1972 (c.59) s.3(3); 1975 s.10(2), Sch.1 para.26.
264(1)	1975 Sch.1 para.22.
(2)	1975 Sch.1 para.23(1), (2).
(3)	1975 Sch.1 para.24.
265(1)	1975 Sch.1 paras.13(1), 25.
(2)	1975 Sch.1 para.35(1).
266(1), (2)	1988 s.19(1).
(3)	1988 Sch.1 para.11.
(4)	1988 Sch.1 para.4(1), (2).
(5)	1988 s.19(3).
267(1)	1988 Sch.1 para.1(3).
(2), (3)	1988 Sch.1 para.1(1), (2).
268 (1) to (5)	1988 Sch.1 para.2(1) to (5).
269(1)	1988 Sch.1 para.3(1), (2).
(2), (3)	1988 Sch.1 para.5(1), (2).
(4)	1988 Sch.1 para.6.
270(1)	1988 Sch.1 para.7(1).
(2)	1988 Sch.1 para.8(1).
(3)	1988 Sch.1 paras.7(2), 8(2).
271(1)	1988 Sch.1 para.10(1), (2).
(2)	1988 Sch.1 para.9(1)(a), (b).
(3)	1988 Sch.1 para.9(1)(c).
(4)	1988 Sch.1 para.9(2).
272	1975 Sch.1 para.35(3); 1988 Sch.1 para.14.
Part VII	
273(1)	1919 s.10(1); 1974 Sch.1 para.33(1); 1975 s.121(1), Sch.16 Pt.IV para.3; 1978 s.138(1); 1988 s.30(3); 1990 Sch.1 para.11(1).
(2)	1975 s.121(1); 1980 Sch.1 para.5; 1984 s.18(7).

TRADE UNION AND LABOUR RELATIONS (CONSOLIDATION) ACT—*continued.*

Section of 1992 Act	Derivation
(3)	1919 s.10(2); 1974 Sch.1 para.33(2); 1975 s.121(2), Sch.16 Pt.III para.33, Pt.IV para.3; 1978 s.138(2); 1988 s.30(3); 1990 Sch.1 para.11(2).
(4)	1974 Sch.1 para.33(3); 1975 s.121(7), Sch.16 Pt.III para.33; 1978 s.138(4), Sch.16 para.23(11).
(5)	1990 Sch.1 para.13.
(6)	drafting.
274(1)	1919 s.10(3); 1974 Sch.1 para.33(2); 1975 s.121(3), Sch.16 Pt.IV para.3; Armed Forces Act 1981 (c.55) Sch.3 para.1(1).
(2)	1919 s.10(3); 1974 Sch.1 para.33(4)(b); 1975 s.121(3), Sch.16 Pt.IV para.3; Interpretation Act 1978 (c.30) s.17(2)(a); Reserve Forces Act 1980 (c.9) Sch.9 para.15; 1990 Sch.1 para.11(3).
275(1), (2)	1919 s.10(4); 1974 Sch.1 para.33(5); 1975 s.121(4), Sch.16 Pt.IV para.3; 1978 s.138(4); 1990 Sch.1 para.11(4).
276(1)	1990 Sch.1 para.18.
(2)	1988 s.30(2).
277(1), (2)	1990 Sch.1 para.12(1), (2).
(3)	1990 Sch.1 para.12(4).
(4)	1990 Sch.1 para.13.
(5), (6)	1990 Sch.1 para.12(5), (6)
278(1), (2)	1975 ss.121(1), 122(1); 1978 ss.138(1), 139(1); 1990 Sch.1 para.12(1).
(3)	1975 s.122(4); 1978 s.139(3); 1990 Sch.1 para.12(3).
(4)	1975 s.122(1); 1978 s.138(1); 1990 Sch.1 para.12(3).
(5)	1990 Sch.1 para.13.
(6)	1975 s.122(5) to (8); House of Commons (Administration) Act 1978 (c.36) Sch.2 para.5; 1978 s.139(4) to (9); 1990 Sch.1 para.12(3).
279	1974 s.30(2); 1975 s.126(1) "worker"; National Health Service Act 1977 (c.49) Sch.15 para.62; National Health Service (Scotland) Act 1978 (c.29) Sch.16 para.39; Health Services Act 1980 (c.53) Sch.1 para.25; Family Practitioner Committees (Consequential Modifications) Order 1985 (S.I. 1985/39) art.7(3,), (9), (11), (13); National Health Service and Community Care Act 1990 (c.19) s.2(1)(b).
280(1)	1974 s.30(1) "employee", "worker"; 1975 s.126(1) "employee, "worker"; 1978 s.146(2); 1990 Sch.1 para.14.
(2)	1974 s.30(1) "police service"; 1978 s.146(3); 1990 Sch.1 para.14.
281(1) to (4)	1978 s.146(4) to (7).
(5)	1978 ss.146(8), 151, Sch.13; 1982 Sch.2 para.8(5).
(6)	1978 s.152, Sch.14 Pt.I.
282(1), (2)	1975 s.119(7); 1982 Sch.2 para.6(1).
283(1)	1975 s.119(12)
(2)	1975 s.119(14).
284	1975 s.119(4); 1978 s.144(2); 1990 Sch.1 para.16(3).
285(1)	1975 s.119(5); 1978 s.141(2); 1990 Sch.1 para.15.
(2)	1975 s.119(6); 1978 s.141(5); 1990 Sch.1 para.16(1), (2).

TRADE UNION AND LABOUR RELATIONS (CONSOLIDATION) ACT—*continued.*

Section of 1992 Act	Derivation
286(1), (2)	1975 s.119(15); 1978 s.149(1), (2).
(3)	1975 s.123(3); 1978 s.154(3).
(4)	1975 s.119(16); 1978 s.149(4).
287(1)	1975 s.127(2); 1978 s.137(2); Employment (Continental Shelf) Act 1978 (c.46) s.1(1); drafting.
(2)	1975 s.127(1)(e) to (fg); 1978 s.137(1); 1980 Sch.1 para.7; 1982 Sch.3 para.13(4); 1990 Sch.1 para.17.
(3)	1975 s.127(3); 1978 s.137(3).
(4)	1975 s.127(4); 1978 s.137(4).
(5)	1978 s.137(5); Employment (Continental Shelf) Act 1978 (c.46) s.2; drafting.
288(1)	1974 Sch.1 para.32(1); 1975 s.118(1); 1978 s.140(1); 1980 s.4(11); 1988 s.4(7); 1990 Sch.1 para.10(1).
(2)	1978 s.140(2)(d), (e), (g); 1980 s.4(11); 1990 Sch.1 para.10(2).
(3)	1975 s.118(2)(a), (d).
289	1974 s.30(6); 1975 s.126(8); 1978 s.153(5).
290	1978 s.133(1); 1980 Sch.1 para.17; 1988 Sch.3 para.2(3); 1990 Sch.1 para.4.
291(1)	1980 s.4(8).
(2)	1978 s.136(1)(c), (e), (g); 1980 ss.2(7), 5(9); 1988 ss.4(5), 5(10); 1990 Sch.1 para.8.
(3)	Tribunals and Inquiries Act 1971 (c.62) s.13(1A); 1978 s.136(5), Sch.16 para.11; 1980 Sch.1 para.19; 1988 Sch.3 para.2(4).
292(1)	1975 Sch.12 para.1; 1978 Sch.12 para.1..
(2)	1975 Sch.12 para.2; 1978 Sch.12 para.2.
(3)	1975 Sch.12 para.3(1), (2); 1978 Sch.12 para.3(1), (2).
(4)	1975 Sch.12 para.5; 1978 Sch.12 para.5.
(5)	1975 Sch.12 para.6; 1978 Sch.12 para.6.
293(1)	drafting.
(2)	1975 s.123(3); 1978 s.154(3).
(3)	1975 s.123(2); 1978 s.154(2).
294(1)	1975 s.128(1); 1978 s.157(1).
(2)	1975 s.128(3); 1978 s.157(3).
(3)	1975 s.123(3); 1978 s.154(3).
(4)	1975 s.128(3); 1978 s.157(3).
(5)	1975 s.128(4); 1978 s.157(4).
(6)	1975 s.123(1), (2); 1978 s.154(1), (2).
295(1) "contract of employment"	1974 s.30(1); 1978 s.153(1); 1988 s.32(1).
"employee"	1974 s.30(1); 1975 s.126(1); 1978 s.153(1).
"employer"	1974 s.30(1) "employer" para.(a); 1975 s.126(1); 1978 s.153(1); 1988 s.32(1).
(2)	drafting.
296(1)	1919 s.8 "worker"; 1974 s.30(1) "worker"; 1975 s.126(1); 1982 Sch.3 para.10; 1988 s.32(1).
(2)	1974 s.30(1) "employer" para.(b); 1975 s.126(1); 1988 s.32(1).

TRADE UNION AND LABOUR RELATIONS (CONSOLIDATION) ACT—*continued.*

Section of 1992 Act	Derivation
297	1974 s.30(5); 1975 s.126(1) "associated employer".
298 "act" and "action" "contravention" "dismiss", &c. "post" "tort"	 1974 s.30(1) "act" and "action"; 1978 s.153(1). 1988 s.32(1) "contravention". 1975 s.126(1); 1978 s.153(1) "effective date of termination", Sch.16 para.23(13). 1913 s.4(1F); 1980 s.2(9); 1984 ss.9(1), 11(11) "post", 13(2); 1988 s.13(6). 1974 s.30(1) "tort"; 1980 s.16(3); 1982 s.19(2).
299	drafting.
300(1) to (3)	drafting.
301(1) (2)(a) (b) (c), (d) (e), (f) (3)	drafting 1974 s.31(5). 1984 s.22(6); 1988 s.34(6); Industrial Relations (Northern Ireland) Order 1992 (S.I. 1992/807 (N.I.5)) art.67(2). 1975 s.129(6); 1978 s.160(3); 1982 s.22(5). drafting. drafting; 1964 s.10(3).
302	drafting.
303	drafting.

TRADE UNION AND LABOUR RELATIONS CONSOLIDATION ACT(c. 52)

TABLE OF DESTINATIONS

Notes:—
1. This Table shows the destination of the provisions proposed to be repealed by the consolidation.

2. The following abbreviations are used in the Table:—

1875	—	Conspiracy and Protection of Property Act 1875 (c. 86).
1913	—	Trade Union Act 1913 (2 & 3 Geo.5 c. 30).
1919	—	Industrial Courts Act 1919 (c. 69).
1964	—	Trade Union (Amalgamations, &c.) Act 1964 (c. 24).
1971	—	Industrial Relations Act 1971 (c. 72).
1974	—	Trade Union and Labour Relations Act 1974 (c. 52).
1975	—	Employment Protection Act 1975 (c. 71).
1976	—	Trade Union and Labour Relations (Amendment) Act 1976 (c. 7).
1978	—	Employment Protection (Consolidation) Act 1978 (c. 44).
1980	—	Employment Act 1980 (c. 42).
1982	—	Employment Act 1982 (c. 46).
1984	—	Trade Union Act 1984 (c. 49).
1988	—	Employment Act 1988 (c. 19).
1989	—	Employment Act 1989 (c. 38).
1990	—	Employment Act 1990 (c. 38).

3. The Table does not give details of amendments made by the Trade Disputes and Trade Unions Act 1927 (c. 22) and undone by the Trade Disputes and Trade Unions Act 1946 (c. 52), or of amendments made by the Industrial Relations Act 1971 (c. 72) and undone by the Trade Union and Labour Relations Act 1974 (c. 52).

Existing provision	Subject matter	Section of 1992 Act	Remarks
	CONSPIRACY AND PROTECTION OF PROPERTY ACT 1875 (c.86)		
3	Amendment of law as to conspiracy in trade disputes.	243(1) to (4)	Amended Trade Disputes Act 1906 (c. 47) s.1, 1974 Sch. 3, para. 1; repealed in part Trade Disputes Act 1906 (c. 47) s. 5(1), 1971 Sch. 9; repealed (EW) Criminal Law Act 1977 (c. 45) Sch. 13.
5	Breach of contract involving injury to persons or property.	240(1), (3)	Repealed in part Criminal Law Act 1977 (c. 45) Sch. 13; words ceased to have effect (EW) Criminal Justice Act 1948 (c. 58) s. 1(2), (S) Criminal Procedure (Scotland) Act 1975 (c. 21) s. 221(2).
7	Penalty for intimidation or annoyance, by violence or otherwise.	241(1) to (3)	Repealed in part Trade Disputes Act 1906 (c. 47) s. 2(2), Criminal Law Act 1977 (c. 45) Sch. 13; words ceased to have effect (EW) Criminal Justice Act 1948 (c. 58) s. 1(2), (S) Criminal Procedure (Scotland) Act 1975 (c. 21) s. 221(2); amended Public Order Act 1986 (c. 64) Sch. 2 para. 1(1).
15	Meaning of "maliciously".	240(2)	Applies Malicious Damage Act 1861 (c. 97) s.58.

TRADE UNION AND LABOUR RELATIONS CONSOLIDATION ACT—*continued.*

Existing provision	Subject matter	Section of 1992 Act	Remarks
	CONSPIRACY AND PROTECTION OF PROPERTY ACT 1875 (c.86)—*continued.*		
16	Saving as to sea service.	241(4)	Substituted Merchant Shipping Act 1970 (c. 36) Sch. 3 para. 1.
	FRIENDLY SOCIETIES ACT 1896 (c. 25)		
22(2), (3)	Contributions to medical societies.	19(3)	Repealed in part and amended Friendly Societies Act 1974 (c. 46) Sch. 9 para. 1, Sch. 11.
	TRADE UNION ACT 1913 (c. 30)		
1	Amendment of law as to objects and powers of trade unions.		Repealed 1971 Sch. 9; 1984 s. 17(3).
2(1)	Definition of "trade union" and "employers' association".	1	Subs. (1), (1A) substituted 1974 Sch. 3 para. 2(2).
(1A)		122	
(2) to (5)		—	Repealed 1971 Sch. 9.
3(1)	Restriction on application of funds for certain political purposes.	71(1), (2), 73(1), 82(1)	Repealed in part 1974 Sch. 5; amended 1975 Sch. 16, Pt. IV para. 2(2).
(2)		82(2) to (4)	Amended 1975 Sch. 16, Pt. IV para. 2(2); repealed in part 1975 Sch. 18.
(3) to (3C)		72(1) to (4)	Substituted 1984 s. 17(1)
(4)		73(2)	
(5)		118(7)	
4(1)	Approval of rules.	74(1), (3)	Repealed in part 1974 Sch. 5; amended 1975 Sch. 16 Pt. IV para. 2(2), 1984 s. 13(1), 1988 Sch. 3 para. 1(1)(a).
(1A)		76	Inserted 1984 s. 13(2).
(1B)		77(1), (2)	Inserted 1984 s. 13(2); amended 1988 Sch. 3 para. 1(1)(b), 1990 s. 5(4).
(1C) to (1F)		77(3) to (5)	Inserted 1984 s. 13(2); subs. (1D) substituted 1988 s. 14(1).
(1F)		298	Inserted 1984 s. 13(2); repealed in part 1988 Sch. 4.
5(1)	Notice of objection to contribute towards political objects.	84(1) to (3)	Amended 1975 Sch. 16 Pt. IV para. 2(2).
(2)		84(4), (5)	
5A	Appeals.	95	Inserted 1975 Sch. 16 Pt. IV para. 2(3); amended 1978 Sch. 16 para. 2.
6	Mode of giving effect to exemption from contribution to political fund.	85(1), (2)	Repealed in part 1984 s. 14(5).
6A	Applications of ss. 3 to 6 to employers' associations.	132	Inserted 1974 Sch. 3 para. 2(5).

TRADE UNION AND LABOUR RELATIONS CONSOLIDATION ACT—*continued.*

Existing provision	Subject matter	Section of 1992 Act	Remarks
	TRADE UNION ACT 1913 (c. 30)—*continued.*		
7	Definition of Certification Officer.	*passim*	Inserted 1975 Sch. 16. Pt. IV para 2(4).
8	Short title and construction.	—	Unnecessary.
Sch.	Form of exemption notice.	84(1)	
	INDUSTRIAL COURTS ACT 1919 (c. 69)		
1 to 3	Industrial Courts.	—	Repealed 1975 Sch. 18.
4(1)	Inquiry into trade disputes.	215(1), (2), 216(3)	Subs. (1) repealed in part 1975 Sch. 16 Pt. IV para. 3(2).
(2), (3)		216(1), (2)	
(4), (5)		216(4), (5)	
5(1), (2)	Reports.	215(2), (3)	
(3)		215(4), (5)	
6	Continuation of certain provisions as to regulation of wages.	—	Repealed Statute Law Revision Act 1927 (c. 42).
7	Remuneration and expenses.	—	Amended 1974 Sch. 3 para 3; repealed in part 1975 Sch. 16 Pt. IV para. 3(2); unnecessary.
8	Interpretation.		Substituted 1975 Sch. 16, Pt. IV para 3(3), 1982 Sch. 3 para. 10.
	"trade dispute".	218	
	"worker".	296(1)	
9	Rules as to apearance by counsel or solicitor.	216(6)	Amended 1974 Sch. 3 para. 3; repealed in part 1975 Sch. 16 Pt. IV para. 3(2).
10(1)	Employment under the Crown.	273(1)	Section substituted 1975 Sch. 16 Pt. IV para. 3(4).
(2)		273(3)	
(3)		274(1), (2)	Reference to women's services unnecessary, see now Armed Forces Act 1981 (c. 55) Sch. 3 para. 1(1); reference to Auxiliary Forces Act 1953 (c. 50) now Reserve Forces Act 1980 (c. 9) Pt. VI, by virtue of Interpretation Act 1978 (c. 30) s. 17(2)(a).
(4)		275(1), (2)	
11	Application of Act to trade disputes in agriculture.	—	Repealed 1975 Sch. 16 Pt. IV para. 3(2).
12	Adaptions for Scotland and Ireland.	—	Repealed 1975 Sch. 16 Pt. IV para. 3(2).
13	Report to Parliament.	215(6)	
14	Short title.	—	Unnecessary.

TRADE UNION AND LABOUR RELATIONS CONSOLIDATION ACT—*continued.*

Existing provision	Subject matter	Section of 1992 Act	Remarks

INDUSTRIAL COURTS ACT 1919 (c. 69)—*continued.*

Existing provision	Subject matter	Section of 1992 Act	Remarks
Sch.	Provisions as to temporary regulation of wages.	—	Repealed Statute Law Revision Act 1927 (c. 42).

TRADE DISPUTES AND TRADE UNIONS ACT 1946 (c. 52)

1	Repeal of 1927 Act and restoration of law in force before that Act.	*passim*	Repealed in part Statute Law (Repeals) Act 1973 (c. 39); effect reproduced in relation to provisions deriving from pre-1927 enactments; see also Sch. 3 paras 2, 3.
2	Short title.	—	Unnecessary.
Sch.	Transitional provisions.	—	Repealed Statute Law (Repeals) Act 1973 (c. 39).

INDUSTRIAL ASSURANCE AND FRIENDLY SOCIETIES ACT 1948 (c. 39)

words in 6(1), (2)	Insurance on life of child under 10.	19(1), 129(3)	Repealed in part Friendly Societies Act 1974 (c. 46) Sch. 11, Companies Act 1967 (c. 81) Sch. 7; amended Industrial Assurance and Friendly Societies Act 1948 (Isle of Man) Order 1948 (S.I. 1948/2578), Industrial Assurance and Friendly Societies Act 1948 (Northern Ireland) Order 1949 (S.I. 1949/598), 1974 Sch. 3 para. 5(2).
16(4)	Offence of failing to comply with s. 6(1).	19(2) 129(3)	Repealed in part Friendly Societies Act 1974 (c. 46) Sch. 11; amended ibid. Sch. 9 para. 12, 1974 Sch. 3 para. 5(3), Criminal Justice Act 1982 (c. 48) s. 38.
23(1)(d)	Meaning of "trade union" and "employers' association".	19(1), (2), 129(3)	Inserted 1974 Sch. 3 para. 5(4).

TRADE UNION (AMALGAMATIONS, &c.) ACT 1964 (c. 24)

1(1)	Conditions necessary for amalgamation or transfer of engagements.	97(1), (2)	Amended 1975 Sch. 16 Pt. IV para. 10(2).
(1A)		133	Inserted 1971 Sch. 8; substituted 1974 Sch. 3 para. 10(3).
(2)		99(1) 100(1)	Amended 1975 Sch. 16 Pt. IV para. 10(2).
(3)		99(2), (3)	
(4)		98(1), (2)	Amended 1975 Sch. 16 Pt. IV para. 10(2)
(5)		101(1), (2)	Amended 1975 Sch. 16 Pt. IV para. 10(2).
(6)		97(3)	

TRADE UNION AND LABOUR RELATIONS CONSOLIDATION ACT—*continued.*

Existing provision	Subject matter	Section of 1992 Act	Remarks
	TRADE UNION (AMALGAMATIONS, &c.) ACT 1964 (c. 24)—*continued.*		
2(1)	Manner of voting and majority required for resolution.	97(4)	
(2)		100(2)	
(3)		100(3), (4)	
3	Power to alter rules of transferee union for purposes of transfer of engagements.	102(1) to (3)	
4(1) to (3)	Complaint as regards passing of resolution.	103(1)	Amended 1975 Sch. 16 Pt. IV para. 10(2).
(4)		103(4)	Amended 1975 Sch. 16 Pt. IV para. 10(2).
(5)		103(3)	Amended 1975 Sch. 16 Pt. IV para. 10(2).
(6)		—	Repealed 1988 Sch. 4.
(7)		103(5)	Amended 1975 Sch. 16 Pt. IV para. 10(2).
(8)		104	Substituted 1975 Sch. 16 Pt. IV para. 10(3); amended 1978 Sch. 16 para. 5.
(9)		—	Unnecessary.
(10)		103(2)	
(11)		—	Repealed 1971 Sch. 9.
5(1)	Disposal of property on amalgamation or transfer.	105(1)	
(2)		105(4)	
(3)		105(2), (3)	
(4)		93(1)	
6(1)	Change of name of trade union.	107(1)	
(2)		107(2), (3)	Substituted 1974 Sch. 3 para. 10(5); amended 1975 Sch. 16 Pt. IV para. 10(2).
(3)		107(4)	
7(1)	Regulations.	108(1)	Function transferred Secretary of State for Employment and Productivity Order 1968 (S.I. 1968/729); amended 1975 Sch. 16 Pt. IV para. 10(2).
(2) to (4)		108(2) to (4)	Subs (2) amended 1975 Sch. 16 Pt. IV para. 10(2).
8	Power to Registrar to delegate functions.	254(4)	
9(1)	Interpretation.		Substituted 1974 Sch. 3 para. 10(8); repealed in part 1975 Sch. 18.
	"amalgamating unions" and "amalgamated union".	*passim*	

TRADE UNION AND LABOUR RELATIONS CONSOLIDATION ACT—*continued.*

Existing provision	Subject matter	Section of 1992 Act	Remarks
	TRADE UNION (AMALGAMATIONS, &c.) ACT 1964 (c. 24)—*continued.*		
	"Certification Officer"	*passim*	Inserted 1975 Sch. 16 Pt. IV para. 10(2).
	"employers' association"	122	
	"Northern Ireland union"	120	
	"trade union"	1	
	"transferor trade union and "transferee trade union".	*passim*	
(2)		—	Unnecessary.
10(1)	Provisions as to Northern Ireland	301	Repealed in part Northern Ireland Constitution Act 1973 (c. 36) Sch. 6 Pt. I.
(2)		106(1)	
(3)		—	Unnecessary.
(4)		—	Repealed Northern Ireland Constitution Act 1973 (c. 36) Sch. 6 Pt. I.
(5), (6)		120(1), (2)	
11(1)	Short title, citation, saving and commencement.	—	Unnecessary
(2), (3)		—	Repealed Statute Law (Repeals) Act 1969 (c.52).
(4)		—	Spent.
Sched. 1	Provisions supplemental to s. 4.	—	Repealed 1988 Sch. 4.
Sched. 2	Modifications of Act where amalgamation or transfer involves Northern Ireland union.		
para. 1		106(5)	
para. 2(1)		106(2)	Amended 1975 Sch. 16 Pt. IV para. 10(2).
(2)		106(4)	
para 3		106(4)	
para. 4		106(3)	Amended 1975 Sch. 16 Pt. IV para. 10(2).
Sched. 3	Repeals.	—	Repealed Statute Law (Repeals) Act 1969 (c. 52).
	MERCHANT SHIPPING ACT 1970 (c. 36)		
42(1)	Application of 1875 (except s. 5) to seamen.	*passim*	Given effect by not excluding seamen from relevant provisions; and see 240(4).
Sched. 3, para. 1	Substitutes new 1875 s. 16.	240(4)	

TRADE UNION AND LABOUR RELATIONS CONSOLIDATION ACT—*continued.*

Existing provision	Subject matter	Section of 1992 Act	Remarks
	ADMINISTRATION OF JUSTICE (SCOTLAND) ACT 1972 (c. 59)		
3(3)	Exclusion of power of arbiter to state case.	217,263 (6)	Repealed in part 1974 Sch. 5; amended 1974 Sch. 3 para. 17, 1975 s. 10(2), 1982 Sch. 3 para. 11(a), (b).
	FRIENDLY SOCIETIES ACT 1974 (c. 46)		
Sched. 9	Amendments of other enactments.		
para. 1		19(3)	Amends Friendly Societies Act 1896 (c. 25) s. 22(2).
para. 12		19(2)	Amends Industrial Assurance and Friendly Societies Act 1948 (c. 39) s. 16(4).
	TRADE UNION AND LABOUR RELATIONS ACT 1974 (c. 52)		
1(1)	Repeal of 1971 and reenactment of certain provisions.		Repealed Statute Law (Repeals) Act 1986 (c.12)
(2)		—	Repealed in part 1978 Sch. 17, Statute Law (Repeals) Act 1986 (c. 12); remainder introduces Sch.
(3)		—	Repealed Statute Law (Repeals) Act 1986 (c. 12).
1A	Charter on freedom of the press.	—	Inserted 1976 s. 2; repealed 1980 s. 19.
2(1)	Status of trade unions.	10(1), (2), 12(1), (2), 117(3)	Para. (c) repealed in part 1982 Sch. 4.
(2)		10(3), 117(3)	Amended Companies Consolidation (Consequential Provisions) Act 1985 (c. 9) Sch. 2.
(3)		10(3)	
(4)		—	Spent.
(5)		11(1),(2) 117(3)	
3(1)	Status of employers' associations.	127(1)	
(2)		127(2), 129(1)(a)	Para. (c) repealed in part 1982 Sch. 4.
(3)		—	Spent.
(4)		127(3)	Amended Companies Consolidation (Consequential Provisions) Act 1985 (c. 9) Sch. 2.
(5)		128(1), (2)	
4(1) to (3)	Supplementary provisions as to property of trade unions and employers associations.	13(1) to (4), 129(1)(b), (c), (2)	

TRADE UNION AND LABOUR RELATIONS CONSOLIDATION ACT—*continued.*

Existing provision	Subject matter	Section of 1992 Act	Remarks

TRADE UNION AND LABOUR RELATIONS ACT 1974 (c. 52)—*continued.*

Existing provision	Subject matter	Section of 1992 Act	Remarks
(4)		14(2), 129(1)(c)	Amended Companies Consolidation (Consequential Provisions) Act 1985 (c. 9) Sch. 2.
(5) to (8)		14(3) to (6), 129(1)(c)	
5	Rights of workers as to arbitrary or unreasonable exclusion or expulsion from trade union.	—	Repealed 1976 s. 1.
6	Provisions as to rules of trade unions and employers' associations.	—	Repealed 1976 s. 1.
7	Right to terminate membership of trade union.	69	Substituted 1976 s. 3(1).
8(1), (2)	Lists of trade unions and employers' associations.	2(1), 123(1)	Amended 1975 Sch. 16 Pt. III para. 1.
(3)		3(1), (3), 124(1), (3)	Amended 1975 Sch. 16 Pt. III para. 1.
(4)		3(2), 124(2)	Amended 1975 Sch. 16 Pt. III para. 1; fee prescribed by Certification Officer (Amendment of Fees) Regulations 1991 (S.I. 1991/484) reg. 4.
(5)		3(4), 124(4)	Amended 1975 Sch. 16 Pt. III para. 1.
(6)		4(1), (2), 125(1), (2)	Repealed in part 1976 s. 1(c); amended 1975 Sch. 16 Pt. III para. 1
(6A)		4(3), 125(3)	Inserted 1975 Sch. 16 Pt. III para. 2.
(7)		9(1), (3), 126(1), (2)	Substituted 1975 Sch. 16 Pt. III para. 3; amended 1978 Sch. 16 para. 18
(8)		—	Repealed 1975 Sch. 18.
(9)		2(2), (3), 123(2), (3)	Amended 1975 Sch. 16 Pt. III paras. 1, 4.
(10)		2(4) to (6), 123(4) to (6)	Amended 1975 Sch. 16 Pt. III paras. 1, 5.
9(1) to (3)	Application of existing Acts referring to registered trade unions, employers' associations, &c.	—	See Sch. 3 para. 4
10(1)	Duty to keep accounting records.	118(4), 135(3)	
(2), (3)		28(1), (2), 131(1)	
(4)		44(1), (2),	

TRADE UNION AND LABOUR RELATIONS CONSOLIDATION ACT—*continued.*

Existing provision	Subject matter	Section of 1992 Act	Remarks

TRADE UNION AND LABOUR RELATIONS ACT 1974 (c. 52)—*continued.*

Existing provision	Subject matter	Section of 1992 Act	Remarks
		(4), 131(1)	
11(1)	Duties as to annual returns, auditors and members' superannuation.	43(1), 131(1), 118(1), (4), 135(1), (3)	
(2)		32(1), 131(1)	Amended 1975 Sch. 16 Pt. III para. 1.
(3)		33(1), 131(1)	
(4)		27, 32(5), 131(1)	
(5)		32(6), 131(1)	Amended 1975 Sch. 16 Pt. III para. 1.
(6), (7)		—	Introduce Schs.
(8)		44(1), (2), (4), 131(1)	
(9)		117(4), 131(2)	Inserted Companies Act 1989 (c. 40) s. 124.
12(1) to (5)	Offences.	45(1) to (5), 131(1)	Applied 1988 s. 6(8); subs. (5) amended Criminal Justice Act 1982 (c. 48) s. 38.
13(1)	Acts in contemplation or furtherance of trade disputes.	219(1)	Substituted 1976 s. 3(2)
(2)		—	Repealed 1982 s. 19(1).
(3)		—	Repealed 1980 s. 17(8).
(4)		219(2)	
14	Immunity of trade unions and employers' associations from actions in tort.	—	Repealed 1982 s. 15(1).
15(1) to (4)	Peaceful picketing.	220(1) to (4)	Section substituted 1980 s. 16; subs. (3) amended 1982 Sch. 3 para. 12
16	No compulsion to work.	236	
17(1)	Restriction on grant of ex parte injunctions and interdicts.	221(1)	Renumbered 1975 Sch. 16 Pt. III para. 6.
(2), (3)		221(2)	Inserted 1975 Sch. 16 Pt. III para. 6.
18(1), (2)	Enforceability of collective agreements.	179(1), (2)	See also Sch. 3 para. 5.
(3)		179(3), (4)	
(4)		180(1) to (3)	
(5)		180(3)	
19	Transitional provisions as to trade unions and employers' associations ceasing to be incorporated.	—	Effect saved in certain respects Sch. 3 para. 6; otherwise spent.

TRADE UNION AND LABOUR RELATIONS CONSOLIDATION ACT—*continued.*

Existing provision	Subject matter	Section of 1992 Act	Remarks
	TRADE UNION AND LABOUR RELATIONS ACT 1974 (c. 52)—*continued.*		
20 to 24	Provisions connected with repeal of provisions of Industrial Relations Act 1971.	—	Repealed Statute Law (Repeals) Act 1986 (c. 12).
25(1) to (3)	Miscellaneous amendments, transitional provisions and repeals.	—	Introduce Schs.
26(1) to (3)	Regulations and orders.	293(1), (2) and *passim*	
(4)		—	Unnecessary.
27	Expenses.	—	Unnecessary.
28(1)	Meaning of trade union and employers' association.	1	
(2)		122	
29(1) to (3)	Meaning of trade dispute.	244(1) to (3)	Amended 1982 s. 18(2) to (4).
(4)		—	Repealed 1982 s. 18(5).
(5), (6)		244(4), (5)	Subs. (6) amended 1982 s. 18(6).
(7)		—	Repealed Criminal Law Act 1977 (c. 45) Sch. 13.
30(1)	General provisions as to interpretation.		
	"act" and "action".	298	
	"Certification Officer".	*passim*	
	"collective agreement".	178(1)	
	"contract of employment".	295(1)	
	"employee".	295(1), 280	
	"employer".	295(1), 296(2)	Inserted 1975 Sch. 16 Pt. III para. 7(2).
	"employers' association".	122(2)	
	"independent trade union".	5	Amended 1975 Sch. 16 Pt. III para. 7(3).
	"individual proprietor".	122(1)(a)	
	"1971 Act".	—	Unnecessary.
	"officer".	119	Inserted 1975 Sch. 16 Pt. III para. 7(5).
	"official".	119	
	"police service".	280	
	"special register body".	117(1)	Amended Companies Consolidation (Consequential Provisions) Act 1985 (c. 9) Sch. 2.
	"tort".	298	Amended 1982 s. 19(2).
	"union membership agreement".	174(2)	Amended 1976 s. 3(3).
	"worker".	296(1), 280	Repealed in part Armed Forces Act 1981 (c. 55) Sch. 5.

TRADE UNION AND LABOUR RELATIONS CONSOLIDATION ACT—*continued.*

Existing provision	Subject matter	Section of 1992 Act	Remarks
	TRADE UNION AND LABOUR RELATIONS ACT 1974 (c. 52)—*continued.*		
(2)		279	Amended National Health Service Act 1977 (c. 49) Sch. 15 para. 61, National Health Service (Scotland) Act 1978 (c. 29) Sch. 16 para. 39, Health Services Act 1980 (c. 53) Sch. 1 para. 25; National Health Service and Community Care Act 1990 (c. 19) s. 2(1)(b); part unnecessary by virtue of Family Practitioner Committee (Consequential Modifications) Order 1985 (S.I. 1985/39) art. 7(3), (9), (11), (13).
(3), (4)	"successor".	—	See Sch. 2 para. 21(2)(d).
(5)	"associated employer".	297	
(5A)		174(2)	Inserted 1976 s. 3(4).
(6)		289	
(7)		—	Unnecessary.
31(1)	Short title, commencement and extent.	—	Unnecessary.
(2)		—	Spent.
(3)		*passim*	
(4)		—	Spent.
(5)		301	Repealed in part House of Commons Disqualification Act 1975 (c. 24) Sch. 3.
Sch. 1	Re-enacted provisions of Industrial Relations Act 1971.		
Paras. 1 to 30		—	Repealed 1975 Sch. 18, Race Relations Act 1976 (c. 74) Sch. 5, 1978 Sch. 17.
Para. 31(1)	Nominations by members of trade unions.	17(1), 18(1)	Para. (b) amended 1975 Sch. 16 Pt. III para. 31, Administration of Estates (Small Payments) (Increase of Limits) Order 1984 S.I. 1984/539).
(2)		17(2), (3)	
(3)		17(4), (5), 18(2)	
(4)		18(4)	Substituted 1975 Sch. 16 Pt. III para. 32.
(5)		—	Repealed 1975 Sch. 16 Pt. III para. 32.
para. 32	Restrictions on contracting out.	288	Remainder repealed 1978 Sch. 17, 1980 Sch. 2.

TRADE UNION AND LABOUR RELATIONS CONSOLIDATION ACT—*continued.*

Existing provision	Subject matter	Section of 1992 Act	Remarks
	TRADE UNION AND LABOUR RELATIONS ACT 1974 (c. 52)—*continued.*		
para. 33(1)	Employment under the Crown.	273(1)	
(2)		273(2), 274(1)	Amendment 1975 Sch. 16 Pt. III. para. 33.
(3)		273(3)	Repealed in part 1978 Sch. 17; para. (e) amended 1975 Sch. 16 Pt. III para. 33.
(4)		274(2)	Para. (a) unnecessary; para. (b) amended Reserve Forces Act 1980 (c.9) para. 15.
(4A)		—	Inserted 1975 Sch. 16 Pt. III para. 34; repealed 1978 Sch. 17.
(5)		275(1), (2)	
Sched. 2	Administrative provisions relating to trade unions and employers' associations.		
para. 1(1),(2)	Annual returns.	32(1),(2), 131(1)	Amended 1975 Sch. 16 Pt. III para. 1.
paras. 2 to 4		32(3), 131(1)	Amended 1975 Sch. 16 Pt. III para. 1.
para. 5.		32(4), 131(1)	Amended 1975 Sch. 16 Pt. III para. 1.
para. 6, 7	Qualifications of auditors.	34(1), 131(1)	Para. 6 amended Companies Consolidation (Consequential Provisions) Act 1985 (c.9) Sch. 2; reference to s.389 of Companies Act 1985 (c.6) now s.25 of Companies Act 1989 (c.40), by virtue of Interpretaton Act 1978 (c.30) s.17(2)(a).
para. 8		—	Amended Companies Consolidation (Consequential Provisions) Act 1985 (c.9) Sch. 2; effect preserved Sch. 3 para. 11(2).
para. 9(1) to (3)		34(2) to (4), 131(1)	Sub-para. (2) amended 1975 Sch. 16 Pt. III para. 1.
para. 10(1)		34(5),	
(2)		131(1)	
para. 11	Appointment and removal of auditors.	35(1), 131(1)	
para. 12		35(1), (2), 131(1)	
para. 13			

TRADE UNION AND LABOUR RELATIONS CONSOLIDATION ACT—*continued.*

Existing provision	Subject matter	Section of 1992 Act	Remarks
	TRADE UNION AND LABOUR RELATIONS ACT 1974 (c. 52)—*continued.*		
(1)		35(1),(3), 131(1)	
(2)		35(4), 131(1)	
(3), (4)		35(5), 131(1)	
para. 14		35(6), 131(1)	
para. 15(1),(2)		35(7),(8), 131(1)	
para. 16	Auditor's rights.	37(1), 131(1)	
para. 17		37(3), 131(1)	
para. 18	Auditor's report.	36(1), 131(1)	
para. 19		36(2) 131(1)	
para. 20		36(3), (4), 131(1)	
para. 21		37(2), 131(1)	
para. 22		*passim*	Amended 1975 Sch. 16 Pt. III para. 1.
para. 23	Examinaton of superannuation schemes.	—	Spent.
para. 24		40(3), 131(1)	
para. 25		39(2), 40(4), 131(1)	
para. 26		40(5), (6), 131(1)	
para. 27		39(1), (2) 131(1)	Amended 1975 Sch 16 Pt. III para. 1.
para. 28		39(3), 40(1), 131(1)	
para. 29		—	Spent.
para. 30		41(1)(a), 131(1)	Amended 1975 Sch. Pt. III para. 1.
para. 31		41(2), 131(1)	Amended 1975 Sch. 16 Pt.III para.1.
para.32	Periodical re-examination of schemes.	40(1), (2), 131(1)	Amended 1975 Sch. 16 Pt. III para. 1.
para. 33		40(3) to (7), 131(1)	

TRADE UNION AND LABOUR RELATIONS CONSOLIDATION ACT—*continued.*

Existing provision	Subject matter	Section of 1992 Act	Remarks
	TRADE UNION AND LABOUR RELATIONS ACT 1974 (c. 52)—*continued.*		
paras. 33A, 33B		41(1)(b), 131(1)	Inserted 1980 Sch. 1 para. 2.
paras. 34, 35	Separate fund for superannuation scheme.	38(2), 131(1)	
para. 36	Interpretation.		
(a)		38(1), 131(1)	
(b)		42,131(1)	Amended 1975 Sch. 16 Pt. III para. 1.
(c)		38(2), 131(1)	
Sch. 3	Consequential amendments.		
para. 1		243(1)	
para. 2			
(1)		—	Introductory words.
(2)		1,122(1)	
(3)		*passim*	Undoes amendments made by 1971 Sch. 8.
(4)		—	Repeals words in 1913 ss. 3(1), 4(1).
(5)		132	
(6)		—	Repealed 1975 Sch. 18.
para. 3		—	Repealed 1975 Sch. 18.
para. 4		—	Repealed 1980 Sch. 2.
para. 5(1) to (4)		19(1), (2)	
para. 6		—	Repealed House of Commons Disqualification Act 1975 (c. 24) Sch. 3, Northern Ireland Assembly Disqualification Act 1975 (c. 25) Sch. 3 Pt. I.
para. 7		—	Amends provision repealed by Insurance Companies Act 1974 (c. 49) Sch. 2.
para. 8		—	Repealed 1975 Sch. 18.
para. 9		—	Repealed 1975 Sch. 18, Wages Councils Act 1979 (c. 12) Sch. 7.
para. 10(1)		—	Introductory words.
(2)		*passim*	Undoes amendments made by 1971 Sch. 8.
(3)		133	
(4)		—	Repealed 1975 Sch. 18.
(5)		107(2), (3), 134(2), (3)	

Tables of Derivations and Destinations

TRADE UNION AND LABOUR RELATIONS CONSOLIDATION ACT—*continued.*

Existing provision	Subject matter	Section of 1992 Act	Remarks

TRADE UNION AND LABOUR RELATIONS ACT 1974 (c. 52)—*continued.*

Existing provision	Subject matter	Section of 1992 Act	Remarks
(6)		—	Repealed 1975 Sch. 18.
(7)		254(4)	
(8)		*passim*	Substitutes new 1964 s. 9(1) (interpretation); see entries for that provision.
11		—	Amends provision repealed by Industrial Relations (Northern Ireland) Order 1992 (S.I. 1992/807 (N.I.5)); and see Sch. 3 para. 12(3).
12		—	Amends provision repealed by Insurance Companies Act 1974 (c. 49) Sch. 2.
13		—	Amends provisions repealed by Insurance Companies (Northern Ireland) Order 1976 (S.I. 1976/59 (N.I.3)).
14		—	Repeals Merchant Shipping Act 1970 (c. 36) s. 42(3); remainder repealed Merchant Shipping Act 1988 (c. 12) Sch. 7.
15		—	Repealed 1975 Sch. 18.
16		—	Repealed 1978 Sch. 17.
17		217, 263 (6)	
Sch. 4	Transitional provisions.	—	Repealed in part (paras. 1, 3, 6(4)) 1978 Sch. 17; any remaining effect saved Sch. 3 paras. 1, 2; otherwise spent.

EMPLOYMENT PROTECTION ACT 1975 (c. 71)

Existing provision	Subject matter	Section of 1992 Act	Remarks
1(1)	Advisory Conciliation and Arbitration Service.	247(1)	
(2)		209	
(3)		—	Introduces Sch.
2(1) to (3)	Conciliation.	210(1) to (3) 211	
(4)		211	
3(1)	Arbitration.	212(1)	
(2)		212(2), (3)	
(3), (4)		212(4)	
(5)		212(5)	
(6)		212(4)(a)	
4(1)	Advice.	213(1),(2)	
(2)		213(3)	

TRADE UNION AND LABOUR RELATIONS CONSOLIDATION ACT —*continued.*

Existing provision	Subject matter	Section of 1992 Act	Remarks
	EMPLOYMENT PROTECTION ACT 1975 (c. 71)—*continued.*		
5(1), (2)	Inquiry.	214(1), (2)	
6(1), (2)	Codes of Practice.	199(1), (2)	Subs. (2) amended 1978 Sch. 16 para. 23(2).
(3), (4)		200(1), (2)	
(5)		200(3), (5)	
(6), (7)		200(4)	
(8)		200(4). (5)	
(9)		200(5)	
(10)		199(4), 200(1)	
(10A)		208(1), (3)	Inserted 1980 Sch. 1 para. 4.
(11)		207(1), (2)	
7(1)	Certification Officer.	254(1), (2)	
(2)		*passim*	Transfer of functions under 1913, 1964 and 1974.
(3)		—	Introduces Sch.
(4)		254(3)	
(5), (6)		254(4)	
8(1), (2)	Certification as independent trade union.	6(1)	Fee presribed by Certification Officer (Amendment of Fees) Regulations 1991 (S.I. 1991/484) reg.5.
(3), (4)		6(2), (3)	
(5)		6(5), (6), 7(4), (5)	
(6)		6(4), 7(3)	
(7)		7(1)	
(8)		7(2) to (5)	
(9)		9(2) to (4)	Amended 1978 Sch. 16 para. 23(3).
(10)		7(6)	
(11)		8(1) to (3)	
(12)		8(4), (5)	
9(1), (2)	Custody of documents.	257(1), (2)	
10(1)	Central Arbitration Committee.	259(1)	
(2)		Sch. 3 para. 7	
(3)		—	Introduces Sch.
17(1) to (5)	General duty of employers to disclose information.	181(1) to (5)	Subs. (2)(b) repealed 1980 Sch. 2.
18(1), (2)	Restrictions on general duty under s.17.	182(1), (2)	
19(1)	Complaint of failure to disclose information.	183(1)	
(2), (3)		183(2)	

TRADE UNION AND LABOUR RELATIONS CONSOLIDATION ACT—*continued.*

Existing provision	Subject matter	Section of 1992 Act	Remarks
	EMPLOYMENT PROTECTION ACT 1975 (c. 71)—*continued.*		
(4) to (7)		183(3) to (6)	
20(1) to (4)	Further complaint arising from failure to disclose information.	184(1) to (4)	
21(1), (2)	Determination of claim and award.	185(1), (2)	
(3), (4)		185(3)	
(5)		185(4)	Paragraph (b) repealed 1980 Sch. 2.
(6) to (8)		185(5) to (7)	
99(1)	Duty of employer to consult trade union representatives on redundancy.	188(1)	
(2)		196	
(3)		188(2)	Amended Employment Protection (Handling of Redundancies) Variation Order 1979 (S.I. 1979/958).
(4) to (9)		188(3) to (8)	
100(1)	Duty of employer to notify Secretary of State of certain redundancies.	193(1), (2), (6)	Amended Employment Protection (Handling of Redundancies) Variation Order 1979 (S.I. 1979/958).
(2), (3)		193(3), (4)	
(4)		193(6)	
(5)		193(5)	
(6)		193(7)	
101(1)	Complaint by trade union and protective award.	189(1)	
(2)		189(6)	
(3) to (6)		189(2) to (5)	
(7)		189(1)	
102(1) to (3)	Entitlement under protective award.	190(1) to (3)	
(4)		190(4)	Amended 1978 Sch. 16, para. 23(4).
(5) to (11)		191(1) to (7)	
103(1) to (3)	Complaint by employee to industrial tribunal.	192(1) to (3)	
104	Reduction of rebate on failure to notify redundancies.	—	Repealed Wages Act 1986 (c. 48) Sch. 5 Pt. I.
105(1)	Offence and proceedings.	194(1)	Amended Criminal Justice Act 1982 (c. 48) s. 38.
(2), (3)		194(2)	

TRADE UNION AND LABOUR RELATIONS CONSOLIDATION ACT—*continued.*

Existing provision	Subject matter	Section of 1992 Act	Remarks
			EMPLOYMENT PROTECTION ACT 1975 (c. 71)—*continued.*
(4), (5)		—	Repealed Wages Act 1986 (c. 48) Sch. 5 Pt. I.
106(1)	Supplementary	—	Repealed 1980 Sch. 2.
(2)		195(3)	
(3)		190(5)	
(4), (5)		197(1), (2)	
107(1)	Power to adapt provisions in case of collective agreement.	198(1), (2)	
(2) to (4)		198(3) to (5)	
108(1)	General provisions as to industrial tribunals and conciliation officers.	192(4)	Amended 1978 Sch. 16 para 23(5); part unnecessary.
(2) to (8)		—	Repealed 1978 Sch. 17.
110	Death of employee or employer.	—	Introduces Sch. 12; see entries for that Schedule.
117(1), (2)	Offences by bodies corporate.	194(3), (4)	
118(1)	Restrictions on contracting out.	288(1)	Part unnecessary.
(2)		288(3)	Repealed in part 1978 Sch. 17, 1980 Sch. 2.
119(1)	Excluded classes of employment.	—	Amended 1978 Sch. 16 para. 23(8); unnecessary.
(2)		—	Repealed 1978 Sch. 17.
(3)		—	Repealed Dock Work Act 1989 (c. 13) Sch. 1.
(4)		284	Repealed in part 1978 Sch. 17.
(5), (6)		285(1)	Subs. (5) repealed in part 1978 Sch. 17.
(7)		282	Repealed in part 1978 Sch. 17; amended 1982 Sch. 2 para. 6(1).
(8) to (11)		—	Repealed 1978 Sch. 17.
(12)		283(1)	Repealed in part 1978 Sch. 17.
(13)		—	Relates to provisions repealed by 1978 Sch. 17.
(14)		283(2)	
(15)		286(1), (2)	
(16)		286(4)	
(17)		—	Added 1978 Sch. 16 para. 23(9); repealed 1982 Sch. 4.
121(1)	Application to Crown.	273(1), (2)	Repealed in part 1978 Sch. 17, 1980 Sch. 2.
(2)		273(3)	
(3)		274(1), (2)	Amended Armed Forces Act 1981 (c. 55) Sch. 5 Part I.
(4)		275(1), (2)	

TRADE UNION AND LABOUR RELATIONS CONSOLIDATION ACT—*continued.*

Existing provision	Subject matter	Section of 1992 Act	Remarks
	EMPLOYMENT PROTECTION ACT 1975 (c. 71)—*continued.*		
(5), (6)		—	Amended 1978 Sch. 16 para. 23(10), (11); relate to provision repealed by National Health Service and Community Care Act 1990 (c. 19) Sch. 10.
(7)		273(5)	Amended 1978 Sch. 16 para. 23(11).
(8)		—	Repealed 1978 Sch. 17.
122(1)	Application of employment legislation to House of Commons staff.	278(1), (2), (5)	Amended House of Commons (Administration) Act 1978 (c. 36) Sch. 2 para. 5(2); repealed in part 1978 Sch. 17.
(2)		Sch. 2 paras. 4(2), 7, 8	Amended Race Relations Act 1976 (c. 74) Sch. 3 para. 1(5).
(3)		—	Substituted House of Commons (Administration) Act 1978 (c. 36) Sch. 2 para. 5(3); repealed 1978 Sch. 17.
(4) to (8)		278(3), (6)	Subs. (4) to (7B) substituted House of Commons (Administration) Act 1978 (c. 36) Sch. 2 para. 5(3); subs. (8) amended ibid. para. 5(4).
(9)		—	Repealed House of Commons (Administration) Act 1978 (c. 36) Sch. 3.
123(1)	Orders, rules and regulations.	*passim*	
(2)		*passim*	Repealed in part 1978 Sch. 17.
(3)	Power to include supplementary, &c. provisions.	*passim*	
(4)		—	Unnecessary (Interpretation Act 1978 (c. 30) s. 14).
words in 124(1)	Financial provisions.	—	Unnecessary.
words in 125(1)	Minor and consequential amendments.	—	Introduce Sch.
126(1)	Interpretation.		
	"associated employer"	297	
	"collective agreement"	178(1), (2)	
	"employee"	280(1), 295(1)	
	"employer"	295(1), 296(2)	
	"independent trade union", "independence" and "independent"	5	
	"official"	119	
	"successor"	—	Spent.

TRADE UNION AND LABOUR RELATIONS CONSOLIDATION ACT—*continued.*

Existing provision	Subject matter	Section of 1992 Act	Remarks
	EMPLOYMENT PROTECTION ACT 1975 (c. 71)—*continued.*		
	"trade union"	1	
	"union membership agreement"	—	Spent.
	"worker"	296(1)	
	"business"	195(2)	
	"collective bargaining"	178(1), (2)	
	"Committee"	*passim*	
	"dismiss", "dismissal" and "effective date of termination".	298	Amended 1978 Sch. 16 para. 23(13).
	"the 1974 Act".	—	Unnecessary.
	"recognition".	178(3)	Amended 1980 Sch. 1 para. 6.
	"Service".	*passim*	
	"trade dispute".	218	Inserted 1982 Sch. 3 para. 13(2).
(2)		122	Part spent.
(3)		—	Repealed 1978 Sch. 17.
(4)		—	Spent.
(5)		—	Repealed 1978 Sch. 17.
(6), (7)		195(1), (2)	
(8)		289	
(9)		—	Unnecessary (Interpretation Act 1978 (c. 30) s. 20(2)).
126A(1) to (6)	Meaning of "trade dispute".	218(1) to (5)	Inserted 1982 Sch. 3 para. 13(3); subs. (5) unnecessary.
127(1)	Power to extend employment legislation.	287(2), Sch. 2 paras. 27, 28	Repealed in part 1978 Sch. 17, Wages Councils Act 1979 (c. 12) Sch. 7; amended 1982 (c. 9) s. 11(3), 1982 (c. 10) Sch. 3 para. 6.
(2)		287(1)	Extended Employment (Continental Shelf) Act 1978 (c. 46) s. 1(1).
(3), (4)		287(3), (4)	Subs. (3)(g) repealed in part 1978 Sch. 17.
128	Reciprocal arrangements with Northern Ireland.	294	Repealed in part 1978 Sch. 17.
129	Short title, commencement and extent.		
words in (5)		—	Refer to repealed sections.
words in (6)		—	Refer to repealed sections.
Sched. 1, Part I	ACAS.		
para. 1	The Council.	247(2), 248(1)	
para. 2(1)		248(1), 249(2)	
(2)		248(2)	

TRADE UNION AND LABOUR RELATIONS CONSOLIDATION ACT—*continued.*

Existing provision	Subject matter	Section of 1992 Act	Remarks
	EMPLOYMENT PROTECTION ACT 1975 (c. 71)—*continued.*		
(3)		248(4), 249(2)	
(4)		248(3)	
para. 3(1)		249(1)	
(2)		249(3)	
(3), (4)		249(2)	
(5) to (9)		249(4), (5)	
para. 4(1), (2)		248(5), (6)	
para. 5		248(7)	
paras. 6, 7	Staff.	251(1) to (3)	Functions transferred by Transfer of Functions (Minister for the Civil Service and Treasury) Order 1981 (S.I. 1981/1670).
para. 7		251(2), (3)	
para. 8		254(5)	
para. 9	Supplementary.	247(6)	
para. 10(1), (2)		251(5)	
para. 11(1), (2)		247(3), (4)	
para. 12		247(5)	
para. 13(1)		253(1), 265(1)	
(2)		258(1)	
(3)		253(1), 258(1)	
Part II	Central Arbitration Committee.		
para. 14(1) to (3)	Constitution.	260(1) to (3)	
para. 15(1) to (4)		261(1) to (4)	
(5) to (7)		261(5)	
para. 16(1), (2)		260(4), (5)	
para. 17(1), (2)	Proceedings.	263(1)	
(3)		263(2)	
paras. 18 to 20		263(3) to (5)	
para. 21		260(6)	
paras. 22, 23		264(1), (2)	
para. 24		264(3)	
para. 25	Supplementary.	265(1)	
para. 26		263(6)	
27		259(2)	

TRADE UNION AND LABOUR RELATIONS CONSOLIDATION ACT—*continued.*

Existing provision	Subject matter	Section of 1992 Act	Remarks
	EMPLOYMENT PROTECTION ACT 1975 (c. 71)—*continued.*		
Part III	Supplementary Provisions.		
para. 28	Remuneration and allowances.	250(1), (4), 255(1), (4), 262(1), (4)	Functions under paras. 28 and 29 transferred Transfer of Functions (Minister for the Civil Service and Treasury) Order 1981 (S.I. 1981/1670).
para. 29		252(2)	
para. 30	Sums payable on retirement.	250(2), (4), 255(2), (4), 262(2), (4)	Functions under paras. 30 to 32 transferred Transfer of Functions (Minister for the Civil Service and Treasury) Order 1981 (S.I. 1981/1670).
para. 31		250(3), (4), 255(3), (4), 262(3), (4)	
para. 32		251(4)	
para. 32A	Expenses and accounts.	256(4)	Inserted 1988 s. 22(3).
para. 33		252(1)	
para. 34		253(2)	
para. 35(1)		253(2), 258(2), 265(2)	
(2)		253(3), (4)	
(3)		272	
Sched. 12	Death of employer or employee.		
Part I, paras. 1 to 3		292(1) to (3)	
para. 4		—	Unnecessary.
paras. 5, 6		292(4), (5)	
para. 7		190(6)	
Part II		—	Repealed 1978 Sch. 17.
Sched. 16	Minor and consequential amendments.		
Part III	Amendments of 1974		
para. 1		*passim*	Translation of references to Registrar of Friendly Societies.
para. 2		4(3)	
para. 3		9(1), (3), (4)	
para. 4		9(2) to (4)	
para 5		2(4), (5)	
para. 6		221(1), (2)	

TRADE UNION AND LABOUR RELATIONS CONSOLIDATION ACT—*continued.*

Existing provision	Subject matter	Section of 1992 Act	Remarks
		EMPLOYMENT PROTECTION ACT 1975 (c. 71)—*continued.*	
para. 7(1)		*passim*	Inserts definition of "Certification Officer".
(2)		295(1), 296(2)	
(3)		5	
(4)		—	Inserts provision repealed 1978 Sch. 17
(5)		119	
paras. 8 to 30		—	Repealed 1978 Sch. 17.
para. 31		18(1)	
para. 32		18(4)	
para. 33		273(3)	
para. 34		—	Repealed 1978 Sch. 17.
para. 35		—	Spent.
Part IV	Miscellaneous amendments.		
para. 2	Amendments of 1913		
(1)		—	Introductory words.
(2)		*passim*	Translation of references to Registrar of Friendly Societies.
(3)		95	
(4)		*passim*	Inserts definition of "Certification Officer".
para. 3	Amendments of 1919		
(1)		—	Introductory words.
(2)		—	Repeals.
(3)		218, 296(1)	
(4)		273(1), (3), 274, 275	
para. 7		—	Amends provision repealed by Public Passenger Vehicles Act 1981 (c. 14) Sch. 8.
para. 10	Amendments of 1964.		
(1)		—	Introductory words.
(2)		*passim*	Relates to transfer of functions to Certification Officer.
(3)		104	
para. 13			
(1)		—	Introductory words.
(2), (3)		Sch. 2 para. 3(3)	Repealed in part Wages Act 1986 (c. 48) Sch. 5 Pt. II, 1986 (c. 59) Sch. Pt. I.
(4), (5)		—	Repealed 1986 (c. 59) Sch. Pt. II.

TRADE UNION AND LABOUR RELATIONS CONSOLIDATION ACT—*continued.*

Existing provision	Subject matter	Section of 1992 Act	Remarks
EMPLOYMENT PROTECTION ACT 1975 (c. 71)—*continued.*			
(6) to (11)		—	Repealed Wages Act 1986 (c. 48) Sch. 5 Pt. II.
para. 16		Sch. 2 para. 4(2), (3)	Repealed in part Employment and Training Act 1981 (c. 57) Sch. 3.
Sched. 17 paras. 1 to 6	Transitional provisions.	—	Any remaining effect saved Sch. 3 para. 2; otherwise spent.
TRADE UNION AND LABOUR RELATIONS (AMENDMENT) ACT 1976 (c. 7)			
1	Repeals of principal Act.	—	Repealed in part 1978 Sch. 17; remainder repeals provisions of 1974.
2	Freedom of the press.	—	Repealed 1980 Sch. 2.
3(1)	Amendments of principal Act.	69	
(2)		219(1)	
(3), (4)		174(2)	
(5), (6)		—	Repealed 1978 Sch. 17.
4(1), (2)	Short title, citation and transitional provisions.	—	Unnecessary.
(3)		—	Spent.
RACE RELATIONS ACT 1976 (c. 74)			
Sched. 3 para. 1(1)	Minor and consequential amendments.	—	Introductory words.
(2) to (4)		—	Repealed 1978 Sch. 17.
(5)		Sch. 2 para. 7	Amends 1975 s. 122.
CRIMINAL LAW ACT 1977 (c. 45)			
1(3)	Restriction of offence of conspiracy.	242(1)	
5(11)		—	Repeals (EW) 1875 s. 3.
words in 63(2)		*passim*	Relate to extent of repeals in 1875.
NATIONAL HEALTH SERVICE ACT 1977 (c. 49)			
Sch. 15 para. 62		279	Amends 1974 s. 30(2)
NATIONAL HEALTH SERVICE (SCOTLAND) ACT 1978 (c. 29)			
Sch. 16 para. 39		279	Amends 1874 s. 30(2).
HOUSE OF COMMONS (ADMINISTRATION) ACT 1978 (c. 36)			
Sched. 2	Supplementary and consequential provisions.		
words in para. 1	Power of Mr Speaker to act after dissolution.	278(5)	Given effect by application of 1978 s. 139(4) to (9).

TRADE UNION AND LABOUR RELATIONS CONSOLIDATION ACT—*continued.*

Existing provision	Subject matter	Section of 1992 Act	Remarks
	HOUSE OF COMMONS (ADMINISTRATION) ACT 1978 (c. 36)—*continued.*		
para. 5(1)	Amendments of 1975.	—	Introductory words.
(2)		278(4)(a) and (b) 278(5)	Amendments of 1975 s. 122; given effect by applying identical provisions of 1978 s. 139.
	EMPLOYMENT PROTECTION (CONSOLIDATION) ACT 1978 (c. 44)		
23(1)	Trade union membership and activities.	146(1)	Repealed in part 1980 s. 15(1); amended 1982 s. 10(4).
(1A), (1B)		146(3), (4)	inserted 1982 s. 10(3).
(2)		146(2)	
(2A), (2B)		—	Inserted 1980; repealed 1988 s.11.
(3) to (6)		—	Repealed 1980 Sch. 2.
(7)		151(1)	Substituted 1988 Sch. 3 para. 2(1).
24(1)	Complaints to industrial tribunal.	146(5)	
(2)		147	
(3)		149(1)	
25(1), (2)	Supplementary provisions as to complaint.	148(1), (2)	Subs. (1) repealed in part 1980 s. 15(3).
26(1) to (5)	Assessment of compensation.	149(2) to (6)	
26A(1) to (3)	Awards against third parties.	150(1) to (3)	
27(1)	Time off for carrying out trade union duties.	168(1),(2)	Amended 1989 (c.38) s. 14
(2)		168(3)	
(3), (4)		169(1) to (3)	
(5), (6)		169(4)	
(7)		169(5)	
28(1) to (4)	Time off for trade union activities.	170(1) to (4)	
58(1), (2)	Dismissal relating to trade union membership.	152(1),(2)	subs. (1) repealed in part 1988 Sch. 4
(3) to (12)		—	Repealed 1988 Sch. 4.
(13)		152(3)	Amended 1988 Sch. 3 para. 2(2)(a).
(14)		152(4)	substituted 1988 Sch. 3 para. 2(2)(b).
words in 59	Dismissal on ground of redundancy.	153	Amended 1982 Sch. 3 para. 17.
62(1)	Dismissal in connection with industrial action.	238(1)	Amended 1982 s. 9(4).

TRADE UNION AND LABOUR RELATIONS CONSOLIDATION ACT—*continued.*

Existing provision	Subject matter	Section of 1992 Act	Remarks
EMPLOYMENT PROTECTION (CONSOLIDATION) ACT 1978 (c. 44)—*continued.*			
(2)		238(2)	Amended 1982 s. 9(2).
(3)		239(3)	Amended 1982 s. 9(4).
(4)		238(3) to (5)	Amended 1982 s. 9(3), Sch. 3 para. 18; repealed in part ibid. Sch. 4.
(5)		238(1), (3)	Added 1990 Sch. 2 para. 1.
62A(1) to (6)	Dismissal of those taking part in unofficial industrial action.	237(1) to (6)	Inserted 1990 s. 9(1).
64(3)	Qualifying period and upper age limit.	154	Amended 1982 Sch. 3 para. 19.
words in 64A(2)	Qualifying period.	154	Section inserted 1980 s. 8; words amended 1982 Sch. 3 para. 20.
67(3)	Extended period for complaining.	239(2)	Substituted 1982 s. 9(5).
72A(1)	Reduction of compensation: matters to be disregarded.	155(1)	Section inserted 1982 s. 6.
(2)		155(1) to (3)	
(3)		155(2)	
73(4A)	Minimum basic award.	156(1)	Inserted 1982 s. 4(1); limit increased Unfair Dismissal (Increase of Limits of Basic and Special Awards) Order 1992 (S.I. 1992/313) art. 2.
(4B)		159(1). (3)	Inserted 1982 s. 4(1).
75A(1) to (6)	Calculation of special award.	158(1) to (6)	Section inserted 1982 s. 5(3); limits in subs.(1), (2) increased Unfair Dismissal (Increase of Limits of Basic and Special Awards) Order 1992 (S.I. 1992/313) art. 2.
76A(1) to (3)	Awards against third parties.	160(1) to (3)	Section inserted 1982 s. 7.
77(1), (2)	Interim relief pending determination of complaint.	161(1), (2)	Subs.(1) substituted 1982 s. 8(1); subs.(2) amended 1982 Sch.3 para. 24(1).
(3)		162(1) to (3)	Amended 1982 s. 8(2). Sch. 3 para. 24(2).
(3A)		162(2), (3)	Inserted 1982 s. 8(2).
(4)		162(4)	
(5)		163(1), (2)	Amended 1982 Sch. 3 para. 24(3).
(6) to (9)		163(3) to (6)	
(10)		161(4), (6)	Repealed in part 1982 Sch. 4.
(11)		161(5)	
78(1)	Order for continuation of contract.	164(1)	

TRADE UNION AND LABOUR RELATIONS CONSOLIDATION ACT—*continued.*

Existing provision	Subject matter	Section of 1992 Act	Remarks
EMPLOYMENT PROTECTION (CONSOLIDATION) ACT 1978 (c. 44)—*continued.*			
(2)		164(2), (3)	
(3) to (6)		164(4) to (7)	
79(1)	Supplementary provisions relating to interim relief	165(1), (2)	
(2)		166(1), (2)	
(3)		166(3) to (5)	
words in 132(1)(-b)	Recoupment of social security benefits.	Sch. 2 para. 19(b)	
passages in 133(1)	Functions of conciliation officers.	290	Amended 1980 Sch. 1 para. 17; 1988 Sch. 3 para. 2(3); 1990 Sch. 1 para. 4.
136(1)(c),(g)	Appeals to Employment Appeal Tribunal.	291(2)	Para.(g) inserted 1990 Sch. 1 para.8.
(2)		95,104	
(3)		9	
words in (5)		291(3)	Amended 1980 Sch.1 para. 19; 1988 Sch.3 para.2(4); part unnecessary.
words in 146(4)	Part-time employment.	281(1)	
words in 149(2)	Power to amend Act.	286	Amended 1980 Sch. 1 para. 21(b).
words in Sched. 2	Maternity: unfair dismissal.	—	Refer to provisions repealed 1988 s. 11, Sch. 4.
Sched. 16	Consequential amendments.		
para. 2	Amendments of 1913.	95	Inserts 1913 s. 5A.
para. 5	Amendment of 1964.	104	Amends 1964 s. 4(8).
para. 18	Amendment of 1974	9(1), (4)	Amends 1974 s. 8(7).
para. 23(1)	Amendments of 1975.	—	Introductory words.
(2)		199(2), (3)	Amends 1975 s. 6(2).
(3)		9(2), (4)	Amends 1975 s. 8(9).
(4)		190(4)	Amends 1975 s. 102(4).
(5)		—	Repealed Wages Act 1986 (c. 48) Sch. 5 Pt. I.
(6)		190(5)	Amends 1975 s. 106(3).
(7)		—	Amends 1975 s.108(1); unnecessary.
(8)		—	Amends 1975 s.119(1); unnecessary.
(9)		—	Repealed 1982 Sch. 4.

TRADE UNION AND LABOUR RELATIONS CONSOLIDATION ACT—*continued.*

Existing provision	Subject matter	Section of 1992 Act	Remarks
EMPLOYMENT PROTECTION (CONSOLIDATION) ACT 1978 (c. 44)—*continued.*			
(10)		—	Refers to provisions repealed by National Health Service and Community Care Act 1990 (c. 19) Sch. 5.
(11)		273(4)(c)	Amends 1975 s. 121(7); remainder refers to spent provisions.
(12)		—	Amends 1975 s.125(1); drafting provision.
(13)		298	Amends 1975 s.126(1) "dismissal", etc.
EMPLOYMENT (CONTINENTAL SHELF) ACT 1978 (c. 46)			
1(1)	Powers to apply employment legislation.	287(1)	Extends power conferred by 1975 s. 127.
RESERVE FORCES ACT 1980 (c. 9)			
Sch. 9 para. 15		274(2)	Amends 1974 Sch. 1 para. 33(4).
EMPLOYMENT ACT 1980 (c. 42)			
1(1)	Payments in respect of secret ballots.	115(1)	
(2), (3)		115(2)	Subs. (3) extended Funds for Trade Union Ballots Order 1982 (S.I. 1982/953) art. 2, amended 1984 s. 20(2).
(3A)		115(2)(d)	Inserted 1984 s. 20(3).
(4)		115(3)	
(5)		115(4)	Repealed in part 1984 s. 20(4).
(6)		254(6)	Part unnecessary.
(7)		115(5)	
(8)		*passim*	Attracts definitions in 1974.
2(1)	Secret ballots on employer's premises.	116(1), (3)	Amended 1988 Sch. 3 para. 3(1)(a).
(2)		116(2)	Repealed in part 1984 s. 20(5).
(3)		116(1), (3)	
(4) to (6)		116(4) to (6)	
(7)		291(2)	
(8)		116(7)	
(9)		298 and *passim*	Attracts definitions in 1974.
3(1)	Issue by Secretary of State of Codes of Practice.	203(1)	Amended 1982 s. 18(1).
(2), (3)		204(1)	
(4)		204(2)	
(5)		204(3), (4)	

TRADE UNION AND LABOUR RELATIONS CONSOLIDATION ACT—*continued*.

Existing provision	Subject matter	Section of 1992 Act	Remarks

EMPLOYMENT ACT 1980 (c. 42)—*continued*.

Existing provision	Subject matter	Section of 1992 Act	Remarks
(6)		203(2)	
(7)		208(2)	
(8)		207(1), (3)	
(9)		1	Inserted 1988 s. 18(2).
4(1)	Unreasonable exclusion or expulsion from trade union.	174(1)	
(3)		177(2), (3)	
(4), (5)		174(5), (6)	
(6)		175	
(7)		176(1)	
(8)		291(1)	
(9)		174(4)	
(10)		174(1), (2) and *passim*	Attracts definitions in 1974.
(11)		288(1), (2)	
5(1), (2)	Compensation.	176(2)	
(3)		176(3)	
(4)		176(4), (5)	
(5), (6)		176(6), (7)	
(7)		176(4)	
(8)		176(5)	Amended 1988 Sch. 3 para. 3(2)(a).
(8A)		176(8)	Inserted 1988 Sch. 3 para. 3(2)(b).
(9)		291(2)	
15(1)	Action short of dismissal relating to trade union membership and activities.	—	Repeals words in 1978 s. 23(1)(c).
(2)		—	Repealed 1988 Sch. 4.
(3)		—	Repeals provisions in 1978 ss. 23, 25.
(4)		—	Repealed 1982 Sch. 4.
16(1)	Picketing.	220(1) to (4)	Substitutes 1974 s. 15.
(2)		219(3)	
(3)		298	
19	Enactments ceasing to have effect.	—	Repeals provisions of 1974 and 1975 and related provisions.
passages in 20(1)		—	Unnecessary.
Sch. 1	Minor and consequential amendments.		
para. 2		—	Repeals 1974 Sch. 1 para. 32(2)(a).
para. 3		41(2) to (4)	Inserts 1974 Sch. 2 paras. 33A, 33B.

TRADE UNION AND LABOUR RELATIONS CONSOLIDATION ACT—*continued.*

Existing provision	Subject matter	Section of 1992 Act	Remarks
	EMPLOYMENT ACT 1980 (c. 42)—*continued.*		
para. 4		208(1), (3)	Inserts 1975 s. 6(10A).
para. 5		—	Removes reference to repealed provision in 1975 s. 121(1).
para. 6		178(3)	Amends 1975 s. 126(1) "recognition".
para. 7		287(2)	Amends 1975 s. 127(1).
words in para. 17		290	Insert 1978 s. 133(1)(d).
para. 19		291(3)	Amends 1978 s. 136(5).
para, 21(b)		—	Inserts reference in 1978 s. 149 to provision repealed by 1982 Sch. 4.
para. 24		—	Inserts references in 1978 Sch. 2 to provisions repealed by 1982 Sch. 4.
	HEALTH SERVICES ACT 1980 (c. 53)		
Sched. 1 para. 25		279	Amends 1974 s. 30(2).
	AGRICULTURAL TRAINING BOARD ACT 1982 (c. 9)		
11(3)		Sch. 2 para. 27	Amends 1975 s. 127(1).
	INDUSTRIAL TRAINING ACT 1982 (c. 10)		
Sched. 3 para. 6		Sch. 2 para. 28	Amends 1975 s. 127(1).
	OIL AND GAS (ENTERPRISE) ACT 1982 (c. 23)		
Sched. 3 para. 25		Sch. 2 para. 29(3), (4)	Provides for amendment of 1975 s. 127.
	EMPLOYMENT ACT 1982 (c. 46)		
2	Compensation for certain dismissals.	—	Spent.
3	Dismissal for non-membership of union.	152(1), (2)	Inserts 1978 s. 58, 58A.
4(1)	Basic Award.	156(1),	Inserts 1978 s. 73 (4A) (4B).
(2)		159(1), (3), 156(2)	Inserts 1978 s. 73 (7C); otherwise makes repeals.
5(1)	New Special Award.	157(2)	Inserts words in 1978 s. 71(2)(b).
(2)		157(1), Sch. 2 para. 16	Substitutes 1978 s. 72.
(3)		158	Inserts 1978 s. 75A.
6	Reduction of compensation: matters to be disregarded.	155	Inserts 1978 s. 72A.
7	Awards against third parties.	160	Inserts 1978 s. 76A.
8(1)	Interim relief.	161(1)	Substitutes 1978 s. 77(1).
(2)		162(2), (3)	Amends 1978 s. 77(3) and insterts subs. (3A).

TRADE UNION AND LABOUR RELATIONS CONSOLIDATION ACT—*continued.*

Existing provision	Subject matter	Section of 1992 Act	Remarks
	EMPLOYMENT ACT 1982 (c. 46)—*continued.*		
9(1)	Dismissal in connection with strike or other industrial action.	—	Introductory words.
(2)		238(2)	Amends 1978 s. 62(2).
(3)		238(3)	Amends 1978 s. 62(4).
(4)		238(1), 239(3)	Amends 1978 s. 62(1), (3).
(5)		239(2)	Substitutes 1978 s. 67(3).
10(1), (2)	Action relating to trade union membership.	—	Repealed 1988 Sch. 4.
(3)		146(3), (4)	Inserts 1978 s. 23(1A), (1B).
(4)		146(1)	Amends 1978 s. 23(1).
11	Awards against third parties.	160	Substitute 1978 s. 26A.
12(1)	Prohibition on union membership requirements.	144	
(2)		145(1) to (4), 187(2)	
(3)		145(3)	
(4)		145(2)	
(5)		145(4)	
(6)		145(3)	
(7)		145(1), (5)	Part unnecessary.
13(1)	Prohibition on union recognition requirements.	186, 187(1)	
(2)		187(1), (2)	
(3)		187(1)	
(4)		187(3)	Part unnecessary.
14(1)	Pressure to impose union membership or recognition requirements.	222(3), 225(1)	
(2)		225(2)	
(3)		225(2)	Substituted for subs. (3) and (4) 1988 Sch. 3 para. 4.
15(1)	Actions in tort against trade unions and employers' associations.	—	Repeals 1974 s. 14.
(2)		20(1)	Amended 1990 s. 6(2).
(3) to (3B)		20(2) to (4)	Substituted 1990 s. 6(3).
(4)		21(1)	Substituted 1990 s. 6(4).
(5) to (5B)		21 (2) to (4)	Substituted 1990 s. 6(5).
(6)		21(5)	Repealed in part 1990 Sch. 3.
(6A)		21(6)	Inserted 1990 s. 6(6).
(7)	Interpretation.		
	"commercial contract"	21(7)	Inserted 1990 s. 6(7).
	"rules"	20(7)	

TRADE UNION AND LABOUR RELATIONS CONSOLIDATION ACT—*continued.*

Existing provision	Subject matter	Section of 1992 Act	Remarks
			EMPLOYMENT ACT 1982 (c. 46)—*continued.*

Existing provision	Subject matter	Section of 1992 Act	Remarks
	other definitions.	119	Definitions of "official" and "employed official" repealed 1990 s. 6(7).
(8)		20(5)	
(9)		20(6)	Inserted 1990 s. 6(8).
16(1)	Limit on damages awarded against trade unions in actions in tort.	22(1), (2)	
(2)		22(1), (5)	Amended Consumer Protection Act 1987 (c. 43) Sch. 4 para. 8.
(3)		22(2)	
(4)		22(3)	
(5)		22(3), (4)	
(6)		22(5)	
(7)		118(3)	
17(1)	Recovery of sums awarded against trade unions and employers' associations.	23(1), 130(1)	
(2)		23(2), 130(2)	
(3)		23(2), (3)	
18(1)	Meaning of "trade dispute".	—	Introductory words.
(2) to (4)		244(1) to (3)	Amend 1974 s. 29(1) to (3).
(5)		—	Repeals 1974 s. 29(4).
(6)		244(5)	Amends 1974 s. 29(6).
(7)		—	Any remaining effect saved Sch. 3 para. 2.
19(1)	Amendment of sections 13 and 30 of 1974 Act.	—	Repeals 1974 s. 13(2).
(2)		298	Amends 1974 s. 30(1) "tort".
22(4)	Transitional provision.	—	Spent.
(5)	Extent of amendment to 1975 s. 127.	301	
Sched. 1	Compensation for certain dismissals.	—	Spent.
Sched. 2, para. 6(1)	Change of basis of computation of continous period of employment.	282	Amends 1975 s. 119(7).
Sched. 3	Minor and consequential amendments.		
para. 10		218, 295(1)	Substitutes 1919 s. 8.
para. 11		217	Amends Administration of Justice (Scotland) Act 1972 (c. 59) s. 3(3).
para. 12		220(3)	Amends 1974 s. 15(3).
para. 13		218	Amends 1975 s. 126(1) and inserts 1975 s. 126A.
para. 17		153	Amends 1978 s. 59(a).

TRADE UNION AND LABOUR RELATIONS CONSOLIDATION ACT—_continued._

Existing provision	Subject matter	Section of 1992 Act	Remarks
	EMPLOYMENT ACT 1982 (c. 46)—_continued._		
para. 18		238(3)	Amends 1978, s. 62(4)(b).
paras. 19, 20		154	Amend 1978 s. 64(3), 64A(2).
para. 24(1)		161(3)	Amends 1978 s. 77(2)(b).
(2)		162(1)	Amends 1978 s. 77(3).
(3)		163(1), (2)	Amends 1978 s. 77(5).
para. 27(2), (3)		—	Refer to provision repealed 1988 s. 11, Sch. 4.
	TRADE UNION ACT 1984 (c. 49)		
1(1)	Duty of trade union to hold elections for certain positions.	46(1), (2), (6)	Repealed in part 1988 s. 12(1); amended ibid. Sch. 3 para. 5(1).
(2)		46(1), (2)	Repealed in part 1988 s. 12(1).
(3)		59	Repealed in part 1988 s. 12(1).
(4)		46(6)	
(5)		119	
(6)		61(2)	
(6A)		46(3)	Inserted 1988 s. 12(1).
(6B)		46(1), (2)	Inserted 1988 s. 12(1).
(6C)		46(4)	Inserted 1988 s. 12(1).
(7)		46(5)	
2(1), (2)	Requirements to be satisfied in relation to elections.	50(1), (2)	
(3)		50(3)	
(4)		50(3), (4)	
(5)		51(1), (2)	Amended 1988 Sch. 3 para. 5(2), 1990 s. 5(4).
(6), (7)		51(3), (4)	
(8)		51(5), (6)	
(9), (10)		47(1), (2)	
(11), (12)		47(3)	
(13)		60(1), (3)	Amended 1988 Sch. 3 para. 5(2).
(14)		53	
3	Modification of section 2 requirements.	—	Repealed 1988 Sch. 4.
4(1), (2)	Register of members' names and addresses.	24(1), (2)	
(2A)		24(3)	Inserted 1988 Sch. 3 para. 5(3).
(3)		24(4)	
5(1)	Remedy for failure to comply with Part. I.	25(1), 26(1), 54(1), (2), 55(1), 56(1)	Amended 1988 Sch. 3 para. 5(4)(a).

TRADE UNION AND LABOUR RELATIONS CONSOLIDATION ACT—*continued.*

Existing provision	Subject matter	Section of 1992 Act	Remarks
	TRADE UNION ACT 1984 (c. 49)—*continued.*		
(2)		54(3)	
(3)		25(2), 55(2) 25(3), 26(3), 55(3), 56(3)	Part unnecessary.
(5) to (7)		26(4), 56(4)	
(8)		56(5)	Amended 1988 Sch. 3. para. 5(4)(b).
(9)		26(4), 56(4)	
(10)		24(6), 54(1)	Amended 1988 Sch. 3 para. 5(4)(a).
(11), (12)		26(5), 56(6)	
(12A)		56(6)	Inserted 1988 Sch. 3 para. 5(4)(c).
(13)		121	
6(1), (2)	Proceedings before Certification Officer: supplementary provisions.	25(4), (5), 55(4), (5)	
(3)		24(6), 54(1)	
(4)		26(2), 56(2)	
(5)		25(2), 55(2)	
(6)		—	Repealed 1988 Sch. 4.
(7), (8)		25(6), (7), 55(6), (7)	
7(1) to (3)	Exemption for certain trade unions.	118(6)	
(4) to (7)		43(2), 57(1)	
(8)		57(2)	
8(1) to (3)	Exemption for certain persons nearing retirement.	58(1) to (3)	Subs. (1) repealed in part and subs. (2)(a) amended 1988 Sch. 3 para. 5(5)(a), (b).
(4), (5)		Sch. 3 paras. 9, 10	First part of subs. (4) spent; remainder inserted 1988 Sch. 3 para. 5(5)(c), (d).
9(1)	Interpretation of Part I and transitional provisions.		
	"merchant seaman"	60(2), 118(6)	
	"offshore worker"	60(2)	
	"overseas member"	60(2)	
	"post"	298	
	"principal executive committee"	119	
	"proper address"	24(5)	
	"section"	119	
	"single transferable vote"	51(7)	
	"special register body"	117	Inserted 1988 Sch. 3 para. 5(6).

TRADE UNION AND LABOUR RELATIONS CONSOLIDATION ACT—*continued.*

Existing provision	Subject matter	Section of 1992 Act	Remarks

TRADE UNION ACT 1984 (c. 49)—continued.

Existing provision	Subject matter	Section of 1992 Act	Remarks
	"trade union"	1	
	other definitions	*passim*	
(2)		61(1)	
(3), (4)		—	Spent transitional provisions.
10(1)	Industrial action authorised or endorsed by trade union without support of a ballot.	226(1)	Substituted for subs. (1) and (2) 1990 Sch. 2 para. 2(2).
(3)		226(2)	Amended 1990 Sch. 2 para. 2(3).
(3A)		226(3)	Inserted 1988 s. 17(2); amended 1990 Sch. 2 para. 2(4).
(4), (4A)		226(2)	Substituted 1988 Sch. 3 para. 5(7); repealed in part 1990 Sch. 2 para. 2(5), (6)
(5)			Repealed in part 1990 Sch. 2 para. 2(7).
	"the 1974 Act"	—	Unnecessary.
	"the date of the ballot"	246	
	"place of work"	246	Inserted 1988 s. 17(3).
	"trade union"	1	
11(1)	Requirements to be satisfied in relation to ballots.	227(1)	Amended 1988 Sch. 3 para. 5(8)(a).
(1A)		228(1)	Inserted 1988 s. 17(1).
(1B)		228(2), (3)	Inserted 1988 s. 17(1).
(2)		227(2)	Amended 1988 Sch. 3 para. 5(8)(b).
(3)		229(1), (4)	Amended 1988 Sch. 3 para. 5(8)(c).
(4)		229(2)	Amended 1988 Sch. 3 para. 5(8)(d).
(4A)		229(3)	Inserted 1990 s. 7(1).
(5)		230(1)	
(6)		230(2), (3)	
(7)		230(4)	
(8)		231	Amended 1988 Sch. 3 para. 5(8)(e).
(9), (10)		231(1), (2)	
(11)	"overseas member"	232(3)	
	"post"	298	
	"working hours"	246	
	"strike"	246	

TRADE UNION AND LABOUR RELATIONS CONSOLIDATION ACT—*continued.*

Existing provision	Subject matter	Section of 1992 Act	Remarks
	TRADE UNION ACT 1984 (c. 49)—*continued.*		
	closing words	226(4)	Inserted 1988 Sch. 3 para. 5(8)(f).
12(1)	Political fund resolutions: periodic ballots.	*passim*	
(2)		73(3), (4)	
(3)		—	Spent transitional provision.
(4)		73(4)	
(5)		93(2)	
13(1)	Ballots: supplementary provisions.	74(3)	Amends 1913 s. 4(1).
(2)		76, 77, 298	Inserts 1913 s. 4(1A) to (1F).
(3)		74(2)	
(4) to (6)		Spent.	
(7), (8)		94(1), (2)	
(9)		84(4)	
(10)	"new resolution"	84(4)	
	"overseas member"	94(3)	
14(1)	Assets and liabilities of political fund.	83(1)	
(2)		83(1), (2)	
(3), (4)		83(3)	
(5)		—	Repeals words in 1913 s. 6.
15(1), (2)	Position where resolution has ceased to have effect.	89(2)	
(3)		90(1), (2)	
(4)		90(3)	
(5)		89(3)	
(6)		91(1)	
(7)		91(1) to (3)	
(8)		91(4)	
(9)		89(5)	
(10)		89(1)	
(11)		*passim*	
16(1)	Remedy for failure to comply with s. 15(3)(a).	90(4)	
(2) to (4)		90(5)	
(5)		90(6)	
(6)		121	
17(1)	Political objects.	72	Substitutes 1913 s. 3(3) to (3C).
(2)		Sch. 3 para. 8	
(3)		—	Repeals 1913 s. 1(6).
18(1) to (3)	Collection of union dues by employer.	86(1) to (3)	
(4)		87(1), (2)	

TRADE UNION AND LABOUR RELATIONS CONSOLIDATION ACT—*continued.*

Existing provision	Subject matter	Section of 1992 Act	Remarks
	TRADE UNION ACT 1984 (c. 49)—*continued.*		
(5), (6)		87(3), (4)	
(7)		273(1), (2)	
19(1)	Interpretation of Part III.	*passim*	Attracts definitions in 1913.
(2)	"the date of the ballot"	96	
	"commencement date"	—	Spent.
	"principal executive committee"	119	
	other definitions.	*passim*	
(3)		*passim*	
(4)		132	
20(1)	Amendments of ss. 1 and 2 of Employment Act 1980.	—	Introductory words.
(2)		115(2)	Amends 1980 s. 1(3).
(3)		115(2)	Inserts 1980 s. 1(3A).
(4)		—	Repeals 1980 s. 1(5).
(5)		—	Repeals word in 1980 s. 2(2)(b).
21	Expenses.	—	Unnecessary.
22(1)	Short title, commencement and extent.	—	Unnecessary.
(2) to (5)		—	Spent.
(6)		301(2)	Amended 1988 Sch. 3 para. 5(9).
	COMPANIES CONSOLIDATION (CONSEQUENTIAL PROVISIONS) ACT 1985 (c. 9)		
entry in Sched. 2		10(3), 30(4), 34(1), 117(1)	Amendments of 1974.
	WAGES ACT 1986 (c. 48)		
words in 1(6)	Deduction of political fund contributions.	88(2)	Inserted 1988 Sch. 3 para. 6(1).
5(3A)		88(3), (4)	Inserted 1988 Sch. 3 para. 6(2).
	PUBLIC ORDER ACT 1986 (c. 64)		
Sched. 2 para. 1		241(2), (3)	Amends 1875 s. 7.
	CONSUMER PROTECTION ACT 1987 (c. 43)		
Sched. 4 para. 8		22(1)	Amends 1982 s. 16(2).
	EMPLOYMENT ACT 1988 (c. 19)		
1(1)	Right to a ballot before industrial action.	62(1)	Amended 1990 Sch. 2 para. 3(2).
(2)		62(3)	Amended and repealed in part 1990 Sch. 2 para. 3(3).
(3)		62(5)	Substituted (for subs. (3) and (4)) 1990 Sch. 2 para. 3(4).

TRADE UNION AND LABOUR RELATIONS CONSOLIDATION ACT—*continued.*

Existing provision	Subject matter	Section of 1992 Act	Remarks
	EMPLOYMENT ACT 1988 (c. 19)—*continued.*		
(5)		62(2)	Amended 1990 Sch. 2 para. 3(5).
(6)		62(6), 226(4)	Applied 1984 s. 11(11) (as amended 1988 Sch. 3 para. 5(8)(f)).
(7)	"industrial action" other definitions.	62(6) —	Extended 1990 s.5(1). Given effect by applying parallel provisions of Pt. V.
(8)		62(9)	
2(1)	Right not to be denied access to the courts.	63(2)	
(2)		63(4)	
(3)		63(3)	
(4)		63(1)	
(5), (6)		63(5), (6)	
3(1)	Right not to be unjustifiably disciplined.	64(1)	
(2)		65(1)	
(3)		65(1) to (5), (7)	
(4)		65(6)	
(5)		64(2)	
(6)		65(2), (7)	
(7)		64(4)	
(8)		64(3)	
4(1)	Complaint of infringement of right under s. 3.	66(1)	
(2), (3)		66(2)	
(4)		66(3)	
(5)		291(2)	
(6)		66(4)	
(7)		288(1)	
5(1) to (9)	Further remedies for infringement of right under s. 3.	67(1) to (9)	
(10)		291(2)	
6(1)	Right to inspect union's accounting records.	29(1)	
(2)		29(3), 30(1)	
(3), (4)		30(2), (3)	
(5), (6)		30(5), (6)	
(7)		31(1), (2)	
(8)		45	
(9)(a)		29(1), (2)	
(b)		118(4)	

TRADE UNION AND LABOUR RELATIONS CONSOLIDATION ACT—*continued.*

Existing provision	Subject matter	Section of 1992 Act	Remarks
	EMPLOYMENT ACT 1988 (c. 19)—*continued.*		
(c)		30(4)	
(10)		30(1)	
7(1)	Right to require employer to stop deductions of union subscriptions.	68(1)	
(2)		68(2), (3)	
(3)		68(4)	
8(1) to (3)	Use of funds for indemnifying unlawful conduct.	15(1) to (3)	
(4)		15(4), (5)	
(5), (6)		15(5), (6)	
9(1) to (4)	Remedy against trustees for unlawful use of property.	16(1) to (4)	
(5)		16(6)	
10(1)	Industrial action to enforce membership.	222(1), (4)	
(2)		222(2), (4)	
(3)(a), (b)		222(4), (5)	
11	Action by employer to enforce membership.	—	Repeals 1978 ss. 23(2A), (2B), 58(3) to (12).
12(1)	Extension to non-voting positions of duty to hold elections.	46(1) to (4)	Amends 1984 s. 1.
(2)		57(2), (3)	
(3), (4)		Sch. 3 para. 9	
(5)		—	Spent.
(6)		119, Sch. 3 para. 9(2)	Definition of "retirement age" spent.
13(1)	Election addresses.	*passim*	Introductory words.
(2)		48(1), (2), (4) to (7)	
(3)		48(3)	
(4)		48(2)	
(5)		48(8)	
(6)	"post"	298	
	"proper address".	—	Applied: see 48(1)(b) and 51(4)(a).
14(1)	Requirement of postal ballot for certain ballots and elections.	77(4)	Amends 1913 s. 4(1D).
(2)		—	Repeals 1984 s. 3.
15(1)	Independent scrutiny of certain ballots and elections.	*passim*	Introductory words.

TRADE UNION AND LABOUR RELATIONS CONSOLIDATION ACT—*continued.*

Existing provision	Subject matter	Section of 1992 Act	Remarks
		EMPLOYMENT ACT 1988 (c. 19)—*continued.*	
(2)		49(1), (4) to (7), 75(1), (4) to (7)	Amended 1990 s. 5(5).
(3), (4)		49(2), (3), 75(2), (3)	
(5)		52(1), (2), 78(1), (2)	
(6)		52(2), 78(2)	
(7)		52(3) to (6), 78(3) to (6)	
(8)		132	
16(1)	Remedy with respect to ballot on use of funds for political purposes.	80(1), 81(1)	
(2), (3)		79(2), (3)	
(4)		79 to 81 *passim*	Applies 1984 ss. 5(3) to (13) and 6.
(5)		132	Applies 1913 s. 6A.
17(1)	Ballots on industrial action affecting different places of work.	228	Inserts 1984 s. 11(1A), (1B).
(2)		226(3)	Inserts 1984 s. 10(3A).
(3)		246	Amends 1984 s. 10(5).
18(1)	Codes of practice as to ballots and elections.	203(1)(b)	Amends 1980 s. 3(1).
(2)		1	Inserts 1980 s. 3(9).
19(1)	Appointment, etc. of the Commissioner.	266(1)	
(2)		—	Introduces Sch.
(3)		266(5)	
20(1)	Assistance by the Commissioner.	110(1)	
(2)		110(5), 111(1)	
(3)		111(3), 114(1)	
(4), (5)		110(2), (3)	
(6)		114(2)	
(7)		109(1), (3)	
(8)		109(3)	
21(1)	Provisions supplementary to s. 20.	113(1), (2)	
(2)		111(4)	
(3)		111(3)	
(4), (5)		111(5), (6)	
(6)		114(3)	
22(1)	Procedure before the Certification Officer.	256(1), (2)	

TRADE UNION AND LABOUR RELATIONS CONSOLIDATION ACT—*continued.*

Existing provision	Subject matter	Section of 1992 Act	Remarks
	EMPLOYMENT ACT 1988 (c. 19)—*continued.*		
(2)		256(3)	
(3)		256(4)	Inserts 1975 Sch. 1 para. 32A.
23(1), (2)	Interlocutory and interim orders.		
(1), (2)		16(5), 26(6), 31(3), 56(7), 62(4), 81(7)	
30(1)	Crown employees and contracts, &c.	62(7), 245	
(2)		276(2)	
(3)		273(3)	
32(1)	Interpretation		
	"branch or section".	119	
	"conduct".	65(7)	
	"contract of employment".	295(1)	
	"employer".	295(1), 296(2)	
	"official".	119	
	"trade union".	1	
	"worker".	296(1)	
	"contravention".	298	
	"the court".	121	
	"member".	15(7), 16(7), 30(7), 70	
	"rules".	119	
(2)		—	Spent.
34(2), (3)	Short title, commencement and extent.	—	Spent.
words in (6)		301(2)	
Sch. 1	Commissioner for the rights of trade union members.		
para. 1(1), (2)		267(2), (3)	
(3)		267(1)	
para. 2(1) to (5)		268(1) to (5)	Closing words of sub-para. (5) unnecessary.
para. 3(1), (2)		269(1)	
para. 4(1), (2)		266(4)	
para. 5(1), (2)		269(2), (3)	
para. 6		269(4)	
para. 7(1), (2)		270(1), (3)	
para. 8(1), (2)		270(2), (3)	
para. 9(1), (2)		271(2), (3) 271(4)	

TRADE UNION AND LABOUR RELATIONS CONSOLIDATION ACT—*continued.*

EMPLOYMENT ACT 1988 (c. 19)—*continued.*

Existing provision	Subject matter	Section of 1992 Act	Remarks
para. 10(1), (2)		271(1)	
para. 11		266(3)	
para. 12		Sch. 2 para. 1	
para. 13		Sch. 2 para. 4(4)	
para. 14		272	
Sched. 3, Part I	Minor and consequential amendments.		
para. 1(1)(a)	Amendments of 1913.	74(3)	Amends 1913 s. 4(1).
(b)		77(2)	Amends 1913 s. 4(1B)
(2)		—	Any remaining effect saved Sch. 3 para. 2.
para. 2(1)	Amendments of 1978.	151(1)	Substitute 1978 s. 23(7).
(2)(a)		152(3)	Amends 1978 s. 58(13).
(b)		152(4)	Substitutes 1978 s. 58(14).
(3)		290	Amends 1978 s. 133(1).
(4)		291(3)	Amends 1978 s. 136(5).
(5)		Sch. 2 para. 25	Amends 1978 Sch. 11.
para. 3(1)(a)	Amendments of 1980.	116(3)	Amends 1980 s. 2(1).
(b)		298	Amends 1980 s. 2(9).
(2)(a)		176(5)	Amends 1980 s. 5(8).
(b)		176(8)	Inserts 1980 s. 5(8A).
para. 4	Amendment of 1982.	225(2)	Substitutes 1982 s. 14(3).
para. 5(1)	Amendments of 1984.	46(1)	Amends 1984 s. 1(1)(a).
(2)(a)		51(2)	Amends 1984 s. 2(5).
(b)		60(3)	Amends 1984 s. 2(13).
(3)		24(3)	Inserts 1984 s. 4(2A).
(4)(a)		24(6), 25(1), 26(1), 54(1), (2), 55(1), 56(1)	Amends 1984 s. 5(1), (10).
(b)		56(5)	Amends 1984 s. 5(8).
(c)		56(6)	Inserts 1984 s. 5(12A).
(5)(a)		—	Repeals word in 1984 s. 8(1).
(b)		58(2)	Amends 1984 s. 8(2)(a).
(c), (d)		Sch. 3 paras. 9, 10	Amends 1984 s. 8(4) and inserts 1984 s. 8(5).
(6)		117	Amends 1984 s. 9(1); part drafting provision.
(7)		226(2)	Substitutes 1984 s. 10(4), (4A).
(8)(a)		227(1)	Amends 1984 s. 11(1)(a).

TRADE UNION AND LABOUR RELATIONS CONSOLIDATION ACT—*continued.*

Existing provision	Subject matter	Section of 1992 Act	Remarks
	EMPLOYMENT ACT 1988 (c. 19)—*continued.*		
(b)		227(2)	Amends 1984 s. 11(2)(b).
(c)		229(4)	Amends 1984 s. 11(3).
(d)		229(2)	Amends 1984 s. 11(4).
(e)		231	Amends 1984 s. 11(8).
(f)		226(4)	Amends 1984 s. 11(11).
(9)		(301)2)	Amends 1984 s. 22(6).
para. 6(1)	Amendments of Wages Act 1986 (c.48).	88(2)	Amends Wages Act 1986 (c.48) s. 1(6).
(2)		88(3), (4)	Inserts Wages Act 1986 (c.48) s. 5(3A).
(3)		—	Any remaining effect saved Sch. 3 para. 2.
	EMPLOYMENT ACT 1989 (c.38)		
14	Trade union duties for which time off must be allowed by employer.	168(1),(2)	Amends 1978 s. 27(1).
Sched. 6, para. 19		173(1), 178(3)	Substitutes 1978 s. 32; see now Sch. 2 para. 14.
Sched. 9, para. 2		—	Spent transitional provision.
	COMPANIES ACT 1989 (c.40)		
124	Audience of trade unions and employers' associations.	117(4), 131(2)	Adds 1974 s. 11(9).
	EMPLOYMENT ACT 1990 (c.38)		
1(1) to (6)	Refusal of employment on grounds related to union membership.	137(1) to (6)	
(7)		137(8)	
2(1) to (5)	Refusal of service of employment agency on grounds related to union membership.	138(1) to (5)	
3(1)	Interpretation and other supplementary provisions.	143(1)	
(2)		137(7)	
(3), (4)		143(2), (3)	
(5)		—	Introduces Sch.
4(1) to (6)	Secondary action.	224(1) to (6)	
(7)		*passim*	Attracts definitions in 1974.
5(1)	Minor amendments relating to ballots.	62(8), 235	
(2), (3)		232(4), (5)	
(4)		51(2)(a), 77(2)(a)	
(5)		49(5), 75(5)	
6(1)	Responsibility of trade union for acts of officials, &c.	—	Introductory words.
(2)		20(1)	Amends 1982 s. 15(2).

TRADE UNION AND LABOUR RELATIONS CONSOLIDATION ACT—*continued.*

Existing provision	Subject matter	Section of 1992 Act	Remarks
	EMPLOYMENT ACT 1990 (c.38)—*continued.*		
(3)		20(2) to (4)	Substitutes 1982 s. 15(3) to (3B).
(4)		21(1)	Substitutes 1982 s. 15(4).
(5)		21(2) to (4)	Substitutes 1982 s. 15(5) to (5B).
(6)		21(6)	Inserts 1982 s. 15(6A).
(7)		21(7)	Amends 1982 s. 15(7).
(8)		20(6)	Inserts 1982 s. 15(9).
7(1)	Calling of industrial action with support of ballot.	229(3)	Inserts 1984 s. 11(4A).
(2)		233(1)	
(3), (4)		233(3), (4)	
(5)	"date of the ballot".	246	
	"specified person".	233(2)	
	"trade union".	1	
8(1) to (6)	Period after which ballot ceases to be effective.	234(1) to (6)	
(7)	"date of the ballot".	246	
	"trade union".	1	
9(1)	Dismissal of those taking part in unofficial industrial action.	237	Inserts 1978 s. 62A.
(2)		223	
(3)		*passim*	Attracts 1974 definitions.
10(1) to (3)	Proceedings in respect of which assistance may be provided.	109(2)	
(4)(a)		1,119	
(b)		109(2)	
(5)		110(4)	
(6)		—	Unnecessary.
11(1), (2)	Title of proceedings where assistance provided.	112(1), (2)	
(3)		—	Unnecessary.
12(1), (2)	Consequential revision or revocation of Codes of Practice.	201(1), 205(1)	
(3)		205(2)	
(4)		201(2)	
(5), (6)		201(3), (4), 205(3), (4)	
(7)		202(1), (3), 206(1), (2)	
(8)		202(2)	
(9)		201(4), 205(4)	
Sched. 1	Further provisions relating to access to employment.		

TRADE UNION AND LABOUR RELATIONS CONSOLIDATION ACT—*continued.*

Existing provision	Subject matter	Section of 1992 Act	Remarks
	EMPLOYMENT ACT 1990 (c.38)—*continued.*		
Part I	Proceedings, remedies and related matters.		
para. 1		—	Introductory words.
para. 2(1), (2)		143(4)	
para. 3(1) to (3)		139(1) to (3)	
para. 4		290	Amends 1978 s. 133(1).
para. 5(1) to (4)		140(1) to (4)	
para. 6(1) to (3)		141(1) to (3)	
para. 7(1) to (4)		142(1) to (4)	
para. 8		291(2)	Amends 1978 s. 136(1).
Part II	Scope of application of provisions.		
para. 9		*passim*	Introductory provisions.
para. 10(1), (2)		288(1), (2)	
para. 11(1)		273(1)	
(2)		273(3)	Part unnecessary.
(3)		274(1), (2)	
(4)		275	
para. 12(1)		277(1), 278(1)	
(2)		277(2)	
(3)		278(3)	
(4)		277(3)	
(5), (6)		277(5), (6)	
para. 13		273(4), 277(4), 278(4)	
para. 14		280(1), (2)	
para. 15		285(1)	
para. 16(1), (2)		285(2)	
(3)		284	
para. 17(1), (2)		287(2)	
para. 18(1), (2)		276(1)	
Sched. 2	Consequential amendments.		
para. 1(2)	Amendment of 1978.	238(3)	Inserts 1978 s. 62(5)
para. 2(1)	Amendments of 1984.	—	Introductory words.
(2)		226(1)	Substitutes 1984 s. 10(1)
(3)		226(2)	Amends 1984 s. 10(3)
(4)		226(3)	Amends 1984 s. 10(3A).

TRADE UNION AND LABOUR RELATIONS CONSOLIDATION ACT—*continued.*

Existing provision	Subject matter	Section of 1992 Act	Remarks
	EMPLOYMENT ACT 1990 (c.38)—*continued.*		
(5)		—	Repeals words in 1984 s. 10(4).
(6)		226(2)	Amends 1984 s. 10(4A).
(7)		—	Repeals definitions in 1984 s. 10(5).
para. 3(1)	Amendments of 1988.	—	Introductory words.
(2)		62(1)	Amends 1988 s. 1(1).
(3)		62(3)	Amends 1988 s. 1(2).
(4)		62(5)	Substitutes 1988 s. 1(3), (4).
(5)		62(2)	
	INDUSTRIAL RELATIONS (NORTHERN IRELAND) ORDER 1992 (S.I. 1992/807 (N.I.5))		
Art. 67(2)	Extent of amendments to 1913.	301(2)(b)	

TRIBUNALS AND INQUIRIES ACT 1992 (c. 53)

TABLE OF DERIVATIONS

(for Table of Destinations see page cdxxvi)

Notes:

1. The following abbreviations are used in this Table:—

1971	= The Tribunals and Inquiries Act 1971 (c. 62)
1972 c. 11	= The Superannuation Act 1972 (c. 11)
1973 c. 36	= The Northern Ireland Constitution Act 1973 (c. 36)
1973 c. 38	= The Social Security Act 1973 (c. 38)
1974 c. 39	= The Consumer Credit Act 1974 (c. 39)
1976 c. 35	= The Police Pensions Act 1976 (c. 35)
1978 c. 30	= The Interpretation Act 1978 (c. 30)
1978 c. 44	= The Employment Protection (Consolidation) Act 1978 (c. 44)
1979 c. 38	= The Estate Agents Act 1979 (c. 38)
1980 c. 20	= The Education Act 1980 (c. 20)
1981 c. 54	= The Supreme Court Act 1981 (c. 54)
1982 c. 10	= The Industrial Training Act 1982 (c. 10)
1982 c. 16	= The Civil Aviation Act 1982 (c. 16)
1983 c. 41	= The Health and Social Services and Social Security Adjudications Act 1983 (c. 41)
1984 c. 35	= The Data Protection Act 1984 (c. 35)
1985 c. 65	= The Insolvency Act 1985 (c. 65)
1986 c. 53	= The Building Societies Act 1986 (c. 53)
1986 c. 60	= The Financial Services Act 1986 (c. 60)
1987 c. 22	= The Banking Act 1987 (c. 22)
1988 c. 33	= The Criminal Justice Act 1988 (c. 33)
1988 c. 48	= The Copyright, Designs and Patents Act 1988 (c. 48)
1990 c. 16	= The Food Safety Act 1990 (c. 16)
1990 c. 27	= The Social Security Act 1990 (c. 27)
1990 c. 41	= The Courts and Legal Services Act 1990 (c. 41)
1991 c. 21	= The Disability Living Allowance and Disability Working Allowance Act 1991 (c. 21)
1991 c. 40	= The Road Traffic Act 1991 (c. 40)
1991 c. 48	= The Child Support Act 1991 (c. 48)
1992 c. 6	= The Social Security (Consequential Provisions) Act 1992 (c. 6)
S.I. 1972/1210	= The Tribunals and Inquiries (Value Added Tax Tribunals) Order 1972
S.I. 1974/1478	= The Tribunals and Inquiries (Industrial Training Levy Exemption Referees) Order 1974
S.I. 1974/1964	= The Tribunals and Inquiries (Misuse of Drugs Tribunals) Order 1974
S.I. 1979/659	= The Tribunals and Inquiries (Vaccine Damage Tribunals) Order 1979
S.I. 1984/1094	= The Tribunals and Inquiries (Dairy Produce Quota Tribunal) Order 1984
S.I. 1984/1247	= The Tribunals and Inquiries (Foreign Compensation Commission) Order 1984
S.I. 1991/2699	= The Tribunals and Inquiries (Specified Tribunals) Order 1991

2. The Table does not show the effect of the Transfer of Functions (Secretary of State and Lord Advocate) Order 1972 (S.I. 1972/2002), which transferred the functions of the Secretary of State under sections 2, 4, 5, 11, 12, 15, 16 and 19 of the Tribunals and Inquiries Act 1971 to the Lord Advocate.

3. The Act consolidates the effect of the current orders under s. 15(1), (2), (3) and (4) of 1971. The power to vary or revoke these orders conferred by s. 16(2) is preserved in relation to the provisions of the Act derived from such orders by clause 13(5).

Section of 1992 Act	Derivation
1(1)	1971 s. 1(1).
(2)	1971 s. 1(2); 1973 c. 36 s. 40(2).
2	1971 s. 2.
3	1971 s. 3.
4	1971 s. 4.
5	1971 s. 5.
6(1), (2)	1971 s. 7(1), (2).
(3)	1971 s. 7(3); Supplementary Benefits Act 1976 (c. 71) Sch. 7 para. 22; Social Security (Miscellaneous Provisions) Act 1977 (c. 5) s. 22(15); 1983 c. 41 Sch. 9 para. 10; 1991 c. 21 Sch. 2 para. 2(1): 1991 c. 48 Sch. 5 para. 1(1); S.I. 1979/659 art. 3.

TRIBUNALS AND INQUIRIES ACT—*continued.*

Section of 1992 Act	Derivation
(4)	Social Security Administration Act 1992 (c. 5) ss: 41. 43. 50.
(5)—(7)	1971 s. 7(4)—(6).
(8)	1971 s. 7(7); Sch. 1 para. 45(a); 1984 c. 58 s. 115(2).
(9)	1971 s. 7(8).
7(1)	1971 s. 8(1).
(2)	1971 s. 8(2); 1979 c. 38 s. 24(1)(a); 1982 c. 16 s. 7(3)(b); 1984 c. 35 Sch. 2 para. 13(a); 1985 c. 65 Sch. 1 para. 5(2); 1986 c. 60 Sch. 6 para. 6(a); 1987 c. 22 Sch. 6 para. 4(1); 1988 c. 33 Sch. 15 para. 37(1); 1990 c. 27 s. 12(2)(b); 1992 c. 6 Sch. 2 para. 8.
(3)	1971 s. 8(3).
8(1)	1971 s. 10(1); S.I. 1984/1247 art. 3.
(2)	1986 c. 53 s. 48(3); 1987 c. 22 s. 30(3).
(3)	1971 s. 10(2); 1987 c. 22 s. 30(4).
(4)	1971 s. 10(3).
9	1971 s. 11.
10(1)—(7)	1971 s. 12.
(8)	1971 s. 16(2)
11(1)	1971 s. 13(1); 1980 c. 20 s. 7(6); 1983 c. 41 Sch. 9 Pt. I para. 11; 1985 c. 65 Sch. 1 para. 5(3); 1986 c. 60 Sch. 6 para. 6(b); Education (Schools) Act 1992 (c. 38) Sch. 4 para 2; S.I. 1972/1210 art. 3; S.I. 1974/1478 art. 3.
(2)	1971 s. 13(1A); 1978 c. 44 Sch. 16 para. 11.
(3)	1971 s. 13(2); 1981 c. 54 Sch. 5.
(4)	1971 s. 13(3).
(5)	1971 s. 13(4).
(6)	1971 s. 13(5A); 1974 c. 39 s. 42(1).
(7)	1971 s. 13(6); 1974 c. 39 s. 42(2); Rating and Valuation (Amendment) (Scotland) Act 1984 (c. 31) Sch. 2 para. 12.
(8)	1971 s. 13(7); 1974 c. 39 s. 42(3); Judicature (Northern Ireland) Act 1978 (c. 23) Sch. 5.
(9)	1971 s. 13(8).
(10)	1971 s. 13(9).
12	1971 s. 14.
13(1)—(4)	1971 s. 15(1)—(4)
(5)	1971 s. 15(5). See Note 3 above.
(6)	1971 s. 15(6).
14(1)	1971 s. 19(4); 1974 c. 39 s. 3(b); 1979 c. 38 s. 24(1)(a); 1984 c. 35 Sch. 2 para. 13(b); S.I. 1984/1247 art. 4.
(2)	1973 c. 38 s. 66(4) and (9).
(3)	1982 c. 16 s. 7(3)(c).
15	1971 s. 16(1).
16	1971 s. 19(1)—(3).
17	Introduces Sch. 2.
18(1)	Introduces Sch. 3
(2)	Introduces Sch. 4.
(3)	1971 Sch. 3.
19	—
Sch. 1 para. 1	1971 Sch. 1 para. 1; Agricultural Holdings Act 1986 (c. 5) Sch. 14 para. 49.
para. 2	1971 Sch. 1 para. 1A; Aircraft and Shipbuilding Industries Act 1977 (c. 3) s. 42(10).
para. 3	1982 c. 16 s. 7(3)(a).
para. 4	1971 Sch. 1 para. 2A; 1987 c. 22 Sch. 6 para. 4(2).
para. 5	1971 Sch. 1 para. 3.
para. 6	S.I. 1991/2699 art. 2(b).
para. 7	1971 Sch. 1 para. 4A; 1991 c. 48 Sch. 5 para. 1(2).
para. 8	1971 Sch. 1 paras. 4, 21A, 28A; 1983 c. 41 Sch. 9 paras. 12, 13. 14; Registered Homes Act 1984 (c. 23) Sch. 1 para. 5(a); Children Act 1989 (c. 41) Sch. 13 para. 30.
para. 9	1971 Sch. 1 para. 5

TRIBUNALS AND INQUIRIES ACT—*continued.*

Section of 1992 Act	Derivation
para. 10	1971 Sch. 1 para. 5AA; 1990 c. 41 Sch. 18 para. 2.
para. 11	1971 Sch. 1 para. 5A; 1988 c. 48 Sch. 7 para. 14.
para. 12	1971 Sch. 1 para. 5B; 1988 c. 33 Sch. 15 para. 37(2).
para. 13	S.I. 1984/1094 art. 2; 1978 c. 30 ss. 17(2)(a), 23.
para. 14	1971 Sch. 1 para. 5B; 1984 c. 35 Sch. 2 para. 13(c); 1988 c. 33 Sch. 15 para. 37(2).
para. 15	1971 Sch. 1 para. 6; 1980 c. 20 s. 7(6); Education Reform Act 1988 (c. 40) Sch. 12 Part I para. 12; Education (Schools) Act 1992 (c. 38) Sch. 4 para. 3.
para. 16	1971 Sch. 1 para. 10; 1982 c. 10 Sch. 3 para. 2.
para. 17	1971 Sch. 1 para. 6A; 1979 c. 38 s. 24(1)(b).
para. 18	1971 Sch. 1 para. 6B; 1986 c. 60 Sch. 6 para. 6(c).
para. 19	1971 Sch. 1 para. 6C; 1990 c. 16 Sch. 3 para. 14(1).
para. 20	S.I. 1984/1247 art. 2.
para. 21	1971 Sch. 1 para. 7; S.I. 1991/2699 art. 2(a).
para. 22	1971 Sch. 1 para. 8; 1978 c. 30 s. 17(2)(a).
para. 23	1971 Sch. 1 para. 9; 1978 c. 30 s. 17(2)(a).
para. 24	S.I. 1974/1478 art. 2.
para. 25	1971 Sch. 1 para. 9A; Industry Act 1975 (c. 68) Sch. 3 para. 10.
para. 26	1971 Sch. 1 para. 10A; 1985 c. 65 Sch. 1 para. 5(4); Insolvency Act 1986 (c. 45) Sch. 14.
para. 27	1971 Sch. 1 para. 12.
para. 28	1971 Sch. 1 para. 12A; Local Government Finance Act 1988 (c. 41) Sch. 12 Pt. III para. 41; Local Government Finance Act 1992 (c. 14) Sch. 13 para. 31.
para. 29	1971 Sch. 1 para. 13.
para. 30	1971 Sch. 1 para. 14; Mental Health Act 1983 (c. 20) Sch. 4 para. 29.
para. 31	1971 Sch. 1 para. 16.
para. 32	S.I. 1974/1964 art. 3.
para. 33	1971 Sch. 1 para. 17; National Health Service Reorganisation Act 1973 (c. 32) Sch. 4 para. 134; National Health Service Act 1977 (c. 49) Sch. 15 para. 53; National Health Service and Community Care Act 1990 (c. 19) s. 2(1)(b).
para. 34	1971 Sch. 1 para. 22; Patents, Designs and Marks Act 1986 (c. 39) Sch. 2 Part I para. 1(2)(d).
para. 35(a), (b)	1971 Sch. 1 para. 23(a), (b).
(c)	1971 Sch. 1 para. 23(d)
(d)	1973 c. 38 s. 66(4), (9).
(e)	1971 Sch. 1 para. 23(e); Social Security Act 1990 (c. 27) s. 12(2)(a).
(f)	1971 Sch. 1 para. 23(c); 1972 c. 11 Sch. 6 para. 91(a); 1976 c. 35 Sch. 2 para. 9.
para. 36	1971 Sch. 1 para. 25; European Communities Act 1972 (c. 68) Sch. 4 para. 5(6).
para. 37	1971 Sch. 1 para. 28(b).
para. 38	1971 Sch. 1 para. 19(e), (f); Reserve Forces (Safeguard of Employment) Act 1985 (c. 17) Sch. 4 para. 3.
para. 39	1971 Sch. 1 para. 29(a), (b), (d); 1978 c. 30 s. 17(2)(a).
para. 40	1971 Sch. 1 para. 30; Transport Act 1985 (c. 67) Sch. 2 Part II para. 2(2); 1991 c. 40 Sch. 7 para. 1.
para. 41	1971 Sch. 1 para. 30A; Social Security (Consequential Provisions) Act 1975 (c. 16) Sch. 2 para. 46; 1992 c. 6 Sch. 2 para. 9.
para. 42	1971 Sch. 1 para. 31; Transport Act 1985 (c. 67) Sch. 7 para. 15.
para. 43	S.I. 1979/659 art. 2.
para. 44	S.I. 1972/1210 art. 2(a).
para. 45	1971 Sch. 1 para. 32.
para. 46	1971 Sch. 1 para. 33; 1978 c. 30 s. 17(2)(a).
para. 47	1971 Sch. 1 para. 34.
para. 48	1971 Sch. 1 para. 35.
para. 49	S.I. 1984/1094 art. 2; 1978 c. 30 s. 17(2)(a), 23(2).

TRIBUNALS AND INQUIRIES ACT—*continued.*

Section of 1992 Act	Derivation
para. 50	1971 Sch. 1 para. 36; 1978 c. 30 s. 17(2)(a); Education (Scotland) Act 1980 (c. 44) s. 28E(7); Education (Scotland) Act 1981 (c. 58) s. 1(1); Self-Governing Schools etc. (Scotland) Act 1989 (c. 39) Sch. 10 para. 4.
para. 51	1971 Sch. 1 para. 38; 1982 c. 10 Sch. 3 para. 2.
para. 52	1971 Sch. 1 para. 36A; 1990 c. 16 Sch. 3 para. 14(2).
para. 53	1971 Sch. 1 para. 37; S.I. 1991/2699 art. 3(a).
para. 54	1971 Sch. 1 para. 39.
para. 55	S.I. 1974/1964 art. 3.
para. 56	1971 Sch. 1 para. 41; National Health Service (Scotland) Act 1972 (c. 58) Sch. 6 para. 152; National Health Service (Scotland) Act 1978 (c. 29) Sch. 16 para. 35; S.I. 1991/2699 art. 3(b).
para. 57	1971 Sch. 1 para. 43; 1972 c. 11 Sch. 6 para. 91(b); 1976 c. 35 Sch. 2 para. 9.
para. 58	Tribunals and Inquiries (Valuation Appeal Committees) Order 1975 (S.I. 1975/1404) art. 3.
para. 59	1971 Sch. 1 para. 45; Rent (Scotland) Act 1984 (c. 58) Sch. 8 Part I para. 1.
para. 60	1971 Sch. 1 para. 46.
para. 61	1971 Sch. 1 para. 47.
para. 62	1971 Sch. 1 para. 48; Civic Government (Scotland) Act 1982 (c. 45) s. 18(11); Transport Act 1985 (c. 67) Sch. 2 part II para. 2(3).
para. 63	S.I. 1972/1210 art. 2(b).
Sch. 2	
paras. 1-4	1988 c. 33 s. 171(1); 1990 c. 41 s. 124(3); 1991 c. 48 s. 58(2).
para. 5	1971 Sch. 2 para. 1.
Sch. 3	—
Sch. 4	—

TRIBUNALS AND INQUIRIES ACT 1992 (c. 53)

TABLE OF DESTINATIONS

Notes:

1. The following abbreviations are used in this Table:—

1971	The Tribunals and Inquiries Act 1971 (c. 62)
1972 c. 11	The Superannuation Act 1972 (c. 11)
1973 c. 36	The Northern Ireland Constitution Act 1973 (c.36)
1973 c. 38	The Social Security Act 1973 (c. 38)
1974 c. 39	The Consumer Credit Act 1974 (c. 39)
1976 c. 35	The Police Pensions Act 1976 (c. 35)
1976 c. 71	The Supplementary Benefits Act 1976 (c. 71)
1977 c. 5	The Social Security (Miscellaneous Provisions) Act 1977 (c. 5)
1978 c. 30	The Interpretation Act 1978 (c. 30)
1978 c. 44	The Employment Protection (Consolidation) Act 1978 (c. 44)
1979 c. 36	The Nurses, Midwives and Health Visitors Act 1979 (c. 36)
1979 c. 38	The Estate Agents Act 1979 (c. 38)
1980 c. 20	The Education Act 1980 (c. 20)
1980 c. 34	The Transport Act 1980 (c. 34)
1980 c. 53	The Health Services Act 1980 (c. 53)
1981 c. 54	The Supreme Court Act 1981 (c. 54)
1982 c. 10	The Industrial Training Act 1982 (c. 10)
1982 c. 16	The Civil Aviation Act 1982 (c. 16)
1983 c. 41	The Health and Social Services and Social Security Adjudications Act 1983 (c. 41)
1984 c. 23	The Registered Homes Act 1984 (c. 23)
1984 c. 35	The Data Protection Act 1984 (c. 35)
1985 c. 65	The Insolvency Act 1985 (c. 65)
1985 c. 67	The Transport Act 1985 (c. 67)
1986 c. 45	The Insolvency Act 1986 (c. 45)
1986 c. 60	The Financial Services Act 1986 (c. 60)
1987 c. 22	The Banking Act 1987 (c. 22)
1988 c. 33	The Criminal Justice Act 1988 (c. 33)
1988 c. 48	The Copyright, Designs and Patents Act 1988 (c. 48)
1990 c. 16	The Food Safety Act 1990 (c. 16)
1990 c. 27	The Social Security Act 1990 (c. 27)
1991 c. 21	The Disability Living Allowance and Disability Working Allowance Act 1991 (c. 21)
1991 c. 48	The Child Support Act 1991 (c. 48)
1992 c. 6	The Social Security (Consequential Provisions) Act 1992 (c. 6)
S.I. 1972/1210	The Tribunals and Inquiries (Value Added Tax Tribunals) Order 1972
S.I. 1974/1478	The Tribunals and Inquiries (Industrial Training Levy Exemption Referees) Order 1974
S.I. 1974/1964	The Tribunals and Inquiries (Misuse of Drugs Tribunals) Order 1974
S.I. 1975/816 (N.I. 7)	The Administration of Justice (Northern Ireland) Order 1975
S.I. 1979/659	The Tribunals and Inquiries (Vaccine Damage Tribunals) Order 1979
S.I. 1984/1094	The Tribunals and Inquiries (Dairy Produce Quota Tribunal) Order 1984.
S.I. 1984/1247	The Tribunals and Inquiries (Foreign Compensation Commission) Order 1984
S.I. 1991/2699	The Tribunals and Inquiries (Specified Tribunals) Order 1991

2. The Table does not show the effect of the Transfer of Functions (Secretary of State and Lord Advocate) Order 1972 (S.I. 1972/2002), which transferred the functions of the Secretary of State under sections 2, 4, 5, 11, 12, 15, 16 and 19 of the Tribunals and Inquiries Act 1971 to the Lord Advocate.

PART I

ENACTMENTS

Section of Act	Subject matter	Section of 1992 Act	Remarks
	THE TRIBUNALS AND INQUIRIES ACT 1971 (c. 62)		
1	Council on Tribunals.	1	Subs. (2) amended 1973 c. 36 s. 40(2)

TRIBUNALS AND INQUIRIES ACT—*continued.*

Section of Act	Subject matter	Section of 1992 Act	Remarks
	THE TRIBUNALS AND INQUIRIES ACT 1971 (c. 62)—*continued.*		
2	Composition of the Council and the Scottish Committee.	2	
3	Tenure of office, remuneration and expenses.	3	
4	Reports of, and references to, Council and Scottish Committee.	4	
5	Recommendations of Council as to appointment of members of tribunals.	5	
6	Right of Council member to attend hearings under Part X of Local Government Act 1933.	—	Repealed Local Government Act 1972 (c. 70) Sch. 30.
7	Chairmen etc. of certain tribunals: provisions as to appointment.	6	Subs. (3) amended 1976 c. 71 Sch. 7 para. 22; 1977 c. 5 s. 22(15); 1983 c. 41 Sch. 9 para. 10; 1991 c. 21 Sch. 2 para. 2(1); 1991 c. 48 Sch. 5 para. 1(1); 1992 c. 6 Sch. 2 para. 8; S.I. 1979/659 art. 3 Subs. (3) repealed in part 1977 c. 5 Sch. 2; Housing Act 1980 (c. 51) Sch. 26. Reference in subs. (3) to para. 19(a) and (b) of Sch. 1 spent. Subsection (7)(b) spent.
8	Concurrence required for removal of members of certain tribunals.	7	Subs. (2) amended 1974 c. 39 s. 3(a); Health Services Act 1976 (c. 83) Sch. 1 para 23(2); 1979 c. 38 s. 24(1)(a); 1984 c. 35 Sch. 2 para. 13(a); 1985 c. 65 Sch. 1 para. 5(2); 1986 c. 60 Sch. 6 para. 6(a); 1987 c. 22 Sch. 6 para. 4(1); 1988 c. 33 Sch. 15 para. 37(1); 1990 c. 27 s. 12(2)(b). Subs. (2) repealed in part 1980 c. 53 Sch. 7.
9	Legal qualifications for certain tribunals.	—	Repealed Statute Law (Repeals) Act 1977 (c. 18) Sch. 1.
10	Procedural rules for tribunals.	8	Subs. (1) amended S.I. 1972/1210 art. 4; S.I. 1984/1247 art. 3.
11	Procedure in connection with statutory inquiries.	9	
12	Reasons to be given for decisions of tribunals and Ministers.	10	
13	Appeals from certain tribunals.		

TRIBUNALS AND INQUIRIES ACT—*continued.*

Section of Act	Subject matter	Section of 1992 Act	Remarks
*	THE TRIBUNALS AND INQUIRIES ACT 1971 (c. 62)—*continued.*		
(1)	—	11(1)	Amended 1980 c. 20 s. 7(6); 1983 c. 41 Sch. 9 Pt. I para. 11; 1985 c. 65 Sch. 1 para. 5(3); 1986 c. 60 Sch. 6 para. 6(b); S.I. 1972/1210 art. 3; S.I. 1974/1478 art. 3. Repealed in part 1983 c. 41 Sch. 10.
(1A)	—	11(2)	Inserted 1978 c. 44 Sch. 16 para. 11.
(2)	—	11(3)	Amended 1981 c. 54 Sch. 5.
(3)	—	11(4)	
(4)	—	11(5)	Repealed in part Administration of Justice Act 1977 (c. 38) Sch. 5 Part IV.
(5)	—	—	Repealed 1980 c. 34 Sch. 9 Part I.
(5A)	—	11(6)	Inserted 1974 c. 39 s. 42(1).
(6)	—	11(7)	Amended 1974 c. 39 s. 42(2); Rating and Valuation (Amendment) (Scotland) Act 1984 (c. 31) Sch. 2 para. 12. Repealed in part 1980 c. 34 Sch. 9 Part I. Reference in para. (b) to para. 42 of Sch. 1 spent.
(7)	—	11(8)	Amended 1974 c. 39 s. 42(3); Judicature (Northern Ireland) Act 1978 (c. 23) Sch. 5.
(8), (9)	—	11(9), (10)	
(10)	—	—	Spent.
14	Extension of supervisory powers of superior courts.		
(1)	—	12(1)	Repealed (N.I.) S.I. 1975/816 (N.I. 7) Sch. 2.
(2)	—	12(2)	
(3)	—	12(3)	Repealed in part British Nationality Act 1981 (c. 61) Sch. 9. Repealed (N.I.) S.I. 1975/816 (N.I. 7) Sch. 2.
15	Power to apply Act to additional tribunals and to repeal or amend certain provisions.		
(1)–(4)	—	13(1)–(4)	

TRIBUNALS AND INQUIRIES ACT—*continued.*

Section of Act	Subject matter	Section of 1992 Act	Remarks
	THE TRIBUNALS AND INQUIRIES ACT 1971 (c. 62)—*continued.*		
(5)	—	13(5)	References to paragraphs 2, 18(a), 27 and 44 of Schedule 1 spent.
(6)	—	13(6)	Amended 1973 c. 36 s. 40(2).
16	Rules and orders.		
(1)	—	15	
(2)	—	10(8)	Unnecessary in part: see 1978 c. 30 s. 14.
17	Introduces Sch. 2.	—	
18	Consequential amendments, repeals and savings.		
(1), (2)	Introduce Schs. 3, 4.	—	
(3)–(5)	Savings.	—	Spent.
19	Interpretation.		
(1)–(3)	—	16(1)–(3)	
(4)	—	14(1)	Amended 1974 c. 39 s. 3(b); 1979 c. 38 s. 24(1)(a); 1984 c. 35 Sch. 2 para. 13(b); S.I. 1984/1247 art. 4. Reference to para. 29(c) of Sch. 1 spent.
20	Short title, commencement and extent.		
(1), (2)	—	—	
(3)	—	19(3)	
Sch. 1	Tribunals under general supervision of Council.		
para. 1	—	Sch. 1 para. 1	Amended Agricultural Holdings Act 1986 (c. 5) Sch. 14 para. 49.
para. 1A	—	Sch. 1 para. 2	Inserted Aircraft and Shipbuilding Industries Act 1977 (c. 3) s. 42(10).
para. 2	—	—	Repealed Statute Law (Repeals) Act 1986 (c. 12) Sch. 1 Part I.
para. 2A	—	Sch. 1 para. 4	Inserted 1987 c. 22 Sch. 6 para. 4(2).
para. 3	—	Sch. 1 para. 5	
para. 4	—	Sch. 1 para. 8	Amended 1983 c. 41 Sch. 9 para. 12; 1984 c. 23 Sch. 1 para. 5(a); Children Act 1989 (c. 41) Sch. 13 para. 30.
para. 4A	—	Sch. 1 para. 7	Inserted 1991 c. 48 Sch. 5 para. 1(2).
para. 5	—	Sch. 1 para. 9	

TRIBUNALS AND INQUIRIES ACT—*continued.*

Section of Act	Subject matter	Section of 1992 Act	Remarks

THE TRIBUNALS AND INQUIRIES ACT 1971 (c. 62)—*continued.*

Section of Act	Subject matter	Section of 1992 Act	Remarks
para. 5AA	—	Sch. 1 para. 10	Inserted Courts and Legal Services Act 1990 (c. 41) Sch. 18 para. 2.
para. 5A	—	Sch. 1 para. 11	Inserted 1988 c. 48 Sch. 7 para. 14. (Previous paragraph 5A inserted 1974 c. 39 s. 3(c) and repealed 1979 c. 38 s. 24(b)).
para. 5B	—	Sch. 1 para. 12	Inserted 1988 c. 33 Sch. 15 para. 37(2).
para. 5B	—	Sch. 1 para. 14	Inserted (as para. 5A) 1984 c. 35 Sch. 2 para. 13(c). Renumbered (as para. 5B) 1988 c. 48 Sch. 7 para. 14.
para. 6	—	Sch. 1 para. 15	Amended 1980 c. 20 s. 7(6); Education Reform Act 1988 (c. 40) Sch. 12 Part I para. 12.
para. 6A	—	Sch. 1 para. 17	Inserted 1979 c. 38 s. 24(1)(b).
para. 6B	—	Sch. 1 para. 18	Inserted 1986 c. 60 Sch. 6 para. 6(c).
para. 6C	—	Sch. 1 para. 19	Inserted 1990 c. 16 Sch. 3 para. 14(1).
para. 7	—	Sch. 1 para. 21	
para. 7A	—	—	Inserted Health Services Act 1979 (c. 83) Sch. 1 para. 23(3). Repealed 1980 c. 53 Sch. 7.
para. 8	—	Sch. 1 para. 22	
para. 9	—	Sch. 1 para. 23	
para. 9A	—	Sch. 1 para. 25	Inserted Industry Act 1975 (c. 68) Sch. 3 para. 10.
para. 10	—	Sch. 1 para. 16	Amended 1982 c. 10 Sch. 3 para.2
para. 10A	—	Sch. 1 para. 26	Inserted 1985 c. 65 Sch. 1 para. 5(4). Amended 1986 c. 45 Sch. 14.
para. 11	—	—	Repealed British Steel Act 1988 (c. 35) Sch. 2 Part I.
para. 12	—	Sch. 1 para. 27	
para. 12A	—	Sch. 1 para. 28	Inserted Local Government Finance Act 1988 (c. 41) Sch. 12 Part III para. 41.
para. 13	—	Sch. 1 para. 29	

TRIBUNALS AND INQUIRIES ACT—*continued.*

Section of Act	Subject matter	Section of 1992 Act	Remarks
\multicolumn{4}{c}{THE TRIBUNALS AND INQUIRIES ACT 1971 (c. 62)—*continued.*}

Section of Act	Subject matter	Section of 1992 Act	Remarks
para. 14	—	Sch. 1 para. 30	Amended Mental Health Act 1983 (c. 20) Sch. 4 para. 29.
para. 15	—	—	Repealed 1990 c. 16 Sch. 3 para. 14(1).
para. 16	—	Sch. 1 para. 31	
para. 17	—	Sch. 1 para. 33	Amended National Health Service Reorganisaton Act 1973 (c. 32) Sch. 4 para. 134; National Health Service Act 1977 (c. 49) Sch. 15 para. 53; 1980 c. 53 Sch. 1 para. 87; National Health Service and Community Care Act 1990 (c. 19) s. 2(1)(b). Repealed in part Health and Social Security Act 1984 (c. 48) Sch. 8 Part I.
para. 18	—	—	Repealed Social Security (Miscellaneous Provisions) Act 1977 (c. 5) Sch. 2.
para. 19	—	Sch. 1 para. 38	Paragraphs (a)–(d) spent: s. 23(3) of, and Schs. 3 and 4 to, National Service Act 1948 repealed Statute Law (Repeals) Act 1977 (c. 18) Sch. 1 Part I. Paragraphs (d), (e) amended Reserve Forces (Safeguard of Employment) Act 1985 (c. 17) Sch. 4 para. 3.
para. 20	—	—	Repealed 1976 c. 71 Sch. 7 para. 22.
para. 21	—	—	Spent: Nurses Act 1957 repealed 1979 c. 36 Sch. 8
para. 21A	—	Sch. 1 para. 8	Inserted 1983 c. 41 Sch. 9 para. 13; amended 1984 c. 23 Sch. 1 para. 5(b).
para. 22	—	Sch. 1 para. 34	Amended Patents, Designs and Marks Act 1986 (c. 39) Sch. 2 Part I para. 1(2)(d).
para. 23	—	Sch. 1 para. 35(a), (b), (c), (e), (f)	Sub-para. (c) amended 1972 c. 11 Sch. 6 para. 91(a); 1976 c. 35 Sch. 2 para. 8(a). Sub-para. (e) inserted 1990 c. 27 s. 12(2)(a).
para. 24	—	—	Repealed 1988 c. 48 Sch. 8.

TRIBUNALS AND INQUIRIES ACT—*continued.*

Section of Act	Subject matter	Section of 1992 Act	Remarks

THE TRIBUNALS AND INQUIRIES ACT 1971 (c. 62)—*continued.*

Section of Act	Subject matter	Section of 1992 Act	Remarks
para. 25	—	Sch. 1 para. 36	Amended European Communities Act 1972 (c. 68) Sch. 4 para. 5(6).
para. 26	—	—	Repealed 1986 c. 60 Sch. 17 Part I.
para. 27	—	—	Spent: General Rate Act 1967 repealed Local Government Finance Act 1988 (c. 41). Sch. 13 Part I.
para. 28	—	Sch. 1 para. 37	Sub-para. (a) repealed Housing Act 1980 (c. 51) Sch. 26.
para. 28A	—	Sch. 1 para. 8	Inserted 1983 c. 41 Sch. 9 para. 14. Amended 1984 c. 23 Sch. 1 para. 5(c).
para. 29	—	Sch. 1 para. 39	Sub-para. (c) spent: Board of Referees dissolved Finance Act 1982 (c. 39) s. 156.
para. 30	—	Sch. 1 para. 40	Substituted 1985 c. 67 Sch. 2 Part II para. 2(2); amended 1991 c. 40 Sch. 7 para. 1.
para. 30A	—	Sch. 1 para. 41	Inserted Social Security (Consequential Provisions) Act 1975 (c. 18) Sch. 2 Part II para. 2(2). Amended 1983 c. 41 Sch. 9 Part I para. 15,1991 c. 21 Sch. 2 para. 2(2). Substituted 1992 c. 6 Sch. 2 para. 9.
para. 30B	—	—	Inserted 1976 c. 71 Sch. 7 para. 22. Repealed 1983 c. 41 Sch. 10.
para. 31	—	Sch. 1 para. 42	Substituted 1985 c. 67 Sch. 7 para. 15.
para. 32	—	Sch. 1 para. 45	
para. 33	—	Sch. 1 para. 46	
para. 34	—	Sch. 1 para. 47	
para. 35	—	Sch. 1 para. 48	
para. 36	—	Sch. 1 para. 50	Amended Education (Scotland) Act 1980 (c. 44) s. 28E(7); Education (Scotland) Act 1981 (c. 58) s. 1; Self-Governing Schools etc. (Scotland) Act 1989 (c. 39) Sch. 10 para. 4.

TRIBUNALS AND INQUIRIES ACT—*continued.*

Section of Act	Subject matter	Section of 1992 Act	Remarks

THE TRIBUNALS AND INQUIRIES ACT 1971 (c. 62)—*continued.*

Section of Act	Subject matter	Section of 1992 Act	Remarks
para. 36A	—	Sch. 1 para. 52	Inserted 1990 c. 16 Sch. 3 para. 14(2).
para. 37	—	Sch. 1 para. 53	
para. 37A	—	—	Inserted Health Services Act 1976 (c. 83) Sch. 1 para. 23(4). Repealed 1980 c. 53 Sch. 7.
para. 38	—	Sch. 1 para. 51	Amended 1982 c. 10 Sch. 3 para. 2.
para. 39	—	Sch. 1 para. 54	
para. 40	—	—	Repealed 1990 c. 16 Sch. 3 para. 14(2).
para. 41	—	Sch. 1 para. 56	Amended National Health Service (Scotland) Act 1972 (c. 58) Sch. 6 para. 152; National Health Service (Scotland) Act 1978 (c. 29) Sch. 16 para. 35.
para. 42	—	—	Spent: Nurses (Scotland) Act 1951 s. 24 repealed 1979 c. 36 Sch. 8.
para. 43	—	Sch. 1 para. 57	Sub-para. (c) inserted 1972 c. 11 Sch. 6 para. 91(b); amended 1976 c. 35 Sch. 2 para. 9.
para. 44	—	—	Repealed Tribunals and Inquiries (Valuation Appeal Committees) Order 1975 (S.I. 1975/1404) art. 4.
para. 45	—	Sch. 1 para. 59	Sub-para. (a) spent: see Rent (Scotland) Act 1984 (c. 58) s. 115(2). Sub-para. (b) amended ibid. Sch. 8 Part I para. 1.
para. 46	—	Sch. 1 para. 60	
para. 47	—	Sch. 1 para. 61	
para. 48	—	Sch. 1 para. 62	Inserted Civic Government (Scotland) Act 1982 (c. 45) s. 18(11). Amended 1985 c. 67 Sch. 2 Part II para. 2(3).
Sch. 2	Transitory provisions.		
para. 1	—	Sch. 2 para. 5	
para. 2	—	—	Spent.

TRIBUNALS AND INQUIRIES ACT—*continued.*

Section of Act	Subject matter	Section of 1992 Act	Remarks
	THE TRIBUNALS AND INQUIRIES ACT 1971 (c. 62)—*continued.*		
Sch. 3	Consequential amendments.	18(3)	
	THE SUPERANNUATION ACT 1972 (c. 11)		
Sch. 6 para. 91	Amends 1971 Sch. 1 paras. 23, 43.	Sch. 1 paras. 35, 57	
	THE NATIONAL HEALTH SERVICE (SCOTLAND) ACT 1972 (c. 58)		
Sch. 6 para. 152	Amends 1971 Sch. 1 para. 41.	Sch. 1 para. 56	
	THE NATIONAL HEALTH SERVICE REORGANISATION ACT 1973 (c. 32)		
Sch. 4 para. 134	Amends 1971 Sch. 1 para 17.	Sch. 1 para. 33	
	THE SOCIAL SECURITY ACT 1973 (c. 38)		
66(4), (9)	Occupational Pensions Board.	14(2), Sch. 1 para. 35(d)	
	THE CONSUMER CREDIT ACT 1974 (c. 39)		
3	Amends 1971 ss. 8(2), 19(4) Sch. 1.		
(a)	—	7(2)	
(b)	—	14(1)(b)	
(c)	—	—	Spent.
42	Further appeal on point of law.	11(6), (7)(a), (8)	
	THE SOCIAL SECURITY (CONSEQUENTIAL PROVISIONS) ACT 1975 (c. 18)		
Sch. 2 para. 46	Inserts 1971 Sch. 1 para. 30A.	Sch. 1 para. 41	
	THE INDUSTRY ACT 1975 (c. 68)		
Sch. 3 para. 10	Inserts 1971 Sch. 1 para. 9A.	Sch. 1 para 25	
	THE POLICE PENSIONS ACT 1976 (c. 35)		
Sch. 2 para. 9	Amends 1971 Sch. 1 paras. 15, 43.	Sch. 1 paras. 35(f), 57(c)	
	THE AIRCRAFT AND SHIPBUILDING INDUSTRIES ACT 1977 (c. 3)		
42(10)	Inserts 1971 Sch. 1 para. 1A.	Sch. 1 para. 2	
	THE NATIONAL HEALTH SERVICE ACT 1977 (c. 49)		
Sch. 15 para. 53	Amends 1971 Sch. 1 para. 17.	Sch. 1 para. 33	

TRIBUNALS AND INQUIRIES ACT—*continued.*

Section of Act	Subject matter	Section of 1992 Act	Remarks
THE JUDICATURE (NORTHERN IRELAND) ACT 1978 (c. 23)			
Sch. 5 Part II, entry relating to 1971	Amends 1971 s. 13(7).	11(8)	
THE NATIONAL HEALTH SERVICE (SCOTLAND) ACT 1978 (c. 29)			
Sch. 16 para. 35	Amends 1971 Sch. 1 para. 41.	Sch. 1 para. 56	
THE EMPLOYMENT PROTECTION (CONSOLIDATION) ACT 1978 (c. 44)			
Sch. 16 para. 11	Inserts 1971 s. 13(1A).	11(2)	
THE ESTATE AGENTS ACT 1979 (c. 38)			
24(1)	Amends 1971 s. 8(2) and inserts Sch. 1 para. 6A.	7(2), 14(b), Sch. 1 para. 17	
THE EDUCATION ACT 1980 (c. 20)			
7(6)	Amends 1971 s. 13(1) and Sch. 1 para. 6.	11(1), Sch. 1 para. 15	
THE EDUCATION (SCOTLAND) ACT 1980 (c. 44)			
28E(7)	Amends 1971 Sch. 1 para. 36.	Sch. 1 para. 50	Inserted Education (Scotland) Act 1981 (c. 58) s. 1(1).
THE SUPREME COURT ACT 1981 (c. 54)			
Sch. 5, entry relating to 1971	Amends 1971 s. 13(2).	11(3)	
THE INDUSTRIAL TRAINING ACT 1982 (c. 10)			
Sch. 3 para. 2	Amends 1971 Sch. 1 paras. 10, 38.	Sch. 1 paras. 16, 51	
THE CIVIL AVIATION ACT 1982 (c. 16)			
7(3)	Application of 1971 to Civil Aviation Authority.	7(2), 14(3), Sch. 1 para. 3	
THE CIVIC GOVERNMENT (SCOTLAND) ACT 1982 (c. 45)			
18(11)	Inserts 1971 Sch. 1 para. 48.	Sch. 1 para. 62	
THE MENTAL HEALTH ACT 1983 (c. 20)			
Sch. 4 para. 29	Amends 1971 Sch. 1 para. 14.	Sch. 1 para. 30	
THE HEALTH AND SOCIAL SERVICES AND SOCIAL SECURITY ADJUDICATIONS ACT 1983 (c. 41)			
Sch. 9	Minor and consequential amendments.		
para. 10	Amends 1971 s. 7(3).	6(3)	
para. 11	Amends 1971 s. 13(1).	11(1)	

TRIBUNALS AND INQUIRIES ACT—*continued.*

Section of Act	Subject matter	Section of 1992 Act	Remarks

THE HEALTH AND SOCIAL SERVICES AND SOCIAL SECURITY ADJUDICATIONS ACT 1983 (c. 41)—*continued.*

Section of Act	Subject matter	Section of 1992 Act	Remarks
para. 15	Amends 1971 Sch. 1 para. 30A(a).	—	Spent: new paragraph 30A substituted 1992 c. 6 Sch. 2 para 9.

THE REGISTERED HOMES ACT 1984 (c. 23)

Sch. 1 para. 5	Amends 1971 Sch. 1 paras. 4, 21A, 28A.	Sch. 1 para. 8	

THE RATING AND VALUATION (AMENDMENT) (SCOTLAND) ACT 1984 (c. 31)

Sch. 2 para. 12	Amends 1971 s. 13(6).	11(7)(c)	

THE DATA PROTECTION ACT 1984 c. 35)

Sch. 2 para. 13	Amends 1971 ss. 8(2), 19(4) and inserts Sch. 1 para. 5B.	7(2), 14(1)(a), Sch. 1 para. 14	

THE RESERVE FORCES (SAFEGUARD OF EMPLOYMENT) ACT 1985 (c. 17)

Sch. 4 para. 3	Amends 1971 Sch. 1 para. 19	Sch. 1 para. 38	

THE INSOLVENCY ACT 1985 (c. 65)

Sch. 1 para. 5	Amends 1971 ss. 8(2), 13(1).	7(2), 11(1)	Sub-para. (4) repealed 1986 c. 45 Sch. 12.

THE TRANSPORT ACT 1985 (c. 67)

Sch. 2, Part II, para. 2	Amends 1971 Sch. 1 paras. 30, 48.	Sch. 1 paras. 40, 62	
Sch. 7 para. 15	Amends 1971 Sch. 1 para. 31.	Sch. 1 para. 42	

THE AGRICULTURAL HOLDINGS ACT 1986 (c. 5)

Sch. 14 para. 49	Amends 1971 Sch. 1 para. 1(b).	Sch. 1 para. 1(b)	

THE PATENTS, DESIGNS AND MARKS ACT 1986 (c. 39)

Sch.2 para. 1(2)(d)	Amends 1971 Sch. 1 para. 22.	Sch. 1 para. 34.	

THE INSOLVENCY ACT 1986 (c. 45)

Sch. 14, entry relating to 1971	Amends 1971 Sch. 1 para. 10A.	Sch. 1 para. 26	

THE BUILDING SOCIETIES ACT 1986 (c. 53)

Words in 48(3)	Consultation with Council on Tribunals.	8(2)(a)	

THE FINANCIAL SERVICES ACT 1986 (c. 60)

Sch. 6 para. 6	Amends 1971 ss. 8(2), 13(1) and inserts Sch. 1 para. 6B.	7(2), 11(1), Sch. 1 para. 18	

TRIBUNALS AND INQUIRIES ACT—*continued.*

Section of Act	Subject matter	Section of 1992 Act	Remarks
	THE BANKING ACT 1987 (c. 22)		
Words in 30(3) and (4)	Consultation with Council on Tribunals.	8(2)(b), (3)(b)	
Sch. 6 para 4	Amends 1971 s. 8(?) and inserts Sch. 1 para. 2A.	7(2), Sch. 1 para. 4	
	THE CRIMINAL JUSTICE ACT 1988 (c. 33)		
Sch. 15 para. 37	Amends 1971 s. 8(2) and inserts Sch. 1 para. 5B.	7(2), Sch. 1 para. 12	
	THE EDUCATION REFORM ACT 1988 (c. 40)		
Sch. 12 para. 12	Amends 1971 Sch. 1 para. 6.	Sch. 1 para. 15	
	THE LOCAL GOVERNMENT FINANCE ACT 1988 (c. 41)		
Sch. 12 para. 41	Inserts 1971 Sch. 1 para. 12A.	Sch. 1 para. 28	
	THE COPYRIGHT, DESIGNS AND PATENTS ACT 1988 (c. 48)		
Sch. 7 para. 14	Amends 1971 Sch. 1 para. 5A and inserts para. 5A.	Sch. 1 paras. 11, 14	
	THE SELF-GOVERNING SCHOOLS ETC. (SCOTLAND) ACT 1989 (c. 39)		
Sch 10 para. 4	Amends 1971 Sch. 1 para. 36.	Sch. 1 para. 50(c)	
	THE CHILDREN ACT 1989 (c. 41)		
Sch. 13 para. 30	Amends 1971 Sch. 1 para. 4.	Sch. 1 para. 8	
	THE FOOD SAFETY ACT 1990 (c. 16)		
Sch. 3 para. 14	Inserts 1971 Sch. 1 para 6C, 36A.	Sch. 1 paras. 19, 52	
	THE SOCIAL SECURITY ACT 1990 (c. 27)		
12(2)	Amends 1971 s. 9(2) and Sch. 1 para. 23.	7(2), Sch. 1 para. 35(e)	
	THE COURTS AND LEGAL SERVICES ACT 1990 (c. 41)		
Sch. 18 para. 2	Inserts 1971 Sch. 1 para. 5AA.	Sch. 1 para. 10	
	THE DISABILITY LIVING ALLOWANCE AND DISABILITY WORKING ALLOWANCE ACT 1991 (c. 21)		
Sch. 2 para. 2(1)	Amends 1971 s. 7(3).	6(3)	
	THE ROAD TRAFFIC ACT 1991 (c. 40)		
Sch. 7 para. 1	Amends 1971 Sch. 1 para. 30.	Sch. 1 para. 40(b)	
	THE CHILD SUPPORT ACT 1991 (c. 48)		
Sch. 5 para. 1	Amends 1971 s. 7(3) and inserts Sch. 1 para 4A.	6(3), Sch. 1 para. 7	

TRIBUNALS AND INQUIRIES ACT—*continued.*

Section of Act	Subject matter	Section of 1992 Act	Remarks
THE SOCIAL SECURITY (CONSEQUENTIAL PROVISIONS) ACT 1992(c.6)			
Sch. 2 paras. 8, 9	Amends 1971 7(3) and Sch. 1 para. 30A.	6(3), Sch. 1 para. 41	
THE LOCAL GOVERNMENT FINANCE ACT 1992 (c. 14)			
Sch. 13 para. 31	Amends 1971 Sch. 1 para. 12A.	Sch. 1 para. 28	
THE EDUCATION (SCHOOLS) ACT 1992 (c. 38)			
Sch. 4 paras. 2, 3	Amends 1971 s. 13(1), Sch. 1 para. 6.	11(1) Sch. 1 para. 15	
PART II ORDERS			
THE TRIBUNALS AND INQUIRIES (VALUE ADDED TAX TRIBUNALS) ORDER 1972 (S.I. 1972/1210)			
2	Adds value added tax tribunals to 1971 Sch. 1.	Sch. 1 para. 44, 63	
3	Amends 1971 s. 13.	11(1), (7)(b)(i)	
4	Amends 1971 s. 10.	—	Unnecessary: see Finance Act 1985 (c. 54) s. 27(3).
THE TRIBUNALS AND INQUIRIES (INDUSTRIAL TRAINING LEVY EXEMPTION REFEREES) ORDER 1974 (S.I. 1974/1478)			
2	Adds to 1971 Sch. 1 referees established by S.I. 1974/1335.	Sch. 1 para. 24	
3	Applies 1971 s. 13.	11(1)	
THE TRIBUNALS AND INQUIRIES (MISUSE OF DRUGS TRIBUNALS) ORDER 1974 (S.I. 1974/1964)			
3	Adds to 1971 Sch. 1 tribunals constituted under Misuse of Drugs Act 1971 Sch. 3 Part I.	Sch. 1 paras. 32, 55	
THE TRIBUNALS AND INQUIRIES (VALUATION APPEAL COMMITTEES) ORDER 1975 (S.I. 1975/1404)			
3	Adds valuation appeal committees to 1971 Sch. 1.	Sch. 1 para. 58	
4	Repeals 1971 Sch. 1 para. 44.	—	Repeal: spent.
THE TRIBUNALS AND INQUIRIES (VACCINE DAMAGE TRIBUNALS) ORDER 1979 (S.I. 1979/659)			
2	Adds to 1971 Sch. 1 tribunals constituted under Vaccine Damage Payments Act 1979.	Sch. 1 para. 43	
3	Applies 1971 s. 7.	6(3)	

TRIBUNALS AND INQUIRIES ACT—*continued.*

Section of Act	Subject matter	Section of 1992 Act	Remarks
THE TRIBUNALS AND INQUIRIES (DAIRY PRODUCE QUOTA TRIBUNALS) ORDER 1984 (S.I. 1984/1094)			
2	Adds to 1971 Sch. 1 dairy produce quota tribunals.	Sch. 1 paras. 13, 49	
THE TRIBUNALS AND INQUIRIES (FOREIGN COMPENSATION COMMISSION) ORDER 1984 (S.I. 1984/1247)			
2	Adds Foreign Compensation Commission to 1971 Sch. 1.	Sch. 1 para. 20	
3	Amends 1971 s. 10.	8(1)	
THE TRIBUNALS AND INQUIRIES (SPECIFIED TRIBUNALS) ORDER 1991 (S.I. 1991/2699)			
2, 3	Add tribunals to 1971 Sch. 1.	Sch. 1 paras. 6, 21, 53, 56(d)	

TABLE VI

Acts and Measures (in chronological order)
repeated, amended or otherwise affected
by those Acts, Measures and Statutory Instruments
which received the Royal Assent or were made during 1992

LIST OF ABBREVIATIONS

am.	amended	ext.	extended	restr.	restricted
appl.	applied	GSM	General Synod Measure	(*retrosp.*)	retrospectively
appt.day/days	appointed day/days	incorp.	incorporated	SI	Statutory Instrument
CAM	Church Assembly Measure	(L.)	local (S.I.)	subst.	substituted
cont.	continued	mod.	modified	(*temp.*)	temporarily
defn/defns. of	definition/definitions of	(mods.)	with modifications	trans	transfer
excl.	excluded	(*prosp.*)	prospectively	spec. provns.	specified provisions
expld.	explained	rep.	repealed	in pt.	in part/partially

Year and Chap. or No. of Measure	Short title	How affected	1992, Chapter of Act or Number of Measure or Statutory Instrument
1662			
(14 Cha. 2) c.4	Act of Uniformity 1662	s.10 excl.	GSM 1, ss.15,16
1791			
(31 Geo. 3) c.85	Neath Canal Act 1791	ss.50,55,73 rep.in pt.	SI 1349(L), art.2
1803			
(43 Geo. 3) c.108	Gifts for Churches Act 1803	rep.	GSM 1, s.17(2), Sch.4, Pt.I
1804			
(44 Geo. 3) c.43	Clergy Ordination Act 1804	s.2 rep.	GSM 1, s.17(2), Sch.4, Pt.I
1817			
(57 Geo. 3) c.93	Distress (Costs) Act 1817	excl.	SI 613, reg.45(9)
		power to excl.	14, s.14(3), Sch.4, para.19(3)
1818			
(58 Geo. 3) c.69	Vestries Act 1818	rep.	GSM 1, s.17(2), Sch.4, Pt.I
1819			
(59 Geo. 3) c.85	Vestries Act 1819	rep.	GSM 1, s.17(2), Sch.4, Pt.I
1827			
(7 & 8 Geo. 4) c.17	Distress (Costs) Act 1827	excl.	SI 613, reg.45(9)
		power to excl.	14, s.14(3), Sch.4, para.19(3)
1828			
(9 Geo. 4) c.xcviii	Aire and Calder Navigation Act 1828	s.117 rep.	iv, s.39(2)
1831			
(1 & 2 Will. 4) c.60	Vestries Act 1831	rep.	GSM 1, s.17(2), Sch.4, Pt.I
1833			
(3 & 4 Will. 4) c.41	Judicial Committee Act 1833	mod.	SI 1716, art.2(2)
		ext.	45, s.2(5)

Year and Chap. or No. of Measure	Short title	How affected	1992, Chapter of Act or Number of Measure or Statutory Instrument
1837			
(7 Will. 4 & 1 Vict.) c.45	Parish Notices Act 1837	s.1 rep.	GSM 1, s.17(2), Sch.4, Pt.I
		s.3 rep.	GSM 1, s.17(2), Sch.4, Pt.I
		s.5 rep.in pt.	GSM 1, s.17(2), Sch.4, Pt.I
1838			
(1 & 2 Vict.) c.106	Pluralites Act 1838	s.35 rep.	GSM 1, s.17(2), Sch.4 Pt.I
		s.45 rep.	GSM 1, s.17(2), Sch.4, Pt.I
		s.46 rep.	GSM 1, s.17(2), Sch.4, Pt.I
		s.50 rep.in pt.	GSM 1, s.17(2), Sch.4, Pt.I
		s.73 rep.	GSM 1, s.17(2), Sch.4, Pt.I
		s.86 rep.	GSM 1, s.17(2), Sch.4, Pt.I
		s.99 rep.	GSM 1, s.17(2), Sch.4, Pt.I
		s.100 rep.	GSM 1, s.17(2), Sch.4, Pt.I
		s.102 rep.in pt.	GSM 1, s.17(2), Sch.4, Pt.I
		s.110 rep.	GSM 1, s.17(2), Sch.4, Pt.I
		s.129 rep.	GSM 1, s.17(2), Sch.4, Pt.I
1839			
(2 & 3 Vict.) c.45	Highway (Railway Crossing) Act 1839	excl.	SI 1113(L), art.3(3)
		excl.	SI 1267(L), art.4(2)
1840			
(3 & 4 Vict.) c.110	Loan Societies Act 1840	s.27 rep.in pt. (*prosp.*)	40, s.120, Sch.21, Pt.I, para.1, Sch.22, Pt.I
1842			
(5 & 6 Vict.) c.55	Railway Regulation Act 1842	excl.	SI 1113(L), art.3(3)
		excl.	SI 1267(L), art.4(2)
		s.17 rep.in pt. (EWS)	42, ss.40,68(1), Sch.4, Pt.I
1844			
(7 & 8 Vict.) c.59	Lecturers and Parish Clerks Act 1844	s.6 rep.	GSM 1, s.17(2), Sch.4, Pt.I
1845			
(8 & 9 Vict.) c.18	Lands Clauses Consolidation Act 1845	excl.	i, s.4(3)
		excl.	3, s.2(5)
		incorp.in pt.(mods.)	iii, ss.3(1)(a),24
		appl.(mods.)	iii, s.22(3)(a)
		excl.	iv, s.4(3)
		excl.	v, s.4(1)(c)
		excl.	xi, s.4(3)
		excl.	xiv, s.3(2)(c)
		excl.	xv, s.3(3)
		excl.	xviii, s.3(3)
c.20	Railways Clauses Consolidation Act 1845	incorp.in pt.(mods.)	SI 1113(L), art.3(1)(2)
		incorp.in pt.(mods.)	i, ss.3,17(6)
		incorp.in pt.(mods.)	iii, s.3(1)(b)
		incorp.(mods.)	iv, s.3(1)

Year and Chap. or No. of Measure	Short title	How affected	1992, Chapter of Act or Number of Measure or Statutory Instrument
1845—*cont.*			
		incorp.in pt.(mods.)	v, s.3
		incorp.in pt.(mods.)	xi, s.3(1)(a)(2)
		incorp.(mods.)	xiv, s.3(1)
		s.6 saved	vii, s.14(6)(b)
		s.6 saved	viii, s.14(5)(b)
		s.6 saved	xi, s.21(6)
		s.43 saved	vii, s.14(6)(b)
		s.43 saved	viii, s.14(5)(b)
		s.75 am. (EW)	42, s.49
c.33	Railway Clauses Consolidation (Scotland) Act 1845	incorp. in pt.	SI 1267(L), art.4(1)
		s.68 am.	42, s.49
1847			
(10 & 11 Vict.) c.27	Harbours, Docks, and Piers Clauses Act 1847	am.	SI 1136(L), art.9(3)
		incorp.in pt.(mods.)	xii, s.1, Sch. s.63, Sch.2
		saved	xii, s.1, Sch., ss.3,33(2)
c.65	Cemeteries Clauses Act 1847	s.27 am.	GSM 1, s.17(1), Sch.3, para.1
c.98	Ecclesiastical Jurisdiction Act 1847	rep.	GSM 1, s.17(2), Sch.4, Pt.I
c.27	Harbours, Docks and Piers Clauses Act 1847	incorp.in pt.(mods.)	SI 1623(L), art.3
1848			
(11 & 12 Vict.) c.vi	Folkestone Waterworks Act 1848	s.1 rep.in pt.	SI 1214(L), art.4, Sch.2, Pt.I
		ss.4,8,10-16 rep.	SI 1214(L), art.4, Sch.2, Pt.I
c.xliii	Bristol Dock Act 1848	saved	xxi, s.5
1849			
(12 & 13 Vict.) c.51	Judicial Factors Act 1849	s.5(1) am. (1.1.1993)	SI 3218, reg.82(1), Sch.10, Pt.I, para.1
c.67	Sequestration Act 1849	s.1 am.	GSM 1, s.17(1), Sch.3, para.2
		s.1 rep.in pt.	GSM 1, s.17(2), Sch.4, Pt.II
c.lxxxi	Manchester, Sheffield and Lincolnshire Railway Act 1849	s.91 rep.in pt.	xi, s.24(2)(a)
		s.92 excl.	xi, s.24(1)
		s.92 rep.	xi, ss.24(2)(b),48, Sch.4, Pt.I
		s.96 rep.in pt.	xi, s.24(2)(a)
		s.97 rep.	xi, ss.24(2)(b),48, Sch.4, Pt.I
1850			
(13 & 14 Vict.) c.98	Pluralities Act 1850	rep.	GSM 1, s.17(2), Sch.4, Pt.I
1851			
(14 & 15 Vict.) c.42	Crown Lands Act 1851	s.21 rep.in pt. (*prosp.*)	27, s.7(5)

Year and Chap. or No. of Measure	Short title	How affected	1992, Chapter of Act or Number of Measure or Statutory Instrument
1851—cont.			
c.vi	Durham Markets Company's Act 1851	s.1 rep.in pt. (*prosp.*)	xx, s.5, Sch.2, Pt.II
		ss.7-9,23,24 rep. (*prosp.*)	xx, s.5, Sch.2, Pt.II
		s.9A added	xx, s.4, Sch.1, para.1
		ss.27,28,56 rep.	xx, s.5, Sch.2, Pt.I
		ss.30,31 rep.in pt.	xx, s.4, Sch.1, paras.2,3
		ss.33,35,36,38,40 am.	xx, s.4, Sch.1, paras.4-8
		Schs.(A),(B),(C) rep.	xx, s.5, Sch.2, Pt.I
c.cxvi	Kensington Improvement Act 1851	s.43 am. (1.4.1993)	SI 3292, art.2, Sch.
		s.51 am. (1.4.1993)	SI 3292, art.2, Sch.
1853			
(16 & 17 Vict.) c.20	Evidence (Scotland) Act 1853	s.3 appl.	5, s.59(4)(b)
c.65	Vestries Act 1853	rep.	GSM 1, s.17(2), Sch.4, Pt.I
1854			
(17 & 18 Vict.) c.91	Lands Valuation (Scotland) Act 1854	appl.	14, s.117(1), Sch.13, para.10 (substituting s.22 in 1956 c.60)
		s.35 saved (*prosp.*)	14, s.111(10)
1855			
(18 & 19 Vict.) c.81	Places of Worship Registration Act 1855	s.5 am.	SI 99, art.2, Sch.
		s.5 am.	SI 2982, Sch.
c.111	Bills of Lading Act 1855	rep.	50, s.6(2)
1856			
(19 & 20 Vict.) c.29	National Gallery Act 1856	rep.	50, s.11(3), Sch.9
1857			
(20 & 21 Vict.) c.44	Crown Suits (Scotland) Act 1857	ext.	52, s.247(4)
c.ii	Price's Patent Candle Company's (Limited) Act 1857	s.1 rep.	xvii, s.5, Sch.2, Pt.I
		s.5 rep. (*prosp.*)	xvii, s.5, Sch.2, Pt.II
		s.8 rep.	xvii, s.5, Sch.2, Pt.I
		ss.10-13 rep.	xvii, s.5, Sch.2, Pt.I
		s.14 subst.	xvii, s.3, Sch.1, para.1
		ss.15-16 rep. (*prosp.*)	xvii, s.5, Sch.2, Pt.II
		s.19 subst.	xvii, s.3, Sch.1, para.2
		ss.20,22,25,28 rep. (*prosp.*)	xvii, s.5, Sch.2, Pt.II
		s.26 rep.	xvii, s.5, Sch.2, Pt.I
		s.29 rep.	xvii, s.5, Sch.2, Pt.I
		s.36 rep.	xvii, s.5, Sch.2, Pt.I
c.xlviii	Tweed Fisheries Act 1857	s.62 rep. (1.1.1993)	SI 1974, art.3
1858			
(21 & 22 Vict.) c.x	Folkestone Waterworks Act 1858	s.21 rep.	SI 1214(L), art.4, Sch.2, Pt.I
c.lxxii	Burry Navigation and Llanelly Harbour Act 1858	excl. (saving)	xix, s.3(1)(3)

Year and Chap. or No. of Measure	Short title	How affected	1992, Chapter of Act or Number of Measure or Statutory Instrument
1859			
(22 & 23 Vict.) c.lxx	Tweed Fisheries Amendment Act 1859	ss.12,13 am. (1.1.1993)	SI 1974, art.10
c.xcix	Eastbourne Waterworks Act 1859	s.3 rep.in pt.	SI 17(L), art.4, Sch.2, Pt.I
		ss.6-9,11,12,14-18,40 rep.	SI 17(L), art.4, Sch.2, Pt.I
1861			
(24 & 25 Vict.) c.45	General Pier and Harbour Act 1861	rep. (EWS)	42, ss.65(1)(a),68(1), Sch.4, Pt.II
1862			
(25 & 26 Vict.) c.19	General Pier and Harbour Act 1861, Amendment Act 1862	rep. (EWS)	42, s.68(1), Sch.4, Pt.II
c.69	Harbours Transfer Act 1862	ss.13,14 rep. (EWS)	42, s.68(1), Sch.4, Pt.II
1863			
(26 & 27 Vict.) c.13	Town Gardens Protection Act 1863	s.1 am. (1.4.1993)	SI 3293, art.2, Sch.
		s.1(2) added (1.4.1993)	SI 3293, art.2, Sch.
c.92	Railways Clauses Act 1863	incorp. in pt.	SI 1113(L), art.3(1)
		incorp. in pt.	xi, s.3(1)(b)
		ss.3-19 (Pt.I) incorp. in pt.	i, s.3(1)(b)
		ss.3-19 (Pt.I) incorp.in pt.(mods.)	iii, s.3(1)(c)(2)
c.cvii	Bristol and Portishead Pier and Railway. Act 1863	excl.	xxi, s.3
		ss.2,3 rep. in pt. (*prosp.*)	xxi, ss.2,7, Sch., Pt.I
		ss.5-18 rep. (*prosp.*)	xxi, ss.2,7, Sch., Pt.I
		s.19 rep.in pt. (*prosp.*)	xxi, ss.2,7, Sch., Pt.I
		s.20, para.1 rep. (*prosp.*)	xxi, ss.2,7, Sch., Pt.I
		s.22 rep. (*prosp.*)	xxi, ss.2,7, Sch., Pt.I
		s.26 rep. (*prosp.*)	xxi, ss.2,7, Sch., Pt.I
		ss.28-30 rep. (*prosp.*)	xxi, ss.2,7, Sch., Pt.I
		s.31 rep.in pt. (*prosp.*)	xxi, ss.2,7, Sch., Pt.I
		ss.32,33 rep. (*prosp.*)	xxi, ss.2,7, Sch., Pt.I
		ss.35-37 rep. (*prosp.*)	xxi, ss.2,7, Sch., Pt.I
		s.39 rep. (*prosp.*)	xxi, ss.2,7, Sch., Pt.I
		ss.41,42 rep. (*prosp.*)	xxi, ss.2,7, Sch., Pt.I
		ss.48-60 rep. (*prosp.*)	xxi, ss.2,7, Sch., Pt.I
		ss.64-76 rep. (*prosp.*)	xxi, ss.2,7, Sch., Pt.I
		s.78 rep. (*prosp.*)	xxi, ss.2,7, Sch., Pt.I
		Schs.B-E rep. (*prosp.*)	xxi, ss.2,7, Sch., Pt.I
c.ccxvii	London and North-western Railway (Additional Powers) Act 1863	rep.in pt.	xi, s.7(3)
1864			
(27 & 28 Vict.) c.v	Folkestone Waterworks Acts Amendment Act 1864	s.19 rep.	SI 1214(L), art.4, Sch.2, Pt.I
1866			
(29 & 30 Vict.) c.39	Exchequer and Audit Departments Act 1866	s.10 mod.	2, s.2(4)
c.lxxxviii	Bristol and Portishead Pier and Railway Act 1866	excl.	xxi, s.3
		s.2 rep.in pt. (*prosp.*)	xxi, ss.2,7, Sch., Pt.I

Year and Chap. or No. of Measure	Short title	How affected	1992, Chapter of Act or Number of Measure or Statutory Instrument
1866—cont.			
		s.3 rep. (*prosp.*)	xxi, ss.2,7, Sch., Pt.I
		s.4 rep.in pt. (*prosp.*)	xxi, ss.2,7, Sch., Pt.I
		ss.6-8 rep. (*prosp.*)	xxi, ss.2,7, Sch., Pt.I
		ss.10-15 rep. (*prosp.*)	xxi, ss.2,7, Sch., Pt.I
		s.20 rep. (*prosp.*)	xxi, ss.2,7, Sch., Pt.I
		s.23 rep. (*prosp.*)	xxi, ss.2,7, Sch., Pt.I
		ss.32-41 rep. (*prosp.*)	xxi, ss.2,7, Sch., Pt.I
		ss.44-68 rep. (*prosp.*)	xxi, ss.2,7, Sch., Pt.I
		Sch.4 rep. (*prosp.*)	xxi, ss.2,7, Sch., Pt.I
1867 (30 & 31 Vict.) c.17	Lyon King of Arms Act 1867	Sch.B am.	SI 305, arts.2,3(1), Sch.1
		Sch.B rep.in pt.	SI 305, arts.2,3(2), Sch.2
c.133	Consecration of Churchyards Act 1867	s.12 rep.	GSM 1, s.17(2), Sch.4, Pt.I
1868 (31 & 32 Vict.) c.37	Documentary Evidence Act 1868	am.	SI 3060, Sch.2, para.6(c)
		ext.	5, s.177, Sch.8, para.3
		am.	38, ss.1(6),5(6), Sch.1, para.7
		Sch. am. (EWS)	SI 3060, Sch.2, para.6(a)(b)
		Sch. am.	38, ss.1(6),5(6), Sch.1, para.7(a)(b)
c.109	Compulsory Church Rate Abolition Act 1868	s.9 rep.	GSM 1, s.17(2), Sch.4, Pt.I
c.114	Ecclesiastical Commission Act 1868	rep.	GSM 1, s.17(2), Sch.4, Pt.I
c.119	Regulation of Railways Act 1868	excl.	SI 1113(L), art.3(3)
		excl.in pt.	SI 1267(L), art.4(2)
		s.22 mod.	SI 1113(L), art.3(4)
c.123	Salmon Fisheries (Scotland) Act 1868	Sch.E rep.in pt. (1.1.1993)	SI 1974, art.11
1869 (32 & 33 Vict.) c.62	Debtors Act 1869	s.5 mod.	5, s.187(3)
c.109	Residence of Incumbents Act 1869	s.2 rep.in pt.	GSM 1, s.17(2), Sch.4, Pt.I
c.115	Metropolitan Public Carriage Act 1869	s.4 (defn. of "hackney carriage") am.	42, s.62(1)
1870 (33 & 34 Vict.) c.78	Tramways Act 1870	s.3 rep. (1.1.1993) (*saving*)	42, ss.65(1)(b),68(1), Sch.4, Pt.I
		ss.4-21 rep. (1-1-1993)	42, ss.65(1)(b),68(1), Sch.4, Pt.I
		ss.22-24 rep. (1-1-1993) (*saving*)	42, ss.65(1)(b),68(1), Sch.4, Pt.I
		ss.22-33 (Pt.I) mod.	xviii, s.10
		s.25 restr.	vii, s.5(5)

Year and Chap. or No. of Measure	Short title	How affected	1992, Chapter of Act or Number of Measure or Statutory Instrument
1870—*cont.*			
		s.25 rep.in pt. (1-1-1993) (*saving*)	42, ss.65(1)(b),68(1), Sch.4, Pt.I
		s.25 rep.in pt. (*prosp.*)	42, ss.65(1)(b),68(1), Sch.4, Pt.I
		ss.26-40 rep. (1-1-1993) (*saving*)	42, ss.65(1)(b),68(1), Sch.4, Pt.I
		ss.34-64 (Pt.III) mod.	xviii, s.10
		ss.41,42 rep. (1-1-1993)	42, ss.65(1)(b),68(1), Sch.4, Pt.I
		ss.43-47 rep. (1-1-1993) (*saving*)	42, ss.65(1)(b),68(1), Sch.4, Pt.I
		s.48 rep. (*prosp.*)	42, ss.65(1)(b),68(1), Sch.4, Pt.I
		ss.49-64 rep. (1-1-1993) (*saving*)	42, ss.65(1)(b),68(1), Sch.4, Pt.I
		Sch.C rep. (1-1-1993) (*saving*)	42, ss.65(1)(b),68(1), Sch.4, Pt.I
		Sch.A, Pts.I,II rep. (1-1-1993) (saving)	42, ss.65(1)(b),68(1), Sch.4, Pt.I
		Sch.A, Pt.III rep. (1-1-1993)	42, ss.65(1)(b),68(1), Sch.4, Pt.I
		Sch.B rep. (1-1-1993)	42, ss.65(1)(b),68(1), Sch.4, Pt.I
1871 (34 & 35 Vict.) c.45	Sequestration Act 1871	s.1 rep.	GSM 1, s.17(2), Sch.4, Pt.II
c.78	Regulation of Railways Act 1871	mod.	xviii, s.10
		s.2 (defn. of "railways") appl. (31-1-1993) (EWS)	42, s.42(1)
		s.3 rep.in pt. (proviso) (31.1.1993) (EWS)	42, ss.42(2),68(1), Sch.4, Pt.I
		s.6 rep. & superseded (EWS) (*prosp.*)	42, ss.43,44(1),68(1), Sch.4, Pt.I
		s.7 am. (EWS) (*prosp.*)	42, s.44(2)
		s.8 am. (EWS) (*prosp.*)	42, s.44(3)
c.xxvi	Folkestone Waterworks Act 1871	s.3 rep.	SI 1214(L), art.4, Sch.2, Pt.I
c.cxlii	Portishead Docks Act 1871	rep. (except ss.1,4 & 41-52) (*prosp.*)	xxi, ss.2,7, Sch., Pt.I
		excl.	xxi, s.3
		ss.41-44 saved	xxi, s.6(1)
		s.41 rep.in pt.	xxi, s.6(3)
		ss.43,44 rep.in pt.	xxi, s.6(3)
		ss.47-50 rep.in pt.	xxi, s.6(3)
		ss.48,49 saved	xxi, s.6(1)
1872 (35 & 36 Vict.) c.24	Charitable Trustees Incorporation Act 1872	s.1 subst. (1.1.1993)	41, s.48, Sch.4, para.1
		s.2 rep.in pt. (1.1.1993)	41, ss.48,78(2), Sch.4, para.2, Sch.7

Year and Chap. or No. of Measure	Short title	How affected	1992, Chapter of Act or Number of Measure or Statutory Instrument
1872—cont.			
		s.3 subst. (1.1.1993)	41, s.48, Sch.4, para.3
		s.4 rep.in pt. (1.1.1993)	41, ss.48,78(2), Sch.4, para.4, Sch.7
		s.5 rep.in pt. (1.1.1993)	41, ss.48,78(2), Sch.4, para.5, Sch.7
		s.6A added (1.1.1993)	41, s.48, Sch.4, para.6
		s.7 rep.in pt. (1.1.1993)	41, ss.48,78(2), Sch.4, para.7, Sch.7
		s.8 am. (1.1.1993)	41, s.48, Sch.4, para.8
		s.12 replaced (by ss.12, 12A) (1.1.1993)	41, s.48, Sch.4, para.9
		s.14 subst. (1.1.1993)	41, s.48, Sch.4, para.10
		Sch. rep. (1.1.1993)	41, ss.48,78(2), Sch.4, para.11, Sch.7
1873			
(36 & 37 Vict.) c.xlvi	Bristol and Portishead Pier and Railway Act 1873	rep. (*prosp.*)	xxi, ss.2,7, Sch., Pt.I
		excl.	xxi, s.
c.lxxiii	Bournemouth Gas and Water Act 1873	ss.2,5,7,16,24,29-31,34, 35 rep.	SI 1988(L), art.4, Sch.2, Pt.I
c.lxxx	Colne Valley Water Act 1873	s.2 rep.in pt.	SI 424(L), art.4, Sch.2, Pt.I
		ss.5,9,13,25,27,28,30 rep.	SI 424(L), art.4, Sch.2, Pt.I
c.clvii	Peterhead Harbours Act 1873	rep.	xii, s.1, Sch. s.63, sch.2
1874			
(37 & 38 Vict.) c.cxxviii	Great Eastern Railway Act 1874	appl.(mods.)	SI 1136(L), art.9(1)
		ss.2,4,8,13,64-68,81-84 appl.(mods.)	SI 1136(L), arts.2(1),9(1), Sch.
1875			
(38 & 39 Vict.) c.17	Explosives Act 1875	saved	iii, s.11(2)
		s.15 am.	SI 1752, reg.10, Sch.9, Pt.II
		s.18 am.	SI 1752, reg.10, Sch.9, Pt.II
		s.21 am.	SI 1752, reg.10, Sch.9, Pt.II
c.86	Conspiracy and Protection of Property Act 1875	s.3 rep.	52, s.300(1), Sch.1
		s.5 rep.	52, s.300(1), Sch.1
		s.7 rep.	52, s.300(1), Sch.1
		ss.15,16 rep.	52, s.300(1), Sch.1
c.xxx	Eastbourne Waterworks Act 1875	s.2 rep.in pt.	SI 17(L), art.4, Sch.2, Pt.I
		ss.11-18,20,26,28 rep.	SI 17(L), art.4, Sch.2, Pt.I
1876			
(39 & 40 Vict.) c.lxxiv	Great Western and Bristol and Exeter Railway Companies Amalgamation Act 1876	s.10 rep. (*prosp.*)	xxi, ss.2,7, Sch., Pt.II
c.clxxiv	Peterhead Harbours Amendment Act 1876	rep.	xii, s.1, Sch. s.63, Sch.2

Year and Chap. or No. of Measure	Short title	How affected	1992, Chapter of Act or Number of Measure or Statutory Instrument
1877			
(40 & 41 Vict.) c.2	Treasury Bills Act 1877	s.8 rep.in pt.	48, ss.79(1)(2),82, Sch.18, Pt.XI
c.lxxiii	East Worcestershire Water Act 1877	s.2 rep.in pt.	SI 2374(L), art.4, Sch.2, Pt.I
		ss.4,5,7,8,11,14-22 rep.	SI 2374(L), art.4, Sch.2, Pt.I
c.lxxix	Bristol and Portishead Pier and Railway Company's Act 1877	rep. (except ss.1,7 & 13) (*prosp.*)	xxi, ss.2,7, Sch., Pt.I
		excl.	xxi, s.3
1878			
(41 & 42 Vict.) c.73	Territorial Waters Jurisdiction Act 1878	s.3 power to excl.	52, s.287(3)(e)
c.xiv	Sevenoaks Waterworks Act 1878	s.2 rep.in pt.	SI 19(L), art.4, Sch.2, Pt.I
		ss.5,18,26,28,29,35,39 rep.	SI 19(L), art.4, Sch.2, Pt.I
c.ccii	Bournemouth Gas and Water Act 1878	ss.2,15,20,24,33 rep.	SI 1988(L), art.4, Sch.2, Pt.I
c.ccxxvi	Portishead Docks Act 1878	rep. (*prosp.*)	xxi, ss.2,7, Sch., Pt.I
		excl.	xxi, s.3
1879			
(42 & 43 Vict.) c.11	Bankers' Book Evidence Act 1879	appl.(mods.) (*prosp.*)	xiii, s.10
		s.9(1) am. (1.1.1993)	SI 3218, reg.82(1), Sch.10, Pt.I, para.2
c.cxcviii	Metropolis Management (Thames River Prevention of floods) Amendment Act 1879	s.5 mod.	iii, s.32(9)
1880			
(43 & 44 Vict.) c.xxii	Portishead Docks Act 1880	rep. (*prosp.*)	xxi, ss.2,7, Sch., Pt.I
		excl.	xxi, s.3
1881			
(44 & 45 Vict.) c.41	Conveyancing Act 1881	defn. of "convey" appl. (*prosp.*)	xiii, s.11(7)
c.l	Eastbourne Waterworks Act 1881	s.2 rep.in pt.	SI 17(L), art.4, Sch.2, Pt.I
		ss.22-28,30,32,36,38 rep.	SI 17(L), art.4, Sch.2, Pt.I
c.civ	Pier and Harbour Orders Confirmation Act 1881	Sch. rep.in pt. (Peterhead Harbours Order 1881 rep.)	xii, s.1, Sch. s.63, Sch.2
1882			
(45 & 46 Vict.) c.42	Civil Imprisonment (Scotland) Act 1882	s.4 mod.	5, s.187(3)
c.50	Municipal Corporations Act 1882	Sch.9, Pt.I rep.in pt. (1-1-1993) (*saving*)	42, s.68(1), Sch.4, Pt.I
c.61	Bills of Exchange Act 1882	s.80 am.	32, s.2
		s.81A added	32, s.1

Year and Chap. or No. of Measure	Short title	How affected	1992, Chapter of Act or Number of Measure or Statutory Instrument
1883			
(46 & 47 Vict.) c.xii	Price's Patent Candle Company (Limited) Act 1883	rep. (*prosp.*)	xvii, s.5, Sch.2, Pt.II
1884			
(47 & 48 Vict.) c.xvii	Rickmansworth Waterworks Act 1884	s.2 rep.in pt.	SI 125(L), art.4, Sch.2, Pt.I
		ss.5,17,19,22-24 rep.	SI 125(L), art.4, Sch.2, Pt.I
c.cclv	Bristol Dock Act 1884	ss.32-34 rep.in pt. (*prosp.*)	xxi, ss.2,7, Sch., Pt.II
		s.35 rep. (*prosp.*)	xxi, ss.2,7, Sch., Pt.II
		ss.37,38 rep.in pt. (*prosp.*)	xxi, ss.2,7, Sch., Pt.II
		s.39 rep. (*prosp.*)	xxi, ss.2,7, Sch., Pt.II
		s.51 rep.in pt. (*prosp.*)	xxi, ss.2,7, Sch., Pt.II
		Sch.4, Pt.III rep. (*prosp.*)	xxi, ss.2,7, Sch., Pt.II
c.cclvi	Great Western and Portishead Railway Companies Act 1884	rep. (*prosp.*)	xxi, ss.2,7, Sch., Pt.I
		excl.	xxi, s.3
1885			
(48 & 49 Vict.) c.54	The Pluralities Acts Amendment Act 1885	s.2 rep.in pt.	GSM 1, s.17(2), Sch.4, Pt.I
		s.9 rep.	GSM 1, s.17(2), Sch.4, Pt.I
		s.11 rep.	GSM 1, s.17(2), Sch.4, Pt.I
		s.13 rep.	GSM 1, s.17(2), Sch.4, Pt.I
c.xx	Rickmansworth and Uxbridge Valley Water Act 1885	ss.3,8 rep.	SI 125(L), art.4, Sch.2, Pt.I
c.cxxxiii	Colne Valley Water Act 1885	s.4 rep.	SI 424(L), art.4, Sch.2, Pt.I
c.clxxxviii	Manchester Ship Canal Act 1885	excl. (*prosp.*)	SI 1268(L), art.3(2)
		s.33 rep.in pt. (*prosp.*)	SI 1268(L), art.3, Sch.
		s.119, paras.15-17 rep. (*prosp.*)	SI 1268(L), art.3, Sch.
1887			
(50 & 51 Vict.) c.40	Savings Banks Act 1887	s.10 am.	SI 99, art.2, Sch.
		s.10 am.	SI 2982, Sch.
		s.10 am.	SI 3216, Sch.
c.65	Military Tramways Act 1887	rep. (1.1.1993)	42, ss.65(1)(c),68(1), Sch.4, Pt.I
1888			
(51 & 52 Vict.) c.xxv	Folkestone Waterworks Act 1888	s.2 rep.	SI 1214(L), art.4, Sch.2, Pt.I
c.clxi	Manchester Ship Canal (Alteration of Works) Act 1888	excl. (*prosp.*)	SI 1268(L), art.3(2)
		s.6 rep.in pt. (*prosp.*)	SI 1268(L), art.3, Sch.
		s.32 rep. (*prosp.*)	SI 1268(L), art.3, Sch.
1889			
(52 & 53 Vict.) c.14	Town Police Clauses Act 1889	s.3 rep.in pt. (*prosp.*)	42, s.68(1), Sch.4, Pt.I

Year and Chap. or No. of Measure	Short title	How affected	1992, Chapter of Act or Number of Measure or Statutory Instrument
1889—*cont.*			
c.57	Regulation of Railways Act 1889	excl.	SI 1113(L), art.3(3)
		excl.in pt.	SI 1267(L), art.4(2)
c.lxxvii	Eastbourne Waterworks Act 1889	s.2 rep.in pt.	SI 17(L), art.4, Sch.2, Pt.I
		ss.14-17,19,24,30,31,33 rep.	SI 17(L), art.4, Sch.2, Pt.I
1891 (54 & 55 Vict.) c.38	Stamp Duties Management Act 1891	power to appl.	4, s.1(4), Sch.1, para.8(3)(b)
		power to appl. (NI)	7, s.1(4), Sch.1, para.8(3)(b)
c.39	Stamp Act 1891	saved	27, s.5(5)
		s.9 power to appl.	4, s.1(4), Sch.1, para.8(3)(b)
		s.9 power to appl. (NI)	7, s.1(4), Sch.1, para.8(3)(b)
		s.14(4) mod. (16-1-1992) (*retrosp.*)	2, s.1(3)
		s.59 am. (NI)	SI 232, art.2
c.43	Forged Transfers Act 1891	s.2(a) replaced (by paras.(a)(aa)(ab)) (EWS) (*prosp.*)	14, s.117(1), Sch.13, para.1
1893 (56 & 57 Vict.) c.iii	Manchester Ship Canal Act 1893	s.28, para.(4) rep. (*prosp.*)	SI 1268(L), art.3, Sch.
c.ccv	West Hampshire Water Act 1893	s.2 rep.in pt.	SI 1993(L), art.4, Sch.2, Pt.I
		ss.5-9,15-17,20-22 rep.	SI 1993(L), art.4, Sch.2, Pt.I
1894 (57 & 58 Vict.) c.28	Notice of Accidents Act 1894	rep. (EWS) (*prosp.*)	42, s.68(1), Sch.4, Pt.I
c.34	British Museum (Purchase of Land) Act 1894	s.2 rep.	44, s.11(2)(3), Sch.8, Pt.I, para.3(1), Sch.9
		s.2A trans.of functions	SI 1311, art.3(1), Sch.1, Pt.I
		s.2A am.	44, s.11(2), Sch.8, Pt.I, para.3(2)
c.60	Merchant Shipping Act 1894	excl.	SI 1293, art.11
		mod.	SI 1294, art.10
		excl.	SI 1294, arts.11-13
		ss.1-91 (Pt.I) restr.	SI 1736, art.3
		ss.8-12 restr.	SI 1293, art.12, Sch.
		s.58 mod.	SI 1293, art.10(2)
		s.59 restr.	SI 1293, art.12, Sch.
		ss.459-461 restr.	SI 1293, art.12, Sch.
		ss.510-571 (Pt.IX) (defn. of "wreck") appl.	vi, s.6(1)
		ss.510-571 (Pt.IX) (defn. of "wreck") appl.	ix, s.1, Sch., s.6(2)

Year and Chap. or No. of Measure	Short title	How affected	1992, Chapter of Act or Number of Measure or Statutory Instrument
1894—*cont.*			
		ss.510-571 (Pt.IX) (defn. of "wreck") appl.	xiv, s.16(1)
		ss.530-534 restr.	SI 1293, arts.8,9
		ss.530-534 restr.	SI 1294, arts.8,9
		ss.552,553 restr.	SI 1293, art.12, Sch.
		ss.557-564 saved	SI 1293, art.9
		ss.557-564 saved	SI 1294, art.9
		ss.567,568 restr.	SI 1293, art.12, Sch.
		ss.634-675 (Pt.XI) (defn. of "local lighthouse authority") appl.	xxi, s.2
		s.692 ext.(mods.)	SI 3, reg.46
		s.692 appl.(mods.)	SI 1564, reg.8
		s.692(1)-(3) appl.(mods.)	SI 2359, reg.25(1)
		s.692(1)(2) appl.(mods.)	SI 98, reg.2
c.clxx	Peterhead Harbours Act 1894	rep.	xii, s.1, Sch. s.63, Sch.2
1895			
(58 & 59 Vict.) c.cxlviii	Manchester, Sheffield and Lincolnshire Railway Act 1895	s.26 rep.in pt.	xi, s.24(2)(a)
1896			
(59 & 60 Vict.) c.25	Friendly Societies Act 1896	saved	52, s.300(3), Sch.3, para.12(4)(a)
		s.22(2)(3) rep.	52, s.300(1), Sch.1
		s.62 rep. (*prosp.*)	40, s.120(2), Sch.22, Pt.I
		ss.63-66 appl.	52, s.19(1)(b)
		ss.64-67 rep. (*prosp.*)	40, s.120(2), Sch.22, Pt.I
c.48	Light Railways Act 1896	rep. (1-1-1993) (EW)	42, s.68(1), Sch.4, Pt.I
c.clxxxvii	Eastbourne Waterworks Act 1896	s.2 rep.in pt.	SI 17(L), art.4, Sch.2, Pt.I
		ss.22-25,27,32,39,40,42 rep.	SI 17(L), art.4, Sch.2, Pt.I
c.cxcvi	Bournemouth Gas and Water Act 1896	s.2 rep.in pt.	SI 1988(L), art.4, Sch.2, Pt.I
		ss.11,45,47,48,51,64 rep.	SI 1988(L), art.4, Sch.2, Pt.I
1897			
(60 & 61 Vict.) c.38	Public Health (Scotland) Act 1897	s.3 (defn. of "ratepayer") subst. (*prosp.*)	14, s.117(1), Sch.13, para.2
c.59	Merchant Shipping Act 1897	restr.	SI 1293, art.12, Sch.
c.cxxiv	Eastbourne Waterworks Act 1897	s.2 rep.in pt.	SI 17(L), art.4, Sch.2, Pt.I
		ss.16-19,21,26,33,34,36 rep.	SI 17(L), art.4, Sch.2, Pt.I
1898			
(61 & 62 Vict.) c.48	Benefices Act 1898	s.10 rep.	GSM 1, s.17(2), Sch.4, Pt.II
		s.11 am.	GSM 1, s.17(1), Sch.3, para.3
		s.12 rep.	GSM 1, s.17(2), Sch.4, Pt.I
c.cxlvii	Folkestone Water Act 1898	s.2 rep.in pt.	SI 1214(L), art.4, Sch.2, Pt.I

Year and Chap. or No. of Measure	Short title	How affected	1992, Chapter of Act or Number of Measure or Statutory Instrument
1900			
(63 & 64 Vict.) c.27	Railways Employment (Prevention of accidents) Act 1900	s.13(2) rep. (EWS) (*prosp.*)	42, s.68(1), Sch.4, Pt.I
c.ccxlii	Rickmansworth and Uxbridge Valley Water Act 1900	s.2 rep.in pt.	SI 125(L), art.4, Sch.2, Pt.I
1902			
(2 Edw. 7) c.8	Cremation Act 1902	s.11 rep.	GSM 1, ss.2(5),17(2), Sch.4, Pt.II
c.lviii	Bournemouth Gas and Water (Poole Gas Transfer) Act 1902	s.2 rep.in pt.	SI 1988(L), art.4, Sch.2, Pt.I
		ss.7,19 rep.	SI 1988(L), art.4, Sch.2, Pt.I
c.cv	West Hampshire Water Act 1902	s.2 rep.in pt.	SI 1993(L), art.4, Sch.2, Pt.I
		ss.14-16,19,24,29,31,32, 40 rep.	SI 1993(L), art.4, Sch.2, Pt.I
c.clv	East Worcestershire Water Act 1902	ss.3,26-29,31,33-35 rep.	SI 2374(L), art.4, Sch.2, Pt.I
1903			
(3 Edw. 7) c.30	Railways (Electrical Power) Act 1903	rep. (1-1-1993) (EWS)	42, ss.65(1)(d),68(1), Sch.4, Pt.I
c.ccix	Bournemouth Gas and Water Act 1903	s.22 rep.	SI 1988(L), art.4, Sch.2, Pt.I
1904			
(4 Edw. 7) c.cviii	Great Eastern Railway (General Powers) Act 1904	ss.2-5,7-18 appl.(mods.)	SI 1136(L), arts.2(1),9(1), Sch.
1906			
(6 Edw. 7) c.14	Alkali, &c., Works Regulation Act 1986	saved	iii, s.11(2)
c.32	Dogs Act 1906	s.3 ext.	SI 901, art.4
c.50	National Galleries of Scotland Act 1906	s.4C(3)(d) am.	44, s.11(2), Sch.8, Pt.II, para.6(2)
		s.4C(3)(c) subst.	44, s.11(2), Sch.8, Pt.II, para.6(1)
		s.4C(4) rep.	44, s.11(3), Sch.9
c.53	Notice of Accident Act 1906	rep. (EWS)	42, s.68(1), Sch.4, Pt.I
c.58	Workmen's Compensation Act 1906	cont.	4, s.111, Sch.8, Pt.I, para.1
		(saving) continued	7, s.111, Sch.8, para.1
c.cc	Bristol Corporation Act 1906	s.14 rep. (*prosp.*)	xxi, ss.2,7, Sch., Pt.II
1907			
(7 Edw. 7) c.24	Limited Partnership Act 1907	excl.	SI 1027, reg.2
c.51	Sheriff Courts (Scotland) Act 1907	Sch.1, rule 9(2B) added	SI 249, rule 2(2)
		Sch.1, rule 10(3) am.	SI 249, rule 2(3)
		Sch.1, rule 15(2) subst.	SI 249, rule 2(4)
		Sch.1, rule 33 am.	SI 249, rule 2(5)
		Sch.1, rule 50A added	SI 249, rule 2(6)
		Sch.1, rule 59A added	SI 249, rule 2(7)

Year and Chap. or No. of Measure	Short title	How affected	1992, Chapter of Act or Number of Measure or Statutory Instrument
1907—*cont.*			
		Sch.1, rule 59A renumbered (As 59B)	SI 249, rule 2(8)
		Sch.1, rule 98(1) am.	SI 249, rule 2(9)
		Sch.1, rule 138(5) subst.	SI 249, rule 2(10)
		Sch.1, Appx., Form B2 rep.in pt.	SI 249, rule 2(11)(a)
		Sch.1, Appx., Forms C3,C4 added	SI 249, rule 2(11)(b)
		Sch.1, Appx., Form E am.	SI 249, rule 2(11)(c)
c.53	Public Health Acts Amendment Act 1907	s.21 am. (1.4.1993) (EW)	14, s.117(1), Sch.13, para.3
c.cxlv	Colne Valley Water Act 1907	ss.2,5 rep.	SI 424(L), art.4, Sch.2, Pt.I
1908			
(8 Edw. 7) c.36	Small Holdings and Allotments Act 1908	s.23(2) am. (1.4.1993)	14, s.117(1), Sch.13, para.4
		s.29(1) am. (1.4.1993)	14, s.117(1), Sch.13, para.5
c.57	Coal Mines Regulation Act	rep. (EWS) (*prosp.*)	17, ss.2,3(3), Sch., Pt.II
c.cxxxiii	Gas and Water Orders Confirmation Act 1908	Sch. rep.in pt. (Sevenoaks Water O, s.4 rep. in pt.)	SI 19(L), art.4, Sch.2, Pt.II
1911			
(1 & 2 Geo. 5) c.27	Protection of Animals Act 1911	s.8(b) mod. (EW)	51, s.10(10)
c.46	Copyright Act 1911	s.15(5) trans.of functions	SI 1311, art.3(1), Sch.1, Pt.I
1912			
(2 & 3 Geo. 5) c.14	Protection of Animals (Scotland) Act 1912	s.7(b) mod.	51, s.10(10)
c.19	Light Railways Act 1912	rep. (1-1-1993) (EW)	42, s.68(1), Sch.4, Pt.I
c.xx	Price's Patent Candle Company Limited Act 1912	ss.3,7,8 rep. (*prosp.*)	xvii, s.5, Sch.2, Pt.II
		s.7 rep.in pt.	xvii, s.3, Sch.1, para.3
		s.7 am.	xvii, s.3, Sch.1, para.3
		ss.9,10 rep.	xvii, s.5, Sch.2, Pt.I
		Sch., para.12A added	xvii, s.3, Sch.1, para.4
1913			
(2 & 3 Geo. 5) c.30	Trade Union Act 1913	rep.	52, s.300(1), Sch.1
		saved	52, s.300(3), Sch.3, para.12(4)(b)
1913			
(3 & 4 Geo. 5) c.li	West Hampshire Water Act 1913	rep.	SI 1993(L), art.4, Sch.2, Pt.I
c.lxv	Bournemouth Gas and Water Act 1913	s.2 rep.in pt.	SI 1988(L), art.4, Sch.2, Pt.I
		ss.6,9-11,39,40,42,43,60 rep.	SI 1988(L), art.4, Sch.2, Pt.I
1915			
(5 & 6 Geo. 5) c.48	Fishery Harbours Act 1915	rep.	42, ss.65(1)(e),68(1), Sch.4, Pt.II

Year and Chap. or No. of Measure	Short title	How affected	1992, Chapter of Act or Number of Measure or Statutory Instrument
1916			
(6 & 7 Geo. 5) c.31	Police, Factories, etc. (Miscellaneous Provisions) Act 1916	rep. (EWS) (*prosp.*)	41, s.78(2), Sch.7
1917			
(7 & 8 Geo. 5) c.8	Coal Mines Regulation (Amendment)	rep. (EWS) (*prosp.*)	17, s.3(3), Sch., Pt.II
c.xxxii	Gas and Water Provisional Orders Act 1917	Sch. rep.in pt. (Rickmansworth and Uxbridge Valley Water Order s.3 rep.)	SI 125(L), art.4, Sch.2, Pt.II
		Sch. rep. (Rickmansworth and Uxbridge Valley Water Order s.39 rep.)	SI 125(L), art.4, Sch.2, Pt.II
1919			
(9 & 10 Geo. 5) c.23	Anthrax Prevention Act 1919	saved	iii, s.11(2)
c.48	Coal Mines Act 1919	rep. (EWS) (*prosp.*)	17, s.3(3), Sch., Pt.II
c.69	Industrial Courts Act 1919	rep.	52, s.300(1), Sch.1
		saved	52, s.300(3), Sch.3, para.12(4)(c)
c.xlviii	Bournemouth Gas and Water Act 1919	ss.3,17,35,37,38-40,43,46- 50 rep.	SI 1988(L), art.4, Sch.2, Pt.I
		Sch.3 rep.	SI 1988(L), art.4, Sch.2, Pt.I
c.xcv	Peterhead Harbours Order Confirmation Act 1919	rep.	xii, s.1, Sch. s.63, Sch.2
c.cix	Water Order Confirmation Act 1919	Sch. rep.in pt. (West Hampshire Water O. Rep.)	SI 1993(L), art.4, Sch.2, Pt.II
1920			
(10 & 11 Geo. 5) c.16	The Imperial War Museum Act 1920	s.2 renumbered s.2(1)	44, s.11(2), Sch.8, Pt.II, para.7(2)(6)
		ss.2,2A,3(2),4 trans.of functions	SI 1311, art.3(1), Sch.1, Pt.I
		s.2(2) added	44, s.11(2), Sch.8, Pt.II, para.7(2)(6)
		s.2(b) am.	44, s.11(2), Sch.8, Pt.II, para.7(1)(a)(6)
		s.2(d) am.	44, s.11(2), Sch.8, Pt.II, para.7(1)(b)(6)
		s.2A added	44, s.11(2), Sch.8, Pt.II, para.7(3)(6)
		s.3(2) rep.in pt.	44, s.11(3), Sch.9
		s.4(1) am.	44, s.11(2), Sch.8, Pt.II, para.7(4)(6)
		s.4(4) am.	44, s.11(2), Sch.8, Pt.II, para.7(5)(6)
		s.4(5) rep.	44, s.11(3), Sch.9
		Sch., para.(1) am.	SI 1311, art.12(2), Sch.2, para.1
		Sch., para.(8) trans.of functions	SI 1311, art.3(1), Sch.1, Pt.I

Year and Chap. or No. of Measure	Short title	How affected	1992, Chapter of Act or Number of Measure or Statutory Instrument
1920—*cont.*			
c.33	Maintenance Orders (Facilities for Enforcement) Act 1920	trans.of functions	SI 709, art.4(1)(a) SI 709, art.4(2)
		am.	
		s.3(1) am. (*prosp.*)	56, s.1, Sch.1, Pt.I, para.1(2)
		s.3(3)-(6) am. (*prosp.*)	56, s.1, Sch.1, Pt.I, para.1(3)-(6)
		s.3(7)(8) added (*prosp.*)	56, s.1, Sch.1, Pt.I, para.1(7)
		s.4(1) am. (*prosp.*)	56, s.1, Sch.1, Pt.I, para.2(1)
		s.4(2) subst. (*prosp.*)	56, s.1, Sch.1, Pt.I, para.2(3)
		s.4(3)-(5) am. (*prosp.*)	56, s.1, Sch.1, Pt.I, para.2(4)-(6)
		s.4(6A)(za) added (*prosp.*)	56, s.1, Sch.1, Pt.I, para.2(7)
		s.4A added (*prosp.*)	56, s.1, Sch.1, Pt.I, para.3
		s.7 renumbered (s.7(1)) (*prosp.*)	56, s.1, Sch.1, Pt.I, para.4
		s.7(2) added (*prosp.*)	56, s.1, Sch.1, Pt.I, para.4
		s.11(d) added (*prosp.*)	56, s.1, Sch.1, Pt.I, para.5
c.65	Employment of Women, Young Persons and Children Act 1920	saved	iii, s.11(2)
c.iv	Price's Patent Candle Company Limited Act 1920	rep. (*prosp.*)	xvii, s.5, Sch.2, Pt.II
		ss.12,17 rep.	xvii, s.5, Sch.2, Pt.I
c.lxiv	Eastbourne Waterworks Act 1920	s.2 rep.in pt.	SI 17(L), art.4, Sch.2, Pt.I
		ss.4,8-10,17,18 rep.	SI 17(L), art.4, Sch.2, Pt.I
1921			
(11 & 12 Geo. 5) c.55	Railways Act 1921	ss.68,69 rep. (1-1-1993) (EW)	42, s.68(1), Sch.4, Pt.I
		s.71 rep. (1-1-1993) (EW)	42, s.68(1), Sch.4, Pt.I
		ss.73-74 rep. (1-1-1993) (EW)	42, s.68(1), Sch.4, Pt.I
c.xxvi	Eastbourne Waterworks Act 1921	s.2 rep.in pt.	SI 17(L), art.4, Sch.2, Pt.I
		ss.20,22-25,27,29,31,34, 37-39 rep.	SI 17(L), art.4, Sch.2, Pt.I
c.xlvii	Sunderland and South Shields Water Act 1921	s.63 rep.	SI 978(L), art.3, Sch., Pt.I
c.xcviii	Peterhead Harbours Order Confirmation Act 1921	rep.	xii, s.1, Sch. s.63, Sch.2
1922			
(12 & 13 Geo. 5) c.35	Celluloid and Cinematograph Film Act 1922	saved	iii, s.11(2)
		s.2(1)(a)(2)(a) am.	SI 1811, regs.3(1),4, Sch.1, Pt.1

Year and Chap. or No. of Measure	Short title	How affected	1992, Chapter of Act or Number of Measure or Statutory Instrument
1922—*cont.*			
		Sch.1, Pt.II, reg.3 am.	SI 1811, regs.3(1),4, Sch.1, Pt.1
		Sch.1, Pt.III, reg.10 am.	SI 1811, regs.3(1),4, Sch.1, Pt.1
		Sch.1, Pt.III, reg.11 am.	SI 1811, regs.3(1),4, Sch.1, Pt.1
c.xxvi	Sunderland and South Shields Water Act 1922	s.21 rep.	SI 978(L), art.3, Sch., Pt.I
c.xxxiii	Colne Valley Water Act 1922	s.2 rep.in pt.	SI 424(L), art.4, Sch.2, Pt.I
		ss.58,71,75-77,80-83 rep.	SI 424(L), art.4, Sch.2, Pt.I
1923 (13 & 14 Geo. 5) c.8	Industrial Assurance Act 1923	defn. of "collecting society" appl.	40, s.119(1)
		s.1(1A) subst. (*prosp.*)	40, s.100, Sch.19, Pt.I, paras.1,2(1)
		s.1(2) (defn. of "industrial assurance business") appl. (*prosp.*)	40, s.43
		s.1(2)(d) am. (*prosp.*)	40, s.100, Sch.19, Pt.I, para.2(2)
		ss.2-4 rep. (*prosp.*)	40, s.120(2), Sch.22, Pt.I
		s.4(2) appl.	52, s.19(1)(b)
		ss.6-8 rep. (*prosp.*)	40, s.120(2), Sch.22, Pt.I
		s.10(1) subst. (*prosp.*)	40, s.100, Sch.19, Pt.I, para.3
		s.10(3) am. (*prosp.*)	40, s.100, Sch.19, Pt.I, para.5(1)(a)
		s.11(2) am. (*prosp.*)	40, s.100, Sch.19, Pt.I, para.4
		ss.15,16 rep. (*prosp.*)	40, s.120(2), Sch.22, Pt.I
		s.17(1)(2) subst. (*prosp.*)	40, s.100, Sch.19, Pt.I, para.6
		s.17(3) am. (*prosp.*)	40, s.100, Sch.19, Pt.I, para.5(1)(b)(2)(a)
		s.18(1) rep.in pt. (*prosp.*)	40, s.120(2), Sch.22, Pt.I
		s.18(1)(3) am. (*prosp.*)	40, s.100, Sch.19, Pt.I, para.5(1)(c)(2)(b)
		s.18(1)(d) rep.in pt. (*prosp.*)	40, s.120(2), Sch.22, Pt.I
		s.18(1)(f)(g) rep.in pt. (*prosp.*)	40, s.120(2), Sch.22, Pt.I
		s.18(1)(c) rep. (*prosp.*)	40, s.120(2), Sch.22, Pt.I
		s.18(3) rep.in pt. (*prosp.*)	40, s.120(2), Sch.22, Pt.I
		s.19(1)-(4) rep.in pt. (*prosp.*)	40, s.120(2), Sch.22, Pt.I
		s.20(1)(b) rep. (*prosp.*)	40, s.120(2), Sch.22, Pt.I
		s.23 subst. (*prosp.*)	40, s.100, Sch.19, Pt.I, para.7
		s.26(1) subst. (*prosp.*)	40, s.100, Sch.19, Pt.I, para.8
		s.31 rep. (*prosp.*)	40, s.120(2), Sch.22, Pt.I
		s.32 subst. (*prosp.*)	40, s.100, Sch.19, Pt.I, para.9

Year and Chap. or No. of Measure	Short title	How affected	1992, Chapter of Act or Number of Measure or Statutory Instrument
1923—*cont.*			
		s.33 subst. (*prosp.*)	40, s.100, Sch.19, Pt.I, para.10
		ss.35,36 rep. (*prosp.*)	40, s.120(2), Sch.22, Pt.I
		s.38 rep. (*prosp.*)	40, s.120(2), Sch.22, Pt.I
		s.39(1) am. (*prosp.*)	40, s.100, Sch.19, Pt.I, para.5(1)(d)
		s.39(5) am. (*prosp.*)	40, s.100, Sch.19, Pt.I, para.11
		s.43 am. (*prosp.*)	40, s.100, Sch.19, Pt.I, para.5(1)(e)
		s.44 rep. (*prosp.*)	40, s.120(2), Sch.22, Pt.I
		s.45(1) (defns. of "the Commission", "friendly society", "incorporated friendly society" and "the relevant authority") added (*prosp.*)	40, s.100, Sch.19, Pt.I, para.12
		s.45(2) rep. (*prosp.*)	40, s.120(2), Sch.22, Pt.I
		Sch.1 rep. (*prosp.*)	40, s.120(2), Sch.22, Pt.I
c.17	Explosives Act 1923	saved	iii, s.11(2)
1925			
(15 & 16 Geo. 5) c.18	Settled Land Act 1925	defn. of "settled land" appl.	12, s.69(3)
		defn(s). appl. (1.1.1993)	41, ss.33(6),35(5)
		s.29(1) excl. (1.1.1993)	41, ss.33(6),35(5)
		s.117(xxx) (defn. of "trust corporation") am. (*retrosp.*)	41, s.14(1)(2) (adding 1960 c.58 s.21A)
c.19	Trustee Act 1925	s.39 mod.	52, s.13(2)(a)
		s.40 mod.	52, s.13(2)(b)
		s.40 mod.	52, s.13(4)
		s.68(18) (defn. of "trust corporation") am. (*retrosp.*)	41, s.14(1)(2) (adding 1960 c.58 s.21A)
c.20	Law of Property Act 1925	defn. of "convey" appl. (*prosp.*)	xiii, ss.11(7),15(2)(c)
		s.53(1)(c) excl.	SI 225, reg.18(2)(b)
		s.136 excl.	SI 225, reg.18(2)(c)
		s.141 excl.	SI 581(L), art.5(2)
		s.205(xxviii) (defn. of "trust corporation") am. (*retrosp.*)	41, s.14(1)(2) (adding s.21A to 1960 c.58)
c.21	Land Registration Act 1925	appl.	SI 613, reg.51(5)
		excl. (31.1.1993)	23, s.5(5)
		ext. (31.1.1993)	23, s.5(6)
		defns. of "prescribed" and "registered disposition" appl. (1.1.1993)	41, s.35(6)
		s.49(1)(g) am.	SI 613, reg.51(5)
		s.49(1)(j) added (31.1.1993)	23, s.5(2)
		s.64(7) added (31.1.1993)	23, s.5(3)

Year and Chap. or No. of Measure	Short title	How affected	1992, Chapter of Act or Number of Measure or Statutory Instrument
1925—*cont.*			
c.23	Administration of Estates Act 1925	s.55(xxvi) (defn. of "trust corporation") am. (*retrosp.*)	41, s.14(1)(2) (adding s.21A to 1960 c.58)
c.84	Workmen's Compensation Act 1925	defn. of "members of the deceased's family" appl.	4, s.111, Sch.8, Pt.I, paras.5(1)(b),6(6)
		defn. of "workman" appl.	4, s.111, Sch.8, Pt.I, para.5(1)(e)
1926			
(16 & 17 Geo. 5) c.16	Execution of Diligence (Scotland) Act 1926	s.2(2)(g) am.	SI 249, rule 5
c.48	Births and Deaths Registration Act 1926	s.12 am.	29, s.1(1)
c.lxxxii	West Hampshire Water Act 1926	s.2 rep.in pt.	SI 1993(L), art.4, Sch.2, Pt.I
		ss.29,31-34,36,41,44,45, 47,48,63,64,66-68,70,74 rep.	SI 1993(L), art.4, Sch.2, Pt.I
1927			
(17 & 18 Geo. 5) c.41	Superannuation and other Trust Funds (Validation) Act 1927	power to cont. certain provisions	6, s.5, Sch.3, Pt.II, para.15
1928			
(18 & 19 Geo. 5) c.32	Petroleum (Consolidation) Act 1928	saved	iii, s.11(2)
		s.1(1)(a)(b) am.	SI 1811, regs.3(1),4, Sch.1, Pt.1
		s.4 am.	SI 1752, reg.10, Sch.9, Pt.II
		s.4 excl.	SI 1752, reg.11
		s.5 rep.in pt.	SI 743, reg.30(1)
		s.17(6) added	SI 1811, reg.12, Sch.3, Pt.I
		s.18 rep.in pt.	SI 743, reg.30(1)
		s.20 rep.	SI 1811, reg.12, Sch.3, Pt.I
		s.23 (defn. of "I.W.G.") rep.	SI 1811, reg.12, Sch.3, Pt.I
		s.23 (defn. of "petroleum-spirit") subst.	SI 1811, reg.12, Sch.3, Pt.I
		Sch.2 rep.	SI 1811, reg.12, Sch.3, Pt.I
c.43	Agricultural Credits Act 1928	s.5(7) am. (1.1.1993)	SI 3218, reg.82(1), Sch.10, Pt.I, para.3
c.xlix	Rickmansworth and Uxbridge Valley Water Act 1928	s.2 rep.in pt.	SI 125(L), art.4, Sch.2, Pt.I
		ss.35,54,56,58-61 rep.	SI 125(L), art.4, Sch.2, Pt.I
c.lxxxvi	Bournemouth Gas and Water Act 1928	ss.3,14,15,49,52 rep.	SI 1988(L), art.4, Sch.2, Pt.I
c.xcvi	Colne Valley Water Act 1928	s.2 rep.in pt.	SI 424(L), art.4, Sch.2, Pt.I
		s.22 rep.	SI 424(L), art.4, Sch.2, Pt.I
1929			
(19 & 20 Geo. 5) c.13	Agricultural Credits (Scotland) Act 1929	s.9(2) am. (1.1.1993)	SI 3218, reg.82(1), Sch.10, Pt.I, para.4
c.28	Industrial Assurance and Friendly Societies Act 1929	rep. (*prosp.*)	40, s.120(2), Sch.22, Pt.I

Year and Chap. or No. of Measure	Short title	How affected	1992, Chapter of Act or Number of Measure or Statutory Instrument
1930			
(20 & 21 Geo. 5) c.ciii	Ministry of Health Provisional Orders Confirmation Ac 1930	Sch. rep.in pt. (Sevenoaks Water O s.3 rep.in pt., ss.8,14-19, 21 rep.)	SI 19(L), art.4, Sch.2, Pt.II
c.cxlix	Ministry of Health Provisional Order Confirmation (Folkestone Water) Act 1930	Sch. rep.in pt. (Folkestone Water O. s.3 rep.in pt, 18-22, 24-33 rep.)	SI 1214(L), art.4, Sch.2, Pt.II
1931			
(21 & 22 Geo. 5) c.27	Coal Mines Act 1931	rep. (EWS) (*prosp.*)	17, s.3(3), Sch., Pt.II
c.xcii	London and North Eastern Railway Act 1931	ss.2,3,18-23,26,47 appl.(mods.)	SI 1136(L), arts.2(1),9(1), Sch.
No.4	Channel Islands (Church Legislation) Measure 1931	defn. of "Channel Islands" appl.	GSM 1, s.19(4)
No.7	The Cathedrals Measure 1931	rep.	GSM 1, s.17(2), Sch.4, Pt.I
1932			
(22 & 23 Geo. 5) c.12	Destructive Imported Animals Act	ss.5(2),6(1)(f) excl.	SI 3324, art.4
		s.6(1) restr.	SI 3324, art.4
		s.11 renumbered as s.11(1)	SI 3302, reg.2
		s.11(2) added	SI 3302, reg.2
c.29	Coal Mines Act 1932	rep. (EWS) (*prosp.*)	17, s.3(3), Sch., Pt.II
1933			
(23 & 24 Geo. 5) c.12	Children and Young Persons Act 1933	s.18(1)(f) rep.in pt.	SI 2793, Sch.2, Pt.I
		Sch.2 trans.of functions	SI 709, art.2(1), Sch.1
		Sch.2 am.	SI 709, art.2(3), Sch.1
c.53	Road and Rail Traffic Act 1933	s.41 rep. (*prosp.*)	42, s.68(1), Sch.4, Pt.I
		s.43 rep. (*prosp.*)	42, s.68(1), Sch.4, Pt.I
No.4	Benefices (Sequestrations) Measure 1933	s.6 rep.	GSM 1, s.17(2), Sch.4, Pt.II
1934			
(24 & 25 Geo. 5) c.36	Petroleum (Production) Act 1934	defn. of "petroleum" defn(s). appl.	15, s.5(7)
		s.2 am.	15, s.3(2)(b)(c)
c.43	The National Maritime Museum Act 1934	s.2 trans.of functions	SI 1311, art.3(1), Sch.1, Pt.I
		ss.4,5 trans.of functions	SI 1311, art.3(1), Sch.1, Pt.I
		s.5(1) am.	44, s.11(2), Sch.8, Pt.II, para.8(1)
		s.5(2) rep.in pt.	44, s.11(2)(3), Sch.8, Pt.II, para.8(2)(a), Sch.9
		s.5(2) am.	44, s.11(2), Sch.8, Pt.II, para.8(2)(b)
		s.6(1) rep.	44, s.11(2)(3), Sch.8, Pt.II, para.8(3)(a)(5), Sch.9
		s.6(2) trans.of functions	SI 1311, art.3(1), Sch.1, Pt.I

Year and Chap. or No. of Measure	Short title	How affected	1992, Chapter of Act or Number of Measure or Statutory Instrument
1934—*cont.*		s.6(2) am.	44, s.11(2), Sch.2, Pt.II, para.8(3)(b)(5)
		s.6(3)(4) rep.	44, s.11(2)(3), Sch.8, Pt.II, para.8(3)(a)(5), Sch.9
		Sch.2, paras.1,3 am.	44, s.11(2), Sch.8, Pt.II, para.8(4)(5)
c.xviii	East Worcestershire Water Act 1934	s.3 rep.in pt.	SI 2374(L), art.4, Sch.2, Pt.I
		ss.15,46,49,51-54,56-72, 74-76 rep.	SI 2374(L), art.4, Sch.2, Pt.I
1935 (25 & 26 Geo. 5) c.li	West Hampshire Water Act 1935	s.3 rep.in pt.	SI 1993(L), art.4, Sch.2, Pt.I
		ss.9,10,15,17-20,22-25,27, 28,31,33-35,37-52 rep.	SI 1993(L), art.4, Sch.2, Pt.I
c.lxxxiii	Bournemouth Gas and Water Act 1935	ss.3,8-11,22,29 rep.	SI 1988(L), art.4, Sch.2, Pt.I
c.cxi	Stoke on Trent Corporation Act 1935	s.68 rep.	SI 117, art.19(1), Sch.
		s.116 rep.in pt.	SI 117, art.2(1)
1936 (26 Geo. 5 & 1 Edw. 8) c.22	Hours of Employment (Conventions) Act 1936	saved	iii, s.11(2)
c.27	Petroleum (Transfer of Licences) Act 1936	saved	iii, s.11(2)
		s.1(4) am.	SI 1752, reg.10, Sch.9, Pt.II
		s.1(4) excl.	SI 1752, reg.11
c.49	Public Health Act 1936	s.276 appl.(mods.)	SI 1492, reg.14(1)
		s.289 appl.(mods.)	SI 1492, reg.14(1)
		s.294 appl.(mods.)	SI 1492, reg.14(1)
		s.324 trans.of functions (as applied by section 10(5) of the Public Libraries and Museums Act 1964)	SI 1311, art.3(1), Sch.1, Pt.I
c.52	Private Legislation Procedure (Scotland) Act 1936	s.1(4) am. (1-1-1993)	42, s.24
c.lvi	Rickmansworth and Uxbridge Valley Water Act 1936	s.2 rep.in pt.	SI 125(L), art.4, Sch.2, Pt.I
		s.44 rep.	SI 125(L), art.4, Sch.2, Pt.I
1937 (1 Edw. 8 & 1 Geo. 6) c.28	Harbours, Piers and Ferries (Scotland) Act 1937	ss.4,5 rep.	42, s.68(1), Sch.4, Pt.II
c.33	Diseases of Fish Act 1937	s.1 excl.	SI 3295, Sch.7
		s.1 excl. (Intra- Community Trade)	SI 3298, Sch.4, Pt.II
c.37	Children and Young Persons (Scotland) Act 1937	s.28(1)(f) rep.in pt.	SI 2793, Sch.2, Pt.I
c.lxxiv	Ministry of Health Provisional Order Confirmation Act 1937	Sch. rep. (Sevenoaks Water O rep.)	SI 19(L), art.4, Sch.2, Pt.II

Year and Chap. or No. of Measure	Short title	How affected	1992, Chapter of Act or Number of Measure or Statutory Instrument
1938			
(1 & 2 Geo. 6) c.69	Young Persons (Employment) Act 1938	s.5 am.	SI 99, art.2, Sch.
		s.5 am.	SI 2982, Sch.
c.73	Nursing Homes Registration (Scotland) Act 1938	s.10(2) (defn. of " nursing home") appl.	14, ss.11(5),79(5), Sch.1, para.8(2)
c.xvi	Bournemouth Gas and Water Act 1938	ss.4,9-13,25,46,47,50-54, 56 rep.	SI 1988(L), art.4, Sch.2, Pt.I
1939			
(2 & 3 Geo. 6) c.31	Civil Defence Act 1939	s.62(1A)(a) am.	14, s.117(1), Sch.13, para.6
c.44	House to House Collections Act 1939	rep. (*prosp.*)	41, s.78(2), Sch.7
c.49	House of Commons Members Fund Act 1939	Sch.1, para.1 subst.	SI 1683
		Sch.1, para.2 subst. (*temp.*)	SI 1683
		Sch.1, para.2A am. (*temp.*)	SI 1683
c.lxxviii	Colne Valley Water Act 1939	s.3 rep.in pt.	SI 424(L), art.4, Sch.2, Pt.I
		ss.31,66-70,73,75-77,82, 84,110-112 rep.	SI 424(L), art.4, Sch.2, Pt.I
c.xcvii	London Building Acts (Amendment) Act 1939	s.151 mod.	SI 1732, art.4(3)
c.cii	Folkestone Water Act 1939	s.3 rep.in pt.	SI 1214(L), art.4, Sch.2, Pt.I
		ss.36-44,46-49,51,52,55, 57-59,63-72 rep.	SI 1214(L), art.4, Sch.2, Pt.I
1940			
(3 & 4 Geo. 6) c.31	War Charities Act 1940	rep.	41, s.78(2), Sch.7
c.xxviii	Bournemouth Gas and Water Act 1940	ss.3(3),33 rep.	SI 1988(L), art.4, Sch.2, Pt.I
1941			
(4 & 5 Geo. 6) c.xvii	East Worcestershire Water Act 1941	s.3 rep.in pt.	SI 2374(L), art.4, Sch.2, Pt.I
		ss.60-64,66,75-85 rep.	SI 2374(L), art.4, Sch.2, Pt.I
1943			
(6 & 7 Geo. 6) No.1	The New Parishes Measure 1943	s.13(1)(bb) am.	GSM 1, s.8(a)(i)
		s.13(1)(e) am.	GSM 1, s.8(a)(ii)
		s.13(1)(f) added	GSM 1, s.8(a)(iii)
		s.16(1A) added	GSM 1, s.8(b)(i)
		s.16(3)(a) am.	GSM 1, s.8(b)(ii)
		s.16(3)(e) added	GSM 1, s.8(b)(ii)
		s.17(1) am.	GSM 1, s.8(c)
1944			
(7 & 8 Geo. 6) c.31	Education Act 1944	expld.	13, s.1(6)
		expld.	13, s.14
		expld.	13, s.62(6)
		defn(s). appl.	13, s.90(5)

Year and Chap. or No. of Measure	Short title	How affected	1992, Chapter of Act or Number of Measure or Statutory Instrument
1944—*cont.*			
		s.7 restr. (1.4.1993)	13, s.93(1), Sch.8, Pt.I, para.2
		s.8(1)(b) subst. (1.4.1993)	13, s.10(1)
		s.8(1A) added (1.4.1993)	13, s.10(2)
		s.8(2) am. (1.4.1993)	13, s.10(3)
		s.8(3) rep. (1.4.1993)	13, s.93, Sch.8, Pt.I, para.3, Sch.9
		s.9(1) am. (1.4.1993)	13, s.93(1), Sch.8, Pt.I, para.4
		s.9(7) added (1.8.1993)	13, s.12(1)
		s.14 excl.	13, s.59(2)(a)
		s.41 subst. (1.4.1993)	13, s.11
		s.41 (defn. of "learning difficulties") appl. (1.4.1993)	13, s.93(1), Sch.8, Pt.I, para.33(a) (amending 1988 c.40 s.124(2)(b))
		s.55(1) subst. (1.4.1993)	13, s.93(1), Sch.8, Pt.I, para.5(a)
		s.55(2)(3) am. (1.4.1993)	13, s.93(1), Sch.8, Pt.I, para.5(b)(c)
		s.55(4) subst. (1.4.1993)	13, s.93(1), Sch.8, Pt.I, para.5(d)
		s.55(5) added (1.4.1993)	13, s.93(1), Sch.8, Pt.I, para.5(e)
		s.56 renumbered s.56(1) (1.4.1993)	13, s.93(1), Sch.8, Pt.I, para.6
		s.56(2) added (1.4.1993)	13, s.93(1), Sch.8, Pt.I, para.6
		s.62(1) am. (1.4.1993)	13, s.93(1), Sch.8, Pt.I, para.7
		s.67(4A) rep. (1.4.1993)	13, s.93, Sch.8, Pt.I, para.8, Sch.9
		s.68 ext.	13, s.93(1), Sch.8, Pt.I, para.9
		s.77 rep.in pt. (*prosp.*)	13, s.93(1), Sch.8, Pt.I, para.10
		s.77(1) rep.in pt. (*prosp.*)	38, s.21(7)(8), Sch.4, para.1(a), Sch.5
		s.77(1) am. (*prosp.*)	38, s.21(7), Sch.4, para.1(b)
		s.77(5)(6) rep. (*prosp.*)	38, s.21(8), Sch.5
		s.81 am. (1.4.1993)	13, s.93(1), Sch.8, Pt.I, para.11(a)
		s.81(c) am. (1.4.1993)	13, s.93(1), Sch.8, Pt.I, para.11(b)
		s.81(c) rep.in pt. (1.4.1993)	13, s.93(1), Sch.8, Pt.I, para.11(b)
		s.85(2)(3) rep.in pt. (1.4.1993)	13, s.93, Sch.8, Pt.I, para.12, Sch.9
		s.93 appl. (1.4.1993)	13, s.57(6)
		s.94(1) am.	SI 99, art.2, Sch.
		s.94(1) am.	SI 2982, Sch.
		s.111 ext.	13, s.89(5)

Year and Chap. or No. of Measure	Short title	How affected	1992, Chapter of Act or Number of Measure or Statutory Instrument
1944—*cont.*			
		s.114(1) (defns. of "part-time senior education" and "post-school age education") rep. (1.4.1993)	13, s.93, Sch.8, Pt.I, para.13(2)(b), Sch.9
		s.114(1) (defn. of "further education") am.	13, s.93(1), Sch.8, Pt.I, para.13(2)(a)
		s.114(1) (defn. of "pupil") subst. (1.4.1993)	13, s.93(1), Sch.8, Pt.I, para.13(2)(d)
		s.114(1) (defn. of "school") subst. (1.4.1993)	13, s.93(1), Sch.8, Pt.I, para.13(2)(e)
		s.114(1) (defn. of "secondary education") subst. (1.4.1993)	13, s.93(1), Sch.8, Pt.I, para.13(2)(f)
		s.114(1) (defn. of "secondary school") subst. (1.4.1993)	13, s.93(1), Sch.8, Pt.I, para.13(2)(g)
		s.114(1) (defn. of "primary school") subst. (1.4.1993)	13, s.93(1), Sch.8, Pt.I, para.13(2)(c)
		s.114(1) (defn. of "agreed syllabus") appl.	38, s.18(1)
		s.114(1A)(1B)(1C) rep. (1.4.1993)	13, s.93, Sch.8, Pt.I, para.13(3), Sch.9
		s.114(2A) am. (1.4.1993)	13, s.93(1), Sch.8, Pt.I, para.13(4)
1945			
(8 & 9 Geo. 6) c.19	Ministry of Fuel and Power Act 1945	saved	iii, s.11(2)
c.42	Water Act 1945	Sch.3, Pt.VI appl.	vii, s.6(2)
1945			
(9 & 10 Geo. 6) c.18	Statutory Orders (Special Procedure) Act 1945	s.3(4A) added (1-1-1993)	42, s.12(2)
		s.11(1)(a) replaced (by paras. (a)(aa))	14, s.117(1), Sch.13, para.7
c.viii	Colne Valley Water Act 1945	s.3 rep.in pt.	SI 424(L), art.4, Sch.2, Pt.I
		ss.44,45,47-50,52,54-58 rep.	SI 424(L), art.4, Sch.2, Pt.I
		s.60(1) rep.in pt.	SI 424(L), art.4, Sch.2, Pt.I
		ss.60(2),63,84-90 rep.	SI 424(L), art.4, Sch.2, Pt.I
1946			
(9 & 10 Geo. 6) c.36	Statutory Instruments Act 1946	appl.	40, s.1, Sch.1, para.11
		s.5 appl. (NI)	8, s.166(5)
c.50	Education Act 1946	Sch.1, para.9 added (1.4.1993)	13, s.93(1), Sch.8, Pt.I, para.14
c.52	Trade Disputes and Trade Unions Act 1946	rep.	52, s.300(1)(3), Schs.1,3, para.3
c.62	National Insurance (Industrial Injuries) Act 1946	power to cont. certain provisions	6, s.5, Sch.3, Pt.II, para.15
c.67	National Insurance Act 1946	power to cont. certain provisions	6, s.5, Sch.3, Pt.II, para.15
1947			
(10 & 11 Geo. 6) c.39	Statistics of Trade Act 1947	s.9 excl.	52, s.247(5)

Year and Chap. or No. of Measure	Short title	How affected	1992, Chapter of Act or Number of Measure or Statutory Instrument
1947—*cont.*			
c.41	Fire Services Act 1947	power to cont. provn.	6, s.5, Sch.3, Pt.II, para.15
		defn. of "fire authority" appl.	14, s.107, Sch.11, Pt.IV, para.38(d) (adding defn. of "fire authority" to s.109(1) of 1980 c.45)
c.42	Acquisition of Land (Authorisation Procedure) (Scotland) Act 1947	appl.(mods.)	37, s.31(1)(6)
c.43	Local Government (Scotland) Act 1947	ss.209-257 (Pt.XI) appl.	14, s.107, Sch.11, Pt.II, para.23(a)
		ss.209-257 (Pt.XI) power to mod.	14, s.107, Sch.11, Pt.II, para.23(a)
c.44	Crown Proceedings Act 1947	ext.	52, s.247(4)
		ss.13-23 (Pt.II) ext.	SI 58, art.41(5)
c.46	Wellington Museum Act 1947	trans.of functions	SI 1311, art.3(1), Sch.1, Pt.I
c.48	Agriculture Act 1947	s.109 (defns. of "agricultural land" and "agricultural unit") appl.	iv, s.25(9)
No.2	Church Commissioners Measure 1947	s.5 am.	GSM 1, s.17(1), Sch.3, para.4
		Sch.1, paras.1,2 am.	GSM 1, s.17(1), Sch.3, para.5
1947 (11 & 12 Geo. 6) c.41	Fire Services Act 1947	am.	19, s.18(4)(b)
		s.6(2) am.	19, s.27, Sch.3, para.1(a)
		s.6(2A) added	19, s.27, Sch.3, para.1(b)
		s.10 am.	19, s.27, Sch.3, para.2(a)-(c)
1948 (11 & 12 Geo. 6) c.29	National Assistance Act 1948	ss.21-36 (Pt.III) (defn. of "local authority") appl.	4, s.135(4)
		s.26(1)(1A) replaced (by (1),(1A)-(1E) (1-4- 1993) (EW)	49, s.1(1)
		s.26A(2) (defn. of "relevant premises") appl.	4, s.135(4)
		s.41 rep.	41, s.78(2), Sch.7
		s.64(1) (defn. of "trade dispute") subst.	6, s.4, Sch.2, para.1
c.39	Industrial Assurance and Friendly Societies Act 1948	ss.1,2 rep. (*prosp.*)	40, s.120(2), Sch.22, Pt.I
		s.4 rep. (*prosp.*)	40, s.120(2), Sch.22, Pt.I
		ss.6,7 rep. (*prosp.*)	40, s.120(2), Sch.22, Pt.I
		s.6(1) appl.	52, s.19(1)(a)
		s.6(1) am.	52, s.19(2)
		s.6(1)(2) rep.in pt.	52, s.300(1), Sch.1
		s.8(2) am. (*prosp.*)	40, s.100, Sch.19, Pt.I, para.13
		ss.10,11 rep. (*prosp.*)	40, s.120(2), Sch.22, Pt.I
		s.13(1) am. (*prosp.*)	40, s.100, Sch.19, Pt.I, para.14

Year and Chap. or No. of Measure	Short title	How affected	1992, Chapter of Act or Number of Measure or Statutory Instrument
1948—*cont.*		s.13(3) rep. (*prosp.*)	40, s.120(2), Sch.22, Pt.I
		s.16(4) rep.	52, s.300(1), Sch.1
		s.17A(1) am. (*prosp.*)	40, s.100, Sch.19, Pt.I, para.15
		s.17A(2) rep. (*prosp.*)	40, s.120(2), Sch.22, Pt.I
		s.23(1)(d) rep.	52, s.300(1), Sch.1
		s.23(1)(e) added (*prosp.*)	40, s.100, Sch.19, Pt.I, para.16(b)
		s.23(1)(c) rep.in pt. (*prosp.*)	40, ss.100,120, Sch.19, Pt.I, para.16(a), Sch.22, Pt.I
		Sch.1 rep. (*prosp.*)	40, s.120(2), Sch.22, Pt.I
		Sch.2 rep. (*prosp.*)	40, s.120(2), Sch.22, Pt.I
		Sch.3, para.(b) rep.in pt. (*prosp.*)	40, s.120(2), Sch.22, Pt.I
		Sch.3, para.(c)(d) rep. (*prosp.*)	40, s.120(2), Sch.22, Pt.I
c.40	Education (Miscellaneous Provisions) Act 1948	s.3(3) rep. (1.4.1993)	13, s.93, Sch.8, Pt.I, para.15, Sch.9
		s.5(3)(aa) added (1.4.1993)	13, s.93(1), Sch.8, Pt.I, para.16
c.41	Law Reform (Personal Injuries) Act 1948	s.2(1)(a)(1A) am.	6, s.4, Sch.2, para.2
(12, 13 & 14 Geo. 6) c.5	Civil Defence Act 1948	s.9(1) (defn. of "local authority") am.	14, s.117(1), Sch.13, para.8
1949			
(12, 13 & 14 Geo. 6) c.16	National Theatre Act 1949	ss.1,2(1) trans.of functions	SI 1311, art.3(1), Sch.1, Pt.I
c.35	British Film Institute Act 1949	s.1 trans.of functions	SI 1311, art.3(1), Sch.1, Pt.I
c.42	Lands Tribunal Act 1949	s.1(3A) excl.	14, s.82(5)
		s.3(12)(a) amdt(s). cont.	53, s.18(3)
c.43	Merchant Shipping (Safety Convention) Act 1949	s.12(1)(b) rep.	SI 3, reg.50
		s.12(1)(ii) rep.	SI 3, reg.50
c.54	Wireless Telegraphy Act 1949	s.12A rep.	SI 2372, reg.2
c.74	Coast Protection Act 1949	ss.1-33 (Pt.I) saved	xii, s.1, Sch., s.62(b)
		s.2(8)(a) am.	42, s.65(2)
		s.17(8)(b) am.	42, s.65(2)
		ss.18,34-36 saved	vi, s.16
		ss.18,34-36 saved	xiv, s.27
		s.35(1)(h) added (1-1- 1993)	42, s.19
		s.35(1)(i) added	42, s.63(3)
		Sch.4, paras.30,31,32 subst.	SI 1549, reg.2
c.76	Marriage Act 1949	s.27(6)(7) am.	SI 99, art.2, Sch.
		ss.27(6)(7),32(5),41(6), 51(1)(2),57(4),63(1)(b), 64(2)(a)(c),65(2)(c) am.	SI 2982, Sch.
		s.32(5) am.	SI 99, art.2, Sch.
		s.41(6) am.	SI 99, art.2, Sch.

Year and Chap. or No. of Measure	Short title	How affected	1992, Chapter of Act or Number of Measure or Statutory Instrument
1949—*cont.*			
		s.51(1)(2) am.	SI 99, art.2, Sch.
		s.57(4) am.	SI 99, art.2, Sch.
		s.63(1)(b) am.	SI 99, art.2, Sch.
		s.64(2)(a) am.	SI 99, art.2, Sch.
		s.64(2)(c) am.	SI 99, art.2, Sch.
		s.65(2)(c) am.	SI 99, art.2, Sch.
c.87	Patents Act 1949	ext.(mods.)	SI 3091, reg.5
1950			
(14 Geo. 6) c.27	Arbitration Act 1950	excl.	5, s.59(7)
		ss.1-34 excl.	52, s.212(5)
		ss.1-34 excl.	52, s.263(6)
c.28	Shops Act 1950	s.35 am.	SI 3216, Sch.
		s.35(1) am.	SI 99, art.2, Sch.
		s.35(1) am.	SI 2982, Sch.
c.37	Maintenance Orders Act 1950	s.4(1)(d) am.	6, s.4, Sch.2, para.3(1)(a)
		s.4(2) am.	6, s.4, Sch.2, para.3(2)
		s.9(1)(d) am.	6, s.4, Sch.2, para.3(1)(b)
		s.9(2) am.	6, s.4, Sch.2, para.3(2)
		s.12(1)(d) am.	6, s.4, Sch.2, para.3(1)(c)
		s.16(2)(a)(viii) am.	6, s.4, Sch.2, para.3(1)(d)
		s.16(2)(b)(ix) am.	6, s.4, Sch.2, para.3(1)(e)
		s.16(2)(c)(viii) am.	6, s.4, Sch.2, para.3(1)(f)
c.39	Public Utilities Street Works Act 1950	defn. of "controlled land" appl.	vii, s.8(3)
		ss.1-20 (Pt.I) excl.	v, s.6(3)
		ss.21-25 (Pt.II) ext.	vii, s.8(3)
		s.26 appl.	i, s.32(4)
		s.26 (defn. of "operating undertakers") appl.	i, s.32(4)
		s.26 appl.	xi, s.39(4)
		Sch.4 ext.	vii, s.8(3)
c.lii	Middlesex County Council Act 1950	s.3 (defn. of "food") rep.	SI 2766, art.3(a)
		s.11 rep.	SI 2766, art.3(b)
1951			
(14 & 15 Geo. 6) c.30	Sea Fish Industry Act 1951	s.21(4) rep. (EWS)	42, s.68(1), Sch.4, Pt.II
		s.21(5)(8) rep.in pt. (EWS)	42, s.68(1), Sch.4, Pt.II
c.58	Fireworks Act 1951	s.4 saved	iii, s.11(2)
		s.7 saved	iii, s.11(2)
c.65	Reserve and Auxiliary Forces (Protection of Civil Interests) Act 1951	ext.	39, s.2(4)
c.xxxii	Bristol Corporation Act 1951	s.32 rep. (*prosp.*)	xxi, ss.2,7, Sch., Pt.II
c.xxxiv	Bournemouth and District Water Act 1951	ss.2,4-14,19-28 rep.	SI 1988(L), art.4, Sch.2, Pt.I

Year and Chap. or No. of Measure	Short title	How affected	1992, Chapter of Act or Number of Measure or Statutory Instrument
1952			
(15 & 16 Geo. 6 & 1 Eliz. 2) c.52	Prison Act 1952	s.39 am.	25, s.2(1)(a)(b)(4)
c.60	Agriculture (Poisonous Substances) Act 1952	saved	iii, s.11(2)
c.1	Essex County Council Act 1952	s.103 rep.	SI 117, art.19(1), Sch.
1953			
(1 & 2 Eliz. 2) c.10	Agricultural Land (Removal of Surface Soil) Act 1953	s.2(3) (saving)	SI 1630, art.3(3)
c.20	Births and Deaths Registration Act 1953	s.13(2) am.	SI 99, art.2, Sch.
		ss.13(2),30(2)(c),31(2)(a) (c),32(c),33(1) am.	SI 2982, Sch.
		s.30(2)(c) am.	SI 99, art.2, Sch.
		s.31(2)(a) am.	SI 99, art.2, Sch.
		s.31(2)(c) am.	SI 99, art.2, Sch.
		s.32(c) am.	SI 99, art.2, Sch.
		s.33(1) am.	SI 99, art.2, Sch.
		s.41 am.	29, s.1(1)
c.34	Finance Act 1953	s.30 trans.of functions	SI 1311, art.3(1), Sch.1, Pt.I
c.36	Post Office Act 1953	s.63 power to appl.	4, s.1(4), Sch.1, para.8(3) (b)
		s.63 power to appl. (NI)	7, s.1(4), Sch.1, para.8(3) (b)
c.37	Registration Service Act 1953	s.20 ext.	5, s.124(1), Sch.10, para.3
c.47	Emergency Laws (Miscellaneous Provisions) Act 1953	s.3 saved	iii, s.11(2)
No.2	Diocesan Stipends Funds Measure 1953	s.4(1)(dd) added	GSM 1, s.17(1), Sch.3, para.6
		s.5(1)(aa) added	GSM 1, s.17(1), Sch.3, para.7
		s.8(1) (defn. of "parsonage house") defn(s). added	GSM 1, s.17(1), Sch.3, para.8
1954			
(2 & 3 Eliz. 2) c.64	Transport Charges &c. (Miscellaneous Provisions) Act 1954	s.9 rep. (*prosp.*)	42, s.68(1), Sch.4, Pt.I
		s.13(1) rep.in pt. (*prosp.*)	42, s.68(1), Sch.4, Pt.I
		s.14(5) rep. (*prosp.*)	42, s.68(1), Sch.4, Pt.I
c.65	The National Gallery and Tate Gallery Act 1954	rep.	44, s.11(3), Sch.9
		ss.2(4),3,4(3)(4) trans.of functions	SI 1311, art.3(1), Sch.1, Pt.I
		s.4(4) am.	SI 1311, art.12(2), Sch.2, para.2
c.70	Mines and Quarries Act 1954	saved	iii, s.11(2)
		ss.81(1),82 rep. (1.9.1993)(1.9.1997)	SI 2932, regs.1(3),27(1), Sch.2, Pt.I

Year and Chap. or No. of Measure	Short title	How affected	1992, Chapter of Act or Number of Measure or Statutory Instrument
1954—*cont.*			
		ss.83,85(1) excl.	SI 3073, reg.33(2)(g)
		s.93 rep.	SI 2793, Sch.2, Pt.I
		s.115 rep.in pt.	SI 2793, Sch.2, Pt.I
		s.187 rep. (EWS) (*prosp.*)	17, s.3(3), Sch., Pt.II
		Sch.4 rep.in pt. (EWS) (*prosp.*)	17, s.3(3), Sch., Pt.II
1955			
(3 & 4 Eliz. 2) c.14	The Imperial War Museum Act 1955	s.2(1) trans.of functions	SI 1311, art.3(1), Sch.1, Pt.I
		s.2(1) rep.in pt.	44, s.11(2)(3), Sch.8, Pt.II, para.9(1), Sch.9
		s.2(3) rep.in pt.	44, s.11(2)(3), Sch.8, Pt.II, para.9(2), Sch.9
c.18	Army Act 1955	cont. (31.8.1993)	SI 1712, art.1
c.19	Air Force Act 1955	cont. (31.8.1993)	SI 1712, art.1
1955			
(4 & 5 Eliz. 2) c.19	Friendly Societies Act 1955	cont. (until 31.8.1992)	SI 1712, art.1
		power to cont. certain provn(s).	6, s.5, Sch.3, Pt.II, para.15
		s.3(2) rep. (*prosp.*)	40, s.120(2), Sch.22, Pt.I
		s.6 rep. (*prosp.*)	40, s.120(2), Sch.22, Pt.I
c.xi	Kent Water Act 1955	s.3(5) rep.in pt.	SI 19(L), art.4, Sch.2, Pt.I
		s.3(5) rep.in pt.	SI 1214(L), art.4, Sch.2, Pt.I
		ss.19,25 rep.	SI 1214(L), art.4, Sch.2, Pt.I
		s.49 rep.	SI 19(L), art.4, Sch.2, Pt.I
1956			
(4 & 5 Eliz. 2) c.49	Agriculture (Safety, Health and Welfare Provisions) Act 1956	saved	iii, s.11(2)
		s.2 rep	SI 2793, Sch.2, Pt.I
		ss.3,5,25(3)(6) rep. (1.1.93, 1.1.96)	SI 3004, Sch.2, Pt.I
c.52	Clean Air Act 1956	s.3(4) am.	SI 36, reg.2(2)
		ss.6(1)(b),7(1)(b)(c) am.	SI 36, reg.2(3)-(5)
c.54	Finance Act 1956	s.26 amdt(s). saved	12, s.290, Sch.11, Pt.II, para.24(1)(a)
		s.34(1) trans.of functions	SI 1311, art.3(1), Sch.1, Pt.I
c.60	Valuation and Rating (Scotland) Act 1956	s.6 (defn. of "rateable value") appl.	14, s.99(1)
		s.6 cont. (*prosp.*)	14, s.111(12)
		s.6(1) mod. (1992-93)	SI 864, arts.5,6
		s.6(1) mod. (1992-93)	SI 865, arts.5,6
		s.6(1) mod.	SI 1782, art.8
		s.6(1) mod.	SI 1783, art.7
		s.6(1) mod.	SI 1784, art.8
		s.6(1) mod.	SI 1785, art.8
		s.6(1) mod.	SI 1786, art.8

Year and Chap. or No. of Measure	Short title	How affected	1992, Chapter of Act or Number of Measure or Statutory Instrument
1956—*cont.*			
		s.6(1) mod.	SI 1787, art.7
		s.6(1) mod.	SI 1788, art.8
		s.6(1) mod.	SI 1789, art.7
		s.6(1) mod.	SI 1790, arts.8,9
		s.6(1) mod.	SI 1790, art.9
		s.6(1) mod.	SI 1791, art.8
		s.6(1) mod.	SI 1792, art.8
		s.6(1) mod.	SI 1793, art.8
		s.6(1) mod.	SI 1795, art.8
		s.6(1) mod.	SI 1796, art.6
		s.20A added (*prosp.*)	14, s.117(1), Sch.13, para.9
		s.22 subst.	14, s.117(1), Sch.13, para.10
No.3	Parochial Church Councils (Powers) Measure 1956	s.6 (defn. of "diocesan authority") appl.	GSM 1, s.10(3)
		s.6(1) excl. (*retrosp.*)	GSM 1, s.10(1)
		s.6(2) excl.	GSM 1, s.10(2)
1957			
(5 & 6 Eliz. 2) c.20	House of Commons Disqualification Act 1957	power to cont. certain provn(s).	6, s.5, Sch.3, Pt.II, para.15
c.26	National Insurance Act 1957	power to cont. certain provn(s).	6, s.5, Sch.3, Pt.II, para.15
c.36	Cheques Act 1957	s.4(2)(a) am.	32, s.3
c.53	Naval Discipline Act 1957	cont. (31.8.1993)	SI 1712, art.1
c.xxxiii	British Transport Commission Act 1957	s.23 rep. (*prosp.*)	xxi, ss.2,7, Sch., Pt.II
No.1	Channel Islands (Church Legislation) Measure 1931 (Amendment) Measure 1957	defn. of "Channel Islands" appl.	GSM 1, s.19(4)
1958			
(6 & 7 Eliz. 2) c.27	Industrial Assurance Act 1948 (Amendment) Act 1958	rep. (*prosp.*)	40, s.120(2), Sch.22, Pt.I
c.45	Prevention of Fraud (Investments) Act 1958	trans.of functions	SI 1315, arts.2(3)(4),6
c.49	Trading Representations (Disabled Persons) Act 1958	s.1(2)(b) rep.	41, s.78(2), Sch.7
c.51	Public Records Act 1958	Sch.1, Table , Pt.II, para.3 am.	13, s.93(1), Sch.8, Pt.II, para.68
c.69	Opencast Coal Act 1958	s.35 am.	SI 46, art.2(1)
		s.51(1) (defn. of "appropriate Minister") am.	SI 1314, art.3(3), Sch., para.1(a)
1959			
(7 & 8 Eliz. 2) c.72	Mental Health Act 1959	s.8(3) rep.	41, s.78(2), Sch.7
c.li	Lee Valley Water Act 1959	ss.3,5-14,17,18,24-31,44, 45,47,51,53-59,61-76 rep.	SI 124(L), art.4, Sch.2, Pt.I
		s.79 rep.in pt.	SI 124(L), art.4, Sch.2, Pt.I
		Sch.3, Pt.II rep.in pt.	SI 124(L), art.4, Sch.2, Pt.I

Year and Chap. or No. of Measure	Short title	How affected	1992, Chapter of Act or Number of Measure or Statutory Instrument
1959—*cont.*			
No.2	The Vacancies in Sees Measure 1959	s.2 rep.	GSM 1, s.17(2), Sch.4, Pt.I
1960			
(8 & 9 Eliz. 2) c.16	Road Traffic Act 1960	Sch.17 rep.in pt. (*prosp.*)	42, s.68(1), Sch.4, Pt.I
c.37	Payment of Wages Act 1960	power to cont. certain provn(s).	6, s.5, Sch.3, Pt.II, para.15
c.39	Dock Workers (Pensions) Act 1960	power to cont. certain provn(s).	6, s.5, Sch.3, Pt.II, para.15
c.58	Charities Act 1960	defns. of "charity" and "charitable purposes" appl.	13, s.27(5)
		am.	13, s.93(1), Sch.8, Pt.II, para.69(1)
		defn. of "a charity" appl. (*prosp.*)	41, s.58(1)
		defns. of "charity" and "charitable purposes" appl. (*prosp.*)	41, s.72(5)
		s.1(2) am.	41, s.47, Sch.3, para.1
		s.4 reprinted as am.	41, s.2(9), Sch.1
		s.4(1) subst.	41, s.2(2)
		s.4(2) am.	41, s.2(3)
		s.4(2A) added	41, s.2(4)
		s.4(4)(c) subst.	41, s.2(5)
		s.4(6) rep.in pt.	41, s.78(2), Sch.7
		s.4(6)(b) saved	41, s.4(5)(9)
		s.4(7A)(7B) added	41, s.2(6)
		s.4(8A)(8B) added	41, s.2(7)
		ss.6,7 ext.	41, s.12(1)(a)
		ss.6,7 am. (1.1.1993)	41, s.18(9)
		s.6(3) am.	41, s.6(2)(a)
		s.6(3)(b) replaced (by paras.(b)(c))	41, s.6(2)(b)
		s.6(5) am.	41, s.6(3)
		s.6(6) rep.	41, ss.6(4),78(2), Sch.7
		s.6(7) subst.	41, s.6(5)
		s.6(9) rep.	41, ss.6(6),78(2), Sch.7
		s.7(1) subst.	41, s.7(2)
		s.7(4) rep.	41, ss.7(3),78(2), Sch.7
		s.7(6) added	41, s.7(4)
		s.8(1)(2) rep. (*prosp.*)	41, ss.47,78(2), Sch.3, para.2(a), Sch.7
		s.8(3)-(6) saved (*prosp.*)	41, s.21(9)
		s.8(3) am. (*prosp.*)	41, s.47, Sch.3, para.2(b)
		s.8(4)(b) am. (*prosp.*)	41, s.47, Sch.3, para.2(c)
		s.8(6)(a) rep. (*prosp.*)	41, ss.47,78(2), Sch.3, para.2(d), Sch.7
		s.8(7) rep. (*prosp.*)	41, ss.47,78(2), Sch.3, para.2(e), Sch.7
		s.9 ext. (*prosp.*)	41, s.25(2)

Year and Chap. or No. of Measure	Short title	How affected	1992, Chapter of Act or Number of Measure or Statutory Instrument
1960—*cont.*			
		s.9(1)(3) replaced (by s.9)	41, s.47, Sch.3, para.3
		s.9(2) replaced (by s.9) (1.1.1993)	41, s.47, Sch.3, para.3
		s.14(1) am. (1.1.1993)	41, s.15(2)
		s.14(1A) added (1.1.1993)	41, s.15(3)
		s.14(4)(b) am. (1.1.1993)	41, s.15(4)
		s.14(4A) added (1.1.1993)	41, s.15(5)
		s.14(5A)(5B) added (1.1.1993)	41, s.15(6)
		s.16(1) subst.	41, s.47, Sch.3, para.4(a)
		s.16(2) rep.	41, ss.47,78(2), Sch.3, para.4(b), Sch.7
		s.17(1) excl.	41, s.30(1)
		s.17(2) am.	41, s.47, Sch.3, para.5(a)
		s.17(2A) added	41, s.47, Sch.3, para.5(b)
		s.17(4)(5) am.	41, s.47, Sch.3, para.5(c)
		s.18 mod.	41, s.31(1)
		s.18(1)(b) am.	41, s.47, Sch.3, para.6
		s.18(4)(c) added	41, s.13(2)
		s.18(5) subst.	41, s.13(3)
		s.18(6) am.	41, s.13(4)
		s.18(6A) added	41, s.13(5)
		s.18(13)(14) added	41, s.13(6)
		s.19(6) rep.in pt.	41, ss.47,78(2), Sch.3, para.7(a), Sch.7
		s.19(6) am.	41, s.47, Sch.3, para.7(b)
		s.20 reprinted as am.	41, s.8(10), Sch.1
		s.20 ext. (except subsection (1A)(ii))	41, s.12(1)(b)
		s.20(1) replaced (by subss.(1)(1A))	41, s.8(2)
		s.20(2) am.	41, s.8(3)
		s.20(3)(a) replaced (by paras.(a)(aa)(ab))	41, s.8(4)
		s.20(7) replaced (by subss.(7)(7A)(7B))	41, s.8(5)
		s.20(8) am.	41, s.8(6)
		s.20(9) am.	41, s.8(7)
		s.20(9A) added	41, s.8(8)
		s.20(10) replaced (by subss.(10)(10A)	41, s.8(9)
		s.20(10) restr.	41, s.55(2)(b)
		s.20A added	41, s.9
		s.20A ext.	41, s.12(1)(c)
		s.21(2)(3) am.	41, s.47, Sch.3, para.8
		s.21A added (*retrosp.*)	41, s.14(1)(2)
		s.21A mod. (*retrosp.*)	41, s.14(1)(2)
		s.22(6) rep.	41, ss.47,78(2), Sch.3, para.9(a), Sch.7
		s.22(9) rep.in pt.	41, ss.47,78(2), Sch.3, para.9(b), Sch.7

Year and Chap. or No. of Measure	Short title	How affected	1992, Chapter of Act or Number of Measure or Statutory Instrument
1960—*cont.*			
		s.22A added	41, s.16
		s.23A added	41, s.17
		s.26A added (1.1.1993)	41, s.28
		s.27 rep. (1.1.1993)	41, s.78(2), Sch.7
		s.27(2)-(8) rep. (1.1.1993)	41, s.37(5)
		s.28(3)(6) am. (1.1.1993)	41, s.47, Sch.3, para.10(a) (b)
		s.28A added	41, s.11
		s.29 rep. (1.1.1993)	41, s.78(2), Sch.7
		s.30 renumbered as s.30(1)	41, s.10(2)
		s.30(2)-(6) added	41, s.10(1)
		s.30A(2)(3) replaced (by subss.(2)-(4)) (1.1.1993)	41, s.40
		ss.30BA,30BB added (1.1.1993)	41, ss.41,42
		s.30C(1)(e) am.	41, s.47, Sch.3, para.11(b)
		s.30C(1)(c) rep.in pt.	41, ss.47,78(2), Sch.3, para.11(a), Sch.7
		s.31 rep.	41, ss.47,78(2), Sch.3, para.12, Sch.7
		s.32(1)(2) saved (*prosp.*)	41, s.24(1)
		s.32(2) am. (*prosp.*)	41, s.47, Sch.3, para.13(a)
		s.32(3) subst. (*prosp.*)	41, s.47, Sch.3, para.13(b)
		s.34(2)(c) am.	41, s.47, Sch.3, para.14
		s.40 appl.(mods.)	41, s.56(4)-(6)
		s.40(1)(2) appl.	41, s.57(2)(a)(4)
		s.40(4) appl.	41, s.57(2)(a)(4)
		s.40A added	41, s.47, Sch.3, para.15
		s.41 ext.	41, s.56(3)
		s.41 appl.	41, s.57(2)(b)(4)
		s.41(a) subst.	41, s.47, Sch.3, para.16
		s.43(2A) added	41, s.47, Sch.3, para.17
		s.44 rep. (1.1.1993)	41, s.78(2), Sch.7
		ss.45,46 appl.	41, s.1(2)
		s.45(3) rep.in pt.	41, ss.47,78(2), Sch.3, para.18(a)(i), Sch.7
		s.45(3) am.	41, s.47, Sch.3, para.18(a) (ii)
		s.45(4) am.	41, s.47, Sch.3, para.18(b)
		s.46 (defn. of "permanent endowment") rep.in pt.	41, ss.47,78(2), Sch.3, para.19(a), Sch.7
		s.46 renumbered as s.46(1)	41, s.47, Sch.3, para.19
		s.46 (defn. of "company") appl. (*prosp.*)	41, s.58(1)
		s.46(2) added	41, s.47, Sch.3, para.19(b)
		Sch.1, para.1(3) rep.in pt.	41, s.78(2), Sch.7
		Sch.1, para.2(1)(2) am.	41, s.47, Sch.3, para.20
		Sch.1, para.3(4) am.	41, s.47, Sch.3, para.21(2)
		Sch.1, para.3(6) am.	41, s.12(1)
		Sch.1, para.3(6) added	41, s.47, Sch.3, para.21(3)

Year and Chap. or No. of Measure	Short title	How affected	1992, Chapter of Act or Number of Measure or Statutory Instrument
1960—*cont.*			
		Sch.2, paras.(ce)-(ch) added	44, s.11(2), Sch.8, Pt.II, para.10(1)
		Sch.2, para.(d) subst.	44, s.11(2), Sch.8, Pt.I, para.4
		Sch.2, paras.(da)-(dd) added (*prosp.*)	41, s.47, Sch.3, para.22
		Sch.2, paras.(da)-(dd) rep. (*prosp.*)	44, s.11(2)(3), Sch.8, Pt.II, para.10(2), Sch.9
		Sch.2, para.(e) ext.	13, s.93(1), Sch.8, Pt.II, para.69(2)
		Sch.6 rep.in pt.	41, s.78(2), Sch.7
c.62	Caravan Sites and Control of Development Act 1960	ss.1-32 (Pt.I) appl. (EW)	14, s.7(6)
		ss.1-32 (Pt.I) (defn. of "caravan") appl. (EW)	14, s.72(3)
		s.29(1) (defn. of "caravan") appl.	35, s.1(2)(a)
c.67	Public Bodies (Admission to Meetings) Act 1960	saved	19, s.6(5)
1961			
(9 & 10 Eliz. 2) c.9	Agricultural Research etc. (Pensions) Act 1961	s.1 am.	SI 1296, art.6(1), Sch., para.1
		s.1(1) trans.of functions	SI 1296, arts.2(4),3
c.33	Land Compensation Act 1961	appl.(mods.)	i, s.28(3)
		appl.(mods.)	iii, s.25(3)
		am.	iv, s.27(2)
		appl.	viii, s.14(6)
		mod.	xi, s.35(3)
		ss.1-3 (Pt.I) appl.	3, s.2, Sch.2, Pt.II, para.4(2)
		ss.1-3 (Pt.I) appl.	3, s.2, Sch.2, Pt.III, para.7(7)(8)
		ss.1-3 (Pt.I) appl.	3, s.3, Sch.3, para.1(6)
		s.21(1) am.	53, s.18(1), Sch.3, para.1
c.34	Factories Act 1961	saved	iii, s.11(2)
		ss.1-7,18,28,29,57-60 rep. (1.1.1993, 1.1.1996)	SI 3004, Sch.2, Pt.I
		ss.12-16,17,19 rep. (pt.1.9.1997)	SI 2932, regs.1(3),27(1), Sch.2, Pt.I
		s.22(2) am.	SI 195, reg.2, Sch.1, Pt.II
		s.22(2)(3) subst.	SI 195, reg.5, Sch.2, para.3(a)(b)
		s.26(1) restr.	SI 3073, reg.33(2)(a)(i)
		s.26(1)(e) am.	SI 195, reg.2, Sch.1, Pt.I
		s.26(1)(e) subst.	SI 195, reg.5, Sch.2, para.3(c)
		s.26(1)(g) am.	SI 195, reg.2(3)
		s.26(1)(g) subst.	SI 195, reg.5, Sch.2, para.3(d)
		s.27(1)(6) excl.	SI 3073, reg.33(2)(a)(ii)

Year and Chap. or No. of Measure	Short title	How affected	1992, Chapter of Act or Number of Measure or Statutory Instrument
1961—*cont.*			
		s.27(2) subst.	SI 195, reg.5, Sch.2, para.3(e)
		s.27(2)(6) am.	SI 195, reg.2, Sch.1, Pt.I
		s.27(6) am.	SI 195, reg.5, Sch.2, para.3(f)
		s.30(6) am.	SI 2966, Sch.2, Pt.I, para.1
		s.65 rep.	SI 2966, reg.14(2)
		s.68(2A) added	SI 1811, reg.6(2)
		s.68(3) rev.in pt. & am.	SI 1811, reg.6(3)(a)
		s.68(3)(a) am.	SI 1811, reg.6(3)(b)
		s.68(3)(b) rep.	SI 1811, reg.6(3)(c)
		s.68(3)(c) rev.in pt. & am.	SI 1811, reg.6(3)(d)
		s.68(3)(d) subst.	SI 1811, reg.6(3)(e)
		s.68(5) am.	SI 1811, reg.6(4)
		s.68(7) am.	SI 1811, reg.6(5)
		s.68(8) rep.in pt.	SI 1811, reg.6(6)
		s.72 rep.	SI 2793, Sch.2, Pt.I
		s.79 rep.	SI 1811, reg.6(7)
		s.178(1) am.	SI 99, art.2, Sch.
		s.178(1) am.	SI 2982, Sch.
c.39	Criminal Justice Act 1961	s.22(1) rep.	25, s.2(3)(4)
		s.22(2)(b) am.	25, s.2(2)(4)
		Sch.4 rep.in pt.	25, s.2(3)(4)
c.57	Trusts (Scotland) Act 1961	s.2(3) restr.	SI 272, rule 16
c.62	Trustee Investment Act 1961	defn(s). appl.	41, s.38(4)
		s.2(1) power to mod.	41, s.38(1)(2)
		s.2(1) excl.	41, s.38(2)
		s.6 power to appl.	41, s.39(3)(b)
		Sch.1, Pt.I, para.1 am.	SI 1738, art.2
		Sch.1, Pt.IV, para.3 am. (EWS)	SI 232, art.4
c.64	Public Health Act 1961	s.73 saved	iii, s.11(2)
c.xiii	Great Ouse Water Act 1961	ss.97,98,100 rep.	SI 124(L), art.4, Sch.2, Pt.I
No.3	Clergy Pensions Measure 1961	power to cont. certain provn(s).	6, s.5, Sch.3, Pt.II, para.15
		s.33 am. (1.1.1993)	41, s.78(1), Sch.6, para.1
1962			
(10 & 11 Eliz. 2) c.9	Local Government (Financial Provisions etc.) (Scotland) Act 1962	s.4(9) rep.in pt.	14, s.117(1), Sch.13, para.11
c.23	South Africa Act 1962	Sch.2, para.2 trans.of functions	SI 709, art.4(1)(b)(i)
		Sch.2, para.2 am.	SI 709, art.4(2)
c.46	Transport Act 1962	ss.4(2),5(2),11(3),12(3), 14(3)(4),17(1),27(3)-(5) restr. (EWS)	SI 3060, reg.4(2)
		s.54 excl.	iii, s.38
		s.56 excl.	iii, s.38
		s.56(6A) added (1-1-1993)	42, s.21(1)

Year and Chap. or No. of Measure	Short title	How affected	1992, Chapter of Act or Number of Measure or Statutory Instrument
1962—*cont.*			
		s.83(1)-(5) rep. (1-1- 1993) (EW)	42, s.68(1), Sch.4, Pt.I
c.58	Pipe-Lines Act 1962	s.83(6) rep. (EWS) (*prosp.*) defn. of "pipe-line" defn(s). appl.	42, s.68(1), Sch.4, Pt.I 15, s.2(4)
		s.2(2)(b) am. (1.1.1995)	SI 449, reg.2(2)(a)(i)
		s.3(1) am. (1.1.1995)	SI 449, reg.2(2)(b)(i)
		s.7(1) am. (1.1.1995)	SI 449, reg.2(2)(b)(ii)
		s.8(1)(b) am. (1.1.1995)	SI 449, reg.2(2)(a)(i)
		ss.20-26 saved	iii, s.11(2)
		ss.27-32 power to rep. or mod.	15, s.2 (amending s.15 of 1974 c.37)
		s.27(1) am. (1.1.1995)	SI 449, reg.2(2)(c)
		s.27(6) am. (1.1.1995)	SI 449, reg.2(2)(c)
		s.31(1) am. (1.1.1995)	SI 449, reg.2(2)(c)
		ss.33,34 saved	iii, s.11(2)
		s.37 power to rep. or mod.	15, s.2 (amending s.15 of 1974 c.37)
		s.42 saved	iii, s.11(2)
		s.66(1) (defn. of "cross-country pipe-line") am. (1.1.1995)	SI 449, reg.2(2)(b)(iii)
		Sch.1, para.1(b) am. (1.1.1995)	SI 449, reg.2(2)(a)(ii)
		Sch.1, para.7 am. (1.1.1995)	SI 449, reg.2(2)(a)(ii)
		Sch.2, para.1(b) am. (1.1.1995)	SI 449, reg.2(2)(a)(iii)
		Sch.2, para.7(1) am. (1.1.1995)	SI 449, reg.2(2)(a)(iii)
		Sch.5 saved	iii, s.11(2)
1963			
c.12	Local Government (Financial Provisions) (Scotland) Act 1963	s.10 rep. s.15 excl.	14, s.117(2), Sch.14 14, s.82(5)
c.18	Stock Transfer Act 1963	s.4(1) (defn. of "local authority") am.	14, s.117(1), Sch.13, para.12
c.24	British Museum Act 1963	s.1(1)(c) trans.of functions	SI 1311, art.3(1), Sch.1, Pt.I
		s.3(4) am.	44, s.11(2), Sch.8, Pt.I, para.5(a)
		s.5(3) am.	44, s.11(2), Sch.8, Pt.I, para.5(b)
		s.8(1)(3) am.	44, s.11(2), Sch.8, Pt.I, para.1(1)(2)(3)(a)
		s.8(2)(b) trans.of functions	SI 1311, art.3(1), Sch.1, Pt.I
		s.8(2)(b) trans.of functions (*prosp.*)	44, s.11(2), Sch.8, Pt.I, para.2(1)(2)
		s.8(2)(b) am.	44, s.11(2), Sch.8, Pt.I, para.2(1)(a)(2)
		s.9(1) rep.in pt.	44, s.11(3), Sch.9

Year and Chap. or No. of Measure	Short title	How affected	1992, Chapter of Act or Number of Measure or Statutory Instrument
1963—*cont.*			
		s.9(2) rep.	44, s.11(3), Sch.9
		s.10(1) am.	44, s.11(2), Sch.8, Pt.I, para.1(1)(2)(3)(a)
		s.10(2) trans.of functions	SI 1311, art.3(1), Sch.1, Pt.I
		s.10(2) trans.of functions	44, s.11(2), Sch.8, Pt.I, para.2(1)(2)
		s.10(2) am.	44, s.11(2), Sch.8, Pt.I, para.2(1)(b)(2)
		s.12 rep.	44, s.11(3), Sch.9
		Sch.2, paras.2,3 rep.	44, s.11(3), Sch.9
		Sch.2, para.4 am.	44, s.11(2), Sch.8, Pt.I, para.1(1)(2)(3)(b)
c.25	Finance Act 1963	s.55 mod. (16-1-1992) (*retrosp.*)	2, s.1(1)
		s.65(2)(a) am.	41, s.78(1), Sch.6, para.2
c.41	Offices, Shops and Railway Premises Act 1963	saved	iii, s.11(2)
		ss.4-16 rep. (saving) (1.1.93, 1.1.96)	SI 3004, Sch.2, Pt.I
		s.17 rep. (pt.1.9.1997) (saving)	SI 2932, regs.1(2)(3),27, Sch.2, Pt.I
		s.23 rep.in pt.	SI 2793, Sch.2, Pt.I
c.xxiv	London Transport Act 1963	ss.10,11 incorp.(mods.)	iii, s.20(1)(2)
		s.15 incorp.	iii, s.20(1)
		s.21 incorp.(mods.)	iii, s.28(1)(2)
		s.28 incorp.	iii, s.28(1)
		s.42 incorp.(mods.)	iii, s.29(1)(2)
No.1	Ecclesiastical Jurisdiction Measure 1963	s.2(3) rep.	GSM 1, s.17(2), Sch.4, Pt.II
		s.55(1)(e) am.	GSM 1, s.17(1), Sch.3, para.9
		s.55(2) rep.in pt.	GSM 1, s.7(a)(i)
		s.55(3) rep.in pt. & am.	GSM 1, s.7(a)(ii)
		s.55(3A) added	GSM 1, s.7(a)(iii)
		s.56(1) rep.in pt. & am.	GSM 1, s.7(b)(i)
		s.56(1A) added	GSM 1, s.7(b)(ii)
No.2	Cathedrals Measure 1963	s.12(3) subst.	GSM 1, s.17(1), Sch.3, para.10
		s.20(2)(iii) am. (1.1.1993)	41, s.78(1), Sch.6, para.3
1964			
c.14	Plant Varieties and Seeds Act 1964	s.10(2) am.	53, s.18(1), Sch.3, para.2
c.24	Trade Union (Amalgamations,c) Act 1964	rep.	52, s.300(1), Sch.1
c.29	Continental Shelf Act 1964	s.1(4) rep. (*prosp.*)	15, ss.3(1)(a),7(2), Sch.2
c.40	Harbours Act 1964	defn. of "harbour authority" appl.	SI 1136(L), art.2(1)
		defn. of "harbour authority" appl.	42, s.67(1)
		s.14(2)(b) am.	42, s.63, Sch.3, para.1(2)

Year and Chap. or No. of Measure	Short title	How affected	1992, Chapter of Act or Number of Measure or Statutory Instrument
1964—*cont.*			
		s.14(2B) added	42, s.63, Sch.3, para.1(3)
		s.14(3) am.	42, s.63, Sch.3, para.1(4)
		s.14(4A) added	42, s.63, Sch.3, para.1(5)
		s.14(5) am.	42, s.63, Sch.3, para.1(6)
		s.14(5A) added	42, s.63, Sch.3, para.1(7)
		s.16(5)-(7) am.	42, s.63, Sch.3, para.2(2)-(4)
		s.16(7A) added	42, s.63, Sch.3, para.2(5)
		s.17(2A)(2B) added	42, s.63, Sch.3, para.3
		s.17(3)(4) rep.	42, s.68(1), Sch.4, Pt.II
		s.18(3) am.	42, s.63, Sch.3, para.4
		s.37(1)(2) am.	42, s.63(2)(a)(b)
		s.37(2A) added	42, s.63(2)(c)
		s.37(3) rep.	42, s.63(2)(d)
		s.42 appl.(mods.) (*prosp.*)	SI (L), para.4(3) Forth Ports Authy Scheme 1992 (as set out in SI 1992/546)
		s.42(2)-(9) appl.(mods.) (*prosp.*)	SI 546(L), art.2, Sch. (Forth Ports Authority Scheme 1992. para.4(3))
		s.47(1A) added	42, s.63, Sch.3, para.5(2)
		s.47(2A) added	42, s.63, Sch.3, para.5(3)
		s.47(3) am.	42, s.63, Sch.3, para.5(4)
		s.48A added	42, s.63, Sch.3, para.6
		s.57 (defn. of "bridleway") added	42, s.63, Sch.3, para.7(2)
		s.57 (defn. of "footpath") added	42, s.63, Sch.3, para.7(3)
		s.57(1) (defn. of "environmental assessment") added (S)	SI 1421, reg.2
		s.57(1) rep.in pt.	42, s.68(1), Sch.4, Pt.II
		s.62 saved	SI 1347, art.4
		s.62 rep.	42, ss.63,68(1), Sch.3, para.8, Sch.4, Pt.II
		Sch.2, para.3(c) am.	42, s.63, Sch.3, para.9(2)
		Sch.2, paras.7A,7B added	42, s.63, Sch.3, para.9(3)
		Sch.2, para.8A added	42, s.63, Sch.3, para.9(4)
		Sch.2, paras.9A,9B added	42, s.63, Sch.3, para.9(5)
		Sch.2, para.16A added	42, s.63, Sch.3, para.9(6)
		Sch.3, Pt.I, para.1A added (S)	SI 1421, reg.2
		Sch.3, Pt.I, para.1A(1)(e) am.	SI 1421, reg.3(2)
		Sch.3, Pt.I, para.3 am. (S)	SI 1421, reg.2
		Sch.3, Pt.I, para.3A added (S)	SI 1421, reg.2
		Sch.3, Pt.I, para.4(5) am. (S)	SI 1421, reg.3(1)
		Sch.3, Pt.I, para.4ZA added (S)	SI 1421, reg.3(1)
		Sch.3, para.1B added	42, s.63, Sch.3, para.10(2)

Year and Chap. or No. of Measure	Short title	How affected	1992, Chapter of Act or Number of Measure or Statutory Instrument
1964—*cont.*			
		Sch.3, para.3(ba) added	42, s.63, Sch.3, para.10(3)
		Sch.3, para.4A(1) am.	42, s.63, Sch.3, para.10(4)
		Sch.3, para.4A(2)-(4) replaced (by subpara.(2)	42, s.63, Sch.3, para.10(4)
		Sch.3, para.4B subst.	42, s.63, Sch.3, para.10(5)
		Sch.3, para.5(a) am.	42, s.63, Sch.3, para.10(6)
		Sch.3, para.5A rep.	42, s.68(1), Sch.4, Pt.II
		Sch.3, paras.8A,8B rep.	42, ss.63,68(1), Sch.3, para.10(7), Sch.4, Pt.II
		Sch.3, para.9 rep.in pt.	42, s.68(1), Sch.4, Pt.II
		Sch.3, para.9A rep.	42, s.68(1), Sch.4, Pt.II
		Sch.3, para.14(3) am.	42, s.63, Sch.3, para.10(8)
c.48	Police Act 1964	ss.1-27 (Pt.I) am. (EW)	19, s.18(4)(a)
		s.23(1) am.	19, s.27, Sch.3, para.3(1)
		s.23(1B) subst.	19, s.27, Sch.3, para.3(2)
		s.23(2)(a)-(c) subst.	19, s.27, Sch.3, para.3(3)
		s.23(3) subst.	19, s.27, Sch.3, para.3(4)
		Sch.1, para.7(a) am.	19, s.27, Sch.3, para.4(a)
		Sch.1, para.7(b) am.	19, s.27, Sch.3, para.4(b)
		Sch.3, para.3 am. (*prosp.*)	19, s.27, Sch.3, para.5(1)
		Sch.3, para.3A added	19, s.27, Sch.3, para.5(2)
c.71	Trading Stamps Act 1964	defn. of "trading stamp scheme" appl. (1.12.1992,1.1.1993)	48, s.14(2), Sch.3, Pt.I, para.37 (substituting 1983 c.55, s.37)
c.75	Public Libraries and Museums Act 1964	trans.of functions	SI 1311, art.3(1), Sch.1, Pt.I
		appl.	14, s.46(4)
		s.8(2)(5)(d) am.	SI 1311, art.12(2), Sch.2, para.3(a)
		s.8(7) rep.in pt.	SI 1311, art.12(2), Sch.2, para.3(b)
c.81	Diplomatic Privileges Act 1964	appl.	12, s.11(2)(4)
		appl.	12, s.11(3)(4)
		s.2(5A) am. (1.12.1992, 1.1.1993)	48, s.14(2), Sch.3, Pt.III, para.87
c.xxvi	London Transport Act 1964	s.12 incorp.(mods.)	iii, ss.22(3)(b),28(1)
		s.14 incorp.(mods.)	iii, s.28(1)
1965			
c.2	Administration Justice Act 1965	Sch.1 rep.in pt. (1-1- 1993) (EW)	42, s.68(1), Sch.4, Pt.I
c.4	Science and Technology Act 1965	ss.2,3 trans.of functions	SI 1296, arts.2(1),3
		ss.2,3 am.	SI 1296, art.6(1), Sch., para.2(1)
		s.5(1) cert. functs. made exercisable concurrently	SI 1296, arts.2(2)(a),3
		s.5(1) am.	SI 1296, art.6(1), Sch., para.2(2)
		s.5(1)(b) cert. functs. made exercisable concurrently	SI 1296, arts.2(2)(b),3

Year and Chap. or No. of Measure	Short title	How affected	1992, Chapter of Act or Number of Measure or Statutory Instrument
1965—*cont.*			
		s.5(1)(b) subst.	SI 1296, art.6(1), Sch., para.2(3)
		s.5(1)(c) am.	SI 1296, art.6(1), Sch., para.2(4)
		Sch.1 trans.of functions	SI 1296, arts.2(1),3
		Sch.1 am.	SI 1296, art.6(1), Sch., para.2(1)
		Sch.3 trans.of functions	SI 1296, arts.2(1),3
		Sch.3 am.	SI 1296, art.6(1), Sch., para.2(1)
c.12	Industrial and Provident Societies Act 1965	am. (*prosp.*)	40, s.95, Sch.16, para.32 (adding s.84A to 1974 c.46)
		restr.	52, s.10(3)(b)
		s.31(a)(i) replaced (by subparas.(i)(ia))	14, s.117(1), Sch.13, para.13
		s.60(2) subst. (*prosp.*)	40, s.83
c.17	The Museum of London Act 1965	trans.of functions	SI 1311, art.3(1), Sch.1, Pt.I
		s.7(1)(2) rep.	44, s.11(2)(3), Sch.8, Pt.II, para.11(a), Sch.9
		s.7(3) am.	44, s.11(2), Sch.8, Pt.II, para.11(b)
		s.7(4) rep.	44, s.11(2)(3), Sch.8, Pt.II, para.11(a), Sch.9
c.19	Teaching Council (Scotland) Act 1965	s.2(2) am.	37, s.62(2), Sch.9, para.1(3)(a)(b)
		ss.5,6 am.	37, s.62(2), Sch.9, para.1(2)
		s.5(1)(a)(b) am.	37, s.62(2), Sch.9, para.1(4)(a)(b)
		s.7(1)(2) subst.	37, s.55(2)
		s.17(3A) added	37, s.55(3)
		Sch.1, paras.1,2,6 am.	37, s.62(2), Sch.9, para.1(2)
		Sch.1, para.1(1)(b)(v) am.	37, s.62(2), Sch.9, para.1(5)(a)
		Sch.1, para.1(3) am.	37, s.62(2), Sch.9, para.1(5)(b)
		Sch.1, para.1(3)(b)(ii) am.	37, s.62(2), Sch.9, para.1(5)(c)
		Sch.1, para.6A added	37, s.62(2), Sch.9, para.1(5)(d)
c.24	Severn Bridge Tolls Act	rep.	3, s.40, Sch.5
		s.12(1) restr.	3, s.21(6)
		s.17(1) restr.	3, s.5(7)
c.25	Finance Act 1965	ss.31,32 saved	12, s.290, Sch.11, Pt.II, para.20
		Sch.6, para.7 mod.	12, s.290, Sch.11, Pt.I, para.5(2)
		Sch.7, para.2 excl.	12, s.35, Sch.2, Pt.I, para.3(1)(b)
c.32	Administration of Estates (Small Payments) Act 1965	s.6(1) ext.	52, s.18(4)

Year and Chap. or No. of Measure	Short title	How affected	1992, Chapter of Act or Number of Measure or Statutory Instrument
1965—*cont.*			
c.49	Registration of Births, Deaths and Marriages (Scotland) Act 1965	s.28B rep. (*prosp.*)	14, s.117(2), Sch.14
		s.54 ext.	5, s.124(1), Sch.10, para.3
		s.56(1) (defn. of "still- born child") am.	29, s.1(2)
c.51	National Insurance Act 1965	power to cont. certain provisions	6, s.5, Sch.3, Pt.II, para.15
		s.36(4) Power to replace	4, s.62(1)(a)
		s.37 power to ext.	4, s.62(1)(b)
c.52	National Insurance (Industrial Injuries) Act 1965	power to cont. certain provn(s).	6, s.5, Sch.3, Pt.II, para.15
c.53	Family Allowances Act 1965	power to cont. certain provn(s).	6, s.5, Sch.3, Pt.II, para.15
c.54	National Health Service Contributions Act 1965	power to cont. certain provn(s).	6, s.5, Sch.3, Pt.II, para.15
c.56	Compulsory Purchase Act 1965	ext.	iv, s.28(2)
		appl.(mods.)	v, s.26(2)(3), Sch.3
		appl.	v, s.31(2)
		appl.(mods.)	xiv, s.5, Sch.
		ext.	xiv, s.9(2)
		appl.(mods.)	xv, s.17(3)
		ss.1-22 (Pt.I) appl.(mods.)	3, s.2(3)(4), Sch.2, para.7(7)
		ss.1-32 (Pt.I) appl.(mods.)	i, ss.4(1)(2),17(6),20(3)(4)(a), Sch.2
		ss.1-32 (Pt.I) appl.(mods.)	iv, ss.4(1)(2),21(3)(4)
		ss.1-32 (Pt.I) appl.(mods.)	v, s.4(1)(a)(b)
		ss.1-32 (Pt.I) incorp.in pt.(mods.)	xi, ss.4(1)(2),27(3)(4), Sch.3
		ss.1-32 (Pt.I) appl.in pt.(mods.)	xiv, s.3(2)(a)(b)
		ss.1-32 (Pt.I) appl.in pt.(mods.)	xv, s.3(1)(2)
		ss.1-32 (Pt.I) appl.(mods.)	xv, s.17(4)(a), Sch.
		ss.1-32 (Pt.I) appl.in pt.(mods.)	xviii, s.3(1)(2)
		s.8(1) excl.	i, s.23(1)
		s.8(1) excl.	iv, s.25(1)
		s.8(1) restr.	xi, s.30(1)
		s.10(2) saved	v, s.27(6)
		s.10(2) saved	vii, s.14(6)(b)
		s.10(2) saved	viii, s.14(5)(b)
		s.10(2) saved	xi, s.21(6)
c.57	Nuclear Installations Act 1965	s.1 saved	iii, s.11(2)
		ss.3-6 saved	iii, s.11(2)
		s.22 saved	iii, s.11(2)
		s.24 saved	iii, s.11(2)
		Sch.2 saved	iii, s.11(2)

Year and Chap. or No. of Measure	Short title	How affected	1992, Chapter of Act or Number of Measure or Statutory Instrument
1965—*cont.*			
c.62	Redundancy Payments Act 1965	power to cont. certain provn(s).	6, s.5, Sch.3, Pt.II, para.15
c.63	Public Works Loans Act 1965	s.2(1)(a)(i) replaced (by sub-paras. (i)(ia))	14, s.117(1), Sch.13, para.14
c.74	Superannuation Act 1965	Sch.8 am.	44, s.11(2), Sch.8, Pt.I, para.1(1)(2)(4)
c.ix	Durham Markets Company Act 1965	s.3 rep.in pt. (*prosp.*)	xx, s.5, Sch.2, Pt.II
		ss.6,7(1)(2) rep.	xx, s.5, Sch.2, Pt.I
		s.7(3) am.	xx, s.4, Sch.1, para.9
		s.7A added	xx, s.4, Sch.1, para.10
		s.8(1)(2) am.	xx, s.4, Sch.1, paras.11, 12
		ss.8(1),9-18 rep. (*prosp.*)	xx, s.5, Sch.2, Pt.II
		s.8A added	xx, s.4, Sch.1, para.13
		ss.19-42 (Pt.IV) rep. (*prosp.*)	xx, s.5, Sch.2, Pt.II
		ss.43-47 (Pt.V) rep. (*prosp.*)	xx, s.5, Sch.2, Pt.II
		Schs.2,3 rep.	xx, s.5, Sch.2, Pt.I
c.xxi	British Railways Act 1965	s.35(3)(8) rep.	42, s.68(1), Sch.4, Pt.I
c.xli	London Transport Act 1965	s.10 incorp.	iii, s.20(1)
		s.13 incorp.	iii, s.28(1)
		s.34(3) rep.	42, s.68(1), Sch.4, Pt.I
c.xlv	Clyde Port Authority Order Confirmation Act 1965	ss.6,9,12,38, Sch.1 rep. (*prosp.*)	SI 304(L), art.2, Sch. (Clyde Port Authority Scheme 1991 Sch. Pt.II)
		ss.50-57,59-66, Schs.4,5 rep. (*prosp.*)	SI 304(L), art.2, Sch. (Clyde Port Authority Scheme 1991 Sch. Pt.I)
1966			
c.6	National Insurance Act 1966	power to cont. certain provn(s).	6, s.5, Sch.3, Pt.II, para.15
		power to cont. (NI)	9, s.5, Sch.3, Pt.II, para.15
c.10	Commonwealth Secretariat Act 1966	Sch., para.10(1A) added (1.12.1992,1.1.1993)	48, s.14(2), Sch.3, Pt.III, para.88
c.28	Docks and Harbours Act 1966	s.37(3) rep.	42, s.68(1), Sch.4, Pt.II
c.36	Veterinary Surgeons Act 1966	Sch.3 (defn. of "recognised institution paragraph (iA)") am. (1.4.1993)	13, s.93(1), Sch.8, Pt.II, para.70
		Sch.3 (defn. of "recognised institution") am. (1-4-1993)	37, s.62(2), Sch.9, para.2(a)
		Sch.3 (defn. of "recognised institution") rep.in pt.	37, s.62(2), Sch.9, para.2(b)
		Sch.3 (defn. of "recognised institution") am.	37, s.62(2), Sch.9, para.2(c)
c.42	Local Government Act 1966	Sch.3, Pt.II, Column 1, para.20 rep.	41, s.78(2), Sch.7
c.45	Armed Forces Act 1966	s.2(1)(i) added	39, s.2(1)
		s.2(1A)(1B) added	39, s.2(2)
c.51	Local Government (Scotland) Act 1966	Sch.1, Pt.I, para.2A rep. (*prosp.*)	14, s.117(2), Sch.14

Year and Chap. or No. of Measure	Short title	How affected	1992, Chapter of Act or Number of Measure or Statutory Instrument
1966—*cont.*			
c.xvii	British Railways Act 1966	ss.2,4,7-9,22-28 appl.(mods.)	SI 1136(L), arts.2(1),9(1), Sch.
c.xxxiii	London Transport Act 1966	ss.13,14 incorp.	iii, s.28(1)
1967			
c.9	General Rate Act 1967	defn. of "rates" appl	5, s.191
		defn. of "rating authority" appl.	5, s.191
		s.70(5) am.	14, s.117(1), Sch.13, para.15
		s.72(1) am.	14, s.117(1), Sch.13, para.16
		s.73(1)(2)(b) am.	14, s.117(1), Sch.13, para.17
		s.74(2)(3) am.	14, s.117(1), Sch.13, para.18
		s.75(b) am.	14, s.117(1), Sch.13, para.19
		s.76(1)(2)(2B)(3)(4) am.	14, s.117(1), Sch.13, para.20
		s.77 am.	14, s.117(1), Sch.13, para.21
		s.78(1) am.	14, s.117(1), Sch.13, para.22
		s.83(8)(9) am.	14, s.117(1), Sch.13, para.23
		s.93(1) am.	14, s.117(1), Sch.13, para.24
		s.108(1)(c) am.	14, s.117(1), Sch.13, para.25
		s.115(1) (defn. of "hereditament") appl.	14, s.3(2)(a)
c.13	Parliamentary Commissioner Act 1967	appl.(mods.)	SI 2257, art.16(2)
		mod. (1-1-1993) (EWS)	42, s.23(10)
		Sch.2 am.	SI 1296, art.6(1), Sch., para.3(a)(c)
		Sch.2 rep.in pt.	SI 1296, art.6(1), Sch., para.3(b)
		Sch.2 am.	SI 1311, art.12(1)(a)
		Sch.2 rep.in pt.	SI 1314, art.5
		Sch.2 am.	SI 2383, Sch., para.9
		Sch.2 am. (EWS)	SI 3060, Sch.2, para.7
		Sch.2 am.	19, s.12, Sch.2, para.11
		Sch.2 am.	38, ss.1(6),5(6), Sch.1, para.8
		Sch.2 am.	40, s.1, Sch.1, para.12
		Sch.2 amdt(s). cont.	52, s.300(2), Sch.2, para.1
		Sch.2, Note 5 am.	SI 1311, art.12(1)(b)
		Sch.2, Note 6 am.	SI 1296, art.6(1), Sch., para.3(d)
c.22	Agriculture Act 1967	s.67(3)(e) am.	6, s.4, Sch.2, para.4

Year and Chap. or No. of Measure	Short title	How affected	1992, Chapter of Act or Number of Measure or Statutory Instrument
1967—*cont.*			
c.25	National Insurance (Industrial Injuries) (Amendment) Act 1967	power to cont. certain provn(s).	6, s.5, Sch.3, Pt.II, para.15
c.34	Industrial Injuries and Diseases (Old Cases) Act 1967	power to cont. certain provn(s).	6, s.5, Sch.3, Pt.II, para.15
c.73	National Insurance Act 1967	power to cont. certain provn(s).	6, s.5, Sch.3, Pt.II, para.15
c.80	Criminal Justice Act 1967	Sch.3, Pt.I rep.in pt.	42, s.68(1), Sch.4, Pt.I
c.81	Companies Act 1967	Sch.6, Pt.II rep. (*prosp.*)	40, s.120(2), Sch.22, Pt.I
c.84	Sea Fish (Conservation) Act 1967	s.4(6) am. (Pt.17.1.1993) (*pt.prosp.*)	60, ss.1(2)(a),11(1)(2)(4)
		s.4(6)(c) added (Pt.17.1.1993) (*pt.prosp.*)	60, ss.1(2)(b),11(1)(2)(4)
		s.4(6B)-(6D) added	60, ss.1(3),11(4)
		s.4(7) am. (17.1.1993)	60, ss.1(4),11(1)(4)
		s.4(9)(b) am. (17.1.1993)	60, ss.1(5),11(1)(4)
		s.4A(7) am. (17.1.1993)	60, ss.3(2),11(1)(4)
		s.4A(10)(b) am. (17.1.1993)	60, ss.3(3),11(1)(4)
		s.4AA added	60, ss.2,11(4)
		ss.4B-4C added	60, ss.4,11(4)
		s.11(1)(a)(b) am. (17.1.1993)	60, ss.5,11(1)(4)
		s.15(3A)-(3B) added	60, ss.6,11(4)
		s.20(5) am.	60, ss.7(2),11(4)
		s.20(5A)-(5B) added	60, ss.7(3),11(4)
		s.22(2)(a) (defn. of "Ministers") appl.	60, ss.10,11(2)(4)
		s.24 ext.	60, ss.11(4),12(2)
c.86	Country (Scotland) Act 1967	ss.30-47 (Pt.III) (defn. of "bridleway") appl.	42, s.63, Sch.3, para.7(2) (adding defn. of "bridleway" to 1964 c.40, s.57)
c.88	Leasehold Reform Act 1967	s.23(4) am. (1.1.1993)	41, s.78(1), Sch.6, para.4
c.90	Family Allowances and National Insurance Act 1967	power to cont. certain provn(s).	6, s.5, Sch.3, Pt.II, para.15
c.xvi	Pittenweem Harbour Order Confirmation Act 1967	Sch. am. (Pittenweem Harbour Order ss. 3,4,7, 8,9,11,12 am.)	ix, s.1, Sch., s.7
c.xli	Forth Harbour Reorganisation Scheme Confirmation (Special Procedure) Act 1967	Sch.1, art.3(2) rep. (*prosp.*)	SI 546(L), Sch., art.2 (Forth Ports Authority Scheme 1992. para.12, sch., Pt.II)
		Sch., art.35 rep. (*prosp.*)	SI 546(L), Sch., art.2 (Forth Ports Authority Scheme 1992. para.12, sch., Pt.I)
No.1	Clergy Pensions (Amendment) Measure 1967	s.3(2A) added	SI 1748, reg.2
No.2	Extra-Parochial Ministry Measure 1967	s.2 saved	GSM 1, s.2(3)

Year and Chap. or No. of Measure	Short title	How affected	1992, Chapter of Act or Number of Measure or Statutory Instrument
1968			
c.7	London Cab Act 1968	s.4 (defn. of "private hire-car") am. (*prosp.*)	42, s.62(2)
c.13	National Loans Act 1968	s.5(8) rep.	48, ss.80(1)(2),82, Sch.18, Pt.XII
		Sch.4, para.1(a)(i) replaced (by subparas.(i)(ia)) (EWS)	14, s.117(1), Sch.13, para.26
c.14	Public Expenditure and Receipts Act 1968	power to cont. certain provn(s).	6, s.5, Sch.3, Pt.II, para.15
		Sch.3, para.1(b) am.	6, s.4, Sch.2, para.5
c.16	New Towns (Scotland) Act 1968	defn. of "a development corporation" appl.	14, s.99(1)
c.18	Consular Relations Act 1968	s.1(8A) am. (1.12.1992, 1.1.1993)	48, s.14(2), Sch.3, Pt.III, para.89(1)
		s.8(1) am. (1.12.1992, 1.1.1993)	48, s.14(2), Sch.3, Pt.III, para.89(2)
c.20	Courts-Martial (Appeals) Act 1968	s.36(1) am.	34, s.7(4)
c.27	Firearms Act 1968	defns. of "ammunition" and "firearm" appl.	51, s.14
		s.5(1A) added (EWS)	SI 2823, reg.3(1)
		s.5(2) am.	SI 2823, reg.3(2)
		s.5(7) added	SI 2823, reg.3(3)
		s.5A added	SI 2823, reg.3(4)
		s.22(1A) added	SI 2823, reg.4(1)
		s.26(3) rep.in pt.	31, s.1(1)(a)
		s.26(3A)-(3C) added	31, s.1(1)(b)
		s.27(1A) added	SI 2823, reg.4(2)
		s.28(1C) added	SI 2823, reg.4(3)
		ss.32A-32C added	SI 2823, reg.5(1)
		s.48(1A) added	SI 2823, reg.7(2)
		s.48(2) am.	SI 2823, reg.7(3)
		s.48(4) added	SI 2823, reg.7(4)
		s.57(4) (defn. of "another member State") added	SI 2823, reg.5(2)(a)
		s.57(4) added	SI 2823, reg.5(2)(b)
		s.57(4) (defns. of "European firearms pass" and "European weapons directive") added	SI 2823, reg.5(2)(c)
		s.57(4A) added	SI 2823, reg.3(5)
		Sch.6, Pt.I am.	SI 2823, reg.3(6)
		Sch.6, Pt.I am.	SI 2823, reg.4(4)
		Sch.6, Pt.I am.	SI 2823, reg.5(3)
		Sch.6, Pt.I am.	SI 2823, reg.7(5)
c.40	Family Allowances and National Insurance Act 1968	power to cont. certain provn(s).	6, s.5, Sch.3, Pt.II, para.15
c.47	Sewerage (Scotland) Act 1968	s.59(1) (defns. of "public sewer" and "public sewage treatment works") appl.	14, s.99(1)

Year and Chap. or No. of Measure	Short title	How affected	1992, Chapter of Act or Number of Measure or Statutory Instrument
1968—*cont.*			
c.48	International Organisations Act 1968	s.2(2)(aa) am. (EWS) (*prosp.*)	14, s.117(1), Sch.13, para.27
		Sch.1, Pt.II, para.9B am. (EWS) (*prosp.*)	14, s.117(1), Sch.13, para.28
		Sch.1, para.19(c) added (1.12.1992,1.1.1993)	48, s.14(2), Sch.3, Pt.III, para.90
		Sch.1, para.24(b) rep.	12, s.290, Sch.12
c.49	Social Work (Scotland) Act 1968	s.1(2) (defn. of "local authority") appl.	4, s.135(4)
		s.86A(2) (defn. of "relevant premises") appl.	4, s.135(4)
c.59	Hovercraft Act 1968	defn. of "hovercraft" appl.	v, s.2(1)
		defn. of "hovercraft" appl.	12, s.155
c.60	Theft Act 1968	s.12A added	11, s.1(1)(3)
		s.12A restr.	11, s.1(3)
		s.12A(4) restr.	11, s.1(2)
		Sch.2, Pt.III rep.in pt. (*prosp.*)	41, s.78(2), Sch.7
c.62	Clean Air Act 1968	ss.2(5),3(1)(b)(c) am.	SI 36, reg.3(1)-(4)
		s.5(3)(a)(b) am.	SI 36, reg.3(5)(6)
c.64	Civil Evidence Act 1968	power to cont. certain provn(s).	6, s.5, Sch.3, Pt.II, para.15
c.65	Gaming Act 1968	s.20(3) am. (EWI)	SI 426, art.2
		s.20(3) am. (S)	SI 751, art.2
		s.21(2)(b) am. (EW)	SI 429, art.2
		s.21(2)(b)(e) am. (S)	SI 751, art.3
		s.21(2)(e) am. (EW)	SI 429, art.2
		s.34(3)(a)-(c)(4)(a)(8)(a) (b) am.	SI 2647, art.2, Sch.
		s.34(3)(a)(c)(4)(a)(8)(a) (b) am.	SI 3022, art.2, Sch.
		s.41(3)(4)(8) am. (EW)	SI 2646, art.2
		s.41(3)(4)(8) am. (S)	SI 2754, art.2
		s.42(1)(d)(e) added	10, s.1(2)
		s.42(1A) added	10, s.1(3)
		s.42(2) am.	10, s.1(4)
		s.42(3)(a) am.	10, s.1(5)
		s.42(3)(d)-(g) added	10, s.1(6)
		s.42(3A)-(3C) added	10, s.1(7)
		s.42(8) subst.	10, s.1(8)
		s.48(3)(a)-(c)(ca)(cb)(d)- (g) am. (EW)	SI 93, art.2, Sch.
		s.48(3)(a)-(c)(ca)(cb)(d)- (g) am. (S)	SI 410, art.2, Sch.
		s.48(4)(a)(b) am. (EW)	SI 93, art.2, Sch.
		s.48(4)(a)(b) am. (S)	SI 410, art.2, Sch.
		s.48(4A) am. (EW)	SI 93, art.2, Sch.
		s.48(4A) am. (S)	SI 410, art.2, Sch.
c.67	Medicines Act 1968	ss.1-5 (Pt.I) mod.	SI 605, regs.2(3),3
		s.1 ext.	SI 605, regs.2(4),3

Year and Chap. or No. of Measure	Short title	How affected	1992, Chapter of Act or Number of Measure or Statutory Instrument
1968—*cont.*			
		ss.6,7(1)(a)(2)(4)-(6) appl.(mods.)	SI 605, reg.2(1)(2), Sch.
		s.7 excl.	SI 2844, art.2
		s.7(5)(b) am.	SI 604, regs.2(2),4
		s.7(6A)(6B) added	SI 604, regs.2(3),4
		s.7(7) am.	SI 604, regs.2(4),4
		s.7(7) (defn. of "ready- made veterinary drug") rep.in pt.	SI 604, regs.2(5),4
		s.8(3)(b) am.	SI 604, regs.3(2),4
		s.8(4) replaced (by sub ss.(4)(5)(6))	SI 604, regs.3(3),4
		s.14 appl.(mods.)	SI 605, reg.2(1)(2), Sch.
		s.18 appl.(mods.)	SI 605, reg.2(1)(2), Sch.
		s.19(1)-(3) appl.(mods.)	SI 605, reg.2(1)(2), Sch.
		ss.20-22 appl.(mods.)	SI 605, reg.2(1)(2), Sch.
		s.24 appl.(mods.)	SI 605, reg.2(1)(2), Sch.
		s.28(1)-(3)(7) appl.(mods.)	SI 605, reg.2(1)(2), Sch.
		ss.29,30 appl.(mods.)	SI 605, reg.2(1)(2), Sch.
		s.40(11) appl.	SI 1520, reg.2(2)
		s.44(1)-(3) appl.(mods.)	SI 605, reg.2(1)(2), Sch.
		s.45(1)(2)(6)-(9) appl.(mods.)	SI 605, reg.2(1)(2), Sch.
		s.46(1) appl.(mods.)	SI 605, reg.2(1)(2), Sch.
		s.47(1)-(4)(6)(7) appl.(mods.)	SI 605, reg.2(1)(2), Sch.
		s.50 appl.(mods.)	SI 605, reg.2(1)(2), Sch.
		s.58(1)(d) added (*prosp.*)	28, s.1(1)
		s.58(4)(a) am. (*prosp.*)	28, s.1(2)
		s.58(5) am. (*prosp.*)	28, s.1(3)
		ss.58A,58B added	SI 3271, reg.2
		s.86 appl.(mods.)	SI 605, reg.2(1)(2), Sch.
		s.91 appl.(mods.)	SI 605, reg.2(1)(2), Sch.
		s.107 appl.(mods.)	SI 605, reg.2(1)(2), Sch.
		ss.108-114 mod.	SI 32, reg.12
		ss.108-114 appl.(mods.)	SI 1520, reg.12
		ss.108-115 mod.	SI 605, regs.2(3),3
		ss.118,119 mod.	SI 605, regs.2(3),3
		s.119 mod.	SI 32, reg.12
		s.119 appl.(mods.)	SI 1520, reg.12
		ss.121,122 appl.(mods.)	SI 605, reg.2(1)(2), Sch.
		s.124(1)(3) appl.(mods.)	SI 605, reg.2(1)(2), Sch.
		s.125 mod.	SI 605, regs.2(3),3
		s.126(4) appl.(mods.)	SI 605, reg.2(1)(2), Sch.
		ss.127,128,129(1)-(3)(5) appl.(mods.)	SI 605, reg.2(1)(2), Sch.
		s.132 ext.	SI 605, regs.2(4),3
		s.132(1) (defns. of "the 1965 Directive" and "the 1981 Directive") added	SI 3271, reg.3
		ss.133,134 appl.(mods.)	SI 605, reg.2(1)(2), Sch.
		Sch.2 appl.(mods.)	SI 605, reg.2(1)(2), Sch.
		Sch.3 mod.	SI 605, regs.2(3),3

Year and Chap. or No. of Measure	Short title	How affected	1992, Chapter of Act or Number of Measure or Statutory Instrument
1968—*cont.*			
c.70	Law Reform (Miscellaneous Provisions) (Scotland) Act 1968	s.17 (defn. of "documents") appl. (*prosp.*)	xiii, ss.9(2),15(3)(d)
c.73	Transport Act 1968	defn. of "new authorities" appl.	12, s.170(12)
		s.9(1) (defn. of " designated area") appl.	12, s.170(14)
		ss.45(5)(6),49,50(1)(2), 144 restr. (EWS)	SI 3060, reg.4(2)
		s.60(2)(c)(d) added	SI 3077, reg.14(2)
		s.60(4A) added	SI 3077, reg.14(3)
		s.63(6) (defn. of "trade union") am.	52, s.300(2), Sch.2, para.2
		ss.116-118 appl.(mods.)	SI 1267(L), art.7
		s.121(4) rep. (1-1-1993) (EW)	42, s.68(1), Sch.4, Pt.I
		s.121(5)(6) rep.in pt. (1.1.1993) (EW)	42, s.68(1), Sch.4, Pt.I
		s.124 rep. (EW) (*prosp.*)	42, ss.50,68(1), Sch.4, Pt.I
		s.125(4) rep. (*prosp.*)	42, s.68(1), Sch.4, Pt.I
		s.144 trans.of functions	SI 1311, art.5(1)
c.xxxii	Port of London Act 1968	appl.(mods.)	SI 284(L), art.2, Sch. (Port of Tilbury Transfer Scheme 1991, para.6,sch.4)
		defn. of "the river Thames" appl.	iii, s.2(1)
		s.3 am.	SI 3011, art.2(1)
		Sch.2, Pt.I, para.2(1) rep.in pt.	SI 3011, art.2(2)(a)
		Sch.2, Pt.I, para.2(2) rep.	SI 3011, art.2(2)(b)
		Sch.2, Pt.I, para.3 subst.	SI 3011, art.2(2)(c)
		Sch.2, Pt.I, para.6(1) am.	SI 3011, art.2(2)(d)
		Sch.2, Pt.I, paras.6(3), proviso am.	SI 3011, art.2(2)(e)
		Sch.2, Pt.I, para.12 subst.	SI 3011, art.2(2)(f)
1969			
c.1	London Transport Act 1969	s.14 incorp.	iii, s.28(1)
c.4	National Insurance &c. Act 1969	power to cont. certain provn(s).	6, s.5, Sch.3, Pt.II, para.15
c.10	Mines and Quarries (Tips) Act 1969	saved	iii, s.11(2)
c.12	Industrial and Provident Societies Act 1969	s.60(3) rep.in pt. (*prosp.*)	40, s.120(2), Sch.22, Pt.I
c.22	Redundant Churches and Other Religious Buildings Act 1969	ss.4,5 subst.	41, s.49, Sch.5, paras.1,2
c.38	Sharing of Church Buildings Act 1969	s.8(3) am. (1.1.1993)	41, s.78(1), Sch.6, para.5
c.44	National Insurance Act 1969	power to cont. certain provn(s).	6, s.5, Sch.3, Pt.II, para.15
c.46	Family Law Reform Act 1969	s.22(1) trans.of functions & am.	SI 709, art.3(2), Sch.2

Year and Chap. or No. of Measure	Short title	How affected	1992, Chapter of Act or Number of Measure or Statutory Instrument
1969—*cont.*			
c.48	Post Office Act 1969	power to cont. certain provn(s).	6, s.5, Sch.3, Pt.II, para.15
		s.74 am.	12, s.290, Sch.10, para.1
c.51	Development of Tourism Act 1969	s.2 ext.	26, s.1(1)(3)
		s.2(3) excl.	26, s.1(1)(3)
		s.2(3) saved	26, s.1(3)(b)
		s.14(2)(a)(i) replaced (by subparas.(i)(ia))	14, s.117(1), Sch.13, para.29
c.57	Employers Liability (Compulsory Insurance) Act 1969	excl.	52, s.269(4)
		s.1(3)(b) am.	SI 2890, reg.11(1)
c.xxxiv	Forth Ports Authority Order Confirmation Act 1969	Sch. rep. (Forth Ports Authority Order ss.28-32,34,37-41,sch.2 rep.) (*prosp.*)	SI 546(L), art.2, Sch. (Forth Ports Authority Scheme 1992. para.12, sch., Pt.I)
		Sch. rep. (Forth Ports Authority Order s.88 rep.) (*prosp.*)	SI 546(L), art.2, Sch. (Forth Ports Authority Scheme 1992. para.12, sch., Pt.II)
No.2	Synodical Government Measure 1969	Sch.3 mod.	GSM 1, s.17(1), Sch.3, para.10 (substituting s.12(3) to 1963 No.2)
1970			
c.9	Taxes Management Act 1970	ext.(mods.)	SI 511, reg.3, Sch.1
		power to mod.	12, s.209(3)
		saved	12, s.290, Sch.11, Pt.II, para.24(1)(b)
		s.1 appl. (NI)	7, s.15(3), Sch.2, para.6(2)
		s.2(5) subst. (1.4.1994)	48, s.76, Sch.16, para.2(1)
		s.3(2) subst. (1.4.1994)	48, s.76, Sch.16, para.2(3)
		s.3(3) am. (1.4.1994)	48, s.76, Sch.16, para.2(4)
		s.7(4) am.	48, s.19(1)(7)
		s.8 mod.	12, s.3(6)(b)
		s.11(1)(b) am.	12, s.290, Sch.10, para.2(2)
		s.12(2) am.	12, s.290, Sch.10, para.2(3)(a)-(e)
		s.17(4) rep.in pt.	48, ss.29(1)(2),82, Sch.18, Pt.VII
		s.17(4A)-(4C) added	48, s.29(1)(2)
		s.21 appl.(mods.)	SI 569, reg.18
		s.21 appl.(mods.)	SI 569, reg.22
		s.21 appl.(mods.)	SI 2074, regs.9(3),12(3)
		s.25(9) am.	12, s.290, Sch.10, para.2(4)
		s.27(1) am.	12, s.290, Sch.10, para.2(2)
		s.28 subst.	12, s.290, Sch.10, para.2(5)
		s.29 excl.	48, s.63, Sch.11, paras.2(2),6 (adding 1988 c.1, sch.3, para.6E)
		s.30 mod.	SI 734, reg.6
		s.30(2)(a)(3)(a) am.	12, s.290, Sch.10, para.2(6)

Year and Chap. or No. of Measure	Short title	How affected	1992, Chapter of Act or Number of Measure or Statutory Instrument
1970—*cont.*			
		s.31(3)(c) am.	12, s.290, Sch.10, para.2(7)
		s.33(1) mod.	SI 511, reg.9, Sch.2
		s.34 excl.	12, s.248(2)
		s.34 mod.	48, s.63, Sch.11, paras.2(2),6 (adding 1988 c.1, sch.3, para.6E)
		s.36(1)(2) mod.	48, s.63, Sch.11, paras.2(2),6 (adding 1988 c.1, sch.3, para.6E)
		s.36(3A) added ('93-94)	48, s.20, Sch.5, paras.9(2),10
		s.37A am. ('93-94)	48, s.20, Sch.5, paras.9(3),10
		s.43(1) mod.	SI 511, reg.9, Sch.2
		s.43A(2A) added ('93-94)	48, s.20, Sch.5, paras.9(4),10
		ss.44-59 (Pt.V) appl.	SI 10, reg.10(3)
		ss.44-59 (Pt.V) appl.	SI 12, reg.10(3)
		ss.44-59 (Pt.V) appl.(mods.) (NI)	7, s.15(3), Sch.2, para.8
		s.46A added	48, s.76, Sch.16, para.3
		s.46A appl.(mods.)	48, s.76, Sch.16, para.8 (adding 1984 c.51 s.225A)
		s.47(1) am.	12, s.290, Sch.10, para.2(2)
		s.56 appl.	SI 511, reg.7(4)
		ss.56B-56D added	48, s.76, Sch.16, para.4
		ss.56B-56D appl.	48, s.76, Sch.16, para.8 (adding 1984 c.51 s.225A)
		s.57(1)(a) am.	12, s.290, Sch.10, para.2(2)
		s.57B rep. & superseded	48, ss.76,82, Sch.16, paras.4,5, Sch.18, Pt.IX
		s.72 restr. (NI)	7, s.15(3), Sch.2, para.5(a)
		s.78(3)(b) am.	12, s.290, Sch.10, para.2(2)
		s.86 appl. (NI)	7, s.15(3), Sch.2, para.6(1)
		s.86(4) am.	12, s.290, Sch.10, para.2(8)
		s.86(4), Table rep.in pt.	48, ss.63,82, Sch.11, paras.3,6, Sch.18, Pt.VII
		s.87A appl.(mods.)	SI 2326, reg.6(5)
		s.87A(3) am. (*prosp.*)	12, s.290, Sch.10, para.2(9)
		s.88(1)(4)(5)(a)(b) appl. (NI)	7, s.15(3), Sch.2, para.6(1)
		s.91(3)(c) am.	48, s.19(2)
		ss.93-107 (Pt.X) appl.(mods.)	4, s.16(1)(b), Sch.2
		s.98 appl.	4, s.1(4), Sch.1, para.6(7)
		s.98 appl. (NI)	7, s.1(4), Sch.1, para.6(7)
		s.98 am.	12, s.290, Sch.10, para.2(10)(a)(i)-(vi)
		s.98 am.	12, s.290, Sch.10, para.2(10)(b)(i)(ii)
		s.98 am.	48, s.63, Sch.11, paras.4, 6

Year and Chap. or No. of Measure	Short title	How affected	1992, Chapter of Act or Number of Measure or Statutory Instrument
1970—*cont.*			
		s.98, Table rep.in pt.	48, ss.28,82, Sch.18, Pt.VII
		s.98, Table am.	48, s.28(4)(6)
		s.98A power to appl.	4, s.1(4), Sch.1, para.7(2)(9)-(12)
		s.98A power to appl. (NI)	7, s.1(4), Sch.1, para.7(2)(9)-(12)
		s.98A(2)(a) restr.	4, s.1(4), Sch.1, para.7(3)
		s.98A(2)(b)(4) mod.	4, s.1(4), Sch.1, para.7(4)(a)
		ss.100-100D power to appl.	4, s.1(4), Sch.1, para.7(2)(b)(9)-(12)
		ss.100-100D power to appl. (NI)	7, s.1(4), Sch.1, para.7(2)(b)(9)-(12)
		s.100 restr. (NI)	7, s.1(4), Sch.1, para.7(4)(b)
		ss.102-104 power to appl.	4, s.1(4), Sch.1, para.7(2)(b)(9)-(12)
		ss.102-104 power to appl. (NI)	7, s.1(4), Sch.1, para.7(2)(b)(9)-(12)
		ss.111,119(4) am.	12, s.290, Sch.10, para.2(2)
		s.113(1B) appl.	SI 511, reg.6
		s.118(1) (defn. of "chargeable gain") am.	12, s.290, Sch.10, para.2(11)(a)
		s.118(1) (defn. of "Taxes Act") am.	12, s.290, Sch.10, para.2(11)(b)
		s.118(1) (defn. of "the 1992 Act") added	12, s.290, Sch.10, para.2(11)(c)
		s.118(1) (defn. of "the Taxes Acts") appl.	48, s.76, Sch.16, para.8 (adding 1984 c.51 s.225A)
c.10	Income and Corporation Taxes Act 1970	appl.(mods.)	4, s.16(1), Sch.2
		power to cont. certain provn(s).	6, s.5, Sch.3, Pt.II, para.15
		appl.	12, s.1(2)
		defns. of "trade", "profession", "vocation", "office" and "employment" appl.	12, ss.158(2),163,164, Sch.6, Pt.I, para.1(2)
		power to mod.	12, s.209(3)
		defn. of "trade" appl.	12, s.288(1)
		rep. (saving)	12, s.290, Sch.11, para.24(1), Sch.12
		ss.267,268A excl.	SI 58, art.9, Sch.2, para.1
		s.268A(6A) added	48, s.49(2)
		ss.269A,269B added (*retrosp.*)	48, s.47
		ss.269C,269D added (*retrosp.*)	48, s.48
		s.272(1F) am.	48, s.24, Sch.6, paras.4,9
		ss.273,273A appl.(mods.)	SI 58, art.33
		s.274(2) excl.	SI 58, art.11(3)

Year and Chap. or No. of Measure	Short title	How affected	1992, Chapter of Act or Number of Measure or Statutory Instrument
1970—*cont.*			
		s.275(1) mod.	48, s.77, Sch.17, paras.6(3)(6),7
		s.275(1A)(1B) am.	48, s.49(3)(a)(b)(9)
		s.278(1) am. (*retrosp.*)	48, s.25(2)
		s.281(2) am.	48, s.49(4)(9)
c.16	National Health Service Contributions Act 1970	power to cont. certain provn(s).	6, s.5, Sch.3, Pt.II, para.15
c.24	Finance Act 1970	ss.27,28 rep.	12, s.290, Sch.12
		s.29(3)(5)-(7)(9) rep.	12, s.290, Sch.12
		Sch.3 rep.	12, s.290, Sch.12
		Sch.6 rep.	12, s.290, Sch.12
c.31	Administration of the Justice Act 1970	power to cont. certain provn(s).	6, s.5, Sch.3, Pt.II, para.15
		Sch.4, para.3A am.	6, s.4, Sch.2, para.6
		Sch.8, para.6 rep.in pt. & am.	6, s.4, Sch.2, para.7
c.35	Conveyancing and Feudal Reform (Scotland) Act 1970	s.1(2) (defn. of "land obligations") appl.	37, s.16, Sch.3, para.1(5)
c.36	Merchant Shipping Act 1970	s.42(1) rep.	52, s.300(1), Sch.1
		Sch.3, para.1 rep.	52, s.300(1), Sch.1
c.39	Local Authorities (Goods and Services) Act 1970	am. (1.4.1993)	13, s.93(1), Sch.8, Pt.II, para.71(1)(2)
		ext.	37, s.12, Sch.2, para.21
c.41	Equal Pay Act 1970	s.1(10A) added	52, s.300(2), Sch.2, para.3(2)
		s.5 amdt(s). cont.	52, s.300(2), Sch.2, para.3(3)
		s.5 am.	52, s.300(2), Sch.2, para.3(3)
		s.7 amdt(s). cont.	52, s.300(2), Sch.2, para.3(3)
		s.7 am.	52, s.300(2), Sch.2, para.3(3)
c.42	Local Authority Social Services Act 1970	Sch.1 rep.in pt.	41, s.78(2), Sch.7
c.44	Chronically Sick and Disabled Persons Act 1970	power to cont. certain provn(s).	6, s.5, Sch.3, Pt.II, para.15
		s.8(2)(aa) subst. (1.4.1993)	13, s.93(1), Sch.8, Pt.II, para.72(a)
		s.8(2)(ba) added (1.4.1993)	13, s.93(1), Sch.8, Pt.II, para.72(b)
		s.8(2)(c) subst.	37, s.62(2), Sch.9, para.3
c.51	National Insurance (Old Persons' and Widows' Pensions and Attendance Allowance) Act 1970	power to cont. certain provn(s).	6, s.5, Sch.3, Pt.II, para.15
1971			
c.10	Vehicles (Excise) Act 1971	s.6 am. (1.12.1992, 1.1.1993)	48, s.14(2), Sch.3, Pt.III, para.91
		s.7(2)(c) rep.in pt. (*prosp.*)	48, s.82, Sch.18, Pt.IV
		s.7(2C)(2D) rep. (*prosp.*)	48, ss.12(1)(b),82, Sch.18, Pt.IV

Year and Chap. or No. of Measure	Short title	How affected	1992, Chapter of Act or Number of Measure or Statutory Instrument
1971—*cont.*			
		s.18A(3) rep.in pt. (1.1.1993)	48, ss.11(10)(11),82, Sch.18, Pt.III
		Sch.1, Pt.II, Table , para.4 replaced (10.3.1992) (*retrosp.*)	20, s.4(2)(5)
		Sch.2, Pt.II, Table am. (10.3.1992) (*retrosp.*)	20, s.4(3)(5)
		Sch.4, Pt.I, para.5(3)(a) am. (1.1.1993)	48, s.11(2)(11)
		Sch.4, Pt.I, para.14A subst. (1.1.1993)	48, s.11(3)(11)
		Sch.4, Pt.II, Table C am. (1.1.1993)	48, s.11(7)(11)
		Sch.4, Pt.II, Table C(1) am. (1.1.1993)	48, s.11(8)(11)
		Sch.4, Pt.II, Table C(2) am. (1.1.1993)	48, s.11(9)(11)
		Sch.4, Pt.II, Table A am. (1.1.1993)	48, s.11(4)(11)
		Sch.4, Pt.II, Table A(1) am. (1.1.1993)	48, s.11(5)(11)
		Sch.4, Pt.II, Table A(2) am. (1.1.1993)	48, s.11(6)(11)
		Sch.5, Pt.II, Table am. (10.3.1992) (*retrosp.*)	20, s.4(4)(5)
c.20	Mines Management Act 1971	saved	iii, s.11(2)
c.29	National Savings Bank Act 1971	ss.10,11 am. (1.1.1993)	40, s.120(1), Sch.21, Pt.I, para.2
		s.10(1) mod. (1.1.1993)	40, s.84(1)(a)
		s.27 (defn. of "the Registrar") replaced (by "the adjudicator" (1.1.1993))	40, s.120(1), Sch.21, Pt.I, para.3
c.32	Attachment of Earnings Act 1971	defn. of "maintenance order" defn(s). appl.	5, s.107(15)
		power to cont. certain provn(s).	6, s.5, Sch.3, Pt.II, para.15
		power to appl.	14, s.14(3), Sch.4, para.19(2)
		s.22(4) am.	SI 1296, art.6(1), Sch., para.4
		Sch.1, para.7 rep.in pt. & am.	6, s.4, Sch.2, para.7
		Sch.2, para.3A am.	6, s.4, Sch.2, para.6
		Sch.3 mod.	SI 613, reg.42(2)(b)
c.40	Fire Precautions Act 1971	s.40 mod.	SI 1732, art.5
c.50	National Insurance Act 1971	power to cont. certain provn(s).	6, s.5, Sch.3, Pt.II, para.15
c.56	Pensions (Increase) Act 1971	trans.of functions	SI 331, art.2(1)(h)(4)
		s.8(1)(b) trans.of functions	SI 331, art.2(1)(b)(4)
		Sch.3, reg.P14 appl.(mods.)	SI 3229, reg.2(1)
		Sch.3, para.1(2) mod.	3, s.18(4)(5)

Year and Chap. or No. of Measure	Short title	How affected	1992, Chapter of Act or Number of Measure or Statutory Instrument
1971—*cont.*			
		Sch.3, para.6(1)(a)(i) replaced (by subparas. (i)(ia)) (EWS)	14, s.117(1), Sch.13, para.30
c.60	Prevention of Oil Pollution Act 1971	saved	v, s.18(3)
c.61	Mineral Workings (Offshore Installations) Act 1971	power to rep. or mod.	15, s.1 (amending s.15 of 1974 c.37)
		defn. of "offshore installation" appl.	15, s.1(4)
		defn. of "offshore installation" appl.	24, s.1(2)
		s.1(4) mod.	15, s.1(5)(a)
c.62	Tribunals and Inquiries Act 1971	power to cont. certain provn(s).	6, s.5, Sch.3, Pt.II, para.15
		appl.(mods.) (1-1-1993) (EWS)	42, s.23(9)
		rep.	53, s.18(2), Sch.4, Pt.I
		s.7(3) am.	6, s.4, Sch.2, para.8
		s.13(1) am. (EW)	38, s.21(7), Sch.4, para.2
		Sch.1, Pt.I, para.6(d) added (EW)	38, s.21(7), Sch.4, para.3
		Sch.1, Pt.I, para.12A am. (EWS)	14, s.117(1), Sch.13, para.31
		Sch.1, para.30A subst.	6, s.4, Sch.2, para.9
c.64	Diplomatic and Other Privileges Act 1971	s.1(5) added (1.12.1992, 1.1.1993)	48, s.14(2), Sch.3, Pt.III, para.92
c.68	Finance Act 1971	power to cont. certain provn(s).	6, s.5, Sch.3, Pt.II, para.15
		s.7 rep. (*prosp.*)	48, ss.12(1)(a),82, Sch.18, Pt.IV
		s.55 rep.	12, s.290, Sch.12
c.73	Social Security Act 1971	power to cont. certain provn(s).	6, s.5, Sch.3, Pt.II, para.15
c.77	Immigration Act 1971	defn. of "Immigration rules" appl.	5, s.78(6)(c)
		defn. of "immigration rules" appl. (NI)	8, s.74(6)(c)
c.lvii	Mersey Docks and Harbour Act 1971	s.5 rep.	x, s.4, Sch.2
		s.7(1) rep.	x, s.4, Sch.2
		s.7(2) rep.in pt.	x, s.4, Sch.2
		s.7(3) rep.in pt.	x, s.4, Sch.2
		s.8(1)(b) rep.	x, s.4, Sch.2
		s.37(2) rep.in pt.	x, s.4, Sch.2
		ss.45-47 rep.	x, s.4, Sch.2
		s.48(1)(c) rep.in pt.	x, s.4, Sch.2
		s.51 rep.	x, s.4, Sch.2

Year and Chap. or No. of Measure	Short title	How affected	1992, Chapter of Act or Number of Measure or Statutory Instrument
1972			
c.4	National Insurance Regulations (Validation) Act 1972	power to cont. certain provn(s).	6, s.5, Sch.3, Pt.II, para.15
c.11	Superannuation Act 1972	power to cont. certain provn(s).	6, s.5, Sch.3, Pt.II, para.15
		s.1 ext.	13, ss.1,9,62,70, Sch.1, para.7(5)
		s.1 ext. (*prosp.*)	37, s.7, Sch.1, para.11
		s.1 ext.	37, s.37, Sch.7, para.7(5)
		s.1 ext.	52, s.269(2)
		ss.1,9,10 am. (1.1.1993)	SI 3218, reg.82(1), Sch.10, Pt.I, para.5
		Sch.1 am.	SI 2383, Sch., para.10(1)
		Sch.1 am.	13, ss.1,9,62,70, Sch.1, para.7(5)
		Sch.1 rep.in pt. (1.4.1993)	13, s.93, Sch.8, Pt.II, para.73, Sch.9
		Sch.1 am. (*prosp.*)	37, s.7, Sch.1, para.11
		Sch.1 am.	37, s.37, Sch.7, para.7(5)
		Sch.1 am.	44, s.11(2), Sch.8, Pt.I, para.1(1)(2)(5)
		Sch.6, para.91 rep.	53, s.18(2), Sch.4, Pt.I
c.18	Maintenance Orders (Reciprocal Enforcement) Act 1972	trans.of functions	SI 709, art.4(3)(a)
		am.	SI 709, art.4(5)
		s.3(1) subst. (*prosp.*)	56, s.1, Sch.1, Pt.II, para.6(2)
		s.3(4) subst. (*prosp.*)	56, s.1, Sch.1, Pt.II, para.6(3)
		s.3(7) subst. (*prosp.*)	56, s.1, Sch.1, Pt.II, para.6(4)
		s.5(3A) added (*prosp.*)	56, s.1, Sch.1, Pt.II, para.7
		s.7(2)(i) am. (*prosp.*)	56, s.1, Sch.1, Pt.II, para.8(2)
		s.7(3)(4) am. (*prosp.*)	56, s.1, Sch.1, Pt.II, para.8(3)(4)
		s.7(6) am. (*prosp.*)	56, s.1, Sch.1, Pt.II, para.8(5)
		s.7(8) added (*prosp.*)	56, s.1, Sch.1, Pt.II, para.8(6)
		s.9(1ZA)(za) added (*prosp.*)	56, s.1, Sch.1, Pt.II, para.9
		s.17(5) am. (*prosp.*)	56, s.1, Sch.1, Pt.II, para.10(2)
		s.17(5A) added (*prosp.*)	56, s.1, Sch.1, Pt.II, para.10(3)
		s.17(7) am. (*prosp.*)	56, s.1, Sch.1, Pt.II, para.10(4)
		s.17(7A) added (*prosp.*)	56, s.1, Sch.1, Pt.II, para.10(5)
		s.18(1A) added (*prosp.*)	56, s.1, Sch.1, Pt.II, para.11

Year and Chap. or No. of Measure	Short title	How affected	1992, Chapter of Act or Number of Measure or Statutory Instrument
1972—*cont.*			
		s.21(1) am. (*prosp.*)	56, s.1, Sch.1, Pt.II, para.12
		ss.27,28,28A replaced (by ss.27A-27C,28,28A- 28C) (*prosp.*)	56, s.1, Sch.1, Pt.II, para.13
		s.29A(1) am. (*prosp.*)	56, s.1, Sch.1, Pt.II, para.14
		s.34(1) am. (*prosp.*)	56, s.1, Sch.1, Pt.II, para.15(2)
		s.34(3A) added (*prosp.*)	56, s.1, Sch.1, Pt.II, para.15(3)
		s.35 replaced (by ss.35, 35A) (*prosp.*)	56, s.1, Sch.1, Pt.II, para.16
		s.36(1) am. (*prosp.*)	56, s.1, Sch.1, Pt.II, para.17
		s.38A added (*prosp.*)	56, s.1, Sch.1, Pt.II, para.18
		s.39 (defns. of "maintenance order", "revoke" and "revocation") added (*prosp.*)	56, s.1, Sch.1, Pt.II, para.19
c.28	Employment Medical Advisory Service Act 1972	saved	iii, s.11(2)
c.36	National Insurance (Amendment) Act 1972	power to cont. certain provn(s).	6, s.5, Sch.3, Pt.II, para.15
c.41	Finance Act 1972	s.128(2) rep. (*prosp.*)	48, s.82, Sch.18, Pt.IV
c.48	Parliamentary and other Pensions Act 1972	s.4(3AA)(d) rep.in pt.	SI 599, reg.4
		s.4(3AA)(e) replaced (by paras. (e)(f))	SI 599, reg.4
c.52	Town and Country Planning (Scotland) Act 1972	appl.	ix, s.1, Sch., s.24(1)
		defn. of "planning permission" appl.	12, s.35, Sch.2, Pt.II, para.10(3)
		appl.	xii, s.1, Sch., s.60
		s.7(1) am.	53, s.18(1), Sch.3, para.7
		s.7(5) am.	53, s.18(1), Sch.3, para.6
		s.7(6) am.	53, s.18(1), para.3, Sch.3
		s.11(1)(b) am.	53, s.18(1), Sch.3, para.4
		s.19(1) (defn. of "development") appl.	51, s.10(1)(d)
		s.46(5) am.	53, s.18(1), Sch.3, para.5
		s.83B(3) excl. (*temp.*)	SI 334, art.5(1)(b)
		s.83B(4)(b) restr. (*temp.*)	SI 334, art.5(2)(3)
		s.84AA(10) ext.(mods.)	SI 478, reg.2, Sch.
		s.84AB ext.(mods.)	SI 478, reg.2, Sch.
		s.85(10) ext.(mods.)	SI 478, reg.2, Sch.
		s.86 ext.(mods.)	SI 478, reg.2, Sch.
		s.87 ext.(mods.)	SI 478, reg.2, Sch.
		s.87A ext.	SI 478, reg.2, Sch.
		s.89 ext.(mods.)	SI 478, reg.2, Sch.
		s.89A(1)(a) ext.	SI 478, reg.2, Sch.

Year and Chap. or No. of Measure	Short title	How affected	1992, Chapter of Act or Number of Measure or Statutory Instrument
1972—*cont.*			
		s.89A(3) ext.(mods.)	SI 478, reg.2, Sch.
		s.166 ext.(mods.)	SI 478, reg.2, Sch.
		s.213(1) am.	SI 1314, art.3(3), Sch., para.1(h)
		s.231(3)(f) ext.(mods.)	SI 478, reg.2, Sch.
		s.270 ext.(mods.)	SI 478, reg.2, Sch.
		s.278 mod.	37, s.31(7)
		Sch.9, para.13 am.	53, s.18(1), Sch.3, para.8
c.54	The British Library Act 1972	trans.of functions	SI 1311, art.3(1), Sch.1, Pt.I
		Sch., para.11(4)(d) added	44, s.11(2), Sch.8, Pt.II, para.12(1)
		Sch., para.11(5)(a) am. (*prosp.*)	44, s.11(2), Sch.8, Pt.II, para.12(2)
		Sch., para.11(6) rep.	44, s.11(3), Sch.9
c.57	National Insurance Act 1972	power to cont. certain provn(s).	6, s.5, Sch.3, Pt.II, para.15
c.58	National Health Service (Scotland) Act 1972	Sch.6, para.152 rep.	53, s.18(2), Sch.4, Pt.I
c.59	Administration of Justice (Scotland) Act 1972	s.3 excl.	52, s.217
		s.3 excl.	52, s.263(6)
		s.3(3) rep.	52, s.300(1), Sch.1
c.61	Land Charges Act 1972	appl.	SI 613, reg.51(5)
		ext. (31.1.1993)	23, s.5(6)
		s.6(1)(d) added (31.1.1993)	23, s.5(1)
c.65	National Debt Act 1972	s.5 subst. (1.1.1993)	40, s.120(1), Sch.21, Pt.I, para.4
		s.5(1) mod. (1.1.1993)	40, s.84(1)(b)
		s.9(3) (defn. of "war savings certificates") appl.	12, s.121(2)(a)
c.70	Local Government Act 1972	defn. of "proper officer" appl.	14, s.68(5)
		defn. of "local government elector" appl.	19, s.1(6)
		saved	19, s.6(5)
		s.6(2)(c) am.	19, s.27, Sch.3, para.6
		s.7(6) am.	19, s.27, Sch.3, para.7(1)
		s.7(7) am.	19, s.27, Sch.3, para.7(2) (a)(b)
		s.9(4) am.	19, s.27, Sch.3, para.8
		s.11(5)(a) am.	19, s.27, Sch.3, para.9
		s.12(2) am.	19, s.27, Sch.3, para.10
		s.30(1)(b)(3) am.	19, s.27, Sch.3, para.11
		ss.46-52 rep.	19, s.29, Sch.4, Pt.II
		s.54(1)(e) am.	19, s.27, Sch.3, para.12
		s.60(1) am.	19, s.27, Sch.3, para.13(1)
		s.60(2)-(7) am.	19, s.27, Sch.3, para.13(2)
		s.60(2)(b) rep.in pt.	19, s.29, Sch.4, Pt.II
		s.61(1) am.	19, s.27, Sch.3, para.14
		ss.62,63 rep.	19, s.29, Sch.4, Pt.II

Year and Chap. or No. of Measure	Short title	How affected	1992, Chapter of Act or Number of Measure or Statutory Instrument
1972—*cont.*			
		s.65(1)(2) am.	19, s.27, Sch.3, para.15(1)(2)
		s.66 rep.	19, s.29, Sch.4, Pt.II
		s.71(1)(2) am.	19, s.27, Sch.3, para.16(1)(2)
		s.73(2) am.	19, s.27, Sch.3, para.17
		s.78(1) (defn. of "substantive change") am.	19, s.27, Sch.3, para.18(1)
		s.78(2) am.	19, s.27, Sch.3, para.18(2)
		ss.94,97 (defn. of "local authority") appl.	14, s.106(6)
		s.97(1)-(3) appl.	14, s.106(5)
		s.97(4) am. (1.4.1993)	14, s.117(1), Sch.13, para.32
		ss.100A-100J (Pt.VA) ext.	14, s.67(4)
		s.101 excl.	SI 1492, reg.10
		s.101 excl.	19, s.5(4)
		s.123 excl.	13, s.39(8)
		s.131(2)(c) rep. (1-1- 1993)	42, s.68(1), Sch.4, Pt.I
		s.131(3) am. (1.1.1993)	41, s.78(1), Sch.6, para.6
		s.150(1) am. (*prosp.*)	14, s.117(1), Sch.13, para.33
		s.168(1)(b) am. (1.4.1993)	14, s.117(1), Sch.13, para.34(1)(a)
		s.168(1)(b)(i) am. (1.4.1993)	14, s.117(1), Sch.13, para.34(1)(b)
		s.168(5)(a) replaced (by paras.(a)(aa) (1.4.1993)	14, s.117(1), Sch.13, para.34(2)
		s.196(7)(8) rep.	19, s.29, Sch.4, Pt.II
		s.197(5) rep.in pt.	19, s.29, Sch.4, Pt.II
		s.210(8) rep.	41, s.78(2), Sch.7
		s.250(2)-(5) appl.(mods.)	vii, s.27
		s.250(2)(3) appl.(mods.)	SI 664, regs.11(16),26(1),27(4),29(5),30(3), Sch.9, para.9
		s.250(2)(3) appl. (1-1- 1993)	42, s.11(5)
		s.250(4) saved	vii, s.24(8)(b)
		s.250(4)(5) appl.(mods.) (1-1-1993)	42, s.11(5)(6)
		s.250(5) appl.(mods.)	SI 664, regs.11(16),26(1),27(4),29(5),30(3), Sch.9, para.9
		s.270 (defn. of "local authority") appl.	52, s.72(4)
		s.270(1) (defn. of "local authority") appl.	5, s.16(4)(a)
		s.270(1) rep.in pt.	19, s.29, Sch.4, Pt.II
		Sch.2, para.7(1)(b)(2) am.	19, s.27, Sch.3, para.19(1)(2)
		Sch.3, para.10 am.	19, s.27, Sch.3, para.20
		Sch.7 rep.	19, s.29, Sch.4, Pt.II

Year and Chap. or No. of Measure	Short title	How affected	1992, Chapter of Act or Number of Measure or Statutory Instrument
1972—*cont.*			
		Sch.9 rep.	19, s.29, Sch.4, Pt.II
		Sch.11 am.	19, s.27(2)
		Sch.12A, Pt.II, para.7 added	SI 1497, art.2
		Sch.29, paras.22,23 rep. (*prosp.*)	41, s.78(2), Sch.7
c.73	Museums and Galleries Admission Charges Act 1972	s.1(1)(b) subst.	44, s.11(2), Sch.8, Pt.I, para.1(1)(2)(6)
c.80	Pensioners' Payments and National Insurance Contributions Act 1972	power to cont. certain provn(s).	6, s.5, Sch.3, Pt.II, para.15
No.3	Benefices Measure 1972	s.1(2A) added	GSM 1, s.17(1), Sch.3, para.11
1973			
c.11	Fire Precautions (Loans) Act 1973	s.1(7) am. (1.1.1993)	41, s.78(1), Sch.6, para.7
c.26	Land Compensation Act 1973	ss.53-56 excl.	iv, s.25(1)
c.32	National Health Service Reorganisation Act 1973	Sch.4, para.134 rep.	53, s.18(2), Sch.4, Pt.I
c.36	Northern Ireland Constitution Act 1973	s.3(2) mod. (*prosp.*)	40, s.124(2)
		s.11 saved	8, s.153(5)
		ss.17-23 (Pt.III) mod.	8, s.167(2)
		Sch.3 mod. (*prosp.*)	40, s.124(2)
c.38	Social Security Act 1973	excl.	6, s.5, Sch.3, Pt.II, para.15
		excl. (NI)	9, s.5, Sch.3, Pt.II, para.15
		s.66(4)(9) rep.	53, s.18(2), Sch.4, Pt.I
c.41	Fair Trading Act 1973	s.130(1) am.	35, s.10, Sch., paras.2(1), 6
c.50	Employment and Training Act 1973	power to cont. certain provn(s).	6, s.5, Sch.3, Pt.II, para.15
		s.11(3) am.	6, s.4, Sch.2, para.10
		s.12(2) am.	6, s.4, Sch.2, para.11
c.51	Finance Act 1973	s.38(1)(3)-(5)(8) rep.	12, s.290, Sch.12
		s.38(2) am.	12, s.290, Sch.10, para.3(1)
		s.46 trans.of functions	SI 1311, art.3(1), Sch.1, Pt.I
		Sch.15, paras.2,4 am.	12, s.290, Sch.10, para.3(2)
c.57	Badgers Act 1973	rep.	51, s.15(2), Sch.
c.62	Powers of Criminal Courts Act 1973	s.30 saved	11, s.1(2)(a)
		s.44 (saving)	SI 1286, art.6(5)(c)
c.65	Local Government (Scotland) Act 1973	defns. of "local authority", "joint board" and "joint committee" appl.	19, s.1(7)(b)
		saved	19, s.6(5)
		defn. of "local authority" appl.	37, s.35(5)
		s.41(1)-(3) appl.	14, s.112(4)
		s.41(4) am. (*prosp.*)	14, s.117(1), Sch.13, para.35

Year and Chap. or No. of Measure	Short title	How affected	1992, Chapter of Act or Number of Measure or Statutory Instrument
1973—*cont.*			
		s.56(6) subst.	14, s.117(1), Sch.13, para.36
		s.74 excl.	37, s.28(6)
		ss.93-122 (Pt.VII) appl.	14, s.107, Sch.11, Pt.II, para.23(b)
		ss.93-122 (Pt.VII) power to mod.	14, s.107, Sch.11, Pt.II, para.23(b)
		ss.93-122 (Pt.VII) saved	19, s.5(7)
		ss.93-122 (Pt.VII) ext.	19, s.29(1)
		s.96(1) saved	14, s.107, Sch.11, Pt.III, para.24
		s.96(1) appl.	14, s.107, Sch.11, Pt.III, para.25
		s.96(2)-(4) appl.	14, s.107, Sch.11, Pt.III, para.25
		s.97A(1) ext.	19, s.3(3)
		s.97A(3) excl.	19, s.3(3)
		s.99(d) added	19, s.3(2)
		s.105(1) appl.	14, s.107, Sch.11, Pt.III, para.25
		s.109 (defn. of "rating authority") appl.	5, s.191
		s.109(1)(a)(b) replaced (by para.(a) (*prosp.*)	14, s.117(1), Sch.13, para.37(1)
		s.109(2) am. (*prosp.*)	14, s.117(1), Sch.13, para.37(2)
		s.110 rep. (*prosp.*)	14, s.117, Sch.13, para.38, Sch.14
		s.110A rep.	14, s.117, Sch.13, para.38, Sch.14
		s.111(1)(a)(b)(d) rep. (*prosp.*)	14, s.117, Sch.13, para.39, Sch.14
		s.118(1)(b) rep.in pt. (*prosp.*)	14, s.117, Sch.13, para.40, Sch.14
		s.192 ext.(mods.)	14, s.83(1), Sch.6, para.3
		s.202(4)-(8)(10)-(12) appl.(mods.)	xii, s.1, Sch., s.42(3)
		ss.202(4)-(8)(10)(12),203 appl.(mods.)	SI 1975(L), art.8
		s.211 saved	14, s.108(2), Sch.12, Pt.I, para.5(b)
		s.235 (defn. of "local authority") appl.	52, s.72(4)
		s.235(1) (defn. of "local authority") appl.	5, s.16(4)(c)
		Sch.19, paras.5,8 rep.	42, s.68(1), Sch.4, Pt.II
c.xxi	Medway Ports Authority Act 1973	ss.49-59 rep.	SI 202(L), art.2, Sch. (Medway Ports Authy. Scheme 1991,para.11(1), sch.,Pt.I)

Year and Chap. or No. of Measure	Short title	How affected	1992, Chapter of Act or Number of Measure or Statutory Instrument
1973—*cont.*			
		s.83 rep.	SI 202(L), art.2, Sch. (Medway Ports Authy. Scheme 1991, para.11(2),sch.,Pt.I)
1974			
c.14	National Insurance Act 1974	s.6(1)(3) rep.	6, s.3, Sch.1
c.28	Northern Ireland Act 1974	s.1(4) interim period cont. (until 16.7.1993)	SI 1702, art.2
		s.1(4) (defn. of "interim period") appl. (NI)	7, s.172(8)
		s.1(4) (defn. of "interim period") appl.	8, s.166(11)
		Sch.1, para.1(4)(5) excl.	15, s.6(a)(b)
		Sch.1, para.1(4)(5) excl.	28, s.4(a)
		Sch.1, para.1(4)(5) excl.	29, s.3(a)
		Sch.1, para.1(4)(5) excl.	31, s.2(2)(a)
		Sch.1, para.1(4)(5) excl.	33, s.2(7)(a)
		Sch.1, para.1(4)(5) excl.	43, s.54(1)(a)
		Sch.1, para.1(4)(5) excl. (NI)	61, s.3
c.30	Finance Act 1974	s.29 rep.	12, s.290, Sch.12
		s.50 rep. (*prosp.*)	48, s.82, Sch.18, Pt.IV
c.37	Health and Safety at Work etc. Act 1974	appl.(mods.)	SI 2415, reg.4(1)
		appl.	SI 2997, reg.6
		appl.(mods.) (EWS)	SI 3060, reg.15(1)
		appl. (EWS)	SI 3217, reg.21(1)
		Pt.I ext. (EWS)	SI 3217, reg.4
		Pt.1 ext.	15, s.2(1)
		ss.1-54 (Pt.I) mod.	SI 2051, reg.16(2)
		ss.1-54 (Pt.I) ext.	15, s.1(1)
		ss.1-54 (Pt.I) am.	15, s.1(1)
		s.3(2) mod. (EWS)	SI 3217, reg.5
		s.6 mod.	SI 1524, reg.3
		s.6(1)(1A) mod.	SI 1524, reg.4
		s.15 ext.	15, ss.1(2),2
		s.15(1) saved	15, ss.1(2),2(2)
		s.15(6)(e) added	15, s.4(1)(6)
		ss.18(6)(7)(b),19-28 mod.	SI 711, reg.28(3)(b)(5)(a)
		ss.19-28,33-35,36(1)(2), 37,38,39,41,42 appl.(mods.)	SI 3073, reg.28, Sch.6, para.1(b)(c)
		s.28 restr. (EWS)	SI 3217, reg.15
		s.33(1)(e)-(o)(2)(3)(4)(d) (e)(5) mod.	SI 711, reg.28(3)(b)(5)(a)
		s.33(1A) added	15, s.4(2)(6)
		s.33(2A) added	15, s.4(3)(6)
		s.33(3) am.	15, s.4(4)(a)(b)(6)
		s.33(4)(d)(5) rep.	15, ss.4(5)(6),7(2), Sch.2
		s.34 appl.(mods.)	SI 3073, reg.28, Sch.6, para.3(e)(i)
		s.34(3) am.	SI 711, regs.4,28(3)(b)

Year and Chap. or No. of Measure	Short title	How affected	1992, Chapter of Act or Number of Measure or Statutory Instrument
1974—*cont.*			
		s.34(3)(4)(5) mod.	SI 711, reg.28(3)(b)(5)(a)
		ss.35-39,41,42 mod.	SI 711, reg.28(3)(b)(5)(a)
		s.44(4) am.	53, s.18(1), Sch.3, para.9
		s.80(1) appl.(mods.)	ix, s.1, Sch., s.22(2)
		s.80(1) appl.	xii, s.1, Sch., s.61
		s.84(5) rep.	15, s.3(1)(b)
		s.84(5) rep.	15, s.7(2), Sch.2
c.39	Consumer Credit Act 1974	defn. of "regulated agreement" appl.	35, s.12(5)
		mod.	35, s.12(5)
		defn. of "credit token" appl. (EW) (*prosp.*)	41, s.58(1)
		s.3 rep.	53, s.18(2), Sch.4, Pt.I
		s.16(1)(h) am. (1.1.1993)	SI 3218, reg.82(1), Sch.10, Pt.I, para.7
		ss.21,39(1),147(1) restr. (1.1.1993)	SI 3218, reg.5(1)(c)
		s.22 am. (1.1.1993)	SI 3218, reg.57(1)
		ss.25,25(2)(b) am. (1.1.1993)	SI 3218, reg.58(1)
		s.26 am. (1.1.1993)	SI 3218, reg.59(1)
		s.35 am. (1.1.1993)	SI 3218, reg.60
		s.40(1) am. (1.1.1993)	SI 3218, reg.61(1)
		s.41 am. (1.1.1993)	SI 3218, reg.18(6), Sch.5, para.5
		s.42 rep.	53, s.18(2), Sch.4, Pt.I
		s.54 am. (1.1.1993)	SI 3218, reg.59(2)
		s.148(1) am. (1.1.1993)	SI 3218, reg.61(2)
		s.149(1)(2) am. (1.1.1993)	SI 3218, reg.61(3)
		s.174(3A) am. (1.1.1993)	SI 3218, reg.62
		s.189(1) (defn. of "friendly society") rep.in pt. (*prosp.*)	40, s.120(2), Sch.22, Pt.I
c.40	Control of Pollution Act 1974	saved	ix, s.1, Sch., s.22(1)(b)
		s.30C am. (S)	SI 574, reg.4(a)
		s.30C mod. (S)	SI 574, reg.4(b)
c.44	Housing Act 1974	s.11 rep.	12, s.290, Sch.12
c.46	Friendly Societies Act 1974	defn. of "registered friendly society" appl.	4, s.1(4), Sch.1, para.11(2)
		restr. (*prosp.*)	40, s.93(1)
		ext. N.I. (*prosp.*)	40, s.96(1)
		defns. of "separately registered" and "registered" appl.	40, s.116
		mod. (*prosp.*)	40, s.124(2)
		restr.	52, s.10(3)(b)
		appl.	52, s.19(2)
		s.4(1) am. (*prosp.*)	40, s.95, Sch.16, para.2(1)(a)
		s.4(1)(a) am. (*prosp.*)	40, s.95, Sch.16, para.2(1)(b)
		s.4(2A) added (*prosp.*)	40, s.95, Sch.16, para.2(2)

Year and Chap. or No. of Measure	Short title	How affected	1992, Chapter of Act or Number of Measure or Statutory Instrument
1974—*cont.*			
		s.4(3) am. (*prosp.*)	40, s.95, Sch.16, para.2(3)
		s.6(2) rep. (*prosp.*)	40, ss.95,120(2), Sch.16, para.3, Sch.22, Pt.I
		s.7 ext. (*prosp.*)	40, s.96(2)
		s.7(1) am. (*prosp.*)	40, s.95, Sch.16, para.4(a)(c)
		s.7(1)(a) am. (*prosp.*)	40, s.95, Sch.16, para.4(b)
		s.8 rep. (*prosp.*)	40, s.120(2), Sch.22, Pt.I
		s.9(2)(3) rep. (*prosp.*)	40, s.120(2), Sch.22, Pt.I
		s.11(1) rep. (*prosp.*)	40, s.120(2), Sch.22, Pt.I
		s.13(1) am. (*prosp.*)	40, s.95, Sch.16, para.5
		s.13(2) rep. (*prosp.*)	40, s.120(2), Sch.22, Pt.I
		s.15 subst. (*prosp.*)	40, s.95, Sch.16, para.6(1)(3)
		s.15(2) saved (*prosp.*)	40, s.95, Sch.16, para.6(3)
		s.16 rep.in pt. (*prosp.*)	40, s.120(2), Sch.22, Pt.I
		s.17 rep. (*prosp.*)	40, ss.95,120(2), Sch.16, para.6(2)(3), Sch.22, Pt.I
		s.17 saved (*prosp.*)	40, s.95, Sch.16, para.6(3)
		s.21 am. (*prosp.*)	40, s.95, Sch.16, para.7
		s.23A added (*prosp.*)	40, s.95, Sch.16, para.8
		s.24 subst. (*prosp.*)	40, s.95, Sch.16, para.9
		s.26 subst. (*prosp.*)	40, s.95, Sch.16, para.10
		ss.27,28 rep. (*prosp.*)	40, ss.95,120(2), Sch.16, para.11, Sch.22, Pt.I
		ss.29-34 rep.in pt. (*prosp.*)	40, s.95, Sch.16, para.12
		s.30(5) rep.in pt. (*prosp.*)	40, s.120(2), Sch.22, Pt.I
		s.35 rep.in pt. (*prosp.*)	40, s.95, Sch.16, para.12
		s.35(5A) added (*prosp.*)	40, s.95, Sch.16, para.13
		ss.36-39 rep.in pt. (*prosp.*)	40, s.95, Sch.16, para.12
		s.40 rep.in pt. (*prosp.*)	40, s.95, Sch.16, para.12
		s.40(3) added (*prosp.*)	40, s.95, Sch.16, para.14
		ss.41-45 rep.in pt. (*prosp.*)	40, s.95, Sch.16, para.12
		s.46(1)(a)(b) rep. (*prosp.*)	40, ss.95,120(2), Sch.16, para.15(1)(2), Sch.22, Pt.I
		s.46(1)(e) saved (*prosp.*)	40, s.95, Sch.16, para.15(2)
		s.46(2A) added (*prosp.*)	40, s.95, Sch.16, para.15(3)
		s.46(3) rep. (*prosp.*)	40, s.120(2), Sch.22, Pt.I
		s.49(b) am. (*prosp.*)	40, s.95, Sch.16, para.16(a)
		s.49(c) am. (*prosp.*)	40, s.95, Sch.16, para.16(b)
		s.50(2A) added (*prosp.*)	40, s.95, Sch.16, para.17
		s.51(2) am. (*prosp.*)	40, s.95, Sch.16, para.18(a)
		s.51(4) am. (*prosp.*)	40, s.95, Sch.16, para.18(b)
		s.52 appl.	52, s.19(3)
		s.53(1) subst. (*prosp.*)	40, s.95, Sch.16, para.19
		s.53(3) rep. (*prosp.*)	40, ss.95,120(2), Sch.16, para.19(2), Sch.22, Pt.I
		s.55(4) am. (*prosp.*)	40, s.95, Sch.16, para.20
		s.57A added (*prosp.*)	40, s.95, Sch.16, para.21

Year and Chap. or No. of Measure	Short title	How affected	1992, Chapter of Act or Number of Measure or Statutory Instrument
1974—*cont.*			
		s.63A added (*prosp.*)	40, s.95, Sch.16, para.22
		ss.65A,65B added (*prosp.*)	40, s.95, Sch.16, para.23
		ss.70-75 rep. (*prosp.*)	40, ss.95,120(2), Sch.16, para.24, Sch.22, Pt.I
		s.76(1) am. (*prosp.*)	40, s.95, Sch.16, para.25(1)(2)(a)
		s.76(1) am.	53, s.18(1), Sch.3, para.10
		s.76(1)(c)-(e) rep.in pt. (*prosp.*)	40, ss.95,120(2), Sch.16, para.25(2)(b), Sch.22, Pt.I
		s.76(3) replaced (by subss.(3A) and (3B)) (*prosp.*)	40, s.95, Sch.16, para.25(3)
		s.76(4)(c) added (*prosp.*)	40, s.95, Sch.16, para.25(4)
		s.76(5) rep.in pt. (*prosp.*)	40, s.120(2), Sch.22, Pt.I
		s.77 rep. (*prosp.*)	40, ss.95,120(2), Sch.16, para.26, Sch.22, Pt.I
		s.78(1) am. (*prosp.*)	40, s.95, Sch.16, para.27
		s.78(1) rep.in pt. (*prosp.*)	40, s.120(2), Sch.22, Pt.I
		s.78(2)(3) rep. (*prosp.*)	40, s.120(2), Sch.22, Pt.I
		s.79(1) rep.in pt. (*prosp.*)	40, s.120(2), Sch.22, Pt.I
		s.80(1) am. (*prosp.*)	40, s.95, Sch.16, para.28(a)
		s.80(1) rep.in pt. (*prosp.*)	40, s.120(2), Sch.22, Pt.I
		s.80(1A) added (*prosp.*)	40, s.95, Sch.16, para.28(b)
		s.82(2) am. (*prosp.*)	40, s.95, Sch.16, para.29(1)(2)
		s.82(3) am. (*prosp.*)	40, s.95, Sch.16, para.29(3)(a)(b)
		s.82(3A)(3B) added (*prosp.*)	40, s.95, Sch.16, para.29(4)
		s.82(4) rep. (*prosp.*)	40, s.120(2), Sch.22, Pt.I
		s.82(5) rep.in pt. (*prosp.*)	40, s.120(2), Sch.22, Pt.I
		s.82(8)(9) added (*prosp.*)	40, s.95, Sch.16, para.29(5)
		s.83(3) am. (*prosp.*)	40, s.95, Sch.16, para.30(1)
		s.83(8) am. (*prosp.*)	40, s.95, Sch.16, para.30(2)
		s.84 rep.in pt. (*prosp.*)	40, s.95, Sch.16, para.31
		s.84A added (*prosp.*)	40, s.95, Sch.16, para.32
		s.86(1) am. (*prosp.*)	40, s.95, Sch.16, para.33(a)
		s.86(2A) added (*prosp.*)	40, s.95, Sch.16, para.33(b)
		s.87 subst. (*prosp.*)	40, s.95, Sch.16, para.34
		s.87(1) ext. (*prosp.*)	40, s.98, Sch.18, Pt.II, para.16 (substituting sch.11, para.26(2) to 1986 c.60)
		ss.88,89 rep. (*prosp.*)	40, ss.95,120(2), Sch.16, para.35, Sch.22, Pt.I
		s.90 rep.in pt. (*prosp.*)	40, s.95, Sch.16, para.36
		s.91(1)(2) ext. (*prosp.*)	40, s.98, Sch.18, Pt.II, para.16 (substituting sch.11, para.26(2) to 1986 c.60)
		s.91(4) am. (*prosp.*)	40, s.95, Sch.16, para.37

Year and Chap. or No. of Measure	Short title	How affected	1992, Chapter of Act or Number of Measure or Statutory Instrument
1974—*cont.*			
		s.93(1)(b)(c) am. (*prosp.*)	40, s.95, Sch.16, para.38(a)(b)
		s.93(3) am. (*prosp.*)	40, s.95, Sch.16, para.38(c)
		s.95 rep.in pt. (*prosp.*)	40, s.95, Sch.16, para.39
		s.95A added (*prosp.*)	40, s.95, Sch.16, para.39
		s.96 am. (*prosp.*)	40, s.95, Sch.16, para.40
		s.97(1)(b) am. (*prosp.*)	40, s.95, Sch.16, para.41
		s.98(1)(e) rep. (*prosp.*)	40, s.120(2), Sch.22, Pt.I
		s.98(1)(g) am. (*prosp.*)	40, s.95, Sch.16, para.42(a)
		s.98(2) am. (*prosp.*)	40, s.95, Sch.16, para.42(b)
		s.98(4) rep.in pt. (*prosp.*)	40, s.120(2), Sch.22, Pt.I
		s.98(8) am. (*prosp.*)	40, s.95, Sch.16, para.42(c)
		s.100(a) am. (*prosp.*)	40, s.95, Sch.16, para.43
		s.102 am. (*prosp.*)	40, s.95, Sch.16, para.44
		s.106 rep. (*prosp.*)	40, ss.95,120(2), Sch.16, para.45, Sch.22, Pt.I
		s.106, Sch.5, para.8 am.	SI 3216, Sch.
		s.106(2) am.	SI 99, art.2, Sch.
		s.106(2), Sch.5(8) am.	SI 2982, Sch.
		s.107(1) rep.in pt. (*prosp.*)	40, s.120(2), Sch.22, Pt.I
		s.107(2A) added (*prosp.*)	40, s.95, Sch.16, para.46
		s.110(2) am. (*prosp.*)	40, s.95, Sch.16, para.47
		s.111(1) (defn. of "collecting society") am. (*prosp.*)	40, s.95, Sch.16, para.48(a)
		s.111(1) (defn. of "Commission") added (*prosp.*)	40, s.95, Sch.16, para.48(b)
		s.111(1) (defn. of "Gazette") am. (*prosp.*)	40, s.95, Sch.16, para.48(d)
		s.111(1) (defn. of "the 1992 Act") added (*prosp.*)	40, s.95, Sch.16, para.48(e)
		s.111(1) (defn. of "the Companies Acts") am. (*prosp.*)	40, s.95, Sch.16, para.48(c)
		s.111(6) rep. (*prosp.*)	40, s.120(2), Sch.22, Pt.I
		s.115 rep. (*prosp.*)	40, ss.95,120(2), Sch.16, para.49, Sch.22, Pt.I
		s.117(3) am. (*prosp.*)	40, s.95, Sch.16, para.50
		s.117(3) rep.in pt. (*prosp.*)	40, s.120(2), Sch.22, Pt.I
		Sch.1 rep. (*prosp.*)	40, s.120(2), Sch.22, Pt.I
		Sch.2, para.3(1) rep.in pt. & am. (*prosp.*)	40, s.95, Sch.16, para.51(1)(a)
		Sch.2, para.3(1) rep.in pt. (*prosp.*)	40, s.120(2), Sch.22, Pt.I
		Sch.2, para.3(3) added (*prosp.*)	40, s.95, Sch.16, para.51(1)(b)
		Sch.2, paras.7,12,15 rep.in pt. (*prosp.*)	40, s.95, Sch.16, para.51(2)
		Sch.2, para.14 rep.in pt. (*prosp.*)	40, s.120(2), Sch.22, Pt.I
		Sch.3 rep. (*prosp.*)	40, s.120(2), Sch.22, Pt.I

Year and Chap. or No. of Measure	Short title	How affected	1992, Chapter of Act or Number of Measure or Statutory Instrument
1974—*cont.*			
		Sch.5 rep. (*prosp.*)	40, s.120(2), Sch.22, Pt.I
		Sch.5, para.8 am.	SI 99, art.2, Sch.
		Sch.6 rep. (*prosp.*)	40, s.120(2), Sch.22, Pt.I
		Sch.6A added (*prosp.*)	40, s.95, Sch.16, para.52
		Sch.9, para.1 rep.	52, s.300(1), Sch.1
		Sch.9, para.2 rep. (*prosp.*)	40, s.120(2), Sch.22, Pt.I
		Sch.9, para.5 rep. (*prosp.*)	40, s.120(2), Sch.22, Pt.I
		Sch.9, para.6 rep. (*prosp.*)	40, s.120(2), Sch.22, Pt.I
		Sch.9, para.8 rep. (*prosp.*)	40, s.120(2), Sch.22, Pt.I
		Sch.9, para.10(1) rep. (*prosp.*)	40, s.120(2), Sch.22, Pt.I
		Sch.9, para.12 rep.	52, s.300(1), Sch.1
c.47	Solicitors Act 1974	s.23(2) am. (1.1.1993)	SI 3218, reg.82(1), Sch.10, Pt.I, para.8(1)
		s.23(2)(i) added (*prosp.*)	40, s.120(1), Sch.21, Pt.I, para.5(1)(2)
		s.23(2B) added (*prosp.*)	40, s.120(1), Sch.21, Pt.I, para.5(3)
		s.87(1) (defns. of "liability insurance business" and "pecuniary loss insurance business") rep.	SI 2890, reg.12(1)
		s.87(1) (defn. of "authorised insurers") replaced by defn.of"authorised insurer"	SI 2890, reg.12(1)
		s.87(1) am. (1.1.1993)	SI 3218, reg.82(1), Sch.10, Pt.I, para.8(2)
c.52	Trade Union and Labour Relations Act 1974	rep.	52, s.300(1), Sch.1
c.viii	Zetland County Council Act 1974	Sch.1 am.	SI 1977(L), art.2
1975			
c.7	Finance Act 1975	Sch.4, para.17 trans.of functions	SI 1311, art.3(1), Sch.1, Pt.I
		Sch.4, para.17(1)(3)(4) am.	SI 1311, art.12(2), Sch.2, para.4(a)(b)
		Sch.4, para.17(5) rep.in pt.	SI 1311, art.12(2), Sch.2, para.4(c)
c.9	Supply Powers Act 1975	Sch.1 rep.in pt. (1-1- 1993) (EWS).	42, s.68(1), Sch.4, Pt.I
c.14	Social Security Act 1975	mod.	SI 812, art.2
		am.	SI 1312, art.2
		rep. (saving)	6, s.3, Sch.1
		ext.	6, s.5, Sch.3, Pt.I, para.5
		power to am.	6, s.5, Sch.3, Pt.II, para.22(3)(4)(a)
		s.58B mod.	SI 1555, regs.3,4
		s.58B(2) mod.	SI 1555, reg.3
		s.64(1B)(a)(b) am.	SI 524, art.2

Year and Chap. or No. of Measure	Short title	How affected	1992, Chapter of Act or Number of Measure or Statutory Instrument
1975—*cont.*			
		ss.93-119 (Pt.III) mod.	SI 728, reg.3 (substituting SI 1991/2891 reg.22, para.(9))
		s.106(2) am.	SI 2982, Sch.
		s.160(2) am.	SI 99, art.2, Sch.
		s.166(1)-(3A) appl.(mods.)	33, s.2(5)
c.15	Social Security (Northern Ireland) Act 1975	rep. (except.ss.97(4), 158.sch.10,paras.5(2),6, 7,7A)	9, s.3, Sch.1
		ext.	9, s.5, Sch.3, Pt.I, para.5
		power to am.	9, s.5, Sch.3, Pt.II, para.21(3)(4)(a)
		s.155(4A) added	6, s.4, Sch.2, para.12
		s.155A added	6, s.4, Sch.2, para.13
		s.158(2) am.	6, s.4, Sch.2, para.14(a)
		s.158(2A) added	6, s.4, Sch.2, para.14(b)
		Sch.10, para.5(3) added	9, s.4, Sch.2, para.10(1)
		Sch.10, paras.6-7A excl.	8, ss.39,41,48-50, Sch.2, para.1(6)
		Sch.10, para.6(1)(a) subst.	9, s.4, Sch.2, para.10(2)
c.16	Industrial Injuries and Diseases (Old Cases) Act 1975	rep.	6, s.3, Sch.1
c.17	Industrial Injuries and Diseases (Northern Ireland old Cases) Act 1975	rep.	9, s.3, Sch.1
c.18	Social Security (Consequential Provisions) Act 1975	s.2(3)(a) am.	6, s.4, Sch.2, para.15
		s.2(3)(b) am. (NI)	9, s.4, Sch.2, para.11
		Sch.2, paras.6,8,9 rep.	6, s.3, Sch.1
		Sch.2, para.11 rep.	6, s.3, Sch.1
		Sch.2, para.26 rep.	53, s.18(2), Sch.4, Pt.I
		Sch.2, para.31 rep.in pt. (NI)	9, s.3, Sch.1
		Sch.2, paras.69,70 rep.	6, s.3, Sch.1
		Sch.2, paras.73,74,77,80, 87,108,110,112 rep. (NI)	9, s.3, Sch.1
		Sch.3, paras.1-20 rep.	6, s.3, Sch.1
c.21	Criminal Procedure (Scotland) Act 1975	s.331 excl.	SI 973, art.4(3)(a)
		s.331 excl.	SI 975, art.16(8)
		s.331 excl.	SI 1302, art.17(8)
		s.331 excl.	SI 1304, art.5(3)(a)
		s.331 excl.	SI 2372, reg.90
		s.331 excl.	5, s.116(7)(a)
		s.331(1) appl. (*prosp.*)	40, s.107(5)
		s.331(3) appl.	SI 2992, reg.14(5)
		s.331(3) appl.	SI 2993, reg.12(5)
		s.331(3) appl.	SI 2994, reg.12(5)
		s.331(3) appl.	5, s.116(7)(b)(ii)
		s.331(3) appl.	35, s.11(3)
		s.452(4)(a)-(e) appl.	SI 2372, reg.95(8)

Year and Chap. or No. of Measure	Short title	How affected	1992, Chapter of Act or Number of Measure or Statutory Instrument
1975—*cont.*			
c.22	Oil Taxation Act 1975	ss.1-12 (Pt.I) appl.	12, s.199(7)(c)
		ss.1-12 (Pt.I) appl.	12, s.276(5)
		s.2(5A) am.	48, s.74, Sch.15, para.1
		s.3(1)(f) am.	48, s.74, Sch.15, para.2(1)
		s.3(4)(c)(i) rep.in pt.	48, ss.74,82, Sch.15, para.2(2)(a), Sch.18, Pt.VIII
		s.3(4)(c)(iv) am.	48, s.74, Sch.15, para.2(2)(b)
		s.3(5)(a)(c) am.	48, s.74, Sch.15, para.2(3)
		s.3(6) am.	48, s.74, Sch.15, para.2(4)
		s.12 appl.	12, s.197(1)(b)
		s.12(1) (defns. of "oil", "licence" and "licensee") appl.	12, s.196(5)
		s.12(1) (defns. of "initial storage" and "initial treatment") rep.in pt.	48, ss.55(3),74,82, Sch.15, para.3(a), Sch.18, Pt.VIII
		s.12(1) (defns. of "initial storage", "land" and "production purposes") am.	48, ss.55(3),74, Sch.15, para.3(b)-(d)
		Sch.2, para.1(1), Table am.	48, s.76, Sch.16, para.6
		Sch.3, para.2(2)(e)(ii) am.	48, s.74, Sch.15, para.4(1)
		Sch.3, para.7, head. rep.in pt.	48, ss.74,82, Sch.15, para.4(2)(a), Sch.18, Pt.VIII
		Sch.3, para.7(a) am.	48, s.74, Sch.15, para.4(2)(b)
c.23	Reservoirs Act 1975	s.1 excl.	v, s.12(2)
c.24	House of Commons Disqualification Act 1975	s.1(1)(c) am	39, s.3(4)
		Sch.1, Pt.I am.	6, s.4, Sch.2, para.16
		Sch.1, Pt.I am. (NI)	9, s.4, Sch.2, para.12(a)
		Sch.1, Pt.II am.	19, s.12, Sch.2, para.12
		Sch.1, Pt.II rep.in pt.	19, s.29, Sch.4, Pt.II
		Sch.1, Pt.II am.	40, s.1, Sch.1, para.6(1)
		Sch.1, Pt.II amdt(s). cont.	52, s.300(2), Sch.2, para.4(2)
		Sch.1, Pt.II am.	60, ss.8(1),11(4)
		Sch.1, Pt.III am. (EWS)	SI 3060, Sch.2, para.8
		Sch.1, Pt.III am.	6, s.4, Sch.2, para.17
		Sch.1, Pt.III am. (NI)	9, s.4, Sch.2, para.12(b)-(d)
		Sch.1, Pt.III am.	13, ss.1,9,62,70, Sch.1, para.6
		Sch.1, Pt.III rep.in pt. (1.4.1993)	13, s.93, Sch.8, Pt.II, para.74, Sch.9
		Sch.1, Pt.III am. (*prosp.*)	16, s.16(1), Sch.2, para.1
		Sch.1, Pt.III am. (*prosp.*)	37, s.7, Sch.1, para.2(3)
		Sch.1, Pt.III am.	37, s.37, Sch.7, para.6

Year and Chap. or No. of Measure	Short title	How affected	1992, Chapter of Act or Number of Measure or Statutory Instrument
1975—*cont.*			
		Sch.1, Pt.III am.	38, ss.1(6),5(6), Sch.1, para.9(1)
		Sch.1, Pt.III am.	52, s.300(2), Sch.2, para.4(3)
		Sch.1, Pt.III amdt(s). cont.	52, s.300(2), Sch.2, para.4(4)
		Sch.1, Pt.III am.	53, s.18(1), Sch.3, para.11
		Sch.1, Pt.IV rep.in pt. (*prosp.*)	16, s.16(2), Sch.3
c.25	Northern Ireland Assembly Disqualification Act 1975	s.1(1)(c) am.	39, s.3(4)
		Sch.1, Pt.I am.	6, s.4, Sch.2, para.18
		Sch.1, Pts.I,II am.	9, s.4, Sch.2, para.13(a) (b)
		Sch.1, Pt.II rep.in pt.	9, s.3, Sch.1
		Sch.1, Pt.II rep.in pt.	9, s.4, Sch.2, para.13(c)
		Sch.1, Pt.II am.	19, s.12, Sch.2, para.12
		Sch.1, Pt.II am.	40, s.1, Sch.1, para.6(2)
		Sch.1, Pt.II am.	60, ss.8(2),11(4)
		Sch.1, Pt.III am. (EWS)	SI 3060, Sch.2, para.8
		Sch.1, Pt.III am.	9, s.4, Sch.2, para.13(d) (e)(f)
		Sch.1, Pt.III am. (*prosp.*)	16, s.16(1), Sch.2, para.2
		Sch.1, Pt.III am.	38, ss.1(6),5(6), Sch.1, para.9(2)
		Sch.1, Pt.III amdt(s). cont.	52, s.300(2), Sch.2, para.4(4)
c.26	Ministers of the Crown Act 1975	defn. of "Minister of the Crown" appl.	61, s.4(2)
c.30	Local Government (Scotland) Act 1975	s.2(1) mod. (1992-93)	SI 864, arts.5,7(2)
		s.2(1) mod. (1992-93)	SI 865, arts.5,7(2)
		s.2(1) mod.	SI 1782, art.9(3)
		s.2(1) mod.	SI 1783, art.8(3)
		s.2(1) mod.	SI 1784, art.9(3)
		s.2(1) mod.	SI 1785, art.9(3)
		s.2(1) mod.	SI 1786, art.9(3)
		s.2(1) mod.	SI 1787, art.8(3)
		s.2(1) mod.	SI 1788, art.9(3)
		s.2(1) mod.	SI 1789, art.8(3)
		s.2(1) mod.	SI 1790, art.10(2)
		s.2(1) mod.	SI 1791, art.9(3)
		s.2(1) mod.	SI 1792, art.9(3)
		s.2(1) mod.	SI 1793, art.9(3)
		s.2(1) mod.	SI 1795, art.9(3)
		s.2(1)(2)(a) mod.	SI 1796, art.7(2)(3)
		s.2(1)(c)(d) mod.	SI 1782, art.9(1)(2)
		s.2(1)(c)(d) mod.	SI 1783, art.8(1)(2)
		s.2(1)(c)(d) mod.	SI 1784, art.9(1)(2)
		s.2(1)(c)(d) mod.	SI 1785, art.9(1)(2)
		s.2(1)(c)(d) mod.	SI 1786, art.9(1)(2)
		s.2(1)(c)(d) mod.	SI 1787, art.8(1)(2)

Year and Chap. or No. of Measure	Short title	How affected	1992, Chapter of Act or Number of Measure or Statutory Instrument
1975—*cont.*			
		s.2(1)(c)(d) mod.	SI 1788, art.9(1)(2)
		s.2(1)(c)(d) mod.	SI 1789, art.8(1)(2)
		s.2(1)(c)(d) mod.	SI 1791, art.9(1)(2)
		s.2(1)(c)(d) mod.	SI 1792, art.9(1)(2)
		s.2(1)(c)(d) mod.	SI 1793, art.9(1)(2)
		s.2(1)(c)(d) mod.	SI 1795, art.9(1)(2)
		s.2(1)(e) am.	14, s.117(1), Sch.13, para.41
		s.2(1)(c) mod. (1992-93)	SI 864, arts.5,7(1)
		s.2(1)(c) mod. (1992-93)	SI 865, arts.5,7(1)
		s.2(1)(c) mod.	SI 1790, art.10(1)
		s.2(1)(c) mod.	SI 1796, art.7(1)
		s.3 ext.	14, s.72(8), Sch.5, para.11
		s.3(2)(4) mod.	SI 1782, art.9(4)(5)
		s.3(2)(4) mod.	SI 1783, art.8(4)(5)
		s.3(2)(4) mod.	SI 1784, art.9(4)(5)
		s.3(2)(4) mod.	SI 1785, art.9(4)(5)
		s.3(2)(4) mod.	SI 1786, art.9(4)(5)
		s.3(2)(4) mod.	SI 1787, art.8(4)(5)
		s.3(2)(4) mod.	SI 1788, art.9(4)(5)
		s.3(2)(4) mod.	SI 1789, art.8(4)(5)
		s.3(2)(4) mod.	SI 1791, art.9(4)(5)
		s.3(2)(4) mod.	SI 1792, art.9(4)(5)
		s.3(2)(4) mod.	SI 1793, art.9(4)(5)
		s.3(2)(4) mod.	SI 1795, art.9(4)(5)
		s.6(1) am.	14, s.117(1), Sch.13, para.42
		s.6(5) mod. (1992-93)	SI 864, art.5
		ss.7-10 appl.	14, s.107, Sch.11, Pt.II, para.23(c)
		ss.7-10 power to mod.	14, s.107, Sch.11, Pt.II, para.23(c)
		s.7A added	14, s.110(1)
		s.7A replaced (by s.7B) (*prosp.*)	14, s.110(2)
		s.9A subst.	14, s.110(4)
		s.30(1B) am.	6, s.4, Sch.2, para.25
		s.33(1A) am.	6, s.4, Sch.2, para.26
		s.35(2ZA) am.	6, s.4, Sch.2, para.27(1)
		s.35(5)(7) am.	6, s.4, Sch.2, para.27(2)
		s.36(6) am.	6, s.4, Sch.2, para.28
		s.37 appl. (*prosp.*)	14, s.99(2)(b)
		s.37 (defn. of "non- domestic rate") am. (*prosp.*)	14, s.110(3)
		s.37 (defn. of "apportionment note") added	14, s.117(1), Sch.13, para.43(a)
		s.37 (defns. of "non-domestic rate" and "part residential subjects") added	14, s.117(1), Sch.13, para.43(b)

Year and Chap. or No. of Measure	Short title	How affected	1992, Chapter of Act or Number of Measure or Statutory Instrument
1975—*cont.*			
		s.37 (defn. of "prescribed") am.	14, s.117(1), Sch.13, para.43(c)
		s.37(1) mod.	SI 1790, art.10(3)
		s.37(1) (defn. of "year of revaluation") appl.	14, s.72(8), Sch.5, para.7
		s.37(1) (defn. of "material change of circumstances") appl.	14, s.111(6)(7)
		s.37(1) (defn. of "rate") rep.	14, s.117(2), Sch.14
		s.37A(7) am.	6, s.4, Sch.2, para.29
		s.41C(4A) am.	6, s.4, Sch.2, para.30
		s.44(6)(a) am.	6, s.4, Sch.2, para.31
		s.45(3)(a) am.	6, s.4, Sch.2, para.30
		s.51A(10) am.	6, s.4, Sch.2, para.32
		s.52D(1) am.	6, s.4, Sch.2, para.33
		s.59(1) am.	6, s.4, Sch.2, para.34
		s.60(1) am.	6, s.4, Sch.2, para.35(a)
		s.60(3) am.	6, s.4, Sch.2, para.35(b)
		ss.60ZB-60ZF added	6, s.4, Sch.2, para.36
		ss.61A,61B added	6, s.4, Sch.2, para.37
		Sch.3, para.6(2)(a) am. (*prosp.*)	14, s.117(1), Sch.13, para.44(a)
		Sch.3, para.20(2) am. (*prosp.*)	14, s.117(1), Sch.13, para.44(b)
		Sch.3, para.22(2) am.	14, s.117(1), Sch.13, para.44(c)
		Sch.3, para.31 (defns. of "community charges" and "community water charges") rep. (*prosp.*)	14, s.117, Sch.13, para.44(d), Sch.14
		Sch.3, para.31 (defns. of "council tax" and "council water charge") added (*prosp.*)	14, s.117(1), Sch.13, para.44(d)
c.45	Finance (No.2) Act 1975	s.47 rep.	12, s.290, Sch.12
		s.58 rep.	12, s.290, Sch.12
c.51	Salmon and Freshwater Fisheries Act 1975	saved	iii, s.32(10)
		ss.9-14 saved	iv, s.16(2)
		s.9 appl.	v, s.5(5)
		s.9 saved	v, s.35(13)
c.53	Public Service Vehicles (Arrest of Offenders) Act 1975	rep. (*prosp.*)	42, s.68(1), Sch.4, Pt.I
c.60	Social Security Pensions Act 1975	excl.	4, s.55, Sch.5, para.2(4) (b)
		ss.1-5 (Pt.I) rep.	6, s.3, Sch.1
		ss.6-10 rep.	6, s.3, Sch.1
		ss.12-16A rep.	6, s.3, Sch.1
		ss.18-21 rep.	6, s.3, Sch.1
		ss.23-25 rep.	6, s.3, Sch.1

Year and Chap. or No. of Measure	Short title	How affected	1992, Chapter of Act or Number of Measure or Statutory Instrument
1975—*cont.*			
		s.26(1)(a) am.	6, s.4, Sch.2, para.20(1)
		s.26(1A) added	6, s.4, Sch.2, para.20(2)
		s.27(2) (defn. of "the contracted-out percentage") am.	SI 795, art.2
		s.27(5) am.	6, s.4, Sch.2, para.21
		s.28(1)(a) am.	6, s.4, Sch.2, para.22(a)
		s.28(1)(b) am.	6, s.4, Sch.2, para.22(b)
		s.29(1)(a) am.	6, s.4, Sch.2, para.23(1)
		s.29(2)(2A) am.	6, s.4, Sch.2, para.23(2)
		s.29(3) am.	6, s.4, Sch.2, para.23(3)
		ss.29A-29C added	6, s.4, Sch.2, para.24
		s.31(8) am.	52, s.300(2), Sch.2, para.5
		ss.35(6),36(3) power to am.	5, ss.150(1)(e)(i),151
		s.37A mod.	5, s.151(4)(a)
		s.51A(13) rep.	6, s.3, Sch.1
		s.60(1)(a) rep.	6, s.3, Sch.1
		s.60A rep.in pt.	6, s.3, Sch.1
		s.62(1)(3) rep.	6, s.3, Sch.1
		s.62(2) subst.	6, s.4, Sch.2, para.38
		s.64(2) rep.in pt.	6, s.3, Sch.1
		s.64(2) am.	6, s.4, Sch.2, para.39
		s.65(4) rep.	6, s.3, Sch.1
		s.66(1) (defn. of "occupational pension scheme") appl.	5, s.191
		s.66(1) (defns. of "the Administration Act" and "the Contributions and Benefits Act") added	6, s.4, Sch.2, para.40(1)
		s.66(2) am.	6, s.4, Sch.2, para.40(2)
		s.66(2)(a)(b) rep.in pt.	6, s.3, Sch.1
		Sch.1 rep.	6, s.3, Sch.1
		Sch.1A, para.8 am.	6, s.4, Sch.2, para.41
		Sch.2, para.6(3)(c) am.	6, s.4, Sch.2, para.42
		Sch.3, para.2(2) am.	SI 795, art.3
		Sch.4, paras.35-46 rep.	6, s.3, Sch.1
		Sch.4, paras.49,50 rep.	6, s.3, Sch.1
		Sch.4, paras.53-64 rep.	6, s.3, Sch.1
		Sch.4, paras.66,67 rep.	6, s.3, Sch.1
		Sch.4, paras.68-70,71(a) (b) rep. (NI)	9, s.3, Sch.1
c.61	Child Benefit Act 1975	rep.	6, s.3, Sch.1
		ss.1-15 (Pt.I) mod.	SI 812, art.2
		ss.1-15 (Pt.I) am.	SI 1312, art.2
c.65	Sex Discrimination Act 1975	s.21(2) rep. (EWS) (*prosp.*)	17, s.3(3), Sch., Pt.II
		s.22, Table , para.5 am.	13, s.93(1), Sch.8, Pt.II, para.76(4)
		s.22, Table , paras.7B-7C added	37, s.62(2), Sch.9, para.4(2)(a)(b)

Year and Chap. or No. of Measure	Short title	How affected	1992, Chapter of Act or Number of Measure or Statutory Instrument
1975—*cont.*			
		s.22, Table , para.4A subst.	13, s.93(1), Sch.8, Pt.II, para.76(3)
		s.22, Table 3B am.	13, s.93(1), Sch.8, Pt.II, para.76(2)
		s.22A added (*prosp.*)	13, s.93(1), Sch.8, Pt.II, para.77
		s.23A added	13, s.93(1), Sch.8, Pt.II, para.78
		s.23B added	37, s.62(2), Sch.9, para.4(3)
		s.25(2) mod.	13, s.93(1), Sch.8, Pt.II, para.79(2)
		s.25(6)(c)(i) am.	13, s.93(1), Sch.8, Pt.II, para.79(1)(a)
		s.25(6)(c)(i) am.	37, s.62(2), Sch.9, para.4(4)
		s.25(6)(d) added	13, s.93(1), Sch.8, Pt.II, para.79(1)(b)
		s.26(4) added (*prosp.*)	13, s.93(1), Sch.8, Pt.II, para.80
		s.27(6) added (1.4.1993)	13, s.93(1), Sch.8, Pt.II, para.81
		s.82(1) (defn. of "further education") am. (1.4.1993)	13, s.93(1), Sch.8, Pt.II, para.82
		s.82(1) (defn. of "Board of management") added	37, s.62(2), Sch.9, para.4(5)
		s.85A added	52, s.300(2), Sch.2, para.6
		Sch.2, para.4 subst. (1.4.1993)	13, s.93(1), Sch.8, Pt.II, para.83
		Sch.2, para.6 am.	37, s.62(2), Sch.9, para.4(6)
c.68	Industry Act 1975	s.9 saved (*retrosp.*)	SI 8, art.3
		Sch.3, para.10 rep.	53, s.18(2), Sch.4, Pt.I
c.71	Employment Protection Act 1975	ss.1-10 rep.	52, s.300(1), Sch.1
		ss.17-21 rep.	52, s.300(1), Sch.1
		ss.99-108 rep.	52, s.300(1), Sch.1
		s.110 rep.	52, s.300(1), Sch.1
		ss.117-119 rep.	52, s.300(1), Sch.1
		ss.121-123 rep.	52, s.300(1), Sch.1
		s.124(1)(b) rep.	52, s.300(1), Sch.1
		s.124(6) am.	6, s.4, Sch.2, para.43
		s.125(1) rep.in pt.	52, s.300(1), Sch.1
		ss.126-128 rep.	52, s.300(1), Sch.1
		s.129(5)(6) rep.in pt.	52, s.300(1), Sch.1
		Sch.1 rep.	52, s.300(1), Sch.1
		Sch.12 rep.	52, s.300(1), Sch.1
		Sch.16, Pt.III rep.	52, s.300(1), Sch.1
		Sch.16, Pt.IV, paras.2,3 rep.	52, s.300(1), Sch.1
		Sch.16, Pt.IV, para.7 rep.	52, s.300(1), Sch.1
		Sch.16, Pt.IV, para.10 rep.	52, s.300(1), Sch.1
		Sch.16, Pt.IV, para.13 rep.	52, s.300(1), Sch.1
		Sch.16, Pt.IV, para.16 rep.	52, s.300(1), Sch.1
		Sch.17, paras.1-6 rep.	52, s.300(1), Sch.1

Year and Chap. or No. of Measure	Short title	How affected	1992, Chapter of Act or Number of Measure or Statutory Instrument
1975—*cont.*			
c.74	Petroleum and Submarine Pipe-lines Act 1975	s.20(2) mod.	15, s.1(5)(b)
		ss.26,27 power to rep. or mod.	15, s.1 (amending s.15 of 1974 c.37)
		s.26(1) (defns. of "pipe-line" and "pipe-line works") defn(s). appl.	15, s.1(4)
		s.28(2)(b) rep.	15, ss.3(1)(c),7(2), Sch.2
		s.29(2) rep.in pt.	15, ss.3(1)(c),7(2), Sch.2
		s.32 power to rep. or mod.	15, s.1 (amending s.15 of 1974 c.37)
c.75	Policyholders Protection Act 1975	s.1(2)(aa) added (*prosp.*)	40, s.97, Sch.17, para.1(1)
		s.1(2)(b) am. (*prosp.*)	40, s.97, Sch.17, para.1(2)
		s.3A added (*prosp.*)	40, s.97, Sch.17, para.2
		s.4(3) added (*prosp.*)	40, s.97, Sch.17, para.3
		s.5, head. am. (*prosp.*)	40, s.97, Sch.17, para.4
		s.5A added (*prosp.*)	40, s.97, Sch.17, para.5
		s.8(1) am. (*prosp.*)	40, s.97, Sch.17, para.6(1)
		s.8(4) am. (*prosp.*)	40, s.97, Sch.17, para.6(2)
		s.8A added (*prosp.*)	40, s.97, Sch.17, para.7
		s.10(1) am. (*prosp.*)	40, s.97, Sch.17, para.8(1)
		s.10(3) added (*prosp.*)	40, s.97, Sch.17, para.8(2)
		s.11(3A) added (*prosp.*)	40, s.97, Sch.17, para.9
		s.11A added (*prosp.*)	40, s.97, Sch.17, para.10
		s.16(10) added (*prosp.*)	40, s.97, Sch.17, para.11
		s.17(8) am. (*prosp.*)	40, s.97, Sch.17, para.12
		s.18(1)(a) am. (*prosp.*)	40, s.97, Sch.17, para.13
		s.19(11) added (*prosp.*)	40, s.97, Sch.17, para.14
		s.21(10) added (*prosp.*)	40, s.97, Sch.17, para.15
		s.25(1) am. (*prosp.*)	40, s.97, Sch.17, para.16
		s.27 am. (*prosp.*)	40, s.97, Sch.17, para.17
		s.32(1) (defns. of "authorised friendly society", "closing society", "the Commission", "friendly society", "incorporated friendly society" and "qualifying society") added (*prosp.*)	40, s.97, Sch.17, para.18(1)(2)
		s.32(2) am. (*prosp.*)	40, s.97, Sch.17, para.18(3)
		s.32(2A)(2B) added (*prosp.*)	40, s.97, Sch.17, para.18(4)
		s.32(4A) added (*prosp.*)	40, s.97, Sch.17, para.18(5)
		Sch.3, paras.4A,4B added (*prosp.*)	40, s.97, Sch.17, para.19(1)
c.xviii	Dundee Port Authority Order Confirmation Act 1975	Sch. am. (Dundee Port Authority O. s.4 rep., Sch.1 Pt.I paras. 6 excl, 1(1)(2) subst, 5 am., Pt.II 1 am.)	SI 1435(L), arts.5(3),7(1)(2)(3),8
c.xxxi	London Transport Act 1975	s.21 incorp.(mods.)	iii, s.29(1)(3)

Year and Chap. or No. of Measure	Short title	How affected	1992, Chapter of Act or Number of Measure or Statutory Instrument
1976			
c.5	Education (School-leaving Dates) Act 1976	s.2(4) rep.	6, s.3, Sch.1
c.7	Trade Union and Labour Relations (Amendment) Act 1976	rep.	52, s.300(1), Sch.1
c.27	Theatres Trust Act 1976	s.2(2)(d) am. (1.1.1993)	41, s.78(1), Sch.6, para.8
		Sch. trans.of functions	SI 1311, art.3(1), Sch.1, Pt.I
c.32	Lotteries and Amusements Act 1976	s.16(3) am. (EW)	SI 425, art.2
		s.16(3)(b) am. (S)	SI 749, art.2
c.35	Police Pensions Act 1976	para.9, Sch.2 rep.	53, s.18(2), Sch.4, Pt.I
c.40	Finance Act 1976	s.54 rep.	12, s.290, Sch.12
		s.131(2) rep.in pt.	12, s.290, Sch.12
c.57	Local Government (Miscellaneous Provisions) Act 1976	s.16 restr.	14, s.117(1), Sch.13, para.45
		s.42 restr.	iii, s.16(1)
		s.80(1) (defn. of "private hire vehicle") am.	42, s.62(3)
c.66	Licensing (Scotland) Act 1976	s.19(1) am.	18, s.1(2)
		s.25(1) rep.in pt.	18, s.1(1)(a)
		s.25(1A)-(1C) subst.	18, s.1(1)(b)
		s.25(1A)(1B)(1C) saved	SI 819, art.4
		s.25(7) am.	18, s.1(1)(c)
c.71	Supplementary Benefits Act 1976	ss.22,23 rep.	6, s.3, Sch.1
		Sch.7, para.36 rep.	6, s.3, Sch.1
c.74	The Race Relations Discrimination Act 1976	s.17, Table , para.3B added	13, s.93(1), Sch.8, Pt.II, para.85(2)
		s.17, Table , para.4A subst.	13, s.93(1), Sch.8, Pt.II, para.85(3)
		s.17, Table , para.5 am.	13, s.93(1), Sch.8, Pt.II, para.85(4)
		s.17, Table , paras.7B-7C added	37, s.62(2), Sch.9, para.5(2)(a)(b)
		s.17A added (*prosp.*)	13, s.93(1), Sch.8, Pt.II, para.86
		s.18A added	13, s.93(1), Sch.8, Pt.II, para.87
		s.18B added	37, s.62(2), Sch.9, para.5(3)
		s.19(2) mod.	13, s.93(1), Sch.8, Pt.II, para.88(2)
		s.19(6)(c)(i) am.	13, s.93(1), Sch.8, Pt.II, para.88(1)(a)
		s.19(6)(c)(i) am.	37, s.62(2), Sch.9, para.5(4)
		s.19(6)(d) added	13, s.93(1), Sch.8, Pt.II, para.88(1)(b)
		s.75A added	52, s.300(2), Sch.2, para.7
		s.78(1) (defn. of "board management") added	37, s.62(2), Sch.9, para.5(5)

Year and Chap. or No. of Measure	Short title	How affected	1992, Chapter of Act or Number of Measure or Statutory Instrument
1976—*cont.*			
		Sch.3 rep.	52, s.300(1), Sch.1
c.76	Energy Act 1976	defn. of "petroleum products" defn(s). appl.	15, s.5(7)
c.80	Rent (Agriculture) Act 1976	defn. of "statutory tenant" appl.	14, s.6(6)
c.xxxvii	London Transport Act 1976	s.13 incorp.(mods.)	iii, s.29(1)(4)
No.1	The Cathedrals Measure 1976	s.3(1) am.	GSM 1, s.9(2)(a)(5)
		s.3(2) am.	GSM 1, s.9(2)(b)(5)
		s.3(3) subst.	GSM 1, s.9(2)(c)(5)
		s.3(4) am.	GSM 1, s.9(2)(d)(5)
		s.4(1) rep.	GSM 1, s.9(3)(a)
		s.4(1) rep.	GSM 1, s.17(2), Sch.4, Pt.II
		s.4(2) am.	GSM 1, s.9(3)(b)
		s.5(1) am.	GSM 1, s.9(4)
No.2	Ecclesiastical Judges and Legal Officers Measure 1976	s.7(2) expld.	GSM 1, s.13
No.3	Church of England (Miscellaneous Provisions) Measure 1976	s.6(2) am.	GSM 1, s.17(1), Sch.3, para.12
No.4	Endowments and Glebe Measure 1976	defn. of "diocesan glebe land" appl.	iii, s.35(4)
		s.20(5)(6) am.	GSM 1, s.17(1), Sch.3, para.13
		s.23(2) am.	GSM 1, s.17(1), Sch.3, para.14
		s.24 am.	GSM 1, s.17(1), Sch.3, para.15
		s.38(3) am.	GSM 1, s.17(1), Sch.3, para.16
		s.45(1) (defn. of "lay worker") added	GSM 1, s.17(1), Sch.3, para.17
1977			
c.3	Aircraft and Shipbuilding Industries Act 1977	s.6(2)(b) am.	52, s.300(2), Sch.2, para.8(2)
		s.42(10) rep.	53, s.18(2), Sch.4, Pt.I
		s.56(1) (defn. of "relevant trade union") am.	52, s.300(2), Sch.2, para.8(3)
c.5	Social Security (Miscellaneous Provisions) Act 1977	ss.1,2,3(1) rep.	6, s.3, Sch.1 6,
		ss.4-6 rep.	s.3, Sch.1
		ss.8-11 rep.	6, s.3, Sch.1
		s.13 rep.	6, s.3, Sch.1
		ss.17,18 rep.	6, s.3, Sch.1
		s.20(1)(2) rep.	6, s.3, Sch.1
		s.20(3)(4) rep. (NI)	9, s.3, Sch.1
		s.21(1)(a) am.	6, s.4, Sch.2, para.44(1)
		s.21(3) subst.	6, s.4, Sch.2, para.44(2)
		s.22(1)-(5) rep.	6, s.3, Sch.1

Year and Chap. or No. of Measure	Short title	How affected	1992, Chapter of Act or Number of Measure or Statutory Instrument
1977—*cont.*			
		s.23(2) rep.in pt.	6, s.3, Sch.1
		s.23(2) am.	6, s.4, Sch.2, para.45(a) (b)
		s.24(1) (defn. of "the Old Cases Act") rep.	6, s.3, Sch.1
		s.24(2)(4) rep.	6, s.3, Sch.1
		s.24(3) am.	6, s.4, Sch.2, para.46
		Sch.1 rep.	6, s.3, Sch.1
c.36	Finance Act 1977	ss.41,42 rep.	12, s.290, Sch.12
c.37	Patents Act 1977	ext.(mods.)	SI 3091, reg.5
		s.40(6) (defn. of "relevant collective agreement") am.	52, s.300(2), Sch.2, para.9
		s.123 ext.	SI 3091, reg.4
c.42	Rent Act 1977	defn. of "statutory tenancy" appl.	14, s.6(6)
		s.72A added	6, s.4, Sch.2, para.47
c.45	Criminal Law Act 1977	s.1(1) mod. (EW)	52, s.242(1)
		s.1(3) rep.	52, s.300(1), Sch.1
		s.5(11) rep.	52, s.300(1), Sch.1
		s.63(2) rep.in pt.	52, s.300(1), Sch.1
c.49	National Health Service Act 1977	mod.	SI 635, reg.25(16)
		defn. of "health service hospital" appl.	14, ss.11(5),79(5), Sch.1, para.6(2)(a)
		s.33(2A) ext.	SI 635, reg.13(1)
		s.41(c) rep.in pt. (*prosp.*)	28, s.2
		s.41(cc) added (*prosp.*)	28, s.2
		Sch.15, para.53 rep.	53, s.18(2), Sch.4, Pt.I
		Sch.15, para.54 rep. (*prosp.*)	48, s.82, Sch.18, Pt.IV
		Sch.15, para.62 rep.	52, s.300(1), Sch.1
		Sch.15, paras.63,64 rep.	6, s.3, Sch.1
		Sch.15, para.67 rep.	6, s.3, Sch.1
c.xii	London Transport Act 1977	Sch. rep.in pt.	42, s.68(1), Sch.4, Pt.I
c.xvii	British Railways Act 1977	Sch.1 rep.in pt.	42, s.68(1), Sch.4, Pt.I
1978			
c.2	Commonwealth Development Corporation Act 1978	s.9A(2) am.	SI 816, art.2
		s.10(1) am.	SI 816, art.3
c.22	Domestic Proceedings and Magistrates' Courts Act 1978	ss.1-35 (Pt.I) appl.(mods.) (*prosp.*)	56, s.1, Sch.1, Pt.II, para.13 (substg. 1972, c.18, ss.28,28A)
		s.2(3) trans.of functions & am.	SI 709, art.3(2), Sch.2
		ss.57,58 rep. (*prosp.*)	56, s.2(2), Sch.3
		s.88 (defn. of "child of the family") appl. (*prosp.*)	56, s.1, Sch.1, Pt.II, para.13 (substg. 1972, c.18, s.28A)
		s.90(3)(b) am. (*prosp.*)	56, s.2(1), Sch.2, para.1
		Sch.2, paras.34,35 rep. (*prosp.*)	56, s.2(2), Sch.3

Year and Chap. or No. of Measure	Short title	How affected	1992, Chapter of Act or Number of Measure or Statutory Instrument
1978—*cont.*			
c.23	Judicature (Northern Ireland) Act 1978	s.87 excl.	SI 225, regs.18(2)(c), 123(b)(ii)
		Sch.5, Pt.II rep.in pt.	9, s.3, Sch.1
		Sch.5, Pt.II rep.in pt.	53, s.18(2), Sch.4, Pt.I
c.29	National Health Service (Scotland) Act 1978	s.27(c) rep.in pt. (*prosp.*)	28, s.3
		s.27(cc) added (*prosp.*)	28, s.3
		s.87D mod.	SI 81, art.3
		s.108(1) (defn. of "health service hospital") appl.	14, ss.11(5),79(5), Sch.1, para.6(2)(a)
		Sch.16, para.35 rep.	53, s.18(2), Sch.4, Pt.I
		Sch.16, para.39 rep.	52, s.300(1), Sch.1
		Sch.16, para.40 rep.	6, s.3, Sch.1
c.30	Interpretation Act 1978	Sch.1 (defn. of "London borough") am.	19, s.27, Sch.3, para.21
c.36	House of Commons (Administration) Act 1978	Sch.1, para.5(6) subst.	52, s.300(2), Sch.2, para.10
		Sch.2, para.1 rep.in pt.	52, s.300(1), Sch.1
		Sch.2, para.5 rep.	52, s.300(1), Sch.1
c.40	Rating (Disabled Persons) Act 1978	s.2(5B)(5C) am.	14, s.117(1), Sch.13, para.46
		s.4(9) am.	6, s.4, Sch.2, para.48
		Sch.1, para.11(2)(3) am.	14, s.117(1), Sch.13, para.47
c.42	Finance Act 1978	s.8(2)(3) rep. (*prosp.*)	48, s.82, Sch.18, Pt.IV
		s.8(4) rep.in pt. (*prosp.*)	48, s.82, Sch.18, Pt.IV
c.44	Employment Protection (Consolidation) Act 1978	defns. of "contract of employment", "employee" and "employer" appl.	13, s.90(1)
		mod.	24, s.1(1)(3)
		defn. of "offshore employee" appl.	24, s.1(2)
		s.15(1) am.	SI 312, arts.2,3
		ss.23-28 rep.	52, s.300(1), Sch.1
		s.29(1)(e) am.	37, s.62(2), Sch.9, para.6(a)
		s.29(1)(e) rep.in pt.	37, s.62(3), Sch.10
		s.29(1)(ef) am.	13, s.93(1), Sch.8, Pt.II, para.89
		s.29(1)(eg) added	37, s.62(2), Sch.9, para.6(b)
		s.29(2)(c) am.	37, s.62(2), Sch.9, para.6(c)
		s.29(4)(b) am.	52, s.300(2), Sch.2, para.11
		s.30(1) am.	52, s.300(2), Sch.2, para.12(a)
		s.30(2) am.	52, s.300(1), Sch.2, para.12(b)
		s.30(3) rep.	52, s.300(1)(2), Schs.1,2, para.12(c)
		s.32 subst.	52, s.300(1), Sch.2, para.13
		ss.54-80 (Pt.V) mod.	52, ss.152(1),153

Year and Chap. or No. of Measure	Short title	How affected	1992, Chapter of Act or Number of Measure or Statutory Instrument
1978—*cont.*			
		ss.54-80 (Pt.V) excl.	52, s.167(1)
		s.55 (defns. of "dismiss dismissal" and "effective date of termination") appl.	52, s.298
		s.55(2)-(7) appl.	4, s.171(1)
		ss.57-61 mod.	52, s.239(3)(a)
		s.57(3) am.	52, s.300(1), Sch.2, para.14
		s.58 rep.	52, s.300(1), Sch.1
		s.59 rep.in pt.	52, s.300(1), Sch.1
		ss.62,62A rep.	52, s.300(1), Sch.1
		ss.64,64A excl.	52, s.154
		s.64(1) rep.in pt.	52, s.300(1), Sch.1
		s.64(3) rep.	52, s.300(1), Sch.1
		s.64A(2) rep.in pt.	52, s.300(1), Sch.1
		ss.67-69 restr.	52, s.167(3)
		s.67(2) excl.	52, s.239(2)
		s.67(3) rep.	52, s.300(1), Sch.1
		s.71(2)(b) excl.	52, s.157(2)
		s.71(2)(b) am.	52, s.300(1), Sch.2, para.15
		s.72 subst.	52, s.300(1), Sch.2, para.16
		s.72A rep.	52, s.300(1), Sch.1
		s.73(4A) am.	SI 313, arts.2,3
		s.73(4A)(4B) rep.	52, s.300(1), Sch.1
		s.73(7C) subst.	52, s.300(1), Sch.2, para.17
		s.75A rep.	52, s.300(1), Sch.1
		s.75A(1)(2) am.	SI 313, arts.2,3
		ss.76A-79 rep.	52, s.300(1), Sch.1
		ss.81-120 (Pt.VI) trans.of functions	SI 331, art.2(1)(g)(4)
		s.81(2) (defn. of "redundancy") appl.	4, ss.27(2)(b),28(4)
		s.122(2)(a) am.	52, s.300(1), Sch.2, para.18(2)
		s.122(4)(c)(d) am.	52, s.300(1), Sch.2, para.18(3)(a)(b)
		s.122(5) am.	SI 312, arts.2,3
		s.123(4) am.	6, s.4, Sch.2, para.49
		s.132(1) am.	52, s.300(1), Sch.2, para.19(d)
		s.132(1)(b) rep.in pt.	52, s.300(1)(2), Schs.1,2, para.19(a)
		s.132(1)(bb) added	52, s.300(1), Sch.2, para.19(b)
		s.132(1)(c) am.	52, s.300(1), Sch.2, para.19(c)
		s.132(4) am.	6, s.4, Sch.2, para.50(1)
		s.132(6) (defn. of "unemployment benefit") am.	6, s.4, Sch.2, para.50(2)
		s.133(1)(a)(b) rep.in pt.	52, s.300(1), Sch.1
		s.133(1)(d) rep.	52, s.300(1), Sch.1

Year and Chap. or No. of Measure	Short title	How affected	1992, Chapter of Act or Number of Measure or Statutory Instrument
1978—*cont.*			
		s.133(1)(f)(g) rep.	52, s.300(1), Sch.1
		s.133(2)-(6) appl.	52, s.290
		s.135(3) am.	52, s.300(1), Sch.2, para.20
		s.136(1)(g) rep.	52, s.300(1), Sch.1
		s.136(1)(c) rep.	52, s.300(1), Sch.1
		s.136(2)(3) rep.	52, s.300(1), Sch.1
		s.136(5) rep.in pt.	52, s.300(1), Sch.1
		s.139 (defn. of "relevant member of the House of Commons staff") appl.	52, ss.278(3),300(2), Sch.2 para.3(2) (adding 1970 c.41 s.1(10A)) para.6 (adding 1975 c.65 s.85A) para.7 (adding 1976 c.74 s.75A)
		s.139(4)-(9) appl.(mods.)	52, ss.278(6),300(2), Sch.2, paras.6,7 para.6 (adding 1975 c.65 s.85A) para.7 (adding 1976 c.74 s.75A)
		s.146(4) rep.in pt.	52, s.300(1), Sch.1
		s.149(2) rep.in pt.	52, s.300(1), Sch.1
		s.151 appl.	52, s.281(5)
		s.151 appl.	52, s.282(2)
		s.153 (defn. of "contract of employment") appl.	35, s.1(3)(b)
		s.153(1) (defns. of "collective agreement", "employers association" and "official") am.	52, s.300(2), Sch.2, para.21(2)(a)-(c)
		s.153(1) (defn. of "successor") subst.	52, s.300(2), Sch.2, para.21(2)(d)
		s.153(1) (defns. of "trade dispute" and "trade union") am.	52, s.300(2), Sch.2, para.21(2)(e)(f)
		s.153(4A) added	52, s.300(2), Sch.2, para.21(3)
		Sch.2, Pt.I, para.2(1) am.	52, s.300(2), Sch.2, para.22
		Sch.2, para.2(2) rep.in pt.	52, s.300(1), Sch.1
		Sch.2, para.2(4) rep.in pt.	52, s.300(1), Sch.1
		Sch.3, para.5 am.	52, s.300(2), Sch.2, para.23
		Sch.9, para.2(1) am.	52, s.300(2), Sch.2, para.24(2)
		Sch.9, para.8 am.	52, s.300(2), Sch.2, para.24(3)
		Sch.11, para.18(aa) am.	52, s.300(2), Sch.2, para.25
		Sch.11, para.18(d) am.	52, s.300(2), Sch.2, para.25(a)
		Sch.11, para.21A(1) am.	52, s.300(2), Sch.2, para.25(b)
		Sch.11, para.21A(3) am.	52, s.300(2), Sch.2, para.25(b)
		Sch.13 mod. (1.4.1993)	13, s.35(2)
		Sch.13 appl.	52, s.281(5)
		Sch.13 appl.	52, s.282(2)
		Sch.13, para.14(1)(b)(ia) added	6, s.4, Sch.2, para.51(1) (a)

Year and Chap. or No. of Measure	Short title	How affected	1992, Chapter of Act or Number of Measure or Statutory Instrument
1978—*cont.*			
		Sch.13, para.14(1)(b)(i) am.	6, s.4, Sch.2, para.51(1) (b)
		Sch.13, para.14(4)(b) am.	6, s.4, Sch.2, para.51(2)
		Sch.13, para.17(3) mod. (EW)	44, s.1(7)
		Sch.13, para.24 (defn. of "strike") appl.	52, s.281(3)(b)
		Sch.14 appl.	52, s.190(5)
		Sch.14, Pt.I appl.	52, s.281(6)
		Sch.14, para.8(1)(a)-(c) am.	SI 312, arts.2,3
		Sch.16, para.2 rep.	52, s.300(1), Sch.1
		Sch.16, para.5 rep.	52, s.300(1), Sch.1
		Sch.16, para.11 rep.	53, s.18(2), Sch.4, Pt.I
		Sch.16, para.18 rep.	52, s.300(1), Sch.1
		Sch.16, para.19 rep.	6, s.3, Sch.1
		Sch.16, para.23 rep.	52, s.300(1), Sch.1
		Sch.16, para.29 rep.	6, s.3, Sch.1
c.46	Employment (Continental Shelf) Act 1978	s.1(1) rep.	52, s.300(1), Sch.1
c.56	Parliamentary Pensions Act 1978	s.2(4) am.	SI 599, reg.5(a)
		s.2(5) rep.	SI 599, reg.5(b)
		s.2(6) am.	SI 599, reg.5(c)
		s.2(7) am.	SI 599, reg.5(d)
		s.2(7)(iii) rep.in pt.	SI 599, reg.5(d)
No.1	Dioceses Measure 1978	s.2(3) am.	GSM 1, s.17(1), Sch.3, para.18
No.2	The Parochial Registers and Records Measure 1978	s.2(3) subst. (1.1.1993)	GSM 1, s.4(1), Sch.1, para.2
		s.3(2) subst. (1.1.1993)	GSM 1, s.4(1), Sch.1, para.3
		s.5 am. (1.1.1993)	GSM 1, s.4(1), Sch.1, para.4
		s.9 subst. (1.1.1993)	GSM 1, s.4(1), Sch.1, para.5
		s.9 mod. (1.1.1993)	GSM 1, s.4(2)
		s.9A added (1.1.1993)	GSM 1, s.4(1), Sch.1, para.6
		s.10(2)(aa) added (1.1.1993)	GSM 1, s.4(1), Sch.1, para.7(a)
		s.10(7) am. (1.1.1993)	GSM 1, s.4(1), Sch.1, para.7(b)
		s.12A added (1.1.1993)	GSM 1, s.4(1), Sch.1, para.8

Year and Chap. or No. of Measure	Short title	How affected	1992, Chapter of Act or Number of Measure or Statutory Instrument
1978—*cont.*		s.20(3A)-(3C) added (1.1.1993)	GSM 1, s.4(1), Sch.1, para.9
		s.25 am. (1.1.1993)	GSM 1, s.4(1), Sch.1, para.10
		Sch.1, Form 2 subst. (1.1.1993)	GSM 1, s.4(1)(3), Sch.1, para.11
		Sch.2 subst. 1.1.1993)	GSM 1, s.4(1), Sch.1, para.12
1979 c.2	Customs and Excise Management Act 1979	defns. of "customs and excise Acts" and "goods" appl.	48, s.1(7)
		defn. of "goods" appl.	48, s.2(5)
		defns. of "the customs and excise Acts" and "goods" appl. (1.1.1993)	48, s.4(5)(6)
		defn. of "assigned matter" appl. (1.12.1992,1.1.1993)	48, s.14(2), Sch.3, Pt.I, para.44 (adding 1983 c.55, s.46B)
		s.1(1) (defn. of "approved route") rev.	SI 3095, reg.3(1)
		s.1(1) (defn. of "perfect entry") am.	SI 3095, Sch.1, para.2
		s.1(1) (defn. of "approved route") rev.	SI 3095, Sch.2
		s.1(1) (defn. of "excise duty point") added (1.12.1992,1.1.1993)	48, s.1(5), Sch.1, para.1
		s.1(1) (defns. of "occupier" and "warehoused") am.	48, s.3, Sch.2, para.1(a) (b)
		s.1(1) (defn. of "the Customs and Excise Acts 1979") rep.in pt. (1.1.1993)	48, s.82, Sch.18, Pt.II
		s.5(3) am.	SI 3095, Sch.1, para.3
		ss.20(3),22(3),25(3),42(3) am.	SI 3095, reg.3(2)
		s.21 restr. (1.1.1993)	48, s.4(3)(a)(6)
		ss.24(2)(b),43(1)(a),51, 67(1)(b),96(1)(a),127, 162 mod.	SI 3152, Pt.IV
		s.25(1) am.	SI 3095, Sch.1, para.4
		ss.26-29 restr. (1.1.1993)	48, s.4(3)(b)-(e)(6)
		s.26(1)(a) rev.	SI 3095, reg.3(3)
		s.26(1)(a)·rev.	SI 3095, Sch.2
		s.27(1) am.	48, s.10(2)
		s.28(1) am.	48, s.10(3)
		s.34 restr. (1.1.1993)	48, s.4(3)(f)(6)
		s.35(1) rev.in pt.	SI 3095, reg.3(4)(a)
		s.35(1) rev.in pt.	SI 3095, Sch.2
		s.35(6) am.	SI 3095, reg.3(4)(b)
		s.35(7) rev.in pt.	SI 3095, reg.3(4)(c)
		s.35(8) rev.	SI 3095, reg.3(4)(d)
		s.35(8) rev.	SI 3095, Sch.2

Year and Chap. or No. of Measure	Short title	How affected	1992, Chapter of Act or Number of Measure or Statutory Instrument
1979—*cont.*			
		ss.37,38,38A rev.	SI 3095, reg.3(5)
		ss.37,38,38A rev.	SI 3095, Sch.2
		s.37A(1) subst.	SI 3095, Sch.1, para.5
		s.37B(6) am.	SI 3095, Sch.1, para.6
		s.43(2) am. (1.12.1992, 1.1.1993)	48, s.1(5), Sch.1, para.2(a)
		s.43(2D) added (1.12.1992, 1.1.1993)	48, s.1(5), Sch.1, para.2(b)
		s.63(1)(2)(7) am.	SI 3095, reg.3(6)(a)(b)(c)
		s.64(1) am.	SI 3095, reg.3(7)
		ss.75A(1),77(1)(a),77A(1) am.	SI 3095, Sch.1, para.7
		ss.75B,75C added	SI 3095, reg.3(8)
		ss.77B,77C added	SI 3095, reg.3(9)
		s.78 restr. (1.1.1993)	48, s.4(3)(g)(6)
		s.78(1B) added	SI 3095, reg.3(10)
		s.78(2A) added (1.1.1993)	48, s.5(1)(2)
		s.93(1) subst.	48, s.3, Sch.2, para.2(1)
		s.93(2) (defn. of "relevant business activity") am.	48, s.3, Sch.2, para.2(2) (e)
		s.93(2)(da)(db) added	48, s.3, Sch.2, para.2(2) (a)
		s.93(2)(ee) am.	48, s.3, Sch.2, para.2(2) (b)
		s.93(2)(fa)-(fc) added	48, s.3, Sch.2, para.2(2) (c)
		s.93(2)(g) am.	48, s.3, Sch.2, para.2(2) (d)
		s.93(2A) am.	48, s.3, Sch.2, para.2(3) (a)(b)
		s.93(3) am.	48, s.3, Sch.2, para.2(4)
		s.93(5A) added	48, s.3, Sch.2, para.2(5)
		s.93(6) am.	48, s.3, Sch.2, para.2(6)
		s.93(7)(b) am.	48, s.3, Sch.2, para.2(7) (a)(b)
		s.94(6) added (1.12.1992, 1.1.1993)	48, s.1(5), Sch.1, para.3
		s.95(1) am. (1.12.1992, 1.1.1993)	48, s.1(5), Sch.1, para.4
		s.96(6) added (1.12.1992, 1.1.1993)	48, s.1(5), Sch.1, para.5
		s.100(2)(a)(b) am.	48, s.3, Sch.2, para.3(a)
		s.100(2)(d) subst.	48, s.3, Sch.2, para.3(b)
		s.100H(1)(f) rep. (1.12.1992,1.1.1993)	48, ss.1(5),82, Sch.1, para.6(1)(a), Sch.18, Pt.I, Note 1
		s.100H(1)(g) am. (1.12.1992,1.1.1993)	48, s.1(5), Sch.1, para.6(1)(b)
		s.100H(1)(h) subst. (1.12.1992,1.1.1993)	48, s.1(5), Sch.1, para.6(1)(c)
		s.100H(1)(ma) added	48, s.3, Sch.2, para.4
		s.117(1) rep.in pt.	48, ss.3,82, Sch.2, para.5(a), Sch.18, Pt.I, Note 2
		s.117(1)(2)(a)(5) rep.in pt.	48, s.82, Sch.18, Pt.I
		s.117(1)(a) am.	48, s.3, Sch.2, para.5(b)

Year and Chap. or No. of Measure	Short title	How affected	1992, Chapter of Act or Number of Measure or Statutory Instrument
1979—*cont.*			
		s.117(2)(a) rep.in pt.	48, ss.3,82, Sch.2, para.5(a), Sch.18, Pt.I, Note 2
		s.117(3) am.	48, s.3, Sch.2, para.5(b)
		s.117(5) rep.in pt.	48, ss.3,82, Sch.2, para.5(a), Sch.18, Pt.I, Note 2
		s.117(8) (defn. of "relevant excise duty") rep.	48, ss.3,82, Sch.2, para.5(c), Sch.18, Pt.I, Note 2
		s.117(8) (defn. of "relevant excise duty") rep.	48, s.82, Sch.18, Pt.I
		s.127A(1) am. (1.12.1992, 1.1.1993)	48, s.1(5), Sch.1, para.7
		s.129(1)(b) am.	48, s.3, Sch.2, para.6(a)
		s.129(1A) added	48, s.3, Sch.2, para.6(b)
		s.163(3) added	48, s.10(4)
		s.164 restr. (1.1.1993)	48, s.4(3)(h)(6)
		ss.167(2)(a),168(2)(a) mod.	SI 2790, reg.12
		s.170(6) added	48, s.3, Sch.2, para.7
		s.170A added	48, s.3, Sch.2, para.8
		s.170B added (pt.prosp.)	48, s.3, Sch.2, para.8
		s.171(5) am.	48, s.3, Sch.2, para.9
		s.178(2) rep.in pt. (1.1.1993)	48, s.82, Sch.18, Pt.II
c.3	Customs and Excise Duties (General Reliefs) Act 1979	ss.10(2)(a),11(1)(a) mod.	SI 3152, Pt.IV
		s.13(3)(a)(b) am. (1.12.1992,1.1.1993)	48, s.1(5), Sch.1, para.8(1)(a)(b)
		s.13(3A)-(3C) added (1.12.1992,1.1.1993)	48, s.1(5), Sch.1, para.8(2)
		s.13(4) (defn. of "conduct") added (1.12.1992,1.1.1993)	48, s.1(5), Sch.1, para.8(3)
		s.13(4) (defn. of "value added tax") am. (1.12.1992,1.1.1993)	48, s.14(2), Sch.3, Pt.III, para.93
		s.13C(5) added	48, s.3, Sch.2, para.10
c.4	Alcoholic Liquor Duties Act 1979	s.1(2) subst.	SI 3158, reg.2(2)
		s.2(1) subst.	SI 3158, reg.2(3)
		s.5 am. (10.3.1992) (*retrosp.*)	20, s.1(1)(5)
		s.6A added	SI 3158, reg.2(4)
		s.9(2)(3) replaced by s.9(2)	SI 3158, reg.3(1)
		s.9(5)(b) rev.	SI 3158, reg.3(2)
		ss.16,21,22(1)(3A)(5),42, 43 mod.	SI 3152, Pt.IV
		s.24(3) am.	SI 1917, art.2(a)
		ss.24(3),69(2) am.	SI 1907,1917
		s.36 am. (10.3.1992) (*retrosp.*)	20, s.1(2)(5)
		s.36(2) am. (*prosp.*)	48, s.1(5), Sch.1, para.9

Year and Chap. or No. of Measure	Short title	How affected	1992, Chapter of Act or Number of Measure or Statutory Instrument
1979—*cont.*			
		s.41A(7)(d) rep. (*prosp.*)	48, ss.1(5),82, Sch.1, para.10(1), Sch.18, Pt.I, Note 3
		s.49(1)(e) subst. (*prosp.*)	48, s.1(5), Sch.1, para.11(1)
		s.52 rep. (*prosp.*)	48, s.82, Sch.18, Pt.I, Note 4
		s.54(1) am. (1.12.1992, 1.1.1993)	48, s.1(5), Sch.1, para.12
		s.55(1) am. (1.12.1992, 1.1.1993)	48, s.1(5), Sch.1, para.13
		s.62(1) am. (10.3.1992) (*retrosp.*)	20, s.1(4)(5)
		s.69(2) am.	SI 1917, art.2(b)
		Sch.1, Table subst. (10.3.1992) (*retrosp.*)	20, s.1(3)(5), Sch.
c.5	Hydrocarbon Oil Duties Act 1979	s.1(4) (defn. of "heavy oil") appl.	48, s.53(2) (adding 1988 c.1 s.158(2A))
		s.6(1) am. (10-3-1992) (*retrosp.*)	20, s.3(1)(5)
		ss.9(4),15(1),17(1),18(1), 19(3),19A(1),20(1) mod.	SI 3152, Pt.IV
		s.11(1) am. (10-3-1992) (*retrosp.*)	20, s.3(2)(5)
		s.13A(1) am. (10.3.1992) (*retrosp.*)	20, s.3(3)(5)
		s.14(1) am. (10.3.1992) (*retrosp.*)	20, s.3(4)(5)
c.6	Matches and Mechanical Lighters Duties Act 1979	rep. (1.1.1993)	48, ss.6(1)(2),82, Sch.18, Pt.II
c.7	Tobacco Products Duty Act 1979	s.5(1)(b) am.	48, s.8(a)
		s.5(1A) added	48, s.8(b)
		Sch.1, Table subst. (10-3-1992) (*retrosp.*)	20, s.2(1)(2)
c.10	Public Lending Right Act 1979	trans.of functions	SI 1311, art.3(1), Sch.1, Pt.I
c.14	Capital Gains Tax Act 1979	rep. (saving)	12, s.290, Sch.11, para.24(2), Sch.12
		am. (*retrosp.*)	48, s.48 (adding s.269C to 1970 c.10)
		s.4(2) mod.	SI 511, reg.9, Sch.2
		ss.19-43 (Pt.II)(Ch.II) appl.	SI 58, art.9, Sch.2, para.8(1)
		s.21(4) mod.	SI 58, art.9, Sch.2, para.2
		s.21(7) excl.	SI 58, art.9, Sch.2, para.2
		s.29A appl.	SI 58, art.18(4)
		s.31(1) excl.	SI 58, art.9, Sch.2, para.3
		s.32(1) appl.(mods.)	SI 58, art.9, Sch.2, para.5(2)
		s.32(1)(a)(b) mod.	SI 58, art.9, Sch.2, paras.4,5(1)
		s.33(1)(2) excl.	SI 58, art.9, Sch.2, para.6

Year and Chap. or No. of Measure	Short title	How affected	1992, Chapter of Act or Number of Measure or Statutory Instrument
1979—*cont.*			
		s.34 mod.	48, s.77, Sch.17, paras.6(2)(5),7
		s.35 appl.	SI 58, art.24(3)
		s.40(2) appl.(mods.)	SI 58, art.9, Sch.2, para.7
		s.41(2) appl.(mods.)	SI 58, art.9, Sch.2, para.7
		s.43(4) appl.(mods.)	SI 58, art.9, Sch.2, para.8(1)
		s.45(2) mod.	SI 511, reg.9, Sch.2
		s.85(1)(c) added (*retrosp.*)	48, s.35(2)
		s.88(2)-(5) appl. (*retrosp.*)	48, ss.47,48 (adding 1970 c.10 s.269B, 269D)
		s.108(4) appl.(mods.)	SI 58, art.9, Sch.2, para.9
		s.111A excl.	SI 58, art.9, Sch.2, para.10
		s.113 excl.	SI 58, art.9, Sch.2, para.11
		ss.115-119 mod.	48, s.77, Sch.17, paras.3, 7
		ss.115-121 excl.	SI 58, art.9, Sch.2, para.10
		s.122(3) excl.	SI 58, art.11(3)
		ss.143A,143B added (*prosp.*)	48, s.56, Sch.9, para.20(1)
		s.149B(6)(a) am. (*prosp.*)	44, s.11(2), Sch.8, Pt.I, para.1(1)(2)(7)
		Sch.1, para.5(2) am.	6, s.4, Sch.2, para.52
		Sch.1, para.5(2) am. (NI)	9, s.4, Sch.2, para.20(a) (b)
		Sch.3 appl.	SI 58, art.26
		Sch.3, para.2(2) appl.(mods.)	SI 58, art.26
c.17	Vaccine Damage Payments Act 1979	s.1(4) am.	6, s.4, Sch.2, para.53
		s.1(4) am. (NI)	9, s.4, Sch.2, para.21
		s.6(4) saved (NI)	8, s.77(3)(d)
		s.12(2) am.	6, s.4, Sch.2, para.54
c.18	Social Security Act 1979	s.2 rep.	6, s.3, Sch.1
		ss.4,5 rep.	6, s.3, Sch.1
		ss.9(1),10 rep.	6, s.3, Sch.1
		s.9(2) rep. (NI)	9, s.3, Sch.1
		ss.14,15 rep.	6, s.3, Sch.1
		ss.19,20(3) rep.	6, s.3, Sch.1
		Sch.1 rep.	6, s.3, Sch.1
		Sch.2 rep.	6, s.3, Sch.1
		Sch.3, paras.4-8 rep.	6, s.3, Sch.1
		Sch.3, paras.10,11 rep.	6, s.3, Sch.1
		Sch.3, para.13 rep.in pt.	6, s.3, Sch.1
		Sch.3, paras.14,15 rep.	6, s.3, Sch.1
		Sch.3, para.23 rep.	6, s.3, Sch.1
		Sch.3, para.29 rep.	6, s.3, Sch.1
		Sch.3, paras.31,32 rep.	6, s.3, Sch.1
c.33	Land Registration (Scotland) Act 1979	appt. day(s) for spec. provns. (1.10.1992) (Clackmannan)	SI 815, art.2
		ss.2(1)(2),3(3) appt. day(s) for (1.4.1993)	SI 2060, art.2

Year and Chap. or No. of Measure	Short title	How affected	1992, Chapter of Act or Number of Measure or Statutory Instrument
1979—*cont.*			
c.34	Credit Unions Act 1974	s.31(1) am. (1.1.1993)	SI 3218, reg.82(1), Sch.10, Pt.I, para.9
c.36	Nurses, Midwives and Health Visitors Act 1979	s.1(2)-(7) replaced (*prosp.*)	16, s.1(1)
		s.2(3) am. (*prosp.*)	16, s.16(1), Sch.2, para.3
		s.3(3) am. (*prosp.*)	16, s.3(a)
		s.3(3) rep.in pt. (*prosp.*)	16, ss.3(b),16(2), Sch.3
		s.4(3)(b) rep. (*prosp.*)	16, ss.10,16(2), Sch.3
		s.5(2)-(10) subst. (*prosp.*)	16, s.4
		s.6(1)(a) am. (*prosp.*)	16, s.5(2)
		s.6(1)(b) am. (*prosp.*)	16, s.16(1), Sch.2, para.4
		s.6(1)(da) added (*prosp.*)	16, s.5(3)
		s.6(1)(e) rep. (*prosp.*)	16, ss.5(4),16(2), Sch.3
		s.6(2) am. (*prosp.*)	16, s.5(5)
		ss.7-9 rep. (*prosp.*)	16, ss.6,16(2), Sch.3
		s.12(1)(ba)(bb) added (*prosp.*)	16, s.7(2)
		s.12(2) am. (*prosp.*)	16, ss.7(3),8(2)
		s.12(3) am. (*prosp.*)	16, s.8(3)(a)
		s.12(3) renumbered part (3A) (*prosp.*)	16, s.8(3)(b)
		s.12(6) added (*prosp.*)	16, s.7(4)
		s.12A added (*prosp.*)	16, s.9
		s.13(1) am. (*prosp.*)	16, s.7(5)
		s.15(2) am. (*prosp.*)	16, s.11
		s.16(2)(b) am. (*prosp.*)	16, s.16(1), Sch.2, para.5
		s.16(5) added (*prosp.*)	16, s.12
		s.17(2) rep. (*prosp.*)	16, s.16(2), Sch.3
		s.17(3) am. (*prosp.*)	16, s.16(1), Sch.2, para.6
		s.17(4) rep.in pt. (*prosp.*)	16, s.16(2), Sch.3
		s.19(3)(a) rep. (*prosp.*)	16, ss.13(2)(a),16(2), Sch.3
		s.19(3)(d) added (*prosp.*)	16, ss.13(2)(b),16(2), Sch.3
		s.19(4) rep. (*prosp.*)	16, ss.13(3),16(2), Sch.3
		s.20(5) am. (*prosp.*)	16, s.16(1), Sch.2, para.7
		s.22(3A) added (*prosp.*)	16, s.14
		s.23(1) (defn. of "elected members") am. (*prosp.*)	16, s.16(1), Sch.2, para.8(2)
		s.23(1) defn(s). added (*prosp.*)	16, s.16(1), Sch.2, para.8(3)
		s.23(2) rep.in pt. (*prosp.*)	16, s.16(2), Sch.3
		Sch.1 subst. (*prosp.*)	16, s.1(2), Sch.1
		Sch.1, para.2(1) excl.	16, s.15(2)
		Sch.1, para.2(2) excl.	16, s.15(1)
		Sch.2, paras.1-4 rep. (*prosp.*)	16, s.16(2), Sch.3
		Sch.2, paras.6-8 rep. (*prosp.*)	16, s.16(2), Sch.3
		Sch.6, para.1 am. (*prosp.*)	16, s.16(1), Sch.2, para.9(2)
		Sch.6, para.1 rep.in pt. (*prosp.*)	16, s.16(2), Sch.3
		Sch.6, para.2, Table am. (*prosp.*)	16, s.16(1), Sch.2, para.9(3)

Year and Chap. or No. of Measure	Short title	How affected	1992, Chapter of Act or Number of Measure or Statutory Instrument
1979—*cont.*			
		Sch.6, para.2, Table , Column 1 rep.in pt. (*prosp.*)	16, s.16(2), Sch.3
		Sch.6, para.2A added (*prosp.*)	16, s.16(1), Sch.2, para.9(4)
		Sch.6, para.3(a) am. (*prosp.*)	16, s.16(1), Sch.2, para.9(5)
		Sch.6, para.4 am. (*prosp.*)	16, s.16(1), Sch.2, para.9(6)
c.38	Estate Agents Act 1979	s.24(1) rep.	53, s.18(2), Sch.4, Pt.I
c.41	Pneumoconiosis etc. (Workers' Compensation) Act 1979	s.2(3) (defns. of "death benefit" and "disablement benefit") am.	6, s.4, Sch.2, para.55(1) (2)
		s.4(3) am.	6, s.4, Sch.2, para.56
		s.10(2) am.	6, s.4, Sch.2, para.57
c.43	Crown Agents Act 1979	s.8(5) am. (1.1.1993)	SI 3218, reg.82(1), Sch.10, Pt.I, para.10
		Sch.1, para.15(2)(b) am.	52, s.300(2), Sch.2, para.26
c.46	Ancient Monuments and Archaeological Areas Act 1979	mod.	SI 1732, art.3(1)
		s.50 mod.	SI 1732, art.3(1)
		s.50 ext.	SI 1732, art.3(1)(a)
		s.50(4)(a) mod.	SI 1732, art.3(2)
		s.55(6)(b) am.	53, s.18(1), Sch.3, para.12
		Sch.1, para.2 mod.	SI 3138, Sch.2, para.1(1)
c.47	Finance (No.2) Act 1979	s.17 rep.	12, s.290, Sch.12
c.53	Charging Orders Act 1979	power to appl.	14, s.14(3), Sch.4, para.19(2)
c.55	Justices of the Peace Act 1979	trans.of functions	SI 709, art.2(1)
		defn. of "inner London area" appl.	14, s.46(4)
		s.38(4) am.	SI 709, art.2(4)(a)
		s.38(4) rep.in pt.	SI 709, art.2(5)
		s.58(2)(b) am.	6, s.4, Sch.2, para.58
		s.65 am.	14, s.117(1), Sch.13, para.48
		Sch.1 am.	SI 709, art.2(4)(a)
c.58	Isle of Man Act 1979	Sch.1, paras.34,35 rep. (1.1.1993)	48, s.82, Sch.18, Pt.II
c.60	Zimbabwe Act 1979	Sch.2, para.3 trans.of functions	SI 709, art.4(1)(b)(ii)
		Sch.2, para.3 am.	SI 709, art.4(2)
1980			
c.9	Reserve Forces Act 1980	s.7 rep.	39, s.3(1)
		s.10(5) appl.(mods.)	39, s.3(2)
		ss.24,25 appl.(mods.)	39, s.3(2)
		s.44 appl.(mods.)	39, s.3(2)(3)
		s.139(1) appl.(mods.)	39, s.3(2)
		s.139(2) rep.	39, s.3(1)
		ss.140-144 appl.(mods.)	39, s.3(2)
		Sch.9, para.15 rep.	52, s.300(1), Sch.1

Year and Chap. or No. of Measure	Short title	How affected	1992, Chapter of Act or Number of Measure or Statutory Instrument
1980—*cont.*			
c.17	National Heritage Act 1980	trans.of functions	SI 1311, art.3(1), Sch.1, Pt.I
		s.2(1) am.	SI 1311, art.12(2), Sch.2, para.5(2)(a)(4)
		ss.4(3),5(3) am.	SI 1311, art.12(2), Sch.2, para.5(2)(b)
		ss.7(1)(2),8(1) am.	SI 1311, art.12(2), Sch.2, para.5(2)(a)
		s.9(1)-(6) am.	SI 1311, art.12(2), Sch.2, para.5(2)(a)-(d)(4)
		s.10(1)-(3) am.	SI 1311, art.12(2), Sch.2, para.5(2)(a)(4)
		s.12(2) am.	SI 1311, art.12(2), Sch.2, para.5(2)(a)
		s.14(1) am.	SI 1311, art.12(2), Sch.2, para.5(2)(e)
		s.16(1) rep.in pt.	44, ss.10(1)(a),11(3), Sch.9
		s.16(1) am.	44, s.10(1)(b)
		s.16(1)(2)(e)(3)-(5) am.	SI 1311, art.12(2), Sch.2, para.5(2)(b)(d)(3)
		s.16(2) am.	44, s.10(1)
		s.16A added	44, s.10(2)
		s.16A(1)(3) am.	SI 1311, art.12(2), Sch.2, para.5(5)
		s.18(2) (defn. of "the Ministers") rep.	SI 1311, art.12(2), Sch.2, para.5(2)
		Sch.1, paras.5(2),6,7(4) am.	SI 1311, art.12(2), Sch.2, para.5(2)(a)
c.20	Education Act 1980	s.7(6) rep.	53, s.18(2), Sch.4, Pt.I
		s.8(5)(6) replaced (by subss.(5)(5A)(5B)(6)) (*prosp.*)	38, s.21(7), Sch.4, para.4(1)
		s.9(2) am. (*prosp.*)	38, s.21(7), Sch.4, para.4(2)
		s.13 appl.(mods.)	13, s.59(2)(b)
		s.13(1A) added (1.8.1993)	13, s.12(2)
		s.16(1)-(3B) appl.(mods.)	13, s.59(2)(b)
		s.22(3B) added (*prosp.*)	13, s.93(1), Sch.8, Pt.I, para.17
c.26	British Aerospace Act 1980	s.12(2) am.	12, s.290, Sch.10, para.4
c.30	Social Security Act 1980	s.2 rep.	6, s.3, Sch.1
		s.3(1)-(3)(11) rep.	6, s.3, Sch.1
		s.4(3)(5)(6) rep.	6, s.3, Sch.1
		s.5(1) rep.	6, s.3, Sch.1
		s.6(2)(4) rep.	6, s.3, Sch.1
		s.9(1)(2) rep.	6, s.3, Sch.1
		s.9(3)(4) rep.in pt.	6, s.3, Sch.1
		s.9(3)(4) rep. (NI)	9, s.3, Sch.1
		s.9(5)(7) rep.	6, s.3, Sch.1
		s.10 rep. (NI)	9, s.3, Sch.1
		s.10(1)-(5) rep. (EWS)	6, s.3, Sch.1
		s.10(9) rep.in pt. (EWS)	6, s.3, Sch.1

Year and Chap. or No. of Measure	Short title	How affected	1992, Chapter of Act or Number of Measure or Statutory Instrument
1980—*cont.*			
		s.11 rep.	6, s.3, Sch.1
		ss.13,14 rep. (NI)	9, s.3, Sch.1
		s.13(1)-(3) rep. (EWS)	6, s.3, Sch.1
		s.13(5)(6) rep. (EWS)	6, s.3, Sch.1
		s.14 rep. (EWS)	6, s.3, Sch.1
		ss.17,18 rep.	6, s.3, Sch.1
		s.19(3) rep.	6, s.3, Sch.1
		s.21(3) am.	6, s.4, Sch.2, para.59
		Sch.1 rep.	6, s.3, Sch.1
		Sch.2, para.21 rep.	6, s.3, Sch.1
		Sch.3 rep. (exc. Pt.II) (N.I.)	6, s.3, Sch.1
		Sch.3, Pt.II rep. (NI)	9, s.3, Sch.1
		Sch.4, para.10 rep.	6, s.3, Sch.1
		Sch.4, para.14 rep.	6, s.3, Sch.1
c.39	Social Security (No.2) Act 1980	rep.	6, s.3, Sch.1
c.42	Employment Act 1980	ss.1-5 rep.	52, s.300(1), Sch.1
		ss.15,16 rep.	52, s.300(1), Sch.1
		s.19 rep.	52, s.300(1), Sch.1
		s.20(1) rep.in pt.	52, s.300(1), Sch.1
		Sch.1, paras.2-7 rep.	52, s.300(1), Sch.1
		Sch.1, para.17 rep.in pt.	52, s.300(1), Sch.1
		Sch.1, para.19 rep.	52, s.300(1), Sch.1
		Sch.1, para.21(b) rep.	52, s.300(1), Sch.1
		Sch.1, para.24 rep.	52, s.300(1), Sch.1
c.43	Magistrates' Courts Act 1980	saved (*prosp.*)	40, s.110(1)
		appl. (*prosp.*)	41, s.71(3)
		s.17 saved	11, s.1(2)(b)
		s.22(12) added	11, s.2(2)
		s.32 ext. (extended to Is. of Man)	SI 2670, reg.2
		s.32 ext.(mods.) (Guernsey) (1.2.1993)	SI 3202, art.2(b)
		s.33(1)(a) am.	11, s.2(3)(a)
		s.33(3) added	11, s.2(3)(b)
		s.59 excl. (*prosp.*)	56, s.1, Sch.1, Pt.II, para.13 (adding.1972, c.18, s.27C)
		s.59(4) appl.(mods.) (*prosp.*)	56, s.1, Sch.1, Pt.II, para.13 (adding. 1972, c.18, s.27C)
		s.59(8)(10)(11) trans.of functions & am.	SI 709, art.3(2), Sch.2
		s.60(1) mod. (*prosp.*)	56, s.1, Sch.1, Pt.II, para.7 (adding subs (3A) to s.5 of 1972 c.18)
		s.65(1)(m) rep.	6, s.3, Sch.1
		s.65(1)(n) added	6, s.4, Sch.2, para.60
		s.68 trans.of functions	SI 709, art.2(1), Sch.1
		s.68 am.	SI 709, art.2(3), Sch.1

Year and Chap. or No. of Measure	Short title	How affected	1992, Chapter of Act or Number of Measure or Statutory Instrument
1980—*cont.*			
		s.77(1) ext.	SI 130, reg.8(3)
		s.77(1) ext.	SI 190, art.5(3)
		s.78 ext.	SI 130, reg.8(3)
		s.78 ext.	SI 190, art.5(3)
		s.94A(1)(2)(6) trans.of functions & am.	SI 709, art.3(2), Sch.2
		s.125(3) appl.	SI 613, reg.48(6)
		s.127 excl.	SI 2372, reg.90
		s.127(1) excl.	SI 613, reg.34(3)
		s.127(1) excl.	SI 975, art.16(7)
		s.127(1) excl.	SI 1302, art.17(7)
		s.137(4) trans.of functions	SI 709, art.2(1), Sch.1
		s.144 saved (*prosp.*)	56, s.1, Sch.1, Pt.I, para.4 (adding subs (2) to s.7 of 1920 c.33)
		s.144 ext. (*prosp.*)	56, s.1, Sch.1, Pt.II, para.11 (adding 1972, c.18, s.18(1A))
		s.144 ext. (*prosp.*)	56, s.1, Sch.1, Pt.II, para.18 (adding 1972, c.18,s.38A)
		s.150(1) (defn. of "court maintenance order") ext.	5, s.106(5)
		Sch.1 saved	11, s.1(2)(b)
		Sch.2, para.3 added	11, s.2(1)
		Sch.6, Pt.I am.	SI 842, art.2, Sch.
		Sch.7, para.108 rep. (*prosp.*)	56, s.2(2), Sch.3
		Sch.7, para.135 rep.	6, s.3, Sch.1
c.44	Education (Scotland) Act 1980	appl.	37, s.36(3)
		s.1(1) am. (1-4-1993)	37, s.2(a)
		s.1(2A) added (1-4-1993)	37, s.2(b)
		s.1(5)(b) (defn. of "further education") appl. (*prosp.*)	37, s.7, Sch.1, para.2(2) (a)
		s.1(5)(b) (defn. of "futher education") appl. (*prosp.*)	37, s.8(3)
		s.1(5)(b) (defn. of "further education") appl.	37, s.12(2)(a)
		s.1(5)(b) (defn. of "futher education") appl. (1-4-1993)	37, s.22(3)(b)
		s.3(1) rep.in pt.	37, s.62(3), Sch.10
		s.3(6)(a) rep.in pt.	37, s.62(3), Sch.10
		s.7(1)-(3) rep.	37, s.62(3), Sch.10
		s.7(7)(8) rep.	37, s.62(3), Sch.10
		s.14ZA added (1-4-1993)	37, s.62(2), Sch.9, para.7(2)
		s.17(1)(3) am. (1-4-1993)	37, s.62(2), Sch.9, para.7(3)(a)
		s.17(6) added (1-4-1993)	37, s.62(2), Sch.9, para.7(3)(b)
		s.28E(7) rep.	53, s.18(2), Sch.4, Pt.I

Year and Chap. or No. of Measure	Short title	How affected	1992, Chapter of Act or Number of Measure or Statutory Instrument
1980—*cont.*			
		ss.28I–28K added (*prosp.*)	38, s.17
		s.65B(6A) added (1-4-1993)	37, s.62(2), Sch.9, para.7(4)
		s.66 am. (1-4-1993)	37, s.62(2), Sch.9, para.7(5)
		s.68 am. (1-4-1993)	37, s.62(2), Sch.9, para.7(6)(a)(b)
		s.77 rep.	37, s.62(3), Sch.10
		s.84 am.	SI 3216, Sch.
		s.135(1) (defns. of "central institution" and "self-governing school") appl.	37, s.62(2), Sch.9, para.6(c) (amending 1978 c.44,s.29(2)(c))
		s.135(1) (defn. of "educational establishment") am.	37, s.62(2), Sch.9, para.7(7)
		s.135(1) (defn. of "educational establishments") appl.	37, s.62(2), Sch.9, para.12(2) (subst,s.1(3)(b) of 1990 c.6)
		s.135(1) (defn. of "educational establishment") appl. (1-4-1993)	37, s.62(2), Sch.9, para.12(3) (amending sch.2,para.2(2) of 1990 c.6)
		s.135(1) rep.in pt.	37, s.62(3), Sch.10
c.45	Water (Scotland) Act 1980	s.2 appl.(mods.)	SI 30(L), art.3, Sch.2
		s.3 (defn. of "water authority") appl.	14, s.99(1)
		s.9(6) rep. (*prosp.*)	14, s.117(2), Sch.14
		s.9A am. (*prosp.*)	14, s.107, Sch.11, Pt.IV, para.29(a)
		s.9A(a)(b) replaced (by paras.(a)-(c))	14, s.107, Sch.11, Pt.IV, para.29(b)
		s.10(3)(4) appl.(mods.)	SI 30(L), art.3, Sch.2
		s.35(1) rep.in pt. (*prosp.*)	14, s.107, Sch.11, Pt.IV, para.30(a)
		s.35(2) am. (*prosp.*)	14, s.107, Sch.11, Pt.IV, para.30(b)
		s.35(5) subst. (*prosp.*)	14, s.107, Sch.11, Pt.IV, para.30(c)
		s.40 appl. (*prosp.*)	14, s.99(2)(c)
		s.40 cont.	14, s.107, Sch.11, Pt.I, para.12
		s.40(2)(a) am.	14, s.107, Sch.11, Pt.IV, para.31(a)
		s.40(4) am.	14, s.107, Sch.11, Pt.IV, para.31(b)
		s.41(2)(2A) rep. (*prosp.*)	14, s.117(2), Sch.14
		s.41A added (*prosp.*)	14, s.107, Sch.11, Pt.IV, para.32
		s.46(2) am. (*prosp.*)	14, s.107, Sch.11, Pt.IV, para.33
		s.49 subst. (*prosp.*)	14, s.107, Sch.11, Pt.IV, para.34
		s.54(3)(b) rep.in pt. (*prosp.*)	14, s.117(2), Sch.14

Year and Chap. or No. of Measure	Short title	How affected	1992, Chapter of Act or Number of Measure or Statutory Instrument
1980—*cont.*			
		s.56A added (*prosp.*)	14, s.107, Sch.11, Pt.IV, para.35
		s.58(3) am. (*prosp.*)	14, s.107, Sch.11, Pt.IV, para.36
		s.61(1)(b) am.	14, s.107, Sch.11, Pt.IV, para.37
		s.109(1) (defn. of "the 1992 Act") added	14, s.107, Sch.11, Pt.IV, para.38(a)
		s.109(1) (defn. of "apportionment note") am. (*prosp.*)	14, s.107, Sch.11, Pt.IV, para.38(b)
		s.109(1) (defn. of "fire authority") added	14, s.107, Sch.11, Pt.IV, para.38(d)
		s.109(1) (defn. of "part residential subjects") am. (*prosp.*)	14, s.107, Sch.11, Pt.IV, para.38(e)
		s.109(1) (defn. of "prescribed") am.	14, s.107, Sch.11, Pt.IV, para.38(f)
		s.109(1) (defn. of "council water charge") added	14, s.107, Sch.11, Pt.IV, para.38(c)
		s.109(1) rep.in pt. (*prosp.*)	14, s.117(2), Sch.14
		Sch.4, paras.2,10(3)(4) appl.(mods.)	SI 393(L), art.3, Sch.2
		Sch.4, paras.2,10(3)(4) appl.(mods.)	SI 998(L), art.3, Sch.2
c.46	Solicitor (S) Act 1980	s.35(2) am. (1.1.1993)	SI 3218, reg.82(1), Sch.10, Pt.I, para.11
		s.44(1)(b)(c) am.	SI 2890, reg.12(2)
		s.44(5) (defn. of "authorised insurer") added	SI 2890, reg.12(3)
c.48	Finance Act 1980	s.61(2) rep.	12, s.290, Sch.12
		ss.77-84 rep.	12, s.290, Sch.12
		s.117 rep.	12, s.290, Sch.12
		Sch.17 appl.	12, s.197(1)(b)
		Sch.18 rep.	12, s.290, Sch.12
		Sch.19, para.5(4) rep.in pt.	6, s.3, Sch.1
c.51	Housing Act 1980	Sch.22 am. para.2.	53, s.18(1), Sch.3, para.13
c.53	Health Services Act 1980	Sch.1, para.25 rep.	52, s.300(1), Sch.1
c.65	Local Government, Planning and Land Act 1980	excl.	v, s.61(1)
		s.2(7)(aa)(ii) subst.	14, s.117(1), Sch.13, para.49
		ss.5-23 (Pt.III) (defn. of "local authority or development body") appl. (14-2-1993)	19, s.10(3)
		s.7(1) restr.	SI 582, reg.3
		s.7(1B) am. (14-2-1993)	19, s.11, Sch.1, para.1
		s.9(2) am. (*prosp.*)	19, s.11, Sch.1, para.2(1)
		s.9(4)(a) am. (14-3-1994)	19, s.11, Sch.1, para.2(2)
		s.9(6) am. (14-3-1994)	19, s.11, Sch.1, para.2(3)
		s.13(2)(c) subst. (*prosp.*)	19, s.11, Sch.1, para.3

Year and Chap. or No. of Measure	Short title	How affected	1992, Chapter of Act or Number of Measure or Statutory Instrument
1980—*cont.*			
		s.13(6) rep. (*prosp.*)	19, s.29, Sch.4, Pt.I
		s.16(1) am. (*prosp.*)	19, s.11, Sch.1, para.4(1)
		s.16(1A) added (*prosp.*)	19, s.11, Sch.1, para.4(2)
		s.16(2)(3) rep. (*prosp.*)	19, s.29, Sch.4, Pt.I
		s.18(2B) am. (*prosp.*)	19, s.11, Sch.1, para.5
		s.19A(1) am. (4-1-1993)	19, s.11, Sch.1, para.6(a)
		s.19A(1)(a) am. (4-1-1993)	19, s.11, Sch.1, para.6(b)
		s.19A(1)(f) rep.in pt. (*prosp.*)	19, s.29, Sch.4, Pt.I
		s.19B(5A) added (4-1-1993)	19, s.11, Sch.1, para.7(1)
		s.19B(6) am. (4-1-1993)	19, s.11, Sch.1, para.7(2)
		s.20(2) am. (14-3-1994)	19, s.11, Sch.1, para.8
		s.23(1) am. (*prosp.*)	19, s.11, Sch.1, para.9
		s.46 rep.	14, s.117(2), Sch.14
		s.138 appl.	v, s.64
		s.154(1) am.	6, s.4, Sch.2, para.61
c.66	Highways Act 1980	mod.	3, s.3, Sch.3, para.5(3)
		defn. of "special road" appl.	3, s.39(1)
		defn. of "trunk road" appl.	3, s.39(1)
		defn. of "bridleway" appl.	3, s.39(1)
		defn. of "cycle track" appl.	3, s.39(1)
		defn. of "footpath" appl.	3, s.39(1)
		defn. of "highway" appl.	3, s.39(1)
		defns. of "bridleway" and "footpath" appl. (31-1-1993)	42, s.48(8)
		defn. of "bridleway" appl.	42, s.63, Sch.3, para.7(2) (adding defn. of "bridleway" to 1964 c.40, s.57)
		defn. of "footpath" appl.	42, s.63, Sch.3, para.7(3) (adding defn. of "footpath" to 1964 c.40, s.57)
		s.6 restr.	3, s.15(6)
		s.12(3) appl.	3, s.3, Sch.3, para.6(3)
		s.36(2)(e) added (31-1-1993)	42, s.64(3)
		s.36(2)(c) rep.in pt. (31-1-1993)	42, ss.64(2),68(1), Sch.4, Pt.I
		s.36(3A) added (31-1-1993)	42, s.64(4)
		ss.62-105 (Pt.V) ext.	3, s.32(2)(a)
		s.62(3)(fg) added	30, s.1(1)
		ss.90G-90I added	30, s.1(2), Sch.1
		s.118(5) am. (31.1.1993)	42, s.47, Sch.2, para.2(2)
		s.118(7) am. (31.1.1993)	42, s.47, Sch.2, para.2(3)
		s.118A added (31.1.1993)	42, s.47, Sch.2, para.3
		s.119A added (31.1.1993)	42, s.47, Sch.2, para.4
		s.120(1)-(3) am. (31.1.1993)	42, s.47, Sch.2, para.5(1)-(4)
		s.120(3A) added (31.1.1993)	42, s.47, Sch.2, para.5(5)

Year and Chap. or No. of Measure	Short title	How affected	1992, Chapter of Act or Number of Measure or Statutory Instrument
1980—*cont.*			
		s.120(4)(5) am. (31.1.1993)	42, s.47, Sch.2, para.5(6)(7)
		s.121(1)-(4) am. (31.1.1993)	42, s.47, Sch.2, para.6(2)-(5)
		s.239(3)(4)(c) appl.	3, s.32(2)
		s.250(4)(5) appl.(mods.)	3, s.2, Sch.2, Pt.II, para.1(3)(a)
		s.251 appl.(mods.)	3, s.2, Sch.2, Pt.II, para.1(3)(b)
		s.251 appl.(mods.)	xiv, s.5(2)
		s.252 appl.(mods.)	3, s.2, Sch.2, Pt.II, para.1(3)(c)
		s.261 mod.	3, s.2, Sch.2, Pt.II, para.6
		s.293(1) am. (31.1.1993)	42, s.47, Sch.2, para.7
		s.325(2)(a) am. (31.1.1993)	42, s.47, Sch.2, para.8
		s.329 (defns. of "street", "bridleway", "cycle track" and "footpath") appl.	vii, s.2(1)
		s.329 (defns. of "bridleway", "cycle track" and "footpath") appl.	viii, s.2(1)
		s.329 (defn. of "traffic calming works") added	30, s.1(3)
		s.329(1) (defns. of "rail crossing diversion order" and "rail crossing extinguishment order") added (31.1.1993)	42, s.47, Sch.2, para.9
		Sch.6, Pt.I, para.3(3)(a) (i) replaced (by subparas.(i)(ia))	14, s.117(1), Sch.13, para.50
		Sch.6, para.1(1)(2)(3A) (3B) am. (31.1.1993)	42, s.47, Sch.2, para.10(2)(a)(b)(c)
		Sch.6, para.2A(1) am. (31.1.1993)	42, s.47, Sch.2, para.10(3)
		Sch.6, para.3(2) am. (31.1.1993)	42, s.47, Sch.2, para.10(4)(a)(b)
		Sch.19, Pt.II appl.(mods.)	3, s.2, Sch.2, Pt.II, para.1(3)(a)
		Sch.24, para.14 rep.	3, s.40, Sch.5
c.i	Ardveenish Harbour Order Confirmation Act 1980	Sch. am. (Ardveenish O s.3, Proviso (iv)(v) subst.)	SI 1975(L), art.9(1), Sch.1
		Sch. am. (Ardveenish O ss.11(2),13(2),14(2) am.)	SI 1975(L), art.9(1), Sch.1
		Sch. am. (Ardveenish O am.)	SI 1975(L), art.9(2)
		Sch. rep.in pt. (Ardveenish O s.2 rep.in pt.)	SI 1975(L), art.9(3), Sch.2
		Sch. rep.in pt. (Ardveenish O ss.18,26 rep.)	SI 1975(L), art.9(3), Sch.2
c.iii	Forth Ports Authority (No.2) Order Confirmation Act 1980	rep. (*prosp.*)	SI 546(L), art.2, Sch. (Forth Ports Authority Scheme 1992. para.12, sch., Pt.II)

Year and Chap. or No. of Measure	Short title	How affected	1992, Chapter of Act or Number of Measure or Statutory Instrument
1980—*cont.*			
c.xi	West Midlands County Council Act 1980	s.97 am.	SI 1831(L), art.2
		ss.116(2),117(2) rep.in pt.	SI 117, art.19(1), Sch.
c.xiii	Cheshire County Council Act 1980	s.22 rep.	SI 117, art.19(1), Sch.
		ss.108(2),109(2) rep.in pt.	SI 117, art.19(1), Sch.
c.xxxvii	South Yorkshire Act 1980	s.20 rep.	SI 117, art.19(1), Sch.
		ss.105(2),106(2) rep.in pt.	SI 117, art.19(1), Sch.
1981			
c.1	Social Security (Contributions) Act 1981	rep.	6, s.3, Sch.1
c.3	Gas Levy Act 1981	s.2(4A) added	SI 450, reg.2(2)
		s.3(3)(4) am. (temp. until 31.12.1999)	SI 450, reg.2(3)
		s.3(3)(4) am. (1.1.2000)	SI 450, reg.2(4)(a)
		s.7(2) (defn. of "therm") rep. (1.1.2000)	SI 450, reg.2(4)(b)
c.7	Parliamentary Pensions Act 1981	s.2(1)(b) subst. (*temp.*)	SI 1683
		s.2(1)(b) am.	SI 1683
c.14	Public Passenger Vehicles Act 1981	s.24(1)(c) added (31-1- 1993)	42, s.61(2)(a)
		s.24(2) am. (31-1-1993)	42, s.61(2)(b)
		s.25(1) am. (31-1-1993)	42, s.61(3)
		s.27(1) am. (31-1-1993)	42, s.61(4)
		s.46(3) am. (1.4.1993)	13, s.93(1), Sch.8, Pt.II, para.90
		s.60(1)(j) am. (31-1-1993)	42, s.61(5)(a)
		s.60(1)(k) am. (31-1-1993)	42, s.61(5)(b)
		s.60(1B) added (31-1-1993)	42, s.61(6)
c.20	Judicial Pensions Act 1981	ss.13,32 excl.	5, ss.41,43,50-52, Sch.2, para.1(6)
		s.21(1)(c)(ii) am.	SI 360, art.2
		Sch.3, para.10 rep.	6, s.3, Sch.1
c.22	Animal Health Act 1981	defns. of "animals" and "poultry" mod.	SI 3303, art.2
		s.32 appl. (1.1.1993)	SI 3159, art.2
		s.64A added	SI 3293, reg.2
		s.87(1) mod.	SI 3304, art.1(2)(a)
		s.87(4) (defn. of "poultry") mod.	SI 3304, art.1(2)(b)
c.33	Social Security Act 1981	ss.5,6 rep.	6, s.3, Sch.1
		s.8(2) rep.	6, s.3, Sch.1
		Sch.1, para.3(a) rep.	6, s.3, Sch.1
		Sch.1, paras.6,7 rep.	6, s.3, Sch.1
		Sch.2, para.2 rep.	6, s.3, Sch.1
c.35	Finance Act 1981	s.3 rep. (1.1.1993)	48, s.82, Sch.18, Pt.II
		s.38(3)(4) rep.	12, s.290, Sch.12
		s.57 appl.	12, s.150(4)
		ss.79-91 rep.	12, s.290, Sch.12

Year and Chap. or No. of Measure	Short title	How affected	1992, Chapter of Act or Number of Measure or Statutory Instrument
1981—*cont.*			
		s.135 rep.in pt.	12, s.290, Sch.12
		s.289(4) (defn. of "eligible shares") appl.	12, s.150(1)
		Sch.6, paras.1-3 rev.	SI 3095, Sch.2
		Sch.8, para.2(d) rep.in pt	48, s.82, Sch.18, Pt.I, Note 5
		Sch.8, para.2(d)(ii) rep.	48, s.82, Sch.18, Pt.I, Note 5
c.38	British Telecommunications Act 1981	s.67(4) am. (1.1.1993)	SI 3218, reg.82(1), Sch.10, Pt.I, para.12
		s.82(1) am.	12, s.290, Sch.10, para.5
c.54	Supreme Court Act 1981	s.16 (defn. of "judgment of the Court") appl.	53, s.11(3)
		s.128 (defn. of "trust corporation") am. (*retrosp.*)	41, s.14(1)(2) (adding 1960 c.58 s.21A)
		Sch.5 rep.in pt.	53, s.18(2), Sch.4, Pt.I
c.56	Transport Act 1981	s.1 rcstr. (EWS)	SI 3060, reg.4(2)
		Sch.6, para.4(4)-(7) rep.	42, s.68(1), Sch.4, Pt.II
c.60	Education Act 1981	s.14(2)(aa) added	13, s.93(1), Sch.8, Pt.I, para.18
c.61	British Nationality Act 1981	s.42 saved (12.3.1992) (*retrosp.*)	45, s.1(3)(4)
c.63	Betting and Gaming Duties Act 1981	s.1(2) am.	20, s.5(1)(2)
		s.22(2) am.	SI 2954, art.3(2)
		Sch.3, para.2(1)(a) subst.	48, s.7(1)(2)(4)
		Sch.3, para.12(1) am.	48, s.7(1)(3)(4)
		Sch.4, para.2(2)(b)(i)-(iii)(3)(4) am.	SI 2954, art.3(3)
c.64	New Towns Act 1981	s.78(1) am.	SI 1314, art.3(3), Sch., para.1(c)
		s.80(1)(a) (defn. of "local authority") am.	14, s.117(1), Sch.13, para.51
c.66	Compulsory Purchase (Vesting Declarations) Act 1981	appl.	v, s.4(3)
c.67	Acquisition of Land Act 1981	defn. of "owner" appl.	3, s.39(1)
		appl.(mods.)	13, s.40(6)
		s.4 mod.	3, s.2, Sch.2, Pt.II, para.5
		s.6 appl.	i, s.17(2)
		s.7(1)(a) (defn. of "local authority") am.	14, s.117(1), Sch.13, para.52
		ss.10-15 (Pt.II) appl.(mods.)	v, s.4(1)(a)(b)
		s.23(3)(b) am.	53, s.18(1), Sch.3, para.14
		Sch.2, Pt.II appl.	3, s.2, Sch.2, Pt.II, para.3(1)
		Sch.2, Pt.II appl.	v, s.4(2)
		Sch.2, Pts.II,III appl.	xiv, s.3(3)
		Sch.2, Pt.III appl.(mods.)	3, s.2, Sch.2, Pt.II, para.3(1)

Year and Chap. or No. of Measure	Short title	How affected	1992, Chapter of Act or Number of Measure or Statutory Instrument
1981—*cont.*			
c.69	Wildlife and Countryside Act 1981	s.73(4) rep.	51, s.15(2), Sch.
		Sch.2, Pt.II rev.in pt.	SI 3010, art.2
		Sch.3, Pt.II rev.in pt.	SI 3010, art.3
		Sch.5 am.	SI 2350, reg.2
		Sch.7, paras.8-12 rep.	51, s.15(2), Sch.
		Sch.8 rev.in pt.	SI 2350, reg.3
		Sch.9, Pt.I am.	SI 2674, art.2
		Sch.9, Pts.I,II am.	SI 320, arts.2,3
c.v	Peterhead Harbours Order Confirmation Act 1981	rep.	xii, s.1, Sch. s.63, Sch.2
c.ix	Greater Manchester Act 1981	ss.31,51 rep.	SI 117, art.19(1), Sch.
		ss.179(2),180(2) rep.in pt.	SI 117, art.19(1), Sch.
c.xviii	County of Kent Act 1981	ss.21,22 rep.	SI 117, art.19(1), Sch.
		ss.128(2),129(2) rep.in pt.	SI 117, art.19(1), Sch.
c.xxiii	British Railways Act 1981	s.9(2)-(5) appl.	xi, s.8(3)
c.xxv	East Sussex Act 1981	s.25 rep.	SI 117, art.19(1), Sch.
		s.102(2) rep.in pt.	SI 117, art.19(1), Sch.
c.xxxii	London Transport Act 1981	s.17 incorp.(mods.)	iii, s.29(1)(5)
c.xxxiv	Derbyshire Act 1981	s.20 rep.	SI 117, art.19(1), Sch.
		s.63(2) rep.in pt.	SI 117, art.19(1), Sch.
		Sch.4 rep.in pt.	SI 117, art.19(1), Sch.
c.xxxv	British Railways (No.2) Act 1981	Pt.V appl.(mods.)	SI 1136(L), arts.2(1),9(1), Sch.
1982			
c.2	Social Security (Contributions) Act 1982	rep.	6, s.3, Sch.1
c.9	Agricultural Training Board Act 1982	s.11(3) rep.	52, s.300(1), Sch.1
		s.12(1A) added	52, s.300(2), Sch.2, para.27
		s.12(2) am.	52, s.300(2), Sch.2, para.27
c.10	Industrial Training Act 1982	s.21(1A) added	52, s.300(2), Sch.2, para.28
		s.21(2) am.	52, s.300(2), Sch.2, para.28
		Sch.3 rep. para.2.	53, s.18(2), Sch.4, Pt.I
		Sch.3, para.6 rep.	52, s.300(1), Sch.1
c.16	Civil Aviation Act 1982	s.7(3) rep.	53, s.18(2), Sch.4, Pt.I
		s.17(1)(c) am.	SI 2992, Sch.2, para.4
		s.23(3)(b) am.	SI 3179, Sch.3, para.1
		s.64(2)(d) added	SI 2992, reg.20
		s.69A added	SI 2992, reg.21
		s.70 am.	SI 2992, Sch.2, para.5
		s.75 saved (EWS) (*prosp.*)	42, s.68(2)
		s.84(1)(a) am.	SI 2992, Sch.2, para.6
		s.84(2) am.	SI 2992, Sch.2, para.7
c.23	Oil and Gas (Enterprise) Act 1982	s.23(2) appl.	4, ss.120(2),175(8)(9)
		s.23(2)(6) appl. (NI)	7, s.166(3)
		s.27(3) rep.in pt.	15, ss.3(1)(d),7(2), Sch.2
		s.38(2) ext.	52, s.300(2), Sch.2, para.29(4)

Year and Chap. or No. of Measure	Short title	How affected	1992, Chapter of Act or Number of Measure or Statutory Instrument
1982—*cont.*			
		Sch.3, para.21 rep.	6, s.3, Sch.1
		Sch.3, para.25 rep.	52, s.300(1), Sch.1
		Sch.3, para.40 subst.	52, s.300(2), Sch.2, para.29(2)
		Sch.3, para.44 rep.	6, s.3, Sch.1
		Sch.3, para.45 added	52, s.300(2), Sch.2, para.29(3)
c.24	Social Security and Housing Benefits Act 1982	defn. of "rebate or allowance" appl.	5, s.135(2)(a)(ii)(4)(a)
		ss.1-7 rep.	6, s.3, Sch.1
		s.9 rep.	6, s.3, Sch.1
		ss.17,18 rep.	6, s.3, Sch.1
		ss.22,23,23A rep.	6, s.3, Sch.1
		ss.26,27 rep.	6, s.3, Sch.1
		s.37 rep.	6, s.3, Sch.1
		s.39(1)-(4) rep.	6, s.3, Sch.1
		s.44 rep.	6, s.3, Sch.1
		s.46(2) rep.	6, s.3, Sch.1
		s.48(2) rep.	6, s.3, Sch.1
		Sch.1 rep.	6, s.3, Sch.1
		Sch.2, paras.1-4 rep.	6, s.3, Sch.1
		Sch.4, paras.7-10 rep.	6, s.3, Sch.1
		Sch.4, paras.12,13 rep.	6, s.3, Sch.1
		Sch.4, paras.15-18 rep.	6, s.3, Sch.1
		Sch.4, paras.30-34 rep.	6, s.3, Sch.1
		Sch.4, para.39 rep.	6, s.3, Sch.1
c.27	Civil Jurisdiction and Judgments Act 1982	s.5(1) trans.of functions	SI 709, art.4(6)(a)
		s.5(1)(a)(b) subst.	SI 709, art.4(7)
		s.37(2) rep. (*prosp.*)	56, s.2(2), Sch.3
		Sch.5, para.5(c) am.	6, s.4, Sch.2, para.62
		Sch.8, para.4(1)(c) rep.in pt. (EWS) (*prosp.*)	14, s.117(2), Sch.14
c.30	Local Government (Miscellaneous Provisions) Act 1982	s.33 appl.(mods.)	v, s.59
		Sch.4, para.1(2)(j) subst. (*prosp.*)	41, s.78(1), Sch.6, para.9
c.32	Local Government Finance Act 1982	ss.11-36 (Pt.III) (defn. of "health service bodies") appl.	19, s.1(8)(c)
		ss.11-36 (Pt.III) saved	19, s.5(7)
		ss.11-36 (Pt.III) ext.	19, s.29(1)
		s.15(1) rep.in pt.	19, s.29, Sch.4, Pt.I
		s.15(1)(d) added	19, s.3(1)
		s.18(3) am.	19, s.5(5)
		s.18(5) saved	19, s.6(5)
		s.26(1) ext.	19, s.3(3)
		s.26(4) excl.	19, s.3(3)
c.34	Forfeiture Act 1982	s.4(2) am.	6, s.4, Sch.2, para.63(1)

Year and Chap. or No. of Measure	Short title	How affected	1992, Chapter of Act or Number of Measure or Statutory Instrument
1982—*cont.*			
		s.4(4) am.	6, s.4, Sch.2, para.63(2)
		s.4(5) rep.in pt.	6, s.3, Sch.1
		s.4(5) (defns. of "Commissioner" and "relevant enactment") am.	6, s.4, Sch.2, para.63(3)
c.39	Finance Act 1982	s.80 rep.	12, s.290, Sch.12
		ss.83-88 rep.	12, s.290, Sch.12
		s.87(2) appl.(mods.)	SI 58, art.9, Sch.2, para.12(1)
		s.129 excl.	13, s.88(2)
		s.148 rep.	12, s.290, Sch.12
		Sch.13 rep.	12, s.290, Sch.12
		Sch.18, para.3(2)(a) am.	48, s.74, Sch.15, para.5
c.45	Civic Government (Scotland) Act 1982	s.18(11) rep.	53, s.18(2), Sch.4, Pt.I
		s.119(6)(d) am.	41, s.78(1), Sch.6, para.10(a)
		s.119(6)(d) am. (*prosp.*)	41, s.78(1), Sch.6, para.10(b)
c.46	Employment Act 1982	ss.2-19 rep.	52, s.300(1), Sch.1
		s.21(1) subst.	52, s.300(2), Sch.2, para.30
		s.22(4)(5) rep.	52, s.300(1), Sch.1
		Sch.1 rep.	52, s.300(1), Sch.1
		Sch.2, para.6(1) rep.	52, s.300(1), Sch.1
		Sch.3, paras.10-13 rep.	52, s.300(1), Sch.1
		Sch.3, paras.17-20 rep.	52, s.300(1), Sch.1
		Sch.3, para.24 rep.	52, s.300(1), Sch.1
		Sch.3, para.27(2)(a) rep.	52, s.300(1), Sch.1
		Sch.3, para.27(3)(a) rep.	52, s.300(1), Sch.1
c.47	Duchy of Cornwall Management Act 1982	s.6(4) am. (1.1.1993)	SI 3218, reg.82(1), Sch.10, Pt.I, para.14
c.48	Crimimal Justice Act 1982	s.37 ext. (extended to Is. of Man)	SI 2670, reg.2
		s.37 ext.(mods.) (Guernsey) (1.2.1993)	SI 3202, art.2(a)
c.49	Transport Act 1982	s.70(2)(a)(i) am.	6, s.4, Sch.2, para.64(a)
		s.70(2)(a)(iA) am.	6, s.4, Sch.2, para.64(b)
		s.70(2)(a)(iii) am.	6, s.4, Sch.2, para.64(c)
c.50	Insurance Companies Act 1982	defn. of "insurance company" appl.	5, s.81(3)(i)
		defn. of "insurance company" appl. (NI)	8, s.77(3)(h)
		defn. of "insurance business" appl. (EWS)	33, s.1(2), Sch., para.1 (adding s.15A to 1992 c.5)
		defn. of "insurance company" appl. (*prosp.*)	40, s.86(1)(d)
		s.2 restr. (1.1.1993)	SI 3218, reg.5(1)(d)
		s.2(2) am.	52, s.300(2), Sch.2, para.31
		s.5(2) am.	SI 2890, reg.2(1)
		s.5(3) added	SI 2890, reg.2(2)

Year and Chap. or No. of Measure	Short title	How affected	1992, Chapter of Act or Number of Measure or Statutory Instrument
1982—*cont.*			
		s.13 am. (1.1.1993)	SI 3218, reg.64
		ss.15-71 (Pt.II) restr. (1.1.1993)	SI 3218, reg.65
		s.15(3) am.	52, s.300(2), Sch.2, para.31
		s.49(1) am. (*prosp.*)	40, s.120(1), Sch.21, Pt.I, para.6(1)
		s.49A added (*prosp.*)	40, s.120(1), Sch.21, Pt.I, para.6(2)
		s.51(4A) am.	SI 2890, reg.3
		s.61(2A) added	SI 2890, reg.4
		s.63A added	SI 2890, reg.5
		s.71(3)(b) am.	SI 2890, reg.6
		s.81A defn(s). appl. (*prosp.*)	40, s.57(9)
		s.81A defn(s). appl. (*prosp.*)	40, s.85, Sch.15, Pt.II, para.18(a)
		s.81A(4) rep.in pt. & am.	SI 2890, reg.7(2)
		s.81B(1)(e) added	SI 2890, reg.7(3)
		s.81B(1A) added	SI 2890, reg.7(4)
		s.81C(2)(c) added	SI 2890, reg.7(5)
		s.81CC added	SI 2890, reg.7(6)
		s.83A added	SI 2890, reg.8
		s.87(2)(a) subst.	SI 3179, Sch.3, para.2
		s.94A , inserted by the Insurance Companies (Amdt.) Regs 1990, renumbered as s.94B	SI 2890, reg.9(2)
		s.96(1) (defns. of "claims representative" and "parent undertaking") added	SI 2890, reg.9(3)
		s.96A defn(s). appl. (*prosp.*)	40, s.57(9)
		s.96A defn(s). appl. (*prosp.*)	40, s.85, Sch.15, Pt.II, para.18(a)
		s.96A(1A)(1B) added	SI 2890, reg.9(4)
		s.96B(1)(c) am.	SI 2890, reg.9(5)
c.53	Administration of the Justice Act 1982	s.46(2)(b)(i)(d) rep. (1-1-1993)	42, s.68(1), Sch.4, Pt.I
		s.46(2)(f) rep.	12, s.290, Sch.12
c.iii	Humberside Act 1982	s.74 rep.	SI 117, art.19(1), Sch.
		ss.94(2),95(2) rep.in pt.	SI 117, art.19(1), Sch.
c.iv	County of Avon Act 1982	s.22 rep.	SI 117, art.19(1), Sch.
		ss.58(2),59(2) rep.in pt.	SI 117, art.19(1), Sch.
c.xv	Cumbria Act 1982	s.2(1) rep.in pt.	SI 117, art.19(1), Sch.
		s.13 rep.	SI 117, art.19(1), Sch.
		ss.63(2),64(2) rep.in pt.	SI 117, art.19(1), Sch.
1983			
c.2	Representation of the People Act 1983	s.76(2)(a)(i) am.	SI 706, art.2
		s.76(2)(a)(ii) am.	SI 706, art.3
		s.76(2)(aa)(i) am.	SI 706, art.4
		s.76(2)(aa)(ii) am.	SI 706, art.5

Year and Chap. or No. of Measure	Short title	How affected	1992, Chapter of Act or Number of Measure or Statutory Instrument
1983—*cont.*			
		s.76(2)(b)(ii) am.	SI 706, art.6
		s.197(1) am.	SI 706, art.7
		s.197(2) am.	SI 706, art.8
c.3	Agricultural Marketing Act 1983	s.3A added	SI 2111, reg.4
c.14	International Transport Convention Act 1983 (Amendment) O	s.1(3)(a) am.	SI 237, art.2
c.16	Level Crossings Act 1983	s.1(11) (defn. of "operator") subst. (31- 1-1993)	42, s.51
c.20	Mental Health Act 1983	defn. of "mental disorder" appl.	12, s.3, Sch.1, para.1(6)
		Sch.4, para.29 rep.	53, s.18(2), Sch.4, Pt.I
		Sch.4, para.49 rep.	12, s.290, Sch.12
c.28	Finance Act 1983	s.34 rep.	12, s.290, Sch.12
		s.36(4)(5) appl.	12, s.196(2)
		Sch.6 rep.	12, s.290, Sch.12
c.40	Education (Fees and Awards) Act 1983	s.1(3)(b) subst. (1.4.1993)	13, s.93(1), Sch.8, Pt.I, para.19(a)
		s.1(3)(ca) added (1.4.1993)	13, s.93(1), Sch.8, Pt.I, para.19(b)
		s.1(3)(cb) added	37, s.62(2), Sch.9, para.8(1)(2)
		s.1(3)(d) am. (1-4-1993)	37, s.62(2), Sch.9, para.8(3)(a)(b)
c.41	Health and Social Services and Social Security Adjudications Act 1983	appt. day(s) for ss.21- 24 (12.4.1993)	SI 2974, art.1(2)
		s.30(3) rep.	41, s.78(2), Sch.7
		Sch.8 rep. (except paras.1(3)(a) and 29.)	6, s.3, Sch.1
		Sch.9, Pt.I, paras.10,11, 15 rep.	53, s.18(2), Sch.4, Pt.I
c.44	National Audit Act 1983	s.6 restr.	37, s.12, Sch.2, para.19
		s.6 restr. (1-4-1993)	37, s.53(2)(b)
		ss.6,8 restr.	13, s.53(2)(b)
		s.6(3)(c) restr.	37, s.12, Sch.2, para.19
		s.6(3)(c) restr. (1-4- 1993)	37, s.53(2)(b)
		s.8 restr.	37, s.12, Sch.2, para.19
		s.8 restr. (1-4-1993)	37, s.53(2)(b)
c.47	National Heritage Act 1983	ss.1-16 trans.of functions	SI 1311, art.3(1), Sch.1, Pt.I
		s.6(3)(c) am.	44, s.11(2), Sch.8, Pt.II, para.13(1)
		s.6(4) rep.	44, s.11(3), Sch.9
		s.8 rep.	44, s.11(3), Sch.9
		s.14(3)(c) am.	44, s.11(2), Sch.8, Pt.II, para.13(1)
		s.14(4) rep.	44, s.11(3), Sch.9
		s.16 rep.	44, s.11(3), Sch.9
		s.18(3) rep.in pt.	44, s.11(3), Sch.9

Year and Chap. or No. of Measure	Short title	How affected	1992, Chapter of Act or Number of Measure or Statutory Instrument
1983—*cont.*			
		s.18(3)(d) added	44, s.11(2), Sch.8, Pt.II, para.13(2)
		s.18(8) added	44, s.11(2), Sch.8, Pt.II, para.13(3)
		s.18A added	44, s.11(2), Sch.8, Pt.II, para.13(4)
		s.20(3)(c) am.	44, s.11(2), Sch.8, Pt.II, para.13(1)
		s.20(4) rep.	44, s.11(3), Sch.9
		s.34 trans.of functions	SI 1311, art.6(1)(a)
		Sch.1, Pts.I,II trans.of functions	SI 1311, art.3(1), Sch.1, Pt.I
		Sch.1, para.9 rep.	44, s.11(3), Sch.9
		Sch.1, para.19 rep.	44, s.11(3), Sch.9
		Sch.4, paras.13,14 rep.	41, s.78(2), Sch.7
		Sch.5, paras.1,2 rep.	44, s.11(3), Sch.9
		Sch.5, para.5 rep.	44, s.11(3), Sch.9
		Sch.5, para.7 rep.	44, s.11(3), Sch.9
c.49	Finance (NO.2) Act 1983	s.7 rep.	12, s.290, Sch.12
c.53	Car Tax Act 1983	s.1(1) am. (1.1.1993)	48, s.18, Sch.4, para.2(1)
		s.1(2) am. (10.3.1992) (*retrosp.*)	20, s.8(1)(2)
		s.1(2A) added	58, s.1
		s.1(3) subst. (1.1.1993)	48, s.18, Sch.4, para.2(2)
		s.4(1)(3) am. (1.1.1993)	48, s.18, Sch.4, para.3(a)(b)
		s.4(1A) added	58, s.2(2)
		s.4(3A) added	58, s.2(3)
		s.5(1) rep.in pt. (1.1.1993)	48, s.82, Sch.18, Pt.VI
		s.5(1)(a)(b) am. (1.1.1993)	48, s.18, Sch.4, para.4(1)(a)(b)
		s.5(1)(ba)(bb) added (1.1.1993)	48, s.18, Sch.4, para.4(1)(c)
		s.5(5A)-(5C) added (1.1.1993)	48, s.18, Sch.4, para.4(2)
		s.5(6) rep. (1.1.1993)	48, s.82, Sch.18, Pt.VI
		s.6(7)(8) added	58, s.2(4)
		s.7 am. (1.1.1993)	48, s.18, Sch.4, para.5(1)
		s.7(1)-(3)(4)(a) am. (1.1.1993)	48, s.18, Sch.4, para.5(2)-(5)
		s.7(4B) am. (1.1.1993)	48, s.18, Sch.4, para.5(6)(b)
		s.7(4B)(b)(c) am. (1.1.1993)	48, s.18, Sch.4, para.5(6)(a)(b)
		s.7(7A) added	58, s.3
		s.9 (defn. of "another member State") added (1.1.1993)	48, s.18, Sch.4, para.6
		Sch.1, para.1A added (1.1.1993)	48, s.18, Sch.4, para.7(1)
		Sch.1, para.2(2)(a) am. (1.1.1993)	48, s.18, Sch.4, para.7(2)

Year and Chap. or No. of Measure	Short title	How affected	1992, Chapter of Act or Number of Measure or Statutory Instrument
1983—*cont.*			
		Sch.1, para.5(2) am.	58, s.2(6)
		Sch.1, para.6(1)(2) am. (1.1.1993)	48, s.18, Sch.4, para.7(3) (a)(b)
		Sch.1, para.6(3)(4) added	58, s.2(7)
		Sch.1, para.7(1) am. (1.1.1993)	48, s.18, Sch.4, para.7(4) (a)
		Sch.1, para.7(2)(aa) added (1.1.1993)	48, s.18, Sch.4, para.7(4) (b)
		Sch.1, para.7(2A) added	58, s.2(8)
		Sch.1, para.8(3)(b) am.	58, s.2(9)
		Sch.1, para.9 am. (1.1.1993)	48, s.18, Sch.4, para.7(5)
		Sch.1, para.10(1)(ba) added (1.1.1993)	48, s.18, Sch.4, para.7(6)
		Sch.1, para.12 am.	58, s.2(10)
		Sch.1, para.12(c)(d) am. (1.1.1993)	48, s.18, Sch.4, para.7(7)
		Sch.1, para.13 rep.	58, s.2(11)
		Sch.1(1A) added	58, s.2(5)
c.55	Value Added Tax Act 1983	Sch.2, para.6 am. (1.1.1993) mod.	48, s.18, Sch.4, para.8 SI 627, art.2(d) (inserting art.5(3A) in S.I.1980/442)
		ext. (1.1.1993)	48, s.14(1)(b)
		s.1 am. (1.12.1992, 1.1.1993)	48, s.14(2), Sch.3, Pt.I, para.2
		s.2(2) rep.in pt. (1.1.1993)	48, ss.14(3),82, Sch.18, Pt.V
		s.2(4)(5) rep. (1.1.1993)	48, ss.14(3),82, Sch.18, Pt.V
		ss.2A-2C added (1.12.1992, 1.1.1993)	48, s.14(2), Sch.3, Pt.I, para.3(1)
		s.3(3) am. (1.12.1992, 1.1.1993)	48, s.14(2), Sch.3, Pt.I, para.4(1)
		s.3(5) am. (1.12.1992, 1.1.1993)	48, s.14(2), Sch.3, Pt.I, para.4(2)
		s.4(1) am. (1.12.1992, 1.1.1993)	48, s.14(2), Sch.3, Pt.I, para.5
		s.5(3A)(3B) added (1.12.1992,1.1.1993)	48, s.14(2), Sch.3, Pt.I, para.6(1)
		s.5(9) am. (1.12.1992, 1.1.1993)	48, s.14(2), Sch.3, Pt.I, para.6(2)
		s.5(10) am. (1.12.1992, 1.1.1993)	48, s.14(2), Sch.3, Pt.I, para.6(3)
		s.6(1) am. (1.12.1992, 1.1.1993)	48, s.14(2), Sch.3, Pt.I, para.7(1)
		s.6(2) am. (1.12.1992, 1.1.1993)	48, s.14(2), Sch.3, Pt.I, para.7(2)
		s.6(3) replaced (by subss.(2A)-(2D)(3) (1.12.1992,1.1.1993))	48, s.14(2), Sch.3, Pt.I, para.7(3)
		s.6(4) am. (1.12.1992, 1.1.1993)	48, s.14(2), Sch.3, Pt.I, para.7(4)

Year and Chap. or No. of Measure	Short title	How affected	1992, Chapter of Act or Number of Measure or Statutory Instrument
1983—*cont.*		s.6(4A) added (1.12.1992, 1.1.1993)	48, s.14(2), Sch.3, Pt.I, para.7(5)
		s.6(6) am. (1.12.1992, 1.1.1993)	48, s.14(2), Sch.3, Pt.I, para.7(6)
		s.7(4)(a) rep. (1.1.1993)	48, ss.14(3),82, Sch.18, Pt.V
		s.7(6) added (1.12.1992, 1.1.1993)	48, s.14(2), Sch.3, Pt.I, para.8
		s.8(1) am. (1.12.1992, 1.1.1993)	48, s.14(2), Sch.3, Pt.I, para.9
		ss.8A-8C added (1.12.1992, 1.1.1993)	48, s.14(2), Sch.3, Pt.I, para.10
		s.9(1) rep.in pt. (1.1.1993)	48, ss.14(3),82, Sch.18, Pt.V
		s.9(1)(aa) added (1.12.1992,1.1.1993)	48, s.14(2), Sch.3, Pt.I, para.11(a)
		s.9(1)(b) am. (1.12.1992, 1.1.1993)	48, s.14(2), Sch.3, Pt.I, para.11(b)
		s.10(1) am.	48, s.14(2), Sch.3, Pt.I, para.12(1)
		s.10(3) subst.	48, s.14(2), Sch.3, Pt.I, para.12(2)
		s.10(6) rep. (1.1.1993)	48, ss.14(3),82, Sch.18, Pt.V
		s.10A added (1.12.1992, 1.1.1993)	48, s.14(2), Sch.3, Pt.I, para.13
		s.11(1) am. (1.12.1992, 1.1.1993)	48, s.14(2), Sch.3, Pt.I, para.14(1)
		s.11(2) am. (1.12.1992, 1.1.1993)	48, s.14(2), Sch.3, Pt.I, para.14(2)
		s.11(2A) added (1.12.1992, 1.1.1993)	48, s.14(2), Sch.3, Pt.I, para.14(3)
		s.11(3)(4) rep. (1.1.1993)	48, ss.14(3),82, Sch.18, Pt.V
		s.14(1) am. (1.12.1992, 1.1.1993)	48, s.14(2), Sch.3, Pt.I, para.15(1)
		s.14(3) am. (1.12.1992, 1.1.1993)	48, s.14(2), Sch.3, Pt.I, para.15(2)(c)(d)
		s.14(3) rep.in pt. (1.1.1993)	48, ss.14(3),82, Sch.18, Pt.V
		s.14(3)(aa) added (1.12.1992,1.1.1993)	48, s.14(2), Sch.3, Pt.I, para.15(2)(a)
		s.14(3)(b) am. (1.12.1992, 1.1.1993)	48, s.14(2), Sch.3, Pt.I, para.15(2)(b)
		s.14(3A) am. (1.12.1992, 1.1.1993)	48, s.14(2), Sch.3, Pt.I, para.15(3)
		s.14(4) am. (1.12.1992, 1.1.1993)	48, s.14(2), Sch.3, Pt.I, para.15(4)(a)(b)
		s.14(9)(a)-(c) am. (1.12.1992,1.1.1993)	48, s.14(2), Sch.3, Pt.I, para.15(5)(a)-(c)
		s.14(10) am. (1.12.1992, 1.1.1993)	48, s.14(2), Sch.3, Pt.I, para.15(6)(a)

Year and Chap. or No. of Measure	Short title	How affected	1992, Chapter of Act or Number of Measure or Statutory Instrument
1983—*cont.*			
		s.14(10)(a) am. (1.12.1992,1.1.1993)	48, s.14(2), Sch.3, Pt.I, para.15(6)(b)(c)
		s.15(1) am. (1.12.1992, 1.1.1993)	48, s.14(2), Sch.3, Pt.I, para.16(1)
		s.15(2)(ba) added (1.12.1992,1.1.1993)	48, s.14(2), Sch.3, Pt.I, para.16(2)
		s.15(2)(c) rep. (1.1.1993)	48, ss.14(3),82, Sch.18, Pt.V
		s.16(3) am. (1.12.1992, 1.1.1993)	48, s.14(2), Sch.3, Pt.I, para.17(1)(a)(b)
		s.16(6)(a) am. (1.12.1992, 1.1.1993)	48, s.14(2), Sch.3, Pt.I, para.17(2)
		s.16(7) am. (1.12.1992, 1.1.1993)	48, s.14(2), Sch.3, Pt.I, para.17(3)
		s.16(8) am. (1.12.1992, 1.1.1993)	48, s.14(2), Sch.3, Pt.I, para.17(4)
		s.16(9)(a) am. (1.12.1992, 1.1.1993)	48, s.14(2), Sch.3, Pt.I, para.17(5)
		s.17(1) am. (1.12.1992, 1.1.1993)	48, s.14(2), Sch.3, Pt.I, para.18
		s.18(3)(a)(b) am. (1.12.1992,1.1.1993)	48, s.14(2), Sch.3, Pt.I, para.19(1)
		s.18(4) am. (1.12.1992, 1.1.1993)	48, s.14(2), Sch.3, Pt.I, para.19(2)
		s.19(1) am. (1.12.1992, 1.1.1993)	48, s.14(2), Sch.3, Pt.I, para.20(1)
		s.19(1A)(a) am. (1.12.1992,1.1.1993)	48, s.14(2), Sch.3, Pt.I, para.20(2)
		s.19(2) am. (1.12.1992, 1.1.1993)	48, s.14(2), Sch.3, Pt.I, para.20(3)(a)(b)
		s.19(3) am. (1.12.1992, 1.1.1993)	48, s.14(2), Sch.3, Pt.I, para.20(4)(a)(b)
		s.20(1) rep.in pt. & am. (1.12.1992,1.1.1993)	48, ss.14(2),82, Sch.3, Pt.I, para.21(1)(a)(b), Sch.18, Pt.V
		s.20(2) am. (1.12.1992, 1.1.1993)	48, s.14(2), Sch.3, Pt.I, para.21(2)
		s.20A added (1.12.1992, 1.1.1993)	48, s.14(2), Sch.3, Pt.I, para.22
		s.21(1) rep.in pt. & am. (1.12.1992,1.1.1993)	48, ss.14(2),82, Sch.3, Pt.I, para.23(1)(a)(b), Sch.18, Pt.V
		s.21(2A) added (1.12.1992, 1.1.1993)	48, s.14(2), Sch.3, Pt.I, para.23(2)
		s.23(1) am. (1.12.1992, 1.1.1993)	48, s.14(2), Sch.3, Pt.I, para.24(1)
		s.23(2)(a) am. (1.12.1992, 1.1.1993)	48, s.14(2), Sch.3, Pt.I, para.24(2)
		s.24(1)-(3) replaced (by subs.(1)(1.12.1992, 1.1.1993))	48, s.14(2), Sch.3, Pt.I, para.25
		s.24(3)(c) rep. (1.1.1993)	48, s.82, Sch.18, Pt.II

Year and Chap. or No. of Measure	Short title	How affected	1992, Chapter of Act or Number of Measure or Statutory Instrument
1983—*cont.*			
		s.25 am. (1.12.1992, 1.1.1993)	48, s.14(2), Sch.3, Pt.I, para.26(a)(b)
		s.26(1) am. (1.12.1992, 1.1.1993)	48, s.14(2), Sch.3, Pt.I, para.27
		s.27(2A)(2B) am. (1.12.1992,1.1.1993)	48, s.14(2), Sch.3, Pt.I, para.28(1)(2)
		s.29(1)(c) am. (1.12.1992, 1.1.1993)	48, s.14(2), Sch.3, Pt.I, para.29
		s.29A(2)(3)(8) am. (1.12.1992,1.1.1993)	48, s.14(2), Sch.3, Pt.I, para.30(1)-(3)
		s.30(1)(2) am. (1.12.1992, 1.1.1993)	48, s.14(2), Sch.3, Pt.I, para.31(1)(2)
		s.30(5) am. (1.12.1992, 1.1.1993)	48, s.14(2), Sch.3, Pt.I, para.31(3)
		s.31(3) am. (1.12.1992, 1.1.1993)	48, s.14(2), Sch.3, Pt.I, para.32(1)
		s.31(6) added (1.12.1992, 1.1.1993)	48, s.14(2), Sch.3, Pt.I, para.32(2)
		s.32(1) rep. (1.1.1993)	48, ss.14(3),82, Sch.18, Pt.V
		s.32(2) subst. (1.12.1992, 1.1.1993)	48, s.14(2), Sch.3, Pt.I, para.33
		ss.32A,32B added (1.12.1992,1.1.1993)	48, s.14(2), Sch.3, Pt.I, para.34
		s.35 subst. (1.12.1992, 1.1.1993)	48, s.14(2), Sch.3, Pt.I, para.35
		s.36(1)(2) am. (1.12.1992, 1.1.1993)	48, s.14(2), Sch.3, Pt.I, para.36(1)(2)
		s.36(3) rep. (1.1.1993)	48, ss.14(3),82, Sch.18, Pt.V
		s.37 subst. (1.12.1992, 1.1.1993)	48, s.14(2), Sch.3, Pt.I, para.37
		s.37B added (exc. s.37B(2))	48, s.16(1)
		s.37B(2) added (1.1.1993)	48, s.16(1)
		s.38 am. (1.12.1992, 1.1.1993)	48, s.14(2), Sch.3, Pt.I, para.38
		s.38A(8A) added	48, s.15(2)(4)
		s.38C added	20, s.6(1)
		s.39(1A)(b) am. (1.12.1992,1.1.1993)	48, s.14(2), Sch.3, Pt.I, para.39(1)(a)
		s.39(1A)(ba) added (1.12.1992,1.1.1993)	48, s.14(2), Sch.3, Pt.I, para.39(1)(b)
		s.39(1A)(ii) am. (1.12.1992,1.1.1993)	48, s.14(2), Sch.3, Pt.I, para.39(1)(c)
		s.39(2B)(a) am. (1.12.1992,1.1.1993)	48, s.14(2), Sch.3, Pt.I, para.39(2)
		s.39(4) am. (1.12.1992, 1.1.1993)	48, s.14(2), Sch.3, Pt.I, para.39(3)
		s.40(1)(b) am. (1.12.1992, 1.1.1993)	48, s.14(2), Sch.3, Pt.I, para.40(a)
		s.40(1)(da) added (1.12.1992,1.1.1993)	48, s.14(2), Sch.3, Pt.I, para.40(b)

Year and Chap. or No. of Measure	Short title	How affected	1992, Chapter of Act or Number of Measure or Statutory Instrument
1983—*cont.*			
		s.40(1)(fa) added (1.12.1992,1.1.1993)	48, s.14(2), Sch.3, Pt.I, para.40(c)
		s.40(1)(hza) added	48, s.16(2)
		s.40(1)(j) rep.in pt. (1.1.1993)	48, ss.14(3),82, Sch.18, Pt.V
		s.40(1)(ja) added (1.12.1992,1.1.1993)	48, s.14(2), Sch.3, Pt.I, para.40(d)
		s.40(1)(m)(iii) added (1.12.1992,1.1.1993)	48, s.14(2), Sch.3, Pt.I, para.40(e)
		s.40(1)(n) am. (1.12.1992, 1.1.1993)	48, s.14(2), Sch.3, Pt.I, para.40(f)
		s.40(1)(o) am. (1.12.1992, 1.1.1993)	48, s.14(2), Sch.3, Pt.I, para.40(g)
		s.41(1) am. (1.12.1992, 1.1.1993)	48, s.14(2), Sch.3, Pt.I, para.41(1)
		s.41(3A) added (1.12.1992, 1.1.1993)	48, s.14(2), Sch.3, Pt.I, para.41(2)
		s.41(6) added (1.12.1992, 1.1.1993)	48, s.14(2), Sch.3, Pt.I, para.41(3)
		s.43(1)(a)(b) am. (1.12.1992,1.1.1993)	48, s.14(2), Sch.3, Pt.I, para.42(1)(a)(b)
		s.43(2)(a)(b) am. (1.12.1992,1.1.1993)	48, s.14(2), Sch.3, Pt.I, para.42(2)(a)(b)
		s.43(3) am. (1.12.1992, 1.1.1993)	48, s.14(2), Sch.3, Pt.I, para.42(3)
		s.45(4)(a) am.	20, s.6(2)
		s.45(4)(e) added	48, s.16(3)
		s.46 am. (1.12.1992, 1.1.1993)	48, s.14(2), Sch.3, Pt.I, para.43
		ss.46A,46B added (1.12.1992,1.1.1993)	48, s.14(2), Sch.3, Pt.I, para.44
		s.47A added (1.12.1992, 1.1.1993)	48, s.14(2), Sch.3, Pt.I, para.45
		s.47A(1)(c)(i) am.	SI 3127, art.2(1)(a)(b)
		s.47A(1A) added	SI 3127, art.2(2)
		s.48(1) (defns. of "another member State" and "subordinate legislation") added (1.12.1992,1.1.1993)	48, s.14(2), Sch.3, Pt.I, para.46(1)(a)(b)
		s.48(1) (defn. of "taxable person") subst. (1.12.1992, 1.1.1993)	48, s.14(2), Sch.3, Pt.I, para.46(1)(d)
		s.48(1) (defn. of "tax") am. (1.12.1992,1.1.1993)	48, s.14(2), Sch.3, Pt.I, para.46(1)(c)
		s.48(1A)(1B) added (1.12.1992,1.1.1993)	48, s.14(2), Sch.3, Pt.I, para.46(2)
		s.48(5) am. (1.12.1992, 1.1.1993)	48, s.14(2), Sch.3, Pt.I, para.46(3)
		s.48(9) added (1.12.1992, 1.1.1993)	48, s.14(2), Sch.3, Pt.I, para.46(4)
		s.49 am. (1.12.1992, 1.1.1993)	48, s.14(2), Sch.3, Pt.I, para.47

Year and Chap. or No. of Measure	Short title	How affected	1992, Chapter of Act or Number of Measure or Statutory Instrument
1983—*cont.*		Sch.1, para.1(1)(2)(4) am. (1.12.1992,1.1.1993)	48, s.14(2), Sch.3, Pt.I, para.48(1)(2)(3)(a)
		Sch.1, para.1(1)(a)(b)(2) (a)(b) am.	SI 629, arts.1,2(a)
		Sch.1, para.1(3) am.	SI 629, arts.1,2(b)
		Sch.1, para.1(4)(a) am. (1.12.1992,1.1.1993)	48, s.14(2), Sch.3, Pt.I, para.48(3)(b)
		Sch.1, para.1(4A)(4B) added (1.12.1992, 1.1.1993)	48, s.14(2), Sch.3, Pt.I, para.48(4)
		Sch.1, para.1(5) am. (1.12.1992,1.1.1993)	48, s.14(2), Sch.3, Pt.I, para.48(5)
		Sch.1, para.1A(1)(4)(b) am. (1.12.1992,1.1.1993)	48, s.14(2), Sch.3, Pt.I, para.49(1)
		Sch.1, para.1A(7)(ba) added (1.12.1992, 1.1.1993)	48, s.14(2), Sch.3, Pt.I, para.49(2)
		Sch.1, para.1B added (1.12.1992,1.1.1993)	48, s.14(2), Sch.3, Pt.I, para.50
		Sch.1, para.2(1)-(3) am. (1.12.1992,1.1.1993)	48, s.14(2), Sch.3, Pt.I, para.51(1)-(3)
		Sch.1, para.2(1)(2) am.	SI 629, arts.1,2(b)
		Sch.1, para.3(3) am. (1.12.1992,1.1.1993)	48, s.14(2), Sch.3, Pt.I, para.52
		Sch.1, paras.5,5A(1) am. (1.12.1992,1.1.1993)	48, s.14(2), Sch.3, Pt.I, para.53
		Sch.1, para.5A(2) rep.in pt. (1.1.1993)	48, ss.14(3),82, Sch.18, Pt.V
		Sch.1, para.5A(2)(b) rep. (1.1.1993)	48, ss.14(3),82, Sch.18, Pt.V
		Sch.1, para.7 am. (1.12.1992,1.1.1993)	48, s.14(2), Sch.3, Pt.I, para.54
		Sch.1, para.7A am. (1.12.1992,1.1.1993)	48, s.14(2), Sch.3, Pt.I, para.55
		Sch.1, para.8A(1) am. (1.12.1992,1.1.1993)	48, s.14(2), Sch.3, Pt.I, para.56(1)
		Sch.1, para.8A(1A)(1B) added (1.12.1992, 1.1.1993)	48, s.14(2), Sch.3, Pt.I, para.56(2)
		Sch.1, para.8A(2) am. (1.12.1992,1.1.1993)	48, s.14(2), Sch.3, Pt.I, para.56(3)
		Sch.1, para.9(1) am. (1.12.1992,1.1.1993)	48, s.14(2), Sch.3, Pt.I, para.57(1)
		Sch.1, para.9(1A)(1B) added (1.12.1992, 1.1.1993)	48, s.14(2), Sch.3, Pt.I, para.57(2)
		Sch.1, para.9(2) am. (1.12.1992,1.1.1993)	48, s.14(2), Sch.3, Pt.I, para.57(3)
		Sch.1, para.11(1)(2) am. (1.12.1992,1.1.1993)	48, s.14(2), Sch.3, Pt.I, para.58(1)(2)
		Sch.1, para.15 rep.in pt. (1.1.1993)	48, ss.14(3),82, Sch.18, Pt.V
		Schs.1A,1B added (1.12.1992,1.1.1993)	48, s.14(2), Sch.3, Pt.I, para.59
		Sch.2, para.5A restr.	SI 3111, art.4

Year and Chap. or No. of Measure	Short title	How affected	1992, Chapter of Act or Number of Measure or Statutory Instrument
1983—*cont.*			
		Sch.2, para.5A added (1.12.1992,1.1.1993)	48, s.14(2), Sch.3, Pt.I, para.60(1)
		Sch.2, para.7(2)(a)(b) am. (1.12.1992,1.1.1993)	48, s.14(2), Sch.3, Pt.I, para.60(2)
		Sch.2, para.7(2A) added (1.1.1993)	48, s.16(4)
		Sch.3, para.8 added	SI 3128, art.2
		Sch.4, paras.2,5 rep. (1.12.1992,1.1.1993)	48, ss.14(2),82, Sch.3, Pt.I, para.61(1)(2), Sch.18, Pt.V
		Sch.4, para.3A added (1.12.1992,1.1.1993)	48, s.14(2), Sch.3, Pt.I, para.61(2)
		Sch.4, para.7 am.	48, s.14(2), Sch.3, Pt.I, para.61(3)(a)(c)
		Sch.4, para.7(b) am.	48, s.14(2), Sch.3, Pt.I, para.61(3)(b)
		Sch.4, para.8A added (1.12.1992,1.1.1993)	48, s.14(2), Sch.3, Pt.I, para.61(4)
		Sch.4, para.11 subst. (1.12.1992,1.1.1993)	48, s.14(2), Sch.3, Pt.I, para.61(5)
		Sch.4, para.13 rep.in pt. (1.1.1993)	48, ss.14(3),82, Sch.18, Pt.V
		Sch.4A added (1.12.1992, 1.1.1993)	48, s.14(2), Sch.3, Pt.I, para.62
		Sch.5, Group 4, Item 1(i) added	SI 628, art.2
		Sch.5, Group 7, Note (8) rep.in pt.	48, ss.17(1)(2),82, Sch.18, Pt.V
		Sch.5, Group 9 subst.	SI 3223, art.2
		Sch.5, Group 10, Item 3(c) added	SI 628, art.3
		Sch.5, Group 10, Item 5 subst.	SI 3223, art.3(a)
		Sch.5, Group 10, Item 10(b) rev.in pt.	SI 3223, art.3(b)
		Sch.5, Group 10, Item 11 rev.	SI 3223, art.3(c)
		Sch.5, Group 10, Item 12 subst.	SI 3223, art.3(d)
		Sch.5, Group 10, Item 14 added	SI 3126, art.2(a)
		Sch.5, Group 10, Note (8) added	SI 3126, art.2(b)
		Sch.5, Group 14, Item 2(i) added	SI 628, art.4
		Sch.5, Group 14, Item 10B added	SI 628, art.4
		Sch.5, Group 14, Item 12A added	SI 3065, art.2
		Sch.5, Group 14, Note 7 am.	6, s.4, Sch.2, para.65
		Sch.5, Group 14, Note 7 am. (NI)	9, s.4, Sch.2, para.28

Year and Chap. or No. of Measure	Short title	How affected	1992, Chapter of Act or Number of Measure or Statutory Instrument
1983—*cont.*			
		Sch.5, Group 14, Note (1) am. (1.12.1992,1.1.1993)	48, s.14(2), Sch.3, Pt.I, para.63(1)
		Sch.5, Group 15, Item 1 am.	SI 3095, Sch.1, para.8
		Sch.5, Group 15, Item 1 rep.in pt. & am. (1.12.1992,1.1.1993)	48, ss.14(2),82, Sch.3, Pt.I, para.63(2), Sch.18, Pt.V
		Sch.5, Group 15, Item 4 am. (1.12.1992,1.1.1993)	48, s.14(2), Sch.3, Pt.I, para.63(3)(a)
		Sch.5, Group 15, Note (6) am. (1.12.1992,1.1.1993)	48, s.14(2), Sch.3, Pt.I, para.63(3)(b)
		Sch.5, Group 15A added	SI 3131, art.2
		Sch.5, Group 16, Item 3 am. (1.12.1992,1.1.1993)	48, s.14(2), Sch.3, Pt.I, para.63(4)
		Sch.6, Group 9, Note 2 am.	52, s.300(2), Sch.2, para.32
		Sch.6, Group 11 am.	12, s.290, Sch.10, para.6
		Sch.7, para.2(1)(2) am. (1.12.1992,1.1.1993)	48, s.14(2), Sch.3, Pt.I, para.64(1)(2)
		Sch.7, para.2(2A)-(2C) added (1.12.1992, 1.1.1993)	48, s.14(2), Sch.3, Pt.I, para.64(3)
		Sch.7, para.2(3B)(3C) added (1.12.1992, 1.1.1993)	48, s.14(2), Sch.3, Pt.I, para.64(4)
		Sch.7, para.3(2A) added (1.12.1992,1.1.1993)	48, s.14(2), Sch.3, Pt.I, para.65
		Sch.7, para.4(2A) am. (1.12.1992,1.1.1993)	48, s.14(2), Sch.3, Pt.I, para.66(1)
		Sch.7, para.4(5)(6) am. (1.12.1992,1.1.1993)	48, s.14(2), Sch.3, Pt.I, para.66(2)(3)
		Sch.7, para.4A added (1.12.1992,1.1.1993)	48, s.14(2), Sch.3, Pt.I, para.67
		Sch.7, para.5(2) am. (1.12.1992,1.1.1993)	48, s.14(2), Sch.3, Pt.I, para.68
		Sch.7, para.6(10) added (1.12.1992,1.1.1993)	48, s.14(2), Sch.3, Pt.I, para.69
		Sch.7, para.7(1) am. (1.12.1992,1.1.1993)	48, s.14(2), Sch.3, Pt.I, para.70
		Sch.7, para.8(2) am. (1.12.1992,1.1.1993)	48, s.14(2), Sch.3, Pt.I, para.71(1)(a)-(c)
		Sch.7, para.8(4) am. (1.12.1992,1.1.1993)	48, s.14(2), Sch.3, Pt.I, para.71(2)
		Sch.7, para.9(1) am. (1.12.1992,1.1.1993)	48, s.14(2), Sch.3, Pt.I, para.72
		Sch.7, para.10(2) am. (1.12.1992,1.1.1993)	48, s.14(2), Sch.3, Pt.I, para.73
		Sch.7, para.11(1)(ba) added (1.12.1992, 1.1.1993)	48, s.14(2), Sch.3, Pt.I, para.74
		Sch.10, para.6 am. (1.12.1992,1.1.1993)	48, s.14(2), Sch.3, Pt.I, para.75
		Sch.10, para.6 rep.in pt. (1.1.1993)	48, ss.14(3),82, Sch.18, Pt.V
c.56	Oil Taxation Act 1983	Sch.1, para.1(4) rep.in pt.	48, ss.74,82, Sch.15, para.6, Sch.18, Pt.VIII

Year and Chap. or No. of Measure	Short title	How affected	1992, Chapter of Act or Number of Measure or Statutory Instrument
1983—*cont.*			
		Sch.1, para.1(4)(c) rep.	48, ss.74,82, Sch.15, para.6, Sch.18, Pt.VIII
		Sch.2, para.12(3) am.	48, s.74, Sch.15, para.7
		Sch.4, para.11(3) rep.in pt.	48, ss.74,82, Sch.15, para.8(a), Sch.18, Pt.VIII
		Sch.4, para.11(4) rep.	48, ss.74,82, Sch.15, para.8(b), Sch.18, Pt.VIII
c.v	Hampshire Act 1983	s.2(1) rep.in pt.	SI 117, art.19(1), Sch.
		s.5 rep.	SI 117, art.19(1), Sch.
c.vi	Parkeston Quay Act 1983	appl.(mods.)	SI 1136(L), arts.2(1),9(1), Sch.
		ss.11-17 appl.(mods.)	SI 1136(L), art.8(1)(3)
		s.29 appl.(mods.)	SI 1136(L), art.8(2)
c.xviii	Staffordshire Act 1983	s.41 rep.	SI 117, art.19(1), Sch.
		Sch.2 rep.	SI 117, art.19(1), Sch.
No.1	Pastoral Measure 1983	defn. of "suspension period" appl.	GSM 1, s.2(6)
		s.29(1) rep.in pt.	GSM 1, s.17(1), Sch.3, para.19
		s.54(3) am.	GSM 1, s.17(1), Sch.3, para.20
		s.67(6)(e) rep.in pt.	GSM 1, s.17(1), Sch.3, para.21
		s.68(1)(2) rep.in pt.	GSM 1, s.17(1), Sch.3, para.22
		Sch.4, para.15(1)(b)(c) am.	GSM 1, s.17(1), Sch.3, para.23(a)(b)
		Sch.4, para.15(2) am.	GSM 1, s.17(1), Sch.3, para.23(c)
		Sch.6, para.3(1) am.	GSM 1, s.17(1), Sch.3, para.24
		Sch.7, para.1 am.	GSM 1, s.17(1), Sch.3, para.25(a)
		Sch.7, para.4 subst.	GSM 1, s.17(1), Sch.3, para.25(b)
1984			
c.12	Telecommunications Act 1984	defn(s). appl.	i, s.33(1)
		defn(s). appl.	xi, s.41(1)
		defn. of "telecommunication apparatus" appl. (EW) (*prosp.*)	41, s.60(10)
		defn. of "telecommunication system" appl.	50, s.5(1)
		s.3(3A) added	43, s.56(6), Sch.1, para.1
		ss.27A,27B added	43, s.1
		s.27C added	43, s.2
		s.27D added	43, s.3

Year and Chap. or No. of Measure	Short title	How affected	1992, Chapter of Act or Number of Measure or Statutory Instrument
1984—*cont.*			
		s.27E added	43, s.4
		s.27F added	43, s.5(1)
		s.27G(1)-(7) added	43, s.6(1)
		s.27G(8) added (*prosp.*)	43, s.6(1)
		ss.27H(1)-(3)(5)-(7),27I added	43, s.7
		s.27H(4) added (*prosp.*)	43, s.7
		s.27J added	43, s.8
		s.27K added	43, s.9
		s.27L added	43, s.10
		s.46A added	43, s.49
		s.53(6) (defn. of "relevant purpose") am.	43, ss.5(2),6(2)
		s.53(6) (defn. of "relevant purpose") am.	43, s.56(6), Sch.1, para.2
		s.72(2) am.	12, s.290, Sch.10, para.7
		s.78 rep.	SI 2372, reg.2
		s.101(2)(bb) added	43, s.56(6), Sch.1, para.3(a)
		s.101(4)(a) am.	43, s.56(6), Sch.1, para.3(b)
		s.104(1) am.	43, s.56(6), Sch.1, para.4
		Sch.2 mod.	xviii, s.10
		Sch.4 (defn. of "telecommunications code system") appl.	ix, s.1, Sch., s.8(3)
		Sch.4, para.7 rep. (1-1-1993) (EWS)	42, s.68(1), Sch.4, Pt.I
c.23	Registered Homes Act 1984	defns. of "mental nursing home" and "nursing home" appl.	14, ss.11(5),79(5), Sch.1, para.7(2)
		defns. of "nursing homes" and "mental nursing homes" appl. (*prosp.*)	40, s.13, Sch.7, para.9(d)
		Sch.1, para.5 rep.	53, s.18(2), Sch.4, Pt.I
c.27	Road Traffic Regulation Act 1984	ss.1-5 appl.(mods.)	ii, s.1, Sch., s.3(2)
		s.1 mod.	SI 1217, regs.3(1)(a),5(1)(a)(2)-(5),11
		s.6 mod.	SI 1217, regs.3(1)(b),5(1)(b)(2)-(5),11
		s.9 mod.	SI 1217, regs.3(1)(c),5(1)(c)(2)-(5),11
		s.14 mod.	SI 1217, regs.4(1)(2),6(1)(2),11
		s.14(2) mod.	3, s.22(1)
		s.17 mod.	3, s.22(3)
		s.18 mod.	SI 1217, regs.3(1)(d),5(1)(d)(2)-(5),11
		ss.64,65 appl.(mods.)	ii, s.1, Sch., s.3(2)
		s.65(1) ext.	xi, s.14(3)(b)
		ss.67,68 appl.(mods.)	ii, s.1, Sch., s.3(2)

Year and Chap. or No. of Measure	Short title	How affected	1992, Chapter of Act or Number of Measure or Statutory Instrument
1984—*cont.*			
		s.89 appl.(mods.)	ii, s.1, Sch., s.3(2)
		s.89 appl.	ii, s.1, Sch., s.3(3)(b)
		s.98 appl.(mods.)	ii, s.1, Sch., s.3(2)
		para.18(2), Sch.4 am.	53, s.18(1), Sch.3, para.15
		Sch.3, para.2 mod.	SI 1218, art.3(2)
		Sch.9 appl.(mods.)	ii, s.1, Sch., s.3(2)
c.31	Rating and Valuation (Amendment)(Scotland) Act 1984	Sch.2, para.12 rep.	53, s.18(2), Sch.4, Pt.I
c.32	London Regional Transport Act 1984	s.41 am. (1-1-1993)	42, s.21(2)
		ss.54-58 rep.	xvi, s.11
		s.68 (defn. of "subsidiary") appl.	xvi, s.2(1)
		Sch.6, paras.7,8 rep.	12, s.290, Sch.12
c.35	Data Protection Act 1984	defn(s). appl.	37, s.59(3)
		s.5(1) excl.	13, s.86(1)
		s.5(1) excl.	37, s.59(1)
		s.30 ext. (EW)	41, s.53
		s.30(1)(2) am. (1.1.1993)	SI 3218, reg.82(1), Sch.10, Pt.I, para.15
		Sch.2, para.13 rep.	53, s.18(2), Sch.4, Pt.I
c.36	Mental Health (Scotland) Act 1984	s.11(1) am. (1-4-1993)	37, s.62(2), Sch.9, para.9(a)
		s.11(1)(b) added (1-4- 1993)	37, s.62(2), Sch.9, para.9(b)
		s.12 (defn. of " private hospital") appl.	14, ss.11(5),79(5), Sch.1, para.8(2)
c.42	Matrimonial and Family Proceedings Act 1984	s.26 rep. (*prosp.*)	56, s.2(2), Sch.3
		Sch.1, para.9 rep. (*prosp.*)	56, s.2(2), Sch.3
c.43	Finance Act 1984	s.44 rep.	12, s.290, Sch.12
		s.50 rep.	12, s.290, Sch.12
		s.56(3)(4) rep.	12, s.290, Sch.12
		ss.63-71 rep.	12, s.290, Sch.12
		s.64 mod. (*retrosp.*)	12, s.290, Sch.11, Pt.II, para.16(4)
		s.70 cont.	12, s.290, Sch.11, Pt.II, para.18(b)
		s.73(4)(5) rep.in pt. (*prosp.*)	40, s.120(2), Sch.22, Pt.I
		ss.79-81 rep.	12, s.290, Sch.12
		s.126(3)(b) rep.in pt.	12, s.290, Sch.12
		Sch.4, Pt.II, para.3 rev.	SI 3095, Sch.2
		Sch.5, para.1 rev.	SI 3095, Sch.2
		Sch.11 rep.	12, s.290, Sch.12
		Sch.13 mod. (*retrosp.*)	12, s.290, Sch.11, Pt.II, para.16(4)
		Schs.13,14 rep.	12, s.290, Sch.12
		Sch.13, para.10(2)(bc) added	48, s.49(5)(10)
		Sch.14 cont.	12, s.290, Sch.11, Pt.II, para.18(b)

Year and Chap. or No. of Measure	Short title	How affected	1992, Chapter of Act or Number of Measure or Statutory Instrument
1984—*cont.*			
		Sch.14, para.12 am.	12, s.290, Sch.11, Pt.II, para.18(b)
		Sch.22, para.4 rep.	48, s.82, Sch.18, Pt.IX
c.48	Health and Social Security Act 1984	ss.11-14 rep.	6, s.3, Sch.1
		ss.16-18 rep.	6, s.3, Sch.1
		Schs.4,5 rep.	6, s.3, Sch.1
		Sch.7, paras.1-3 rep.	6, s.3, Sch.1
		Sch.7, paras.6-8 rep.	6, s.3, Sch.1
c.49	Trade Union Act 1984	rep.	52, s.300(1), Sch.1
c.51	Inheritance Tax Act 1984	defn. of "chargeable transfer" appl.	12, s.260(2)(a)
		s.8(1) excl.	48, s.72(2)
		s.24 appl.	12, s.264(8)
		s.31(4G)(b) am.	12, s.290, Sch.10, para.8(2)
		s.74(4)(b)(c) am.	6, s.4, Sch.2, para.66(1) (2)
		s.74(4)(b)(c) am. (NI)	9, s.4, Sch.2, para.29(1) (2)
		s.79(2) am.	12, s.290, Sch.10, para.8(3)
		s.89(4)(b)(c) am.	6, s.4, Sch.2, para.66(1) (2)
		s.89(4)(b)(c) am. (NI)	9, s.4, Sch.2, para.29(1) (2)
		s.97 amdt(s). saved	12, s.290, Sch.10, para.8(4)(a)
		s.97 am.	12, s.290, Sch.10, para.8(4)(b)
		ss.103-159 (Pt.V)(Ch.I) mod.	48, s.73, Sch.14, para.9(4)
		s.104(1)(a)(b) am.	48, s.73, Sch.14, paras.1, 8,9
		s.105(1)(b) am.	48, s.73, Sch.14, paras.2(2),8,9
		s.105(1)(cc) added	48, s.73, Sch.14, paras.2(3),8,9
		s.105(1ZA) added	48, s.73, Sch.14, paras.2(4),8,9
		s.105(2) am.	48, s.73, Sch.14, paras.2(5),8,9
		ss.105(7),234(4) am.	SI 3181, reg.4
		ss.107(4),113A(6),124A(6) am.	12, s.290, Sch.10, para.8(5)
		ss.113A,113B am.	48, s.73, Sch.14, para.9(2)
		s.113A(3B) added	48, s.73, Sch.14, paras.3, 8,9
		s.116(2)(4) am.	48, s.73, Sch.14, paras.4, 8,9
		s.135 am.	12, s.290, Sch.10, para.8(6)
		s.138 am.	12, s.290, Sch.10, para.8(7)
		s.165 am.	12, s.290, Sch.10, para.8(8)
		s.183 am.	12, s.290, Sch.10, para.8(9)
		s.187 am.	12, s.290, Sch.10, para.8(10)
		s.194 am.	12, s.290, Sch.10, para.8(11)

Year and Chap. or No. of Measure	Short title	How affected	1992, Chapter of Act or Number of Measure or Statutory Instrument
1984—*cont.*			
		s.225A added	48, s.76, Sch.16, para.8
		s.227(1AA) added	48, s.73, Sch.14, paras.5, 8,9
		s.228(5) added	48, s.73, Sch.14, paras.6, 8,9
		s.230 trans.of functions	SI 1311, art.3(1), Sch.1, Pt.I
		s.230(1)(3)(4)(a)(b) am.	SI 1311, art.12(2), Sch.2, para.6(2)-(4)
		s.230(5) (defn. of "Ministers") rep.	SI 1311, art.12(2), Sch.2, para.6(5)
		s.270 am.	12, s.290, Sch.10, para.8(12)
		s.272 am.	12, s.290, Sch.10, para.8(13)
		Sch.1, Table am.	SI 625, art.2
		Sch.1, Table subst.	48, s.72(1)(2)
		Sch.8, paras.9-12,23 rep.	12, s.290, Sch.12
c.54	Roads (Scotland) Act 1984	defn. of "road" appl.	ii, s.1, Sch., s.3(1)(a)
		appl.	42, s.63, Sch.3, para.7(3) (adding defn. of "footpath" to 1964 c.40, s.57)
		defn. of "carriageway" appl.	42, s.67(1)
		ss.39A-39C added	30, s.2(1), Sch.2
		s.40 am.	30, s.2(2)(a)(c)
		s.40 rep.in pt.	30, s.2(2)(b)
		s.139(3) am.	53, s.18(1), Sch.3, para.16
		Sch.9, para.6 rep. (1-1- 1993) (saving)	42, s.68(1), Sch.4, Pt.I
		Sch.9, para.12 rep. (1-1-1993)	42, s.68(1), Sch.4, Pt.I
c.55	Building Act 1984	ss.1-46 (Pt.I) mod.	SI 1732, art.4(1)
		s.44 ext.	SI 1732, art.4(1)(a)
		s.87 mod.	SI 1732, art.4(2)
c.58	Rent (Scotland) Act 1984	defn. of "statutory tenant" appl.	14, s.75(5)
c.60	Police and Criminal Evidence Act 1984	ext.	SI 975, art.16(13)
		am.	SI 1302, art.17(13)
		appt. day(s) for s.60(1) (b) (Thames Valley Police Area) (9.11.1992)	SI 2802, art.2
		s.24(2) ext.	SI 975, art.16(13)
		s.24(2) ext.	SI 1302, art.17(13)
c.62	Friendly Societies Act 1984	s.3 rep. (*prosp.*)	40, s.120(2), Sch.22, Pt.I
1985			
c.6	Companies Act 1985	defn. of "a company" appl.	12, s.170(9)(a)
		defn. of "companies" appl.	37, s.12(2)(i)

Year and Chap. or No. of Measure	Short title	How affected	1992, Chapter of Act or Number of Measure or Statutory Instrument
1985—*cont.*			
		defn. of "company" appl. (*prosp.*)	40, s.13(11)
		defn. of "company" appl. (*prosp.*)	40, s.75(6)(a)
		defn. of "company" appl. (*prosp.*)	40, s.86(1)(c)
		restr.	52, s.10(3)(a)
		s.1(3A) added	SI 1699, reg.2, Sch., para.1
		s.6(3) appl. (adding 1960 c.58 s.30A(4)) (1.1.1993)	41, s.40
		s.14 mod.	SI 225, reg.119(1)
		s.18(3) ext.	SI 225, reg.119(3)
		s.21(3A) added	SI 1083, reg.3
		s.24 mod.	SI 225, reg.61(7)
		s.24 am.	SI 1699, regs.2,3, Sch., para.2
		s.26(3) appl.(mods.) (EW)	41, s.4(7)(9)
		ss.56-79 (Pt.III) trans.of functions	SI 1315, arts.2(3)(4),6
		s.182(1)(b) excl.	SI 225, reg.18(2)(a)
		s.183 excl.	SI 225, reg.18(2)(a)
		ss.185,186 excl.	SI 225, reg.48(1)(2)
		s.191 mod.	SI 225, reg.16, Sch.2, para.2
		s.191(4) ext.	SI 225, reg.91(2)
		ss.198-220 (Pt.VI) excl.	SI 225, reg.23(1)(a)
		ss.198-220 (Pt.VI) mod.	SI 225, reg.121, Sch.8, para.1(a)
		s.209(1)(c) am.	41, s.78(1), Sch.6, para.11(a)
		s.223 appl. (EW) (*prosp.*)	41, s.1(1)
		s.228(2)(b) am.	SI 3178, reg.4
		s.242(1) am.	SI 1083, reg.2(2)
		s.242B added	SI 2452, reg.3
		s.243(4) am.	SI 1083, reg.2(3)
		s.246(1)(b) am.	SI 2452, reg.4(2)(a)
		s.246(1A)(1B) added	SI 2452, reg.4(1)
		s.246(2) rep.	SI 2452, reg.4(2)(b)
		s.246(3) am.	SI 2452, reg.4(2)(c)
		s.247(2)(a) am.	SI 2452, reg.5(2)
		s.247(3) am.	SI 2452, reg.5(3)(4)
		s.249(2)(a) am.	SI 2452, reg.6(2)
		s.249(3) am.	SI 2452, reg.6(3)(4)
		s.250(1)(a) rev.in pt.	SI 3003, reg.2(2)
		s.250(1)(b) subst.	SI 3003, reg.2(3)
		s.251(1) am.	SI 3003, reg.3(2)
		s.251(2) am.	SI 3003, reg.3(4)
		s.251(7) am.	SI 3003, reg.3(5)
		s.255A(4)(b)(ii) am.	SI 3178, reg.5
		s.255B(1) am.	SI 3178, reg.6

Year and Chap. or No. of Measure	Short title	How affected	1992, Chapter of Act or Number of Measure or Statutory Instrument
1985—*cont.*			
		s.255E added	SI 1083, reg.2(4)
		s.262(1) (defn. of "credit institution") subst.	SI 3178, reg.7
		s.312 mod. (*prosp.*)	40, s.27, Sch.11, Pt.II, para.8(1)
		s.316(3) mod. (*prosp.*)	40, s.27, Sch.11, Pt.II, para.8(1)
		s.322B added	SI 1699, reg.2, Sch., para.3(1)
		ss.324-326 excl.	SI 225, reg.23(1)(b)
		ss.324-326 mod.	SI 225, reg.121, Sch.8, para.1(b)
		s.328 excl.	SI 225, reg.23(1)(b)
		s.328 mod.	SI 225, reg.121, Sch.8, para.1(b)
		s.346 excl.	SI 225, reg.23(1)(b)
		s.346 mod.	SI 225, reg.121, Sch.8, para.1(b)
		s.346(2) appl.	37, s.12, Sch.2, para.14(5)
		s.352 mod.	SI 225, reg.16, Sch.2, para.1(1)
		s.352(5) appl.(mods.)	SI 225, reg.56(5)
		s.352A added	SI 1699, reg.2, Sch., para.4(1)
		s.353(1)(2)(4) appl.	SI 225, reg.26(1)
		s.353(4) appl.(mods.)	SI 225, reg.26(1)
		s.356 appl.	SI 225, reg.26(2)
		s.356(6) ext.	SI 225, reg.26(3)
		s.357 appl.	SI 225, reg.26(3)
		s.358 excl.	SI 225, reg.16, Sch.2, para.1(3)
		s.359 excl.	SI 225, reg.73(2)
		s.359(1)(a)(2)-(4) appl.(mods.)	SI 225, reg.73(1)
		s.360 am.	SI 225, reg.67(2)
		s.364A mod.	SI 225, reg.121, Sch.8, para.3
		s.370A added	SI 1699, reg.2, Sch., para.5
		s.380 appl. (EW)	41, s.5(2)
		s.380(6) ext.	SI 225, regs.77(2),89(4)
		s.382B added	SI 1699, reg.2, Sch., para.6(1)
		s.402 excl.	SI 225, reg.91(1)
		s.425 (defn. of "arrangement") appl.	12, s.180(7)
		ss.428-430F (Pt.XIIIA) mod.	SI 225, reg.121, Sch.8, para.9(3)
		s.430(3)(a) mod.	SI 225, reg.121, Sch.8, para.9(9)
		s.430(5) mod.	SI 225, reg.121, Sch.8, para.9(5)

Year and Chap. or No. of Measure	Short title	How affected	1992, Chapter of Act or Number of Measure or Statutory Instrument
1985—*cont.*		s.430(6) excl.	SI 225, reg.121, Sch.8, para.9(4)
		s.430A(1)(2) mod.	SI 225, reg.121, Sch.8, para.9(9)
		s.446(4)(c)-(c) am. (1.1.1993)	SI 3218, reg.82(1), Sch.10, Pt.I, para.16
		s.449(1)(d) am.	SI 1315, art.10(1), Sch.4, para.1
		s.449(1)(de)(df) added (*prosp.*)	40, s.120(1), Sch.21, Pt.I, para.7(1)
		s.449(3)(j)(k) rep.in pt. (*prosp.*)	40, s.120(2), Sch.22, Pt.I
		s.449(3)(jj) added (*prosp.*)	40, s.120(1), Sch.21, Pt.I, para.7(2)
		s.651 appl.(mods.) (EW)	41, s.10(1) (adding 1960 c.58 s.30(3))
		s.653(2) appl.(mods.) (EW)	41, s.10(1) (adding 1960 c.58 s.30(4))
		ss.654,655 appl.(mods.) (*prosp.*)	40, s.23, Sch.10, Pt.IV, para.68(1)-(3)
		ss.656-658 appl. (*prosp.*)	40, s.23, Sch.10, Pt.IV, para.68(1)-(3)
		s.680(1A) added	SI 1699, reg.2, Sch., para.7
		ss.690A,690B added	SI 3179, Sch.2, para.2
		ss.691,692 mod. (transtl)	SI 3179, Sch.4, para.1(5)
		s.692A added	SI 3179, Sch.2, para.4
		s.693 am.	SI 3179, Sch.2, para.6
		s.693(2)-(4) added	SI 3179, Sch.2, para.6
		s.694 am.	SI 3179, Sch.2, para.7(2)
		s.694(3) rep.in pt.	SI 3179, Sch.2, para.7(3)
		s.694(3A)(3B) added	SI 3179, Sch.2, para.7(4)
		s.694A added	SI 3179, Sch.2, para.8
		s.695(1) am.	SI 3179, Sch.2, para.9
		s.695A added	SI 3179, Sch.2, para.10
		s.696(1)(3)(4) am.	SI 3179, Sch.2, para.11(a) (b)(c)
		s.696(3) am.	SI 3179, Sch.3, para.4
		s.697(3) added	SI 3179, Sch.2, para.12
		s.698 am.	SI 3179, Sch.2, para.13
		s.698(1) rep.in pt.	SI 3179, Sch.2, para.13
		s.698(2) added	SI 3179, Sch.2, para.13
		s.699(1) am.	SI 3179, Sch.2, para.14
		ss.699A,699B added	SI 3179, reg.2
		s.699AA added	SI 3179, Sch.2, para.16
		s.699B am.	SI 3179, Sch.2, para.17
		ss.700,703 mod. (transtl)	SI 3179, Sch.4, para.4(2)
		ss.703O-703R added	SI 3179, Sch.2, para.19
		s.704(5) am.	SI 225, reg.121, Sch.8, para.10
		s.705(5)(za) added	SI 3179, Sch.3, para.5
		s.705A added	SI 3179, reg.3

Year and Chap. or No. of Measure	Short title	How affected	1992, Chapter of Act or Number of Measure or Statutory Instrument
1985—*cont.*			
		s.706(1) am.	SI 225, reg.121, Sch.8, para.10
		ss.706(2)(a),707(4)(a) am.	SI 3179, Sch.3, para.6
		s.707(1) am.	SI 225, reg.121, Sch.8, para.10
		s.707A(1) am.	SI 225, reg.121, Sch.8, para.10
		s.708(1)(a)(4) am.	SI 225, reg.121, Sch.8, para.10
		s.709(1)(3) am.	SI 225, reg.121, Sch.8, para.10
		s.711(1)(u)-(z) added	SI 3179, Sch.3, para.7
		s.714(1)(aa) added	SI 3179, Sch.3, para.8
		s.716 excl.	52, s.127(3)
		s.716(1) am.	SI 1028, reg.2
		s.723A appl.(mods.)	SI 225, reg.26(2)
		s.727 appl. (*prosp.*)	40, s.106(4)
		s.727 appl. (EW) (*prosp.*)	41, s.22(3)
		s.735 (defn. of "company") appl.	48, s.66, Sch.12, para.2(2)(a)
		s.736 (defn. of "subsidiary") appl.	12, s.239(7)
		s.741(3) rep.in pt.	SI 1699, reg.2, Sch., para.3(2)
		s.741(3) am.	SI 1699, reg.2, Sch., para.3(2)
		s.744 am.	SI 1315, art.10(1), Sch.4, para.2
		Sch.7, para.6(d) added	SI 3178, reg.3
		Sch.8, Pt.I subst.	SI 2452, reg.4(3), Sch., paras.1(3),2
		Sch.8, Pts.I,II,III , made respectively, sections A-C of Pt.III.	SI 2452, reg.4(3), Sch., para.1(1)
		Sch.8, Pt.II subst.	SI 2452, reg.4(3), Sch., paras.1(4),3
		Sch.8, Pt.III subst.	SI 2452, reg.4(3), Sch.8, para.1(5)
		Sch.8, paras.1-10 renumbered as paras.17- 26	SI 2452, reg.4(3), Sch., para.1(2)
		Sch.8, para.3(1) am.	SI 2452, reg.4(3), Sch., para.4(2)
		Sch.8, para.3(4) added	SI 2452, reg.4(3), Sch., para.4(3)
		Sch.8, paras.7(1)(1)(a)(2), 8(1) am.	SI 2452, reg.4(3), Sch., para.4(4)-(6)
		Sch.8, para.9 am.	SI 2452, reg.4(3), Sch., para.4(7)
		Sch.8, para.10(1)-(3) am.	SI 2452, reg.4(3), Sch., para.4(4)(8)
		Sch.9, Pt.II, para.7(3) am.	SI 1083, reg.2(5)
		Sch.13 excl.	SI 225, reg.23(1)(b)

Year and Chap. or No. of Measure	Short title	How affected	1992, Chapter of Act or Number of Measure or Statutory Instrument
1985—*cont.*			
		Sch.13 mod.	SI 225, reg.121, Sch.8, para.1(b)
		Sch.13, Pt.I appl. (1.1.1993) (EW)	41, s.32(2), Sch.2, para.4(2)
		Sch.13, para.11(b) am.	41, s.78(1), Sch.6, para.11(b)
		Sch.14, para.2(2) mod.	SI 225, reg.121, Sch.8, para.5(3)
		Sch.21, para.6(2) ext.	xvii, s.4
		Sch.21A added	SI 3179, Sch.2, para.3
		Sch.21A, para.1(2) mod. (transtl)	SI 3179, Sch.4, para.8(2)
		Sch.21B added	SI 3179, Sch.2, para.5
		Sch.21C added	SI 3179, reg.2
		Sch.21C mod. (transtl)	SI 3179, Sch.4, para.4(3)
		Schs.21C,21D mod. (transtl)	SI 3179, Sch.4, para.8(2)
		Sch.21C, paras.10,12(1) mod. (transtl)	SI 3179, Sch.4, para.5(2)
		Sch.21C, paras.11(a),13(2) mod. (transtl)	SI 3179, Sch.4, para.5(4)
		Sch.21D added	SI 3179, Sch.2, para.18
		Sch.21D mod. (transtl)	SI 3179, Sch.4, para.6(3)
		Sch.21D, paras.8,10(1) mod. (transtl)	SI 3179, Sch.4, para.7(2)
		Sch.21D, paras.9(a),12(2) mod. (transtl)	SI 3179, Sch.4, para.7(4)
		Sch.24 am.	SI 1699, reg.2, Sch., paras.3(3),4(2),6(2)
		Sch.24 am.	SI 3179, Sch.3, para.9
c.7	Business Names Act 1985	ss.2,3 restr.	SI 1196, reg.3(1)(2)
c.8	Company Securities (Insider Dealing) Act 1985	trans.of functions am. (1.1.1993)	SI 1315, arts.2(1)(a),6 SI 3218, reg.82(1), Sch.10, Pt.I, para.17
c.9	Companies Consolidation (Consequential Provisions) Act 1985	Sch.2 rep.in pt. (*prosp.*) Sch.2 rep.in pt.	41, s.78(2), Sch.7 52, s.300(1), Sch.1
c.16	The National Heritage (Scotland) Act 1985	s.3(2)(e) am.	44, s.11(2), Sch.8, Pt.II, para.14(1)
		s.8(3)(d) am.	44, s.11(2), Sch.8, Pt.II, para.14(3)
		s.8(3)(c) subst.	44, s.11(2), Sch.8, Pt.II, para.14(2)
		s.8(4) rep.	44, s.11(3), Sch.9
		s.23 am.	44, s.11(2), Sch.8, Pt.II, para.14(4)
		Sch.2, para.2 rep.	44, s.11(3), Sch.9
c.17	Reserve Forces (Safeguard of Employment) Act 1985	ext.	39, s.2(3)
		Sch.4, para.13 rep.	53, s.18(2), Sch.4, Pt.I
c.20	Charities Act 1985	rep. (except s.2, rep. prosp.)	41, s.78(2), Sch.7
c.21	Films Act 1985	Sch.1, para.1 appl.	48, s.43(2)(a)

Year and Chap. or No. of Measure	Short title	How affected	1992, Chapter of Act or Number of Measure or Statutory Instrument
1985—*cont.*			
c.23	Prosecution of Offences Act 1985	s.20(5) am.	SI 709, art.2(3)(b)
c.31	Wildlife and Countryside (Amendment) Act 1985	s.1 rep.	51, s.15(2), Sch.
c.35	Gaming (Bingo) Act 1985	defn. of "Multiple bingo" appl.	10, s.1(8)
		s.2(4) rep.	10, s.1(9)
c.47	The Further Education Act 1985	s.1(4) added (1.4.1993)	13, s.93(1), Sch.8, Pt.I, para.20
		s.2(2)(a)-(d) replaced (by paras.(a)-(c))	13, s.93(1), Sch.8, Pt.I, para.21(1)
		s.2(8) am.	13, s.93(1), Sch.8, Pt.I, para.21(2)
c.48	Food and Environment Protection Act 1985	ss.5-15 saved	ix, s.1, Sch., s.22(1)(a)
		ss.5-15 saved	xii, s.1, Sch., s.62(a)
		ss.5-15 saved	xv, s.25
c.50	Representation of the People Act 1985	s.6(2)(b) mod.	SI 834, reg.3 (substituting S.I.1986/1111 reg.62, para.(5))
c.51	Local Government Act 1985	ss.46,47 trans.of functions	SI 1311, art.3(1), Sch.1, Pt.I
		s.46(1) am.	SI 1311, art.12(2), Sch.2, para.7(a)
		s.46(2) rep.	SI 1311, art.12(2), Sch.2, para.7(b)
		s.47(2)(3) am.	SI 1311, art.12(2), Sch.2, para.7(a)
		s.47(4) rep.	SI 1311, art.12(2), Sch.2, para.7(b)
		s.48(4A) added	14, s.105
		s.57(3) am.	SI 3325, art.2
		Sch.13, para.3(2) trans.of functions	SI 331, art.2(2)(4)
		Sch.16, paras.4-6 rep. (*prosp.*)	19, s.29, Sch.4, Pt.II
c.53	Social Security Act 1985	s.5(1)(c) added	6, s.4, Sch.2, para.67(1)
		s.5(2) am.	6, s.4, Sch.2, para.67(2)
		s.7 rep.	6, s.3, Sch.1
		s.8(1) rep.	6, s.3, Sch.1
		ss.9-13 rep.	6, s.3, Sch.1
		s.18 rep.	6, s.3, Sch.1
		s.20 rep.	6, s.3, Sch.1
		s.27 rep.	6, s.3, Sch.1
		s.30 rep.	6, s.3, Sch.1
		s.32(8) am.	6, s.4, Sch.2, para.68
		Sch.3, para.1 rep.	6, s.3, Sch.1
		Sch.4, paras.3-7 rep.	6, s.3, Sch.1
		Sch.5, para.5 rep.	6, s.3, Sch.1
		Sch.5, paras.8,9 rep.	6, s.3, Sch.1
		Sch.5, para.11 rep.	6, s.3, Sch.1
		Sch.5, paras.13-15 rep.	6, s.3, Sch.1

Year and Chap. or No. of Measure	Short title	How affected	1992, Chapter of Act or Number of Measure or Statutory Instrument
1985—*cont.*			
c.54	Finance Act 1985	s.13(2)(b) am. (1.12.1992, 1.1.1993)	48, s.14(2), Sch.3, Pt.II, para.77(1)(a)
		s.13(2)(ba) added (1.12.1992,1.1.1993)	48, s.14(2), Sch.3, Pt.II, para.77(1)(b)
		s.13(3)(b) am. (1.12.1992, 1.1.1993)	48, s.14(2), Sch.3, Pt.II, para.77(2)
		s.14(1) am.	20, s.7(1)(3)(4)
		s.14(5B)(b) am. (1.12.1992,1.1.1993)	48, s.14(2), Sch.3, Pt.II, para.78
		s.14B added (1.12.1992, 1.1.1993)	48, s.14(2), Sch.3, Pt.II, para.79
		s.15(1)(a) am. (1.12.1992, 1.1.1993)	48, s.14(2), Sch.3, Pt.II, para.80(1)(a)
		s.15(1)(aa) added (1.12.1992,1.1.1993)	48, s.14(2), Sch.3, Pt.II, para.80(1)(b)
		s.15(3) am. (1.12.1992, 1.1.1993)	48, s.14(2), Sch.3, Pt.II, para.80(2)(a)
		s.15(3)(a)(b) am. (1.12.1992,1.1.1993)	48, s.14(2), Sch.3, Pt.II, para.80(2)(b)(c)
		s.15(3)(ba) added (1.12.1992,1.1.1993)	48, s.14(2), Sch.3, Pt.II, para.80(2)(d)
		s.15(3A)(a)(b) am. (1.12.1992,1.1.1993)	48, s.14(2), Sch.3, Pt.II, para.80(3)(a)(b)
		s.15(3B)(3C) added (1.12.1992,1.1.1993)	48, s.14(2), Sch.3, Pt.II, para.80(4)
		s.15(3D) added (1.1.1993)	48, s.16(5)
		s.17(1)(a) am. (1.12.1992, 1.1.1993)	48, s.14(2), Sch.3, Pt.II, para.81(a)
		s.17(1)(aa) added (1.12.1992,1.1.1993)	48, s.14(2), Sch.3, Pt.II, para.81(b)
		s.17A added (1.12.1992, 1.1.1993)	48, s.14(2), Sch.3, Pt.II, para.82
		s.18(1)(c) am. (1.12.1992, 1.1.1993)	48, s.14(2), Sch.3, Pt.II, para.83
		s.19(5) am.	20, s.7(2)(5)
		s.20(3A) added	48, s.15(1)(3)
		s.21(1) am. (1.12.1992, 1.1.1993)	48, s.14(2), Sch.3, Pt.II, para.84(1)
		s.21(4A) added (1.12.1992, 1.1.1993)	48, s.14(2), Sch.3, Pt.II, para.84(2)
		s.21(5)(6) am. (1.12.1992, 1.1.1993)	48, s.14(2), Sch.3, Pt.II, para.84(3)(4)(a)(c)
		s.21(6)(a) am. (1.12.1992, 1.1.1993)	48, s.14(2), Sch.3, Pt.II, para.84(4)(b)
		s.22(1) am. (1.12.1992, 1.1.1993)	48, s.14(2), Sch.3, Pt.II, para.85(1)(b)
		s.22(1)(a) am. (1.12.1992, 1.1.1993)	48, s.14(2), Sch.3, Pt.II, para.85(1)(a)
		s.22(2) am. (1.12.1992, 1.1.1993)	48, s.14(2), Sch.3, Pt.II, para.85(2)
		s.22(7) am. (1.12.1992, 1.1.1993)	48, s.14(2), Sch.3, Pt.II, para.85(3)

Year and Chap. or No. of Measure	Short title	How affected	1992, Chapter of Act or Number of Measure or Statutory Instrument
1985—*cont.*			
		s.22(7) rep.in pt. (1.1.1993)	48, ss.14(3),82, Sch.18, Pt.V
		s.26(2)(a) am.	53, s.18(1), Sch.3, para.17
		s.33(5)(a) am. (1.12.1992, 1.1.1993)	48, s.14(2), Sch.3, Pt.II, para.86
		ss.67-72 rep.	12, s.290, Sch.12
		s.68(4) excl.	SI 58, art.9, Sch.2, para.12(2)
		s.68(7A)(a) am. (*prosp.*)	48, s.56, Sch.9, para.20(2)(a)
		s.68(7A)(b) am.	48, s.49(6)(10)
		s.68(7A)(j) added	48, s.77, Sch.17, paras.5(7),7
		s.81 am.	12, s.290, Sch.10, para.9
		s.95(1)(b) rep.	12, s.290, Sch.12
		Schs.19-21 rep.	12, s.290, Sch.12
c.57	Sporting Events (Control of Alcohol etc.) Act 1985	s.4(1) am.	57, s.1
c.58	Trustee Savings Bank Act 1985	Sch.2, para.2 am.	12, s.290, Sch.10, para.10(1)(a)(b)
		Sch.2, para.3 am.	12, s.290, Sch.10, para.10(2)(a)(b)
		Sch.2, para.4 am.	12, s.290, Sch.10, para.10(3)(a)(b)(c)
		Sch.2, para.9(1) (defn. of "the 1992 Act") added	12, s.290, Sch.10, para.10(4)(a)
		Sch.2, para.9(2) am.	12, s.290, Sch.10, para.10(4)(b)
c.61	Administration of Justice Act 1985	s.21(5) subst.	SI 2890, reg.12(4)
c.65	Insolvency Act 1985	Sch.1, para.5 rep.	53, s.18(2), Sch.4, Pt.I
c.66	Bankruptcy (Scotland) Act 1985	defn. of "permanent trustee" appl.	12, s.66(5)
		s.31(8) restr.	5, s.89(2)
		s.31(8) am.	6, s.4, Sch.2, para.69
		s.73(1) am. (1.1.1993)	SI 3218, reg.82(1), Sch.10, Pt.I, para.18
c.67	Transport Act 1985	defn. of "local service" appl.	iv, s.10(6)(b)
		s.34(2) (defn. of "bus service") appl.	xvi, s.2(1)
		s.130(3)(4) am.	12, s.290, Sch.10, para.11(a)(b)
		Sch.2, para.2, Pt.II rep.	53, s.18(2), Sch.4, Pt.I
		Sch.7, para.15 rep.	53, s.18(2), Sch.4, Pt.I
c.68	Housing Act 1985	ss.79-117 (Pt.IV) (defn. of "secure tenant") appl.	14, s.6(6)
		s.425(2)(b) am.	6, s.4, Sch.2, para.70
		s.622 am. (1.1.1993)	SI 3218, reg.82(1), Sch.10, Pt.I, para.19
		Sch.1, para.12 subst.	41, s.78(1), Sch.6, para.12
		Sch.4, para.5A(a) mod.	SI 1709, reg.2(a)

Year and Chap. or No. of Measure	Short title	How affected	1992, Chapter of Act or Number of Measure or Statutory Instrument
1985—*cont.*			
		Sch.4, para.5A(a) am.	SI 1709, reg.2(a)
		Sch.4, para.7(1) mod.	SI 1709, reg.2(b)
		Sch.4, para.7(1) am.	SI 1709, reg.2(b)
		Sch.14, Pt.I, Item 4 am.	6, s.4, Sch.2, para.71
		Sch.14, Pt.IV, para.3 am.	6, s.4, Sch.2, para.72
c.69	Housing Associations Act 1985	defn. of "housing association" appl.	12, s.218(2)
		defns. of "registered housing association" and "unregistered self- build society" appl.	12, s.219(4)
		defn. of "registered housing association" appl.	12, s.259(3)
		s.10(1) am. (1.1.1993)	41, s.78(1), Sch.6, para.13(1)
		s.26(2) am. (*prosp.*)	41, s.78(1), Sch.6, para.13(2)
		s.35(2)(c) am. (1.1.1993)	41, s.78(1), Sch.6, para.13(3)
		s.106(1) am. (1.1.1993)	SI 3218, reg.82(1), Sch.10, Pt.I, para.20
c.71	Housing (Consequential Provisions) Act 1985	Sch.2, para.18 rep.	12, s.290, Sch.12
c.72	Weights and Measures Act 1985	appt. day(s) for s.43 (1.4.1994)	SI 770, art.2
		expld.	SI 1579, reg.3(3)
		mod.	SI 1591, art.2
		mod.	SI 1592, art.2
		mod.	SI 1593, art.2
		s.11 mod.	SI 1591, art.2
		s.11 mod.	SI 1592, art.2
		s.11 mod.	SI 1593, art.2
c.73	Law Reform (Miscellaneous Provisions) (Scotland) Act 1985	s.8 restr.	37, s.16, Sch.3, para.3(2)
		s.8 restr.	37, s.16, Sch.3, para.4(5)
		s.8 restr. (1-4-1993)	37, s.17(7)
c.xiii	Worcester City Council Act 1985	s.35 rep.	SI 117, art.19(1), Sch.
c.xvii	Leicestershire Act 1985	s.22 rep.	SI 117, art.19(1), Sch.
		s.106(2) rep.in pt.	SI 117, art.19(1), Sch.
		Sch.2 rep.	SI 117, art.19(1), Sch.
c.xxxiv	Oxfordshire Act 1985	s.18 rep.	SI 117, art.19(1), Sch.
		s.46(2) rep.in pt.	SI 117, art.19(1), Sch.
c.xlii	Hereford City Council Act 1985	s.9 rep.	SI 2766, art.2
1986			
c.5	Agricultural Holdings Act 1986	Sch.11, para.21 am.	53, s.18(1), Sch.3, para.18
		Sch.14, para.49 rep.	53, s.18(2), Sch.4, Pt.I
c.14	Animal (Scientific Procedures) Act 1986	Sch.3, para.9 rep. (EWS)	51, s.15(2), Sch.

Year and Chap. or No. of Measure	Short title	How affected	1992, Chapter of Act or Number of Measure or Statutory Instrument
1986—cont.			
c.31	Airports Act 1986	s.29(1) added	SI 2992, Sch.2, para.1
		s.31(2) am.	SI 2992, Sch.2, para.2
		s.32(3) am.	SI 2992, Sch.2, para.3
		s.77(2) am.	12, s.290, Sch.10, para.12
c.33	Disabled Persons (Services, Consultation and Representation) Act 1986	s.5(3)(4) replaced (by subss.(3)(3A)(3B)(3C)(4)) (1.4.1993)	13, s.93(1), Sch.8, Pt.II, para.91(1)(2)
		s.5(5) am. (1.4.1993)	13, s.93(1), Sch.8, Pt.II, para.91(3)
		s.5(6) am. (1.4.1993)	13, s.93(1), Sch.8, Pt.II, para.91(4)
		s.5(9) (defn. of "child") am. (1.4.1993)	13, s.93(1), Sch.8, Pt.II, para.91(5)(a)
		s.5(9) (defn. of "responsible authority") am. (para.(b) replaced by paras.(b)(c)) (1.4.1993)	13, s.93(1), Sch.8, Pt.II, para.91(5)(b)
		s.5(9) am. (1.4.1993)	13, s.93(1), Sch.8, Pt.II, para.91(5)(c)(d)
		s.6(1) subst. (1.4.1993)	13, s.93(1), Sch.8, Pt.II, para.92
c.39	Patents, Designs and Marks Act 1986	Sch.2, Pt.I, para.1(2)(d) rep.	53, s.18(2), Sch.4, Pt.I
c.40	Education Act 1986	s.1(1)(a) cert. functs. made exercisable concurrently	SI 1296, arts.2(3)(a),3
		s.1(1A) added	SI 1296, art.6(1), Sch., para.5(1)
		s.1(2)(3) am.	SI 1296, art.6(1), Sch., para.5(2)
		s.5 am.	SI 1296, art.6(1), Sch., para.5(2)
c.41	Finance Act 1986	defn. of "personal equity plans" appl. (*prosp.*)	40, s.13, Sch.7, para.1
		s.8(5)(g) rep. (1.1.1993)	48, s.82, Sch.18, Pt.II
		s.9(3)(aa) added (1.12.1992,1.1.1993)	48, s.14(2), Sch.3, Pt.III, para.94(a)
		s.9(5) am. (1.12.1992, 1.1.1993)	48, s.14(2), Sch.3, Pt.III, para.94(b)
		s.33 rep.	41, s.78(2), Sch.7
		ss.58-60 rep.	12, s.290, Sch.12
		s.81(3) subst. (*prosp.*)	SI 3286, reg.2
		s.89(3) subst. (*prosp.*)	SI 3286, reg.3
		s.108(5) appl.	48, s.74(4)
		Sch.3, paras.2,6 rep.	48, s.82, Sch.18, Pt.I, Note 6
		Sch.5, para.5 rep. (1.1.1993)	48, s.82, Sch.18, Pt.II
		Sch.6, para.2, Table A subst.	SI 733, art.2
		Sch.6, para.3, Table B subst.	SI 733, art.3
		Sch.20, para.8(1A)(a) am.	48, s.73, Sch.14, paras.7- 9
		Sch.21, para.5(1) am.	48, s.74, Sch.15, para.9
c.44	Gas Act 1986	Pt.1 (defn. of "gas"). appl.	15, s.2(4)

Year and Chap. or No. of Measure	Short title	How affected	1992, Chapter of Act or Number of Measure or Statutory Instrument
1986—*cont.*			
		ss.1-48 (Pt.I) (defn. of "public gas supplier") appl.	viii, s.2(1)
		s.4(1A) added	43, s.38(1)
		s.4(2)(d) am. (1.1.2000)	SI 450, reg.3(5)(a)(i)
		s.4(2)(d) am.	SI 1751, art.2(a)
		s.4(4) added	43, s.56(6), Sch.1, para.5
		s.6(1) am. (1.1.2000)	SI 450, reg.3(5)(b)
		s.7(7)(a) rep.in pt.	43, ss.38(2),56(7), Sch.2
		s.7(9) am. (1.1.1995)	SI 450, reg.3(3)(a)
		s.7(12) am. (1.1.2000)	SI 450, reg.3(5)(a)(ii)
		s.8(5) am. (1.1.1995)	SI 450, reg.3(3)(a)
		s.8(5)(b) am. (1.1.2000)	SI 450, reg.3(5)(a)(iii)
		s.8(5)(b) am.	SI 1751, art.2(b)
		s.8A added	43, s.37
		s.10(1)(a) am. (1.1.1995)	SI 450, reg.3(3)(a)
		s.10(3)(b) am. (1.1.1995)	SI 450, reg.3(3)(b)
		s.10(5) am. (1.1.2000)	SI 450, reg.3(5)(a)(iv)
		s.12(1) am. (temp. until 31.12.1999)	SI 450, reg.3(4)(a)
		s.12(1) am. (1.1.2000)	SI 450, reg.3(5)(c)
		s.13(1)(2)(c) am. (temp. until 31.12.1999)	SI 450, reg.3(4)(a)
		s.13(1)(2)(c) am. (1.1.2000)	SI 450, reg.3(5)(c)
		s.13(7) am.	SI 1314, art.3(3), Sch., para.2(a)
		s.14(3) am. (1.1.2000)	SI 450, reg.3(5)(d)
		s.14(4)(b) am. (1.1.2000)	SI 450, reg.3(5)(a)(v)
		s.14(4)(b) am.	SI 1751, art.2(c)
		s.14A added	43, s.16
		s.15A added (*prosp.*)	43, s.17
		s.15B added	43, s.15
		s.16 power to rep. or mod. (*prosp.*)	15, s.2 (amending s.15 of 1974 c.37)
		s.16(7) am.	SI 1314, art.3(3), Sch., para.2(a)
		s.18(1) rep.	15, ss.3(3)(a),7(2), Sch.2
		s.19(8) rep.	43, ss.38(3),56(7), Sch.2
		s.20(1) am. (1.1.1995)	SI 450, reg.3(3)(c)
		s.20(2)(a) am. (1.1.1995)	SI 450, reg.3(3)(d)
		s.24(1)(a) subst.	43, s.38(4)
		s.27(a)(c) am.	43, s.38(5)
		s.28(1)(2)(4) am.	43, s.48(2)
		s.28(5)(aa) added	43, s.48(3)
		s.28(8) (defn. of "relevant requirement") am.	43, s.56(6), Sch.1, para.6(a)(b)
		s.32A added	43, s.18
		ss.33A,33B added	43, s.11
		s.33C added	43, s.12
		s.33D added	43, s.13

Year and Chap. or No. of Measure	Short title	How affected	1992, Chapter of Act or Number of Measure or Statutory Instrument
1986—*cont.*			
		s.33E added	43, s.14
		s.38(1) am.	43, s.56(6), Sch.1, para.7
		s.42(2)(cc) added	43, s.56(6), Sch.1, para.8(a)
		s.42(4)(a) am.	43, s.56(6), Sch.1, para.8(b)
		s.47(1)(c)(d) am.	43, s.56(6), Sch.1, para.9(2)(a)(b)
		s.47(3)(4) power to rep. or mod. (*prosp.*)	15, s.2 (amending s.15 of 1974 c.37)
		s.47(3)(aa) added	43, s.56(6), Sch.1, para.9(3)
		s.47(5) rep.in pt. (*prosp.*)	15, ss.3(3)(b),7(2), Sch.2
		s.48(1) (defn. of "kilowatt hour") added	SI 450, reg.3(2)
		s.48(1) am. (temp. until 31.12.1999)	SI 450, reg.3(4)(b)
		s.48(1) (defn. of "therm") rep. (1.1.2000)	SI 450, reg.3(5)(e)
		s.48(1) (defn. of "prescribed") am.	43, s.56(6), Sch.1, para.10
		s.60(2) am.	12, s.290, Sch.10, para.13
		Sch.5, para.3(4) added	43, s.53(1)
		Sch.5, para.7(5A) added	43, s.19
		Sch.7, para.2(9) am.	SI 1314, art.3(3), Sch., para.1(d)
		Sch.8, para.6(2) am.	15, s.3(3)(c)
		Sch.8, para.6(2A) added	15, s.3(3)(d)
c.45	Insolvency Act 1986	excl.	3, s.20(4)
		excl.	5, ss.89(1),93(1)
		ss.73-219 (Pt.IV) appl.(mods.) (*prosp.*)	40, ss.21(1),22,23, Sch.10
		ss.73-219 (Pt.IV) mod. (*prosp.*)	40, s.23, Sch.10
		s.122(1)(e) am.	SI 1699, reg.2, Sch., para.8
		s.122(1)(f) ext.	SI 613, reg.49(2)
		s.122(1)(f) power to mod. (EW)	14, s.14(3), Sch.4, para.10(1)
		s.177(5) appl. (*prosp.*)	40, s.24(4)
		ss.220-229 (Pt.V) ext. (*prosp.*)	40, s.52(1)(9)
		s.220 (defn. of "unregistered company") appl.	48, s.66, Sch.12, para.2(2)(b)
		s.220(1) rep. (1-1-1993)	42, s.65(1)(f)
		s.220(1)(a) rep. (1-1- 1993) (EWS)	42, s.68(1), Sch.4, Pt.I
		s.221(5)(b) ext.	SI 613, reg.49(2)
		ss.230-246 (Pt.VI) appl.(mods.) (*prosp.*)	40, ss.21(1),22,23, Sch.10
		ss.230-246 (Pt.VI) mod. (*prosp.*)	40, s.23, Sch.10
		ss.247-251 (Pt.VII) appl.(mods.) (*prosp.*)	40, ss.21(1),22,23, Sch.10

Year and Chap. or No. of Measure	Short title	How affected	1992, Chapter of Act or Number of Measure or Statutory Instrument
1986—*cont.*			
		ss.247-251 (Pt.VII) mod. (*prosp.*)	40, s.23, Sch.10
		s.267 ext.	SI 613, reg.49(1)
		s.267 power to mod.	14, s.14(3), Sch.4, para.9(1)
		ss.386-387 (Pt.XII) appl.(mods.) (*prosp.*)	40, ss.21(1),22,23, Sch.10
		ss.386-387 (Pt.XII) mod. (*prosp.*)	40, s.23, Sch.10
		ss.388-398 (Pt.XIII) appl.(mods.) (*prosp.*)	40, ss.21(1),22,23, Sch.10
		ss.388-398 (Pt.XIII) mod. (*prosp.*)	40, s.23, Sch.10
		s.414 ext. (*prosp.*)	40, s.23, Sch.10, Pt.IV, para.69(2)
		s.430 appl. (*prosp.*)	40, ss.21(1),22,23, Sch.10
		s.430 mod. (*prosp.*)	40, s.23, Sch.10
		s.432 appl. (*prosp.*)	40, ss.21(1),22,23, Sch.10
		s.432 mod. (*prosp.*)	40, s.23, Sch.10
		Sch.6, para.6 am.	6, s.4, Sch.2, para.73
		Sch.6, para.13(2)(c)(d) am.	52, s.300(2), Sch.2, para.33(a)(b)
		Sch.7, para.1(2) am.	53, s.18(1), para.19, Sch.3
		Sch.10 appl. (*prosp.*)	40, ss.21(1),22,23, Sch.10
		Sch.10 mod. (*prosp.*)	40, s.23, Sch.10
		Sch.14 rep.in pt.	53, s.18(2), Sch.4, Pt.I
c.46	Company Directors Disqualification Act 1986	s.22B added (*prosp.*)	40, s.120(1), Sch.21, Pt.I, para.8
c.47	Legal Aid (Scotland) Act 1986	appt. day(s) for s.30 (1.7.1992)	SI 1226, art.2
		s.6(2) am.	53, s.18(1), Sch.3, para.20
		s.8 am.	SI 1587, reg.3
		s.8(a) am.	SI 1587, reg.2
		s.11(2)(a) am.	SI 1587, reg.4
		s.15(1)(2)(a) am.	SI 1586, regs.2,3
		s.17(2)(a) am.	SI 1586, reg.4
c.48	Wages Act 1986	ss.1-11 (Pt.I) mod.	52, s.68(4)
		s.1 mod.	52, s.88(2)
		s.1(6) rep.in pt.	52, s.300(1), Sch.1
		s.5 restr.	52, s.88(3)
		s.5(2) mod.	52, s.88(4)
		s.5(3A) rep.	52, s.300(1), Sch.1
		s.7(1)(c)(d) am.	52, s.300(2), Sch.2, para.34(2)(a)(b)
		s.7(1)(e) am.	6, s.4, Sch.2, para.74(a)
		s.7(1)(f) am.	6, s.4, Sch.2, para.74(b)
		Sch.2, para.2(1)(b) am.	52, s.300(2), Sch.2, para.34(3)
		Sch.4, paras.1-3 rep. (*prosp.*)	17, s.3(3), Sch., Pt.II
c.50	Social Security Act 1986	s.3(4) am.	6, s.4, Sch.2, para.76
		s.4(1) am.	6, s.4, Sch.2, para.77
		s.7(5) am.	6, s.4, Sch.2, para.78

Year and Chap. or No. of Measure	Short title	How affected	1992, Chapter of Act or Number of Measure or Statutory Instrument
1986—*cont.*		s.9(5) am.	6, s.4, Sch.2, para.79
		s.16(4)(a) am.	6, s.4, Sch.2, para.80
		s.17A(1) am.	6, s.4, Sch.2, para.81
		ss.18-29 rep.	6, s.3, Sch.1
		s.30(1)-(9)(11) rep.	6, s.3, Sch.1
		ss.31-36 rep.	6, s.3, Sch.1
		ss.37(1),38 rep.	6, s.3, Sch.1
		ss.40-51 rep.	6, s.3, Sch.1
		s.50(1) am. (*contingently*)	29, s.2(2)(b)
		ss.51-65 (Pt.VI) power to am.	6, s.5, Sch.3, Pt.II, para.22(3)(4)(b)
		s.51C added (temp. until 1.7.1992)	33, s.1(1)(2)
		s.52(2) am.	6, s.4, Sch.2, para.82
		s.52(3)-(10) rep.	6, s.3, Sch.1
		s.53 rep.	6, s.3, Sch.1
		s.56(2)(3) rep.in pt.	6, s.3, Sch.1
		s.56(4)-(4B) rep.	6, s.3, Sch.1
		s.58 rep.	6, s.3, Sch.1
		s.59(3)(c) am.	6, s.4, Sch.2, para.83
		s.61(1)(3)-(5) rep.in pt.	6, s.3, Sch.1
		s.61(7)-(9) rep.	6, s.3, Sch.1
		s.61(10) (defns. of "the Committee" and "the Council") rep.	6, s.3, Sch.1
		ss.62-69 rep.	6, s.3, Sch.1
		s.64(2) restr.	SI 469, reg.2
		s.70(1) rep.	6, s.3, Sch.1
		ss.73,74 rep.	6, s.3, Sch.1
		s.79(3)(4) rep.	6, s.3, Sch.1
		s.80(1) rep.in pt.	6, s.3, Sch.1
		s.81 rep.	6, s.3, Sch.1
		s.83(1) am.	6, s.4, Sch.2, para.84
		s.83(2)(3)(b)-(e) rep.	6, s.3, Sch.1
		s.83(5) rep.in pt.	6, s.3, Sch.1
		s.84(1) (defn. of "the benefit Acts") rep.in pt.	6, s.3, Sch.1

Year and Chap. or No. of Measure	Short title	How affected	1992, Chapter of Act or Number of Measure or Statutory Instrument
1986—*cont.*			
		s.84(1) (defns. of "dwelling", "housing authority", "housing benefit scheme", "Housing Revenue Account dwelling", "income-related benefit", "local authority", "long-term benefit", "new town corporation", "primary Class 1 contributions", "secondary Class 1 contributions", "qualifying benefit", "rate rebate", "rent rebate", "rent allowance", "rates", "rating authority", "trade dispute", "war disablement pension" war widow's pension" and "applicable amount") rep.	
		s.84(3) rep.	6, s.3, Sch.1
		s.85(1)(a)-(c)(f)(3)(c)(d) (4) rep.	6, s.3, Sch.1
		s.85(5) rep.in pt.	6, s.3, Sch.1
		s.85(7) rep.	6, s.3, Sch.1
		s.85(8) rep.in pt.	6, s.3, Sch.1
		s.85(9)-(12) rep.	6, s.3, Sch.1
		Sch.3 rep. (exc. para. 17)	6, s.3, Sch.1
		Sch.3, para.4 excl.	4, s.111, Sch.8, Pt.III, para.8(6)
		Sch.4 rep.	6, s.3, Sch.1
		Sch.5, Pt.II, paras.(b), (c) rep.	6, s.3, Sch.1
		Sch.5, paras.2-20 rep.	6, s.3, Sch.1
		Schs.6,7 rep.	6, s.3, Sch.1
		Sch.8, paras.1-3 rep.	6, s.3, Sch.1
		Sch.8, paras.5-7 rep.	6, s.3, Sch.1
		Sch.9, paras.1,3(1)(c),(2) (a)-(g)(j) rep. (NI)	9, s.3, Sch.1
		Sch.9, paras.11,12 rep. (NI)	9, s.3, Sch.1
		Sch.10, para.10 rep.	6, s.3, Sch.1
		Sch.10, para.34 rep.	6, s.3, Sch.1
		Sch.10, para.40 rep.	6, s.3, Sch.1
		Sch.10, para.48 rep.	6, s.3, Sch.1
		Sch.10, para.54 rep.	6, s.3, Sch.1
		Sch.10, paras.62-67 rep.	6, s.3, Sch.1
		Sch.10, para.68(2) rep.	6, s.3, Sch.1
		Sch.10, paras.69,70 rep.	6, s.3, Sch.1
		Sch.10, para.72 rep.	6, s.3, Sch.1
		Sch.10, para.74 rep.	6, s.3, Sch.1
		Sch.10, para.77 rep.	6, s.3, Sch.1
		Sch.10, paras.83-88 rep.	6, s.3, Sch.1

Year and Chap. or No. of Measure	Short title	How affected	1992, Chapter of Act or Number of Measure or Statutory Instrument
1986—*cont.*			
		Sch.10, paras.90-92 rep.	6, s.3, Sch.1
		Sch.10, para.95 rep.	6, s.3, Sch.1
		Sch.10, paras.97-100 rep.	6, s.3, Sch.1
		Sch.10, para.103(a)(b) rep.	6, s.3, Sch.1
		Sch.10, paras.104-107 rep.	6, s.3, Sch.1
		Sch.10, para.108(a) rep.	6, s.3, Sch.1
c.53	Building Societies Act 1986	appl.(mods.)	SI 1547, arts.5,6, Sch.2
		defn. of "building society" appl.	12, s.288(1)
		s.5(1) am. (1.1.1993)	SI 3218, reg.67
		s.7(4) am. (1.1.1993)	SI 3218, reg.82(1), Sch.10, Pt.I, para.22(a)
		s.7(4)(c)(ii) rep.in pt. (*prosp.*)	40, s.120(2), Sch.22, Pt.I
		s.7(4)(c)(iii) am.	52, s.300(2), Sch.2, para.35
		s.9(4)(cc) added (1.1.1993)	SI 3218, reg.68(1)
		s.9(13) (defn. of "the prescribed minimum") am. (1.1.1993)	SI 3218, reg.68(2)(a)
		s.9(13) (defn. of "qualifying holding") added (1.1.1993)	SI 3218, reg.68(2)(b)
		s.25(5) am. (1.1.1993)	SI 3218, reg.82(1), Sch.10, Pt.I, para.22(b)
		s.41(6)(a) am. (1.1.1993)	SI 3218, reg.83, Sch.11, Pt.IV, para.18(2)(a)
		s.41(6)(dd) added (1.1.1993)	SI 3218, reg.69
		s.42(5)(d) added (1.1.1993)	SI 3218, reg.70
		s.43(1A) added (1.1.1993)	SI 3218, reg.71(1)
		s.43(4) am. (1.1.1993)	SI 3218, reg.71(2)
		s.43(5) am. (1.1.1993)	SI 3218, reg.71(3)
		s.43(9A) added (1.1.1993)	SI 3218, reg.71(4)
		s.44(4)(a) am. (1.1.1993)	SI 3218, reg.83, Sch.11, Pt.IV, para.18(2)(a)
		s.44(4)(dd) added (1.1.1993)	SI 3218, reg.72(1)
		s.44(9A) added (1.1.1993)	SI 3218, reg.72(2)
		s.45(3) am. (1.1.1993)	SI 3218, reg.73
		s.45(3) am. (1.1.1993)	SI 3218, reg.83, Sch.11, Pt.IV, para.18(2)(b)
		s.45A added (1.1.1993)	SI 3218, reg.74
		s.46(1) am. (1.1.1993)	SI 3218, regs.22(6),23(7), Sch.6, para.9(1), Sch.7, para.5(1)
		s.47 am. (1.1.1993)	SI 3218, regs.22(6),23(7), Sch.6, para.9(2), Sch.7, para.5(2)
		s.48(3) restr.	53, s.8(2)(a)
		s.48(3) rep.in pt.	53, s.18(2), Sch.4, Pt.I
		s.52(1) am. (1.1.1993)	SI 3218, reg.75
		s.53(2)(g) rep. (1.1.1993)	SI 3218, reg.76(1)
		s.53(2A) added (1.1.1993)	SI 3218, reg.76(2)
		s.53(4)(a)(6)(7)(8)(9)(a) am. (1.1.1993)	SI 3218, reg.76(3)(5)-(8)

Year and Chap. or No. of Measure	Short title	How affected	1992, Chapter of Act or Number of Measure or Statutory Instrument
1986—*cont.*			
		s.53(5)(b) subst. (1.1.1993)	SI 3218, reg.76(4)
		s.53(11A) added (1.1.1993)	SI 3218, reg.76(9)
		s.53(13A)(13B) added (1.1.1993)	SI 3218, reg.76(10)
		s.53(15)(16) added (1.1.1993)	SI 3218, reg.76(11)
		s.54(3A)(3B) added (1.1.1993)	SI 3218, reg.77(1)
		s.54(6) am. (1.1.1993)	SI 3218, reg.77(2)
		ss.62-64 mod. (*prosp.*)	40, s.27, Sch.11, Pt.II, para.9(1)(a)-(c)(2)
		s.65 mod. (*prosp.*)	40, s.27, Sch.11, Pt.II, para.9(1)(d)(2)(3)
		s.66 mod. (*prosp.*)	40, s.27, Sch.11, Pt.II, para.9(1)(e)(2)
		s.68 mod. (*prosp.*)	40, s.27, Sch.11, Pt.II, para.9(1)(f)(2)
		s.69 mod. (*prosp.*)	40, s.27, Sch.11, Pt.II, para.9(1)(g)(2)(4)
		s.70 mod. (*prosp.*)	40, s.27, Sch.11, Pt.II, para.9(1)(h)(2)
		s.71(10A) added (1.1.1993)	SI 3218, reg.78
		s.78 excl. (1.1.1993)	SI 359, reg.9(4)
		s.98(3) am. (1.1.1993)	SI 3218, reg.82(1), Sch.10, Pt.I, para.22(c)
		s.115(1A) added (1.1.1993)	SI 3218, reg.79
		s.118A added (1.1.1993)	SI 3218, reg.80
		s.119(2A) added (1.1.1993)	SI 3218, reg.81
		Sch.8, Pt.II, para.1(b) replaced (by sub-para.(b)(i)(ii))	SI 509, art.3
		Sch.8, Pt.IV, para.7 am. (1.1.1993)	SI 3218, reg.82(1), Sch.10, Pt.I, para.22(d)
c.56	Parliamentary constituencies Act 1986	s.3(1) am.	55, s.2(1)(2)
		s.3(2) am.	55, s.2(2)(3)
		s.3(2A) added	55, s.2(4)
		s.3(7) mod.	55, s.3(2)(3)
		s.3(7)(8) added	55, s.3(1)
		Sch.1, para.4A added	55, s.1(1)-(3)
		Sch.1, para.4A expld.	55, s.1(3)
		Sch.1, para.8 am.	55, s.1(4)
		Sch.3, para.6 rep.	12, s.290, Sch.12
c.59	Sex Discrimination Act 1986	s.6 am.	52, s.300(2), Sch.2, para.36
c.60	Financial Services Act 1986	trans.of functions	SI 1315, arts.2(1)(b),6
		defn. of "unit trust scheme" appl.	12, s.99(2)(a)
		appl.	12, s.102(3)(b)
		defn. of "authorised person" appl.	12, s.143(4)
		defn. of "authorised person" appl.	12, s.144(8)(c)(i)

Year and Chap. or No. of Measure	Short title	How affected	1992, Chapter of Act or Number of Measure or Statutory Instrument
1986—*cont.*		defn. of "collective investment scheme" appl.	12, s.288(1)
		defn. of "unit trust schemes" appl. (*prosp.*)	40, s.13, Sch.7, para.2
		ss.1-128 (Pt.I)(Ch.IX) appl.(mods.)	SI 225, reg.96(7)
		ss.3,4 restr. (1.1.1993)	SI 3218, reg.5(1)(b)
		s.5(1)(b)(i) am. (1.1.1993)	SI 3218, reg.55, Sch.9, para.2
		s.7 am. (1.1.1993)	SI 3218, reg.48(1)
		s.10(3) am. (1.1.1993)	SI 3218, reg.55, Sch.9, para.3
		s.13(2) am. (1.1.1993)	SI 3218, reg.55, Sch.9, para.4
		s.23 subst. (*prosp.*)	40, s.98, Sch.18, Pt.I, para.1
		ss.26,27 am. (1.1.1993)	SI 3218, regs.49,50
		s.26(2)(5) appl.(mods.)	SI 225, reg.95(2)
		ss.28,29 cert. functs. made exercisable jointly	SI 1315, arts.4,6, Sch.2, para.4(c)
		s.28(1)(a) am. (1.1.1993)	SI 3218, reg.55, Sch.9, para.5
		s.29 appl.(mods.)	SI 225, reg.96(5)(6)
		s.31 am. (1.1.1993)	SI 3218, reg.51
		s.32(2)(a) am. (1.1.1993)	SI 3218, reg.55, Sch.9, para.6
		ss.33,34 cert. functs. made exercisable jointly	SI 1315, arts.4,6, Sch.2, para.4(c)
		s.33(1) cert. functs. made exercisable jointly	SI 1315, arts.4,6, Sch.2, para.2
		s.43 am. (1.1.1993)	SI 3218, reg.52
		s.43 (defn. of "a listed institution") appl.	12, s.144(8)(c)(i)
		s.44 am. (1.1.1993)	SI 3218, reg.55, Sch.9, para.7
		s.45(1)(j) am.	41, s.78(1), Sch.6, para.14
		s.45(2) am. (1.1.1993)	SI 3218, reg.55, Sch.9, para.8
		s.47A cert. functs. made exercisable jointly	SI 1315, arts.4,6, Sch.2, para.3
		ss.47A,47A(1)(4) am. (1.1.1993)	SI 3218, reg.55, Sch.9, para.9
		ss.48,48(1)(2) am. (1.1.1993)	SI 3218, reg.55, Sch.9, para.10
		ss.49,49(2) am. (1.1.1993)	SI 3218, reg.55, Sch.9, para.11
		s.51(1) am. (1.1.1993)	SI 3218, reg.55, Sch.9, para.12
		s.52 am. (1.1.1993)	SI 3218, reg.55, Sch.9, para.13
		s.53 appl.(mods.)	SI 225, reg.111

Year and Chap. or No. of Measure	Short title	How affected	1992, Chapter of Act or Number of Measure or Statutory Instrument
1986—*cont.*			
		s.53(1) am. (1.1.1993)	SI 3218, reg.55, Sch.9, para.14
		ss.54,54(2) am. (1.1.1993)	SI 3218, reg.55, Sch.9, para.15
		s.54(1)(2)(6) appl.(mods.)	SI 225, reg.105(6)
		s.55 am. (1.1.1993)	SI 3218, reg.55, Sch.9, para.16
		s.57 am. (1.1.1993)	SI 3218, reg.55, Sch.9, para.17
		s.59 am. (1.1.1993)	SI 3218, reg.55, Sch.9, para.18
		ss.60,60(1)(3) am. (1.1.1993)	SI 3218, reg.55, Sch.9, para.19
		ss.60,61 cert. functs. made exercisable jointly	SI 1315, arts.4,6, Sch.2, para.4(c)
		s.64(1) am. (1.1.1993)	SI 3218, reg.55, Sch.9, para.20
		s.65(1) am. (1.1.1993)	SI 3218, reg.55, Sch.9, para.21
		ss.66,66(1) am. (1.1.1993)	SI 3218, reg.55, Sch.9, para.22
		s.67 am. (1.1.1993)	SI 3218, reg.55, Sch.9, para.23
		s.67(1)(b) am. (1.1.1993)	SI 3218, reg.16(3)
		s.69 appl.	SI 225, reg.96(5)(6)
		s.70(2)-(6) appl.	SI 225, reg.96(5)(6)
		s.75 (defn. of "collective investment scheme") appl.	35, s.1(3)(c)
		s.75(6) am. (1.1.1993)	SI 3218, reg.55, Sch.9, para.24
		s.76 am. (1.1.1993)	SI 3218, reg.55, Sch.9, para.25
		s.93(1) am. (1.1.1993)	SI 3218, reg.55, Sch.9, para.26
		ss.97-101 cert. functs. made exercisable jointly	SI 1315, arts.4,6, Sch.2, para.4(c)
		s.97 am. (1.1.1993)	SI 3218, reg.15(5), Sch.4, para.2
		s.98(2)(a)(b) am. (1.1.1993)	SI 3218, reg.15(5), Sch.4, para.3(1)
		s.98(3)(b) am. (1.1.1993)	SI 3218, reg.15(5), Sch.4, para.3(2)
		s.100(2) am. (1.1.1993)	SI 3218, reg.15(5), Sch.4, para.4(1)
		s.101(5) ext.	SI 225, reg.101
		s.102 am. (1.1.1993)	SI 3218, reg.55, Sch.9, para.27
		ss.104,104(1) am. (1.1.1993)	SI 3218, reg.55, Sch.9, para.28
		ss.105,106 appl.	SI 225, reg.110
		s.106 am. (1.1.1993)	SI 3218, reg.55, Sch.9, para.29

Year and Chap. or No. of Measure	Short title	How affected	1992, Chapter of Act or Number of Measure or Statutory Instrument
1986—*cont.*		ss.107,108 appl.(mods.)	SI 225, reg.98
		s.107(3) am. (1.1.1993)	SI 3218, reg.55, Sch.9, para.30
		s.109(1) appl.(mods.)	SI 225, reg.98
		s.109(1) am. (1.1.1993)	SI 3218, reg.55, Sch.9, para.31
		s.110 appl.(mods.)	SI 225, reg.98
		s.110(3) am. (1.1.1993)	SI 3218, reg.55, Sch.9, para.32
		s.113 am. (1.1.1993)	SI 3218, reg.55, Sch.9, para.33
		s.113(3) subst. (*prosp.*)	40, s.98, Sch.18, Pt.I, para.2
		s.115 mod.	SI 1315, art.6
		s.119(1)(2) am. (1.1.1993)	SI 3218, reg.55, Sch.9, para.34
		s.121(1)(2) am. (1.1.1993)	SI 3218, reg.55, Sch.9, para.35
		s.128B cert. functs. made exercisable jointly	SI 1315, arts.4,6, Sch.2, para.5
		ss.128C,128C(2) am. (1.1.1993)	SI 3218, reg.55, Sch.9, para.36
		s.128C(1)(4)(5) cert. functs. made exercisable jointly	SI 1315, arts.4,6, Sch.2, para.5
		s.132 ext.	SI 2890, reg.10
		s.139(3)(4) rep. (*prosp.*)	40, s.120(2), Sch.22, Pt.I
		s.139(5) rep.in pt. (*prosp.*)	40, s.120(2), Sch.22, Pt.I
		s.141(2) am. (*prosp.*)	40, s.98, Sch.18, Pt.I, para.3
		s.152(4A) added	SI 232, art.3
		ss.154,154(3) am. (1.1.1993)	SI 3218, reg.55, Sch.9, para.37
		ss.171,171(3) am. (1.1.1993)	SI 3218, reg.55, Sch.9, para.38
		ss.178,178(3)-(5) am. (1.1.1993)	SI 3218, reg.55, Sch.9, para.39
		s.178(10) am.	SI 1315, art.10(1), Sch.4, para.3
		ss.179,180 ext.(mods.)	SI 225, reg.113(2)-(4)
		s.179(2) am. (1.1.1993)	SI 3218, reg.55, Sch.9, para.40
		s.179(3)(aa) added	SI 1315, art.10(1), Sch.4, para.4
		s.179(3)(e) subst. (*prosp.*)	40, s.98, Sch.18, Pt.I, para.4
		ss.180,181 cert. functs. made exercisable concurrently	SI 1315, arts.5,6, Sch.3, para.1
		s.180(1)(bb) added	SI 1315, art.10(1), Sch.4, para.5
		s.180(1)(g) am. (1.1.1993)	SI 3218, reg.55, Sch.9, para.41

Year and Chap. or No. of Measure	Short title	How affected	1992, Chapter of Act or Number of Measure or Statutory Instrument
1986—*cont.*			
		s.180(1)(h) subst. (*prosp.*)	40, s.98, Sch.18, Pt.I, para.5
		s.181 ext.	SI 225, reg.113(5)
		ss.183,184 cert. functs. made exercisable jointly	SI 1315, arts.4,6, Sch.2, para.4(a)(b)
		s.186 cert. functs. made exercisable jointly	SI 1315, arts.4,6, Sch.2, para.4(d)
		s.186(7) am.	SI 1315, art.10(1), Sch.4, para.6
		s.187(4) ext.	SI 225, reg.94(6)
		s.187(4) ext.	SI 225, reg.117(1)
		s.189 am.	SI 225, reg.115
		s.189(5)(c) rep.in pt. (*prosp.*)	40, s.120(2), Sch.22, Pt.I
		s.190 am.	SI 225, reg.114
		s.191 am. (1.1.1993)	SI 3218, reg.55, Sch.9, para.42
		s.192(1)(4)(6) ext.	SI 225, reg.6(7)
		s.199(7) am.	SI 1315, art.10(1), Sch.4, para.3
		s.201(4) am.	SI 1315, art.10(1), Sch.4, para.3
		s.204(1) am. (*prosp.*)	40, s.98, Sch.18, Pt.I, para.6
		s.205 am.	SI 1315, art.10(1), Sch.4, para.7
		s.205A(1) am.	SI 1315, art.10(1), Sch.4, para.8
		s.206(1) am. (1.1.1993)	SI 3218, reg.55, Sch.9, para.43
		s.207(1) (defn. of "prescribed") am.	SI 1315, art.10(1), Sch.4, para.9
		s.207(1) (defns. of "friendly society", "incorporated friendly society" and "registered friendly society") added (*prosp.*)	40, s.98, Sch.18, Pt.I, para.7
		s.207(1) (defn. of "registered friendly society") rep. (*prosp.*)	40, s.120(2), Sch.22, Pt.I
		s.210(3) am. (*prosp.*)	40, s.98, Sch.18, Pt.I, para.8
		Sch.1, paras.17,18(2),26 am. (1.1.1993)	SI 3218, reg.55, Sch.9, para.44
		Sch.1, para.25A subst.	SI 273, art.2(1)
		Sch.2, para.2 am. (1.1.1993)	SI 3218, reg.48(2)
		Sch.2, paras.2,3,3(3),7 am. (1.1.1993)	SI 3218, reg.55, Sch.9, para.45
		Sch.5, Pt.I, para.2(2) am. (1.1.1993)	SI 3218, reg.82(1), Sch.10, Pt.I, para.23
		Sch.6 ext.	SI 225, reg.103(6)
		Sch.6, para.6 rep.	53, s.18(2), Sch.4, Pt.I

Year and Chap. or No. of Measure	Short title	How affected	1992, Chapter of Act or Number of Measure or Statutory Instrument
1986—*cont.*			
		Sch.7, para.1(2) am.	SI 1315, art.10(1), Sch.4, para.10
		Sch.7, paras.4,5 am. (1.1.1993)	SI 3218, reg.55, Sch.9, para.46
		Sch.8 am. (1.1.1993)	SI 3218, reg.55, Sch.9, para.47
		Sch.9, para.13 cert. functs. made exercisable concurrently	SI 1315, arts.5,6, Sch.3, para.2
		Sch.10, para.8(2)-(5) cert. functs. made exercisable jointly	SI 1315, arts.4,6, Sch.2, para.6
		Sch.11 am. (*prosp.*)	40, s.98, Sch.18, Pt.II, para.10
		Sch.11, para.1 (defn. of "a recognised self- regulating organis. for friendly societies") am. (*prosp.*)	40, s.98, Sch.18, Pt.II, para.11(1)
		Sch.11, para.1 (defn. of "a member society") rep.in pt. & am.	40, s.98, Sch.18, Pt.II, para.11(2)(a)(b)
		Sch.11, para.1 (defn. of "the Registrar") replaced (by defns. of "the Commission" and "recognition order") (*prosp.*)	40, s.98, Sch.18, Pt.II, para.11(3)
		Sch.11, para.1 (defn. of "a member society") rep.in pt. (*prosp.*)	40, s.120(2), Sch.22, Pt.I
		Sch.11, para.3(1) am. (*prosp.*)	40, s.98, Sch.18, Pt.II, para.12
		Sch.11, para.4(2) am. (*prosp.*)	40, s.98, Sch.18, Pt.II, para.13
		Sch.11, para.7(1) am. (*prosp.*)	40, s.98, Sch.18, Pt.II, para.14
		Sch.11, para.13A(6) am. (*prosp.*)	40, s.98, Sch.18, Pt.II, para.15
		Sch.11, para.26(1) rep.in pt. (*prosp.*)	40, s.120(2), Sch.22, Pt.I
		Sch.11, para.26(2) subst. (*prosp.*)	40, s.98, Sch.18, Pt.II, para.16
		Sch.11, para.26(3) rep. (*prosp.*)	40, s.120(2), Sch.22, Pt.I
		Sch.11, para.27 rep. (*prosp.*)	40, s.120(2), Sch.22, Pt.I
		Sch.11, para.28(6) am. (*prosp.*)	40, s.98, Sch.18, Pt.II, para.17
		Sch.11, para.29(1)(a)(b) am. (*prosp.*)	40, s.98, Sch.18, Pt.II, para.18(a)(b)
		Sch.11, para.31A added (*prosp.*)	40, s.98, Sch.18, Pt.II, para.19
		Sch.11, para.37(1) am. (*prosp.*)	40, s.98, Sch.18, Pt.II, para.20(1)

Year and Chap. or No. of Measure	Short title	How affected	1992, Chapter of Act or Number of Measure or Statutory Instrument
1986—*cont.*			
		Sch.11, para.37(1A) added (*prosp.*)	40, s.98, Sch.18, Pt.II, para.20(2)
		Sch.11, para.38(1)(a) rep.in pt. (*prosp.*)	40, s.120(2), Sch.22, Pt.I
		Sch.11, para.40A added (*prosp.*)	40, s.98, Sch.18, Pt.II, para.21
		Sch.11, para.43 rep. (*prosp.*)	40, s.120(2), Sch.22, Pt.I
		Sch.11, para.45 subst. (*prosp.*)	40, s.98, Sch.18, Pt.II, para.22
		Sch.14 am.	SI 225, reg.115
		Sch.14, Pt.I, para.5 am. (*prosp.*)	40, s.98, Sch.18, Pt.I, para.9(1)(a)
		Sch.14, Pt.I, para.6 am. (*prosp.*)	40, s.98, Sch.18, Pt.I, para.9(2)
		Sch.14, Pt.II, para.7 am. (*prosp.*)	40, s.98, Sch.18, Pt.I, para.9(1)(b)
		Sch.14, Pt.III, para.4 am. (*prosp.*)	40, s.98, Sch.18, Pt.I, para.9(1)(c)
		Sch.15, para.14(1) rep.in pt. (*prosp.*)	40, s.120(2), Sch.22, Pt.I
		Sch.15, para.14(3) rep.in pt. (*prosp.*)	40, s.120(2), Sch.22, Pt.I
c.61	Education (No.2) Act 1986	s.16A (Pt.III) added (1.8.1993)	13, s.12(3)
		s.30(5) added	38, s.21(7), Sch.4, para.5
		s.43(5)(aa) subst. (1.4.1993)	13, s.93(1), Sch.8, Pt.I, para.22(a)(i)
		s.43(5)(ba) added (1.4.1993)	13, s.93(1), Sch.8, Pt.I, para.22(a)(ii)
		s.43(5)(c) rep. (1.4.1993)	13, s.93, Sch.8, Pt.I, para.22(a)(iii), Sch.9
		s.43(7) rep.in pt. (1.4.1993)	13, s.93, Sch.8, Pt.I, para.22(b), Sch.9
		s.43(7)(b) rep. (1.4.1993)	13, s.93, Sch.8, Pt.I, para.22(b), Sch.9
		s.49(3)(d)(da) rep. (1.4.1993)	13, s.93, Sch.8, Pt.I, para.23(a), Sch.9
		s.49(3)(db) added (1.4.1993)	13, s.93(1), Sch.8, Pt.I, para.23(b)
		s.49(3)(e) am. (1.4.1993)	13, s.93(1), Sch.8, Pt.I, para.23(c)
		s.51(2)(b) rep.in pt. (1.4.1993)	13, s.93, Sch.8, Pt.I, para.24(a), Sch.9
		s.51(5)(6) rep. (1.4.1993)	13, s.93, Sch.8, Pt.I, para.24(b), Sch.9
		s.51(8) am. (1.4.1993)	13, s.93(1), Sch.8, Pt.I, para.24(c)
		s.51(13) added (1.4.1993)	13, s.93(1), Sch.8, Pt.I, para.24(d)
		s.52(1)(a) am. (1.4.1993)	13, s.93(1), Sch.8, Pt.I, para.25

Year and Chap. or No. of Measure	Short title	How affected	1992, Chapter of Act or Number of Measure or Statutory Instrument
1986—*cont.*			
		s.52(3) am. (1.4.1993)	13, s.93(1), Sch.8, Pt.I, para.25
		s.58(3)(4)(5)(a) rep. (1.4.1993)	13, s.93, Sch.8, Pt.I, para.26(a), Sch.9
		s.58(5)(ab) rep.in pt. (1.4.1993)	13, s.93, Sch.8, Pt.I, para.26(b), Sch.9
c.62	Salmon Act 1986	s.21 appt. day(s) for (1.1.1993)	SI 1973, art.3
c.63	Housing and Planning Act 1986	appt. day(s) for spec. provns. (13.7.1992, 17.8.1992)	SI 1753, art.2
		Sch.5, para.29 restr.	SI 1753, art.2(2), Sch., para.2
		Sch.5, para.34 restr.	SI 1753, art.2(2), Sch., para.3
		Sch.5, paras.35-38 restr.	SI 1753, art.2(2), Sch., para.4
		Sch.5, para.40(2)-(4) restr.	SI 1753, art.2(2), Sch., para.5
c.64	Public order Act 1986	Sch.2, para.1 rep.	52, s.300(1), Sch.1
c.ii	Berkshire Act 1986	s.20 rep.	SI 117, art.19(1), Sch.
c.iii	British Railways Act 1986	s.30 am.	xi, s.37
c.xxv	Mersey Docks and Harbour Act 1986	Sch. am.	x, s.5
No.3	Patronage (Benefices) Measure 1986	s.9(1)(2) am.	GSM 1, s.17(1), Sch.3, para.26
		Sch.2, para.4 am.	GSM 1, s.17(1), Sch.3, para.27
1987			
c.3	Coal Industry Act 1987	s.3(4)(a) am.	17, s.1(2)
		s.3(6) am.	17, s.1(3)
		s.5(8) replaced (by subss.(8)(8A))	41, s.78(1), Sch.6, para.15
c.7	Social Fund (Maternity and Funeral Expenses) Act 1987	rep.	6, s.3, Sch.1
c.12	Petroleum Act 1987	ss.11(2)(a),21-24 power to rep. or mod.	15, s.1 (amending s.15 of 1974 c.37)
		ss.16(1),21(7) mod.	15, s.1(5)(c)
c.15	Reverter of Sites Act 1987	s.4(4) am.	41, s.78(1), Sch.6, para.16
c.16	Finance Act 1987	s.12(3) rep. (1.1.1993)	48, ss.14(3),82, Sch.18, Pt.V
		s.13(2)(3) rep. (1.1.1993)	48, ss.14(3),82, Sch.18, Pt.V
		s.40 rep.	12, s.290, Sch.12
		s.68(3) rep.	12, s.290, Sch.12
c.18	Debtors (Scotland) Act 1987	s.1(5)(e)(ee) replaced (by para.(e)) (*prosp.*)	14, s.117(1), Sch.13, para.53(1)
		s.1(9) added (*prosp.*)	14, s.117(1), Sch.13, para.53(2)
		s.5(4)(e)(ee) replaced (by para.(e)) (*prosp.*)	14, s.117(1), Sch.13, para.54(1)

Year and Chap. or No. of Measure	Short title	How affected	1992, Chapter of Act or Number of Measure or Statutory Instrument
1987—*cont.*			
		s.5(9) added (*prosp.*)	14, s.117(1), Sch.13, para.54(2)
		s.68 rep.	6, s.3, Sch.1
		s.106 (defn. of "maintenance order") appl.	5, s.107(15)
		s.106 (defn. of "levying authority") rep. (*prosp.*)	14, s.117, Sch.13, para.55(a), Sch.14
		s.106 (defn. of "summary warrant") am. (*prosp.*)	14, s.117(1), Sch.13, para.55(b)
		Sch.5, paras.25-34 saved	14, s.97(5), Sch.8, para.4
		Sch.5, para.35 (defn. of "creditor") am. (*prosp.*)	14, s.117(1), Sch.13, para.56
c.22	Banking Act 1987	defn. of "authorised institution" appl. (EWS)	33, s.1(2), Sch., para.1 (adding s.15A to 1992 c.5)
		defn. of "deposit-taking business" appl.	48, s.66, Sch.12, para.1(1)(b)
		s.1(3)(4) am. (1.1.1993)	SI 3218, reg.47, Sch.8, para.2
		s.2(3) am. (1.1.1993)	SI 3218, reg.47, Sch.8, para.3
		s.3 restr. (1.1.1993)	SI 3218, reg.5(1)(a)
		s.5(3) am. (1.1.1993)	SI 3218, reg.47, Sch.8, para.4
		s.8(1) am. (1.1.1993)	SI 3218, reg.25
		s.9(7) added (1.1.1993)	SI 3218, reg.26
		s.10(5) am. (1.1.1993)	SI 3218, reg.32(2)(a)
		s.11(1A) added (1.1.1993)	SI 3218, reg.28(1)
		s.11(3A) added (1.1.1993)	SI 3218, reg.28(2)
		s.11(10) added (1.1.1993)	SI 3218, reg.28(3)
		s.12(4) appl. (1.1.1993)	SI 3218, reg.10(4)
		s.12(4) appl. (1.1.1993)	SI 3218, reg.23(3)
		s.12A added (1.1.1993)	SI 3218, reg.29
		s.13(3A) added (1.1.1993)	SI 3218, reg.30(1)
		s.15(4) added (1.1.1993)	SI 3218, reg.30(2)
		s.16(2) appl. (1.1.1993)	SI 3218, regs.9(7),23(7), Sch.3, para.5(2), Sch.7, para.6(2)
		ss.17,17(1)-(3) am. (1.1.1993)	SI 3218, reg.47, Sch.8, para.5
		s.18(1)(2) am. (1.1.1993)	SI 3218, reg.47, Sch.8, para.6
		s.21(1) am. (1.1.1993) (*saving*)	SI 3218, regs.31(1),46(a)
		s.22(1A) added (1.1.1993)	SI 3218, reg.31(2)
		s.23(1)(a) am. (1.1.1993)	SI 3218, reg.32(2)(b)
		s.26A added (1.1.1993)	SI 3218, reg.32(1)
		s.27(1) am. (1.1.1993)	SI 3218, regs.22(6),23(7), Sch.6, para.8(1), Sch.7, para.4
		s.27(1)(4) am. (1.1.1993)	SI 3218, reg.9(7), Sch.3, para.4(1)

Year and Chap. or No. of Measure	Short title	How affected	1992, Chapter of Act or Number of Measure or Statutory Instrument
1987—*cont.*			
		s.27(1)(a) am. (1.1.1993)	SI 3218, reg.32(2)(c)
		s.29 am. (1.1.1993)	SI 3218, reg.22(6), Sch.6, para.8(2)
		s.29(2)(a) am. (1.1.1993)	SI 3218, reg.9(7), Sch.3, para.4(2)
		s.30 restr.	53, s.8(2)(b)
		s.30(3) rep.in pt.	53, s.18(2), Sch.4, Pt.I
		s.30(4) rep.in pt.	53, s.18(2), Sch.4, Pt.I
		s.33(1) am. (1.1.1993)	SI 3218, reg.47, Sch.8, para.7
		s.36A added (1.1.1993)	SI 3218, reg.33
		s.37(2) subst. (1.1.1993) (*saving*)	SI 3218, regs.34,46(a)
		s.37A added (1.1.1993)	SI 3218, reg.35
		s.39 am. (1.1.1993)	SI 3218, reg.47, Sch.8, para.8
		s.39(6)(7) replaced (by subss.(6)(7)(7A)) (1.1.1993) (*saving*)	SI 3218, regs.36,46(a)
		ss.40,40(2) am. (1.1.1993)	SI 3218, reg.47, Sch.8, para.9
		s.41 am. (1.1.1993)	SI 3218, reg.47, Sch.8, para.10
		s.41(2)(3) replaced (by subss.(2)(3)(3A)) (1.1.1993) (*saving*)	SI 3218, regs.37,46(a)
		s.45(1) am. (1.1.1993)	SI 3218, reg.47, Sch.8, para.11
		ss.47,47(1)(7) am. (1.1.1993)	SI 3218, reg.47, Sch.8, para.12
		s.50(2) am. (1.1.1993)	SI 3218, reg.47, Sch.8, para.13
		s.52(1) am. (1.1.1993)	SI 3218, reg.47, Sch.8, para.14
		s.58(1) am. (1.1.1993)	SI 3218, reg.47, Sch.8, para.15
		s.60(6) am. (1.1.1993)	SI 3218, reg.47, Sch.8, para.16
		s.68(3) am. (1.1.1993)	SI 3218, reg.47, Sch.8, para.17
		s.69(1) am. (1.1.1993)	SI 3218, reg.47, Sch.8, para.18
		s.70(1)-(3)(3)(b) am. (1.1.1993)	SI 3218, reg.47, Sch.8, para.19
		s.71(1) am. (1.1.1993)	SI 3218, reg.47, Sch.8, para.20
		s.74(1) am. (1.1.1993)	SI 3218, reg.47, Sch.8, para.21
		s.79(2)(aa) added	SI 3179, Sch.3, para.10
		s.79(5) am.	SI 3179, Sch.3, para.10
		s.82 am. (1.1.1993)	SI 3218, reg.47, Sch.8, para.22

Year and Chap. or No. of Measure	Short title	How affected	1992, Chapter of Act or Number of Measure or Statutory Instrument
1987—*cont.*			
		s.83 am. (1.1.1993)	SI 3218, reg.47, Sch.8, para.23
		s.83(1) am. (1.1.1993) (*saving*)	SI 3218, regs.38,46(b)
		s.84(1), Table am.	SI 1315, art.10(1), Sch.4, para.11(1)
		s.84(1), Table , (Entries in table numbered 1-19) (1.1.1993)	SI 3218, reg.39(1)
		s.84(1), Table am. (*prosp.*)	40, s.120(1), Sch.21, Pt.I, para.9
		s.84(1), Table rep.in pt. (*prosp.*)	40, s.120(2), Sch.22, Pt.I
		s.84(5) replaced (by subss.(5)(5A)) (1.1.1993) (*saving*)	SI 3218, regs.39(2),46(b)
		s.84(5A)(a) am. (1.1.1993)	SI 3218, reg.47, Sch.8, para.24
		s.84(6)(a)(i) am. (1.1.1993) (*saving*)	SI 3218, regs.39(3),46(b)
		s.84(6)(a)(ii) am.	SI 1315, art.10(1), Sch.4 para.11(2)
		s.84(7)-(10) added (1.1.1993) (*saving*)	SI 3218, regs.39(4),46(b)
		s.85(1)(g) rep. (1.1.1993) (*saving*)	SI 3218, regs.40(1),46(b)
		s.85(1A) added (1.1.1993) (*saving*)	SI 3218, regs.40(2),46(b)
		s.86 subst. (1.1.1993) (*saving*)	SI 3218, regs.41,46(b)
		s.86(1)-(3) am. (1.1.1993)	SI 3218, reg.47, Sch.8, para.25
		s.87(3A) added (1.1.1993) (*saving*)	SI 3218, regs.42,46(b)
		s.87(3A) am. (1.1.1993)	SI 3218, reg.47, Sch.8, para.26
		s.93(1) am. (1.1.1993)	SI 3218, reg.47, Sch.8, para.27
		s.94(1)(3) am. (1.1.1993)	SI 3218, reg.47, Sch.8, para.28
		s.95(4) am. (1.1.1993)	SI 3218, reg.47, Sch.8, para.29
		s.96(7) rep.in pt. (*prosp.*)	40, s.120(2), Sch.22, Pt.I
		s.99(1) am. (1.1.1993)	SI 3218, reg.47, Sch.8, para.30
		s.100(4) am. (1.1.1993)	SI 3218, reg.47, Sch.8, para.31
		s.101(1) am. (1.1.1993)	SI 3218, reg.47, Sch.8, para.32
		s.103(6)(b) am. (EWS)	19, s.27, Sch.3, para.22
		s.105(3)(e) added (1.1.1993) (*saving*)	SI 3218, regs.43(1),46(a)

Year and Chap. or No. of Measure	Short title	How affected	1992, Chapter of Act or Number of Measure or Statutory Instrument
1987—*cont.*			
		s.105(3)(c) am. (1.1.1993) (*saving*)	SI 3218, regs.43(1),46(a)
		s.105(4) replaced (by subss.(3A)(4)) (1.1.1993) (*saving*)	SI 3218, regs.43(2),46(a)
		s.105(5A) added (1.1.1993) (*saving*)	SI 3218, regs.43(3),46(a)
		s.105(9)(10) subst. (1.1.1993) (*saving*)	SI 3218, regs.43(4),46(a)
		s.105A(1) subst. (1.1.1993) (*saving*)	SI 3218, regs.44(1),46(a)
		s.105A(2) am. (1.1.1993) (*saving*)	SI 3218, regs.44(2),46(a)
		s.106(1) , defn. of "shareholder controller" and related definitions subst. (1.1.1993) (*saving*)	SI 3218, regs.45(1)(c), 46(a)
		s.106(1) (defn. of "parent controller") added (1.1.1993) (*saving*)	SI 3218, regs.45(1)(a), 46(a)
		s.106(1) (defn. of "relevant supervisory authority") subst. (1.1.1993) (*saving*)	SI 3218, regs.45(1)(b), 46(a)
		s.106(1) (defn. of "former authorised institution") am. (1.1.1993)	SI 3218, reg.47, Sch.8, para.33
		s.106(2A) added (1.1.1993) (*saving*)	SI 3218, regs.45(2),46(a)
		Sch.2, para.6(1) rep.in pt. (*prosp.*)	40, s.120(2), Sch.22, Pt.I
		Sch.3 appl.(mods.) (1.1.1993)	SI 3218, reg.23(3)
		Sch.3, para.4(2) am. (1.1.1993) (*saving*)	SI 3218, regs.27(1),46(a)
		Sch.3, para.4(3) replaced (by subparas.(3)(3A)) (1.1.1993) (*saving*)	SI 3218, regs.27(2),46(a)
		Sch.3, para.4(3A) am. (1.1.1993)	SI 3218, reg.83, Sch.11, Pt.II, para.4(2)
		Sch.3, para.4(10) subst. (1.1.1993) (*saving*)	SI 3218, regs.27(3),46(a)
		Sch.3, para.6 subst. (1.1.1993) (*saving*)	SI 3218, regs.27(4),46(a)
c.26	Housing (Scotland) Act 1987	ss.44-84 (Pt.III) (defn. of "secure tenancy") appl.	14, s.75(5)
		ss.61-69 mod.	SI 325, regs.3,5,7
		ss.71-75 mod.	SI 325, regs.3,5,7
		ss.78,79 mod.	SI 325, regs.3,5,7
		s.81A(1) mod.	SI 325, regs.3,5,7
		ss.82-84A mod.	SI 325, regs.3,5,7
		s.216 mod.	SI 325, regs.3,5,7
		s.338(1) am. (1.1.1993)	SI 3218, reg.82(1), Sch.10, Pt.I, para.26

Year and Chap. or No. of Measure	Short title	How affected	1992, Chapter of Act or Number of Measure or Statutory Instrument
1987—*cont.*			
c.42	Family Law Reform Act 1987	s.1 appl.	5, s.78(7)(8)
		s.2(1)(g) rep.	6, s.3, Sch.1
		Sch.2, para.46 rep. (*prosp.*)	56, s.2(2), Sch.3
		Sch.2, para.59 rep.	6, s.3, Sch.1
		Sch.2, paras.91-93 rep.	6, s.3, Sch.1
c.43	Consumer Protection Act 1987	ext.	SI 711, reg.30
		s.13 appl. (1.1.1993)	SI 3139, reg.3(2)(a)
		ss.14,15,28-35,37,38,39, 40,44,47 appl.(mods.)	SI 3073, reg.28, Sch.6, para.3(c)(d)
		s.22 am. (1.1.1993)	SI 3218, reg.82(1), Sch.10, Pt.I, para.27
		s.24(2) appl.	SI 316, reg.9(3)(a)
		s.24(2) appl.	SI 737, reg.9(3)(a)
		ss.27-35 (Pt.IV) appl. (1.1.1993)	SI 3139, reg.3(2)(c)
		s.39 appl.	SI 316, reg.9(3)(b)
		s.39 appl.	SI 737, reg.9(3)(b)
		s.40(1)-(3) appl.	SI 316, reg.9(3)(c)
		s.40(1)(2)(3) appl.	SI 737, reg.9(3)(c)
		Sch.4, para.8 rep.	52, s.300(1), Sch.1
c.47	Abolition of Domestic Rates Etc. (Scotland) Act 1987	defn. of "levying authority" appl.	4, s.137(1)
		power to excl.	5, s.6(2)
		power to am.	5, s.138(9)
		defn. of "levying authority" appl.	5, s.191
		rep.in pt. (1.4.1992, 1.10.1992)	14, s.117(2), Sch.14
		rep. (residue) (*prosp.*)	14, s.117(2), Sch.14
		s.9(7) am.	6, s.4, Sch.2, para.86
		s.20B(2)(a) am.	6, s.4, Sch.2, para.87
		s.26 (defns. of "community charge" and "community water charge") appl. (*prosp.*)	14, s.117(1), Sch.13, para.53(2) (adding subs.(9) to s.1 of 1987 c.18)
		s.26 (defns. of "community charge" and "community water charge") appl. (*prosp.*)	14, s.117(1), Sch.13, para.54(2) (adding subs.(9) to s.5 of 1987 c.18)
		s.26(2)(a) (defn. of "rates") appl.	5, s.191
		Sch.1A, para.4(2)(a)(b)(d) (e) replaced by paras. (a)(b)(e)	6, s.4, Sch.2, para.88(a)
		Sch.1A, para.4(2)(g)(h) subst.	6, s.4, Sch.2, para.88(b)
		Sch.1A, para.4(2)(k)(l) added	SI 503, reg.2
		Sch.1A, para.5 am.	6, s.4, Sch.2, para.89
		Sch.1A, para.6A(1A) added	14, s.101(2)
		Sch.2, para.4(7) am.	6, s.4, Sch.2, para.90(a)
		Sch.2, para.4(12) am.	6, s.4, Sch.2, para.90(b)

Year and Chap. or No. of Measure	Short title	How affected	1992, Chapter of Act or Number of Measure or Statutory Instrument
1987—*cont.*			
		Sch.2, para.5(1)(7)(c) am.	6, s.4, Sch.2, para.91
		Sch.2, para.7A(1) am.	6, s.4, Sch.2, para.92
c.51	Finance (No.2) Act 1987	appt. day(s) for ss.85, 86,88,91 and sch.6, para.7 (30.9.1993)	SI 3066, art.2(2)(a)
		appt. day(s) for ss.82, 83 (31.12.1993)	SI 3066, art.3(2)
		s.64 rep.	12, s.290, Sch.12
		s.73 rep.	12, s.290, Sch.12
		ss.79-81 rep.	12, s.290, Sch.12
		Sch.6, para.2 rep.	12, s.290, Sch.12
		Sch.6, paras.4,5 rep.	12, s.290, Sch.12
c.53	Channel Tunnel Act 1987	Sch.6, para.3 rep.in pt. (EWS) (*prosp.*)	42, s.68(1), Sch.4, Pt.I
1988			
c.1	Income and Corporation Taxes Act 1988	appl.	SI 97, reg.18 (substituting 1979/591, sch.1, reg.28)
		appt. day(s) for ss.8(3), 10,252(2)(3),419(1)(3), 584(1)(2)(5)-(10),826 (30.9.1993)	SI 3066, art.2(2)(b)
		defns. of "year" and "year of assessment" appl. (NI)	7, s.15(3), Sch.2, para.1
		defns. of "resident" and "ordinarily resident" appl.	12, s.9(1)
		excl.	48, s.66, Sch.12, paras.6(2),7
		mod.	48, s.77, Sch.17, para.9(1)(2)
		s.1(2) am.	SI 622, art.2(1)
		s.1(2)(a) am.	20, s.9(1)(3)(10)(11)
		s.1(2)(aa) added	20, s.9(1)(2)(10)(11)
		s.1(2)(b) am. (1992-1993)	20, s.10(2)(5)
		s.1(2A) added	20, s.9(1)(4)(10)(11)
		s.1(3) am.	20, s.9(1)(5)(10)(11)
		s.1(4) am.	20, s.9(1)(6)(10)(11)
		s.1(4) excl. (1992-1993)	20, s.10(2)(5)
		s.1(6) am.	20, s.9(1)(7)(10)(11)
		s.1(6A) added	20, s.9(1)(8)(10)(11)
		s.6 appl.	12, s.1(2)
		s.11(2)(b) subst.	12, s.290, Sch.10, para.14(2)
		s.13(2) am.	48, s.22(b)
		s.15(1)4 subst.	48, s.58(1)(2)
		s.18, Sch.D ext. (Case VI)	48, s.66, Sch.12, paras.3(1),7
		ss.33A,33B added	48, s.57(1)(2)
		s.38(1)(a)(4) excl.	48, s.77, Sch.17, paras.5(4)(6),6(1),7
		s.56(5) am.	12, s.290, Sch.10, para.14(3)

Year and Chap. or No. of Measure	Short title	How affected	1992, Chapter of Act or Number of Measure or Statutory Instrument
1988—*cont.*			
		s.56A added	48, s.34, Sch.8, paras.1,6
		s.59 restr. (NI)	7, s.15(3), Sch.2, para.5(b)
		s.65(6)-(9) appl.	12, s.12(2)
		s.68(4) (defns. of "settlement" and "settlor") appl.	12, s.97(7)
		s.76(7) mod.	SI 1655, regs.1,4(1)
		s.96(8) mod.	SI 511, reg.9, Sch.2
		s.98(2) appl.	12, s.156(4)
		s.100(2) (defn. of "trading stock") appl.	12, s.288(1)
		s.100(2) (defn. of "trading stock") appl.	48, s.42(8)
		ss.111-115 appl.(mods.) (NI)	7, s.15(3), Sch.2, para.4(2)
		s.112(1)(2) appl.	12, s.59(c)
		s.119(1) excl.	12, s.201(2)
		s.119(1) am.	12, s.290, Sch.10, para.14(4)
		s.122(1) rep.in pt.	12, s.290, Sch.12
		s.122(1)(b) rep.	12, s.290, Sch.12
		s.122(3)(8) rep.	12, s.290, Sch.12
		s.122(4)(a) am.	12, s.290, Sch.10, para.14(5)
		s.122(5)(7) appl.	12, s.203(1)
		s.123(2) am.	48, s.63, Sch.11, paras.1(2),6
		s.123(3) rep.in pt.	48, ss.63,82, Sch.11, paras.1(3),6, Sch.18, Pt.VII
		s.123(3A) added	48, s.63, Sch.11, paras.1(4),6
		s.123(7)(8) added	48, s.30
		s.126A added	12, s.290, Sch.10, para.14(6)
		s.128 am.	12, s.290, Sch.10, para.14(7)
		s.129(4) am.	12, s.290, Sch.10, para.14(8)
		s.135 appl.	12, s.120(7)
		s.137(1)(b)(2) am.	12, s.290, Sch.10, para.14(9)
		s.138 appl.	12, s.120(7)
		s.139(14) am.	12, s.290, Sch.10, para.14(10)
		ss.140(3),162(10)(d) am.	12, s.290, Sch.10, para.14(11)
		ss.157,158 appl.	4, s.10(4)
		s.158(2) replaced (by subs.(2),Tables A,AB & B and subss.(2A)(2B))	48, s.53(2)(4)
		s.158(2), Tables A-B subst.	SI 732, art.2

Year and Chap. or No. of Measure	Short title	How affected	1992, Chapter of Act or Number of Measure or Statutory Instrument
1988—*cont.*			
		s.158(4) am.	48, s.53(3)(4)
		s.162 appl.	12, s.120(7)
		s.167A(2A) am.	48, s.19(3)
		s.185 appl.	12, s.120(7)
		s.185(3)(b)(7) am.	12, s.290, Sch.10, para.14(12)(a)(b)
		s.187 (defn. of "participant and the trust instrument") appl.	12, s.238(3)
		s.187(2) am.	12, s.290, Sch.10, para.14(13)
		s.203 saved	20, ss.9(11),10(5)
		s.207 appl.	12, s.9(2)
		s.209(2)(e)(vii) added	48, s.31(1)(4)
		s.209(9)-(11) added	48, s.31(2)(4)
		s.212(1)(b) am.	48, s.31(3)(4)
		s.214(2) (defn. of "chargeable payment") appl.	12, s.192(5)
		s.220(2)(9) am.	12, s.290, Sch.10, para.14(14)
		s.233(1)(c) am.	48, s.19(4)
		s.233(2) am.	48, s.19(3)
		s.234(1) am.	48, s.32(2)(a)(4)
		s.234(3) excl.	SI 569, reg.16
		s.234(3)(4) rep.	48, ss.32(2)(b)(4),82, Sch.18, Pt.VII
		s.234A added	48, s.32(1)(4)
		s.245B(1)(c) am.	12, s.290, Sch.10, para.14(15)
		s.249(4)(c) am.	48, s.19(4)
		s.251 am.	12, s.290, Sch.10, para.14(16)
		s.254(1) (defn. of "security") appl.	12, s.35, Sch.3, para.7(3)(a)
		s.254(1) (defn. of "security") appl.	12, s.276(2)(d)
		ss.256-278 (Pt.VII) (Ch.I) excl. (NI)	7, s.15(3), Sch.2, para.3(2)(a)
		ss.257,257A am.	SI 622, art.2(1)
		s.257A(1) am. (1992-1993)	20, s.10(3)(5)
		s.257B replaced (by ss.257BA,257BB)('93-94)	48, s.20, Sch.5, paras.2, 10
		s.257C(1) excl. (1992-1993)	20, s.10(3)(5)
		s.257D(10) am. ('93-94)	48, s.20, Sch.5, paras.3, 10
		s.257F am. ('93-94)	48, s.20, Sch.5, paras.4, 10
		s.259(2) am. ('93-94)	48, s.20, Sch.5, para.5(2)
		s.259(3A) added ('93-94)	48, s.20, Sch.5, para.5(3)
		s.261A added ('93-94)	48, s.20, Sch.5, paras.6, 10
		s.262 renumbered 262(1) ('93-94)	48, s.20, Sch.5, paras.7, 10
		s.262(2)-(4) added ('93-94)	48, s.20, Sch.5, paras.7, 10

Year and Chap. or No. of Measure	Short title	How affected	1992, Chapter of Act or Number of Measure or Statutory Instrument
1988—*cont.*			
		s.265(3)(b) am. ('93-94)	48, s.20, Sch.5, paras.8(2),10
		s.265(4) rep.in pt. ('93- 94)	48, ss.20,82, Sch.5, paras.8(3),10, Sch.18, Pt.VII
		s.265(6) am. ('93-94)	48, s.20, Sch.5, paras.8(4),10
		s.266(2)(a)(iii) am. (*prosp.*)	48, s.56, Sch.9, para.2(2)
		s.266(6)(a) am. (*prosp.*)	48, s.56, Sch.9, para.2(2)
		s.266(13) added (*prosp.*)	48, s.56, Sch.9, para.2(3)
		ss.279-288 (Pt.VII) (Ch.II) appl. (1989- 1990 and previous years of assessment) (NI)	7, s.15(3), Sch.2, para.9(1)
		s.279 mod. (NI)	7, s.15(3), Sch.2, para.9(3)
		s.282 appl.	12, s.288(3)
		s.288(1) mod.	SI 511, reg.9, Sch.2
		s.288(3) mod.	SI 511, reg.9, Sch.2
		s.289(1)(a)(b)(d) am.	48, s.38(a)-(c)
		ss.299,305 am.	12, s.290, Sch.10, para.14(17)
		s.306(1)(b) mod.	SI 511, reg.9, Sch.2
		s.312 am.	12, s.290, Sch.10, para.14(18)
		s.322 (defn. of "consular officer or employee") appl.	12, s.271(1)(f)
		s.333(2)(5) appl.(mods.)	12, s.151(2)
		s.339(3A) am.	48, s.26(1)(3)
		s.343(2) excl.	48, s.67 (adding s.152B to 1990 c.1)
		ss.345-347 rep.	12, s.290, Sch.12
		s.347A(5) am.	48, s.60(1)(2)
		s.347B(1)(a) am.	48, s.61(1)(a)(b)(2)
		s.347B(8)-(12) added (6.4.1993)	48, s.62(1)(4)(6)
		s.349(3A)(a) am.	48, s.34, Sch.8, paras.2(2),6
		s.349(4) (defn. of "qualifying deposit right") added	48, s.34, Sch.8, paras.2(3),6
		s.350(1) excl.	SI 569, reg.13(2)(d)
		s.352 excl.	SI 569, reg.21
		s.352 mod.	SI 569, rcg.23
		s.353 excl. (NI)	7, s.15(3), Sch.2, para.3(2)(b)
		s.353(5) am.	48, s.19(3)
		s.356(3)(b)(5) appl.	12, s.222(9)
		s.356B(5) mod.	SI 511, reg.9, Sch.2
		s.356B(7) mod.	SI 511, reg.9, Sch.2
		s.367(5) am. (1992-1993)	20, s.10(4)(5)
		s.369(3) am.	48, s.19(5)(7)
		s.369(3B) am.	48, s.19(3)

Year and Chap. or No. of Measure	Short title	How affected	1992, Chapter of Act or Number of Measure or Statutory Instrument
1988—*cont.*			
		s.369(5A)(5B) added	48, s.19(5)(7)
		s.376(4)(g) subst. (*prosp.*)	48, s.56, Sch.9, para.3(2)
		s.376(4A) added (*prosp.*)	48, s.56, Sch.9, para.3(3)
		ss.380-381 appl. (NI)	7, s.15(3), Sch.2, para.3(1)(a)
		s.380(1) mod.	SI 511, reg.9, Sch.2
		s.381(1) mod.	SI 511, reg.9, Sch.2
		s.383 appl. (NI)	7, s.15(3), Sch.2, para.3(1)(b)
		s.385 appl. (NI)	7, s.15(3), Sch.2, para.3(1)(c)
		s.387 excl. (NI)	7, s.15(3), Sch.2, para.3(2)(c)
		ss.388-389 appl. (NI)	7, s.15(3), Sch.2, para.3(1)(d)
		s.390 excl. (NI)	7, s.15(3), Sch.2, para.3(2)(d)
		s.399(1)(5) am.	12, s.290, Sch.10, para.14(19)(a)(b)
		s.400(2)(a)(c)(d) (defn. of "tax losses") appl.	48, s.77, Sch.17, para.2(3)
		s.400(2)(e)(6) am.	12, s.290, Sch.10, para.14(20)(a)(b)
		s.404 (defn. of "dual resident investing company") appl.	12, s.288(1)
		s.409(2) mod.	12, s.179(4)(a)
		ss.414,415 (defn. of "close company") appl.	12, s.288(1)
		s.416 appl.	12, s.86, Sch.5, para.2(8)(9)
		s.416 appl.	12, s.86, Sch.5, para.8(8)
		s.416 appl.	12, s.86, Sch.5, para.9(9)(10)
		s.416 appl.	12, s.288(1)
		s.416(2)-(6) appl.	12, s.184(1)(b)
		s.417(1) (defn. of "participator") appl.	12, s.86, Sch.5, para.2(10)
		s.417(1) (defn. of "participator") appl.	12, s.86, Sch.5, para.8(9)
		s.417(1) (defn. of "participartor") appl.	12, s.86, Sch.5, para.(9)(11)
		s.417(1) (defn. of "participator") appl.	12, s.239(7)
		s.421(1)(c) am.	48, s.19(6)(7)
		ss.431-458 (Pt.XII)(Ch.I) (defns. of "life assurance business" and "insurance company") appl.	12, s.204(4)
		ss.431-458 (Pt.XII)(Ch.I) appl.	12, s.212(7)(b)
		s.431(2) mod.	SI 1655, regs.1,5(1)

Year and Chap. or No. of Measure	Short title	How affected	1992, Chapter of Act or Number of Measure or Statutory Instrument
1988—*cont.*			
		s.432A mod.	SI 1655, regs.1,6(1),7(1), 8(1)
		s.432A(8)(9) appl.	12, s.212(6)
		ss.432B-432E excl.	SI 1655, regs.1,10
		s.432B mod.	SI 1655, regs.1,9(1)
		s.434(2) restr.	48, s.65(2)(a)(5)
		s.438(8) am.	12, s.290, Sch.10, para.14(21)
		s.440(3)(5) am.	12, s.290, Sch.10, para.14(22)(a)(b)
		s.440(4) mod.	SI 1655, regs.1,11(1),12(1)
		s.440(4)(d) excl.	SI 1655, regs.1,13
		s.440A(2) mod.	SI 1655, regs.1,14(1),15(1)
		s.440A(2)(d) excl.	SI 1655, regs.1,16
		s.440A(5) am.	12, s.290, Sch.10, para.14(23)(a)
		s.440A(6) subst.	12, s.290, Sch.10, para.14(23)(b)
		s.442 am.	12, s.290, Sch.10, para.14(24)
		s.442(3) excl. (*retrosp.*)	48, s.48 (adding ss.269C, 269D to 1970 c.10)
		s.444A(8) am.	12, s.290, Sch.10, para.14(25)
		ss.450-456 appl.	12, s.209(1)
		s.450(6) am.	12, s.290, Sch.10, para.14(26)
		s.459 am. (*prosp.*)	48, s.56, Sch.9, para.4
		s.460(1) am. (*prosp.*)	48, s.56, Sch.9, para.5(2)
		s.460(2)(a) am. (*prosp.*)	48, s.56, Sch.9, para.5(3)(a)
		s.460(2)(aa) added (*prosp.*)	48, s.56, Sch.9, para.5(3)(b)
		s.460(5)-(10) am. (*prosp.*)	48, s.56, Sch.9, para.5(4)
		s.460(11) am. (*prosp.*)	48, s.56, Sch.9, para.5(5)
		s.461(4)(a) am. (*prosp.*)	48, s.56, Sch.9, para.6
		s.461(6)-(8) am. (*prosp.*)	40, s.120(1), Sch.21, Pt.I, para.10(a)
		s.461(8A) added (*prosp.*)	40, s.120(1), Sch.21, Pt.I, para.10(b)
		s.461(9) rep.in pt. (*prosp.*)	40, s.120(2), Sch.22, Pt.I
		ss.461A-461C added (*prosp.*)	48, s.56, Sch.9, para.7
		s.462(2)(3) am. (*prosp.*)	48, s.56, Sch.9, para.8(2)(3)
		s.462A(9) added (*prosp.*)	48, s.56, Sch.9, para.9
		s.463(1) am. (*prosp.*)	48, s.56, Sch.9, para.10
		s.464(1)(3) am. (*prosp.*)	48, s.56, Sch.9, para.11(2)
		s.464(5)(d)(ii) am. (*prosp.*)	48, s.56, Sch.9, para.11(3)
		s.464(7) am. (*prosp.*)	48, s.56, Sch.9, para.11(4)
		s.465(6) added (*prosp.*)	48, s.56, Sch.9, para.12
		s.465A added (*prosp.*)	48, s.56, Sch.9, para.13

Year and Chap. or No. of Measure	Short title	How affected	1992, Chapter of Act or Number of Measure or Statutory Instrument
1988—*cont.*			
		s.466(1)-(3) am. (*prosp.*)	48, s.56, Sch.9, para.14(2) (7)(8)
		s.466(2) (defn. of "registrar") rep. (*prosp.*)	40, s.120(2), Sch.22, Pt.I
		s.466(2) (defns. of "friendly society" and "incorporated friendly society") added (*prosp.*)	48, s.56, Sch.9, para.14(4)
		s.466(2) (defn. of "new society") subst. (*prosp.*)	48, s.56, Sch.9, para.14(5)
		s.466(2) (defns. of "registered branch" and "registered friendly society") added (*prosp.*)	48, s.56, Sch.9, para.14(6)
		s.466(5) added (*prosp.*)	48, s.56, Sch.9, para.14(9)
		s.467(4)(a)(b) am.	52, s.300(2), Sch.2, para.37(a)(b)
		s.467(4)(ba) replaced (by subparas.(ba)(bb))	SI 808, art.2
		s.468(3) am.	48, s.32(3)(4)
		s.468(6) (defn. of "authorised unit trust") appl.	12, s.99(2)(b)
		s.473(2)(5)(6)(7) am.	12, s.290, Sch.10, para.14(27)(a)-(c)
		s.477A(1A)(3A) am.	48, s.34, Sch.8, paras.3(2) ,6
		s.477A(10) am.	48, s.34, Sch.8, paras.3(3) ,6
		s.477B(5) am.	12, s.290, Sch.10, para.14(28)
		s.481(5A) added	48, s.34, Sch.8, paras.4,6
		s.484(2) am.	12, s.290, Sch.10, para.14(29)
		s.486 (defn. of "registered industrial and provident society") appl.	12, s.170(9)(c)
		s.492(1)(a)(b) appl.	12, s.198(5)(b)
		s.502(1) (defn. of "ring fence profits") am.	12, s.290, Sch.10, para.14(30)
		s.502(1)(c) (defn. of "oil extraction activities") rep.in pt. & am.	48, ss.55(1)(2),82, Sch.18, Pt.VII
		s.502(1A) added	12, s.290, Sch.10, para.14(30)
		s.504 appl.	12, s.241(2)
		s.505(3)(5)(b)(6) am.	12, s.290, Sch.10, para.14(31)
		s.507(1)(d) am.	44, s.11(2), Sch.8, Pt.I, para.1(1)(2)(8)
		s.507(1)(e) added	SI 2383, Sch., para.11
		s.513(3) am.	12, s.290, Sch.10, para.14(32)

Year and Chap. or No. of Measure	Short title	How affected	1992, Chapter of Act or Number of Measure or Statutory Instrument
1988—*cont.*			
		ss.519,519A (defns. of "local authority association" and "health service body") appl.	12, s.271(3)
		s.539(3) (defn. of "friendly society") added (*prosp.*)	48, s.56, Sch.9, para.15
		s.547(5)(c) am.	48, s.19(4)
		s.549(2) am.	48, s.19(3)
		s.550(3) am.	48, s.19(2)
		s.574(1) mod.	SI 511, reg.9, Sch.2
		s.574(1) am.	12, s.290, Sch.10, para.14(33)
		s.575(1)(c)(2)(3) am.	12, s.290, Sch.10, para.14(34)(a)-(c)
		s.576(2) am.	12, s.290, Sch.10, para.14(35)(a)
		s.576(5) (defn. of "holding") subst.	12, s.290, Sch.10, para.14(35)(b)(i)
		s.576(5) (defns. of "new consideration" and "spouse") am.	12, s.290, Sch.10, para.14(35)(ii)(iii)
		ss.590-612 (Pt.XIV)(Ch.I) (defns. of "exempt approved schemes" and "statutory schemes") appl.	12, s.3, Sch.1, para.2(8)
		ss.590-659 (Pt.XIV) (defns. of "exempt approved scheme" and "approved personal pension scheme") appl.	12, s.271(1)
		s.590C am.	SI 624, art.2
		s.599(8)(b) subst. (*prosp.*)	48, s.56, Sch.9, para.16
		s.599A(7) am.	48, s.19(2)
		s.617(1) am.	6, s.4, Sch.2, para.93(1) (2)
		s.617(1) am. (NI)	9, s.4, Sch.2, para.33(1) (2)
		s.617(2)(a) am.	6, s.4, Sch.2, para.93(3) (a)
		s.617(2)(a)(aa) am. (NI)	9, s.4, Sch.2, para.33(3) (a)(b)
		s.617(2)(aa) am.	6, s.4, Sch.2, para.93(3) (b)
		s.617(3)(a) am.	6, s.4, Sch.2, para.93(4)
		s.617(3)(b)(4)(5) am. (NI)	9, s.4, Sch.2, para.33(4)- (6)
		s.617(4) am.	6, s.4, Sch.2, para.93(5)
		s.617(5) am.	6, s.4, Sch.2, para.93(6)
		s.617(5) excl. (NI)	7, s.15(3), Sch.2, para.3(2)(e)
		ss.619-620 excl. (NI)	7, s.15(3), Sch.2, para.3(2)(f)
		s.624 (defn. of "sponsored superannuation scheme") appl.	12, s.3, Sch.1, para.2(8)

Year and Chap. or No. of Measure	Short title	How affected	1992, Chapter of Act or Number of Measure or Statutory Instrument
1988—*cont.*		s.630 (defn. of "authorised insurance company") am. (*prosp.*)	48, s.56, Sch.9, para.17
		s.671(2) am.	48, s.27(1)(2)
		s.681(4) (defn. of "settlor") appl.	12, s.3, Sch.1, para.2(7)
		s.683(2) am.	48, s.19(3)
		s.684(2) am.	48, s.19(3)
		s.689(2) am.	48, s.19(3)
		s.699(2) am.	48, s.19(3)
		s.701(4) (defn. of "personal representative") appl.	12, s.288(1)
		s.710 (defn. of "securities") appl.	12, s.108(1)(a)
		s.710 (defn. of "transfer of securities") appl.	12, s.119(1)
		s.710(2A)(13) am.	12, s.290, Sch.10, para.14(36)(a)(b)
		s.710(3)(da) added	48, s.34, Sch.8, paras.5,6
		s.711 (defn. of "accrued interest") appl.	12, s.119(2)
		s.711 (defn. of "accrued interest") appl.	12, s.119(3)
		s.715(1)(a) restr.	48, s.65(2)(b)(5)
		s.715(2)(a) restr.	48, s.65(2)(c)(5)
		s.715(8) am.	12, s.290, Sch.10, para.14(37)
		s.716 (defn. of "unrealised interest") appl.	12, s.119(5)(a)
		s.723(8) am.	12, s.290, Sch.10, para.14(38)
		s.727(2) am.	12, s.290, Sch.10, para.14(39)
		s.731(4B) am.	12, s.290, Sch.10, para.14(40)
		s.734(2) am.	12, s.290, Sch.10, para.14(41)
		s.737 appl.(mods.)	SI 2074, reg.14(1)
		s.737(1) mod.	SI 569, reg.13(2)
		s.737(5A) mod.	SI 569, reg.14(1)(2)
		s.740(6)(a) am.	12, s.290, Sch.10, para.14(42)
		s.745(2)-(5) appl.(mods.)	12, s.98(2)
		s.757(1)-(7) am.	12, s.290, Sch.10, para.14(43)(a)-(f)
		s.758(5)(6) am.	12, s.290, Sch.10, para.14(44)(a)(b)
		s.759(9) am.	12, s.290, Sch.10, para.14(45)
		s.760(4) am.	12, s.290, Sch.10, para.14(46)

Year and Chap. or No. of Measure	Short title	How affected	1992, Chapter of Act or Number of Measure or Statutory Instrument
1988—*cont.*			
		s.761(2)(3)(5)(6)(7)(a)(b) am.	12, s.290, Sch.10, para.14(47)(a)-(d)
		s.761(4) rep.	12, s.290, Sch.12
		s.762(1)(2) am.	12, s.290, Sch.10, para.14(48)(a)(b)
		s.762(2)(a)-(d) am.	12, s.290, Sch.10, para.14(48)(b)(ii)-(v)
		s.762(3) am.	12, s.290, Sch.10, para.14(48)(c)
		s.762(4) am.	12, s.290, Sch.10, para.14(48)(d)
		s.763(1)-(6) am.	12, s.290, Sch.10, para.14(49)(a)-(g)
		s.776(9) am.	12, s.290, Sch.10, para.14(50)
		s.777(11)(12) am.	12, s.290, Sch.10, para.14(51)
		ss.788-806 (Pt.XVIII) (Chs.I,II mod.)	12, s.277(1)
		s.808A added	48, s.52(1)(2)
		s.815A appl. (*retrosp.*)	48, s.45 (adding s.140C to 1992 c.12)
		s.815A appl. (*retrosp.*)	48, s.48 (adding 1970 c.10 s.269C)
		s.815A added	48, s.50
		s.815B added	48, s.51(1)
		s.815B(4) (dcfn. of "the Arbitration Convention") appl.	48, s.51(6)
		s.816 appl.	12, s.277(4)
		s.816(2A) added	48, s.51(2)
		s.819(2) am.	48, s.19(3)
		s.824 appl.(mods.) (NI)	7, s.15(3), Sch.2, para.6(1)
		s.824(8) am.	12, s.290, Sch.10, para.14(52)
		s.827(1)(a) am. (1.12.1992,1.1.1993)	48, s.14(2), Sch.3, Pt.III, para.95
		s.831(3) (defn. of "the 1992 Act") added	12, s.290, Sch.10, para.14(53)(a)
		s.831(5) am.	12, s.290, Sch.10, para.14(53)(b)
		s.832 (defn. of "year of assessment") appl. (NI)	7, s.15(3), Sch.2, para.9(4)
		s.832(1) (defn. of "ordinary share capital") appl.	12, s.135(1)(a)
		s.832(1) (defn. of "chargeable gain") am.	12, s.290, Sch.10, para.14(54)
		s.832(1) (defn. of "lower rate") added	20, s.9(9)(10)(11)
		s.838 defn(s). appl.	12, ss.163,164, Sch.6, Pt.II, para.8(5)

Year and Chap. or No. of Measure	Short title	How affected	1992, Chapter of Act or Number of Measure or Statutory Instrument
1988—*cont.*			
		s.838 (defn. of "75 per cent. subsidiary") defn(s). mod.	12, s.170(2)(c)
		s.838 appl.	12, s.184(1)(a)
		s.838 defn(s). appl.	12, Sch.7, Pt.II, para.7(4)
		s.839 appl. (1.12.1992, 1.1.1993)	48, s.14(2), Sch.3, Pt.I, para.62 (adding 1983 c.55, sch.4A)
		s.839(2)-(8) appl.	SI 58, art.8(9)(b), Sch.1, para.3
		s.841 (defn. of "recognised stock exchange") appl.	12, s.288(1)
		s.842 (defn. of "investment trust") appl.	12, s.288(1)
		s.842(4) am.	12, s.290, Sch.10, para.14(55)
		s.842A (defn. of "local authority") appl.	12, s.288(1)
		s.842A(2)(a)-(c) subst. (1.4.1993) (EWS)	14, s.117(1), Sch.13, para.57
		s.843(2) am.	12, s.290, Sch.10, para.14(56)
		Sch.3, para.6(2) rep. & superseded	48, ss.63,82, Sch.11, paras.2(2)(3),6, Sch.18, Pt.VII
		Sch.3, paras.6A-6F added	48, s.63, Sch.11, paras.2(2),6
		Sch.3, para.6B appt. day(s) for (14.11.1992)	SI 2073, art.2
		Sch.3, paras.7-9 rep. & superseded	48, ss.63,82, Sch.11, paras.2(2)(3),6, Sch.18, Pt.VII
		Sch.3, para.10 rep.	48, ss.63,82, Sch.11, paras.2(3),6, Sch.18, Pt.VII
		Sch.3, para.11 am.	48, s.63, Sch.11, paras.2(4),6
		Sch.3, para.13(1) rep.in pt.	48, ss.63,82, Sch.11, paras.2(5)(a),6, Sch.18, Pt.VII
		Sch.3, para.13(1) am.	48, s.63, Sch.11, paras.2(5)(b),6
		Sch.3, para.15(2) rep.	48, ss.63,82, Sch.11, paras.2(3),6, Sch.18, Pt.VII
		Sch.4, paras.1(8),19,20 am.	12, s.290, Sch.10, para.14(57)(a)
		Sch.4, para.2(4) am.	12, s.290, Sch.10, para.14(57)(b)
		Sch.4, para.7 am.	12, s.290, Sch.10, para.14(57)(c)
		Sch.4, para.12 am.	12, s.290, Sch.10, para.14(57)(d)
		Sch.6 appl.	4, s.10(4)

Year and Chap. or No. of Measure	Short title	How affected	1992, Chapter of Act or Number of Measure or Statutory Instrument
1988—*cont.*			
		Sch.6, Pt.I, Tables A-C subst.	SI 731, art.2
		Sch.7, para.19(1) (defn. of "excess liability") am.	48, s.19(3)
		Schs.9,10 excl.	12, s.238(2)(c)(4)
		Sch.9, para.2(2) excl.	12, s.238(1)
		Sch.10, para.5(7) am.	12, s.290, Sch.10, para.14(58)
		Sch.12, para.1A added	48, s.54(1)(2)
		Sch.13 excl.	SI 569, reg.17
		Sch.14, paras.2(1)(b),3(1) (3)(a) am. (*prosp.*)	48, s.56, Sch.9, para.18(2) (3)
		Sch.15, para.3(1)(2)(c)(4) (c) am. (*prosp.*)	48, s.56, Sch.9, para.19(2) - (4)
		Sch.15, para.3(4A) added (*prosp.*)	48, s.56, Sch.9, para.19(5)
		Sch.15, para.4(3)(b) rep.in pt. (*prosp.*)	40, s.120(2), Sch.22, Pt.I
		Sch.15, para.4(3)(b)(i) subst. (*prosp.*)	48, s.56, Sch.9, para.19(6)
		Sch.15, para.6(1) am. (*prosp.*)	48, s.56, Sch.9, para.19(7)
		Sch.16 excl.	SI 569, reg.13(2)(d)
		Sch.16 appl.(mods.)	SI 2074, reg.14(5)
		Sch.18 appl.	SI 58, art.35(5)
		Sch.18 appl.(mods.)	12, s.170(8)
		Sch.18 appl.(mods.)	12, s.228(10)
		Sch.18, para.1(5) (defn. of "normal commercial loan") appl.	12, s.117(1)
		Sch.18, para.5(5) replaced (by para.5A)	48, s.24, Sch.6, paras.1,6
		Sch.18, paras.5B-5E added	48, s.24, Sch.6, paras.2,7
		Sch.18, para.6 am.	48, s.24, Sch.6, paras.3,8
		Sch.19A mod.	SI 511, regs.5(1),8
		Sch.19A, para.2B mod.	SI 511, reg.5(2)
		Sch.20, para.3A added	41, s.78(1), Sch.6, para.17
		Sch.20, para.12(2) am.	12, s.290, Sch.10, para.14(59)
		Sch.22, para.7 am.	12, s.290, Sch.10, para.14(60)
		Sch.22, para.7(3)(d) mod.	12, s.271(10)
		Sch.23A am.	12, s.290, Sch.10, para.14(61)
		Sch.23A, para.2(3)(b) mod.	SI 569, reg.23
		Sch.23A, para.3(2) mod.	SI 2074, reg.5(1)
		Sch.26, para.3 am.	12, s.290, Sch.10, para.14(62)
		Sch.28, para.2 am.	12, s.290, Sch.10, para.14(63)(a)
		Sch.28, para.3 am.	12, s.290, Sch.10, para.14(63)(b)(i)(ii)

Year and Chap. or No. of Measure	Short title	How affected	1992, Chapter of Act or Number of Measure or Statutory Instrument
1988—*cont.*			
		Sch.28, para.3(3) am.	12, s.290, Sch.10, para.14(63)(b)(iii)-(v)
		Sch.28, paras.4(3)(b),8(3) am.	12, s.290, Sch.10, para.14(63)(c)
		Sch.28, para.8(4)(5) rep.	12, s.290, Sch.12
		Sch.29, para.10(4)(b) rep.	12, s.290, Sch.12
		Sch.29, para.11 rep. (*prosp.*)	40, s.120(2), Sch.22, Pt.I
		Sch.29, para.12 rep.	12, s.290, Sch.12
		Sch.29, para.14 rep.in pt.	6, s.3, Sch.1
		Sch.29, paras.14,32 rep.in pt. (NI)	9, s.3, Sch.1
		Sch.29, paras.15-28 rep.	12, s.290, Sch.12
		Sch.29, para.32 rep.in pt.	6, s.3, Sch.1
		Sch.29, para.32, Table rep.in pt.	12, s.290, Sch.12
c.7	Social Security Act 1988	ss.1-8 rep.	6, s.3, Sch.1
		ss.10,11 rep.	6, s.3, Sch.1
		s.13(4)(e) am.	6, s.4, Sch.2, para.94
		s.15(2) am.	6, s.4, Sch.2, para.95
		s.15A(1) am.	6, s.4, Sch.2, para.96
		s.17 rep.	6, s.3, Sch.1
		s.18(2) rep.in pt.	6, s.3, Sch.1
		Sch.1 rep.	6, s.3, Sch.1
		Sch.2, para.1(1) rep.	6, s.3, Sch.1
		Sch.3 rep.	6, s.3, Sch.1
		Sch.4, paras.3-20 rep.	6, s.3, Sch.1
		Sch.4, paras.23-30 rep.	6, s.3, Sch.1
c.9	Local Government Act 1988	ss.1-16 (Pt.I) power to mod. (*prosp.*)	19, s.8(5)
		ss.1-16 (Pt.I) (defn. of "defined authority") appl. (14-2-1993)	19, s.10(3)
		ss.1-16 (Pt.I) (defn. of "defined activity") appl.	37, s.62(1), Sch.8, Pt.I, para.1(3)
		s.1(3)(a) (defn. of "local authority") appl.	37, s.62(1), Sch.8, Pt.I, para.1(3)
		s.2(2) restr.	SI 583, art.3
		s.2(3) am. (*prosp.*)	19, s.11, Sch.1, para.10
		s.4(6) am. (14-2-1993)	19, s.11, Sch.1, para.11
		s.6 appl.	SI 9, reg.2(2)
		s.6(1) appl.	37, s.62(1), Sch.8, Pt.I, para.1(3)
		s.6(3) am. (*prosp.*)	19, s.11, Sch.1, para.12
		s.7(2)(b)(d) power to mod. (4-1-1993)	19, s.9(3)(c)
		s.7(3)(a) rep.in pt. (*prosp.*)	19, s.29, Sch.4, Pt.I
		s.8 saved (4-1-1993)	19, s.9(3)
		s.13(1)(b) replaced (by para(b)(ba)) (4-1-1993)	19, s.11, Sch.1, para.13
		s.14(4A)-(4C) added (4-1-1993)	19, s.11, Sch.1, para.14

Year and Chap. or No. of Measure	Short title	How affected	1992, Chapter of Act or Number of Measure or Statutory Instrument
1988—*cont.*			
		s.15(8)(a) saved (*prosp.*)	19, s.8(6)
		s.17(8) am.	52, s.300(2), Sch.2, para.38
		s.17(8) (defn. of "industrial dispute") am.	52, s.300(2), Sch.2, para.38(a)(b)
c.19	Employment Act 1988	ss.1-23 rep.	52, s.300(1), Sch.1
		s.27 rep.	6, s.3, Sch.1
		s.30 rep.	52, s.300(1), Sch.1
		s.32(1) rep.in pt.	52, s.300(1), Sch.1
		s.32(2) rep.	52, s.300(1), Sch.1
		s.34(2)(3) rep.	52, s.300(1), Sch.1
		s.34(6) rep.in pt.	52, s.300(1), Sch.1
		s.34(6)(a)(b) rep.	52, s.300(1), Sch.1
		Sch.1 rep.	52, s.300(1), Sch.1
		Sch.3, paras.1-6 rep.	52, s.300(1), Sch.1
c.26	Finance Act 1988	s.38(9) am.	48, s.60(1)(2)
c.33	Criminal Justice Act 1988	s.81(8)(9) trans.of functions & am.	SI 709, art.2(1), Sch.1
		s.81(8)(9) am.	SI 709, art.2(3), Sch.1
		Sch.15, para.37 rep.	53, s.18(2), Sch.4, Pt.I
c.34	Legal Aid Act 1988	defn. of "assisted party" appl.	5, s.108(7)(a)(ii)
		s.34(6) am.	6, s.4, Sch.2, para.97
		s.34(14) rep.	6, s.3, Sch.1
		s.43 (defn. of "statutory inquiry") am.	53, s.18(1), Sch.3, para.21
c.35	British steel Act 1988	s.11(2) am.	12, s.290, Sch.10, para.15
c.39	Finance Act 1988	s.14(8)(a) rep. (1.1.1993)	48, ss.14(3),82, Sch.18, Pt.V
		s.21 restr.	SI 1844, reg.7(4)
		s.36(5A) added (6.4.1993)	48, s.62(2)(4)(6)
		s.38(8A) added (6.4.1993)	48, s.62(3)(4)(6)
		s.50(4) am.	12, s.290, Sch.10, para.16(2)
		ss.62-64 rep.	12, s.290, Sch.12
		s.68(4) am.	12, s.290, Sch.10, para.16(3)
		ss.77-89 (Pt.III)(Ch.II) appl.	12, s.120(1)
		s.80(2) replaced (by subss.(1A)(2))	48, s.37(2)(6)
		s.80(3)(a)(c) am.	48, s.37(3)(4)(6)
		s.80(3A) added	48, s.37(5)(6)
		s.82(3) am.	12, s.290, Sch.10, para.16(4)(a)(b)
		s.84 am.	12, s.290, Sch.10, para.16(5)
		ss.96-104 rep.	12, s.290, Sch.12
		ss.96,97 excl.	SI 58, art.9, Sch.2, para.13
		s.105(1)-(5) rep.	12, s.290, Sch.12
		ss.106-116 rep.	12, s.290, Sch.12
		s.118 rep.	12, s.290, Sch.12

Year and Chap. or No. of Measure	Short title	How affected	1992, Chapter of Act or Number of Measure or Statutory Instrument
1988—*cont.*		s.132(6) am.	12, s.290, Sch.10, para.16(6)
		Sch.3, para.31 rep.in pt.	6, s.3, Sch.1
		Sch.3, para.31 rep. (NI)	9, s.3, Sch.1
		Sch.4, Pt.I, para.11 subst. (*retrosp.*)	48, s.39
		Sch.4, Pt.II, para.15(1) am.	48, s.40(2)
		Sch.4, Pt.II, para.15(1A)-(1C) added	48, s.40(3)(5)
		Sch.4, Pt.II, para.15(3)- (5) added	48, s.40(4)(5)
		Sch.6, para.4(4) mod.	SI 511, reg.9, Sch.2
		Sch.6, para.6(5) rep.	12, s.290, Sch.12
		Schs.8-11 rep.	12, s.290, Sch.12
		Schs.8,9 excl.	SI 58, art.9, Sch.2, para.13
		Sch.8, para.1(3)(a) am. (*prosp.*)	48, s.56, Sch.9, para.20(2) (b)
		Sch.8, para.1(3)(b) am.	48, s.49(7)(10)
		Sch.8, para.1(3)(j) added	48, s.77, Sch.17, paras.5(8),7
		Sch.11, para.5 rep.in pt. & am.	48, ss.49(8)(a)-(c)(11),82, Sch.18, Pt.VII
		Sch.12, paras.4,5,7(b) rep.	12, s.290, Sch.12
		Sch.12, para.6(2) am.	12, s.290, Sch.10, para.16(7)
		Sch.13, paras.16,17,18 rep.	12, s.290, Sch.12
c.40	Education Reform Act 1988	defn. of "financial year" appl. (1.4.1993)	13, s.37(7)
		defn. of "higher education" appl.	13, s.90(1)
		s.3(2)(a) rep.in pt.	SI 1548, art.2(a)
		s.3(2)(aa) added	SI 1548, art.2(b)
		s.9(1A) added (1.8.1993)	13, s.12(4)
		s.9(4) (defn. of "nursery school") appl.	38, s.18(1)
		s.22(2) rep.in pt.	38, s.21(8), Sch.5
		s.22(2)(d) added	38, s.21(7), Sch.4, para.6(1)(2)
		s.22(5) rep.in pt.	38, s.21(7)(8), Sch.4, para.6(4)(b), Sch.5
		s.22(5) am.	38, s.21(7), Sch.4, para.6(1)(4)(a)
		s.22(5)(aa)(ab) added	38, s.21(7), Sch.4, para.6(1)(3)
		s.24(1)(b) am. (1.4.1993)	13, s.93(1), Sch.8, Pt.I, para.28(a)
		s.24(1)(b)(ii) am. (1.4.1993)	13, s.93(1), Sch.8, Pt.I, para.28(b)
		s.24(1)(b)(iii) added (1.4.1993)	13, s.93(1), Sch.8, Pt.I, para.28(c)
		ss.33-51 (Pt.I) (Ch.III) mod.	SI 164, reg.2(3)

Year and Chap. or No. of Measure	Short title	How affected	1992, Chapter of Act or Number of Measure or Statutory Instrument
1988—*cont.*			
		s.33(4)(a) am. (1.8.1993)	13, s.12(5)
		s.34(4) am.	SI 164, reg.4(2)
		s.36 (defn. of "delegated budget") appl.	38, s.18(1)
		s.36(5A) added (1.8.1993)	13, s.12(6)
		s.38(3A) added (1.8.1993)	13, s.12(7)
		s.57(5) am. (1.8.1993)	13, s.13(1)
		s.79(13) added (1.8.1993)	13, s.13(2)
		s.81(8)(b) am. (1.4.1993)	14, s.117(1), Sch.13, para.58(1)
		s.81(8A) rep. (1.4.1993)	14, s.117, Sch.13, para.58(2), Sch.14
		s.89(1A) added (1.8.1993)	13, s.13(3)
		s.100(1A) added (*prosp.*)	13, s.93(1), Sch.8, Pt.I, para.29
		s.105 (defns. of "city technical college" and "city college for the technology of the arts") appl.	38, s.18(1)
		s.105(2)(b) rep.in pt. (1.8.1993)	13, s.12(8)
		s.106(1A) added (1.8.1993)	13, s.12(9)
		ss.120-161 (Pt.II) mod.	13, s.84(2)
		s.120(2) rep. (1.4.1993)	13, s.93, Sch.8, Pt.I, para.30(a), Sch.9
		s.120(3)(b) am. (1.4.1993)	13, s.93(1), Sch.8, Pt.I, para.30(b)
		s.120(4) am. (1.4.1993)	13, s.93(1), Sch.8, Pt.I, para.30(c)
		s.120(6)-(8) rep. (1.4.1993)	13, s.93, Sch.8, Pt.I, para.30(d), Sch.9
		s.120(9)(a)(ii)(b) rep. (1.4.1993)	13, s.93, Sch.8, Pt.I, para.30(d), Sch.9
		ss.121-138 (Pt.II) (Ch.II) mod. (*temp.*)	13, s.64(1)
		s.122(2)-(5) rep.	13, s.93, Sch.8, Pt.I, para.31, Sch.9
		s.122A added (1.4.1993)	13, s.74(1)
		s.123 (defn. of "transfer date") appl.	13, s.91(6)(a)
		s.123(1) am. (1.4.1993)	13, s.93(1), Sch.8, Pt.I, para.32(a)
		s.123(3) replaced (by subss.(3)(4))	13, s.93(1), Sch.8, Pt.I, para.32(b)
		s.124(2)(b) am. (1.4.1993)	13, s.93(1), Sch.8, Pt.I, para.33(a)
		s.124(4) rep. (1.4.1993)	13, s.93, Sch.8, Pt.I, para.33(b), Sch.9
		ss.124A-124D added	13, s.71(1)
		s.124B(7) power to excl.	13, s.78(2)
		s.124D ext.	13, s.76(7)

Year and Chap. or No. of Measure	Short title	How affected	1992, Chapter of Act or Number of Measure or Statutory Instrument
1988—*cont.*			
		s.125 am.	13, s.71(2)
		s.127 appl.(mods.)	SI 1849(L), art.4
		s.127 appl.(mods.)	SI 2151(L), art.4
		s.128(1)(b)(iii)(iv) replaced (by subpara. (iii))	13, s.93(1), Sch.8, Pt.I, para.34(a)(i)
		s.128(1)(b)(v) added	13, s.93(1), Sch.8, Pt.I, para.34(a)(ii)
		s.128(4)(b) subst.	13, s.93(1), Sch.8, Pt.I, para.34(b)
		s.128(6) added	13, s.93(1), Sch.8, Pt.I, para.34(c)
		s.129 ext. (1.4.1993)	13, s.74(2)
		s.129(1)(2) subst.	13, s.72(1)(a)
		s.129(3)(4) rep.	13, ss.72(1)(b),93(2), Sch.9
		ss.129A-129B added	13, s.73(1)
		ss.131-132 rep. (1.4.1993)	13, s.93, Sch.8, Pt.I, para.35, Sch.9
		s.132(6) appl.	13, s.90(4)
		s.133 am. (*retrosp.*)	13, s.67(5)
		s.133(1) subst. (1.4.1993)	13, s.67(1)
		s.133(2)(a) am.	13, s.67(2)
		s.133(3) am.	13, s.67(3)
		s.133(4)(aa)(ab) added	13, s.67(4)
		s.134 rep. (1.4.1993)	13, s.93, Sch.8, Pt.I, para.35, Sch.9
		s.134(10) excl.	SI 427, art.6
		s.134(10) excl.	SI 428, art.6
		s.135(1)(c) subst.	13, s.93(1), Sch.8, Pt.I, para.36(a)
		s.135(2) am. (1.4.1993)	13, s.93(1), Sch.8, Pt.I, para.36(b)
		s.136(2) am. (1.4.1993)	13, s.93(1), Sch.8, Pt.I, para.37(a)
		s.136(3)-(7) rep.	13, s.93, Sch.8, Pt.I, para.37(b), Sch.9
		s.137(2) rep.in pt.	13, s.93, Sch.8, Pt.I, para.38, Sch.9
		ss.139-155 (Pt.II) (Ch.III) rep. (1.4.1993)	13, ss.85(1),93(2), Sch.9
		s.156 rep.in pt.	13, ss.73(2),85(1)
		s.156 rep. (1.4.1993)	13, s.93(2), Sch.9
		s.157(1)-(3) subst.	13, s.75
		s.157(4) rep.in pt. (1.4.1993)	13, s.93, Sch.8, Pt.I, para.39(a)(i), Sch.9
		s.157(4) am. (1.4.1993)	13, s.93(1), Sch.8, Pt.I, para.39(a)(ii)(iii)
		s.157(5)(b) rep. (1.4.1993)	13, s.93, Sch.8, Pt.I, para.39(b), Sch.9
		s.157(6)(b) am. (1.4.1993)	13, s.93(1), Sch.8, Pt.I, para.39(c)

Year and Chap. or No. of Measure	Short title	How affected	1992, Chapter of Act or Number of Measure or Statutory Instrument
1988—*cont.*			
		s.158(2)(a)(i)(iii)(b) rep. (1.4.1993)	13, s.93, Sch.8, Pt.I, para.40, Sch.9
		s.159(2)(b) rep. (1.4.1993)	13, s.93, Sch.8, Pt.I, para.41, Sch.9
		s.161(1)(c) rep. (1.4.1993)	13, s.93, Sch.8, Pt.I, para.42, Sch.9
		s.177(2)(3) restr.	SI 501, art.4(1)(2)
		s.179 trans.of functions	SI 331, art.2(1)(e)(4)
		s.181 trans.of functions	SI 331, art.2(1)(f)(4)
		s.197(4) am.	13, s.93(1), Sch.8, Pt.I, para.43(a)
		s.197(6) am.	13, s.93(1), Sch.8, Pt.I, para.43(b)
		s.197(7A)(7B) added	13, s.93(1), Sch.8, Pt.I, para.43(c)
		s.198(5) am. (1.4.1993)	13, s.93(1), Sch.8, Pt.I, para.44
		s.205(2)(d) subst. (1.4.1993)	13, s.93(1), Sch.8, Pt.I, para.45(a)
		s.205(6) rep. (1.4.1993)	13, s.93, Sch.8, Pt.I, para.45(b), Sch.9
		s.210(1)(3)(d) am. (1.4.1993)	13, s.93(1), Sch.8, Pt.I, para.46
		s.211(ba) added (1.4.1993)	13, s.93(1), Sch.8, Pt.I, para.47(a)
		s.211(c) rep. (1.4.1993)	13, s.93, Sch.8, Pt.I, para.47(b), Sch.9
		s.213(1) cert. functs. made exercisable concurrently	SI 1296, arts.2(3)(b),3
		s.213(1) am.	SI 1296, art.6(1), Sch., para.6(1)
		s.214(2)(a) am.	13, s.93(1), Sch.8, Pt.I, para.48
		s.218(1)(f) am. (1.4.1993)	13, s.93(1), Sch.8, Pt.I, para.49(a)
		s.218(7)(b) am. (1.4.1993)	13, s.93(1), Sch.8, Pt.I, para.49(b)
		s.218(10)(aa) added (1.4.1993)	13, s.93(1), Sch.8, Pt.1, para.49(c)(i)
		s.218(10)(b) rep. (1.4.1993)	13, s.93, Sch.8, Pt.I, para.49(c)(ii), Sch.9
		s.218(11) am. (1.4.1993)	13, s.93(1), Sch.8, Pt.I, para.49(d)
		s.219(1)(b) rep. (1.4.1993)	13, s.93, Sch.8, Pt.I, para.50, Sch.9
		s.219(2)(d) rep. (1.4.1993)	13, s.93, Sch.8, Pt.I, para.50, Sch.9
		s.219(2)(e) rep.	13, s.93, Sch.8, Pt.I, para.50, Sch.9
		s.219(3)(c)(ii) rep. (1.4.1993)	13, s.93, Sch.8, Pt.I, para.50, Sch.9

Year and Chap. or No. of Measure	Short title	How affected	1992, Chapter of Act or Number of Measure or Statutory Instrument
1988—*cont.*			
		s.220(1) am.	13, s.93(1), Sch.8, Pt.I, para.51(2)
		s.220(2)(a)(b) subst.	13, s.93(1), Sch.8, Pt.I, para.51(3)(a)
		s.220(2)(ba)(bb) added	13, s.93(1), Sch.8, Pt.I, para.51(3)(b)
		s.220(3) subst.	13, s.93(1), Sch.8, Pt.I, para.51(4)
		s.220(4) am. (*prosp.*)	13, s.93(1), Sch.8, Pt.I, para.51(5)
		s.221(1)(c) rep. (1.4.1993)	13, s.93, Sch.8, Pt.I, para.52, Sch.9
		s.221(3) (defn. of "relevant institution") rep. (1.4.1993)	13, s.93, Sch.8, Pt.I, para.52, Sch.9
		s.222(2)(b) rep. (1.4.1993)	13, s.93, Sch.8, Pt.I, para.53, Sch.9
		s.222(3)(c) rep.in pt. (1.4.1993)	13, s.93, Sch.8, Pt.I, para.53, Sch.9
		s.226(2)(b) am.	38, s.21(7), Sch.4, para.7
		s.227(2)-(4) rep.	13, s.93, Sch.8, Pt.I, para.54, Sch.9
		s.230(1) rep.in pt. (1.4.1993)	13, s.93, Sch.8, Pt.I, para.55(a), Sch.9
		s.230(3)(b) subst. (1.4.1993)	13, s.93(1), Sch.8, Pt.I, para.55(b)(i)
		s.230(3)(c)(ii) rep. (1.4.1993)	13, s.93, Sch.8, Pt.I, para.55(b)(ii), Sch.9
		s.230(3)(ca) added (1.4.1993)	13, s.93(1), Sch.8, Pt.I, para.55(b)(iii)
		s.232(2) rep.in pt. (1.4.1993)	13, s.93, Sch.8, Pt.I, para.56(a), Sch.9
		s.232(3) rep.in pt.	13, s.93, Sch.8, Pt.I, para.56(b), Sch.9
		s.232(4)(b) rep.in pt.	13, s.93, Sch.8, Pt.I, para.56(c), Sch.9
		s.233(a) am.	SI 1296, art.6(1), Sch., para.6(2)
		s.234(1) am. (1.4.1993)	13, s.93(1), Sch.8, Pt.I, para.57(a)
		s.234(2)(b) rep. (1.4.1993)	13, s.93, Sch.8, Pt.I, para.57(b), Sch.9
		s.235(2)(a)(h) rep. (1.4.1993)	13, s.93, Sch.8, Pt.I, para.58, Sch.9
		s.235(5A) added	37, s.62(2), Sch.9, para.10
		Sch.1, para.5 rep.	38, s.21(8), Sch.5
		Sch.4, para.2(2)-(10) ext.	SI 164, reg.2(4)(a)
		Sch.4, para.4(3) am.	SI 164, reg.4(3)
		Sch.4, para.4(6)(a) ext.	SI 164, reg.2(4)(b)(i)
		Sch.4, para.7(2) ext.	SI 164, reg.2(4)(b)(ii)
		Sch.7, para.1(4) subst.	13, s.93(1), Sch.8, Pt.I, para.59(a)
		Sch.7, para.8 added	13, s.71(3)(a)

Year and Chap. or No. of Measure	Short title	How affected	1992, Chapter of Act or Number of Measure or Statutory Instrument
1988—*cont.*			
		Sch.7, para.18 power to excl.	13, s.78(2)
		Sch.7, para.18(2)(b) am.	13, s.93(1), Sch.8, Pt.I, para.59(b)(i)
		Sch.7, para.18(2A) added	13, s.71(3)(b)
		Sch.7, para.18(5) subst.	13, s.93(1), Sch.8, Pt.I, para.59(b)(ii)
		Sch.7, para.19 rep.	13, s.93, Sch.8, Pt.I, para.59(c), Sch.9
		Sch.7A added	13, s.71(4), Sch.6
		Sch.8 rep.in pt. (1.4.1993)	13, s.93(1), Sch.8, Pt.I, para.60
		Sch.8, para.17 mod.	13, s.64(4)
		Sch.10, para.3 saved	SI 831, art.4
		Sch.10, para.3 mod.	13, s.93(1), Sch.8, para.61
		Sch.10, para.4 am.	13, s.93(1), Sch.8, Pt.I, para.65
		Sch.12, Pt.I, para.12 rep.	53, s.18(2), Sch.4, Pt.I
		Sch.12, para.68 rep. (1.4.1993)	13, s.93, Sch.8, Pt.I, para.66, Sch.9
		Sch.12, para.69(2) rep. (1.4.1993)	13, s.93, Sch.8, Pt.I, para.66, Sch.9
		Sch.12, para.70 rep. (1.4.1993)	13, s.93, Sch.8, Pt.I, para.66, Sch.9
		Sch.12, para.100(2) rep. (1.4.1993)	13, s.93, Sch.8, Pt.I, para.66, Sch.9
		Sch.12, para.101(4) rep. (1.4.1993)	13, s.93, Sch.8, Pt.I, para.66, Sch.9
c.41	Local Government Finance Act 1988	defn. of "charging authority" appl.	4, s.137(1)
		power to excl.	5, s.6(2)
		power to am.	5, s.138(9)
		ss.1-40 (Pts.I,II) rep.	14, s.117(2), Sch.14
		s.9 (defn. of "contribution period") appl.	4, s.137(1)
		s.26 appl.	14, s.27(8)
		s.41(1) am.	14, s.117(1), Sch.13, para.59
		s.43 mod.	SI 557, art.3(a)
		s.43(7) am.	14, s.117(1), Sch.13, para.60
		s.44(5) am.	14, s.117(1), Sch.13, para.61
		s.44A mod.	SI 557, art.3(a)
		s.44A(1) am.	14, s.117(1), Sch.13, para.62(1)
		s.44A(6)(a)(8)(a) am.	14, s.117(1), Sch.13, para.62(2)
		s.45 mod.	SI 557, art.3(a)
		s.45(7) am.	14, s.117(1), Sch.13, para.63
		s.46(4) am.	14, s.117(1), Sch.13, para.64

Year and Chap. or No. of Measure	Short title	How affected	1992, Chapter of Act or Number of Measure or Statutory Instrument
1988—*cont.*		s.47(1)(a)(3) am.	14, s.117(1), Sch.13, para.65(1)
		s.47(9) am.	14, s.117(1), Sch.13, para.65(2)
		s.49(1) am.	14, s.117(1), Sch.13, para.66(1)
		s.49(2)(b) am.	14, s.117(1), Sch.13, para.66(2)
		s.55(1)(a) am.	14, s.117(1), Sch.13, para.67(1)
		s.55(5) am.	14, s.117(1), Sch.13, para.67(2)
		s.55(7)(a)(b) replaced (by para.(a))	14, s.104, Sch.10, Pt.I, para.1
		s.55(7A)(a) am.	14, s.117(1), Sch.13, para.67(3)
		s.58(9) am.	14, s.117(1), Sch.13, para.68
		s.61(1)(a) am.	14, s.117(1), Sch.13, para.69
		s.64(3A)-(3B) added	14, s.104, Sch.10, Pt.I, para.2(1)
		s.64(12) added	14, s.104, Sch.10, Pt.I, para.2(2)
		s.66(2D) rep.in pt.	14, s.117, Sch.13, para.70(1), Sch.14
		s.66(3)(b)(4) rep.in pt.	14, s.117, Sch.13, para.70(2), Sch.14
		s.67(2) am.	14, s.117(1), Sch.13, para.71
		ss.68-73 rep.	14, s.117(2), Sch.14
		s.74(4)(a)(b) subst.	14, s.117(1), Sch.13, para.72(1)
		s.74(5) subst.	14, s.117(1), Sch.13, para.72(2)
		ss.74A,75A rep.	14, s.117(2), Sch.14
		s.75(2)(a)(b) am.	14, s.117(1), Sch.13, para.73(1)
		s.75(4)(c)(5) am.	14, s.117(1), Sch.13, para.73(2)
		s.75(6)(a) subst.	14, s.117(1), Sch.13, para.73(3)
		s.75(7) subst.	14, s.117(1), Sch.13, para.73(4)
		s.76(2)(3) replaced (by subs.(2))	14, s.104, Sch.10, Pt.II, para.8
		s.78(1) (defn. of "revenue support grant") appl.	14, s.69(1)
		s.78(6)(7) rep.	14, ss.104,117(2), Sch.10, Pt.II, para.9, Sch.14
		s.78A added	14, s.104, Sch.10, Pt.II, para.10

Year and Chap. or No. of Measure	Short title	How affected	1992, Chapter of Act or Number of Measure or Statutory Instrument
1988—*cont.*			
		s.79(1) am.	14, s.104, Sch.10, Pt.II, para.11(1)
		s.79(2)(3) mod.	SI 2996, reg.4(1)
		s.79(4) am.	14, s.104, Sch.10, Pt.II, para.11(2)
		ss.80,81 rep.	14, ss.104,117(2), Sch.10, Pt.II, para.12, Sch.14
		s.82 subst.	14, s.104, Sch.10, Pt.II, para.13
		s.83(1)-(5) mod.	SI 2996, reg.4(1)
		s.84 rep.	14, ss.104,117(2), Sch.10, Pt.II, para.14, Sch.14
		ss.84A-84C added	14, s.104, Sch.10, Pt.II, para.15
		s.84C mod.	SI 2996, reg.4(1)
		s.85(1) am.	14, s.104, Sch.10, Pt.II, para.16(1)
		s.85(2) (defn. of "additional grant") appl.	14, s.69(1)
		s.85(7) am.	14, s.104, Sch.10, Pt.II, para.16(2)
		s.86(2)(3) mod.	SI 2996, reg.4(1)
		s.86(4)-(6) rep.	14, ss.104,117(2), Sch.10, Pt.II, para.17, Sch.14
		s.88A replaced (by ss.88A, 88B)	14, s.104, Sch.10, Pt.II, para.18
		s.89(1) am.	14, s.104, Sch.10, Pt.III, para.19
		s.90 subst.	14, s.104, Sch.10, Pt.III, para.20
		ss.95,96 rep.	14, ss.104,117(2), Sch.10, Pt.III, para.21, Sch.14
		s.95(3)(d) added	SI 287, art.2
		ss.97-98 restr.	14, s.62(2)
		s.97 subst.	14, s.104, Sch.10, Pt.III, para.22
		s.98(1)(2) rep.	14, ss.104,117(2), Sch.10, Pt.III, para.23(1)(a), Sch.14
		s.98(3)(a)(c) rep.in pt.	14, ss.104,117(2), Sch.10, Pt.III, para.23(1)(b), Sch.14
		s.98(3)(d) rep.	14, ss.104,117(2), Sch.10, Pt.III, para.23(1)(b), Sch.14
		s.98(4) rep.in pt.	14, ss.104,117(2), Sch.10, Pt.III, para.23(1)(c), Sch.14
		s.98(4)(5) am.	14, s.104, Sch.10, Pt.III, para.23(2)

Year and Chap. or No. of Measure	Short title	How affected	1992, Chapter of Act or Number of Measure or Statutory Instrument
1988—*cont.*			
		s.98(5) rep.in pt.	14, ss.104,117(2), Sch.10, Pt.III, para.23(1)(d), Sch.14
		s.98(6) am.	14, s.104, Sch.10, Pt.III, para.23(3)
		s.99 subst.	14, s.104, Sch.10, Pt.III, para.24
		ss.100-110 (Pt.VII) rep.	14, s.117(2), Sch.14
		ss.114-116 saved	19, s.5(7)
		s.117 restr.	SI 2903, reg.12
		s.118(1)(c) am.	14, s.117(1), Sch.13, para.74
		s.128(1C) am.	14, s.117(1), Sch.13, para.75
		s.129 rep.	14, s.117(2), Sch.14
		ss.133,134 rep.	14, s.117(2), Sch.14
		s.138(2)(a)-(d) rep.	14, s.117, Sch.13, para.76(1), Sch.14
		s.138(2)(g) rep.	14, s.117, Sch.13, para.76(1), Sch.14
		s.138(3) subst.	14, s.117(1), Sch.13, para.76(2)
		s.139(2)(a)-(c) rep.	14, s.117(2), Sch.14
		s.139A(5)(a) am.	14, s.117(1), Sch.13, para.77(1)
		s.139A(6) subst.	14, s.117(1), Sch.13, para.77(2)
		s.139A(7A) added	14, s.117(1), Sch.13, para.77(3)
		s.139A(8) rep.	14, s.117, Sch.13, para.77(4), Sch.14
		s.140(1) am.	14, s.117(1), Sch.13, para.78(1)
		s.140(2)(d)-(g) replaced (by paras.(d)-(e))	14, s.117(1), Sch.13, para.78(2)
		s.140(3) am.	14, s.117(1), Sch.13, para.78(3)
		s.141(6)-(8) subst.	14, s.117(1), Sch.13, para.79(1)
		s.141(9) rep.	14, s.117, Sch.13, para.79(2), Sch.14
		ss.141A,141B rep.	14, s.117(2), Sch.14
		s.143(3) am.	14, s.117(1), Sch.13, para.80(1)
		s.143(6) rep.in pt.	14, s.117, Sch.13, para.80(2), Sch.14
		s.143(7)(9B) rep.	14, s.117, Sch.13, para.80(3), Sch.14
		s.144 (defn. of "combined police authority") appl.	14, s.19(3)(f)

Year and Chap. or No. of Measure	Short title	How affected	1992, Chapter of Act or Number of Measure or Statutory Instrument
1988—*cont.*			
		s.144 (defns. of "combined police authority" and "combined fire authority") appl.	14, s.117(1), Sch.13, para.7 (amdg. 1945 c.18, s.11(1))
		s.144 (defns. of "combined police authority" and "combined fire authority") appl.	14, s.117(1), Sch.13, para.12 (amdg. 1963 c.18 s.4(1))
		s.144 (defns. of "combined police authority" and "combined fire authority") appl.	14, s.117(1), Sch.13, para.13 (amdg. 1965 c.12 s.31((a))
		s.144 (defns. of "combined fire authority" and "combined police authority") appl.	14, s.117(1), Sch.13, para.14 (amdg. 1965 c.63 s.2(1)(a))
		s.144(1) appl. (EW)	14, s.27(8)
		s.144(2) subst.	14, s.117(1), Sch.13, para.81(1)
		s.144(6) am.	14, s.117(1), Sch.13, para.81(2)
		s.145A rep.	14, s.117(2), Sch.14
		s.146(1) rep.	14, s.117, Sch.13, para.82, Sch.14
		Sch.1, para.4(2) subst.	6, s.4, Sch.2, para.98
		Sch.1, para.4(2)(h) rep.	SI 494, art.2(a)
		Sch.1, para.4(2)(k)(l) added	SI 494, art.2(b)
		Sch.1, para.5A added	14, s.101(1)
		Sch.2, para.14(2)(a) am.	6, s.4, Sch.2, para.99
		Sch.4, para.6(1) am.	6, s.4, Sch.2, para.100
		Sch.4, para.7(3A) added	14, s.102(2)
		Sch.4, para.8(1)(a) am.	14, s.102(3)
		Sch.4, para.13A added	14, s.102(4)
		Sch.4, para.15 am.	14, s.102(5)
		Sch.4, para.28(2) rep.in pt.	6, s.3, Sch.1
		Sch.4, para.28(2) am.	6, s.4, Sch.2, para.101
		Sch.4A appl.(mods.)	14, s.17(1)
		Sch.4A, para.1(1)-(3) am.	14, s.117(1), Sch.13, para.83(1)
		Sch.4A, para.4(1) am.	14, s.117(1), Sch.13, para.83(2)
		Sch.4A, para.6(3)(a)(b) replaced (by para.(a))	14, s.117(1), Sch.13, para.83(3)
		Sch.4A, para.7(1)-(3) am.	14, s.117(1), Sch.13, para.83(4)
		Sch.4A, para.10(2) am.	14, s.117(1), Sch.13, para.83(5)
		Sch.5, para.11(2) replaced (by subparas.(2)(3))	14, s.104, Sch.10, Pt.I, para.3
		Sch.6, para.2(6A) subst.	14, s.104, Sch.10, Pt.I, para.4

Year and Chap. or No. of Measure	Short title	How affected	1992, Chapter of Act or Number of Measure or Statutory Instrument
1988—*cont.*			
		Sch.7, Pt.II, para.9(3)(4) replaced (by subparas.(3)(4)(5))	14, s.104, Sch.10, Pt.I, para.5
		Sch.7, para.5(13) am.	14, s.117(1), Sch.13, para.84(1)
		Sch.7, para.6(1) am.	14, s.117(1), Sch.13, para.84(2)(a)
		Sch.7, para.6(4)(a) am.	14, s.117(1), Sch.13, para.84(2)(b)
		Sch.7A mod.	SI 559, reg.2(2)
		Sch.7A, para.2 mod.	46, ss.1,8(1)
		Sch.7A, para.5(2A) added	46, ss.2(1),8(1)
		Sch.7A, para.5(7)-(9) excl.	46, ss.3(3),8(1)
		Sch.7A, para.5(9) am.	14, s.117(1), Sch.13, para.85
		Sch.7A, para.8 excl.	46, ss.3(3),8(1)
		Sch.8, Pt.II, para.4(1) am.	14, s.104, Sch.10, Pt.I, para.6(2)
		Sch.8, Pt.II, para.4(3)(a) am.	14, s.104, Sch.10, Pt.I, para.6(3)
		Sch.8, Pt.II, para.4(4) rep.	14, ss.104,117(2), Sch.10, Pt.I, para.6(4), Sch.14
		Sch.8, Pt.II, para.4(5A) added	14, s.104, Sch.10, Pt.I, para.6(5)
		Sch.8, Pt.II, para.5(2) am.	14, s.104, Sch.10, Pt.I, para.6(6)
		Sch.8, Pt.II, para.5(6)(b) (c) subst.	14, s.104, Sch.10, Pt.I, para.6(7)
		Sch.8, Pt.II, para.5(6A) added	14, s.104, Sch.10, Pt.I, para.6(8)
		Sch.8, Pt.II, para.5(8)(9) am.	14, s.104, Sch.10, Pt.I, para.6(9)
		Sch.8, Pt.II, para.5(10) replaced (by subparas.(10)-(15))	14, s.104, Sch.10, Pt.I, para.6(10)
		Sch.8, Pt.II, para.6(2) subst.	14, s.104, Sch.10, Pt.I, para.6(11)
		Sch.8, Pt.III subst.	14, s.104, Sch.10, Pt.I, para.7
		Sch.8, para.2 mod.	SI 2996, reg.4(2)
		Sch.8, para.2(1) mod.	46, ss.5(1),8(1)
		Sch.8, para.2(1)(c) am.	14, s.117(1), Sch.13, para.86(1)
		Sch.8, para.2(2)(a)(b) am.	14, s.117(1), Sch.13, para.86(2)
		Sch.8, para.5(4)(5)(7)(9) (10)(b)(14) mod.	SI 2996, reg.4(1)
		Sch.8, para.6(6) mod.	46, ss.5(2),8(1)
		Sch.8, para.6(7)(c) am.	14, s.117(1), Sch.13, para.86(3)
		Sch.8, para.9 mod.	46, ss.4,8(1)
		Sch.8, para.12 mod.	SI 2996, reg.4(1)

Year and Chap. or No. of Measure	Short title	How affected	1992, Chapter of Act or Number of Measure or Statutory Instrument
1988—*cont.*			
		Sch.8, para.15 mod.	SI 2996, reg.4(1)
		Sch.9, para.2(1)(c) am.	14, s.117(1), Sch.13, para.87(1)
		Sch.9, para.3(1)(3) am.	14, s.117(1), Sch.13, para.87(2)
		Sch.9, para.4(1)(b) am.	14, s.117(1), Sch.13, para.87(3)
		Sch.9, para.4A(1) am.	14, s.117(1), Sch.13, para.87(3)
		Sch.9, para.6(1)(1A) am.	14, s.117(1), Sch.13, para.87(4)
		Sch.9, para.6A added	14, s.117(1), Sch.13, para.87(5)
		Sch.9, para.8(2)(4) am.	14, s.117(1), Sch.13, para.87(6)
		Sch.10 rep. (exc. paras.1, 9(1)(5))	6, s.3, Sch.1
		Sch.11, para.1(1) am.	14, s.117(1), Sch.13, para.88(1)
		Sch.11, para.2(d)-(f) added	14, s.117(1), Sch.13, para.88(2)
		Sch.11, para.5(1)(p) am.	14, s.117(1), Sch.13, para.88(3)
		Sch.11, para.6(4) am.	14, s.117(1), Sch.13, para.88(4)
		Sch.11, para.6(6) rep.	14, s.117, Sch.13, para.88(5), Sch.14
		Sch.11, para.8(3)(e) replaced (by paras. (e) (ea))	14, s.117(1), Sch.13, para.88(6)
		Sch.11, para.8(4)(f) replaced (by paras.(f) (fa)(fb)(fc)(fd)(fe))	14, s.117(1), Sch.13, para.88(7)
		Sch.11, para.9(1)(a)-(c) replaced (by paras.(a)- (d))	14, s.117(1), Sch.13, para.88(8)
		Sch.11, para.10A added	14, s.117(1), Sch.13, para.88(9)
		Sch.11, para.11(1)(a)(b) am.	14, s.117(1), Sch.13, para.88(10)
		Sch.11, para.11(2)(d) subst.	14, s.117(1), Sch.13, para.88(11)
		Sch.11, para.14(a) rep.	14, s.117, Sch.13, para.88(12)(a), Sch.14
		Sch.11, para.14(b)(c) am.	14, s.117(1), Sch.13, para.88(12)(b)
		Sch.11, para.15(b) am.	14, s.117(1), Sch.13, para.88(13)
		Sch.11, para.16(1) am.	14, s.117(1), Sch.13, para.88(14)
		Sch.11, para.18 subst.	14, s.117(1), Sch.13, para.88(15)
		Sch.12, Pt.III, para.41 rep.in pt.	53, s.18(2), Sch.4, Pt.I

Year and Chap. or No. of Measure	Short title	How affected	1992, Chapter of Act or Number of Measure or Statutory Instrument
1988—*cont.*			
		Sch.12, para.5 rep.	14, s.117, Sch.13, para.89, Sch.14
		Sch.12, paras.8,15,17-36, 38 rep. (*prosp.*)	14, s.117(2), Sch.14
		Sch.12, paras.10,13 rep.	14, s.117(2), Sch.14
		Sch.12A rep.	14, s.117(2), Sch.14
c.43	Housing (Scotland) Act 1988	defn. of "statutory assured tenant" appl.	14, s.75(5)
		s.48A added	6, s.4, Sch.2, para.102
c.45	Firearms (Amendment) Act 1988	s.11(1) am.	31, s.1(2)
		s.17(1) am.	SI 2823, reg.6(1)
		s.17(1A) added	SI 2823, reg.6(1)
		s.17(3A) added	SI 2823, reg.7(1)
		s.18(1A) added	SI 2823, reg.8(1)
		s.18(4) am.	SI 2823, reg.8(2)
		s.18(6) added	SI 2823, reg.8(3)
		s.18A added	SI 2823, reg.9
		s.42A added	SI 2823, reg.6(2)
		Sch.6, Pt.I am.	SI 2823, reg.6(3)
c.47	School Boards (Scotland) Act 1988	s.1(1) (defn. of "school board") appl.	37, s.62(2), Sch.9, para.6(c) (amending 1978 c.44,s.29(2)(c))
		s.8(4)(b) rep. (1-4-1993)	37, s.62(3), Sch.10
		s.22(2) rep.in pt. (1-4- 1993)	37, s.62(3), Sch.10
c.48	Copyright, Design and Patents	s.3(1) (defn. of "literary work") am. (1.1.1993)	SI 3233, reg.3
		s.18(2) am. (1.1.1993)	SI 3233, reg.4(1)
		s.18(3) added (1.1.1993)	SI 3233, reg.4(2)
		s.21(3)(a) am. (1.1.1993)	SI 3233, reg.5(1)
		s.21(3)(ab) added (1.1.1993)	SI 3233, reg.5(2)
		s.21(4) rev.in pt. (1.1.1993)	SI 3233, reg.5(3)
		s.27(3) am. (1.1.1993)	SI 3233, reg.6
		s.27(3A) added (1.1.1993)	SI 3233, reg.6
		s.29(4) added (1.1.1993)	SI 3233, reg.7
		ss.50A-50C added (1.1.1993)	SI 3233, reg.8
		ss.153-156 ext.	SI 1313, art.2
		s.179 am. (1.1.1993)	SI 3233, reg.9
		s.296(2A) added (1.1.1993)	SI 3233, reg.10
		s.296A added (1.1.1993)	SI 3233, reg.11
		Sch.7, para.14 rep.	53, s.18(2), Sch.4, Pt.I
		Sch.7, para.26 rep.	12, s.290, Sch.12
c.49	Health and Medicines Act 1988	s.6(2) am.	12, s.290, Sch.10, para.17
c.50	Housing Act 1988	appt. day(s) for spec. provns. (21.2.1992)	SI 324, art.2
		s.41A added	6, s.4, Sch.2, para.103
		s.121(4)-(6) rep.	6, s.3, Sch.1
		s.121(7) subst.	6, s.4, Sch.2, para.104

Year and Chap. or No. of Measure	Short title	How affected	1992, Chapter of Act or Number of Measure or Statutory Instrument
1988—*cont.* c.52	Road Traffic Act 1988	defns. of "motor vehicle", "the Road Traffic Acts" and "the Traffic Acts" appl.	ii, s.1, Sch., s.2
		ss.1-8 appl.(mods.)	ii, s.1, Sch., s.3(2)
		s.11 appl.(mods.)	ii, s.1, Sch., s.3(2)
		ss.14-16 appl.(mods.)	ii, s.1, Sch., s.3(2)
		s.14(2)(aa)(bb) added (EWS)	SI 3105, reg.2(2)
		s.14(4) am. (EWS)	SI 3105, reg.2(3)
		s.14(7) added (EWS)	SI 3105, reg.2(4)
		s.15(3A) added (EWS)	SI 3105, reg.3(2)
		s.15(4) am. (EWS)	SI 3105, reg.3(3)
		s.15(5)(a)(b) am. (EWS)	SI 3105, reg.3(4)
		s.15(5A) added (EWS)	SI 3105, reg.3(5)
		s.15(6) subst. (EWS)	SI 3105, reg.3(6)
		s.15(9) (defns. of "maximum laden weight", "passenger car" and "the seat belt directive") added (EWS)	SI 3105, reg.3(7)
		s.22 appl.(mods.)	ii, s.1, Sch., s.3(2)
		ss.24-26 appl.(mods.)	ii, s.1, Sch., s.3(2)
		ss.28-30 appl.(mods.)	ii, s.1, Sch., s.3(2)
		ss.35-37 appl.(mods.)	ii, s.1, Sch., s.3(2)
		s.40A restr.	SI 1217, regs.7,9,11
		s.41 appl.(mods.)	ii, s.1, Sch., s.3(2)
		s.47 appl.(mods.)	ii, s.1, Sch., s.3(2)
		s.57(1A) added (1.1.93) (EWS)	SI 3107, reg.16, Sch.2, para.5(1)
		s.63(1A) added (1.1.93) (EWS)	SI 3107, reg.16, Sch.2, para.1(1)
		s.64A added (1.1.96) (EWS)	SI 3107, reg.16, Sch.2, para.2
		s.65(1A) added (1.1.93) (EWS)	SI 3107, reg.16, Sch.2, para.1(2)
		s.65A added (1.1.96) (EWS)	SI 3107, reg.16, Sch.2, para.3
		s.66(4A) added (1.1.93) (EWS)	SI 3107, reg.16, Sch.2, para.4
		s.66A ext.	SI 1286, art.3
		s.67 appl.(mods.)	ii, s.1, Sch., s.3(2)
		ss.68-73 restr.	SI 1217, regs.7,11
		s.68 appl.(mods.)	SI 1217, reg.10
		ss.75,76 restr.	SI 1217, regs.7,11
		ss.77-79 restr.	SI 1217, regs.7,9,11
		s.81 appl.(mods.)	ii, s.1, Sch., s.3(2)
		s.83 restr.	SI 1217, regs.7,11
		s.85 (defn. of "EC certificate of conformity") added (1.1.93) (EWS)	SI 3107, reg.16, Sch.2, para.5(2)(a)

Year and Chap. or No. of Measure	Short title	How affected	1992, Chapter of Act or Number of Measure or Statutory Instrument
1988—*cont.*			
		s.85 (defn. of "light passenger Vehicle") added (1.1.93) (EWS)	SI 3107, reg.16, Sch.2, para.5(2)(b)
		s.86 am. (1.1.93) (EWS)	SI 3107, reg.16, Sch.2, para.5(3)
		s.87 appl.(mods.)	SI 1217, regs.8,11
		s.87 appl.(mods.)	ii, s.1, Sch., s.3(2)
		s.103 appl.(mods.)	ii, s.1, Sch., s.3(2)
		ss.110-114 appl.(mods.)	ii, s.1, Sch., s.3(2)
		ss.143,144 appl.(mods.)	ii, s.1, Sch., s.3(2)
		s.145(3)(aa) added	SI 3036, reg.2(1)
		s.145(3)(b) am.	SI 3036, reg.2(2)
		s.145(4)(4A) added	SI 3036, reg.2(3)
		ss.157(2),158(2) am.	SI 2402, arts.2,3
		ss.163-165 appl.(mods.)	ii, s.1, Sch., s.3(2)
		ss.170-172 appl.(mods.)	ii, s.1, Sch., s.3(2)
		s.178 appl.(mods.)	ii, s.1, Sch., s.3(2)
		s.180 appl. (1.1.93)	SI 3107, reg.13(4)
		s.180 mod. (N.I.)(1.1.93)	SI 3107, reg.13(5)
		s.183(2) am. (1.1.96) (EWS)	SI 3107, reg.16, Sch.2, para.6
		s.185 (defn. of "motor car") appl.	3, s.8(2)
		ss.190,191 restr.	SI 1217, regs.7,11
		s.192A added	42, s.39
		s.195(3)(4) am. (EWS)	SI 3105, reg.4
c.53	Road Traffic Offenders Act 1988	s.20(4) ext.	SI 1286, art.4(1)
		s.29 mod.	SI 1286, art.6(3)
		ss.34-37 (saving)	SI 1286, art.6(5)(a)
		s.34(1A) added	11, s.3(2)
		s.45(5) mod.	SI 1286, art.6(4)
		s.53(2)(a)(b) am. (S)	SI 435, arts.2,3
		s.82 trans.of functions	SI 709, art.2(1), Sch.1
		s.82 am.	SI 709, art.2(3), Sch.1
		s.82(2) trans.of functions	SI 709, art.2(1), Sch.1
		s.82(2) am.	SI 709, art.2(3), Sch.1
		Sch.2 (saving)	SI 1286, art.6(5)(b)
		Sch.2, Pt.I am. (1.1.96) (EWS)	SI 3107, reg.16, Sch.2, para.7
		Sch.2, Pt.II am.	11, s.3(1)
		Sch.3 am.	SI 345, art.2
c.i	Greater Manchester (Light Rapid Transit System) Act 1988	ss.5-35 (Pt.II) appl.in pt.(mods.)	xviii, s.11(1)(2)
		s.23 restr.	xviii, s.20(3)
		s.42 am.	xviii, s.17(20)
c.ii	Greater Manchester (Light Rapid Transit System) (No.2) Act 1988	s.9 am.	xviii, s.11(3)

Year and Chap. or No. of Measure	Short title	How affected	1992, Chapter of Act or Number of Measure or Statutory Instrument
1988—*cont.*			
c.xi	British Railways (London) Act 1988	s.9(1)(b)(f) rep.in pt.	xi, ss.46(4),48, Sch.4, Pt.II
c.xxviii	Harwich Parkeston Quay Act 1988	appl.(mods.)	SI 1136(L), arts.2(1),9(1), Sch.
No.3	Church of England (Ecumenical Relations) Measure 1988	s.5(2)(b) am.	GSM 1, s.6
1989			
c.4	Prevention of Terrorism (Temporary Provisions) Act 1989	spec. provns. cont. (to 21.3.1993)	SI 495, art.3
c.6	Official Secrets Act 1989	ext.(mods.) (Hong Kong)	SI 1301, art.2, Schs.1,2
c.8	National Maritime Museum Act 1989	ss.1(5),2(2) trans.of functions	SI 1311, art.3(1), Sch.1, Pt.I
c.15	Water Act 1989	s.95(4)-(6) am.	12, s.290, Sch.10, para.18(a)-(c)
c.24	Social Security Act 1989	ss.1-3 rep.	6, s.3, Sch.1
		ss.4(1)-(4),5(1)-(4),6(1) rep.	6, s.3, Sch.1
		s.6(7) am.	6, s.4, Sch.2, para.105(1)
		s.6(9) am.	6, s.4, Sch.2, para.105(2)(a)(b)
		s.7(1)-(5) rep.	6, s.3, Sch.1
		ss.9-19 rep.	6, s.3, Sch.1
		s.21 rep.	6, s.3, Sch.1
		s.22(1)-(6)(8) rep.	6, s.3, Sch.1
		s.25 (defn. of "war pension scheme") appl.	4, s.137(1)
		s.25(4) (defn. of "war pension") appl.	5, s.123, Sch.4, Pt.II, para.5
		s.25(4) (defn. of "war pensions") appl. (NI)	7, s.133(1)
		s.27 rep.	6, s.3, Sch.1
		s.28(2) rep.in pt.	6, s.3, Sch.1
		s.28(3)(4) rep.	6, s.3, Sch.1
		s.29(1) am.	6, s.4, Sch.2, para.106
		s.29(2)(5) rep.	6, s.3, Sch.1
		s.30(1) (defns. of "the 1982 Act" and "the Old Cases Act") rep.	6, s.3, Sch.1
		s.32 rep.	6, s.3, Sch.1
		Sch.1, paras.1-10 rep.	6, s.3, Sch.1
		Schs.2,3 rep.	6, s.3, Sch.1
		Sch.4, paras.1-21 rep.	6, s.3, Sch.1
		Sch.4, para.24 rep.	6, s.3, Sch.1
		Sch.7 rep. (exc. paras.1, 14,21 and 27)	6, s.3, Sch.1
		Sch.8, paras.1-7 rep.	6, s.3, Sch.1
		Sch.8, paras.9,10(1) rep.	6, s.3, Sch.1
		Sch.8, paras.11,12(2)(5)(6) rep.	6, s.3, Sch.1

Year and Chap. or No. of Measure	Short title	How affected	1992, Chapter of Act or Number of Measure or Statutory Instrument
1989—*cont.*			
		Sch.8, paras.14-18,19(a) (b) rep.	6, s.3, Sch.1
c.26	Finance Act 1989	appt. day(s) for s.102 (30.9.1993)	SI 3066, art.2(2)(c)
		s.11(2)(f) subst.	48, s.13(1)(a)
		s.11(3) am.	48, s.13(1)(b)
		s.11(3A) added	48, s.13(1)(c)
		s.11(6) (defn. of "the principal section") am.	48, s.13(1)(d)
		s.12(3)(a) am.	48, s.13(2)(a)
		s.12(3)(f) subst.	48, s.13(2)(b)
		s.12(3)(ja) added	48, s.13(2)(c)
		s.12(5) am.	48, s.13(2)(d)
		s.33(10) rep.in pt.	48, s.82, Sch.18, Pt.VII
		s.57(4) rep.in pt.	48, s.82, Sch.18, Pt.VII
		s.69 (defn. of "chargeable event") appl.	12, s.228(7)
		s.69 (defn. of "chargeable event") appl.	12, s.232(9)
		s.69(3A) added	48, s.36(1)(2)
		s.69(9) am.	12, s.290, Sch.10, para.19(1)
		s.70(2) am.	12, s.19(2)
		s.82 mod.	SI 1655, regs.1,17(1)
		s.83(1) restr.	48, s.65(2)(d)(5)
		s.83(2) mod.	SI 1655, regs.1,18(1)
		s.91(2) rep.	12, s.290, Sch.12
		s.92(3) rep.	12, s.290, Sch.12
		s.92(4) rep.in pt.	12, s.290, Sch.12
		s.96(3) rep.	12, s.290, Sch.12
		s.122 rep.	12, s.290, Sch.12
		s.123(1)(a) rep.	12, s.290, Sch.12
		ss.124-141 rep.	12, s.290, Sch.12
		s.127(3) excl. (*retrosp.*)	48, s.47 (adding s.269A to 1970 c.10)
		s.158(2)(a) am.	12, s.19(3)
		s.170(2) rep.	48, ss.32,82, Sch.18, Pt.VII
		s.178(2) am.	12, s.290, Sch.10, para.19(4)
		s.178(2)(gg) am.	6, s.4, Sch.2, para.107
		s.178(2)(m) am.	48, s.63, Sch.11, paras.5, 6
		s.179(1)(a)(vi) rep.	12, s.290, Sch.12
		s.182A added	48, s.51(3)
		Sch.5 appl.	12, s.228(7)
		Sch.5 appl.	12, s.235(8)
		Sch.5, paras.8,11 am.	12, s.290, Sch.10, para.19(5)
		Sch.11, para.1(3A) replaced (by sub- paras.(3A)-(3G)) (*retrosp.*)	48, s.33, Sch.7, paras.2,7, 8

Year and Chap. or No. of Measure	Short title	How affected	1992, Chapter of Act or Number of Measure or Statutory Instrument
1989—*cont.*			
		Sch.11, paras.1(8)(c),19 am.	12, s.290, Sch.10, para.19(6)(a)(b)
		Sch.11, para.2(13)(c)(d) replaced (by paras.(c)(d)(c)) (*retrosp.*)	48, s.33, Sch.7, paras.3,7, 8
		Sch.11, para.19A added (*retrosp.*)	48, s.33, Sch.7, paras.4,7, 8
		Sch.11, para.21(3) am. (*retrosp.*)	48, s.33, Sch.7, paras.5(1) ,7,8
		Sch.11, para.21A added (*retrosp.*)	48, s.33, Sch.7, paras.5(2) ,7,8
		Sch.11, para.22C added (*retrosp.*)	48, s.33, Sch.7, paras.6-8
		Sch.12, para.6 rep.	12, s.290, Sch.12
		Schs.14,15 rep.	12, s.290, Sch.12
c.29	Electricity Act 1989	defn. of "electrical plant" appl.	i, s.32(1)(a)
		defns. of "electricity undertakers", "electricity lines" and "electricity plant" appl.	v, s.49(1)(a)
		defn. of "electrical plant" appl.	xi, s.39(1)
		s.23(1A) added	43, s.56(6), Sch.1, para.11
		s.23(2) ext.	43, s.25(1)
		s.23(2) rep.in pt.	43, ss.25(2),56(7), Sch.2
		s.25(8) (defn. of "relevant requirement") am.	43, s.56(6), Sch.1, para.12
		s.28(1) am.	43, s.56(6), Sch.1, para.13
		s.37 excl.	vii, s.10(3)
		s.37(1) excl.	SI 3074, reg.3
		s.39(1) rep.in pt.	43, s.56(7), Sch.2
		s.39(1)(c) added	43, s.20(1)
		s.39(5A) added	43, s.56(6), Sch.1, para.14
		s.40(1) rep.in pt.	43, ss.20(2),56(7), Sch.2
		s.40(1A) added	43, s.20(2)
		s.40(3) added	43, s.24
		s.41(3) added	43, s.56(6), Sch.1, para.15
		s.42A added	43, s.21
		s.42B added	43, s.22
		s.44A added (*prosp.*)	43, s.23
		s.100(6) added	SI 232, art.5
		Sch.7, para.1(2) replaced (by sub-paras. (2)(2A))	43, s.56(6), Sch.1, para.16
		Sch.11, para.2 am.	12, s.290, Sch.10, para.20(1)
		Sch.11, para.2A added	12, s.290, Sch.10, para.20(1)
		Sch.11, para.3 am.	12, s.290, Sch.10, para.20(2)

Year and Chap. or No. of Measure	Short title	How affected	1992, Chapter of Act or Number of Measure or Statutory Instrument
1989—*cont.*			
		Sch.11, paras.4,5 am.	12, s.290, Sch.10, para.20(3)
		Sch.16, para.3(1) am.	SI 1314, art.3(3), Sch., para.1(e)
c.33	Extradition Act 1989	appl.(mods.)	SI 3200, art.4
		s.1(2) ext.(mods.) (British Antarctic Territory)	SI 1300, art.2, Sch.
		ss.2,5 ext.(mods.) (British Antarctic Territory)	SI 1300, art.2, Sch.
		s.6(1)(3)-(10) ext.(mods.) (British Antarctic Territory)	SI 1300, art.2, Sch.
		s.7(1)-(5) ext.(mods.) (British Antarctic Territory)	SI 1300, art.2, Sch.
		ss.8,9(1)(2)(5)(6)(8)-(10) ext.(mods.) (British Antarctic Territory)	SI 1300, art.2, Sch.
		s.10(1)-(7)(9)-(12) ext.(mods.) (British Antarctic Territory)	SI 1300, art.2, Sch.
		s.11(1)-(5) ext.(mods.) (British Antarctic Territory)	SI 1300, art.2, Sch.
		s.12(1)-(3)(5)(6) ext.(mods.) (British Antarctic Territory)	SI 1300, art.2, Sch.
		s.14(1)(2)(4) ext.(mods.) (British Antarctic Territory)	SI 1300, art.2, Sch.
		ss.16,17 ext.(mods.) (British Antarctic Territory)	SI 1300, art.2, Sch.
		ss.19-21 ext.(mods.) (British Antarctic Territory)	SI 1300, art.2, Sch.
		s.23 ext.(mods.) (British Antarctic Territory)	SI 1300, art.2, Sch.
		s.25 ext.(mods.) (British Antarctic Territory)	SI 1300, art.2, Sch.
		ss.27,28 ext.(mods.) (British Antarctic Territory)	SI 1300, art.2, Sch.
		s.35 ext.(mods.) (British Antarctic Territory)	SI 1300, art.2, Sch.
		Sch.1 appl.(mods.)	SI 3200, arts.2,3
c.38	The Employment Act 1989	s.5(6)(ba) added (1.4.1993)	13, s.93(1), Sch.8, Pt.II, para.93(a)
		s.5(6)(c) subst.	13, s.93(1), Sch.8, Pt.II, para.93(b)
		s.14 rep.	52, s.300(1), Sch.1
		Sch.6, para.19 rep.	52, s.300(1), Sch.1
		Sch.9, para.2 rep.	52, s.300(1), Sch.1
c.39	Self-Governing Schools etc.(Scotland) Act 1989	defn. of "college of further education" appl.	37, s.26(1)
		appl.	37, s.36(3)

Year and Chap. or No. of Measure	Short title	How affected	1992, Chapter of Act or Number of Measure or Statutory Instrument
1989—*cont.*			
		ss.54-66 rep. (1-4-1993)	37, s.62(3), Sch.10
		ss.54-67 (Pt.II) saved	37, s.34(1)(5)
		ss.54(4)(5),55(2)(a)-(c) restr.	37, s.34(8)(a)
		s.58 excl.	37, s.34(1)(6)
		s.70(1)(d) subst. (1-4- 1993)	37, s.62(2), Sch.9, para.11
		s.80(1) rep.in pt. (1-4- 1993)	37, s.62(3), Sch.10
		Sch.10, para.4 rep.	53, s.18(2), Sch.4, Pt.I
c.40	Companies Act 1989	s.52 (defn. of "associate") appl. (*prosp.*)	40, s.72, Sch.14, para.5(4)
		s.82(3) cert. functs. made exercisable concurrently	SI 1315, arts.5,6, Sch.3, para.3
		s.87(4) am.	SI 1315, art.10(1), Sch.4, para.12
		s.87(4), Table am. (*prosp.*)	40, s.120(1), Sch.21, Pt.I, para.11
		s.87(4), Table rep.in pt. (*prosp.*)	40, s.120(2), Sch.22, Pt.I
		s.124 rep.	52, s.300(1), Sch.1
		ss.154-191 (Pt.VII) trans.of functions	SI 1315, arts.2(1)(c),6
		s.158(4)(5) cert. functs. made exercisable jointly	SI 1315, arts.4,6, Sch.2, para.7
		s.160(5) cert. functs. made exercisable jointly	SI 1315, arts.4,6, Sch.2, para.7
		s.168(3) mod.	SI 1315, art.6
		ss.170-174 cert. functs. made exercisable jointly	SI 1315, arts.4,6, Sch.2, para.7
		s.171(6) am.	SI 1315, art.10(1), Sch.4, para.13(a)
		s.172(3) am.	SI 1315, art.10(1), Sch.4, para.13(b)
		s.173(6) am.	SI 1315, art.10(1), Sch.4, para.13(c)
		s.174(5) am.	SI 1315, art.10(1), Sch.4, para.13(d)
		s.176 cert. functs. made exercisable jointly	SI 1315, arts.4,6, Sch.2, para.7
		s.176(2) am. (1.1.1993)	SI 3218, reg.82(1), Sch.10, Pt.I, para.29
		s.176(6) am.	SI 1315, art.10(1), Sch.4, para.13(e)
		s.181 cert. functs. made exercisable jointly	SI 1315, arts.4,6, Sch.2, para.7
		ss.185,186 cert. functs. made exercisable jointly	SI 1315, arts.4,6, Sch.2, para.7
		s.203(3) trans.of functions	SI 1315, arts.2(2)(a),6
		s.206(2) trans.of functions	SI 1315, arts.2(2)(b),6
		s.207 (Pt.IX) trans.of functions	SI 1315, arts.2(1)(c),6
		s.215(2)(3)(4) trans.of functions	SI 1315, arts.2(2)(b),6
		Schs.15,703E(1)(2)(4) am.	SI 3179, Sch.3, para.15

Year and Chap. or No. of Measure	Short title	How affected	1992, Chapter of Act or Number of Measure or Statutory Instrument
1989—*cont.*		Sch.15, s.703A(3) am.	SI 3179, Sch.3, para.12
		Sch.15, s.703B(2)(a) subst.	SI 3179, Sch.3, para.13
		Sch.15, s.703D(1) am.	SI 3179, Sch.3, para.14
		Sch.15, s.703D(1A) added	SI 3179, Sch.3, para.14
		Sch.16, para.1A added	SI 3179, Sch.3, para.16
		Sch.18, para.20 rep.	12, s.290, Sch.12
		Sch.19, para.13 am. (new s.696 of 1989 c.40)	SI 3179, Sch.3, para.17
		Sch.21A, para.1(1) mod. (transtl)	SI 3179, Sch.4, para.1(3)
c.41	Children Act 1989	s.17(9) am.	6, s.4, Sch.2, para.108(a)
		s.29(3) am.	6, s.4, Sch.2, para.108(b)
		s.97(4) trans.of functions & am.	SI 709, art.3(2), Sch.2
		Sch.1 (defn. of "child") appl. (*prosp.*)	56, s.1, Sch.1, Pt.II, para.13 (adding.1972, c.18, s.27A)
		Sch.1, para.5(2) trans.of functions & am.	SI 709, art.3(2), Sch.2
		Sch.2, Pt.III, para.21(4) am.	6, s.4, Sch.2, para.108(c)
		Sch.13, para.30 rep.	53, s.18(2), Sch.4, Pt.I
c.42	Local Government and Housing Act 1989	appt. day(s) for spec. provns. (8.5.1992)	SI 760, art.2
		s.5 saved	19, s.5(7)
		s.12(2) (defn. of "member") subst.	52, s.300(2), Sch.2, para.39(2)
		s.12(2) (defns. of "official" and "trade union") am.	52, s.300(2), Sch.2, para.39(3)
		ss.39-66 (Pt.IV) excl.	SI 581(L), art.5(4)
		s.39(3)(c)(d) replaced (by paras.(c)(d)(e))	14, s.117(1), Sch.13, para.90
		s.41(3) appl.	14, ss.32(11),43(8),50(6)
		s.43(2) am. (1.1.1993)	SI 3218, reg.82(1), Sch.10, Pt.I, para.30
		s.81 rep.	6, s.3, Sch.1
		ss.140-144 rep. (*prosp.*)	14, s.117(2), Sch.14
		s.146 rep. (1.4.1993)	14, s.117(2), Sch.14
		Sch.5, paras.2-18,43,49-54,55(3),56,58,59,61,63-65,70,71,73,74,76(3),77, 78 rep. (1.4.1993)	14, s.117(2), Sch.14
		Sch.5, para.30(4) rep.	14, s.117(2), Sch.14
		Sch.6, para.8 rep.	14, s.117(2), Sch.14
		Sch.6, paras.10-15,20-22, 24-29 rep. (*prosp.*)	14, s.117(2), Sch.14
		Sch.11, para.98 rep. (1.4.1993)	14, s.117(2), Sch.14
		Sch.11, para.113 rep.	6, s.3, Sch.1
c.46	Consolidated Fund (No. 2) Act 1989	rep.	22, s.4, Sch.(C)

Year and Chap. or No. of Measure	Short title	How affected	1992, Chapter of Act or Number of Measure or Statutory Instrument
1989—*cont.*			
c.xv	Midland Metro Act 1989	defns. of "the Act of 1845", "the Act of 1950", "the Act of 1965", "enactment", "the Executive", "land", "the railways board", "statutory undertakers", "telecommunications system", "traffic sign" and "the tribunal" appl.(mods.)	vii, s.2(1)
		defns. of "the Act of 1845", "the Act of 1965", "enactment", "the Executive", "land" and "the railways board" appl.	viii, s.2(1)
		s.2(1) (defn. of "sewerage undertaker") added	vii, s.26(1)(a)(i)
		s.2(1) (defn. of "statutory undertakers") am.	vii, s.26(1)(a)(ii)
		s.2(1) (defn. of "water authority") rep.	vii, s.26(1)(a)(iii)
		ss.3-6 am.	viii, s.3
		ss.3,4,5,6 am.	vii, s.3
		s.9 appl.(mods.)	vii, s.11
		s.9 appl.(mods.)	viii, s.11(1)(2)
		s.12 appl.(mods.)	vii, s.11
		s.12 appl.(mods.)	viii, s.11(1)(2)
		s.15 appl.(mods.)	vii, s.11
		s.15 appl.(mods.)	viii, s.11(1)
		s.17 appl.(mods.)	viii, s.11(1)
		ss.17,18 appl.(mods.)	vii, s.11
		s.18 appl.(mods.)	viii, s.11(1)(2)
		ss.20-24 appl.(mods.)	vii, s.11
		ss.20-25 appl.(mods.)	viii, s.11(1)(2)
		s.23 reprinted as am.	vii, s.26(2), Sch.7
		s.23(1)(2) am.	vii, s.26(1)(b)(i)
		s.23(5) am.	vii, s.26(1)(b)(i)
		s.25 appl.(mods.)	vii, s.11
		ss.27-31 appl.(mods.)	vii, s.15
		s.27 appl.(mods.)	viii, s.15(1)
		s.28 appl.(mods.)	viii, s.15(1)(2)
		ss.29,30 appl.(mods.)	viii, s.15(1)
		s.31 appl.(mods.)	viii, s.15(1)(2)
		s.33 appl.(mods.)	vii, s.15
		s.33 appl.(mods.)	viii, s.15(1)(2)
		ss.36,37 appl.(mods.)	vii, s.19
		ss.36,37 appl.(mods.)	viii, s.17(1)
		ss.40-43 appl.(mods.)	vii, s.19
		ss.40,41 appl.(mods.)	viii, s.17(1)(2)
		s.40(1) am.	vii, s.26(1)(c)

Year and Chap. or No. of Measure	Short title	How affected	1992, Chapter of Act or Number of Measure or Statutory Instrument
1989—*cont.*		s.41(1)(a) subst.	vii, s.26(1)(d)(i)
		s.41(1)(c) am.	vii, s.26(1)(d)(ii)
		ss.42,43 appl.(mods.)	viii, s.17(1)
		Sch.5 appl.(mods.)	vii, s.15
		Sch.5 appl.(mods.)	viii, s.15(1)
1990			
c.1	Capital Allowances Act 1990	s.1(10) rep.in pt.	48, ss.70,82, Sch.13, paras.3,14, Sch.18, Pt.VII
		s.1(11) added	48, s.70, Sch.13, para.11
		s.4(9) (defn. of "the capital expenditure") am.	48, s.70, Sch.13, paras.13, 17
		s.6(4A) added	48, s.70, Sch.13, para.12
		s.6(5) rep.	48, ss.70,82, Sch.13, paras.4,14, Sch.18, Pt.VII
		s.10(1) am.	48, s.70, Sch.13, paras.5, 14
		s.10(1A) added	48, s.70, Sch.13, paras.6, 14
		s.10(3A) added	48, s.70, Sch.13, paras.7, 14
		s.10(4) am.	48, s.70, Sch.13, paras.9, 15
		s.10A added	48, s.70, Sch.13, paras.2, 14
		s.10B added	48, s.70, Sch.13, paras.8, 15
		s.11 mod.	48, s.77, Sch.17, paras.5(4),6(1),7
		s.11(3) mod.	SI 511, reg.9, Sch.2
		s.17A added	48, s.70, Sch.13, paras.10, 16
		s.22(6)(a) am.	6, s.4, Sch.2, para.109(a)
		ss.22(6)(a),36(4)(a) am. (NI)	9, s.4, Sch.2, para.38(a) (b)
		s.24 restr.	48, s.59, Sch.10, paras.9(3),11(6),13
		s.24(6) am.	48, s.68(2)(9)
		s.24(6A) added	48, s.68(3)(9)
		s.24(8) am.	48, s.68(4)(9)
		s.25(3) mod.	SI 511, reg.9, Sch.2
		s.26(1)(ea)-(ec) added	48, s.68(5)(9)
		s.26(2AA) added	48, s.68(6)(9)
		s.31(3) mod.	SI 511, reg.9, Sch.2
		s.33(1) mod.	SI 511, reg.9, Sch.2
		s.34(1)(3) am.	48, s.71(2)(3)(6)
		s.35(1) am.	48, s.71(4)(7)
		s.35(2) am.	48, s.71(5)(8)
		s.36(4)(a) am.	6, s.4, Sch.2, para.109(b)
		s.37(2) mod.	SI 511, reg.9, Sch.2
		s.37(5) am. (10.3.1992) (*retrosp.*)	48, s.68(7)(10)
		s.53(2) mod.	SI 511, reg.9, Sch.2
		s.55(3) mod.	SI 511, reg.9, Sch.2
		s.55(4)(a) excl.	48, s.77, Sch.17, paras.5(5)(c),7

Year and Chap. or No. of Measure	Short title	How affected	1992, Chapter of Act or Number of Measure or Statutory Instrument
1990—*cont.*			
		s.67A added	48, s.68(1)(8)
		s.68(3) (defn. of "relevant period") appl.	48, s.43(1)
		s.68(6A)(6B) added	48, s.69(2)
		s.68(9) am.	48, s.69(3)(5)
		s.68(9A)-(9C) added	48, s.69(4)(5)
		s.68(10) (defn. of "expenditure of a revenue nature") appl.	48, s.43(1)
		s.77(3) mod.	SI 511, reg.9, Sch.2
		s.118A added	12, s.290, Sch.10, para.21(1)
		s.121 appl.	12, s.35, Sch.3, para.7(8)(a)
		s.129(2) mod.	SI 511, reg.9, Sch.2
		s.137 (defn. of "relevant chargeable period") appl.	12, s.195(3)
		s.137 restr.	12, s.195(6)(a)
		s.138(3) restr.	12, s.195(6)(b)
		s.138(7A) added	12, s.290, Sch.10, para.21(2)
		s.152B added	48, s.67
		ss.157,158 excl.	48, s.77, Sch.17, paras.5(4),6(1),7
		Sch.1, para.2 rep. (EWS)	6, s.3, Sch.1
		Sch.1, para.2 rep. (NI)	9, s.3, Sch.1
		Sch.1, paras.3,9(1)-(3) rep.	12, s.290, Sch.12
c.4	Consolidated Fund Act 1990	rep.	22, s.4, Sch.(C)
c.5	Criminal Justice (International Co-operation) Act 1990	Sch.2, Table I am.	SI 2873, art.2(a)
		Sch.2, Table II am.	SI 2873, art.2(b)
		Sch.3, para.1(a)(b) ext.	SI 77, art.2
c.6	Education (Student Loans) Act 1990	s.1 am. (*temp.*)	SI 817, art.4, Sch.5
		s.1(3)(a) am. (1.4.1993)	13, s.93(1), Sch.8, Pt.I, para.67
		s.1(3)(b) subst.	37, s.62(2), Sch.9, para.12(2)
		Sch.2, para.2(2) am. (1-4-1993)	37, s.62(2), Sch.9, para.12(3)
c.8	Town and Country Planning Act 1990	trans.of functions (Scilly)	SI 1620, art.2
		mod.	SI 1620, art.4(a)(b)
		(saving)	SI 1630, art.3(1)
		mod.	SI 1732, art.2(1)
		restr.	3, s.35
		defn. of "planning permission" appl.	12, s.35, Sch.2, Pt.II, para.10(3)
		s.16(3) am.	53, s.18(1), Sch.3, para.22
		s.20(7) am.	53, s.18(1), Sch.3, para.23

Year and Chap. or No. of Measure	Short title	How affected	1992, Chapter of Act or Number of Measure or Statutory Instrument
1990—*cont.*			
		ss.29-54 (Pt.II) (Ch.II) trans.of functions (Scilly)	SI 1620, art.3
		s.35(8) am.	53, s.18(1), Sch.3, para.23
		s.42(6) am.	53, s.18(1), Sch.3, para.24
		ss.55-106 (Pt.III) appl.(mods.)	SI 1492, reg.2(1)(b)
		s.55(1) (defn. of "development") appl.	51, s.10(1)(d)
		s.70A appl.(mods.)	SI 666, reg.13(1)(c), Sch.4, Pts.I,II
		s.72(1)(a) mod.	SI 2683, Sch., para.2
		s.76(1)(d) am. (1.4.1993)	13, s.93(1), Sch.8, Pt.II, para.94(a)
		s.76(1)(f) added (1.4.1993)	13, s.93(1), Sch.8, Pt.II, para.94(b)
		ss.78,79 appl.(mods.)	SI 666, reg.15(1)(3), Sch.4, Pts.III,IV,V
		s.90(2A) added (1-1-1993)	42, s.16(1)
		ss.172-196 (Pt.VII) appl.(mods.)	SI 1492, reg.2(1)(b)
		s.173(10) appl.(mods.)	SI 1562, reg.2, Sch.
		s.173A appl.(mods.)	SI 1562, reg.2, Sch.
		ss.174,175(3) appl.(mods.)	SI 656, reg.18(1)
		s.175(5)(7) appl.(mods.)	SI 1562, reg.2, Sch.
		s.175(6) appl.(mods.)	SI 656, reg.18(1)
		ss.176,177 appl.(mods.)	SI 656, reg.18(1)
		ss.178-181 appl.(mods.)	SI 656, reg.20(1)
		s.179 appl.(mods.)	SI 1562, reg.2, Sch.
		s.180(1)(3) appl.(mods.)	SI 1562, reg.2, Sch.
		s.181 appl.(mods.)	SI 1562, reg.2, Sch.
		ss.183,184 appl.(mods.)	SI 1562, reg.2, Sch.
		ss.186-188 appl.(mods.)	SI 1562, reg.2, Sch.
		s.188 appl.(mods.)	SI 656, reg.21(1)
		s.192(4) (saving)	SI 1630, art.3(2)
		ss.197-225 (Pt.VIII) appl.(mods.)	SI 1492, reg.2(1)(b)
		ss.197-225 (Pt.VIII) appl.(mods.)	SI 1492, reg.2(2)
		s.251 restr.	SI 1492, reg.15(5)
		s.254(1)(b) restr.	SI 1492, reg.15(3)
		s.265(1)(2) am.	SI 1314, art.3(3), Sch., para.1(f)
		s.285 appl.(mods.)	SI 656, reg.22(1)
		s.285(1)(2) appl.(mods.)	SI 1562, reg.2, Sch.
		s.288(9) am.	53, s.18(1), Sch.3, para.25
		s.289 appl.(mods.)	SI 656, reg.22(1)
		s.289 appl.(mods.)	SI 1562, reg.2, Sch.
		ss.293-302 (Pt.XIII) mod.	SI 1732, art.2(1)(2)
		ss.293-302 (Pt.XIII) ext.	SI 1732, art.2(1)(a)
		s.293(2)(b) mod.	SI 1732, art.2(4)(a)

Year and Chap. or No. of Measure	Short title	How affected	1992, Chapter of Act or Number of Measure or Statutory Instrument
1990—*cont.*			
		s.317(1) am.	SI 1314, art.3(3), Sch., para.1(f)
		s.322 appl.(mods.)	SI 1562, reg.2, Sch.
		s.322A appl.(mods.)	SI 1562, reg.2, Sch.
		s.323(1) am.	53, s.18(1), Sch.3, para.26
		s.336(1) (defn. ot "local authority") am.	14, s.117(1), Sch.13, para.91
		Sch.2, Pt.II, para.9(1)(b) am.	53, s.18(1), Sch.3, para.27
		Sch.6, para.8(1) am.	53, s.18(1), Sch.3, para.28
		Sch.7, para.8(6) am.	53, s.18(1), Sch.3, para.29
		Sch.8, para.5(3) am.	53, s.18(1), Sch.3, para.30
		Sch.13, para.23 added (1-1-1993)	42, s.16(2)
c.9	Planning (Listed Buildings and Conservation Areas) Act 1990	mod.	SI 1732, art.2(3)
		excl.	iii, s.16(1)(a)
		defn(s). appl.	iii, s.16(3)
		s.1(5) (defn. of "listed building") appl.	iii, s.34(1)
		s.10 mod.	SI 3138, Sch.1, para.1
		s.12(3A) added (1-1-1993)	42, s.17
		s.63(6) am.	53, s.18(1), Sch.3, para.31
		ss.81-90 (Pt.III) mod.	SI 1732, art.2(3)(a)
		s.83(7)(b) mod.	SI 1732, art.2(4)(b)
		s.85(1) am.	SI 1314, art.3(3), Sch., para.1(g)
		Sch.3, para.7(1) am.	53, s.18(1), Sch.3, para.32
c.10	Planning (Hazardous Substances) Act 1990	appt. day(s) for power or duty to make regulations (11.3.1992) and for residue of Act (1.6.1992)	SI 725, arts.2,3
		s.9 appl.	SI 656, reg.26(4)
		s.12(2A) added (1-1-1993)	42, s.18
		s.22 mod.	SI 656, reg.26(5)
		s.22(4) am.	53, s.18(1), Sch.3, para.33

Year and Chap. or No. of Measure	Short title	How affected	1992, Chapter of Act or Number of Measure or Statutory Instrument
1990—*cont.*		s.23 restr.	SI 725, art.44(1)
		s.23 mod.	SI 725, art.4(2)(3)
		s.25(2) restr.	SI 656, reg.22(2)
		para.7(1), Sch. am.	53, s.18(1), Sch.3, para.34
c.11	Planning (Consequential Provisions) Act 1990	Sch.2, para.3(2) (saving) (*temp.*)	SI 1630, art.3(3)
c.16	Food Safety Act 1990	appt. day(s) for spec. provns. (3.4.1992)	SI 57, art.2
		ss.2,3 appl.(mods.)	SI 496, reg.7(1)(a)(b)
		ss.2,3 appl.(mods.)	SI 1971, reg.9
		ss.2,3 appl.(mods.)	SI 1978, reg.7
		ss.2,3,20,21,30(8),33,36, 44 appl.(mods.)	SI 3236, reg.11(1)
		ss.3,20,21,30,32-34,36 appl.(mods.) (15.1.1993)	SI 3163, reg.18(1)
		ss.3,20,21,30(8),32,33,34, 36 appl.(mods.)	SI 3164, reg.19(1)
		ss.3,20,21,33,36 appl.(mods.)	SI 2037, reg.23
		s.3(4) appl. (1.1.1993)	SI 3145, reg.11(2)
		s.6(3) appl.	SI 3163, reg.18(2)
		ss.6(3),37(1)(c) appl.	SI 3164, reg.19(2)(3)
		s.8(3) appl.(mods.)	SI 496, reg.7(2)
		s.8(3) appl.	SI 3236, reg.11(2)
		s.9 appl.(mods.)	SI 496, reg.7(3)
		s.9 appl.	SI 3236, reg.11(3)
		ss.20-22 appl.(mods.)	SI 1971, reg.9
		ss.20-22 appl.(mods.)	SI 1978, reg.7
		s.20 appl.	SI 1122, reg.4
		s.20 appl.	SI 1601, reg.4
		ss.20,21 appl.(mods.)	SI 496, reg.7(1)(c)(d)
		ss.20,21,30(8),33,36 appl.(mods.) (E)	SI 3165, reg.7(2)
		s.21(1)(5)(6) appl.	SI 1122, reg.4
		s.21(1)(5)(6) appl.	SI 1601, reg.4
		ss.29,30 mod. (1.1.1993)	SI 3145, reg.11(3)
		s.30 appl.(mods.)	SI 3236, reg.11(4)
		s.30(8) appl.(mods.)	SI 496, reg.7(1)(e)
		s.30(8) appl.	SI 1122, reg.4
		s.30(8) appl.	SI 1601, reg.4
		ss.30(8),36 appl.(mods.)	SI 1971, reg.9
		ss.30(8),36 appl.(mods.)	SI 1978, reg.7
		s.33 appl.	SI 1122, reg.4
		s.33 appl.	SI 1601, reg.4
		s.36 appl.(mods.)	SI 496, reg.7(1)(f)
		s.36 appl.	SI 1122, reg.4
		s.36 appl.	SI 1601, reg.4
		s.37(1)(c) appl. (15.1.1993)	SI 3163, reg.18(3)
		s.58(1) appl.(mods.)	SI 496, reg.7(1)(g)
		Sch.3, para.14 rep.	53, s.18(2), Sch.4, Pt.I
c.19	National Health Service and Community Care Act 1990	appt. day(s) for spec. provns. (6.4.1992)	SI 567, art.2

Year and Chap. or No. of Measure	Short title	How affected	1992, Chapter of Act or Number of Measure or Statutory Instrument
1990—*cont.*			
		appt. day(s) for spec. provns. (10.12.1992) (1.4.1993) (12.4.1993)	SI 2975, art.2
		s.42(2) rep.	49, s.1(2)(a)
		s.42(3) am. (EW)	49, s.1(2)
		Sch.9, para.15 rep.	6, s.3, Sch.1
c.25	Horses (Protective Headgear for Young Riders) Act 1990	appt. day for residue (30.6.1992)	SI 1200, art.2
c.27	Social Security Act 1990	appt. day(s) for spec. provns. (6.4.1992)	SI 632, art.2
		appt. day(s) for spec. provns. (29.6.1992)	SI 1532, art.2
		ss.1-5 rep.	6, s.3, Sch.1
		s.6(1)-(3) rep.	6, s.3, Sch.1
		ss.8-10 rep.	6, s.3, Sch.1
		s.12(2) rep.	53, s.18(2), Sch.4, Pt.I
		s.16 rep.	6, s.3, Sch.1
		s.17(1)-(7) rep.	6, s.3, Sch.1
		s.17(8)(9) rep. (EWS)	6, s.3, Sch.1
		s.17(8)(9) rep. (NI)	9, s.3, Sch.1
		s.18(2) am.	6, s.4, Sch.2, para.110
		s.19(1) am.	6, s.4, Sch.2, para.111
		s.20 (defns. of "the 1982 Act", "the 1986 Act", "the 1989 Act" and "the Old Cases Act") rep.	6, s.3, Sch.1
		s.22(1) rep.	6, s.3, Sch.1
		Sch.1, paras.1-4 rep.	6, s.3, Sch.1
		Sch.1, paras.5(1)(2),6 rep.	6, s.3, Sch.1
		Sch.1, para.5(4) rep. (NI)	9, s.3, Sch.1
		Sch.5 rep.	6, s.3, Sch.1
		Sch.6, para.1 rep.	6, s.3, Sch.1
		Sch.6, paras.3,4(1)(2) rep.	6, s.3, Sch.1
		Sch.6, paras.5-7 rep.	6, s.3, Sch.1
		Sch.6, para.8(1)(3)(5)(7)(8)(11) rep.	6, s.3, Sch.1
		Sch.6, paras.9-12 rep.	6, s.3, Sch.1
		Sch.6, paras.14-26 rep.	6, s.3, Sch.1
		Sch.6, paras.27(2),28 rep.	6, s.3, Sch.1
		Sch.6, para.27(3) am.	6, s.4, Sch.2, para.112(1)
		Sch.6, para.27(5) am.	6, s.4, Sch.2, para.112(2)
		Sch.6, paras.30,31(a)(b) rep.	6, s.3, Sch.1
c.28	Appropriation Act 1990	rep.	22, s.4, Sch.(C)
c.29	Finance Act 1990	s.25(2)(g) am.	48, s.26(2)(4)
		s.28(3) rep.	12, s.290, Sch.12
		ss.31-40 rep.	12, s.290, Sch.12
		s.46 mod.	SI 1655, regs.1,19(1)
		ss.46,47 rep.	12, s.290, Sch.12
		s.54 rep.	12, s.290, Sch.12

Year and Chap. or No. of Measure	Short title	How affected	1992, Chapter of Act or Number of Measure or Statutory Instrument
1990—_cont._			
		s.57 rep. (_retrosp._)	48, ss.33,82, Schs.7,18, Pt.VII
		s.58(6) rep.in pt. (_retrosp._)	48, ss.33,82, Schs.7,18, Pt.VII
		s.58(6)(b) rep. (_retrosp._)	48, ss.33,82, Schs.7,18, Pt.VII
		ss.63-65 rep.	12, s.290, Sch.12
		s.70 rep.	12, s.290, Sch.12
		s.72 rep.	12, s.290, Sch.12
		s.81(3) rep.	12, s.290, Sch.12
		s.81(6) rep.	12, s.290, Sch.12
		ss.83-86 rep.	12, s.290, Sch.12
		s.94 rep.	48, ss.28(5)(6),82, Sch.18, Pt.VII
		s.116(5) am.	12, s.290, Sch.10, para.22(2)
		s.120 am.	12, s.290, Sch.10, para.22(3)
		s.123(3)(b) am.	48, s.78
		s.127(2) rep.	12, s.290, Sch.12
		s.128 ext.	48, s.13(3)
		Sch.6, para.10 rep.	12, s.290, Sch.12
		Sch.8 rep.	12, s.290, Sch.12
		Sch.9, paras.1,2 rep.	12, s.290, Sch.12
		Sch.10, para.24 am.	12, s.290, Sch.10, para.22(4)
		Sch.10, paras.28,29(2)(3) rep.	12, s.290, Sch.12
		Sch.12, para.2 am.	12, s.290, Sch.10, para.22(5)(a)(i)(ii)(iii)
		Sch.12, para.2(2) rep.	12, s.290, Sch.12
		Sch.12, paras.4,5,6,7 am.	12, s.290, Sch.10, para.22(5)(b)(c)
		Sch.12, para.10 (defn. of "1979 Act") subst.	12, s.290, Sch.10, para.22(5)(d)
		Sch.14, paras.17,18,19(2)(3)(4) rep.	12, s.290, Sch.12
		Sch.18, para.3 rep.	12, s.290, Sch.12
c.35	Enterprise and New Towns (Scotland) Act 1990	s.23(3) power exercised (Highlands and Islands Development Board dissolved) (21.7.1992)	SI 1764, arts.1,2
		s.31(1) am. (_retrosp._)	SI 8, art.2
c.37	Human Fertilisation and Embryology Act 1990	s.33(6)(d) rep.in pt.	54, s.1(1)(2)(5)
		s.33(6)(f)(g) added	54, s.1(1)(2)(5)
		s.33(6)(h) added (EWS)	54, s.1(1)(2)(5)
		s.33(6A)-(6G) added	54, s.1(1)(3)(5)
		s.33(9) added	54, s.1(1)(4)(5)
		s.45(4) am.	54, s.2(2)
		s.48(1) am.	54, s.2(4)
		Sch.4, para.2 rep.	6, s.3, Sch.1

Year and Chap. or No. of Measure	Short title	How affected	1992, Chapter of Act or Number of Measure or Statutory Instrument
1990—*cont.*			
		Sch.4, para.3 rep. (NI)	9, s.3, Sch.1
c.38	Employment Act 1990	ss.1-12 rep.	52, s.300(1), Sch.1
		s.18(1) rep.in pt.	52, s.300(1), Sch.1
		Sch.1 rep.	52, s.300(1), Sch.1
		Sch.2, para.1(2) rep.	52, s.300(1), Sch.1
		Sch.2, paras.2,3 rep.	52, s.300(1), Sch.1
c.40	Law Reform (Miscellaneous Provisions)(Scotland) Act 1990	appt. day(s) for spec. provns. (4.7.1992) (20.7.1992) (27.7.1992) (30.9.1992)	SI 1599, arts.3,4,5,6
		ss.1-15 (Pt.I) (defn. of "recognised body") appl.	41, s.12(6)
		s.1(7) (defn. of "recognised body") appl.	41, ss.38(5),39(7)
		ss.16-44 (Pt.II) (defn. of "executry services") appl. (*prosp.*)	40, s.13, Sch.7, para.8
		s.51(2)(a) rep.	18, s.1(3)
		s.51(3) rep.	18, s.1(3)
c.41	Courts and Legal Services Act 1990	appt. day(s) for spec. provns. (1.6.1992)	SI 1221, art.2
		defn. of "seven year general qualification" appl. (*prosp.*)	40, s.59(3)(a)
		defn. of "seven year general qualification" appl.	40, s.84(2)(a)
		s.37(8) am. (1.1.1993)	SI 3218, reg.82(1), Sch.10, Pt.I, para.31(a)
		s.48(4) am. (1.1.1993)	SI 3218, reg.82(1), Sch.10, Pt.I, para.31(b)
		s.52(6) am. (1.1.1993)	SI 3218, reg.82(1), Sch.10, Pt.I, para.31(c)
		s.71 appl.	5, s.191
		s.71 (defn. of "10 year general qualification") appl.	8, s.50(2)(b)
		s.119(1)(c) (defn. of "court") am.	53, s.18(1), Sch.3, para.35
		Sch.10, paras.36,37 rep.	6, s.3, Sch.1
		Sch.10, para.46 rep.	6, s.3, Sch.1
		Sch.11 rep.in pt.	6, s.3, Sch.1
		Sch.16, para.39(1)(2) rep. (*prosp.*)	56, s.2(2), Sch.3
		Sch.18, para.2 rep.	53, s.18(2), Sch.4, Pt.I
		Sch.18, para.24 rep.	6, s.3, Sch.1
c.42	Broadcasting Act 1990	defn. of "programme service" appl. (EW)	34, s.6(1)
		defn. of "programme service" appl. (EW) (*prosp.*)	41, s.58(1)
		Sch.20, para.14 rep.	10, s.1(9)

Year and Chap. or No. of Measure	Short title	How affected	1992, Chapter of Act or Number of Measure or Statutory Instrument
1990—*cont.*			
c.43	Environmental Protection Act 1990	appt. day(s) for spec. provns. (14.2.1992, 1.4.1992)	SI 266, arts.2,3
		appt. day(s) for s.108(10) (1.1.1993)	SI 3253, art.2
		appt. day(s) for spec. provns. (1.2.1993)	SI 3253, art.3
		ss.29-78 (Pt.II) ext.(mods.)	SI 588, reg.8
		s.98(2)(a) rep. (1.4.1993)	13, s.93, Sch.8, Pt.II, para.95(a), Sch.9
		s.98(2)(d) subst. (1.4.1993)	13, s.93(1), Sch.8, Pt.II, para.95(b)
		s.98(2)(da) added (1.4.1993)	13, s.93(1), Sch.8, Pt.II, para.95(c)
		s.98(3)(d) subst.	37, s.62(2), Sch.9, para.13(b)
		s.98(3)(f) am.	37, s.62(2), Sch.9, para.13(c)
		s.98(3)(c) replaced (by, para(c)(cc)) (1-4-1993)	37, s.62(2), Sch.9, para.13(a)
		s.111(6A) added	SI 3280, reg.13(1)
		s.112(1) rev.in pt.	SI 2617, reg.2
		s.112(5)(b) subst.	SI 3280, reg.9
		s.118(1)(e) am.	SI 3280, reg.13(2)
		s.149 ext.	SI 901, art.4
		s.153(1)(p) added	SI 654, art.2
		Sch.9, para.6 rep.	51, s.15(2), Sch.
		Sch.15, para.1 rep. (*prosp.*)	14, s.117(2), Sch.14
c.44	Caldey Island Act 1990	s.2 am.	14, s.117(1), Sch.13, para.92
No.2	Care of Cathedrals Measure 1990	trans.of functions	SI 1311, art.6(1)(b)
1991			
c.2	Caravans (Standard Community Charge and Rating) Act 1991	s.2 rep. (*prosp.*)	14, s.117(2), Sch.14
c.3	Statutory Sick Pay Act 1991	ss.1,2,3(1)(a)(b)(3)-(5) rep.	6, s.3, Sch.1
		s.4(5) rep.	6, s.3, Sch.1
c.5	Ministerial and other Pensions and Salaries Act 1991	s.6(1)(2)(3) am.	SI 599, reg.6
c.8	Community Charges (Substitute Setting) Act 1991	rep. (1.4.1993)	14, s.117(2), Sch.14
c.12	Civil Jurisdiction and Judgments Act 1991	appt. day(s) for Act (1.5.1992)	SI 745, art.2
c.17	Maintenance Enforcement Act 1991	appt. day(s) for residue (except Sch.1, paras.15- 17 and s.10 in part)	SI 455, art.2
		s.9 rep.	6, s.3, Sch.1
		Sch.1, paras.15,16,17,20 rep. (*prosp.*)	56, s.2(2), Sch.3

Year and Chap. or No. of Measure	Short title	How affected	1992, Chapter of Act or Number of Measure or Statutory Instrument
1991—*cont.*			
c.18	Crofter Forestry (Scotland) Act 1991	appt. day(s) for Act (1.4.1992)	SI 504, art.2
c.20	Registered Homes (Amendment) Act 1991	appt. day(s) for Act (1.4.93)	SI 2240, art.2
		s.2(5)(a) rep. (EW)	49, s.1(2)(b)
c.21	Disability Living Allowance and Disability Working Allowance Act 1991	ss.1,2(1),3,4(1) rep.	6, s.3, Sch.1
		ss.5,6,7(1) rep.	6, s.3, Sch.1
		ss.8,9 rep.	6, s.3, Sch.1
		ss.11-14 rep.	6, s.3, Sch.1
		Sch.1 rep.	6, s.3, Sch.1
		Sch.2, para.2(1) rep.	53, s.18(2), Sch.4, Pt.I
		Sch.2, paras.2(2),3-5 rep.	6, s.3, Sch.1
		Sch.2, para.8 rep.	6, s.3, Sch.1
		Sch.2, para.9 rep.	12, s.290, Sch.12
		Sch.2, paras.10,11 rep.	6, s.3, Sch.1
		Sch.2, paras.15-17 rep.	6, s.3, Sch.1
		Sch.2, para.19 rep.	6, s.3, Sch.1
		Sch.3, Pt.I rep.	6, s.3, Sch.1
c.22	New Roads and Street Works Act 1991	appt. day(s) for spec. provns. (14.7.1992)	SI 1671, art.2
		appt. day(s) for spec. provns. (14.7.1992)	SI 1686, art.3
		appt. day(s) for spec. provns. (28.11.1992) (1.1.1993) (1.4.1993)	SI 2984, art.2
		appt. day(s) for spec. provns. (30.11.1992) (1.1.1993) (1.4.1993)	SI 2990, art.2, Schs.1-3
		ss.48-106 excl. (Pt.III)	v, s.6(3)
		s.48 (defn. of "street") appl.	42, s.67(1)
		s.107 (defn. of "road") appl.	42, s.67(1)
c.23	Children and Young Persons (Protection from Tobacco) Act 1991	appt. day(s) for spec. provns. (1.3.1992)	SI 332, art.2
		appt. day(s) for s.4(3) (9) (17.12.1992)	SI 3277,3227
		appt. day(s) for remaining provns. of s.4 (20.12.1992)	SI 3277,3227
c.24	Northern Ireland (Emergency Provisions) Act 1991	appt. day(s) for spec. provns. (1.6.1992)	SI 1181, art.2
		spec. provns. cont. (to 15.6.1993)	SI 1413, art.3
		s.34 cont. (to beginning of 16.6.1992)	SI 1390, art.2
		Sch.2 am.	SI 1958, art.2
		Sch.3 cont. (to beginning of 16.6.1992)	SI 1390, art.2
c.26	Road Traffic (Temporary Restrictions) Act 1991	appt. day(s) for Act (1.7.1992)	SI 1218, art.2
		restr.	SI 1218, art.4

Year and Chap. or No. of Measure	Short title	How affected	1992, Chapter of Act or Number of Measure or Statutory Instrument
1991—*cont.*			
c.28	Natural Heritage (Scotland) Act 1991	Sch.2, para.5 rep.	51, s.15(2), Sch.
		Sch.7, para.6 am. (*prosp.*)	14, s.117(1), Sch.13, para.93
c.31	Finance Act 1991	appt. day(s) for spec. provns. (26.2.1992)	SI 173, reg.2
		appt. day(s) for spec. provns. (30.6.1992)	SI 1346, reg.2
		appt. day(s) for s.49 (2.10.1992)	SI 1746, art.2
		s.33(4) rep.in pt.	48, s.82, Sch.18, Pt.VII
		s.57(4) rep.	12, s.290, Sch.12
		s.67 rep.	12, s.290, Sch.12
		s.72(4) am.	12, s.290, Sch.10, para.23
		s.77(2) rep.	12, s.290, Sch.12
		s.78(2)(3)(6)(7) rep.	12, s.290, Sch.12
		ss.83-102 rep.	12, s.290, Sch.12
		Sch.2, para.17 rep. (*prosp.*)	48, s.82, Sch.18, Pt.I, Note 4
		Sch.2, para.21A added	48, s.9(2)
		Sch.2, para.22A added	48, s.9(3)
		Sch.3, para.5(1)(b)(3) rep. (*prosp.*)	48, s.82, Sch.18, Pt.IV
		Sch.6, para.6 rep.	12, s.290, Sch.12
		Sch.7, para.6 mod.	SI 1655, regs.1,20(1)
		Sch.7, paras.14,15 rep.	12, s.290, Sch.12
		Sch.10, para.1 rep.	12, s.290, Sch.12
		Sch.10, para.4 rep.	12, s.290, Sch.12
		Schs.16-18 rep.	12, s.290, Sch.12
		Sch.17, para.2 appl.	12, s.92(2)
c.34	Planning and Compensation Act 1991	appt. day(s) for spec. provns. (24.1.1992)	SI 71, art.2
		appt. day(s) for spec. provns. (24.2.1992, 26.3.1992)	SI 334, arts.3,4
		appt. day(s) for spec. provns. (6.9.1992)	SI 665, art.2
		appt. day(s) for spec. provns. (27.7.1992)	SI 1279, art.2
		appt. day(s) for spec. provns. (17.7.1992)	SI 1491, art.2
		appt. day(s) for spec. provns. (27.7.1992)	SI 1630, art.2(1)
		appt. day(s) for spec. provns. (10.8.1992) (25.9.1992)	SI 1937, arts.3,4
		appt. day(s) for s.28 (residue) (9.11.92)	SI 2413, art.2
		appt. day(s) for spec. provns. (9.11.1992)	SI 2831, art.2
		s.10(1) excl.	SI 1630, art.3(2)

Year and Chap. or No. of Measure	Short title	How affected	1992, Chapter of Act or Number of Measure or Statutory Instrument
1991—*cont.*			
		s.13 restr.	SI 1279, art.3
		s.20 restr.	SI 1491, art.3
		Sch.7, para.1 restr.	SI 1630, art.3(3)
		Sch.7, para.52(2)(c) restr.	SI 1279, art.3
c.35	Badgers (Further Protection) Act 1991	rep.	51, s.15(2), Sch.
c.36	Badgers Act 1991	rep. (EWS)	51, s.15(2), Sch.
c.38	Medical Qualifications (Amendment) Act 1991	appt. day(s) for Act (30.3.1992)	SI 804, art.2
c.40	Road Traffic Act 1991	appt. day(s) for spec. provns. (2.3.1992, 1.4.1992)	SI 199, art.3
		appt. day(s) for spec. provns. (1.4.1992)	SI 421, art.2
		appt. day(s) for spec. provns. (1.7.1992)	SI 1286, art.2 (Pt.II amended by 1992/1410)
		appt. day(s) for spec. provns. (30.6.1992)	SI 1410, art.2
		appt. day(s) for spec. provns. (1.9.1992)	SI 2010, art.2
		ss.23,24 restr.	SI 1286, arts.4(2),5
		s.39 restr.	SI 1286, art.6(6)
		Sch.4, para.102 excl.	SI 199, art.4
		Sch.7, para.1 rep.	53, s.18(2), Sch.4, Pt.I
c.41	Arms Control and Disarmament (Inspections) Act 1991	appt. day(s) for ss.1-5 (17.7.1992)	SI 1750, reg.2
c.42	Social Security (Contributions) Act 1991	rep.	6, s.3, Sch.1
c.47	Mental Health (Detention) (Scotland) Act 1991	appt. day(s) for Act (9.3.1992)	SI 357, art.2
c.48	Child Support Act 1991	appt. day(s) for spec. provns. (17.6.1992)	SI 1431, art.2
		appt. day(s) for ss.13, 21(1)(4)(Part),22(1)(2)(5),23,24(9),58(13)(Part),sch.3(Part),sch.4,sch.5,paras.1-4(Part), (1.9.1992)	SI 1938, art.2
		appt. day(s) for spec. provns. (5.4.1993)	SI 2644, art.2
		s.4(6) mod.	SI 1813, reg.52(8)
		s.18 appl.	SI 1813, reg.52(4)(5)
		s.18(5)-(8) ext.(mods.)	SI 1813, reg.9(6)(7)
		s.18(5)-(9) appl.(mods.)	SI 1813, reg.52(4)(5)
		s.18(5)-(9)(11) appl.(mods.)	SI 1816, reg.12(1)(3)
		s.18(11) appl.(mods.)	SI 1813, reg.52(4)(5)
		s.20 appl.	SI 1813, reg.42(7)
		ss.29(2)(3),31-40 appl.(mods.) (EW)	SI 2643, reg.3
		ss.29(2)(3),31,32 appl.(mods.) (S)	SI 2643, reg.4

Year and Chap. or No. of Measure	Short title	How affected	1992, Chapter of Act or Number of Measure or Statutory Instrument
1991—*cont.*			
		s.43(2) am.	6, s.4, Sch.2, para.113
		s.45 (defns. of "benefit Acts" and "disability living allowance") am.	6, s.4, Sch.2, para.114(a) (b)
		Sch.1 mod.	SI 1815, reg.21(2)
		Sch.1, para.2(1) mod.	SI 1815, reg.23(4)
		Sch.2, para.2(2) am. (EWS) (*prosp.*)	14, s.117(1), Sch.13, para.94(a)
		Sch.2, para.2(4) (defn. of "appropriate authority") am. (*prosp.*)	14, s.117(1), Sch.13, para.94(b)
		Sch.3, para.1(1) rep.in pt.	6, s.3, Sch.1
		Sch.3, para.3(2)(c) rep.in pt.	6, s.3, Sch.1
		Sch.5, para.1 rep.	53, s.18(2), Sch.4, Pt.I
c.49	School Teachers' Pay and Conditions Act 1991	appt. day(s) for spec. provns. (6.3.1992)	SI 532, arts.3,4
		appt. day(s) for s.2(9) (30.3.1992)	SI 988, art.2
		appt. day(s) for s.2(7) (4.12.1992)	SI 3070, art.2
		defns. of "pay and conditions order" and "school teacher" appl. (1.4.1993)	13, s.48(4)(a)
c.51	Local Government Finance and Valuation Act 1991	rep. (*prosp.*)	14, s.117(2), Sch.14
c.52	Ports Act 1991	appt. day(s) for s.32 (1.4.93)	SI 2381, art.2
		s.16 am.	12, s.290, Sch.10, para.24(1)
		s.17 mod.	SI 58, art.34
		s.17 am.	12, s.290, Sch.10, para.24(2)(a)
		s.17(6) am.	12, s.290, Sch.10, para.24(2)(b)
		s.17(7)(a) subst.	12, s.290, Sch.10, para.24(2)(c)(i)
		s.17(7)(b) am.	12, s.290, Sch.10, para.24(2)(c)(ii)
		s.17(13) am.	12, s.290, Sch.10, para.24(2)(d)
		s.18(2)(4)(8) am.	12, s.290, Sch.10, para.24(3)(a)(b)
		s.18(8)(a) rep.	12, s.290, Sch.12
		s.20 am.	12, s.290, Sch.10, para.24(4)
		s.35(3)(6) am.	12, s.290, Sch.10, para.24(5)(a)(b)
		s.40(1) (defn. of "the 1992 Act") added	12, s.290, Sch.10, para.24(6)

Year and Chap. or No. of Measure	Short title	How affected	1992, Chapter of Act or Number of Measure or Statutory Instrument
1991—*cont.*			
c.53	Criminal Justice Act 1991	appt. day(s) for spec. provns. (1.4.1992, 1.10.1992)	SI 333, art.2
		s.26(3) rep.	51, s.15(2), Sch.
		s.35 mod.	SI 1829, art.3
		s.37 mod.	SI 1829, art.3
		s.39 mod.	SI 1829, art.3
		ss.73-92 (Pt.IV) (defn. of "contracted out prison") appl.	25, s.1(6)
		s.76(4) trans.of functions	SI 709, art.2(1), Sch.1
		s.76(4) am.	SI 709, art.2(3), Sch.1
		s.76(5) trans.of functions	SI 709, art.2(1), Sch.1
		s.76(5) am.	SI 709, art.2(3), Sch.1
		s.84(1) am.	SI 1656, art.2
		s.84(1)(b) rep.	SI 1656, art.2(b)
		s.87 am.	SI 1656, art.3
		s.87(5) rep.	SI 1656, art.3
c.56	Water Industry Act 1991	defn. of "public sewers" appl.	iv, s.35(1)
		defn. of "sewerage undertaker" appl.	vii, s.2(1)
		defn. of "public sewer" appl.	xi, s.40(1)
		s.2(3)(bb) added	43, s.50
		s.7(4) am.	43, s.40(1)
		s.7(4)(bb) added	43, s.40(1)
		s.7(5)(6) added	43, s.40(2)
		s.8(2)(a)(4)(b)(5)(b) am.	43, s.56(6), Sch.1, para.17(a)(b)
		s.8(7) added	43, s.40(3)
		s.9(3) am.	43, s.40(4)
		s.10 renumbered s.10(1)	43, s.42
		s.10(2)-(5) added	43, s.42
		s.30A added	43, s.34
		s.34(3)(a) subst.	43, s.39(1)(3)
		s.35(3) rep.	43, ss.39(2)(3),56(7), Sch.2
		s.36(3)(a)(ii)(b)(ii) rep.	43, ss.40(5)(a)(b),56(7), Sch.2
		s.38(5) added	43, s.56(6), Sch.1, para.18
		s.38A added	43, s.27
		s.39(1)(b) subst.	43, s.56(6), Sch.1, para.19(2)
		s.39(1)(c)(ii) am.	43, s.56(6), Sch.1, para.19(3)
		s.39(1)(d) am.	43, s.26(2)
		s.39(1A) added	43, s.26(3)
		s.39(2)(bb) added	43, s.26(4)
		s.39A added	43, s.28
		s.40 replaced (by ss.40 and 40A)	43, s.44

Year and Chap. or No. of Measure	Short title	How affected	1992, Chapter of Act or Number of Measure or Statutory Instrument
1991—*cont.*			
		s.45(1) rep.in pt.	43, ss.43(1),56(7), Sch.2
		s.45(6A) added	43, s.35(2)
		s.46(7) am.	43, s.35(3)
		s.47(2)(b)(ii) am.	43, s.51(2)
		s.47(2A) added	43, s.51(3)
		s.47(3A)(3B) added	43, s.51(4)
		s.49(3) subst.	43, s.35(4)
		s.52(2) rep.in pt.	43, ss.41,56(7), Sch.2
		s.52(3)(a) am.	43, s.56(6), Sch.1, para.20
		s.53(2)(a)(ii) am.	43, s.51(5)
		s.53(2A) added	43, s.35(5)
		s.53(2A) added	43, s.51(5)
		s.64(1) rep.in pt.	43, s.56(6)(7), Sch.1, para.21(a), Sch.2
		s.64(2) am.	43, s.56(6), Sch.1, para.21(b)
		s.64(2A) added	43, s.35(6)
		s.65(9) am.	43, s.56(6), Sch.1, para.22
		s.79(6) am.	43, s.56(6), Sch.1, para.23
		s.86A added	43, s.29
		s.95(5) added	43, s.56(6), Sch.1, para.24
		s.95A added	43, s.31
		s.96(1)(b) subst.	43, s.56(6), Sch.1, para.25(2)
		s.96(1)(c)(ii) am.	43, s.56(6), Sch.1, para.25(3)
		s.96(1)(d) am.	43, s.30(2)
		s.96(1A) added	43, s.30(3)
		s.96(2)(bb) added	43, s.30(4)
		s.96A added	43, s.32
		s.98(4) am.	43, s.56(6), Sch.1, para.26
		s.105 am.	43, s.35(7)
		s.106(1) subst.	43, s.43(2)
		s.106(6) am.	43, s.35(8)(a)
		s.106(7) rep.	43, ss.35(8)(b),56(7), Sch.2
		s.106(8)(b) am.	43, s.35(8)(c)
		s.107(1)(b) am.	43, s.35(9)
		s.107(4A) added	43, s.35(9)
		s.110A added	43, s.45
		s.110A (defn. of "main connection") appl.	43, s.46(2)(3) (adding 1991 c.57 s.87(4))
		s.112(2)(3) am.	43, s.35(10)
		s.113(4) am.	43, s.35(11)(a)
		s.113(5) rep.	43, ss.35(11)(b),56(7), Sch.2
		s.116(4) added	43, s.35(12)
		s.116A added	43, s.33
		s.148(1A) added	43, s.53(2)
		s.148(4A) added	43, s.53(3)
		s.149(2)(aa) added	43, s.53(4)

Year and Chap. or No. of Measure	Short title	How affected	1992, Chapter of Act or Number of Measure or Statutory Instrument
1991—*cont.*			
		s.150A added (*prosp.*)	43, s.36
		s.158(8)-(11) added	43, s.40(6)
		s.192(3A)(3B) added	43, s.47
		s.206(4)(a) am.	43, s.56(6), Sch.1, para.27
		s.213(2)(dd) added	43, s.56(6), Sch.1, para.28
		s.213(2A)(2B) added	43, s.52
		Sch.12, para.1(3) am.	43, s.56(6), Sch.1, para.29
		Sch.12, para.4(2) am.	43, s.56(6), Sch.1, para.30
		Sch.12, para.4(3) am.	43, s.56(6), Sch.1, para.31(a)(b)
		Sch.12, para.4(4) rep.	43, s.56(7), Sch.2
c.57	Water Resources Act 1991	saved	iii, s.32(10)
		saved	v, s.18(5)
		s.11(5) rep.in pt.	14, s.117, Sch.13, para.95(1)(b), Sch.14
		s.11(5)(b) subst.	14, s.117(1), Sch.13, para.95(1)(a)
		s.11(5A) added	14, s.117(1), Sch.13, para.95(2)
		s.11(7)(a)(b) subst.	14, s.117(1), Sch.13, para.95(3)
		s.11(8) (defns. of "relevant area" and "relevant population") rep.	14, s.117, Sch.13, para.95(4), Sch.14
		s.24(1) restr.	iv, s.17(2)
		s.25 appl.	v, s.12(1)
		s.27(4) mod.	SI 1096, arts.3,4, Sch.
		s.57 mod.	SI 1096, art.4
		s.57(1)(2)(4) mod.	SI 1096, arts.3,4, Sch.
		s.83 am.	SI 337, reg.4
		ss.85-87 appl.(mods.)	v, s.18(6)
		s.85 appl.	i, s.18(3)(a)
		s.85 appl.	iii, s.12(2)(a)
		s.85 appl.(mods.)	iv, s.18(4)(a)
		s.85 appl.(mods.)	xi, s.22(4)(a)
		s.87(1) replaced (by subss.(1)(1A)-(1C))	43, s.46(1)(3)
		s.87(4) added	43, s.46(2)(3)
		ss.98-104 (Pt.IV) (defn. of "main river") appl.	iv, s.15(1)
		s.104 (defn. of "controlled waters") appl.	i, s.18(3)(a)
		s.104 (defn. of "controlled waters") appl.	iii, s.12(2)(a)
		s.104 (defn. of "controlled waters") appl.	iv, s.18(4)(a)
		s.104 (defn. of "controlled waters") appl.	xi, s.22(4)(a)
		s.109 mod.	iii, s.32(9)
		s.109 am.	iv, s.33(12)
		s.109 am.	vii, s.21(9)

Year and Chap. or No. of Measure	Short title	How affected	1992, Chapter of Act or Number of Measure or Statutory Instrument
1991—*cont.*			
		s.109 am.	xi, s.42(8)
		s.113 (defn. of "main river") appl.	i, s.18(3)(b)
		s.113 (defn. of "banks") appl.	iii, s.12(2)(b)
		s.113 (defn. of "banks") appl.	iv, s.18(4)(b)
		s.113 (defn. of "banks") appl.	xi, s.22(4)(b)
		s.125(2) mod.	SI 1096, arts.3,4, Sch.
		s.127(1)(4) mod.	SI 1096, arts.3,4, Sch.
		s.135(2) rep.in pt.	14, s.117, Sch.13, para.96(1), Sch.14
		s.135(2) rep.in pt.	14, s.117(2), Sch.14
		s.135(3)(a) rep.in pt.	14, s.117, Sch.13, para.96(2), Sch.14
		s.135(7) added	14, s.117(1), Sch.13, para.96(3)
		s.136 rep.	14, s.117, Sch.13, para.97, Sch.14
		s.165(1)(a)(b) expld.	v, s.7(4)
		s.194(5) excl.	iv, s.15(3)
		Sch.15, para.12(1) am.	14, s.117(1), Sch.13, para.98
		Sch.21, para.5(1)(2) appl.	v, s.7(5)
c.59	Land Drainage Act 1991	defn. of "drainage body" appl.	3, s.33(1)
		saved	iii, s.32(10)
		defn. of "watercourse" appl.	v, s.51(1)
		defn. of "watercourse" appl.	vii, s.21(1)
		s.37(5)(d) replaced by s.37(5)(d)(e)	SI 3079, reg.3
		s.45(6)(7)(a) am.	14, s.117(1), Sch.13, para.99
		s.46(1) am.	14, s.117(1), Sch.13, para.100(1)
		s.46(3)(4) am.	14, s.117(1), Sch.13, para.100(1)
		s.46(6) am.	14, s.117(1), Sch.13, para.100(2)
		s.72 (defn. of "watercourse") appl.	iii, s.32(1)
		s.72 (defn. of "watercourse") defn(s). appl. watercourse	iv, s.33(1)
		s.72 (defn. of "watercourse") appl.	vi, s.21(1)
		s.72 (defn. of "watercourse") appl.	xi, s.42(1)
		s.109 excl.	v, s.5(4)
		Sch.1, para.6(1)(b) am.	SI 3079, reg.4(a)

Year and Chap. or No. of Measure	Short title	How affected	1992, Chapter of Act or Number of Measure or Statutory Instrument
1991—*cont.*			
		Sch.1, para.6(2)(b) am.	SI 3079, reg.4(b)
		Sch.1, para.6(4) am.	SI 3079, reg.4(c)
c.66	British Technology Group Act 1991	s.12(2) am.	12, s.290, Sch.10, para.25
		s.17(2) excl. (*retrosp.*)	SI 8, art.3
		Sch.2 excl. (*retrosp.*)	SI 8, art.3
1992			
c.3	Severn Bridges Act 1992	appt. day(s) for Act (26.4.1992)	SI 578, art.2
		s.8(2) (defn. of "motor car") subst.	SI 1207, art.2(a)
		s.8(2) (defn. of "motor cycle") added	SI 1207, art.2(b)
		s.8(3) rep.in pt.	SI 1207, art.3
		s.8(3)(c) added	SI 1207, art.3
c.4	Social Security Contributions and Benefits Act 1992	mod.	SI 1735, art.2
		mod. (EWS)	SI 3209, art.2
		mod. (EWS)	SI 3210, art.2
		mod. (EWS)	SI 3211, art.2
		mod. (EWS)	SI 3212, art.2
		mod. (EWS)	SI 3213, art.2
		mod.	5, s.32(10)
		mod.	5, s.121(5)
		power to am.	5, ss.177(5)(a),189(11)
		power to am.	5, ss.178(3)(a),189(11)
		power to am.	5, ss.179(4)(a),189(11)
		excl.	5, s.185, Sch.9, para.1(6)
		am.	6, s.2(3)
		expld.	6, s.5, Sch.3, Pt.I, para.1(2)
		power to rep. or am.	6, s.5, Sch.3, Pt.I, para.7(1)
		power to am.	6, s.5, Sch.3, Pt.II, paras.12-14
		power to am.	6, s.5, Sch.3, Pt.II, para.22(3)(4)(c)
		defn. of "income support" appl. (EW)	14, s.14(3), Sch.4, para.6(1)
		defn. of "income support" appl. (S)	14, s.97(5), Sch.8, para.6(1)
		ss.1-9 power to mod.	5, s.61(1)(a)(iii)
		ss.1-19 (Pt.I) power to am.	5, ss.141(4),143(1)(4)
		s.8(2)(a)(b) power to am.	5, s.145(1)(a)(b)
		ss.11(1),13(1) power to am.	5, s.145(4)(a)(b)
		s.11(4) power to am.	5, s.143(3)
		s.18(1) power to am.	5, ss.141(5),143(2)
		ss.20-62 (Pt.II) mod.	5, s.155(2)
		s.20(1)(e) appl.	5, s.191
		s.34 mod.	6, s.4, Sch.2, para.24 (adding ss.29A-29C to 1975 c.60)

Year and Chap. or No. of Measure	Short title	How affected	1992, Chapter of Act or Number of Measure or Statutory Instrument
1992—*cont.*			
		s.34(7) mod.	6, s.4, Sch.2, para.24 (adding ss.29A-29C to 1975 c.60)
		s.35(6) am.	29, s.2(1)(a)(2)(a)
		s.44(4) power to am.	5, ss.150(1)(a)(ii),151
		s.44(6) am. (*temp.*)	6, s.6, Sch.4, Pt.I, paras.1,2
		s.44(7A) added (*temp.*)	6, s.6, Sch.4, Pt.I, paras.1,3
		s.47 mod.	6, s.4, Sch.2, para.24 (adding ss.29A-29C to 1975 c.60)
		s.47(1) mod.	6, s.4, Sch.2, para.24 (adding ss.29A-29C to 1975 c.60)
		ss.63-79 (Pt.III) mod.	5, s.155(2)
		s.64 mod.	6, s.5, Sch.3, Pt.II, para.20
		s.64 (defn. of "attendance allowance") appl.	12, s.3, Sch.1, para.1(6)
		s.66(2) (defn. of "terminally ill") appl.	5, s.32(5)
		s.71 appl.	12, s.3, Sch.1, para.1(6)
		s.72(2) (defn. of "dwelling") am.	SI 2955, reg.3
		ss.80-93 (Pt.IV) mod.	5, s.155(2)
		s.80(4) power to am.	5, ss.150(1)(f),151
		ss.94-110 (Pt.V) mod.	5, s.155(2)
		s.94(2)(a) appl.	5, s.191
		s.122 (defn. of "benefit") appl.	5, s.1(4)
		s.122 (defn. of "benefits") appl.	5, s.20(6)(a)
		s.122 (defn. of "benefit") appl.	5, s.61(4)(a)
		s.122 (defn. of "benefit") appl.	5, s.68(4)
		s.122 (defn. of "benefits") appl.	5, s.71(11)(a)
		s.122 (defn. of "benefit") appl.	5, s.73(1)
		s.122 power to mod.	5, s.73(4)
		s.122 (defn. of "benefit") appl.	5, s.184(c)
		s.122 (defn. of "benefit") appl.	5, s.187(1)(a)
		s.122 (defn. of "benefits") appl.	33, s.1(2), Sch., para.1 (adding s.15A to 1992 c.5)
		ss.123-137 (Pt.VII) power to am.	5, s.150(7)
		s.123 restr.	14, s.103, Sch.9, para.11
		s.123(1)(e) subst.	14, s.103, Sch.9, para.1(1)
		s.123(4)-(6) replaced (by subs.(4))	14, s.103, Sch.9, para.1(2)

Year and Chap. or No. of Measure	Short title	How affected	1992, Chapter of Act or Number of Measure or Statutory Instrument
1992—*cont.*			
		s.129(2) mod.	6, s.6, Sch.4, Pt.II, para.21
		s.129(2)(a) am.	14, s.103, Sch.9, para.2
		s.130(2) am.	14, s.103, Sch.9, para.3
		ss.131-137 restr.	14, s.103, Sch.9, para.11
		s.131 subst.	14, s.103, Sch.9, para.4
		s.131(6) restr.	SI 1814, reg.55
		s.132(1) am.	14, s.103, Sch.9, para.5(1)
		s.132(5) am.	14, s.103, Sch.9, para.5(2)
		s.132(7) am.	14, s.103, Sch.9, para.5(3)
		s.132(9)(b) subst.	14, s.103, Sch.9, para.5(4)
		s.133(3) am.	14, s.103, Sch.9, para.6
		s.134(3) rep.	14, ss.103,117(2), Sch.9, para.7, Sch.14
		s.135(3)(4) mod. (*temp.*)	6, s.6, Sch.4, Pt.I, paras.1,4
		s.135(5) am.	14, s.103, Sch.9, para.8
		s.137(1) (defns. of "contribution period", "the 1987 Act" and "the 1988 Act") rep.	14, ss.103,117(2), Sch.9, para.9(b), Sch.14
		s.137(1) (defn. of "charging authority") replaced (by definition of "billing authority")	14, s.103, Sch.9, para.9(a)
		s.137(1) (defn. of "week") am.	14, s.103, Sch.9, para.9(d)
		s.137(1) (defn. of "levying authority") subst.	14, s.103, Sch.9, para.9(c)
		s.138(1)(b) restr.	5, s.12(1)
		s.143(3)(c)(i)-(iii) subst. (*temp.*)	6, s.6, Sch.4, Pt.I, paras.1,5
		s.148 am.	5, s.67(1)
		s.150 defn(s). appl.	5, s.67(4)
		ss.151-163 (Pt.XI) (defn. of "employer") appl.	5, s.94(5)
		s.171(1) (defn. of "confinement") am.	29, s.2(1)(b)(2)(a)
		s.175(6) am.	14, s.103, Sch.9, para.10
		Sch.1, para.6(2)-(4) mod. (*temp.*)	6, s.6, Sch.4, Pt.I, paras.1,6
		Sch.1, para.6(8) subst. (*temp.*)	6, s.6, Sch.4, Pt.I, paras.1,7
		Sch.2, para.6(1) subst. (*temp.*)	6, s.6, Sch.4, Pt.I, paras.1,8
		Sch.2, para.6(2) mod. (*temp.*)	6, s.6, Sch.4, Pt.I, paras.1,9
		Sch.4 power to am.	5, ss.150(1)(a)(i),151
		Sch.4, Pt.I power to am.	5, s.150(3)(a)
		Sch.4, Pt.I, para.6 power to am.	5, s.154(2)(a)
		Sch.4, Pt.III, paras.1,2, 4,5,6 power to am.	5, s.150(3)(a)

Year and Chap. or No. of Measure	Short title	How affected	1992, Chapter of Act or Number of Measure or Statutory Instrument
1992—*cont.*			
		Sch.4, Pt.III, para.5 power to am.	5, s.154(2)(b)
		Sch.4, Pt.IV power to am.	5, s.154(2)(c)
		Sch.4, Pts.IV,V power to am.	5, s.150(3)(a)
		Sch.4, Pt.V, paras.7,12 power to am.	5, s.154(2)(d)(e)
		Sch.5 power to am.	5, ss.150(1)(d),151
		Sch.7, para.3 mod.	6, s.4, Sch.2, para.24 (adding ss.29A-29C to 1975 c.60)
		Sch.7, para.11(12A) added (*temp.*)	6, s.6, Sch.4, Pt.I, paras.1,10
		Sch.7, para.12(7) added (*temp.*)	6, s.6, Sch.4, Pt.I, paras.1,11
		Sch.7, para.13(4) power to am.	5, ss.150(1)(g),151
		Sch.8 excl.	5, s.185, Sch.9, para.2(2)
		Sch.8, paras.2(6)(c),6(2)(b) power to am.	5, ss.150(1)(a)(iii),151
c.5	Social Security Administration Act 1992	mod.	SI 1735, art.2
		mod. (EWS)	SI 3209, art.2
		mod. (EWS)	SI 3210, art.2
		mod. (EWS)	SI 3211, art.2
		mod. (EWS)	SI 3212, art.2
		mod. (EWS)	SI 3213, art.2
		excl.	4, ss.45(7),55, Sch.5, para.2(4)(b)
		power to am.	4, s.109(2)(3)(4)
		mod.	4, ss.116(1)(b),175(8)(9)
		power to mod.	4, s.175(8)
		am.	6, s.2(3)
		expld.	6, s.5, Sch.3, Pt.I, para.1(2)
		power to rep. or am.	6, s.5, Sch.3, Pt.I, para.7(1)
		power to am.	6, s.5, Sch.3, Pt.II, paras.12-14
		power to am.	6, s.5, Sch.3, Pt.II, para.22(3)(4)(d)
		ss.6,7 restr.	14, s.103, Sch.9, para.26
		s.6(1) am.	14, s.103, Sch.9, para.12(1)(a)
		s.6(1)(d) rep.in pt.	14, ss.103,117(2), Sch.9, para.12(1)(b), Sch.14
		s.6(1)(j)(n)(o)(r)(s)(t) rep.in pt.	14, ss.103,117(2), Sch.9, para.12(1)(c), Sch.14
		s.6(2) am.	14, s.103, Sch.9, para.12(2)
		s.6(3) subst.	14, s.103, Sch.9, para.12(3)
		s.7(3) am.	14, s.103, Sch.9, para.13
		s.15A added (*retrosp.*)	33, s.1(2), Sch., para.1
		ss.17-70 (Pt.II) power to mod.	4, ss.116(2),117(1),119, 120(1),175(8)(9)

Year and Chap. or No. of Measure	Short title	How affected	1992, Chapter of Act or Number of Measure or Statutory Instrument
1992—*cont.*			
		ss.17-70 (Pt.II) power to appl. (EW)	14, s.14(3), Sch.4, para.19(2)
		s.24(1) am. (*temp.*)	6, s.6, Sch.4, Pt.I, paras.1,12(a)
		s.24(5A) added (*temp.*)	6, s.6, Sch.4, Pt.I, paras.1,12(b)
		s.41(4)(c) am.	53, s.18(1), Sch.3, para.36
		s.43(5)(c) am.	53, s.18(1), Sch.3, para.36
		s.50(4)(c) am.	53, s.18(1), Sch.3, para.36
		s.63 restr.	14, s.103, Sch.9, para.26
		s.63(1)(b)(c) replaced (by para.(b))	14, s.103, Sch.9, para.14(1)
		s.63(3) am.	14, s.103, Sch.9, para.14(2)
		ss.76,77 restr.	14, s.103, Sch.9, para.26
		s.76(1) am.	14, s.103, Sch.9, para.15(1)
		s.76(2) rep.in pt.	14, ss.103,117(2), Sch.9, para.15(2), Sch.14
		s.76(3) am.	14, s.103, Sch.9, para.15(3)
		s.76(4)(5)(7) rep.	14, ss.103,117(2), Sch.9, para.15(4), Sch.14
		s.77(1) am.	14, s.103, Sch.9, para.16(1)
		s.77(2)(3) rep.	14, ss.103,117(2), Sch.9, para.16(2), Sch.14
		s.101 excl. (NI)	8, ss.89(1),92(1)
		s.104 mod. (*temp.*)	6, s.6, Sch.4, Pt.I, paras.1,13
		s.107(5) mod. (*temp.*)	6, s.6, Sch.4, Pt.I, paras.1,14
		s.107(9)-(11) mod. (*temp.*)	6, s.6, Sch.4, Pt.I, paras.1,15
		s.107(15) (defn. of "maintenance order") am. (*temp.*)	6, s.6, Sch.4, Pt.II, para.22
		s.116(2) am.	14, s.103, Sch.9, para.17(1)
		s.116(5) am.	14, s.103, Sch.9, para.17(2)
		s.124(3) am.	SI 3216, Sch.
		s.128 restr.	14, s.103, Sch.9, para.26
		s.128(1) am.	14, s.103, Sch.9, para.18(1)
		s.128(2) am.	14, s.103, Sch.9, para.18(2)
		s.128(3) am.	14, s.103, Sch.9, para.18(3)
		ss.138,139 restr.	14, s.103, Sch.9, para.26
		s.138(1)(2) replaced (by subs.(1))	14, s.103, Sch.9, para.19(1)
		s.138(3)(4) rep.	14, ss.103,117(2), Sch.9, para.19(2), Sch.14
		s.138(5) am.	14, s.103, Sch.9, para.19(3)
		s.138(6)-(8) rep.	14, ss.103,117(2), Sch.9, para.19(4), Sch.14
		s.138(9) rep.in pt.	14, ss.103,117(2), Sch.9, para.19(5), Sch.14
		s.138(9) am.	14, s.103, Sch.9, para.19(5)

Year and Chap. or No. of Measure	Short title	How affected	1992, Chapter of Act or Number of Measure or Statutory Instrument
1992—*cont.*			
		s.139(1) am.	14, s.103, Sch.9, para.20(1)
		s.139(2)(3) replaced (by subs.(2))	14, s.103, Sch.9, para.20(2)
		s.139(4) am.	14, s.103, Sch.9, para.20(3)
		s.139(5) am.	14, s.103, Sch.9, para.20(4)
		s.139(6) am.	14, s.103, Sch.9, para.20(5)
		s.139(6)(7) power to am.	4, s.132(6)
		s.139(7) am.	14, s.103, Sch.9, para.20(6)
		s.139(9) am.	14, s.103, Sch.9, para.20(7)
		s.139(10) am.	14, s.103, Sch.9, para.20(8)
		s.140(1) am.	14, s.103, Sch.9, para.21(1)
		s.140(2) am.	14, s.103, Sch.9, para.21(2)
		s.140(3) am.	14, s.103, Sch.9, para.21(3)
		s.140(4) am.	14, s.103, Sch.9, para.21(4)
		s.140(5) am.	14, s.103, Sch.9, para.21(5)
		s.140(6) am.	14, s.103, Sch.9, para.21(6)
		s.140(7) am.	14, s.103, Sch.9, para.21(7)
		s.153 mod. (*temp.*)	6, s.6, Sch.4, Pt.I, paras.1,16
		s.162(4) mod. (*temp.*)	6, s.6, Sch.4, Pt.I, paras.1,17
		s.163(2)(d) am.	14, s.103, Sch.9, para.22
		s.163(5) mod. (*temp.*)	6, s.6, Sch.4, Pt.I, paras.1,18
		s.164(6) am.	33, s.1(2), Sch., para.2(1)
		s.164(7) added (*temp.*)	6, s.6, Sch.4, Pt.I, paras.1,19
		s.164(7) added	33, s.1(2), Sch., para.2(2)
		s.176(1) am.	14, s.103, Sch.9, para.23
		s.189(7) am.	14, s.103, Sch.9, para.24
		s.191 (defns. of "chargeable financial year" and "charging authority") replaced (by definition of "billing authority")	14, s.103, Sch.9, para.25(a)
		s.191 (defn. of "financial year") added	14, s.103, Sch.9, para.25(b)
		s.191 (defn. of "levying authority") subst.	14, s.103, Sch.9, para.25(d)
		s.191 (defn. of "income-related benefit") am.	14, s.103, Sch.9, para.25(c)
		Sch.7, paras.9,14 am.	53, s.18(1), Sch.3, para.37
c.6	Social Security (Consequential Provisions) Act 1992	Sch.2, paras.8,9 rep. Sch.2, paras.12-14 rep. (NI)	53, s.18(2), Sch.4, Pt.I 9, s.3, Sch.1
		Sch.2, para.51 rep.	12, s.290, Sch.12
		Sch.3 am. (*temp.*)	6, s.6, Sch.4, Pt.I, paras.1,20(a)
		Sch.3, para.17A added (*temp.*)	6, s.6, Sch.4, Pt.I, paras.1,20(b)

Year and Chap. or No. of Measure	Short title	How affected	1992, Chapter of Act or Number of Measure or Statutory Instrument
1992—*cont.* c.7	Social Security Contributions and Benefits (Northern Ireland) Act 1992	power to am. mod.	5, ss.177(5)(b),189(11) 8, s.30(10)
		mod.	8, s.115(4)
		power to mod.	8, s.155(4)(5)
		excl.	8, s.161, Sch.6, para.1(7)
		defn. of "benefit" appl.	8, s.167(1)
		am.	9, s.2(3)
		expld.	9, s.5, Sch.3, Pt.I, para.2
		power to rep. or am.	9, s.5, Sch.3, Pt.I, para.7(1)
		power to am.	9, s.5, Sch.3, Pt.II, paras.12(c),13,14
		power to am.	9, s.5, Sch.3, Pt.II, para.21(3)(4)(c)
		ss.20-121 (Pts. II -VI) power to appl.	8, s.161, Sch.6, para.1(3)(a)
		s.20(1)(e) (defn. of "widow's benefit") appl.	8, s.167(1)
		s.44(6) am. (*temp.*)	9, s.6, Sch.4, Pt.I, paras.1,2
		s.44(7A) added (*temp.*)	9, s.6, Sch.4, Pt.I, paras.1,3
		s.64 mod.	9, s.5, Sch.3, Pt.II, para.19
		s.94(2)(a) appl.	8, s.167(1)
		s.121 (defn. of "benefit") appl.	8, s.1(4)(a)
		s.121 (defn. of "benefit") appl.	8, s.5(2)(a)
		s.121 (defn. of "benefit") appl.	8, s.18(6)(a)
		s.121 (defn. of "benefit") appl.	8, s.71(1)
		s.121 (defn. of "benefit") appl.	8, s.160(1)(c)
		s.128(1)(b) mod.	8, s.9(2)
		s.128(2) mod.	9, s.6, Sch.4, Pt.II, paras.1,16
		s.131(3)(4) mod. (*temp.*)	9, s.6, Sch.4, Pt.I, paras.1,4
		s.133 (defn. of "prescribed circumstances") appl.	8, s.74(5)
		s.146 defn(s). appl.	8, s.65(4)
		ss.147-159 (Pt.XI) (defn. of "employer") appl.	8, s.90(5)
		s.171(2) am. (*prosp.*)	40, s.120(1), Sch.21, Pt.I, para.18
		Sch.1, para.6(2)-(4) mod. (*temp.*)	9, s.6, Sch.4, Pt.I, paras.1,5
		Sch.1, para.6(8) subst. (*temp.*)	9, s.6, Sch.4, Pt.I, paras.1,6
		Sch.1, para.10(2) am. (*prosp.*)	40, s.120(1), Sch.21, Pt.I, para.19(1)
		Sch.1, para.10(3) subst. (*prosp.*)	40, s.120(1), Sch.21, Pt.I, para.19(2)

Year and Chap. or No. of Measure	Short title	How affected	1992, Chapter of Act or Number of Measure or Statutory Instrument
1992—*cont.*			
		Sch.2, para.6(1) subst. (*temp.*)	9, s.6, Sch.4, Pt.I, paras.1,7
		Sch.2, para.6(2) mod. (*temp.*)	9, s.6, Sch.4, Pt.I, paras.1,8
		Sch.7, para.12 added (*temp.*)	9, s.6, Sch.4, Pt.I, paras.1,10
		Sch.7, para.(12A) added (*temp.*)	9, s.6, Sch.4, Pt.I, paras.1,9
		Sch.8 mod.	8, s.161, Sch.6, para.1(4)
		Sch.8, para.2 am.	8, s.161, Sch.6, para.1(1)
		Sch.8, para.2 ext.	8, s.161, Sch.6, para.2(1)
		Sch.8, para.2 ext.	8, s.161, Sch.6, para.3
c.8	Social Security Administration (Northern Ireland) Act 1992	power to am.	5, ss.177(5),189(11)
		excl.	7, s.55, Sch.5, para.2(4)(b)
		excl.	7, s.55, Sch.5, para.7(2)(b)
		mod.	7, s.95(4)(5)(c)
		am.	9, s.2(3)
		expld.	9, s.5, Sch.3, Pt.I, para.2
		power to rep. or am.	9, s.5, Sch.3, Pt.I, para.7(1)
		power to am.	9, s.5, Sch.3, Pt.II, paras.12(c),13,14
		power to am.	9, s.5, Sch.3, Pt.II, para.21(3)(4)(d)
		ss.1-3 appl.	7, s.121(1)
		ss.15-17 saved	7, s.1(4), Sch.1, para.7(12)
		ss.15-68 (Pt.II) power to mod.	7, ss.116(2),171(8)
		ss.15-68 (Pt.II) power to mod.	7, ss.117(1),171(8)
		ss.15-68 (Pt.II) power to mod.	7, ss.119,171(8)
		s.66 appl.	7, s.121(1)
		s.99 mod. (*temp.*)	9, s.6, Sch.4, Pt.I, paras.1,11
		s.130 ext.	7, s.44(8)
		s.142(4) mod. (*temp.*)	9, s.6, Sch.4, Pt.I, paras.1,12
		s.143(5) mod. (*temp.*)	9, s.6, Sch.4, Pt.I, paras.1,13
		s.144 added (*temp.*)	9, s.6, Sch.4, Pt.I, paras.1,14
c.9	Social Security (Consequential Provisions)(Northern Ireland)	Sch.3, para.18 am. (*temp.*)	9, s.6, Sch.4, Pt.I, paras.1,15(a)
		Sch.3, para.(17A) added (*temp.*)	9, s.6, Sch.4, Pt.I, paras.1,15(b)
c.11	Aggravated Vehicle-Taking Act 1992	appt. day(s) for Act (1.4.1992)	SI 764, art.2
c.12	Taxation of Chargeable Gains Act 1992	appt. day(s) for ss.137(5),139(8)179,189, 190 (30.9.1993)	SI 3066, art.2(2)(d)
		s.4(1A)(1B) am.	48, s.23(1)(3)

Year and Chap. or No. of Measure	Short title	How affected	1992, Chapter of Act or Number of Measure or Statutory Instrument
1992—*cont.*			
		s.6(1) am.	48, s.23(2)(a)-(c)(3)
		s.35(3)(d) rep.in pt. (*retrosp.*)	48, ss.77,82, Sch.17, paras.5(9),7, Sch.18, Pt.X
		s.35(3)(d)(i) am. (*retrosp.*)	48, s.46(2)
		s.35(3)(d)(i) am. (*prosp.*)	48, s.56, Sch.9, para.21(2)
		s.35(3)(d)(viii) added (*retrosp.*)	48, s.77, Sch.17, paras.5(9),7
		s.37(1) restr.	48, s.65(2)(e)(5)
		s.41 mod.	48, s.77, Sch.17, paras.6(2)(5),7
		s.116(11) am. (*retrosp.*)	48, s.46(3)
		s.135(1)(c) added (*retrosp.*)	48, s.35(1)
		s.140(6A) added (*retrosp.*)	48, s.46(4)
		ss.140A,140B added (*retrosp.*)	48, s.44
		ss.140C,140D added (*retrosp.*)	48, s.45
		ss.152-156 mod.	48, s.77, Sch.17, paras.3, 7
		s.170(8) am. (*retrosp.*)	48, s.24, Sch.6, paras.5, 10
		s.174(1) mod.	48, s.77, Sch.17, paras.6(3)(6),7
		s.174(2)(3) am. (*retrosp.*)	48, s.46(5)(a)(b)
		s.177(2) am. (*retrosp.*)	48, s.46(6)
		s.178(1) am. (*retrosp.*)	48, s.25(1)
		s.179(1) am. (*retrosp.*)	48, s.25(1)
		s.184(2) am. (*retrosp.*)	48, s.46(7)(a)(b)
		s.212 mod.	SI 1655, regs.1,21(1)
		ss.217A-217C added (*prosp.*)	48, s.56, Sch.9, para.21(3)
		s.271(6)(a) am.	44, s.11(2), Sch.8, Pt.I, para.1(1)(2)(9)
c.13	Further and Higher Education Act 1992	appt. day(s) for spec. provns. (6.5.1992, 1.9.1992, 30.9.1992, 1.4.1993, 1.8.1993)	SI 831, arts.2,3
		appt. day(s) for s.9(4) (1.4.93)	SI 2377, art.2
		appt. day(s) for sch.8, para.10 (W)(pt.)(1.9.92) ; (W.)(residue) (1.4.93)	SI 2377, art.3
		appt. day(s) for spec. provns. (7.12.1992) (E)	SI 3057, art.2
		s.48(4)(b) mod.	SI 831, art.5
c.14	Local Government Finance Act 1992	appt. day(s) for spec. provns. (7.3.1992, 1.4.1992)	SI 473, arts.2,3
		appt. day(s) for spec. provns. (1.4.1992)	SI 818, art.2
		appt. day(s) for sch.10, para.1 (18.6.1992)	SI 1460, art.2
		appt. day(s) for spec. provns. (1.8.1992)	SI 1755, art.2

Year and Chap. or No. of Measure	Short title	How affected	1992, Chapter of Act or Number of Measure or Statutory Instrument
1992—*cont.*			
		appt. day(s) for sch.13, paras.36,38(Pt.),43,49, 75 (1.10.1992)	SI 2183, art.2(c)
		appt. day(s) for s.110(1) (4) (1.10.1992)	SI 2183, art.2(a)
		appt. day(s) for sch.11, paras.31(b),37,38(a)(c) (1.10.1992)	SI 2183, art.2(b)
		appt. day(s) for sch.14(Pt.) (1.10.1992)	SI 2183, art.2(d)
		appt. day(s) for sch.13 (pt.) (2.11.1992)	SI 2454, art.2
		appt. day(s) for sch.13 (pt.), sch.14 (pt.) (1.4.1993)	SI 2454, art.3
		am.	SI 3079, reg.12
		ss.1-69 (defn. of "particulars delivered documents") appl.	14, s.117(1), Sch.13, para.88(6) (amdg. 1988 c.41, Sch.11, para.8(3) (e))
		ss.1-69, Pt.I mod.	SI 549, art.3
		ss.1-69, Pt.I mod.	SI 550, arts.3,4
		ss.1-69, Pt.I mod.	19, s.18(1)(a)(b)
		ss.1-99 (Pts.I, II) (defns. of "dwelling" and "resident") appl.	14, s.103, Sch.9, para.4 (substituting s.131 of 1992 c.4)
		s.8(3) mod.	SI 551, art.3
		s.16(1) restr.	SI 613, reg.30
		s.32(2)(e) am.	SI 2429, reg.3(1)
		s.32(3)(b) am.	SI 2429, reg.3(2)
		s.33(3) am.	SI 2429, reg.4
		s.35(2)(a) appl.	SI 3079, reg.11(7)
		s.69 (defns. of "billing authority" and "precepting authority") appl.	14, s.117(1), Sch.13, para.12 (amdg. 1963 c.18 s.4(1))
		s.69 (defns. of "billing authority" and "precepting authority") appl.	14, s.117(1), Sch.13, para.13 (amdg. 1965 c.12 s.31((a))
		s.69 (defns. of "billing authority" and "precepting authority") appl.	14, s.117(1), Sch.13, para.14 (amdg. 1965 c.63, s.2(1)(a))
		s.71 appl.(mods.)	SI 1203, reg.2, Sch.
		s.72(2) (defn. of "dwelling") appl. (*prosp.*)	14, s.107, Sch.11, Pt.IV, para.34 (substituting s.49 of 1980 c.45)
		ss.75-81 appl.(mods.)	SI 1203, reg.2, Sch.
		ss.96,97 appl.(mods.)	SI 1203, reg.2, Sch.
		s.99(1) (defns. of "council tax" and "council water charge") appl. (*prosp.*)	14, s.117(1), Sch.13, para.53(2) (adding 1987 c.18, s.1(9))

Year and Chap. or No. of Measure	Short title	How affected	1992, Chapter of Act or Number of Measure or Statutory Instrument
1992—*cont.*			
		s.99(1) (defns. of "council tax" and "council water charge") appl. (*prosp.*)	14, s.117(1), Sch.13, para.54(2) (adding subs.(9) to s.5 of 1987 c.18)
		s.99(3) appl.(mods.)	SI 1203, reg.2, Sch.
		s.136 saved	SI 1755, art.2(2)(c)
		Sch.13, para.31 rep.	53, s.18(2), Sch.4, Pt.I
c.18	Licensing (Amendment) (Scotland) Act 1992	appt. day(s) for s.1 (15.4.1992)	SI 819, art.3
c.19	Local Government Act 1992	appt. day(s) for spec. provns. (31.10.92)	SI 2371, art.2
		appt. day(s) for ss.9, 11 (Pt.) (4.1.1993)	SI 3241, art.2
		appt. day(s) for ss.10, 11 (Pt.) (14.2.1993)	SI 3241, art.3
		appt. day(s) for s.11 (Pt.) (14.3.1994)	SI 3241, art.4
c.23	Access to Neighbouring Land Act 1992	appt. day for Act (31.1.1993)	SI 3349, art.2
c.27	Parlimentary Corporate Bodies Act 1992	appt. day(s) for s.7(5) (1.4.1992)	SI 902, art.2
c.35	Timeshare Act 1992	appt. day(s) for Act (12.10.1992)	SI 1941, art.2
c.37	Further and Higher Education (Scotland) Act 1992	appt. day(s) for spec. provns. (25.4.1992, 16.5.1992, 1.6.1992, 1.9.1992 and 1.4.1993)	SI 817, art.3
c.38	Education (Schools) Act 1992	appt. day(s) for spec. provns. (16.5.1992, 31.8.1992)	SI 1157, art.2
		Sch.4, paras.2,3 rep.	53, s.18(2), Sch.4, Pt.I
c.40	Friendly Societies Act 1992	appt. day(s) for spec. provns. (8.6.1992)	SI 1325, art.2
		appt. day(s) for ss.84, 120(1)(Pt.), sch.21, Pt.I, paras. 2-4 (1.1.1993)	SI 3117, art.2
		defn. of "friendly society" appl. (*prosp.*)	48, s.56, Sch.9, para.2(3) (adding 1988 c.1, s.266(13))
		s.64(3A) added	SI 1315, art.10(1), Sch.4, para.14
c.41	The Charities Act 1992	appt. day(s) for spec. provns. (1.9.1992) (1.11.1992) (1.1.1993)	SI 1900, arts.2,3
		s.3(1) mod. (*temp.*)	SI 1900, art.4(2)
		s.18(8) am. (1.1.1993)	SI 3218, reg.82(1), Sch.10, Pt.I, para.33
		s.43(1) am. (*temp.*)	SI 1900, art.2(3)
		s.44(1) am. (*temp.*)	SI 1900, art.2(3)
		Sch.3, para.22 rep.	44, s.11(3), Sch.9
c.42	Transport and Works Act 1992	appt. day(s) for spec. provns. (15.7.1992)	SI 1347, art.2

Year and Chap. or No. of Measure	Short title	How affected	1992, Chapter of Act or Number of Measure or Statutory Instrument
1992—*cont.*			
		appt. day(s) for spec. provns. (1.1.1993)	SI 2784, art.2
		appt. day(s) for s.47(1) (Pt.), sch.2 (Pt.) (22.12.1992)	SI 3144, art.2
		appt. day(s) for spec. provns. (31.1.1993)	SI 3144, art.3, Sch.
		Pt.II, Ch.I appt. day(s) for (7.12.1992)	SI 2043, art.2(a)
		s.23(10) am.	SI 1314, art.3(3), Sch., para.2(b)
		s.68(1) appt. day(s) for (7.12.1992)	SI 2043, art.2(b)
		Sch.4, Pt.I appt. day(s) for (7.12.1992)	SI 2043, art.2(c)
c.43	Competition and Service (Utilities) Act 1992	appt. day(s) for spec. provns. (30.5.1992, 1.7.1992, 1.9.1992)	SI * The Competition and Service (Utilities) Act 1992 (Commencement No.1) Order 1992, Dated 29.5.1992.(Note: this is not an SI)
c.44	Museums and Galleries Act 1992	trans.of functions	SI 1311, art.3(1), Sch.1, Pt.I
		appt. day(s) for spec. provns. (1.9.1992) (1.4.1993)	SI 1874, arts.2,3
		s.6(6) rep.in pt.	SI 1311, art.12(2), Sch.2, para.8(2)
		s.9(1)(2)(5)-(7) am.	SI 1311, art.12(2), Sch.2, para.8(3)(b)
		s.9(9) (defn. of "the appropriate Minister") rep.	SI 1311, art.12(2), Sch.2, para.8(3)(a)
		Sch.8, para.2 rep.	SI 1311, art.12(2), Sch.2, para.8(4)
c.46	Non-Domestic Rating Act 1992	appt. day(s) for spec. provns. (23.6.1992)	SI 1486, art.2
		appt. day for residue (16.7.1992)	SI 1642, art.2
c.48	Finance (No.2) Act 1992	appt. day(s) for spec. provns. (1.8.1992) (1.1.1993)	SI 1867, arts.3,4
		appt. day(s) for s.62 (6.4.1993)	SI 2642, art.2
		appt. day(s) for ss.1(1)-(4)(6)(7), 2(1.12.1992)	SI 2979, Sch., Pt.I
		appt. day(s) for ss.1(5) (pt.), 14(2) (Pt.) and Sch.1 (Except paras.9- 11) (Pt.), and Sch.3 (Pt.) (1.12.1992)	SI 2979, Sch., Pt.II
		appt. day(s) for s.3 and sch.2(Pt.) (9.12.1992)	SI 3104, art.2

Year and Chap. or No. of Measure	Short title	How affected	1992, Chapter of Act or Number of Measure or Statutory Instrument
1992—*cont.*			
		appt. day(s) for spec. provns. (1.1.1993)	SI 3261, art.3, Sch.
		s.18 rep. (*retrosp.*)	58, s.4
		Sch.4 rep. (*retrosp.*)	58, s.4
		Sch.18, Pt.VI rep. (*retrosp.*)	58, s.4
c.49	Community Care (Residential Accommodation) Act 1992	appt. day(s) for s.1 (1.4.1993)	SI 2976, art.2
c.52	Trade Union and Labour Relations (Consolidation) Act 1992	mod.	24, s.1(1)(3)
		s.19(1) subst. (*prosp.*)	40, s.120(1), Sch.21, Pt.I, para.17
		s.19(2) rep. (*prosp.*)	40, s.120(2), Sch.22, Pt.I
		s.287(5) rep.	52, s.300(2), Sch.3, para.29(3) (adding 1982 c.23 sch.3 para.45)
c.53	Tribunals and Inquiries Act 1992	s.7(2) am. (*prosp.*)	40, s.120(1), Sch.21, Pt.I, para.13
		s.8(2)(c) added (*prosp.*)	40, s.120(1), Sch.21, Pt.I, para.14(1)
		s.8(3) am. (*prosp.*)	40, s.120(1), Sch.21, Pt.I, para.14(2)
		s.11 excl.	52, s.291(3)
		s.11(1) am.	60, ss.9(2),11(4)
		s.11(1)(3)-(5)(10) ext.(mods.) (Isle of Man) (1.1.1993)	SI 3205, art.2(1)
		Sch.1, Pt.I am.	60, ss.9(3),11(4)
		Sch.1, para.21A added (*prosp.*)	40, s.120(1), Sch.21, Pt.I, para.15
		Sch.1, para.33A added (*prosp.*)	40, s.120(1), Sch.21, Pt.I, para.16
c.vii	Midland Metro Act 1992	s.4(3) appl.	viii, s.11(1)
		s.5(2)-(7) appl.	viii, s.11(1)
		s.6 appl.(mods.)	viii, s.11(1)(2)
		s.8(3) appl.(mods.)	viii, s.11(1)(2)
		s.12 appl.	viii, s.11(1)
		s.13(a) restr.	viii, s.13(2)
		s.16 restr.	viii, s.13(2)
		ss.22,23 appl.(mods.)	viii, s.17(1)
		Sch.4, Pt.I am.	viii, s.12(2)
		Sch.4, Pt.II rep.in pt.	viii, s.12(2)
		Sch.6 restr.	viii, s.13(2)
c.xv	River Humber (Upper Pyewipe Outfall) Act 1992	s.23(3)(a) subst.	vII, s.26(1)(b)(II)
		s.23(3)(b) rep.in pt. & am.	vii, s.26(1)(b)(iii)
		s.23(5) rep.in pt.	vii, s.26(1)(b)(iv)
		s.23(6) added	vii, s.26(1)(b)(v)

INDEX

TO THE

PUBLIC GENERAL ACTS

AND

GENERAL SYNOD MEASURES 1992

B

C

PART I

CHARITIES

Preliminary

D

DIRECTOR OF PUBLIC PROSECUTIONS *See* PUBLIC PROSECUTOR

E

EDUCATION (SCHOOLS) ACT (c. 38) ...   . III, p. 1743.

Her Majesty's Inspectorate for England

§ 1 and Sch. 1. Her Majesty's Inspectorate of Schools in England, III, pp. 1743, 1757.
    2. Functions of the Chief Inspector for England, III, p. 1744.
    3. Power of Chief Inspector for England to arrange for inspections, III, p. 1744.
    4. Annual and other reports of the Chief Inspector for England, III, p. 1745.

Her Majesty's Inspectorate for Wales

5 and Sch. 1. Her Majesty's Inspectorate of Schools in Wales, III, pp. 1745, 1757.
    6. Functions of the Chief Inspector for Wales, III, p. 1746.
    7. Power of Chief Inspector for Wales to arrange for inspections, III, p. 1746.
    8. Annual and other reports of the Chief Inspector for Wales, III, p. 1747.

Inspections by registered inspectors

9 and Sch. 2. Inspection of certain schools, III, pp. 1747, 1759.
    10. Registration of inspectors, III, p. 1748.
    11. Removal from register and imposition or variation of conditions, III, p. 1749.
12 and Sch. 3. Appeals in relation to registration, III, pp. 1749, 1764.
13 and Sch. 2. Religious education, III, pp. 1750, 1759.
    14. Provision of inspection services by local education authorities, III, p. 1750.
    15. Power of local education authority to inspect maintained school for specific purpose, III, p. 1751.

Information about schools

    16. Power of Secretary of State to require information, III, p. 1751.
    17. Information as to schools and pupils: Scotland, III, p. 1753.

Miscellaneous

    18. Interpretation, III, p. 1755.
    19. Regulations and orders, III, p. 1756.
    20. Financial provisions, III, p. 1756.
21 and Schs. 4, 5. Short title, commencement, extent etc.: III, pp. 1756, 1765, 1767.

Schedule 1—Her Majesty's Chief Inspectors, III, p. 1757.
Schedule 2—School Inspections, III, p. 1759.
    Part I—Inspections Under Section 9, III, p. 1759.
    Part II—Inspections of Denominational Education, III, p. 1763.
Schedule 3—Tribunals Hearing Appeals under Section 12, III, p. 1764.
Schedule 4—Minor and Consequential Amendments, III, p. 1765.
Schedule 5—Repeals, III, p. 1767.

ENTRY. Powers of, Under—

Access to Neighbouring Land Act (c. 23, ss. 1-3, 8)   ...   . III, pp. 1609, 1616
Education (Schools) Act (c. 38, ss. 9(7), 13(9), sch. 2, para. 7) ...   ... III, pp. 1748, 1750, 1760
Local Government Finance Act (c. 14, ss. 26, 89)   ...   . II, pp. 1332, 1375
Severn Bridges Act (c. 3, s. 2, sch. 2, Pt. III, para. 7)   ...   . I, pp. 5, 37
Social Security Administration Act (c. 5, ss. 110, 111) ...   . I, pp. 353, 356
Social Security Administration (Northern Ireland) Act (c. 8, ss. 104, 105)   ... II, pp. 776, 778
Transport and Works Act (c. 42, s. 53) ...   . III, p. 2089

EVIDENCE PROVISIONS. Under

Charities Act (c. 41, ss. 6(2), 11) ...   . III, pp. 1973, 11978
Education (Schools) Act (c. 38, sch. 1, para. 7) ...   . III, p. 7158
Friendly Societies Act (c. 40, ss. 59(4)(5), 60, 111)   ...   . III, pp. 1814, 1816, 1860
Local Government Finance Act (c. 14, ss. 82(1), 102(4))   ...   . II, pp. 1370, 1385
Protection of Badgers Act (c. 51, s. 11) ...   . IV, p. 2406
Sexual Offences (Amendment) Act (c. 34, s. 3(4)(a))   ...   . III, p. 1657
Social Security Administration Act (c. 5, ss. 116, 118, 120, 121)   ...   ... I, pp. 357, 359, 361

F

PART IV

AUTHORISATION OF FRIENDLY SOCIETIES' BUSINESS

Restriction on carrying on unauthorised business

Authorisation to carry on business

Restrictions on business of certain authorised societies

Powers of Commission in relation to authorised societies

Supplementary

PART V

REGULATION OF FRIENDLY SOCIETIES' BUSINESS

Preliminary

Actuarial investigations

Margins of solvency

Criteria of prudent management

Powers of Commission

Covering of risks situated in another member State

Appeals

Information

Inspections etc.

FURTHER AND HIGHER EDUCATION ACT (c.13).   ...   .   II, p. 1211

PART I

FURTHER EDUCATION

RESPONSIBILITY FOR FURTHER EDUCATION

The new funding councils

CHAPTER II

INSTITUTIONS WITHIN THE FURTHER EDUCATION SECTOR

The further education corporations

FURTHER AND HIGHER EDUCATION (SCOTLAND) ACT (C. 37)   ...   .   III, p. 1673

PART I

FURTHER EDUCATION

CHAPTER I

DUTIES IN RELATION TO FURTHER EDUCATION

CHAPTER II

SCOTTISH FURTHER EDUCATION FUNDING COUNCIL

CHAPTER III

COLLEGES OF FURTHER EDUCATION

Management of colleges

H

I

L

PART I

CITIZEN'S CHARTER PROVISIONS

Performance standards of local authorities etc.

PART II

LOCAL GOVERNMENT CHANGES FOR ENGLAND

The Local Government Commission

PART III

GENERAL

M

N

The Central Council

§ 1 and Sch. 1.   Changes to constitution, III, pp. 1499, 1506.
    2.   Section 1: preparatory, III, p. 1500.
    3.   Constitution of standing committees, III, p. 1501.

The National Boards

    4.   Changes to constitution, III, p. 1501.
    5.   Functions, III, p. 1502.
    6.   Committees, III, p. 1502.

Registration

    7.   Suspension, III, p. 1503.
    8.   Proceedings about the register: procedure, III, p. 1503.
    9.   Cautions, III, p. 1503.

Provisions relating to midwifery

    10.   Midwifery practice rules: consultation, III, p. 1504.
    11.   Notices of intention: notification of receipt, III, p. 1504.
    12.   Advice under section 16(4) of the 1979 Act: standards, III, p. 1504.

Miscellaneous

    13.   Finances of Central Council and National Boards, III, p. 1504.
    14.   Central Council rules: consultation, III, p. 1504.

General and supplementary

    15.   Transitional provisions, III, p. 1504.
    16 and Schs. 2, 3.   Amendments and repeals, III, pp. 1505, 1508, 1510.
    17.   Short title etc, III, p. 1505.

Schedule   1—Substituted Schedule 1 to the 1979 Act, III, p. 1506.
Schedule   2—Minor and consequential amendments, III, p. 1508.
Schedule   3—Repeals, III, p. 1510.

O

S

PART I

CONSTRUCTION OF NEW SEVERN BRIDGE

PART II

OPERATION OF SEVERN BRIDGES

Introductory

Tolls

PART I

CLAIMS FOR AND PAYMENTS AND GENERAL ADMINISTRATION OF BENEFIT

Necessity of Claim

Widowhood benefits

Claims and payments regulations

Community charge benefits etc.

Industrial injuries benefit

Disability working allowance

The social fund

Child benefit

Statutory sick pay

Statutory maternity pay

Emergency payments

PART II

ADJUDICATION

Adjudication by the Secretary of State

Adjudication by adjudication officers

Appeals from adjudication officers—general

Reviews—general

Attendance allowance, disability living allowance and disability working allowance

The Disability Living Allowance Advisory Board

Housing benefit and community charge benefits.

Part XIV

Social Security Systems Outside Great Britain

Co-ordination

Reciprocity

Part XV

Miscellaneous

Travelling expenses

Offences

Industrial injuries and diseases

Workmen's compensation etc.

Supplementary benefit etc.

Miscellaneous

Part XVI

General

Subordinate legislation

Supplementary

PART III

OVERPAYMENTS AND ADJUSTMENTS OF BENEFIT

Misrepresentation etc.

PART IV

RECOVERY FROM COMPENSATION PAYMENTS

PART V

INCOME SUPPORT AND THE DUTY TO MAINTAIN

Rate of payment, etc.

PART XII

STATUTORY MATERNITY PAY

PART XIII

GENERAL

Interpretation

Subordinate legislation

Short title, commencement and extent

T